THE PUZZLED CENSUS TAKER

"GOT any boys?" the Marshal said
To a lady from over the Rhine;
And the lady shook her flaxen head,
And civilly answered, "*Nein!*"

"Got any girls?" the Marshal said
To the lady from over the Rhine;
And again the lady shook her head,
And civilly answered, "*Nein!*"

"But some are dead?" the Marshal said
To the lady from over the Rhine;
And again the lady shook her head,
And civilly answered, "*Nein!*"

"Husband of course?" the Marshal said
To the lady from over the Rhine;
And again she shook her flaxen head,
And civilly answered, "*Nein!*"

"The devil you have!" the Marshal said
To the lady from over the Rhine;
And again she shook her flaxen head,
And civilly answered, "*Nein!*"

"Now what do you mean by shaking your head,
And always answering 'Nine'?"
"*Ich kann nicht Englisch!*" civilly said
The lady from over the Rhine.

John Godfrey Saxe [1816–1887]

INDEX TO
THE 1810 CENSUS
OF VIRGINIA

Compiled by

ELIZABETH PETTY BENTLEY

Baltimore
GENEALOGICAL PUBLISHING CO., INC.
1980

FOREWORD

This index consists of an alphabetical list of the heads of households in the 1810 Federal Census of Virginia. First the family name of the head of household is given, followed by the Christian name, then the county of residence (abbreviated), and finally the page number of the census schedule. Table I, in the front matter, contains a list of the counties, the abbreviations used in this index, and the roll number of the National Archives' microfilm copy. Table II lists the counties in the order they appear on the census film, the page numbers covered, and other information essential to the reader.

The researcher will undoubtedly want to consult the original source material. Microfilm copies of the census may be purchased from the Publication Sales Branch (NATS), National Archives (GSA), Washington, D.C. 20408. Their catalogue lists the Virginia 1810 returns as Micropublication number M252, rolls 66-71. The microfilm can also be obtained on interlibrary loan from the Regional Branches of the National Archives. For the address of the branch serving your region, request the National Archives' free pamphlet, GS DC 75-8250. The branch libraries of the Church of Jesus Christ of Latter-day Saints can also order microfilm copies of the census to be viewed at their branches. For the address of the branch nearest you, write to The Genealogical Department, 50 E. North Temple, Salt Lake City, Utah 84150. Photocopies of single pages of the census may be obtained from either of these agencies.

Along with the name of the head of household, in the original census, the following twelve columns were filled in with an appropriate entry by the enumerator, left to right: white males under 10 years of age, white males from 10-16 years of age, white males from 16-26 years of age, white males from 26-44 years of age, white males from 45 and upwards (then the same five categories for white females), all other free persons (except Indians, who were not taxed), and slaves. These headings do not generally appear at the top of every page.

The Virginia 1810 films are generally clear, with the notable exception of Bedford County. Where the film is illegible, the public is permitted to use the bound negative photostatic copies on deposit at the Central Search Room of the National Archives in Washington. It should be noted that the film copies were made from the original returns, and some tears in the originals may have occurred after the photostats were made. Unfortunately, some attempts were made at writing over names on the photostats and some of the page numbers were added after these copies were made.

Every effort has been made, using both the film and the photostatic copies, to interpret questionable names. No visible entry, including names which were crossed out, has been intentionally omitted from this index. When one or more illegible letters has been omitted, the gap is filled with elipses (. . .), for example C . . ., which appears before names beginning with Ca. Totally illegible surnames appear before names beginning with A. They are preceded by entries for which no surname was given. These are designated by three hyphens (- - -).

iii

An attempt has been made in the case of questionable interpretations of handwriting to refer the reader to alternative index entries. For example, "see Janes" appears at the conclusion of the *Jones* entries. Similar notations refer the reader to alternative phonetic spellings such as *Pflanigan* for *Flanigan*, or to entries where the surname was used as a given name or the order of the names had been inverted and it is unclear which is the surname. The reader should also be aware that some enumerators employed the British order of inversion: last name, middle name, first name, instead of the usual American form: last name, first name, middle name.

In addition, the enumerator may have made no attempt whatever to discover the correct spelling of a name, simply spelling it as he heard it pronounced. The reader ought to try to imagine possible misinterpretations by substituting double letters for single ones, and vice versa, and replacing letters with similar sounds such as *d* for *t*, *y* for *i*, and *a* for *er*, or with similar shapes such as *e* for *i*, *L* for *S*, and *R* for *B*. Since *I* and *J* are practically indistinguishable when written as initials, they have been consistently indexed as *J*. No attempt has been made in this index to correct spellings. Abbreviations, too, have been transcribed as they appear. Superscript abbreviations such as *Jon*^{n} appear as Jonn. in the index. And "Brown, John [his] estate" is the convention adopted to handle the census reading "John Brown's estate."

There are many reasons why a particular individual might not appear in the census. Among others, the reader will note that the returns of several counties are missing (Cabell, Grayson, Greenbrier, Halifax, Hardy, Henry, James City, King William, Lee, Louisa, Mecklenburg, Nansemond, Northampton, Orange, Patrick, Pittsylvania, Russell, and Tazewell). Then, since the 1810 Federal Census listed only heads of families by name, other family members do not appear in the returns. Also, an individual may be listed with a family of a different surname as a boarder, laborer, or student. He may have avoided enumeration out of fear or superstition, or he may simply have been left out because of his remote residence or temporary absence from home.

Multiple listing in the index of the same person may occur because the names of the enumerators are included as well as clerks, marshalls, assistants, and owners of establishments where the returns were posted for public inspection. These names generally appear in affidavits at the end of each county's list. In addition, some people owned land in more than one county and appear in both lists or are shown as overseers, quartermasters, executors of estates, or as heads of companies employing groups of people who lived on the premises.

In compiling this index I have intentionally refrained from consulting other published indexes of these same returns in order to preserve the integrity of the work, but I recommend these indexes to the reader as alternative interpretations.

Thanks are due my family, who spent hours putting the names in alphabetical order and encouraged me to finish the work. Again, thanks to Dr. Michael Tepper, editor-in-chief of Genealogical Publishing Company, for his patience.

Elizabeth Petty Bentley

TABLE I

County	Abbreviation	Roll no.
Accomack	Acc	66
Albemarle	Alb	66
Amelia	Aml	66
Amherst	Amh	66
Augusta	Ags	66
Bath	Bth	66
Bedford	Bdf	67
Berkeley (W. Va.)	Brk	66
Botetourt	Btt	66
Brooke (W. Va.)	Br	66
Brunswick	Brn	66
Buckingham	Bck	66
Cabell (W. Va.)		missing
Campbell	Cmp	68
Caroline	Crl	67
Charles City	Chc	68
Charlotte	Chr	68
Chesterfield	Chs	67
Culpeper	Clp	68
Cumberland	Cmb	68
Dinwiddie	Dnw	67
Elizabeth City	Elc	68
Essex	Ess	68
Fairfax	Frf	68
Fauquier	Fqr	68
Fluvanna	Flv	68
Franklin	Frn	68
Frederick	Frd	68
Giles	Gls	68
Gloucester	Glc	68
Goochland	Gch	68
Grayson		missing
Greenbrier (W. Va.)		missing
Greensville	Grn	68
Halifax		missing
Hampshire (W. Va.)	Hmp	69
Hanover	Hnv	69
Hardy (W. Va.)		missing
Harrison (W. Va.)	Hrr	69

v

Henrico	Hnr	69
Richmond City	Hnr	70
Henry		missing
Isle of Wight	Isw	69
James City		missing
Jefferson (W. Va.)	Jff	69
Kanawah (W. Va.)	Knw	69
King and Queen	Knq	69
King George	Kng	69
King William		missing
Lancaster	Lnc	69
Lee (recapitulation only)		69
Loudoun	Ldn	69
Louisa		missing
Lunenburg	Lnn	69
Madison	Mds	69
Mason (W. Va.)	Msn	69
Mathews	Mth	69
Mecklenburg		missing
Middlesex	Mdd	69
Monongalia (W. Va.)	Mnn	69
Monroe (W. Va.)	Mnr	70
Montgomery	Mnt	70
Nansemond		missing
Nelson	Nls	70
New Kent	Nwk	70
Norfolk	Nrf	70
Norfolk Borough	Nrf	67
Northampton		missing
Northumberland	Nrt	70
Nottoway	Ntt	70
Ohio (W. Va.)	Oho	70
Orange		missing
Patrick		missing
Pendleton (W. Va.)	Pnd	70
Pittsylvania		missing
Powhatan	Pwh	70
Prince Edward	Pre	70
Prince George	Prg	70
Prince William	Prw	70
Princess Anne	Pra	70
Randolph (W. Va.)	Rnd	70
Richmond	Rch	70
Rockbridge	Rck	70
Rockingham	Rcm	67
Russell		missing

vi

TABLE II

ROLL 66

Accomack Co., pp. 2, 1, 3-139. St. George Parish, pp. 2, 1, 3-71. Accomack Parish, pp. 72-138.

Albemarle Co., pp. 147-215. St. Ann's Parish, pp. 147-178 (part); pp. 166A, 166B, and 166C are all indexed as 166. Town of Charlottesville, pp. 178 (part)-180 (part). Town of New York, p. 180 (part). Town of Warren, pp. 180 (part)-181. Town of Milton, p. 182. Town of N. Milton, p. 183. Fredericksville Parish, pp. 184-213.

Amelia Co., pp. 221, 222, 224, 223, 248-225 (backwards), 249-254.

Amherst Co., pp. 255-306.

Augusta Co., pp. 307, 312-410. Waynesboro, pp. 406 (part)-409 (part). Greenville, pp. 409 (part)-410 (part). Middlebrook, p. 410 (part).

Bath Co., pp. 450-412 (backwards).

Berkeley Co., pp. 599-493 (backwards). Martinsburg, pp. 599-591 (part).

Botetourt Co., pp. 602-671.

Brooke Co., pp. 673-699. Page 698a is indexed as 698.

Brunswick Co., pp. 701-770. St. Andrews Parish, pp. 701-741. Mehersin Parish, pp. 742-769 (part). Freetown, pp. 769 (part)-770.

Buckingham Co., pp. 773-847. Pages 773a and 773b are indexed as 773; p. 775a is indexed as 775.

ROLL 67

Bedford Co., pp. 452-491. Note that there are two columns of names on each page. The unnumbered pages following pp. 457 and 458 are indexed as 457 and 458 respectively.

Caroline Co., pp. 885-935.

Chesterfield Co., pp. 52-70, machine stamped on every other page. Connected leaves are indexed by the number in the lower left hand corner of the second leaf. Town of Manchester, pp. 67-68. In the Hundred Neck, p. 69.

Dinwiddie Co., pp. 137-171. Pages 143 and 144, 147 and 148 are reversed. All names beginning with A and many beginning with B appear to be missing from these returns. Also note that Petersburg Town follows Norfolk Co. on this roll.

Norfolk Co., Norfolk Borough, pp. 886-929. The final unnumbered page is indexed as 929. Note that the remainder of Norfolk Co. appears on roll 70.

Dinwiddie Co., Petersburg Town, pp. 325-336. The "a" and "b" pages are indexed with their number only, that is, 326, 328, 330, 332, 334, and 336. Note that the remainder of the county precedes Norfolk Co. on this roll.

Rockingham Co., pp. 1-44. Harrisonburg, pp. 1-3 (part). Port Republic, p. 3 (part). New Haven, p. 3 (part). Keezletown, p. 12 (part).

ROLL 68

Campbell Co., pp. 847-885. The two unnumbered pages following p. 869 are indexed as 869. Lynchburg, pp. 847-855 (part).

Charles City Co., pp. 938-962.

Charlotte Co., pp. 39-72, machine stamped on every other page. The unnumbered pages are indexed with the number of the preceding page.

Culpeper Co., pp. 1-96.

Cumberland Co., pp. 97-135. The two unnumbered pages following p. 105 are indexed as 105.

Elizabeth City Co., pp. 174-193. Hampton, pp. 176-181.

Essex Co., pp. 194-225.

Fairfax Co., pp. 228-324. No numbers are visible on pp. 228 and 229, but they are indexed in sequence. The two unnumbered pages following p. 245 are indexed as 245.

Fauquier Co., pp. 339-423.

Fluvanna Co., pp. 448-429 (backwards). No number is visible on p. 448, but it is indexed in sequence. Bernardsburg, p. 447 (part). Columbia, pp. 439 (part)-438 (part).

Franklin Co., pp. 450-503.

Frederick Co., pp. 506-609. Winchester, pp. 506-517. Stephensburg, pp. 518-521. Front Royal, pp. 522-523. Middletown, pp. 524-525. Berryville, p. 526. Millwood, p. 527. Kernstown, p. 528. Pughtown, p. 529.

Giles Co., pp. 614-644.

Gloucester Co., pp. 646-679. The few persons from Gloucester Town and Botetourt listed throughout this partially alphabetical list are noted in the index entry.

Goochland Co., pp. 682-723.

Greensville Co., pp. 444-457, machine stamped on every other page. The unnumbered page is indexed with the number of the page following it. Note that the second leaf of p. 451 and the first leaf of p. 452 are reversed.

ROLL 69

Hampshire Co., pp. 756-839. Romney, pp. 756-757 (part). Frankfort, pp. 757 (part)-759 (part). Springfield, pp. 759 (part)-760 (part).

Hanover Co., pp. 844-902.

Harrison Co., pp. 904-967.

Henrico Co., pp. 111-133, handwritten in the upper right hand corner on every other page. The unnumbered pages are indexed with the number of the preceding page. Also note that Richmond City appears on roll 70.

Isle of Wight Co., pp. 2-47.

Jefferson Co., pp. 54-110. Charlestown, pp. 54-58 (part). Smithfield, pp. 59 (part)-61 (part). Harper's Ferry, pp. 68 (part)-72 (part). Shepherdstown, p. 99-?; no end point is indicated for Shepherdstown.

Kanawha Co., pp. 1-14, handwritten at the center top of every other page. The unnumbered or "A" page is indexed with the number of the preceding page. The final unnumbered page is indexed as 14.

King and Queen Co., pp. 154-182. Page numbers 155-164 are not visible on the film, but they are indexed in sequence.

King George Co., pp. 188-225. Note British inversion.

Lancaster Co., pp. 336-369.

Lee Co., p. 227. This is only a statistical summary. No names are given.

Loudoun Co., pp. 232-325. Pages 321 and 322 are reversed. Town of Hillsboro, p. 301 (part). Middleburg, pp. 301 (part)-302 (part). Leesburg, pp. 302 (part)-306. Waterford, pp. 307-308 (part).

Lunenburg Co., pp. 327, 330-367, 370, 371.

Madison Co., pp. 374, 373, 376, 375, 377-418. Note British inversion.

Mason Co., pp. 420-434.

Mathews Co., pp. 435-454. Pages 435 and 436 are reversed.

Middlesex Co., pp. 458-474. The few persons from Urbanna listed throughout this partially alphabetical list are noted in the index entry.

Monongalia Co., pp. 478, 487, 488, 479-486, 489-558.

ROLL 70

Monroe Co., pp. 562-600, 603, 602. The two unnumbered pages following p. 602 are indexed as 602.

Montgomery Co., pp. 606-671. The few persons from Christiansburg are noted in the index entry.

Nelson Co., pp. 676-740.

New Kent Co., pp. 742-775. The first page is unnumbered and is indexed as 742. Note British inversion.

Norfolk Co., pp. 788-842. The two unnumbered pages following p. 842 are indexed as 842. Parish of St. Bride's, pp. 788-809. Elizabeth River Parish, pp. 810-813 and 838-841. Parish of Portsmouth, not including the town, pp. 814-825. Town of Portsmouth, Parish of Portsmouth, pp. 826-835. Town of Gosport, Parish of Portsmouth, pp. 836-837. Note that Norfolk Borough appears on roll 67.

Northumberland Co., pp. 970-978, 981-1000, 1002, 1001, 979, 980.

Nottoway Co., pp. 1-23, handwritten in the upper left hand corner.

Ohio Co., pp. 1-26, handwritten in the upper left hand corner of every other page. The unnumbered page is indexed with the number of the page preceding it. Wheeling, pp. 1-3 (part). West Liberty, p. 3 (part). Elizabeth Town, p. 3 (part).

Pendleton Co., pp. 214-228, handwritten in the upper right hand corner of every other page. The unnumbered page is indexed with the number of the preceding page. Franklin Town, pp. 226 (part)-227.

Powhatan Co., pp. 1-15, handwritten along the right edge, not the original numbers in the lower left hand corner.

Prince Edward Co., pp. 554-594.

Prince George Co., pp. 529-551.

Prince William Co., pp. 527-497 (backwards). Haymarket, p. 513 (part). Buckland, p. 513 (part). Occoquan, p. 501 (part). Dumfries, pp. 501 (part)-498.

Princess Anne Co., pp. 436-487, 490.

Randolph Co., pp. 416-431. Beverly, pp. 416-?; the end point for Beverly is not clear.

Richmond Co., pp. 390-413.

Henrico Co., City of Richmond, pp. 1-36, handwritten in the upper left hand corner of every other page. The unnumbered page is indexed with the number of the preceding page. The remainder of Henrico Co. appears on roll 69.

Rockbridge Co., pp. 262-300, 304, 303, 302, 301, 305-311. Lexington, pp. 262-265 (part). A partially illegible location, . . . field, p. 265 (part).

ROLL 71

Shenandoah Co., pp. 163-261. Page 163 is a typed copy of p. 164 and part of p. 165; some names on p. 163 do not appear twice in the index because of differences in interpretation of the handwritten copy. Woodstock, pp. 246-251. New Market, pp. 252-254. Strasburg, pp. 255-257.

Southampton Co. pp. 148-162 (161A and 161B are indexed as 161); 126-132, 137-146; 844-860, 864; 866-882. This county's returns are divided into four groups labeled A, B, D, and C.

Spotsylvania Co., pp. 66-120. Corporation of Fredricksburg, pp. 107-120.

Stafford Co., pp. 20-63. The unnumbered page following p. 63 is indexed as 63. Aquia, pp. 21 (part)-22 (part). Falmouth, pp. 34-36 (part).

Surry Co., pp. 398-621.

Sussex Co., pp. 624-676. The unnumbered page following p. 674 is indexed as 674, and the unnumbered page following p. 676 is indexed as 676.

Warwick Co., pp. 678-685. Pages 681A and 681B are indexed as 681. The names on p. 685 are all crossed out and supply no data; it appears to duplicate names on pp. 678-680. A nearly duplicate list visible to the left of the primary list is much fainter, possibly erased. Where the given name is written in full there, it is indexed in full even though the primary list gives only an abbreviation. There seems to be one additional name on the left hand list on p. 678.

Washington Co., pp. 688-761.

Westmoreland Co., pp. 766-791.

Wood Co., pp. 1-19.

Wythe Co., pp. 818-863.

York Co., pp. 870-872, 872A, 873, 875-886, 888, 887, 889, 890. The unnumbered page following p. 890 is indexed as 890. Page 872A is indexed as 872. Residents of Williamsburg and York Town are noted throughout this partially alphabetical list. In the index, this is noted with a (W) for Williamsburg or a (Y) for York Town following the given name of the individual.

INDEX TO THE 1810 CENSUS
OF VIRGINIA

INDEX TO THE 1810 CENSUS
OF VIRGINIA

---, ---, Ann Smith
  Acadamy 265 Rck
---, D.S.C. Company 814 Nrf
---, Do [Ditto for Peter
  Crutchfield?] Public
  Guard 18 Hnr
---, Fort Powhatan 540 Prg
---, George & William
  Mine 28 Hnr
---, In Jail 517 Frd
---, In the Poor
  house 517 Frd
---, Lewis Fort 860 Sth
---, Manchester Turnpike
  Co. 61 Chs
---, Negroes of Colour,
  Li...in H. Martin 685 Nls
---, Overseer of
  Poor 306 Ldn
---, Parish of St.
  Brides 915 Nrf
---, Poor House 326 Dnw
---, Poor House 765 Nwk
---, Poor House 915 Nrf
---, Poor House 535 Prg
---, Poor House 471 Pra
---, Poor of the
  County 412 Fqr
---, Poore House 133 Hnr
---, Poors house 32 Isw
---, The poor of Sd.
  [said] County 510 Prw
---, Washing... ...damy
  [Washington Acad-
  emy?] 265 Rck
Aaron 251 Ldn
Aaron, (FB) 436 Pra
Aaron, F.N. 624 Sss
Abigale, (F. Negroe) 343 Fqr
Ablinia 6 Hnr
Abraham, (F. Negroe) 380 Fqr
Adam, free negro 646 Glc
Aggy, free negro 646 Glc
Agnis, a free negro 970 Nrt
Allens 520 Prw
Amey 742 Nwk
Amey, (free) 498 Prw
Ambrose, free negro 231 Frf
Amey, free negro 70 Chs
Anakey, free negro 70 Chs
Anthony, a free negro 977 Nrt
Bazil 815 Hmp
Beck of Tynew, (F.N.) 30 Isw
Beck of Watkins,
  (F.N.) 21 Isw
Belinda, F.N. 625 Sss
Bengamin 794 Hmp
Betty 743 Nwk
Betty 210 Shn
Betty, a free negro 973 Nrt
Betty, free negro 235 Frf

Billey, free negro 235 Frf
Black James 575 Frd
Black John 508 Prw
Black Mingo 514 Frd
Black Simon 514 Frd
Black Simon 577 Frd
Blackwell's Lucy
  (F.N.) 9 Clp
Bob, (F. Negroe) 15 Clp
Bridget 871 Yrk
Brown's Harry (F.N.) 9 Clp
Brum, (FB) 437 Pra
Cain 872 Yrk
Cambridge 243 Ldn
Cate, f. negro 245 Frf
Cato 445 Bth
Cesar 277 Ldn
Charity, (free) 860 Hnv
Charles, a free negro 974 Nrt
Charles, f. negro 246 Frf
Charles, (free) 855 Hnv
Charles (free negro) 650 Glc
Charles, (Free
  Negroe) 393 Fqr
Charlotte, a free
  negro 975 Nrt
China, (F.B.) 448 Pra
Clem 268 Ldn
Cooper George, F.N. 165 Knq
Cupid 3 Hnr
Daniel 820 Hmp
Daniel, a free negro 977 Nrt
Danl., f. negro 248 Frf
Daphney 435 Bth
David, (free N.) 533 Brk
Diannah 2 Hnr
Dick 771 Wst
Diley, (free) 144 Dnw
Dinah 769 Hmp
Dolly 771 Hmp
Egbon, & Son 8 Hnr
Elizabeth 197 Shn
Ellenor 595 Brk
Emanuel, a free
  negro 978 Nrt
Embrow 2 Hnr
Esam 422 Bth
Esther 793 Hmp
Esther, (free) 527 Brk
Fanny, F.N. 637 Sss
Fanny, Free 386 Mds
Fanny, (free) 501 Prw
Fanny, (free Neg) 509 Brk
Fellis 772 Wst
Fitzwilson 31 Hnr
Flora, (F. Black) 461 Bdf
Flora, f. negro 255 Frf
Frank 772 Wst
Frank, (free negro) 654 Glc
Free Adam 598 Frd
Free Aggy 870 Yrk

Free Alse 579 Frd
Free Ben 583 Frd
Free Cansea 548 Frd
Free Charles 849 Hnv
Free Cinthia 534 Frd
Free Cuffa 128 Cmb
Free Esther 872 Yrk
Free Godfrey 875 Yrk
Free Isaac 529 Frd
Free Jack 877 Yrk
Free Jemmy 146 Dnw
Free Jenny 839 Wyt
Free Joseph 583 Frd
Free Joshua 583 Frd
Free Marks 235 Aml
Free Molly 815 Nrf
Free Ned 371 Ags
Free Patty 584 Frd
Free Philip 534 Frd
Free Primace 453 Mth
Free Richard 527 Brk
Free Sally 883 Yrk
Free Sampson 849 Hnv
Free Sarah 513 Prw
Free Sarah 890 Yrk
Free Suckey 890 Yrk
Free Tom 453 Mth
Free Will 439 Flv
Free Will 596 Frd
Free William 583 Frd
Freeborn Susan 117 Spt
Gilbert, (free Neg) 509 Brk
Godfrey 754 Nwk
Grace 592 Brk
Grace, F.N. 165 Knq
Hachley's Liddy,
  (F.N.) 41 Clp
Hager, (Free) 579 Brk
Hannah, (free) 149 Dnw
Hannah, (free) 868 Hnv
Harris, F.N. 640 Sss
Harry 258 Ldn
Harry 774 Wst
Harry, free negro 70 Chs
Harry, 3rd. 288 Ldn
Harvey 590 Brk
Hary 309 Ldn
Herman's (Plant.) 457 Pra
Hinah, free negro 261 Frf
Iddy 592 Brk
Indian Fanny 545 Prg
Isaac, freeman 855 Hnv
Isaac's Isaac 103 Acc
Ismenard 30 Hnr
Israel 877 Yrk
Jack, (free) 855 Hnv
Jacob 508 Prw
Jacob, (FB) 460 Pra
James, (free negro) 660 Glc
Jane 776 Wst
Jeffery 757 Nwk

Jeffery, (free) 514 Prw
Jenny, (free negro) 660 Glc
Jess, (free Neg.) 519 Brk
Jesse, f. negro 272 Frf
Jessee 508 Prw
Jessee, (free) 511 Prw
Jessee, (free negro) 660 Glc
Jim Boy, f. negro 271 Frf
Jno., (frenchman) 269 Frf
Joseph 820 Hmp
Joseph, a free negro 987 Nrt
Lamb, (F.B.) 463 Pra
Lett 223 Shn
Levinia, a free woman
  of couler 721 Wsh
Lewis 71 Clp
Lewis 14 Hnr
Lucas, f. negro 279 Frf
Lucindia 15 Hnr
Lucretia, f. negro 275 Frf
Lucy 422 Bth
Lucy 32 Hnr
Lucy, (fre) 547 Brk
Lucydia 14 Hnr
Lydda, & Daughters
  (Sampsons) 406 Mds
Mary, (F.Negroe) 412 Fqr
Mathews' Wm., F.N. 57 Clp
Matildia 18 Hnr
Michael R. 174 Shn
Milley, f. negro 285 Frf
Milly, F.N. 651 Sss
Molly, (FB) 469 Pra
Molly, (fre) 547 Brk
Murcah, (free negro) 665 Glc
Nancey, free negro 286 Frf
Nancy, (FB) 469 Pra
Nanny, free negro 665 Glc
Nat. 19 Hnr
Nat, free negro 286 Frf
Negro Caty, free 105 Jff
Nelly, f. negro 287 Frf
Neptune 847 Wth
Nero, a free Negro 991 Nrt
Nutty, (free) 898 Hnv
Old Psalter 510 Prw
Owen, (FB) 470 Pra
Parson's Eliza 471 Pra
Patience, (F. Negroe) 412 Fqr
Pattey 766 Nwk
Patty, (FB) 470 Pra
Peg of Jordan, (F.N.) 28 Isw
Peggy 782 Wst
Peggy, a free negro 992 Nrt
Pelino 329 Dnw
Peter, (fre) 547 Brk
Philis, a free negro 992 Nrt
Phil, F.N. 174 Knq
Phillip 30 Hnr
Phillis, (free) 157 Dnw
Pleasant, a free
  negro 992 Nrt
Pompey 916 Nrf
Priscilla Kit, f.
  negro 289 Frf
Rachael 445 Bth
Rachael, (free N.) 513 Brk
Rachael, (free N.) 517 Brk
Rachel 784 Wst
Rachel, free 855 Hnv
Rachell 17 Hnr
Ralph, F.N. 661 Sss
Rebecca, F.N. 660 Sss
Rhodahdaugh 28 Hnr
Richard, f. negro 295 Frf
Rose 241 Ldn
Rose 784 Wst
Rose, a free negro 993 Nrt
Rose, (free) 863 Hnv
Rosiener 237 Shn

Ruth 28 Hnr
Sackey, free negro 300 Frf
Salley, F.N. 178 Knq
Salley, (free) 856 Hnv
Sally 190 Shn
Sally, belonging to
  Geo. Blow 890 Yrk
Sam, (F.Negro) 54 Clp
Sampsons Lydda, &
  Daughters 406 Mds
Sarah 881 Cmp
Sarah, a free negro 996 Nrt
Sarah, Free Negro 876 Sth
Scipio, (F.Negroe) 15 Clp
Sencho, (F.Negroe) 420 Fqr
Sharlot 28 Hnr
Silvia 33 Hnr
Simon, (F.Negroe) [2] 994 Nrt
Spencer 309 Ldn
Stephen, bound for a
  term of years 447 Bth
Sukey, a free negro
  [2] 994 Nrt
Sute [Seste?] 216 Pnd
Tarr 445 Bth
Tiller, free negro 307 Frf
Tiller, free negro 308 Frf
Tom 208 Shn
Toney 788 Wst
Venus, free 849 Hnv
Vilett 19 Hnr
Viniah, (FB) 477 Pra
Violet 593 Brk
Watters Ned, f. negro 317 Frf
Will, f. negro 312 Frf
William 544 Brk
William [no numbers
  filled in] 880 Sth
Winnifred, a free
  negro 998 Nrt
Winny, (free) 518 Prw
York 591 Brk
see John, Jube, Old
..., ... 234 Aml
... 882 Cmp
... 54 Chs
... 65 Chs
... [2] 67 Chs
... 68 Chs
... 757 Hmp
... 758 Hmp
... 451 Mth
... 454 Mth
... 838 Nrf
... 970 Nrt
... [4] 303 Rck
... [2] 304 Rck
... 165 Shn
...jah [?] 166 Shn
Co... 756 Hmp
D... [crossed out] 10 Knw
Elizabeth, of C. 42 Stf
J... 304 Rck
Jam... 756 Hmp
Jas. 756 Hmp
Nancy 454 Mth
Sally 453 Mth
Samuel 58 Chs
William 847 Cmp
Wm. 454 Mth
...adey, Thomas 865 Cmp
...amp...on, Peter 7 Isw
...ampbell, John 271 Rck
...ang, Mary 273 Rck
...anham, Edward 303 Amh
...ard, Hugh 304 Amh
...atterson, ... 300 Rck
...avis, ... 835 Bck
...d, Joseph [crossed
  out] 267 Rck

...der..., John 841 Nrf
...e, Polly 336 Dnw
...ens, James 509 Prw
...id, William 848 Cmp
...ime, George 562 Mnr
...imon see Miller
...inich, ... 303 Rck
...kslager, Jacob 758 Hmp
...law, Michl. 301 Rck
...ller, ... 757 Hmp
...m see ...msen
...msen, Benjamin 3 Isw
...ner see Powner
...ns, Henry 41 Stf
...olph, John 12 Wod
...oman, ... 759 Hmp
...oover, Elender 447 Bth
...oway, Elizabeth 43 Stf
...p, Francis 18 Oho
...rim, George 562 Mnr
...s, ... 758 Hmp
...therling, ... 164 Shn
...thop see Shop
...tt, ... 303 Rck
  Elizabeth 69 Chs
  Joh... 304 Rck
  Sarah 223 Ess
...udd, ... 58 Chs
...w, Anthony 454 Mth
...well, Robt. L. 262 Rck
...x, ... 64 Chs

--- A ---

A..., ... [2] 452 Bdf
  ... [all names beginning with
  A are missing] 138 Dnw
  John 452 Bdf
  T... 452 Bdf
  Thomas 452 Bdf
A...de..., William 452 Bdf
A...der..., ... 452 Bdf
A...enger see Arlenger
A...rs, ... 452 Bdf
Aaims, John 680 Br
Abbey, David 56 Chs
  Dean 330 Dnw
Abbit, Abner 938 Hrr
  Jacob 938 Hrr
Abbot, Andrew 604 Btt
  Benjamin 801 Bck
  John 604 Btt
  John 565 Mnr
  Joseph 567 Mnr
  Lucy 119 Spt
  Thos. 604 Btt
  see Bundwick
Abbott, Ann 72 Acc
  Anna 3 Clp
  Elijah 24 Stf
  Feilding 42 Stf
  Garland 845 Hnv
  George 823 Bck
  James 567 Mnr
  James 887 Nrf
  James 198 Shn
  Jno. 4 Clp
  John 48 Stf
  Joseph 888 Crl
  Lucy 848 Hnv
  Mary 290 Ldn
  Molly 20 Stf
  Paul 5 Oho
  Samuel 198 Shn
  Thomas 72 Acc
  William 578 Frd
  Wm. 2 Clp
Abdel, Revel 2 Acc

Abel, Alexander	354	Fqr	Jonathan, Sr.	437	Pra	Green	445	Grn
Christ.	284	Ldn	Thomas	437	Pra	Hannah	232	Frf
Cunrod	267	Ldn	Ackles, Abram	13	Oho	Henry	452	Bdf
Geo.	267	Ldn	James	7	Oho	Henry	954	Chc
Isbel	818	Wth	Acklin, Christopher [2]	714	Wsh	Henry	252	Ldn
John	83	Jff	Jas. V.	714	Wsh	Henry	267	Ldn
Lewis	819	Wth	John	714	Wsh	Henry	625	Sss
Michael	819	Wth	Acles see Ackes			Henry	743	Wsh
Abell, James	511	Prw	Acom, Solomon	2	Acc	Hugh	303	Rck
John	148	Alb	Acra, James	646	Glc	Humphrey	15	Rcm
William	506	Prw	Jno.	646	Glc	Isaac	625	Sss
Abercromby see Acromby			Mary	646	Glc	Jack	56	Chs
Aberdeen, Henry	826	Nrf	Acre, Achilles	154	Knq	Jacob	73	Acc
Abernathy, Ann	759	Hmp	Sarah	742	Nwk	Jacob	758	Hmp
David	330	Lnn	Seaton	154	Knq	Jacob	936	Hrr
Elisha	702	Brn	Acred, Alexr.	188	Kng	Jacob	23	Oho
Elizabeth	702	Brn	William	189	Kng	James	41	Chr
Frederick	702	Brn	Acree, Jno.	880	Hnv	James	105	Cmb
Henry	702	Brn	Joshua	880	Hnv	James	230	Frf
James	573	Brk	Thos.	879	Hnv	James	392	Fqr
James	702	Brn	Acres, Agnes	870	Cmp	James	614	Gls
Jarratt	702	Brn	Burwell 476 Frn			James	445	Grn
Jno., Sen.	702	Brn	Daniel	475	Frn	James	288	Ldn
John	759	Hmp	Gasper	290	Ldn	James	527	Prw
John	798	Hmp	James	475	Frn	James	598	Srr
John, 1st.	702	Brn	James	521	Prw	James	624	Sss
Martha	702	Brn	Jesse	273	Ldn	Jessee	702	Brn
Miles	702	Brn	John	479	Frn	Jno.	4	Clp
Samuel	759	Hmp	Nathaniel	475	Frn	Jno.	230	Frf
Samuel	798	Hmp	Samuel	476	Frn	Jno.	879	Hnv
William	445	Grn	Thomas	474	Frn	Jno.	260	Ldn
William	759	Hmp	Thomas Tom	210	Ess	Jno.	849	Sth
Wm.	574	Brk	Walter	244	Ldn	Jno., President	232	Frf
Abernethy, Jos.	821	Nrf	William	475	Frn	John	73	Acc
Able, Antho.	478	Mnn	William, Sr.	476	Frn	John	224	Aml
John	604	Btt	Acromby, Robt.	479	Mnn	John	452	Bdf
Martin	478	Mnn	Acton, John	262	Rck	John	603	Btt
Abney, Isabella	398	Ags	Joshua	603	Btt	John	860	Cmp
Wm.	314	Ags	Ad..., Anny	452	Bdf	John	947	Chc
Abnick, Jacob	221	Shn	Adair, Cors.	314	Ags	John	232	Frf
Aboot, James	70	Jff	James	267	Rck	John	411	Fqr
Abrahams, Daniel	693	Br	James, Jr.	611	Mnt	John	441	Flv
Jacob L.	801	Bck	James, Sr.	611	Mnt	John	564	Frd
Abrahem, Levi	313	Ags	Jas.	478	Mnn	John	743	Nwk
Abram, Adam	769	Brn	John	282	Rck	John	21	Oho
Abrams, Charles	1	Hnr	Mary	73	Acc	John	411	Rch
Depy	29	Hnr	Saml.	282	Rck	John	14	Rcm
Lemwel	848	Sth	William	563	Mnr	John, Sr.	948	Chc
Abrel, Joseph	831	Hmp	Adam, Jas.	336	Lnc	Jonathan	919	Hrr
Abrey, Eve	9	Rcm	Adams, Abednego	3	Clp	Jonathan	726	Wsh
Absheir, Abram	477	Frn	Absolom	467	Frn	Jordan	624	Sss
Edward	472	Frn	Amos	784	Hmp	Joshua	730	Wsh
Isaac	473	Frn	Amos	624	Sss	Josiah	341	Fqr
James	473	Frn	Ann H.	598	Srr	Leonard	108	Spt
Luke	472	Frn	Bartholomew	614	Gls	Leonnah	41	Chr
Peter	473	Frn	Betcy	487	Frn	Lewis	11	Hnr
Abslom, James	436	Pra	Charity	73	Acc	Littleton, Jr.	376	Fqr
John	436	Pra	Charles	397	Fqr	Littleton, Senr	341	Fqr
Aby, Jonas	507	Frd	Charles	500	Prw	Margaret	868	Sth
Abzey see Abrey			Christopher	7	Oho	Mary	293	Amh
Accinelly, John	830	Nrf	Claiborne	545	Prw	Mary	41	Chr
Acers, Adam	661	Mnt	Dancy	224	Aml	Mary	877	Sth
Austin	641	Mnt	Dancy	702	Brn	Mathew	236	Ldn
Blackburn	661	Mnt	Daniel	425	Rnd	Milly	208	Ess
Clayburn	630	Mnt	David	702	Brn	Nathl	919	Hrr
Jacob	613	Mnt	David	863	Cmp	Nelson	888	Crl
John	661	Mnt	David	41	Chr	Patsey	2	Hnr
Jonathan	661	Mnt	David	758	Hmp	Pellathiel	554	Pre
Solomon	661	Mnt	Davy	398	Ags	Peter	341	Fqr
William	661	Mnt	Edward	233	Frf	Peter	743	Nwk
see Áckes, Acres			Edward	535	Prg	Polley	124	Hnr
Acherd, Andrew	432	Msn	Edwin	445	Grn	Polly	849	Sth
Acheson, James	13	Oho	Elizabeth	702	Brn	Prudence	13	Ntt
John	13	Oho	Elizabeth	154	Knq	Rebecca	248	Aml
Ackes, Wm.	653	Mnt	Epaphroditus	742	Nwk	Richard	791	Bck
see Acres, Acles			Francis	232	Frf	Richard	682	Gch
Ackiss, Elizabeth	436	Pra	Francis	341	Fqr	Richd.	258	Ldn
Francis, Jr.	436	Pra	George	880	Hnv	Richd.	161	Sth
Francis, Sr.	437	Pra	Gersham	824	Hmp	Richd., Col.	132	Hnr
Jonathan, Jr.	436	Pra	Gray E.	598	Srr	Robert	303	Ldn

Name	Page	Co.
Robert	857	Sth
Robert	818	Wth
Saml	231	Frf
Saml.	19	Hnr
Saml.	10	Rcm
Samuel	452	Bdf
Samuel	674	Br
Samuel	364	Fqr
Samuel	257	Ldn
Samuel	500	Prw
Sarah	879	Hnv
Stephen	72	Acc
Stephen	84	Spt
Susanna	510	Prw
Susannah	232	Frf
Tamor	849	Sth
Thomas	888	Crl
Thomas	41	Chr
Thomas	104	Cmb
Thomas	130	Cmb
Thomas	341	Fqr
Thomas	497	Frn
Thomas	445	Grn
Thomas	154	Knq
Thomas	330	Lnn
Thomas	532	Prg
Thomas	503	Prw
Thomas	10	Rcm
Thomas	625	Sss
Thomas F.	68	Chr
Thos.	879	Hnv
Thos.	467	Mnn
Turner	376	Fqr
Victory	478	Mnn
Walter	4	Clp
Walter	880	Hnv
Wesley	230	Frf
William	452	Bdf
William	674	Br
William	694	Br
William	131	Cmb
William	352	Fqr
William	529	Frd
William	598	Srr
William, (Son Jams)	42	Chr
William B.	41	Chr
Williams	181	Shn
Willm.	603	Btt
Wily	248	Aml
Withers	542	Prg
Wm.	398	Ags
Wm.	192	Elc
Wm.	276	Ldn
Wm.	297	Ldn
Wm.	304	Rck
Wm., (Overseer for Saml. White)	603	Btt
Wright	131	Cmb
Adcock, Jos.	742	Wsh
Joseph, (S Jo)	808	Bck
Samuel	130	Cmb
William	460	Frn
William, Sr.	825	Bck
see Edcock		
Adcocke, Amos	809	Bck
Asa	808	Bck
Carter	804	Bck
George, Jr.	808	Bck
George, Senr.	808	Bck
Henry	795	Bck
Henry	804	Bck
Henry	808	Bck
Henry	832	Bck
Hezekiah	808	Bck
John	804	Bck
John	808	Bck
Joseph	800	Bck
Joseph	804	Bck
Joseph	808	Bck
Joshua	804	Bck

Name	Page	Co.
Joshua	808	Bck
Matthew	831	Bck
Molley	832	Bck
Adcocky, Carter	808	Bck
Addams, Philip	857	Hnv
see Adams		
Adde, Peter	886	Nrf
Adderson, Anthony	37	Isw
John	189	Isw
Robert	436	Pra
Thomas	37	Isw
William, Jun.	37	Isw
William, Sen.	37	Isw
Addeson, Levi	812	Nrf
Addington, J. C.	886	Nrf
Addison, Arthur	73	Acc
Levi	886	Nrf
Obed	2	Acc
Richard	73	Acc
Richard	809	Hmp
William	2	Acc
William	3	Acc
William, senr.	3	Acc
Addy, William	85	Jff
Adelblue, Chas.	479	Mnn
Adell, Eli	517	Brk
Adelman, Elizabeth	313	Ldn
Adie, Benjamin	509	Prw
Benjamin	40	Stf
Elizabeth	21	Stf
William	21	Stf
Adire, William	590	Mnr
Adkerson, Thomas	452	Bdf
Thomas	10	Knw
Adkesson, James	148	Alb
Adkin, Bartholomew	614	Gls
Adkins, Abr.	270	Ldn
Absalom, G.	702	Brn
Benjamin	624	Sss
David	614	Gls
Edmund	603	Btt
James	615	Gls
John	624	Sss
Joshua	614	Gls
Moses	615	Gls
Noah	818	Wth
Randolp	614	Gls
Reuben	615	Gls
Reubin	614	Gls
Richard	702	Brn
Samuel	615	Gls
Sheard	614	Gls
Thos. T.	615	Gls
William [2]	624	Sss
William, (EN)	42	Chr
William, Jr.	624	Sss
Willis	624	Sss
Adkinson, Jno.	11	Hnr
Johnston	624	Sss
Maryann	119	Cmb
Samuel	119	Cmb
Thos.	132	Cmb
William	820	Hmp
Adney, Daniel	474	Frn
Thomas	474	Frn
Adoms, Jno.	450	Mth
John	33	Hnr
Richard	33	Hnr
Aeijener, George	286	Rck
Jacob	286	Rck
Jno., Sr.	286	Rck
John	286	Rck
Aere, Jacob	20	Bck
Aestoop, Hennery	330	Lnn
Aeyener see Aeijener		
Afford, Ben.	832	Nrf
Africa, Kedor	802	Nrf
Sally	802	Nrf
Wroght	801	Nrf
Agan, Thomas	374	Mds

Name	Page	Co.
Agar, Henry	646	Glc
Agee, A. J.	501	Frn
Ephriem	452	Frn
Herculus	778	Bck
Jacob	804	Bck
James, (Sr.)	824	Bck
Jesse	450	Frn
John	802	Bck
Joseph	824	Bck
Matthew	457	Frn
Thomas	Bck	824
see Ahee		
Ager, John	78	Jff
John	818	Wth
Saml.	230	Frf
Aggy, Free	870	Yrk
Agnew, John	679	Br
Agnue, ...	452	Bdf
Robert	72	Acc
Agy, Wm.	755	Wsh
Ahart, Abraham	374	Mds
Abram	615	Gls
John	374	Mds
Ahee, Benjamin	825	Bck
Aheman, John	439	Bth
Aib, Jacob	933	Hrr
Aid, James	604	Btt
Aider, Adam	487	Frn
Aikeen, James	106	Cmb
Aiken, ...l.	299	Rck
Aikers, Elijah	800	Bck
Elijah	813	Bck
Elijah	828	Bck
William	800	Bck
Aikman, Adam	795	Hmp
Ailen, Geo., Sen	312	Ags
Ailor, Fred.	313	Ags
George	312	Ags
Ailshite, Christian	190	Shn
John	182	Shn
Ailworth, James	72	Acc
William	73	Acc
Aimes, Benj., of L	3	Acc
Benjamin	2	Acc
Bridget	4	Acc
Chu...chwell	3	Acc
Elijah	4	Acc
James	2	Acc
Jesse	3	Acc
John	2	Acc
Joseph	3	Acc
Levi	2	Acc
Levin	3	Acc
Margaret	3	Acc
Richard	3	Acc
Shadrach	2	Acc
Thomas	3	Acc
Thomas	3	Oho
see Annis		
Aims see Aaims		
Ainot, John	563	Mnr
Ainsworth, Robert	68	Chs
Airbough, Jacob	4	Rcm
Jacob	5	Rcm
Airbuckle, Joseph	277	Amh
Aires, Francis	436	Pra
Tully	436	Pra
Airey, Philip	27	Rcm
Airhart, Henry	25	Rcm
Jaccob	25	Rcm
John	644	Mnt
Philip	25	Rcm
Airley, Henry	38	Rcm
Jacob	6	Rcm
John	38	Rcm
Airman, George	37	Rcm
John	8	Rcm
Michael	8	Rcm
Michael, (Jr.)	8	Rcm
Airs, Samuel	118	Cmb

William	766	Wst	Hezekiah	41	Chr	John	878	Cmp
Airy, Charles	24	Rcm	James	577	Mnr	John	330	Dnw
George	28	Rcm	James	398	Rch	John	583	Frd
George	41	Rcm	Jeremiah	330	Lnn	John	948	Hrr
William	28	Rcm	Jeremiah	397	Rch	John	517	Prw
Aisquith, Edward	99	Jff	Jno.	14	Knw	John	273	Rck
Aiter, Henry	32	Rcm	John	122	Cmb	John	290	Rck
Aits, John	927	Hrr	John	577	Mnr	Joseph	148	Alb
William	927	Hrr	John	412	Rch	Joseph	551	Brk
Wm.	928	Hrr	John S.	330	Lnn	Joseph	569	Brk
see Ates, Ats			Joseph	587	Mnr	Joseph	13	Oho
Aka, Martin	287	Ldn	Josiah	330	Lnn	Joseph	392	Rch
Martin, J.	287	Ldn	Richard	330	Lnn	Joseph	290	Rck
Simon	287	Ldn	Sally	585	Mnr	Lewis	34	Stf
Akard, John	614	Gls	Thomas	604	Btt	Lucy	189	Kng
Aker, Andrew	818	Wth	Thomas	563	Mnr	Mathew	577	Mnr
John	818	Wth	William	41	Chr	Michael	577	Mnr
Jonathan	818	Wth	William	398	Rch	Minor	154	Knq
Michael [2]	818	Wth	Alderton, William	773	Hmp	Phil. T.	188	Kng
Philip [2]	818	Wth	Aldrege, Thomas	275	Amh	Philip	517	Prw
Akerd, Fredrick	756	Wsh	Aldridge, Adam	547	Frd	Reuben	184	Alb
Akers, Hezekiah	94	Spt	Elizabeth	544	Prg	Richard	399	Fqr
John	773	Hmp	Ezekiel	634	Mnt	Richard	522	Prw
John	81	Spt	James	615	Gls	Richd.	154	Knq
Peter	41	Chr	Jeremiah	531	Prg	Robert	882	Cmp
William	865	Cmp	Jno.	652	Mnt	Robert	888	Crl
see Ackes			John	509	Frd	Robert	498	Prw
Akin, Joel	330	Lnn	Leonard	634	Mnt	Robt.	154	Knq
Joseph	330	Lnn	Michal	515	Frd	Robt.	298	Rck
Joseph, Sen.	861	Cmp	Susanna	545	Prg	Samuel	148	Alb
Js.	60	Chs	Wm.	634	Mnt	Sarah	535	Frd
Nancy	60	Chs	Wm.	539	Prg	Sarah	60	Stf
Pleasant	60	Chs	Ale, Valentine	599	Brk	Thomas	602	Frd
Pleasant	336	Dnw	Ale..., James	562	Mnr	Thomas	970	Nrt
Robt.	59	Chs	Alenberger, John	580	Brk	Thomas	33	Stf
Thomas	64	Chs	Alender, Jacob	535	Frd	Thos. P.	188	Kng
Thomas	69	Chs	Aleshere, Benedock	430	Msn	William	184	Alb
see Arms, Kers			Alestock, Absolom	446	Bth	William	330	Lnn
Akins, Alexander	20	Rcm	Alexande, Vincent	963	Hrr	William	517	Prw
John	588	Mnr	Wm. [2]	298	Rck	William	35	Stf
Willm.	647	Mnt	Alexander, Ambrose,			Wm.	312	Ags
Akinson, Mary	39	Isw	jr.	154	Knq	Wm.	315	Ags
Akles, Richd.	479	Mnn	Ambrose, ser.	154	Knq	Wm.	398	Ags
Alban, Joseph	924	Hrr	And.	279	Rck	Wm.	574	Brk
Albert, Arthur	15	Oho	And., (S. R.)	290	Rck	Wm.	293	Rck
Emanuel	9	Hnr	Andw.	582	Mnr	see Ale..., Alexead,		
George	508	Frd	Ann	61	Stf	Allexander		
Jacob	615	Gls	Archerbald	275	Amh	Alexandra, Betsey	73	Acc
James	614	Gls	Archibald D., Dr.	42	Chr	Alexeand, Edmund	791	Nrf
Michal	580	Frd	Charles	14	Knw	Alfford, George	598	Mnr
William	538	Frd	Charles	576	Mnr	John	577	Mnr
Alberton, Jesse	568	Mnr	Chs.	277	Ldn	John	818	Wth
Albin, Andrew	605	Frd	David	332	Dnw	Joseph	577	Mnr
James	555	Frd	Eli	184	Alb	Nancey	36	Rck
John	931	Hrr	Elisha	154	Knq	Thos.	581	Mnr
Robert	555	Frd	Ewel	970	Nrt	Alfred, Henry	587	Mnr
William	542	Frd	Feilding	39	Stf	Jno.	336	Lnc
Albright, Jno.	281	Rck	Gab.	314	Ags	Margt.	336	Lnc
Jno.	298	Rck	Gab., L. M.	314	Ags	Nathan	336	Lnc
Albrite, Philip	17	Oho	Gerard, Jr.	517	Prw	Saml.	336	Lnc
Albriton, Jno.	233	Frf	Gerard, Sr.	517	Prw	Alfreid, Geo.	312	Ags
Nancey	232	Frf	Hannah	154	Knq	Algier, Abraham	33	Rcm
Alburtis, John	595	Brk	Hatoway	262	Ldn	Algood, Danl.	18	Ntt
Alcock, Thomas	39	Stf	Hector	499	Prw	Wm.	17	Ntt
Alcocke, Wm.	3	Clp	Henry	888	Crl	Alison, Jos.	289	Rck
Aldane, Thomas	886	Nrf	Henry	562	Mnr	Wm.	313	Ags
Alday, Perrin	41	Chr	Hugh	312	Ags	Alkier, Adam	949	Hrr
Alder, ---, Hawkins &	22	Hnr	James	313	Ags	John	962	Hrr
George	591	Frd	James	683	Br	Mones	949	Hrr
James	270	Ldn	James	206	Ess	All, James	647	Mnt
Jno.	273	Ldn	James	13	Oho	James, Sr.	669	Mnt
John	818	Wth	Jane	148	Alb	Jeremiah [Jounnah?]	645	Mnt
Lattimore	314	Ldn	Jane	517	Prw	Johan	287	Rck
Markis	89	Jff	Jesse	970	Nrt	John	647	Mnt
Alderman, Elizabeth	424	Bth	Jno.	885	Hnv	Nancy	646	Mnt
Ezekiel	423	Bth	Jno.	272	Rck	see Ale		
Alders, Geo.	273	Ldn	John	148	Alb	Allamong, Christian	67	Jff
Alderson, Booker	122	Cmb	John	184	Alb	Allan, Carlton	886	Nrf
Bur	602	Btt	John [2]	314	Ags	Daniel A.	105	Cmb
Davis	594	Mnr	John	692	Br			

Name	Pg	Pl	Name	Pg	Pl	Name	Pg	Pl
Isham	112	Hnr	Hamlin	446	Grn	Judiah	12	Hnr
Margte.	886	Nrf	Hannah	299	Amh	Kewen	13	Hnr
Patsy	122	Hnr	Henry	2	Clp	Landon	3	Clp
Sally	115	Hnr	Henry	374	Mds	Levi	511	Prw
Thos.	886	Nrf	Heny	230	Frf	Lims	41	Chr
Wm.	573	Brk	Howell	742	Brn	Littlebury	122	Hnr
see Aller			Hugh	602	Btt	Malcolm, Jr.	604	Btt
Allason, David	374	Fqr	Isaac	516	Frd	Malcolm, Sr.	604	Btt
Allbeart, Peter	32	Rcm	Issabella	189	Kng	Mary	834	Bck
Allbright, Frederick	4	Rcm	James	248	Aml	Mary	350	Fqr
John	4	Rcm	James	307	Ags	Moses	602	Btt
Allcock, John	278	Amh	James	312	Ags	Moses	165	Shn
Joseph	280	Amh	James	2	Clp	Moses	738	Wsh
Richard	291	Amh	James	113	Cmb	Moss	230	Frf
Allcocke, Robert	148	Alb	James	126	Cmb	Nathaniel	888	Crl
Westin	184	Alb	James	208	Ess	Patty	888	Yrk
Alldaffer, John	7	Rcm	James	219	Ess	Peter	759	Wsh
Joseph	7	Rcm	James	908	Hrr	Polly	72	Acc
Allder, Barbara	35	Rcm	James	953	Hrr	Polly	676	Nls
Allegree, Daniel	447	Flv	James	189	Kng	Reubin	42	Chr
Wm.	26	Hnr	James	330	Lnn	Richard	121	Hnr
Allemong, Elizabeth	556	Frd	James	251	Ldn	Richard	742	Nwk
William	556	Frd	James	584	Mnr	Richard	23	Oho
Allen, ---, Ellis &	21	Hnr	James	742	Nwk	Richard	505	Prw
Abner	8	Hnr	James	554	Pre	Richd.	224	Aml
Amos	23	Hnr	James	193	Shn	Richd.	312	Ags
Andrew, (Overseer)	418	Fqr	James	706	Wsh	Richd.	21	Ntt
Andw.	590	Mnr	James A.	120	Cmb	Richd.	681	Wrw
Ann	185	Elc	James, free negro	231	Frf	Richd., ser.	681	Wrw
Archebald	178	Shn	James, jr.	312	Ags	Richmond	99	Cmb
Archer	554	Pre	James, jr.	3	Clp	Robert	279	Amh
Aron	199	Shn	James, Junr.	742	Nwk	Robert	602	Btt
Arthur	769	Brn	James, senr.	3	Clp	Robert	66	Chs
Barns	958	Hrr	Jane	18	Hnr	Robert	788	Hmp
Benja.	151	Sth	Jeconiah	677	Br	Robert	821	Hmp
Benjamin	107	Cmb	Jeremiah	703	Brn	Robert	188	Kng
Benjamin	114	Cmb	Jesse	802	Bck	Rodam	232	Frf
Benjamin	237	Shn	Jessee	504	Prw	Sally	452	Bdf
Charles	452	Bdf	Jessee	176	Shn	Saml.	224	Aml
Charles	98	Cmb	Jincy	326	Dnw	Saml., [his] est.	154	Knq
Charles	554	Pre	Jno.	3	Clp	Samuel	835	Bck
Charles C.	2	Clp	Jno.	230	Frf	Samuel	581	Mnr
Chas.	4	Clp	Jno., free negro	232	Frf	Samuel	677	Nls
Chloe	506	Prw	John	73	Acc	Samuel	554	Pre
Christian	122	Hnr	John	602	Btt	Samuel	9	Wod
Cynthia	887	Nrf	John	703	Brn	Samuel H.	299	Amh
Daniel	2	Acc	John	185	Elc	Samuel V.	554	Pre
Daniel	350	Fqr	John	540	Frd	Samul	23	Oho
Daniel, Jr.	224	Aml	John	445	Grn	Sarah	889	Crl
Daniel, Sr.	248	Aml	John	955	Hrr	Saunders	682	Gch
Daniel A.	554	Pre	John	6	Hnr	Silvanus	202	Ess
Danl.	314	Ags	John	9	Hnr	Simeon	133	Cmb
Danl.	10	Ntt	John	132	Hnr	Simon	595	Frd
David	230	Frf	John [2]	420	Msn	Thomas	3	Acc
David	534	Frd	John	433	Msn	Thomas	302	Amh
David	11	Hnr	John	434	Msn	Thomas	695	Br
David	28	Hnr	John	25	Oho	Thomas	888	Crl
Davis	193	Shn	John	534	Prg	Thomas	3	Clp
Dicy	326	Dnw	John	275	Rck	Thomas	821	Hmp
E. Nos	28	Hnr	John	295	Rck	Thomas	836	Hmp
Edward C.	554	Pre	John	176	Shn	Thomas, jr.	2	Clp
Edwd.	887	Nrf	John	199	Shn	Thomas, jr.	154	Knq
Edwd.	436	Pra	John	680	Wrw	Thomas, Junr.	163	Shn
Elijah	183	Shn	John	688	Wsh	Thomas, Junr.	164	Shn
Eliza	19	Hnr	John, Jun.	773	Hmp	Thomas, senr.	3	Clp
Eliza.	187	Elc	John, Sen.	773	Hmp	Thomas, Senr.	163	Shn
Elizabeth	447	Flv	John, Senr.	42	Chr	Thomas, Senr.	164	Shn
Elizabeth	785	Hmp	John A.	554	Pre	Thomas G.	154	Knq
Elizabeth B.	222	Ess	John C.	98	Cmb	Thos., senr.	2	Clp
Enoch	314	Ags	John G.	742	Nwk	Wesley	196	Shn
Erasmus	888	Crl	Jones	26	Hnr	William	224	Aml
Eunice	199	Shn	Jos.	478	Mnn	William	452	Bdf
Ezekiel	198	Shn	Joseph	401	Fqr	William	778	Bck
Fielding	2	Clp	Joseph	676	Nls	William	834	Bck
Francis	189	Kng	Joseph	9	Rck	William	888	Crl
Geo. N.	444	Flv	Joseph	165	Shn	William	109	Cmb
George	802	Bck	Joseph	199	Shn	William	446	Grn
George	543	Frd	Joseph, esq.	279	Rck	William	676	Nls
George	573	Mnr	Joseph, (of J)	177	Shn	William	743	Nwk
George, H.	374	Mds	Joshua	504	Prw	William	970	Nrt

Name	Pg	Code
William	198	Shn
William	116	Spt
William	50	Stf
William	598	Srr
William, Sr.	452	Bdf
William A.	554	Pre
William C.	98	Cmb
William M.	121	Cmb
Wilson	888	Crl
Winney	224	Aml
Wm.	55	Chs
Wm.	682	Gch
Wm.	17	Hnr
Wm.	277	Ldn
Wm.	317	Ldn
Wm.	582	Mnr
Wm. C.	97	Cmb
Wm. C.	135	Cmb
Wm. G.	2	Clp
Wm. L., has slaves in		
York County	888	Yrk
Wm. T.	703	Brn
Wyatt	703	Brn
Zachariah	504	Prw
Zachariah	505	Prw
Allender, James	763	Hmp
Thomas	549	Brk
William	773	Hmp
Wm.	479	Mnn
see Aleander		
Allens, ---	520	Prw
Allensworth, Butler	592	Frd
Catharine	593	Frd
James	559	Frd
John	594	Frd
Philip	594	Frd
Reuben	593	Frd
Simon	593	Frd
Wm., [his] Est.	188	Kng
Aller, Peter	778	Hmp
Alexander, Elias	426	Rnd
Alley, Abram	542	Prg
D.A.	112	Hnr
David	544	Prg
Elr.	479	Mnn
Hamlin	544	Prg
Isaiah	272	Amh
James	742	Brn
John	116	Hnr
Milly	544	Prg
Rebecca	742	Brn
Reuben	112	Hnr
Stephen	542	Prg
Stephen H.	6	Hnr
Thomas	271	Amh
Thomas	35	Hnr
Thos.	116	Hnr
Wm.	116	Hnr
Wm.	544	Prg
Allford, Salley, (F. Negroe)	358	Fqr
Allhighser, Jno.	682	Gch
Alligree, David	148	Alb
Allin, George	697	Wsh
James	452	Frn
John	330	Lnn
William	490	Frn
William	330	Lnn
Winney	451	Frn
Allington, John	222	Shn
Allins, David	116	Spt
Allion, Isaac	701	Wsh
James	701	Wsh
see Allon		
Allison, And.	288	Rck
Andw.	312	Ags
Charles	691	Br
Eliza	886	Nrf
Fanny	313	Ags
Frederick	766	Wst
James	312	Ags
James	691	Br
Jno.	3	Clp
Jno.	546	Prg
John	336	Dnw
John	231	Frf
John	376	Fqr
John	718	Wsh
John, jr.	315	Ags
Jonathan	691	Br
Mary	742	Wsh
Mary D.	28	Stf
Mathew	742	Wsh
Polly	691	Br
Richard	361	Fqr
Richd	290	Ldn
Robert	720	Wsh
Robt.	26	Rcm
Samuel	696	Br
Simpson	521	Prw
Thomas	691	Br
Thomas	231	Frf
Thomas	232	Frf
William	361	Fqr
William	720	Wsh
Wm.	312	Ags
Wm.	247	Ldn
Wm., jr.	315	Ags
Wm. C.	231	Frf
see Alison		
Allkire, Peter	819	Hmp
Allman, Easter	886	Nrf
Harrison	886	Nrf
Lucy	179	Shn
Martha	886	Nrf
William	909	Hrr
Allmond see Dunston		
Allon, Eli	701	Wsh
see Allion		
Alloway, John	398	Rch
Mary A.	394	Rch
Allport, John	888	Crl
William	888	Crl
Alls, Robert	436	Pra
Allwell, Judy	398	Rch
Ally, Thos., Jr.	625	Mnt
Thos , Senr.	608	Mnt
Alman, Alice	646	Glc
Jenny	646	Glc
Jenny, younger	646	Glc
Mildred	646	Glc
Sally	646	Glc
Almand, Jno.	646	Glc
Wm.	646	Glc
Almon, Edward	330	Lnn
Almond, David	120	Spt
Edwd. OK.	41	Chr
Elisha	42	Chr
Henry	85	Spt
James	32	Isw
John	94	Spt
John	103	Spt
Randal, (F.N.)	38	Isw
William	869	Cmp
Alphin, Elizabeth	184	Alb
John	184	Alb
Alpin, Thos.	895	Hnv
Alson, Richee	766	Wst
Alsop, Benjamin	72	Spt
George [2]	888	Crl
James	99	Spt
John	89	Spt
Robert	188	Kng
Samuel [2]	89	Spt
William	188	Kng
William	70	Spt
Alstott, Jacob	603	Btt
John	64	Jff
see Aulstott		
Alt, Jacob	70	Jff
Altar, Daniel	549	Frd
Frederick	180	Shn
Frederick	181	Shn
John	180	Shn
Altaver, George	205	Shn
Altick, Abram	476	Frn
Daniel	463	Frn
Jacob	477	Frn
John	463	Frn
John, Jr.	476	Frn
John, Sr.	476	Frn
Joseph	472	Frn
Solomon	477	Frn
Altizer, David	655	Mnt
Emeriah, jr.	660	Mnt
Emeriah, Sr.	660	Mnt
John	660	Mnt
Altoff see Altop		
Altoop, John	912	Hrr
Altop, Mary	913	Hrr
see Altoop		
Alts, Adam	10	Knw
see Aits, Alt		
Alverson, John	602	Btt
Zachariah	766	Wst
Alvis, Adam	870	Yrk
Dabney	859	Hnv
David	819	Bck
Elijah	682	Gch
Elizabeth	856	Hnv
Israel	870	Yrk
James	68	Chs
James	888	Yrk
John	870	Yrk
Judith	682	Gch
Robert	860	Hnv
Stanley	682	Gch
Zachariah	682	Gch
Alzey see Abrey		
Amack, John	6	Knw
Amager, Moses, free		
negro	233	Frf
see Ammager		
Amberson, Jos.	479	Mnn
Ambler, Jno.	32	Hnr
John	540	Frd
John	119	Hnr
Lewis	244	Ldn
Squire	19	Hnr
Wm.	244	Ldn
Ambrose, Amey	624	Sss
Daniel	598	Brk
Henry	567	Brk
Jacob	572	Brk
Jno.	479	Mnn
John	567	Brk
John	624	Sss
Matthias	571	Brk
Reaps	530	Prg
Wm.	573	Brk
Wm.	646	Glc
Ambrous, Elijah	404	Rch
William	399	Rch
Ambrus, William	330	Lnn
Amelia, James	682	Gch
Amen, Daniel	602	Btt
David	602	Btt
John	602	Btt
Michl.	603	Btt
Amens, Peter	443	Bth
America, Walker	887	Nrf
Amers, Lewis	248	Shn
Ames, James	11	Isw
Jerry	13	Oho
Michael	888	Crl
Amey, ---	742	Nwk
Amich, Saml.	285	Ldn
Saml.	298	Ldn
Amick, Philip	605	Frd
Amis, Ann	3	Clp

7

Gabl., jr.	2	Clp	Beverly	154	Knq	James	742	Nwk
Gabl., senr.	2	Clp	Caleb	742	Brn	James	10	Oho
John	2	Clp	Catharine	148	Alb	James	285	Rck
Philip N.	2	Clp	Catharine	131	Cmb	James	20	Rcm
Thos.	3	Clp	Caty	117	Spt	James	193	Shn
Amix, James	604	Btt	Charles	41	Chr	James	707	Wsh
Mattw., jr.	602	Btt	Charles	114	Cmb	James, Jr.	603	Btt
Mattw., Sr.	604	Btt	Charles	844	Hnv	James, Jr.	604	Btt
Saml., Sr.	604	Btt	Charles	676	Nls	James, Sr.	604	Btt
see Amyx			Chas.	478	Mnn	James C.	738	Wsh
Ammager, James, free			Churchill	154	Knq	Jane	1	Hnr
negro	231	Frf	Cornelius	3	Clp	Jas.	869	Cmp
Uriah, free negro	231	Frf	Cornelius	534	Frd	Jas.	302	Rck
see Amager			Dan	479	Mnn	Jenn	537	Brk
Ammerly, Wm.	304	Ldn	Daniel	336	Dnw	Jesse, Jr.	569	Frd
Ammond, Christopher	28	Rcm	Daniel	176	Shn	Jesse, Senr.	569	Frd
Peter	28	Rcm	Davd.	710	Wsh	Jessee	126	Cmb
Ammonds, Abm.	478	Mnn	David	813	Bck	Jno.	3	Clp
Isc.	478	Mnn	David	3	Clp	Jno.	231	Frf
Jno.	478	Mnn	David	328	Dnw	Jno.	867	Hnv
Ammons, John	952	Chc	David	569	Frd	Jno.	878	Hnv
Martha	944	Chc	David	597	Frd	Jno.	444	Mth
William	943	Chc	David	886	Hnv	Jno.	479	Mnn
Amold see Arnold			David	554	Pre	Jno.	17	Ntt
Amole, Jacob	306	Rck	David	520	Prw	Jno. D.	442	Mth
Amonet, Charles	10	Pwh	E.	33	Hnr	Jno. F.	5	Ntt
James	3	Pwh	Edmund	148	Alb	Jno., K.	858	Hnv
Reuben	830	Bck	Eli	2	Knw	Jno., O. F.	848	Hnv
William	830	Bck	Eli	241	Ldn	Jno., (son of Elijah)	4	Clp
Amonett, Thomas	184	Alb	Eliakim	598	Frd	John	452	Bdf
Amory, Thos. C.	646	Glc	Elijah	3	Clp	John	582	Brk
Amos, Charles	837	Bck	Elijah	262	Ldn	John	603	Btt
Charles	676	Nls	Eliza.	2	Clp	John	809	Bck
Clough S.	830	Bck	Elizabeth	511	Prw	John [2]	888	Crl
Francis	830	Bck	Elizath.	886	Nrf	John	2	Clp
James	831	Bck	Ezekiel	4	Clp	John	111	Cmb
James	469	Frn	Fanny	115	Spt	John	112	Cmb
James	497	Frn	Francis	224	Aml	John	331	Dnw
Joseph	676	Nls	Francis, jr.	224	Aml	John	538	Frd
Pleasant	555	Pre	Garland	869	Hnv	John	569	Frd
William	811	Bck	Garland, Jnr.	878	Hnv	John	588	Frd
William	118	Cmb	Geo.	540	Brk	John	904	Hrr
William	457	Frn	Geo. K.	16	Hnr	John	57	Jff
Wilson	469	Frn	George	314	Ags	John	676	Nls
Amoss, Henry, Jnr.	478	Mnn	George	129	Cmb	John	742	Nwk
Henry, Snr.	478	Mnn	George	230	Frf	John	820	Nrf
Stephn.	478	Mnn	George	442	Flv	John	970	Nrt
Ampey, Nancy	30	Hnr	George	669	Mnt	John	22	Oho
Ampy, Betty, persons of			George	307	Rck	John	554	Pre
colour			George, Christians-			John	266	Rck
William	192	Shn	burg	619	Mnt	John	304	Rck
Amus, George	703	Brn	George, Jr.	442	Flv	John	250	Shn
Nancy	330	Lnn	George, Sr.	314	Ags	John	151	Sth
Amy, George	683	Br	Gracee, & Co.	332	Dnw	John	727	Wsh
Amyx, Andrew, Jr.	602	Btt	Hall	942	Chc	John	737	Wsh
Anans, Susanah	744	Wsh	Hannah	26	Hnr	John	738	Wsh
Ancel, George	313	Ags	Henry [2]	224	Aml	John, Colo.	758	Wsh
Wm.	313	Ags	Henry	864	Hnv	John, J.	812	Bck
Ancois, Arthur	249	Ldn	Henry	4	Pwh	John, Jr.	810	Bck
Anders, Frederick	260	Ldn	Hetty	886	Nrf	John, Jr.	856	Cmp
Jno.	308	Ldn	Isaac	737	Wsh	John, Senr.	856	Cmp
Andersan, Nancy	9	Hnr	J.B.	32	Hnr	John B.	888	Crl
Anderson, ...key, free			Jack	916	Hrr	John S.	795	Bck
negro	70	Chs	Jacob	514	Frd	Joseph	4	Clp
Aaron	690	Br	Jacob	640	Mnt	Joseph	354	Fqr
Abraham	535	Frd	Jacob	738	Wsh	Joseph	534	Frd
Agney	4	Hnr	James	313	Ags	Joseph	615	Gls
Alexander	875	Hnv	James	314	Ags	Joseph	894	Hnv
Alexander	519	Prw	James	452	Bdf	Joseph	17	Rcm
Alexr.	314	Ags	James	503	Brk	Joshua	531	Brk
Andrew	30	Rcm	James	596	Brk	Joshua	816	Bck
Andw.	312	Ags	James	787	Bck	Josias	603	Btt
Ann	503	Brk	James	814	Bck	Judith	970	Nrt
Ann	539	Frd	James	41	Chr	Larkin [2]	554	Pre
Arch.	479	Mnn	James	469	Frn	Lawrance	682	Gch
Benja.	682	Gch	James	508	Frd	Lawrence	111	Cmb
Benjamin	442	Flv	James	798	Hmp	Lea	816	Nrf
Benjamin	374	Mds	James	76	Jff	Leroy	854	Cmp
Benjamin, Sr.	442	Flv	James	10	Knw	Lewis	129	Cmb
Betsy	77	Spt	James	330	Lnn	Lewis	9	Hnr

Name	Page	Co.
Lewis	742	Wsh
Maria	123	Hnr
Mary	646	Glc
Mary	61	Jff
Mary	521	Prw
Mary	250	Shn
Mason	330	Lnn
Mat	8	Hnr
Mat.	682	Gch
Matthew	828	Bck
Matthew	829	Bck
McDowell	625	Sss
Meredth.	682	Gch
Nancey	7	Hnr
Nancy	688	Br
Nancy	959	Hrr
Nathan	56	Chs
Nathan	508	Frd
Nathaniel	148	Alb
Nathaniel	75	Spt
Natthaniel	829	Bck
Nelly	549	Frd
Nelson	677	Nls
Obediah	374	Mds
Olive	828	Bck
Partrick	894	Hnv
Paulin	7	Ntt
Paylon	4	Clp
Peter	514	Frd
Peter	2	Wod
R.C., Est.	54	Chs
Rachel, (W)	870	Yrk
Richard	783	Bck
Richard	798	Bck
Richard	111	Cmb
Richard	127	Cmb
Richard	833	Hmp
Richard	885	Hnv
Richard	13	Hnr
Richard	21	Stf
Richd.	31	Hnr
Ro., (W)	870	Yrk
Robert	841	Bck
Robert	212	Shn
Robert, Jr.	602	Btt
Robt.	549	Prg
Robt.	266	Rck
Robt.	272	Rck
Salley	67	Chs
Sally	108	Cmb
Sally	334	Dnw
Sally	27	Hnr
Saml.	3	Oho
Samuel	148	Alb
Samuel	121	Cmb
Samuel	514	Prw
Samuel, jr.	292	Amh
Sarah	856	Cmp
Sarah	511	Prw
Sarah	176	Shn
Spencer	513	Prw
Susan	442	Mth
Susanna	886	Nrf
Synthia	178	Shn
Taliafo.	4	Clp
Thomas	241	Ldn
Thomas	310	Ldn
Thomas	330	Lnn
Thomas	970	Nrt
Thomas F.	796	Bck
Thos.	57	Chs
Thos.	737	Wsh
Vincent	362	Fqr
Walter	970	Nrt
Walter G.	836	Nrf
William	224	Aml
William	690	Br
William	786	Bck
William	888	Crl
William	124	Cmb
William	586	Frd
William	829	Hmp
William	431	Msn
William	11	Oho
William	554	Pre
William	766	Wst
William, [his] Estate	889	Crl
William, jr.	810	Bck
William, jr.	970	Nrt
William, senr.	830	Bck
William, sr.	970	Nrt
Willis	55	Stf
Wilson	15	Hnr
Wilson	887	Nrf
Wim.	878	Hnv
Wm.	314	Ags
Wm.	561	Brk
Wm.	815	Nrf
Wm., Jr.	603	Btt
Wm., Major	602	Btt
Wm., Sr.	603	Btt
Worsham	42	Chr
see A...rson, A...de..., Andison, Bagley, Bunett, Gathwright, Rowe, Scott		
Anderton, Isaac	646	Glc
Isaac	445	Grn
Isack	449	Mth
Mildred	440	Mth
William	445	Grn
Wm.	441	Mth
Andes, Andrew	4	Rck
Andison, Elay	545	Prg
Andre..., Sarah	624	Sss
Andres, John	743	Wsh
Andrew, Abram	299	Amh
James	871	Hnv
William	299	Amh
Andrews, ---	326	Dnw
A.	326	Dnw
Aaron	62	Chs
Adam	62	Chs
Alexandrew	330	Lnn
Ann M.	3	Acc
Anny	330	Lnn
Anthony	859	Sth
Ballard	54	Chs
Bartho.	598	Srr
Benjamin	330	Lnn
Benjamin	598	Srr
Cammel	148	Alb
Charity	598	Srr
Drury	330	Lnn
Eleana	73	Acc
Eliza.	200	Ess
Elizabeth	60	Chs
Elizabeth	783	Hmp
Elizabeth	86	Spt
Elizabeth	625	Sss
Frederick	55	Chs
Garnett	555	Pre
George	312	Ags
George	330	Lnn
Henry	598	Srr
Isaac	646	Glc
Jacob	2	Acc
Jacob	387	Fqr
James	888	Crl
James	334	Dnw
Jane	245	Ldn
Jessee	330	Lnn
Jno.	314	Ags
Joel	55	Chs
John	605	Frd
John	554	Pre
John	624	Sss
John, Senr.	554	Pre
Joseph	73	Acc
Joseph	245	Ldn
Joseph	374	Mds
Joseph	624	Sss
Js.	887	Nrf
Lucy	625	Sss
Mark	201	Ess
Mark	554	Pre
Miles	57	Chs
Nancy	62	Chs
Nathaniel	625	Sss
Nathaniel S.	554	Pre
Patsy	40	Isw
Peggy	624	Sss
Polley	65	Chs
Richard	624	Sss
Robt.	546	Prg
Sally	848	Sth
Sally	598	Srr
Saml.	42	Rcm
Samuel	698	Br
Stephen	624	Sss
Thomas	452	Bdf
Thomas	461	Frn
Thos.	546	Prg
William	73	Acc
Wm.	55	Chs
Wm.	214	Ess
see Andre..., Andrws		
Andrick, Fred...ck	228	Shn
George	228	Shn
Andrws, Patrick	547	Prg
Rebecca	624	Sss
Aneram, Jacob	22	Oho
Richard	21	Oho
Thomas	21	Oho
Angel, John	970	Nrt
John D.	224	Aml
Robert	970	Nrt
Robert J.	224	Aml
Rodam	444	Flv
Thomas	444	Flv
William	129	Hnr
William	970	Nrt
Angell, Baker	336	Lnc
Eliza.	336	Lnc
Wm.	812	Nrf
Angle, Jacob	462	Frn
John	463	Frn
Peter	462	Frn
Anglea, Bartlett	98	Cmb
Burton	100	Cmb
James	100	Cmb
John	100	Cmb
Joseph	100	Cmb
William	100	Cmb
Anglen, Samuel	911	Hrr
Anglin, Adam	931	Hrr
Angst, George	17	Rcm
Angus, Abraham	334	Dnw
Anington see Arrington		
Ankram, James	6	Oho
Ankrum, Aaron	21	Oho
Archabald	100	Jff
Annandale, David	766	Wst
Samuel	766	Wst
Annanias, Betsy	886	Nrf
Annes, John B.	386	Fqr
Anness, Sarah	509	Prw
William	509	Prw
William	517	Prw
Annin, Daniel	526	Frd
Samuel	72	Jff
Annis, Custis	72	Acc
Levi	72	Acc
Michajah	4	Acc
Nancy	72	Acc
Arnold, James	932	Hrr
Annot, John, bound for a term of years	447	Bth
Ansell, Frederick	436	Pra
John	436	Pra
Anselm, Bailey, junr.	744	Nwk

Ansil, Leonard	291	Ldn	Michal	225	Pnd	Christopher	32	Rcm
Anthoney, Christopher	452	Bdf	Peter	225	Pnd	Elizabeth	11	Rcm
Christopher	851	Cmp	see Armoncost			George	24	Rcm
James	197	Ess	Arbuckle, Edwar	73	Acc	Henry	19	Rcm
Jno.	547	Prg	William	420	Msn	Jacob	26	Rcm
John	881	Cmp	see Airbuckle			Jno.	24	Rcm
Joseph	862	Hnv	Arburthnot, James	886	Nrf	John	26	Rcm
Mark	452	Bdf	Arbuthnott, James	24	Oho	John, (Jr.)	37	Rcm
Samuel	849	Cmp	Samuel	16	Oho	Nancey	19	Rcm
Anthony, Billy	115	Hnr	Archbold, James	908	Hrr	Nicholas	26	Rcm
Eliza.	4	Hnr	Archdacon, Michael	439	Bth	Peter	19	Rcm
Garland	866	Hnv	Archer, Allen	332	Dnw	Peter, (Jr.)	19	Rcm
Hardeman	860	Hnv	Amas	742	Brn	Philip	19	Rcm
Jas. C.	11	Hnr	Aron	478	Mnn	Philip	25	Rcm
Jesee	866	Hnv	Ebenezer	693	Br	Armbrister, Phillip	818	Wth
Jno.	899	Hnv	Edward	64	Chs	Armenteval, Peter	313	Ags
Jno., Jnr.	851	Hnv	Elisha	874	Hnv	Armes see Aimes, Arms		
Judith	899	Hnv	Field	326	Dnw	Armestead, ---	327	Dnw
Mark	313	Ags	George	676	Br	Robert	876	Cmp
Nathl.	863	Hnv	Isaac	695	Wsh	William	268	Amh
Patty	123	Hnr	J.	658	Btt	Armfeild, Betty	870	Yrk
Sally	32	Isw	Jesse	446	Grn	Matt	870	Yrk
Anton, Robert	766	Wst	Jno.	69	Chs	Warren	870	Yrk
Stephen	766	Wst	Jno. H.	56	Chs	Armintrout, Charls	276	Rck
Antrim, John	580	Frd	John	886	Nrf	George	276	Rck
Joshua	562	Frd	John, (SC)	248	Aml	Henry	276	Rck
Anyan, George	224	Aml	John, Sr.	224	Aml	Armistead, Anthy.	187	Elc
Apler, Peter	75	Jff	John R.	248	Aml	Francis M.	186	Elc
Apley, John	288	Rck	Joseph	21	Oho	Geo.	186	Elc
Aplin, Thomas	304	Amh	Obadiah	874	Hnv	Guy	742	Nwk
William	676	Nls	Oliff	794	Nrf	Hampt.	184	Elc
Apperson, Daniel, jr.	330	Lnn	Peter F., jr.	14	Pwh	Hy.	887	Nrf
Daniel, Sr.	330	Lnn	Peter F., Majr.	1	Pwh	Jno.	13	Hnr
David	330	Lnn	Richd., Est.	224	Aml	John B.	396	Fqr
Edmund	743	Nwk	Robt. P.	66	Chs	Moss	886	Nrf
Eliza.	4	Clp	Saml., & family	886	Nrf	Petr. F.	2	Clp
Jacob	840	Bck	Samuel	694	Br	Prisca.	184	Elc
Jacob, Jr.	840	Bck	Sary	374	Mds	Rob.	179	Elc
James	834	Bck	Tho., (Y)	870	Yrk	Robert	242	Ldn
John	870	Yrk	Thos.	819	Nrf	Robert B.	742	Nwk
Jonathan	330	Lnn	William	248	Aml	Sarah	192	Elc
Litleberry	742	Nwk	William	697	Br	Theodk.	886	Nrf
Martha	330	Lnn	William	10	Pwh	Thos.	886	Nrf
Mildred	870	Yrk	Wm.	64	Chs	William	742	Nwk
Peter	106	Spt	Wm. H.	335	Dnw	William	521	Prw
Polly	743	Nwk	see Coleman, Franklin, Goff,			Willm.	176	Elc
Richard	742	Nwk	Jones, Robertson			Willm., sr.	184	Elc
Thomas	128	Hnr	Ardis, Daniel	72	Acc	Wm.	886	Nrf
William	954	Chc	James	72	Acc	Wm.	887	Nrf
William	743	Nwk	William	72	Acc	Wm., S.Sp.	187	Elc
Apple, Michael	439	Bth	Ardon, Aaron	260	Ldn	Wm., (W)	870	Yrk
Michl.	409	Ags	Areson, Frederick	550	Frd	Wm. B.	187	Elc
Paul	406	Ags	Arete, Michl.	581	Mnr	Wm. M.	186	Elc
Appleberry, Absolum	439	Flv	Argabright, George,			Armitage, James	230	Frf
Elizabeth	148	Alb	(Jr.)	6	Rcm	Armoncost, Benjamin	224	Pnd
James	436	Flv	George, (sen.)	6	Rcm	see Arbocost		
Wm., Sr.	439	Flv	Jacob	24	Rcm	Armone see Armour		
Appleby, Caty	3	Clp	Jno.	665	Mnt	Armontroub, Fredk.	604	Btt
Fanny	3	Clp	John	604	Btt	George	604	Btt
Jno.	4	Clp	Jos.	665	Mnt	Armontrout, Jacob	216	Pnd
Robert	416	Fqr	Argenbright, Augustine	312	Ags	Armour, Joseph	606	Mnt
Robt.	2	Clp	Fred.	312	Ags	Arms, Akin James	554	Pre
William	970	Nrt	Jacob	313	Ags	James	554	Pre
Applegate, Joseph	683	Br	Argotte, Villabos	886	Nrf	John	554	Pre
Applewaite see Applwaite			Argyle, Fredrick	682	Gch	Richard W.	554	Pre
Applewhaite, George	31	Isw	Arinbright, Geo.	398	Ags	Walter	336	Lnc
Henry W.	25	Isw	Arington, Adler	804	Bck	Arms Akin see Arms		
Applewhite, Frs.	887	Nrf	Daniel	464	Frn	Armshpoker, John	689	Br
Thos.	138	Sth	John	494	Frn	Armstead, Betsy	813	Nrf
Applewite, Jno.	145	Sth	Thomas	471	Frn	Francis	115	Cmb
Applwaite, Charllotte	851	Sth	William	305	Amh	Francis	437	Mth
Aramgosh, Michl.	313	Ags	see Arrington			Henry	952	Chc
Arbaugh, Thomas	71	Jff	Arion, Philip	23	Rck	James A.	116	Cmb
Arbocost, Adam	224	Pnd	Arisman, Jacob	676	Nls	John	42	Chr
David	217	Pnd	Arlenger, C.	313	Ags	John	117	Cmb
George	225	Pnd	Jac.	314	Ags	Robert	111	Cmb
Henry	217	Pnd	Arlington, James	886	Nrf	Robt.	438	Mth
Henry	225	Pnd	John	3	Acc	Robt.	831	Nrf
John	225	Pnd	Thomas	2	Acc	Thadeus	129	Cmb
Michal	218	Pnd	Armantrout, Augustine	24	Rcm	Thos.	810	Nrf

Name	Pg	Co.
William	117	Cmb
William, Jur.	41	Chr
William, Senr.	42	Chr
see Arnstead, Goodwyn		
Armstong, Cathorine	960	Hrr
Rebeca	834	Nrf
Armstrong, Abel	314	Ags
Alexr.	423	Msn
Amos	218	Pnd
Andw.	312	Ags
Andw.	479	Mnn
Baker	757	Wsh
Ban...	799	Nrf
Benja.	880	Cmp
Charles	887	Nrf
Charles	33	Rcm
David	593	Frd
Elizabeth	102	Jff
Ellis	196	Ess
Fieldg.	2	Clp
George	522	Frd
George	597	Frd
George, 106 years old	690	Br
Hugh	690	Br
James	692	Br
James	522	Frd
James	234	Ldn
James	53	Stf
Jane	970	Nrt
Jas.	314	Ags
Jas.	2	Clp
Jeremiah	559	Frd
Jeremiah	582	Frd
Jerrot	218	Pnd
Jesse	415	Fqr
Jesse	188	Kng
Jno.	2	Clp
Jno.	330	Rck
John	314	Ags
John	214	Ess
John	941	Hrr
John	801	Nrf
John	18	Oho
John	218	Pnd
John	272	Rck
John, (W. C.	313	Ags
Joseph	189	Kng
Joseph	53	Stf
Js. A. D.	188	Kng
Lucy	13	Hnr
Mary	689	Br
Mary	469	Frn
Pattey	410	Fqr
Rachel	848	Cmp
Rawleigh	4	Clp
Rebeca	801	Nrf
Richard E.	874	Hnv
Robert	431	Rnd
Tho.	336	Lnc
Thomas	602	Btt
Thomas	369	Lnc
Thomas	554	Pre
Thomas	818	Wth
William	457	Frn
William	810	Hmp
William	821	Hmp
William	79	Jff
William	24	Oho
William	217	Pnd
William	218	Pnd
Wm.	313	Ags
Wm.	230	Frf
Wm.	189	Kng
Wm.	9	Oho
Wm. D.	604	Btt
see Ross		
Arnal, Henry	579	Brk
Jacob	581	Brk
Arnedd, Wm.	261	Ldn
Arnet, Andw.	478	Mnn
Dan	478	Mnn
Jas.	478	Mnn
Jno.	478	Mnn
Jonathn.	478	Mnn
Arnett, Daniel	722	Wsh
Henry	590	Mnr
Wm.	584	Mnr
Arney, Henry	818	Wth
Mary	818	Wth
Tobias	818	Wth
Arnholt, Adam	807	Hmp
Arnish, Wm.	721	Wsh
Arnoe, Lewis	886	Nrf
Arnol, George	933	Hrr
James, Jur.	41	Chr
Arnold, Andrew	768	Hmp
Anthony	66	Spt
Benjamin	39	Rcm
Daniel	602	Btt
Daniel	762	Hmp
David	554	Pre
Edward	233	Frf
Enoch	188	Kng
George	375	Fqr
George	11	Rcm
George	81	Spt
Gerard	231	Frf
Henry	897	Hnv
Isaac	411	Fqr
James	510	Prw
James, Senr.	41	Chr
Jessee	522	Prw
Jno.	4	Clp
Jno. [?]	479	Mnn
John	868	Cmp
John	569	Frd
John	763	Hmp
John	768	Hmp
John	910	Hrr
John	188	Kng
John	654	Mnt
John	13	Oho
John	554	Pre
Joseph	602	Btt
Joseph	675	Br
Lettice	508	Prw
Levi	768	Hmp
Lewis	4	Clp
Moses	125	Cmb
Richard	7	Wod
Robert	676	Nls
Saml.	4	Clp
Samuel	602	Btt
Samuel	803	Hmp
Simon	923	Hrr
Thomas	39	Rcm
Wiatt	867	Cmp
William	232	Frf
William	188	Kng
William	510	Prw
Wim.	865	Hnv
Zachariah	803	Hmp
see Annold, Arnol		
Arnott, Kitty	334	Dnw
Arnstead, Jesse	827	Nrf
Aroerbastis, Michael	553	Brk
Arontz, James	446	Mth
Arrington, Adler	882	Cmp
Charles	871	Cmp
John	858	Cmp
John	819	Nrf
Richard	503	Prw
Richard	504	Prw
Thomas	507	Prw
Walter	504	Prw
Arrisse, J. P.	886	Nrf
Arrowsmith, James	356	Fqr
Arselle, John	887	Nrf
Arson see Asson		
Arters, William	418	Rnd
Arther, Barnabas	452	Bdf
Barnabas	868	Cmp
Chanler	614	Gls
James	452	Bdf
Jeremiah	452	Bdf
Joel	614	Gls
John, B. R.	452	Bdf
John, Junr.	452	Bdf
Lewis	452	Bdf
Nancy	452	Bdf
Nimrod	614	Gls
Sally	452	Bdf
Thomas	452	Bdf
William	452	Bdf
William, Sr.	452	Bdf
Arthur, Hugh	694	Br
Isham	869	Cmp
James	603	Btt
John	258	Shn
John, Jr.	470	Frn
John, Sr.	469	Frn
Joseph	868	Cmp
Joseph	193	Shn
Thomas	464	Frn
see Arther		
Artis, Matthew	847	Sth
Artist, Absalom	155	Sth
Ann	149	Sth
Charles	161	Sth
Dick	128	Sth
Edmond	846	Sth
Edward	150	Sth
George	148	Sth
Joe	850	Sth
John	159	Sth
Joshua	161	Sth
Lydia	870	Sth
Mildred	137	Sth
Patience	869	Sth
Artrip, Hannah	35	Rcm
Arturs, Joseph	712	Wsh
Arundle, Isaac	231	Frf
Jno.	230	Frf
Asberry, Henry	406	Rch
John	958	Hrr
Asbey, James	28	Hnr
Asbury, George	471	Frn
Henry	777	Hmp
James	452	Bdf
Jeremiah	834	Hmp
Joseph	232	Frf
Joseph	763	Hmp
Joseph	3	Knw
Thomas	232	Frf
Thomas	946	Hrr
Aschew, Christopher	484	Frn
John	484	Frn
Aschill see Asdill		
Aschue, Phillip	484	Frn
Asdill, John	564	Frd
Sarah	516	Frd
Aseger, Simeon	251	Shn
Ash, Adam	915	Hrr
Anne	342	Fqr
Betty	330	Dnw
Billey	326	Dnw
Christopher	946	Hrr
Elizabeth	342	Fqr
Francis	566	Frd
George	341	Fqr
Jacob	581	Brk
Jno.	260	Ldn
Milley	589	Frd
Nanny	870	Yrk
Rebecca 646 Glc		
Thornton	342	Fqr
William	342	Fqr
Viney	330	Dnw
Ashbeny, Joseph	446	Mth
Ashberry see Ashbeny		

Name	No.	Abbr.
Ashbrook, Eli	765	Hmp
James	57	Chs
Jeremiah	65	Chs
Peter	65	Chs
Thos.	59	Chs
Ashburn, Geo.	336	Lnc
Hannah	970	Nrt
Haynie	970	Nrt
Luke	336	Lnc
Thomas	970	Nrt
Ashby, A.	888	Yrk
Alfred	589	Frd
Bengamin	799	Hmp
Geo.	479	Mnn
George	3	Acc
James	2	Acc
James	410	Ags
James	870	Yrk
Jeremiah	799	Hmp
John	42	Stf
John	870	Yrk
John, Junr.	404	Fqr
John, Senr.	341	Fqr
Joseph	42	Stf
Matt	888	Yrk
Nathn.	479	Mnn
Nimrod	342	Fqr
Robert	342	Fqr
Sally	42	Stf
Samuel	2	Acc
Samuel	404	Fqr
Sarah	597	Frd
Thomas	2	Acc
Thompson	342	Fqr
William	2	Acc
Wm.	2	Clp
Wm.	436	Pra
Ashbye, John	12	Oho
Ashcraft, Ezekiel	950	Hrr
John	925	Hrr
John	950	Hrr
Levi	907	Hrr
Uriah	907	Hrr
Ashdon, Jno.	314	Ldn
Ashe, Nat.	816	Nrf
Ashefelter, Thomas	31	Rcm
Jacob	10	Rcm
John	13	Rcm
Ashenhust, John	682	Br
William	682	Br
Asher, Anto.	478	Mnn
Charles	3	Clp
Eliza.	3	Clp
Jas.	478	Mnn
John	858	Cmp
John	478	Mnn
Wm., (Free Mo.)	3	Clp
Ashfad, Judy	231	Frf
Ashford, Francis	231	Frf
Geo.	231	Frf
Wm.	291	Rck
Ashinhurst, Ralph	492	Frn
Ashley, Benjamin	589	Frd
Cas.	148	Alb
Edmd.	870	Sth
John	599	Frd
Warren	886	Nrf
Wim.	870	Hnv
Ashlin, Augustine	435	Flv
John	439	Flv
Ashmore, William	514	Prw
Ashton, Bendett, jr.	189	Kng
Bendett, sr.	189	Kng
Charles, jr.	188	Kng
Chas., Senr.	189	Kng
George D.	188	Kng
Hannah	189	Kng
James	603	Btt
Jno. W.	232	Frf
John, Sr.	188	Kng
Joseph	794	Hmp
Laurence	366	Fqr
Laurence	189	Kng
Mary	188	Kng
Richd. W.	189	Kng
Samuel	511	Prw
West	188	Kng
Ashurst, Jacob	224	Aml
Ashwell, Mary	743	Nwk
Nancy	15	Hnr
see Askwill		
Ashwood, John	13	Rck
Ashworth, Harrison	42	Chr
Joel	456	Frn
John	455	Frn
Jonathan	42	Chr
Samuel	455	Frn
William C.	453	Frn
Ask see Ax		
Asken, Aaron	12	Isw
Askew, James	869	Cmp
Joshua	14	Oho
Mills	10	Isw
Thomas, Jun.	5	Isw
Askin, George	603	Btt
George	231	Frf
Jno.	230	Frf
William	862	Cmp
William	231	Frf
Askins, Benjamin	766	Wst
Berryman	523	Frd
Posey	591	Frd
Reubn.	478	Mnn
Thomas	766	Wst
Thos.	313	Ags
Vincent	230	Frf
William	766	Wst
Wm.	4	Clp
Askue, Jno.	858	Hnv
Askwill, James	941	Hrr
James	947	Hrr
Aslin, Francis, Est.	224	Aml
Laurence	742	Brn
Asson, Edward H.	677	Nls
Asten, Blane	766	Wst
Jacob	766	Wst
Laurence	766	Wst
Mima	766	Wst
William	766	Wst
Willoughby	766	Wst
Winney, Junr.	766	Wst
Winney, Senr.	766	Wst
Astin, Isaac	604	Btt
Aston, John	313	Ags
John	409	Ags
John	15	Pwh
Astrop, Jessee	42	Chr
Aswald, James A.	32	Hnr
Atcher, Christ.	296	Ldn
Christ. [erased]	313	Ldn
Cornelius	297	Ldn
Cornelius [erased]	313	Ldn
Atcheson, Hugh	46	Stf
Atcheston, Arnold	33	Stf
Atchiston, George	49	Stf
Ates, Martin	928	Hrr
see Aits		
Athan, Leslie F.	306	Rck
Wilson	287	Rck
Athay, Elisha	585	Brk
Ather, Joseph	298	Rck
Athey, Benedict	212	Shn
Ebenezer	514	Prw
Elijah	506	Prw
Elizabeth	232	Frf
Hezekiah W.	257	Ldn
Hezh.	251	Ldn
John	515	Prw
Josias	502	Prw
Samuel	249	Ldn
Thomas	232	Frf
Thos.	722	Wsh
Townley	73	Jff
Wilford	252	Ldn
Athy, Bazil	784	Hmp
James	13	Wod
John	784	Hmp
John	722	Wsh
Thomas	808	Hmp
Thomas	810	Hmp
Walter	808	Hmp
Atkenson, Joseph	140	Sth
Atkerson, Edward	2	Clp
George	3	Knw
Joel	703	Brn
Joel	625	Sss
John	703	Brn
Lewis	703	Brn
Robert	5	Knw
Sarah	703	Brn
Thomas	625	Sss
Atkins, Ambrose	3	Clp
Benjamin	42	Chr
Clayton	154	Knq
Elisha	139	Sth
Frank	770	Brn
George	742	Brn
James	331	Dnw
Jane	852	Hnv
Jesse	858	Sth
Jno.	41	Chr
John	154	Knq
John	108	Spt
Joseph	818	Wth
Joseph, Senr.	818	Wth
Judith	852	Hnv
Judith, Jnr.	852	Hnv
Lewis	154	Knq
Liston	970	Nrt
Martha	328	Dnw
Mary	154	Knq
Milly	208	Ess
Sally	42	Chr
Spencer	3	Clp
Thomas	41	Chr
Willm.	872	Sth
Atkinson, Absalom	445	Grn
Celia	36	Isw
Charles [2]	888	Crl
Daniel	888	Crl
Elizabeth	36	Isw
Elizabeth	14	Ntt
George	693	Br
Guy	230	Frf
Hardy	598	Srr
James	224	Aml
James	883	Hnv
James	25	Isw
James	742	Nwk
James	151	Sth
Jno.	478	Mnn
John	693	Br
Joseph	12	Isw
Josiah	853	Hnv
Mary	742	Nwk
Nancy	36	Isw
Nathaniel	888	Crl
Patcy	31	Isw
Patcy	36	Isw
Reuben	200	Ess
Roger	65	Chs
Samuel	598	Srr
Thomas	686	Br
Tim.	844	Sth
William	888	Crl
William	445	Grn
William W.	9	Pwh
Wm.	800	Nrf
Wm.	887	Nrf
Wm.	162	Sth

see Akinson, Attki...		
Whitfeild		
Aton, John	688	Br
Ats, Lewis	928	Hrr
see Aits		
Attki..., Michael	442	Flv
Attkisson, Isaiah	276	Amh
Pleasant	682	Gch
Rachal	298	Amh
Winifred	682	Gch
Attwell, Francis	766	Wst
John	188	Kng
William	766	Wst
Attwood, Eliza.	189	Kng
Thomas	593	Frd
Atwel, Samuel	42	Chr
Atwell, Jesse	310	Ldn
Thomas	76	Jff
Thomas	235	Ldn
Thomas	970	Nrt
Wm.	398	Ags
see Johnston		
Atwood, Caty	2	Clp
Edwd.	436	Pra
Edwin	165	Shn
James	2	Clp
Jno.	437	Pra
John	244	Shn
•Sinnett	177	Shn
Thomas	436	Pra
William	170	Shn
William	177	Shn
Wm.	4	Clp
Wm.	436	Pra
Auche, Abram	406	Ags
Aucubo, John	887	Nrf
Auderton see Anderton		
Augden, Peter	13	Oho
Augdon, Andrew	19	Oho
Aughes, Harmon	36	Rcm
Augier, Lewis	886	Nrf
Augustin, Ashble	478	Mnn
Jno.	478	Mnn
Mary	478	Mnn
Augustus, Ceaser	72	Acc
Auker, Peter	16	Rcm
Aul see All		
Aulbourn, Chs.	312	Ags
Aulich, Charles	509	Frd
Aullaback, John	833	Hmp
Aulnutt, Jesse	78	Jff
Aulstott, Daniel	68	Jff
Jacob	61	Jff
see Alstott		
Ault, Jacob	84	Jff
Jacob, Jnr.	84	Jff
Wm.	286	Ldn
Ausbourn, George	117	Cmb
James	130	Cmb
William	129	Cmb
Auslin, Samuel	121	Cmb
Austin, Agnes	805	Bck
Alexander	861	Cmp
Archibald	841	Bck
Bekey	407	Fqr
Betsy	14	Hnr
Chapman	390	Rch
David	495	Frn
Henry [2]	184	Alb
James	452	Bdf
Jno. ["Jno." crossed out]	883	Hnv
Jno.	479	Mnn
Jno., Jnr.	899	Hnv
Jno., Snr.	873	Hnv
John	184	Alb
John	2	Knw
John	742	Nwk
Julius H.	743	Nwk
Levi	599	Brk

Lucy	68	Chr
Mary	118	Cmb
Mary	122	Hnr
Molly	122	Hnr
Nancy	184	Alb
Nancy	68	Chr
Ransome	888	Yrk
Rheubin	116	Cmb
Richard	868	Hnv
Richard	743	Nwk
Richd.	37	Rck
Samuel	184	Alb
Thomas	184	Alb
Thomas	452	Bdf
Thomas	405	Fqr
William	452	Bdf
Wim.	883	Hnv
Z...heriah	742	Nwk
Auston, John T.	118	Cmb
Moris	314	Ags
Auther, Patsey	14	Hnr
Avary, Nathan	8	Ntt
Avent, Durham	445	Grn
Henry	445	Grn
John, Jr.	445	Grn
John, Sr.	445	Grn
Peter	445	Grn
Samuel	445	Grn
Thomas	445	Grn
see Massey		
Aversole, Abraham	82	Jff
Daniel	82	Jff
Avery, Elizabeth	625	Sss
Frs.	887	Nrf
John	445	Grn
John [2]	625	Sss
Peter	330	Lnn
Randolph	540	Prg
Richard H.	446	Grn
Richard H.	625	Sss
Richd.	540	Prg
Rudd	330	Lnn
Wm.	540	Prg
see Avey		
Avey, Edward	548	Prg
Avie, Christian	603	Btt
Avis, David	91	Jff
John	817	Nrf
Robert	69	Jff
Avory, Barrington	702	Brn
George	224	Aml
John	702	Brn
Tillman	703	Brn
Wm.	703	Brn
Avriss, William	598	Srr
Awbrey, Thos.	292	Ldn
Wm.	287	Ldn
Awtrey see Awbrey		
Ax, William	584	Brk
see Ash		
Axline, David	283	Ldn
Jacob	285	Ldn
Jno.	283	Ldn
Axtead, Thomas	436	Pra
Wm.	436	Pra
Ayers, Elisha	924	Hrr
Jacob	818	Wth
Ayles, David	14	Wod
Ayliff, Thomas	452	Bdf
William	452	Bdf
William	349	Fqr
Aylor, Absolom	374	Mds
Henry	374	Mds
Jacob	374	Mds
Lewis	374	Mds
Michael	374	Mds
Aylstock, Absolem	604	Btt
Ayres, Biddy	797	Bck
Charles	360	Fqr
Danl.	277	Rck

Hannah	452	Bdf
Henry	73	Acc
Henry	287	Rck
Isaac	72	Acc
James	452	Bdf
John	888	Crl
John, Jr.	777	Bck
John, senr.	831	Bck
John C.	743	Nwk
Levin	73	Acc
Mary	831	Bck
Matthias	780	Bck
Nathan, Jr.	791	Bck
Nathan, senr.	841	Bck
Peg...y	4	Acc
Ritche	449	Mth
Rosanna	198	Ess
Samuel	392	Fqr
William	667	Bck
see Mason, Staton, Tatham		

--- B ---

B..., ... [8]	453	Bdf
... [several]	138	Dnw
... [3]	140	Dnw
...	334	Dnw
...	840	Nrf
Alexr.	140	Dnw
Charrity	453	Bdf
John	453	Bdf
John	454	Bdf
John	970	Nrt
Math	453	Bdf
Nathan	453	Bdf
Robert	453	Bdf
Sarah	455	Bdf
Talaiferro	140	Dnw
Thomas [2]	453	Bdf
William	453	Bdf
B...a...ter, William	454	Bdf
B...es, William	454	Bdf
B...h, Valentin	688	Wsh
B...n, Joseph	140	Dnw
William	454	Bdf
B...nwell, John, of D.	9	Acc
B...oin, Elizabeth	140	Dnw
B...ow, Charles	524	Brk
B...tler, Mabeth	140	Dnw
Ba..., ...	453	Bdf
...o...	453	Bdf
Ba...t..., Isaac	454	Bdf
Bab, Jacob	225	Shn
Babb, Abner	553	Frd
David	578	Frd
Jas.	733	Wsh
John	550	Frd
John	24	Isw
Lemuel	2	Isw
Peter	578	Frd
Sampson	578	Frd
Thomas	581	Frd
William	47	Isw
Babbetti, Calvin	9	Oho
Babbington, Wme.	890	Nrf
Babel, Chs.	318	Ldn
Baber, Edward	777	Bck
Caleb	798	Bck
George	186	Alb
Isaac	798	Bck
Killis	680	Nls
Jessee	149	Alb
John	819	Wth
Lidda	180	Alb
Peter	890	Crl
Rhody	890	Crl
Robert	149	Alb
Thomas	783	Bck

Thomas	437	Flv	
William	453	Bdf	
William	821	Wth	
Wm.	445	Flv	
Baccus, Hennery	946	Hrr	
John	191	Kng	
Sarah	681	Nls	
Bacher see Bucher			
Back, Aaron	35	Rcm	
Joseph	377	Mds	
Backeday, Frank	767	Wst	
Backer see Barker			
Backes, Wm.	946	Hrr	
Backet, James	12	Knw	
Backhouse, Ann	82	Jff	
Joseph	436	Bth	
Richd.	811	Nrf	
Backhurst, John B. S.	29	Isw	
Backinttoe, John	398	Ags	
Backman, Jacob	184	Shn	
Michl.	186	Elc	
Backouse, Peggy	183	Elc	
Backster, Roger	608	Btt	
Backus, George	248	Aml	
Bacon, Drury	333	Lnn	
Edmun P.	333	Lnn	
Elisabeth	746	Nwk	
Isaac	562	Brk	
Izard	900	Hnv	
Izard	112	Hnr	
John	818	Nrf	
John G.	44	Chr	
Langston	43	Chr	
Lydal	43	Chr	
Mary	150	Alb	
Mary	333	Lnn	
Peter [2]	890	Nrf	
Richard	333	Lnn	
T. G.	16	Ntt	
William	150	Alb	
William	42	Chr	
see Burwell			
Bacus, Sanfort	956	Hrr	
Badden, James	241	Frf	
Badder, Thomas	289	Amh	
Thomas, jr.	289	Amh	
Baddon, Rogel	3	Oho	
Baden, John	71	Jff	
Badger, Ann, Mrs.	331	Dnw	
Ezekel	7	Acc	
Jesse	8	Clp	
Nathaniel	9	Acc	
Rose	9	Acc	
Sarah	8	Acc	
Badget, John	140	Dnw	
Milley	797	Bck	
Badgett, Richd.	601	Srr	
Thos.	681	Wrw	
Badkins, Sally	744	Nwk	
Bael, Harrison	887	Hnv	
Baele, John B.	834	Nrf	
Bagant, Wm.	267	Ldn	
Bagbey, Matthew	116	Cmb	
Bagby, Clayton	557	Pre	
Daniel	825	Bck	
Daniel	840	Bck	
Henry	785	Bck	
Henry	156	Knq	
Henry, Senr.	777	Bck	
Hezekiah	809	Bck	
James	819	Bck	
James	129	Cmb	
James	7	Pwh	
John	786	Bck	
John	825	Bck	
John	154	Knq	
John	273	Rck	
Josiah	815	Bck	
Richard	156	Knq	
Robert	154	Knq	

Thomas	156	Knq	
William	809	Bck	
William	556	Pre	
Bage, Eliza.	601	Srr	
George	265	Rck	
Bagent, John	557	Frd	
Bagg, Polly	9	Acc	
Baggerly, Charles	169	Shn	
Baggot, George	109	Spt	
George	110	Spt	
Mary	110	Spt	
Baggott, Robert	236	Frf	
Thomas	234	Frf	
Townshend	234	Frf	
William	237	Frf	
Bagley, Anderson	331	Lnn	
Anderson, jr.	332	Lnn	
Benajah	3	Wod	
John	6	Wod	
Lucy	601	Srr	
Reuben	283	Ldn	
Woodson	473	Frn	
Bagnal, Charles	27	Isw	
Matilda	12	Isw	
Nancy	12	Isw	
William	8	Isw	
Bagnall, Jos.	888	Nrf	
Richd.	888	Nrf	
Bagnell, William	180	Alb	
Bags, Caleb	606	Btt	
Bagsdale, ... lliam	335	Dnw	
Bagwell, Charles	76	Acc	
Daniel	80	Acc	
Danl.	11	Acc	
George	82	Acc	
George P.	76	Acc	
Isaiah	11	Acc	
Saml.	1	Ntt	
Thomas	7	Acc	
see Bagnell			
Baham, Sarah	928	Hrr	
Baher, John	30	Rcm	
Baib see Barb			
Baicin see Bricin			
Bail see Barb			
Bailes, John	7	Knw	
Solomon	8	Knw	
Thomas	7	Knw	
Bailey, ...	454	Bdf	
Andrew	42	Chr	
Ans., Doctr.	599	Srr	
Anselmn, Senr.	745	Nwk	
Armager	628	Sss	
Benjamin	815	Bck	
Brittain	626	Sss	
Caleb, New Port	15	Wod	
Carr	519	Prw	
Charles	186	Alb	
Charles	455	Bdf	
Charles	846	Sth	
Chas.	336	Lnc	
David	454	Bdf	
David	683	Gch	
David	535	Prg	
David	629	Sss	
Dempsy	127	Sth	
Edmon	33	Hnr	
Edmund	627	Sss	
Edward	600	Srr	
Edwd.	128	Sth	
Eliza	609	Btt	
Elizabeth	130	Cmb	
Frances	139	Dnw	
Francis	890	Crl	
George	593	Frd	
George	582	Mnr	
George	889	Nrf	
George	844	Sth	
Harrison	334	Dnw	
Henry	827	Bck	

Henry	600	Srr	
Henry	626	Sss	
Hermon	626	Sss	
Isaac	859	Sth	
Isaac	601	Srr	
Ishmael	785	Bck	
J. C.	676	Sss	
Jacob	132	Sth	
James [2]	869	Cmp	
James	678	Nls	
James	745	Nwk	
James	263	Rck	
James	600	Srr	
James C.	627	Sss	
James H.	767	Wst	
Jane	192	Kng	
Jane	744	Nwk	
Jeremiah	191	Kng	
Jesse	336	Lnc	
Jesse	844	Sth	
Jesse	627	Sss	
John	565	Brk	
John	744	Brn	
John	43	Chr	
John	927	Hrr	
John	678	Nls	
John	173	Shn	
John	179	Shn	
John	628	Sss	
John	766	Wst	
John, Junr.	768	Wst	
Jonathan	626	Sss	
Joseph	62	Chs	
Joseph	375	Fqr	
Joseph	126	Hnr	
Joshua	142	Sth	
Joshua	627	Sss	
Josiah	454	Bdf	
Js., jun.	58	Chs	
Js., Senr.	58	Chs	
Laban	627	Sss	
Lucy	334	Dnw	
Lucy	677	Nls	
Margret	185	Elc	
Martain	15	Wod	
Mary	243	Ldn	
Mathew	443	Mth	
Moses	387	Fqr	
Oley	58	Chs	
Parke	105	Cmb	
Philip	454	Bdf	
Philip	820	Bck	
Phillip	627	Sss	
Phillip	630	Sss	
Phoebe	627	Sss	
Pierce	239	Frf	
Precilla	332	Dnw	
Quinton	579	Mnr	
R. W.	889	Nrf	
Reuben	827	Bck	
Richard	334	Dnw	
Robert	629	Sss	
Robert	791	Wst	
Robert S.	600	Srr	
Sally	600	Srr	
Saml.	239	Frf	
Saml.	816	Nrf	
Saml.	846	Sth	
Samuel	239	Frf	
Samuel	678	Nls	
Samuel	745	Nwk	
Samuel	600	Srr	
Samuel D.	43	Chr	
Sarah	334	Dnw	
Sarah	679	Nls	
Sarah	599	Srr	
Spencer	12	Hnr	
Stephan	928	Hrr	
Stephen	375	Fqr	
Stephen	766	Wst	

14

Name	No.	Abbr.	Name	No.	Abbr.	Name	No.	Abbr.
Susanna	766	Wst	James R.	625	Sss	James	604	Frd
Thomas	565	Brk	John	743	Brn	James	962	Hrr
Thomas	691	Br	John	330	Dnw	James	888	Nrf
Thomas	373	Fqr	John	9	Oho	James	889	Nrf
Thomas	628	Sss	Moses	481	Mnn	James	709	Wsh
Thomas, jr.	600	Srr	Robt.	298	Rck	Jane	555	Pre
Thomas, Sr.	600	Srr	Thomas	3	Oho	Jemima	77	Acc
Washington	627	Sss	Thos.	540	Prg	Jesman	99	Cmb
William	261	Amh	Washington	813	Bck	Joànna	460	Mdd
William	410	Fqr	Wm.	550	Prg	John	453	Bdf
William	559	Frd	Wm.	294	Rck	John	681	Br
William	448	Grn	Bairs, Jesse	756	Wsh	John	695	Br
William	126	Hnr	Baish, Thos.	889	Nrf	John	509	Frd
William	677	Nls	Baity, Jno.	281	Ldn	John	539	Frd
William	744	Nwk	Baizden, Saml.	846	Sth	John	564	Frd
William	844	Sth	Bajett, Wm.	16	Hnr	John	683	Gch
William	600	Srr	Bakech, Isaac	378	Mds	John	764	Hmp
William, Corpr.	745	Nwk	John	378	Mds	John	809	Hmp
William, junr.	746	Nwk	Robert [2]	378	Mds	John	102	Jff
William, (O. field)	407	Fqr	Baken, Wm.	268	Rck	John	103	Jff
William, (Overseer)	346	Fqr	Baker, Abraham	453	Bdf	John	480	Mnn
William M.	677	Nls	Abram	14	Knw	John	745	Nwk
Wm.	58	Chs	Adam	585	Mnr	John	22	Oho
Wm.	10	Clp	Adam	225	Shn	John	555	Pre
Wm.	800	Nrf	Amy	865	Hnv	John	423	Rnd
Wm.	833	Nrf	Andrew	506	Frd	John	397	Rch
Wm.	889	Nrf	Andrew	556	Pre	John	7	Rcm
Wm.	274	Rck	Andw.	710	Wsh	John	19	Rcm
Wm. S.	283	Rck	Bazdel	453	Bdf	John	24	Rcm
Wright	375	Fqr	Benjamin	438	Pra	John	30	Rcm
see Baly, Storke			Betsey	315	Ags	John C.	24	Rcm
Bailis, John	15	Clp	Betsey	890	Hnv	Jonathan	788	Hmp
Bailor, Christer.	318	Ags	Brooks	42	Chr	Jos.	289	Rck
Geo.	319	Ags	Caleb, Junr.	556	Pre	Joseph	554	Frd
Jacob	320	Ags	Caleb, Senr.	558	Pre	Joseph	809	Hmp
Martin	320	Ags	Catharine	555	Pre	Joseph	37	Isw
Bails, Hugh	570	Mnr	Caty	222	Shn	Joseph [2]	822	Wth
John	606	Btt	Christain W.	151	Alb	Joshua	812	Hmp
Jonathan	604	Btt	Christena	222	Pnd	Josiah	609	Mnt
Thomas, Jr.	598	Frd	Christina	8	Pwh	Leah	77	Acc
Thomas, Senr.	598	Frd	Cilas, (F.N.)	35	Isw	Leakim	98	Jff
Thos.	570	Mnr	Cunrod	285	Ldn	Lewis	177	Shn
Baily, Bob.	871	Yrk	Daniel	7	Acc	Marcy	709	Wsh
Charles	139	Dnw	Daniel	180	Shn	Martin	851	Hnv
Edward	808	Hmp	Davd.	690	Wsh	Martin [Marlen?]	10	Hnr
Exum	139	Dnw	Douglas	822	Wth	Martin	26	Rcm
George	34	Hnr	Eleanor	797	Hmp	Mary	131	Hnr
George	376	Mds	Elias	565	Brk	Mary	555	Pre
Henry	10	Knw	Elijah	75	Acc	Mathew	13	Pwh
Joseph	913	Hrr	Elisabeth	232	Ldn	Matthew	425	Rnd
Richard	125	Hnr	Elizabeth	30	Rcm	Matthias	821	Wth
Robert	819	Wth	Elizabeth P.	512	Frd	Mechech	22	Oho
Robt.	316	Ags	Elliott	555	Pre	Michael	815	Hmp
Thomas	916	Hrr	Evan	22	Oho	Michael	6	Knw
Thornbury	916	Hrr	Francis	531	Brk	Micheal	428	Rnd
William	940	Hrr	Fredk.	593	Mnr	Nathan	695	Br
see B..., Brent			Geo.	485	Mnn	Nicholas	789	Hmp
Bain, Edwd.	291	Rck	George	453	Bdf	Overton	698	Wsh
Quinton	303	Ldn	George	122	Hnr	Patrick	788	Hmp
Quiton	254	Ldn	George	18	Oho	Perrygrine	796	Hmp
Bainbridge, Wm.	486	Mnn	George	15	Rcm	Peter	278	Rck
Baine, Nancy	25	Hnr	George	743	Wsh	Philip	322	Ags
Baines, Benjamin	627	Sss	Grafton	695	Br	Philip	5	Rcm
Coleman	74	Acc	Hance	888	Nrf	Philip P.	220	Shn
Edw.	180	Elc	Hannah	809	Hmp	Pierce	507	Brk
James	626	Sss	Henry	610	Btt	Presilla	4	Hnr
Jesse	627	Sss	Henry	813	Hmp	Prieston	80	Acc
John	627	Sss	Henry	8	Oho	Prisela	484	Mnn
Lemuel	628	Sss	Henry	278	Rck	Richard	75	Acc
Littleberry	155	Sth	Henry	215	Shn	Richard	419	Fqr
Matt.	185	Elc	Henry, Sr.	609	Btt	Richard	743	Nwk
Samuel	628	Sss	Henry W.	514	Frd	Richard	746	Nwk
Stephen	744	Brn	Hezekiah	77	Acc	Robert	610	Btt
Zacheriah	628	Sss	Hugh	21	Rcm	Robert	839	Nrf
Baird, Ephraim	531	Prg	Isaac	702	Wsh	Rudolph	184	Shn
Hamlin	625	Sss	Jac.	486	Mnn	Ruth	888	Nrf
Henry	19	Oho	Jacob	322	Ags	Saml.	610	Btt
Jacob	256	Shn	Jacob	577	Frd	Saml.	281	Ldn
James	16	Oho	Jacob	39	Rcm	Saml. H.	522	Prw
James H.	535	Prg	James	690	Br	Samuel	453	Bdf

Samuel	576	Frd	Balenger, Francis	254	Ldn	Jno.	307	Ldn
Samuel	191	Kng	Bales, David	297	Ldn	John	281	Amh
Samuel	199	Shn	David	311	Ldn	John	234	Frf
Samuel	768	Wst	Edmund	602	Frd	John	926	Hrr
Sebostian	222	Pnd	Baley, Abraham	332	Lnn	John	62	Stf
Sharlotte	220	Shn	Ansel	149	Alb	John S.	567	Frd
Solonon	418	Rnd	Duanna	500	Frn	Joseph	468	Frn
Stephen	77	Acc	Hugh	616	Gls	Joseph, Jr.	971	Nrt
Tho.	483	Mnn	Ison	148	Alb	Joseph, Sr.	970	Nrt
Thomas	797	Hmp	Jno. R.	442	Pra	Lewis	678	Nls
Thos.	10	Hnr	John	149	Alb	Mary	298	Ldn
Timothy	180	Elc	John	151	Alb	Moses	218	Ess
Walter	91	Jff	John	7	Clp	Motram	972	Nrt
William	77	Acc	John E.	939	Chc	Motty	196	Ess
William	507	Frd	Lewis	149	Alb	Osborn	361	Fqr
William	14	Oho	Martin	896	Hnv	Parkes	745	Nwk
William	820	Wth	Peter	333	Lnn	Peter	20	Oho
William, of Ish.	75	Acc	Pheby	333	Lnn	Reuben	36	Stf
Wm.	14	Clp	Pleasant	148	Alb	Richard	208	Ess
Wm.	962	Hrr	Presley	43	Chr	Richard	680	Nls
Wm.	486	Mnn	Saml.	7	Clp	Richard M.	973	Nrt
see Angell, Baher, Bakes,			Samuel	881	Hnv	Robert	288	Ldn
Barker, Moore			Sarah	428	Bth	Salley	14	Hnr
Bakes, Wm.	958	Hrr	Thomas	151	Alb	Salley	973	Nrt
Bakewel, Samuel R.	684	Br	William	148	Alb	Saml.	82	Acc
Samuel R.	698	Br	William	150	Alb	Samuel	5	Hnr
Bakewell, Robt.	814	Nrf	William	331	Lnn	Samuel	426	Rnd
Bakir, Peter	226	Shn	Woodliff	150	Alb	Sarah	417	Fqr
Balaner, Richard	34	Hnr	Balfour, George	890	Nrf	Sarah	677	Nls
Balden, John	482	Mnn	John	943	Chc	Spencer	239	Frf
Jonah	483	Mnn	Balger, James	526	Frd	Spencer	587	Mnr
Th...	482	Mnn	Baling, Nelson	482	Mnn	Spencer	972	Nrt
William	148	Alb	Balinger, James	11	Clp	Spencer	523	Prw
Balderson, Ebenezer	402	Rch	John	668	Mnt	Stephen	219	Ess
Gilbert	402	Rch	Saml.	13	Clp	Stephen	239	Frf
John	402	Rch	Saml.	15	Clp	Stephen	313	Ldn
William	402	Rch	Balis, John	70	Jff	Taliaferro	402	Fqr
Baldick, Fanny	12	Clp	Thos.	855	Hnv	Tho. P.	338	Lnc
Francis	14	Clp	Ball, Aaron	203	Ess	Thomas	583	Frd
Joseph	8	Clp	Alseley	678	Nls	Thomas	970	Nrt
Mary	15	Clp	Ann	338	Lnc	Valentine	13	Pwh
Baldin, Isaac	480	Mnn	Ann	308	Ldn	William	416	Bth
Joseph	533	Brk	Anne	404	Fqr	William	234	Frf
Lucas	5	Knw	Archd.	58	Chs	William	349	Fqr
Wm.	480	Mnn	Baldy	585	Brk	William	378	Fqr
Balding, John	25	Oho	Benjamin	346	Fqr	William	507	Frd
Joseph	3	Oho	Chaney	395	Rch	William	678	Nls
Baldwin, Benjamin	555	Pre	Charlotte	8	Clp	William	970	Nrt
Charles	556	Pre	Chilton	404	Fqr	William	971	Nrt
Cornelius	507	Frd	Christopher	74	Acc	William, major	972	Nrt
Cornelius	540	Frd	Cleary	769	Wst	William, of Muddy		
Geo.	8	Ntt	Custis	5	Acc	Creek	33	Stf
George	248	Aml	Cyrus	336	Lnc	Wm.	66	Chs
Henry	17	Oho	David	346	Fqr	Wm.	7	Clp
Jabin	599	Mnr	David	604	Frd	Wm.	218	Ess
James	555	Pre	David, jr.	970	Nrt	Wm.	219	Ess
Jno.	260	Ldn	David, Sr.	971	Nrt	Wm.	298	Ldn
John	248	Aml	Edward	535	Frd	see Bael, Bell		
John	557	Pre	Edwd. P.	338	Lnc	Ballad, Benjamin	73	Spt
John	11	Wod	Eliza.	214	Ess	Benjamin	101	Spt
John, Jun.	555	Pre	Elizabeth	971	Nrt	Charles	101	Spt
John, Senr.	557	Pre	Enoch	366	Fqr	James	92	Spt
Joseph	240	Ldn	Francis	973	Nrt	Susanna	890	Crl
Joseph	167	Shn	Geo.	337	Lnc	Susanna	893	Crl
Joseph C.	605	Frd	Geo.	480	Mnn	William	101	Spt
Little John	556	Pre	George	596	Frd	see Ballard		
Lucy	10	Ntt	George	646	Glc	Ballade see Battaile		
Mahlon	234	Ldn	George	746	Nwk	Ballah, Jas.	483	Mnn
Pleasant	558	Pre	Hanah	567	Mnr	Ballance, Ahaz	797	Nrf
Reos	537	Frd	Hannah	406	Fqr	Cary	791	Nrf
Samuel	556	Pre	Heny	241	Frf	Elizabeth	797	Nrf
Stacey	234	Ldn	Isaac	299	Ldn	Ephraham	799	Nrf
Thomas	538	Frd	Isham	5	Pwh	Francis	442	Pra
William	362	Fqr	James	690	Br	Henry	795	Nrf
William	538	Frd	James	234	Frf	Mons	796	Nrf
William	555	Pre	James	547	Frd	Thos.	788	Nrf
William	556	Pre	James	423	Msn	Willis	890	Nrf
Wm.	16	Ntt	James	20	Oho	Wm.	820	Nrf
Bale, William, of A.			Jas., Do. [ditto, i.e.	John		Ballard, Betsey	572	Mnr
[of t. ?]	55	Stf	Turner] for	470	Mdd	Birkley	455	Bdf

16

David	184 Alb	
Edward	185 Alb	
Elijah	4 Knw	
Elijah, Jur.	4 Knw	
Eliza.	580 Mnr	
Fielding	4 Knw	
Francis	185 Alb	
Garland	185 Alb	
James	79 Acc	
James	184 Alb	
James	493 Frn	
James	564 Mnr	
Jeremiah	593 Mnr	
John	185 Alb	
John	280 Amh	
John	317 Ags	
John	406 Ags	
John	4 Knw	
John	377 Mds	
John	580 Mnr	
Johnson	185 Alb	
Joseph W.	46 Isw	
Lewis	680 Nls	
Mary	887 Nrf	
Mildred	893 Crl	
Moses	82 Acc	
Phillip, Junr.	4 Knw	
Phillip, Senr.	4 Knw	
Richard	93 Spt	
Thomas	4 Knw	
Thomas	576 Mnr	
William	184 Alb	
William	185 Alb	
William	454 Bdf	
William	563 Mnr	
see Ballad, Sherman		
Balle, Jesse	10 Clp	
Jno.	10 Clp	
Ballenger, Francis	242 Frf	
George	567 Mnr	
Henry	287 Amh	
Henry	567 Mnr	
James	235 Frf	
James, Junr.	242 Frf	
Joseph	235 Frf	
William	237 Frf	
Wm.	14 Clp	
Ballentine, Jas.	833 Nrf	
Jos.	823 Nrf	
Mary	811 Nrf	
Ballet, Elizabeth	428 Bth	
Ballew, Ann	319 Ags	
Ballinger, Edward	415 Fqr	
Edward	103 Spt	
Henson	393 Fqr	
Ballow, Jordan	13 Pwh	
Leonard	11 Pwh	
Ballowe, Fanney	797 Bck	
John	812 Bck	
Thomas	782 Bck	
Balltrip, Sharp	929 Hrr	
Balls, Thos.	889 Nrf	
Balmain, Alexander	517 Frd	
Balman, Evin	192 Shn	
Balmane, Nancy	234 Frf	
Balmer, Mildred	873 Sth	
Balser, Dan.	480 Mnn	
Geo.	479 Mnn	
Balsley, George	321 Ags	
Balsom, Sarah	889 Nrf	
Wm.	890 Nrf	
Balson, David	926 Hrr	
Balthazer, Henry	11 Rcm	
Balthrop, Jeremiah	393 Fqr	
John	398 Fqr	
Reuben	190 Kng	
Baltimore, Ann	115 Cmb	
Balton, James	704 Wsh	
Baltzell, Michal	514 Frd	
Baltzer, Abrm.	297 Rck	
Benj.	297 Rck	
Baly, John	924 Hrr	
Joseph	924 Hrr	
Menter	963 Hrr	
Bamer see Barner		
Bamton, Andrew	234 Shn	
Bandy, Caleb	12 Acc	
James	611 Btt	
John	611 Btt	
Reuben	455 Bdf	
Thomas	611 Btt	
Willm.	606 Btt	
Bane, Abraham S.	585 Frd	
George	333 Lnn	
Hugh	679 Br	
James, Junr.	616 Gls	
James, Senr.	616 Gls	
John	679 Br	
Robert	304 Rck	
William	688 Br	
Banes, Henry	583 Brk	
Banester, Bennett	432 Msn	
Thos. B.	248 Aml	
Bangey, Geo.	317 Ags	
Banham, Aaron	271 Ldn	
Baning, John	606 Btt	
Banister, ---, & Co.	334 Dnw	
James	455 Bdf	
Jno. M.	334 Dnw	
Jno. M.	336 Dnw	
John M.	326 Dnw	
Oliver, (F.N.)	7 Clp	
Bankest, Jacob	479 Mnn	
Bankhead, Christian	892 Crl	
John	892 Crl	
Banks, Adam	376 Mds	
Andrew, [his] est.	158 Knq	
Baylor	6 Clp	
Benjamin	601 Srr	
Betty	595 Frd	
Betty	871 Yrk	
Betty	888 Yrk	
Caty	216 Ess	
Clemment	87 Jff	
David	83 Acc	
Duey	438 Flv	
Edward	783 Hmp	
Elizabeth	743 Brn	
Elizabeth	124 Hnr	
Elizabeth, (F. Negroe)	398 Fqr	
Garrard	376 Mds	
George	32 Stf	
George W.	222 Ess	
Gerrard	120 Spt	
Godfrey	871 Yrk	
H.	66 Chs	
Harrison	438 Pra	
Henry	13 Hnr	
Jacob	684 Gch	
James	777 Bck	
James	179 Elc	
James	155 Knq	
James	436 Mth	
James	452 Mth	
Jeremiah	598 Srr	
Jno.	648 Glc	
Jno.	452 Mth	
Jno., Jr.	442 Pra	
John	332 Dnw	
John	179 Elc	
John	684 Gch	
John	18 Hnr	
John	84 Jff	
John	656 Mnt	
John	438 Pra	
John	888 Yrk	
Joshua	681 Wrw	
Judith	595 Frd	
Lucy	871 Yrk	
Maria	124 Hnr	
Mary	232 Ldn	
Mary	681 Wrw	
Molly, (Y)	870 Yrk	
Richd. P.	206 Ess	
Samuel	84 Jff	
Tho.	871 Yrk	
William	96 Clp	
Wm.	1 Clp	
Wm.	6 Clp	
Wm.	222 Ess	
Wm.	441 Flv	
Wm.	442 Pra	
Wm.	870 Yrk	
Wm., (B)	205 Ess	
see Michem		
Bann see Banes		
Bannin see Bauin		
Banning, Asa	275 Rck	
Bannion, James	53 Stf	
William	54 Stf	
Bannister, Augustine	361 Fqr	
Oliver	284 Rck	
Banns, John	816 Nrf	
Banon, Jno.	866 Hnv	
Banton, George	677 Nls	
William	784 Bck	
Banty, Henry	150 Sth	
Baptestter, Sally	192 Kng	
Baptist, Ann	888 Yrk	
Edwd.	870 Yrk	
Elizabeth	44 Chr	
Franky	120 Spt	
Jno.	680 Wrw	
Bar..., ...l, free		
negro	971 Nrt	
John	524 Prw	
John, jr.	743 Brn	
Barachman, Hen.	480 Mnn	
Baran, Eliza	4 Hnr	
Barb, Abraham	224 Shn	
Adam	224 Shn	
Adam	225 Shn	
Adam	226 Shn	
David	226 Shn	
Henry	231 Shn	
Jacob	746 Wsh	
John	224 Shn	
William	230 Shn	
see Bab		
Barba, Susan	49 Stf	
Barbee, Andrew	405 Fqr	
Andrew, Jr.	410 Fqr	
Chandler	363 Fqr	
Haws	166 Shn	
James	342 Fqr	
John	407 Fqr	
John A.	183 Shn	
Joseph A.	364 Fqr	
Sampson	381 Fqr	
Thomas	411 Fqr	
Thos.	7 Clp	
Turner	363 Fqr	
Wm.	13 Clp	
see Barber		
Barber, Clotsworthy	334 Dnw	
Edward	24 Stf	
Edward, jr.	51 Stf	
Elisha	611 Btt	
Harry	34 Stf	
James	330 Dnw	
James	363 Fqr	
Jas.	831 Nrf	
John	563 Frd	
John	24 Isw	
John	888 Nrf	
Joseph	880 Cmp	
Joseph	52 Stf	
Judy	330 Dnw	
Mordecia	326 Dnw	
Samuel	887 Nrf	

Name	No.	Code
Thomas	357	Fqr
William	110	Spt
William	29	Stf
see Barbee, Harber		
Barbie see Barbee		
Barbour, Gabl.	11	Clp
Philip, Qr.	378	Mds
Barbow, Agnis	940	Chc
Barby, Molley	156	Knq
Barclay, Jacob	19	Rcm
Jingo	12	Acc
Rot.	826	Nrf
Barden, Benj., Jun.	42	Isw
Margaret	757	Hmp
Samuel	602	Frd
Bardett, Eliza.	589	Mnr
Barding, William	247	Aml
Bardle, John	794	Hmp
Bare, Adam	795	Hmp
H.	484	Mnn
Jacob	295	Rck
Jno.	295	Rck
Joseph	295	Rck
Suzan	795	Hmp
Barecroft, John	409	Rch
Thomas	972	Nrt
William	972	Nrt
Bareford, James	240	Frf
Barey, Jeremiah	529	Brk
Barfoot, Eunic	800	Nrf
James	156	Knq
Richd.	157	Knq
William	154	Knq
Barge see Barger		
Barger, Adam	1	Knw
Adam	285	Rck
Christn.	318	Ags
Elias	642	Mnt
Jacob	324	Ags
Jacob	284	Rck
John	608	Btt
John	823	Hmp
John	273	Rck
Bargerhoof, Nicholas	226	Pnd
Bargerhuff, William	440	Bth
Barham, Benja.	126	Sth
Burwell	601	Srr
Fathy	601	Srr
Howel	140	Sth
John	127	Sth
Joseph, sr.	601	Srr
Sally	602	Srr
Saml.	161	Sth
Stephen	131	Sth
Barhaw, John	430	Flv
Barick, Phillip	698	Wsh
Bariger, John	630	Mnt
Baringer, Adam	631	Mnt
Danl.	624	Mnt
Isaac S.	662	Mnt
John S.	639	Mnt
Barkahizer, Barbara	15	Rcm
Barkdale, Goodman	149	Alb
Barkelow, Elizabeth	760	Hmp
Barker, Anis	127	Hnr
Ann	132	Cmb
Anne	235	Frf
Aron	481	Mnn
Barbara	237	Frf
Burwele	742	Brn
Carroll	234	Frf
Charity	885	Hnv
Charles	368	Fqr
Charles	191	Shn
Charles	628	Sss
Charles, Senr.	753	Wsh
Daniel	525	Prw
Daniel	767	Wst
Dav.	481	Mnn
David	629	Sss

Name	No.	Code
Edmund	884	Hnv
Edward	700	Wsh
Elijah	455	Bdf
Fanny	499	Prw
Feabah	8	Hnr
George	12	Acc
George	879	Hnv
Gray	628	Sss
Isaac	4	Knw
James	627	Sss
Jane	237	Frf
Jane	507	Prw
Jane	525	Prw
Jas.	480	Mnn
Jas.	483	Mnn
Jas., Jnr.	484	Mnn
Jno.	888	Hnv
Jno.	483	Mnn
Jno., Snr.	879	Hnv
Jno. B.	240	Frf
John	565	Brk
John	42	Chr
John	419	Fqr
John	745	Nwk
John	507	Prw
John	627	Sss
John	753	Wsh
John	767	Wst
Jos.	481	Mnn
Jos., Jr.	481	Mnn
Joseph	768	Wst
Kenelm	238	Frf
Leonard	233	Frf
Leonard	972	Nrt
Mary	881	Hnv
Mary	545	Prg
Merit	4	Pwh
Moses	520	Frd
Nancy	629	Sss
Nathan	884	Hnv
Nathaniel	240	Frf
Parker	75	Acc
Prieston	83	Acc
Rebecca W.	115	Cmb
Richd.	868	Sth
Rivers	848	Sth
Salley	745	Nwk
Sarah	484	Mnn
Thomas	437	Flv
Thomas	24	Oho
Thomas	214	Shn
Thos.	742	Brn
Thos.	753	Wsh
William [2]	233	Frf
William	368	Fqr
William	122	Hnr
William	113	Spt
William H.	5	Pwh
William W.	114	Cmb
Wim.	879	Hnv
Wm.	684	Gch
Zach.	480	Mnn
see Baker, Basker		
Barkerville, John	819	Bck
Barkett, Abm.	441	Flv
Jesse	440	Flv
Wm.	438	Flv
Barkhart, Geo.	487	Mnn
Barkill, Jno.	23	Hnr
Barkley, Sarah	156	Knq
Wm.	551	Brk
Barkman, Andrew	225	Shn
Barks, Jacob	798	Hmp
Barksdale, Claiborne	43	Chr
Claiborne, Sr.	68	Chr
Dudley	555	Pre
Duglass	149	Alb
Grief	42	Chr
Jonathin	150	Alb
Nelson	185	Alb

Name	No.	Code
Samuel	150	Alb
see Barkdale		
Barkshier, Ott	26	Oho
Barkshire, Corns.	480	Mnn
Jno.	481	Mnn
Barkwell, Thomas	744	Nwk
Barlett, John	611	Btt
Thomas	918	Hrr
Barley, David	546	Frd
James	10	Rcm
John	549	Frd
Barlow, Anna	855	Hnv
Benj.	13	Isw
Cary	601	Srr
David	893	Crl
Dolly	446	Grn
George	33	Isw
Harrisson	28	Isw
Jacob	708	Wsh
James	30	Isw
James	289	Ldn
James	709	Wsh
John	441	Bth
John	743	Brn
John	889	Crl
John [2]	893	Crl
John	702	Wsh
Joseph	708	Wsh
Lucy	601	Srr
Maria	36	Isw
Robt. T.	684	Gch
Samuel	890	Crl
Thomas	347	Fqr
Willis W.	946	Chc
Barmore, Geo.	482	Mnn
Barn, Abner	826	Hmp
Barnard, Notley	817	Hmp
Barnatt, Hannah	682	Gch
Barnell see Barnett		
Barner, Harerson	742	Brn
Jacob	42	Chr
John, Sr.	744	Brn
William	9	Pwh
Barnerd, Benjamin	501	Frn
Peter, Jr.	452	Frn
Peter, Sr.	501	Frn
Walter	481	Frn
Barnes, Ann	678	Wrw
Archibald	74	Acc
Armisted	8	Clp
Arthur	78	Acc
Arthur	442	Pra
Asa	333	Lnn
Benja.	129	Sth
Benja.	151	Sth
Bennett	446	Grn
Bennett	161	Sth
Bracket	44	Chr
Britain	160	Sth
Charles	564	Frd
Charles	439	Pra
Charles	393	Rch
Drury	744	Brn
Eliza.	871	Sth
Ezekiel	8	Wod
Francis	440	Pra
Francis, Capt.	42	Chr
Francis, Senr.	44	Chr
Gabriel	42	Chr
George	331	Lnn
George P.	75	Acc
Hannah	567	Frd
Hannah	584	Frd
Henry	375	Mds
Jacob	868	Sth
James	706	Brn
James	44	Chr
James	140	Dnw
James	591	Frd
James	333	Lnn

Jaob	158	Sth	Joshua	455	Bdf	Barraud, ---, Doctr.	889	Nrf
Jeremh., f. negro	237	Frf	Lewis	516	Frd	---, Madm.	887	Nrf
Jeremh., f. negro	242	Frf	Milley	533	Frd	Barrel, John	597	Brk
Jesse	334	Dnw	Nathan	681	Nls	Barret, Danl.	480	Mnn
Jno.	10	Clp	Nicoles	705	Wsh	Henry	820	Wth
Jno.	239	Frf	Reason	605	Btt	James	684	Gch
John	5	Acc	Salley	8	Hnr	John	572	Mnr
John	76	Acc	Sally	7	Clp	Mary	108	Spt
John	44	Chr	Thos.	614	Mnt	Samuel	8	Wod
John	446	Grn	Timothy	883	Cmp	William	10	Wod
John	331	Lnn	William	425	Msn	Wm.	486	Mnn
John	439	Pra	see Grimsley			Barrett, Anderson	35	Hnr
John	151	Sth	Barney, Thomas	567	Brk	Benjamin	582	Frd
Joseph	442	Pra	Barnhart, George	7	Rcm	Charles L.	269	Amh
Leonard	67	Chr	Henry	86	Jff	Danl.	840	Nrf
Leonard	375	Mds	Peter	7	Rcm	David	578	Frd
Leond., Este.	7	Clp	Philip	106	Jff	James	12	Knw
Marten	375	Mds	see Burnhart			James	148	Sth
Martha Joy	869	Sth	Barnheart, John	478	Frn	Jesse	148	Sth
Mary	950	Chc	Barnhouse, Jacob	809	Hmp	John	123	Cmb
Mary	859	Sth	John	809	Hmp	John	498	Frn
Michael	583	Brk	John	430	Rnd	John	779	Hmp
Newman B.	36	Stf	Barnitt, Bettey	151	Alb	Joseph	781	Hmp
Ome	80	Acc	Barns, Abm. [Jno. crossed			Mary	488	Frn
Richard	206	Ess	out]	480	Mnn	Nathan	779	Hmp
Robert	8	Wod	Abm.	483	Mnn	Presley	880	Sth
Samuel	10	Acc	Anderson	120	Hnr	Saml.	29	Hnr
Silvanes	7	Wod	Daniel	927	Hrr	Thomas	578	Frd
Spencer	11	Acc	David	34	Hnr	Thomas	888	Nrf
Stephen	566	Frd	Edward	506	Frd	Thomas	525	Prw
Stephen	20	Oho	Elisha	5	Knw	William	487	Frn
Telitha	83	Acc	Geo. D.	480	Mnn	William	498	Frn
Thomas	611	Btt	Hannah	972	Nrt	Wm.	834	Nrf
Thomas	42	Chr	Henry	486	Mnn	Barrick, Bailey	459	Mdd
Thos.	870	Sth	Isc.	480	Mnn	David	459	Mdd
Tully, Jr.	441	Pra	J.S.	482	Mnn	David	391	Rch
Tully, Sr.	441	Pra	James	831	Bck	George	516	Frd
Vachel	11	Clp	James	489	Frn	George	391	Rch
William	514	Prw	Nancy	133	Hnr	Griffin G.	394	Rch
Wm.	146	Sth	Reason	1	Wod	Jacob	31	Rcm
Wm.	683	Wrw	Robt.	27	Hnr	John	458	Mdd
see Baines, Banes, Bar...,			Samuel, Jr.	972	Nrt	John B.	459	Mdd
Barner			Samuel, Sr.	971	Nrt	Newby	396	Rch
Barnet, Barret	442	Bth	Samuel G.	972	Nrt	Robert	459	Mdd
Edwd.	281	Rck	Stephen	972	Nrt	Barricks, John	22	Rcm
Elizabeth	150	Alb	Thomas	573	Mnr	Barringer, George	431	Msn
Elizabeth	151	Alb	Travers	13	Rcm	Barrington, Mary	813	Nrf
Isaac	432	Bth	Uz	484	Mnn	Robert	807	Nrf
Jno.	484	Mnn	William, Jr.	971	Nrt	William	914	Hrr
Judah	114	Hnr	William, Sr.	972	Nrt	Barriot, John	503	Brk
Lucy	185	Alb	Wm.	950	Hrr	Barris see Barns		
Robert	430	Bth	Wm.	481	Mnn	Barrock, Moore	855	Cmp
Thomas	432	Bth	see Barn, Barnes, Borns			William	458	Mdd
William	116	Spt	Barnsfield, Jno.	683	Gch	Barron, Ezer	524	Frd
Zachariah	432	Bth	Baron, Sally	145	Sth	Hendly	516	Prw
see Basnet			Barp, Isaa	485	Mnn	James	192	Elc
Barnett, Achilles G.	564	Frd	Barr, Adam	238	Ldn	Jessee	518	Prw
Allan	123	Hnr	Francis	216	Shn	Robt.	890	Nrf
Ambrose	533	Frd	Geo.	235	Ldn	Saml.	192	Elc
Benja. N.	7	Clp	George	398	Fqr	see Bar...		
Brightwell	555	Pre	Hugh	237	Ldn	Barrot, James	768	Wst
David	614	Mnt	James	558	Frd	Luke	606	Btt
Francis, F. Negroe	412	Fqr	Jno.	7	Clp	Barrott, Benja.	137	Sth
Hutchens	441	Flv	John	423	Rnd	Burwell	855	Sth
James	149	Alb	Michl.	482	Mnn	Edmund	869	Sth
James	438	Flv	Nancey	398	Fqr	George	971	Nrt
James	378	Mds	Peter	527	Frd	Giles	161	Sth
James	614	Mnt	Philip	210	Shn	Jacob	132	Sth
Jane	296	Amh	Richard	693	Br	Jordan	151	Sth
Jas.	9	Clp	Richd.	827	Nrf	Luke	606	Btt
John	324	Ags	Robert	558	Frd	Millisent	971	Nrt
John	617	Mnt	Robert	578	Frd	Rawley	18	Isw
John	678	Nls	Wm.	544	Prg	Reuben	870	Sth
John	680	Nls	Barrach, Geo.	481	Mnn	Thomas	43	Chr
John	767	Wst	Jas.	481	Mnn	Wm.	144	Sth
John	768	Wst	Barrachman, Jno.	480	Mnn	Barrow, Ben	849	Sth
John	2	Wod	Barrack, Russel	878	Cmp	Benjamin	944	Chc
John	888	Yrk	Vincent	767	Wst	David	704	Brn
Joseph	617	Mnt	Barrat, ---, Miss	890	Nrf	Denis	704	Brn
Joseph	501	Prw	Wm.	139	Dnw	Elizabeth	952	Chc

Israel	12	Hnr	Jacob	639	Mnt	Lerina	873	Sth
John	941	Chc	James	274	Ldn	Martha	13	Pwh
John	564	Frd	John	371	Fqr	Mary	248	Aml
John	602	Frd	John	23	Oho	Partin	705	Brn
John	869	Sth	Joseph	347	Fqr	Peter	14	Ntt
John, Sr.	704	Brn	Joseph	639	Mnt	Thos.	705	Brn
Phillip	941	Chc	Levi	274	Ldn	Thos.	56	Chs
Sarah	849	Sth	Lucy	157	Knq	Wm.	57	Chs
Solomon	503	Brk	Mary	581	Frd	Wm.	65	Chs
Thomas	603	Frd	Richard P.	542	Frd	Zachariah	447	Grn
William, Jr.	602	Frd	Seth	105	Spt	Basse, Joseph	822	Nrf
William, Senr.	602	Frd	Thos.	588	Brk	Welles	822	Nrf
Wm., Jr.	704	Brn	Valentine	521	Prw	Wm.	822	Nrf
Wm., Sr.	704	Brn	William	606	Btt	Wm., jr.	822	Nrf
see Burrow			William, (M)	178	Shn	Bassett, Burwell	744	Nwk
Barrtlett, Joseph	767	Wst	William W.	76	Acc	Jno.	886	Hnv
Barruck, Jno.	283	Ldn	Wm., (Fleet)	217	Ess	Bassham, John	469	Frn
Barrus see Barnes			see Barlow, Burton			William	467	Frn
Barry, Andw.	398	Ags	Barum, Nathan	597	Mnr	William	469	Frn
James	888	Nrf	Barwell see Bar...			Bassin, Dominica	888	Nrf
Thomas	677	Nls	Basebeech, Archer	3	Ntt	Bastable, George	407	Fqr
William	242	Frf	Jno., jr.	3	Ntt	Baster, William B.	847	Cmp
Barrycraft, Jno.	293	Ldn	Basey, Benja.	6	Clp	Bastian, John	890	Crl
Nancy	288	Ldn	Henry	6	Clp	Bastin, Sarah	196	Ess
Nancy	293	Ldn	Isaac	6	Clp	Baswell, Mary	437	Pra
Barrymore, Mary	836	Nrf	James	8	Clp	Batchelder, Henry	460	Mdd
Bartee, Anna	791	Nrf	Johnice [?]	8	Oho	Batcheldor, Mary	460	Mdd
Bryt.	799	Nrf	Josiah	368	Fqr	Batchelor, Peter	610	Btt
George	611	Btt	Kitty	6	Clp	Bate, Richard	334	Dnw
John	804	Nrf	Nancy	6	Clp	Batee see Batte		
Lemuel	804	Nrf	Thomas P.	240	Frf	Bateman, Jesse	609	Mnt
Saml.	793	Nrf	Basha, Daniel	680	Nls	Thomas	266	Ldn
Saml., jr.	840	Nrf	Bashal, Thos.	813	Nrf	William	39	Rcm
Thos.	788	Nrf	Bashan see Barhaw			Wm.	266	Ldn
William	795	Nrf	Bashaw, Elijah	406	Fqr	Batemon, Benjamin	454	Bdf
Wm.	799	Nrf	Mary	840	Nrf	Elizabeth	454	Bdf
Barter, David	43	Chr	Peter	12	Clp	Bater, Samuel R.	206	Shn
John	67	Chr	Rawlh.	13	Clp	Bates, Ann	154	Knq
Barteson, James	588	Brk	Bashm, John C.	831	Nrf	Benjamin	862	Hnv
Bartholemy, Moses	687	Br	Basick, Samuel	548	Frd	Caroline	683	Gch
Bartle, John, jr.	600	Srr	Basil, John	81	Jff	Charles	822	Wth
Bartles, Robert	245	Shn	Baskaw, George	438	Pra	Cyrus	508	Prw
Bartlet, James	871	Yrk	Basker, Charles	881	Hnv	David	333	Lnn
Tho.	486	Mnn	Wm.	281	Rck	David	2	Ntt
Thomas	932	Hrr	Basket, Abriham	213	Ess	Edward	236	Frf
see Cole			Elizabeth	156	Knq	Elisha	871	Yrk
Bartlett, Anny	956	Hrr	Rewben	156	Knq	Elizh.	871	Yrk
Benj.	931	Hrr	Baskins, Charles	315	Ags	Emily	22	Oho
Elisha	398	Rch	John C.	315	Ags	Fleming	972	Nrt
Eppa	918	Hrr	Baskit, James	607	Btt	Fleming	501	Prw
Garnet	633	Mnt	James	156	Knq	Hannah	871	Yrk
George	535	Frd	Basnet, Booz	480	Mnn	James	943	Chc
Henry	527	Frd	Jno.	480	Mnn	James	365	Fqr
Isacc	402	Rch	S.	483	Mnn	James	375	Mds
James	432	Flv	see Barnet			James	60	Stf
James	588	Frd	Bason see Basore			John	890	Crl
James	940	Hrr	Basore, John	588	Brk	John	375	Mds
James	276	Ldn	Michl.	520	Brk	John	508	Prw
Jams	956	Hrr	Peter	520	Brk	Patsy	891	Crl
Jno.	265	Ldn	Bass, Archd.	64	Chs	Reuben	375	Mds
John	929	Hrr	Arthur	52	Chs	Reuben	679	Nls
John	405	Rch	Benjamin	705	Brn	Robert, Jur.	148	Alb
Nancy	954	Hrr	Edward	53	Chs	Robert, Senr.	148	Alb
Patty	556	Pre	Edwd., Est.	248	Aml	Stephen	888	Yrk
Reubin	633	Mnt	Edwin	146	Sth	Thomas	237	Frf
Samuel	232	Ldn	Elizabeth	16	Ntt	Thomas	261	Ldn
Sanford	932	Hrr	Ephraim	705	Brn	Thomas	273	Ldn
Thomas	274	Ldn	Frederick S.	878	Cmp	William	275	Amh
William	927	Hrr	Hartwell H.	705	Brn	William	154	Knq
William	171	Shn	Henry	628	Sss	William	59	Stf
William	768	Wst	Henry R.	873	Sth	William	822	Wth
Wm.	958	Hrr	Howel	847	Sth	Willis	375	Mds
see Barlett, Blake,	Edwards		James, jr.	705	Brn	Batey, Robert	531	Frd
Bartley, George	149	Alb	James, Sr.	705	Brn	Bathale, Wm.	813	Nrf
Phiby	447	Flv	Jno. M.	67	Chs	Batkins, Jno., Jnr.	881	Hnv
Bartly, Ben., (FN)	68	Chr	John	248	Aml	Batley, Fielding	374	Fqr
Barton, Benja.	13	Clp	John W.	7	Pwh	John	325	Dnw
Benjn., Jr.	639	Mnt	John, Senior	52	Chs	Baton, William	513	Frd
Burr	454	Bdf	Joseph	130	Hnr	Batson, James	234	Ldn
Elisha	455	Bdf	Joshua	626	Sss	Jno.	234	Ldn

20

Richd.	15	Clp	John	53	Chs	Bayley, James	20	Oho
Thomas	234	Ldn	John	3	Pwh	Jno.	251	Ldn
Batt, Alexander W.	744	Brn	John	9	Pwh	Sydnor	232	Ldn
Fredric	447	Grn	Js., Est.	59	Chs	William	20	Oho
Gardner	446	Grn	Julia	117	Hnr	Baylie, John, (M)	178	Shn
Henry	446	Grn	Leonard	591	Brk	Baylis, Henry	573	Frd
Jas.	336	Lnc	Littleberry	704	Brn	William	537	Frd
Jno. B.	330	Dnw	Martha	531	Prg	Bayliss see Baytiss		
John	446	Grn	Martin	6	Pwh	Baylor, Abrm., Christians-		
Miles	247	Aml	Michael	821	Wth	burg	618	Mnt
Moses	509	Brk	Michael, Senr.	821	Wth	Frederk.	563	Brk
Richard B.	334	Dnw	Polley	141	Dnw	James	767	Wst
Sarah	446	Grn	Rd.	57	Chs	John	889	Crl
Wm.	744	Brn	Richard	8	Pwh	Lucy	99	Jff
Wm., Senr.	541	Prg	Robinson	246	Aml	Richard	93	Jff
see Ball, Butt			Robt.	56	Chs	Robert	198	Ess
Battaile, ...	893	Crl	Salley	60	Chs	Bayly, Bowman	9	Acc
John	890	Crl	Samuel	531	Prg	Edward	12	Acc
Laurence	891	Crl	Sarah	68	Chs	Elijah	83	Acc
Lawe., Este.	6	Clp	Siller	704	Brn	Isma	10	Acc
Batte, Archibald	545	Prg	William	630	Sss	James	11	Acc
Fanny	545	Prg	Wm.	60	Chs	Jenny	10	Acc
Fred.	547	Prg	see B...h			John	6	Acc
Jno.	545	Prg	Baughan, Benjamin, jr.	890	Crl	Joseph	1	Oho
Kitty	545	Prg	James	131	Cmb	Major	4	Acc
Sarah	534	Prg	John	120	Cmb	Nancy	11	Acc
Battell, J.B.	890	Nrf	Peyton	557	Pre	Rachel	12	Acc
Batten, Cabeb	800	Nrf	Tucker	120	Cmb	Richard, Col.	6	Acc
Elizabeth	438	Pra	Warner	123	Cmb	Richard D.	6	Acc
George	441	Pra	Baugher, Danl.	29	Rcm	Robert	76	Acc
Wm.	441	Pra	Nicholas	35	Rcm	Robert, M	80	Acc
Battin, Clements	34	Isw	Baughman, Henry	605	Btt	Robert, of R	79	Acc
Samuel	18	Isw	Baughn, James	864	Hnv	Sarah	75	Acc
Thom	955	Hrr	Jno.	863	Hnv	Shadrach	79	Acc
Willey	40	Isw	John	117	Hnr	Southey	81	Acc
William	34	Isw	Joseph	117	Hnr	Thomas	7	Acc
Battle, Jesse	128	Sth	Sammul	846	Hnv	Thomas M.	5	Acc
Battles, Betsy	115	Hnr	Wm.	116	Hnr	Thomas S.	5	Acc
Elizabeth	180	Alb	Bauin, John	20	Stf	Tom	77	Acc
Juanna	9	Hnr	Baulden, Samuel	67	Chr	William P.	23	Stf
Milly	115	Hnr	Bauldin, Mary	69	Chr	Zadock	80	Acc
Nancy	3	Hnr	Bawcatt, William	515	Frd	Bayn, Griffin	455	Bdf
Robert	185	Alb	Bawen, Thomas	399	Rch	Bayne, Charles	611	Btt
Shadrick	151	Alb	see Bowen			George	607	Btt
Turner	180	Alb	Bawgis, John [2]	955	Hrr	Jesse	823	Hmp
Batton, Henry	482	Mnn	Baws, Patsy	811	Nrf	Jos.	832	Nrf
John	377	Mds	Baxley, Andrew	609	Btt	Nancey	647	Glc
John	482	Mnn	Baxter, Allen	2	Knw	Sarah	78	Acc
Batts, Andra	942	Hrr	Eve	536	Prg	Wm.	828	Nrf
Benjamin	626	Sss	Geo. A., Rev.	264	Rck	Baynes, Henry	888	Nrf
Chambling	69	Chs	Greenberry	689	Brk	Baynham, Wm.	202	Ess
Thomas	64	Chs	Hardy	146	Sth	Bayrd, Adam	13	Hnr
Thos.	65	Chs	James	819	Wth	Mary	15	Hnr
Baty, Alexander	938	Hrr	John	413	Bth	Baysee, John	178	Shn
David	290	Ldn	John	190	Kng	Baysie, Elesinon	337	Lnc
John	910	Hrr	John	13	Rcm	Isaac	971	Nrt
John	944	Hrr	Joseph	13	Rcm	Baytiss, Jno.	13	Clp
John	953	Hrr	Mary	413	Bth	Bayton, Beverly	834	Nrf
Robert	23	Stf	Michael	820	Wth	Jno.	879	Sth
Samu.	939	Hrr	Samuel	694	Br	Baytop, James	647	Glc
Batz, Conrad	472	Frn	Samuel	767	Wst	James, jr.	647	Glc
Baucher, Henry	328	Dnw	William	696	Br	Thomas	646	Glc
Baudy see Bandy			William	534	Prg	Bazden, Lewis	601	Srr
Baugh, ... F.	15	Pwh	Wilie	534	Prg	Bazell, John	719	Wsh
Adam	738	Wsh	see Baster			Bazzle, Andw.	26	Rcm
Ann	11	Pwh	Baxtor, Alexr.	13	Clp	Michael	17	Rcm
Archabald	334	Dnw	Bayles, Aden	483	Mnn	Beaber, Hannah C.	768	Wst
Bartlett	860	Cmp	Enoch	187	Alb	Beach, James B.	43	Chr
Frederick	223	Shn	Jesse	357	Fqr	John	179	Shn
George	821	Wth	Joseph	187	Alb	Lodowich B.	43	Chr
George	822	Wth	M. [crossed out]	481	Mnn	Mary	333	Lnn
Henry	821	Wth	Wm.	577	Brk	Molly, of R	12	Acc
Jacob	821	Wth	Wm.	481	Mnn	Nathan B.	43	Chr
James	246	Aml	Wm.	485	Mnn	Samuel	10	Knw
James	743	Brn	Bayless, Dudley	390	Fqr	Thomas	27	Stf
James	532	Prg	Joanna	238	Frf	Beacham, Ann	888	Nrf
Jeremiah	59	Chs	Milley	239	Frf	Bushard	972	Nrt
Jno.	69	Chs	Thomas	238	Frf	John	972	Nrt
Joanna	544	Prg	William	235	Frf	Levi	681	Wrw
Joel	704	Brn	William	390	Fqr	Parker	972	Nrt

Name	No.	Abbr	Name	No.	Abbr	Name	No.	Abbr
Thomas	972	Nrt	Joseph W.	9	Oho	Lucinda	39	Rcm
Beacy, Sarah	333	Lnn	Theodore	68	Jff	Marton	745	Wsh
Beadle, Rhody	14	Ntt	Thomas	66	Jff	Matthew	74	Acc
Thomas	14	Ntt	Zephaniah	16	Oho	Peter	323	Ags
Beadles, H. D.	888	Nrf	Bealle, Eli	834	Hmp	Peter, jr.	321	Ags
Jeftian	155	Knq	Beam, Benjamin	221	Shn	Peter, sr.	323	Ags
William	43	Chr	Christley	16	Rcm	Robert	453	Bdf
Beagle, Joel	37	Stf	Daniel	221	Shn	Robert	479	Frn
John	27	Stf	Jacob	181	Shn	Robert	543	Frd
William	46	Stf	Samuel	221	Shn	Robt.	409	Ags
Beagles, Edmund	890	Crl	Beaman, Nathl.	876	Sth	Saml.	319	Ags
Beake, Isaa	6	Oho	Beamer, Nicholas	27	Hnr	Samuel	453	Bdf
Beaker, Fredk.	605	Btt	Zadock	517	Brk	Samuel	466	Frn
Beal, Abey	41	Isw	Beamon, Rebecca	460	Mdd	Sarah	466	Frn
Alexander	693	Br	Beamot, Ann	888	Nrf	Step.	246	Ldn
Alpheus	676	Br	Beamus, Margte.	888	Nrf	Thomas	23	Rcm
Burten	24	Isw	Bean, Edward	607	Mnt	William	678	Br
Burwell	140	Sth	George	971	Nrt	William	7	Rcm
Burwell	144	Sth	Henry	667	Mnt	William	172	Shn
C. L.	887	Nrf	James	571	Frd	Wm.	324	Ags
Dorcas	161	Sth	John	605	Btt	Wm., sr.	319	Ags
Drewry	144	Sth	John	607	Btt	see Biard		
Edwin	157	Sth	John	190	Elc	Beardshere, Peter	238	Shn
Elias	23	Isw	John	971	Nrt	Bease, Thos.	824	Nrf
Eliza.	162	Sth	John	558	Pre	Beaser, Jno.	268	Ldn
Eliza.	852	Sth	John, Jun.	192	Elc	Beasey, Micage	79	Acc
Elizabeth	46	Isw	Joseph	768	Wst	Beasley, Conelius	192	Kng
Jacob	46	Isw	Joseph, (F. Negroe)	420	Fqr	Cornelias	66	Jff
Jacob	157	Sth	Josiah	607	Btt	Edwin	328	Dnw
Jas.	486	Mnn	Mordecai	571	Frd	Elizabeth C.	56	Chs
Jeremh.	156	Sth	Saml.	272	Rck	John	207	Ess
Jesse	151	Sth	see Bear, Beau			John	556	Pre
Jno.	886	Hnv	Beanard, Fredk.	638	Mnt	Liberty	8	Ntt
Jno.	139	Sth	Beane, Edwin	338	Lnc	Peter	743	Brn
John	573	Brk	Jno.	338	Lnc	Richard	452	Frn
John	24	Hnr	Joseph	98	Jff	Robertson	63	Chs
Jordan	162	Sth	Opie	338	Lnc	Smith	9	Acc
Martha	128	Sth	Peter	337	Lnc	Stephen	3	Ntt
Mary	688	Br	Tho., Jr.	337	Lnc	Thomas	150	Alb
Mingo	878	Sth	Tho., Sen.	337	Lnc	William	908	Hrr
Ninian	674	Br	Beans, Amos	316	Ldn	Wm.	60	Chs
Peggy	46	Isw	James	309	Ldn	see Kent		
Robert	378	Mds	Mathew	314	Ldn	Beasly, Isaac	931	Hrr
Saml.	289	Ldn	Wm. [2]	314	Ldn	Beaten, Richd.	822	Nrf
Shad.	852	Sth	Bear, Andw.	17	Rcm	Beath, Joseph	610	Btt
Shad.	879	Sth	Chry	317	Ags	Willm.	610	Btt
Silas	156	Sth	Cutlip	610	Btt	Beatles, James	435	Bth
William	689	Br	Frederick	545	Frd	Beatman, Robt.	16	Isw
William	557	Frd	Henry	605	Btt	Beats, John	728	Wsh
Beale, Bazill	799	Hmp	Henry	32	Rcm	Peter	285	Rck
Charles	605	Btt	Jacob	319	Ags	Beatty, Charles	794	Hmp
Henry	766	Wst	Jacob	324	Ags	Henry	508	Frd
James	606	Btt	Jacob	31	Rcm	Isaac	802	Hmp
Jno. E.	888	Nrf	Jacob	32	Rcm	John	26	Rcm
John	12	Rcm	Jacob, (ST)	316	Ags	John, (Jr.)	26	Rcm
John	766	Wst	John	18	Rcm	Levi	486	Mnn
John H.	211	Ess	John	20	Rcm	Robert	526	Frd
Lolly, f. negro	236	Frf	Michl.	317	Ags	Robt.	486	Mnn
Madison	605	Btt	Peter	780	Hmp	Stephen	486	Mnn
Nancy	767	Wst	Philip	18	Rcm	William	562	Frd
Reuben	390	Rch	Samuel	248	Shn	Beaty, Andrw	234	Ldn
Rhoda	606	Btt	Thomas	22	Rcm	Davd.	730	Wsh
Richard	393	Rch	Tobias	27	Rcm	Davd., Junr.	730	Wsh
Richard E.	367	Fqr	Valentine	29	Rcm	David	525	Brk
Samuel, Junr.	767	Wst	William	14	Rcm	Elisa.	234	Ldn
Samuel, Senr.	767	Wst	see Baher, Bean			Geo.	20	Hnr
Sinah	400	Rch	Beard, Charles	242	Frf	James	730	Wsh
William	414	Fqr	Charles	25	Rcm	Jno.	287	Rck
William	767	Wst	Christer.	319	Ags	John	696	Br
see Bell			David	5	Rcm	John	695	Wsh
Bealer, George	31	Rcm	Dickie	279	Rck	Mahlon	241	Ldn
Beall, Bazil	7	Oho	Francis	39	Rcm	Mary	277	Ldn
Eli	506	Frd	George	823	Hmp	Websents	693	Br
Ezera	334	Dnw	Jabez	454	Bdf	William	693	Br
Hezekiah	93	Jff	James	677	Br	Wm.	517	Brk
James	8	Oho	James	8	Rcm	Wm.	546	Brk
John	76	Jff	Jesse	599	Mnr	Wm., Capt.	717	Wsh
John R.	424	Rnd	Jno.	293	Rck	Beau, Henry	820	Wth
Joseph	66	Jff	Jos.	319	Ags	Jacob	821	Wth
Joseph	74	Jff	Jos.	305	Ldn	Beauchamp, David	6	Wod

Elijah	6	Acc
Manlove	4	Wod
Martha	11	Wod
William	6	Wod
Beaugh, Jacob	300	Ldn
Beavans, Cathern.	12	Acc
Lott	81	Acc
William H.	75	Acc
Beaver, Abraham	178	Shn
Davd.	296	Rck
George	27	Rcm
Jno.	296	Rck
Mary	682	Br
Michael	807	Hmp
Mos.	485	Mnn
Matthias	27	Rcm
Peter	27	Rcm
Peter, Jun.	807	Hmp
Peter, Sen.	807	Hmp
Beavers, Alexr.	664	Mnt
Gabriel	251	Ldn
Jno.	278	Ldn
John	384	Fqr
John	596	Frd
Mary	272	Ldn
Moses	664	Mnt
Samuel	596	Frd
Wm.	251	Ldn
Beavours, Alexander	617	Gls
Beazley, Ann	891	Crl
Anna	221	Ess
Charles	67	Spt
Daniel	892	Crl
Edmund	889	Crl
Edmund	893	Crl
Ephraim	86	Spt
Fanny	892	Crl
Frances	890	Crl
Gabriel	43	Chr
Henry	86	Spt
Larkin	889	Crl
Nancy	69	Chr
Nathan	835	Bck
Philip	889	Crl
Reuben	5	Clp
Sarah	889	Crl
William	889	Crl
William	891	Crl
William	86	Spt
Winnefred	86	Spt
Wm.	5	Clp
Beazly, Laskin	90	Spt
Bebber, Jessee V.	421	Msn
John V.	429	Msn
Beberidge, Wm.	234	Ldn
Bechnor, Henry, Sr.	605	Btt
Bechtell, Rachel	200	Shn
Beck, Chs., & C.	21	Hnr
James	113	Spt
Jesse	291	Amh
John	12	Oho
Nicholas	186	Alb
Pheby	917	Hrr
Polly	706	Brn
Samuel	677	Br
Samuel	260	Ldn
Susanna	239	Frf
Beckam, Polley	398	Fqr
William	523	Prw
Becke see Beeke		
Beckers see Bockers		
Becket, Humphrey	185	Alb
John	587	Brk
Michael	573	Mnr
Rachel	12	Acc
Richard	482	Frn
Salley	120	Hnr
Beckett, John	636	Mnt
Sarah	60	Acc
Thos.	658	Mnt

Beckham, Abner	6	Clp
Archelaus	891	Crl
Elijah	13	Clp
James	378	Mds
James, Jr.	818	Bck
Jas., Este.	7	Clp
Thos.	6	Clp
William	818	Bck
Beckhorn, John	807	Hmp
Beckley, Jacob	284	Ldn
Jas.	545	Prg
John	190	Elc
John	831	Nrf
Nelly	498	Prw
Susannah	297	Amh
Beckman, Michael	746	Wsh
Becknal, Jessee	677	Nls
John	681	Nls
Lucy	682	Nls
Nancy	677	Nls
William	677	Nls
Beckner, Danl.	608	Btt
David	611	Btt
Jacob	607	Btt
John, Sr.	610	Btt
Becknor, Jacob	472	Frn
Jno., (the Younger)	607	Btt
John, Jr.	605	Btt
Jonathan	607	Btt
Josh., Sr.	605	Btt
Becks, Reuben	186	Alb
Beckwith, Barnes	392	Rch
Jona.	412	Rch
Jonathan	506	Frd
Lewis	241	Frf
Lewis	244	Ldn
Newman	811	Hmp
Richard	36	Stf
Samuel	769	Hmp
Tapley	233	Frf
see Bickwith		
Bedders, Fanny	767	Wst
Beddingfield, John	629	Sss
Beddo, John	405	Rch
Lawrence	405	Rch
Bedford, Stephen	42	Chr
William	115	Spt
Bedgod, Mary	830	Nrf
Bedinger, Daniel	98	Jff
Henry	528	Brk
Jacob	87	Jff
Bedlock, Peter	139	Dnw
Bedwel, James	679	Brk
Bedwell, William	540	Brk
Bee, Fras.	337	Lnc
Gabriel, a free mulatto	973	Nrt
Massy	339	Lnc
Beebe, Isaac	9	Wod
John	7	Wod
Beech, Amey	10	Acc
Ann	12	Acc
Chs., Jr.	235	Frf
Chs., Senr.	235	Frf
James	233	Frf
Jno.	236	Frf
Kendall	8	Acc
Loderick	558	Pre
Mary	559	Pre
Molly	10	Acc
Pearce	558	Pre
Soloman	236	Frf
Thomas	240	Frf
Thomas	241	Frf
William	235	Frf
William B.	559	Pre
Beecks, James	681	Brk
Rachel	681	Brk
Beede, Wm.	445	Mth
Beedle, Andw., Junr.	241	Frf

Andw., Senr.	241	Frf
Beegle, Dick	549	Prg
Beeke, William	610	Mnt
Beeland, William	6	Rcm
Beeler, Benjamin	80	Jff
Beem, John	799	Hmp
Beemer, Benjamin	528	Frd
Chaty	251	Shn
Hannah	528	Frd
Been, Jane	618	Gls
Walter	799	Hmp
Walter	610	Mnt
William	618	Gls
Beery, Abraham	40	Rcm
George	9	Rcm
John	40	Rcm
Nicholas	20	Rcm
Beesley, Bennet	35	Rcm
Henry	13	Acc
James	35	Rcm
Jeremiah	35	Rcm
Beesly, John	953	Hrr
Wm.	953	Hrr
Beeson, Edwd.	503	Brk
Jacob	15	Wod
Jonas	1	Wod
Micajah	507	Brk
Beeter, Benjn.	511	Brk
Beetle, Joseph	39	Rcm
Beetley, Betsey	972	Nrt
Butcher	973	Nrt
Francis	973	Nrt
George	972	Nrt
John	973	Nrt
Beezeley, Charles	178	Shn
Begal, Susan	929	Hrr
Begarley, James	238	Ldn
Beggard, Robt.	129	Hnr
Begleton, Jane	681	Nls
Begs, Thomas	281	Rck
Beham, Tobias	13	Clp
Behaney, Henry	889	Nrf
Behealer, George	449	Frn
Isaac	449	Frn
Beilee, Mary	691	Wsh
Beime, Thomas	562	Mnr
see ...ime, Beirne		
Beirne, Andw.	586	Mnr
Oliver	563	Mnr
see Beime		
Beissey, William	51	Stf
Belber, Matthias V.	8	Knw
Belcher, Benjamin	481	Frn
Danl.	64	Chs
Eliza.	246	Aml
Frances	492	Frn
Isham	62	Chs
Isham	492	Frn
Isham, Sr.	55	Chs
Jno.	4	Ntt
Jno. T.	59	Chs
Joel	326	Dnw
John	43	Chr
Mary	247	Aml
Mary	330	Dnw
Morriss	55	Chs
Moses	62	Chs
Obadiah	43	Chr
Richd.	248	Aml
Robert	62	Chs
William	501	Frn
Belches, James	646	Glc
Belchy, Sarah	822	Wth
Bele see Bell		
Beleridge see Beberidge		
Belew, Battersby	129	Cmb
Eliza	102	Cmb
Howard	681	Nls
Peter	187	Alb
Belfield, Ann H.	411	Rch

John	397	Rch	Jeremh.	537	Brk	William	8	Acc
John W.	411	Rch	Jeremiah	606	Mnt	William	553	Brk
Belfild, Sydnor	411	Rch	Jno.	332	Dnw	William	891	Crl
Belfour, John	34	Stf	Jno.	480	Mnn	William	391	Fqr
Sarah	706	Wsh	Jno.	283	Rck	William	418	Fqr
Bell, Adam	333	Lnn	Jno. R.	1	Ntt	William	454	Frn
Adam	555	Pre	John	247	Aml	William	123	Hnr
Alexa.	334	Dnw	John	398	Ags	William	99	Spt
Ann	8	Acc	John	141	Dnw	William	35	Stf
Ann	832	Hmp	John	332	Dnw	William, MC	81	Acc
Ann	972	Nrt	John	198	Ess	Winny	336	Dnw
Barton	509	Prw	John	399	Fqr	Wm.	593	Brk
Bayley F.	53	Stf	John	510	Frd	Wm.	332	Dnw
Benja., junr.	599	Srr	John	517	Frd	Wm.	623	Mnt
Benjamin, Senr.	599	Srr	John	629	Mnt	Wm., (Capt.)	323	Ags
Benjn.	511	Brk	John	806	Nrf	Wm., (MT)	317	Ags
Betty	11	Acc	John	838	Nrf	Wm., Senr.	320	Ags
Bramly	875	Sth	John	890	Nrf	see Ball, Beale		
Caty	115	Spt	John	971	Nrt	Bellamy, Benjamin	455	Bdf
Charles	418	Fqr	John	7	Oho	John	9	Hnr
Charles	390	Rch	John	11	Oho	Jos.	647	Glc
Charles	25	Stf	John	425	Rnd	Richard	106	Cmb
Chas.	338	Lnc	John	34	Stf	Bellar, Mary	96	Jff
Claiborne	247	Aml	John	599	Srr	Bellard, Jno.	301	Ldn
Coleman	338	Lnc	John	871	Yrk	Bellemy, William	105	Cmb
Daniel	25	Stf	John, (LG)	324	Ags	Beller, Eli	545	Brk
Danl.	410	Ags	John, (MT)	322	Ags	Bellett, Susan, (W)	870	Yrk
David	246	Aml	John, of E	5	Acc	Bellimey, Bradley	682	Gch
David	322	Ags	John, Senr.	9	Acc	John	685	Gch
David	67	Chr	John D.	523	Prw	Bellomy, Mathew	869	Cmp
David	316	Ldn	John H.	599	Srr	Bells, John E.	431	Rnd
David	14	Oho	Jos., jr.	323	Ags	Ruth	484	Mnn
Dolly, f. negro	236	Frf	Joseph	945	Hrr	Belmire, Jacob	597	Brk
Drury	276	Amh	Joseph	820	Wth	Martin	89	Jff
Edmund	74	Acc	Joseph, (ST)	316	Ags	Michael	597	Brk
Edward	7	Acc	Joseph, Ser.	315	Ags	Belnap, Thomas	762	Hmp
Elijah	28	Stf	Josiah	439	Pra	Belote, Caleb	6	Acc
Eliza.	337	Lnc	Kaziah	75	Acc	Hancock	6	Acc
Esther	11	Acc	L. G.	305	Ldn	James, Junr.	5	Acc
Fanney	454	Frn	Leah	556	Pre	James, Senr.	5	Acc
Farguson	544	Frd	Lewis	393	Fqr	Jesse	11	Acc
Feilding	2	Oho	Lewis	768	Wst	John	6	Acc
Fielden	599	Srr	Luran...	817	Nrf	Laben	10	Acc
Francis	320	Ags	Michl. [2]	599	Srr	Peggy	11	Acc
Francis	322	Ags	Nancy	7	Acc	Belsches, Hugh C.	625	Sss
Geo.	806	Nrf	Nancy	940	Chc	Belt, Humphrey	126	Cmb
Geodiah	9	Acc	Nancy	68	Chr	John	373	Fqr
George	7	Acc	Nancy	3	Hnr	John G.	183	Alb
George	80	Acc	Nancy, of G	9	Acc	Loyd	610	Btt
George	454	Frn	Nathaniel	5	Acc	W. S.	238	Frf
George	559	Pre	Richard	556	Pre	William	368	Fqr
George	520	Prw	Robert	609	Btt	Belvin, Aaron	648	Glc
George W.	555	Pre	Robert	606	Mnt	Jno.	648	Glc
Graham	326	Dnw	Robert	6	Oho	Jno., Senr.	648	Glc
Graham	336	Dnw	Robert W.	178	Alb	Lewis	648	Glc
Hannah	40	Stf	Robt.	21	Hnr	Martha	888	Yrk
Henry	838	Bck	Robt.	663	Mnt	Ralph	648	Glc
Isaac	8	Acc	Robt., Jr.	645	Mnt	Wm.	648	Glc
Jack, f. negro	236	Frf	Saml.	319	Ags	Bemard see Bernard		
Jacob	254	Shn	Saml.	21	Hnr	Ben, Alex.	326	Dnw
James	150	Alb	Saml., (Majr.	320	Ags	Robert	369	Fqr
James	315	Ags	Samuel	299	Amh	Benaugh, James	850	Cmp
James	533	Brk	Samuel	544	Frd	Bendall, Isaac	626	Sss
James	869	Cmp	Samuel	599	Srr	James	893	Crl
James	67	Chr	Sarah	882	Hnv	James	629	Sss
James	391	Fqr	Sarah A.	53	Stf	Jesse	627	Sss
James	458	Frn	Southey	78	Acc	Jno.	849	Hnv
James	6	Oho	Southy	556	Pre	Jno.	680	Wrw
James	7	Oho	Susannah	811	Bck	Wm.	683	Wrw
James	265	Rck	Thomas	455	Bdf	Bendit see Burdit		
James	280	Rck	Thomas	889	Crl	Bendle, Thos.	21	Hnr
James	154	Sth	Thomas	558	Frd	Benear, Julin	362	Fqr
James	820	Wth	Thomas	972	Nrt	Beneger, David	193	Shn
James, junr.	599	Srr	Thomas, Senr.	891	Crl	Beneham, Richard	392	Rch
James M.	83	Spt	Thornton	768	Wst	Bener, James	593	Frd
James P.	599	Srr	Thos., jr.	315	Ags	Benford, Catharine	120	Hnr
Jas., Esq.	323	Ags	Thos., (LG)	322	Ags	Chappell	534	Prg
Jas., ([his] Quarter)	340	Fqr	Turlenton	618	Gls	Equilla	545	Prg
Jas. E.	485	Mnn	Victor	605	Btt	George	746	Nwk
Jason	555	Frd	Walter	506	Prw	James	131	Hnr

Jas.	547	Prg
Jenny	130	Hnr
Robert	746	Nwk
Saml.	547	Prg
Sharod	131	Hnr
Thomas	131	Hnr
Wm.	119	Hnr
Bengamon, A.	485	Mnn
Benges see Burges		
Benham, Joel	753	Wsh
Benjham, Wm.	540	Prg
Benn, George	10	Isw
Thomas	162	Sth
Bennatt, Walker	5	Ntt
Bennehan see Beneham		
Benner, Henry	681	Nls
Saml.	320	Ags
Bennet, Abraham	946	Hrr
Abram	951	Hrr
Charles C.	37	Stf
Elizabeth	705	Brn
Howard	872	Cmp
Isaac	429	Rnd
Jacob	609	Btt
Jacob	934	Hrr
Jas.	486	Mnn
Joel	182	Alb
John	28	Hnr
John	132	Hnr
John	267	Rck
Mary	484	Mnn
Patey	459	Frn
Petsey	30	Hnr
Richard	453	Bdf
Thomas	114	Hnr
Wm.	951	Hrr
Wm.	429	Rnd
see Drumwright		
Bennett, Charles	24	Hnr
Charles	297	Ldn
Chs.	312	Ldn
Cossom	191	Kng
Eli	328	Dnw
Eliza.	13	Clp
Elizabeth	30	Isw
George	192	Kng
Griffin	17	Ntt
Horashia	281	Amh
Isaac	608	Btt
Jacob	947	Hrr
James	263	Amh
James	580	Frd
James	785	Hmp
James	556	Pre
James, jr.	601	Srr
James, sr.	601	Srr
Jane	768	Wst
Jesse	601	Srr
Jessee	424	Msn
John	930	Hrr
John	766	Wst
Joseph	233	Frf
Joseph	951	Hrr
Joseph, Jr.	242	Frf
Mary	602	Srr
Mason	58	Jff
Moses	608	Btt
Moses	911	Hrr
Rees	579	Frd
Richard	331	Lnn
Richd.	10	Hnr
Sam.	178	Elc
Sarah	190	Kng
Sylvanus	827	Hmp
Thomas	332	Dnw
Thomas	785	Hmp
Thomas, Jur.	785	Hmp
Van	88	Jff
William	543	Frd
William	447	Grn
William	20	Oho
William	846	Sth
William	601	Srr
Wm.	17	Hnr
see Barnes		
Bennington, Job	270	Rck
Bennit, Hannah	222	Pnd
John	940	Hrr
John	221	Pnd
John	222	Pnd
Joseph	221	Pnd
William	925	Hrr
Bennitt, Tho.	192	Elc
Benno, John	890	Nrf
Benns, William	511	Brk
see Burns		
Benott see Burott		
Benskin see Bosman		
Benson, Alexander	432	Bth
Amos	438	Pra
Azariah	678	Wrw
Betsey	82	Acc
Chas.	7	Clp
Daniel	74	Acc
Erwin	598	Mnr
Fra.	827	Nrf
Hamilton	436	Bth
Isabella	584	Frd
James	892	Crl
James	31	Stf
John	10	Acc
John	108	Spt
Margaret	436	Bth
Mary Ann	816	Nrf
Mathew	432	Bth
Nancy	10	Acc
Nathaniel	82	Acc
Sarah	74	Acc
Scarburgh	78	Acc
Stephen	246	Aml
Willis	31	Stf
Wm.	319	Ags
Wm.	8	Clp
Wm.	484	Mnn
see Bensons, Brown		
Bensons, James, Este.	7	Clp
Benston, James	4	Acc
Bent, Lemuel	515	Frd
Benter, William	803	Bck
Benthal, Caleb	189	Elc
Benthale, Mary	825	Nrf
Wm.	826	Nrf
Benthall, Chs.	888	Nrf
Joseph	438	Pra
Robert	439	Pra
Wm.	437	Pra
Bentley, Efford	247	Aml
Robert	333	Lnn
Solomon	14	Oho
William, Colo.	7	Pwh
Wm.	590	Brk
Wm.	648	Glc
Bently, George	13	Knw
Joseph	303	Ldn
Saml.	17	Ntt
Benton, Danl.	116	Hnr
John	820	Wth
see Burton		
Bentz see Benns		
Berauld, Etropius	889	Nrf
Berbour, Phil	485	Mnn
Berch, John	113	Hnr
Thos.	487	Mnn
Bereheart, Lewis, Snr.	235	Shn
see Rineheart		
Bergess, John	398	Ags
Berkeley, Carter	863	Hnv
Carter B.	459	Mdd
Charles	3	Oho
Edmund	850	Hnv
Elizabeth W. C.	867	Hnv
Landen C.	867	Hnv
Lewis	861	Hnv
Lewis	521	Prw
William	3	Pwh
Berkhamer, Henry	958	Hrr
Berkins, Jno.	273	Ldn
Berkley, Benja.	238	Frf
Geo.	248	Ldn
George	43	Chr
Jno. L.	258	Ldn
John	694	Br
John	68	Chr
William	559	Pre
Berkly, Alexander	68	Chr
Berleneyer, John O.	743	Nwk
Berlin, Isaac	543	Frd
Jacob	584	Frd
Bernard, Allen	433	Flv
Allen	447	Flv
Anne	435	Flv
Fanny	682	Gch
Gabl.	889	Nrf
John	446	Flv
John	685	Gch
John, Sr.	431	Flv
Josuah M.	117	Cmb
Thomas	190	Kng
Thornton	100	Spt
William	190	Kng
Bernet, Elizabeth	115	Spt
John	114	Spt
Bernett, Geo.	311	Ldn
Berrey, Wm.	233	Ldn
Berrick, Reubin	336	Lnc
Berriman, Jane	972	Nrt
Joseph	600	Srr
Nathl., jr.	600	Srr
Nathl., sr.	600	Srr
Newton	768	Wst
Berry, Aaron	9	Clp
Ann	690	Wsh
Anthony	10	Clp
Anthony	375	Mds
Austin	558	Pre
Ben	483	Mnn
Benj.	15	Hnr
Benjamin	598	Frd
Benjamin	21	Rcm
Benjn.	590	Mnr
Betsey	140	Dnw
Charles	319	Ags
Charles	441	Pra
Davd.	716	Wsh
David	10	Rcm
Enock	14	Rcm
Geo.	319	Ags
George	75	Acc
George	590	Frd
George	17	Rcm
Henry	15	Rcm
Henry, & o & e	20	Rcm
Hillary	439	Pra
Houlder	458	Mdd
Hugh	750	Wsh
Huldah	587	Frd
Isaac	401	Fqr
Isaac	641	Mnt
James	74	Acc
James	425	Bth
James	892	Crl
James	375	Mds
James	440	Pra
Jane	323	Ags
Jno.	649	Glc
Johana	427	Bth
John	320	Ags
John	332	Dnw
John	96	Jff

Name	No.	Code
John	972	Nrt
John	558	Pre
John	716	Wsh
John	822	Wth
John, [his] Est.	190	Kng
Joseph	589	Frd
Joseph	558	Pre
Joshua	375	Mds
Julias	330	Dnw
Laurence	190	Kng
Leah	83	Acc
Lewis	149	Alb
Lucindia	9	Hnr
Margaret	17	Rcm
Mary	375	Mds
Mary	108	Spt
Mary	699	Wsh
Michael S.	375	Mds
Nancy	102	Jff
Ned	871	Yrk
Peter	559	Pre
Polley	140	Dnw
Polly	878	Sth
Richard	61	Stf
Richd.	482	Mnn
Robert	648	Glc
Robt.	320	Ags
Rowland	375	Mds
Samuel	396	Fqr
Samuel	17	Oho
Sarah	12	Hnr
Thomas	598	Frd
Thomas	800	Hmp
Thomas	973	Nrt
Thomas	20	Oho
Thomas	558	Pre
Thomas	441	Rcm
Thornly	598	Frd
Thos.	699	Wsh
Thos.	716	Wsh
Washington	206	Ess
William	235	Frf
William	776	Hmp
William	826	Hmp
William	55	Jff
William	375	Mds
William	458	Mdd
Wm.	55	Chs
see Beery		
Berryhill, Alexander	3	Oho
John	267	Rck
Berryman, Anderson	837	Bck
James [2]	359	Fqr
James	190	Kng
John	190	Kng
Lucy	117	Spt
Maximillian	359	Fqr
Newton	892	Crl
Richd.	337	Lnc
Sarah	837	Bck
Thomas N.	767	Wst
William	836	Bck
see Askins, Berriman		
Bersons see Persons		
Berton, Ann	744	Brn
Robert	180	Alb
Thomas	972	Nrt
Bertre, Lewis	888	Nrf
Berts, John	575	Brk
Bery, Adasom	681	Nls
John	681	Nls
Besacker, Adam	608	Btt
Besh, Peter	9	Rcm
Besick, Peter	517	Frd
Besom, Ann	888	Nrf
Bess, William	607	Btt
Best, Henry	818	Nrf
James	316	Ags
James	280	Ldn
John	315	Ags

Name	No.	Code
John	454	Bdf
Levi	454	Bdf
Michael	32	Rcm
William	536	Prg
Wm.	317	Ldn
Bestpitch, Peter	648	Glc
Bethael, George	780	Hmp
Bethard, Rhode	12	Acc
Bethel, Carter	121	Hnr
Claiborn	121	Hnr
Edward	409	Fqr
Henry	44	Stf
Isham	121	Hnr
Jenny	121	Hnr
John [2]	679	Nls
John, Jur.	679	Nls
Robt.	121	Hnr
Thomas	122	Hnr
William	122	Hnr
William	25	Stf
Bethell, John	819	Wth
Bett see Belt		
Bettel, Davd.	754	Wsh
Bettenger, Andw.	242	Frf
Betters, Jno.	482	Mnn
Bettey, Harriss	192	Kng
John	191	Kng
Marshall	192	Kng
Roger	192	Kng
Sukey	192	Kng
Bettice, Beverly	51	Stf
Bettiss, Thomas	354	Fqr
Bettle, Francis	592	Brk
Betton, Solomon	236	Ldn
Betts, Barby	332	Lnn
Charles	332	Lnn
Drury	629	Sss
Elisha	606	Btt
George	439	Pra
John	566	Frd
John	229	Shn
John	819	Wth
Jourdon	971	Nrt
Martin	228	Shn
Nancy	971	Nrt
Peter	265	Ldn
Roston	331	Lnn
Royston	973	Nrt
Tabitha	629	Sss
Tellus	973	Nrt
Thomas	973	Nrt
Bettsy see Bettey		
Betty, Elizabeth	743	Brn
Beuford, Ab.	18	Ntt
Benjamin	838	Bck
John	631	Mnt
Joseph	555	Pre
Bevan, Samuel	758	Hmp
Bevans, Peter	9	Acc
Soloman	9	Acc
Thomas	10	Acc
William	79	Acc
Bevard, James	32	Rcm
Bevars, Walter	833	Nrf
Bevelle, Jas.	5	Ntt
Beventin, John	965	Hrr
Beverage, John	10	Hnr
John	217	Pnd
John	523	Prw
Thomas	523	Prw
Wm.	115	Hnr
Beverege, Henry	217	Pnd
Beveridge, John	516	Frd
Noble	302	Ldn
Wm. M.	648	Glc
Beverley, C.	324	Ags
McKenzie	891	Crl
Mumford	6	Clp
Peter	236	Frf
Beverly, Betty	775	Bck

Name	No.	Code
Carter	399	Ags
Charles	775	Bck
Cill	493	Frn
Elizabeth	190	Kng
Herod	486	Frn
Jenney	776	Bck
Jonathan	776	Bck
Jonathan	820	Bck
Lucy	115	Spt
Major	290	Rck
McKinsey	767	Wst
Pricella	823	Bck
William	775	Bck
Beverrege, John	390	Fqr
Bevil, Robert	141	Dnw
Bevill, William	247	Aml
Beville, Archer	21	Ntt
Benjn.	2	Ntt
Carter	2	Ntt
Gerald	15	Ntt
Nancy	15	Ntt
Bevington, Francis	768	Wst
Bevours, Saml.	236	Frf
Bew, Christopher	155	Knq
Jane	158	Knq
John	155	Knq
Major	156	Knq
Beymer, Frederick	1	Oho
Biadly see Bradly		
Biar, Jacob, (HC)	315	Ags
Biard, Thos.	756	Wsh
Bias, Elizabeth	301	Amh
James	267	Amh
John	265	Amh
Larkin	266	Amh
Lucy	301	Amh
Rolin	265	Amh
Bibb, Branch H.	42	Chr
David	891	Crl
Elizabeth	828	Bck
Fleming	893	Crl
Garrett	890	Crl
Henry	679	Nls
Henry, Jur.	678	Nls
Jno.	42	Chr
John	891	Crl
John	679	Nls
Martin	298	Amh
Randolph	292	Amh
Richard	439	Flv
Thomas	678	Nls
William	680	Nls
Bibber, Zenith	680	Nls
see Bebber		
Bibbey, Betsey	326	Dnw
William	430	Msn
see Bibby		
Bibbs, Jas.	320	Ags
Bibby, William	430	Msn
see Bobby		
Bibee, Peter	681	Nls
Bible, Adam	30	Rcm
George	215	Pnd
Biby, Jolly	260	Amh
Joseph	880	Cmp
Bice, John, Jr.	606	Btt
John, Sr.	610	Btt
Morrel	935	Hrr
Stephen	485	Mnn
William	926	Hrr
see Rice		
Bickel, Christopher	418	Rnd
Bickers, Jane	377	Mds
Nancey	377	Mds
Susan	377	Mds
William	377	Mds
Bickerstieff, Mary	320	Ags
Bickerton, Thomas	27	Rcm
Bicketon, Wim.	896	Hnv
Bickle, George	417	Rnd

Jacob	322	Ags
Bickwith, Sybell	239	Frf
Bidaman, Dedrick	59	Jff
Bidders Thomas	187	Alb
Biddle Jacob	755	Wsh
Jno. P. [?]	442	Pra
John	442	Pra
Saml.	305	Rck
Wm.	889	Nrf
Bideler, Barbary	206	Shn
Jacob	205	Shn
Bidenbaugh, Michael	70	Jff
Bidgood, Benjamin	15	Isw
Josiah	34	Isw
Margt.	328	Dnw
Micajah	19	Isw
Nancy	28	Isw
Richard	8	Isw
Sally	29	Isw
Bidwell, Rezen	23	Oho
Spenser	23	Oho
Biedler see Bideler		
Bierer, John	7	Rcm
Joseph	7	Rcm
Martha	6	Rcm
Sarah	6	Rcm
Biern see Beime		
Bigaby, Teackle	82	Acc
Bigbee, Jno.	11	Clp
Ralls	11	Clp
Bigbie, William	789	Bck
Bigers, James	484	Frn
Bigger, Andrew	556	Pre
James	557	Pre
John	556	Pre
John, Junr.	555	Pre
Peggy	556	Pre
Biggerstaff, Nancy	787	Hmp
Rachel	787	Hmp
Bigges, John	419	Fqr
Biggins, Bagland	327	Dnw
Marsha	328	Dnw
Biggleston, Alexr. , overseer		
for Doctr. Gilliam	141	Dnw
Biggs, Benjamin	10	Oho
Daniel	75	Jff
David	824	Nrf
Ep... [Ephm. ?]	483	Mnn
James	617	Gls
John	605	Btt
John	609	Btt
John	618	Gls
Noah	483	Mnn
Peter	608	Btt
Peter	43	Chr
Richard	706	Brn
Thomas	606	Btt
Thomas	292	Rck
Zachariah	686	Br
see Briggs, Bugg		
Bigham, John	787	Hmp
Josiah	8	Hnr
Bigle see Rigle		
Bigler, Jacob	924	Hrr
Mark	925	Hrr
Bigles, Marks	610	Btt
Bigsby, Darkess	247	Ldn
Bilbow, Peter	860	Hnv
Bilbre, Aggay	6	Hnr
John	605	Btt
Mary	605	Btt
Bilbro, Benjamin	600	Srr
Bernard	600	Srr
Bile see Bell		
Biles, Thomas	12	Oho
Tony	558	Pre
Biley, Edward	872	Cmp
Bill, Betsy	822	Nrf
Henry	829	Nrf
see Bell		

Billhimer, Henry	32	Rcm
Jacob	22	Rcm
Joseph	11	Rcm
Michael	29	Rcm
Billiler, Calob	725	Wsh
Edward	725	Wsh
Billings, Hannah	768	Wst
Newman	678	Br
Billingsby, Clement	51	Stf
James	22	Stf
Billingsley, James	401	Fqr
John A.	102	Spt
Billingsly, Cyres	482	Mnn
Fras.	480	Mnn
S.	482	Mnn
Wm.	481	Mnn
Billington, Josiah	111	Hnr
Billinsley, Robt.	587	Brk
Billips, Edward	614	Mnt
Richard	475	Frn
Thomas	475	Frn
Bills, Lewis	745	Wsh
William	25	Oho
Billups, Ann	887	Nrf
Auguse.	141	Dnw
Chris.	437	Mth
Chris. , Sr.	449	Mth
Edward	611	Btt
Hugh G.	649	Glc
Humphrey	436	Mth
Jno.	448	Mth
Jno. , jr.	449	Mth
John	331	Lnn
Bilsley, Chrn.	321	Ags
Bimis see Binns		
Bims, Elizabeth	950	Chc
Binder, Geo.	259	Ldn
Binear, Henry	408	Fqr
Binford, Abram	940	Chc
Amey	939	Chc
Ann	959	Chc
David	334	Dnw
Isaac	959	Chc
Jesse	326	Dnw
John	947	Chc
Mosby	950	Chc
Robert	956	Chc
S. H.	888	Nrf
Thomas	948	Chc
Thos.	684	Gch
Bing, Henry K.	227	Shn
Bingess, Rachael	788	Nrf
Bingham, Henry	36	Rcm
John	829	Nrf
Bingley, Matthew	832	Nrf
Binion, Martin, Jr.	501	Frn
Martin, Sr.	501	Frn
Binkly, Peter	820	Wth
Binneger, Saml.	916	Hrr
Binns, Cate	290	Ldn
Charles	744	Nwk
Chs.	303	Ldn
Daniel	745	Nwk
David	745	Nwk
Jeremiah	744	Nwk
Jeremiah, junr.	746	Nwk
Jno. A.	313	Ldn
John	1	Hnr
John	745	Nwk
Marston	745	Nwk
Martha	745	Nwk
Peter	683	Gch
Richard	746	Nwk
Simon	279	Ldn
Thos.	306	Ldn
Will	957	Chc
William	601	Srr
Wm.	303	Ldn
Bins, Wilcher	247	Aml
Birce, Francis	756	Wsh

Birch, Christopher	716	Wsh
Elizabeth	557	Pre
James	238	Frf
John	83	Acc
Jonathan	791	Hmp
Joseph	83	Acc
Littleberry	684	Gch
Mary	744	Nwk
Milley	744	Nwk
Reuben	744	Nwk
Thos. E.	638	Mnt
Birchett, Drury	535	Prg
Edward	327	Dnw
Peter	535	Prg
Robert	330	Dnw
Bird, Aaron	62	Stf
Adam	419	Bth
Andrew	234	Shn
Ann	157	Knq
Ann B.	157	Knq
Anthony A.	155	Knq
Bartley	496	Frn
Braxton	459	Mdd
Daniel T.	81	Acc
Danl.	287	Rck
David	430	Bth
Elijah	460	Mdd
Eliwin	8	Acc
Esther	76	Acc
Fanny	77	Acc
Frederick	430	Bth
Geo.	479	Mnn
George	196	Shn
George	236	Shn
Henry, F.N.	628	Sss
Jacob	11	Acc
Jacob	224	Pnd
James	496	Frn
James	498	Frn
Joanna	157	Knq
Johannas	81	Acc
John	316	Ags
John	415	Bth
John [2]	453	Bdf
John	199	Ess
John	498	Frn
John	236	Shn
John, Junr.	76	Acc
John, Jur.	431	Bth
John, Senr.	76	Acc
John, Ser.	431	Bth
John, Sr.	495	Frn
Lewis	30	Stf
Luke	453	Bdf
Luke	501	Frn
Major	81	Acc
Mary	157	Knq
Mounts	194	Shn
Nancey	34	Hnr
Parker	77	Acc
Peggy	10	Acc
Peter	233	Shn
Robert	845	Hnv
Sam.	744	Nwk
Samuel	495	Frn
Samuel, (free)	893	Hnv
Samuel, Sr.	498	Frn
Stephen	764	Hmp
Tho.	486	Mnn
Thomas	416	Bth
Thomas	461	Frn
Volentine	224	Pnd
William	76	Acc
William	412	Bth
William	430	Bth
William	851	Cmp
William	105	Cmb
William	459	Frn
William	492	Frn
William	155	Knq

William	504	Prw	John	395	Fqr	Bla...well, Wm.	691	Wsh
see Creasey, George			John	649	Mnt	Blachewell, Nimrod	323	Ags
Birdsall, Whitson	316	Ldn	John	532	Prg	Black, Alex.	301	Rck
Wm.	315	Ldn	John	602	Srr	Alexr.	921	Hrr
Birdsong, Benjamin	626	Sss	John	629	Sss	Anthony	316	Ags
Cherry	628	Sss	John	711	Wsh	Archibald	912	Hrr
George	626	Sss	Jonathan	5	Clp	Ben	271	Rck
John	628	Sss	Jonathan	711	Wsh	Catharine	303	Rck
John	629	Sss	Jonathan, Jur.	736	Wsh	Christn., Jr.	606	Btt
John M.	744	Brn	Jos.	740	Wsh	Christn., Sr.	606	Btt
Judith	705	Brn	Joseph	185	Alb	Daniel	819	Wth
Lucy	628	Sss	Joseph	499	Frn	Eave	610	Btt
Merritt	705	Brn	Joshua	539	Frd	Elenor	823	Wth
Robert	626	Sss	Josiah	5	Clp	Fredk., Jr.	606	Btt
Sally	869	Sth	Landon	499	Frn	Fredk., Sr.	606	Btt
Samuel	628	Sss	Levi	711	Wsh	George	83	Acc
Thomas	628	Sss	Levi	712	Wsh	George	599	Frd
William	628	Sss	Lloyd	606	Frd	George	271	Rck
Wm. M.	705	Brn	Lucy	629	Sss	George	214	Shn
Bire see Rire			Luman	68	Chs	George	248	Shn
Bires, Isaac	90	Jff	Martha	704	Brn	Hugh	52	Stf
John	106	Jff	Marticia	704	Brn	Isaac	17	Rcm
Sarah	98	Jff	Mary	704	Brn	James	315	Ags
Birk, Wm.	8	Clp	Mason	600	Srr	James	322	Ags
Birkhedde, Abram S.	21	Oho	Noah	736	Wsh	James	323	Ags
Birlhart, John	315	Ags	Pelig	736	Wsh	James	912	Hrr
Biror, Jacob	323	Ags	Peter	819	Wth	James	556	Pre
Birry see Berry			Peter, Junr.	820	Wth	James	287	Rck
Birthright, Peter	706	Brn	Polley	328	Dnw	John	318	Ags
Birton, William	187	Alb	Richd., Ser.	546	Prg	John [2]	687	Br
Birtt, Edward	627	Sss	Richd. J.	546	Prg	John	868	Cmp
Harwood	629	Sss	Rosanna	499	Frn	John	139	Dnw
Biscoe, Ann	3	Pwh	Sarah	598	Srr	John	783	Hmp
H. L., Est.	67	Chs	Southey	75	Acc	John	665	Mnt
Jno.	338	Lnc	Stephen	602	Srr	John	266	Rck
Thomas	372	Fqr	Susanna	601	Srr	John	6	Rcm
Wm.	336	Lnc	Thomas	553	Frd	John	42	Rcm
Bise, Aaron	420	Fqr	Thomas	600	Srr	John	217	Shn
John	349	Fqr	William	184	Alb	John	256	Shn
Biset, Dublin	313	Ldn	William	551	Frd	John	699	Wsh
Bish, Frederick	31	Rcm	William	533	Prg	John	819	Wth
Bishop, Ann	127	Sth	William	436	Pra	John	823	Wth
Anne	395	Fqr	William	437	Pra	Jonathan	438	Flv
Asa	326	Dnw	William	490	Pra	Joseph	50	Stf
Augustine	822	Wth	William	600	Srr	Laml.	323	Ags
Beall	539	Frd	Wm.	139	Dnw	Leonard	219	Shn
Brice	539	Frd	Wm.	487	Pra	Margaret	592	Brk
Catharine	609	Btt	Wm.	490	Pra	Martin	216	Shn
Charles	335	Dnw	Wm.	711	Wsh	Nancy	327	Dnw
Chris	485	Mnn	Wm., Jr.	437	Pra	Peter	216	Shn
David	600	Srr	Bishup, George	610	Btt	Peter, Junr.	206	Shn
Ebenezer P.	18	Oho	Jacob	607	Btt	Peter, sen.	214	Shn
Eliza.	8	Clp	Jeremiah	608	Btt	Robert	287	Rck
Elizabeth	499	Frn	John	607	Btt	Sally	332	Ags
Elizabeth	646	Mnt	Stephen	794	Bck	Sally	201	Ess
George	100	Jff	Bisphan, Ann	411	Rch	Saml.	316	Ags
George	104	Jff	Bisshop, Edmond	332	Lnn	Saml.	608	Btt
Greenbury	558	Frd	John	331	Lnn	Samuel	150	Alb
Griffin	76	Acc	Bithshears, Jessee	744	Brn	Samuel	922	Hrr
Henry	485	Mnn	Bitser, Harman	234	Ldn	Turner	446	Flv
Henry	661	Mnt	Bittle, Ben.	152	Sth	William [2]	150	Alb
Henry	138	Sth	Geo.	324	Ags	William	858	Cmp
Hermon, jr.	600	Srr	Henry	873	Sth	William	587	Mnr
Hubbard	532	Prg	Lucy	145	Sth	William	556	Pre
Jacob	76	Acc	Peggy	873	Sth	William	56	Stf
Jacob	597	Brk	William	866	Sth	Willm.	665	Mnt
Jacob	661	Mnt	Bitzer, Cunrod	314	Ldn	Wm.	316	Ags
Jacob	546	Prg	Biven, T. A.	399	Ags	Wm.	722	Wsh
Jacob	437	Pra	Bivin, Jno.	438	Pra	Wm., sr.	316	Ags
James	187	Alb	Bivins, Edmond	946	Chc	Blackbourn, Nath.	16	Hnr
James	305	Amh	John	683	Gch	Blackbourne, Royal	442	Flv
James	140	Dnw	Bixby, N. R.	333	Dnw	Blackbun, William	7	Pwh
James	889	Nrf	Bixler, Chrisr.	483	Mnn	Blackburn, Absom.	112	Hnr
James	533	Prg	Saml.	483	Mnn	Ambrose	199	Ess
James	160	Sth	Bixton, Thos.	887	Nrf	Ann	900	Hnv
James	600	Srr	Bizard, Jac.	482	Mnn	Christian	504	Prw
Jereh.	139	Dnw	Robt.	482	Mnn	Christopher	891	Crl
Jerry	446	Grn	Bizer, Jacob	804	Hmp	Christopher	29	Stf
Jno.	486	Mnn	Nicholas	825	Hmp	David	863	Hnv
John	704	Brn	Bl..., Joseph	454	Bdf	Jesse	113	Hnr

Joseph	119	Hnr	John	170	Shn	Patsey	649	Glc
Joseph	68	Jff	Laml.	317	Ags	Peter	616	Gls
Nathiel	35	Hnr	Thomas	170	Shn	Ralph C.	325	Dnw
P. A.	458	Mdd	Bladen, Thomas	237	Frf	Salley	411	Fqr
Rogr.	681	Wrw	William	235	Frf	Samuel	460	Mdd
Rowland	116	Hnr	Blades, Camel	35	Hnr	Stephen	128	Sth
Saml.	113	Hnr	Bladley, Mary P.	113	Cmb	Thomas	459	Mdd
Saml.	157	Sth	Blagg, John	218	Pnd	Thos.	12	Clp
Samuel	445	Bth	William	218	Pnd	Warner	459	Mdd
Smith	115	Hnr	Blailock, H...h.	682	Gch	William	616	Gls
Thomas	892	Crl	Jeremh.	682	Gch	William	679	Nls
Thomas	236	Frf	Blain, Alexander	149	Alb	William	521	Prw
Thomas	805	Hmp	Danl., Rev.	266	Rck	William, Junr.	44	Chr
Thomas	268	Ldn	George	681	Nls	William, Senr.	43	Chr
Thomas	502	Prw	James	427	Msn	Wm.	12	Clp
Thos.	112	Hnr	John	149	Alb	Wm.	213	Ess
Wm.	112	Hnr	John	284	Rck	Wm.	649	Glc
Wm.	55	Jff	John	40	Rcm	see Harris		
Wm.	190	Kng	Nathan	149	Alb	Blakeley, John	324	Ags
Wm., jr.	112	Hnr	William	2	Knw	Wm.	274	Ldn
Blackburne, Edwd. L.	241	Frf	William	20	Rcm	Blakely, George	321	Ags
John	435	Flv	William	36	Rcm	Blakemon, George	323	Ags
Robert	241	Frf	Blaine, Mathw.	582	Mnr	Blakemoor, Caleb	18	Oho
Blacker, Henry	569	Frd	Blair, Alexr.	322	Ags	James	17	Oho
Jacob	569	Frd	Allen	301	Amh	George	533	Frd
Joseph	569	Frd	Archer	31	Hnr	James	566	Frd
Luke	569	Frd	Duncan	7	Clp	Marcus	533	Frd
Blackerbe, Gregory	349	Fqr	E., Mrs.	889	Nrf	Blaker, John	243	Ldn
Blackerby, Chloe	970	Nrt	James [2]	679	Br	Blakewell, Rancel	317	Ags
Hettry	971	Nrt	James	4	Oho	Blakey, Churchhill	460	Mdd
William	971	Nrt	James	264	Rck	Churchill	378	Mds
Blackhead, Ben	880	Sth	John	432	Bth	Churchill, Jr.	378	Mds
Blackley, James	464	Frn	John	679	Br	George	119	Hnr
Mary	460	Mdd	John	704	Wsh	Henry	459	Mdd
Reuben	185	Alb	John, Senr.	746	Wsh	Jemima	24	Hnr
Blackman, Saml.	880	Sth	John D.	33	Hnr	John, & mother	378	Mds
Blackmore, Charles	687	Br	Margaret	322	Ags	Robert	801	Bck
Edwd.	337	Lnc	Mary	611	Btt	Robert	459	Mdd
William	181	Shn	Mary	890	Nrf	William	378	Mds
Blackshins, Dick	871	Sth	Mathew	322	Ags	see Blakus		
Blackstone, James	890	Crl	Nancy, (F.N.)	32	Isw	Blakinship, H.	18	Hnr
Jenny	891	Crl	Peggy, (F.N.)	31	Isw	Blakley, John R.	328	Dnw
see Engledew			Randal	679	Br	Blakus, Reubin	126	Hnr
Blackwell, Anne	413	Fqr	Sarah	617	Mnt	Blalock, Elizabeth	743	Brn
Armistead	359	Fqr	Sarah	116	Spt	Blamire, Elzabeth	832	Nrf
Benja.	6	Clp	Willm.	607	Btt	Blancett, Rhodham	392	Fqr
Benjamin	414	Fqr	Willm.	668	Mnt	Blanch, Ezekiel	744	Brn
Catharine	886	Hnv	Wm.	318	Ags	Sanuel	744	Brn
Chap... [Chapman?]	331	Lnn	Wm.	8	Clp	Blanchard, Frs.	890	Nrf
David	523	Prw	Blake, Alice	459	Mdd	Thos.	889	Nrf
George	971	Nrt	Allen	584	Frd	Blanchet, Elizabeth	820	Wth
Heritage	179	Shn	Augustine	647	Glc	Bland, Alexdr.	584	Mnr
Hiram	971	Nrt	Bartlett S.	459	Mdd	Allen	505	Prw
Job	332	Lnn	Benjamin	206	Ess	Amey	219	Ess
John	187	Alb	Benjamin	446	Mth	Ann	890	Nrf
John	352	Fqr	Beverly A.	13	Knw	Ann	12	Ntt
John	330	Lnn	Charles	111	Cmb	Edward	12	Ntt
Joseph	6	Clp	Chas.	647	Glc	Eliza. R.	12	Ntt
Joseph, Jr.	358	Fqr	E. G.	332	Dnw	Henry	222	Pnd
Joseph, (of Jos.)	418	Fqr	Elijah	13	Clp	James	381	Fqr
Joseph, Senr.	419	Fqr	Eliza	647	Glc	James	157	Knq
Marth	541	Prg	Exum	868	Sth	John	248	Aml
Moses	455	Bdf	George	82	Acc	John	140	Dnw
Robert	706	Brn	George	241	Frf	John	335	Dnw
Robert	819	Wth	George	616	Gls	John	389	Fqr
Robert, Est.	332	Lnn	George	13	Knw	John	505	Prw
Saml.	6	Clp	George	460	Mdd	John	525	Prw
Samuel	357	Fqr	Harmon	83	Acc	John, jr.	155	Knq
Samuel	973	Nrt	Isaac	616	Gls	John, Senr.	155	Knq
Sarah	19	Hnr	James	1	Knw	John D.	154	Knq
Thomas	332	Lnn	James	16	Oho	John Y.	157	Knq
Thomas	971	Nrt	Jno.	12	Clp	Joshua	584	Mnr
Thos.	10	Clp	Jno.	647	Glc	Mary	155	Knq
Wm., jr.	6	Clp	John	6	Knw	Mary	157	Knq
Wm., senr.	6	Clp	John	459	Mdd	Mary	548	Prg
Zachariah	819	Wth	L.	31	Hnr	Peter	16	Ntt
see ---, Bla...well, Chilton			Lemwriah	43	Chr	Peter R.	4	Ntt
Blackwill, Lewis	519	Prw	Margarett	648	Glc	Peter R., jr.	12	Ntt
Blackwood, Alexr.	122	Hnr	Mary	444	Bth	Richd. Y.	18	Ntt
James	170	Shn	Patience	82	Acc	Robert	155	Knq

Name		
Robert	156	Knq
Robert	569	Mnr
Salley D.	12	Ntt
Sarah	157	Knq
Susan	534	Prg
Thomas	222	Pnd
Warner	155	Knq
William, jr.	157	Knq
William, Ser.	157	Knq
Blane, James	836	Nrf
Blanford, Francis D.	442	Pra
Blankenbeker, Christena	376	Mds
Elisebeth	376	Mds
Jahob	376	Mds
John, Jr.	376	Mds
Jonas	376	Mds
Lewis	376	Mds
Nicholas	376	Mds
Samuel	376	Mds
Blankenship, Abel	557	Pre
Ann	62	Chs
Archabald	856	Cmp
Danl.	55	Chs
David	43	Chr
Hesakiah	499	Frn
Hudson	860	Cmp
John	456	Frn
John	480	Frn
Josiah	535	Prg
Legun	481	Frn
Max	56	Chs
Pleasant	60	Chs
Pleasant	472	Frn
Salley	798	Bck
Smith	463	Frn
Zachariah	856	Cmp
Blankenson, John N.	783	Bck
Blankinship, Abraham	453	Bdf
Archibald	615	Gls
Arther	618	Gls
Barnet	450	Frn
Benj.	454	Bdf
Benjamin	455	Bdf
Bland	60	Chs
Drury	55	Chs
Eda	617	Gls
Emanuel	64	Chs
Ephraim	62	Chs
Francs.	684	Gch
Haley	54	Chs
Hilrey	617	Gls
James	54	Chs
Jesse	616	Gls
Jessee	549	Prg
Jno.	5	Ntt
John	443	Bth
Joseph	455	Bdf
Lydia	54	Chs
Nathan	54	Chs
Patience	292	Amh
Peter	617	Gls
Richd.	615	Gls
Stephen	54	Chs
Wm.	54	Chs
Wm.	59	Chs
Blanknship, Stanton	247	Aml
Blankpicker, Zacheriah	821	Wth
Blanks, Allen	43	Chr
David	949	Chc
Ingram	446	Grn
James	446	Grn
Jane	811	Bck
John	43	Chr
Mary	942	Chc
Thomas	43	Chr
Blantain, Nancy	102	Spt
Blanton, Charles	890	Crl
David	109	Cmb
James	106	Cmb
James	556	Pre

Name		
John	109	Cmb
John	573	Mnr
John	558	Pre
Joshua	557	Pre
Lawrence	106	Cmb
Sally	107	Cmb
Thomas	559	Pre
William	575	Mnr
Blarney, Edward	12	Oho
Blassingham, James	871	Yrk
John	601	Srr
Tho.	871	Yrk
Blassingime, Johannah	648	Glc
Wm.	648	Glc
Blatchford, John C.	683	Gch
Blauser, Abraham	191	Shn
Blaydes, John C.	76	Spt
Blaze, Willm.	607	Btt
Blazer, Christian	4	Rcm
Bleasor, Barey L.	726	Wsh
Bledso, Loven	754	Wsh
Bledsoe, Anthoney	755	Wsh
Elijah	442	Flv
Gaven	754	Wsh
Isaac	754	Wsh
Vallentine	754	Wsh
Blenise, Joseph	238	Frf
Bless, Christian	611	Btt
Blessing, Abm.	423	Msn
Jacob	737	Wsh
John	821	Wth
Lewis	199	Shn
Blevins, Davd.	715	Wsh
Hardin	715	Wsh
Blew, Betsey	28	Hnr
Billey	28	Hnr
Jesse	82	Jff
Joel	94	Jff
John S.	96	Jff
Mary	54	Jff
Michael	789	Hmp
Michael	94	Jff
Blexton see Janney		
Blick, George, jr.	141	Dnw
George, Senr.	141	Dnw
James	705	Brn
James	141	Dnw
John, jr.	141	Dnw
John, Senr.	140	Dnw
Joshua	140	Dnw
Blincoe, Mark	249	Ldn
Sampson	304	Ldn
Thos.	232	Ldn
Wm.	232	Ldn
Blind, Michael	219	Shn
Peter	209	Shn
Blink, Betty	100	Spt
Blinker, George	972	Nrt
Mark	972	Nrt
Blizard, Burten	215	Pnd
James	215	Pnd
Blizzard, Ezekiah	126	Sth
Sucky	601	Srr
Block, Jacob	21	Hnr
Simon	21	Hnr
Simon, (W)	870	Yrk
Wm.	19	Hnr
Blocksom, Thomas	273	Ldn
Blodgett, Abisha	15	Oho
Bloodson, James	109	Cmb
Blos, Adam	421	Bth
Blose, Adam	34	Rcm
Blosser, Jacob	5	Rcm
Jacob	185	Shn
John	38	Rcm
Peter	180	Shn
Blount, Jos.	795	Nrf
Blout, Adam	819	Wth
Blow, Alexander	626	Sss
Geo.	890	Yrk

Name		
George	126	Sth
George	630	Sss
Henry	148	Sth
Henry	626	Sss
James	130	Sth
Jno. T.	161	Sth
Peter	161	Sth
Rebecca	628	Sss
Richd.	827	Nrf
Thos.	888	Nrf
Will.	876	Sth
Bloxam, Anderson	8	Acc
Ezekel	75	Acc
Levin	75	Acc
Woodman	74	Acc
Bloxham, Dennis	76	Acc
James	234	Frf
Scarbr.	189	Elc
Bloxom, George	8	Acc
George	81	Acc
Hazariah	81	Acc
Jacob [2]	80	Acc
James	82	Acc
Major	80	Acc
Molly	80	Acc
Rachel	81	Acc
Richard, of W	80	Acc
Richard, Sen.	82	Acc
Southey	8	Acc
Stephen	81	Acc
Stephen, Sen.	81	Acc
Bloxon, Elijah	76	Acc
Bloxton, Abraham	56	Stf
Joseph	24	Stf
Samuel	27	Stf
Blu, William	14	Oho
Blue, Cupid, (F. Negroe)	419	Fqr
Daniel	792	Hmp
Garrett	792	Hmp
Isaac	792	Hmp
John	762	Hmp
Michael	792	Hmp
Michael	800	Hmp
Michael, Jur.	792	Hmp
Nathan	510	Brk
Richard	778	Hmp
Uriah	509	Brk
Uriah	799	Hmp
see Blu		
Bluefoot, Sally	648	Glc
Thos.	648	Glc
Bluer, William	909	Hrr
Bluford, James	184	Elc
John M.	972	Nrt
Spencer	973	Nrt
Blundel, Elija	971	Nrt
John	971	Nrt
Moses, a free mulatto	973	Nrt
Samuel	971	Nrt
Westley	973	Nrt
Blundell, Thomas	767	Wst
Blundon, Elijah	241	Frf
Blunhall, Patsey	852	Hnv
Blunt, Ann	868	Hnv
Bartholomew	850	Hnv
Benja.	151	Sth
Benja.	162	Sth
Charles	861	Cmp
Frances	151	Sth
Francis	868	Hnv
Francis	375	Mds
George	856	Sth
Henry	850	Sth
James	893	Crl
Jno.	867	Hnv
John	2	Isw
Molley	889	Crl
Nathl.	610	Btt
Richd.	161	Sth
Saml.	127	Sth

Susana	850	Hnv	Bococke, John, sr.	787	Bck	Wm.	870	Yrk
Thomas, Jr.	629	Sss	John T.	788	Bck	Bohart, Philip	95	Jff
Thomas, Sr.	601	Srr	Boddington, Helena	829	Nrf	Boher, ---, & Hubner	22	Hnr
Thomas, Sr.	630	Sss	Bodeman, James	543	Brk	Bohn see Boher		
Thompson	61	Chs	Boden, Wm.	519	Brk	Bohon, Joseph C.	5	Clp
Walter	626	Sss	Bodine, Francis	237	Frf	Thos.	5	Clp
William	31	Isw	John	785	Hmp	Wm.	5	Clp
Wilson	610	Btt	Bodkin, James	536	Frd	Boice, Mary	528	Frd
Blutcher, Benjamin	187	Alb	Thomas	267	Rck	Robert	938	Hrr
Bly, Adam	204	Shn	Bodkins, Chas.	284	Rck	Boid, Alexr.	315	Ags
George	211	Shn	Bodley, Wm.	482	Mnn	John	7	Clp
John	536	Frd	Bog, Jos.	487	Mnn	Sally	14	Clp
Blytchender, Charles	223	Pnd	Bogan, Andw., Sr.	287	Rck	Boin, John	148	Alb
Blythe, Dinah	890	Nrf	Benj.	305	Rck	Micajah	148	Alb
Eliza.	139	Sth	John	605	Btt	Boisnard, John	6	Acc
Geo.	890	Nrf	Willm.	611	Btt	Boiss see Bass		
John	376	Fqr	Bogar, Michael	298	Ldn	Boisseau, ---	329	Dnw
John [2]	126	Sth	Bogard, Daniel	797	Hmp	---	332	Dnw
Maryann	882	Hnv	Bogas, Enoch	584	Mnr	Benj. P.	139	Dnw
Polly	589	Mnr	Nimrod	427	Msn	Benjamin	333	Dnw
Boadridge, Prescilla	13	Clp	Boger, David	300	Ldn	Benjn., jr.	139	Dnw
Boady, Frederick	29	Rcm	Fredr.	285	Ldn	Benjn., Senr.	140	Dnw
Boals, Henry	139	Dnw	Boges, Samuel	937	Hrr	David	139	Dnw
James	139	Dnw	Bogges, Thomas	446	Bth	Joseph	141	Dnw
Boar, Matthias	40	Rcm	Boggess, Henry, Jr.	605	Btt	Mary	628	Sss
Board, Frances	454	Bdf	Henry, Sr.	608	Btt	Wm.	139	Dnw
John	404	Fqr	Linsy	486	Mnn	Boitnetts, Justis	472	Frn
Pat	483	Mnn	Maryam	240	Frf	Boke, John	536	Brk
Stephen	453	Bdf	Robert	241	Frf	Wm.	554	Brk
Boarer, Isaac	556	Frd	Robert, Junr.	240	Frf	Boker see Baker		
Jacob	556	Frd	Samuel	276	Ldn	Boland, Betsey	594	Brk
Boashand, Ths.	757	Wsh	Wm.	280	Ldn	John	690	Br
Boashill, Thos.	800	Nrf	Boggs, Ann	507	Brk	Stephen	425	Rnd
Boasley, Wm.	63	Chs	Arthur	5	Acc	Boler, Charles	37	Stf
Boast, John	333	Dnw	Charles	7	Knw	Boles, Fleming	57	Chs
Boatman, Jno.	338	Lnc	Francis	4	Acc	John	453	Bdf
Wm., jr.	337	Lnc	Francis	8	Acc	Thomas	677	Br
Wm., Senr.	338	Lnc	Francis	7	Knw	Boley, Benjamin	454	Bdf
Boaton see Beaton			Francis	11	Oho	Elij...h	454	Bdf
Boatright, Benjn.	7	Pwh	George	10	Knw	Elizabeth	67	Jff
Charles	110	Cmb	Hugh C.	82	Spt	Jacob	597	Brk
James, jr.	128	Cmb	James	6	Knw	John	454	Bdf
James, snr.	128	Cmb	James	7	Knw	John	76	Jff
Jessee	110	Cmb	John	6	Acc	Bolin, John	409	Fqr
Jessee	128	Cmb	John	7	Knw	Nancy	503	Prw
John	129	Cmb	Margarett	101	Jff	William	369	Fqr
Samuel	115	Cmb	Wm.	559	Brk	Boling, Edwd.	302	Rck
Samuel	128	Cmb	Bogle, Andrew	616	Gls	Gane	925	Hrr
Valentine	126	Cmb	James	616	Gls	James	283	Rck
Boatwright, James	880	Cmp	John	616	Gls	Jemima	508	Frd
John	684	Gch	Mary	808	Hmp	Jeremiah	510	Frd
John	557	Pre	Ralph	819	Wth	Jesse	11	Clp
Reuben	829	Bck	Robert	819	Wth	Jesse	617	Gls
Richd.	685	Gch	Bogs, John	216	Pnd	John	150	Alb
Wade	455	Bdf	Bogue, Jno.	254	Ldn	Nathl.	14	Clp
Boaz, Daniel	555	Pre	Bohanan, Charity	508	Prw	William	524	Frd
Meshack	556	Pre	Bohannan, Joseph	217	Ess	Wm.	12	Clp
Boaze, Daniel	881	Hnv	Joseph	449	Mth	Bolinger, David	572	Frd
Elizabeth	813	Bck	Wm.	155	Knq	Elizabeth	610	Btt
Gedion	882	Hnv	Bohannon, Ambrose	647	Glc	Peter	11	Rcm
Jno.	881	Hnv	Benja.	647	Glc	William	542	Frd
Meshack	813	Bck	John	10	Hnr	Boll..., ...	68	Chs
Thos.	894	Hnv	John	14	Hnr	Bollar, John	415	Bth
Boazley, Ephraim	206	Ess	Joseph	331	Lnn	John, Ser.	439	Bth
Boazman, Micajh.	154	Sth	Leonard	647	Glc	Boller, Thomas	124	Cmb
Bob, F.N.	156	Knq	Mary	375	Mds	Bolling, ..., residing in		
Bobbett, John	283	Amh	Mary	450	Mth	Petersburg	140	Dnw
John	630	Sss	Nathaniel	332	Lnn	Archabald, Jr.	863	Cmp
Uriah	292	Amh	Sary	375	Mds	Archabald, Senr.	863	Cmp
Bobbins see Robbins			Thomas	413	Fqr	B.	65	Chs
Bobbitt, John	655	Mnt	Thomas	375	Mds	Betty	64	Chs
Bobby, Joseph	430	Msn	Thos.	23	Hnr	Edmund	67	Chr
Bobinson, John	3	Wod	William	332	Lnn	Edwd.	683	Gch
Boblits, Michael	455	Bdf	William	12	Wod	Eliza.	64	Chs
Bobo, Jesse	6	Wod	Wilshire	331	Lnn	George	97	Spt
Bobson, Israel	869	Cmp	Wm.	450	Mth	Hall	331	Dnw
Bocaman, Christn.	605	Btt	see Bookhannon			John	140	Dnw
Bocheny see Buchang			Bohanon, Henry	871	Yrk	Jonathn.	242	Frf
Bockers, Van	515	Brk	John	871	Yrk	Laneaus	786	Bck
Bocock, Samuel	454	Bdf	Quarles	870	Yrk	Mary	326	Dnw

Mary	336	Dnw	Thomas	946	Hrr	Wm., (of Nathn.)	440	Pra
Mary, in Petersburg	139	Dnw	William	549	Frd	Bonny, Henry	813	Nrf
Robert	326	Dnw	Wright	455	Bdf	Bonsal, ---, & Co.	890	Nrf
Robt.	4	Ntt	Bonds, Sarah	629	Sss	Joseph	771	Hmp
Robt., jr.	141	Dnw	Bondurant, Darby	790	Bck	Bonsey, John	243	Shn
Saml. P.	139	Dnw	David	790	Bck	Bonsten, Matthias	218	Pnd
Stith	19	Ntt	James	804	Bck	Bonts, Jacob	285	Ldn
Thos. T.	247	Aml	John	785	Bck	Valentine	285	Ldn
Wm.	685	Gch	Judith	841	Bck	Bonum, David	400	Fqr
see Walker, Wells			Noah	794	Bck	Bonwell, Betty	5	Acc
Bollingbrook, Betty	332	Dnw	Thomas	794	Bck	Betty, of Jas.	7	Acc
Bollings, Charles	163	Shn	Thomas, Jr.	792	Bck	Caleb	192	Elc
Bolls, Jessy	8	Hnr	Bone, Hezekiah	745	Nwk	Clement	6	Acc
Bolon, Alexander	521	Prw	Bonecutter, George	554	Frd	Elijah	5	Acc
Margt.	264	Ldn	Bonefield, Gregery	425	Rnd	George	79	Acc
Bolt, John	439	Pra	Samuel	425	Rnd	Jesse	7	Acc
Maxx	439	Pra	Bonenis, Moses	758	Wsh	John, Senr.	8	Acc
Philip	525	Brk	Boner, David	6	Oho	Levi	11	Acc
see Boult			Jno., Ser.	480	Mnn	McKeel, Junr.	11	Acc
Bolten, Aaron	815	Nrf	Joseph	616	Gls	Molly	8	Acc
Bolter see Boller			William	681	Br	Rachel	81	Acc
Boltess, Eve	255	Shn	see Bonner			Robert	5	Acc
William	255	Shn	Bones, James	663	Mnt	Susannah	13	Acc
Bolton, Anthony	806	Nrf	Joseph	663	Mnt	see B...nwell		
Coonrod	609	Btt	Bonham, Benja.	588	Frd	Bony, John	415	Bth
James	7	Hnr	Hezekiah	736	Wsh	Booby, John	87	Jff
John	801	Bck	Jeremiah	598	Frd	Louis	890	Nrf
John	706	Wsh	Jises	15	Oho	Peter	889	Nrf
Lydia	818	Nrf	Martin	821	Wth	Booher, Henry	924	Hrr
Noah	704	Wsh	Nehemiah	616	Gls	Book, Phillip	611	Btt
Wm.	292	Ldn	Oney	820	Wth	Booker, Andrew	605	Btt
Wm., Estate of	817	Nrf	Samuel	533	Frd	Benj.	703	Wsh
Boman, David	229	Shn	Samuel	270	Ldn	Daniel, Sr.	247	Aml
Francis	958	Chc	Bonnardell, J.	2	Hnr	Edith C.	103	Cmb
George	812	Hmp	Bonneau, John	890	Nrf	Edmond	556	Pre
Jacob	241	Shn	Bonnegent, P.	890	Nrf	Edward	119	Cmb
John	239	Shn	Bonnen, Smith	529	Brk	Edward	559	Pre
John	240	Shn	see Borren			Eliza.	246	Aml
John	693	Wsh	Bonner, Amos	481	Mnn	Eliza.	248	Aml
Kien	243	Shn	Edmund	647	Glc	Frances	332	Lnn
Ralph	148	Alb	Geo.	542	Prg	Geo.	188	Elc
Rebecka	557	Pre	Harry, F.N.	628	Sss	George	555	Pre
Thos.	552	Brk	J.	484	Mnn	Henry	247	Aml
Wiley	957	Chc	James	541	Prg	Henry	23	Oho
William	230	Shn	John	446	Grn	Jacob	961	Hrr
Bomgarden, Jacob	318	Ags	Jos., Jr.	481	Mnn	Jacob	377	Mds
Bomgardner, Frederick	821	Wth	Josh.	480	Mnn	James	449	Mth
Jacob	318	Ags	Reub.	484	Mnn	Jane	648	Glc
Bomgarner, Chrn.	318	Ags	Robert	530	Prg	Jno. C.	437	Mth
Henry	322	Ags	Samuel	418	Rnd	John	248	Aml
Robt.	322	Ags	William	414	Bth	John	158	Knq
Bomin, Benjamin	248	Shn	Williamson	446	Grn	John	376	Mds
Catharine	248	Shn	see Boner			John	558	Pre
Bomon, Jacob	321	Ags	Bonnett, Jacob	937	Hrr	John S.	247	Aml
Joseph	321	Ags	John	14	Oho	Jonathan	332	Lnn
Bonafield, Arnold	173	Shn	Lewis	952	Hrr	Lewis	217	Ess
Bonair, James, Jr.	26	Oho	Lewis	14	Oho	Lowry	331	Lnn
Bonar, James	17	Oho	Peter	952	Hrr	Lucy	28	Hnr
Bonas, Moses, (F.N.)	13	Isw	Saml.	952	Hrr	Parham	246	Aml
Sampson, (F.N.)	36	Isw	William	420	Msn	Pink D.	248	Aml
Bond, Abel	936	Hrr	Bonney, Anna	441	Pra	Richard	103	Cmb
Abel	943	Hrr	Diana	440	Pra	Richard	120	Cmb
Adam	180	Shn	Edwd., of Jno.	440	Pra	Richd.	187	Elc
Allen	149	Alb	Henry	441	Pra	Samuel	557	Pre
Benjamin	22	Oho	Jas.	438	Pra	Sarah	289	Rck
Isaac	453	Bdf	Jno., (of Jno.)	439	Pra	Thos.	649	Glc
James	679	Br	Jno., (of Jona.)	441	Pra	William	43	Chr
Jno.	272	Ldn	Jno., Sr.	440	Pra	William	113	Cmb
John	294	Amh	Jonathan	441	Pra	see Bockers, Booher, Foster		
John	582	Frd	Martha	441	Pra	Bookhannon, Wm. [crossed		
Joseph	65	Jff	Mary	440	Pra	out]	453	Mth
Joseph	209	Shn	Moses	437	Pra	Bookover, Jno.	483	Mnn
Levy	964	Hrr	Nathan	440	Pra	William	98	Jff
Lewis	961	Hrr	Richard	441	Pra	Booling, Joseph	454	Frn
Richard	693	Br	Thomas	442	Pra	Boolling, Peter	769	Brn
Richard	945	Hrr	Tully	438	Pra	Boolon, Ambrose	186	Shn
Richard	955	Hrr	V.	887	Nrf	Bools, Thomas, f. negro	235	Frf
Robert	483	Frn	V., 2nd.	891	Nrf	Boon, Abraham	9	Rcm
Ruth	521	Prw	Wm.	442	Pra	Abram	476	Frn
Thomas	810	Hmp	Wm., (of Edwd.)	440	Pra	Jacob	473	Frn

Jacob, Jr.	479	Frn	Peter	153	Sth	Joseph	460	Mdd
James	161	Sth	William	453	Bdf	Lewis	460	Mdd
John	585	Mnr	Bootman, John	522	Prw	Peter	305	Ldn
John	655	Mnt	Booton, William	421	Msn	Thos., senr.	60	Chs
Peter	474	Frn	Bootright, Benjamin	882	Hnv	see Bots		
Sarah	336	Dnw	James	1	Hnr	Bossel, Betty	271	Ldn
Boone, Humphry	13	Oho	Jno.	882	Hnv	Bossemon, C., jr.	320	Ags
Nicholas	13	Oho	Boots, Isaac	682	Br	Chista.	320	Ags
Richard	13	Oho	see Bools			Bosserman, Jacob	215	Shn
Boones, Lawrence	108	Spt	Bootts, Joseph	179	Shn	William	204	Shn
Boontz, Jacob	234	Frf	Booz, Philip	887	Nrf	William, Jr.	205	Shn
Boosh, Agness	735	Wsh	Booze, David	608	Btt	Bossermon, Frederick	206	Shn
Henry	943	Hrr	Paul	482	Mnn	Henry	207	Shn
Booten, John	377	Mds	Peter	608	Btt	Michael	207	Shn
William	377	Mds	Boozer, Fredk.	610	Btt	Bossler, Hennery	931	Hrr
Booth, Abijah	658	Mnt	Boram, Edy.	889	Nrf	Bost, Samuel	298	Ldn
Abner	635	Mnt	Hezekiah	44	Chr	Boste see Botle		
Asahel	2	Oho	Isaac	427	Msn	Boster, Jno.	893	Hnv
Benjamin	471	Frn	John	427	Msn	Bostian, Adam	584	Frd
Benjn.	1	Ntt	W. T.	889	Nrf	Bostick, John	584	Mnr
Beverly	600	Srr	William	837	Bck	Mary	584	Mnr
Daniel	426	Rnd	Bord...y, John	956	Chc	Peggy	584	Mnr
Danl.	659	Mnt	Borden, Abraham	217	Shn	Thos.	584	Mnr
David	501	Frn	Augustine	217	Shn	Boston, Abel	483	Mnn
David	600	Srr	George	217	Shn	Daniel	78	Acc
Edwd.	871	Yrk	Philip	217	Shn	Ease... [Easer?]	83	Acc
Eliza.	247	Aml	Border, Daniel	68	Jff	George	15	Oho
Enoch	751	Wsh	Borders, Jacob	617	Gls	James	186	Alb
Franky	706	Brn	Bordin, John	642	Mnt	Philip	2	Rcm
Frederick	971	Nrt	Bordoin, Nicholas	243	Shn	Bostwick, Lanson	679	Br
George	139	Dnw	Bordon, Henry	278	Rck	Boswel, John	4	Wod
George	659	Mnt	Borer, Adam	564	Brk	Boswell, Barney	454	Bdf
George	626	Sss	Bores, Paul	693	Br	Elizt.	319	Ags
Gilliam	8	Ntt	Borgoin, Thomas	227	Pnd	George	506	Prw
Glanville	871	Yrk	Borham, John	186	Elc	J. L.	399	Ags
Isaac, Jr.	635	Mnt	Borher see Bosher			Jno.	647	Glc
Isaac, Sr.	635	Mnt	Boring, Abraham	675	Br	John	332	Lnn
James	283	Ldn	Absolom	934	Hrr	John	746	Nwk
James	971	Nrt	James	694	Br	Suson	704	Brn
James	22	Oho	Nicholous	932	Hrr	Thos., Botetourt	647	Glc
James	426	Rnd	Thomas	934	Hrr	William	744	Nwk
Jno., J.	283	Ldn	Borne, Rachel	850	Hnv	William [erased]	745	Nwk
Jno., Sn.	284	Ldn	Borns, Jacob	950	Hrr	William C.	332	Dnw
John	83	Acc	see Barns			see Boxwell		
John	139	Dnw	Boroker see Bowker			Bosworth, Jos.	14	Knw
John	971	Nrt	Boroughs, Joseph	285	Amh	Bother see Botken, Botler		
Joseph	971	Nrt	Borren, Chariot	921	Hrr	Botken, James	434	Bth
Lucy B.	647	Glc	Borrer, Adam	567	Brk	James, Snr.	435	Bth
Mark	601	Srr	Borring, Ians	954	Hrr	Botkin, John	217	Pnd
Matthew	247	Aml	Borton, Nancy	326	Dnw	John	218	Pnd
Matthew	602	Srr	Borum, Benjamin	555	Pre	Thomas	219	Pnd
Mordecai	508	Frd	James, jr.	7	Ntt	William	217	Pnd
Nancy	139	Dnw	Jno. W.	9	Ntt	Botle, Thalache	803	Nrf
Peter	470	Frn	John	559	Pre	Botler, Joseph	416	Fqr
Richard	166	Shn	Judith	8	Ntt	Botner, Joseph	329	Dnw
Richard	626	Sss	Wm.	4	Ntt	Bots, Judith	308	Ldn
Robert	600	Srr	Bosang, Wm.	398	Ags	see Boss		
Robt. C.	140	Dnw	Bosden, Michael	832	Nrf	Bott, Archd.	54	Chs
Rodham	971	Nrt	Bose, Adam	387	Fqr	Edwd. B.	610	Btt
Stephin	630	Mnt	Bosel, John	587	Brk	Frederick	455	Bdf
Thomas	630	Sss	Bosely, James	808	Hmp	James	246	Aml
Thos.	742	Brn	Boseman, Milly	629	Sss	Joel	614	Mnt
William	426	Rnd	Boshan, Jacob, jr.	321	Ags	John	747	Wsh
Willm.	611	Btt	Bosher, Charles	18	Hnr	Lucy	140	Dnw
Winnifred	971	Nrt	Gideon	1	Hnr	Thomas	54	Chs
Wm.	139	Dnw	Gidion	127	Hnr	Botter see Boller		
Wm.	648	Glc	John	922	Hrr	Bottle, George	254	Shn
see Woodson			Lenord	105	Cmb	Bottom, Bolling	629	Sss
Boothe, Alexr.	315	Ags	Wm.	874	Cmp	Elizabeth	129	Hnr
Caleb	536	Brk	see Bowsher			Enis	128	Hnr
Caleb, jr.	536	Brk	Bosick see Basick			Hazelwood	128	Hnr
Coventon	83	Acc	Bosisters, Philip	647	Mnt	Joel	128	Hnr
George	441	Pra	Bosley, Alexr.	520	Brk	Mary	247	Aml
James	447	Grn	Bosman, Benskin	746	Nwk	Mildred	128	Hnr
James	856	Sth	Edward	676	Br	Miles	44	Chr
John	556	Pre	James	745	Nwk	Bottoms, Tho.	339	Lnc
John	856	Sth	John	9	Hnr	Botts, Ann	157	Knq
Jonathan	536	Brk	Boson, Milly, f. negro	238	Frf	Ann	41	Stf
Nathaniel	557	Pre	Boss, James	460	Mdd	Benj.	35	Hnr
Obediah	397	Rch	John	458	Mdd	Bernard	515	Prw

James	9	Clp	William	156	Knq	Jas.	339	Lnc
Joseph	11	Clp	William	517	Prw	Jesse	75	Jff
Joshua	240	Frf	Boush, Ann	890	Nrf	Jesse	401	Rch
Samuel	41	Stf	Bennett	887	Nrf	Jno.	870	Yrk
Seth	514	Prw	Caleb	437	Pra	John	581	Frd
Thomas	275	Ldn	Michl.	889	Nrf	John	431	Msn
Thomas	506	Prw	Nat	888	Nrf	John	401	Rch
Boucher see Baucher			Nathanl.	874	Sth	John	404	Rch
Bouchiers, Monsr.	889	Nrf	Reuben	890	Crl	John, Sr.	607	Btt
Bouden, Jesse	144	Sth	Wilson	890	Nrf	Joshua	404	Rch
Boudett, St. Aubin	68	Chs	Wm., Jr.	437	Pra	Lucrecy	59	Jff
Boughan, Lewis	217	Ess	Wm., [his] (Plantn.)	438	Pra	Mary	59	Jff
Major	220	Ess	Wm., Sr.	438	Pra	Nancy	870	Sth
Nancy	220	Ess	see Butt			Phinehas	575	Frd
Sarah	221	Ess	Boushe, Jas.	805	Nrf	Sarah	60	Jff
Boughon, Eve	10	Clp	Boushong, ---, Capt.	889	Nrf	Stephen	387	Fqr
Jeremh.	10	Clp	Bouslog, John	479	Mnn	William	411	Rch
Jno.	13	Clp	Boutwell, Burkenhead	892	Crl	see Bawen		
Richd.	9	Clp	John	892	Crl	Bowens, Phillip	610	Btt
Vincent	11	Clp	Rowe	871	Yrk	Bower, Andw.	16	Rcm
Boughton, Alexr.	211	Ess	Bovan, George	601	Srr	Christr.	605	Btt
Benja.	396	Rch	Robert	601	Srr	George	292	Rck
Jane	158	Knq	Bovell, John	690	Wsh	Henry	541	Brk
John	213	Ess	Stephen, Revd.	691	Wsh	Henry	105	Jff
John	155	Knq	Bow, John	186	Alb	Jacob	537	Brk
Joshua	210	Ess	Levi	750	Wsh	William	359	Fqr
Richd.	211	Ess	Nathl.	874	Hnv	Bowers, Adam	511	Frd
Wm.	211	Ess	see Bowe			Balaam	447	Grn
Wm.	156	Knq	Bow..., Margaret	209	Shn	Carr	138	Sth
Wm. B.	156	Knq	Bowan, Ann	27	Hnr	Charity	17	Hnr
Bouldin, Ephraim	67	Chr	Arthur	737	Wsh	Christian	232	Shn
James	42	Chr	Jos.	12	Clp	Christian	236	Shn
Joannah	44	Chr	Joseph	713	Wsh	David	820	Nrf
John	43	Chr	Thos.	13	Clp	Eliza	820	Nrf
Richard	42	Chr	Wm.	10	Clp	Elizabeth	249	Shn
Thomas T.	43	Chr	Wm.	13	Clp	Frederick	88	Jff
William, Senr.	43	Chr	Wm., jr.	13	Clp	George	234	Shn
Boule, Leroy D.	222	Ess	Bowas, Henry, Junr.	224	Shn	George	236	Shn
Boulevare, Musco	889	Crl	Henry, Senr.	224	Shn	Jac.	480	Mnn
Bouls, Betsey	742	Brn	John	224	Shn	Jacob	132	Hnr
Boult, Willoughby	439	Pra	Bowcher, Ezekiel	703	Wsh	Jno.	138	Sth
see Bolt			Bowcock, Henry	768	Wst	John	606	Btt
Boultin, Jacob	227	Pnd	Matthew	460	Frn	John	88	Jff
Boulton, Abrahaham	17	Rcm	Peter, F.N.	39	Isw	John	744	Nwk
David	20	Rcm	William	460	Frn	John	220	Pnd
Henry	610	Btt	Bowcocke, Douglas	186	Alb	Jonathan	75	Jff
Isaac	19	Rcm	Jason	187	Alb	Lenard	28	Hnr
James	19	Rcm	Bowden, Benj.	10	Isw	Laurence	16	Rcm
Jonathan	17	Rcm	Danger, jr.	156	Knq	Michael	23	Stf
Mary	43	Chr	Eliza	157	Knq	Noah	22	Rcm
Valentine	4	Rcm	J.F.	888	Nrf	Robert	690	Br
Boulware, Andrew	892	Crl	James	18	Isw	Sarah	511	Fnd
Caleb	893	Crl	John	18	Isw	Siles	331	Lnn
Elizabeth	891	Crl	Joshua	626	Sss	Tamar	819	Nrf
Joel	158	Knq	Lydia	900	Hnv	Thos.	9	Clp
Lee	156	Knq	Mary	100	Spt	William	879	Cmp
Mark, junr.	892	Crl	Richd.	889	Nrf	William	27	Rcm
Mark, senr.	892	Crl	Robert	157	Knq	Willis	876	Sth
Mary	891	Crl	Stephen	97	Jff	Young	331	Lnn
Purdie D.	893	Crl	Thomas	127	Hnr	see Bowes, Bowez		
Saml.	156	Knq	Thomas, Jun.	19	Isw	Bowerset, John	364	Fqr
Thomas	197	Ess	Thomas, Sen.	19	Isw	Bowerss, Lewis	231	Shn
Thomas	158	Knq	William	330	Dnw	Bowes, Danl.	132	Hnr
William	891	Crl	William	331	Dnw	Thos.	114	Hnr
see Dyke, Vawter			William	155	Knq	Boweyer, Adam	583	Mnr
Bounce, Susan	105	Spt	Bowdey see Bord...y			Christan	594	Mnr
Bounds, Thomas	5	Oho	Bowe, Thomas	881	Cmp	Jacob	596	Mnr
Bourdon, Nicholas J.	139	Dnw	Wim.	873	Hnv	Bowez, John	232	Shn
Bourland, Andrew	416	Bth	Boweess see Bowerss			Bowie, Cintha	15	Clp
Bourn, Frederick	893	Crl	Bowen, Alexr.	66	Jff	James	892	Crl
Bourne, David	684	Gch	Alexr.	233	Ldn	John	404	Fqr
George	295	Amh	B...ket	61	Stf	Sarah	892	Crl
Henry	290	Amh	Berket	118	Spt	William	604	Frd
Jesse	274	Amh	Charles	544	Frd	Bowin, James	259	Amh
Jessee	156	Knq	Daniel	829	Hmp	James	64	Jff
John	305	Amh	Elizabeth	396	Fqr	John	610	Btt
Mary	156	Knq	Francis	393	Fqr	Willm.	647	Mnt
Miles	156	Knq	George	5	Isw	see Bauin, Bowm		
Stephen	684	Gch	Greenbery	519	Brk	Bowis, Jesse Scott	746	Nwk
William	582	Frd	James	416	Fqr	William	746	Nwk

Name	No.	Place
Bowker, Adam	185	Shn
Martin	185	Shn
Bowler, Walker	13	Pwh
Wm.	503	Brk
Wm.	9	Hnr
Wm.	14	Hnr
Bowles, ...	246	Aml
Anderson	853	Hnv
Bartlett	432	Flv
Bartlett	683	Gch
Ben	112	Hnr
Benjamin	441	Flv
Benjamin, B.	860	Hnv
Charles	279	Amh
Charles K.	853	Hnv
Elisha	685	Gch
Fitzhugh	598	Srr
Geo.	683	Gch
Henry	246	Aml
Hezekiah	882	Hnv
Isaac	12	Hnr
Isaac	302	Rck
Jno.	61	Chs
Jno.	851	Hnv
John	683	Gch
Knight	433	Flv
Lyal	111	Hnr
Lyddall	123	Hnr
Magret	698	Wsh
May	698	Wsh
Obadiah	191	Kng
Peter	875	Hnv
Polley	263	Amh
R. C.	685	Gch
Salley	899	Hnv
Sarah	684	Gch
Seth	683	Gch
Stephen	257	Amh
T.	316	Ags
Thomas	112	Hnr
Thomas	6	Isw
Thomas P.	10	Pwh
Thos.	698	Wsh
Thos., H.	851	Hnv
Thos., P.	848	Hnv
Thos., (S)	57	Chs
Thos. P.	899	Hnv
William	13	Pwh
Wim.	851	Hnv
see Bowes		
Bowlesby, Jas.	482	Mnn
Bowley, Simon	378	Fqr
Bowlin, James S.	375	Mds
Jesse	2	Rcm
Mary	681	Nls
William	15	Rcm
Bowling, Bailey	303	Amh
Benjamin	42	Stf
Charles	29	Stf
James	277	Amh
John	290	Amh
John	855	Cmp
John	54	Stf
Lawrence	66	Spt
Nancy	853	Cmp
Simon	380	Fqr
Spencer	46	Stf
Thomas	66	Spt
William	29	Stf
see Clark, Smith		
Bowls, Betsey	493	Frn
Caty	185	Alb
Daniel	679	Nls
David	821	Wth
Francis	498	Frn
George	487	Frn
George, Jr.	487	Frn
Jabel	493	Frn
James	240	Ldn
John	82	Acc
John	182	Alb
John	547	Frd
Joseph	488	Frn
Lucy	185	Alb
Matthew C.	653	Mnt
Sarah	498	Frn
William	470	Frn
Zachariah	185	Alb
Bowm, Creshey	129	Hnr
Bowman, Abraham	196	Shn
Adam	801	Hmp
Benjamin	40	Rcm
Benjamin	202	Shn
Benjamin	229	Shn
Charles	657	Mnt
Daniel, Jun.	204	Shn
Daniel, Ser.	203	Shn
David	21	Rcm
Eliza.	247	Aml
Elizabeth	479	Frn
Eve	205	Shn
Geo.	485	Mnn
George	587	Brk
George	32	Rcm
Gilbert	678	Nls
Godfrey	317	Ags
Henry	12	Pwh
Isaac	203	Shn
Isaac	208	Shn
Jacob	200	Shn
Jno., (Jr.)	32	Rcm
John	593	Brk
John	681	Br
John	333	Dnw
John	815	Hmp
John	202	Shn
John, (sen.)	32	Rcm
Jonathan	827	Hmp
Jos.	613	Mnt
Joseph	21	Rcm
Margaret	834	Hmp
Marshal	12	Knw
Ned	129	Hnr
Peter	414	Fqr
Peter	20	Rcm
Peter	215	Shn
Phebe	558	Pre
Philip	208	Shn
Polly	129	Hnr
Robert	674	Br
Saml.	13	Rcm
Saml.	21	Rcm
Stephen	202	Shn
Theddeus	438	Pra
William	820	Bck
William	678	Nls
see Bayly		
Bowme see Bourne		
Bown, Saml.	316	Ags
Bownd, Thomas	14	Isw
Bowry, John G.	947	Chc
Bows, Russel	865	Cmp
Bowser, Adam	846	Sth
Billy	871	Yrk
William	882	Sth
Bowsher, John	8	Hnr
see Bosher		
Bowsman, Adam	471	Frn
George	450	Frn
Lawrance	284	Rck
Mary	472	Frn
Philip	454	Bdf
Bowyer, Adam	432	Bth
David	609	Btt
Engle	11	Clp
Henry	605	Btt
Philip	323	Ags
Phillip, (F.N.)	15	Isw
Reuben	589	Mnr
Thomas	298	Rck
Thos.	321	Ags
William	289	Rck
see Bowzer		
Bowyers, John	605	Btt
Bowzer, Jno., esqr. [?]	271	Rck
Boxley, George	82	Spt
William	82	Spt
Boxuarde, Gabl.	328	Dnw
Boxwell, John	776	Hmp
Joseph	786	Hmp
Robert	786	Hmp
Boy, Jeremiah	735	Wsh
Boyakin, Julia	851	Sth
Shadrach	153	Sth
Boyce, Bartlet	722	Wsh
Danl.	485	Mnn
Henry	205	Shn
Jno.	20	Hnr
John	187	Alb
Jos.	20	Hnr
Joseph	12	Hnr
Peter	215	Shn
Richard	399	Fqr
S.	483	Mnn
Wm.	484	Mnn
see Boyer, Royce		
Boyd, An.	485	Mnn
Andrew	605	Btt
Anw.	484	Mnn
Augustin, a free mulatto	973	Nrt
Cathne.	890	Nrf
Daniel	736	Wsh
Doctor	326	Dnw
Elisha	599	Brk
Eliz.	317	Ags
Elizabeth	301	Ldn
Enice	888	Nrf
Hannah	257	Ldn
Harrison	500	Frn
Henry	494	Frn
Henry	735	Wsh
James	579	Mnr
Jeremiah	823	Bck
Jeremiah	735	Wsh
Jno.	236	Frf
Jno.	301	Ldn
John	494	Frn
John	616	Gls
John	157	Knq
John	192	Kng
John	169	Shn
John	757	Wsh
Mary	186	Alb
Patrick	589	Mnr
Philip	565	Mnr
Robert	157	Knq
Robert	743	Nwk
Robt.	546	Brk
Saml.	534	Brk
Sina	377	Fqr
Spencer	11	Ntt
Thomas	155	Knq
Thomas	819	Wth
William	149	Alb
William	154	Knq
William	743	Nwk
William	182	Shn
Wm.	323	Ags
Wm.	338	Lnc
Wm.	268	Ldn
see Boy		
Boyde, William	90	Jff
Boydstone, Benjaman	102	Jff
Boyel, William	187	Alb
Boyer, Ada..., jr.	455	Bdf
Adam	12	Rcm
Adam, Sr.	455	Bdf
Frs.	887	Nrf
John, (Jr.)	24	Rcm

Joseph	455	Bdf
Margaret	3	Rcm
Michel.	454	Bdf
Peter	31	Rcm
see Boyce		
Boyers, Conrod	224	Pnd
Jacob	522	Frd
John	12	Rcm
Mary	247	Shn
Peter	24	Rcm
Sameul	217	Pnd
see Royer		
Boykin, Britain	844	Sth
Daniel	143	Sth
David	142	Sth
Edwin	139	Sth
Francis M.	22	Isw
John	871	Sth
Saml. G.	143	Sth
Simon	882	Sth
see Boyakin		
Boyl, Edward	69	Jff
Boyle, David	501	Prw
Frances	329	Dnw
Francis	326	Dnw
James	329	Dnw
Boyles, Abram	617	Gls
Charles	428	Rnd
Gilbert	422	Rnd
Gilbert	427	Rnd
Henry	828	Hmp
John	453	Bdf
William	617	Gls
Boyres, Joseph	89	Jff
Boys, David	261	Ldn
Wm.	398	Ags
Bozaph, Joshua	923	Hrr
Boze, Richd.	12	Rcm
Bozel, Lewis	238	Frf
Bozorth, George	909	Hrr
Bozwell, George	504	Prw
Henry	237	Frf
James	505	Prw
Matthew	234	Frf
Polly	505	Prw
William	505	Prw
Bozzel, Gilbert	457	Frn
John	501	Frn
Thomas	456	Frn
William	456	Frn
Br..., ...	453	Bdf
Braadley, Saml.	826	Nrf
Brabham, Thomas	258	Ldn
Bracey, Champeon	19	Isw
Drury	42	Isw
Jesse	879	Sth
John	158	Sth
Joseph	158	Sth
Mills	4	Isw
Nancy	16	Isw
Brachet, Ludwell	248	Aml
Bracken, James	849	Cmp
Jno.	648	Glc
John, has Slaves in York		
County	888	Yrk
Brackenridge, Thos.	58	Jff
Bracket, Jonathan	130	Hnr
Thomas	104	Cmb
Brackett, Jno.	5	Ntt
Joseph	4	Pwh
Brackley, David	22	Hnr
Brackney, Rachel	34	Rcm
Reuben	8	Clp
Bracston, Ellizabeth	7	Hnr
Bracy, Tabitha	743	Brn
Bradberry, Jas.	338	Lnc
Bradbourn, John	428	Msn
Jos.	422	Msn
Bradbury, William	43	Chr
Bradby, Smaalwood	959	Chc

Bradchaw, Joseph	301	Amh
Bradely, Henry	940	Chc
Braden, Geo.	317	Ags
Jno.	312	Ldn
Joseph	301	Ldn
Robert	312	Ldn
Sarah	312	Ldn
Bradenham, Robert	744	Nwk
Bradey, Elizabeth	381	Fqr
James	237	Ldn
Bradfield, Benj.	315	Ldn
Daniel	527	Prw
George	525	Prw
James	309	Ldn
Jno.	308	Ldn
Joseph	527	Prw
Saml.	527	Prw
Thomas	526	Prw
Bradford, Abel	10	Acc
Arthur	6	Acc
Baldwin	411	Fqr
Charles	8	Acc
David	14	Clp
David	890	Nrf
Elizabeth	9	Acc
Fielding	850	Cmp
Henry	518	Frd
Henry, f. negro	240	Frf
Jacob	10	Acc
Jno.	10	Clp
John	9	Acc
John	605	Btt
John	609	Btt
John	402	Fqr
John	905	Hrr
John	376	Mds
Joseph	376	Mds
Josh.	12	Clp
Nancy	10	Acc
Peggy J.	376	Mds
Rachel	608	Btt
Richard	12	Acc
Saml. K.	8	Clp
Sarah	9	Acc
Simon	361	Fqr
Thomas	10	Acc
Thomas H.	7	Acc
William	678	Br
William	366	Fqr
William	376	Mds
William	178	Shn
Wm.	609	Btt
see Breedfott		
Bradfute, D.	11	Hnr
Bradley, Abram	702	Wsh
Absalom	892	Crl
Anne	744	Nwk
Augustine	377	Mds
Benjn.	102	Cmb
Cisley	556	Pre
Clement	130	Cmb
Collins	857	Cmp
Daniel	102	Cmb
Danl.	237	Frf
Danl.	240	Frf
Edward	678	Br
Edward	745	Nwk
Elizabeth	32	Isw
Emanuel	416	Fqr
Gideon	190	Kng
Henry	55	Stf
James	893	Crl
James	947	Chc
James	234	Frf
James	237	Frf
James	760	Wsh
Jas.	20	Hnr
John	818	Bck
John	938	Chc
John	119	Cmb

John	486	Mnn
John	706	Wsh
Joseph	247	Aml
Joshua	606	Btt
Joshua	14	Ntt
Littleton	950	Chc
Martha	942	Chc
Mary	424	Bth
Mary	880	Cmp
Mary	946	Chc
Micajah	615	Gls
Mical	944	Chc
Michiel	743	Brn
Phenias	130	Cmb
Pleasant	746	Nwk
Porterfeild	950	Chc
Richard	818	Bck
Richard	375	Fqr
Samuel B.	130	Cmb
Sarah	892	Crl
Tenas M.	35	Hnr
Thomas	617	Gls
William	817	Bck
William	947	Chc
William	124	Cmb
William	469	Frn
William	470	Frn
William	617	Gls
William	556	Pre
Wm.	266	Rck
Wm.	723	Wsh
Wm.	734	Wsh
see Bellimey, Brady		
Bradly, Jno. O.	338	Lnc
Reuben	707	Wsh
Brads, James	271	Rck
Bradshaw, Allin	468	Frn
Benja.	683	Gch
Benja.	867	Sth
Benjamin	46	Isw
Benjamin	558	Pre
Dysey	21	Ntt
Elias	858	Sth
Elisha	17	Isw
Francess	41	Isw
Harberson	22	Stf
Jacob	41	Isw
Jacob	854	Sth
James	432	Bth
James	246	Ldn
Jemima	858	Sth
Jeremiah	41	Isw
Jno.	16	Ntt
John	441	Bth
John	683	Gch
John, jr.	433	Bth
Jonas	41	Isw
Jos.	858	Sth
Joseph	58	Jff
Larner	683	Gch
Lucy	558	Pre
Margret	558	Pre
Milley	442	Flv
Polly	41	Isw
Richd.	144	Sth
Richd.	852	Sth
Susan [2]	854	Sth
Unity	20	Ntt
William	41	Isw
Zachariah	46	Stf
see Bradchaw		
Brady, Barnabas	682	Br
Barnet	399	Ags
Benjn.	542	Brk
Benjn. H.	399	Ags
Caleb	574	Frd
Edward	614	Mnt
Elizabeth	512	Frd
Israel	567	Brk
James	680	Br

Jno.	6	Clp	Rodolph	889	Nrf	Brandham, Thos.	14	Clp
John	321	Ags	Branaman, Abraham	16	Rck	Brandican, Henry	192	Kng
John	130	Cmb	Christian	698	Br	Reuben	192	Kng
John	909	Hrr	Danl.	7	Rcm	Brandingburg, Jacob	930	Hrr
John	236	Ldn	Malachi	14	Rcm	Brandley, Jno. R.	63	Chs
John	678	Nls	Branan, Henry	889	Nrf	Brandon, ---, Madm.	889	Nrf
Joshua	534	Brk	Wm.	424	Rnd	Abm.	484	Mnn
McCord	273	Rck	see Branam, Braumen			Alexa.	484	Mnn
Michael	780	Hmp	Branby, William	12	Isw	James	276	Ldn
Patrick	323	Ags	see Brantley			Jona.	484	Mnn
Patrick	378	Fqr	Branch, Archibald	787	Bck	Rich.	484	Mnn
Thomas	522	Prw	Awstin	860	Sth	Wm.	484	Mnn
see Brody			Benja.	846	Sth	Brandt, Nichs.	888	Nrf
Brafford, Martha	67	Chr	Bolling	840	Bck	Brandum, Peter	334	Dnw
Samuel	68	Chr	Burwell	141	Sth	Suckey	335	Dnw
Braford, Hugh	289	Rck	Charles	9	Pwh	Branee, Franky	378	Mds
Brag see Bray			Daniel	9	Pwh	Brangel, Bina	544	Frd
Bragg, Ann	890	Nrf	Drew	144	Sth	Branham, Benjamin	767	Wst
David	332	Lnn	E.O.	65	Chs	Ezekiel	10	Clp
Dozier	349	Fqr	Edward	706	Brn	Marmaduke	151	Alb
Elius	149	Alb	Edward	61	Chs	Nimrod	187	Alb
Evans	10	Clp	Edwd.	63	Chs	Reuben	195	Shn
James	330	Lnn	Edwd.	65	Chs	William	192	Shn
Jno.	56	Chs	Edwd.	138	Sth	Branigan, Nicolas	333	Lnn
Joel	62	Chs	Elizabeth	558	Pre	Branimon, David	321	Ags
Joel	331	Lnn	Francis	151	Sth	Brann, Reuben	769	Wst
John	544	Frd	George	144	Sth	Samuel	767	Wst
John	397	Rch	George	162	Sth	Stephen	768	Wst
John, jr.	437	Flv	Goodman	845	Sth	William, Junr.	767	Wst
John, Sr.	439	Flv	Henry	65	Chs	William, Senr.	768	Wst
Joseph	14	Clp	Jesse	141	Sth	Brannan, James	893	Crl
Joseph	328	Dnw	Jesse	848	Sth	John	890	Crl
Joseph	332	Dnw	Jno.	68	Chs	Thomas	890	Crl
Mary	435	Flv	Jonathan	777	Bck	Branner, John	233	Shn
Richard	446	Flv	Joseph	853	Sth	Philip	29	Rcm
Ruth R. [X. ?]	412	Rch	Lucy	58	Chs	Brannin, Joseph	258	Shn
Tapley	336	Fqr	Mary	142	Sth	Thos.	5	Clp
Thomas	64	Chs	Mary Ann	65	Chs	Branon, Daniel	806	Bck
Thomas	333	Lnn	Matthew	785	Bck	Susan	592	Brk
Thos.	247	Aml	Matthew	11	Ntt	Branrd, Benjamin	893	Hnv
Thos.	10	Clp	Matthew	558	Pre	Branscomb, Edmund	447	Grn
William	420	Fqr	Olive	786	Bck	Richard	447	Grn
William	332	Lnn	Olive	792	Bck	Thomas	447	Grn
William K.	400	Rch	Olive	61	Chs	Bransford, Abraham	111	Cmb
Wm.	65	Chs	Peter, (F.N.)	40	Isw	Benjamin	103	Cmb
Bragwell, Jessee, Sr.	742	Brn	Polly	5	Pwh	Francis, Capt.	5	Pwh
Braham, James	521	Frd	Pompey, (F.N.)	40	Isw	Jacob	104	Cmb
Jas.	485	Mnn	Richd.	64	Chs	Judith	812	Bck
Tho.	485	Mnn	Samuel	42	Chr	Martha	13	Pwh
Brahan, William	357	Fqr	Stephen	65	Chs	Robert	779	Bck
Brahen, Thomas	362	Fqr	Susanna	454	Bdf	Samuel	819	Bck
Braim, Melchisadic	44	Chr	Thomas	784	Bck	Bransom, John	436	Flv
Brain, Ben	486	Mnn	Thomas	804	Bck	Tabby	436	Flv
Wm.	958	Hrr	Thomas	685	Gch	Bransome, John	892	Crl
Braithwait, William	554	Frd	Thomas	556	Pre	Branson, Ann	562	Frd
Brake, Abram	958	Hrr	Thomas	558	Pre	Brisco	755	Wsh
Jacob	910	Hrr	Thos., (Col)	58	Chs	John	50	Stf
John	932	Hrr	Thos., (Wood)	58	Chs	Leonerd	755	Wsh
Bramble, ---, & Colley's			William	332	Lnn	Newyear	766	Wst
(Plantn.)	438	Pra	see Hatcher			Rebecca	593	Frd
John	889	Nrf	Brancon, Vincent	15	Clp	Rees	599	Brk
Bramblett, Reuben	453	Bdf	Brand, David	316	Ags	Vincent	768	Wst
Bramel, Philomel	22	Stf	Geo.	481	Mnn	Branston see Turner		
Bramell, Nancy	504	Prw	Jacob	519	Frd	Brant, John	70	Jff
Bramer, John, Jr.	487	Frn	James	316	Ags	Brantley, Cordall	130	Sth
Noah	487	Frn	Jas.	480	Mnn	Francess	26	Isw
Bramford, Thomas	780	Bck	Jno.	481	Mnn	John	816	Nrf
Bramhall, Peter	57	Jff	John	317	Ags	Thomas, Sen.	36	Isw
Bramham, Benja.	391	Rch	Joseph	186	Alb	Valentine	11	Isw
James	5	Clp	Thomas	387	Fqr	Willis	849	Sth
Vincent	412	Rch	see Branrd			see Branby		
Bramill, Jeremiah	525	Prw	Branden, John	551	Brk	Brantly, Thomas	29	Isw
Zephaniah	525	Prw	Rebecca	551	Brk	Brantner, Frederick	87	Jff
Bramwell, Thomas	680	Nls	Wm.	531	Brk	Branton, Wm.	139	Dnw
Bran, John, Jnr.	482	Mnn	Brander, Daniel	330	Dnw	Brashears, Colmore	291	Ldn
Thomas	972	Nrt	Jacob	331	Dnw	Brass, Benja., Senr.	238	Frf
Branader, Blythe	508	Prw	John	65	Chs	Benjamin, f. negro	239	Frf
Branam, Daniel	350	Fqr	Moses	330	Dnw	Sarah, f. negro	239	Frf
John	350	Fqr	Mourning	333	Dnw	Brassfield, Leonard	522	Prw
John	423	Rnd	Shadrick	330	Dnw	Brasswell, Jessee, jr.	744	Brn

John	743	Brn	Breeding, Bryant	819	Wth	Benjamin	447	Grn
see Bragwell			John	746	Nwk	Biddy	706	Brn
Braswell, Benjamin	35	Isw	Julius	746	Nwk	Buckner	447	Grn
George	3	Isw	Preston	15	Rcm	David	20	Oho
Brattan, Wm.	321	Ags	Robert H.	71	Jff	Henry	742	Brn
Brattens, Elizt.	323	Ags	Breedlove, Armstead	2	Rcm	Henry	15	Hnr
Bratton, James	442	Bth	Charles	562	Frd	Howell	877	Sth
Jas., Christiansburg	642	Mnt	Cornelius	187	Alb	Irby	447	Grn
Jno.	888	Nrf	Isaac	196	Shn	James	743	Brn
John	295	Rck	Nathaniel	42	Chr	James	767	Wst
Robert	433	Bth	Sarah	216	Ess	Jno.	242	Frf
Robert	819	Wth	see Breadlove			Jno.	545	Prg
Robert	820	Wth	Breedwell, Mary	2	Rcm	John	743	Brn
Thos., Christians-			Breefield, John	520	Brk	John	951	Chc
burg	642	Mnt	Breelove, Philip	7	Clp	John	526	Prw
Braughton, Jas.	796	Nrf	Breese, Wm.	398	Ags	Jordan	36	Isw
Braugton, Lovey	442	Pra	Breeze, Joshua	588	Frd	Kinchen	447	Grn
Braumen, Thomas	424	Rnd	Luke	588	Frd	Nancy	455	Bdf
see Branan			Brelford, David	832	Hmp	Sackfeild	459	Frn
Braunan see Braumen			Margarom	834	Hmp	Shadrick	706	Brn
Brawford, James	318	Ags	see Brelsford			Snoden	192	Shn
John	318	Ags	Brell see Brill			Susanah	957	Chc
Saml.	283	Rck	Brelsford, Barney	831	Hmp	Suson	744	Brn
Brawly, James	820	Wth	Daniel	800	Hmp	Thomas	523	Prw
John	820	Wth	David	831	Hmp	Thomas	524	Prw
Brawn, ---	327	Dnw	see Brelford			Vincent	447	Grn
Joel	325	Dnw	Bremam see Branam			William	241	Frf
John	328	Dnw	Bremar, Dennis	889	Nrf	Wm.	743	Brn
Letty	326	Dnw	Bremeaugh, Wm.	425	Msn	Wm.	438	Pra
Patty	328	Dnw	Brenbury see Bunbury			see Brown		
Walke	489	Bdf	Brennemon, Daniel	195	Shn	Brewington, William	83	Acc
Brawner, Basil	526	Prw	Brenner, Casper	32	Rcm	Brewshaw, Gidian	149	Alb
Benedicter	507	Prw	Philip	32	Rcm	Brewster, Wm.	889	Nrf
Emily	514	Prw	Brenor, Jno.	15	Hnr	see Bruster		
Henry	514	Prw	Brent, ---, & Cooke	22	Stf	Brezeal, John H.	246	Aml
Ignatius	514	Prw	Baily G.	338	Lnc	Brezendine see Brizendine		
John	371	Fqr	Charles, Jr.	605	Frd	Brian, Andrew	424	Msn
Sarah	502	Prw	Charles, Senr.	547	Frd	Dennis	569	Brk
William	526	Prw	Chas.	337	Lnc	James	663	Mnt
Zaphaniah	527	Prw	Daniel C.	20	Stf	Briant, Ambrous	653	Mnt
Brawnes, Basnett, (Over-			Eliza.	337	Lnc	Andrew M.	858	Cmp
seer)	381	Fqr	Elizabeth	47	Stf	Bill	189	Shn
Brawns see Browns			Ellen	337	Lnc	David	454	Bdf
Brawton see Bracston			Geo., Jr.	337	Lnc	Elisha	873	Cmp
Braxton, Abram	744	Nwk	Geo., Senr.	339	Lnc	Finney	266	Amh
Carter, [his] est.	156	Knq	Hannah	366	Fqr	Hanah	742	Wsh
Elizh.	119	Hnr	Henry	236	Frf	James	609	Btt
see Bracston, James			Hugh	337	Lnc	James	428	Rnd
Bray, George	155	Knq	James	43	Chr	Jas., (Fidler)	607	Btt
Isaac	972	Nrt	James	572	Frd	John	610	Btt
James	155	Knq	James	678	Nls	John	860	Cmp
John	163	Shn	James D.	679	Nls	John	865	Cmp
John	164	Shn	Jas., Jr.	339	Lnc	John	488	Frn
Jonah	831	Nrf	Jas., Senr.	339	Lnc	John	767	Wst
Peter	155	Knq	Jed.	339	Lnc	Levy	767	Wst
Thomas	460	Mdd	Jno.	337	Lnc	Littlebery	266	Amh
Timothy	348	Fqr	Martin	70	Spt	Luke	428	Rnd
William	163	Shn	Richard	517	Prw	Owin	741	Wsh
William	164	Shn	Thomas	366	Fqr	Reuben	766	Wst
see Broy			William	416	Fqr	Richard	12	Knw
Breadlove, Richard	679	Nls	Willis	233	Ldn	Richard	245	Ldn
William	679	Nls	Wm.	338	Lnc	Richd.	611	Btt
Bream, Frences	893	Crl	Brett, ---, Madam	889	Nrf	Robert	593	Frd
Jemima	890	Crl	Richard	521	Prw	Saml., (F.Negro)	7	Clp
Joseph, (North Wales)	890	Crl	Brew, Henry	26	Rcm	Tapley	766	Wst
Breane, James	23	Hnr	Brewbaker, Abraham	607	Btt	Thomas	454	Bdf
Breathwate, Jas.	442	Pra	Abraham	217	Shn	William	295	Amh
Breckenridge, Jas.	607	Btt	Barbara	189	Shn	William	858	Cmp
Brecker, David	196	Shn	Emanuel	217	Shn	William	42	Chr
Breckett, John	12	Knw	Jacob	221	Shn	Briants, Hawkins	729	Wsh
Breden, James	377	Mds	John	189	Shn	Briarly, Ann	547	Frd
Jobe	377	Mds	Peter	189	Shn	Robert	605	Frd
William	377	Mds	Rebecca	220	Shn	Samuel	584	Frd
Bredy, Charles	333	Lnn	Samuel	189	Shn	Brice, Benja. J.	923	Hrr
Breeden, Edwin	820	Wth	Brewbeck, Joseph	218	Ags	David	250	Shn
Enoch	73	Spt	see Brubeck			Wm.	262	Rck
James	820	Wth	Brewen, Mary	370	Fqr	see Brue		
Jno.	875	Hnv	Brewer, ---	328	Dnw	Bricin, Thomas	50	Stf
Wm.	11	Hnr	---	336	Dnw	Brick, James	565	Frd
Breedfott, Wm.	822	Nrf	Amey	41	Isw	Brickard, Jacob	377	Mds

Brickell, John H.	839	Nrf
Brickers see Bickers		
Brickey, Gerard	400	Rch
Peter	609	Btt
William	769	Wst
Willm.	609	Btt
Brickhouse, Wm.	812	Nrf
Bricking, J.	68	Chs
Brickman, Wm.	398	Ags
Bridenhart, Jane	94	Jff
Bridgband, Patty	296	Amh
Bridge, James	316	Ags
Bridgeford, Mary	888	Nrf
Bridgeforth, John	704	Brn
Bridgeland, John	852	Cmp
Bridgeman, Francis	83	Jff
Franklin	819	Wth
Rhody	21	Stf
William	83	Jff
Bridger, Polly	40	Isw
Bridgers, Rachel	427	Bth
Bridges, Ann	41	Stf
Anna E.	646	Glc
Dennis	237	Frf
Jno.	240	Frf
Jno.	249	Ldn
Matthew	42	Rcm
Richard	890	Crl
Robinson	646	Glc
Sally	205	Ess
William	41	Rcm
Bridget, Charles	157	Knq
James	302	Rck
Bridgforth, Benjn., jr.	2	Ntt
Elizabeth	6	Ntt
Thomas, Est.	332	Lnn
Bridgland, Alexander	853	Cmp
Bridgman, Francis	542	Frd
Joseph	971	Nrt
Unsa	971	Nrt
William	820	Wth
Bridgmon, Wm.	139	Dnw
Bridgwater, Charles	680	Nls
Danl.	121	Hnr
Dicey	58	Chs
Hannah	680	Nls
Nathaniel	679	Nls
Richard	782	Bck
William	681	Nls
Zac	129	Hnr
Bridiwell, James	252	Ldn
Bridlove, Frany	252	Shn
Isaac	254	Shn
Bridwell, Annanias	7	Clp
Benjamin	512	Prw
Charles	44	Stf
Henry	42	Stf
Isaac	512	Prw
Isaac	42	Stf
John	384	Fqr
John	512	Prw
Lewis, of A. [of t.?]	44	Stf
Lewis, of C.	43	Stf
Rebecca	43	Stf
Samuel	43	Stf
William	42	Stf
Willis	512	Prw
Brierly, Richard	528	Brk
Robert	527	Brk
Brigendine, Bowler	555	Pre
Briggs, ---, Vowles &	35	Stf
David	9	Clp
David	39	Stf
Edmd. L., (W)	871	Yrk
Elizabeth	706	Brn
Frederick	706	Brn
Henry	128	Sth
James	629	Sss
Jane	860	Sth
John	6	Pwh

John	626	Sss
Robert	377	Mds
Susanna	867	Sth
Thomas	34	Stf
William	50	Stf
Wm.	138	Sth
see Biggs, Brigs		
Bright, Armstrong	797	Nrf
Charles	454	Bdf
Charles, Sr.	454	Bdf
Curtis	8	Oho
Frank	870	Yrk
Geo.	317	Ags
Geo. A.	318	Ags
George	611	Btt
Jas.	438	Pra
John	317	Ags
John	235	Frf
John	441	Pra
John	19	Rcm
Joseph	454	Bdf
Joshua	454	Bdf
Levi	484	Mnn
Lovey	798	Nrf
Matthew	800	Nrf
Nancy	797	Nrf
Peter	41	Rcm
Rachel	21	Rcm
Reuben	610	Btt
Uras	798	Nrf
Wm.	800	Nrf
Wm.	438	Pra
Brightberry see Brown		
Brightwell, Absalom	85	Spt
Anderson	557	Pre
Charles	557	Pre
Druciller	559	Pre
Mary	84	Spt
Thomas	84	Spt
William	559	Pre
William	84	Spt
William, Senr.	559	Pre
Wm.	68	Chs
see Rather		
Brigs, Elisha	485	Mnn
Brill, George	212	Shn
Henry	453	Bdf
Henry	572	Frd
Henry	770	Hmp
Henry, Senr.	572	Frd
Jacob	24	Rcm
Michael	568	Brk
Thomas	10	Rcm
Brillhart, John	16	Rcm
Brimm, Leonard	459	Mdd
Brimmer, Isaac	38	Stf
John, Jr.	33	Stf
John, sr.	32	Stf
Lucy	114	Spt
Brindley, George	427	Bth
James	414	Bth
John	425	Bth
Bringam, Saml.	430	Rnd
Bringham, Henry	797	Hmp
Brining, Hannah	99	Spt
Brinker, George	563	Frd
Henry	759	Hmp
Jacob	199	Shn
Jacob	200	Shn
John	199	Shn
Nancey	27	Rcm
Brinkley, John	417	Bth
Robert	416	Bth
William	416	Bth
Brinn, Eliza	768	Wst
Winney	768	Wst
Brinnan, William	400	Rch
Brinney, Ochar	77	Acc
Brinnon, Fanny	768	Wst
Sarah	768	Wst

Brinsen, Henry	890	Nrf
Brinson, Nathan	441	Pra
Brint, Hugh	389	Fqr
Brintle, James	706	Brn
Susannah	331	Lnn
Brinton, Robt.	318	Ags
Weldon	56	Jff
Brion, Solomon	221	Ess
Briquet, Claudius	888	Nrf
Brisco, Aquila	236	Ldn
Briscoe, Alexr. M.	61	Jff
Daniel	767	Wst
George	768	Wst
Isaac	431	Bth
John	61	Jff
Reuben	767	Wst
Reuben, Senr.	767	Wst
Brisendens, John	155	Knq
Brison, Barney	83	Jff
Benjamin	521	Frd
Brissie, Standly	191	Kng
Brister, Rachel	157	Knq
Thomas	234	Ldn
Bristoe, John	846	Sth
Polly	109	Spt
Briston, Benn.	881	Sth
William	881	Sth
Bristow, Alexander	458	Mdd
Bartho.	458	Mdd
Benjn.	458	Mdd
Charles	139	Dnw
Charles	460	Mdd
Elizabeth	649	Glc
Geo.	647	Glc
James	458	Mdd
John, (Piddy)	459	Mdd
Josiah	458	Mdd
Leonard	458	Mdd
Lucy	647	Glc
Mary	458	Mdd
Brite, Elizabeth	248	Ldn
see Britt		
Briton, Tollis	964	Hrr
see Briston		
Britt, Archelus	151	Alb
Athington	142	Sth
Beasant	882	Sth
Brittain	42	Isw
Harrison	143	Sth
Isaac	744	Brn
James	137	Sth
Jesse	870	Sth
John	369	Fqr
John	142	Sth
Joseph	882	Sth
Nancy	844	Sth
Nathan	160	Sth
Nelson	13	Knw
Obediah	149	Alb
Obediah	794	Bck
Presley	447	Grn
Willm.	643	Mnt
Wm.	684	Gch
Wm. H.	685	Gch
Wylie	629	Sss
Brittain, Bennel	127	Hnr
Jesse	127	Hnr
Brittan, George	190	Shn
Britten, John	227	Pnd
Brittingham, Jno.	82	Acc
Levi	74	Acc
Polly	79	Acc
see Brittinham, Brittinhan,		
Henderson		
Brittinham, John	190	Elc
Brittinhan, Purll.	179	Elc
Brittle, Brittain	627	Sss
James	860	Sth
James	876	Sth
Jesse	626	Sss

William	627	Sss	Joseph	79	Acc	William	539	Prg
Britton, Eliza	822	Nrf	Joshua	80	Acc	William, jr.	536	Prg
Henry	482	Mnn	Robert.	81	Acc	Wm.	602	Srr
Hosey	487	Mnn	Savage	78	Acc	Brodie, David	191	Elc
Jno.	10	Hnr	Southey	79	Acc	Brodnax, Wm. E.	704	Brn
Jonathn.	696	Wsh	William	79	Acc	Brodshaw, John	757	Wsh
Nancy	398	Ags	see Hill			Brody, Hezekiah, a free parson		
Rachel	35	Rcm	Broadwaters, Guy	250	Ldn	of couler	721	Wsh
Saml.	739	Wsh	Broadway, John	557	Pre	John, a free parson of		
Sarah	809	Nrf	Joseph	557	Pre	couler	721	Wsh
Tim.	323	Ags	Thos.	248	Aml	Jonathan, a free man of		
William	55	Jff	Broady, Eliza	335	Dnw	couler	721	Wsh
Wilson	486	Mnn	John	461	Frn	Brofee, Christopr.	8	Clp
Wm.	318	Ags	Brocius, Jacob	300	Rck	Brogan, Robert	491	Frn
Britz, John	611	Btt	Brock, Ann	98	Spt	Brogdon, William, (FN)	44	Chr
Britze, Adam	609	Btt	Benjamin	33	Isw	Brokenborogh, J.B.	34	Hnr
Henry	609	Btt	Charles	441	Pra	Brome, John	513	Brk
Brizendine, Ann	44	Chr	Cornilius	441	Pra	Bronauch, Nancy	238	Frf
Banester	450	Frn	Eliza	5	Hnr	Bronaugh, Benjamin	513	Prw
Bartlett	211	Ess	Frederick	5	Rcm	George	66	Spt
Isaac, Jr.	454	Frn	Gaskins	442	Pra	John	414	Fqr
Isaac, Sr.	454	Frn	Henry	442	Pra	John	499	Prw
John	44	Chr	Humphry	873	Hnv	Rebeca	263	Ldn
Joshua	458	Frn	Jacob	5	Rcm	Samuel	378	Mds
Lankford	456	Frn	Jehua	500	Frn	Wm.	264	Ldn
Leroy	454	Frn	Jno. P.	892	Hnv	Bronson, Abraham	538	Frd
Patsey	216	Ess	John	186	Alb	Broocke, James	211	Ess
Philup	43	Chr	John	6	Rcm	Mary	217	Ess
Randal	216	Ess	John	141	Sth	Reuben	222	Ess
Reubin	67	Chr	John	71	Spt	Spencer	211	Ess
Vincent	210	Ess	Joseph	377	Mds	Thos.	219	Ess
William	458	Frn	Margaret	93	Spt	Wm.	211	Ess
Wm.	215	Ess	Mary	186	Alb	Wm.	222	Ess
Young	44	Chr	Mary	33	Isw	Broockes, James	216	Ess
Brizindine, William, Jr.	454	Frn	Mary	101	Spt	Philip	211	Ess
Brizley, Godfrey	218	Ess	Michael	680	Nls	Samuel	216	Ess
Bro..., Sally	455	Bdf	Moses	437	Pra	Thomas	216	Ess
Broach, Benoni	156	Knq	Nancy	101	Spt	Broocks, Robt.	442	Mth
John	155	Knq	Noah	441	Pra	Brook, Anne, ([her]		
William	155	Knq	Ransum	441	Pra	Quarter)	419	Fqr
Broadbelt, Sarah	374	Fqr	Robert	94	Spt	Benjn.	859	Sth
Broaddus, Andrew	889	Crl	Rudolph	5	Rcm	Caty	339	Lnc
James	150	Alb	Sarah	441	Pra	Edwd.	243	Ldn
John	890	Crl	Tubal	500	Frn	George	237	Frf
Mordicai	891	Crl	William	187	Alb	Lucy	143	Sth
P...	156	Knq	William	25	Stf	Richard	437	Bth
Reuben	889	Crl	see Brook			Samuel	240	Ldn
Richard	890	Crl	Brockenborough, Austin	767	Wst	Brookbank, Chs.	280	Ldn
Thomas	890	Crl	Brockenbrh., Arther	207	Ess	Jno.	240	Frf
William	156	Knq	Brockenbro., Thomas	207	Ess	Brooke, Ame	237	Frf
Broades, Joseph	238	Frf	Brockenbroh., Austin	207	Ess	Anne	421	Fqr
Broadfeilds, Charles	33	Isw	Brockenbrough, Champ	891	Crl	Edmund	525	Prw
Broadhead, Jonathan	186	Alb	Moore F.	401	Rch	Frances T.	88	Spt
Thomas	186	Alb	New.	211	Ess	Isaac	214	Ess
William	186	Alb	Wim.	892	Hnv	John	874	Cmp
Broadhurst, James	17	Rcm	Brockheart, Mary	758	Hmp	John	133	Hnr
Broadnex, Lydia	9	Hnr	Brockman, Ambros	187	Alb	John, [his] Lot	117	Spt
Broadridge see Boadridge			Amey	186	Alb	John T.	60	Stf
Broads, Michael	239	Frf	David	664	Mnt	Matthew W.	365	Fqr
Broadus, Edmd.	14	Clp	Elijah	480	Frn	Reuben	210	Ess
James	14	Clp	James	186	Alb	Richard	158	Knq
Robert	647	Glc	Joseph	187	Alb	Richd.	1	Hnr
Thos.	12	Clp	Robert	186	Alb	Walter D.	237	Frf
Wm.	649	Glc	William	186	Alb	William	399	Rch
Wm., jr.	7	Clp	see Taylor			William	109	Spt
Wm., Senr.	8	Clp	Brockwell, Carter	549	Prg	William H.	391	Rch
Broadwater, Breeche	80	Acc	Elisha	539	Prg	Wm.	11	Clp
Charles	610	Btt	Evy [David crossed			Wm. T.	197	Ess
Chs. G.	236	Frf	out]	543	Prg	Brookes, Charles	683	Gch
Chs. L., & wife	239	Frf	James	535	Prg	Isaac	649	Glc
Derry	79	Acc	James	599	Srr	Jessee	157	Knq
Edward	74	Acc	Jamima	550	Prg	Major	156	Knq
Elias	77	Acc	Jamimah	535	Prg	Meriman	155	Knq
Esther	78	Acc	Jas., jr.	545	Prg	Peter	157	Knq
Henry	74	Acc	Jesse	545	Prg	Robert	156	Knq
Heny.	82	Acc	Jno.	539	Prg	Sam	744	Nwk
James	78	Acc	John	630	Sss	Thomas	158	Knq
John	78	Acc	Joseph, sr.	535	Prg	Thos.	683	Gch
John, senr.	79	Acc	Littleberry	547	Prg	William	157	Knq
Joseph	74	Acc	Sarah	535	Prg	Wm., Sr.	316	Ags

Wm. D.	155	Knq	Sammuel	8	Hnr	Jones	139	Dnw
Brookhart, Abraham	12	Wod	Samuel	562	Frd	Joseph	704	Brn
David	25	Rcm	Samuel, senr.	460	Mdd	Littlebury	140	Dnw
John	13	Wod	Sarah	892	Crl	Urius	704	Brn
Brooking, Betty L.	460	Mdd	Sarah	889	Nrf	Brower, Daniel	477	Frn
Charles	649	Glc	Sarah	558	Pre	Henry, Jr.	480	Frn
Charles	458	Mdd	Tarleton	821	Wth	Henry, Sr.	480	Frn
Edward	649	Glc	Tho.	452	Mth	Browing, Saml.	114	Hnr
Francis	248	Aml	Thomas	876	Cmp	Browmore, H.	484	Mnn
Mary	649	Glc	Thomas	889	Crl	Brown, ---, & Vass &		
Robert	378	Mds	Thomas	44	Chr	Co.	156	Knq
Robert E.	247	Aml	Thomas	69	Chr	..., for James Calla-		
William	378	Mds	Thomas	356	Fqr	way's Exs.	462	Frn
Brookins, Charles	574	Mnr	Thos.	18	Hnr	...m	300	Rck
William	574	Mnr	Thos.	827	Nrf	...n, for Macons		
Brookover, Mary	525	Frn	Traverse	43	Chr	Estate	105	Cmb
Brooks, Absm.	398	Ags	William [2]	876	Cmp	Aaron	703	Brn
Ann	29	Stf	William	43	Chr	Abe.	233	Ldn
Anthony	12	Ntt	William	327	Dnw	Able	427	Msn
Armistead	558	Pre	William [2]	356	Fqr	Abram	957	Chc
Barnabas	304	Ldn	William	453	Frn	Abram	285	Ldn
Barshaba	451	Mth	William	828	Hmp	Abram	153	Sth
Bartlett	556	Pre	William	99	Jff	Adam	777	Hmp
Benj.	239	Ldn	William	555	Pre	Adam	510	Frd
Bibby	44	Chr	William	513	Prw	Adam	54	Jff
Bluford	891	Crl	Winney	356	Fqr	Adam	481	Mnn
Catharine	611	Btt	Winney	377	Mds	Alex.	2	Hnr
Chas.	297	Rck	Wm., (Guardian)	458	Mdd	Alexander	42	Chr
Dabney	77	Spt	Wm., jr.	315	Ags	Alexander	44	Chr
Davd.	825	Nrf	Wm., Jr.	609	Btt	Alexander	328	Dnw
David	889	Nrf	Wm., Sr.	609	Btt	Alexander	792	Hmp
Edward	888	Nrf	Zach.	67	Chs	Alexander	6	Knw
Edwd.	870	Yrk	Zachariah	876	Cmp	Alexander	562	Mnr
Elias	558	Pre	Zeb	831	Nrf	Alexr.	695	Wsh
Elijah	288	Ldn	see Baker, Brooke			Alxander	9	Oho
Elisabeth	240	Ldn	Broombach, Martain	5	Wod	Ambrose	881	Cmp
Elisha	9	Knw	Broombock, Henry	182	Shn	Amos	167	Shn
Elizabeth	893	Crl	John	180	Shn	Anderson	148	Alb
Elizabeth	680	Nls	Broomfield, William	515	Frd	Andrew	19	Oho
Geo.	320	Ags	Broscius, George	545	Brk	Andrew	819	Wth
Geo.	13	Ntt	Jacob	545	Brk	Andrew	822	Wth
George	119	Hnr	Broshus, Abram	315	Ags	Andrew C.	155	Knq
George	453	Mth	Brotherhood, Joshua	115	Hnr	Ann	893	Crl
George	742	Wsh	Brothers, John [2]	674	Br	Ann	6	Clp
Hanah	873	Sth	Thomas	608	Btt	Ann	140	Dnw
Hezekiah	559	Pre	Brott..., Robt.	295	Rck	Ann	13	Hnr
James	150	Alb	Brouck, Chaty	234	Shn	Ann	260	Ldn
James	876	Cmp	Brough, Emely	180	Elc	Ann	118	Spt
James	893	Crl	Harman	608	Btt	Ann	119	Spt
James	43	Chr	Hepple	281	Rck	Anna	407	Ags
James	345	Fqr	Robert	890	Nrf	Anthony	235	Frf
James	30	Rcm	Willm.	179	Elc	Anthy.	440	Pra
Jane	822	Wth	Broughman, John	608	Btt	Archer	125	Cmb
Jesse	1	Ntt	Broughton, Mary	871	Yrk	Archibald	557	Pre
Jessee	819	Wth	Nehemiah	78	Acc	Armistead	9	Clp
Jno.	61	Chs	T. G.	889	Nrf	Armistead	534	Prg
Jno.	8	Clp	Brougman, Jacob	583	Brk	Armstead	141	Dnw
Jno.	891	Hnv	Broun, Andrew	564	Brk	Augustine [2]	648	Glc
Jno.	438	Mth	Brounley, Elizabeth	560	Frd	Bazaleel (Bezaleel)	147	Alb
John	876	Cmp	Elizabeth, Senr.	587	Frd	Ben	483	Mnn
John	889	Crl	Foster	454	Mth	Benja.	320	Ags
John	330	Dnw	Isac	436	Mth	Benajah, Senr.	838	Bck
John	678	Nls	James	438	Mth	Benjamin	150	Alb
John	833	Nrf	James	445	Mth	Benjamin	694	Br
Laurence, bound for a term			Jno.	445	Mth	Benjamin	519	Prw
of years	448	Bth	Jno.	454	Mth	Benjamin	194	Shn
Letty	295	Ldn	Johanon	453	Mth	Benjm.	958	Chc
Levy	44	Chr	Wm.	436	Mth	Bentley	866	Hnv
Martin	61	Chs	Wm.	454	Mth	Bernard	184	Alb
Moses	708	Wsh	Brounly, Archad.	440	Mth	Bernis	187	Alb
Nancy	871	Yrk	Phillip	441	Mth	Betsy	333	Dnw
Nelson	876	Cmp	Broushe, Geo.	324	Ags	Betsy	2	Hnr
Nicholous	929	Hrr	Brow..., John	562	Mnr	Betty	953	Chc
Overton	82	Spt	Browbeck, Philip	297	Rck	Bezaleel	184	Alb
Philip	891	Crl	Browder, David	139	Dnw	Bezaleel	185	Alb
Phillip	863	Hnv	George	742	Brn	Bezaleel	218	Alb
Polly	377	Mds	Jereh.	140	Dnw	Bezaleel	220	Alb
Reed	841	Bck	John	705	Brn	Bignal	545	Prg
Richard	47	Stf	John, jr.	141	Dnw	Bob	550	Prg
Robert	180	Alb	John, Senr.	141	Dnw	Brackston	793	Hmp

Brightberry	187	Alb	Fleming	844	Hnv	James	13	Clp
Burgess	337	Lnc	Fr...cis	834	Nrf	James	105	Cmb
Burwel	332	Lnn	Francis	322	Ags	James	125	Cmb
Cathr.	229	Rck	Francis	388	Fqr	James	130	Cmb
Charles	211	Ess	Francis	59	Stf	James	561	Frd
Charles	69	Jff	Franky	890	Crl	James	583	Frd
Charles	1	Knw	Freeman	959	Chc	James	790	Hmp
Chas.	648	Glc	Garland	841	Bck	James	800	Hmp
Christopher	820	Wth	Garott	63	Chs	James	904	Hrr
Christopher	821	Wth	Geo.	648	Glc	James	942	Hrr
Christopher [2]	822	Wth	Geo.	271	Ldn	James	2	Hnr
Clement	121	Cmb	Geo.	308	Ldn	James	107	Jff
Cornelious	940	Chc	Geo.	317	Ldn	James	237	Ldn
Cornelious	606	Mnt	Geo. A.	811	Nrf	James	266	Ldn
Cornelius	398	Ags	George	507	Brk	James	317	Ldn
Cornelius	217	Ess	George	607	Btt	James	332	Lnn
Daniel	453	Bdf	George	125	Cmb	James	449	Mth
Daniel	857	Cmp	George	332	Dnw	James	566	Mnr
Daniel	62	Chs	George	394	Fqr	James	404	Rch
Daniel	196	Ess	George	441	Mth	James	244	Shn
Daniel	399	Fqr	George	663	Mnt	James	45	Stf
Daniel	455	Frn	George, jr.	333	Lnn	James	6	Wod
Daniel	232	Ldn	George, L.	333	Lnn	James	819	Wth
Daniel	254	Ldn	George, Sr.	662	Mnt	James, (CC)	69	Chr
Danl.	4	Clp	George M.	287	Amh	James, (Capt.)	42	Chr
Danl.	12	Clp	George N.	524	Prw	James, jr.	814	Nrf
Danl., jr.	5	Clp	Gideon	4	Clp	James, jr., & Co.	127	Hnr
Danl., jr.	12	Clp	Govy	788	Hmp	James, post master and inn		
Danl. C.	11	Clp	Gracy	648	Glc	keeper, Shepherds		
Daphne	38	Stf	Hannah	425	Bth	Town	110	Jff
David	455	Bdf	Hannah	17	Hnr	James, (S.H.)	320	Ags
David	561	Frd	Hannah	27	Hnr	James M.	276	Amh
David	678	Nls	Henry	261	Amh	Jamima	877	Hnv
David	183	Shn	Henry	866	Cmp	Jamima	885	Hnv
Davis	703	Brn	Henry	868	Cmp	Janings	468	Frn
Denis	484	Mnn	Henry	879	Cmp	Jas.	485	Mnn
Dixon	24	Stf	Henry	310	Sld	Jas.	830	Nrf
Dixon	678	Wrw	Henry	811	Nrf	Jas.	440	Pra
Dixon, Jr.	938	Chc	Henry	889	Nrf	Jas., Jur.	22	Hnr
Dixon, Ser.	938	Chc	Henry	199	Shn	Jas., (Mjr.)	320	Ags
Eazral	226	Pnd	Henry	219	Shn	Jas., Sr.	814	Nrf
Ebenezor	611	Btt	Henry	627	Sss	Javis	946	Hrr
Ebinezer	614	Mnt	Henry, jr.	156	Knq	Jeremh.	14	Clp
Edmond	881	Cmp	Henry, Snr.	158	Knq	Jeremiah	5	Clp
Edmund	791	Bck	Henry A.	156	Knq	Jeremiah	198	Ess
Edward	957	Chc	Herbert	56	Chs	Jeremiah, jr.	9	Clp
Edward	944	Hrr	Hillary	440	Pra	Jerremiah	59	Stf
Edward	393	Rch	Hugh	322	Ags	Jerry	972	Nrt
Edwd.	262	Rck	Hugh	36	Stf	Jesse	454	Bdf
Edwd., (of Ed.)	437	Pra	Innis	26	Stf	Jesse	56	Chs
Edwd., (of Moss.)	441	Pra	Isaac	959	Chc	Jesse	356	Fqr
Edwd., (of Smith)	439	Pra	Isaac	582	Frd	Jesse	516	Frd
Edwd. B.	197	Ess	Isaac	260	Ldn	Jesse	526	Frd
Edwin C.	972	Nrt	Isaac	271	Ldn	Jesse	734	Wsh
Elias	799	Hmp	Isaac	823	Wth	Jessee	130	Cmb
Elias	59	Jff	Isaack	108	Cmb	Jno.	648	Glc
Elijah	185	Alb	Isaack	109	Cmb	Jno.	266	Ldn
Elijah	380	Fqr	Isacher	317	Ldn	Jno.	271	Ldn
Elinder	962	Hrr	Isham	141	Dnw	Jno.	287	Ldn
Elisha	436	Bth	Isom	575	Brk	Jno.	308	Ldn
Eliz.	161	Sth	Issabella	54	Jff	Jno.	311	Ldn
Eliza	768	Wst	J.G.	889	Nrf	Jno.	314	Ldn
Eliza.	5	Clp	Jabed	483	Mnn	Jno., (blk. Smith)	14	Clp
Eliza.	393	Rch	Jacky	779	Bck	Jno., (DB)	439	Pra
Elizabeth	184	Alb	Jacob	316	Ags	Jno., free negro	70	Chs
Elizabeth	453	Bdf	Jacob	20	Hnr	Jno., Jr.	483	Mnn
Elizabeth	351	Fqr	Jacob	114	Hnr	Jno., (of Hezakiah)	439	Pra
Elizabeth	826	Nrf	Jacob	311	Ldn	Jno., senr. (near		
Elizabeth	542	Prg	Jacob	19	Oho	M.P.)	6	Clp
Elizabeth	510	Prw	Jacob	206	Shn	Jno. F.	13	Clp
Elizabeth	440	Pra	Jacob	880	Sth	Jno. T.	878	Hnv
Elliot	609	Btt	James	316	Ags	Joel	772	Hmp
Ellis W., Charleston	2	Knw	James	320	Ags	Joel	378	Mds
Enoch	322	Ags	James [2]	321	Ags	John	185	Alb
Enoch	9	Clp	James	608	Btt	John	266	Amh
Evan	5	Clp	James	692	Br	John	273	Amh
Ezekiel	967	Hrr	James	891	Crl	John	320	Ags
Fanney	333	Lnn	James	959	Chc	John	399	Ags
Felix	557	Pre	James	5	Clp	John	406	Ags
Fielding	277	Ldn	James	9	Clp	John	415	Bth

Name	Page	Co.
John	455	Bdf
John	545	Brk
John	609	Btt
John	675	Br
John	684	Br
John	697	Br
John	704	Brn
John	869	Cmp
John	893	Crl
John	958	Chc
John	101	Cmb
John	121	Cmb
John	131	Cmb
John	326	Dnw
John	330	Dnw
John	178	Elc
John	205	Ess
John	340	Fqr
John	350	Fqr
John	460	Frn
John	515	Frd
John	561	Frd
John	578	Frd
John	683	Gch
John	760	Hmp
John	789	Hmp
John	939	Hrr
John	6	Hnr
John	22	Hnr
John	114	Hnr
John	331	Lnn
John	333	Lnn
John	431	Msn
John	459	Mdd
John	482	Mnn
John	566	Mnr
John	582	Mnr
John	746	Nwk
John	890	Nrf
John	24	Oho
John	26	Oho
John	219	Pnd
John	14	Pwh
John	557	Pre
John	521	Prw
John	525	Prw
John	408	Rch
John	33	Stf
John	58	Stf
John	627	Sss
John	819	Wth
John	821	Wth
John	871	Yrk
John, (C)	788	Bck
John, Jr.	447	Grn
John, Junr.	768	Wst
John, Senr.	287	Amh
John, Senr.	873	Cmp
John, Senr.	768	Wst
John, sr.	323	Ags
John, Sr.	447	Grn
John, (tanner)	510	Frd
John B.	767	Wst
John C.	190	Kng
John F.	945	Chc
John G.	378	Mds
John H.	330	Dnw
John T., persons of coulour	132	Cmb
Jonah	422	Bth
Jonathan	945	Chc
Jonathan	542	Frd
Jos.	14	Knw
Jos.	295	Ldn
Jos.	234	Shn
Joseph	429	Bth
Joseph	692	Br
Joseph	788	Bck
Joseph	67	Chs
Joseph	360	Fqr
Joseph	576	Frd
Joseph	129	Hnr
Joseph	56	Jff
Joseph	12	Knw
Joseph	505	Prw
Joseph	527	Prw
Joseph C.	43	Chr
Joshua	357	Fqr
Joshua	681	Wrw
Joshua G.	442	Mth
Josiah	9	Oho
Kidar	440	Pra
Kimmy	816	Nrf
Letty	334	Dnw
Lewis	784	Bck
Lewis	828	Bck
Lewis	199	Ess
Lewis	648	Glc
Lewis	156	Knq
Lewis	626	Sss
Lodwick	8	Ntt
Loe	615	Gls
Lucretia	601	Srr
Lucy	444	Mth
Lucy	38	Stf
Manley	397	Fqr
Marian	575	Brk
Marmaduke	465	Frn
Marshall	352	Fqr
Martin	11	Clp
Martin	427	Msn
Mary	148	Alb
Mary	599	Brk
Mary	879	Cmp
Mary	67	Chr
Mary	9	Clp
Mary	17	Hnr
Mary	27	Hnr
Mary	813	Nrf
Mary	890	Nrf
Mary	59	Stf
Mason	331	Lnn
Matthew	149	Alb
Matthew	700	Wsh
Meriwether	151	Alb
Micajah	117	Hnr
Michael	553	Brk
Michael [2]	820	Wth
Michael	821	Wth
Michl.	642	Mnt
Michl.	662	Mnt
Miletus	838	Bck
Miller	878	Hnv
Milley	955	Chc
Molley	326	Dnw
Molly	17	Hnr
Moses	260	Ldn
Moses	657	Mnt
Moses	131	Sth
Moses, Sr.	441	Pra
Murphey, & C.	679	Nls
Mymy	329	Dnw
Nancey	757	Wsh
Nancy	437	Bth
Nancy	683	Gch
Nancy	31	Hnr
Nancy	127	Hnr
Nancy	338	Lnc
Nath.	16	Hnr
Nathan	117	Hnr
Nathan	311	Ldn
Nelly	339	Lnc
Nicholas	5	Clp
Nimrod	643	Mnt
Oliver	686	Br
Pattes	331	Lnn
Patty	334	Dnw
Patty	114	Hnr
Pheby	9	Clp
Peter	319	Ags
Peter	11	Clp
Peter	38	Stf
Rachael	890	Crl
Rachal	278	Amh
Rachal	77	Jff
Rachel	192	Elc
Rachel	338	Lnc
Rachel	871	Yrk
Raleigh	703	Brn
Randolph	822	Wth
Rane P.	891	Crl
Rebecca	533	Brk
Rebecca	326	Dnw
Rebecca	869	Sth
Reuben	440	Pra
Reuben S.	454	Bdf
Reupard R.	744	Brn
Rhoda	17	Oho
Richard	686	Br
Richard	692	Br
Richard	238	Ldn
Richard	314	Ldn
Richard T.	768	Wst
Richardson	703	Brn
Richd.	323	Ags
Richd.	189	Elc
Robert	150	Alb
Robert	185	Alb
Robert	647	Glc
Robert	779	Hmp
Robert	944	Hrr
Robert	331	Lnn
Robert	429	Msn
Robert	4	Oho
Robert	8	Oho
Robert	520	Prw
Robert	38	Stf
Robt.	318	Ags
Robt.	611	Btt
Rodham	454	Bdf
Rubin	483	Mnn
Saml.	318	Ags
Saml.	116	Hnr
Saml.	157	Knq
Saml.	293	Rck
Saml.	299	Rck
Saml.	759	Wsh
Saml. W.	438	Mth
Samuel	604	Btt
Samuel	131	Cmb
Samuel	479	Frn
Samuel	510	Frd
Samuel	578	Mnr
Samuel	439	Pra
Samuel	58	Stf
Scarburgh	82	Acc
Schrimshaw	42	Chr
Scipio	601	Srr
Sifax	556	Pre
Soloman S. J.	190	Kng
Solomon	427	Bth
Sp., Junr.	339	Lnc
Stephen	788	Bck
Stephen	331	Lnn
Stephen	264	Rck
Stephen, Ser.	264	Rck
Susan	971	Nrt
Susana	13	Clp
Susanna	459	Frn
Talton	453	Frn
Tarlton	185	Alb
Thomas	425	Bth
Thomas	455	Bdf
Thomas	611	Btt
Thomas	692	Br
Thomas	704	Brn
Thomas	854	Cmp
Thomas	43	Chr
Thomas	118	Cmb
Turner	122	Cmb

Name	No.	Loc
Thomas	341	Fqr
Thomas	521	Frd
Thomas	550	Frd
Thomas	579	Frd
Thomas	114	Hnr
Thomas	233	Ldn
Thomas	377	Mds
Thomas	970	Nrt
Thomas	439	Pra
Thomas	73	Spt
Thomas	599	Srr
Thomas	629	Sss
Thomas	768	Wst
Thomas	12	Wod
Thomas	821	Wth
Thomas, jr.	73	Spt
Thomas H.	187	Alb
Thos.	317	Ags
Thos.	320	Ags
Thos.	447	Flv
Thos.	12	Hnr
Thos.	486	Mnn
Thos., (bro. of Danl.)	11	Clp
Thos., Capt.	10	Clp
Thos., (G.N. Fork)	14	Clp
Thos., jr.	4	Clp
Thos., (son of Garfield	8	Clp
Thos. W.	607	Btt
Timothy	505	Brk
Toby	871	Sth
Travers	186	Alb
Tyree H.	13	Knw
Walker	605	Btt
Walter	50	Stf
Wendle	487	Mnn
Wiley	156	Knq
Will	958	Chc
William	79	Acc
William	150	Alb
William	180	Alb
William	454	Bdf
William	677	Br
William	692	Br
William	776	Bck
William	236	Frf
William	547	Frd
William	555	Frd
William	556	Frd
William	563	Frd
William	616	Gls
William	4	Knw
William	190	Kng
William	330	Lnn
William	331	Lnn
William	377	Mds
William	503	Prw
William	80	Spt
William	108	Spt
William	60	Stf
William	689	Wsh
William	767	Wst
William, of R.	33	Stf
William, of W.	45	Stf
William, Senr.	157	Knq
William B.	107	Spt
William J.	767	Wst
Willis	258	Amh
Willm.	605	Btt
Willm.	182	Elc
Wilson	105	Cmb
Wm.	317	Ags
Wm.	406	Ags
Wm.	531	Brk
Wm.	703	Brn
Wm.	61	Chs
Wm.	130	Cmb
Wm.	14	Hnr
Wm.	18	Hnr
Wm.	116	Hnr
Wm.	118	Hnr
Wm.	253	Ldn
Wm.	291	Ldn
Wm.	312	Ldn
Wm.	317	Ldn
Wm.	566	Mnr
Wm.	592	Mnr
Wm.	9	Oho
Wm.	442	Pra
Wm.	692	Wsh
Wm., [his] Est.	339	Lnc
Wm., Jr.	337	Lnc
Wm., N.F.	723	Wsh
Wm., (Son of Danl.)	5	Clp
Wm., (son of Dl.)	12	Clp
Wm. A.	11	Clp
Wm. P.	310	Ldn
Wm. S.	440	Pra
Zach.	9	Clp
see ---, B...n, Benson, Bown, Brawn, Browns, Robinson		
Browne, Abbridgton	823	Nrf
Catharine	234	Frf
Coleman	240	Frf
Cretia	877	Sth
Elizabeth	817	Nrf
James	18	Rcm
Jesse	875	Sth
Jesse	599	Srr
John	7	Rcm
John	18	Rcm
Lucy	35	Isw
Lucy	599	Srr
Peter	6	Rcm
Rebecca	601	Srr
Saml.	155	Sth
Sarah	602	Srr
Temperance	11	Isw
Tony	857	Sth
William	24	Rcm
William	28	Rcm
Willis	858	Sth
Wm., Estate	599	Srr
Brownfield, Katty	324	Ags
Browning, Caleb	453	Bdf
Charles	821	Wth
Chs.	11	Clp
Chs., (of the River)	9	Clp
Edmon	723	Wsh
Elias	798	Hmp
Enos	723	Wsh
Francis	150	Alb
Francis	185	Alb
Jas.	684	Gch
Jno.	11	Clp
Jno.	892	Hnv
John	150	Alb
Jonathin	150	Alb
Joseph	192	Shn
Nich.	10	Clp
Robt.	112	Hnr
Shadk.	12	Clp
Thomas	209	Shn
Wm.	12	Clp
Wm.	14	Clp
see Browing		
Brownlaw, Cathr.	264	Rck
Brownlee, Alexr.	318	Ags
James	318	Ags
James	610	Btt
John	693	Br
Mary	316	Ags
Walter	696	Br
Brownley, Archibald	531	Prg
see Brounley		
Brownllee, Wm.	316	Ags
Brownlow, John	110	Spt
Brownly, Robert	334	Dnw
Browns, ---, & Co.	328	Dnw
James	744	Brn
Brows, John	667	Mnt
Broy, Elijah	178	Shn
see Bray		
Broyles, Barbara	376	Mds
Benjamin	376	Mds
Delila	376	Mds
Epharim	571	Mnr
James	376	Mds
John	571	Mnr
John	34	Rcm
Peter	571	Mnr
Solomon	568	Mnr
Solomon	573	Mnr
Thomas	376	Mds
Broyte, Cath.	485	Mnn
Jno.	485	Mnn
Broyter, Wm.	485	Mnn
Brubaker, Jacob	611	Btt
John	611	Btt
Brubeck, Jacob	318	Ags
see Brewbeck		
Bruce, Agness	19	Ntt
Alexander	399	Fqr
Armistreat	65	Chs
Charles	25	Stf
Elijah	14	Clp
Elizabeth	601	Srr
Frederick	102	Jff
Garland	621	Mnt
George	551	Frd
George	768	Wst
George, Jr.	551	Frd
Hannah	192	Kng
Henry	887	Nrf
James	705	Brn
James	43	Chr
James	580	Frd
Jas., jr.	9	Clp
Jas., Senr.	6	Clp
Joel	6	Clp
Joseph	684	Gch
Joseph	817	Nrf
Joshua	819	Wth
Leftridge	191	Kng
Nelson	44	Chr
Rachel	551	Frd
Rebecca	438	Flv
Reuben	684	Gch
Richard	186	Alb
Sarah	191	Kng
Vinson	616	Gls
William	83	Acc
William	454	Bdf
William	893	Crl
William	615	Gls
Wm.	817	Nrf
Bruch, John, Sr.	607	Btt
see Brugh		
Bruden, Bartlett	120	Hnr
Brue, Joseph, f. negro	241	Frf
Bruemer, George	609	Btt
see Brunemer, Brunermer		
Bruen, Daniel	88	Spt
Bruffee, Margoreet	151	Alb
Bruffey see Brofee		
Bruffy, James	442	Bth
John	417	Bth
Robt.	399	Ags
Bruggs, William	420	Rnd
Brugh, Daniel	606	Btt
Peter	607	Btt
see Bruch		
Bruice, Mary	333	Lnn
Bruin see Bricin		
Brullen, Peter	321	Ags
Brumage, Jno.	480	Mnn
Jno.	482	Mnn
Jos. [Isaac crossed out]	483	Mnn

Name			Name			Name		
Brumbalew, Fanny	706	Brn	Wilson	3	Hnr	Buchanan, Andw.	692	Wsh
Brumby, Elizabeth	892	Crl	Wm.	870	Yrk	Fade	608	Btt
William	370	Fqr	see Brion			Jack A.	608	Btt
Brumfield, David	16	Rcm	Bryant, Alexander	394	Rch	John	697	Br
Humphrey	617	Gls	Allen	774	Bck	Jonathan	676	Br
John	561	Brk	Austin	796	Bck	R.	484	Mnn
Micajah	616	Gls	Bailey	154	Sth	Robt.	730	Wsh
Brumley, Ann	156	Knq	Baily	877	Sth	Sally	887	Nrf
Arechl.	704	Wsh	Betsy	409	Rch	Theodore	606	Btt
John	437	Pra	Britain	877	Sth	Thomas	676	Br
Robert	156	Knq	Charles	836	Bck	Buchang, Jacob	324	Ags
Samuel	972	Nrt	Charles	149	Sth	Buchannan, Alexr.	725	Wsh
Brummel, Wm.	682	Wrw	Dabney	679	Nls	Archibald	7	Oho
Brummet, H.	29	Hnr	Dabney P.	680	Nls	Archl.	725	Wsh
James	56	Stf	David	796	Bck	Davd.	693	Wsh
John	52	Stf	David	837	Bck	Hugh	297	Rck
Brumwell, D.	25	Hnr	Drew	151	Sth	James	12	Oho
Brunder, Aaron	330	Dnw	Edward	377	Mds	Jas.	730	Wsh
see Brander			Elizabeth	14	Isw	Jno.	9	Clp
Brundige, Timothy	501	Prw	Hanah	712	Wsh	Jno.	297	Rck
Brundt, George	819	Nrf	Isaac	804	Bck	Jno., Jur.	730	Wsh
Brunemer, John	609	Btt	Isaack	127	Cmb	John	12	Oho
Peter	609	Btt	James	127	Cmb	John	16	Oho
see Bruemer			James	681	Nls	John	22	Oho
Bruner, George	569	Frd	Jesse	558	Pre	Margaret	23	Oho
Henry	784	Hmp	Jesse	628	Sss	Rebeca	23	Oho
Jacob	776	Hmp	John	791	Bck	Samul	9	Oho
Peter	785	Hmp	John	820	Bck	Thomas	14	Oho
Brunermer, Coonrod	608	Btt	John	892	Crl	Walter	7	Oho
see Bruemer			John	441	Flv	Buchannen, John	730	Wsh
Brunk, Jacob	4	Rcm	John	680	Nls	Buchanno, Matthw	693	Wsh
Brunswick, Charles	331	Dnw	John	409	Rch	Buchannon, Andw.	710	Wsh
Brunton, Susanna	516	Prw	John	410	Rch	James	822	Wth
Brushwood, Geo.	157	Knq	John [2]	157	Sth	Jas.	693	Wsh
Jas.	155	Knq	John	58	Stf	Jos.	731	Wsh
William	157	Knq	John	713	Wsh	Matthew	697	Wsh
Bruster, John	821	Wth	Jonas	150	Sth	Moses	692	Wsh
Thos.	15	Hnr	Joseph	408	Rch	Robt.	698	Wsh
Brutus, George	595	Frd	Joshua	157	Sth	Saml.	697	Wsh
Samuel	595	Frd	Lewis	161	Sth	Thos.	15	Clp
Silvia	595	Frd	Martha	557	Pre	William	701	Wsh
Bryan, Benjamin	191	Kng	Martin	820	Bck	Wm. E.	699	Wsh
Benjamin	16	Rcm	Mary	129	Cmb	Buchanon, Alexander	821	Wth
Charles	419	Fqr	Mary	559	Pre	George	822	Wth
Charles	73	Jff	Mich.	850	Sth	John [2]	822	Wth
Chas.	321	Ags	Nelson	628	Sss	Moses, Senr.	692	Wsh
Cornelius	16	Rcm	Oliver	43	Chr	Patrick	822	Wth
Daniel	1	Rcm	Permenous	682	Nls	William	821	Wth
Dorcas A.	871	Yrk	Rawligh	409	Rch	Wm.	302	Rck
Edward	93	Jff	Rebecca	601	Srr	Bucher, Jacob	574	Frd
Elezabeth	187	Alb	Richard	678	Nls	John	574	Frd
Elizh., (Y)	870	Yrk	Richd.	300	Rck	Len.	481	Mnn
Ellen	971	Nrt	Samuel	5	Knw	Margarett	520	Frd
James	774	Hmp	Silas, Capt.	12	Pwh	Philip P.	572	Frd
James	424	Msn	Silvanous [2]	679	Nls	Robt.	481	Mnn
James, Jur.	701	Wsh	Silvanous, jr.	678	Nls	Buck, Anthony	108	Spt
Jas.	10	Clp	Stephon	12	Pwh	Charles, Sen.	208	Shn
Jesse	972	Nrt	Stinson	784	Bck	Christian	821	Wth
Jno.	12	Clp	Susanna	681	Nls	Cornelius	68	Chs
John	239	Frf	Thadecas	397	Rch	Debra	797	Hmp
John	358	Fqr	Thomas	399	Rch	John	719	Wsh
John	795	Hmp	Thos. B.	535	Prg	Jonathan	776	Bck
John	61	Jff	William	678	Nls	Joseph	565	Mnr
John	191	Kng	William	681	Nls	Martin	18	Rcm
John	20	Rcm	William	557	Pre	Patty	847	Sth
John	871	Yrk	William	396	Rch	Robert	563	Brk
John, Junr.	823	Wth	William	57	Stf	Samuel	208	Shn
John, Senr.	822	Wth	Wm.	888	Nrf	Samuel	130	Sth
Letty	12	Clp	Wm.	126	Sth	Sipio	235	Ldn
Lovell	190	Kng	see Byant			Thomas	593	Frd
Milly	10	Clp	Bryarly, David	582	Frd	Thomas	208	Shn
Nathaniel	822	Wth	Bryce, Mary	685	Gch	Thos.	848	Sth
Stephen	588	Brk	Bryer, John	17	Oho	William	163	Shn
Susann	399	Ags	Bryont, Wm.	431	Flv	William	164	Shn
Thomas	16	Rcm	Bryson, ---, & Parkill	11	Hnr	Buckalew, George	820	Wth
Thomas	20	Rcm	Rebecca	566	Mnr	Buckan, Thomas	61	Stf
William	240	Frf	Buaterg, Jereh.	809	Nrf	Buckanan, Peggy	336	Dnw
William	191	Kng	Bucey, Thomas	681	Br	Buckels, Abraham	86	Jff
William, (Jr.)	42	Rcm	Buch, Phil	481	Mnn	Henry	86	Jff
William, (sen.)	42	Rcm	see Berch			James	90	Jff

Name	No.	Co.
Buckelue, S.	481	Mnn
Buckey, Jno.	241	Frf
Peter	416	Rnd
Valentine	675	Br
Buckeys, John	253	Shn
Buckhanan, Alexr.	319	Ags
David	319	Ags
James	319	Ags
Jas., sr.	319	Ags
John	133	Hnr
Nancy	123	Hnr
Buckhannon, Wm.	446	Mth
Buckhanon, John	241	Ldn
Buckies, Danl.	599	Brk
Buckingham, John	696	Br
Thomas	286	Ldn
Buckland, Susanna, Colour	598	Mnr
Thomas	578	Mnr
Buckle, John	5	Knw
Sarah R.	329	Dnw
Buckler, Abram	755	Wsh
John	780	Hmp
Sally	79	Acc
Buckles, William	90	Jff
see Buckies		
Bucklew, George	920	Hrr
John	920	Hrr
Buckley, Ann	317	Ags
Caty	545	Frd
Isaac	428	Bth
Jno. H.	233	Frf
John	428	Bth
John	706	Brn
Joseph	431	Bth
Joshua	424	Bth
Joshua	233	Frf
Mary Ann	238	Frf
Richard	552	Frd
Bucklue, P.	485	Mnn
Wm.	485	Mnn
see Buckelue		
Buckmaster, Nathaniel	58	Jff
Zacariah	56	Jff
Buckner, Aris	243	Ldn
Charles	889	Crl
Eliza	768	Wst
Elizabeth	331	Lnn
Francis	156	Knq
Geo.	155	Knq
Geo., Este.	5	Clp
George	890	Crl
George M.	86	Spt
Horace	5	Clp
James H.	332	Lnn
Jno. D.	647	Glc
John	105	Cmb
Judith	892	Crl
Monroe	889	Crl
Richard	892	Crl
Susan	26	Hnr
Thomas	889	Crl
Thornton	362	Fqr
William	889	Crl
William	42	Chr
William A.	892	Crl
Wm.	706	Brn
see Wells		
Bucknner, James	333	Lnn
Bucknor, Antony	7	Wod
Buckstone, Jacob	689	Br
Budd, Elijah	6	Acc
John	8	Acc
Major	9	Acc
Undrel	563	Mnr
William	7	Acc
William, of Mj.	7	Acc
Zerobabel	8	Acc
Buff, Jno.	8	Clp
John	594	Frd
Buffin, Chesley	330	Dnw
Buffington, Abraham	430	Msn
David	821	Hmp
Jacob	430	Msn
Joel	430	Msn
Jonathin	962	Hrr
Joshua	554	Frd
Richard	805	Hmp
William	805	Hmp
Bufkin, Alice	818	Nrf
Buford, Abraham	455	Bdf
Hennery	331	Lnn
Henry, Sr.	455	Bdf
Jo...n	454	Bdf
Peter	141	Dnw
Thomas	331	Lnn
William, jr.	331	Lnn
William, Sr.	332	Lnn
see Bufurd		
Bufurd, Henry, Jr.	455	Bdf
Bug, Toney, F.N.	628	Sss
Bugg, Allen	281	Amh
John	331	Lnn
Pleasant, (M)	707	Brn
Sherod	285	Amh
Woodson	443	Flv
Bukey, Hezekiah	6	Wod
John	5	Oho
Bukham see Beckham		
Bulger, Edward	203	Shn
James	548	Frd
John	406	Rch
John, Junr.	399	Rch
Bulington, Elizabeth	939	Chc
Bull, Betsey	11	Acc
Betty	77	Acc
Daniel	5	Acc
George	7	Acc
Isaac	198	Shn
John	2	Acc
John	146	Acc
John, Junr.	12	Acc
John, Carter	5	Acc
John, Senr.	12	Acc
Jonah	532	Brk
Michal	576	Frd
Molly	11	Acc
Nathan	531	Brk
Polly, of B	12	Acc
Richard	5	Acc
Southey	7	Acc
Susannah	77	Acc
William	83	Acc
see Butt		
Bullack, Obadiah	13	Isw
Bullar, Griffin	186	Alb
Bullard, Charles, [his] plantation	94	Spt
Geo. H.	190	Kng
Richard	891	Crl
Buller, Frederick	24	Oho
Bullery, Thos.	695	Wsh
Bullett, Baersheba	384	Fqr
Bullifant, Edward	945	Chc
James	943	Chc
John	946	Chc
Major	942	Chc
Reba.	888	Yrk
Sarah	951	Chc
Turner	890	Nrf
Bullington, Howard	126	Hnr
Judith	126	Hnr
Bullman, Ann	157	Knq
Thomas	155	Knq
Bullock, Abner	87	Spt
David	34	Hnr
Elizabeth	87	Spt
Hannah	280	Rck
James	182	Alb
James	87	Spt
John	849	Cmp
John	859	Cmp
John	5	Isw
John	87	Spt
Joseph	5	Isw
Joseph	89	Spt
Josiah	814	Nrf
Margt.	183	Elc
Samuel	174	Shn
William	889	Crl
Willis	5	Isw
Bulls, Nancy	846	Sth
William P.	446	Grn
Bully, Andrew	192	Elc
John	178	Elc
Tho.	191	Elc
Tho., Jur.	190	Elc
Bumbaugh, Michael	244	Shn
Thomas	244	Shn
Bumgainer, Christeen	191	Shn
Bumgardner, David	424	Msn
Bumgarner, Agnes	769	Hmp
Adam	431	Bth
Christian	182	Shn
Henry	172	Shn
Fredk.	9	Clp
Fredric	932	Hrr
Geo.	9	Clp
John	561	Brk
Peter	181	Shn
Philip	643	Mnt
Rebecca	769	Hmp
Bumpass, Ann	901	Hnv
George	870	Hnv
Nathan	856	Hnv
Nathan, Jnr.	860	Hnv
Samuel	856	Hnv
Wim.	856	Hnv
Bunburg, Ester	889	Nrf
Bunbury, Eliza.	191	Kng
Henry	191	Kng
Richard	191	Kng
Thomas	192	Kng
Bunch, Da	324	Ags
James	455	Bdf
see Branch		
Bunckley, Tristram	12	Isw
Buncrut, Leanard	803	Hmp
Bunda, Fras., (F.N.)	7	Clp
Nancy, (F.N.)	8	Clp
Sally, (F. Molatte)	8	Clp
Thos., (F.Ne.)	14	Clp
Wm., (F.M.)	8	Clp
Wm., Senr., (F.N.)	9	Clp
Bunday, Ann	202	Ess
Catharine	202	Ess
Henry, jr.	202	Ess
Henry, Sr.	202	Ess
John	202	Ess
Lelly	202	Ess
Lewis	202	Ess
Nelson	202	Ess
Sarah	202	Ess
Usler	202	Ess
Bundich, Geo., Aswm.	81	Acc
Bundrant, William	123	Cmb
Bundurant, Benjamin	680	Nls
Jacob	500	Frn
John	454	Bdf
Bundwick, Abbot	81	Acc
Elizabeth	12	Acc
George	75	Acc
John	10	Acc
John A.	6	Acc
John S.	13	Acc
Joseph	77	Acc
Justice	75	Acc
Rachel	9	Acc
Richard	74	Acc
Richd., of G.	80	Acc

Sally	82	Acc
Sarah	78	Acc
Tabitha	77	Acc
William	75	Acc
Bundy, Betty	119	Spt
Sylvia	119	Spt
Bunett, Anderson	878	Hnv
Bunganna, Jacob	932	Hrr
Bunn, Ezekiel	683	Br
George	511	Brk
Rhoda	881	Sth
Bunnal, John	932	Hrr
Bunnel, Daniel	261	Ldn
Bunnell, Jont.	264	Ldn
Luther	69	Spt
Bunough, William	892	Crl
Bunt see Brent		
Bunter, Jas.	12	Clp
Bunting, Ben	824	Nrf
Eliza	824	Nrf
George	6	Acc
George	74	Acc
George, Junr.	78	Acc
George, sen.	76	Acc
Isma	78	Acc
Jas.	814	Nrf
Jonathan	77	Acc
Luther	6	Acc
Severn	79	Acc
Smith	10	Acc
Solomon	11	Acc
Thos.	828	Nrf
William	7	Acc
William	76	Acc
Willm. R.	7	Acc
Bunton, Alexr.	302	Rck
Jno.	302	Rck
Moses	272	Rck
Moses	279	Rck
Smith	441	Mth
Buntz, John	820	Wth
Burbridge, Mary	821	Hmp
Moses	375	Mds
Burch, Ann	19	Hnr
Ann	157	Knq
Benjamin	849	Hnv
Cheadle	248	Aml
Eli	868	Cmp
Eliza.	157	Knq
Evander	15	Oho
Henry	886	Hnv
James	259	Amh
Jesse	4	Oho
John	185	Alb
John, Jnr.	185	Alb
John, jr.	287	Amh
John, Senr.	261	Amh
Levi	712	Wsh
Peter	868	Hnv
Philip	489	Bdf
Richard	186	Alb
Shepherd	156	Knq
Simon	820	Bck
Thomas	676	Br
Thos.	487	Mnn
William	151	Alb
Zephaniah	15	Oho
see Berch		
Burchart, David	591	Brk
Burchell, Jno.	18	Hnr
John	535	Frd
John	192	Kng
Burcher, Elizh., (Y)	888	Yrk
Wm.	682	Wrw
Burchet, John	139	Dnw
Burchett, Burwell	140	Dnw
Jno.	541	Prg
Lucy	541	Prg
Burchfield, John	42	Chr
Burchnal, Jas.	482	Mnn

Burckley see Bunckley		
Burd, John	151	Alb
Burden, Archibald	74	Spt
Burdet, Betsey	573	Mnr
Giles	577	Mnr
Isham	580	Mnr
John	577	Mnr
John	588	Mnr
Willis	585	Mnr
Burdett, Charles	588	Mnr
James	361	Fqr
Wm.	585	Mnr
see Bardett		
Burdit, Stephen	12	Clp
William	513	Prw
Burditt, Jarvis	452	Frn
Burens, Joshua	304	Rck
Burfoot, Lawson	60	Chs
Thomas, Jr.	52	Chs
Thomas, jr.	66	Chs
Thos., senr.	59	Chs
Burford, Ambrose	290	Amh
Daniel, jr.	260	Amh
Daniel, Minr.	272	Amh
Daniel, Senr.	261	Amh
Daniel L.	297	Amh
James	272	Amh
John	271	Amh
John L.	291	Amh
Tandy	8	Pwh
William	148	Alb
William	289	Amh
Burgass, Jas.	838	Nrf
Burge, Beverley	706	Brn
Bradford	705	Brn
Drury	328	Dnw
Frances	543	Prg
Frances	550	Prg
Frederick, Snr.	703	Brn
Hambleton	530	Prg
Henry	67	Chr
James	706	Brn
Littlebury	139	Dnw
Robt.	327	Dnw
Sally	543	Prg
Thos.	705	Brn
William	629	Sss
Wood	532	Prg
Wooden	332	Lnn
Burger, Adam	479	Mnn
Fredrick	738	Wsh
Henry	608	Btt
Michael	740	Wsh
S.	481	Mnn
Burges, Elizabeth	429	Bth
Frans.	12	Clp
James	454	Bdf
James	406	Rch
John	501	Frn
John	665	Mnt
John, Ju.	426	Bth
John, Ser.	427	Bth
John P.	558	Pre
John W.	563	Frd
John W.	601	Frd
Nancy	429	Bth
Nathan	426	Bth
Samuel	822	Wth
Tho.	179	Elc
Thos.	722	Wsh
Burgess, Ann	890	Nrf
Charles	439	Pra
Daniel	853	Cmp
Daniel	766	Wst
Edmund	455	Bdf
Edward	387	Fqr
George W.	797	Bck
Henry	1	Rcm
James	3	Rcm
John	854	Cmp

John	387	Fqr
John	443	Flv
John R.	601	Srr
Joseph	848	Cmp
Lanfair	437	Pra
Lucretia	602	Srr
Miles	600	Srr
Molly	768	Wst
Nathl.	889	Nrf
Thomas	869	Cmp
Thomas	616	Gls
William	234	Frf
William	171	Shn
Wm.	320	Ags
Wm.	683	Gch
Wright	399	Ags
see Bergess, Brown, Kern,		
Moody		
Burgher, Charles	681	Nls
Burgis, Wm.	721	Wsh
Wm.	730	Wsh
Burgner, Christian	248	Shn
Burgoine, John	79	Jff
Joseph	307	Ldn
Burgur, Benjamin	149	Alb
David	149	Alb
John	149	Alb
Burk, Ann	99	Spt
Betsey	684	Br
Clara	617	Gls
Cornelius	558	Frd
Ed.	317	Ags
Edmd.	13	Clp
Edward	68	Spt
Elisebeth	755	Wsh
Elizabth.	504	Brk
Enoch	308	Ldn
Geo.	14	Clp
Henry	647	Glc
Isaac	509	Frd
James	580	Frd
James	723	Wsh
Jas.	744	Wsh
Jas.	752	Wsh
Jno.	647	Glc
Jno.	680	Wrw
John	585	Brk
John	616	Gls
John	828	Hmp
John	273	Rck
John	29	Rcm
John	744	Wsh
John	753	Wsh
Jonathan	628	Mnt
Joshua	717	Wsh
Josiah	615	Gls
Margt.	640	Mnt
Michael	827	Hmp
Richard	10	Clp
Richard	820	Wth
Saml.	665	Mnt
Susanna	408	Fqr
Thomas	581	Frd
Thomas	583	Frd
Thos.	647	Glc
Thos.	721	Wsh
William	513	Frd
William	617	Gls
William	828	Hmp
Wm.	317	Ags
Wm.	10	Clp
Wm.	309	Ldn
see Bush		
Burkby, Thomas	306	Ldn
Burke, Benjamin	239	Frf
Elizabeth	460	Mdd
Graves	203	Ess
Jackey M.	206	Ess
James	182	Elc
James	235	Frf

Jno. 14 Knw
John, & Co., Urbanna 460 Mdd
Nancy 221 Ess
Nancy 102 Jff
Polly 507 Prw
Redmn. 890 Nrf
William 459 Mdd
Burkes, Geo. 6 Ntt
Burket, Danl. 315 Ags
Natl. 321 Ags
Burkett, Leamick 219 Pnd
Michael 90 Jff
Thomas 778 Hmp
  see Carder
Burkham see Burkimn
Burkhammer, Henry 557 Frd
Burkhead, Francis 186 Alb
John 185 Alb
Richard 187 Alb
Burkheart, Henry 821 Wth
John 821 Wth
Burkholder, Christley 17 Rcm
David 14 Rcm
Henry 14 Rcm
Isaac 606 Btt
Jacob, (Jr.) 40 Rcm
Jacob, (sen.) 40 Rcm
John 40 Rcm
Martin 40 Rcm
Peter 28 Rcm
Burkilt, John 178 Elc
Burkimn, Stephen 6 Oho
Burks, Charles 820 Bck
Charles, Senr. 268 Amh
Charles M. 268 Amh
David, jr. 267 Amh
David, Senr. 268 Amh
David J. 266 Amh
George 783 Bck
George 839 Bck
Isham 834 Bck
James 557 Pre
Jessee 679 Nls
John 182 Alb
John 677 Nls
John 679 Nls
John 558 Pre
John, jr. 267 Amh
John P. 270 Amh
Judith 820 Bck
Lindsay 261 Amh
Nathaniel D. 266 Amh
Richard 264 Amh
Richard 558 Pre
Richard, (SD) 266 Amh
Samuel 264 Amh
Samuel 820 Bck
Samuel 826 Bck
Samuel, (SD) 265 Amh
William 557 Pre
Burkshire, R. 480 Mnn
Burley, Alexdr. 684 Gch
Ann 834 Nrf
Jacob 25 Oho
James 407 Ags
Thomas 294 Amh
Burlin, Abraham 70 Jff
Thos. 12 Hnr
Burn, Thos. 487 Mnn
Wm. 487 Mnn
Burndrum, Joseph 868 Cmp
Burner, Abraham 224 Pnd
Abraham 204 Shn
Adam 420 Bth
Daniel 224 Pnd
Henry 175 Shn
Isaa 9 Rcm
Jacob 174 Shn
Jacob, Senr. 175 Shn
Jane 421 Bth

John 175 Shn
Jonas 204 Shn
Joseph 190 Shn
Litha 187 Shn
Samuel 183 Shn
Burnes, Robert 43 Chr
Burnet, Jerimiah 331 Lnn
  see Bennet
Burnett, Curnelius 860 Hnv
David 877 Hnv
Dugga 743 Brn
Edmund 455 Bdf
Elizabeth 878 Hnv
Elizabeth 879 Hnv
Elizabeth 333 Lnn
Fanney 885 Hnv
Jacob 259 Amh
James 455 Bck
James 776 Bck
Jeremiah 331 Lnn
Jessee 684 Gch
Jno. 878 Hnv
John 623 Mnt
Joseph 219 Ess
Joshua 140 Dnw
Joshua 876 Hnv
Kelly 877 Hnv
Leonard 220 Ess
Leroy 333 Lnn
Lewis 742 Brn
Mary 878 Hnv
Nathan 878 Hnv
Philip 332 Lnn
Reuben 891 Crl
Richard 884 Hnv
Richmond 679 Nls
Robert 331 Lnn
Robert 223 Pnd
Sanders 888 Hnv
Thomas R. 776 Bck
Thos., overseer for F.
  Muir's Estate 141 Dnw
William 867 Cmp
Williamson 455 Bdf
Wim. 885 Hnv
  see Bunett, Burnnett
Burnham, Jno. 680 Wrw
Joseph 381 Fqr
Lockey 681 Wrw
Burnhart, Geo., sr. 324 Ags
George 324 Ags
Burnhouse, Christ. 284 Ldn
Geo. 284 Ldn
Burnit, William 77 Jff
Burnitt, Johns 744 Brn
Burnley, Ann 186 Alb
Harriet 21 Hnr
Mary 898 Hnv
Nathaniel 182 Alb
Nicholas 185 Alb
Burnly, Elizabeth 127 Hnr
Burnnett, Eliz. 157 Knq
Burns, Archd. 598 Brk
Archd. 888 Nrf
Barny 486 Mnn
Edward 767 Wst
George 459 Mdd
George 188 Shn
Henry 501 Prw
Hugh 10 Rcm
James 677 Br
Jeremiah 414 Bth
Jno., (Millwright) 606 Btt
John 434 Bth
John 511 Brk
John 678 Brk
John 617 Gls
John, jr. 511 Br
Joseph 434 Bth
Magnus 593 Mnr

Mary 434 Bth
Nancy 322 Ags
Pat 486 Mnn
Patrick 69 Jff
Payton 951 Hrr
Philip 73 Jff
Polley 123 Hnr
Richard 680 Nls
Saml. 406 Ags
Samuel 417 Rnd
Thos. 318 Ags
Thos. 593 Mnr
Wm. 437 Flv
Wm. 31 Hnr
  see Benns, Bunn
Burnside, Jem 322 Ags
John 426 Msn
Patrick 949 Hrr
Burnsides, Alexander 428 Bth
Andw. 35 Rcm
Jonathan 4 Rcm
Mary 428 Bth
William 19 Rcm
Burnsids, John 942 Hrr
Wm. 941 Hrr
Burott, Allexander 35 Hnr
Buroult see Benoutt
Burr, D.J. 11 Hnr
James 94 Jff
Moses 83 Jff
William 94 Jff
Burrage, Charles 85 Spt
Burras, Edward 432 Bth
Isaac 123 Hnr
Michl. 10 Clp
Wim. 872 Hnv
Burrass, Benjamin 79 Spt
Bolling 79 Spt
Clement 79 Spt
Burrell, Eliza 768 Wst
Nathl. 604 Btt
Burress, Thomas 583 Brk
William 454 Bdf
Burris, Anderson 637 Mnt
Isabelha 299 Rck
ISack 28 Hnr
Jesse 972 Nrt
John 637 Mnt
Micajah 612 Mnt
William 973 Nrt
William H. 973 Nrt
Willm. 621 Mnt
Burriss, John 378 Mds
Burrohs, Elza 439 Mth
Jno. 438 Mth
Burron, Ann 486 Mnn
Burroughs, George 20 Stf
John, jr. 42 Stf
John, sr. 41 Stf
Philip 403 Fqr
Rachel 78 Spt
Samuel 40 Stf
Thomas 403 Fqr
Thomas 21 Stf
Burrougs, John 350 Fqr
Burrow, Grey 141 Dnw
James 545 Prg
Nimrod 140 Dnw
Thos. 532 Prg
Willie 706 Brn
Burrows, Anthy. 437 Pra
Booz 480 Mnn
David 5 Oho
Edd. 480 Mnn
Elijah 23 Oho
Ezl. 481 Mnn
Ezry 890 Nrf
Travy 438 Pra
Wm. 438 Pra
Burrus, Charles 185 Alb

Name	No.	Co.
George	890	Crl
Harry	893	Crl
Henry	889	Crl
Joshua	283	Amh
Mary	890	Crl
Nelson	186	Alb
Pleasant	893	Crl
Samuel	889	Crl
Thomas	889	Crl
Walter	150	Alb
William	889	Crl
William	892	Crl
Burry, John	253	Shn
Burson, Aaron	263	Ldn
Geo.	263	Ldn
James	675	Br
James	264	Ldn
Jesse	263	Ldn
John	235	Ldn
Jont.	264	Ldn
Jos.	263	Ldn
Joseph	300	Ldn
Levi	264	Ldn
Moses	264	Ldn
Burt, Ann	888	Yrk
J. M.	887	Nrf
John N.	600	Srr
Lewis	870	Yrk
Tho.	888	Yrk
Wm.	7	Clp
Burthonad, John	12	Wod
Burtis, Samuel	178	Alb
Burton, ...	760	Hmp
Abraham	247	Aml
Alexander	455	Bdf
Allen	246	Aml
B.	482	Mnn
Benjamin	238	Frf
Campbell	157	Knq
Caty	155	Knq
Charles	8	Rcm
Douglas	837	Bck
Edwd.	684	Gch
Elias	617	Gls
Elias	157	Knq
Eliza	123	Hnr
Elizabeth	829	Bck
Frances	157	Knq
George	191	Kng
Helin	6	Acc
Henry	648	Glc
Huldey	821	Hmp
Isaac	617	Gls
Isaac	26	Stf
Isham	791	Bck
James	381	Fqr
James	39	Stf
James H.	677	Nls
Jeremiah	112	Hnr
Jesse	881	Cmp
Jno.	54	Chs
Jno.	648	Glc
Jno.	877	Hnv
Jno., jr.	61	Chs
John	5	Acc
John	78	Acc
John	247	Aml
John	827	Bck
John	880	Cmp
John	116	Hnr
John	557	Pre
John, Snr.	119	Hnr
John Y.	155	Knq
Joshua	93	Jff
Judith	493	Frn
Levi	556	Frd
Lucy	107	Cmb
Lucy	125	Hnr
Marshall	617	Gls
Molly	458	Mdd
Nancy	14	Hnr
Nathaniel	38	Stf
Natthaniel	791	Bck
Peter	247	Aml
Rachael	37	Stf
Reuben	112	Hnr
Robert	455	Bdf
Saml.	6	Clp
Sarah	155	Knq
Simon	647	Glc
Thomas	12	Acc
Thomas	184	Alb
Thomas	116	Hnr
Thos.	744	Brn
Thos.	752	Wsh
William	149	Alb
William	248	Aml
William	453	Bdf
William	791	Bck
William	104	Cmb
William	117	Cmb
William	131	Cmb
William	334	Dnw
William	332	Lnn
William	632	Mnt
William	18	Oho
William	38	Stf
William	57	Stf
William, Sr.	455	Bdf
Wilshere	99	Cmb
Wim.	877	Hnv
Wm., Jr.	119	Hnr
Wm., Snr.	119	Hnr
Zachariah	556	Frd
see Barton, Benton, Berton, Birton		
Burus see Burns		
Burwell, ... S., for A.		
Lewes	458	Frn
Armstead	140	Dnw
Bacon	527	Frd
Clarissa	330	Dnw
Hanna	549	Prg
James B.	413	Rch
John S.	458	Frn
Lewis	149	Alb
Lewis	604	Frd
Lewis	333	Lnn
Nathaniel, Jr.	584	Frd
Nathaniel, Senr.	604	Frd
Nathl.	647	Glc
Natt, Colol., has slaves in York County	871	Yrk
Patty	123	Hnr
Philip	604	Frd
Robert C.	559	Frd
Thomas	605	Btt
William A.	457	Frn
see Acres, Hamlet, Innes, Law, Walker		
Bury, James	820	Wth
Wm.	748	Wsh
Busbie, Patsey, Gloucester Town	647	Glc
Busby, Elizabeth	31	Isw
Isaac	581	Mnr
John	765	Hmp
Robert	155	Knq
William	756	Hmp
see Bushby		
Busch, Francis	878	Cmp
Nichodemus	878	Cmp
Thomas	372	Fqr
Busey, Jane	226	Shn
Bush, Abraham	223	Pnd
Aron	590	Mnr
Charlotte	18	Hnr
David	321	Ags
Dennis	520	Frd
Edmund	28	Rcm
Edward	8	Hnr
George	913	Hrr
George	595	Mnr
George	258	Shn
Henry	507	Frd
Jas.	336	Lnc
John	321	Ags
John	611	Btt
John	212	Ess
John	629	Sss
Joshua	375	Mds
Leonard	223	Pnd
Margret	961	Hrr
Martin	321	Ags
Michael	949	Hrr
Nathan	594	Mnr
Peter	606	Btt
Peter	949	Hrr
Philip	513	Frd
Rebecca	560	Frd
Regina	516	Frd
Salley	398	Ags
Vance	603	Frd
William	512	Frd
William	4	Knw
Wm.	683	Gch
Wm.	939	Hrr
see Rush		
Bushby, Joseph	234	Frf
Bushel, Holmes	532	Prg
Wm.	188	Elc
Bushell, Baldwin	189	Elc
Joe.	189	Elc
John	189	Elc
Bushman, David	61	Jff
Bushrong, Andrew	207	Shn
Henry	234	Shn
John	205	Shn
Peter	234	Shn
Busick, Sammuel	853	Hnv
Buskett, David	626	Mnt
Buskey, Cornelius	438	Pra
John	439	Pra
Mary	442	Pra
Buskil, Richd.	662	Mnt
Buskirk, Aram.	270	Ldn
John V.	574	Frd
see V. Buskirk		
Buskitt, Jacob	1	Oho
Busky, Josha.	888	Nrf
Busler, John	150	Alb
Busmot, Ann	888	Nrf
Bussa, Hezekiah	809	Hmp
Bussel, John	53	Stf
Mary	32	Stf
Randal	56	Stf
Robert	169	Shn
Vincent	53	Stf
Bussell, Benjaman	91	Jff
John, for	458	Mdd
Mathew	378	Mds
William	378	Mds
Bussey, Jessee	481	Mnn
John	429	Rnd
Bussle, Adam	331	Lnn
Busswell see Buzwell		
Bussy, John	607	Btt
Buster, Claudius	406	Ags
Claudius	9	Knw
John	68	Chr
Thos. S.	14	Knw
see Busler		
Bustin, David	440	Pra
Thomas	440	Pra
Busy, Peter	226	Shn
Butcher, Alexander	241	Frf
Balse	931	Hrr
Ely	422	Rnd
George	961	Hrr
Jacob	609	Btt

Name	Page	Code
James	767	Hmp
James	613	Mnt
Jno. M.	19	Ntt
John	767	Hmp
John	961	Hrr
John	2	Rcm
John	9	Wod
Nicholas	214	Pnd
Nicholas, J.	223	Pnd
Sally	418	Bth
Samuel	608	Btt
Samuel	420	Rnd
Thomas	421	Rnd
Willm.	608	Btt
Buter, Christopher, Jnr.	851	Hnv
Butlar, Lawrence	412	Rch
Butler, Aaron	8	Clp
Allen	46	Isw
Amelia	888	Nrf
Armestd.	11	Clp
Armistead	15	Clp
Barnet	150	Alb
Barnet	810	Bck
Benja.	11	Clp
Betsey	538	Prg
Caleb	684	Gch
Christopher	62	Stf
Christopher, Snr.	848	Hnv
Chs.	11	Clp
Dangerfield	889	Hnv
Daniel, free negro	70	Chs
Danl.	128	Hnr
Deborah	527	Brk
Douglas	523	Brk
Edward	178	Alb
Edwd.	129	Sth
Edwin	822	Wth
Elijah	485	Mnn
Eliza.	12	Clp
Elizabeth	851	Hnv
Epaphroditus	23	Isw
Faithy	856	Sth
Fielding	13	Clp
Fielding	14	Clp
George	606	Btt
George	679	Nls
Harrison	14	Clp
Henry	694	Br
Henry	237	Frf
Henry	887	Nrf
Isaac	248	Aml
Jacob	18	Isw
Jacob	292	Ldn
Jacob	297	Ldn
Jacob, (F.N.)	43	Isw
James	178	Alb
James	879	Cmp
James	18	Isw
James	50	Stf
James	59	Stf
James	767	Wst
James, F.N.	627	Sss
James, Sr.	767	Cmp
Jane	192	Kng
Jas.	10	Clp
Jesse	9	Ntt
Jessee	768	Wst
Jno.	5	Clp
Jno.	12	Clp
Jno.	233	Frf
Jno., Jnr.	855	Hnv
Jno., jr.	7	Ntt
Jno., Senr.	3	Ntt
Jno. O.	887	Nrf
Joel	542	Prg
John	891	Crl
John	110	Cmb
John	140	Dnw
John	900	Hnv
John	487	Mnn
John	1	Oho
John	538	Prg
John	768	Wst
John A.	626	Sss
Jonathan	859	Cmp
Jonathan	139	Dnw
Joseph	140	Dnw
Joseph	43	Isw
Joseph	522	Prw
Josh., Senr.	11	Clp
Josha.	13	Clp
Lamma	141	Dnw
Latilia	826	Nrf
Laurence	368	Fqr
Laurence	546	Frd
Lawrence	233	Frf
Mary	891	Crl
Mary	893	Crl
Matthew	880	Sth
Micajah	141	Dnw
Molly	768	Wst
Nancy	869	Cmp
Nancy	767	Wst
Nicholas	694	Br
Paul	302	Rck
Peter	78	Acc
Reuben	599	Srr
Robert	532	Frd
Robt.	8	Isw
Robt. H.	139	Dnw
Sammuel	844	Hnv
Samuel	889	Crl
Samuel	599	Srr
Samuel	767	Wst
Samuel, (M)	707	Brn
Sion	743	Brn
Solomon	9	Isw
Spencer	7	Clp
Stephen	882	Cmp
Stephen, Jun.	42	Isw
Susanna	591	Brk
Taliafo.	11	Clp
Tho.	486	Mnn
Thomas	857	Cmp
Thomas	893	Crl
Thomas	553	Frd
Thomas	684	Gch
Thomas	93	Jff
Thomas	972	Nrt
Thomas	602	Srr
Thos.	535	Brk
Thos.	854	Hnv
Thos.	112	Hnr
Tilmon	141	Dnw
Townzend	8	Clp
Tristm.	890	Nrf
William	881	Cmp
William	93	Jff
William	527	Prw
William	57	Stf
William, Jr.	767	Wst
William, Junr.	527	Prw
William, jr.	60	Stf
William, Senr.	767	Wst
William, Sr.	247	Aml
William, Younger	766	Wst
Willis	42	Isw
Wim.	871	Hnv
Wm.	743	Brn
Wm.	5	Clp
Wm.	15	Clp
Wm.	890	Nrf
Wm., (son of Spr.)	13	Clp
see B...tler, Buter, Washington		
Buts see Berts		
Butt, Abiah	797	Nrf
Adam	18	Rcm
Anthy.	439	Pra
Archd.	517	Brk
Archd.	610	Btt
Arthur	801	Nrf
Barrick	582	Brk
Bassett	804	Nrf
Benj.	800	Nrf
Benja.	581	Brk
Boush	440	Pra
Cabeb	800	Nrf
Caleb	798	Nrf
Chas.	557	Brk
Chas.	800	Nrf
Conrod	803	Hmp
David	437	Pra
Dorcas	887	Nrf
Ezekiel	257	Shn
Frances	801	Nrf
Frdrck.	821	Nrf
Frs.	889	Nrf
George	440	Pra
Henry	557	Brk
Henry	807	Nrf
Henry	219	Pnd
Henry	6	Rcm
Henry, (Jr.)	799	Nrf
Hezekiah	78	Jff
Horatio	34	Isw
Isaac	515	Brk
Isaah	799	Nrf
Jacob	20	Rcm
James	548	Frd
Jas. B.	827	Nrf
Jeremiah	796	Nrf
Jeremiah	439	Pra
Jno., (of Willis)	440	Pra
John	518	Brk
John	25	Rcm
John	720	Wsh
John, (E)	804	Nrf
John, (N.W.)	804	Nrf
John E.	818	Nrf
John N.	792	Nrf
John W.	789	Nrf
Jos.	821	Nrf
Joshua	799	Nrf
Lemuel	805	Nrf
Mary	514	Brk
Malichi	797	Nrf
Miles	797	Nrf
Nancy	790	Nrf
Nancy, (jr.)	806	Nrf
Nat.	799	Nrf
Richard	605	Btt
Ricd.	517	Brk
Rignal	607	Btt
Robt.	800	Nrf
Samuel	792	Nrf
Sol.	800	Nrf
Susan	515	Brk
Thomas N.	99	Spt
W. G.	792	Nrf
William	216	Pnd
Willis	439	Pra
Wilson	798	Nrf
Wm.	557	Brk
Wm.	438	Pra
Wm., (S)	800	Nrf
see Bull		
Butter see Butler		
Butterfield, Ann	538	Frd
James	530	Brk
Jas.	529	Brk
John	538	Frd
Thos.	559	Brk
Butterworth, Benja.	881	Cmp
Benjamin	868	Cmp
Jereh.	141	Dnw
Jno.	140	Dnw
Littlebury	141	Dnw
Buttery see Bullery		
Buttler, William, jr.	246	Aml

Button, Harmon	7	Clp	Byrne, James	328	Dnw	Julius, (FB)	17	Ntt
see Britton			James	550	Prg	Caffee, Elizabeth	824	824
Butts, Alfred	535	Prg	John	191	Kng	Caffery, Rebekah	489	Bdf
Charles	101	Jff	Mary	336	Dnw	Caffey, Wm.	650	Glc
Charles	598	Srr	William	190	Kng	Caffrey, Judith	874	Hnv
Daniel	154	Sth	Byrns, Thos.	486	Mnn	Caga, Abraham	194	Shn
Danl. C.	139	Dnw	Byrnside, James	563	Mnr	Cage, Andrew	590	Brk
Edward	129	Sth	John	575	Mnr	Fielder	45	Chr
Elianor	10	Clp	Bywaters, Henry	5	Clp	Cagy, Christian	196	Shn
Jesse	446	Grn	Jno., jr.	8	Clp	Henry	195	Shn
Samuel	37	Stf	Robt.	9	Clp	Jacob	195	Shn
Thomas	857	Sth	Thos.	5	Clp	John	195	Shn
William	522	Prw	William	541	Frd	Rudolph	195	Shn
William	145	Sth				Rudolph	230	Shn
Wm.	129	Sth				Rudolph	239	Shn
Buxton, Joseph	852	Sth	--- C ---			Cahal, Griffith	686	Br
Mary	877	Sth				Cahell, John	824	Wth
Patsey	813	Bck				Cahill, Dennis	568	Frd
Thos.	813	Nrf	C..., ...	456	Bdf	William	568	Frd
see Burton			... [2]	457	Bdf	Caho, Elizabeth	511	Prw
Buzard, Henry	225	Pnd	...	459	Bdf	John	508	Prw
Lewis	225	Pnd	... [2]	142	Dnw	William	507	Prw
Buzwell, George	191	Shn	James	457	Bdf	Cahoe, Bartholomew	18	Clp
Buzzard, Frederick	760	Hmp	Jasper	457	Bdf	Cahoon, Charles	613	Btt
Frederick	771	Hmp	Jesse	457	Bdf	James W.	501	Prw
Jacob	772	Hmp	L...	457	Bdf	Mark	298	Amh
John	771	Hmp	Leonard	457	Bdf	William	302	Amh
Leonard	440	Bth	Samuel, Sr.	457	Bdf	Caib, David	444	Bth
Martin	441	Bth	Waddy	457	Bdf	Cail see Caib		
Reuben	441	Bth	William	457	Bdf	Cain, Allen	631	Sss
Solomon	440	Bth	Wmson., ...r	142	Dnw	Carnelias	955	Hrr
Byant, John C.	44	Chr	C...alter, Robert	562	Mnr	Claiborne	328	Dnw
Byars, Flemen	708	Wsh	C...l...y, William, Sr.	456	Bdf	Claiborne	630	Sss
George	735	Wsh	C...le, France...	457	Bdf	Cor.	326	Ags
James	713	Wsh	C...le, John B.	142	Dnw	Daniel	769	Brn
Jno., Jur.	736	Wsh	C...perton, Hugh	562	Mnr	David	959	Hrr
John	319	Ags	C...rie, John	60	Stf	Edmond	936	Hrr
John	737	Wsh	C...rter, ...	458	Bdf	George	447	Grn
Leonrd	319	Ags	C...twood, John	457	Bdf	Henry	769	Brn
William, Capt.	717	Wsh	C...w, Lovel H.	457	Bdf	Isaac	936	Hrr
Byass see Byerss			Ca...er, James, Sr.	456	Bdf	Isham	630	Sss
Bybe, Pleasant	447	Flv	Caalt see Coalt			James	336	Dnw
Bybee, John	447	Flv	Cabaniss, Cassamer	480	Frn	Jessee	489	Mnn
Byers, Jno.	14	Clp	Courtland	472	Frn	John	447	Grn
Joseph	515	Frd	Cabbage see Cubbage			John	936	Hrr
Byerss, James	868	Hnv	Cabble, Ben	855	Cmp	John	633	Sss
Byne, Mary A.	156	Knq	Cabel, John	855	Cmp	Peter	769	Brn
Bynear, Elizabeth	514	Prw	Cabell, Federick	682	Nls	Peter	839	Nrf
Bynum, Britain	447	Grn	George	682	Nls	Peter	530	Prg
Byram, Fielding	525	Prw	George, Senr.	849	Cmp	Ricd.	492	Mnn
John	96	Spt	Jno. S., Est. in			Richd.	191	Elc
John	16	Wod	Bedford	489	Bdf	Ruffin	633	Sss
Nimrod	510	Prw	John	809	Bck	Shadk.	178	Elc
Peter	52	Stf	Joseph	827	Bck	Tho.	190	Elc
Sendte [Senate?]	23	Stf	Joseph C.	684	Nls	Thomas	974	Nrt
William	52	Stf	Landon	682	Nls	Thos.	492	Mnn
William	16	Wod	Nicholas, Est. of	683	Nls	Walter	680	Br
Byrd, Aaron	161	Sth	Robt.	26	Hnr	Walter	491	Mnn
Andw.	22	Rcm	Samuel	683	Nls	William	325	Dnw
David	159	Sth	William	683	Nls	William	103	Jff
Francis	541	Frd	William H., Bucking-			Caine, Micajah	457	Bdf
James	201	Ess	ham	683	Nls	Cairy, Edy	326	Dnw
Jesse	326	Dnw	William S.	684	Nls	Caiver, William	194	Kng
Mary	941	Chc	Cabeness, Asa	336	Lnn	Cake, Cloe	651	Glc
Nelly	601	Srr	Charles	336	Lnn	David	439	Mth
Peggy, (FN)	44	Chr	Cabler, Frederick	869	Cmp	Geo.	651	Glc
Reuben	330	Dnw	Cabrick, Peter	814	Hmp	Lewis	651	Glc
Richard W.	27	Isw	Cache, Charles	243	Aml	Calacoat, Elizabeth	456	Frn
Sally	332	Dnw	Cachley, Valentine	426	Bth	Calahan, John	823	Wth
Samuel, (free Negroe)	351	Fqr	Cade, Jacob	817	Hmp	Calamel, Moses	548	Frd
Thomas	402	Fqr	Moses	422	Rnd	Calan, Mary	305	Amh
Thomas	583	Frd	see Cave			Calaway, ---	481	Frn
Thomas	160	Sth	Cadell, Saml.	637	Mnt	Abner	479	Frn
William	154	Sth	Cadwallader, Elizabeth	513	Frd	Henry T.	482	Frn
William, (FN)	44	Chr	Cadwalleder, Malon	855	Cmp	James	478	Frn
Wm. P.	649	Glc	Cadwallender see Jones			John	457	Frn
Byrn, Chas.	484	Mnn	Cadwallider, ...	458	Bdf	Calbert, Nathaniel	101	Jff
James	398	Fqr	Mary	456	Bdf	Calbreath, John	614	Btt
Uriah	392	Fqr	Thomas	456	Bdf	Caldwel, Alexander	683	Br
see Burn			Caesar, Squire	689	Gch	Caldwell, Anna Linney	866	Cmp

Annas	331	Ags	Wm.	340	Lnc	Reuben	510	Prw
David	331	Ags	Callam see Collans			Robert	766	Hmp
David	917	Hrr	Callaun, William	896	Crl	Rolls	21	Clp
David	31	Rcm	Callaway, Dudley	278	Amh	Samuel	132	Sth
Elizabeth	26	Rcm	Francis	857	Cmp	Thomas	443	Pra
Henry	621	Gls	James	569	Mnr	Vincent	502	Prw
Hugh	613	Btt	James, [his] Exs.	462	Frn	William	516	Prw
Hugh	615	Btt	John	861	Cmp	Williams	489	Bdf
James	3	Oho	Joseph	866	Cmp	Calvin, Gabl.	20	Clp
James	283	Rck	Nancy	301	Amh	James	20	Clp
Jane	509	Frd	Zah.	569	Mnr	John	714	Wsh
John	331	Ags	Calleham, David	861	Cmp	Thomas	542	Brk
John	4	Oho	Stephen	868	Cmp	Calwell, Archibald	615	Btt
John	7	Oho	Callehan, Jas.	504	Brk	John	444	Bth
John	11	Oho	John	614	Btt	John	110	Cmb
John	181	Shn	Callen, Patrick	697	Wsh	John, Sr.	615	Btt
John	195	Shn	Callender, Saml., free			Mary	614	Btt
John, Jr.	615	Btt	Negro	614	Btt	Stephen	615	Btt
Joseph	551	Frd	Thomas	2	Oho	Thomas	106	Cmb
Joseph	2	Oho	Callenger, Wm.	893	Nrf	Wm.	615	Btt
Katty	331	Ags	Calley, John	28	Hnr	Cambell, Elizt.	410	Ags
Margaret	27	Rcm	see Colley			Camblin, Dav.	492	Mnn
Patrick	3	Wod	Callicoates, James,			Cambridge, ---	243	Ldn
Robert	612	Btt	(Est.)	46	Chr	Camden, Henry	287	Amh
Robert	328	Dnw	Califfe, Jeremh.	893	Nrf	Jabaz	280	Amh
Samuel	19	Oho	Callihan, John	826	Hmp	James	256	Amh
Sarah	296	Ldn	Callis, Abel	334	Lnn	Jno. W.	274	Rck
Smith	614	Btt	Ambros	450	Mth	John	686	Nls
William	620	Gls	Ambrose	445	Mth	John F.	256	Amh
William	181	Shn	Emanuel, Est.	335	Lnn	Leroy	261	Amh
William	107	Spt	Henry	334	Lnn	Micajah	282	Amh
Wm.	329	Ags	James	444	Mth	William	294	Amh
Wm.	747	Wsh	John	708	Brn	William W.	684	Nls
Wm., Sr.	614	Btt	John	440	Mth	Wyatt	686	Nls
see Calamell, Calwell			Richard	334	Lnn	see Gamdin		
Cale, Chrr.	492	Mnn	Robt.	442	Mth	Camdon, Washington	303	Rck
James	438	Bth	Wm.	863	Hnv	Camel, Andrew	950	Hrr
Jno.	492	Mnn	Wm.	444	Mth	see Commel		
see Cole, Kale			Callison, Anthony	427	Bth	Cameron, Allen	291	Rck
Calendine, Daniel	682	Br	Daniel	426	Bth	Charles	418	Bth
Daniel	698	Br	Daniel, sr.	423	Bth	Daniel	827	Wth
Martin	675	Br	Edward	426	Bth	Donald	541	Prg
Caler, Ann	114	Spt	Hiram	328	Ags	Evender	14	Acc
Mathias	619	Gls	Isaac	425	Bth	James	688	Br
Caleste see McCaleste			James	425	Bth	James	827	Wth
Calfee, Henry	823	Wth	Mary	427	Bth	Jno.	22	Clp
James	824	Wth	Robt.	328	Ags	John	690	Br
John	823	Wth	Calliss, Richd. N.	196	Ess	Meleno	892	Nrf
Mary	824	Wth	Calliway, Elijah	619	Gls	Robert	287	Amh
William	824	Wth	Isiah	619	Gls	Sophia	598	Brk
Calhoon, Adam	559	Pre	Calloms, James	193	Kng	Thomas	690	Br
George, Dr.	45	Chr	Calloway, Achilles	457	Bdf	Wm.	891	Nrf
James	559	Pre	Jeremiah	456	Bdf	Camm, John	284	Amh
Jno.	18	Clp	Joel	457	Bdf	Thos., [his] Este.	682	Wrw
Mark	825	Wth	Joshua	566	Mnr	Cammac, Wm.	891	Nrf
Wm.	399	Ags	Mary	456	Bdf	Cammack, George	102	Spt
Calhoun see Collawn			William	457	Bdf	Cammel, Sharlot	117	Spt
Calliff, James	799	Bck	William, ...	457	Bdf	Cammell, Ann	891	Nrf
Caliham, Daniel	736	Wsh	see C...l...y			Ann	892	Nrf
Caliman, Moses	546	Frd	Callthorp, Will.	874	Sth	Charles	891	Nrf
Calimus, George	817	Hmp	Calmes, Spencer	168	Shn	Fanny	115	Spt
Calky, Thomas	274	Rck	Calt see Coalt			Nancy	105	Spt
Call, Adam	326	Dnw	Calvan, Joshua	789	Hmp	Cammer see Commer		
Charles	830	Bck	Luther	790	Hmp	Cammeron, John	336	Lnn
Daniel	35	Hnr	Robert	775	Hmp	Camnitz, John	2	Oho
Isaac, [his] Est.	194	Kng	Samuel	778	Hmp	Camonel, James	219	Pnd
James	826	Wth	Calvart, George	245	Frf	Sameul	219	Pnd
John	825	Wth	Calvert, ---, Mrs.	891	Nrf	Camp, ---, Mrs.	63	Clp
Mac.	35	Hnr	Catharine	507	Prw	Abrm.	298	Rck
Maurice L.	830	Bck	Enoch	565	Frd	Adam	488	Mnn
Trissy	328	Dnw	Francis	503	Prw	Eliza.	23	Clp
William	541	Prg	George	245	Frf	G.W.	893	Nrf
Callaghan, Charles	429	Bth	Hannah	447	Pra	Geo.	860	Sth
Dennis	417	Bth	Hanse	400	Ags	Hansford	891	Nrf
John	418	Bth	Jesse	567	Frd	Isaac	488	Mnn
Callaham, Moses	334	Lnn	John	510	Prw	James M.	953	Hrr
Sam,(free)	334	Lnn	John	524	Prw	Jno.	650	Glc
Callahan, Charles	769	Wst	Margaret	443	Pra	John	745	Brn
Griffin	18	Acc	Margte.	892	Nrf	John	891	Nrf
Jane	861	Hnv	Matt	126	Sth	Jordon	453	Frn

Name	Page	Co.
Matthew	880	Sth
Miles	650	Glc
Miles, Gloucester		
Town	650	Glc
Richard	894	Crl
Robert	454	Frn
Robert	269	Ldn
Robt., & Mother	17	Clp
Steven	19	Oho
Thomas	452	Frn
Thos.	156	Sth
William	453	Frn
William	686	Nls
Willis	19	Clp
Wm.	19	Clp
Wm.	650	Glc
Wm. G.	891	Nrf
Wm. S.	650	Glc
see Canep		
Camp...ll, ...hn	458	Bdf
Campaign, John	118	Spt
Campbel, Alexander	690	Br
James	690	Br
John	677	Br
John	686	Br
John	568	Mnr
John	10	Oho
Joseph	689	Br
Richard	16	Oho
Robert	698	Br
Robert	583	Mnr
William	688	Br
Campbell, ...ary	168	Shn
...hn	458	Bdf
...s	458	Bdf
A. A.	1	Ntt
Abraham	188	Shn
Abrm.	304	Rck
Alex, Snr.	159	Knq
Alexand., jr.	159	Knq
Alexander	419	Bth
Ambrose	275	Amh
Ambrous	682	Nls
Andrew	579	Frd
Andrew	259	Ldn
Andw.	24	Rcm
Anthony	457	Bdf
Archibald	347	Fqr
Archibd.	889	Yrk
Charles	297	Rck
Collin	334	Dnw
Collin	513	Prw
Colon	719	Wsh
Cornelius	878	Cmp
Danl.	616	Btt
David	598	Brk
David	688	Wsh
Dolley	328	Dnw
Dugal	539	Brk
Duncan	293	Rck
Edward	616	Btt
Edwd.	291	Rck
Edwd.	690	Wsh
Elias	23	Clp
Elijah	22	Clp
Elizabeth	278	Amh
Elizabeth	461	Mdd
Elliott	894	Crl
Finley	510	Brk
Francis	685	Nls
Francis, Ju.	685	Nls
Geo.	22	Clp
Geo.	341	Lnc
George	303	Amh
George	718	Wsh
Harroway	21	Clp
Henry	458	Bdf
Henry	910	Hrr
Henry	683	Nls
Henry	686	Nls
Hugh	326	Ags
Hugh	218	Ess
Hugh K.	420	Fqr
Isaac	360	Fqr
Iver	510	Frd
J. W.	332	Dnw
Jack	332	Dnw
Jael	685	Nls
James	259	Amh
James	326	Ags
James	457	Bdf
James [2]	539	Brk
James	65	Chs
James	158	Knq
James	273	Ldn
James	311	Ldn
James	685	Nls
James	686	Nls
James	974	Nrt
James	520	Prw
James	40	Rcm
James	707	Wsh
James	728	Wsh
James	825	Wth
Jane	300	Rck
Jane	2	Rcm
Jno.	15	Clp
Jno.	268	Ldn
Jno.	288	Ldn
Jno.	306	Ldn
Jno.	20	Ntt
Jno., Capt.	726	Wsh
Joel	299	Amh
Joel	291	Rck
John	259	Amh
John	325	Ags
John	613	Btt
John	347	Fqr
John	463	Frn
John	530	Frd
John	552	Frd
John	563	Frd
John	574	Frd
John	600	Frd
John	7	Knw
John	336	Lnn
John	685	Nls
John	6	Oho
John	10	Oho
John	15	Oho
John	25	Oho
John	518	Prw
John	280	Rck
John	21	Rcm
John	706	Wsh
John	769	Wst
John, jur.	690	Wsh
John H.	196	Shn
Jos.	487	Mnn
Larrance	399	Amh
Lewis	869	Cmp
Lewis	878	Cmp
Margret	591	Mnr
Mary	825	Wth
Matthew	895	Crl
Morgan	22	Clp
Moses	799	Hmp
Nathaniel	380	Fqr
Owin	21	Clp
Parker	457	Bdf
Patk.	614	Btt
Patrick	616	Btt
Patrick	738	Wsh
Patty	521	Prw
Peter	682	Nls
Price	908	Hrr
Reuben	20	Clp
Richard	23	Oho
Robert	457	Bdf
Robert	3	Knw
Robert	279	Ldn
Robt.	326	Ags
Robt.	544	Brk
Robt.	691	Wsh
Robt., (F. Mo.)	19	Clp
Rogers	499	Frn
Rosanna	509	Frd
Runy	804	Hmp
Salley	974	Nrt
Saml.	299	Rck
Saml.	748	Wsh
Saml. L.	263	Rck
Samuel	804	Hmp
Samuel	686	Nls
Sarah	592	Mnr
Sarah	500	Prw
Sarah	717	Wsh
Susan	770	Wst
Susanh.	616	Btt
Tandy	328	Ags
Thomas	458	Bdf
Thomas	459	Bdf
Thomas	498	Frn
Thomas	553	Frd
Thomas	974	Nrt
Thos.	331	Ags
Thos.	489	Mnn
Thos.	795	Nrf
Thos.	448	Pra
Whitaker	160	Knq
Wiley	258	Amh
Willey	159	Knq
William	441	Bth
William	457	Bdf
William	458	Bdf
William	870	Cmp
William	895	Crl
William	460	Frn
William	488	Frn
William	575	Frd
William	932	Hrr
William	12	Isw
William	74	Jff
William	571	Mnr
William	686	Nls
William	2	Rcm
William	8	Rcm
William	726	Wsh
William	824	Wth
William, jr.	159	Knq
Willm.	612	Btt
Wm.	612	Btt
Wm.	259	Ldn
Wm.	489	Mnn
Wm.	583	Mnr
Wm.	591	Mnr
Wm.	444	Pra
Wm.	293	Rck
Wm., Sen.	159	Knq
Wm. C.	612	Btt
Zachariah	896	Crl
see ...ampbell, Burton,		
Cambell, Camp...ll,		
Campell, Daniel, McCamp-		
bell, Nance		
Campble, Cornelius	243	Shn
Campbll, John	6	Oho
Campell, ---, & Paul	21	Hnr
Camper, Elice	614	Btt
Harman	616	Btt
Harmon	456	Bdf
James	612	Btt
Jessee	614	Btt
Jno., Sr.	612	Btt
John, Jr.	614	Btt
Simond	613	Btt
Solomon	614	Btt
see Carper		
Campher, Michal	581	Frd
Camran, Judith	899	Hnv

Name	Page	Co.
Camron, Daniel	101	Jff
Duncan	685	Nls
Salley	123	Hnr
William	75	Jff
see Cannon		
Camuck, James	824	Wth
John	824	Wth
Canada, Jno.	1	Hnr
Martin	870	Hnv
Moses	6	Knw
Canaday, Mary	247	Shn
Caty	379	Mds
Fauntley	195	Kng
John	45	Chr
John	933	Hrr
John	973	Nrt
Joseph	188	Alb
Leroy	379	Mds
Susin	33	Hnr
Whorton	379	Mds
Canaggy, Eliza.	17	Clp
Canby, Benj.	305	Ldn
Samuel	810	Hmp
Sarah	892	Nrf
Cance see Lance		
Candler, Penelope	853	Cmp
Cane, Jeremiah	813	Nrf
Jeremiah	444	Pra
John	4	Wod
Mary	293	Ldn
Canelee, Henry	15	Oho
Canep, James	827	Wth
Caney, Jas., (G.)	817	Nrf
see Carney		
Canfield, Daniel	430	Rnd
Canidy, George, Jr.	457	Bdf
George, sr.	457	Bdf
Cann, John	784	Hmp
Sarah	834	Nrf
Cannady, Daniel	17	Clp
David	17	Ntt
Isaac	917	Hrr
James	17	Clp
William	159	Knq
Cannafax, Edward	859	Cmp
Radford	859	Cmp
William	871	Cmp
Canniel see Canelee		
Cannifax, Wm.	582	Mnr
Canning, George	781	Hmp
Cannon, Elizabeth	444	Pra
Fanny	410	Rch
Francis	508	Prw
George	897	Crl
Henry	332	Dnw
Jacob	785	Hmp
James	19	Clp
James	7	Hnr
Jas., Senr.	19	Clp
Jno.	23	Clp
Jno.	444	Pra
Jno., (Pungo)	446	Pra
John	513	Prw
Leanard	804	Hmp
Luke	509	Prw
Robert	677	Br
Stephen	894	Crl
Wm.	447	Pra
Canody, Ians	955	Hrr
Jams	963	Hrr
Canon, James	409	Fqr
Canor, James	361	Fqr
see Caron		
Canson see Carrson		
Canter, Henry	745	Wsh
John	573	Frd
R.	29	Hnr
Canterberry, Joel	621	Gls
John	572	Mnr
Canterbery, Joseph	619	Gls
Canterbury, John	3	Knw
Saml.	567	Mnr
Cantley, James	564	Mnr
Cantly, Rebecca	565	Mnr
Cantrell, John	426	Msn
Cantsill, John	13	Knw
Capeheart, Philip	424	Msn
Capel, Wilkinson	145	Sth
Capell, Robertson	130	Sth
Thomas	877	Sth
Caperton, Adam	569	Mnr
Hugh	621	Gls
see C...perton		
Capharte, Dolley	8	Hnr
Capito, Daniel	227	Pnd
Caplin, Cristopher	3	Wod
Isaac	930	Hrr
Caplinger, Adam	220	Pnd
Christley	30	Rcm
George	220	Pnd
George	421	Rnd
George	30	Wod
John	15	Wod
Leonard	14	Wod
Capparl, David	115	Hnr
Jonas	115	Hnr
Cappelar, Wm.	23	Clp
Capper, Sarah	776	Hmp
Cappermage, J.B.	892	Nrf
Capps, Andrew	443	Pra
Anna	446	Pra
Anna	447	Pra
Argin	448	Pra
Avarilla	447	Pra
Batson	446	Pra
Charles	446	Pra
Denis	446	Pra
Dinnis	443	Pra
Frances	444	Pra
Francis	444	Pra
Henry	445	Pra
Hillary	443	Pra
Hillary	446	Pra
Jesse	443	Pra
Jno.	446	Pra
Joel	447	Pra
Lancaster	448	Pra
Lydia	443	Pra
Lydia	448	Pra
Mary	446	Pra
Maryan	446	Pra
Morris	447	Pra
Moses	446	Pra
Moses, (of Ml.[?])	447	Pra
Rody, (wd. Wm.)	447	Pra
Sally	443	Pra
Sarah	447	Pra
Solo., (of Jno.)	444	Pra
Willoughby	443	Pra
Willoughby	446	Pra
Capron, Elizth.	892	Nrf
Carahoof, J.F.	326	Ags
John	326	Ags
Carbaugh, Christian	5	Rcm
Card see Curd		
Carden, Archer	688	Gch
David	687	Gch
Juriah	687	Gch
Reuben	687	Gch
Robt.	328	Ags
Robt.	687	Gch
Carder, Abbott	757	Hmp
Benja.	23	Clp
Burkett	380	Mds
French	778	Hmp
George, Jur.	789	Hmp
George, Ser.	789	Hmp
James	20	Clp
John	926	Hrr
Larrence	904	Hrr
Lucy	18	Clp
Mildred	18	Clp
Uriah	16	Clp
William	618	Gls
William	913	Hrr
William	380	Mds
Wm., (R. Oak)	24	Clp
Wm. J.	21	Clp
Cardin, Jesse	7	Pwh
Joseph	612	Btt
Cardon, Robert	631	Mnt
Cardozo, Aaron	10	Pwh
Abraham	123	Hnr
Jacob W.	111	Cmb
Moses N.	10	Pwh
Cardwell, Francis	14	Ntt
George	244	Aml
George	559	Pre
James	158	Knq
John	158	Knq
Kitty	873	Yrk
Peter, ([his] Est.)	45	Chr
Richd.	244	Aml
Richd.	142	Dnw
Wilcher	45	Chr
Wm., jr.	18	Clp
Care, Philip	896	Crl
Carell, John	523	Brk
Carey, Diana	770	Wst
John	828	Hmp
Miles	440	Flv
Obidiah	891	Nrf
Richard	46	Chr
Sarah	46	Chr
Soloman	684	Nls
William	801	Bck
Wilson J.	440	Flv
Wilson M.	440	Flv
Wm.	891	Nrf
Cargill, John	634	Sss
Nathaniel	630	Sss
Cargoe, William	17	Wod
Carick, Saml.	283	Rck
William	896	Crl
Carier, Bailey	652	Mnt
see Caiver		
Carius see Carnes		
Carler see Carter		
Carley, Allen	456	Bdf
James S.	11	Wod
see Corley		
Carlile, David	542	Frd
John	434	Bth
John	688	Gch
Robert	434	Bth
Samuel	692	Br
William	689	Br
Carlin, Mary	242	Frf
Carline, Margte.	892	Nrf
Carlisle, Robert	317	Ldn
Robert	578	Mnr
Carlow, Francis	69	Jff
Carlten see Cartlen		
Carlton, Ambrose	895	Crl
Ann	160	Knq
Archibald	158	Knq
Baylor	212	Ess
Benonie	159	Knq
Christopher, jr.	159	Knq
Christopher, Snr.	158	Knq
Elijah	158	Knq
Frances	160	Knq
Henry	616	Btt
Humphrey	158	Knq
James	616	Btt
Jas.	160	Knq
Joel	158	Knq
John, jr.	160	Knq
John, Snr.	160	Knq
John S.	160	Knq

Name	No.	Co.	Name	No.	Co.	Name	No.	Co.
Lewis, Sen.	159	Knq	John	25	Rcm	Isaac	568	Mnr
Martha	159	Knq	Neven	27	Hnr	Jacob	615	Btt
Mary	160	Knq	Nicholas	25	Rcm	John	638	Mnt
Nathan	159	Knq	Peter	424	Rnd	Joseph	823	Wth
Noah	159	Knq	Carnwell, William	603	Srr	Nicholas	615	Btt
Robert	895	Crl	Carny, John	951	Hrr	Philip	546	Frd
William	158	Knq	John	821	Nrf	William	546	Frd
Wm., Jr.	616	Btt	Wm.	444	Mth	Willm.	638	Mnt
Wm., Sr.	616	Btt	Caron, William	361	Fqr	see Camper		
Carly, Davd.	692	Wsh	see Coram			Carpinter, David	935	Hrr
Carlyle, George	832	Hmp	Carpenter, Abraham	381	Mds	John	745	Brn
William	832	Hmp	Amelia	1	Oho	Willis	746	Brn
William, sen.	832	Hmp	Andrew	381	Mds	Wm.	719	Wsh
Carmack, John	705	Wsh	Angelana	23	Clp	Carr, Abram	880	Sth
John, Jur.	705	Wsh	Aron	381	Mds	Abrm.	126	Sth
William	705	Wsh	Benjamin	258	Amh	Anderson B.	189	Alb
Wm., R.V.	746	Wsh	Benjamin	380	Mds	Andrew	42	Isw
Carman, Henry	106	Jff	Benjn.	14	Ntt	Arthur	159	Sth
Carmichael, Daniel	770	Wst	Charles	84	Acc	Dabney	188	Alb
Daniel	833	Hmp	Charles	88	Acc	Dabny	152	Alb
Hugh	26	Oho	Christopher	3	Wod	Daniel	498	Prw
James	116	Spt	Cornelias	380	Mds	Daniel	507	Prw
John	6	Oho	Eaton	258	Amh	David	42	Isw
John	17	Oho	Elijah	708	Wsh	Elizabeth	10	Pwh
Judy	195	Kng	Elizabeth	93	Spt	Garland	189	Alb
Thomas	23	Oho	Enoch	300	Amh	George	32	Rcm
Carmichel, John	629	Mnt	Ephraham	381	Mds	Gideon	152	Alb
Carmikle, Thomas	824	Wth	George	11	Rcm	Hardy	43	Isw
Carmine, Smith	13	Acc	George	769	Wst	Jacob	581	Frd
Carminy, John	329	Ags	Henry	86	Spt	Jacob	44	Isw
Carna, Jno.	305	Ldn	Hensley	300	Amh	Jacob	220	Pnd
Carnagie, Mary	19	Clp	Isaac	745	Brn	James	152	Alb
Carnagy, William	601	Frd	Jacob	88	Acc	James	279	Ldn
Carnal, Achilles	894	Crl	Jacob	426	Rnd	James	3	Ntt
Ann	898	Crl	James	278	Amh	James	561	Pre
Elizabeth	896	Crl	James	576	Frd	James	420	Rnd
James	897	Crl	James	274	Ldn	John	152	Alb
James S.	897	Crl	James	272	Rck	John	457	Bdf
Nancy	896	Crl	James	770	Wst	John	22	Isw
Patrick	896	Crl	James, a free mulatto	974	Nrt	John	600	Mnr
Pleasant	896	Crl	Jane	434	Bth	John	685	Nls
Richmond	894	Crl	Jerremiah	418	Rnd	John	812	Nrf
William	896	Crl	Jno.	339	Lnc	John	1	Oho
Carnan see Carvan			Jno.	488	Mnn	John	503	Prw
Carnavan, William	522	Frd	Jno., Jr.	488	Mnn	John	431	Rnd
Carne, Barbary	285	Ldn	Joel	380	Mds	John	16	Rcm
Jacob	285	Ldn	John	4	Oho	John	152	Sth
Wm.	292	Ldn	John	770	Wst	John	161	Sth
Carnel, George	90	Spt	John C. A.	403	Rch	John, Sen.	42	Isw
Carner, David	457	Bdf	Jonas	381	Mds	Joseph	240	Ldn
William	457	Bdf	Joseph	413	Bth	Larkin	509	Prw
see Casner			Joseph	380	Mds	Leah	827	Wth
Carnes, Abram	284	Ldn	Joseph	62	Stf	Lucy	152	Alb
George	615	Btt	Joseph	711	Wsh	Marcus	582	Frd
Joseph	188	Alb	Martial	708	Brn	Mary	189	Alb
Carney, Banabas	817	Nrf	Mary	745	Brn	Mary	893	Nrf
Benjamin	512	Prw	Mary	381	Mds	Meekins	188	Alb
George	512	Prw	Mathew	18	Clp	Micajah	188	Alb
Iveson	649	Glc	Pleasant	188	Alb	Mills	24	Isw
Jas., (B.H.)	817	Nrf	Richd.	745	Brn	Nelly	508	Prw
Jas., (jr.)	817	Nrf	Robert	413	Bth	Peter	188	Alb
Jno.	649	Glc	Saml.	613	Btt	Peter	295	Ldn
Jno.	650	Glc	Saml.	6	Ntt	Rebecca	33	Isw
John	816	Nrf	Samuel	381	Mds	Richard	574	Frd
John	817	Nrf	Samuel, Jr.	380	Mds	Robert	151	Sth
Joshua	41	Stf	Samul	17	Oho	Samuel	188	Alb
Silas	512	Prw	Simeon	381	Mds	Samuel	569	Frd
Thomas	911	Hrr	Solomon	381	Mds	Samuel	305	Ldn
Thos.	817	Nrf	Solomon	430	Rnd	Seaborn	532	Frd
Wm.	649	Glc	William	7	Rcm	Thomas	457	Bdf
Wright	817	Nrf	William	769	Wst	Thomas	573	Frd
see Caney			William, Rt.	381	Mds	Thomas	44	Isw
Carnine, Philip	519	Brk	Wm.	339	Lnc	Thomas	294	Ldn
Richd.	519	Brk	Wm.	273	Ldn	William	457	Bdf
Carnohan, John	76	Spt	Wm.	274	Ldn	William	581	Frd
Joseph	82	Spt	Carper, Abram	913	Hrr	William	143	Sth
Carns, Ann	22	Rcm	Benjn.	612	Btt	Willis	23	Isw
Billey	123	Hnr	Frederick	546	Frd	Wm.	329	Ags
Jacob	615	Btt	Fridk	638	Mnt	Wm.	294	Ldn
John	12	Rcm	Henry	474	Frn	see Bowers		

Carrall, Sterling	746	Brn	Carruthers, Thos.	538	Brk	David	654	Mnt
Carraway, Sarah	442	Pra	Carry, Mil.	492	Mnn	Dorathy	443	Mth
Thos.	443	Pra	Carseley, Elizabeth	603	Srr	E.	8	Hnr
Carrel, Jno.	488	Mnn	Hartwell	603	Srr	Eden	260	Ldn
Robt.	653	Mnt	Lucy	603	Srr	Edmund	546	Frd
Samuel, Sr.	606	Mnt	Richard	603	Srr	Edward	266	Amh
Sarah	151	Alb	William	603	Srr	Edward	949	Chc
Wm.	400	Ags	Carson, Abram	326	Ags	Edward	396	Fqr
Carrell, Elizabeth	152	Alb	Andrew	799	Nrf	Edward	728	Wsh
Jesse	577	Frd	Beatty	514	Frd	Edward, decd.	520	Prw
John	423	Msn	Charles S.	760	Wsh	Edward H.	270	Amh
John	602	Srr	Davd.	696	Wsh	Edwd.	239	Ldn
Lewis	152	Alb	David	456	Bdf	Elijah	84	Spt
Martha	603	Srr	Elizabeth	602	Frd	Eliza.	16	Clp
Peter	603	Srr	George	112	Cmb	Elizabeth	298	Amh
Sarah	859	Sth	George	365	Fqr	Elizabeth	896	Crl
Valintine	328	Ags	James, Sr.	862	Cmp	Elizabeth	128	Hnr
W...	602	Srr	John	807	Bck	Elizabeth	892	Nrf
William	153	Alb	John	595	Mnr	Elizabeth	523	Prw
Wm.	262	Ldn	John	561	Pre	Elizabeth	118	Spt
Carren, Jane	839	Nrf	John	166	Shn	Elizabeth	604	Srr
Carrico, James	243	Ldn	Joseph	98	Cmb	Ephraim	253	Ldn
P.	490	Mnn	Joseph	769	Wst	Ezekiel	541	Frd
Carricoe, Barton	520	Prw	Martin	283	Rck	Fanny	642	Mnt
William, Jr.	521	Prw	Richard	44	Isw	Fitzhugh	245	Frf
William, Sr.	521	Prw	Richard	17	Oho	Fleming	299	Amh
Carrida, John, F.N.	632	Sss	Robert	44	Chr	Francis	129	Hnr
Carrier, Edmund	242	Shn	Robet.	805	Nrf	Freeman [crossed		
Henry	173	Shn	Robt.	328	Ags	out]	753	Wsh
Richd.	32	Rcm	Saml.	328	Ags	Geo.	341	Lnc
Solomon	174	Shn	Saml.	280	Rck	Geo.	263	Ldn
Carrington, Benjamin	116	Cmb	Saml.	696	Wsh	Geo. [2]	309	Ldn
Clement	44	Chr	Samuel	688	Br	Geo., [his] Est.	341	Lnc
Colly	124	Cmb	Samuel	864	Cmp	George	820	Bck
Edwd.	117	Hnr	Simon	566	Frd	George	885	Hnv
Francis	607	Brn	Thomas	523	Frd	George	770	Wst
Jenny	891	Nrf	Thomas	103	Jff	George, (of Jno.)	367	Fqr
John	534	Frd	William	864	Cmp	George, Senr.	375	Fqr
Joseph	124	Cmb	Wm.	801	Nrf	Hamlin	603	Srr
Littleberry	116	Cmb	Wm., jr.	805	Nrf	Harris	630	Sss
Nancy	132	Hnr	Carsons, William	163	Shn	Harrison	561	Pre
Patrick	708	Brn	William	164	Shn	Henry	268	Amh
Paul, Junr., Hon.	44	Chr	Carstaphen, Purkins	19	Isw	Henry	240	Ldn
Paul, Senr.	44	Chr	Cart, Conrad	591	Mnr	Henry	642	Mnt
Paul J.	110	Cmb	George	583	Mnr	Henry	56	Stf
Timothy	246	Frf	Cartar, Joseph	547	Frd	Henry	753	Wsh
William	128	Cmb	Carten see Carter			Henry, (FN)	46	Chr
Wm.	1	Pwh	Carter, ...	603	Srr	Hesikiah	115	Cmb
Carrol, Booker	689	Gch	Abner	770	Wst	Hill	298	Amh
Daniel	688	Gch	Abram	262	Amh	Isaac	347	Fqr
David	689	Gch	Agness	239	Ldn	Isaac	513	Frd
Joseph	5	Knw	Alexander	541	Frd	Isham	128	Cmb
Lance.	491	Mnn	Ammon	788	Bck	Jack	258	Amh
Malachi	447	Pra	Ann	549	Frd	Jacob	328	Dnw
Mary	891	Nrf	Anthony, F.N.	633	Sss	Jacob	129	Hnr
Peggy	195	Kng	Arthur	7	Oho	James	188	Alb
Samuel	28	Isw	Arthur W.	549	Frd	James	456	Bdf
William	5	Knw	Asa	261	Ldn	James	895	Crl
William	448	Pra	Benjamin	803	Bck	James	122	Cmb
Wm.	616	Btt	Bernard	365	Fqr	James	549	Frd
Carroll, Anth.	491	Mnn	Betty	328	Dnw	James	689	Gch
Charles	786	Hmp	Bob, F.N.	630	Sss	James	193	Kng
David	786	Hmp	Burwell	142	Dnw	James	238	Ldn
Dorathy	245	Frf	Charles	212	Ess	James	261	Ldn
Grey	47	Isw	Charles	535	Frd	Jane	245	Frf
Henry	632	Sss	Charles	428	Msn	Jane	824	Wth
James	35	Isw	Charles	173	Shn	Jas.	340	Lnc
Jas.	491	Mnn	Charles	66	Spt	Jas., Jr.	341	Lnc
Jesse	433	Flv	Charles, decd.	521	Prw	Jessee	117	Cmb
Jno.	245	Frf	Charles L.	377	Fqr	Jno.	20	Clp
Joseph	13	Isw	Charles L.	112	Spt	Jno.	4	Hnr
Mark	632	Sss	Cloe	342	Lnc	Jno.	341	Lnc
Mary	391	Fqr	Curtis	3	Hnr	Jno.	253	Ldn
Thomas	244	Frf	Dabney	460	Frn	Jno.	304	Rck
Thomas	25	Isw	Dandon	522	Prw	Jno., Jr.	342	Lnc
Warren	51	Stf	Daniel	897	Hnv	Jno. F., Estate	245	Frf
William	152	Alb	Daniel	560	Pre	Joanna	207	Ess
William	632	Sss	Daniel	404	Rch	Job	489	Frn
Wm.	244	Frf	Davd.	713	Wsh	John	457	Bdf
Carrson, Michael	8	Oho	Davd., R.V.	728	Wsh	John	803	Bck

John	816	Bck	Richard	2	Oho	Henry	13	Knw
John	894	Crl	Richard	9	Oho	James	4	Knw
John	895	Crl	Richard	632	Sss	Cartmill, John, Sr.	612	Btt
John	896	Crl	Richd.	127	Hnr	Joseph	573	Frd
John	897	Crl	Robert	200	Ess	Martin	575	Frd
John	44	Chr	Robert	934	Hrr	Nathaniel	575	Frd
John	211	Ess	Robert	93	Jff	Cartnael, Jno.	305	Ldn
John	385	Fqr	Robert	583	Mnr	Cartright, Jesse	564	Mnr
John	408	Fqr	Robert	683	Nls	Jno.	290	Rck
John	548	Frd	Robert	561	Pre	Jno. S.	247	Frf
John	563	Frd	Robert	514	Prw	Cartwell, Henry, Sr.	612	Btt
John	830	Hmp	Robert	770	Wst	Cartwright, Eliza	443	Pra
John	131	Hnr	Robert C.	382	Mds	Carty, Danl.	246	Frf
John	160	Knq	Robt. C., Este.	18	Clp	Carus see Carns		
John	490	Mnn	St. Leger Landon	193	Kng	Caruthers, David	331	Ags
John	652	Mnt	Salley	67	Chs	George	792	Hmp
John	682	Nls	Sally	769	Wst	George	805	Hmp
John	683	Nls	Samuel	576	Frd	Hannah	590	Brk
John	684	Nls	Samuel	281	Ldn	James	3	Knw
John	748	Nwk	Samuel	561	Pre	James	262	Rck
John	561	Pre	Sandon, Este.	18	Clp	Jane	537	Brk
John	509	Prw	Sarah	891	Nrf	John	576	Mnr
John	403	Rch	Sarah	509	Prw	John	262	Rck
John	92	Spt	Sarahah	24	Clp	Joseph	306	Rck
John	109	Spt	Shadrach	683	Nls	Robt.	293	Rck
John, jr.	118	Cmb	Solomon	728	Wsh	Thos.	329	Ags
John, Snr.	118	Cmb	Sooky	634	Sss	Wm.	262	Rck
John C.	685	Nls	Thadeus	974	Nrt	Carvan, Adam	616	Btt
John W.	686	Nls	Theodere K.	125	Hnr	Carvel, Dempe.	937	Hrr
Jonathan	236	Ldn	Theoderick	129	Hnr	Carvender, Molly	770	Wst
Jos.	2	Hnr	Tho., Jr.	340	Lnc	Thomas	769	Wst
Jos.	340	Lnc	Tho., Senr.	341	Lnc	Carver, Anchilles	190	Alb
Jos., Jr.	340	Lnc	Thomas	152	Alb	Cornelius	188	Alb
Jos., Jr., Shff.	368	Lnc	Thomas	616	Btt	Enoch	189	Alb
Joseph	456	Bdf	Thomas	796	Bck	Henry	689	Gch
Joseph	457	Bdf	Thomas	372	Fqr	Henry	908	Hrr
Joseph	895	Crl	Thomas	846	Hnv	James	153	Alb
Joseph	551	Frd	Thomas	194	Kng	James	189	Alb
Joseph	764	Hmp	Thomas N.	505	Prw	Jarrel	189	Alb
Joseph	277	Ldn	Thompson	824	Wth	Jasper	518	Frd
Joseph	45	Stf	Thos.	21	Clp	John	193	Kng
Joseph, sr.	457	Bdf	W. B.	242	Frf	Johnson E.	182	Alb
Josiah	457	Bdf	Walker	500	Frn	Lorrence	189	Alb
Judeah	15	Hnr	Walker R.	86	Spt	Mary	195	Kng
Katy	894	Crl	William	456	Bdf	Reubin	279	Amh
Keziah	875	Hnv	William [2]	457	Bdf	Richard	189	Alb
Landon	193	Kng	William	372	Fqr	Thomas	846	Hnv
Landon	342	Lnc	William	687	Gch	Townshd.	193	Kng
Landon	244	Ldn	William	127	Hnr	Valentine	548	Frd
Landon	973	Nrt	William	382	Mds	William	182	Alb
Landon	399	Rch	William	682	Nls	William	189	Alb
Laudon	243	Frf	William	973	Nrt	Wim.	869	Hnv
Lewis	194	Kng	William	561	Pre	see Caiver, Crven		
Loyal	20	Stf	William	509	Prw	Carvil, William	931	Hrr
Lucey	6	Hnr	William	514	Prw	Carvin, Edwd.	613	Btt
Mahlon	239	Ldn	William, senr.	560	Pre	Richard	616	Btt
Maria	9	Oho	Winnefred	83	Spt	Carwell, Michl.	330	Ags
Martha	116	Hnr	Wm.	31	Hnr	Carwiles, Jacob, Jr.	882	Cmp
Martin	342	Lnc	Wm.	261	Ldn	Jacob, Sr.	882	Cmp
Mary	244	Aml	Wm.	588	Mnr	Sally	68	Chr
Mary	90	Spt	Wm.	7	Ntt	Carwood, John	14	Wod
Mary E.	152	Alb	Wm., (S.S.)	16	Clp	Cary, Ann	678	Wrw
Miles	46	Chr	Wm. C.	17	Clp	Bartlett	10	Hnr
Millinder	22	Stf	Wm. F.	36	Hnr	Benjamin	329	Dnw
Mitchel	824	Wth	Wormly	523	Prw	Chrisr.	595	Frd
Moore F.	377	Fqr	see Adcocky, Berkeley,			David	959	Chc
Nathon	740	Wsh	Beverly, Bull, Ca...er,			Eliza.	138	Sth
Peggy	896	Crl	Caiter, Carder, Casler,			Frances	68	Spt
Peter	270	Amh	Collins, Gilliam, Hamlet,			Frs., (F. Negro)	22	Clp
Peter	973	Nrt	Little, Longest, Moody,			George	769	Wst
Philip	898	Crl	Williams			Harwood	559	Pre
Phillip	500	Frn	Carthrae, John, (Sen.)	36	Rcm	Henry	490	Mnn
Pledge	560	Pre	Carthrea, Jack, (FN)	36	Rcm	Isabellai	243	Frf
Poval	560	Pre	John	3	Rcm	Jno. R., Gloucester		
Presley	898	Crl	William	8	Rcm	Town	650	Glc
Presley	379	Fqr	Cartie, Jno.	19	Clp	Jack	335	Dnw
Rawley	335	Lnn	Cartlage, Lucey	406	Fqr	John	180	Elc
Rawley, Senr.	19	Ntt	Cartlen, John	127	Hnr	Joseph	603	Srr
Richard	45	Chr	Cartling, Andrew	115	Hnr	Lidia	292	Amh
Richard	974	Nrt	Cartmell, David	2	Knw	Lowdon	327	Dnw

Name	No.	Abbr.	Name	No.	Abbr.	Name	No.	Abbr.
Mason	326	Dnw	Casley, Pheeby	222	Pnd	Cateton, Mily	189	Alb
Miles	956	Chc	Casner, Vandle	430	Rnd	William	189	Alb
Miles	191	Elc	Cason, Andw.	329	Ags	Cather, Jasper	576	Frd
Miles	10	Pwh	Bartlett	870	Hnv	Joseph	675	Br
Nancy	543	Frd	Batson	446	Pra	Margaret	905	Hrr
Nancy	14	Hnr	Edward	76	Spt	William	332	Dnw
Sarah	681	Wrw	Erasmus	446	Pra	Catherwood, Charles	906	Hrr
Sarah, (Y)	872	Yrk	Hillary	443	Pra	Cathon, Calia	161	Sth
Soloman, Ju.	684	Nls	Jacamine	446	Pra	Josiah W.	870	Sth
Susan	186	Elc	James	859	Hnv	Will.	870	Sth
Thomas	110	Spt	John	69	Spt	Cathwright, Anderson	122	Hnr
Thos., Gloucester			Larkin	90	Spt	Thomas	795	Bck
Town	650	Glc	Nelly	446	Pra	Wm.	87	Spt
William	327	Dnw	Noah	445	Pra	Catlet, Clarke	565	Brk
William	559	Pre	Reuben	433	Flv	Catlett, Calmes	598	Frd
Wilson M.	68	Spt	Sarah	443	Pra	Charles	561	Frd
Casan, John	803	Nrf	Stephan	445	Pra	Elizabeth	897	Crl
Casay, Thomas	28	Hnr	Thomas	79	Spt	Elizabeth	403	Fqr
Casbey see Cosbey			William	805	Bck	Geo.	650	Glc
Casdorph, Henry	1	Knw	William	81	Spt	George	897	Crl
Thomas	2	Knw	William, jr.	81	Spt	George	560	Frd
Case, Betty	87	Acc	Casper, Henry	399	Ags	Hetty	650	Glc
Bridget	17	Acc	Peter	19	Clp	James	97	Jff
George	16	Acc	Wm.	22	Clp	John	564	Brk
Peter	778	Hmp	see Carper			John	590	Frd
Casebolt, Asael	428	Bth	Cassada, William	857	Cmp	John, (N. R.)	592	Frd
Hannah	429	Bth	Cassady, Bengamin	798	Hmp	John, (T. Ridge)	557	Frd
Henry	426	Bth	John	491	Mnn	John G.	895	Crl
Casels, Nicholas	484	Frn	Mary	274	Rck	Kemp	153	Alb
Casey, Danl.	284	Ldn	Ruth	326	Dnw	Laurence	407	Fqr
Edwd.	18	Hnr	Casseday, Lehr	628	Mnt	Mary	17	Clp
Edwd.	14	Ntt	Cassedy, John	640	Mnt	Nimrod	24	Oho
James	456	Bdf	Wm.	620	Mnt	Peter	403	Fqr
James	7	Isw	Cassel, Mary	216	Pnd	Robert	897	Crl
Jno.	271	Ldn	Cassels, Armistead	143	Dnw	Robert	402	Fqr
John	457	Bdf	William	246	Aml	Thomas	894	Crl
John	419	Fqr	Cassity, Betty, a free			Thomas	24	Oho
John	10	Knw	mulatto	973	Nrt	William	401	Fqr
John	701	Wsh	Jas.	341	Lnc	Cato, Harriss	448	Grn
Richd.	824	Nrf	Patty, a free mulatto	975	Nrt	John	448	Grn
Samuel	300	Ldn	Cast see Cart			Sterling	447	Grn
Samuel	975	Nrt	Caster, David	923	Hrr	Temperance	447	Grn
Spencer	612	Btt	see Carter			Caton, ---	923	Nrf
Susannah	612	Btt	Castero, ---	892	Nrf	Aaron	520	Prw
William	457	Bdf	Castian, Thomas	444	Pra	Hillary	445	Pra
William	19	Isw	Castile, Jno.	492	Mnn	John	952	Hrr
William, Jr.	366	Fqr	Shadk.	492	Mnn	Leanard	760	Hmp
Willis	6	Knw	Castle, Andrew	824	Wth	Thomas	398	Fqr
see Cayc			Henry	826	Wth	William	835	Hmp
Cash, Archdell	195	Kng	John	823	Wth	Catrine see Cattron, Katron		
Barnett	280	Amh	John	824	Wth	Catro, Elizabeth	86	Jff
Bartlett	280	Amh	Michael	824	Wth	Jacob	86	Jff
Elijah	245	Frf	Michael	825	Wth	Cattell see Catlett		
Geo.	327	Ags	Castleman, Benja.	586	Frd	Cattin, Edward	124	Hnr
James	302	Amh	David, Senr.	586	Frd	Catting, Joshua	7	Rcm
James F.	894	Crl	Edward	524	Frd	Cattle, Hannah	588	Mnr
Jesse	278	Amh	John	535	Frd	Cattlet, Alexander	828	Hmp
John	286	Amh	Thomas	594	Frd	David	786	Hmp
John	504	Prw	William, Jr.	535	Frd	Cattron, Phillip	694	Wsh
Joseph	245	Frf	William, Senr.	549	Frd	Catts, Conrad	1	Oho
Peter	300	Amh	Casleton see Harper			Caty, Negro, free	105	Jff
Randolph	258	Amh	Casto, David	913	Hrr	Caudle, Archer	143	Dnw
Samuel	259	Amh	David	922	Hrr	David	448	Grn
Stephen	300	Amh	George	910	Hrr	Dolley	143	Dnw
Thomas	291	Rck	John	913	Hrr	Elizabeth	142	Dnw
Thomas	104	Spt	William	910	Hrr	John	143	Dnw
William	276	Amh	William	417	Rnd	Jos.	143	Dnw
William	245	Frf	Castoe, Andw.	489	Mnn	Mary	143	Dnw
Cashman, Chrisley	520	Brk	Castor, James	923	Hrr	Nancy	142	Dnw
Cashner, Rob.	544	Brk	Sarah	891	Nrf	Sally	330	Dnw
Cashwell, Catharine	295	Amh	Caswel, James	689	Br	Sterling	143	Dnw
Henry	285	Amh	Robert	698	Br	Caudy, Evan	775	Hmp
Casidy, Wm.	251	Ldn	Samuel	689	Br	James	776	Hmp
see Caudy			Casweles, Zachariah	861	Cmp	John	833	Hmp
Caskey, John	695	Br	Cate, James	327	Dnw	Caugfland see Caugsland		
Casky, James	289	Rck	Jane	756	Wsh	Caughern, Thomas	824	Wth
Casleigh, Alexr.	908	Hrr	John	534	Prg	Caughman, Chris G. [?]	284	Rck
Casler, Chiney	119	Hnr	Mary	534	Prg	Caughron, James	721	Wsh
John	762	Hmp	Nancy	532	Prg	Caugsland, Eliza.	160	Knq
John	827	Hmp	Wm.	891	Nrf	Caulfield, Wm.	60	Chs

Causby, David	8	Pwh
Docia	8	Pwh
William	8	Pwh
Causley, Joel	823	Wth
Causner, Jacob	330	Ags
Cauthorn, Caty	209	Ess
Edmd.	209	Ess
Godfrey	209	Ess
James	209	Ess
John	209	Ess
Reuben	209	Ess
Richd.	210	Ess
Thomas	209	Ess
Vincent F.	160	Knq
Cauthron, Fanny	382	Mds
Cavan, James	14	Oho
James	23	Oho
Cavanaugh, Thos.	198	Ess
Cavans, Sarah	308	Ldn
Cave, Benjamin	382	Mds
John	187	Shn
John, & Father	382	Mds
Lucey	382	Mds
Reuben	186	Shn
Richard, & Father	382	Mds
William	759	Hmp
William	41	Rcm
William	186	Shn
Wm.	20	Clp
Cavenda, John	3	Knw
Cavender, Henry	444	Pra
James	446	Pra
Mary	444	Pra
Thos. S.	24	Clp
William	560	Pre
Caver, Mary	221	Shn
Caverler, Isaac	965	Hrr
Caves, Maryanne	500	Prw
Caveter, John	929	Hrr
Caw, Matthias	563	Brk
Matthias	569	Brk
Nicholas	563	Brk
Cawhard, Reuben	457	Bdf
Cawley, John	415	Bth
Sarah	560	Pre
Cawood, Saml.	526	Prw
Cawson, Lawson	733	Wsh
Patcy	27	Isw
Cawthon, Leroy	461	Mdd
Richd.	431	Flv
Robt.	439	Flv
Wm.	431	Flv
Cawthorn, Ann	160	Knq
James	159	Knq
Polley	113	Hnr
Thos.	112	Hnr
Cayc, Maryan	123	Hnr
Cayce, Archibald	9	Pwh
Cayer, William	603	Srr
Cayes, Peasant	45	Chr
Cayhill, Edwd.	29	Hnr
Caykendall, Jacob	416	Rnd
Caylor, George	28	Rcm
Henry	21	Rcm
John	36	Rcm
Caynor, Jno.	18	Clp
Cayse, Flemming	114	Cmb
Cayton, Moses	245	Frf
Caytor, Thomas	898	Crl
see Claytor		
Caywood, John	531	Frd
Thomas	247	Frf
Cearsey, Edward	303	Amh
Cease, Henry	399	Ags
Cecil, Isaac	894	Crl
John	895	Crl
Nancy	506	Prw
Cecill, Saml., Sr.	640	Mnt
see Cicell, Cisell		
Celeham, Jas.	696	Wsh

Celey, Willm.	182	Elc
Celly, Charles	752	Wsh
Celsey, Joel	748	Wsh
Cemby, Emanuel	876	Cmp
see Cumby		
Cennby see Cumby		
Cenningham, Elijah	18	Wod
Center, Drury	736	Wsh
Cesner, Elisebeth	750	Wsh
Henry	734	Wsh
Jacob M.	750	Wsh
John, Jur.	750	Wsh
John, Senr.	760	Wsh
Cetcham see Celeham		
Cetty, Jacob	459	Bdf
Cewing, William	682	Nls
Chabol, Joseph, (W)	882	Yrk
Chace, Leah	87	Acc
Robert	86	Acc
Chaddux, William	371	Fqr
Chaduck, Chas.	22	Clp
Chadwell, Bettey	344	Fqr
Bryan	363	Fqr
Bryan	47	Stf
James	70	Stf
John	410	Fqr
Willm.	615	Btt
Willm.	193	Kng
Chaffers, Ben	493	Frn
Chaffin, ...eph	458	Bdf
...ph	459	Bdf
Coleman	45	Chr
Joshua	246	Aml
Reub.	487	Mnn
Robert	742	Wsh
Solo.	488	Mnn
Thomas, Junr.	44	Chr
Thomas, Senr.	45	Chr
Chafin, Rebecca	623	Mnt
Chaimberlain, Zillar	64	Jff
Chalkley, Archer, jr.	63	Chs
Archer, sen.	63	Chs
Danl.	63	Chs
Elijah	63	Chs
Hobson	63	Chs
Isiah	63	Chs
Obed	63	Chs
Seth	63	Chs
Challis, Saml.	872	Yrk
Chalmers, Sarah	504	Prw
Chamberlain, Edwd.	893	Nrf
Elijah	65	Jff
George	891	Nrf
James	60	Jff
John	691	Br
John	807	Hmp
John	393	Rch
Joseph	189	Shn
William	814	Bck
Chamberlane, Feby	19	Wod
Chamberlayne, William	749	Nwk
Wm.	111	Hnr
Wm. B.	119	Hnr
Chamberlin, John	586	Frd
John	904	Hrr
Joseph	530	Brk
see Chaimberlain		
Chambers, Aaron	56	Jff
Allen	99	Cmb
Ann	399	Ags
Asa	25	Oho
Clopton	796	Bck
David	676	Br
David	25	Hnr
Edward	814	Bck
Edward	334	Lnn
Edward	25	Oho
Geo.	444	Flv
Jacob	577	Mnr
James	15	Isw

Jas.	589	Mnr
John	693	Br
John	795	Bck
John	490	Frn
John	98	Spt
John	99	Spt
Joseph	591	Brk
Joseph	592	Brk
Josiah	561	Pre
Josias	795	Bck
Major	889	Yrk
Mary	283	Ldn
Polly	100	Spt
Rhoda	470	Frn
Robert	572	Mnr
Samuel	697	Br
Samuel	470	Frn
Susannah	142	Dnw
Thomas	823	Wth
Thos.	18	Clp
Vincent	527	Brk
William	470	Frn
Willson	823	Wth
Wm.	517	Brk
Wm.	142	Dnw
Chambes, Wilkes	151	Alb
Chambless, Boling	448	Grn
Lewis	447	Grn
Littleton	447	Grn
Lucy	448	Grn
Rebecca	708	Brn
Chamblin, Aaron	599	Frd
Charles	317	Ldn
Ezekiel	267	Ldn
George	599	Frd
James	269	Ldn
Jno.	265	Ldn
Jno.	272	Ldn
Moses	599	Frd
Thomas	599	Frd
Wm.	261	Ldn
Chambliss, Elizabeth	633	Sss
Henry	631	Sss
James	538	Prg
James	631	Sss
Nathaniel	633	Sss
Theodrick	633	Sss
Thomas	633	Sss
see Owen		
Champ, Christopher	621	Gls
George	615	Btt
John	621	Gls
Champion, Celia	145	Sth
Cuthbert	432	Flv
Elizabeth	973	Nrt
Samuel	633	Sss
William	631	Sss
Champman, Mary	182	Alb
Chanalt, John	158	Knq
Saml.	159	Knq
Sarah	159	Knq
Steven	159	Knq
Chance, Elijah	17	Acc
Saml.	313	Ldn
Chancellar, Thomas	789	Bck
Cooper	345	Fqr
Thomas	914	Hrr
Chancellor, Robt.	685	Gch
Chancy, Samuel	334	Dnw
Chandceller, Andrew	411	Fqr
Chand'er, Henry	143	Dnw
Chandlee, Goldsmith	517	Frd
Chandler, Abraham	560	Pre
Benjamin	512	Frd
Boswel	143	Dnw
Carter B.	533	Frd
Edmund	898	Crl
Elisha	14	Acc
Elizabeth	821	Hmp
Gildiroy	649	Glc

Henry 504 Prw
James 15 Acc
James 121 Hnr
James 750 Nwk
Jemima 898 Crl
Jeremiah 101 Spt
Jno. 306 Rck
John 898 Crl
John 436 Flv
John 769 Wst
Laben 13 Acc
Martin, Sr. 336 Lnn
Mary 891 Nrf
Polly 614 Btt
Reuben 895 Crl
Richard 151 Alb
Richard 750 Nwk
Robert 898 Crl
Sally 196 Ess
Saml. 17 Rcm
Samuel 898 Crl
Sarah 328 Ags
Sterling 334 Lnn
Tabby 897 Crl
Thomas 14 Acc
Thomas 336 Lnn
Thomas 769 Wst
Thomas B. 749 Nwk
Timothy 894 Crl
William 13 Acc
William 245 Aml
William 894 Crl
William 750 Nwk
Williamson 55 Stf
Woodson 142 Dnw
see Barber, Chand'er,
    Chandlin, Chanler, Peyton
Chandlin, Jesse 453 Frn
Chandoin, Francis 827 Bck
Reuben 790 Bck
Chaney, Abel 825 Wth
Hesakiah, Jur. 825 Wth
Hesakiah, Ser 825 Wth
Chanler, Sarah 684 Nls
Channel, Arthur 11 Isw
Martha 160 Sth
Samuel 419 Rnd
Channell, James 302 Ldn
Jerremiah 419 Rnd
Channeller, Samuel 141 Dnw
Chansiller, Wm. 20 Clp
Chany, John 11 Oho
Samuel 964 Hrr
Chap...n, Leroy [?] 847 Cmp
Chapel, James 943 Chc
John 142 Dnw
Thomas 141 Sth
Chaplain, Abraham 88 Jff
Isaac 88 Jff
Chaple, Betty 448 Pra
Geo. 447 Pra
Joseph 448 Pra
Rody 446 Pra
Thomas 232 Ldn
Chaplin, Joseph 37 Rcm
Chapline, Josiah 4 Oho
Moses 2 Oho
Wm. 8 Oho
Chapman, ---, Mrs. 893 Nrf
Abner 894 Crl
Abraham 582 Frd
Amos 532 Frd
Anthony 894 Crl
Benjamin 44 Chr
Benjamin, Sen. 36 Isw
Benjm. 243 Aml
Caty, (free negro) 651 Glc
Elias 547 Frd
Elizh. 873 Yrk
Francis 25 Isw

George 615 Btt
George 687 Br
George 695 Br
George 896 Crl
George 386 Fqr
George 620 Gls
George, Jr. 348 Fqr
George, Sr. 365 Fqr
Harrisson 15 Isw
Henley 621 Gls
Henry 649 Glc
Isaac 620 Gls
Isaac 721 Wsh
James 854 Hnv
James 381 Mds
Jane 160 Knq
Jane 194 Kng
Jas., a free man of
    couler 689 Wsh
Jesse 604 Srr
John 243 Aml
John 614 Btt
John 894 Crl
John 552 Frd
John 589 Frd
John 619 Gls
John 24 Isw
John 522 Prw
John 733 Wsh
John, Jun. 4 Isw
John, Senr. 897 Crl
John, Ser. 621 Gls
John H. 745 Brn
Joseph 548 Frd
Joseph 27 Isw
Joseph 12 Knw
Joshua 535 Frd
Lewis 28 Isw
Philip 522 Prw
Reuben 897 Crl
Richard 897 Crl
Robert 895 Crl
Robert 898 Crl
Robert 893 Nrf
Robert, Senr. 897 Crl
Samuel 28 Isw
Saul 502 Prw
Simeon 381 Mds
Sydney 350 Fqr
Tim. 325 Ags
Thomas 514 Frd
Thomas 536 Frd
Thomas 959 Hrr
Thomas 381 Mds
Thomas 500 Prw
Thomas 508 Prw
Thos. 649 Glc
Thos. 580 Mnr
Valentine 947 Hrr
William 88 Acc
William 687 Br
William 698 Br
William 542 Frd
William 545 Frd
William 8 Isw
William 381 Mds
William 522 Prw
Wm. 407 Ags
see Grant
Chapmon, Lucy 854 Cmp
Chappalier, Zach. 23 Clp
see Cappelar
Chappel, Ann 880 Hnv
Benjamin 748 Nwk
Elizabeth 881 Hnv
Jno., Revd. 45 Chr
Silvia 336 Dnw
Thomas 143 Dnw
Winchester 749 Nwk
Wm., jr. 142 Dnw

Wm., Senr. 142 Dnw
Chappelier, Jas. 23 Clp
Chappell, Anne 61 Chs
Benjamin 632 Sss
David 604 Srr
Henry 631 Sss
Henry 634 Sss
James 149 Sth
James 631 Sss
John 246 Aml
John 244 Frf
John 532 Prg
John 631 Sss
Littleberry 603 Srr
Peter, F.N. 630 Sss
Rebecca 632 Sss
Robbert 336 Lnn
Silas 836 Nrf
Thomas 631 Sss
Thomas, Sr. 630 Sss
William 631 Sss
William 632 Sss
Charaner, Antne. 893 Nrf
Chard, John 298 Rck
Charis see Pharis
Charity, David 604 Srr
Elijah 604 Srr
John 604 Srr
Sally 603 Srr
Squire 603 Srr
Sterling 546 Prg
Winney 213 Ess
Charle, ---, Madme. 893 Nrf
Charles, Edmond 942 Chc
Henry 872 Yrk
John W. 707 Brn
Kemp 872 Yrk
Kemp, Junr. 872 Yrk
Lewis 872 Yrk
Mary 872 Yrk
Travis 461 Mdd
William 880 Sth
Wm. 682 Wrw
Wm. K. 872 Yrk
Charleson, John 850 Cmp
Charleton, Samuel 119 Cmb
Charley, Robert 651 Glc
Charlotte see Chirtottee
Charlton, Elizabeth 507 Prw
Francis 629 Mnt
James 629 Mnt
Jno. 644 Mnt
John 107 Cmb
John 579 Mnr
John J. 780 Bck
Joseph 579 Mnr
Joseph 580 Mnr
Martha, (W) 873 Yrk
Robt. 796 Nrf
Sol. 790 Nrf
Thos. 579 Mnr
Thos. 580 Mnr
Thos., Sr. 580 Mnr
William 576 Frd
Charnock, Edward 16 Acc
John 14 Acc
Owen 16 Acc
Owen 18 Acc
Robert 17 Acc
William 16 Acc
see Churrick
Charnocks, Mary 892 Nrf
Charrier, Abraham 6 Oho
Charter, Geo. 24 Hnr
Jonathan 466 Frn
Nath 24 Hnr
Rausell 34 Hnr
Chasser, John 855 Cmp
Chastain, John 46 Chr
Rane 831 Bck

Name	No.	Co.	Name	No.	Co.	Name	No.	Co.
Stephen	831	Bck	Saml.	539	Brk	John	113	Spt
William	245	Aml	Saml., jr.	539	Brk	Samuel	107	Spt
Chasteen, Lewis	14	Rcm	Chenoweth, Arthur	524	Brk	Tinsley	112	Spt
Chatham, Bernard	46	Chr	John [2]	524	Brk	William	102	Spt
Reuben	382	Mds	John	421	Rnd	Chice, John	460	Frn
Chatwell, Isaiah	825	Wth	Wm.	533	Brk	Chichester, D. P.	247	Frf
Chaudoin, Lewis	687	Gch	Chenowith, William	555	Frd	Danl. M.	244	Frf
Chavers, Betsy, (FN)	46	Chr	William	568	Frd	Nancy	304	Ldn
Jacob, (FN)	45	Chr	William	423	Rnd	Richard M.	365	Fqr
John, (FN)	46	Chr	Chenwith, Arthur	698	Br	Sarah	245	Frf
John, (FN)	68	Chr	Cherce, Lewis	810	Nrf	Chick, Charles	510	Prw
Sarah, (FN)	46	Chr	Cherricks, Arthur	84	Acc	Corbin	456	Bdf
Thomas, (FN)	68	Chr	Cherry, Alexr.	791	Nrf	Dudly	457	Bdf
Chavis, Jack	851	Sth	Amos	823	Nrf	Elijah	246	Frf
John	330	Dnw	Arthur	823	Nrf	Elisha	246	Frf
Fanny	145	Sth	Bryan	814	Nrf	Nancy	515	Prw
Cheadle, John	560	Pre	David, jr.	823	Nrf	Reuben	517	Prw
Cheanault, John	808	Bck	Densy	829	Nrf	William	246	Frf
John	838	Bck	Edward	823	Nrf	Wim.	858	Hnv
Cheaney, Phillip	46	Chr	Eli	814	Nrf	Wm.	253	Ldn
Reubin	46	Chr	Fairo	819	Nrf	Chiders, Stephen	617	Mnt
Cheatham, Abijah	58	Chs	Hilary, Sr.	821	Nrf	Chieves, Anne	531	Prg
Danl.	57	Chs	Isaac	614	Btt	Joel	531	Prg
Eliazar	335	Lnn	Isaac	835	Hmp	Child, James	17	Clp
Elizabeth	6	Ntt	Isaah	823	Nrf	Wm.	17	Clp
Francis	58	Chs	James, Son of Rachel			Childers, Andw.	617	Mnt
Isham	56	Chs	Cherry	613	Btt	Archibald	823	Wth
James	457	Bdf	John	823	Nrf	Jessee	8	Knw
James	602	Srr	Mary	825	Nrf	John	110	Cmb
John	688	Gch	Peter	814	Nrf	John	947	Hrr
Josiah	682	Nls	Rachel	613	Btt	John	428	Msn
Margaret	52	Chs	Saml.	823	Nrf	John	279	Rck
Peter	859	Cmp	Thes.	823	Nrf	Moseby	428	Msn
Robert	152	Alb	Thos.	893	Nrf	Nathl.	67	Chs
Robinson	855	Cmp	Thos., jr.	823	Nrf	Robert	465	Frn
Samuel	59	Chs	Thos., Sr.	823	Nrf	Samuel	964	Hrr
Thomas	334	Lnn	Willis	797	Nrf	William	469	Frn
Thos.	58	Chs	Cherryholmes, Green	20	Rcm	William	428	Msn
William	45	Chr	William	29	Rcm	Wm.	939	Hrr
Wm.	688	Gch	Cheshire, Benjn. B.	104	Cmb	see Chiders, Childs, Chrilders		
Cheatwood, Allexander	124	Cmb	Betty	86	Acc	Childres, Betsey	835	Bck
Daniel	276	Amh	Chloe	507	Prw	Drury	805	Bck
Joel	463	Frn	Eli	86	Acc	Jno. G.	847	Hnv
John	462	Frn	Ephraim	85	Acc	John	814	Bck
Polley	61	Chs	Jabes	85	Acc	John	847	Hnv
Squire	464	Frn	John	85	Acc	Mary	151	Alb
William	464	Frn	John	776	Hmp	Nancey	836	Bck
Cheaves, John	244	Aml	Obadiah	791	Hmp	Richard	852	Hnv
Check, William L.	382	Mds	Purnell	86	Acc	Wim., Jnr.	852	Hnv
Chedester, Peter	556	Brk	Samuel	791	Hmp	Wim., Snr.	852	Hnv
see Chotester			Thomas	86	Acc	Childress, ...all	458	Bdf
Chedicks, Eb	724	Wsh	Uriah	764	Hmp	Abram	125	Hnr
Cheek, James	522	Frd	William	86	Acc	Alexander	120	Hnr
see Check			Chesley, Mary A.	517	Prw	Andrew	120	Hnr
Cheeke, Elijah	22	Clp	Chesman, Mary	180	Elc	Bowlin	632	Mnt
Francis	20	Clp	Chesney, Ben	488	Mnn	Elizabeth	873	Cmp
Geo.	20	Clp	Chesnut, Jane	331	Ags	Jenny	122	Hnr
James	20	Clp	John	331	Ags	John	298	Amh
Luke	23	Clp	John	430	Bth	John	122	Hnr
Cheely, Charles	707	Brn	Chesterman, Jno.	859	Hnv	Joseph	287	Amh
John	707	Brn	Chevallie, J. A.	1	Hnr	Joseph	125	Hnr
Joseph	707	Brn	Chevallier, Jas.	650	Glc	Mary	125	Hnr
Cheesman, John B.	541	Brk	Chevice, Molly	650	Glc	Meredith	54	Chs
William	826	Hmp	Chevis, David T.	193	Kng	Meredith	687	Gch
William, Jur.	826	Hmp	Henry	894	Crl	Molly	126	Hnr
Cheetam, James	440	Flv	John	85	Spt	Nelson	685	Gch
Wm.	442	Flv	Margarett	898	Crl	Obadiah	560	Pre
Cheffen, Christopher	728	Wsh	Chew, Ann	109	Spt	Patrick	431	Flv
Christopher, Jur.	728	Wsh	Colby	761	Hmp	Philip	685	Gch
Cheffey, John	11	Oho	James	760	Hmp	Polley	131	Hnr
Chelp, Ann	379	Mds	Jno.	272	Ldn	Reuben	6	Knw
Chelph, Elias	379	Mds	Joseph	91	Spt	Robert	10	Knw
Philip	379	Mds	Joshua	578	Brk	Sarah	561	Pre
Chelton, Cyrus	407	Rch	Richd.	489	Mnn	Shadrack	6	Knw
Cheney, Ezl.	492	Mnn	Robert S.	116	Spt	Stephen	561	Pre
Chennault, William	869	Cmp	Wm.	270	Ldn	Susanah	126	Hnr
Chenoth, James	504	Brk	Chewning, Fanney	884	Hnv	William	560	Pre
Jos.	539	Brk	George	450	Frn	William, Jr.	560	Pre
Philemon	539	Brk	John	189	Alb	Wm.	687	Gch
Richd.	566	Brk	John	81	Spt	see Childrey		

Childrey, Charles	119	Hnr
Jeremiah	45	Chr
John	120	Hnr
Thomas	119	Hnr
Wm.	125	Hnr
Childris, Benjamin	152	Alb
Samuel	152	Alb
Childs, Benjamin	539	Frd
David	243	Frf
Elizabeth	246	Frf
Isaac	489	Mnn
Jas.	492	Mnn
Robert	964	Hrr
see Childers		
Chiles, Ann	897	Crl
Dabney	898	Crl
Fleming	894	Crl
Henry	153	Alb
Henry	753	Wsh
John [2]	898	Crl
Lucy	76	Spt
Paul	753	Wsh
Richard	76	Spt
Sally	896	Crl
Samuel	894	Crl
Samuel	895	Crl
Sarah	895	Crl
Tarlton W.	895	Crl
William	806	Bck
William	895	Crl
see Hackett		
Chilton, Andw.	341	Lnc
Blackwell	366	Fqr
Caty	341	Lnc
Erwin	340	Lnc
Geo., jr.	21	Clp
George	367	Fqr
Henry	457	Bdf
Jesse	340	Lnc
Joseph	368	Fqr
Mark A.	386	Fqr
Mer.	340	Lnc
Moses	341	Lnc
Rawleigh	858	Cmp
Richard	880	Cmp
Richd.	342	Lnc
Richd.	307	Ldn
Samuel	357	Fqr
Stephen	374	Fqr
Stephen	341	Lnc
Susan	291	Ldn
Thomas	408	Fqr
Wm.	20	Clp
Wm.	303	Ldn
see Roszel		
Chimney, Willm.	621	Mnt
Chinaweth, Absalom	835	Hmp
Chineau, Wm.	30	Hnr
Chinn, Charles	391	Fqr
Cirus	275	Rck
Hugh	389	Fqr
John Y.	400	Rch
Joseph	58	Stf
Robert	369	Fqr
Robt.	339	Lnc
Rolly	234	Ldn
Thomas	236	Ldn
Thos.	301	Ldn
Chinoweth, Elias	767	Hmp
James	615	Btt
John	767	Hmp
Chinwith, Arthur	683	Br
Arthur	698	Br
Chipley, James	249	Shn
William	542	Frd
Chipmell, John	332	Dnw
Chipps, John	489	Mnn
Wm.	487	Mnn
Chirtottee, Moses	723	Wsh
Chisben, David	897	Crl
Chiser, John	589	Frd
Chisholm, Alexander	834	Hmp
Isham	153	Alb
Nimrod	846	Hnv
Walter	845	Hnv
Chisler, Michal	516	Frd
Chisley, Robert	384	Fqr
Chism, Brison	73	Spt
James	561	Frd
Chisman, Elias	872	Yrk
Miles C.	872	Yrk
Thos.	872	Yrk
Chiveral, George	194	Kng
Willm.	194	Kng
Chivis see Chevis		
Chopeland, Michael	747	Nwk
Chopper, Philip	102	Jff
Chotester, Holdridge	942	Hrr
Chowning, Garrett	894	Crl
J.	458	Mdd
James	461	Mdd
Jno.	339	Lnc
Jno., Jr.	339	Lnc
John	473	Mdd
John, (Sailor)	461	Mdd
William	769	Wst
Wm.	339	Lnc
see Cowning		
Chrilders, Thomas	682	Nls
see Smith		
Chrisley, Mary	823	Wth
Chrisman, Charles	18	Rcm
George	18	Rcm
Jacob	42	Rcm
John	432	Msn
John	42	Rcm
Jonathn.	609	Mnt
Peter	601	Frd
Christ, Danl.	331	Ags
Jacob	324	Ags
John	328	Ags
Peggy	332	Ags
Christain, Andrew	561	Pre
Christian, ---	332	Dnw
Abner	279	Amh
Adam	11	Hnr
Agness	749	Nwk
Anthoney	872	Cmp
Archer	750	Nwk
Billy	27	Hnr
Charles	285	Amh
Charles	683	Nls
Charles H.	275	Amh
Collier	750	Nwk
David	939	Chc
Drury	282	Amh
Eaton	952	Chc
Edmond	939	Chc
Edmund	941	Chc
Edward	56	Jff
Elijah	282	Amh
Elizabeth	261	Amh
Ellison	618	Gls
George	789	Bck
Gideon	750	Nwk
Gilbert	11	Knw
Henry	258	Amh
Henry B.	938	Chc
Isam	939	Chc
Jacob	856	Hnv
James	283	Amh
James, (SG)	257	Amh
John	331	Ags
John	950	Chc
John	618	Gls
John	336	Lnn
John	439	Mth
John, B.	282	Amh
John, Jr.	789	Bck
John H.	750	Nwk
Jones R.	750	Nwk
Joseph	951	Chc
Martha	789	Bck
Mary	888	Hnv
Mourning	847	Cmp
Patrick	331	Ags
Peter	860	Hnv
Peter	825	Nrf
Raughley C.	974	Nrt
Robert	848	Cmp
Robert	2	Knw
Robert	747	Nwk
Robt.	328	Ags
Saml.	334	Dnw
Samuel P.	803	Bck
Thomas	792	Bck
Thomas	953	Chc
Turner	873	Hnv
Walter	284	Amh
William	619	Gls
William A.	947	Chc
William C.	296	Amh
Wm.	636	Mnt
Wm. M.	443	Pra
Christie, Charles	360	Fqr
Easter	893	Nrf
Elijah	879	Cmp
James	893	Nrf
Nancy	545	Frd
Robert	566	Frd
Christman, Phillip	774	Hmp
Christopher, Betty	89	Acc
George	87	Acc
George	770	Wst
John	334	Lnn
John	974	Nrt
Opulas	85	Acc
Robert	975	Nrt
Robt.	296	Rck
Thomas	975	Nrt
Wm.	872	Yrk
Christy, James	894	Hnv
James [2]	584	Mnr
John, jr.	38	Stf
John, sr.	38	Stf
Joseph	99	Spt
Martin	788	Hmp
Robert	584	Mnr
Saml.	542	Brk
Thos.	892	Hnv
William	759	Hmp
Chriswell, James	526	Brk
John	537	Brk
Chrouch, Joseph	244	Frf
Chumbley, James	560	Pre
John	560	Pre
Robert	561	Pre
Chunn, Andrew	407	Fqr
Celia	56	Stf
Church, Charity	88	Acc
Elijah	2	Oho
Henry	489	Mnn
James	15	Acc
Jonathan M.	715	Wsh
Luke	245	Frf
Samuel	974	Nrt
Stephen	15	Acc
Stephen	88	Acc
Wm.	342	Lnc
Wm.	489	Mnn
Wm.	490	Mnn
Churchell, Sarah	507	Frd
Churchhill, Dorotha	461	Mdd
E., Ditto for	459	Mdd
see Blakey		
Churchill, Charles	589	Frd
Richd.	18	Clp
Samuel	410	Rch
see Blakey, Gibbs		
Churchman, Elijah	324	Ags

Churchwell, Lydia	326	Dnw	Ambrose	380	Mds	John	276	Rck
Churn, John	15	Acc	Amey	19	Clp	John, jr.	276	Rck
Thomas	87	Acc	Andrew	613	Btt	John, Jun.	17	Isw
William	15	Acc	Anthony	571	Mnr	John, Sen.	30	Isw
Churrick, Arthur	14	Acc	Archer	9	Hnr	John, Senr.	856	Cmp
see Charnock			Barw.	489	Mnn	John, T.C.	871	Cmp
Cibels, Salley	6	Hnr	Benjamin	103	Cmb	John D.	160	Knq
Cicell, John	639	Mnt	Benjamin	12	Isw	John E.	604	Srr
Thos.	639	Mnt	Benjamin	120	Spt	Johnson	907	Hrr
see Cecill			Benjm.	947	Chc	Jos.	685	Gch
Cillaspy,. Nathan	189	Alb	Betsey	434	Flv	Joseph	516	Brk
Cimmons, Thomas	295	Ldn	Bowlling	867	Cmp	Joseph	894	Hnv
Cincilo, Daniel	954	Hrr	Catharine	17	Oho	Joseph	816	Nrf
Circle, Andrew	615	Btt	Charles	447	Grn	Joseph, Mother &		
Peter, Jr.	614	Btt	Charles	264	Rck	Brother	380	Mds
Peter, Sr.	612	Btt	Charles	117	Spt	Joshua	448	Grn
Cisell, Philip	637	Mnt	Charlotte	447	Grn	Joshua	917	Hrr
Rebecca	640	Mnt	Christopher	447	Flv	Josias	19	Clp
Saml., Jr.	622	Mnt	Daniel	513	Frd	Leonard	290	Rck
Willm., Jr.	622	Mnt	Daniel	922	Hrr	Littleberry	631	Sss
Willm., Sr.	622	Mnt	David	894	Hnv	Lucy	881	Cmp
Zachariah	622	Mnt	Edith	45	Chr	Lucy	448	Grn
Cisler, Ann	85	Jff	Edmund	896	Crl	Lucy	5	Hnr
Citty, Jacob	458	Bdf	Edwd.	45	Chr	Mary	434	Flv
City, Peter	20	Rcm	Edwin	448	Grn	Mary	140	Sth
Cizer, Richd.	61	Chs	Elias	23	Clp	Mathew J.	247	Shn
Cla...kston, William	457	Bdf	Elias	233	Ldn	Micajah	263	Amh
Claborn, John	329	Ags	Elijah	203	Shn	Micajah	302	Amh
Clabourn see Lowry			Elijah, Capt.	45	Chr	Michl.	613	Btt
Claburn, Robt.	616	Btt	Eliza	892	Nrf	Nathl.	326	Ags
Clack, Amy	707	Brn	Elizabeth	188	Alb	Norry	45	Chr
Clackston, Wm.	687	Gch	Elizabeth	939	Chc	Paulet	863	Cmp
see Cla...kston			Elizabeth	448	Grn	Perry	129	Hnr
Claflyn, Ephraim	23	Oho	Elizabeth	1	Oho	Petus	447	Grn
Clag, James	613	Btt	Fanny	893	Nrf	Ralph	785	Hmp
James	15	Oho	Filmer	679	Wrw	Ralph	572	Mnr
see Clagg			Frances	898	Crl	Rebecca	604	Srr
Claget, Richard	514	Brk	Frances	603	Srr	Reuben	603	Frd
Clagg, Thomas	15	Oho	Francis	104	Cmb	Reuben	380	Mds
see Claig			Francis, jr.	105	Cmb	Reuben, Jr.	380	Mds
Claggett, Henry	304	Ldn	George	615	Btt	Richard	632	Sss
Samuel	407	Fqr	George	578	Frd	Richd.	264	Ldn
Claiborne, Auguse.	142	Dnw	George	447	Grn	Rob.	490	Mnn
Devereux	447	Grn	George	336	Lnn	Robert	68	Chs
Herbert	142	Dnw	George	380	Mds	Robert	974	Nrt
John H.	142	Dnw	Henry	448	Grn	Robert	426	Rnd
Phill	708	Brn	Henry	17	Oho	Robert, Dr.	44	Chr
Richard C.	142	Dnw	Jacob	432	Flv	Robt.	276	Rck
Sterling	282	Amh	James	189	Alb	Sally	380	Mds
Thomas	331	Dnw	James	298	Amh	Saml.	399	Ags
Thomas	749	Nwk	James [2]	45	Chr	Saml.	11	Hnr
Claibourn, Francis	13	Hnr	James	448	Grn	Saml.	573	Mnr
Claig, Alexander	614	Btt	James	818	Hmp	Saml.	576	Mnr
Samuel	612	Btt	James	380	Mds	Samuel	448	Grn
Thomas	176	Shn	James	191	Shn	Samuel	957	Hrr
Thomas, Junr.	15	Oho	James, (SM)	380	Mds	Samuel	974	Nrt
see Clag			James B.	893	Hnv	Samul	23	Oho
Clair, John	727	Wsh	James S.	602	Srr	Sary	380	Mds
Clanton, Elizabeth	633	Sss	Jane	399	Ags	Shadrack	334	Lnn
John	633	Sss	Jane	11	Knw	Solomon	544	Brk
Joseph	632	Sss	Jno.	29	Hnr	Susan	839	Nrf
Nancy	631	Sss	Jno.	302	Rck	Susannah	566	Mnr
Nathaniel	632	Sss	Jno.	140	Sth	Thomas	44	Chr
Robert	631	Sss	John	299	Amh	Thomas	620	Gls
William	633	Sss	John	555	Brk	Thomas	632	Sss
Clapdore, Jacob	330	Dnw	John	616	Btt	Thomas K.	178	Alb
Clapham, Samuel	291	Ldn	John	895	Crl	Turner	327	Ags
Clapp, Erl B.	707	Wsh	John	940	Chc	Walker	194	Kng
Clapper, Frederick	63	Jff	John	947	Chc	Walter	573	Brk
Clapsaddle, George	613	Btt	John	333	Dnw	William	258	Amh
Clapton, Benjamin	781	Bck	John	550	Frd	William	896	Crl
Benjamin	839	Bck	John	448	Grn	William	45	Chr
Clardy, Archer	46	Chr	John	777	Hmp	William	769	Hmp
James	143	Dnw	John	924	Hrr	William	808	Hmp
Pleasant	21	Ntt	John	956	Hrr	William	812	Hmp
Clare, Jacob	615	Btt	John	158	Knq	William	914	Hrr
James	531	Frd	John	461	Mdd	William	921	Hrr
Clarey, Jno.	293	Ldn	John	575	Mnr	William	63	Jff
Clark, Alexander	565	Mnr	John	8	Oho	William	159	Knq
Ambrose	571	Brk	John	422	Rnd	William	380	Mds

Name	No.	Pl.	Name	No.	Pl.	Name	No.	Pl.
William	562	Mnr	Lewis	142	Dnw	Peter	188	Alb
William	2	Oho	Lewis	197	Ess	Reuben	152	Alb
William	602	Srr	Linsey	461	Mdd	Thos.	204	Ess
William	716	Wsh	Littleberry	560	Pre	William	411	Fqr
William, Jr.	332	Dnw	Lucy	396	Rch	Clary, Archibald	631	Sss
William, Jr.	380	Mds	Margaret	438	Bth	Benjamin	745	Brn
William, Qr.	380	Mds	Mary	687	Gch	Benjamin	631	Sss
Wm.	513	Brk	Mary	121	Hnr	James	632	Sss
Wm.	489	Mnn	Mary	892	Nrf	John	745	Brn
Wm.	719	Wsh	Mary	855	Sth	John, Sr.	746	Brn
Wm., (F. Mo.)	18	Clp	Molly	199	Ess	Mary	631	Sss
see Clerk, Clork			Nancy	854	Sth	Miles	149	Sth
Clarke, ...	457	Bdf	Peter, jun.	59	Chs	Thomas	632	Sss
Abner	555	Frd	Peter, senr.	59	Chs	Timothy	245	Frf
Agness	560	Pre	Polley	326	Dnw	William	632	Sss
Alexr.	893	Nrf	Presley	401	Rch	Clasby, Sauny	189	Alb
Ann	190	Elc	Priscilla	891	Nrf	Thomas	293	Amh
Ann	3	Ntt	Randall	401	Rch	William	683	Nls
Benja.	121	Hnr	Reubin	395	Rch	Clasen, Jas.	696	Wsh
Benjamin	389	Fqr	Richard	840	Bck	William	696	Wsh
Catharine	200	Ess	Richard	245	Frf	Wm.	696	Wsh
Charles	206	Ess	Richard	116	Hnr	Clasfell, Robert	574	Frd
Charles	750	Nwk	Ritchie	199	Ess	Clasp see Clark		
Chas.	59	Chs	Robert	457	Bdf	Claspell, David	71	Jff
D. R.	129	Hnr	Robert	206	Ess	Claten, John	332	Ags
Daniel	686	Gch	Robert	461	Mdd	Clator, ...	458	Bdf
David	748	Nwk	Robert	397	Rch	...	459	Bdf
David	391	Rch	Robin	221	Ess	Clatter, Mary	19	Clp
Edmond	435	Flv	Sally	200	Ess	Clatterbuck, Gabl.	23	Clp
Edward	120	Hnr	Samuel	438	Bth	James	382	Mds
Eleanor	245	Frf	Samuel	456	Bdf	Landrom	382	Mds
Elisha	685	Gch	Samuel C.	208	Shn	Lucy	897	Crl
Elisha B.	708	Brn	Spencer	461	Mdd	Sarah	897	Crl
Ell...	59	Chs	Stephen	199	Ess	William	897	Crl
Ellison, Est.	59	Chs	Susanna	199	Ess	William	382	Mds
Feald	334	Lnn	Susannah	396	Rch	Clauco, Jos.	892	Nrf
Gaiter	11	Pwh	Thomas	188	Alb	Claud, Charlotte	868	Sth
Gardner	59	Chs	Thomas	205	Ess	Jesse	127	Sth
Hannah	394	Rch	Thomas	216	Ess	John	868	Sth
Henry	536	Frd	Thomas	389	Fqr	Claughton, Catharine	974	Nrt
Isaac	13	Oho	Thomas	17	Ntt	Foushea	560	Pre
Isham	456	Bdf	Thomas	560	Pre	John	974	Nrt
Isham	560	Pre	Thomas	510	Prw	Nancy	408	Rch
James	332	Dnw	Thomas	2	Rcm	Pemberton, Jr.	974	Nrt
James	649	Glc	Thomas	770	Wst	Pemberton, Sr.	974	Nrt
James, Colo.	7	Pwh	Thos.	212	Ess	Clawson, Cornelius	562	Frd
Jesse	457	Bdf	Turner	686	Gch	Isaac	551	Brk
Jesse	814	Bck	Vincent	413	Rch	John	520	Brk
Jesse	59	Chs	William	35	Hnr	John	758	Hmp
Jesse	749	Nwk	William	125	Hnr	Claxton, David	15	Hnr
Jessee F.	218	Ess	William	748	Nwk	Nelson	331	Ags
Jincy	222	Ess	William	3	Pwh	Pope	354	Fqr
Jno.	242	Frf	William	398	Rch	Clay, Charles [?]	457	Bdf
Jno.	20	Hnr	William T.	410	Rch	Charles	143	Dnw
Jno.	892	Nrf	Wim.	857	Hnv	Charles	621	Gls
Jno., Senr.	8	Ntt	Wim.	892	Hnv	Charles, Jr.	244	Aml
Jno. B.	2	Ntt	Wm.	65	Chs	Charles, Sr.	244	Aml
Jno. S.	893	Hnv	Wm.	686	Gch	Charlotte	26	Hnr
Joel	389	Fqr	Wm.	688	Gch	David	245	Aml
John	708	Brn	Wm.	115	Hnr	Edward	20	Ntt
John	402	Fqr	Wm.	120	Hnr	Eleazar	62	Chs
John	536	Frd	Wm.	891	Nrf	Elijah	623	Mnt
John	686	Gch	Wm., Sr.	199	Ess	Jesse	244	Aml
John	29	Hnr	Wm. B.	67	Chs	Jno.	296	Ldn
John	132	Hnr	Wm. H.	685	Gch	John	245	Aml
John	748	Nwk	Clarkson, Anselm	863	Cmp	John	456	Frn
John	560	Pre	Anslem	279	Amh	Larkin	2	Ntt
John	561	Pre	David R.	684	Nls	Levi	334	Lnn
John	523	Prw	Elizabeth	686	Nls	Mitchel, Jur.	619	Gls
John	524	Prw	James	153	Alb	Mitchel, Sen.	619	Gls
John	3	Rcm	James	189	Alb	Obediah	335	Lnn
John	855	Sth	James	205	Ess	Phineas	59	Chs
John H.	342	Fqr	James	686	Nls	Priscilla	143	Dnw
Joseph	456	Bdf	James F.	863	Cmp	Sally	445	Pra
Joseph	800	Bck	Jessee	686	Nls	Saml.	2	Ntt
Josiah	245	Frf	John	188	Alb	Samuel	65	Chs
Josiah	34	Rcm	Julius	188	Alb	Sarah	245	Aml
Josiah, Jr.	245	Frf	Lucy	189	Alb	Thomas	142	Dnw
Lemuel	142	Dnw	Menoah	153	Alb	Thomas	336	Lnn
Lemuel	848	Sth	Nelson	863	Cmp	William, Sn.	458	Frn

Willm.			Jacob	175	Shn	John	824	Wth
see MClay			John [2]	175	Shn	Ozza	295	Ldn
Clayborne, Nathaniel H.	492	Frn	John, (of M)	176	Shn	Samuel	372	Fqr
Claybough, Nicholas	16	Rcm	Michael, Junr.	175	Shn	Samuel	552	Frd
Claybrook, Edwd.	244	Aml	Michael, Senr.	176	Shn	Clemonts, Eliza.	208	Ess
Isaiah	45	Chr	Teter	175	Shn	Lucy	334	Dnw
Jno.	868	Hnv	Cleland, Jas.	492	Mnn	see Cleaments		
Lucy	45	Chr	Jno.	490	Mnn	Clemount, Joseph	736	Wsh
Obadiah, (Est.)	45	Chr	Cleling, Larking	930	Hrr	Clendenen, Alexander	422	Msn
Peter	45	Chr	Clem, Henry	183	Shn	Wm.	422	Msn
Saml.	246	Aml	John	613	Btt	Clendening, Jno.	490	Mnn
Thos. V. [?]	868	Hnv	Mary	183	Shn	Saml.	301	Ldn
Claycom, Henry	581	Brk	see Clein			Wm.	300	Ldn
Henry	584	Brk	Cleman see Green			Clendennen, Robert	619	Gls
Claycomb, Conrod	577	Brk	Clemens, Christ.	327	Ags	William	426	Bth
Claypole, Joseph	14	Knw	Elizabeth	384	Fqr	Clendinen, Mary	680	Br
Clayton, Abel	15	Acc	Gasper	327	Ags	Clenmons, Sally	707	Brn
Amos	272	Ldn	John [2]	326	Ags	Clere, George	898	Crl
David	8	Oho	James	327	Ags	Thomas	896	Crl
Dennis	85	Acc	Stephen	326	Ags	Clerk, Benj.	714	Wsh
E., Jur.	489	Mnn	Thos.	326	Ags	Fugate	823	Wth
Elisha	489	Mnn	Clements, Adam	872	Cmp	George	719	Wsh
Geo.	16	Clp	Austin	46	Chr	Jacob	756	Wsh
George	2	Isw	Bartlett	258	Amh	James	24	Clp
Jacob	220	Pnd	Benjamin	868	Cmp	James	731	Wsh
James	34	Isw	Benjamin	437	Flv	John	823	Wth
James	159	Knq	Benjamin	448	Grn	Joseph	733	Wsh
James	142	Sth	Benjn.	143	Dnw	Lucy	541	Prg
Jasper S.	453	Mth	Charles	431	Flv	Mathias	756	Wsh
Jno.	60	Chs	Claiborne	45	Chr	Mathuas	756	Wsh
John	457	Bdf	Danl.	834	Nrf	Patcey	747	Wsh
John	520	Brk	Ewen	222	Ess	Peter	719	Wsh
John	707	Brn	Francis	300	Amh	Susanna	470	Frn
John	104	Jff	George	294	Amh	William	957	Hrr
John	161	Sth	George	19	Isw	William	427	Msn
John	92	Spt	George	532	Prg	see Cleck, Cleek, Taylor		
Leonard	55	Chs	Hannah	78	Spt	Clerkson, David	452	Frn
Milly	892	Nrf	Isham	45	Chr	John	471	Frn
Philip	17	Clp	Jas.	687	Gch	Clevand, Mary	152	Alb
Rewben	160	Knq	Jeremiah	281	Amh	Cleveland, Alexander	65	Jff
Stephen	685	Br	Jeremiah	531	Prg	Elijah, ... O. B. Washing-		
Stephen	300	Ldn	Jesse	265	Amh	ton's (O. S.)	63	Jff
Tabitha	87	Acc	Jessee	689	Gch	Harrison	552	Frd
Thos.	24	Clp	John	283	Amh	Jesse	65	Jff
William	574	Frd	John	872	Cmp	Johnston	248	Ldn
William	159	Knq	John	143	Dnw	Levi	62	Jff
William B.	749	Nwk	John	687	Gch	see Cleavland		
Wm.	707	Brn	John H.	295	Amh	Clevenger, Margaret	914	Hrr
Wm.	273	Ldn	Joice	301	Amh	Miner	916	Hrr
Claytor, ...mul	458	Bdf	Lucreaca	544	Prg	Clever, Frederick	826	Wth
John	456	Bdf	Mahlen	274	Amh	Clevinger, George	573	Frd
Sally	895	Crl	Patt	871	Sth	Jacob	563	Frd
Thomas	895	Crl	Polly C.	246	Aml	John	507	Brk
see Caytor			Robert	500	Prw	John	573	Frd
Cleage, Saml.	613	Btt	Sarah	245	Aml	Mahlon	562	Frd
Cleaments, James	649	Glc	Stephen	265	Amh	Clews, Joseph	311	Ldn
Jno. C.	650	Glc	Stephen	433	Flv	Nancy	311	Ldn
Wm.	649	Glc	Thomas	297	Amh	Thomas	311	Ldn
Clear, George, Christians-			William	282	Amh	Clibon, John	840	Bck
burg	630	Mnt	William	872	Cmp	Leonard	840	Bck
Thomas, Senr.	461	Mdd	William	143	Dnw	Cliborne, Geo.	4	Ntt
Cleatham see Cheatham			William W	302	Amh	Jno.	2	Ntt
Cleavland, Oliver	153	Alb	Wm.	442	Flv	Js.	58	Chs
see Clevand			Clemins, Henry	827	Wth	see Clyborne		
Cleavley, Thomas	159	Knq	Clemmens, John	949	Hrr	Clice, Adam	271	Rck
Cleck, George	415	Bth	Clemmer, Andw.	37	Rcm	George	592	Brk
Jacob	433	Bth	David	12	Rcm	Henry	593	Brk
John	433	Bth	Geo. L.	330	Ags	Jno.	267	Ldn
Michael	424	Bth	Clemmins, Freneis	649	Mnt	Click, Frederick	16	Rcm
Peter	444	Bth	Clemmons, Betsey	456	Frn	John	196	Shn
Cleek, Mathias	757	Wsh	Charles	247	Frf	John	231	Shn
see Clerk			Jno.	860	Sth	see Clerk		
Cleets, Jacob	490	Frn	Mary	245	Frf	Cliff, Sally	110	Cmb
Cleg, Alex	489	Mnn	Mary, f. negro	245	Frf	Clifferd, Elizabeth	305	Ldn
Isaiah	158	Knq	Patsy	849	Sth	Clifford, Samuel	674	Br
Mary	160	Knq	Richd.	849	Sth	Clift, Chandler	195	Kng
Cleghorn, Robert	824	Wth	Sally	244	Frf	Jane	193	Kng
Clein, David, Junr.	175	Shn	see Clenmons			Jenny	195	Kng
David, (of T)	173	Shn	Clemons, Hezekiah	296	Ldn	Joseph	193	Kng
David, Senr.	175	Shn	John	245	Aml	Miles	193	Kng

Robert	194	Kng
Sally	897	Crl
Sandford	195	Kng
William	896	Crl
Clifton, Chs.	17	Clp
John	642	Mnt
John	662	Mnt
John	418	Rnd
Samuel	827	Wth
Thomas	37	Rcm
Wm.	648	Mnt
Clighorn, Mary	742	Wsh
Clime, John	103	Jff
Climer, Isaac	85	Jff
Joseph	84	Jff
Clinch, James	602	Srr
Liddy	19	Clp
Mary	19	Clp
Cline, ...ob	299	Rck
Abram	960	Hrr
Andrew	743	Wsh
Casper	201	Shn
Catharine	302	Ldn
Conrad	577	Brk
Fredk., Senr.	17	Clp
George	963	Hrr
George	14	Rcm
Henry	248	Shn
Jacob	536	Brk
Jacob	544	Brk
John	943	Hrr
John	611	Mnt
John	206	Shn
John	213	Shn
John	826	Wth
Lewis	308	Ldn
Michael	223	Shn
Michl.	608	Mnt
Nicholas	306	Ldn
Nicholas, Jur.	826	Wth
Nicholas, Senr.	826	Wth
Peter	611	Mnt
Peter	825	Wth
Peter	826	Wth
Samuel	428	Msn
Wm.	967	Hrr
Wm.	302	Ldn
Cliner, Henry	694	Wsh
Clinetirch, Michael	241	Shn
see Cloutirck		
Clinger, Mary	590	Brk
Clingingpeal, John	616	Btt
Clinginpeel, John	479	Frn
Joseph	479	Frn
Clinkscales, Saml.	507	Prw
William	298	Amh
Clip, Jno.	270	Ldn
Clipliver, Henry	10	Oho
Clippard, John	172	Shn
Clise, Elizabeth	824	Wth
Clisor, Matthias	179	Shn
Cloe, David	365	Fqr
Elizabeth	54	Stf
Cloninger, Henry	88	Jff
Cloomger, Dav.	491	Mnn
Clopton, Abner	949	Chc
David	119	Hnr
Edwin	17	Hnr
Edwin	749	Nwk
James	747	Nwk
Jane	26	Hnr
John	747	Nwk
John, Senr.	747	Nwk
Patsy	583	Frd
Thomas	111	Hnr
Waldergrave	748	Nwk
William, (B)	747	Nwk
William, (R)	748	Nwk
Clore, Ephraham	379	Mds
Gideon	379	Mds
Izarel	379	Mds
Jacob	379	Mds
Jeremiah	379	Mds
John	379	Mds
John, B. S.	379	Mds
Levie	379	Mds
Michael	379	Mds
Moses	379	Mds
Peter	379	Mds
Peter, Jr.	379	Mds
Clork, Alison	964	Hrr
James	951	Hrr
Wm.	950	Hrr
Close, Peter	696	Br
see Clore		
Closen see Clasen		
Closs, Daniel	614	Btt
Clothier see Clothyear		
Clothyear, John	526	Frd
Cloud, Daniel	167	Shn
Jeremiah	315	Ldn
John	553	Frd
Nathanial	224	Pnd
Noah	23	Clp
Cloudas, Beverley	461	Mdd
John	461	Mdd
Wm.	651	Glc
Cloudass, Letty	212	Ess
Clough, Jno.	862	Hnv
Mary	849	Hnv
Robert	870	Hnv
Clounch, Denis	11	Knw
Clouse, Micl.	488	Mnn
Cloutirck, Michael	247	Shn
see Clinetirch		
Clover, Philip	569	Brk
Clow, John	522	Prw
David	384	Fqr
Clowers, Jacob	478	Frn
John	482	Frn
Clowser, Henry	571	Frd
Cloyd, David	663	Mnt
Elizh.	145	Sth
Gordon	638	Mnt
Joseph	616	Btt
Joseph	639	Mnt
Mitchel	612	Btt
Cloyer, George	248	Shn
Clubb, John	834	Nrf
Cluff, Geo.	687	Gch
Matt.	891	Nrf
Saml.	827	Nrf
see Glass		
Clum, Jacob	87	Jff
Clune, James	282	Ldn
Clutter, Jacob	443	Bth
John	422	Bth
Joseph	770	Hmp
Saml.	492	Mnn
Suzan	769	Hmp
William	19	Oho
Clutton, Jno.	340	Lnc
Cluverius, Atwood	651	Glc
Joseph	650	Glc
Thos.	650	Glc
Cly, Merritt	707	Brn
Clyborne, Js.	57	Chs
see Cliborne		
Clybourn, Archibald	620	Gls
Iona	620	Gls
John	621	Gls
Lemuel	620	Gls
Lovey	620	Gls
Clyburn, Wm.	688	Gch
Clyce, Christo.	280	Rck
Clyne, Philip	11	Oho
Coakley, Benjamin	61	Stf
James	57	Stf
John	107	Spt
Reuben	194	Kng
William	193	Kng
Wm., jr.	195	Kng
Coal, Abrm.	522	Brk
Aggay	6	Hnr
Barney	522	Brk
Coals, Philip	34	Hnr
William	896	Crl
Coalt, Robert	25	Oho
Coalter, Edward	17	Oho
Saml.	616	Btt
see C...alter		
Coartney, Fielding	287	Rck
John	395	Rch
Lenard	395	Rch
Sarah	395	Rch
Coates, Edward	6	Oho
Jno.	65	Chs
Jno.	651	Glc
Jno., jr.	651	Glc
Mary	651	Glc
Thomas	214	Ess
Coatney, John	33	Hnr
Rossma	245	Shn
Rosamond	171	Shn
William	525	Prw
Coatny, John	824	Wth
Coats, ---, Mrs.	342	Lnc
Edne	769	Wst
James	583	Frd
James	403	Rch
James, Junr.	403	Rch
Jeremiah	286	Amh
Lewis	69	Spt
Moses	553	Frd
Raw.	340	Lnc
Samuel	402	Rch
William	92	Spt
William	769	Wst
Cobb, Benja.	154	Sth
Burgoin	848	Sth
David	898	Crl
Fedh.	848	Sth
Fleming	11	Knw
George	614	Btt
Hardy	153	Sth
Jeffery	457	Bdf
Jeremh.	156	Sth
Josiah	139	Sth
Kinchen	137	Sth
Lazarus	162	Sth
Leond.	162	Sth
Nicholas	878	Sth
Robin [2]	898	Crl
Solomon	852	Sth
Thomas	2	Knw
William	15	Acc
William	2	Knw
Cobbs, ...	456	Bdf
Charles	876	Cmp
Charles R.	457	Bdf
Ed...d	457	Bdf
Jno.	45	Chr
Jno.	68	Chs
John	456	Bdf
John	855	Cmp
John L.	457	Bdf
John P.	270	Amh
Robert	874	Cmp
Thomas	781	Bck
Thomas	865	Cmp
Thomas	17	Hnr
Thos. M.	246	Aml
Tilghman A.	456	Bdf
Warner	457	Bdf
William	790	Bck
William	865	Cmp
William	876	Cmp
see Cobb, Cobs		
Coben, James	917	Hrr
Cobern, Elizabeth	923	Hrr

Jonathan	921	Hrr
Jonathan	923	Hrr
see Coben		
Cobin, Gawin L.	873	Yrk
Coble, George	527	Frd
Jacob	527	Frd
Cobler, John	381	Mds
Coblin, Wm.	24	Clp
Cobourn, Jeremiah	620	Gls
Cobs, David	151	Alb
Samuel	189	Alb
Coburn, A.	491	Mnn
Jas.	491	Mnn
Jas., Jur.	491	Mnn
Robert	551	Frd
Coby, Hezekiah	526	Prw
Cochran, Alexr.	584	Brk
And.	490	Mnn
David	418	Bth
David	425	Bth
Edward, Jr.	494	Frn
Edward, Sr.	494	Frn
Elizabeth	923	Hrr
George	591	Brk
Henry	689	Gch
Isham	494	Frn
James	326	Ags
James	568	Frd
James	3	Rcm
John	423	Bth
Nathan	494	Frn
Nelley	427	Bth
Samuel	455	Frn
Thomas	424	Bth
William	548	Frd
William	3	Rcm
William	42	Rcm
William	603	Srr
Zacheriah	22	Oho
see Cohcran, Croachran		
Cochrane, James	271	Ldn
Richard	242	Ldn
Cochrum, William	471	Frn
Cock, Charles	6	Ntt
Drury W.	861	Cmp
George	857	Cmp
Henry	15	Clp
John	869	Cmp
John H.	433	Flv
Thomas	856	Cmp
Thomas	857	Cmp
Thomas J.	861	Cmp
Thomas W.	855	Cmp
William	857	Cmp
William	500	Prw
Wim.	848	Hnv
Cockaran see Croachran		
Cockarill, John	974	Nrt
Joshua	975	Nrt
Littleton	976	Nrt
Cockburn, Robert	595	Brk
Cockburne, Martin	247	Frf
Cocke, Ann C.	602	Srr
Archd.	602	Srr
Benja., jr.	685	Gch
Benja., Senr.	686	Gch
Benjamin	603	Srr
Bowler, Jr.	130	Hnr
Bowler, Snr.	130	Hnr
David	603	Srr
David P.	687	Gch
Elizabeth	550	Prg
Geo.	546	Prg
James [2]	685	Gch
James ...	151	Alb
James P.	152	Alb
James P.	246	Aml
James P., Jr.	152	Alb
Jane	246	Aml
Jno.	20	Ntt

John	127	Hnr
John	1	Pwh
Jos., Est.	246	Aml
Martha	11	Pwh
Peter	549	Prg
Presley T.	22	Clp
R. H.	891	Nrf
Richard	686	Gch
Richard	29	Isw
Richard, jr.	118	Hnr
Richard, jr.	602	Srr
Richard, Snr.	118	Hnr
Robert	632	Sss
Saml.	686	Gch
Sherwood	123	Cmb
Thomas	118	Hnr
Thos.	550	Prg
Washington	391	Fqr
William	123	Cmb
William A.	9	Pwh
William B.	44	Chr
Winefred	23	Clp
Wm., Doctr.	602	Srr
Cockenoer, Jacob	250	Shn
Cockenour, Jacob, Junr.	223	Shn
Cockenows see Cokenows		
Cockerham, Edward	749	Nwk
Cockerill, Catharine	245	Frf
George	245	Frf
James	247	Frf
Jeremiah	245	Frf
Samuel	805	Hmp
Sarah	244	Frf
Saufd.	244	Frf
Thomas	243	Frf
Thomas	824	Hmp
William	823	Hmp
Cockons, Nancy	597	Brk
Cockram, Cicily	45	Chr
Cockran, Elizabeth	858	Hnv
Nathan	377	Fqr
see Cochran, Coconon, Coughran		
Cockrell, Hezekiah	348	Fqr
John	373	Fqr
John	61	Jff
Peter	64	Jff
William	379	Fqr
Cockrill, Elias	267	Ldn
Franc...	525	Prw
Geo.	266	Ldn
George	500	Prw
Hannah	267	Ldn
James	271	Ldn
John	525	Prw
Moses	525	Prw
Richd.	248	Ldn
Sanford	249	Ldn
Cocks, Banester	336	Lnn
Benjamin, jr.	602	Srr
Benjamin, sr.	602	Srr
Flemmin	335	Lnn
John	602	Srr
Mary	188	Alb
Mary	604	Srr
Robert	224	Pnd
Thomas, jr.	602	Srr
Thomas, sr.	602	Srr
Wm.	602	Srr
Cocksum, John	853	Cmp
Coconon, Jacob	329	Ags
Cocram see Pettus		
Coddler, Stephen	613	Btt
Cody, Ann	559	Pre
Coe, Catharine	587	Frd
Ebenezer	3	Oho
Edward	8	Wod
Edwd.	258	Ldn
Eli	266	Ldn
Elijah	674	Br

Henry	535	Frd
Jesse	631	Sss
Nathan	674	Br
Philip	7	Oho
Samuel	1	Wod
Walter [2]	8	Wod
William	557	Frd
William H.	544	Frd
Wm.	291	Ldn
Coecane, Samuel	18	Oho
Coeur, Ralf	537	Brk
Cofer, Elizabeth	602	Srr
Esther	38	Isw
George	457	Bdf
Jacob	457	Bdf
Jesse	457	Bdf
John	33	Isw
John	609	Mnt
John, Jun.	38	Isw
John, Sen.	38	Isw
Joseph	458	Bdf
Josias	457	Bdf
Moodey	38	Isw
Samuel	32	Isw
Thomas	603	Srr
Coff, Eliza., free negro	70	Chs
Coffee, Abner	560	Pre
Edmond, Jur.	686	Nls
Edward	685	Nls
James	834	Bck
James	628	Mnt
Nancy	685	Nls
Reuben	685	Nls
Thomas	561	Pre
William	685	Nls
William [2]	686	Nls
Coffeild, Willis	20	Isw
Coffel, Henry	278	Rck
Coffell, Adam	224	Shn
Daniel	239	Shn
George	224	Shn
Coffelt, Agustus	330	Ags
Coffenberger, Geo.	519	Brk
Geo. L.	501	Brk
Coffer, Francis	245	Frf
Thomas	245	Frf
Coffett, George	199	Shn
Jacob	239	Shn
see Coffell		
Coffield, Graham	851	Sth
James	422	Msn
Coffin, Richd.	891	Nrf
John	190	Elc
Cofflan, James	532	Frd
Coffle, Steeffle	225	Shn
Cofflinger, Adam	104	Jff
Coffman, Adam	240	Shn
Adolph	242	Shn
Andrew	243	Shn
Andrew, (of J)	242	Shn
Andw.	17	Rcm
Augustine	241	Shn
Barberry	241	Shn
Christian	14	Rcm
David	16	Rcm
David	38	Rcm
David	186	Shn
David	231	Shn
David	254	Shn
George	217	Shn
George	224	Shn
George	243	Shn
Henry	614	Btt
Henry	490	Mnn
Jacob	613	Btt
Jacob	428	Rnd
Jacob	18	Rcm
Jacob	186	Shn
Jacob	205	Shn
Jacob	248	Shn

Name	Page	Place
John	620	Gls
John	20	Rcm
John	190	Shn
John	238	Shn
John	252	Shn
Martin	186	Shn
Mary	191	Shn
Michael	196	Shn
Paul	781	Hmp
Peter	207	Shn
Saml.	5	Rcm
Saml.	25	Rcm
Samuel	185	Shn
Samuel	254	Shn
see Caughman		
Cofland, Elizabeth	292	Amh
Cofman, Betsey	329	Ags
Danl.	407	Ags
Henner	938	Hrr
Jacob	329	Ags
John	326	Ags
Stophel	329	Ags
Cogan, Edward	522	Prw
John	31	Hnr
Cogar, Peter	474	Frn
William	474	Frn
Cogbill, George	63	Chs
Hill	65	Chs
Jesse	63	Chs
Jno.	63	Chs
Thomas	62	Chs
Cogborn, James	447	Grn
Cogboune, Joseph	887	Hnv
Cogbourne, Mary	887	Hnv
Coggin, Benjamin	16	Isw
Henry	17	Isw
John	18	Isw
Jonathan	143	Sth
Joshua	18	Isw
Lewis	19	Isw
Willie	881	Sth
Coghill, Alwell	894	Crl
James	896	Crl
John	197	Ess
Thos.	198	Ess
William	896	Crl
William	770	Wst
Cogle, Josiah	403	Fqr
see Coogle		
Cogwell, Wm.	131	Hnr
Cohagin, Thomas	247	Frf
William	246	Frf
Cohcran, Chas.	270	Rck
Wm.	301	Rck
Cohen, Robert	334	Dnw
Thomas	851	Cmp
Cohenaur, Joseph	2	Rcm
Cohenour, Jacob	18	Rcm
Cohenower, Christ.	296	Rck
Christ	297	Rck
Cohoran, Thomas	19	Oho
Coil, Sameul	223	Pnd
Thos.	326	Dnw
Coile, George	214	Pnd
Henry	226	Pnd
Jacob	214	Pnd
Coiner, Christn.	331	Ags
Geo., jr.	327	Ags
Geo. M.	329	Ags
George, Sr.	325	Ags
Jacob	327	Ags
John	331	Ags
John, jr.	331	Ags
Philip	327	Ags
Sarah	490	Mnn
see Conner		
Coke, Jno., (W)	872	Yrk
John	218	Shn
Mathias	250	Shn
Richard	85	Acc
Richd.	872	Yrk
Cokely, Danl.	15	Rcm
Cokenour, Abraham	213	Shn
Daniel	206	Shn
Henry	213	Shn
John	189	Shn
John	206	Shn
John	213	Shn
Cokenows, John	216	Pnd
Coker, James	631	Sss
Jonathan	631	Sss
Jordan	631	Sss
Joseph	827	Wth
Coks, Isaac	941	Hrr
Colony, Kendal	85	Acc
Colbert, Francis	457	Bdf
James, Senr.	17	Clp
James D., jr.	17	Clp
Jno.	19	Clp
John	60	Jff
Robert	17	Clp
Saml.	16	Clp
Wm.	17	Clp
Colby see Colly		
Coldman, John	17	Wod
Cole, Bartlet	334	Lnn
Benja.	18	Clp
Benjamin	511	Prw
Chrisn.	490	Mnn
Coverdale	487	Mnn
Danl.	16	Clp
David	508	Prw
Dennis	288	Ldn
Eliezor	624	Mnt
Fanny	209	Ess
Francis	245	Aml
George	45	Chr
Haley	61	Chs
Hambling	64	Chs
Hanson	488	Mnn
Henry	490	Mnn
Henry	508	Prw
Hugh	709	Wsh
Isaac	619	Gls
Jacob	19	Rcm
Jacob	736	Wsh
Jacob	740	Wsh
Jacob S.	767	Hmp
James	419	Fqr
James	437	Flv
James	482	Frn
James	20	Hnr
James	11	Rcm
James	711	Wsh
James S.	767	Hmp
Jno.	56	Chs
Jno., f.negro	243	Frf
Jobe	118	Hnr
John	457	Bdf
John	612	Btt
John	947	Chc
John	377	Fqr
John	668	Mnt
John	510	Prw
John	632	Sss
John	698	Wsh
John, Junr.	84	Acc
John, Senr.	84	Acc
Jos.	58	Chs
Jos.	488	Mnn
Joseph	668	Mnt
Joseph, Jur.	712	Wsh
Joseph, Senr.	708	Wsh
Joshua	386	Fqr
Josiah	336	Lnn
Josiah	893	Nrf
Letty	770	Wst
Major	939	Chc
Martin	284	Ldn
Mary	243	Frf
Mary	336	Lnn
Matthew	511	Prw
Nelly	508	Prw
Nun	334	Lnn
Peggy	769	Wst
Rachel	558	Frd
Richard	439	Bth
Richard	513	Prw
Roscon	872	Yrk
Saml.	123	Hnr
Sampson	711	Wsh
Samuel	508	Prw
Susanna	152	Alb
Thomas	446	Bth
Thomas	160	Knq
Thomas	335	Lnn
Thos.	711	Wsh
Wesley	189	Alb
William	386	Fqr
William	520	Frd
William	508	Prw
William B.	632	Sss
Wm.	60	Chs
Wm.	945	Hrr
Coleband, P.	489	Mnn
Coleburn, Abel	86	Acc
Elizabeth	86	Acc
George [2]	14	Acc
Isaac	87	Acc
James	895	Crl
John	17	Acc
William, of Wm.	15	Acc
Colejin see Colgin		
Coleman, ---	332	Dnw
...y	336	Dnw
Aggy	328	Dnw
Ann	399	Ags
Ann	207	Ess
Ann	649	Glc
Archer	245	Aml
Archer, jr.	244	Aml
Benjamin	71	Spt
Benjamin W.	897	Crl
Bob	550	Prg
Charles	975	Nrt
Charles	678	Wrw
Chs.	249	Ldn
Daniel	245	Aml
Daniel	895	Crl
Ebena.	245	Aml
Edmund T.	276	Amh
Elenor	679	Br
Eliza.	19	Clp
Eliza.	20	Clp
Elizabeth	265	Amh
Elizabeth	776	Bck
Elliott	112	Cmb
Eward T.	105	Cmb
Fanney	858	Hnv
Farish	898	Crl
Francis	70	Spt
Frs.	892	Nrf
Furna	245	Aml
Hawes	898	Crl
Hawes	685	Nls
Henry	112	Cmb
Henry C.	895	Crl
Henry C.	871	Hnv
Henry E.	46	Chr
Isham	142	Dnw
J.Elmur	106	Cmb
Jacob	176	Shn
James	245	Aml
James	457	Bdf
James	142	Dnw
James	246	Frf
James	248	Ldn
James	84	Spt
James, Sr.	457	Bdf
Jesse	244	Aml

Name	Page	Code
Jesse, Jr.	244	Aml
Jno.	246	Frf
John	188	Alb
John	244	Aml
John	265	Amh
John	278	Amh
John	817	Bck
John	895	Crl
John	474	Frn
John, D.	814	Bck
Joseph	152	Alb
Joseph	583	Brk
Joseph	975	Nrt
Julia E.	105	Cmb
Julius	825	Bck
Lewis	216	Ess
Lindsay	270	Amh
Lindsay	895	Crl
Littleberey	264	Amh
Lucy	286	Amh
Lucy	326	Dnw
Mary	245	Aml
Millesent	894	Crl
Nancy	114	Spt
Nathaniel	708	Brn
Ned	770	Wst
Nehemiah	831	Bck
Patsey	812	Bck
Rachul	332	Dnw
Rd.	245	Frf
Rebeckah	82	Spt
Reuben	221	Ess
Reubin	276	Amh
Richard	708	Brn
Richard	401	Rch
Richard	770	Wst
Richd.	650	Glc
Robert	268	Amh
Robert	818	Bck
Robert	845	Hnv
Robert	80	Spt
Robert H.	283	Amh
Robert S.	457	Bdf
Robert S.	84	Spt
Robert S.	91	Spt
Saml.	15	Hnr
Saml.	115	Hnr
Saml.	659	Mnt
Saml.	892	Nrf
Samuel	271	Amh
Samuel, junr.	898	Crl
Samuel, Senr.	897	Crl
Solomon	244	Aml
Spencer	78	Spt
Spilsby	80	Spt
Standfield	142	Dnw
Susanna	219	Ess
Thadecas	409	Rch
Thomas	264	Amh
Thomas	820	Bck
Thomas	246	Frf
Thomas	92	Spt
Thomas B.	894	Crl
Thos.	221	Ess
Thos.	649	Glc
Thos.	650	Glc
Vincent	220	Ess
William	188	Alb
William	244	Aml
William	269	Amh
William	685	Br
William	814	Bck
William	861	Cmp
William	866	Cmp
William	121	Cmb
William	132	Cmb
William	382	Mds
William	684	Nls
William	67	Spt
William B.	78	Spt
Eillm.	616	Btt
Wilson	46	Chr
Wm.	221	Ess
Wm.	650	Glc
Wm.	249	Ldn
Wm.	872	Yrk
see Baines, Browne, Lump-kin, Stowers, Wells		
Colemon, James	456	Bdf
Coles, Edward, Albe-marle	686	Nls
Elizabeth	975	Nrt
George	974	Nrt
Isaac H.	45	Chr
John	153	Alb
Lucy	975	Nrt
Rebecca	152	Alb
Rhoda	975	Nrt
Richard	975	Nrt
Sally	975	Nrt
Samuel	41	Stf
Walter	152	Alb
Walter	845	Hnv
Winnifred	973	Nrt
Coleter see Coteter		
Coley, Ann	688	Gch
Francis	688	Gch
John	950	Chc
Peggy	688	Gch
Polly	688	Gch
Wm.	688	Gch
Colgin, John	941	Chc
William	951	Chc
Colhoun, Mark	283	Rck
Colins see Dowdle		
Colip, John	224	Pnd
Collans, Danil	618	Gls
Mary	620	Gls
Millenton	620	Gls
Saml.	618	Gls
Soloman	620	Gls
Collard, Saml.	243	Frf
Collawn, Margaret	650	Glc
College, John, Ju.	570	Brk
Collens, Frances	91	Jff
Coller, Edward	906	Hrr
Eliza	19	Hnr
G.F.	27	Hnr
Rivers	961	Chc
Colles, John	492	Mnn
Collett, Daniel	63	Jff
Isaac	399	Ags
James	253	Ldn
James	257	Ldn
Wm.	253	Ldn
Collette, Cathne.	893	Nrf
Colley, ---, Bramble &, [their] (Plantn.)	438	Pra
Ann	328	Dnw
Charles, Jnr.	845	Hnv
Charles, Snr.	846	Hnv
Jane	399	Ags
Martin, (F.N.)	13	Rcm
Nancy	901	Hnv
Nathaniel	550	Prg
Thos.	723	Wsh
W. [?]	22	Hnr
Wm.	892	Nrf
Wm., Sr.	810	Nrf
see Corley		
Colliar, George	448	Grn
John	447	Grn
Nancy	447	Grn
Richard	334	Dnw
Vincent	448	Grn
William	447	Grn
Collie, William	158	Knq
Collier, Archd.	603	Srr
Benja.	159	Knq
Benjamin	604	Srr
Berjanin	746	Brn
Charles	745	Brn
Chas. M.	181	Elc
Elizabeth	245	Frf
Emelia	603	Srr
Frances	953	Chc
Frances	46	Chr
Frances	651	Glc
Francis	159	Knq
George C.	603	Srr
Howell	604	Srr
Isaac	633	Sss
Jack	188	Elc
Jane	335	Lnn
John	603	Srr
John	630	Sss
Joseph	159	Knq
Mary	707	Brn
Mary	561	Pre
Michael	745	Brn
Moody	139	Sth
Nathl.	143	Dnw
Rivers	949	Chc
Stephen	603	Srr
Thomas	45	Chr
William	949	Chc
William	8	Pwh
Wm.	7	Ntt
Wm. G.	707	Brn
Wm. S.	745	Brn
see Collie		
Colliet, Thomas	431	Rnd
Collingham, Melby	852	Cmp
Collings, Charles	165	Shn
see Bollings		
Collingsworth, John	770	Wst
William	770	Wst
Collins, Andrew	441	Bth
Andw.	16	Clp
Betsey	326	Dnw
Bristo	577	Frd
Carter	133	Hnr
Catharine	268	Rck
Charles	429	Bth
Christopher J.	193	Kng
Clarissa	898	Crl
Cornelius	910	Hrr
Daniel	817	Hmp
Danl.	619	Mnt
David	355	Fqr
Edmund	898	Crl
Francis	382	Mds
Francis	490	Mnn
Gabriel	160	Knq
Geo.	834	Nrf
George	84	Acc
George	189	Alb
George	910	Hrr
George	951	Hrr
George	963	Hrr
George	160	Knq
George	189	Shn
George, (FN)	13	Rcm
Hezekiah	642	Mnt
Hezekiah	664	Mnt
Isaac	717	Wsh
Jacob	770	Hmp
Jacob	551	Hrr
James	85	Acc
James	327	Ags
James	382	Mds
James	577	Mnr
James	444	Pra
James	286	Rck
Jane	595	Brk
Jane	893	Nrf
Jas.	16	Clp
Jas.	488	Mnn
Jno.	16	Clp
Jno.	849	Hnv

Name	No.	Co.	Name	No.	Co.	Name	No.	Co.
Joel	46	Chr	Colls, Wm.	893	Nrf	Jos.	488	Mnn
John	87	Acc	Colly, Matthew	244	Aml	Joseph	757	Hmp
John	88	Acc	Wm.	399	Ags	Mahlon	264	Ldn
John	325	Ags	Colman, Abram	8	Oho	Mary	44	Stf
John	427	Bth	John	735	Wsh	Mary	751	Wsh
John	326	Dnw	John	744	Wsh	Nimrod	2	Knw
John	222	Ess	Laborn	334	Lnn	Robert	371	Fqr
John	816	Hmp	Patrick	824	Wth	Robert	250	Ldn
John	904	Hrr	Thomas	334	Lnn	Sarah	382	Fqr
John	910	Hrr	William	335	Lnn	Sarah	873	Yrk
John	160	Knq	see Jeffres			Seth	48	Stf
John	827	Nrf	Colony, Benjamin	14	Acc	Thomas	777	Hmp
John	268	Rck	Comfort	16	Acc	Wm.	873	Yrk
John	76	Spt	Elijah	84	Acc	Come, James	13	Knw
John, jr.	160	Knq	James	18	Acc	Comegyes, William	95	Jff
John, jr.	824	Nrf	Lettleton	840	Nrf	Comegys, Abm.	488	Mnn
John, Ju.	428	Bth	Major	16	Acc	Benjn.	513	Brk
John, (ST)	325	Ags	Major, Junr.	16	Acc	Comel, William	942	Hrr
John, Senr.	431	Bth	Peggy	16	Acc	see Connel		
Joix	159	Knq	Rachel	17	Acc	Comer, Auge	569	Mnr
Joseph	399	Fqr	William	14	Acc	Christopher	33	Rcm
Joseph	795	Hmp	Colours, Mary	174	Shn	Christopher, (Sen.)	33	Rcm
Joshua	84	Acc	Colquett, John	104	Cmb	John	185	Shn
Josiah	100	Spt	Colquhoun, Robt.	328	Dnw	John, (of M)	185	Shn
Kinner, (FB)	445	Pra	Thos.	332	Dnw	Martin	185	Shn
Kitty	15	Hnr	W.	332	Dnw	Mary	185	Shn
Levi	288	Ldn	Walter	332	Dnw	Michael	185	Shn
Levi	318	Ldn	Colson, James	326	Dnw	Philip	185	Shn
Lewis	79	Spt	Colston, Rawleigh	587	Brk	Thomas	4	Ntt
Littleberry	744	Brn	William T.	566	Frd	Thomas	530	Prg
Luke	328	Ags	Colt see Coalt			Comett see Cornett		
Mason, Mulo.	160	Knq	Colter, Corbin	541	Brk	Comick see Cornick		
Micajah	327	Ags	John	538	Brk	Comitee, Jno.	293	Ldn
Minton	15	Hnr	Colton, Ann	180	Elc	Commack, William	621	Gls
Nancy	84	Acc	Coltrider, Heny	329	Ags	Commel, Robert	950	Hrr
Nelley	391	Fqr	Colvert, Geo., jr.	22	Alp	see Camel		
Peter	448	Grn	Geo., Senr.	21	Clp	Commer, John	709	Wsh
Presley	456	Bdf	Jesse	24	Clp	John, Senr.	709	Wsh
Presley	794	Nrf	Lanta	346	Fqr	Richd.	709	Wsh
Reubin	475	Frn	Obediah	65	Jff	Commerford, James	616	Btt
Richard	577	Frd	Colvin, Alexander	188	Alb	Patk.	616	Btt
Ries	751	Wsh	Anica	328	Dnw	Comnell see Cornnell		
Robert	87	Acc	Benja.	22	Clp	Company, D.S.C.	814	Nrf
Robert W.	416	Rnd	Charles	49	Stf	Comphor, Jno. [2]	287	Ldn
Samuel	579	Frd	Isaac	826	Wth	Peter	288	Ldn
Sarah	593	Brk	James	208	Shn	Compton, Alexander	543	Frd
Skinner	88	Acc	Jno.	17	Clp	Alexander	524	Prw
Solomon	922	Hrr	John	208	Shn	Edwd.	23	Clp
Southey	16	Acc	John	43	Stf	Elijah	244	Frf
Sterling	84	Acc	John	826	Wth	Garriot	24	Clp
Thomas	46	Chr	Mason	22	Clp	Geo.	21	Clp
Thomas	556	Frd	Nelson	21	Clp	George	36	Rcm
Thomas	762	Hmp	Richard	385	Fqr	Henrietta	23	Clp
Thomas	159	Knq	Samuel	188	Alb	Howard	21	Clp
Thomas	309	Ldn	Colwel, Mary	677	Br	Isaac	559	Brk
Thomas	382	Mds	Robert	698	Br	James	244	Frf
Thos.	821	Nrf	Colwell, Peggy	457	Bdf	Jas.	24	Clp
Timothey	445	Pra	Robt.	715	Wsh	Jno.	19	Clp
Toms.	88	Acc	Colwig, Jacob L.	251	Clp	Jno.	244	Frf
William	88	Acc	Comaga, David	3	Knw	John	560	Brk
William	45	Chr	Coman, William H.	632	Sss	Mathew	19	Clp
William	363	Fqr	Comb, Peter	30	Hnr	Richd.	23	Clp
William	397	Fqr	Combo, Turner	958	Chc	Sarah	45	Chr
William	21	Oho	see Combs, Cumbo			Steapkin	21	Clp
William, of R	88	Acc	Combs, Amus	653	Mnt	Stephen J.	516	Prw
William A.	507	Frd	Betsy	873	Yrk	Thomas	827	Wth
Wm.	16	Clp	Daniel	815	Hmp	Turner	21	Clp
Wm.	213	Ess	David	789	Hmp	Walter	21	Clp
Wm.	834	Nrf	David, (F.Negroe)	359	Fqr	Willm.	616	Btt
see Collons			Ennis	382	Fqr	Wm.	19	Clp
Collinsworth, Elizbth.	626	Mnt	Gilbert	18	Clp	Zebedee	243	Frf
Collip, Adam	739	Wsh	Israel	237	Ldn	see Crompton, Cumpton		
Collis, George	374	Fqr	James	789	Hmp	Coms see Coeur		
Mary	518	Prw	Jesse	488	Mnn	Comton, James	13	Wod
Collison, Jesse	729	Wsh	Jno.	258	Ldn	Meredith	456	Bdf
Colloms, Samuel	425	Msn	John	789	Hmp	Con, John	225	Shn
Collon see Cotton			John	832	Hmp	Conauff, James	714	Wsh
Collons, John	951	Hrr	John	873	Yrk	Conaway, Edward	466	Frn
Collop, Frederick	825	Wth	John H.	47	Stf	John	61	Jff
Collopp, Henry	740	Wsh	Jonas	789	Hmp	Conch, James	826	Bck

Concle, Jacob	410	Ags	Danl.	634	Mnt	John	1	Wod
Conden, James M.	577	Mnr	David	306	Ldn	Stephen	28	Rcm
Condiff, Elijah	457	Bdf	Edmond	820	Bck	Wolsey	214	Pnd
Elisha	456	Bdf	Eleanor	820	Bck	Conroy, Edward	785	Hmp
George	456	Bdf	Fortune	13	Acc	Consolve, Wm. P.	811	Nrf
Isaac	456	Bdf	Hannah	21	Rcm	Consolver, Charles	750	Wsh
Isaac	458	Bdf	James	327	Ags	Martin	16	Clp
Jesse	456	Bdf	James	590	Frd	Milley	750	Wsh
John	458	Bdf	James	948	Hrr	Consolvo, Wm.	893	Nrf
John	459	Bdf	James	212	Shn	Constable, Job	492	Mnn
Condrey, Claiborne	56	Chs	James	30	Stf	Job	500	Mnn
Jno.	56	Chs	Jno.	20	Clp	Rob.	491	Mnn
Conduff, Jas.	699	Wsh	John	327	Ags	Thos.	892	Nrf
Conduit, Daniel	896	Crl	John	809	Bck	Wm.	914	Hrr
Nathaniel	897	Crl	John	820	Bck	Constantine, Patrick	427	Bth
Cone, Hillary	444	Pra	John	839	Bck	Conts, George	694	Wsh
John	840	Nrf	John	176	Shn	Convert, Lewis	22	Hnr
Joshua	444	Pra	John	39	Stf	Conwall, Wm.	594	Mnr
Mary	840	Nrf	Jonathan	633	Mnt	see Cornwal		
Conely, Edward	822	Hmp	Joseph	543	Brk	Conway, Aggy	325	Ags
Coney, L.	36	Hnr	Joseph	302	Ldn	Archer	143	Dnw
Congleton, Moses	685	Br	Lewis	20	Clp	Benjn.	143	Dnw
Congoe, William	6	Wod	M.	490	Mnn	Caleb	489	Mnn
Conington, Eliz.	32	Hnr	Mil.	488	Mnn	Edward	973	Nrt
Conklin, Henry	93	Jff	Paul, [his] Plantation	89	Spt	Elizabeth	694	Br
Conley, Danl.	688	Gch	Peter	104	Jff	Febe	974	Nrt
Danl.	612	Mnt	Rachel	89	Acc	Hannah	116	Hnr
David	331	Ags	Richard	939	Hrr	James	545	Prg
David	35	Rcm	Richd.	300	Ldn	Jeh.	489	Mnn
Francis	796	Hmp	Samuel	533	Frd	John	142	Dnw
George	974	Nrt	Thomas	278	Ldn	John	117	Hnr
Henry	919	Hrr	Urial	18	Clp	John M.	20	Stf
John	332	Ags	William	782	Bck	Joseph	975	Nrt
John	922	Hrr	William	800	Bck	Judy	398	Rch
John	974	Nrt	William	403	Fqr	Lazarus	401	Rch
John	35	Rcm	William C.	851	Cmp	Peter	355	Fqr
Lewis	708	Brn	Willm.	635	Mnt	Peter, Jr.	358	Fqr
Mary	974	Nrt	Wm.	490	Mnn	Saml.	489	Mnn
Thornton	770	Wst	Zadock	245	Shn	Thomas	975	Nrt
Timothy	35	Rcm	Conners, Charles	801	Bck	Thomas B.	45	Stf
Wm.	708	Brn	Connll, William	957	Hrr	Wiley	143	Dnw
Conlon see Coulon			Connollee, Mary	397	Rch	William	143	Dnw
Conly, Arthur	329	Ags	Connor, Dennis, jr.	304	Rck	William	64	Jff
George	955	Hrr	Douglas	527	Prw	Conwell, Hannah	7	Wod
Jerimiy	954	Hrr	George	894	Crl	Shephard	1	Wod
Conn, Alexander	692	Br	James	401	Fqr	Conwey, Thomas	489	Mnn
Betty	690	Br	Patrick	290	Rck	Conyers, Enoch	31	Stf
George	715	Wsh	Paul	894	Crl	John	420	Fqr
Gerrard T.	749	Wsh	Terrance	514	Prw	John	31	Stf
James	79	Jff	Thomas	403	Fqr	Sarah	179	Elc
James	492	Mnn	Thomas [Hanias?]	272	Rck	Cooch, ---, & Hollings-		
Jas.	490	Mnn	William	894	Crl	worth	99	Spt
Jno. F.	749	Wsh	Connoway, Daniel	758	Hmp	Coock, Mary	227	Pnd
Richard J.W.	94	Jff	Conoley, Larkin	200	Ess	Coocke, John	216	Pnd
Susannah	246	Frf	Sally	200	Ess	Coode, Susannah	194	Kng
Thomas	71	Jff	Conolly, Asher	895	Crl	Cooe, Presly	523	Prw
Wm. Y.	760	Wsh	Patrick	46	Chr	Cooglar, George	15	Rcm
Connalley, John	618	Gls	Conous, John	328	Ags	Coogle, S.	490	Mnn
Thomas	447	Grn	Conquest, Elizabeth	896	Crl	Coogler, George	39	Rcm
Connally, Ann	343	Lnc	James	86	Acc	John	39	Rcm
Peggy	18	Ntt	Joseph	86	Acc	Cook, Adam	381	Mds
Wm.	342	Lnc	Thomas	86	Acc	Adam	827	Wth
Connard, Thomas	2	Oho	William	84	Acc	Ama	687	Gch
Connel, Abraham	942	Hrr	Conrad, ---	328	Dnw	Ambrose	381	Mds
James	674	Br	David	330	Ags	Ann	872	Yrk
John	698	Br	Edward	512	Frd	Aron	381	Mds
Margaret	326	Ags	Henry	247	Shn	Barbara	381	Mds
Mary	109	Spt	John	540	Frd	Barlow	491	Mnn
Robert	708	Brn	Jos.	540	Frd	Benjamin	450	Frn
Solomon	684	Br	Joseph, Senr.	594	Frd	Bennet	5	Wod
Wm. T.	745	Brn	William	561	Frd	Daniel	564	Mnr
see Comel			Conrod, Christopher	8	Wod	Edwin	448	Grn
Connell, Joseph	60	Jff	Henry	257	Shn	Eliza.	877	Sth
Richar	957	Hrr	Jacob	559	Brk	Elizabeth	630	Sss
see Conwall			Jacob	18	Rcm	Elizh.	873	Yrk
Connelley, Daniel	141	Dnw	Jacob	30	Rcm	Epharim	569	Mnr
Conner, Andw.	635	Mnt	Jacob, J.	220	Pnd	Foster	447	Grn
Arthur	809	Bck	Jacob, Jun.	257	Shn	Foster	633	Sss
Charles	58	Jff	Jacob, S.	223	Pnd	Foster, Jr.	448	Grn
Dan.	490	Mnn	Jacob, Sen.	257	Shn	Giles	98	Jff

Henry	178	Shn	Abraham	109	Cmb	Crisley	85	Jff
Hugh	8	Oho	Adam	108	Spt	George	924	Hrr
Hyran	491	Mnn	Alexr.	21	Clp	Isaac	963	Hrr
Isabella	487	Frn	Aylee	120	Spt	Jacob	616	Btt
Jacob	612	Btt	Catharine B.	649	Glc	Jacob	941	Hrr
Jacob	84	Jff	Charles	358	Fqr	Jacob, Jr.	614	Btt
Jacob	564	Mnr	Charles, (free negro)	650	Glc	Jacob, Sr.	614	Btt
Jacob	8	Rcm	David	11	Rcm	John	613	Btt
Jacob	245	Shn	Dawson	158	Knq	Joseph	924	Hrr
Jacob	255	Shn	Eliza	160	Knq	Joseph	925	Hrr
James	142	Dnw	Eliza	893	Nrf	Michal	613	Btt
James	619	Gls	Elizabeth	358	Fqr	Michl., Jr.	613	Btt
James	872	Yrk	Elizabeth	651	Glc	Michl., Sr.	614	Btt
James, (FN)	68	Chr	Evy	160	Knq	Thomas	34	Stf
James S.	769	Wst	Francis W.	679	Glc	Coones, James	17	Clp
Jincy	331	Dnw	Giles	650	Glc	Jesse	18	Clp
Jno.	882	Sth	Jno.	23	Clp	Jno.	16	Clp
John	324	Ags	Jno.	649	Glc	Joseph	16	Clp
John	615	Btt	Jno., (free negro)	651	Glc	Wm.	16	Clp
John	786	Bck	John	15	Isw	Cooney, Sarah	244	Frf
John	499	Frn	John	28	Rcm	Coonrod, Benj.	952	Hrr
John	516	Frd	John	20	Stf	Daniel	952	Hrr
John	17	Hnr	John E.	513	Prw	Harrison	421	Bth
John	71	Jff	Mord.	649	Glc	John	952	Hrr
John	621	Mnt	Mordicae	833	Nrf	John	955	Hrr
John	624	Mnt	Moses	160	Knq	Coons, Henry	519	Brk
John	560	Pre	Polly	119	Spt	Jacob	78	Jff
John	5	Wod	Reuben	160	Knq	Coonts, Henry	267	Ldn
John	889	Yrk	Rhoda	160	Knq	Cooper, Abm.	893	Nrf
John, Jun.	619	Gls	Samuel	301	Ldn	Abraham	571	Frd
John, Junr.	872	Yrk	Sarah	651	Glc	Abraham	840	Nrf
John, (S. T.)	331	Ags	Simon	650	Glc	Adam	783	Hmp
John, Sen.	618	Gls	Stephen	288	Ldn	Alexr.	596	Brk
Joseph	538	Prg	Sybel	246	Frf	Ann	24	Clp
Joseph	5	Wod	Whiting	243	Frf	Archer	853	Cmp
Josiah	443	Pra	William	604	Frd	Ava	686	Gch
Judy	330	Dnw	William, jr.	160	Knq	Baylis	4	Knw
Letty	329	Dnw	William D.	159	Knq	Benjamin	515	Prw
Lodwick	153	Alb	Wm.	17	Clp	Betty, (W)	889	Yrk
Lucy	745	Brn	Wm.	236	Ldn	Catherine	826	Nrf
Mary	183	Elc	Wm.	282	Ldn	Charles	616	Btt
Mary	4	Rcm	Wm., (free negro)	651	Glc	Chloe	686	Gch
Mathias	616	Btt	see Cocke			Christopher	791	Hmp
Mildred	872	Yrk	Cookes, Eliza	836	Nrf	Clarissa	686	Gch
Miles	853	Sth	Cookman, Ezekiel	401	Rch	Collin	631	Sss
Nancy	331	Dnw	George	974	Nrt	Cupid	686	Gch
Paul	329	Ags	Wm.	952	Hrr	Dabney	616	Btt
Peter	598	Brk	Cooks, James	251	Ldn	Daniel	689	Gch
Peter	572	Mnr	Phlip	942	Hrr	Daniel	282	Ldn
Peter	7	Rcm	Cooksey, Hezekiah	447	Grn	Daphny	686	Gch
Plato	330	Dnw	Jack, f. negro	245	Frf	David	444	Pra
Rebecca	633	Sss	Leven	402	Fqr	Drury	631	Sss
Richd.	453	Mth	Miles	273	Amh	Edmon	466	Frn
Robert	740	Wsh	Obedh.	247	Frf	Edwd.	686	Gch
Sam	187	Elc	Philip	402	Fqr	Edwin	630	Sss
Saml.	547	Brk	Thomas	447	Grn	Eleanor	579	Frd
Solomon	698	Br	Walter	447	Grn	Elisha	498	Frn
Stephen	75	Jff	Warren	540	Frd	Eliza	20	Hnr
Susanna	9	Ntt	Cookus, Henry	756	Hmp	Elizabeth	812	Nrf
Sybell	244	Frf	Henry	104	Jff	Elizabeth	603	Srr
Thomas	44	Chr	Michl.	515	Brk	Ezekiel	329	Ags
Thomas	619	Gls	Cool, John	226	Pnd	Francis	20	Clp
Thomas	158	Knq	John	12	Rcm	Francis	461	Frn
Thomas	616	Mnt	Cooler, Jacob	225	Pnd	Frederick	536	Frd
Uriah	448	Grn	Cooley, Clark	2	Oho	Frederick	298	Ldn
William	153	Alb	Joseph	517	Frd	Geo.	282	Ldn
William	618	Gls	Peter	575	Frd	Geo.	872	Yrk
William	20	Hnr	Robt.	32	Hnr	Geo., F.N.	159	Knq
William	616	Mnt	Cooll, Herbert, Junr.	830	Hmp	George	562	Frd
William	750	Nwk	Herbert, senr.	830	Hmp	George	572	Frd
William	14	Oho	Jacob	790	Hmp	George	256	Shn
William	446	Pra	Phillip	790	Hmp	He.	491	Mnn
William	560	Pre	Coolley, Elijah	460	Frn	Henry	160	Knq
William	428	Rnd	James	460	Frn	Henry	18	Wod
Wm.	58	Chs	Nancy	460	Frn	Howell	632	Sss
Wm.	22	Hnr	Cooly, Abraham	708	Brn	Isaac	685	Br
Wm.	600	Mnr	John	827	Wth	Isles	466	Frn
see Cock, Kook			Thedious	827	Wth	Jachonias	621	Gls
Cookas, Michael	105	Jff	Coon, Anthony	924	Hrr	Jacob	447	Flv
Cooke, ---, Brent &	22	Stf	Coonrod	925	Hrr	Jacob	513	Frd

72

Name	No.	Co.
Jacob	686	Gch
Jacob	282	Ldn
Jacob	608	Mnt
Jacob	255	Shn
James [2]	330	Ags
James	420	Bth
James	216	Ess
James	594	Mnr
James	789	Nrf
James	9	Oho
James	503	Prw
James	632	Sss
Jeremiah	208	Shn
Jesse	569	Mnr
Jesse	750	Nwk
Jno.	892	Hnv
Jno.	487	Mnn
Job	778	Hmp
John	284	Amh
John	302	Amh
John	400	Ags
John	687	Br
John	897	Crl
John	188	Elc
John	215	Ess
John	466	Frn
John	783	Hmp
John	807	Nrf
John	891	Nrf
John	892	Nrf
John [2]	893	Nrf
John	298	Rck
John	49	Stf
John, Jr.	572	Frd
John, Jr.	668	Mnt
John, Jr.	633	Sss
John, Senr.	571	Frd
John, Sr.	188	Elc
John, Sr.	640	Mnt
John B.	180	Elc
Jonas	66	Jff
Jonathan	812	Nrf
Jonathan, Sr.	812	Nrf
Jos.	298	Rck
Joseph	852	Cmp
Joseph	515	Frd
Joseph	789	Nrf
Leonard	2	Knw
Leonard	427	Msn
Leonard	172	Shn
Leonard B.	22	Rcm
Martin	572	Frd
Michael	298	Ldn
Michl.	282	Ldn
Michl., J.	282	Ldn
Miles	686	Gch
Nathan	20	Oho
Nathan, Jr.	20	Oho
Peggee	825	Nrf
Peter	282	Ldn
Philip	299	Ldn
Phillip	3	Knw
Polley, a woman of couler	760	Wsh
Racael	329	Dnw
Rachel	48	Stf
Rawleigh	367	Fqr
Rebec.	188	Elc
Rebecca	806	Hmp
Reighney	461	Frn
Reuben	708	Brn
Richard	380	Fqr
Richard	3	Knw
Richd.	251	Ldn
Richd.	445	Pra
Robert	22	Clp
Robert	684	Nls
Robert	685	Nls
Robt.	330	Ags
Roger	686	Gch

Name	No.	Co.
Roger	688	Gch
Salley	6	Hnr
Sarah	616	Btt
Sarah	81	Jff
Simon, Mulo.	160	Knq
Starling	461	Frn
Thomas	121	Cmb
Thomas	466	Frn
Thomas	579	Frd
Thomas	797	Hmp
Thomas	47	Stf
Thomas	632	Sss
Valentine	5	Wod
Washington	668	Mnt
William	189	Alb
William	458	Bdf
William	461	Mdd
William	826	Nls
William, Sr.	458	Bdf
Willoughby	445	Pra
Wm.	330	Ags
Wm.	616	Btt
Wm.	16	Clp
Wm.	4	Hnr
Wm.	812	Nrf
Wm.	891	Nrf
Wm., a free man of coller etc.	707	Wsh
see ---, Copper, George		
Coopper, James	335	Lnn
Coore see Coon		
Coorons see Conous		
Cooter, Abram	823	Wth
Laurence	823	Wth
Cootre, Philip	824	Wth
Cootright, George	889	Hnv
Cop, Christian	612	Btt
George	613	Btt
George	204	Shn
Copage, Hannah	105	Spt
Cope, John	530	Brk
Joseph	538	Frd
Joshua	530	Frd
Joshua, Jr.	530	Frd
Samuel	552	Frd
Copeland, Charles	242	Ldn
Isham	27	Isw
James	280	Ldn
Jno.	297	Ldn
Martin	587	Mnr
Richd.	115	Hnr
Richd.	269	Ldn
William	574	Frd
Wm.	298	Ldn
Copelin, James	212	Shn
Willis	3	Rcm
Copenberger, William	827	Wth
Copenhaver, John	511	Frd
Michal	506	Frd
Copenkeeper, Thomas	825	Wth
Copes, Cretia	84	Acc
Daniel	87	Acc
Major	88	Acc
Parker	14	Acc
Peter	86	Acc
Revel	88	Acc
Sally	84	Acc
Selby	14	Acc
Southey	13	Acc
William	89	Acc
Copihaver, Fredrick	739	Wsh
Copin, George	512	Prw
William	511	Prw
Zaacus	961	Hrr
Coplan, Phebe	538	Brk
Copland, Charles	32	Hnr
Coplen, Benj.	948	Hrr
David	948	Hrr
Copley, James	619	Gls

Name	No.	Co.
John	621	Gls
Joseph	619	Gls
Joshua	620	Gls
Thomas	620	Gls
Coplin, Benj.	963	Hrr
Henry	153	Alb
Jacob	938	Hrr
William	153	Alb
Copp, John	217	Shn
Coppage, Charles	273	Amh
Cyrus	973	Nrt
Mary	381	Fqr
Thomas	291	Amh
Travis	18	Clp
William	369	Fqr
see Coppedge		
Coppedg, Thomas	353	Fqr
Coppedge, Jno.	18	Clp
Copper, David	569	Frd
Copperstone, Henry	175	Shn
Henry	195	Shn
Jacob	175	Shn
Coppyberger, Paul	825	Wth
Copsey, John	764	Hmp
Coram, Catharine	49	Stf
Elizabeth	412	Fqr
Jane	49	Stf
Sarah	357	Fqr
Traverse	382	Fqr
see Canon, Canor, Crom		
Corban, Coventon	85	Acc
George	85	Acc
Ralph	85	Acc
Robert	85	Acc
Savage	84	Acc
William	84	Acc
Corbbin, Rebecca	548	Prg
Corbell, Daniel	974	Nrt
John, Jr.	975	Nrt
John, Sr.	974	Nrt
Josiah	803	Nrf
Malachi	803	Nrf
Malachi	447	Pra
Nancy	975	Nrt
Richd.	803	Nrf
Sally	447	Pra
William	975	Nrt
Willis	11	Isw
Wm.	443	Pra
Corbet, Wm.	326	Ags
Corbett, Elias	881	Sth
Johnson	41	Isw
Joshua	875	Sth
Mills	882	Sth
Samuel	880	Sth
Shadrach	41	Isw
Corbin, Adam	943	Hrr
Anderson	943	Hrr
Ann	29	Stf
Armead., (son of Wm.)	16	Clp
Benja.	15	Clp
David	761	Hmp
David, jr.	15	Clp
David, Senr.	15	Clp
Early	22	Clp
Ephraim, (son of Davd.)	15	Clp
Francis	895	Crl
Gavin	342	Lnc
Geo.	21	Clp
Hannah	381	Mds
Henry E., [his] (este.)	460	Mdd
Isaiah	15	Clp
Jane	338	Fqr
Jesse, (son of Davd.)	15	Clp
Jno.	15	Clp
Jno. P.	17	Clp
John	793	Hmp
John	922	Hrr
John	381	Mds

John, Senr.	24	Clp	Jno.	342	Lnc	Thos.	651	Glc
Joseph	828	Hmp	Molly	342	Lnc	Corran, Michl.	893	Nrf
Josh.	21	Clp	Robert	518	Frd	Wm.	892	Nrf
Juliet	460	Mdd	Tho.	341	Lnc	Correll, Andrew	548	Frd
Phoeby	19	Clp	Wm.	342	Lnc	Michael	21	Rcm
Reubn., (son of Davd.)	16	Clp	Cornell, Jacob	22	Oho	Corrick, George	422	Rnd
Richard	158	Knq	Cornelon, Conrad	503	Brk	John	419	Rnd
Richd., Do. [ditto] for	463	Mdd	Corner, Daniel	683	Nls	Corthan, Jas.	851	Hnv
Richd., Do. for	464	Mdd	Gasper	325	Ags	Wim.	863	Hnv
Thomas	190	Shn	Martin	325	Ags	Corthron, Betty	84	Spt
Thomas	201	Shn	see Coiner			John	84	Spt
Wm., Senr.	15	Clp	Cornett, Allen	118	Hnr	Thomas	84	Spt
Wm., (Son of Davd.)	23	Clp	Elizabeth	122	Hnr	Cortney, R.	490	Mnn
Wm., (Son of Wm.)	22	Clp	Frank	118	Hnr	Stephen	747	Wsh
Corbit, Samuel	413	Bth	Jesse	127	Hnr	see Courtney		
Samuel	567	Frd	John	703	Wsh	Coruthers, James	18	Acc
see Corbett			Joseph	36	Stf	John	491	Mnn
Corbly, Andw.	490	Mnn	Richd. R.	16	Clp	John	492	Mnn
Corbon, Nicholas	4	Oho	Sarah	633	Sss	Cosbey, Ann	182	Alb
Corcoran, Thomas	88	Jff	Susanah	119	Hnr	Cosby, Charles	749	Nwk
Cord, John	88	Acc	Wm.	119	Hnr	Charles	83	Spt
Parker	88	Acc	Wm.	756	Wsh	Constance	872	Yrk
William	13	Acc	Cornick, Adam	444	Pra	Dabney	330	Ags
William, Junr.	88	Acc	Elizabeth	444	Pra	Edmond	32	Isw
Cordel, Adam	287	Ldn	Endymian	444	Pra	Garland	868	Hnv
Geo.	302	Ldn	Henry, Jr.	444	Pra	Jack	149	Sth
Presly	304	Ldn	Henry, Sr.	443	Pra	Jack	159	Sth
Cordell, George	170	Shn	Jno.	442	Pra	Jno. L.	891	Nrf
John	244	Shn	Joel	810	Nrf	John	683	Nls
Martin	302	Ldn	Lemuel	442	Pra	John	747	Nwk
Corder, Benjamin	588	Frd	Nancy	444	Pra	Mark	872	Yrk
Elisha	363	Fqr	Polly	447	Pra	Pleasant	687	Gch
James	541	Frd	Thomas	444	Pra	Rebeca	330	Dnw
John	363	Fqr	Wm. B.	443	Pra	Thos.	685	Gch
John, Junr.	401	Fqr	Cornish, Daniel	348	Fqr	Thos. E.	137	Sth
Patty	541	Frd	Richard	975	Nrt	Wm.	330	Ags
Vincent	363	Fqr	Cornnell, William P.	852	Cmp	Cosiamie, Jno.	245	Frf
William	170	Shn	Cornpher, John	232	Shn	Cosier, Sarah	246	Ldn
Cordery, Thos.	488	Mnn	Corns see Conn			Cosley, Wm.	551	Brk
Cordial, Thomas	10	Oho	Cornwal, Francies	594	Mnr	Cosloe, Robert	410	Fqr
Cordle, Charles	745	Brn	see Conwall			Coslow, Saml.	492	Mnn
Lorania	329	Dnw	Cornwall, John [2]	588	Mnr	Thos.	492	Mnn
Martha	707	Brn	Jos.	143	Dnw	Coss, Jno.	489	Mnn
Cordson, Joseph	542	Frd	Loveless	277	Ldn	Cossey, Abel, a free		
Core, Chrisr.	488	Mnn	Payton	20	Clp	mulatto	975	Nrt
M.	487	Mnn	Robert	599	Frd	Bill, a free mulatto	975	Nrt
Mary	87	Acc	William	543	Frd	James, a free mulatto	975	Nrt
William	17	Acc	William	825	Wsh	Cossle, Michael	747	Wsh
Corey, Nancy	461	Mdd	Cornwell, Anne	391	Fqr	Cost, Catharine	286	Ldn
Corgan, Seymour	17	Acc	Archer, (F.N.)	37	Isw	Jacob	300	Ldn
Corgin, Frs.	891	Nrf	Fielding	400	Fqr	Peter	281	Ldn
Cork, George	959	Hrr	Jacob	400	Fqr	Peter	301	Ldn
Corker, Daniel	858	Hnv	John	800	Nrf	Costa, John, 1st.	891	Nrf
Corklyn, David	552	Frd	Samuel	631	Sss	Jno., 2nd.	891	Nrf
Corle, Andrew	224	Pnd	Cornwill, Charles	515	Prw	Costley, Andrew	59	Chs
Corley, Austin	868	Hnv	Constance	516	Prw	Cot see Cox		
Beverley	457	Bdf	Elijah	521	Prw	Cotes, Ann	36	Stf
George	98	Cmb	John	514	Prw	Coteter, John	577	Brk
James	98	Cmb	Peter	515	Prw	Cother, Charlotte	407	Ags
Nathan	864	Hnv	Rabbi	507	Prw	John	937	Hrr
Temperance	98	Cmb	Saml.	512	Prw	Cothom, Jams	930	Hrr
Thomas	116	Cmb	William	510	Prw	Cotman, James	943	Chc
Ursula	868	Hnv	William	516	Prw	James, Sr.	946	Chc
William	98	Cmb	Corprew, Durant	445	Pra	Cotrall, Thos.	422	Msn
Corling, Charles	326	Dnw	Elizabeth	446	Pra	Cotrell, Ford	798	Bck
Wm.	326	Dnw	Jona.	445	Pra	Jno.	342	Lnc
Cormany, Henry	825	Wth	Joseph	447	Pra	Lydda	458	Bdf
Jacob	826	Wth	Saml.	792	Nrf	Cotril, Thommas	935	Hrr
Michael	825	Wth	Thomas, (WN)	443	Pra	Cotrill, Andrew	921	Hrr
Michael, sen.	826	Wth	Thos., (BW)	445	Pra	Richd.	921	Hrr
Corn, Amey	142	Dnw	Wm.	802	Nrf	Cottain, Richard	328	Dnw
Jno.	64	Chs	see Wickins			Cotten, Edmund	868	Sth
Polly	330	Dnw	Corr, Billey	159	Knq	Jno.	153	Sth
Timothy	805	Hmp	Charles	894	Crl	Cotter, William	5	Rcm
Corne, ...gy	335	Dnw	Jas., Sen.	159	Knq	Cotterell, John	432	Msn
Sally	335	Dnw	Jesse	461	Mdd	Robert	835	Hmp
Cornelis, John	5	Oho	Jno.	651	Glc	Cottle, John	597	Mnr
Cornelison, John	915	Hrr	Sterling	158	Knq	William	7	Knw
Cornelius, Charles	688	Gch	Thomas, jr.	159	Knq	Cottom, Charles	107	Spt
Daniel	685	Br	Thomas R.	159	Knq	Cotton, Frederick	630	Sss

Hardy	633	Sss
Henry	745	Brn
Howell	633	Sss
Jas.	489	Mnn
Jas.	548	Mnn
John	537	Prg
Judath, (FB)	446	Pra
Mary	143	Dnw
Nancy	630	Sss
Polly	537	Prg
Wm.	489	Mnn
Cottrel, Charles	117	Hnr
Charles, jr.	111	Hnr
Peter	117	Hnr
Peter, Jr.	118	Hnr
Richd.	116	Hnr
Saml.	111	Hnr
Saml.	117	Hnr
Wm.	117	Hnr
Cottril, John	935	Hrr
Cottsiter, John	457	Bdf
Couch, Ann	16	Hnr
Anne	785	Bck
Daniel	457	Bdf
Daniel	687	Gch
James	812	Bck
Jas.	723	Wsh
Jesse E.	785	Bck
Jessee	812	Bck
John	854	Cmp
John, Jr.	795	Bck
John, Senr.	795	Bck
Martha	724	Wsh
Marton	723	Wsh
Thomas	330	Dnw
William	325	Dnw
see Conch		
Couchman, Henry	540	Brk
Coughran, Jacob	687	Br
Jane	674	Br
John	687	Br
Joseph [2]	687	Br
Coulon, --- Widow	893	Nrf
Coulter, David	331	Ags
John	331	Ags
John, Esqr.	324	Ags
John, (S. R.)	332	Ags
Peter	245	Frf
Thomas	810	Bck
William	218	Pnd
Wm.	407	Ags
see Couter		
Counce, Abraham	91	Jff
Jacob, Jnr.	92	Jff
Jacob, Snr.	92	Jff
John	92	Jff
Council, Amos	159	Sth
Beth	858	Sth
Edwin	857	Sth
Jesse	881	Sth
Joel	881	Sth
Lemuel	159	Sth
Samuel	19	Wod
see Vick		
Councill, David	8	Isw
Counsil, Benjamin	45	Isw
Cutchin	45	Isw
Godwin	44	Isw
Hardy	43	Isw
James	45	Isw
Jesse	45	Isw
Pennina	44	Isw
Countis, Henry	751	Wsh
Peter	751	Wsh
Coupland, David	836	Bck
Phillip	68	Chr
Wm. R.	861	Cmp
Courd, Peter	418	Rnd
Coursey, James	329	Ags
James	296	Rck

Courten see Carter		
Courtner, Anthony	439	Bth
Courtney, Benjamin	769	Wst
Christopr.	20	Clp
Daniel	355	Fqr
Elijah	354	Fqr
Elzey	340	Fqr
Jacob	580	Brk
Jesse	702	Wsh
Jno.	488	Mnn
John	24	Stf
John	769	Wst
Linsey	769	Wst
M.	488	Mnn
Patsey	354	Fqr
Phil	132	Hnr
Robert	158	Knq
Robt.	488	Mnn
Samuel	817	Bck
Samuel	354	Fqr
Thos.	116	Hnr
William	769	Wst
Wm.	243	Frf
Wm.	489	Mnn
see Cortney, Hollawell		
Courtny, William C.	158	Knq
Courts, Prescilla, Este.	17	Clp
Cousins, Betsey [2]	686	Gch
Bill	400	Ags
Charles, (FB)	17	Ntt
Charles A.	245	Aml
Francis	687	Gch
Henry	143	Dnw
Henry	685	Gch
Jno.	64	Chs
John	244	Aml
John	438	Flv
John C.	246	Aml
Josiah	828	Bck
Richd.	245	Aml
Robert, Jr.	245	Aml
Robert, Sr.	245	Aml
Sally	689	Gch
William	561	Pre
Couter, John, Sr.	331	Ags
Coutts, Ann	128	Hnr
Patrick	68	Chs
Wm.	111	Hnr
Covington, Royston B.	973	Nrt
Coverdale see Cole		
Coverley, Thos.	246	Aml
Covey, Isaac	623	Btt
Joseph	608	Mnt
Saml., Jr.	624	Mnt
Saml., Sr.	624	Mnt
Covington, Francis	20	Clp
Jenny	896	Crl
Jno., (Son of Fk.)	22	Clp
Margt.	20	Clp
Martin	45	Chr
Mildred	20	Clp
Richard	896	Crl
Richd.	213	Ess
Sally, of L.	215	Ess
Sarah	213	Ess
Tho.	158	Knq
Thomas	896	Crl
William	895	Crl
William	896	Crl
William	330	Dnw
Wm.	213	Ess
see Couvington		
Cowan, Alexander	420	Fqr
And.	305	Rck
And.	307	Rck
Betty	80	Spt
Davd.	307	Rck
David	67	Jff
Elizabeth	456	Bdf
Henry	27	Rcm

Hugh	691	Brk
Israil	269	Rck
James	827	Wth
John	20	Rcm
Joseph	399	Ags
Mary	335	Lnn
Thomas	533	Frd
William	335	Lnn
William	73	Spt
Wm.	23	Hnr
Coward, Jno.	242	Frf
Samuel	16	Acc
Cowardin, Francis	412	Bth
John	418	Bth
Mary	418	Bth
Peter	415	Bth
Cowdan, Robert, Ser.	826	Wth
Cowden, James	773	Hmp
John	506	Prw
Joseph	773	Hmp
Joseph	826	Wth
Robert, Junr.	826	Wth
Cowdry, Jno. B.	892	Nrf
Margte.	892	Nrf
Cowell, John	151	Alb
Cowen, Jno.	490	Mnn
Robt.	490	Mnn
William	822	Hmp
Cowgar, Henry	216	Pnd
John, J.	222	Pnd
John, S.	222	Pnd
Cowgell, Ewin	828	Hmp
Isaac	17	Clp
Cowger, John	215	Pnd
Cowgil, Isaac	261	Ldn
Cowgill, George	567	Frd
Henry	552	Frd
John	520	Frd
John	553	Frd
John, Jr.	553	Frd
Cowhard, John	457	Bdf
Cowhen, Susanna	347	Fqr
Cowing, Ann	1	Oho
Cowles, Ann, (W)	873	Yrk
James	406	Fqr
Nathanial	951	Chc
Thomas	24	Hnr
Cowley, Beverly	13	Hnr
Margaret	128	Hnr
William	87	Acc
Cowman, Molly	299	Rck
Peter	297	Rck
Cowne, Robt.	18	Clp
Cowning, Samuel, Senr.	894	Crl
see Chowning		
Cowper, Abm.	192	Elc
Elizabeth	335	Lnn
James	191	Elc
John	185	Elc
William	27	Isw
Cox, Abner	216	Ess
Abm.	489	Mnn
Abram	749	Wsh
Abrm.	286	Rck
Absolum	872	Yrk
Ambrous	649	Mnt
Aminadab	292	Ldn
Ann	892	Nrf
Anna	789	Nrf
Ansell	447	Pra
Carter	654	Mnt
Catharine	618	Gls
Charles	345	Fqr
Charls	34	Hnr
Charney	57	Stf
Can.	492	Mnn
David	61	Chs
Drewry	686	Nls
Edward	802	Bck
Edward, Capt.	6	Pwh

Name	No.	Co.
Edwd.	688	Gch
Elias, jr.	645	Mnt
Elias, Sr.	640	Mnt
Eliza.	342	Lnc
Ezekiel	645	Mnt
Ezekiel	443	Pra
Ezl.	488	Mnn
Fintress	446	Pra
Fleet	342	Lnc
Fleet	769	Wst
Francis	65	Jff
Fransinai	7	Pwh
Frederick	9	Pwh
George	682	Br
George	793	Bck
George	107	Spt
Godfrey	892	Nrf
Henry	126	Hnr
Henry, jr.	65	Chs
Henry, junr.	56	Chs
Henry, Senr.	56	Chs
Higgason	61	Chs
Isaac	681	Br
James	875	Cmp
James	382	Fqr
James	443	Flv
James	160	Knq
James	193	Kng
James	382	Mds
James	769	Wst
James	827	Wth
James L.	196	Ess
Jerremima	61	Stf
Jessee	826	Wth
Jno.	340	Lnc
Jno.	488	Mnn
Jno.	444	Pra
Jno., (of Geo.)	444	Pra
Joanna	38	Isw
Joel	872	Yrk
John	329	Ags
John	612	Btt
John	791	Bck
John	327	Dnw
John	219	Ess
John	442	Flv
John	618	Gls
John	688	Gch
John	69	Jff
John	195	Kng
John	826	Nrf
John	893	Nrf
John	561	Pre
John	61	Stf
John	510	Prw
John, jr.	219	Ess
John, L.	57	Stf
Joseph	683	Br
Joshua	872	Yrk
Josiah	122	Cmb
Leander	107	Cmb
Lues, (Widow	615	Btt
Margt.	873	Yrk
Martin	827	Wth
Mary	203	Ess
Matthew	108	Cmb
Michael	12	Oho
Michael, Jr.	12	Oho
Millinor	292	Amh
Mirna	341	Lnc
Molly	447	Pra
Moses	489	Mnn
Nancy, free negro	70	Chs
Newton	60	Stf
Obadiah	17	Clp
Peter	975	Nrt
Peter P.	769	Wst
Philip	330	Ags
Precilla	448	Grn
Presley	57	Stf
Presley	769	Wst
Pugh P.	8	Pwh
Rebecca	974	Nrt
Redford	561	Pre
Reuben	209	Ess
Reuben	216	Ess
Reubin	290	Amh
Robert	818	Nrf
Saml.	716	Wsh
Samuel	563	Brk
Samuel	401	Fqr
Samuel	71	Jff
Samuel	57	Stf
Sarah	59	Stf
Stephen	328	Ags
Susanah	560	Pre
Tapla	894	Crl
Temperance	328	Dnw
Tho.	342	Lnc
Tho.	873	Yrk
Thomas	44	Chr
Thomas	686	Nls
Thomas	974	Nrt
Thos.	790	Nrf
Valentine	457	Bdf
Vincent	59	Stf
White	105	Spt
William	457	Bdf
William	98	Cmb
William	826	Wth
William	827	Wth
William, Jr.	974	Nrt
William, Sr.	974	Nrt
Willison	748	Wsh
Wm.	121	Hnr
Wm.	258	Ldn
Wm.	447	Pra
Zachariah	381	Fqr
see Coks, Coxe, Coxs		
Coxe, David J.	21	Clp
Lidda	24	Clp
Solomon	6	Oho
Coxell, Robert	892	Nrf
Coxon, William H.	14	Acc
Coxs, Jacob	645	Mnt
Coxsin, Levi W.	248	Ldn
Coy, Anthony	305	Amh
Charles, F. B.	13	Pwh
Coyl, James	93	Jff
Coyle, David	109	Spt
James	541	Frd
Michal	508	Frd
Richard	119	Spt
Robert	510	Frd
Cozard, Antho.	490	Mnn
John	491	Mnn
Cozens, Jacob, (FN)	45	Chr
Cr...w, David	456	Bdf
Crab, Isaac	555	Brk
William	553	Brk
Samuel	566	Frd
William M.	769	Wst
Crable, Richard K.	336	Lnn
Crabtree, Gaberal	726	Wsh
Jas.	725	Wsh
John	724	Wsh
Solomon	724	Wsh
Wm.	725	Wsh
Wm.	729	Wsh
Cracraft, Eunice	3	Oho
Craddick, Nathaniel	488	Frn
Craddler, Nelson	770	Wst
Craddock, Asael	246	Aml
Braxton	19	Hnr
Claiborne	244	Aml
James	245	Aml
Jno. C.	6	Ntt
John	17	Hnr
John H.	561	Pre
Moses	873	Cmp
Nancy	189	Alb
Obedience	244	Aml
Pleasant	334	Lnn
Richard	561	Pre
Robert	244	Aml
Robt.	126	Hnr
Cradlebaugh, Fredrick	2	Wod
Cradock, Edmund	605	Frd
Jennet	615	Btt
Thomas	151	Alb
Thomas	189	Alb
Crae, Allexander M.	33	Hnr
Craffiee see Cruffice		
Crafford, Henry	602	Srr
Jenny	604	Srr
Nancy	852	Cmp
see Rush		
Craft, George	613	Btt
Jacob	99	Jff
John	614	Btt
John	447	Pra
Joshua	447	Pra
Michael	676	Br
see Barrycraft		
Crafton, Frederick	335	Lnn
James	335	Lnn
John	160	Knq
John	336	Lnn
John, jr.	336	Lnn
Staples	334	Lnn
Thomas	160	Knq
Thomas	335	Lnn
Thomas	336	Lnn
William, jr.	335	Lnn
William, L. [?]	335	Lnn
Crage, William	227	Shn
Cragelon, John	215	Shn
Cragen, James	794	Hmp
Cragg, Thos., (FN)	18	Clp
Cragge, Robt.	330	Ags
Craghead, George	334	Lnn
Robert	456	Bdf
T.	334	Lnn
William	334	Lnn
Craghill, Hanry	538	Brk
John B.	542	Brk
Cragwall, Saml.	686	Gch
Craig, ---, Mrs.	26	Hnr
...am	458	Bdf
Alexr.	326	Ags
Andrew	519	Brk
Benjn.	659	Mnt
Betty	614	Btt
D.	761	Wsh
Davd.	760	Wsh
David	188	Alb
David	618	Mnt
David	688	Wsh
Elisebeth	755	Wsh
George	336	Lnn
George	420	Msn
George	636	Mnt
George, Sr.	659	Mnt
Henry, (F. Mo.)	24	Clp
James	679	Br
James	310	Ldn
James	630	Mnt
James	18	Oho
James	2	Rcm
James	166	Shn
James, J.	310	Ldn
Jane	327	Ags
Jno., John Michell &,		
& Co.	707	Wsh
John	8	Rcm
John	54	Stf
John	824	Wth
Josiah, Jr.	585	Frd
Josiah, Senr.	585	Frd

Mary	127	Hnr	Cravan, Wm. H.	22	Hnr	Sarah	15	Rcm
Mary	812	Nrf	Craven, Cornelius	312	Ldn	Sarah	700	Wsh
Mary	824	Wth	Giles	309	Ldn	Thomas	549	Frd
Mary, in Richmond has slaves			James	310	Ldn	Thos.	837	Nrf
in York County	872	Yrk	Joseph	279	Ldn	William	445	Bth
Moses	456	Bdf	Joseph	289	Ldn	William	676	Br
Penina	55	Jff	Josiah	290	Ldn	William	686	Nls
Robert	550	Frd	Sarah	289	Ldn	William	17	Rcm
Robert, Jur.	749	Wsh	Cravens, John	489	Mnn	William	80	Spt
Robt.	707	Wsh	Joseph	14	Rcm	William	824	Wth
Salley, (F. Negroe)	386	Fqr	William	36	Rcm	William S.	284	Amh
Saml.	271	Rck	Cravins, James	325	Ags	Wm.	11	Hnr
Samuel	153	Alb	Crawford, Aaron	20	Clp	Wm., Jr.	614	Btt
Samuel	585	Frd	Alexander	676	Br	Wm., Jr.	615	Btt
Samuel	310	Ldn	Alexander	684	Br	Wm., Sr.	612	Btt
Thomas	450	Frn	Alexer.	330	Ags	Wm., Sr.	615	Btt
Thomas	165	Shn	Alexr.	294	Rck	Wm. A.	143	Dnw
Thomas, (F. Negroe)	359	Fqr	Andrew	615	Btt	Zachariah	35	Rcm
Wm.	327	Ags	Andrew	827	Wth	Crawley, Anderson	879	Cmp
Craige, Hugh	15	Wod	Anne	676	Br	Aquilla	563	Frd
Susanna	325	Ags	Archelaus	576	Mnr	Austin	23	Clp
William	496	Frn	Byars	685	Gch	Beverley	879	Cmp
Craighill, Nathaniel	64	Jff	Charles	265	Amh	Curtice	23	Clp
William P.	64	Jff	Dorathy	80	Spt	Garland	21	Clp
Craik, James	243	Frf	Edward, Revd.	760	Wsh	Geo.	21	Clp
Crail, William	693	Br	Eleanor	305	Rck	Henry P.	603	Srr
Crain, James	456	Bdf	Elizabeth	692	Br	Lewis	22	Clp
Craine, James	390	Fqr	Elizabeth	440	Mth	Lyndsay	864	Cmp
John	390	Fqr	Euphomia	446	Bth	Malicia	22	Clp
Cralle, Kenner	975	Nrt	Geo.	327	Ags	Manoah	410	Fqr
Kenner	12	Ntt	Gideon	592	Mnr	Susannah	244	Aml
Jno.	12	Ntt	James	324	Ags	William	44	Chr
John, Jr.	974	Nrt	James	616	Btt	William	747	Nwk
John, Sr.	975	Nrt	James	675	Br	see Manard		
Samuel	974	Nrt	James	618	Gls	Cray, James	9	Oho
Wm.	12	Ntt	James	8	Pwh	Jno.	444	Mth
see Crable			James	80	Spt	William	14	Oho
Cram, John	835	Hmp	James, jr.	75	Spt	Crayden, Eliza.	19	Clp
Cramer, Ambrose	530	Frd	James, (NM)	330	Ags	Crayton, Edward	6	Oho
Frederick	102	Jff	Jane	329	Ags	John	9	Oho
John	830	Hmp	Jerimiah	592	Mnr	Cre...dindon, James	132	Hnr
Peter	100	Jff	Jno.	243	Frf	Creacy, Elizabeth	303	Amh
Samuel J.	58	Jff	Jno.	245	Frf	Creagh, Mary	893	Nrf
Thomas	573	Frd	Jno.	278	Rck	Creaghead, Betsey	451	Frn
Cramlett, Michael	4	Oho	Jno.	305	Rck	Isaiah	451	Frn
Cramlit, Frederic	26	Oho	Jno. [crossed out]	311	Rck	Polley	451	Frn
Crandell, Dudley	893	Nrf	John	266	Amh	Creal, Jno.	20	Clp
Crandle, Esekiah	607	Mnt	John	675	Br	Creamer, Geo.	575	Brk
Ezeriah	613	Mnt	John	676	Br	Jacob	292	Ldn
John	182	Elc	John	143	Dnw	Jno.	892	Nrf
Nathl.	626	Mnt	John	686	Nls	John	255	Shn
Nathl.	641	Mnt	John	111	Spt	Mary	583	Brk
Crandol, John	680	Wrw	John	712	Wsh	Mary	891	Nrf
Thos.	681	Wrw	John	714	Wsh	see Crusen		
Crane, Amos	16	Clp	John, (Majr.)	329	Ags	Creasey, Bird	457	Bdf
John	434	Bth	John, (NM)	326	Ags	Charles	118	Cmb
John	158	Knq	John D.	297	Amh	Clabion	457	Bdf
John	238	Ldn	John R.	528	Frd	Edmund	456	Bdf
Joseph	76	Jff	Josiah, Jr.	615	Btt	John	457	Bdf
M.	32	Hnr	Josiah, Sr.	615	Btt	Pleasant	457	Bdf
Nathaniel	158	Knq	Lathey	242	Frf	Thomas	457	Bdf
Saml.	490	Mnn	Martin	35	Rcm	Thomas F.	457	Bdf
Tarlton	782	Bck	Mary	327	Ags	William	456	Bdf
see Cram			Moses	142	Dnw	Wm. W.	443	Flv
Craney, Sarah, a free			Nathan	445	Bth	Creasy, Franklin	457	Bdf
negro	996	Nrt	Nathan	684	Nls	Sally	561	Pre
Crank, John	151	Alb	Nelson	270	Amh	Crebell, Christn.	331	Ags
Lipscomb	438	Flv	Nelson	685	Nls	Crebs, Conrad	506	Frd
William	256	Amh	Nimrod	615	Btt	Creddendon, Wm.	111	Hnr
Cranks, Stephen	440	Flv	Oliver	13	Oho	Credit, George, a free		
Cranston, Robert	823	Wth	Reuben	512	Prw	mulatto	976	Nrt
Crapper, Ben	893	Nrf	Reubin	269	Amh	John, a free mulatto	976	Nrt
Crask, Griffin	769	Wst	Robert	432	Bth	Sally, a free mulatto	976	Nrt
Joel	769	Wst	Robert	674	Br	Creeck, Sol.	819	Nrf
John	770	Wst	Robt.	327	Ags	Creed, Jno.	447	Pra
Mark	769	Wst	Ruben	248	Shn	Creedland, Eliza.	200	Ess
Richard	769	Wst	Sally	891	Nrf	Creegar, George	825	Wth
William	770	Wst	Saml.	327	Ags	Michael	826	Wth
Craugh, Mary	707	Brn	Saml.	19	Clp	Creeger, Devaut	826	Wth
Craunch, Walter	279	Ldn	Saml., Sr.	615	Btt	Henry	826	Wth

Jacob	826	Wth	Nicholas	18	Clp	Christopher	584	Frd
John	823	Wth	Reuben	687	Gch	Jacob	380	Mds
Peter	826	Wth	Sanders	4	Ntt	Jas.	22	Clp
see Cregar			Thomas	188	Alb	Leanah	24	Clp
Creekabarger, David	7	Rcm	Thos.	856	Hnv	Lewis	380	Mds
John	5	Rcm	Walter	856	Hnv	Reub.	21	Clp
Creekman, Leek	445	Pra	William	188	Alb	Wm.	19	Clp
Creekmur, Anne	790	Nrf	Wm.	612	Btt	Crim, Chs.	281	Ldn
Arthur	789	Nrf	Wm.	10	Ntt	Harman	491	Mnn
Benj.	797	Nrf	see Fretwell, White			Jacob	327	Ags
Charles	790	Nrf	Cresap, Michael	18	Oho	Jacob	281	Ldn
Diana	799	Nrf	Creshmond, Charles	770	Wst	Joseph	401	Fqr
Edward, Sr.	799	Nrf	Cresiper, Anthy.	542	Brk	Michael	94	Jff
Eli	797	Nrf	Cress, George	277	Rck	William	906	Hrr
Edwd., jr.	799	Nrf	Henry	491	Mnn	Crimes, Elizabeth	334	Lnn
Forman	797	Nrf	Henry	288	Rck	Kezia	335	Lnn
Hilary	790	Nrf	Isaac	491	Mnn	Leonard	335	Lnn
Irby	790	Nrf	Jac.	491	Mnn	Crimp, ---, Murphy &	22	Hnr
Jas.	790	Nrf	Jno.	288	Rck	Cringan, Ann	20	Hnr
Jas.	798	Nrf	Lucy	849	Hnv	Crinker, John	529	Brk
Joel	789	Nrf	Cresswell, Richard	4	Oho	Crinn see Crum		
Joel	796	Nrf	Creswell, Abraham	767	Hmp	Crippin, Abel	87	Acc
John	790	Nrf	Cretia, Parthenia	877	Sth	Joshua	87	Acc
Josiah	790	Nrf	Cretini, Casimere	326	Dnw	Savage	84	Acc
Matthew	790	Nrf	Cretser, Henry	92	Jff	Spencer	88	Acc
Nathan	796	Nrf	Crettenden, Wm.	16	Clp	Stephen	86	Acc
Pal	797	Nrf	Crettendon see Cre...dindon			Thomas	87	Acc
Pal, jr.	790	Nrf	Creusier, Mary	22	Clp	see Delastatious		
Paul, Sr.	790	Nrf	Crew, Elijah	953	Chc	Cripping, Saml.	85	Acc
Peter	795	Nrf	Elisha	957	Chc	Cris, Michle	954	Hrr
Sarah	789	Nrf	Elisha	959	Chc	Crise, Fredrick	326	Dnw
Sarah	790	Nrf	Elizabeth	940	Chc	Crisell, Rebecca	59	Jff
Seth	790	Nrf	Gatley	857	Hnv	Criseman, Hannah	178	Alb
Stephen	791	Nrf	James	749	Nwk	Criser, John	684	Nls
Thos.	797	Nrf	Jesse	457	Bdf	Crislep, Jacob	920	Hrr
Tucker	788	Nrf	Jesse	749	Nwk	Crisler, Adam	382	Mds
Willis	790	Nrf	Jessee	857	Hnv	George, & Son	382	Mds
Wm.	790	Nrf	Jno.	650	Glc	Henry	382	Mds
Wm.	797	Nrf	Micajah	859	Hnv	William	382	Mds
Wm., Sr.	805	Nrf	Micajah, Jnr.	844	Hnv	Crislet, George	919	Hrr
Creeknur, John	789	Nrf	Mirum	956	Chc	Crisman, George	394	Fqr
Creel, Clarisy	11	Wod	Nicholass	859	Hnv	Isaac	541	Frd
David	521	Prw	Peggy	114	Hnr	John	527	Frd
George	346	Fqr	Peter	940	Chc	John	505	Prw
George	10	Wod	Robert	955	Chc	Crismon, Thomas	383	Fqr
Harrison	349	Fqr	Saley	856	Hnv	Crismond, Burnett	195	Kng
Philip	540	Brk	Thos.	650	Glc	Ignatious	332	Dnw
Thomas	1	Wod	see C...w			Jno., Senr.	194	Kng
William	407	Fqr	Crewdson, Ellen	206	Ess	John, jr.	194	Kng
William, Jr.	408	Fqr	Ellen	437	Flv	Wm.	194	Kng
Creely, Ann	686	Gch	Reuben	438	Flv	Crisp, John	682	Nls
Patrick	824	Wth	Wm.	435	Flv	John, Snr.	108	Cmb
Creemer see Crumer			Crewer, Nancy	840	Nrf	Lucy	682	Nls
Cregar, Jacob	825	Wth	Crews, Anderson	264	Amh	Crispin, Thomas	23	Oho
Michael	825	Wth	Archerlus	272	Amh	Criss, John	692	Br
Michael	826	Wth	David	456	Bdf	Moses	924	Hrr
Michael	827	Wth	James	615	Btt	Peter	950	Hrr
Peter	825	Wth	John	256	Amh	Crissap, Thomas	795	Hmp
Peter	827	Wth	Joseph	457	Bdf	Crisso, Jacob	457	Bdf
see Creeger			Josiah	882	Cmp	Crist, Adam	615	Btt
Cregg, John	17	Acc	Mary	890	Hnv	Phillip	613	Btt
Creighton, John	947	Chc	Peach	828	Bck	Cristie, Joseph	115	Spt
Cremans, Elijah	11	Knw	Thomas	273	Amh	Cristman, Jacob	773	Hmp
Crenshaw, Allin	335	Lnn	Crick, Jacob	330	Ags	Cristy, Robert	80	Jff
Ann	855	Hnv	Criddle, Jessee	117	Cmb	Criswell, Joseph	106	Jff
Buchner	873	Yrk	John	131	Cmb	Critcher, George	396	Rch
Charles	901	Hnv	Crider, Abraham	200	Shn	John, Estate	769	Wst
Charles, Snr.	845	Hnv	Jacob	330	Ags	Critchfield, Hennery	926	Hrr
Daniel	336	Lnn	Jacob	247	Frf	Critchlow, John	877	Sth
David	856	Hnv	Jacob	518	Frd	Lucy	844	Sth
David	769	Wst	Jacob, 2d.	520	Frd	William	633	Sss
Jno., B.H.	850	Hnv	Jno.	541	Prg	Critchton, James	745	Brn
Joel	850	Hnv	John	519	Frd	Crites, Mary	614	Btt
John	688	Gch	John	525	Frd	Critezer, Catherine	695	Br
John, B.	845	Hnv	John	602	Frd	Peter	692	Br
Joseph	335	Lnn	John, 2d.	519	Frd	Crittenden, Frances F.	158	Knq
Mary	871	Hnv	Margret	751	Wsh	Frances T. M.	159	Knq
Mary [?]	336	Lnn	Martin	542	Frd	James H.	158	Knq
Moses	334	Lnn	Peter	595	Mnr	Jane	461	Mdd
Nat.	870	Sth	Crigler, Aron	380	Mds	Richd.	158	Knq

Sally	748	Nwk	George	222	Pnd	Richard	926	Hrr
Thomas G.	461	Mdd	Cromley, James	576	Frd	Richard	258	Ldn
Wm.	650	Glc	see Crumly			Richard	10	Oho
Z.U.	461	Mdd	Crompton, Ezekiel	559	Brk	Salley	871	Hnv
Zacharia	159	Knq	Cromwell, John	87	Acc	Saml.	245	Frf
Crittendon, John, [his]			Sanel.	830	Nrf	Thomas	612	Btt
Est.	872	Yrk	Cron, Fergus	452	Frn	Wiley	305	Ldn
John F.	205	Ess	Joseph	452	Frn	William	194	Kng
Lemuel	205	Ess	Crone, Adam	646	Mnt	William	10	Oho
Wm.	222	Ess	Henry	575	Brk	Willm.	612	Btt
see Cre...dindon			Croney, Michl.	492	Mnn	Wm.	245	Ldn
Crittenton, John	245	Aml	Thomas	593	Brk	see Crop		
Richard	708	Brn	Cronk, Henry	656	Mnt	Crossfield, James	460	Mdd
Critton, James	13	Wod	Jacob	205	Shn	John	212	Ess
Critz, Abram	911	Hrr	Jacob, (O.Spoor) [Over-			Leonard	460	Mdd
John	909	Hrr	seer of Poor?]	207	Shn	Crossley, Cathne.	892	Nrf
Michael	911	Hrr	Cronshorn, Jacob	216	Pnd	George	14	Acc
Philip	922	Hrr	Crook, Betty, (M)	707	Brn	James	612	Btt
Critzer, Lennard	925	Hrr	Giles	707	Brn	Margte.	892	Nrf
Croachran, William	683	Nls	Henry	752	Wsh	Crosslin, Jonas	157	Sth
Croaghead, John	470	Frn	Joseph	62	Stf	Crosslow, Jane	916	Hrr
Croake, Richard	245	Frf	Micheal	463	Frn	Crosson, James	1	Oho
Croan, Fred.	325	Ags	Robert, (M)	708	Brn	Crosswell, Susannah	86	Acc
Henry	328	Ags	Sarah	707	Brn	Wm.	188	Elc
Michael	328	Ags	William	823	Hmp	Crosthwait, John	189	Alb
Crobarger, Elizabeth	11	Rcm	Crooks, Charles	301	Ldn	Croston, Travis D.	833	Hmp
Croch, Andrew	418	Rnd	Robert	594	Mnr	Croswell, Wm.	650	Glc
see Crouch			Crookshank, John	326	Ags	Crouch, Francis	504	Prw
Crocker, Drury	33	Isw	Jno.	11	Rcm	Jacob	567	Brk
Jesse	161	Sth	Croomer, Saml.	326	Ags	Jacob	418	Rnd
John	161	Sth	Crooper, Richd.	235	Ldn	James	160	Knq
Johnson	37	Isw	Crop, James	28	Stf	John	188	Alb
Milner	2	Isw	Jas.	21	Clp	John	457	Bdf
Milner, for the Poors			John	29	Stf	John	370	Fqr
house	32	Isw	see Cross			John	419	Rnd
William	8	Isw	Cropper, Edmund	14	Acc	Joseph	457	Bdf
Crocket, Asher	618	Gls	James	872	Yrk	Lucy	685	Gch
Joseph	889	Yrk	John, Junr.	17	Acc	Rebecca	567	Brk
Robert	975	Nrt	John, Senr.	13	Acc	Stephen	244	Aml
William	332	Dnw	John S.	13	Acc	Thomas	966	Hrr
Crockett, Andrew	823	Wth	Joshua	15	Acc	Walter	288	Ldn
Elizebeth [2]	827	Wth	Luke	15	Acc	William	457	Bdf
Hugh	617	Mnt	Thomas	16	Acc	Wm.	686	Gch
James	823	Wth	Crosbie, Hannah	893	Nrf	see Chrouch, Croch		
John	741	Wsh	Crosby, Ann	892	Nrf	Croucher, Charles	153	Alb
John	823	Wth	George	328	Ags	Coleman	189	Alb
Joseph	13	Acc	Lewis	506	Prw	William	280	Amh
Joseph	818	Wth	Mary	510	Prw	Croughan, William	693	Br
Joseph	826	Wth	Croshard, Sebastian	326	Dnw	Crous see Crone		
Robert	556	Frd	Crosley, ...ph [Joseph?]	759	Hmp	Crouse, Christian	567	Brk
Robert [2]	823	Wth	Dacid	218	Pnd	Danl.	328	Ags
Saml.	629	Mnt	Crosly, Thomas	119	Spt	Jas.	330	Ags
Saml.	760	Wsh	Crosmuck, Michl.	892	Nrf	John	2	Rcm
Samuel [2]	823	Wth	Cross, ---	247	Frf	Metthias	826	Wth
Thomas	13	Acc	Anderson	332	Ags	Nicholas	911	Hrr
Zadock	13	Acc	Ann	892	Nrf	Crout, Daniel	101	Jff
Crockwell, John	514	Frd	Asial	27	Rcm	Crow, Anthony	749	Nwk
John, Jr.	514	Frd	Benja.	245	Frf	Ben.	828	Nrf
Croddy, John	284	Rck	Charles	6	Ntt	Dennis, & mother	379	Mds
Croel, Jno.	891	Nrf	Gabriel	9	Rcm	Edward	825	Wth
Wm.	892	Nrf	Geo.	492	Mnn	George	825	Wth
Croerbastis see Aroerbastis			Jacob	3	Oho	Hilan	243	Ldn
Croffard, Andrew	420	Rnd	James	193	Kng	Jacob	331	Ags
Crofford, Rhody	801	Hmp	James	278	Ldn	James	594	Mnr
Thomas	336	Lnn	James	10	Oho	James	716	Wsh
Croft, David	69	Jff	Jno.	245	Frf	James, Jur.	825	Wth
Lewis	8	Rcm	Jno.	247	Frf	James, Ser.	825	Wth
Philip	107	Jff	Jno.	900	Hnv	John	328	Ags
Thomas	505	Brk	Jno.	492	Mnn	John	215	Ess
Crofton see Crafton			Joel	896	Hnv	John	221	Ess
Croker, Actious	6	Hnr	John	612	Btt	John	159	Knq
Crokton, Thomas	769	Wst	John	336	Dnw	John	637	Mnt
Croley, Elizabeth	895	Crl	John	558	Frd	John E.	219	Ess
Hannah	897	Crl	John	10	Oho	Joseph	676	Br
Crom see Coram			Jos.	295	Ldn	Judy	221	Ess
Cromeline, Elizabeth	892	Nrf	Joseph	896	Hnv	Katy	328	Ags
Cromer, Martin	40	Rcm	Joseph	160	Knq	Leonard	564	Frd
Cromet, Christopher	226	Pnd	Mordecai	262	Rck	Lewis	716	Wsh
Conrod	226	Pnd	Nathl.	871	Hnv	Linzey	613	Btt
Frederick	226	Pnd	Reason	85	Jff	Moses	221	Ess

Name	Pg	Dist	Name	Pg	Dist	Name	Pg	Dist
Peter	24	Oho	Crozier, Andw.	600	Mnr	Crumton, Elijah	561	Brk
Philip	328	Ags	Cruch, Richd.	32	Hnr	Crumwell, Demsey	848	Sth
Phillip	697	Br	Cruchfield, Robt.	307	Rck	Crupper, Cloe	372	Fqr
Richard	57	Jff	Cruffice, John	819	Hmp	John	372	Fqr
Robert	711	Wsh	Cruidson, Henry	400	Rch	John	588	Frd
St. Albin	219	Ess	Crum, Anthony, Jr.	531	Frd	Thos., (F.N.)	24	Clp
Thomas	825	Wth	Anthony, Senr.	531	Frd	Cruse, John	38	Isw
Thos.	220	Ess	Christian, Jr.	551	Frd	Crusen, Isaac	583	Brk
William	677	Br	Christian, Senr.	552	Frd	Richd.	583	Brk
William	45	Chr	Christian, 3d.	532	Frd	see Creamer		
William	54	Jff	Henry	532	Frd	Crush, Henry	612	Btt
William	379	Mds	Crumb, Abraham	456	Bdf	Peter	613	Btt
Wm.	214	Ess	Gilbert	456	Bdf	Willm.	613	Btt
Wm.	961	Hrr	Crumdol, Mary	271	Ldn	Crusin, Elizabeth	77	Jff
see Crowfielding			Crumer, Catherine	627	Mnt	Jacob	71	Jff
Crowbarger, Geo.	332	Ags	Crumley, Henry	531	Brk	James	13	Oho
Crowder, Ananias	141	Dnw	Thos.	531	Brk	James B.	78	Jff
Bartholewmew	334	Lnn	Crumly, Aaron M.	578	Frd	Crusinberry, Fridk.	649	Mnt
Batt	335	Lnn	see Cromley			Jas.	18	Clp
Daniel	141	Dnw	Crummell, Stephen	92	Jff	Crutcher, James	70	Jff
Eliza.	244	Aml	Crump, Abner	747	Nwk	James	78	Jff
Elizabeth	143	Dnw	Anderson	748	Nwk	Reubin	45	Chr
Elizabeth	973	Nrt	Anne	747	Nwk	Robert	25	Stf
George	141	Dnw	Benedict	749	Nwk	William	352	Fqr
George	336	Lnn	Benj.	18	Hnr	Crutchfed., Wm. F.	682	Wrw
Herbert	19	Ntt	Benjamin	350	Fqr	Crutchfeild, Jane	441	Bth
Herod T.	244	Aml	Beverley	749	Nwk	John	947	Chc
Jesse	974	Nrt	Charles	457	Bdf	Milly	954	Chc
John	143	Dnw	Christopher	747	Nwk	William	33	Hnr
John	975	Nrt	Crawford	29	Isw	Crutchfield, Francis	447	Bth
Joseph	143	Dnw	Edmund	747	Nwk	John	749	Nwk
Laban	142	Dnw	F. P.	112	Hnr	John	73	Spt
Larkin	11	Knw	Fendall	456	Bdf	John S.	846	Hnv
Leonard	141	Dnw	George	380	Fqr	Mary	220	Ess
Moses	973	Nrt	George	459	Frn	Peter	18	Hnr
Nancy	975	Nrt	George	619	Gls	R.	4	Hnr
Nelson	141	Dnw	George	748	Nwk	Robert	67	Spt
Shadrach	537	Prg	George W.	245	Aml	Sarah	688	Gch
Stephen	975	Nrt	James	748	Nwk	Stapleton	88	Spt
Susan	143	Dnw	James O.	102	Cmb	Staplton.	687	Gch
Thomas, Jr.	975	Nrt	Jesse	747	Nwk	Walker	326	Dnw
Thomas, Sr.	975	Nrt	Jno.	243	Frf	Wm.	688	Gch
Wesley	142	Dnw	John	358	Fqr	see Cruchfield, Crutchfed.		
William	974	Nrt	John	747	Nwk	Crutchfielf, Jno.	877	Hnv
William, Jr.	975	Nrt	John	111	Spt	Crutchinger, John	205	Shn
William, Sr.	975	Nrt	John	120	Spt	Crute, John L.	560	Pre
Crowdus, Catharine	651	Glc	John C.	748	Nwk	Willis	559	Pre
Crowfielding, S.	160	Knq	John P.	748	Nwk	Cruthis, James	294	Ldn
Crowl, Catherine	582	Brk	Josiah	747	Nwk	Crutsinger, Conrod	222	Shn
Duval	480	Frn	Nathaniel	747	Nwk	George	218	Shn
Henry	581	Brk	Richard	448	Grn	Crven, John H.	189	Alb
Jacob	589	Brk	Richard [2]	748	Nwk	Cryder, Henry	825	Wth
Jacob	70	Jff	Richard, Colo.	6	Pwh	Cryer, Stephen	142	Dnw
Jacob	103	Jff	Thomas	747	Nwk	Cryner, Andrew	618	Gls
Micheal	462	Frn	Traverse	350	Fqr	Cubaniss, Martha	9	Ntt
Crowle, Henry	613	Btt	Walker	614	Mnt	Cubbage, Archd.	23	Clp
Crown, Elisha	682	Br	Will	749	Nwk	Thomas	381	Mds
John	328	Ags	William	243	Frf	Cubberle, Job	414	Bth
Joseph	170	Shn	William	492	Frn	Thomas	421	Bth
Crownover, Wm.	513	Brk	William	748	Nwk	Cuberly, Levy	423	Rnd
Crowson, Bernard	524	Prw	Wm.	243	Frf	Cublerly, Isaac	222	Pnd
Elijah	204	Shn	see Crimp			Cucher, Jacob	647	Mnt
John	17	Acc	Crumpecher, John	456	Bdf	Cudden, John	409	Ags
Levin	84	Acc	Crumpicker, Abraham	456	Bdf	Cuddy, James	824	Wth
Thomas	524	Prw	Jacob	457	Bdf	Cudmore, Paul	38	Stf
Warren	526	Prw	John	457	Bdf	Cuff, Will	474	Frn
William	85	Acc	Crumpler, Arthur	17	Isw	Cuffee, Aaron	794	Nrf
William	524	Prw	Beasant	141	Sth	Abby	802	Nrf
Croxton, Carter	214	Ess	Benj.	17	Isw	Chas., (FB)	445	Pra
Isaac	215	Ess	Eley	23	Isw	Fancy	795	Nrf
James	220	Ess	Jno.	882	Sth	Fynny [?]	795	Nrf
John	215	Ess	John	162	Sth	Geo. [2]	795	Nrf
Milly	208	Ess	Matthew	23	Isw	Geo., F. B.	445	Pra
Sarah	217	Ess	Sally	44	Isw	Jas.	795	Nrf
William	695	Br	William	847	Sth	John	794	Nrf
Wm.	215	Ess	Crumpton, David	456	Bdf	John, jr.	795	Nrf
Croy, Adam	664	Mnt	David, Sr.	456	Bdf	Lemuel	804	Nrf
Henry	664	Mnt	John	827	Hmp	Lovey	794	Nrf
Jacob	664	Mnt	Penney	258	Ldn	Nancy	795	Nrf
Crozel, ---, Spindler &	2	Hnr	Samuel	780	Hmp	Nancy	802	Nrf

Saml.	795	Nrf	John	272	Rck	George	507	Brk
William	794	Nrf	Jos., Sr.	647	Mnt	Hugh	577	Brk
Willis	795	Nrf	Lettice	381	Fqr	Israel	765	Hmp
Cuffy, Fanny	687	Gch	Martin	445	Pra	James	360	Fqr
Cuhill see Cutrill			Mary	445	Pra	James	800	Hmp
Culley, Hannah	253	Shn	Moses, (Jr.)	27	Rcm	James	682	Nls
Culling, Matthew	692	Br	Moses, (Sen.)	27	Rcm	James	891	Nrf
Richard	692	Br	Robert	676	Br	James	222	Pnd
Cullison, Jeremiah	253	Ldn	Robt.	583	Mnr	James	96	Spt
William	770	Wst	Simon	383	Fqr	James	732	Wsh
Wm.	253	Ldn	Thomas	6	Rcm	Jas.	586	Brk
Culloms, David	194	Kng	William	686	Br	Jas.	67	Chs
John	194	Kng	William	24	Rcm	Jas.	185	Elc
Cullony, James	892	Nrf	Willis	381	Fqr	Jno.	31	Hnr
Cullumber, Jesse	95	Jff	Wm.	234	Ldn	Jno.	269	Rck
Culp, Christian	324	Ags	Wm.	274	Rck	Jno.	297	Rck
Frederick	571	Brk	see Cummus			John	329	Ags
George	815	Hmp	Cummons, Robert	716	Wsh	John	407	Fqr
Henry	4	Rcm	Cummus, Enoch	262	Ldn	John	762	Hmp
John	815	Hmp	Cump, Henry	769	Hmp	John	22	Hnr
Philip	220	Shn	Cumpston, Jacob	792	Hmp	John	12	Isw
Culpason, John	462	Frn	Cumpton, Danl.	22	Clp	John	4	Oho
Culpepper, Asa	798	Nrf	Joseph	625	Mnt	John	276	Rck
Asa	821	Nrf	Cunard, Edward	79	Jff	Jonathan	620	Gls
Daniel	789	Nrf	Cundiff, Griffin	461	Mdd	Josh.	19	Clp
Daniel	891	Nrf	Isaac	523	Prw	Js.	195	Kng
Jas.	445	Pra	James	332	Ags	Lovica	10	Isw
Jereah.	825	Nrf	James	461	Mdd	Margte.	891	Nrf
Peter	823	Nrf	Jno., Jr.	342	Lnc	Mary	965	Hrr
Robt.	821	Nrf	Jno., yr.	341	Lnc	Nancy	688	Gch
Rot.	825	Nrf	Lettice	394	Fqr	Nancy	307	Rck
Thos.	789	Nrf	Nelley	973	Nrt	Phil.	193	Kng
Thos.	796	Nrf	Richd.	340	Lnc	Phil., jr.	195	Kng
Thos.	821	Nrf	William	461	Mdd	Richard	874	Cmp
Willis	829	Nrf	William	523	Prw	Richard	114	Cmp
Wm.	821	Nrf	Cunduff, Bengamin	806	Hmp	Richd.	330	Ags
Culton, Abr.	293	Rck	John	807	Hmp	Robt.	330	Ags
Robt.	294	Rck	John	812	Hmp	Robt.	487	Mnn
see Cutton			Cuningham, Adam	958	Hrr	Robt.	98	Spt
Culverhouse, Cloe	389	Fqr	Andrew	616	Btt	Sam.	184	Elc
James	236	Ldn	Edward	947	Hrr	Saml.	329	Ags
William	393	Fqr	Eliz.	487	Mnn	Saml.	577	Brk
Cumagam, Stephen	419	Rnd	Geo.	490	Mnn	Sarah	332	Dnw
see Cunnagam			Jacob	560	Pre	Sarah	180	Elc
Cumberfoot, Jno.	445	Pra	James	457	Bdf	Sarah	965	Hrr
Cumbo, Anderson	958	Chc	Jno.	489	Mnn	Thomas	270	Rck
John	958	Chc	John	960	Hrr	Timoy.	21	Clp
Nelson	748	Nwk	John	223	Pnd	William	779	Bck
Thomas	45	Chr	John M.	560	Pre	William	340	Fqr
see Combo			Joseph	451	Frn	William	11	Knw
Cumby, Peter	876	Cmp	Joseph	958	Hrr	William	15	Oho
see Cemby			Robert	690	Br	William	222	Pnd
Cumins, James	307	Rck	Ruth	240	Shn	William	18	Wod
Saml.	305	Rck	Thomas	483	Frn	Wim.	886	Hnv
Cummin, Samuel	443	Bth	Thomas	484	Frn	Wm.	937	Hrr
Cumming, James	336	Dnw	Thomas	947	Hrr	Wm.	266	Rck
William	332	Dnw	Walter	946	Hrr	Wm.	270	Rck
Cummings, Geo., Senr.	246	Frf	William	152	Alb	Wm.	280	Rck
George	244	Frf	William	682	Br	Wm.	292	Rck
James	718	Wsh	Cunliffe, Jno.	66	Chs	Wm.	723	Wsh
Jane	542	Prg	Cunnagam, John	419	Rnd	Wm.	758	Wsh
Jno.	300	Ldn	Cunnard, Ant.	292	Ldn	Wm., Jur.	723	Wsh
Jos., Jr.	641	Mnt	Edwd.	272	Ldn	see Cenningham		
Robert	322	Ldn	James	766	Hmp	Cunninghm, John	191	Elc
Cummins, Aaron	794	Hmp	Jno.	266	Ldn	Cunshaw see Crenshaw		
Alexander	383	Fqr	Jont.	267	Ldn	Cup, Henry	422	Bth
And.	290	Rck	Cunningham, ---	920	Nrf	Cupp, Chrisr.	487	Mnn
Charl.	583	Mnr	Adam	916	Hrr	Leo.	490	Mnn
Charles [2]	576	Mnr	Adam	965	Hrr	Leo., Jur.	492	Mnn
Chas., Revd.	718	Wsh	Adam	18	Wod	Cuppy, John	698	Br
Daniel	372	Fqr	Ann	24	Clp	Margaret	680	Br
David	6	Rcm	Bengamin	818	Hmp	Cups, Danl.	325	Ags
George	353	Fqr	Benja.	193	Kng	Jacob	329	Ags
Gideon	836	Hmp	David	330	Ags	Marcus	325	Ags
Gideon	280	Ldn	Edward	124	Cmb	Curb see Curle		
Hugh	595	Mnr	Elizabeth	123	Cmb	Curby, Wm.	833	Nrf
James	679	Br	Elizabeth	965	Hrr	Curd, Charles	792	Bck
Jno.	262	Ldn	Elizabeth	891	Nrf	Edward	814	Bck
John	330	Ags	Elizet.	893	Nrf	Jessee	685	Gch
John	535	Frd	Francis	343	Fqr	John	686	Gch

Name	No.	Code
John	561	Pre
Joseph	787	Bck
Richard	127	Hnr
Curkman, Elizabeth	464	Frn
Curle, ---, Mrs.	893	Nrf
Bennet	749	Nwk
Bridget	893	Nrf
David	748	Nwk
James	582	Frd
James	271	Ldn
John	750	Nwk
John, junr.	747	Nwk
Julius	852	Cmp
Littleton	840	Nrf
Lockey	681	Wrw
Richardson	748	Nwk
Susan	333	Dnw
William	328	Dnw
Curlet, Thomas	513	Frd
William	797	Hmp
Curley, John	683	Nls
Joseph	522	Prw
Walter	194	Kng
Curlin, Lemuel	445	Pra
Curling, Arthur	805	Nrf
Daniel	807	Nrf
James	792	Nrf
John, jr.	792	Nrf
John, Sr.	800	Nrf
Portlock	806	Nrf
Willis	799	Nrf
Wm.	799	Nrf
Curlley, David	770	Wst
Curmagam see Cunnagam		
Curmickle, Wm.	934	Hrr
Curran, Robt.	23	Clp
Currant, Jas.	491	Mnn
Currell, Dolly	341	Lnc
Edwd.	340	Lnc
Fleet	340	Lnc
Jacob	341	Lnc
Jas.	341	Lnc
Raw.	340	Lnc
Tho.	341	Lnc
Currence, John	418	Rnd
William	419	Rnd
Current, Enoch	491	Mnn
Jas., Jur.	491	Mnn
John	491	Mnn
Martin	491	Mnn
Currey, Isaac	293	Ldn
John	747	Wsh
Currie, Armd.	340	Lnc
Elleson	340	Lnc
see C...rie		
Currier, Samul	4	Oho
Currin, James	437	Flv
Wm.	642	Mnt
Wm.	671	Mnt
Curry, Adam	420	Bth
Alexr.	325	Ags
Barnabas	600	Mnr
Benjn.	325	Ags
Charles	839	Bck
Daniel	420	Bth
Dav.	490	Mnn
Isaiah	325	Ags
Isaih	421	Bth
James	325	Ags
James	929	Hrr
James	564	Mnr
James [2]	218	Pnd
Jane	208	Ess
Jesse	535	Brk
John	929	Hrr
John	158	Knq
John	581	Mnr
Margt.	490	Mnn
Mary	301	Amh
Richard	430	Bth
Richd.	650	Glc
Robt.	326	Ags
Saml.	325	Ags
Saml., (Capt.)	325	Ags
Samuel	428	Bth
Thomas	279	Amh
Thomas	425	Bth
Thomas	506	Brk
Thomas	538	Frd
Thomas	91	Jff
Thomas	8	Rcm
William	420	Bth
Wm.	325	Ags
Currys, George	776	Bck
Curtin, William	462	Frn
Curtis, Barnabas	270	Ldn
Betsey	326	Ags
Charles	973	Nrt
Chichester	72	Spt
Chloe, (F.N.)	24	Clp
Christian	457	Bdf
Christopher	81	Spt
D.M.	892	Nrf
David	577	Brk
Edmd.	872	Yrk
Edmond	120	Spt
Elijah	16	Clp
Elijah	72	Spt
Elijah	59	Stf
Eliza.	651	Glc
George	959	Hrr
George	28	Stf
George	769	Wst
Henry	958	Hrr
Jacob	560	Brk
James	288	Ldn
James	11	Oho
James	57	Stf
Jesse	933	Hrr
Jesse	54	Stf
John	511	Frd
John	98	Spt
John, of C.C.	22	Stf
John, of W.O.	59	Stf
Jonathan	326	Dnw
Joshua	547	Brk
Littleberry	633	Sss
Mary	547	Brk
Munson	120	Spt
Richard	39	Stf
Sally	342	Lnc
Theodisus	102	Spt
Thomas	275	Ldn
Thomas	973	Nrt
Thomas	40	Stf
Thornton	61	Stf
Thos., jr.	681	Wrw
Thos., sr.	681	Wrw
William	102	Spt
Wm.	16	Clp
Curtois, Jenny	892	Nrf
Curtz, Jacob	828	Hmp
Peter	831	Hmp
Cusic, Walter	282	Ldn
Cusick, Robert	722	Wsh
Custalo, Jas.	31	Hnr
Custard, Abram	463	Frn
George	507	Brk
George	613	Btt
Isaac	616	Btt
Jacob	616	Btt
John, Jr.	613	Btt
John, Jr.	614	Btt
John, Sr.	614	Btt
Peter	508	Brk
Custer, Conrod	16	Rcm
Jacob	16	Rcm
Paul	30	Rcm
Richd.	30	Rcm
Custice, Elisha	346	Fqr
Custis, Caty	17	Acc
Charles	245	Frf
John, BS	17	Acc
George	17	Acc
George P.W.	749	Nwk
Henry B.	13	Acc
Patience	14	Acc
Revel	16	Acc
Thomas, of Only	15	Acc
Thomas, of R	17	Acc
Thomas, Senr.	15	Acc
William R.	15	Acc
William S.	15	Acc
Custor, Joseph	937	Hrr
Cutchin, Robert	836	Nrf
Cutchins, Anne	45	Isw
Esther	26	Isw
Joseph	26	Isw
Josiah	24	Isw
Josiah, Sen.	26	Isw
Richd.	45	Isw
see Counsil		
Cuthbert, William	386	Hmp
Wm.	891	Nrf
Cuthburt, Wm., [his]		
(Plantn.)	443	Pra
Cutherel, Elu	809	Nrf
Murg [?]	809	Nrf
Cutherell, Ben.	808	Nrf
Jas.	807	Nrf
Joshua	805	Nrf
Reuben	808	Nrf
Saml.	828	Nrf
Wm.	829	Nrf
Cutlar, Stephen	613	Btt
Cutler, Andrew	2	Rcm
John	85	Acc
Richard	15	Acc
Wm.	143	Dnw
Cutloaf, Francis	781	Hmp
Cutright, Abram	948	Hrr
Andrew	911	Hrr
Hanner	906	Hrr
Isaac	909	Hrr
Jacob	911	Hrr
John	911	Hrr
Cutrill, Wm.	892	Nrf
Cuttillo, Abram	873	Yrk
Edwd.	872	Yrk
Cutting, John B.	50	Stf
Cuttler, ---	332	Dnw
Elizabeth	825	Hmp
Cutton, James	294	Rck
see Culton		
Cuzack, Elizabeth	100	Jff
Cyphax, Betty, Urbanna	461	Mdd
Cyphers, William	404	Fqr
Cyphert, Isaac	16	Rcm
Cypress, John	799	Nrf
Rebecca	604	Srr
Czegen, Jno.	491	Mnn

--- D ---

Name	No.	Code
D..., ... [3]	458	Bdf
...s	458	Bdf
Francis	458	Bdf
Saml.	336	Dnw
Daar, John	829	Wth
Dabbs, George	46	Chr
Isaiah	46	Chr
James	46	Chr
Richard, Revd.	47	Chr
William, (Son Richd.)	47	Chr
William, (Surveyer)	47	Chr
Dabney, ---	332	Dnw
Benjn.	144	Dnw
Betsy	88	Spt

C.	24	Hnr	Dale, Joseph	399	Rch	Wm.	130	Hnr
Charles	458	Bdf	Mary	822	Nrf	Dandrige, Eliza	4	Hnr
Charles	859	Hnv	Richard	458	Frn	Danebery, Mary	13	Hnr
Cornelius	458	Bdf	Saml.	270	Rck	Danee see Dance		
George	857	Hnv	Daley, John	337	Lnn	Danell, Jane	296	Ldn
George	35	Hnr	John	19	Oho	Danes, John	20	Hnr
George	655	Mnt	Dalles, John	459	Bdf	Daney, John	22	Hnr
Gwathmey	462	Mdd	Dalley, John	162	Knq	Danford see Densord		
Isham E.	144	Dnw	Dallis, ...bert	460	Bdf	Danfort, Joseph	16	Hnr
Jacob	848	Cmp	John	460	Bdf	Danfossy, B.	330	Dnw
James	651	Glc	Daltin, ...	458	Bdf	Dangerfield, Henry	507	Frd
James, (M)	710	Brn	Dalton, Michael	518	Prw	London	869	Cmp
John	863	Cmp	Susan	334	Dnw	see Daingerfield		
John	144	Dnw	Thos.	836	Nrf	Daniel, ---	328	Dnw
John	655	Mnt	Daly, Arthur	710	Brn	Abram	436	Flv
John	562	Pre	Dame, David	619	Btt	Alexander	617	Btt
John, Junr.	563	Pre	George	248	Frf	Ann	211	Ess
Nathl.	144	Dnw	Jacob	619	Btt	Benj.	316	Ldn
Sarah	652	Glc	Jno.	251	Frf	Beverley	462	Mdd
William	154	Alb	John	462	Frn	Bivion	462	Mdd
William	33	Hnr	Margaret	617	Btt	Campbel	47	Chr
Dacus, William	337	Lnn	Nicholas	252	Frf	Chesley	46	Chr
Dade, Alexander G.	500	Prw	Salley	161	Knq	Elias	24	Isw
Elizabeth	36	Stf	Damerin, William	18	Acc	Elij.	27	Clp
Henry C.	197	Kng	Dameron, ---, Capt.	894	Nrf	Elizabeth	47	Chr
Jno.	251	Frf	Alexander	710	Brn	Elizabeth	877	Hnv
Jno. B.	26	Clp	Holland	813	Nrf	Elizabeth	462	Mdd
Langhorn	197	Kng	James	895	Nrf	Ephram	334	Dnw
Laughorn	520	Prw	John	303	Amh	Geo. S.	462	Mdd
Susannah	196	Kng	Martha	894	Nrf	George	770	Wst
Thomas	192	Shn	Tho.	344	Lnc	George [Garnett?]	462	Mdd
Townshd. S.	196	Kng	Damewood, John	242	Ldn	Harlow	144	Dnw
Wm.	25	Clp	James	618	Btt	Harrison	900	Crl
Daes, Mary	183	Elc	Damrell, John	595	Mnr	Henry	5	Pwh
Daffan, Vincent	771	Wst	Damron, Amnofolis	425	Rnd	Henry	735	Wsh
William	900	Crl	Betsey	976	Nrt	Henry.	28	Clp
Dagg, Robert	302	Ldn	Charles	687	Nls	Hezekiah	709	Brn
Dagger, Peter	619	Btt	Charles	976	Nrt	Hezekiah	562	Pre
Daggs, Purnell	10	Knw	Christopher	976	Nrt	Hezekiah	47	Chr
Reuel	11	Knw	Dunmore	687	Nls	Icabud	690	Gch
Daggy, John	332	Ags	James	154	Alb	James	899	Crl
Peter	332	Ags	Joshua	976	Nrt	James	127	Cmb
Dagnal, Bartlet	873	Yrk	Littlepage	154	Alb	James	113	Hnr
Richard	562	Pre	Luke	977	Nrt	James	537	Prg
Dags, Hezekah	226	Pnd	Mary	976	Nrt	James	27	Stf
Dague, Frederick	15	Oho	Mary	977	Nrt	James, Junr.	46	Chr
Dailey, Elizabeth	759	Hmp	Robert	976	Nrt	Jno.	250	Ldn
Enock	789	Nrf	Roger	410	Rch	John	46	Chr
Hanna	621	Gls	Samuel, Jr.	977	Nrt	John	328	Dnw
Jesse	304	Ldn	Samuel, Sr.	976	Nrt	John	415	Fqr
Jno.	308	Ldn	Thomas	976	Nrt	John	462	Mdd
John	797	Nrf	William	977	Nrt	John	564	Pre
Ralph	98	Jff	William	410	Rch	John	538	Prg
Saml.	536	Brk	William R.	687	Nls	John, snr.	126	Cmb
Thomas	252	Frf	Damrun, Mikel	129	Cmb	John G.	124	Cmb
Wm.	797	Nrf	Damull see Dannell			Joseph	332	Ags
Daily, James	115	Hnr	Danby, John	494	Mnn	Joseph	709	Brn
John	760	Hmp	Dance, Ezekiel	54	Chs	Joseph	47	Chr
Thomas	919	Hrr	Harrison	34	Hnr	Joseph	536	Prg
Wren ['&" crossed			Henry	144	Dnw	Joshua	17	Isw
out]	21	Hnr	Lucy	54	Chs	Josiah	860	Cmp
Daingerfeld, London	549	Prg	Mary	144	Dnw	Leonard	128	Cmb
Bland	88	Spt	Mathew	338	Lnn	Lucy	536	Prg
Charles	549	Prg	Wm.	447	Mth	Mabry	337	Lnn
Edwin	89	Spt	Dancy, Isaac	144	Dnw	Martha	709	Brn
John	207	Ess	William	449	Grn	Martha	144	Dnw
Leroy	579	Frd	Dandrage, ---, Mr. ['Mr."			Mary	879	Sth
Mary	90	Spt	crossed out]	34	Hnr	Mildred	462	Mdd
Samson	549	Prg	Dandridge, Adam S.	96	Jff	Nathaniel	536	Prg
Willis	73	Spt	Alex. S.	690	Gch	Parke	751	Nwk
Dainty, Jonathan	249	Frf	Archd. B.	846	Hnv	Peggy	462	Mdd
Daives, Hugh	21	Hnr	Bartholomew	751	Nwk	Peter	619	Btt
Daiya see Danja			Bat	124	Hnr	Peter	536	Prg
Dakings, Joseph	1	Hnr	Mildred	853	Hnv	Peter V.	133	Hnr
Dakins, John	494	Mnn	Nathaniel W.	847	Hnv	Pheobe	462	Mdd
Dalby, James	19	Acc	Nathl. W.	853	Hnv	Reuben	25	Clp
Jno. A.	5	Ntt	Richard A.	853	Hnv	Reuben	26	Clp
Joseph	576	Frd	Robert	133	Hnr	Reuben	105	Spt
Thos.	60	Chs	Robert H.	854	Hnv	Richard	860	Cmp
William	515	Frd	William T.	847	Hnv	Robert	535	Brk

Robert, 3d.	536	Brk	Daring, John	507	Frd	Daughity, Elizabeth	977	Nrt
Robt.	527	Brk	Darks, Joshua	815	Nrf	James	976	Nrt
Robt.	343	Lnc	Darley, James	619	Btt	John	977	Nrt
Saml.	25	Clp	Darling, Benjamin	1	Knw	William	976	Nrt
Saml.	28	Clp	Donl.	833	Nrf	Daughtrey, Absalem	45	Isw
Samuel	46	Chr	Eliza.	162	Knq	David	45	Isw
Samuel	652	Glc	Timothy	3	Wod	Honour	45	Isw
Stephen	252	Frf	see Dauling			Mary	45	Isw
Thomas	180	Alb	Darlington, David	529	Frd	Mathew	45	Isw
Thomas	538	Prg	Merdeth	576	Frd	Richard	45	Isw
Traverse, jr.	56	Stf	William	574	Frd	Sally	45	Isw
Traverse, Sr.	47	Stf	Darmsdate, Jas.	23	Hnr	Solomon	46	Isw
William	111	Cmb	Darnaby, Edward	67	Spt	Theophilus	45	Isw
William	113	Cmb	Wm.	196	Kng	Daughtry, William	459	Bdf
William, Sr.	129	Cmb	Darnal, Henry, Senr.	746	Wsh	Daul, Samuel	28	Hnr
William, Sr.	536	Prg	S.	494	Mnn	Dauling, John	4	Knw
William P.	46	Chr	Wm.	494	Mnn	Daulton, Peggy	191	Alb
Winefred	536	Prg	Darnall, Catey	416	Fqr	William [2]	191	Alb
Wm.	709	Brn	Jeremiah	26	Clp	Davaughn see Devaughn		
Wm.	690	Gch	Jeremiah	361	Fqr	Davenport, Abraham	67	Jff
see McDaniel			Jno.	25	Clp	Absalom	4	Pwh
Daniels, Dennis	758	Hmp	Rawleigh	409	Fqr	Antony	873	Yrk
James	578	Frd	Thomas	3	Oho	Benja.	63	Jff
John	578	Frd	William	386	Fqr	Birket	26	Clp
John	84	Jff	Darne see Dame			Chapman	689	Nls
William	420	Rnd	Darnel, Jeremiah	653	Glc	D. D.	343	Lnc
Zachariah	656	Mnt	Darnell, Thomas	191	Alb	Daniel	47	Chr
Danja, M. L.	894	Nrf	Wm.	795	Nrf	Elizabeth	69	Chr
Danks, George	771	Wst	Darnes, Henry	250	Frf	Glover	861	Cmp
Dann, Thomas	521	Frd	Penelope	249	Frf	Glover	563	Pre
Thomas	161	Knq	Sarah	248	Ldn	Henry	834	Bck
Dannall, Joshua	14	Oho	Thomas P.	546	Frd	Henry	873	Yrk
Dannell, Saml.	271	Ldn	Thos., quarter	252	Frf	James	77	Spt
Danner, David	174	Shn	Wm.	289	Ldn	James S.	564	Pre
George	829	Wth	Darr, Ann	318	Ldn	Jesse	816	Bck
Jacob	524	Frd	Coonrod	28	Clp	Jessee	120	Cmb
Jacob	174	Shn	George	392	Fqr	Joel	619	Btt
Samuel	174	Shn	Leond.	28	Clp	John	508	Frd
Danolds, Wm.	531	Brk	Joseph	617	Btt	John	66	Jff
Dans, Henry	251	Frf	Darracoot, Polley	861	Hnv	John	104	Spt
Danson, Wm.	343	Lnc	Darracoott, Susan, Jnr.	861	Hnv	John, jr.	68	Spt
Darby, Adam	113	Spt	Darracott, Susanna [second			John P.	562	Pre
Edward	126	Hnr	"n" crossed out]	861	Hnv	Raw	343	Lnc
Edward, Snr.	120	Hnr	Darsonville, Nichs.	894	Nrf	Rebecca	105	Cmb
George	11	Isw	Darst, Benj.	262	Rck	Richard	279	Amh
Jeddiah	3	Wod	Dart, Mary	495	Mnn	Richard	900	Crl
John	18	Acc	Wm.	495	Mnn	Richard	47	Chr
John	463	Mdd	Darter, Jacob	829	Wth	Richard, Senr.	304	Amh
Joseph	144	Dnw	John	828	Wth	Samuel	92	Jff
Nathan	120	Hnr	Nicholas	828	Wth	Sarah	873	Yrk
Peggy	20	Acc	Darus, John	23	Hnr	Thomas	75	Jff
Richardson	120	Hnr	Darvel, Judy	332	Dnw	William	976	Nrt
Richd.	120	Hnr	Dasheil, George	894	Nrf	Wm.	591	Brk
Saml.	495	Mnn	Dashner, Catharine	26	Rcm	Wm.	873	Yrk
Saml., Jr.	495	Mnn	Michael	3	Wod	see Debenport		
Shadrach	20	Acc	Daubens, Boler	338	Lnn	Daverson, Phillip, The		
Thomas, (free black)	458	Bdf	Daubings, Abner	458	Bdf	Estate of	125	Cmb
William	398	Rch	Griffin, Jr.	458	Bdf	Robt.	648	Mnt
Darcey, Henry	894	Nrf	Griffin, Sr.	458	Bdf	Daves, Mary	692	Wsh
James	894	Nrf	Jonah	458	Bdf	Jonathan	493	Mnn
Darden, Benjamin, Sen.	41	Isw	Joseph	458	Bdf	Daveson, Benj.	749	Wsh
David	3	Isw	Daubins, John	338	Lnn	Davess, Jessee	113	Cmb
Holland	22	Isw	Daudoct, Tho.	325	Dnw	Davey, John	894	Nrf
Honor	154	Sth	Daudoor see Dundoor			John, Jun.	801	Hmp
Jacob	15	Isw	Dauge, Zach.	794	Nrf	John, Sen.	801	Hmp
Jacob	156	Sth	Daugh, Letty	124	Hnr	William	802	Hmp
John, (of Hardy)	24	Isw	Rhodah	28	Hnr	Davice, D.W.	335	Ags
John, (of Jacob [?])	7	Isw	Daugherty, Daniel	828	Wth	Elizt.	334	Ags
Leml.	126	Sth	David L.	16	Hnr	Jacob	334	Ags
Patience	154	Sth	E.	493	Mnn	Jerre	334	Ags
Solomon	41	Isw	Henry	574	Mnr	Nancy	334	Ags
Thomas	4	Isw	Jno.	643	Mnt	Wm.	334	Ags
Thos.	826	Nrf	John	107	Jff	Wm., (HC)	335	Ags
William	4	Isw	John	575	Mnr	Wm., (MT)	335	Ags
Dare, Charles	571	Mnr	John	828	Wth	Wm., sr.	335	Ags
John	586	Frd	Patrick	54	Jff	David, Abram	452	Frn
John	571	Mnr	Patrick	86	Jff	Caleb M.	116	Hnr
Parks	571	Mnr	Salley	459	Bdf	Davis	251	Frf
Sussex	651	Glc	William	534	Frd	Edwd.	248	Frf
Dariacoott, Jno.	854	Hnv	Wm.	643	Mnt	Eli	576	Brk

Name	No.	Co.
Richd.	818	Nrf
Davidson, Abner	563	Pre
Alex T.	20	Hnr
Alexander	870	Cmp
Andw. B.	42	Rck
Arthur	20	Rcm
Daniel	602	Frd
Daniel	904	Hrr
Daniel	910	Hrr
David	878	Cmp
David	907	Hrr
Edward	788	Bck
George	871	Cmp
George	563	Pre
Giles	302	Amh
James	570	Frd
James	267	Rck
Jno.	266	Rck
John	806	Bck
John	798	Hmp
John	914	Hrr
John	917	Hrr
John	896	Nrf
John	270	Rck
John	279	Rck
Jos.	808	Nrf
Joseph	563	Pre
Josiah	788	Bck
Josiah	904	Hrr
Josiah	907	Hrr
Josiah	217	Shn
Lewis	816	Bck
Majr.	873	Hnv
Matthew	329	Dnw
Mathew	336	Dnw
Richard	570	Frd
Robert	287	Rck
Sally	563	Pre
Samuel	869	Cmp
Samuel	870	Cmp
Stephen	788	Bck
Stephen	807	Bck
Thomas	674	Br
Wm.	618	Btt
Wm.	266	Rck
Wm., (NR.)	274	Rck
Davies, Arthur L.	652	Glc
Charles	895	Nrf
Jacob	598	Mnr
James	40	Rcm
John	594	Mnr
Joseph	584	Mnr
Lydia	589	Mnr
Nancey	40	Rcm
Nicholas C.	262	Amh
Peter	593	Mnr
Richd.	598	Mnr
Samuel	588	Mnr
Walter	40	Rcm
William F. R.	393	Fqr
Wm.	598	Mnr
Davis, ... [George?]	15	Pwh
Aaron	545	Frd
Abel	311	Ldn
Able	495	Mnn
Abraham	520	Prw
Absalom	845	Sth
Acquilla	829	Wth
Adam	252	Frf
Albinus	24	Oho
Alen	3	Wod
Alexander	445	Flv
Alexr.	619	Btt
Allen	604	Srr
Ann	689	Gch
Ann	828	Nrf
Ann	896	Nrf
Anne	449	Grn
Ant.	287	Ldn
Anthony	742	Nwk

Name	No.	Co.
Anthony	750	Nwk
Aquilla	250	Frf
Archd.	604	Srr
Armsd.	441	Mth
Asa	495	Mnn
Asa	8	Ntt
Augustin	10	Hnr
Augustine	129	Hnr
Austin M.	256	Amh
Azariah	853	Cmp
Baalis	584	Frd
Bartelott	192	Alb
Bartlet	837	Bck
Baxter	634	Sss
Bazilla	896	Nrf
Banj.	959	Hrr
Benja. R.	249	Frf
Benjamin	155	Alb
Benjamin	689	Brk
Benjamin	709	Brn
Benjamin	871	Cmp
Benjn.	617	Btt
Benjn.	130	Cmb
Benjn.	894	Nrf
Benson	506	Prw
Betsey	828	Bck
Betsey	209	Ess
Betsy	338	Lnn
Caleb	144	Dnw
Caleb	950	Hrr
Caleb	493	Mnn
Caleb	248	Shn
Carter	218	Ess
Catey	191	Alb
Catharin	222	Ess
Catharine	852	Cmp
Catharine	900	Crl
Catharine	563	Pre
Cathe., (Widow)	618	Btt
Catherine	689	Br
Charles	266	Amh
Charles	527	Prw
Charles	3	Rcm
Charles	635	Sss
Clement	950	Hrr
Cornelias	104	Jff
Dan	493	Mnn
Daniel	179	Alb
Daniel	621	Gls
Daniel	299	Ldn
David	549	Frd
David	959	Hrr
David	236	Ldn
David	499	Prw
David	859	Sth
David, jr.	604	Srr
David W.	592	Brk
Deborah	894	Nrf
Dolly	209	Ess
E. C.	33	Hnr
E. C.	35	Hnr
Eave	154	Alb
Edith	548	Prg
Edmond	687	Nls
Edmond	399	Rch
Edmund	191	Alb
Edward	161	Knq
Edward	514	Prw
Edward	4	Wod
Edwd.	303	Ldn
Edwd.	449	Mth
Edwd.	200	Ess
Edwd. G.	448	Grn
Edwin	866	Sth
Eleanor	251	Frf
Eli	756	Hmp
Elias	944	Hrr
Elias	516	Prw
Eligah	770	Hmp

Name	No.	Co.
Elijah	155	Alb
Elijah	246	Ldn
Eliz.	179	Elc
Eliza Ann	617	Btt
Eliza.	161	Knq
Elizabeth	190	Alb
Elizabeth	448	Grn
Elizabeth	338	Lnn
Etheldred	634	Sss
Evan	828	Wth
Ewell	771	Wst
Franky	107	Spt
Fanny	408	Rch
Frances	438	Mth
Francis	396	Fqr
Garey	596	Frd
Garey	920	Hrr
Geo.	268	Ldn
Geo.	301	Ldn
George	694	Br
George	565	Frd
George	876	Hnv
George	931	Hrr
George	946	Hrr
George	954	Hrr
George	966	Hrr
George	7	Pwh
George	562	Pre
George	391	Rch
George	58	Stf
George [2]	828	Wth
George, Senr.	829	Wth
George W.	829	Wth
Gideon	311	Ldn
Giles	144	Dnw
Godfrey	215	Ess
Hannah	605	Srr
Henry	458	Bdf
Henry	810	Bck
Henry	854	Cmp
Henry	449	Grn
Henry	803	Hmp
Henry	950	Hrr
Henry	383	Mds
Henry	563	Pre
Henry	448	Pra
Henry	829	Wth
Hezekiah	709	Brn
Hezekiah	813	Hmp
Hiram	621	Gls
Hollen	709	Brn
Horatio	449	Pra
Howell	310	Ldn
Hudson	383	Mds
Hugh	515	Prw
Humphrey	439	Mth
Isaac	436	Bth
Isaac	918	Hrr
Isaac	30	Hnr
Isaac	494	Mnn
Isaac	976	Nrt
Isaac	14	Oho
Isaac, S.	495	Mnn
Isabel	856	Sth
Isack	441	Mth
Isreal	472	Frn
J. S.	894	Nrf
Jachob	154	Alb
Jacob	574	Brk
Jacob	966	Hrr
Jacob	285	Ldn
Jacob	829	Wth
James	89	Acc
James	267	Amh
James	436	Bth
James	617	Btt
James	746	Brn
James	47	Chr
James	182	Elc
James	402	Fqr

James	559	Frd	John	17	Isw	Lewis	689 Nls
James	570	Frd	John	33	Isw	Lindsay	218 Ess
James	621	Gls	John	64	Jff	Linzey	622 Gls
James	652	Glc	John	5	Knw	Linzey	977 Nrt
James	449	Grn	John	197	Kng	Lucey	815 Bck
James	808	Hmp	John	337	Lnn	Lucy	218 Ess
James	872	Hnv	John	440	Mth	Lucy	896 Hnv
James	253	Ldn	John	628	Mnt	Lucy	7 Pwh
James	383	Mds	John	493	Mnn	Lucy	635 Sss
James	688	Nls	John	751	Nwk	Lucy [2]	634 Sss
James	814	Nrf	John	815	Nrf	Lucy W.	853 Cmp
James	894	Nrf	John	831	Nrf	Luke	494 Mnn
James	3	Oho	John	976	Nrt	Maco	622 Gls
James	226	Pnd	John	214	Pnd	Major	91 Acc
James	141	Sth	John	215	Pnd	Margary	62 Chs
James	604	Srr	John	228	Pnd	Martha	604 Srr
James	634	Sss	John	506	Prw	Martin	828 Bck
James	735	Wsh	John	515	Prw	Martin	56 Chs
James	8	Wod	John	161	Sth	Mary	191 Alb
James	828	Wth	John	856	Sth	Mary	651 Glc
James	829	Wth	John	85	Spt	Mary	652 Glc
James, Jr.	383	Mds	John	52	Stf	Mary	856 Hnv
James, (W)	873	Yrk	John	604	Srr	Mary	29 Hnr
Jane	894	Nrf	John	704	Wsh	Mary	337 Lnn
Jane	527	Prw	John	742	Wsh	Mary	804 Nrf
Janis	964	Hrr	John	771	Wst	Mary	742 Wsh
Janous	688	Nls	John	828	Wth	Mat.	494 Mnn
Jas.	448	Pra	John	829	Wth	Matthew	448 Grn
Jeduthan	854	Hnv	John, 1st.	894	Nrf	Matthew	516 Prw
Jehu	493	Mnn	John, 4th	894	Nrf	Matthew	635 Sss
Jeremiah	527	Prw	John, jr.	604	Srr	Melinda	434 Flv
Jeremiah, Sr.	664	Mnt	John, Junr.	771	Wst	Micajah	459 Bdf
Jeronias	190	Alb	John, S.	900	Hnv	Mildred	439 Mth
Jervis C.	28	Stf	John, Senr.	144	Dnw	Mitchel	871 Hnv
Jesse	442	Bth	John, Senr.	771	Wst	Morris	81 Jff
Jesse	28	Clp	John, (son of Job	394	Rch	Moses	29 Hnr
Jesse	963	Hrr	John, Sr.	977	Nrt	Moses	527 Prw
Jesse	196	Kng	John, 3d.	394	Nrf	Moton	107 Cmb
Jesse	867	Sth	John B.	777	Hmp	Mw.	247 Frf
Jessee	503	Prw	John C.	374	Fqr	Nancy	461 Mdd
Jessee	510	Prw	John C.	563	Frd	Nancy	977 Nrt
Jincy	856	Sth	John G.	336	Dnw	Nathan	946 Hrr
Jno.	247	Frf	John P.	853	Cmp	Nathan	967 Hrr
Jno.	248	Frf	John R.	634	Sss	Nathaniel	267 Amh
Jno.	252	Ldn	John S.	689	Gch	Nathaniel	24 Oho
Jno.	257	Ldn	Jona	493	Mnn	Nathaniel	604 Srr
Jno.	281	Ldn	Jonathan	499	Frn	Nathl.	896 Hnv
Jno.	285	Ldn	Jonathan	829	Wth	Nicholas	899 Crl
Jno.	296	Ldn	Jos., jr.	812	Nrf	OEn	934 Hrr
Jno.	298	Ldn	Jos., Sr.	811	Nrf	Parker	809 Hmp
Jno.	493	Mnn	Joseph	848	Cmp	Paschal	436 Bth
Jno., B	854	Hnv	Joseph	47	Chr	Paschas	337 Lnn
Jno., 2nd.	894	Nrf	Joseph	807	Hmp	Patsey	197 Kng
Jno. D.	897	Hnv	Joseph	809	Hmp	Patty	746 Brn
Job	216	Ess	Joseph	967	Hrr	Peggy	204 Ess
Job	503	Prw	Joseph	611	Mnt	Peter	828 Bck
Joel	272	Amh	Joseph	222	Pnd	Peter	847 Hnv
Joel	562	Pre	Joseph	12	Rcm	Peter	959 Hrr
John	243	Aml	Joseph	828	Wth	Peter	770 Wst
John	418	Bth	Joseph E.	144	Dnw	Peter, jr.	144 Dnw
John	460	Bdf	Joseph W.	56	Jff	Peter, Senr.	144 Dnw
John	572	Brk	Joshua	472	Frn	Peter B.	162 Knq
John	618	Btt	Joshua	963	Hrr	Phebe	554 Brk
John	694	Br	Joshua	16	Ntt	Phillip	717 Wsh
John	709	Brn	Judith	409	Fqr	Phillip	748 Wsh
John	796	Bck	Judith	10	Hnr	Pleasant	302 Rck
John	144	Dnw	Judy	434	Flv	R.	493 Mnn
John	176	Elc	Katharine	28	Isw	Ransome	873 Yrk
John	250	Frf	Larkin	900	Crl	Redman	377 Fqr
John	410	Fqr	Lemuel	197	Kng	Rezen	14 Oho
John	446	Flv	Leonard Y.	91	Jff	Richard	190 Alb
John	540	Frd	Leroy	209	Ess	Richard [2]	442 Bth
John	543	Frd	Leroy	976	Nrt	Richard	796 Bck
John	545	Frd	Lettleton	828	Nrf	Richard	689 Gch
John	570	Frd	Levi	393	Fqr	Richard	132 Hnr
John	597	Frd	Lewis	190	Alb	Richard	501 Prw
John	651	Glc	Lewis	267	Amh	Richard	516 Prw
John	690	Gch	Lewis	554	Brk	Richd.	343 Lnc
John	449	Grn	Lewis	206	Ess	Richd.	448 Pra
John	927	Hrr	Lewis	487	Frn	Richd.	681 Wrw

Name	No.	Co.
Ridgeway	404	Fqr
Rob.	493	Mnn
Robert	90	Acc
Robert	190	Alb
Robert	792	Bck
Robert	837	Bck
Robert	35	Isw
Robert	383	Mds
Robert	976	Nrt
Robert	216	Pnd
Robert	604	Srr
Robert	747	Wsh
Robert	829	Wth
Robt., f.negro	249	Frf
Ruth	506	Prw
Sally	840	Nrf
Sam.	494	Mnn
Saml.	218	Ess
Saml.	652	Glc
Saml.	832	Nrf
Saml. B.	459	Bdf
Samuel	774	Bck
Samuel	816	Bck
Samuel	329	Dnw
Samuel	403	Fqr
Samuel	812	Hmp
Samuel	908	Hrr
Samuel	76	Jff
Samuel	196	Kng
Samuel	287	Ldn
Samuel	977	Nrt
Samuel	562	Pre
Samuel	500	Prw
Samuel	604	Srr
Samuel H.	108	Spt
Samul	234	Ldn
Sarah	91	Acc
Sarah	596	Frd
Sarah	771	Wst
Savage	19	Acc
Sheppard	634	Sss
Silas	646	Mnt
Smithson	471	Frn
Sol.	493	Mnn
Sol., jr.	838	Nrf
Solomon	299	Ldn
Spencer	92	Acc
Spencer	599	Frd
Spencer	338	Lnn
Staige	463	Mdd
Stapleton H.	462	Mdd
Stephen	561	Frd
Stephen	946	Hrr
Susan	528	Brk
Susannah	47	Chr
Sussan, (F.N.)	28	Isw
Tamberlin W.W.	459	Bdf
Temple	69	Chr
Thomas	458	Bdf
Thomas	782	Bck
Thomas	249	Frf
Thomas	597	Frd
Thomas [2]	448	Grn
Thomas	764	Hmp
Thomas	770	Hmp
Thomas	959	Hrr
Thomas	2	Isw
Thomas	92	Jff
Thomas	281	Ldn
Thomas	286	Ldn
Thomas	288	Ldn
Thomas	298	Ldn
Thomas	462	Mdd
Thomas	976	Nrt
Thomas	26	Oho
Thomas	223	Pnd
Thomas	562	Pre
Thomas	506	Prw
Thomas	514	Prw
Thomas	448	Pra
Thomas	57	Stf
Thomas, jr.	977	Nrt
Thomas H.	251	Frf
Thomas S.	390	Rch
Thomson	191	Alb
Thos.	652	Glc
Thos.	839	Nrf
Thos.	547	Prg
Thos.	873	Yrk
Thos., Sr.	445	Mth
Thos. G.	709	Brn
Thos. J.	689	Gch
Toby, (F.N.)	28	Isw
Upshaw	205	Ess
Van	935	Hrr
Vincent	398	Rch
Walker	383	Mds
Walter	155	Alb
Walter	795	Hmp
Warren	248	Frf
Wilkinson	496	Frn
William	91	Acc
William	190	Alb
William	191	Alb
William	287	Amh
William	444	Bth
William	527	Brk
William	692	Br
William [2]	144	Dnw
William	335	Dnw
William	249	Frf
William	559	Frd
William	622	Gls
William	905	Hrr
William	5	Knw
William	197	Kng
William [2]	337	Lnn
William	462	Mdd
William	689	Nls
William	222	Pnd
William	563	Pre
William [2]	506	Prw
William	448	Pra
William	604	Srr
William	770	Wst
William	17	Wod
William	829	Wth
William, (Est.)	47	Chr
William, (M)	338	Lnn
William, of Rt.	90	Acc
William, of Sam	92	Acc
William, S.	337	Lnn
William, Senr.	855	Cmp
William, Senr.	771	Wst
William, Ser.	622	Gls
William C.	287	Amh
William M.	604	Srr
Willm.	186	Elc
Wilson	14	Isw
Wilson	75	Spt
Wilson	829	Wth
Wim.	873	Hnv
Winnifred	977	Nrt
Wm.	618	Btt
Wm.	250	Frf
Wm.	434	Flv
Wm.	653	Glc
Wm.	939	Hrr
Wm.	964	Hrr
Wm.	966	Hrr
Wm.	344	Lnc
Wm.	438	Mth
Wm.	495	Mnn
Wm.	895	Nrf
Wm.	450	Pra
Wm.	267	Rck
Wm.	291	Rck
Wm.	296	Rck
Wm.	140	Sth
Wm.	750	Wsh
Wm., Ser.	709	Brn
Wm. E.	653	Glc
Wt.	493	Mnn
Zachariah	337	Lnn
Zachariah	611	Mnt

see ...avis, Allen, D...,

Name	No.	Co.
Dans, David		
Davison, ---, Mrs.	28	Hnr
Andrew	938	Hrr
Andw.	713	Wsh
Danniel	954	Hrr
Edward, Jr.	952	Chc
Edward, Sr.	945	Chc
Flemin	18	Oho
George J.	964	Hrr
James	756	Wsh
Jeddiah	932	Hrr
John	668	Mnt
Jonathan	291	Ldn
Joseph	930	Hrr
Joseph	828	Wth
Sarah	946	Chc
Sarah	706	Wsh
Thos.	617	Btt
William	954	Chc
William	508	Frd
Wm.	956	Hrr
see Dovison		
Daviss, Robert	924	Hrr
Davisson, Amasiah	939	Hrr
John	928	Hrr
John	953	Hrr
Joseph	942	Hrr
Josiah	936	Hrr
Sarah	953	Hrr
Wm.	962	Hrr
Davit, James	692	Brk
Davmillion, George	10	Oho
Davy, Jacob	937	Hrr
Notly	934	Hrr
Wm.	496	Mnn
Dawden, Thos.	545	Prg
Dawe, William	500	Prw
Dawel see Dowel		
Dawley, Caleb	448	Pra
Caleb, Sr.	450	Pra
David	449	Pra
Dennis	895	Nrf
Elizabeth	810	Nrf
Gideon	450	Pra
James	894	Nrf
Jas.	449	Pra
John	896	Nrf
Wm.	450	Pra
Dawney, Alexr.	25	Clp
Dawnman, Richard	407	Rch
Dawns, Benjamin	304	Amh
Dawny, Michael	11	Knw
Daws, Abraham	398	Fqr
Ezekiel	176	Elc
Henry	301	Ldn
John	180	Elc
see Davis		
Dawson, Abraham	784	Hmp
Allen	155	Alb
Anica	893	Hnv
Bayley	46	Stf
Benjamin	340	Fqr
Benjamin	687	Nls
Benjamin	520	Prw
Christopher	977	Nrt
Daniel	977	Nrt
David	688	Nls
Elijah	154	Alb
Elizh.	873	Yrk
Fleming	47	Chr
Geo.	494	Mnn
George	458	Bdf
George	576	Frd
George	976	Nrt

Henry	565	Brk	Jessee	746	Brn	Dealey, Henry	180	Shn
Henry	688	Nls	Jno.	26	Clp	Henry	181	Shn
Henry	562	Pre	Jno.	282	Ldn	Dealon, James	55	Chs
Hudson	280	Amh	John	617	Btt	Deals, Jacob	690	Gch
Isaac	786	Hmp	John	788	Bck	Dealy, Jas.	495	Mnn
Isaac	568	Mnr	John	399	Fqr	Dean, Christopher	943	Chc
James	252	Ldn	John	913	Hrr	Daniel	216	Pnd
James	305	Ldn	John	562	Pre	Elizabeth	34	Rcm
Jerry	976	Nrt	John	241	Shn	Jane	808	Hmp
Jesse	24	Oho	John	149	Sth	Jno. W.	494	Mnn
Jno., Botetourt	652	Glc	John	82	Spt	John	417	Bth
John	249	Frf	John	634	Sss	John	945	Chc
John	376	Fqr	John, jr.	144	Dnw	John	808	Hmp
John	555	Frd	Judith, a free mulatto	977	Nrt	John	494	Mnn
John	812	Hmp	Lewis	900	Hnv	John	226	Pnd
John	10	Knw	Lucy	746	Brn	John, Jr.	361	Fqr
John	493	Mnn	Lucy	197	Ess	John, Senr.	413	Fqr
John	494	Mnn	Mary	155	Alb	Philip	690	Gch
John	976	Nrt	Nancy [?]	252	Shn	Pleasant	944	Chc
John	409	Rch	Paul	417	Fqr	Reuben	70	Spt
John	83	Spt	Phillip	190	Alb	Robt.	710	Brn
John	118	Spt	Polly	746	Brn	Thomas	682	Br
John	30	Stf	Ramsom	764	Hmp	William	417	Bth
John, for Marshall	342	Fqr	Richd.	548	Prg	William	594	Frd
John S.	687	Nls	Robertson	563	Pre	Wm.	494	Mnn
Jonathan	290	Amh	Samuel	551	Frd	Deane, Benjamin	521	Prw
Lewis	274	Amh	Samuel	861	Hnv	Biddy	132	Cmb
Martin	154	Alb	Samuel	688	Nls	Catharine	132	Cmb
Nancy	252	Ldn	Samuel	82	Spt	Charles	11	Oho
Nelson C.	271	Amh	Samuel	771	Wst	Elizabeth	131	Cmb
Pleasant	154	Alb	Sarah	111	Spt	Francis	124	Cmb
Pleasant	290	Amh	Simon Peter, f. negro	252	Frf	Jno.	161	Knq
Rachel	976	Nrt	Stephen, a free mulatto	976	Nrt	John	11	Pwh
Ro.	873	Yrk	Stephin	643	Mnt	Peter	11	Pwh
Samuel	383	Fqr	Tempy	617	Btt	Philip	11	Pwh
Sarah	687	Nls	Thomas	277	Amh	Susan	11	Hnr
Solomon	876	Sth	Thomas	542	Frd	Thos. M.	126	Cmb
Tho.	493	Mnn	William	939	Chc	William	162	Knq
Tho.	494	Mnn	William	762	Hmp	see Doane		
Thomas	572	Brk	William W.	751	Nwk	Deanor, Christian H.	875	Cmp
Thomas	376	Fqr	Wim.	898	Hnv	Deans, Betsy	817	Nrf
Thomas	977	Nrt	Wm.	27	Clp	Elizabeth	816	Nrf
Thos.	443	Mth	Wm.	28	Clp	Geo.	815	Nrf
William	828	Bck	see Scott			Joeph	825	Nrf
William	544	Frd	Daye, John	225	Pnd	Josiah L.	653	Glc
William	687	Nls	Zeakle	224	Pnd	Leml.	817	Nrf
William	977	Nrt	Dayl, Chasey	859	Sth	Dear, Simeon	27	Clp
William	520	Prw	Dayley, Abner	2	Wod	Deardoff, Henry, J.	458	Bdf
William, Jr.	384	Fqr	Mary	896	Nrf	Henry, W)	459	Bdf
William, Jr.	977	Nrt	Saley	5	Hnr	John	459	Bdf
William, Sr.	384	Fqr	Daylong, Cath.	100	Jff	Peter	459	Bdf
William, Sr.	977	Nrt	James	8	Wod	Samuel	459	Bdf
Wm.	25	Clp	Dayton, William	616	Mnt	Dearduff, Jacob	618	Btt
Wm.	268	Ldn	Deabnam, Robt.	436	Mth	Sam	495	Mnn
Dawsy, James	192	Alb	Deacon, ...th...	460	Bdf	Dearen, Rowlett	243	Aml
Day, Arnry	776	Hmp	Deadman, Dickson	154	Alb	William	243	Aml
Ben	618	Btt	Deafabough, Geo.	335	Ags	Dearing, Bailess	411	Fqr
Benjamin	789	Bck	Deafenbough see Deafabough			Elias	343	Fqr
Benjamin	110	Spt	Deagle, Absolom	462	Mdd	George	376	Fqr
Charles	179	Alb	Jno.	652	Glc	Jemimah	458	Bdf
Charles	358	Fqr	Nelson	652	Glc	Jere.	344	Fqr
Cossum	415	Fqr	Deakons, Jno., [his]			Jno.	28	Clp
Daniel	291	Amh	Est.	197	Kng	Joel	458	Bdf
Davis	29	Isw	Deal, Abraham, (Jr.)	8	Rcm	John	340	Fqr
Edward	3	Rcm	Abraham, (Sen.)	8	Rcm	John	773	Hmp
Elice	26	Clp	Elias	28	Clp	Lewis	459	Bdf
Elizabeth	257	Ldn	Frederick	106	Jff	Lewis	344	Fqr
Evan	617	Btt	George	619	Btt	Lewis	364	Fqr
Francis	521	Prw	Henry	618	Btt	Richard	459	Bdf
George	472	Mdd	Jacob	8	Rcm	Dearman, John	42	Rcm
George, a free negro	976	Nrt	James	653	Glc	Dearmont, Mary	588	Frd
George, (Jr.)	15	Rcm	Jarvas	437	Mth	Peter	588	Frd
George, (Sen.)	15	Rcm	Jno.	27	Clp	Deary, John	253	Shn
Henry	298	Ldn	Peter	26	Clp	Deaten, Elijah	9	Ntt
Isaac	41	Rcm	Peter	27	Clp	Deatherage, Wm.	27	Clp
Jacob	299	Ldn	Peter, Sr.	618	Btt	Deatley, Thomas	504	Prw
Jacob	15	Rcm	Philip	284	Rck	Deatly, Christopher	771	Wst
James	144	Dnw	William	597	Frd	George	771	Wst
James	525	Frd	Wm.	27	Clp	James, Junr.	771	Wst
James	422	Msn	Deale, Molly	216	Ess	James, Senr.	771	Wst

Deaton, Benjn.	619	Btt
James	619	Btt
John	619	Btt
John W.	243	Aml
Levy	619	Btt
Martha C.	619	Btt
Temprance	243	Aml
Deavenport, George	396	Rch
Joseph	408	Rch
Nancy	408	Rch
William H.	408	Rch
Deaver, Richard	774	Hmp
see Dever		
Deavers, John	519	Prw
Debell, Jeremiah	399	Fqr
Jno.	250	Frf
John	245	Ldn
Mary	250	Frf
Debenport, Judith	889	Hnv
Debery, Eli	495	Mnn
John	495	Mnn
Debety, Zacariah	17	Wod
Debill, William	396	Fqr
Debnom, Francis	338	Lnn
Philip	337	Lnn
Debo, ...	460	Bdf
Deboard, Elijah	383	Mds
Debostian, Elizabeth	76	Jff
Debow, Henry	452	Frn
Deboy, Abrm.	600	Mnr
John	574	Mnr
Deboys, Conrad	576	Mnr
Debricks, John	219	Pnd
Thomas	219	Pnd
Thomas, S.	219	Pnd
Debrix, David, Sr.	605	Srr
John	605	Srr
Debush, Daniel	698	Wsh
Elijah	697	Wsh
Elisha	697	Wsh
John	697	Wsh
Debyty, Hevey	9	Wod
Decamp, Jacob	684	Br
Zachariah	665	Mnt
Decature, Commodre	896	Nrf
Dechamps, J. B.	895	Nrf
Dechart, Michl.	759	Wsh
Deck, Chaty	189	Shn
see Deek		
Deckard, Peter	828	Wth
Decker, Adam	191	Shn
Andw.	333	Ags
David	190	Shn
Henry	592	Frd
Henry	303	Rck
James	294	Rck
James	172	Shn
John	800	Hmp
Joseph	172	Shn
Deckey, James	251	Frf
John	869	Cmp
Deckinson, John	707	Wsh
Deckman see Dishman		
Declasby, Alexander	689	Nls
Decodry, Israel	328	Dnw
Decormis, Lewis	895	Nrf
Decrisa, Charles	688	Nls
Dedimon, Christian	664	Mnt
Dedmon, John	691	Wsh
Deeds, Geo.	333	Ags
George	34	Rcm
John	618	Btt
Peter	619	Btt
Philip	19	Rcm
Philip	34	Rcm
Deegs, Isaac	451	Mth
see Deggs		
Deek, Michael	28	Rcm
Deel, John	407	Ags
Peter	598	Brk

Deem, Adam	15	Wod
Adam	18	Wod
David	12	Wod
Jacob	2	Wod
Deen, Amis	737	Wsh
Andrew	34	Hnr
Ezekiel	55	Jff
John	260	Amh
John	196	Kng
John	3	Wod
Richd.	698	Wsh
Thornton	196	Kng
Deenn see Dunn		
Deenos, Job	423	Bth
see Deever		
Deer, Andrew	383	Mds
Daniel	243	Aml
John	383	Mds
John, Jr.	383	Mds
Marten	383	Mds
Moses	383	Mds
Susannah	383	Mds
William	243	Aml
Deering, James	863	Cmp
Deever, James	422	Bth
see Deenos		
Deeweese, Polley	483	Frn
Defenbough, John	333	Ags
Deford, Robt.	788	Nrf
Defore, Zacheriah	458	Bdf
Defries, John	290	Rck
Jos.	301	Rck
Joseph	290	Rck
Degart, Mary	894	Nrf
Degernett, Walker	459	Bdf
Deggs, Anthony	451	Mth
Augustin	451	Mth
Bailey	448	Mth
Bailey	452	Mth
David	445	Mth
David	451	Mth
Isack	445	Mth
Jessee	448	Mth
Jno.	445	Mth
Jno.	451	Mth
Jno., (SW)	452	Mth
Joel	451	Mth
Johanna	451	Mth
John	445	Mth
John	976	Nrt
Joseph	441	Mth
Josiah	445	Mth
Wm.	451	Mth
Wm., Sr.	451	Mth
Wm., Sr.	452	Mth
see Deegs		
Degraffenred, Francis	562	Pre
DeGraffenried, Boswell		
B.	338	Lnn
Elizabeth	337	Lnn
Francis	338	Lnn
Joseph B.	338	Lnn
Tscharner	337	Lnn
Dehart, Cornelius	7	Oho
Saml.	6	Rcm
Wm.	7	Oho
Dehaven, Abraham	853	Cmp
John	553	Frd
Jonathan	553	Frd
Peter	553	Frd
Sally	553	Frd
Deheart, John	468	Frn
Deheaven, Isaac	454	Frn
Jesse	454	Frn
Deinom see Dienom		
Deison, Charles	850	Cmp
Deitrick, Jacob D.	400	Ags
Dejarnatt, Daniel	899	Crl
John	899	Crl
Joseph [2]	899	Crl

Dejarnatte, Wm. Y.	860	Hnv
Dejarnett, Bowler	563	Pre
Mumford	47	Chr
Richard	47	Chr
Stephen	563	Pre
Dejernatt, John	330	Dnw
Dejernett, Bowler	16	Ntt
Elias	16	Ntt
Dekins, Thomas	354	Fqr
Dekyrell, Demard	896	Nrf
DeLaCroix, Josephe	836	Nrf
Delaney, Benjn.	657	Mnt
Cloe	617	Btt
David	243	Aml
Edward	895	Nrf
Eliab	27	Clp
Elijah	657	Mnt
Saml.	243	Aml
Samuel	478	Frn
Wm.	300	Ldn
Wm.	660	Mnt
Zachh.	27	Clp
Delany, Anthony	252	Frf
Martin	427	Bth
Saml.	636	Mnt
Delap, William	716	Wsh
Delapp, Robert	696	Wsh
Saml.	730	Wsh
Delastatious, Ann	91	Acc
Crippin	91	Acc
Edmund	90	Acc
James	91	Acc
Delatarte, Wm. W.	830	Nrf
Delauney, James	26	Isw
Delayea, William	86	Jff
Delbridge, Benjamin	710	Brn
Peggy	746	Brn
Robt.	618	Btt
Thos.	746	Brn
Delevas, Daniel	98	Spt
Delinger, Frederick	203	Shn
see Dillinger		
Delk, Dawson	31	Isw
Eliza.	852	Sth
Martha	604	Srr
Moreland	24	Isw
Willie	141	Sth
Dellaplane, Isaac	792	Hmp
Dellard, William	285	Amh
Dellastatious, William	90	Acc
Delleplaine, Jesse	541	Brk
Dellis, Marmaduke	458	Bdf
Deloach, Mildred	844	Sth
Deloatch, Nancy	847	Sth
Delong, George	617	Btt
John	512	Frd
Joseph	619	Btt
Nicholas	602	Frd
Ormon	660	Mnt
Deloram, John	578	Mnr
Delph, Adam	383	Mds
Aron	383	Mds
Conner	383	Mds
Moses	383	Mds
Saml.	26	Clp
Sary	383	Mds
Solomon	383	Mds
Delworth, Joseph	325	Dnw
William	427	Rnd
Delzell, James	617	Btt
Robt.	619	Btt
Dembar, Robert	509	Frd
Dement, Benajah	12	Oho
Henry	4	Oho
William	12	Oho
Demeritt, Mary	396	Rch
Demine, Adam	598	Frd
Demmitt, Bealle	786	Hmp
Demortiers, Jean B.	894	Nrf
Demoss, Jas.	495	Mnn

Nancy	526	Frd
Wm.	495	Mnn
Demoval, Griffin	4	Ntt
Dempsey, James	900	Crl
William	296	Amh
Demsey, Hugh	617	Btt
John	622	Gls
Mildred	617	Btt
Demsy, Tandy	286	Rck
Demwell, Samuel	941	Chc
Denby, Leml.	812	Nrf
Sally	840	Nrf
Wm.	812	Nrf
Deneal, George	399	Fqr
Deneale, James	250	Frf
James	508	Prw
Deneall, William	250	Frf
Denegree, John	161	Sth
Denham, David B.	938	Hrr
Lewis	543	Frd
Lucy	1	Hnr
Denhart, Shadrach	534	Prg
Willium	535	Prg
Denick, Jacob, f. negro	250	Frf
Denis, Richard	708	Brn
Denisa see Decrisa		
Denison, John	333	Ags
John, Sr.	333	Ags
Thomas	57	Jff
Thomas	12	Knw
Deniston, Andw.	703	Wsh
Margret	728	Wsh
Denitty, Dianna	327	Dnw
Denlevy, Peter	3	Hnr
Denne, Patrick	509	Brk
Dennea, Willis	141	Sth
Dennet, James	750	Nwk
Peggy	449	Pra
Dennett, Catherine	751	Nwk
Richard	751	Nwk
Denney, Alexr.	706	Wsh
Richard	976	Nrt
William	817	Hmp
Dennias, Elizabeth	246	Shn
James	30	Hnr
Dennis, Benj.	30	Hnr
Edward	481	Frn
Francis	243	Aml
Isaac	345	Fqr
Jas. F.	16	Hnr
Jessee	688	Nls
Jno.	234	Ldn
John	46	Chr
John	895	Nrf
John	390	Rch
Richd.	20	Ntt
Saml.	27	Clp
Tenny	19	Acc
Thomas	234	Ldn
William	363	Fqr
William	688	Nls
Wm.	234	Ldn
Dennisen, Elisha	920	Hrr
James	10	Oho
Dennison, Elisha	921	Hrr
James	921	Hrr
James	935	Hrr
William	252	Frf
William	448	Grn
Denniston, George	741	Wsh
Robert	828	Wth
Robt.	741	Wsh
Thomas	364	Fqr
William	828	Wth
Dennus, Henry	919	Hrr
Denny, David	587	Frd
Edmd.	251	Frf
Richard	33	Hnr
Samuel	687	Nls
Walter	17	Oho
William	849	Cmp
William	521	Frd
see Denne		
Denom see Derrom		
Denoon, Hanson	100	Jff
James	7	Hnr
Denover, James	589	Brk
Denson, John	157	Sth
Josh.	880	Sth
Mary	157	Sth
Mills	157	Sth
Mills	852	Sth
Minah, (F.N.)	23	Isw
Pacience	42	Isw
Densord, Henry	16	Hnr
see Danfort		
Dent, Charles	458	Bdf
Jno.	493	Mnn
John	458	Bdf
John, Sr.	45	Stf
John, Sr.	53	Stf
Mark	635	Mnt
Peter	458	Bdf
Thomas C.	530	Frd
Walter, Jr.	497	Frn
Walter, Sr.	497	Frn
William [2]	458	Bdf
Denton, Archabald	461	Frn
Augustin	337	Lnn
Benjamin	18	Rcm
Davd.	737	Wsh
Davd., Senr.	740	Wsh
Jero	734	Wsh
Jno.	25	Clp
John	846	Hnv
John	562	Pre
Lucy	338	Lnn
Nathaniel	442	Flv
Phebe	194	Shn
Richd.	282	Rck
Theofilus	337	Lnn
Wm.	441	Flv
Wyatt	337	Lnn
Denver, Patrick	573	Frd
Denwiddie, John	420	Bth
William	432	Bth
Depew, James	458	Bdf
Depoy, Christopher	18	Rcm
Conrod	18	Rcm
Isaac	19	Rcm
Jacob	19	Rcm
John	10	Rcm
Depp, John	12	Pwh
Thomas	10	Pwh
Depreas, Molly	434	Flv
Depreast, Wm.	120	Hnr
Depu, Henry	947	Hrr
Depue, Elijah	617	Btt
Jacob	617	Btt
John	617	Btt
Derah see Dorah		
Derben, Nicholas	817	Hmp
Derby, Custis	18	Acc
Elizabeth	834	Nrf
Hew	338	Lnn
John	337	Lnn
Polly	19	Acc
Derham, James	814	Bck
John	784	Hmp
Derick, Jonathan	618	Btt
Dering, G. S.	492	Mnn
Dernell, Hiram	759	Hmp
Dero...cercet, John W.	958	Chc
Derr, Jacob	289	Rck
Derrett, Robt.	437	Flv
Derrey, Jacob	284	Ldn
Philip	267	Ldn
Derring, Emelius	12	Isw
John	29	Isw
Derrom, James	689	Nls
Thomas [2]	689	Nls
Derry, Peter	283	Ldn
Derum, Catharine	305	Ldn
Desears, B.O.	69	Chs
Desert, Elisabeth	529	Brk
Deshazar, Henry	777	Bck
John	563	Pre
Martha	564	Pre
Deshazo, Jno.	161	Knq
Larkin	161	Knq
Unity	162	Knq
Wm.	162	Knq
Deshealds, Richd.	439	Mth
Desher, John	895	Nrf
Deshields, Joseph	977	Nrt
Deshler, Mary	19	Rcm
Desnoe, Peter	895	Nrf
Desponett, Barnett	572	Frd
Dessiness, Eliz.	180	Elc
Detimore, Christian	9	Rcm
Detives, Frederick	180	Shn
Detro, Jacob	234	Ldn
Detter, Catharine	223	Shn
Dettor, John	155	Alb
Nicholas	688	Nls
Deuccolo, Mary	332	Dnw
Deupree, Thomas	46	Chr
William	47	Chr
Devall, Isaac	683	Br
Jacob	757	Wsh
Lewis	930	Hrr
Devaughn, William	248	Frf
Devaugn, Jas.	244	Shn
Devears, Richard	409	Fqr
Deveese, Abraham	424	Bth
Devenport, ...eph	458	Bdf
...ph, Sr.	458	Bdf
David	854	Hnv
Edmund	458	Bdf
Edward	542	Prg
John	9	Hnr
Jos.	32	Hnr
Dever, Basel	283	Ldn
Isaac	106	Jff
James	828	Wth
Joshua	760	Wsh
Michael	1	Rcm
William	776	Hmp
see Deaver		
Devereaux see Jarrett		
Devereux, John	332	Dnw
Devers, Henry	1	Rcm
Deviers, Hugh	41	Rcm
James	39	Rcm
James	41	Rcm
John	39	Rcm
William	42	Rcm
Devinport, Claiborn	733	Wsh
John	733	Wsh
Julius T.	733	Wsh
Osborn	732	Wsh
Thos.	733	Wsh
Devioms, Gilbert	250	Frf
see Devours		
Devo, David	544	Frd
Devore, William	690	Br
Devors, James	928	Hrr
James	934	Hrr
Robert	928	Hrr
Devours, Ann	250	Frf
see Devioms		
Dew, Ann	832	Hmp
Betty	587	Mnr
Robert	750	Nwk
Sarah	617	Btt
Thomas	161	Knq
William	161	Knq
Wm.	587	Mnr
Dewasher, John	270	Amh
John C.	270	Amh
Dewaye, Joel	2	Wod

Name	Page	Code
Dewbre, Holmes	185	Elc
James	188	Elc
John	189	Elc
Tho.	182	Elc
Dewell, Ann	605	Srr
Henry	604	Srr
Littleberry	605	Srr
Richard	605	Srr
William	605	Srr
Wyatt	605	Srr
Dewes, John	589	Frd
Dewese, Peter	658	Mnt
Dewey, George	18	Acc
Joseph	16	Wod
Joshua	15	Wod
Dewise, Hannah	634	Mnt
Dewit, ...hn	458	Bdf
James	459	Bdf
Jesse	459	Bdf
John	459	Bdf
John	430	Msn
Mary R.	459	Bdf
Thomas	459	Bdf
Dewitt, Peter	495	Mnn
Dewoy see Duvoy		
Dews, Carter	31	Isw
Dolphin	28	Isw
Frances	652	Glc
Nathl.	844	Sth
Thomas	32	Isw
Dewsing, Jacob	646	Mnt
Dey, Lewis	450	Pra
Wm. Lewis	449	Pra
Dibrel, Anthony	778	Bck
Dicason, Gais	942	Hrr
Joseph	942	Hrr
Dice, Christian	297	Rck
Frederick	297	Rck
George	215	Pnd
John	223	Pnd
Matthias	215	Pnd
Philip	28	Hnr
William	215	Pnd
Dicenson, John	191	Alb
Dichart, Peter	716	Wsh
Wm.	716	Wsh
Dick, Adam	746	Wsh
Anne	15	Isw
Archibald, junr.	900	Crl
Archibald, Senr.	901	Crl
David	598	Mnr
David, jr.	598	Mnr
Grace	53	Stf
Henry	543	Frd
John	506	Frd
John	549	Frd
John	598	Mnr
John	17	Oho
John	7	Rcm
Joseph	53	Stf
Mary	558	Frd
Mary	896	Nrf
Michael	746	Wsh
Nathaniel	562	Pre
Nicholas	72	Jff
Peter	556	Frd
Thomas	580	Frd
William	563	Mnr
Dickard, Jacob	829	Wth
Dicken, Joseph N.	899	Crl
Norment	901	Crl
Dickenson, Asa M.	900	Crl
Austin	900	Crl
Benjamin	900	Crl
Chas.	333	Ags
David	901	Crl
David	492	Frn
Henry H.	899	Crl
James [2]	191	Alb
James	899	Crl
James	900	Crl
John [2]	191	Alb
John	442	Bth
Jonathan	899	Crl
Tarpley	46	Chr
Thomas	899	Crl
Wiley [2]	191	Alb
William	899	Crl
Wm.	198	Ess
see Dicenson		
Dickerson, ...ons	460	Bdf
...ph	460	Bdf
Bartlett	460	Bdf
Benjamin	562	Pre
Charles	564	Mnr
Elijah	197	Kng
Elijah, Jr.	659	Mnt
Elizabeth	562	Pre
Griffey, jr.	649	Mnt
Griffith	660	Mnt
Jacob	564	Mnr
James	562	Pre
Jno.	1	Ntt
John	564	Mnr
John	688	Nls
Jonathin	154	Alb
Judith	462	Mdd
Leonard	650	Mnt
Lucy	198	Ess
Morril	659	Mnt
Moses, Jr.	660	Mnt
Moses, Sr.	659	Mnt
Obediah	622	Mnt
Patsey	458	Bdf
Peggy	562	Pre
Peter	562	Pre
Robt.	11	Ntt
Saml.	564	Mnr
Thomas C.	176	Shn
Thos.	9	Ntt
Thurston	688	Nls
William	458	Bdf
William, M)	459	Bdf
Williamson	4	Ntt
Dickey, Ametia	26	Rcm
James	26	Rcm
John	9	Hnr
John	26	Rcm
Joseph	303	Rck
Samuel	861	Cmp
Dickie, Barbary	162	Knq
James	162	Knq
Thomas	288	Rck
Dickins, Jno.	450	Pra
Thomas	338	Lnn
William	338	Lnn
see Dekins		
Dickinson, Adam	415	Bth
Amy	896	Nrf
Barnet	67	Spt
Dabney	865	Hnv
David	867	Hnv
Edward	519	Prw
Hannah	507	Prw
James	20	Oho
Jno.	866	Hnv
John	91	Acc
John	430	Flv
John	525	Prw
John J.	689	Gch
Jos.	837	Nrf
Kinrey	19	Oho
Lewis	513	Prw
Lewis	717	Wsh
Mary	894	Nrf
Nancy	84	Spt
Nathaniel	83	Spt
Nathl., Jnr.	870	Hnv
Richard	83	Spt
Samuel	215	Pnd
Thomas	434	Flv
W. W.	3	Hnr
Wm.	690	Gch
see Deckinson, Wod		
Dickinston, Nathl., Snr.	870	Hnv
Dickkins, Joseph	338	Lnn
Dickonson, Humphry	751	Wsh
Dicks, James	337	Lnn
Levin	182	Elc
Peter	577	Frd
Steven	936	Hrr
Tandy	337	Lnn
William	337	Lnn
Dickson, Austin	853	Cmp
Fanny [Tamey?]	545	Prg
Henry	830	Nrf
Jessee	179	Alb
John [2]	858	Cmp
John	332	Dnw
John	836	Nrf
Polly M.	617	Btt
Reubin	47	Chr
Thomas	865	Cmp
Thos.	895	Nrf
William, Junr.	771	Wst
William, Senr.	771	Wst
William C.	865	Cmp
Wm.	825	Nrf
Wm.	836	Nrf
see Deadman		
Dicky see Dickie		
Didawick, Jacob	220	Shn
Diddep, Thos.	21	Hnr
Diddle, John	335	Ags
Wm.	332	Ags
Didenhover, Rachel	54	Jff
Didlake, Benja.	652	Glc
Jas.	161	Knq
John	161	Knq
Philip	161	Knq
Philip	462	Mdd
Royston	161	Knq
Didrell, E.	894	Nrf
Diehl, George	283	Rck
Saml.	283	Rck
Diell see Dull		
Dienom, Amos	318	Ldn
Dierduff, Jacob	617	Btt
Dieterich, J. P.	895	Nrf
Jacob	300	Rck
Dietrick, Philip	333	Ags
Diffendaffer, Geo.	518	Brk
Diffendurf, P.	496	Mnn
Digges, Dudley	418	Fqr
Edward, Jr.	420	Fqr
Edward, Senr.	362	Fqr
Elizabeth	688	Nls
Isaac	751	Nwk
John	688	Nls
Whiting	409	Fqr
William H.	688	Nls
Wm.	682	Wrw
Diggs, Dudley	161	Knq
Edwd.	449	Pra
Frances	162	Knq
Jno. T.	344	Lnc
Josiah, free negro	70	Chs
Maj	1	Hnr
Mary	653	Glc
Digman, Chs.	495	Mnn
Phil	494	Mnn
Dike, Mungo	302	Ldn
Diley see ---		
Dilinger, George	227	Shn
Dill, Cristin	8	Hnr
Henry	618	Btt
William	922	Hrr
Dilla, Jesse	277	Ldn
Dillard, Abram	828	Wth
Ann	25	Clp

Name	Ref	Co.
Ann	161	Knq
Charles	899	Crl
Edward	751	Nwk
Francis	635	Sss
Geo.	161	Knq
George	899	Crl
George	634	Sss
James	276	Amh
James	350	Fqr
James	653	Glc
James	687	Nls
James	635	Sss
John	900	Crl
John	687	Nls
John	76	Spt
Joseph	268	Amh
Joseph S.	807	Bck
Mary	28	Clp
Matthias	829	Wth
Nicholas	162	Knq
Stephen	899	Crl
Thomas	899	Crl
Thomas	900	Crl
Thomas	75	Spt
Thomas A.	161	Knq
Thos.	652	Glc
Thos.	892	Hnv
Thos.	162	Knq
William	899	Crl
Wim.	896	Hnv
Dillars, Richard	161	Knq
Dillehay, Charles	449	Grn
Dillen, James	285	Rck
Dilley, Catharine	415	Bth
Henry	415	Bth
Martin	415	Bth
Dillian, Henry	622	Gls
James	622	Gls
Dilliard, Ruhm	130	Sth
William	771	Wst
Dillin, Eliza.	26	Clp
Thomas	929	Hrr
Dillinger, Ann	203	Shn
Christeen	227	Shn
David	227	Shn
David	246	Shn
George	208	Shn
Manuel	228	Shn
Martin	228	Shn
see Delinger		
Dillion, Henry	59	Stf
Jn., free negro	70	Chs
Dillman, Christopher	828	Wth
Dillon, Abden	280	Ldn
Asa	471	Frn
Daniel	280	Ldn
Edward	564	Pre
Henry	471	Frn
Henry	562	Pre
James	333	Ags
James	376	Fqr
James	562	Pre
Jesse, Jr.	471	Frn
Jesse, Sr.	464	Frn
Jno.	280	Ldn
Jno.	316	Ldn
John	480	Frn
Meridith	480	Frn
Robert	464	Frn
Samuel	455	Frn
Squire	456	Frn
Thomas	23	Oho
Thos.	690	Gch
William	128	Cmb
William	456	Frn
William, Jr.	464	Frn
Dillow, John	73	Jff
John	78	Jff
Joseph	73	Jff
Peter	78	Jff
Thomas	73	Jff
William	58	Jff
Dillworth, George	330	Dnw
Dilly, Christian	7	Knw
John	513	Prw
Dillyhunt, Jane	302	Ldn
Dilman, Danl., Jr.	617	Btt
Dilmon, Danl.	618	Btt
Danl., Sr.	618	Btt
Dilmor, Jacob, Jr.	617	Btt
Jacob, Sr.	617	Btt
Jacob, (the Younger)	617	Btt
Dils, Henry	5	Wod
John	11	Wod
Mary	5	Wod
William	6	Wod
Dilworth see Delworth		
Dimford see Dunford		
Dimmitt, John	62	Jff
Dimom see Dienom		
Dimond, Jesse	622	Gls
Melinda	622	Gls
Dimue, Larose	690	Gch
Dingas, George	567	Frd
Peter	520	Frd
Dinger, Willm.	617	Btt
Dingess, Mary	622	Gls
Dinguid, George E.	789	Bck
William S.	784	Bck
Dinkins, Mary	829	Wth
Dinmer see Drinner		
Dinn, John	188	Elc
Dinon see Dienom		
Dinquid, George	818	Bck
Dinsmore, James	689	Nls
Mary	582	Frd
Dinwiddie, Robert	687	Nls
Dinwidie, Francis	872	Cmp
Joseph	862	Cmp
Dirnell, Wm.	746	Wsh
Dirtiller, Ned	513	Prw
Dirting, Adam	828	Wth
Catharine	829	Wth
Dish, William	418	Bth
Disher, Danl.	619	Btt
Jacob	618	Btt
John	618	Btt
Peter, Jr.	619	Btt
Peter, Sr.	618	Btt
Dishman, Danl.	55	Chs
David	199	Ess
David	100	Spt
Jas.	196	Kng
Jas. D.	196	Kng
Jno.	55	Chs
John	196	Kng
John, jr.	199	Ess
John, Sr.	199	Ess
Philip	196	Kng
Saml.	196	Kng
Samuel	234	Ldn
Sterling	55	Chs
William	771	Wst
William, Senr.	771	Wst
Wm.	196	Kng
Dishorn, Henry	472	Frn
Dismukes, Paul	690	Gch
William	93	Spt
Disnay, Jane	503	Prw
Dispen, John	17	Wod
Disshue, Lewis	62	Stf
Ditimore, Henry	6	Rcm
Ditty, John	828	Wth
Divers, Ananias	470	Frn
Christopher	465	Frn
Equilla	465	Frn
George	190	Alb
Jno.	260	Ldn
Mary	471	Frn
Divine, Aaron	303	Ldn
Wm.	307	Ldn
Dix, Catharin	217	Ess
Eliza	161	Knq
George	90	Acc
Isaac, Junr.	90	Acc
Isaac, Senr.	90	Acc
Leven	816	Nrf
Levi	90	Acc
Lewis	221	Ess
Revel	90	Acc
Richard	92	Acc
Simond	90	Acc
Thomas, Sr.	220	Ess
Thomas E.	220	Ess
William	18	Acc
Dixan, John	333	Ags
Dixin, James, Sr.	293	Rck
Dixon, Alexr.	291	Ldn
Ann	942	Chc
Archd.	333	Ags
Christopher	20	Oho
Edward	750	Nwk
Eliza.	651	Glc
Enoch	268	Amh
George	5	Knw
George	829	Wth
George W.	690	Wsh
Henry	959	Chc
Henry St. John	690	Wsh
Isabella	815	Hmp
J...	460	Bdf
James	268	Amh
James	10	Oho
James	281	Rck
James	111	Spt
Jno.	651	Glc
Job	20	Oho
John	458	Bdf
John	710	Brn
John	798	Hmp
John	54	Jff
John	688	Nls
John	825	Nrf
John	563	Pre
John	751	Wsh
John	6	Wod
John, jr.	333	Ags
John, sr.	333	Ags
Joseph	798	Hmp
Joseph	688	Nls
Lucy	19	Hnr
Mary	444	Mth
Michl.	443	Mth
Moses, (F. Negroe)	340	Fqr
Nathaniel	488	Frn
Peter	5	Knw
Polly	335	Ags
Randal	47	Isw
Richd.	596	Mnr
Robt.	302	Rck
Sally	563	Pre
Sarah	30	Hnr
Tho.	179	Elc
Thomas	458	Bdf
Thos.	333	Ags
Turner	343	Fqr
William	432	Bth
William	2	Isw
William	3	Knw
William	688	Nls
William	730	Wsh
William, Jur.	730	Wsh
Wm.	291	Ldn
Wm. M.	873	Yrk
see Hall, Hutton, Smith		
Dixson, Thos.	287	Ldn
William	913	Hrr
Dizard, Stephen	422	Bth
Doaghtery, Etheldrd.	132	Sth
Robt.	132	Sth

Doak, David	334	Ags	John, Jr.	417	Fqr	Lidy	771	Wst
David	829	Wth	Joseph	269	Amh	Thomas	770	Wst
Jane	334	Ags	Joseph	771	Wst	William	770	Wst
John	334	Ags	Mason B.	771	Wst	Doler, Martin	34	Hnr
John	828	Wth	Nathaniel	417	Fqr	Doles, Allen	162	Sth
Robt., Coln	334	Ags	Nicholas	9	Ntt	Elizh.	882	Sth
Saml.	334	Ags	Rebecka	477	Frn	Willie	162	Sth
Thos.	334	Ags	Reuben	196	Kng	Willis	161	Sth
Doane, Wm.	438	Flv	Sally	567	Frd	Doleway, William	210	Shn
Dobb see Doble			Thomas	900	Crl	Dolhous, John	335	Ags
Dobbin, George	689	Nls	Thos.	619	Btt	Doling, Jarrott	774	Bck
James	691	Br	William	689	Nls	John	774	Bck
Samuel	814	Hmp	William	563	Pre	Dolittle, Moses	493	Mnn
Dobbins, Bowler	746	Brn	Wm.	312	Ldn	Moses, Jr.	493	Mnn
Daniel	491	Frn	Wm., Jr.	619	Btt	see Doolittle		
Dura	215	Ess	Wm., Sr.	619	Btt	Doll, Jacob	807	Hmp
John	494	Mnn	Doddridge, Benj.	3	Oho	Dollard, William	458	Bdf
Robert	213	Ess	Joseph	685	Br	Dollens, Richard	154	Alb
Wm.	189	Elc	Phillip	684	Br	Dollins, Elizabeth	155	Alb
Wm.	212	Ess	William	7	Knw	Presley	155	Alb
see Dobyns, Dolbyns			Dodridge, George	424	Bth	Wm.	196	Ess
Dobbs, Katharine	29	Isw	Dodson, Alex.	397	Rch	Dolly, Heny A.	838	Nrf
Kedar	796	Nrf	Ann	41	Stf	John	222	Pnd
Patcy	29	Isw	Charles	409	Rch	Dolten, William	179	Shn
Thomas	383	Mds	Charles	49	Stf	Dolton, ...	305	Rck
Dobie, James	26	Clp	Chas.	344	Lnc	John	265	Rck
Nathaniel	634	Sss	Daniel	330	Dnw	Margret	218	Pnd
William	634	Sss	Jacob	230	Shn	Doman, Jacob	789	Hmp
Dobins, Abner	625	Mnt	James	563	Pre	Jacob	831	Hmp
Dangerfield	664	Mnt	James	398	Rch	John	795	Hmp
John	625	Mnt	James B.	396	Rch	William	789	Hmp
John	417	Rnd	Jane	250	Frf	Domaniel, Winnifred	449	Grn
Samuel	417	Rnd	Jas.	28	Clp	Donafranks, Abraham	225	Shn
Thos.	625	Mnt	Joel	27	Clp	Donaghe, John	332	Ags
Washington	627	Mnt	Joseph	230	Shn	Donahey, John	759	Wsh
Doble, Joseph	619	Btt	Josh.	27	Clp	Donahoe, Mary	900	Crl
Dobson, Edward	652	Glc	Lucy	26	Clp	Patty	900	Crl
Jno.	653	Glc	Nancy	26	Clp	Reuben	900	Crl
Nicholas, Christians-			Rawligh	399	Rch	Saml.	333	Ags
burg	619	Mnt	Stephen	27	Clp	Wm.	333	Ags
Richard	751	Nwk	Thomas	399	Rch	Donahower, John	476	Frn
Robt.	177	Elc	Walter	247	Frf	Donald, Janus	282	Rck
Saml.	55	Jff	Wm.	28	Clp	Mathew	297	Rck
William O.	858	Cmp	Doe, ---, Madam	895	Nrf	Richard	832	Bck
Wm.	652	Glc	Dofflemire, Henry	36	Rcm	Donaldson, Adam	110	Spt
Dobtson, Daniel	99	Cmb	Michael	33	Rcm	Andrew	16	Oho
Edith	99	Cmb	Dofre, Robt.	817	Nrf	Charles	894	Nrf
Dobyns, Abner	394	Rch	Dogan, Chs., (F. Mo.)	25	Clp	Elizabeth	20	Hnr
Charles	394	Rch	Henry	523	Prw	Isaac	550	Prg
Chichester	412	Rch	Dogett, Judith	976	Nrt	James	793	Hmp
Christo. L.	395	Rch	Wm.	834	Nrf	Jno.	25	Clp
Henry M.	393	Rch	Doggett, Ann	26	Clp	Saml.	546	Prg
Jesse	393	Rch	Ann	39	Stf	Stephen	308	Ldn
Leroy	412	Rch	Ben.	343	Lnc	Thomas	251	Frf
Leroy, Junr.	393	Rch	Coleman	343	Lnc	William	251	Frf
Thomas	392	Rch	Daniel B.	32	Stf	William	796	Hmp
William	393	Rch	Dennis	344	Lnc	Wm.	586	Brk
Dockerty, Wm.	619	Btt	Geo.	344	Lnc	Wm.	249	Frf
Docketty, Garvy	214	Shn	Jane	900	Crl	Donally, Andrew, Senr.	10	Knw
Dockey, Peter	91	Acc	Jas.	343	Lnc	Andrew, Senr.	14	Knw
Dockings, John	1	Wod	Jno.	343	Lnc	John	335	Ags
Doco, Jannet	278	Ldn	Jno. G.	344	Lnc	Donalson, Jane	334	Ags
Doctor, Martin	167	Shn	Jud.	344	Lnc	John	334	Ags
Dodd, Alexr.	295	Rck	Reubn., Ser.	25	Clp	John A.	71	Jff
Benjamin	416	Fqr	Richd. T.	28	Clp	Js.	495	Mnn
Benjn.	655	Mnt	Sarah	26	Clp	Polly	496	Mnn
Edwd., Junr. (Quarter)	346	Fqr	Thos.	25	Clp	Saml.	562	Brk
Elizabeth	144	Dnw	Doggins, Ann	217	Ess	Stephens	71	Jff
Francis	15	Oho	Doggit, John	47	Chr	Donavan, Danl.	333	Ags
George	197	Kng	Dogo see Doco			James	62	Stf
Griffin	46	Chr	Doherly see Doherty			Donavon, Charles	441	Bth
James	257	Amh	Doherty, Alexr.	501	Brk	Dondal, Moses	183	Shn
James	197	Kng	John	584	Brk	Done, James	724	Wsh
Jno.	312	Ldn	John	16	Rcm	John	710	Wsh
Jno.	295	Rck	Michael	424	Bth	Donelson, Thos.	702	Wsh
John	256	Amh	Thos.	521	Brk	Donely, Isaiah	550	Frd
John	346	Fqr	Doke see Doco			Donen, Darby	201	Shn
John	477	Frn	Dolbyns, Thomas	423	Msn	Doner, Michl.	618	Btt
John	689	Nls	Dold, Philip	332	Ags	Donerla, Jno.	867	Hnv
John	770	Wst	Doleman, John H.	770	Wst	Partrick	896	Hnv

Donevan, Cornelias	618	Btt	Dorrow, John	493	Mnn	John	128	Sth
Donihou, Jno.	281	Rck	Dorset, Queris	28	Clp	Joseph	169	Shn
Jno.	298	Rck	Dorsey, Edwd.	308	Ldn	Josiah	89	Acc
Doniphan, Alexr.	197	Kng	Geo.	495	Mnn	Matthew	18	Acc
Eliza.	196	Kng	Jeremiah	894	Nrf	Robert	401	Fqr
Thornton A.	196	Kng	John	675	Br	Thomas	591	Frd
Donivant, Eldred	338	Lnn	John	62	Jff	William	19	Acc
Donivin, Peter	738	Wsh	Levin	896	Nrf	Doughurty, Jesse	304	Rck
Donley, Hugh	786	Hmp	Michael	236	Ldn	Douglas, ---, Jordan and	757	Nwk
Donnald, Sarah	173	Shn	Sarah	63	Jff	Achellis	192	Alb
Donnall, William	349	Fqr	Sevin	894	Nrf	Achilles	869	Cmp
Donnally, Andrew	117	Spt	Dorss, James	459	Bdf	Benjn., Sr.	618	Btt
Donnalson, Magreth	621	Gls	Lydda	459	Bdf	Charles	190	Alb
Donnehey, John	895	Nrf	Dorton, H.	495	Mnn	David	459	Bdf
Donnely, Patrick	585	Mnr	Joseph	131	Hnr	George	459	Bdf
Donnen, William	201	Shn	Levi	495	Mnn	Hugh	289	Ldn
Donner, Jacob	618	Btt	Dosier see Dozier			James	190	Alb
Donnigan, Patric	18	Oho	Doss, Edward	817	Bck	James	436	Bth
Donnison, Sally	206	Ess	Edward	820	Bck	James	332	Dnw
Donnitt, Lucy	217	Ess	Hartwell	871	Cmp	Jelson	437	Bth
Donoho, ...ard	459	Bdf	Jacob	818	Bck	Jeremiah	516	Prw
Ingree	430	Rnd	James	817	Bck	John	191	Alb
Donohoe, James	113	Spt	James	100	Cmb	John	459	Bdf
Joshua	198	Ess	John	819	Bck	John	617	Btt
Stephen	249	Frf	Joshua	488	Frn	John	828	Wth
Donohower, George	479	Frn	Littleberry	821	Bck	Levi	251	Ldn
Donovan, Daniel	7	Oho	Micajoh	621	Gls	Murphy	458	Bdf
Lydia	12	Oho	Noah	492	Frn	Ralph	5	Oho
Matthew	712	Wsh	Doster, John	576	Frd	Robert	458	Bdf
Donwer, Peter, a man of			William	516	Frd	Thomas	191	Alb
couler	759	Wsh	Doswell, James	868	Hnv	Walter	89	Acc
Dood see Dodd			Jno.	8	Ntt	William	89	Acc
Dooley, George	459	Bdf	John	337	Lnn	William	415	Bth
James B.	459	Bdf	John	563	Pre	William	458	Bdf
John, (B)	459	Bdf	Payton	337	Lnn	William	334	Dnw
John, (L.S.)	458	Bdf	Thomas	563	Pre	Eilliam	750	Nwk
John, Sr.	459	Bdf	William	563	Pre	Wm.	298	Ldn
Moses	458	Bdf	Wm.	20	Ntt	see Dugglis, Duglas		
Thomas	458	Bdf	Dotie, Cage	18	Oho	Douglass, Adam	271	Rck
Val	270	Rck	Dotimore, Jacob	333	Ags	Francis	196	Kng
Doolittle, Tho.	492	Mnn	Dotson, Emanuel	19	Wod	George	586	Frd
see Dolittle			James	191	Alb	Henry	581	Mnr
Dooly, Samuel	539	Frd	Richard	19	Wod	James	860	Cmp
William	539	Frd	Thomas	223	Shn	James	249	Ldn
Doom, Conrad	407	Ags	William	19	Wod	James	274	Rck
Doome, ---, Widow	332	Ags	Dotten see Dolten			Jno.	653	Glc
Jacob	332	Ags	Dotton, Andw., a free man			John	354	Fqr
Doores, Eliza. [2]	26	Clp	of couler	721	Wsh	John	533	Frd
James	24	Clp	Dotts, Boston	94	Jff	John	161	Knq
Jno.	28	Clp	George	97	Jff	Jonas	805	Hmp
Mary	26	Clp	Doty, Abraham	693	Br	Joseph	15	Rcm
Dopson, George	952	Hrr	John	4	Oho	Mouring	55	Stf
Pitman	893	Hnv	Peter	693	Br	Neil	495	Mnn
Dorah, John	494	Mnn	Doubt, Matthias	8	Rcm	Patrick	253	Ldn
Rob.	494	Mnn	Doudge, Batson	450	Pra	Thomas	161	Knq
Doram, Terrance	828	Wth	Francis	450	Pra	Thos.	653	Glc
Doran, Alexander	763	Hmp	Daniel	450	Pra	William	596	Frd
Jas.	493	Mnn	Henry	450	Pra	William	3	Rcm
Jas.	743	Wsh	Nathan	450	Pra	Wm.	266	Rck
John	473	Frn	Reuben, Sr.	450	Pra	Dougles, Chs., (fr.N.)	26	Clp
Mary	473	Frn	Richd.	450	Pra	Dougless, Francis	685	Brk
Mary	527	Frd	Ruben	448	Pra	Robert	297	Amh
Sam	493	Mnn	Tully	449	Pra	Doulan, Christo.	517	Brk
Dorch, William	11	Knw	Tully, (of Joab)	448	Pra	Doumagin, Richd.	161	Knq
Dore, Alexander	250	Frf	William	448	Pra	Dountin, James	976	Nrt
Doreman, Andrew	12	Rcm	Willo.	450	Pra	William	977	Nrt
Doring, Terry	494	Mnn	Willoughby	448	Pra	Douthat, Robt.	617	Btt
Dorington, David	13	Hnr	Doudoct see Daudoct			Robt.	284	Rck
Dorman, Corns.	263	Rck	Dougharty, Wm.	16	Oho	Dovall, John	33	Rcm
Matthew	90	Acc	Dougherty, Davd. M.	291	Rck	Dove, Aaron	30	Rcm
Richard	836	Hmp	David	285	Rck	Benjamin	248	Frf
Dorney, Daniel	895	Nrf	Henry	583	Mnr	David	154	Alb
Dornson, Samuel	13	Knw	Hugh	334	Ags	Frederick	30	Rcm
Dorrell, Jno.	305	Ldn	John	334	Ags	George	30	Rcm
John	432	Flv	John	879	Cmp	Jacob	30	Rcm
Phillip	190	Alb	Robert	778	Hmp	James	249	Frf
Thomas	280	Ldn	Doughtery, James	159	Sth	Jno.	248	Frf
Dorrington, David	114	Hnr	Sally	879	Sth	Thomas	249	Frf
Js.	895	Nrf	Doughty, George	348	Fqr	William	249	Frf
Dorrins, Joseph	896	Nrf	Jephtha	19	Acc	see Dore		

Dovell, Daniel	188	Shn	Francis	19	Acc	John	493	Mnn
Dovison, Andrew	960	Hrr	Green	340	Fqr	P., Jr.	494	Mnn
Dow, Fulton	457	Frn	Henry H.	406	Fqr	Peter	493	Mnn
see Dore			James	597	Frd	Wm.	495	Mnn
Dowdall, James	895	Nrf	James	13	Oho	Drain, Davd.	276	Rck
Margarett	510	Frd	Jesse	91	Acc	Drainer, Conrod	86	Jff
Dowden, Ellenor	544	Brk	John	19	Acc	Drake, ...muel	15	Pwh
George	635	Sss	John, Jr.	977	Nrt	Amos	157	Sth
James B.	605	Srr	John, Sr.	977	Nrt	Andrew	619	Btt
John	824	Hmp	Nancy	977	Nrt	Ann	622	Gls
Dowdle, Colins	24	Hnr	Nanney	91	Acc	Arthur	157	Sth
Jno.	235	Ldn	Rezin	597	Frd	Baldy	158	Sth
Mary	28	Clp	Samuel	20	Acc	Barna.	154	Sth
Moses	293	Ldn	Samuel	977	Nrt	Briscoe	159	Sth
Dowdy, Benjamin	5	Pwh	Samuel	13	Oho	Charles	622	Gls
Eseakel	465	Frn	Solomn.	19	Acc	Chloe	853	Sth
Francis	103	Cmb	Thomas, Colo.	976	Nrt	Drew	148	Sth
Hunley	458	Bdf	William	91	Acc	Edwin	875	Sth
Jessee	105	Cmb	William	12	Oho	Elisebeth	749	Wsh
Jessee	126	Cmb	see Glascock			Francis	547	Frd
John	458	Bdf	Downman, Geo.	334	Lnc	Frs.	894	Nrf
John	103	Cmb	Olevia	343	Lnc	Gabriel	592	Mnr
John, (SM)	458	Bdf	R. W.	343	Lnc	George	18	Wod
Martha	562	Pre	R. W., for	462	Mdd	Gershom	562	Frd
Mary	16	Ntt	Raw.	399	Rch	Hardy	132	Sth
Moses	459	Bdf	Raw., Senr.	399	Rch	James	243	Aml
Richard	106	Cmb	Robert	634	Sss	James	144	Dnw
Thomas	105	Cmb	William	396	Rch	James	403	Rch
Thomas	112	Cmb	Downs, Benjaman	57	Jff	Jerem.	145	Sth
William	458	Bdf	Henry	372	Fqr	Jno.	140	Sth
Dowel, Ambros	190	Alb	Henry	311	Ldn	John	619	Btt
C.	493	Mnn	James	293	Ldn	John	531	Frd
Harrison	190	Alb	James	312	Ldn	John	571	Frd
James	190	Alb	John	88	Jff	John	126	Hnr
James	191	Alb	John	98	Jff	John	450	Pra
John [2]	190	Alb	John	495	Mnn	John	18	Wod
John	191	Alb	Richd.	495	Mnn	Jont.	260	Ldn
Majer	190	Alb	Robt.	494	Mnn	Kerby, & Taylor[?]	11	Hnr
Mary M.	28	Hnr	Susanna	417	Fqr	Martha	158	Sth
Richard	190	Alb	see Dawns			Mildred	26	Clp
Thomas	877	Cmp	Downy, John	495	Mnn	Molly	14	Pwh
William	190	Alb	Dowthat, Suzanna	806	Hmp	Patty	879	Sth
William [2]	191	Alb	Dowton, John	482	Frn	Pleasant	243	Aml
Dowell, Elisha	389	Fqr	Doyeal, John	243	Aml	Ridley	156	Sth
Francis	458	Bdf	Doyl, Amos	872	Sth	Robert	946	Chc
Isaac	526	Frd	Elias	872	Sth	Robert	290	Ldn
Jessee	502	Prw	Jere.	158	Sth	Sally	894	Nrf
John	458	Bdf	John	158	Sth	Samuel	548	Frd
John	540	Frd	Olive	879	Sth	Sarah	690	Gch
John	578	Frd	Philip	881	Sth	Simmons	857	Sth
Major	332	Ags	Shadrach	872	Sth	Thomas	690	Gch
Mary	594	Frd	William	854	Sth	Thomas	274	Ldn
Mary	514	Prw	Zachariah	449	Grn	Thomas, J.	274	Ldn
Nehemiah	458	Bdf	Doyle, Alexander	198	Shn	Thomas R.	687	Nls
Nehemiah	411	Fqr	Amos	496	Mnn	William	243	Aml
Reuben	458	Bdf	Catharine	507	Prw	William	468	Frn
Dowelle, Mecaijah	260	Ldn	David	2		William	3	Pwh
Dowlan, John	537	Brk	Isaac	368	Fqr	William	771	Wst
Dowler, Edward	4	Oho	James	511	Brk	Drakes, John	873	Yrk
Dowles, Elizabeth	900	Crl	Martn.	896	Nrf	Draper, Abraham	663	Mnt
Thomas	899	Crl	Ph...	757	Hmp	Benjn.	617	Btt
Thomas	900	Crl	Polly	27	Hnr	David	191	Alb
Dowlin, Hugh	591	Mnr	Sarah	132	Hnr	Eli	153	Sth
Dowling, Elizabeth	120	Hnr	Simon	511	Brk	Elizh.	880	Sth
John	536	Brk	Theophilus	512	Prw	George	828	Wth
John	271	Ldn	Doyles, Charles	791	Hmp	Isaac	252	Frf
Wm.	536	Brk	Dozier, Allen S.	770	Wst	James	334	Ags
Wm.	205	Ess	Conway	396	Rch	John	630	Mnt
Downer, Walker	899	Crl	James	771	Wst	John	828	Wth
Downes, James	896	Nrf	Richard	395	Rch	Robert	113	Spt
John	895	Nrf	Richard	770	Wst	Sarah	880	Sth
Downey, Edmond	80	Jff	Tho.	344	Lnc	Thos.	880	Sth
Jane	526	Brk	Thomas	771	Wst	Drawbond, Conrod	4	Rcm
John	80	Jff	Thomas, Junr.	771	Wst	Drayton, Lewis	449	Pra
Rachel	212	Ess	William	770	Wst	Samuel	449	Pra
Samuel	444	Bth	Drace, Peter	221	Pnd	Drean, Jno.	304	Ldn
Downinan see Downman			Draffin, Robert	190	Alb	Drew, Ann	5	Hnr
Downing, Arthur	91	Acc	Drage see Drago			Benja.	879	Sth
Edward	976	Nrt	Drago, Epm.	494	Mnn	Cary	777	Bck
Elizabeth	32	Isw	Jac.	494	Mnn	Dolphin	183	Elc

Name	Page	County
Dolphin	535	Frd
Hannah	25	Clp
Susanna	132	Sth
Winnifred	869	Sth
Drewbree, Rob.	681	Wrw
Drewry, Amos	162	Sth
Dolphin	678	Wrw
Edmund	141	Sth
Eliza	808	Nrf
Henry	873	Yrk
Humpy.	851	Sth
James	867	Sth
Jno.	680	Wrw
John	186	Elc
John	789	Nrf
John	808	Nrf
John	875	Sth
John	873	Yrk
Johnson	680	Wrw
Joseph	127	Sth
Lucy	850	Sth
Matthw.	681	Wrw
Nancy	681	Wrw
Richd.	681	Wrw
Richd., Senr.	604	Srr
Saml.	144	Sth
Sarah	681	Wrw
Thos.	681	Wrw
Wm.	794	Nrf
Drinane, John	832	Nrf
Drinkard, Archibald	821	Bck
Davd.	4	Hnr
Francis	562	Pre
George	941	Chc
James	821	Bck
John	15	Hnr
William	751	Nwk
Wim. H.	885	Hnv
Drinnan, James	113	Spt
Drinner, Christina	420	Bth
John	420	Bth
Drish, Jno.	303	Ldn
Wm.	304	Ldn
Driskell, Adam	875	Cmp
Daniel	869	Cmp
Daniel	874	Cmp
William	869	Cmp
Driskle, Dennis	415	Bth
Elizabeth	415	Bth
Driver, Barbara	4	Rcm
Betsey	210	Ess
Charlotte	20	Isw
Edmund	453	Mth
Jack	453	Mth
Jemima	4	Isw
Lewis	25	Rcm
Peter	13	Rcm
Priscilla	27	Isw
Thos.	291	Ldn
Wm.	453	Mth
Dromgoole, Elizabeth	517	Frd
Drommo, Thomas	956	Hrr
Drouns, Jno.	248	Frf
Druen, Danl.	117	Hnr
Druin, David	793	Bck
John	801	Bck
William	803	Bck
Drum, John	333	Ags
Drumgold, Alexr.	743	Wsh
Drumgoole, Edward	746	Brn
Thos.	747	Brn
Drumheller, Adam	154	Alb
George	154	Alb
Jachob	154	Alb
Leonard	154	Alb
Drummen, Thornton	227	Shn
Drummon, Nancy	459	Bdf
Samuel	237	Shn
Thos.	430	Flv
Drummond, Aaron	378	Fqr
Athey	90	Acc
Bill	19	Acc
C.	26	Hnr
Charles	90	Acc
Chars.	19	Acc
Daniel	20	Acc
Geo.	188	Elc
George	18	Acc
George	618	Btt
Grief	746	Brn
Henry	413	Fqr
James	347	Fqr
James	378	Fqr
John	92	Acc
John, jr.	746	Brn
John, Sr.	746	Brn
Joshua	401	Fqr
Mary B.	687	Nls
Peggy	375	Fqr
Richd.	895	Nrf
Robert	20	Acc
Robert	91	Acc
Spencer	90	Acc
Stephen	184	Elc
Thomas	342	Fqr
see Welburn		
Drummound, Isabella	161	Knq
Drumwright, Bennet	689	Gch
Geo.	689	Gch
John	689	Gch
Washton.	689	Gch
Wm.	689	Gch
Drurey, Mary	448	Pra
Drury, John	832	Nrf
Polly	809	Nrf
Raphael	505	Prw
William	460	Bdf
Dryden, Mary	59	Stf
James	288	Rck
James	305	Rck
Drydon, Davd.	749	Wsh
Thos.	749	Wsh
Wm.	749	Wsh
Duayne, Charles	13	Wod
Dubarey, John	808	Nrf
Duberry, Irby	449	Grn
Duchanon, Jas.	305	Rck
Duck, Allen	22	Isw
Demsey	23	Isw
Demsey	44	Isw
Jacob	200	Shn
John, Jun.	46	Isw
John, Sen.	24	Isw
John, Sen.	44	Isw
Joseph	9	Isw
William	23	Isw
Ducker, Thoms., f.		
negro	250	Frf
William	67	Jff
Duckwall, Frdk.	572	Brk
Henry	578	Brk
Lewis	573	Brk
Lewis, jr.	572	Brk
see Ducwall		
Duckwiler, Danl.	619	Btt
Ducoing, P.	894	Nrf
Ducwall, John	570	Brk
Dudden, Joseph	618	Btt
Dudding, John	13	Knw
William	3	Knw
Dudgeon, M.A.	896	Nrf
Dudley, Ann	162	Knq
Armistead	882	Cmp
Asa	493	Mnn
Benja.	653	Glc
Eliza.	652	Glc
Fancy	18	Hnr
George	154	Alb
George	449	Pra
George E.	442	Mth
Gwyn	461	Frn
Henrey F.	161	Knq
Henry	570	Frd
Jacob	449	Pra
James	154	Alb
James	461	Frn
James	976	Nrt
Jas.	161	Knq
John	154	Alb
John	869	Cmp
John	462	Mdd
John	401	Rch
Joseph	977	Nrt
Landon	976	Nrt
Levy	461	Frn
Molley	977	Nrt
Peter	849	Cmp
Peter	89	Spt
Ransom	562	Pre
Robert	462	Mdd
Robert	145	Sth
Robt.	449	Pra
Robt., (KJ)	449	Pra
Sam	494	Mnn
Sarah	162	Knq
Thomas	501	Frn
Thomas	161	Knq
Thos.	449	Pra
William	859	Cmp
Wm. [2]	652	Glc
Wm.	653	Glc
Wm.	449	Pra
Duerson, Henry, jr.	66	Spt
Henry, Sr.	87	Spt
John	70	Spt
Joseph	79	Spt
Joseph, jr.	78	Spt
Thomas	102	Spt
Thomas, jr.	78	Spt
William	81	Spt
William, jr.	69	Spt
Duesbery, James	895	Nrf
Duff, Elizabeth	273	Ldn
George	416	Fqr
Hugh	746	Brn
James	1	Rcm
John	553	Frd
John	699	Wsh
John, Jun.	716	Wsh
Joshua	383	Mds
Margret	716	Wsh
Nathl.	25	Clp
Peter	553	Frd
Saml.	716	Wsh
Samuel	699	Wsh
Thomas	80	Jff
William	716	Wsh
William, Capt.	715	Wsh
Duffee, Asa	47	Chr
Austin	47	Chr
Edmund	47	Chr
Edmund, Jur.	48	Chr
Fleming	47	Chr
Isaac	47	Chr
John	47	Chr
John	894	Nrf
Mary	449	Pra
William	448	Pra
Duffeild, John	127	Cmb
Richard	83	Jff
Robert	415	Bth
Duffel, Edward	849	Cmp
James	849	Cmp
Duffey, Allen	509	Prw
Isaac	91	Acc
John	74	Jff
Moses	509	Prw
Polley	385	Fqr
Duffield, Mary	516	Frd
Duffle, Isaac	420	Rnd

Name	No.	Co.
Duffy, Patrick	594	Brk
Dufield, Abraham	7	Knw
Benjamin	7	Knw
John	7	Knw
Duford, ---, Doctr.	896	Nrf
Dugan, James	543	Brk
John	589	Brk
William	773	Hmp
Dugard, James	28	Hnr
John	28	Hnr
Dugger, Armon	709	Brn
James, jr.	709	Brn
James, S. J.	709	Brn
Mary	734	Sss
Richmond	709	Brn
Wm.	709	Brn
Duggin, Joshua	13	Isw
Dugglis, Ann	934	Hrr
Duggliss, Levy	934	Hrr
Duglas, Edward	392	Rch
Jacob	622	Gls
John, Jr.	410	Rch
Lucy	409	Rch
William	410	Rch
William S.	410	Rch
Duglass, ---	952	Chc
Abra.	1	Hnr
Abra., (Penitiny) [Penitentiary?]	1	Hnr
John	13	Wod
Thomas S.	900	Crl
William	180	Alb
Duke, Aggay	34	Hnr
Alexr.	548	Brk
Burnley	870	Hnv
Clevins	190	Alb
Edwd.	27	Clp
Edwd.	690	Gch
Eliza	334	Dnw
Fontaine	690	Gch
Francis	679	Br
James	334	Ags
James	365	Fqr
James	54	Jff
Jno.	860	Hnv
John	618	Btt
John	94	Jff
Joseph	79	Jff
Martin	17	Hnr
Masten	31	Hnr
Richard	191	Alb
Richd.	27	Clp
Robert	5	Knw
Sarah	690	Gch
Thos.	690	Gch
Thos.	897	Hnv
Washington	169	Shn
Wm.	28	Clp
Wm. L.	27	Clp
Dukes, Ann	27	Clp
Elizabeth	807	Nrf
Robert	691	Wsh
Dulaid, Jas.	825	Nrf
Dulan, Rachael	578	Brk
Dulaney, ---	46	Clp
Abijah	26	Clp
French	25	Clp
James	25	Clp
Jno.	25	Clp
Joseph	24	Clp
Leroye	24	Clp
Walter	166	Shn
Dulany, Benja.	248	Frf
Daniel	249	Frf
Gabriel	383	Mds
Larken	383	Mds
Dulen, Joseph	977	Nrt
Duley, Thomas	911	Hrr
Dulin, Charles	345	Fqr
Collin	807	Hmp
Edward	346	Fqr
Edward	248	Frf
Edwd.	26	Clp
Edwd.	290	Ldn
George	396	Fqr
George, Jr.	368	Fqr
Jno.	248	Frf
Jno.	254	Ldn
John, Jr.	344	Fqr
John, Senr.	407	Fqr
Susannah	251	Frf
William	363	Fqr
William	808	Hmp
William	811	Hmp
William	813	Hmp
Wm.	290	Ldn
Duling, Achilles	901	Crl
Jessee	161	Knq
Larkin	899	Crl
Larkin	161	Knq
Spencer	28	Clp
Wm.	26	Clp
Dull, Chaty	205	Shn
Frederick	219	Shn
Geo., jr.	334	Ags
Geo., se.	334	Ags
George	593	Brk
John	334	Ags
Philip	335	Ags
Dulon, Lewis	916	Hrr
Dultie, John	2	Oho
Duman, Charles	295	Amh
Dumass, Benjamin	330	Dnw
Dumkin, Benjn.	117	Cmb
John	129	Cmb
Dun, Aaron	711	Wsh
Henry	441	Mth
James	192	Alb
John	440	Mth
Jonathan	711	Wsh
Valentine	806	Nrf
William	711	Wsh
Zacharah	190	Alb
Dunagin, Absalom	829	Wth
Dunaha, William	346	Fqr
Dunahaw, Eliza.	391	Rch
Dunahoo, Amos	278	Ldn
Jno.	310	Ldn
Mary	304	Ldn
Saml.	279	Ldn
Dunam, Arklas	930	Hrr
Dunaper, George	225	Shn
Dunarat, Daniel	828	Wth
Dunavant, Abner	243	Aml
Archer	3	Ntt
Philip	243	Aml
Thos.	243	Aml
William	243	Aml
Dunaway, Ann	343	Lnc
Chat.	343	Lnc
Eppa.	189	Elc
Ezekiel	520	Prw
Isaac	26	Clp
Jno.	27	Clp
Jno.	343	Lnc
John	944	Hrr
Jos.	344	Lnc
Joseph	511	Prw
Leana	519	Prw
Opie	343	Lnc
Raw	343	Lnc
Samuel	586	Frd
Samuel	398	Rch
Dunbar, David	162	Knq
David	448	Pra
Jonathan	6	Knw
Robert	592	Mnr
Robert	36	Stf
Sarah	447	Mth
Dunbor, John	20	Stf
Duncall, Jacob	8	Oho
Duncan, Abey	130	Sth
Alexander	113	Spt
Blanch	648	Mnt
Charles	415	Fqr
Charles	622	Gls
Charles, Jr.	370	Fqr
Christopher	397	Fqr
Fleming H.	289	Amh
Fleming W.	806	Bck
Fredk.	27	Clp
Geo. [2]	27	Clp
Gollop	25	Clp
Henry	648	Mnt
Jacob	824	Bck
James	91	Acc
James	28	Clp
Jas. M.	28	Clp
Jesse	90	Acc
Jno.	25	Clp
Jno., Jr.	648	Mnt
John	283	Amh
John	541	Brk
John	431	Flv
John	188	Shn
John, Sr.	648	Mnt
John N.	687	Nls
Joseph	293	Amh
Joseph C.	793	Bck
Josh.	25	Clp
Leroy	357	Fqr
Mary	25	Clp
Moses	415	Fqr
Patrick	571	Frd
Robert	622	Gls
Robt.	25	Clp
Rosamond	27	Clp
Salley	289	Amh
Seth	629	Mnt
Solo., (FB)	450	Pra
Thos.	330	Dnw
Thos.	648	Mnt
Wiatt	257	Amh
William	277	Amh
William	899	Crl
William	622	Gls
Wm.	28	Clp
Wm.	272	Rck
Wm.	305	Rck
Dunchum, John	154	Alb
William	155	Alb
Duncum, Lucy	114	Spt
Dundoor, John	3	Rcm
Mary	17	Rcm
Dunfield, John	275	Rck
John	281	Rck
Dunford, John	828	Wth
Susan	652	Glc
William	110	Cmb
Dungam, David	977	Nrt
Dungan, John	566	Brk
Dungans, Elijah	736	Wsh
Hellin	711	Wsh
John	712	Wsh
Dungar, George	522	Prw
Dungay, Charles	527	Prw
Dungee, James	562	Pre
Mary	463	Mdd
Dungey, Isabella	751	Nwk
Reuben	751	Nwk
Dungy, William	114	Cmb
Dunham, Abel	515	Brk
Dav.	493	Mnn
David	553	Brk
James	591	Brk
John	72	Jff
Maj.	36	Hnr
Samuel	553	Brk
Dunick, James	293	Ldn
Dunington, Henry	17	Hnr

Name	Page	Co.
Dunivant, Abraham	563	Pre
Daniel	563	Pre
Dudley	563	Pre
Shadrick	564	Pre
Dunkan, John	748	Wsh
Dunken, John	709	Wsh
Dunkeson, Thomas	40	Rcm
Dunkin, Caleb	89	Acc
Charles	251	Ldn
Frank	89	Acc
Jno.	259	Ldn
John	750	Wsh
Nancy	747	Brn
Samuel	264	Ldn
Susanna	251	Ldn
Dunkinfield, Feris	2	Hnr
Dunkisor, David	131	Cmb
Dunkle, Ealizabeth	215	Pnd
George	215	Pnd
John	215	Pnd
Dunkley, Fanny	709	Brn
Dunlap, Alexan...	562	Mnr
Alexander	679	Br
Alexr.	294	Rck
Archd.	334	Ags
Catharine	21	Rcm
James	296	Rck
Jno.	294	Rck
John	332	Ags
Jos.	493	Mnn
Joseph	332	Ags
Josie...	5	Oho
Mary	430	Msn
Moses	615	Mnt
Robert	551	Brk
Robt.	332	Ags
Robt.	334	Ags
Robt.	17	Rcm
Thomas	292	Rck
William	679	Br
William	771	Hmp
William	11	Oho
Wm.	296	Rck
Dunlavy, Wm.	437	Mth
Dunlevy, Braxton	462	Mdd
Elizabeth	462	Mdd
George H.	462	Mdd
Dunlop, Augt.	197	Kng
Ester	4	Hnr
James	336	Dnw
James, Jr.	332	Dnw
John	332	Dnw
Lidia	197	Kng
Mary	10	Hnr
Nancy	10	Hnr
Sarah	197	Kng
William	900	Crl
Dunlow see Dunton		
Dunman, John	461	Frn
Dunmon, Joseph	337	Lnn
Dunn, Agrippa	462	Mdd
Amis	711	Wsh
Anthy.	896	Nrf
Bellington	337	Lnn
Benjamin	47	Chr
Burwell	157	Sth
Cuddy	896	Nrf
Curtis	463	Mdd
Dabney	214	Ess
David	505	Brk
Dianna	217	Ess
Drewry	448	Grn
Drury	634	Sss
Edmund	570	Mnr
Ephram	820	Hmp
Geo.	188	Elc
Henry	161	Knq
Hinde	681	Wrw
Hugh	688	Br
Ishmuel	709	Brn
Jackson	162	Knq
Jacob	819	Hmp
James	284	Amh
James	210	Ess
James	448	Grn
James	533	Prg
James	635	Sss
Jas.	494	Mnn
Jno.	315	Ldn
John	900	Crl
John	210	Ess
John	218	Ess
John	550	Frd
John	690	Gch
John	448	Grn
John	121	Hnr
John	570	Mnr
John	896	Nrf
John	635	Sss
John	680	Wrw
John, (D)	214	Ess
John, j.	569	Mnr
John, (T)	221	Ess
Joshua	161	Knq
Levi	302	Rck
Lewis	819	Hmp
Lucritia	47	Chr
Mary	802	Nrf
Mary	838	Nrf
Mary	828	Wth
Patsy	635	Sss
Peachy	462	Mdd
Reuben	568	Mnr
Richard	797	Hmp
Richard	338	Lnn
Richd.	681	Wrw
Rob.	681	Wrw
Saml.	681	Wrw
Thomas	205	Ess
Thomas	501	Frn
Thomas	550	Frd
Thomas	758	Hmp
Thomas	570	Mnr
Thomas	635	Sss
Thomas L.	205	Ess
Thos.	681	Wrw
Tolly	217	Ess
Waters	208	Ess
William	900	Crl
William	448	Grn
William	571	Mnr
William	26	Rcm
Wm.	505	Brk
Wm.	65	Chs
Wm.	758	Wsh
see Dinn		
Dunnahaw see McDunnahaw		
Dunnahoe, Anna	5	Oho
Dunnapin, Isaac	207	Shn
Dunnavan, Davis	5	Rcm
Jacob	20	Rcm
John	5	Rcm
Thomas	18	Rcm
Timothy	14	Rcm
Dunnavant, Josiah	54	Chs
Wm.	62	Chs
Dunnevant, Wm.	11	Ntt
Dunning, William	695	Wsh
Dunnington, Francis	501	Prw
Hezekiah	519	Prw
John P.	357	Fqr
William	500	Prw
William	510	Prw
Dunnivan, Thos.	690	Gch
Dunnom, Oliver	302	Ldn
Dunnom see Dienom		
Dunsan, John	578	Brk
Dunscomb, J.	896	Nrf
Nancy	16	Hnr
Dunscombe, Dick	116	Hnr
Dunsmore, James	577	Mnr
Jno.	13	Hnr
Dunstan, Hezekiah	43	Isw
John	92	Acc
Dunston, Allmond	653	Glc
James	333	Ags
James	652	Glc
Jno.	652	Glc
Lewis	653	Glc
Thos.	653	Glc
Dunton, Carvey	19	Acc
Danl.	344	Lnc
George	20	Acc
Isaac	18	Acc
Molly	19	Acc
Sally	334	Lnc
Dunway, Mary	494	Mnn
Richard	977	Nrt
Dunwin, Daniel	261	Amh
Dunwoody, Rob.	496	Mnn
Duparge, Fris	895	Nrf
Duperier, J.B.	895	Nrf
Dupp see Duff		
Dupray, Joseph	338	Lnn
Dupree, Benja. D.	448	Grn
E.	894	Nrf
Henry	144	Dnw
Henry	448	Grn
Lewis	448	Grn
Robert	449	Grn
Thomas	448	Grn
Thomas, Jr.	449	Grn
William	449	Grn
Willie	448	Grn
Dupriest, John	871	Cmp
Nathan	11	Ntt
Wm.	19	Hnr
Dupuy, Edmd.	13	Ntt
Henry	562	Pre
Jas., jr.	4	Ntt
Jas., Senr.	13	Ntt
Jas. W.	7	Ntt
Jesse L.	1	Ntt
John	562	Pre
Peter	8	Pwh
Stephen	563	Pre
Durant, L.E.	895	Nrf
Durbin, John	690	Br
Dure, Wm.	237	Ldn
Durell, James	325	Dnw
Duren, Joseph	570	Brk
Durfey, Cornelious	944	Chc
Durgen, Barnabas	586	Mnr
Durham, ...illiam	460	Bdf
Ambrose	161	Knq
Caleb	47	Chr
Eliza.	161	Knq
Griffen	161	Knq
Jacob	99	Cmb
James	217	Ess
John	161	Knq
John	4	Oho
Joseph	161	Knq
Larkin	899	Hnv
Nicholas	100	Cmb
Samuel	46	Chr
William	458	Bdf
see Derham		
Duringburger, Peter	2	Wod
Durk, John	831	Hmp
Durkin, Patrick	326	Dnw
see Henderson		
Durmon, Peter	635	Mnt
Wm.	635	Mnt
Durney, James	292	Rck
Durr, Katy	895	Nrf
Durran, Thomas	132	Hnr
Durrer, William	5	Rcm
Durret, Jonathan	74	Spt
Richard	154	Alb

Durrett, Claiborne	899 Crl	Thomas	807 Hmp	Eager, Robt.	279 Rck
Elizabeth	899 Crl	Thomas	17 Wod	Eagle, Chrn.	335 Ags
George	899 Crl	Vincen	15 Wod	Edwd.	576 Brk
Henry	899 Crl	William	4 Oho	George	576 Brk
Isaac W.	190 Alb	Dyer, Batson	449 Pra	Henry	336 Ags
James	154 Alb	Elizabeth	757 Hmp	John	337 Ags
John D.	190 Alb	Gilbert	251 Frf	Jonathan	337 Ags
Marhal	154 Alb	Isaac	597 Frd	Peter	400 Ags
Richard	191 Alb	Isham	55 Chs	Philip	337 Ags
Richard	458 Bdf	James	252 Frf	Philip	400 Ags
Robbin	82 Spt	James	448 Pra	Eagles, Edward	47 Chr
William	458 Bdf	James	418 Rnd	John	337 Ags
Wyatt	901 Crl	John	869 Cmp	Eagon, Samson	400 Ags
Durrum, David	154 Alb	John	252 Frf	Eaken, Sarah	708 Wsh
Durry, Levy	23 Rcm	John	588 Frd	Thos.	700 Wsh
Durt see Dust		John	224 Pnd	Thos.	701 Wsh
Duryarre, ---, Madame	896 Nrf	John	450 Pra	William	701 Wsh
Dusein, Agustus	895 Nrf	Mary	450 Pra	Eakin, James	758 Wsh
Dussey, Peggy	332 Dnw	Matthew	216 Pnd	Nathan, Sr.	620 Btt
Dust, Elizabeth	204 Shn	Roger	216 Pnd	Eakins, Alexr.	718 Wsh
Gasper	818 Hmp	Samuel	154 Alb	Joseph	620 Btt
Peter	560 Brk	Susanah	215 Pnd	Thos., Sr.	620 Btt
Valentine	84 Jff	Suzanna	823 Hmp	Eakles, Joseph	620 Btt
Duton, Mary	204 Shn	Thomas	249 Frf	Ealam, Walter	622 Gls
Dutro, Michael	54 Jff	Thos. B.	304 Ldn	Ealey, Ezekiah	945 Chc
Dutting, Adam	829 Wth	William	325 Dnw	Ealy see Ealy	
Dutton, David	534 Brk	William	336 Dnw	Eamen, Henry	337 Ags
Eleanor, f.negro	251 Frf	William [2]	216 Pnd	Eames, Joel	752 Nwk
James, jr.	652 Glc	Willo.	449 Pra	John, junr.	752 Nwk
James, Senr.	652 Glc	Wm.	449 Pra	John, Senr.	751 Nwk
Lewis	652 Glc	Zebulon	227 Pnd	William	751 Nwk
Richd.	652 Glc	Dyerly, Abraham	616 Mnt	Eamicke, Henry	215 Pnd
Robert	537 Frd	Charles	615 Mnt	Eanes, Danl.	60 Chs
Thos.	652 Glc	John	616 Mnt	Edwd.	55 Chs
Wm.	652 Glc	Peter	615 Mnt	Ephraim	60 Chs
Duty, Elizabeth	585 Frd	Dyke, Boulware	213 Ess	Frances ["Evans"	
Duval, Benja.	690 Gch	Catharine	204 Ess	crossed out]	145 Dnw
Daniel	899 Crl	Elinor	326 Dnw	George	58 Chs
Eliza	894 Nrf	George	29 Clp	Henry	54 Chs
James	899 Crl	Hester	29 Clp	see Eaves	
John	505 Prw	Jack	204 Ess	Eanix, Shadick	155 Alb
Joseph	689 Gch	Vinceat	205 Ess	Earhart, Chrs.	336 Ags
M.	495 Mnn	Walker	652 Glc	John	585 Frd
Philip	803 Bck	Dykes, Davd.	28 Clp	Mary	585 Frd
Rezin	550 Frd	James	895 Nrf	Peter	336 Ags
Samuel .	789 Bck	Dyles, Peter	575 Brk	see Airhart	
William	789 Bck	Dyson, Ann	896 Nrf	Earheart, Jacob	620 Btt
William	504 Prw	Aquilla	536 Frd	Michael	171 Shn
Duvall, Benj.	16 Hnr	Francis	144 Dnw	Earickson, Matthew	623 Gls
Brooke	144 Dnw	Francis	6 Ntt	Earle, Esaias	601 Frd
Danl.	25 Clp	James	144 Dnw	John B.	544 Frd
Elizabeth	116 Hnr	James	894 Nrf	Earles, Jeremiah	522 Frd
John	867 Cmp	Jennet	449 Pra	Earley, ---	481 Frn
Lewis	861 Cmp	Jno.	62 Chs	Abner	856 Cmp
Stephen	116 Hnr	Manor	900 Crl	Andw.	336 Ags
William	68 Spt	Mark	55 Mnr	Coats	483 Frn
DuVall, Benja.	116 Hnr	Mary	894 Nrf	Danl.	336 Ags
Benja.	121 Hnr	Mary	1 Ntt	Jabez L.	459 Bdf
Duvoy, Michael	72 Jff	Williem	19 Oho	Jno., [his] Estate	620 Btt
Dwier, Miles	251 Frf	Wm. N.	838 Nrf	Joel	459 Bdf
Dwimon see Durmon				John	337 Ags
Dwire, Willm.	617 Btt			Joshua	459 Bdf
Dwyer, Isam	896 Nrf	--- E ---		Joshua, sr.	460 Bdf
Joseph	618 Btt			Polley	466 Frn
William	144 Dnw			Sam	478 Frn
see Dwire		E..., ...	459 Bdf	Thomas	460 Bdf
Dyar, Andrew	3 Wod	Mitchell	460 Bdf	Tubel	459 Bdf
Edward	9 Wod	Eaches, Daniel	261 Ldn	Earlis, John	17 Oho
Elisabeth	726 Wsh	Eacock see Edcock		Earls, John	222 Shn
Thos.	725 Wsh	Eaden, Crew	978 Nrt	Earlsizer see Eirlsizer	
Dycher, ---	895 Nrf	Eades, Abraham	156 Alb	Early, George	591 Brk
Dye, Amos	527 Prw	James	446 Flv	Jacover	615 Mnt
Frances	524 Prw	Joseph	155 Alb	James	192 Alb
George	416 Fqr	Shepherd	155 Alb	Jane, and Son	384 Mds
Jno.	442 Mth	Eadin, John	650 Mnt	John	830 Wth
Jno. H.	248 Frf	Eadings, Benjamin	460 Bdf	Paschal	384 Mds
John	14 Wod	James	460 Bdf	Sauck [?]	576 Mnr
Reuben	248 Frf	Jesse	460 Bdf	William	384 Mds
Reuben	196 Kng	see Eddnings		Earlywine, Abraham	15 Oho
Ruben	11 Wod	Eads, Bartlett	292 Amh	Barney	24 Oho

Jacob	24	Oho
Earnest, Dolley	877	Hnv
George L.	878	Hnv
Earnist, Geo.	280	Ldn
Earsom, Jacob	762	Hmp
John	797	Hmp
Simon	797	Hmp
Earson, John	793	Hmp
Eashum, George	93	Acc
Easley see Earley		
Eason, Saml.	703	Wsh
Samuel	510	Frd
Easson, John	15	Isw
East, Charles	335	Ags
James	21	Acc
James	691	Nls
Parker	21	Acc
Severn, Junr.	21	Acc
Severn, of Sout.	21	Acc
Severn, Senr.	21	Acc
Southey	20	Acc
Thomas	795	Bck
Thomas	689	Nls
see Oast		
Eastburn, Tho.	496	Mnn
Easten, William	192	Alb
Easter, Mathew	869	Cmp
Sally	751	Nwk
Welchen	769	Brn
Wm.	653	Glc
Eastes, Andrew	865	Hnv
Eastham, Bird	30	Clp
Edward	384	Mds
George	412	Fqr
Lawson	356	Fqr
Easton, John	805	Hmp
Sarah	881	Cmp
Eastridge, Thomas	564	Pre
Eastrood see Eastwod		
Eastup, Thomas	226	Shn
Eastus, Henry	3	Ntt
Eastwod, Cornelius	817	Nrf
Joshua	819	Nrf
Willis	819	Nrf
Eastwood, Jupiter	897	Nrf
Eaton, Catharine	622	Gls
David	623	Gls
Eaphram	214	Pnd
Elizabeth	451	Pra
Henry	872	Yrk
Jas.	30	Clp
Jas.	451	Pra
John [2]	33	Rcm
John, (W)	872	Yrk
Joseph	442	Mth
Joseph	759	Wsh
Moses	451	Pra
Richd.	451	Pra
Sarah	897	Nrf
Thomas	19	Oho
William	688	Br
William	8	Rcm
William, (Sen.)	12	Rcm
Eaty, Jacob	518	Brk
Sebastian	60	Jff
William	101	Jff
Eavans, Geo.	897	Nrf
Eave, George	878	Cmp
Eavens, Joseph	335	Ags
Eaves, Arthur	48	Chr
Edward	48	Chr
Wm.	747	Brn
Eavin, George	305	Rck
Ebert, Christian	598	Brk
Eblin, Isaac	279	Ldn
Michael	261	Ldn
Samuel	302	Ldn
Echart, James	185	Shn
Michael	106	Jff
Echo, John	121	Hnr

Wm.	121	Hnr
Eckart, Adam	427	Rnd
Eckerley, Paul	336	Ags
Eckert, Jacob	16	Rcm
see Ecort		
Eckholes, James	459	Bdf
Eckiss, Henry	620	Btt
Michl.	620	Btt
Ecklebarger, George	105	Jff
Eckles, Edwd.	15	Ntt
Ephraim	12	Ntt
Jas., Senr.	17	Ntt
Freeman	8	Ntt
Thomas	2	Ntt
Eckolch, John	623	Gls
Eckoles, Jacob	460	Bdf
Eckols, Joel	636	Sss
William	636	Sss
Eckord, Christian	336	Ags
Jacob	336	Ags
John	409	Ags
Ecort, Abraham	226	Pnd
Henry	222	Pnd
Philip	226	Pnd
Ecton, Henry	300	Ldn
Edcock, George	742	Wsh
see Adcock		
Eddens, Benja.	29	Clp
Langley B.	447	Mth
Saml.	447	Mth
Thos.	436	Mth
Eddins, Abraham	384	Mds
Abram.	30	Clp
Blakey	384	Mds
Elijah	384	Mds
Joel	384	Mds
Joseph	384	Mds
Theophalis	384	Mds
Eddleton, Frances	855	Hnv
Eddings, Alexander	460	Bdf
see Eadings		
Edds, Jesse	873	Cmp
John	873	Cmp
Joseph A.	873	Cmp
Thomas	873	Cmp
Thomas	76	Spt
Eddy, Danl.	29	Clp
Guyan	496	Mnn
John	695	Br
John	583	Frd
Wm.	497	Mnn
Edenfield, William	852	Cmp
Edenton, Benjamin	75	Spt
John, jr.	68	Spt
John, Sr.	67	Spt
Edes, Abram	591	Mnr
Jacob	582	Mnr
Jacob	593	Mnr
Thomas	691	Gch
William	578	Mnr
Edgar, David	620	Btt
George	264	Rck
James	459	Bdf
James	685	Br
Sarah	620	Btt
Thomas	459	Bdf
Thos.	10	Hnr
Edge, Fosacur	30	Clp
Jane	95	Spt
John	901	Crl
Lot	30	Clp
Mary	901	Crl
Obediah	877	Cmp
Phillip	95	Spt
Simon	30	Clp
Edgington, Geo.	3	Hnr
John	696	Br
Thomas	686	Br
Edington, John	512	Prw
Phillip	620	Btt

Thomas	414	Bth
Edkins, John	693	Wsh
Edlen, Robert	1	Wod
Edloe, Frank	548	Prg
Jno.	546	Prg
William	943	Chc
see Thompson		
Edlow, ...	335	Dnw
Edmends, Edward	790	Nrf
Edmiston, Andrew	427	Bth
Davd.	697	Wsh
Davd.	699	Wsh
James	427	Bth
John	695	Wsh
John	697	Wsh
John, Esq.	694	Wsh
Moses	712	Wsh
Robt.	276	Rck
Robt.	700	Wsh
Saml.	697	Wsh
Thos.	720	Wsh
William	427	Bth
Wm.	697	Wsh
Wm., Colo.	697	Wsh
Edmond, William, Jur.	690	Nls
see Edmonds		
Edmonds, Benjaman	61	Jff
Daniel	173	Shn
Edmund	8	Oho
Edward	167	Shn
Elias	344	Lnc
Elias, (of Elias)	407	Fqr
Elias, (of Jno.)	397	Fqr
Elias, Senr.	418	Fqr
Henry	450	Pra
James	418	Fqr
James	690	Nls
James	771	Wst
Jeremiah	771	Wst
Jno.	423	Fqr
Jno.	345	Lnc
Jno.	451	Pra
John	339	Fqr
John	952	Hrr
John	8	Oho
John, Senr.	400	Fqr
Margarett	397	Fqr
Ralph	345	Lnc
Rowlin	690	Nls
Samuel	690	Nls
Samuel, Jur.	690	Nls
Thomas	219	Pnd
Vincent	771	Wst
William	690	Nls
William, Jr.	418	Fqr
William, (of Jno.)	400	Fqr
William, Senr.	418	Fqr
Wm.	451	Pra
see Edmond		
Edmondson, Ann	539	Frd
Betsey	848	Cmp
Cathae.	162	Knq
Edmons, Esom	495	Frn
Peter	219	Pnd
William	480	Frn
Edmonson, Lucy	400	Ags
Edmonsun, Benjamin	339	Lnn
Edmudsun, Thomas	819	Hmp
Edmunds, Etheld.	151	Sth
Hevy	710	Brn
James	21	Acc
John	636	Sss
Jonas	127	Sth
Mary	747	Brn
Nicholas	48	Chr
Phill, F.N.	636	Sss
Rebecca	748	Brn
Thomas	20	Acc
Thomas	339	Lnn
Thomas	870	Sth

Thomas, Col.	48	Chr
Thos., Jr.	710	Brn
William	21	Acc
William	264	Amh
William	8	Oho
Wyatt	747	Brn
see Ednunds		
Edmundson, David, jr.	274	Rck
David, Sr.	274	Rck
Hy, Christiansburgs	619	Mnt
John	47	Chr
Martha	145	Dnw
Robt.	300	Rck
William	901	Crl
Edmuns, Cain	339	Lnn
Edmunson, John	568	Brk
Joseph	882	Hnv
Thomas	338	Lnn
Upton	339	Lnn
Ednix see Eanix		
Ednunds, Benjamin	710	Brn
Benjamin, (M)	711	Brn
James	710	Brn
John	747	Brn
Thos., Sr.	710	Brn
Upton	710	Brn
Wm.	710	Brn
Edrington, Benja.	29	Clp
Jas.	29	Clp
John L.	22	Stf
Joseph	29	Clp
Mary	198	Kng
Edsler, George	620	Btt
Edson, Brice	460	Bdf
Henry	335	Ags
Edward, Richd.	30	Hnr
Edwards, Alb.	158	Sth
Ann	978	Nrt
Arnold	415	Fqr
Anthony	835	Hmp
Arther	426	Msn
Baker	22	Stf
Bartlett	654	Glc
Benja.	148	Sth
Benjamin	47	Chr
Benjamin	356	Fqr
Benjamin, Sr.	486	Frn
Bramley	710	Brn
Brice	494	Frn
Burwell	38	Isw
Charles	449	Grn
Charles	690	Nls
Charles C.	162	Knq
Cuffee	384	Mds
D. C.	345	Lnc
Daniel	978	Nrt
Danl.	114	Hnr
David	871	Hnv
David	24	Isw
David	141	Sth
Edmd.	206	Ess
Edward	741	Wsh
Edwd.	252	Ldn
Edwin	978	Nrt
Edwin	142	Sth
Edwin	606	Srr
Eli	868	Sth
Elias	4	Isw
Elias	132	Sth
Elijah	356	Fqr
Eliza	128	Sth
Elizabeth	339	Lnn
Elizabeth	531	Prg
Elizabeth	548	Prg
Elizabeth	53	Stf
Ellis	978	Nrt
Eve	280	Ldn
Fanney	356	Fqr
Fanny	148	Sth
Fanny	772	Wst
Flemstead	105	Cmb
Francis	747	Brn
Geo.	129	Sth
George	978	Nrt
Gideon	580	Frd
Griffen	977	Nrt
Henry	451	Pra
Henry	82	Spt
Henry	605	Srr
Henry	606	Srr
Herbert	26	Isw
Hezekiah	67	Jff
Hezekiah	35	Stf
Honour	39	Isw
Isaac	426	Msn
Isaac	978	Nrt
Isham	747	Brn
Isham	43	Isw
Jacob	21	Acc
James	481	Frn
James	3	Isw
James	126	Sth
James	158	Sth
James, Jur.	690	Nls
James, Sr.	605	Srr
Jas.	497	Mnn
Jemima	356	Fqr
Jeremiah	417	Bth
Jesse	29	Isw
Jesse	663	Mnt
Jesse, Jun.	12	Isw
Jesse, Sen.	3	Isw
Jessee	711	Brn
Jessee	747	Brn
Jessee, jr.	747	Brn
Jno.	654	Glc
Jno.	345	Lnc
Jno., Jr.	345	Lnc
Joel	137	Sth
John	351	Fqr
John	409	Fqr
John	415	Fqr
John	33	Isw
John	162	Knq
John	198	Kng
John	424	Msn
John	497	Mnn
John	689	Nls
John	792	Nrf
John M.	460	Bdf
Jonas	18	Isw
Jonathan	798	Hmp
Jordan	152	Sth
Jordan	636	Sss
Jos.	252	Ldn
Joseph	61	Jff
Joseph	978	Nrt
Joseph	636	Sss
Joseph, Sr.	978	Nrt
Js., Jr.	198	Kng
Js., Senr.	198	Kng
Judith	131	Cmb
Judith	132	Cmb
Kinchen	128	Sth
L. S.	112	Hnr
Laben	20	Acc
Lancelot L.	978	Nrt
Langhorn	828	Bck
Lear	349	Fqr
Lee	606	Srr
Levi	852	Sth
Levy	43	Isw
Lewis	203	Ess
Littleberry	711	Brn
Lucey	369	Fqr
Lucy	711	Brn
Lydda	117	Spt
Martha	828	Bck
Martha	39	Isw
Martin G.	407	Ags
Mary	192	Alb
Mary	711	Brn
Mary	343	Fqr
Mary	654	Glc
Mary	792	Nrf
Mary	872	Yrk
Mary, jr.	654	Glc
Meriday	901	Crl
Michael	38	Isw
N...hemiah	812	Bck
Nehemiah	564	Pre
Newet	127	Sth
P. F.	65	Chs
Pacience	39	Isw
Patrick H.	605	Srr
Peter	522	Frd
Phey	830	Nrf
Philip	30	Clp
Phillip	34	Isw
Rebecca	950	Chc
Richard	828	Bck
Richard, Capt.	978	Nrt
Richard, Jr.	978	Nrt
Richard, Sr.	977	Nrt
Richard H.	605	Srr
Robert	690	Nls
Robert [2]	978	Nrt
Robert, gent.	978	Nrt
Robert, Sen.	39	Isw
Robt.	691	Gch
Robt., Jun.	4	Isw
Sarah	711	Brn
Silvinus	732	Wsh
Skelton	605	Srr
Spencer	29	Clp
Tho.	162	Knq
Thomas	192	Alb
Thomas	279	Amh
Thomas	832	Hmp
Thomas	306	Ldn
Thomas	978	Nrt
Thomas	605	Srr
Thomas D.	605	Srr
Thos.	747	Brn
Thos.	792	Nrf
Thos.	822	Nrf
William	21	Acc
William	145	Dnw
William	326	Dnw
William	449	Grn
William	765	Hmp
William [2]	978	Nrt
William	536	Prg
William	21	Stf
William [2]	605	Srr
William	606	Srr
William, Sr.	978	Nrt
William C.	978	Nrt
Wm.	30	Clp
Wm.	653	Glc
Wm.	344	Lnc
Wm.	384	Mds
Wm.	897	Nrf
Wm.	152	Sth
Wm., jr.	691	Gch
Wm., senr.	691	Gch
Zachariah	8	Isw
see Iveson		
Edwars, Benjamin	332	Dnw
Edy, Samuel	445	Bth
Eeash, Walter	547	Brk
Eekiss see Eckiss		
Eelback, Major	328	Dnw
Eevy, Peter	31	Rcm
Efan, Eliz.	496	Mnn
Effenger, John	248	Shn
Effinger, Michael	249	Shn
Efford, Eliza.	394	Rch
Samuel	396	Rch
Sarah	394	Rch

William	413	Rch	Jemima	42	Isw	James	20 Acc
Eflice, James	301	Rck	John	16	Isw	John	20 Acc
Egan, Margaret	444	Bth	John, (of David)	43	Isw	John [2]	192 Alb
Egbon, ---, & Son	8	Hnr	John M.	22	Isw	John	438 Bth
Egburn, Jacob	30	Clp	Robt.	22	Isw	John	688 Br
Egernan see Eyeman			Susanna	43	Isw	Js.	496 Mnn
Eggai, Jacob	33	Hnr	Tabitha	45	Isw	Moses	692 Br
Eggleston, ...	242	Aml	Elgan, George	347	Fqr	Sally	451 Pra
Edmund	99	Cmb	Jesse	348	Fqr	Samuel	192 Alb
Edwd.	243	Aml	John	459	Bdf	Stephen, (F.N.)	43 Isw
Elizabeth	125	Cmb	William	348	Fqr	Thomas	20 Acc
Elizabeth	870	Hnv	Elgar, Samuel	463	Mdd	William	21 Acc
Joseph	242	Aml	Elgin, Gustavus	534	Frd	William	867 Cmp
Matthew J.	861	Hnv	Eliffe, George	406	Rch	William, Senr.	21 Acc
Richd.	242	Aml	Eliot, Abm.	497	Mnn	Elliott, ...	299 Rck
William T.	243	Aml	John	336	Ags	Abraham	804 Hmp
Eggmon, Christopher	752	Nwk	Thos.	336	Ags	Alexr.	344 Lnc
Egmon, Cornelious	951	Chc	Elison, Peyton	484	Frn	Allen W.	564 Pre
Egmond, ---, Mrs.	326	Dnw	Elkins, Benjamin	198	Kng	Ann	48 Chr
Egnew, William	471	Frn	Davd., Senr.	29	Clp	Becky	330 Dnw
Egypt, Farney	128	Hnr	David	24	Stf	Benjamin	400 Fqr
Eidson, Henry	460	Bdf	James	570	Brk	Benjamin	547 Frd
Henry, Senr.	865	Cmp	Jemima	411	Fqr	Bernard	872 Yrk
John	392	Rch	Jeremiah	198	Kng	Billy	815 Nrf
Jos.	257	Ldn	Jno.	252	Frf	Caleb	200 Ess
Eilbeck, Jonathn.	897	Nrf	John	568	Brk	Curtis	624 Mnt
Ekridge see Eskridge			John	623	Mnt	David	291 Ldn
Elam, Edward	48	Chr	Lorenzo	411	Fqr	Edward	330 Dnw
Edward, (Est.)	48	Chr	Nathl.	29	Clp	Eliza.	198 Kng
Essex	3	Pwh	Wm.	585	Mnr	Gabriel	653 Glc
Frances	6	Pwh	Wm., jr.	29	Clp	Geo.	290 Ldn
Joel	564	Pre	Wm., Senr.	29	Clp	Geo., J.	290 Ldn
Mary	15	Pwh	Ellegood, Wm.	450	Pra	George	358 Fqr
Rd.	57	Chs	Eller, David	620	Btt	Henry	330 Dnw
Robert	334	Dnw	Jacob	620	Btt	Henson	271 Ldn
Robert	564	Pre	Elles, David	880	Cmp	Hy.	897 Nrf
Robt., (Kerr)	57	Chs	Richard	880	Cmp	James	296 Rck
Sally	15	Pwh	Elleton, John	156	Alb	James	772 Wst
Samuel	48	Chr	Richard	155	Alb	Jane	333 Dnw
Solomon H.	48	Chr	Ellett, Benja.	690	Gch	Jno.	18 Hnr
Thomas	47	Chr	Benjaman	83	Jff	John	710 Brn
William	47	Chr	Elizabeth	852	Hnv	John	829 Hmp
Wm.	67	Chs	Jno.	850	Hnv	John	198 Kng
Wm. B.	57	Chs	Jno.	852	Hnv	John	624 Mnt
see Farmer			Robert	844	Hnv	John	564 Pre
Elane, Peter	57	Chs	Robert	886	Hnv	John	268 Rck
Elburn, Reubin	830	Wth	Thomas	856	Cmp	Mary	306 Ldn
Elcan, Lion	840	Bck	Thomas P.	844	Hnv	Moreton	901 Crl
Eld, Henry	897	Nrf	William	844	Hnv	Nancy	817 Nrf
Elder, Claiborne	145	Dnw	Elley, Edwd., Senr.	29	Clp	Peter	3 Hnr
Danl., jr.	145	Dnw	Ellgin, Francis	278	Ldn	Peter	897 Nrf
Danl., Senr.	145	Dnw	Gustavus	278	Ldn	Reezen	253 Frf
James	47	Chr	Rebecca	278	Ldn	Reuben	576 Frd
John	925	Hrr	Walter	278	Ldn	Richard	339 Lnn
Peter	145	Dnw	Wm.	236	Ldn	Ro.	653 Glc
Thomas	145	Dnw	Elliatt, Javish	941	Hrr	Robert	901 Crl
Travis	339	Lnn	Ellice, Thos.	251	Ldn	Robert	618 Mnt
Wm.	145	Dnw	Zachariah	252	Ldn	Samuel	358 Fqr
Wm., Senr.	145	Dnw	Ellicee, Wm.	451	Pra	Sarah	815 Nrf
Wm. M.	145	Dnw	Ellicot, Richard	897	Nrf	Seaton	872 Yrk
Eldridge, Bolling	710	Brn	Ellicott, Nathaniel	501	Prw	Sukey	198 Kng
Howell	710	Brn	Elligood, Margte.	897	Nrf	Thomas C., Dr.	47 Chr
J.R.B.	691	Gch	Elligott, Wm.	23	Hnr	Thos.	29 Clp
Payton R.	29	Clp	Ellington, Elizabeth	564	Pre	Thos.	335 Dnw
R., jr.	841	Bck	Grief	15	Ntt	Thos.	3 Hnr
Robert	635	Sss	Hezekiah	564	Pre	William	747 Brn
Rolfe, Senr.	824	Bck	Jesse	564	Pre	William	901 Crl
Tho.	497	Mnn	Jno.	13	Ntt	William	530 Frd
Thomas	636	Sss	Joel	34	Stf	William	816 Nrf
Thos.	710	Brn	John	565	Pre	William	564 Pre
Thos.	29	Clp	Milly	9	Ntt	Willm.	624 Mnt
Thos., jr.	691	Gch	Mourning	564	Pre	Wm.	288 Rck
Eleston, Francis	978	Nrt	Pleasant	564	Pre	Wm.	296 Rck
John S.	978	Nrt	Ridley	565	Pre	see Ellicott	
Salley	978	Nrt	William	412	Bth	Elliotte, ...	460 Bdf
Eley, Eliz., (of Wm.)	43	Isw	Elliot, Archibald	21	Acc	James	460 Bdf
Elizabeth	20	Isw	Charles	188	Elc	John	459 Bdf
Exum	16	Isw	Henry H.	278	Rck	Robert	459 Bdf
Hanah	848	Sth	Hugh	190	Elc	Ellis, ---, & Allen	21 Hnr
Horatio	43	Isw	Jacob			Abraham	586 Brk

Name			Name			Name		
Ambrose	340	Lnn	Thomas, Senr.	605	Srr	Elsworth, Eligah	947	Hrr
Ann	635	Sss	Thomas B.	339	Lnn	Elsy, Martin	830	Wth
Bartelott	192	Alb	Thos. [2]	30	Clp	William	830	Wth
Benjamin	95	Spt	William	951	Chc	Elum, Lewallen	872	Cmp
Benjamin	636	Sss	William	117	Hnr	Elvin, Jane	336	Ags
Benjamin, Sr.	605	Srr	William	128	Hnr	Elwood, George	272	Rck
Betsey	891	Hnv	William	339	Lnn	Robt.	272	Rck
Bolling	636	Sss	William	521	Prw	Ely, ...well	460	Bdf
Caleb	690	Gch	William, jr.	340	Lnn	Jane	549	Prg
Calvin	340	Lnn	William, Sr.	340	Lnn	Josiah	875	Sth
Celia	13	Knw	Wm.	497	Mnn	Victor	878	Sth
Dabney	192	Alb	Wright	636	Sss	William	830	Hmp
David	773	Hmp	Zackariah	453	Frn	Elzy, Nicholaus	937	Hrr
David	117	Hnr	see Redford			Emack, William	107	Spt
Edwd.	821	Nrf	Ellisen, Zachariah	911	Hrr	Emanl., Solomon	212	Ess
Eliasa	691	Gch	Ellison, Amos	471	Frn	Emanuel see Emanl.		
Elijah	543	Frd	Assa	566	Mnr	Embersom, Ezekiah	288	Amh
Elisha	117	Hnr	Cloe	565	Pre	Emberson, Abel	821	Hmp
Eliza	26	Hnr	Holbert	830	Wth	Equlla	253	Frf
Elizabeth	891	Hnv	James	565	Mnr	John	101	Jff
Ellis	550	Brk	James	830	Wth	William	253	Frf
Ellison	339	Lnn	James, Jr.	565	Mnr	William	115	Spt
Enos	587	Mnr	John	597	Mnr	Embly, John	690	Nls
Evan	524	Frd	John	830	Wth	Embrey, George	351	Fqr
Fielding	16	Ntt	Matt	565	Mnr	Jesse	355	Fqr
Hennery	340	Lnn	Thomas	2	Oho	John	352	Fqr
Henry	635	Sss	Wm.	897	Nrf	John, Senr.	355	Fqr
Hezekiah	101	Spt	Elliss, Wm.	58	Chs	Joseph	352	Fqr
Jacob	117	Hnr	Ellit, Elijah	483	Frn	Judey	341	Fqr
Jacob	588	Mnr	Ellmore, Edwd.	246	Ldn	Richard	352	Fqr
James	691	Gch	James R.	590	Frd	Robert, Jr.	353	Fqr
James	564	Pre	John	247	Ldn	Robert, Senr.	352	Fqr
James, Junr.	348	Fqr	John	771	Wst	Robert, son of Jno.	353	Fqr
James, Senr.	405	Fqr	Joseph	771	Wst	Salley	352	Fqr
Jane	543	Prg	Ellor, Henry	830	Wth	Rhomas, Jr.	353	Fqr
Jno.	30	Clp	Ellot, Saml.	590	Brk	Thomas, Sr.	352	Fqr
Jno. W.	849	Hnv	Ellston see Elleton			William, (son of Thos.)	352	Fqr
Joanna	332	Dnw	Elly, Edward	94	Spt	William, Sr.	355	Fqr
Joel	253	Frf	Ellyson, Agness	752	Nwk	Embrow, ---	2	Hnr
John	297	Amh	David	752	Nwk	Embry, Chs.	30	Clp
John	942	Chc	Gideon	752	Nwk	James	44	Stf
John	339	Lnn	Jesse	751	Nwk	John	28	Rcm
John	609	Mnt	Jonathan	751	Nwk	Joseph	30	Clp
John	510	Prw	Margaret	751	Nwk	Thos.	30	Clp
John	605	Srr	Sam	752	Nwk	Wm.	30	Clp
John	635	Sss	William	752	Nwk	Emerson, Edward D.	88	Jff
John, Jr.	872	Yrk	see Martin			Phillis	93	Acc
John, (W)	872	Yrk	Ellzey, Alice	257	Ldn	Emery, Anne	449	Grn
John B.	192	Alb	John	594	Frd	Charles	605	Srr
Joseph	588	Mnr	Lewis	316	Ldn	Danl.	286	Ldn
Joseph	180	Shn	Thomazin	253	Frf	David	605	Srr
Josiah	327	Lnn	William	603	Frd	Drewry	606	Srr
Leonard	578	Frd	Wm.	257	Ldn	Hannah	606	Srr
Leroy. [Lucy?]	32	Hnr	see Elzey			Hezekiah	606	Srr
Lewis	326	Dnw	Elmore, Charles	978	Nrt	John	605	Srr
Lucy	117	Hnr	Fanny	409	Rch	John, jr.	606	Srr
Maggy	117	Hnr	George	399	Rch	Lemuel	606	Srr
Martha	635	Sss	Henry	874	Hnv	Martha	185	Elc
Mary	117	Hnr	James	864	Cmp	Nathan	605	Srr
Mary	36	Isw	James	339	Lnn	Sally	605	Srr
Michl.	161	Sth	John	620	Btt	Emison, Thomas	299	Ldn
Morris	783	Hmp	Rebeccah	339	Lnn	Emmerson, Arthur	832	Nrf
Nathan	362	Fqr	Richard	409	Rch	Henry	690	Nls
Northton.	128	Sth	Thomas	394	Rch	Mary	439	Mth
Owen	581	Mnr	William, Jnr.	844	Hnv	William	81	Spt
Philip	29	Clp	Wim.	861	Hnv	see Emnesson		
Philip	575	Mnr	Wim., C.h.	883	Hnv	Emmesson, Zachariah	155	Alb
Philip	585	Mnr	Wm.	711	Brn	Emmet, Josiah	3	Rcm
Richard	605	Srr	Elom, William	830	Wth	Emmett, Jacob	782	Hmp
Richard, (L)	339	Lnn	Elright, Adam	3	Rcm	Emminger, David	587	Brk
Richard C.	339	Lnn	Elsbury, Thomas	21	Isw	Emmit, Richard	830	Wth
Robert	198	Kng	Elsey, Mary	907	Hrr	Emmitt, Jacob	765	Hmp
Robert	605	Srr	Thomas	613	Mnt	Emmons, Elizabeth	145	Dnw
Samuel	605	Srr	Elson, Hansen	696	Br	James	352	Fqr
Sarah	901	Crl	John	696	Br	James	622	Gls
Smith	117	Hnr	Reuben	155	Alb	Joel	561	Frd
Stephen	747	Brn	William	155	Alb	Joseph	351	Fqr
Stephen	691	Gch	William	696	Br	Peter	145	Dnw
Stephen	606	Srr	Elstob, Edwd.	897	Nrf	William	328	Dnw
Thomas, jr.	605	Srr	Elswick, Jonathn.	624	Mnt	Emmorie, John	7	Oho

Name	No.	Co.	Name	No.	Co.	Name	No.	Co.
Nicholas	21	Oho	Ennis, James	15	Hnr	Peter	145	Dnw
Emnesson, Elizabeth	155	Alb	John	679	Br	Peterson	145	Dnw
Emonds, Laml.	335	Ags	William	868	Cmp	Thomas	636	Sss
Emory, Hezekiah	60	Jff	William	690	Nls	Wm., residing in P.		
Empty, Wm.	297	Rck	William	771	Wst	George	145	Dnw
Emrick, George	647	Mnt	Winney, (F. Negroe)	420	Fqr	see Spain		
Emrie, Simon	932	Hrr	Enock, Isaac	7	Wod	Epps, Catharine	339	Lnn
Enders, John	25	Hnr	Isaac	9	Wod	Elizabeth	339	Lnn
Enderson, ---, Robins &	11	Hnr	Enos, Henry	653	Glc	George	449	Grn
Frank	29	Hnr	Jno.	653	Glc	Hamlin	53	Chr
Endres, Adams	620	Btt	Lewis, jr.	653	Glc	John	938	Chc
Endsley, Thomas [2]	59	Jff	Lewis, Senr.	653	Glc	John W.	791	Bck
Endsworth, William	99	Jff	Samuel	653	Glc	Peter	950	Chc
Enever, Joseph	62	Stf	see Eonos			see Tucker		
Englan, Henry	416	Rnd	Enox, David	690	Nls	Eppse, Joshua	242	Aml
England, Anney	303	Amh	Elizabeth	689	Nls	Eps, Thomas	34	Hnr
Catharine	848	Hnv	Polly	690	Nls	Eranshaw, Ellenda	252	Frf
Edward	564	Pre	Ensey, Caty	210	Ess	Erby, William	340	Lnn
Jacob	567	Brk	Ensly see Ennasly			William, (R)	338	Lnn
James [2]	430	Rnd	Ensminger, Henry	814	Hmp	Erick, Fancis	912	Hrr
John	32	Stf	Ensor, Elizabeth	412	Fqr	Erle, James	17	Wod
Robert	102	Cmb	William	55	Stf	Errett, Christopher	775	Hmp
William	110	Cmb	Entler, Daniel	104	Jff	Erskine, Michael	574	Mnr
William	113	Cmb	Martin	100	Jff	Michael	596	Mnr
William	848	Hnv	Philip	101	Jff	Reub.	497	Mnn
Wm.	497	Mnn	William	757	Hmp	William	378	Fqr
Engle, Andrew	786	Hmp	see ...ller			William	574	Mnr
George	91	Jff	Entsminger, Davd.	277	Rck	Erskins, Alexander,		
Jacob	70	Jff	Entsninger, Joshua	12	Knw	Est.	340	Lnn
John	91	Jff	Enzey, Dennis	274	Amh	Ervens, Thomas	172	Shn
Joseph	832	Hmp	William	278	Amh	Ervin, Cristerpher	7	Hnr
Joseph	95	Jff	Eoff, John	7	Oho	Eleaner	82	Jff
Levi	780	Hmp	Eonos, Michl.	620	Btt	Elias	82	Jff
Martin	421	Bth	Epes, Archbald	548	Prg	Isaac	497	Mnn
Mathias	786	Hmp	Charles	327	Dnw	Jas.	497	Mnn
Michael	90	Jff	Charles	542	Prg	Jas.	735	Wsh
Philip	84	Jff	Daniel	325	Dnw	Saml.	336	Ags
Philip	91	Jff	Daniel	334	Dnw	Wm.	655	Mnt
Samuel	94	Jff	Daniel	543	Prg	Wm.	724	Wsh
William	1	Wod	Edmond	548	Prg	see Ewin		
Engledew, Blackstone	468	Bdf	Francis	17	Ntt	Ervits, Sammuel	6	Hnr
Engledow, James	830	Wth	Francis	547	Prg	Erwin, Andrew	429	Bth
John	830	Wth	Francis, jr.	538	Prg	Charles	436	Bth
Robert	830	Wth	Francis, Senr.	538	Prg	Edw., jr.	337	Ags
William	830	Wth	Jno., jr.	1	Ntt	Edw., (LG)	336	Ags
Engleheart, Geo., Jr.	620	Btt	John, jr.	534	Prg	Edw., Sr.	337	Ags
Engleman, Peter	337	Ags	John, Senr.	17	Ntt	Edward	420	Bth
Philip	337	Ags	John, Senr.	538	Prg	Francis	336	Ags
Wm.	335	Ags	Lucy	537	Prg	George	217	Pnd
Wm., jr.	335	Ags	Mary	538	Prg	James	337	Ags
Engles, John	16	Wod	Peter, jr.	534	Prg	James	437	Bth
Engleton, Anthony	400	Ags	Peter, Snr.	541	Prg	John	336	Ags
Wm.	400	Ags	Richd.	16	Ntt	John	278	Rck
Englin, Jobe	922	Hrr	Thomas	17	Ntt	John, Jur.	429	Bth
Englis, Tebethe	702	Wsh	William	540	Prg	Peggy	335	Ags
English, Elkanah	451	Pra	Woodlief	2	Ntt	Robert	420	Bth
Geo.	27	Hnr	Wyatt	328	Dnw	Saml.	620	Btt
George	462	Frn	see Fatum, Temple			Thos.	336	Ags
Harrison	53	Stf	Epperd, Matthias	684	Br	Wm.	336	Ags
James	459	Bdf	Epperly, Christn.	657	Mnt	see Ewin		
James	605	Frd	George	657	Mnt	Esau see Efan		
James	771	Wst	Jacob	658	Mnt	Esbey, James	421	Fqr
Job	10	Rcm	Epperson, Gaberal	728	Wsh	Escue, John	155	Alb
John	503	Prw	James	564	Pre	Esene, Maryanne	509	Prw
John	395	Rch	John	732	Wsh	Eshon, Nathan	832	Nrf
John	276	Rck	Joseph	858	Hnv	Nathaniel	944	Chc
Joseph	80	Jff	Lidral	28	Hnr	Esillmon, Peter	210	Shn
Margarett	415	Fqr	LittleBery	874	Cmp	Eskridge, Burdit	771	Wst
Noah	518	Prw	Littlebery, Jr.	874	Cmp	George	786	Hmp
Robert	48	Stf	Mary	48	Chr	Hecktor R.	13	Wod
Salley	386	Fqr	Richd.	732	Wsh	John	356	Fqr
Saml., (Overseer for Col.			William	861	Cmp	Thomas	978	Nrt
Jno. Tayloe)	620	Btt	Wm.	874	Cmp	Thomas	772	Wst
Stephen	454	Frn	Eppert, Christiana	34	Rcm	William	568	Frd
William	454	Frn	Enock	33	Rcm	William	978	Nrt
Wm.	29	Clp	George	34	Rcm	Wm.	305	Ldn
Woden	521	Prw	Philip	34	Rcm	Esleck, Thomas	949	Hrr
Zephh. R.	29	Clp	Eppes, Jane	145	Dnw	Esly, Joseph	941	Hrr
see Inglish			Laban	145	Dnw	Essecks, Thomas	155	Alb
Ennasly, William	551	Frd	Lucey	145	Dnw	Essen see Eseae		

Essex, Benjamin	850	Cmp	see Etherede			Charles	289	Amh
Thomas	503	Prw	Etinger, Michael	16	Rcm	Charles	564	Pre
Estave, Mary	330	Dnw	Etsal, Ben	291	Rck	Charles J.	8	Ntt
Estell, Benj.	688	Wsh	Etter, Henry	830	Wth	Charlotte	449	Grn
John	337	Ags	John [3]	830	Wth	Claiborne	125	Hnr
Wm.	497	Mnn	Mary	830	Wth	David	904	Hrr
Ester, Frs.	897	Nrf	Peter	666	Mnt	David	496	Mnn
Jacob	897	Nrf	Peter	830	Wth	David L.	813	Bck
John	773	Hmp	Samuel	830	Wth	Drury	620	Mnt
Estes, Aaron	901	Crl	Etwater, Anslana	335	Ags	Dudley	497	Mnn
Abraham	338	Lnn	Eubank, Ambross	460	Bdf	E., Jr.	496	Mnn
Ann	901	Crl	Ann	155	Alb	Ed.	496	Mnn
Bartlet	47	Chr	Carlton	162	Knq	Edward	509	Prw
Benjamin	460	Bdf	Charles	155	Alb	Edwd.	897	Nrf
Benjamin	338	Lnn	Daniel	156	Alb	Elijah	176	Shn
Bottom	460	Frn	Elias	460	Bdf	Elisha	795	Bck
Coleman	183	Alb	George	156	Alb	Elisha B.	513	Prw
David	901	Crl	George	459	Bdf	Elizabeth	901	Crl
Dorrity	493	Frn	George	129	Hnr	Elizabeth	78	Jff
Elijah	74	Spt	Henry	162	Knq	Enoch	496	Mnn
Elisha	339	Lnn	Hesekiah	459	Bdf	Evan	337	Ags
Elisha	691	Nls	James	156	Alb	Evan, jr.	336	Ags
Jesse	501	Frn	James	114	Hnr	Foster	302	Amh
Joel	459	Bdf	James	116	Hnr	Francis	747	Brn
Joel	470	Frn	John [2]	156	Alb	Francis	399	Rch
John	901	Crl	John	262	Amh	Frankey	292	Amh
John	339	Lnn	John	901	Crl	George	92	Acc
Jonathan	901	Crl	John	114	Hnr	George	59	Jff
Mathew	339	Lnn	Mary	156	Alb	Gerd.	496	Mnn
Moses	384	Mds	Philip	162	Knq	Griffeth	429	Bth
Nancy	901	Crl	Richard	155	Alb	Guy	253	Frf
Richard	91	Spt	Richard, jr.	162	Knq	Harry	115	Hnr
Samuel	339	Lnn	Richard, Snr.	162	Knq	Helen	375	Fqr
Thomas	339	Lnn	Richeson	162	Knq	Henry	302	Amh
Triplet T.	179	Alb	Royal	901	Crl	Henry	636	Sss
Woolfolk	901	Crl	Thomas	162	Knq	Heston	757	Wsh
Estham, John	192	Alb	Thomas N.	266	Amh	Hezekiah	176	Shn
Esther, Rachel	551	Frd	Thos.	876	Hnv	Howell	449	Grn
Estill, Isaac	564	Mnr	Warner	162	Knq	Hugh	497	Mnn
William C.	1	Knw	William	155	Alb	Isaac	549	Brk
Estinghausen, Lewis	676	Br	William	460	Bdf	Isaac	265	Ldn
Estis, Rowland	431	Flv	William	129	Hnr	Isaac, jr.	549	Brk
Thos.	30	Clp	William, Sr.	460	Bdf	Jac.	497	Mnn
Esum, Robt.	337	Ags	Wm. D.	162	Knq	Jack	810	Bck
Etcher, Peter	257	Ldn	see Gibson			Jacob	439	Bth
Ethel, Anthony	390	Fqr	Eubanks, Garland	400	Ags	James	336	Ags
Etherede, Jas.	451	Pra	Giles	344	Lnc	James	810	Hmp
Etheredge, Amos	451	Pra	John	620	Btt	James	752	Nwk
Andrew	451	Pra	Polley	17	Hnr	James G.	499	Prw
Archd.	897	Nrf	Eudailey, Elisha	48	Chr	Jane	287	Amh
Asa	451	Pra	Moses	48	Chr	Jane	4	Oho
Basett	791	Nrf	Eudres see Endres			Jeremiah	595	Brk
Chas.	807	Nrf	Eunis, Ezekiel	171	Shn	Jeremiah	715	Wsh
Dimpsey	451	Pra	Herbert	243	Aml	Jerry	182	Shn
Donms	790	Nrf	Eustace, Anne	358	Fqr	Jerry	202	Shn
Elijah	799	Nrf	Hancock	23	Stf	Jesse	337	Ags
Elizabeth	796	Nrf	Isaac	383	Fqr	Jesse	330	Dnw
Enoch	799	Nrf	John	977	Nrt	Jesse	269	Ldn
Enoch	801	Nrf	Mary S.	978	Nrt	Jesse, Junr.	830	Wth
Enos	805	Nrf	Thomas	383	Fqr	Jesse, Senr.	830	Wth
Franceis	805	Nrf	William, Jr.	358	Fqr	Jessee	498	Prw
Geo.	818	Nrf	William, Sr.	358	Fqr	Jessee	515	Prw
Henry	800	Nrf	Wm.	345	Lnc	Jno.	253	Frf
Jno.	450	Pra	Ev..., Mitch...	460	Bdf	Jno.	269	Ldn
Jonathan	800	Nrf	Evans, Abraham	413	Bth	Jno.	310	Ldn
Julia	791	Nrf	Agnes	537	Prg	Jno. [2]	496	Mnn
Mary	808	Nrf	Ambrose	302	Amh	Jno.	8	Ntt
Mary	451	Pra	Anderson	287	Amh	Jno., Jr.	496	Mnn
Mathias	788	Nrf	Anne	509	Prw	Joe	93	Acc
Max	809	Nrf	Anthoney	460	Bdf	John	511	Brk
Moses	790	Nrf	Anthony	635	Sss	John	545	Brk
Nancy	803	Nrf	Arthur	93	Acc	John	145	Dnw
Neal	789	Nrf	Bazil	18	Oho	John	191	Elc
Neal, jr.	789	Nrf	Becky	15	Hnr	John	404	Fqr
Richd.	792	Nrf	Ben	496	Mnn	John	439	Flv
Robt.	451	Pra	Benj.	289	Ldn	John	482	Frn
Saml.	808	Nrf	Benja.	154	Sth	John	904	Hrr
Simeon	797	Nrf	Betsey	93	Acc	John	938	Hrr
Thos.	796	Nrf	Caleb	781	Hmp	John	67	Jff
Willes	800	Nrf	Caleb	451	Pra	John	643	Mnt

Name	No.	Co.	Name	No.	Co.	Name	No.	Co.
John	798	Nrf	Willie	449	Grn	Charles	92	Acc
John	14	Oho	Wm.	269	Ldn	Charles	519	Prw
John	23	Oho	Wm. T.	162	Knq	Charles	524	Prw
John	247	Shn	see Eanes, Ervens, Ev...,			Charlotte	506	Prw
John	695	Wsh	Thompson			Edward	93	Acc
John	772	Wst	Eveland, David	295	Ldn	Elizabeth	897	Nrf
John	830	Wth	Evelsizer, Jacob	14	Rcm	Elizth., 2nd.	897	Nrf
John, CT	93	Acc	John	22	Rcm	Ezekiel	451	Pra
John, Jur.	695	Wsh	Even, Allen	711	Wsh	George	92	Acc
Joseph	335	Ags	Everedge, Hilary	817	Nrf	George H.	92	Acc
Joseph	824	Bck	Hy.	897	Nrf	Grace	93	Acc
Joseph	834	Nrf	Luke	818	Nrf	James	451	Pra
Joseph	202	Shn	Wm.	818	Nrf	Jesse, Senr.	516	Prw
Joseph	209	Shn	Everegde, Demsey	818	Nrf	Jessee	192	Alb
Joseph	830	Wth	Everet, Simeon	460	Bdf	Jessee	897	Nrf
Joshua, jr.	336	Ags	Thomas	460	Bdf	Jessee	518	Prw
Levin	92	Acc	Everett, Charles	179	Alb	Jno.	451	Pra
Littleton	93	Acc	Everhart, Casper	265	Ldn	John	838	Nrf
Lucey	145	Dnw	Danl.	568	Brk	Mark	92	Acc
Lucy	100	Spt	Geo.	569	Brk	Sarah	520	Prw
Manuit	757	Wsh	Henry	569	Brk	Soloman, BS	93	Acc
Margaret	504	Prw	Jacob	80	Jff	Soloman, SS	93	Acc
Mark	620	Btt	Michael	283	Ldn	Solomon	518	Prw
Mark	339	Lnn	Michal	531	Frd	Solomon	519	Prw
Mark, f. negro	253	Frf	Philip	298	Ldn	Tho.	497	Mnn
Mary	620	Btt	Wm.	283	Ldn	William	21	Acc
Mary	253	Frf	Everidge, Finch	443	Mth	William	92	Acc
Mary	16	Hnr	Everit, John	689	Br	William, Senr.	92	Acc
Mason	537	Prg	John, Jur.	12	Knw	Ewen, James	278	Rck
Mathew	29	Clp	Everitt, Exum	159	Sth	James	288	Rck
Matt	154	Sth	John, Ser.	12	Knw	Ewers, Bartin	275	Ldn
Molley	286	Amh	Lemuel	6	Isw	Jno.	263	Ldn
Msagan	582	Mnr	Mary	20	Isw	John	279	Amh
N.	496	Mnn	Sally	148	Sth	Jonathan	275	Ldn
Nancy	653	Glc	Thomas	160	Sth	Jont.	315	Ldn
Nathan	11	Oho	Zachariah	5	Isw	Joseph	304	Amh
Nathan	221	Shn	Everley, Elizabeth	256	Shn	Stephen	284	Amh
Overton	869	Cmp	Jeremiah	256	Shn	Thomas	690	Nls
Overton	876	Cmp	P.	497	Mnn	Thos.	275	Ldn
Peggy	114	Spt	P., Jr.	497	Mnn	Ewin, James	337	Ags
Philis	9	Hnr	Saml.	496	Mnn	Jane	336	Ags
Rawley	496	Mnn	Simon	496	Mnn	John, (Sen.)	40	Rcm
Rhoda	776	Bck	Everong, George	225	Shn	John D.	42	Rcm
Rice	145	Dnw	Eversole, Abram	407	Ags	Joseph	336	Ags
Richard	145	Dnw	Abram, jr.	407	Ags	see Elvin, Ervin		
Richd.	222	Ess	Emanuel	548	Brk	Ewing, Anny	459	Bdf
Robert	798	Bck	Henry	74	Jff	Elizabeth	603	Frd
Robt.	695	Wsh	Jacob	620	Btt	George	830	Wth
Saml.	30	Clp	Jacob	17	Rcm	Henry C.	9	Knw
Saml.	13	Hnr	John	40	Rcm	Israel	518	Frd
Sampson	869	Cmp	Peter	830	Wth	James	15	Oho
Samuel	404	Fqr	Everson, David	521	Brk	James	830	Wth
Samuel	301	Ldn	Evert, Mary	907	Hrr	James, Junr.	564	Pre
Sarah	212	Ess	Nathan	907	Hrr	James, Senr.	564	Pre
Shelton	700	Wsh	Eves, George	460	Bdf	John	1	Oho
Stephen	799	Bck	Hannah	48	Stf	John, Ser.	425	Bth
Tarlton	757	Wsh	Eveston, Rosanna	553	Brk	John S.	412	Bth
Thomas	92	Acc	Evic, John	967	Hrr	Joseph	586	Mnr
Thomas	268	Amh	Eviche, Eve	222	Pnd	Joshua	428	Bth
Thomas	879	Cmp	Evick, Adam	227	Pnd	Moses	429	Bth
Thomas	362	Fqr	Catherine	227	Pnd	Oliver	591	Mnr
Thomas	78	Jff	Evilsison, William	337	Ags	Robert	603	Frd
Thomas	162	Knq	Evilsizer, Henry	4	Knw	Saml.	575	Mnr
Thomas	17	Oho	Evin, Jos.	247	Shn	Samuel	603	Frd
Thomas, jr.	210	Ess	Evington, Lewis	67	Chs	Thomas	424	Bth
Thomas, Sr.	211	Ess	Evins, Charles	690	Nls	Thomas	560	Frd
Thomas B.	72	Jff	Charles	691	Nls	William	412	Bth
Thos.	653	Glc	James	691	Nls	William	427	Bth
Thos.	623	Mnt	Javes	254	Shn	William, Ser.	423	Bth
Thos., (Manager for Col.			Jeremiah	253	Shn	see Ewen		
Jno. Tayloe)	620	Btt	Minerva	9	Hnr	Ewit, Hannah	227	Pnd
Unity	303	Amh	Robert	946	Chc	Ewitt, Charles	789	Hmp
Wilkinson	757	Wsh	Saimuel	241	Shn	Exum, Rebecca	141	Sth
William	280	Amh	see Evin			Robert	144	Sth
William	879	Cmp	Evitt, Nehemiah	726	Wsh	Robert	846	Sth
William	583	Frd	Thos.	726	Wsh	Eyeman, Henry	18	Rcm
William	573	Mnr	Wm.	733	Wsh	Eyers, Robert	530	Brk
William	505	Prw	Ewart, Esther	19	Oho	Eyre, Wm.	287	Rck
William	209	Shn	Ewbanks, John	340	Lnn	Eze, Saml.	25	Hnr
William	636	Sss	Ewell, Ann	192	Alb	Ezell, Abell	636	Sss

Benjamin	747	Brn
Buckner	747	Brn
Davis	747	Brn
Robert	635	Sss
Timoth	336	Dnw
Zacheus	635	Sss

--- F ---

F...an, William	461	Bdf
F...azell, ...	462	Bdf
F...d, Burwell	146	Dnw
F...guson, Wm.	146	Dnw
F...il, John	19	Oho
F...ing, ...	461	Bdf
F...mer, Thomas	341	Lnn
F...wler, Simmons	146	Dnw
Faasnought, John	565	Brk
Fabre, Peter	899	Nrf
Face, Frances	180	Elc
Willm.	177	Elc
Facewell see Tracewell		
Fachler, Elizt.	340	Ags
Fachon, Jacob	522	Brk
Fackle, George	214	Shn
Michael	175	Shn
Fackler, Ann	338	Ags
Jacob	400	Ags
Fadeley, Jacob	304	Ldn
Fadely, Catharine	39	Rcm
Faedley, Elizabeth	241	Shn
Fagaly, Michael	25	Rcm
Fagan, Ann	334	Dnw
Jane	11	Pwh
Peter	847	Sth
Fagans, Jno.	34	Clp
Peter [2]	334	Dnw
Fagg, Daniel	157	Alb
John	183	Alb
Joseph	77	Spt
William	93	Spt
Faggan, Peter	769	Brn
Faha, Murty	256	Frf
Faidly, Jacob	228	Shn
Michael	228	Shn
Fair, Edmund	516	Prw
Mary	503	Prw
Thomas	958	Hrr
Thomas	12	Wod
Fairbairn, Robt.	339	Ags
Wm.	341	Ags
Fairchild, Hezekiah	714	Wsh
William H.	24	Oho
Faircloth, John	875	Sth
Matt	161	Sth
Fairfax, Ferdanando	80	Jff
Guy	522	Frd
Henry	509	Prw
Hezekiah	503	Prw
Jno.	500	Mnn
Thomas	256	Frf
William	503	Prw
William	506	Prw
Fairow, John	244	Shn
Fale, George	834	Hmp
George, Sen.	810	Hmp
Faleaferro see Taliaferro		
Falia see Faha		
Falk, Jacob	546	Brk
Falkner, Samuel	103	Spt
Fall, Danl.	341	Ags
Geo.	338	Ags
Geo., jr.	338	Ags
Fallen, John H.	978	Nrt
Fallenash, Mary	913	Hrr
Wm.	924	Hrr
Fallin, Tho.	345	Lnc
William	49	Chr

Falliss, Thomas	354	Fqr
Falls, Danl.	18	Rcm
James, Sr.	622	Btt
Jno.	622	Btt
Jno.	5	Rcm
Peter	621	Btt
Falwell, John	783	Bck
Richard	816	Bck
William	816	Bck
Fanack see Hanack		
Fanceler see Fandler		
Fancher, John	498	Mnn
Fandler, Henry	424	Rnd
Fane, Danl.	339	Ags
Fannan, Bryan	624	Gls
Fanning, John	831	Wth
Josias	349	Fqr
Fannon, Achilis	623	Gls
Acles	831	Wth
Fanny, Free	386	Mds
Fansher, Daniel	904	Hrr
Fanshur, David	25	Oho
Fansler see Fausler		
Fant, Elias	30	Stf
Feilding	29	Stf
George	29	Stf
James	51	Stf
James	15	Wod
John	28	Stf
John P.	51	Stf
Joseph	39	Stf
Nelson	24	Stf
William	101	Spt
Farass, John	694	Nls
Farchild, Abind	714	Wsh
Farding, Aaron	580	Brk
James	77	Jff
Fare, Bazel	757	Hmp
Farence, Henry	916	Hrr
Farer, Arthur	560	Brk
Fargeier see Farquer		
Fargusan, John	460	Bdf
Farguson, Horatio	340	Lnn
William	340	Lnn
see Bell		
Fargusson, Asa	242	Aml
Faringhottz, David	163	Knq
Farinholtz, Ro.	654	Glc
Faris, Adam	23	Oho
Anderson	460	Bdf
Emeriah	660	Mnt
Jacob	753	Nwk
Jane	458	Frn
John	128	Hnr
John	11	Oho
John	566	Pre
Oney	122	Hnr
Richard	566	Pre
Thomas	811	Bck
Thomas	583	Frd
Wm.	10	Oho
Farish, Frances	903	Crl
Hazlewood	110	Spt
James	902	Crl
Littleton	74	Spt
Nancy	74	Spt
Stevens	902	Crl
Thos. B.	32	Clp
Fariss, Bowler	242	Aml
Callam	241	Aml
Jacob	101	Cmb
John	48	Chr
Joseph	4	Pwh
Martin	115	Cmb
Martin	124	Cmb
Farler, David	781	Bck
Edward	341	Lnn
James	566	Pre
John J.	566	Pre
Sith	341	Lnn

William	565	Pre
Farley, Adam	623	Gls
Ann	48	Chr
Arthur	12	Pwh
Berkeley	13	Pwh
Drury	566	Mnr
Edward	461	Bdf
Edward	880	Cmp
Forest	565	Pre
Francis	623	Gls
George	623	Gls
Giddian	623	Gls
Henry	6	Ntt
Jno.	58	Chs
John [2]	623	Gls
Lewellin	565	Pre
Martha	242	Aml
Matt	565	Mnr
Matthew	242	Aml
Peter, Jr.	242	Aml
Peter, Sr.	242	Aml
Pleasant	13	Pwh
Sarah	567	Pre
Stith	567	Pre
Thomas [2]	623	Gls
William	242	Aml
William, Est.	565	Pre
Wm. N.	1	Ntt
Farlow, John	814	Hmp
Joseph	146	Dnw
Farmar, Robt.	898	Nrf
Farmer, Absalom	565	Pre
Barnett	623	Mnt
Benjamin	340	Lnn
Bird	104	Cmb
Catharin	197	Ess
Charles	241	Aml
Conrad	461	Bdf
Daniel	603	Frd
Danl.	30	Clp
Eben	63	Chs
Elam	57	Chs
Elam	692	Gch
Francis	233	Ldn
Frederick	902	Crl
Frederick	1	Oho
Henry	58	Chs
Henry	569	Frd
Henry	649	Mnt
Hezekiah	57	Chs
James	121	Cmb
James	130	Cmb
James	341	Lnn
Jesse	466	Frn
John	828	Bck
John	902	Crl
John	49	Chr
John	453	Frn
John	555	Frd
John	692	Gch
John	623	Mnt
John	707	Wsh
John	714	Wsh
Lewis	197	Ess
Lodwick	341	Lnn
Mark	62	Chs
Mary	341	Lnn
Matthew	452	Frn
Oratio	63	Chs
Ralph	163	Knq
Skelton	866	Hnv
Thomas	832	Wth
Thompson	619	Mnt
William	125	Cmb
William	453	Frn
William	555	Frd
Wm.	32	Clp
see F...mer, Farner		
Farmers see Farmer		
Farner, Abm.	617	Mn.

Jacob	461	Bdf	Farthaly, Athalion	452	Pra	Fawns, Danl. B.	199	Kng
Farnesworth, Jno.	272	Ldn	Farthing, Thomas	876	Cmp	Fawver, Henry	565	Brk
Faro, Samuel	79	Jff	William	865	Cmp	John	35	Rcm
Farquahr, William	3	Oho	Fason, Laurence	637	Sss	Fay, George	9	Oho
Farquer, John	898	Nrf	Richard	637	Sss	see Traylor		
Wm.	899	Nrf	Thomas	637	Sss	Fayman, George	105	Jff
Farr, Cyrus	546	Brk	Fastus, James	899	Nrf	Feagans, Francis	373	Fqr
Edward	546	Brk	Fatcher see Hatcher			James	400	Fqr
Isaac	546	Brk	Fate see Tate			John	389	Fqr
Joseph	64	Jff	Fatherly, Mary	822	Nrf	John	394	Fqr
M.	35	Hnr	Wm.	191	Elc	John	400	Fqr
Nicholas	254	Frf	Fatig, John	242	Shn	Latham	372	Fqr
Saml.	256	Frf	Fatum, Epes	536	Prg	Rawleigh	378	Fqr
William	25	Hnr	Fauber, Chn.	338	Ags	Richardson	364	Fqr
Wm.	899	Nrf	Felty	341	Ags	William	373	Fqr
see Fair, Furr			Jacob	338	Ags	Feagin, Edward	520	Prw
Farrar, Ann	693	Nls	Jacob	339	Ags	George	519	Prw
Betsy	691	Nls	John	338	Ags	Isaac	520	Prw
Field	66	Chs	John, jr.	338	Ags	Fealt, Jacob	15	Oho
Francess	691	Gch	Joseph	340	Ags	Fear, William	330	Dnw
Jno.	66	Chs	Peter	340	Ags	Fearn, George	788	Bck
John	156	Alb	Faucet, Wm.	500	Mnn	Fears, Absalom	566	Pre
John	693	Nls	Faucett, Jno.	266	Ldn	John	49	Chr
Joseph	156	Alb	Faudry, Thomas	691	Gch	Thomas	566	Pre
Landon	694	Nls	Fauger, Adam	497	Mnn	William	566	Pre
Mary	691	Nls	Faught, George	424	Msn	William, Revd.	49	Chr
Perrin	694	Nls	Faukner, James	386	Mds	Feasel, Philip	273	Rck
Robert S.	691	Nls	Faulcon, John	606	Srr	Feaster, Henry	30	Rcm
Saml.	242	Aml	Nicholas	606	Srr	Feather, George	200	Shn
Stephen	433	Flv	Walter	606	Srr	Featheringill, George	210	Shn
Susannah	156	Alb	Faulconer, Nicholas	196	Ess	John	540	Frd
Thomas	691	Nls	Wm. A.	196	Ess	Thomas	208	Shn
Thos.	443	Flv	Faulkener, James	463	Mdd	Feathers, Henry P.	460	Bdf
Thos. B.	691	Gch	Faulkner, Amos	463	Mdd	Jacob	609	Mnt
Wm. [2]	691	Gch	Benja.	163	Knq	Featherston, Carolus	48	Chr
see Turren			Daniel	831	Wth	Charles	242	Aml
Farrell, Wm.	567	Mnr	James	596	Brk	Hezekiah	48	Chr
Farrer, Charles	566	Pre	Jno.	163	Knq	Joshua	2	Ntt
Fdk.	561	Brk	Josiah	903	Crl	Lewis	5	Ntt
Farrier, Robt.	622	Btt	Thomas, jr.	163	Knq	Robert	48	Chr
Farris, Christ.	307	Ldn	Thomas, Snr.	163	Knq	Wm.	20	Ntt
Geo.	315	Ldn	Faulks, John	831	Wth	Wylie	49	Chr
Gidion	714	Wsh	Samuel	831	Wth	Featherstone, Wm.	146	Dnw
Isaac	722	Wsh	William	831	Wth	Feazell, Jacob	461	Bdf
John	857	Cmp	Fauls, Joseph	462	Bdf	Jacob, Jr.	462	Bdf
John	881	Cmp	Fauntleroy, D.	345	Lnc	Joshua	462	Bdf
John	752	Nwk	Joseph	584	Frd	Philip	462	Bdf
Robert	715	Wsh	Joseph	393	Rch	Feazle, Chrestena	216	Pnd
Samuel	694	Wsh	Robert	398	Rch	Fedeman, Saml.	127	Hnr
Sylvanus	752	Nwk	Saml. G.	162	Knq	Feely, Alexander	210	Shn
William	857	Cmp	Thos.	163	Knq	John	832	Wth
William	875	Cmp	Thos., [his] (este.)	463	Mdd	Feezle, Michael	19	Rcm
William	752	Nwk	Fause, Phillip	764	Hmp	Feggat, James	772	Wst
William	693	Wsh	Fausher, Daniel	460	Bdf	Feild, Daniel	385	Mds
Wm.	703	Wsh	Fausler, Adam	19	Rcm	John	385	Mds
Wm.	723	Wsh	Frederick	22	Rcm	Mary	385	Mds
Wm.	740	Wsh	Peter	22	Rcm	Richard	711	Brn
Farros, Willm.	622	Btt	Fautt, Adam	12	Rcm	Susan	711	Brn
Farrow, Ann	463	Mdd	Fauver, Henry	786	Hmp	Feilder, John	566	Pre
Benjamin	403	Fqr	Lucy, (F.Neg.)	34	Clp	Robert	108	Cmb
Betty	431	Flv	Favor, Eliza.	32	Clp	Feilds, John	5	Hnr
Drury, (FB)	461	Bdf	Favus, Umphry	925	Hrr	Richard	471	Frn
George	399	Fqr	Fawcet, Rob.	499	Mnn	Thomas	347	Fqr
Hanah	6	Hnr	Fawcett, Benjamin	445	Bth	Felkner, Henry	341	Fqr
Jacob	600	Frd	Charles	443	Bth	Fellaws, James	326	Dnw
Jno.	33	Clp	Elijah	567	Frd	Feller, Ulrich	339	Ags
John	402	Fqr	Isbell	219	Ess	Fellips, Peter T.	114	Cmb
Mary	69	Chr	John	567	Frd	Fellow, John, Junr.	217	Shn
Nimrod	404	Fqr	Joseph	1	Rcm	John, Senr.	217	Shn
Polley	163	Knq	Joseph, (sen.)	39	Rcm	Joseph	341	Ags
Reuben	193	Alb	Thomas, Jr.	567	Frd	Manuel	216	Shn
Sarah	117	Hnr	Thomas, Senr.	567	Frd	Fellows, Henry	592	Brk
William	514	Prw	Vincent W.	463	Mdd	John	451	Frn
Wm.	33	Clp	see Fowcett			Lawrance	623	Btt
Farrver see Farrow			Fawer, Boston	536	Brk	see Fellaws		
Farry, Geo.	655	Glc	Fawley, Anthony	29	Rcm	Fells, Jacob	115	Hnr
Ro.	655	Glc	George	29	Rcm	Lucy	334	Dnw
Wm.	655	Glc	Henry	297	Ldn	Tabethy	334	Dnw
Fart, Adam	498	Mnn	Jacob	286	Ldn	Felton, John	499	Mnn
Celia	145	Sth	Jno.	298	Ldn	Felts, Amey	637	Sss

Name	Page	Co.	Name	Page	Co.	Name	Page	Co.
Augustin	637	Sss	Frances	68	Chr	Edmd.	205	Ess
Fred.	867	Sth	Fergurson, James	100	Spt	Hen.	498	Mnn
Gray	636	Sss	William	83	Spt	Jas.	499	Mnn
Kinchen	637	Sss	Ferguson, Andw., Sr.	623	Btt	John	206	Ess
Molly [crossed out]	637	Sss	Ann	898	Nrf	Mary	332	Dnw
Nathal.	146	Sth	Benja.	31	Clp	Robt.	499	Mnn
Phillip	849	Sth	Berry	60	Chs	Robt., Jr.	499	Mnn
Susan	849	Sth	Daniel	61	Chs	Sally	206	Ess
Felty, Nicholas	832	Wth	Daniel	465	Frn	Stephen	622	Btt
Fen, Joseph	146	Dnw	David	622	Btt	William	72	Jff
Fencer, Wm.	32	Clp	Dongald	775	Bck	Ferrell, Calup	948	Chc
Fendall, Mary	254	Frf	Ebenezer	841	Nrf	Edward L.	463	Mdd
Fendley, Sarah	345	Lnd	Elaxander	465	Frn	Elender	89	Jff
Wm.	60	Chs	Ely	450	Frn	George	193	Shn
Fenfford, James	804	Nrf	Finley	899	Nrf	Giles	32	Hnr
Fenley, James, F.B.	10	Pwh	George	495	Frn	Jacob	37	Rcm
Fenn, Allen	531	Prg	George	34	Stf	Joseph	300	Ldn
Francis	543	Prg	Holland	3	Rcm	Lettice	392	Fqr
Jno.	541	Prg	Isham	477	Frn	Susan	606	Srr
Peter	532	Prg	Jacob	816	Bck	Ferrer, Hubert	830	Nrf
Sarah	544	Prg	James	488	Frn	Ferrier, William	624	Gls
Thos.	544	Prg	James	526	Prw	Ferril see F..il		
Wm.	544	Prg	Jeffery	816	Bck	Ferrile, James	157	Alb
Fennel, John	338	Ags	Jeremiah	488	Frn	Ferrill, John	15	Wod
John	48	Chr	Jesse	31	Clp	Joseph	11	Oho
Fennell, Bryant	637	Sss	Jno.	18	Ntt	Thomas	578	Frd
Charity	449	Grn	Joel, Senr.	777	Bck	Thomas	604	Frd
James C.	449	Grn	John	525	Brk	Ferriman, John	783	Hmp
Fenner, Benja.	534	Prg	John	775	Bck	Stephen	783	Hmp
Jacob	573	Brk	John	812	Bck	Ferrior, John	621	Btt
Thomas	449	Grn	John	821	Bck	Ferrol, Abner	621	Btt
Fennimore, Samuel	4	Wod	John	451	Frn	Ferroll, Thomas	174	Shn
Fenning, John	367	Fqr	John	526	Prw	William	11	Oho
Fenoll, John	25	Oho	John, Jr.	478	Frn	William	20	Oho
Fensley, Thomas, free			John, Sr.	480	Frn	Ferry, Charles	1	Wod
negro	70	Chs	John D.	588	Frd	Ferte, ---, Dr.	898	Nrf
Fenter, Martin	296	Rck	Joseph	501	Frn	Fertig, Henry	339	Ags
Fenton, Enoch	400	Ags	Josiah	400	Fqr	Ferver, Jacob	563	Brk
Ephraim	539	Frd	King	62	Chs	Fesler, Michl.	622	Btt
Frederick	292	Rck	Lewis	623	Btt	Fester, John	499	Mnn
Judith	539	Frd	Manoah	472	Frn	Feth see Firth		
Samuel	203	Ess	Martha	551	Frd	Fethers, Jac.	499	Mnn
Fentress, Aby	452	Pra	Moses	821	Bck	Fetro, Joseph	966	Hrr
David	811	Nrf	Moses	59	Chs	Martin	933	Hrr
Edwd.	452	Pra	Nancy	465	Frn	Fetter, John	799	Hmp
Emanul	452	Pra	Peter	898	Nrf	Michael	250	Shn
Isaih	454	Pra	Priscilla	9	Ntt	Fetters, George	697	Br
Jane	803	Nrf	Robert	786	Bck	Fetts, John	832	Wth
Jeremiah	454	Pra	Saml.	620	Btt	Joseph	832	Wth
Jno., (of Geo.)	452	Pra	Saml.	447	Flv	Wm.	500	Mnn
Jno., (of Jno.)	453	Pra	Saml.	448	Flv	Fetty, John	498	Mnn
Jno., (of Josha.)	453	Pra	Samuel	360	Fqr	Saml.	498	Mnn
Jona.	453	Pra	Stephen	465	Frn	Fetzer, George	250	Shn
Joshua	453	Pra	Thomas	821	Bck	Henry	249	Shn
Joshua, Jr.	452	Pra	Thomas	450	Frn	Joakum	250	Shn
Lemuel	453	Pra	Thomas	480	Frn	Jos.	246	Shn
Lititia	454	Pra	Thos.	898	Nrf	Fever, Enoch	32	Clp
Major	452	Pra	William	450	Frn	Feverio, ---	892	Nrf
Malachi	453	Pra	Wm.	59	Chs	Fewel, Landen W.	34	Clp
Moses, (of Jno.)	454	Pra	Wm.	31	Clp	Fewell, James	346	Fqr
Moses, Sr.	453	Pra	Zachariah	254	Frf	James	526	Prw
Nathl., Jr.	453	Pra	see F...guson, Ferqueron			Tacey	498	Prw
Peter	454	Pra	Fergusson, Robert	394	Rch	Wm.	31	Clp
Thos.	452	Pra	William	393	Rch	Fewqua, Dudley	539	Prg
Wm.	802	Nrf	Feri see Fen			Liddy	539	Frg
Fenwich, James	156	Alb	Feribee, Sarah	790	Nrf	see Fuquay		
Fenwick, Wm.	68	Chs	Ferkletine, Philip	235	Shn	Fey, John	201	Shn
Fereba, Sarah	800	Nrf	Fernahae, Edward	193	Alb	Feys, Stephen	13	Knw
Ferebee, Alexr.	800	Nrf	Fernando, Mary	544	Prg	Fichpatrick, Jas.	341	Ags
Matt.	898	Nrf	Ferneyhough, Caty	120	Spt	Saml.	340	Ags
Fereber, Willis	814	Nrf	Fernsworth, Daniel	695	Br	Fickle, Gabl.	500	Mnn
Fergason, Daniel	193	Alb	Henry	264	Amh	Gabriel	831	Wth
David	193	Alb	Henry	691	Br	John	499	Mnn
James	422	Rnd	Samuel	695	Br	Jos.	499	Mnn
Larrence [2]	193	Alb	Ferqueron, Bartley	61	Chs	Matthias	831	Wth
Robert	416	Rnd	see Ferguson			Molley	707	Wsh
Wiley [2]	193	Alb	Ferr, James	11	Oho	Ficklin, Benjamin	573	Frd
William	193	Alb	Ferrel, Austin	199	Kng	Benjamin	44	Stf
Fergerson, Danl.	56	Chs	Catharine	624	Gls	Charles	354	Fqr
Eliza.	199	Ess	Dianah	325	Dnw	Eliza.	34	Clp

Name	No.	Co.
Famus	393	Rch
John D.	978	Nrt
Lewis	46	Stf
Strother	24	Stf
Fiddler, Eliza.	162	Knq
Elizabeth	902	Crl
Fidler, Churchill	202	Ess
Jacob	802	Hmp
Jessee	691	Nls
Jno.	33	Clp
Noah	42	Rcm
Pitmond	163	Knq
Field, Ann	654	Glc
Benja.	31	Clp
Danl.	31	Clp
Ellsey	330	Dnw
Henry, jr.	31	Clp
Henry, (son of Danl.)	31	Clp
John	156	Alb
Joseph	157	Alb
Joseph	31	Clp
Ralph H.	156	Alb
Rob.	182	Elc
Robert	156	Alb
Thomas	146	Dnw
Thos., (F. Mo.)	31	Clp
William	146	Dnw
Wm.	654	Glc
Fielding, Anazetta	460	Bdf
Edwin	449	Grn
Mary	33	Clp
Thomas	449	Grn
see Brown, Foalding, Samuel		
Fields, Ben	500	Mnn
Betty	789	Bck
Betty	799	Bck
Daniel	656	Mnt
David	849	Cmp
Dysey	899	Nrf
James	902	Crl
Jas.	726	Wsh
John	806	Bck
John	237	Ldn
John	752	Nwk
John	426	Rnd
Luke	256	Frf
Major	717	Wsh
Nancey, (M)	806	Bck
Robert	95	Acc
Rosy	902	Crl
Sall	881	Cmp
Salley	799	Bck
Samuel	461	Bdf
William	594	Brk
William	255	Frf
William	706	Wsh
see Feilds		
Fiett, Charles	303	Ldn
Fife, Edwd.	595	Mnr
Thomas	582	Mnr
Fifer, Barbara	31	Rcm
Dorathy	39	Rcm
Geo.	337	Ags
John	337	Ags
John	593	Mnr
Fifthorn, John	223	Pnd
Philip	214	Pnd
Figg, Benja.	532	Prg
James	542	Prg
Jno.	655	Glc
Tenable	637	Sss
Wm.	654	Glc
Figgatt, John	2	Hnr
Figget, Spencer	283	Rck
Figgins, Edward	592	Frd
Fihney, Sally	548	Prg
Filar, Frederic	937	Hrr
Filbert, Archer	341	Lnn
John	341	Lnn
Josiah	341	Lnn
Filcolm, Henry	115	Spt
Files, Jacob	529	Frd
John	513	Brk
John	518	Brk
Filler, Fridk.	287	Ldn
Fridk., J.	287	Ldn
Jacob	285	Ldn
Fillin, Catharine	823	Hmp
Fillinger, Mary	627	Mnt
Fillips, Robert	340	Lnn
Filson, George	622	Btt
James	461	Bdf
John	521	Brk
Robert	521	Brk
Robert	13	Knw
Robt.	621	Btt
Thomas	696	Br
Thos.	590	Brk
Filvert, Archibal	340	Lnn
Fin, Solomon	728	Wsh
Finch, Agness	741	Wsh
B...ickdon	870	Cmp
Bernard, Sr.	865	Cmp
Enoch	772	Wst
Frances	526	Prw
Geo.	898	Nrf
Geo., [his] (Plantation)	452	Pra
Henry	957	Chc
James	752	Nwk
John	289	Amh
John	872	Cmp
John	393	Fqr
John	692	Gch
Jones	938	Chc
Nancy	335	Dnw
Richard	29	Hnr
Samuel	753	Nwk
Thomas	48	Chr
William	368	Fqr
William	753	Nwk
Wm.	748	Brn
Zachariah	49	Chr
Fincham, Jas.	33	Clp
Jno.	34	Clp
Wm.	32	Clp
Wm., jr.	33	Clp
Fincks, Elijh.	33	Clp
Finder, Lucy	13	Rcm
Findes, James	59	Stf
Findlay, Susanna	254	Ldn
Findley, Connaley	759	Wsh
Fanney, free negro	70	Chs
Hugh	899	Nrf
James	12	Oho
James	831	Wth
John	213	Shn
Robert	255	Frf
Saml.	409	Ags
Saml.	821	Nrf
Thomas	253	Frf
William	832	Wth
Wm.	340	Ags
Findly, Mary [2]	832	Wth
Samuel	12	Oho
Fink, Daniel	750	Wsh
Danl.	581	Mnr
Frederick	823	Hmp
Gaspe [?]	581	Mnr
Godfrit	3	Oho
Wm.	287	Rck
Finks, Andrew	384	Mds
Andrew	418	Mds
Elias	384	Mds
Elliott	384	Mds
James	384	Mds
Jno.	33	Clp
Joel	385	Mds
John	384	Mds
Mark	384	Mds
William	385	Mds
Finlay, Archibald	536	Frd
Finley, ...d.	300	Rck
James	18	Oho
Jno.	654	Glc
John	592	Brk
Michl.	299	Rck
Salley	461	Bdf
Wm.	288	Rck
Wm., j.	267	Rck
Finn, Henry	832	Wth
John	899	Nrf
Finnal, John	57	Stf
Jonathan	45	Stf
Robert	58	Stf
Finnell, Jno.	33	Clp
Reuben	34	Clp
Reubin	32	Clp
Robt.	32	Clp
Finnerty, Andrew	40	Rcm
Finney, Abraham	94	Acc
Catharine	621	Btt
Charles	281	Rck
Euphamy	22	Acc
Joe	548	Prg
John	22	Acc
John	490	Frn
John, Jr.	500	Frn
John, Sr.	500	Frn
Lewis	500	Frn
Nancy, of Jno.	95	Acc
Phillip	23	Acc
Thos.	59	Chs
William	22	Acc
William	242	Aml
William, SS	94	Acc
see Fihney, Fnney, Terr...		
Finnley, Adam	918	Hrr
Finny, Abraham	23	Acc
William	461	Bdf
Fipps, Thomas	85	Spt
Fips, John	139	Sth
Firbush, Thomas	753	Nwk
Firebough, Adam	40	Rcm
Betsey	40	Rcm
Philip	40	Rcm
Fires, Thomas	870	Sth
Wm.	127	Sth
Firestone, Evey	622	Btt
John	284	Rck
Mathias	284	Rck
Firk see Fisk		
Firneyhough, John	88	Spt
Firth, Geo.	260	Ldn
John	753	Nwk
Samuel	753	Nwk
Wm.	511	Brn
Fisbender, J.H.	13	Hnr
Fiser, John	489	Bdf
Michael	586	Brk
Fish, Benjamin	18	Oho
Francis	253	Frf
Robert	597	Frd
William, Junr.	168	Shn
William, Senr.	168	Shn
Fishback, Christena	385	Mds
Jacob T.	832	Wth
James C.	692	Nls
Jno., (G)	32	Clp
Jno., (Son of Jas.)	32	Clp
John	385	Mds
Martin	31	Clp
Wm.	32	Clp
Fishbeck, Anne	369	Fqr
James N.	388	Fqr
Philip, Jr.	370	Fqr
Phillip, Senr.	370	Fqr
Sarah	369	Fqr
Fishbourn, Teter	338	Ags
Fishburn, Frederick	496	Frn

Name	Page	Co.
Jacob	496	Frn
John	496	Frn
Peter	496	Frn
Phillip	476	Frn
Fishell, Frederick	770	Hmp
Fisher, Abraham	452	Pra
Abraham	9	Rcm
Adam	11	Rcm
Anthony	338	Ags
Barak	604	Frd
Benjamin	74	Spt
Benjm.	340	Lnn
Catharine	255	Frf
Caty	578	Frd
Caty	171	Frd
Charles	966	Hrr
Charles	107	Spt
Comfort	23	Acc
Conrod	578	Mnr
Danl.	341	Ags
David	214	Shn
David	832	Wth
Dunlop	416	Fqr
Eliza.	405	Rch
Elizabeth	519	Frd
Elizabeth	555	Frd
Elizabeth	107	Jff
Fenwick	22	Acc
Frederick	26	Rcm
George	94	Acc
George	156	Alb
George	394	Fqr
George	931	Hrr
George	955	Hrr
George	33	Hnr
George	223	Pnd
George	217	Shn
George	240	Shn
George	256	Shn
George, (F. Negroe)	379	Fqr
George S.	22	Acc
Hannah	251	Shn
Henry	339	Ags
Isaac	572	Mnr
Isriel	453	Pra
Jacob	338	Ags
Jacob	522	Brk
Jacob	87	Jff
Jacob	417	Rnd
Jacob	206	Shn
Jacob [2]	832	Wth
James	711	Brn
James	210	Ess
James	621	Mnt
James	94	Spt
James	772	Wst
Jane	449	Grn
John	340	Ags
John	341	Ags
John	409	Ags
John	461	Bdf
John	597	Brk
John	622	Btt
John	329	Dnw
John	201	Ess
John	400	Fqr
John	578	Frd
John	624	Gls
John	449	Grn
John	199	Kng
John	498	Mnn
John	8	Oho
John	225	Pnd
John	233	Shn
John	832	Wth
John, S. [2]	216	Pnd
John C.	177	Shn
John F.	94	Acc
John R.	22	Acc
Leonard	581	Mnr
Lewis	680	Br
Lewis	201	Ess
Maddocks	95	Acc
Martha	145	Dnw
Martha	112	Spt
Martin	288	Rck
Mary	156	Alb
Mary	813	Nrf
Mickle	955	Hrr
Nancy	201	Ess
Nancy	31	Hnr
Peter	525	Brk
Peter	480	Frn
Peter	966	Hrr
Peter	105	Jff
Philip	582	Mnr
Philip	215	Pnd
Philip	13	Rcm
Phillip	23	Acc
Richd.	209	Ess
Robert	421	Fqr
Robert, Jr.	407	Fqr
Ryley	94	Acc
Samuel	853	Cmp
Samuel	368	Fqr
Simon	6	Oho
Stephen	680	Br
Susannah	25	Hnr
Sylvanus	85	Spt
Teackle	95	Acc
Thomas	419	Fqr
Thomas	604	Frd
Thos.	880	Hnv
Thos.	840	Nrf
Thos. D.	17	Ntt
Tully	94	Acc
William	95	Acc
William	680	Br
William	127	Hnr
William	340	Lnn
William	981	Nrt
Wm.	341	Ags
Wm.	711	Brn
Wm.	64	Chs
Wm.	32	Clp
Wm.	196	Ess
Wm.	200	Ess
Wm.		
Fishneck, Judith, F.B.	10	Pwh
Fisk, Elizabeth	836	Nrf
Henry	581	Mnr
James	796	Nrf
Martin	898	Nrf
Saml.	794	Nrf
Fister, Philip	23	Hnr
Fisth see Firth		
Fitch, Charles	863	Cmp
Elizabeth	193	Alb
James	514	Brk
James	308	Ldn
Samuel	863	Cmp
William	182	Alb
William [2]	193	Alb
Fitchel, William	94	Acc
Fitcher, Geo.	288	Ldn
Geo.	306	Ldn
Fitchet, Jonathan	94	Acc
Fitchett, Daniel	441	Mth
Daniel, [his] Est.	444	Mth
Daniel D.	436	Mth
Randolph	606	Srr
Richd.	443	Mth
Rob.	184	Elc
Selathiel	449	Mth
Thos.	441	Mth
Wm.	435	Mth
Fitchpatrick, Anthoney	732	Wsh
Caleb	400	Ags
Fiterman, Henry	94	Acc
Joseph	94	Acc
Major	95	Acc
Meshack	94	Acc
William	94	Acc
Fiterow, William	224	Shn
Fitsammons, Wm.	637	Mnt
Fittsmoyers, John	237	Shn
Susanah	237	Shn
Fitz, Henry	146	Dnw
Nathl.	332	Dnw
Fitzew, Wm. C.	241	Ldn
Fitzgarrel, Thomas	90	Spt
Fitzgearld, Thomas	757	Hmp
Thomas	762	Hmp
Fitzgerald, Francis	361	Fqr
Francis, jr.	3	Ntt
Fras., Senr.	8	Ntt
Jno.	17	Ntt
Robt.	5	Ntt
Saml.	621	Btt
Wm., jr.	8	Ntt
Wm., Senr.	5	Ntt
Fitzgerall, Juden	694	Nls
Fitzgerrald, Alexander	693	Nls
Barlett	694	Nls
Elisha	693	Nls
John [2]	691	Nls
John	692	Nls
S., jr.	432	Flv
Stephen	440	Flv
Fitzgerrall, Barlett	693	Nls
James	693	Nls
John	694	Nls
Fitzgrrall, Benjamin	693	Nls
Fitzhugh, Alexander	34	Stf
Battaile	772	Wst
Daniel	902	Crl
Danl. McCarty	199	Kng
Edward	380	Fqr
Francis	199	Kng
Geo.	32	Clp
Geo.	899	Nrf
George	365	Fqr
George	517	Prw
George	772	Wst
Giles	253	Frf
Henry	198	Kng
Henry	61	Stf
John	815	Nrf
John	852	Sth
John, ([his] Quarter)	385	Fqr
Lenaugh H.	517	Prw
M. C.	253	Frf
Margaret	517	Prw
Mary	841	Nrf
Mary, (W)	872	Yrk
Nicholas	253	Frf
Raemond	811	Nrf
Rd.	254	Frf
Sarah	198	Kng
Thomas	340	Fqr
Thomas [2]	517	Prw
Thomas	866	Sth
Thomas	60	Stf
Thos., Este.	32	Clp
William	256	Frf
William	386	Fqr
William	512	Prw
Wm.	33	Clp
Wm.	129	Sth
see Carter, Fitzew, Fitzuh		
Fitzjareld, Hugh	275	Amh
Fitzjarrald, John	482	Frn
Fitzpatrick, Alexander	692	Nls
Daniel	766	Hmp
John	686	Br
John	761	Hmp
John	693	Nls
John E.	691	Nls
Joseph	693	Nls
Rebecah	693	Nls
Sarah	831	Wth

Name	No.	Code
Thomas	692	Nls
Thomas, Jur.	692	Nls
William	693	Nls
William	95	Spt
William, Ju.	692	Nls
see Fichpatrick, Fitchpatrick		
Fitz Randolph, Jesse	959	Hrr
Jonathan	959	Hrr
Saml.	959	Hrr
Fitzs, Nathl.	898	Nrf
Sarah	586	Frd
Fitzsimonds, Judith	1	Pwh
Fitzsimons, Mary	279	Ldn
Fitzuh, Priscilla	851	Sth
Fitzwater, George	30	Rcm
William	30	Rcm
Fitzwaters, George	6	Knw
John	7	Knw
Thomas	7	Knw
Fitzwilson, ---	31	Hnr
Fiveash, John	35	Isw
Joseph	34	Isw
Fix, Jacob	338	Ags
Philip	338	Ags
Fizer, Adam	622	Btt
George	624	Gls
Henry	621	Btt
Henry	624	Gls
Henry	101	Jff
Jacob	95	Jff
Jno., Sr.	621	Btt
Fizing, Peter	238	Shn
Flack, Benjamin	422	Bth
John	400	Ags
John	3	Oho
John	19	Rcm
L. B.	332	Dnw
Mary	407	Ags
Flagg, Josiah	513	Brk
Martha	594	Brk
Flake, Robert	36	Isw
William	24	Isw
Flamming, Thos.	898	Nrf
Flanagan, Ambrose	436	Flv
Anna	453	Pra
Ebenezer	431	Rnd
Enoch	452	Pra
Frankey	453	Pra
George	542	Frd
James	447	Flv
Jas.	453	Pra
Joshua	453	Pra
Moses	453	Pra
Nathn.	452	Pra
Peter	452	Pra
Reuben	452	Pra
Speake	511	Frd
Thomas	438	Flv
Wm.	452	Pra
Flanagin, Jeremiah	832	Wth
Flanagum, John	959	Hrr
Flanajin, Betsey	22	Acc
Flander, Lewis	562	Mnr
Flanders, John	146	Dnw
Flanigan, Charles	193	Alb
Danl.	622	Btt
see Pflanigan		
Flaninigan, Levy	612	Mnt
Flaninigan, James	460	Bdf
Flannagan, James	441	Flv
Flannery, Michal	981	Nrt
Flannigan, Nicholas	588	Mnr
Flara, James	592	Mnr
Flaroty, John	516	Prw
Flatford, Thomas	503	Prw
Fleager, George	652	Mnt
see Fleger		
Flecher, Azael	551	Brk
Fleece, John	564	Brk
Fleecy, Charles	654	Glc
Fleeharty, S.	498	Mnn
Fleek, Adam	814	Hmp
Henry, Jun.	814	Hmp
Henry, Ser.	814	Hmp
Jacob	814	Hmp
John	814	Hmp
Fleener see Fluner		
Fleer, Francis	452	Pra
Fleet, Baylor	163	Knq
Henry, jr.	443	Mth
William	163	Knq
see Smith		
Fleger, Abraham	656	Mnt
Michl., Jr.	657	Mnt
see Fleager		
Fleharty, Ann	500	Mnn
Fleiger, John	338	Ags
Fleman, Joseph	78	Spt
Fleming, Alex	498	Mnn
Ann	692	Gch
Archibald	599	Frd
Ben.	498	Mnn
Booz	498	Mnn
James	832	Wth
Jams	926	Hrr
Jams	929	Hrr
Jane	792	Hmp
Jas.	345	Lnc
John	559	Frd
John	564	Frd
Jchn	926	Hrr
John Rf.	423	Bth
Margaret	597	Brk
Mat	498	Mnn
Patrick	825	Hmp
Robt.	8	Ntt
Sally	654	Glc
Sally	116	Spt
Samuel	869	Cmp
Samuel	544	Frd
Samuel	16	Oho
Sarah	654	Glc
Sarah	567	Pre
Thomas	592	Frd
Thos.	498	Mnn
William	574	Frd
William	163	Knq
William	401	Rch
William G.	575	Frd
Wm.	621	Btt
Wm. R.	692	Gch
Flemings, William	244	Shn
Flemming, Andrew	432	Msn
Archd.	240	Ldn
Isaac	341	Ags
James	195	Sth
John	240	Ldn
Robert	394	Fqr
Thomas	904	Hrr
Flemmon, Jesse	183	Shn
John	194	Shn
William	195	Shn
Flemon, Saml.	534	Brk
Flennor, Jchn	908	Hrr
Flesher, Adam	961	Hrr
Hennery	961	Hrr
Henry	218	Pnd
John	966	Hrr
Peter	961	Hrr
Fleshman, Michael	569	Mnr
Peter	569	Mnr
Zachariah	386	Mds
Fletcher, Aaron	362	Fqr
Aaron	623	Gls
Abram	14	Knw
Andrew	627	Mnt
Casper	20	Hnr
Catharine	254	Frf
Cloe	334	Dnw
Daniel	654	Glc
Elijah	365	Fqr
Frs.	898	Nrf
George	592	Frd
George	779	Hmp
James	902	Crl
James	19	Isw
James	741	Wsh
James H.	532	Prg
James N.	748	Brn
Jas.	31	Clp
Jas.	1	Ntt
Jesse	410	Fqr
Jno.	623	Btt
Jno., jr.	33	Clp
John	748	Brn
John	872	Yrk
John, (F. Negroe)	398	Fqr
Joseph	772	Hmp
Joshua	396	Fqr
Lewis	654	Glc
Mary	902	Crl
Midleton	748	Brn
Milly	254	Frf
Molly	711	Brn
Moses	367	Fqr
Nathan	748	Brn
Peter	94	Acc
Polly	844	Sth
Racheal	654	Glc
Rawligh	362	Fqr
Richard	367	Fqr
Richd.	748	Brn
Robert	396	Fqr
Rowland	623	Gls
Sarah	367	Fqr
Stephen	23	Acc
Thomas	902	Crl
Thomas	367	Fqr
Thomas	18	Oho
Thomas, Junr.	95	Acc
Thomas, Senr.	94	Acc
Thos. C.	338	Ags
Washington	94	Spt
William	902	Crl
William	397	Fqr
William	413	Fqr
William	8	Fcm
William	85	Spt
Wm.	31	Clp
Wm.	654	Glc
Wm.	590	Mnr
Wm.	742	Wsh
see Flutcher		
Flick, Henry	28	Rcm
Flin, John	2	Wod
Fling, George	256	Frf
George	46	Stf
William	256	Frf
Flinn, Alexander	827	Hmp
Daniel	394	Rch
Danl.	32	Clp
Eliza.	393	Rch
John	340	Lnn
Mary	222	Pnd
Valentine	33	Clp
Flint, Agness	193	Alb
Betsy	307	Rck
Ester	13	Hnr
James	193	Alb
John	981	Nrt
Joseph	948	Hrr
Lewis	948	Hrr
Richard	981	Nrt
Tho.	345	Lnc
Wm.	621	Btt
Flippen, Robert	105	Cmb
Flippin, Francis	122	Cmb
Jacob	112	Cmb
John	123	Cmb

Name	No.	Code
John M.	113	Cmb
Phillip	123	Cmb
Polly	654	Glc
Robert	565	Pre
Thomas	126	Cmb
William	123	Cmb
Flippo, John	902	Crl
Joseph	902	Crl
May	902	Crl
Flisher, Henry	216	Pnd
John	216	Pnd
Flo..., Joseph	461	Bdf
Floed, Charles	691	Nls
John	268	Amh
Floid, Adam	123	Hnr
Mary	545	Prg
Sudy	340	Lnn
Floide, Ambe.	33	Clp
Flood, Charles	816	Hmp
Charles, (F.N.)	37	Isw
Henry	789	Bck
James	255	Frf
James	898	Nrf
John	816	Hmp
John, jr.	787	Bck
John, Senr.	787	Bck
Molly, (FN)	49	Chr
Moses	794	Bck
Noah	787	Bck
Thomas	254	Frf
William	839	Bck
William P.	95	Jff
Flook, Henry	19	Rcm
Floor, George	832	Wth
Flora, Wm.	832	Nrf
Florance, George	516	Prw
James	527	Prw
John	517	Prw
Rowland	525	Prw
Saml.	503	Prw
William	525	Prw
Florence, William	813	Hmp
Florenoy, James	460	Bdf
Florey, John	38	Rcm
Floro, Adolph	831	Wth
David	831	Wth
Elizabeth	305	Amh
John	831	Wth
Florow, Jacob	474	Frn
John	477	Frn
Samuel	479	Frn
see Flowro		
Fournay, David	9	Pwh
Gideon	12	Pwh
Jordan	9	Pwh
Flournoy, David	567	Pre
Francis	58	Chs
John J.	567	Pre
Nelson	67	Chs
Thomas, Est.	567	Pre
Wm.	58	Chs
see Florenoy		
Flours, Jams	957	Hrr
Lambert	957	Hrr
Flower, David	521	Prw
Flowerrie, Daniel, Jr.	394	Fqr
Daniel, Senr.	394	Fqr
French	394	Fqr
John	347	Fqr
William	388	Fqr
Flowers, Absalem	637	Sss
Adam	12	Rcm
Andrew	819	Bck
Benjamin, F.N.	636	Sss
David	567	Pre
George	906	Hrr
Isham, F.N.	636	Sss
James	785	Bck
James	806	Bck
Jno.	345	Lnc
John	906	Hrr
Mary	538	Frd
Mary	898	Nrf
Roland	803	Bck
Samuel	460	Bdf
Thomas	958	Hrr
Thomas	431	Msn
Thos.	289	Ldn
William	858	Cmp
Flowro, Abram	478	Frn
Joseph	478	Frn
see Florow		
Floyd, Fredk.	23	Acc
Gideon	461	Bdf
Henry	386	Mds
Henry	498	Mnn
James	461	Bdf
John, Christiansburg	619	Mnt
Michl.	498	Mnn
Obediah	902	Crl
Richd.	32	Rcm
Sarah	23	Acc
Thos.	498	Mnn
William	22	Acc
William	461	Bdf
William	952	Chc
William	106	Spt
Wm.	277	Ldn
Wm.	18	Ntt
Floy'd, Allen	748	Brn
Ann	748	Brn
Drury	748	Brn
Jordin	748	Brn
Josiah	748	Brn
Fluck, Peter	621	Btt
Fluhartie, Steven	3	Oho
Fluharty, James	3	Oho
Fluheart, George	23	Acc
Fluner, Abram	745	Wsh
Adam	743	Wsh
Adam	744	Wsh
Benj.	753	Wsh
Christey	743	Wsh
Daniel	746	Wsh
Gasper	744	Wsh
George	752	Wsh
Henry	744	Wsh
Isaac	745	Wsh
Isaac	752	Wsh
Isaac, Jur.	753	Wsh
Jacob	744	Wsh
John	744	Wsh
John	753	Wsh
Michael	718	Wsh
Nicholes	745	Wsh
Robt.	752	Wsh
Flurranee, George	4	Wod
Flurray, Ruth, (FB)	453	Pra
Flurrey, Henry	254	Ldn
Flurry, Godwin	21	Stf
Flutcher, Jno.	33	Clp
Fluther, Henry	117	Hnr
Flynn, John, Senr.	370	Fqr
William	370	Fqr
Fnney, Page P.	114	Cmb
Fo..., Jno. S.	293	Rck
Foalding, Adam	460	Bdf
James, Jr.	460	Bdf
see Fielding		
Foalks, Edward	953	Chc
see Folks		
Foalley, Mary	491	Frn
Foalon, John B.	830	Nrf
Josiah	306	Rck
Foard, Allison	401	Fqr
Anderson	2	Ntt
Betsey	355	Fqr
Geo.	11	Ntt
Richard	361	Fqr
Saml.	10	Ntt
Thomas	344	Fqr
Wm. S.	10	Ntt
Foart, Benjamin	8	Oho
Joseph	8	Oho
Fober, Jacob	216	Shn
John	213	Shn
see Forber		
Fochs, Michal	218	Pnd
Fodderry, John	847	Hnv
Foddery, Majr.	862	Hnv
Foemsted, Elizabeth	436	Bth
Foesee, Rebecca	58	Chs
Fogall, William	26	Rcm
Fogerson, David	691	Nls
Samuel	693	Nls
Fogg, Frederick	163	Knq
James	163	Knq
John	203	Ess
Major	32	Clp
Nathaniel	163	Knq
Obadia	163	Knq
Parker	655	Glc
Thomas	163	Knq
Wm. U.	202	Ess
Fogle, Phillip	794	Hmp
Foglemon, Peter	743	Wsh
Foglesong, Charles	832	Wth
Charistian	832	Wth
Fogson, Neice	95	Acc
Fogus, Henrey	156	Alb
Henry	11	Rcm
Foist, John	544	Brk
Foland, Catharine	25	Rcm
Jacob	235	Shn
Valentine	25	Rcm
Fold see Ford		
Foley, Andrew	359	Fqr
Bryan	371	Fqr
Bryan	403	Fqr
Enoch	365	Fqr
Enoch, Jr.	370	Fqr
Henry	209	Shn
Jacob	10	Rcm
James	410	Fqr
John	376	Fqr
John	803	Hmp
Mary	6	Wod
Presly	513	Prw
Sebby	593	Frd
Thomas, (Overseer)	360	Fqr
Thomas, Senr.	386	Fqr
Thos.	593	Brk
William	376	Fqr
William	800	Hmp
Willis	234	Ldn
Folio, Upshur	22	Acc
William	22	Acc
Folk, Christ.	513	Brk
Daniel	103	Jff
Frederick	105	Jff
George	98	Jff
Folke, Stephen	292	Rck
Folks, Catharine	953	Chc
Joel	57	Chs
Robert	542	Prg
Susanna	69	Chs
William	957	Chc
see Foalks, Fulks		
Foller, Thos.	313	Ldn
Follett, Francis	328	Dnw
George	529	Frd
Isaac	776	Hmp
William	770	Hmp
Folley, Moses	744	Wsh
Folly, James	754	Wsh
Fololer see Fowler		
Folwell, E.G.	330	Dnw
Fones, Bathsheba	403	Rch
Charles	404	Rch

John	156	Alb
John	411	Rch
John, Sr.	432	Flv
Joseph	405	Rch
Thomas	397	Rch
Fontaine, Abraham	692	Gch
Wim.	897	Hnv
Fontress, Henry	838	Nrf
see Fentress		
Fontune, Sarah	692	Nls
Food see F...d		
Fooks, Elizabeth	277	Ldn
Wm.	273	Ldn
Foot, Andrew	12	Oho
Elijah	12	Oho
John	10	Oho
see Foart		
Foote, Richard	517	Prw
Richard H.	381	Fqr
W.H.	255	Frf
William	381	Fqr
William	518	Prw
Footeet, Wm.	788	Nrf
Footil, Peggy	26	Isw
Fop, William	565	Pre
Forber, Chrisley	217	Shn
see Fober		
Forbes, Geo.	339	Ags
John	557	Brk
John	430	Flv
John	470	Frn
John	834	Nrf
John	17	Oho
Murray	34	Stf
William	470	Frn
Wm.	400	Ags
Wm.	291	Rck
Wm., jr.	291	Rck
Forbush, Alexander	825	Bck
Force, David	579	Brk
Forcennan see Forecanan		
Ford, Abner	68	Chr
Austin	845	Hnv
Bal.	773	Bck
Ballard	775	Bck
Ballard	846	Bck
Benjamin	385	Mds
Boaz	806	Bck
Chesley	794	Bck
Chs. F.	256	Frf
Clary	198	Kng
Culbirth	123	Hnr
Edward, Junr.	255	Frf
Elisha	806	Bck
Elizabeth	48	Stf
Francis	82	Spt
Geo.	440	Flv
George	928	Hrr
George	385	Mds
George	300	Rck
George	772	Wst
Granvil	112	Hnr
Harwood	118	Hnr
Henry	944	Hrr
Henry	948	Hrr
Hezekiah	48	Chr
Hezekiah	851	Hnv
Hezekiah	566	Pre
James	271	Rck
Jas.	541	Prg
Joel	801	Bck
John	241	Aml
John	691	Gch
John [2]	112	Hnr
John	118	Hnr
John	385	Mds
John [2]	898	Nrf
John	522	Prw
John	276	Rck
John, jr.	101	Cmb
John, snr.	103	Cmb
John, snr	104	Cmb
John T.	26	Stf
Joseph	806	Bck
Kesikiah	100	Cmb
Langston	850	Hnv
Lewis	624	Gls
Nancey	797	Bck
Nancy	146	Dnw
Newton	101	Cmb
Noah	944	Hrr
Obadiah	848	Hnv
Pascal	101	Cmb
Reuben	385	Mds
Reubin, Jnr.	844	Hnv
Rubin	849	Hnv
Rubin	858	Hnv
Ryland	114	Hnr
Saml.	241	Aml
Saml.	115	Hnr
Samuel	899	Hnv
Sarah	446	Flv
Susanah	113	Hnr
Tandy	447	Flv
Tho. N.	345	Lnc
Thomas	68	Chr
Thomas	7	Pwh
Walter	221	Aml
Walter	222	Aml
Walter	253	Aml
Watson	10	Hnr
William	101	Cmb
William	624	Gls
William	691	Gch
William	692	Gch
William	123	Hnr
William	199	Kng
Wm.	500	Mnn
Wm.	276	Rck
Zachariah	118	Hnr
Zachariah	385	Mds
see F...d, Foart		
Forde, Ellison	589	Mnr
Fordham, Edward	463	Mdd
Fords see Ford		
Fore, Charles	566	Pre
George	69	Chr
James	68	Chr
John	876	Cmp
Nancy	622	Btt
Peter	68	Chr
Peter	565	Pre
Reubin	68	Chr
Stephen	826	Bck
Susanna	69	Chr
Foreacres James	32	Stf
Forebee, John	823	Nrf
Forecanan, Jacob	428	Rnd
Forehan, John	270	Rck
Wm.	269	Rck
Foreman, Euphen	805	Nrf
Jacob	94	Acc
John	569	Frd
John	833	Nrf
Reuben	10	Oho
Forest, ---	926	Nrf
Sarah	567	Pre
Forgason, Charles	567	Pre
Charles	296	Ldn
Chs.	312	Ldn
Hugh	19	Wod
Jethro	566	Pre
John	566	Pre
Josiah	623	Gls
Peter	565	Pre
Forgay, Daniel	500	Prw
Forgison, Amos	236	Ldn
Frank	954	Hrr
Jurdin	726	Wsh
Saml.	954	Hrr
Forguson, Robt.	618	Mnt
Forister, Robt.	345	Lnc
Forker, Thomas	692	Br
Forknee see Forkner		
Forkner, Nicholas	110	Cmb
Spencer	692	Nls
Susannah	131	Cmb
Forks, Davd. Snodgrass	717	Wsh
Forlines, Josiah	1	Pwh
William	10	Pwh
Forman, Alice	797	Nrf
Bengamin	785	Hmp
Catharine	835	Hmp
Constant	823	Nrf
David	779	Hmp
Edwd. R.	521	Brk
Henry	516	Brk
Isaac	499	Mnn
Israel	797	Nrf
Jacob	338	Ags
James	521	Brk
John	499	Mnn
John	798	Nrf
Jos.	499	Mnn
Joseph	521	Brk
Nehemiah	792	Nrf
Patsy	798	Nrf
Richd.	499	Mnn
Richd.	798	Nrf
Rob.	499	Mnn
Sam	499	Mnn
Wm.	801	Nrf
Forrer, Chrisley	187	Shn
Henry	189	Shn
see Furror		
Forrest, George, (S)	448	Mth
Josiah	12	Ntt
Matt	447	Mth
Thos.	445	Mth
Thos., jr.	448	Mth
Thos. Sr.	448	Mth
see Hunter		
Forrester, James	978	Nrt
William	397	Rch
Forrister, James	358	Fqr
Robert	839	Nrf
Forsee, Frances	12	Pwh
William	833	Bck
Forses see Forrer		
Forster, John	585	Frd
John	500	Mnn
Sarah	500	Mnn
Forsyth, Willm.	184	Elc
Wm.	831	Nrf
Forsythe, Elijah	287	Rck
Nancy	526	Prw
Robert	500	Prw
Saml.	339	Ags
Saml.	292	Rck
William	521	Prw
Fort, Chessire	37	Stf
Edwin	711	Brn
Jesse	637	Sss
Joshua	148	Sth
see Fout		
Forte see Ferte		
Fortescue, Wm.	711	Brn
Forth, Ealizabeth	219	Pnd
Fortin, Robert	901	Hnv
Fortner, Henry	708	Wsh
Nathaniel	831	Wth
Dan	500	Mnn
Dan, Senr.	500	Mnn
H., of Dan	500	Mnn
Henry	500	Mnn
Peter	72	Jff
Peter	500	Mnn
Fortress, Lovett	792	Nrf
Fortson, Frederick	903	Crl
Fortune, Benjamin	500	Frn

Name	No.	Abbr.	Name	No.	Abbr.	Name	No.	Abbr.
Eddy	692	Nls	Isaac	389	Fqr	Saml.	212	Ess
Elisha	692	Nls	James	535	Brk	Sarah	125	Hnr
Elizabeth	692	Nls	James	517	Frd	Sarah	447	Mth
Garner	523	Prw	James	571	Mnr	Selby	22	Acc
Hanah	115	Hnr	James	565	Pre	Seth	899	Nrf
Humpy.	196	Ess	James	497	Prw	Seth B.	178	Elc
James, Snr.	845	Hnv	James	297	Rck	Tabitha	385	Mds
John	223	Ess	James, (C)	447	Mth	Thomas	163	Knq
John	460	Frn	James J.	109	Cmb	Thomas	71	Spt
John	692	Nls	Janet	831	Wth	Ursula	902	Crl
Lawce.	898	Nrf	Jeremiah	872	Yrk	Valentine	167	Shn
Lucy	902	Crl	Jesse	833	Bck	William	157	Alb
Major	95	Acc	Jesse	752	Nwk	William	281	Amh
Milley	900	Hnv	Jno.	654	Glc	William	48	Chr
Nicholas	693	Nls	Jno.	10	Hnr	William	49	Chr
Polly	223	Ess	Jno.	23	Hnr	William	125	Hnr
Thomas	145	Dnw	Jno., jr.	9	Ntt	William	606	Srr
Thomas E.	691	Nls	Jno., R.	447	Mth	William	831	Wth
Williamson	500	Frn	Jno., Senr.	8	Ntt	William, Junr. (Son Wil)	48	Chr
Zachariah	692	Nls	Jno., Sr.	448	Mth	William S.	48	Chr
see Fontune			Jno. J.	1	Ntt	William V.	367	Fqr
Forward, Dan	109	Spt	Jno. T.	13	Ntt	Williamson	566	Pre
Fosch, Robert	436	Bth	Joel	193	Alb	Wm.	341	Ags
Fosdick, George	880	Cmp	Joel	567	Pre	Wm.	31	Clp
Foshure, Thomas	25	Oho	John	23	Acc	Wm.	442	Mth
Thomas, Jr.	25	Oho	John	157	Alb	Wm.	815	Nrf
Fosnought, Geo.	338	Ags	John	193	Alb	Wm., jr.	32	Clp
Fosque, George	22	Acc	John	242	Aml	Zeno G.	49	Chr
John	22	Acc	John	461	Bdf	see Cook, Fister, James,		
John, WM	23	Acc	John	445	Mth	Fosters see Foster		
Fossee, Chas.	57	Chs	John	500	Mnn	Fouch, Amos	277	Ldn
Fosset, Lewis	34	Clp	John	587	Mnr	Jno.	288	Ldn
Saml.	340	Ags	John	827	Nrf	Hugh	569	Brk
Wm.	33	Clp	John	899	Nrf	John	14	Wod
Fossett, Obadiah	894	Hnv	John	689	Wsh	Mary	278	Ldn
Foster, ---, & Satchell	23	Hnr	John	831	Wth	Nancy	302	Ldn
... [James?]	454	Mth	John, Senr.	48	Chr	Thomas	278	Ldn
A.	23	Hnr	John, (son Josiah)	49	Chr	Fouchee, Wm., Jun.	20	Hnr
Aaron	678	Br	John, (Son of Jno.)	48	Chr	Fought, Margaret	239	Shn
Achilles	902	Crl	John, Sr.	461	Bdf	Fouglesong, George	622	Btt
Alexander	371	Fqr	John H.	748	Brn	Fouk, Christian	107	Jff
Alexander	831	Wth	John L.	783	Bck	Fouke, Charles	56	Jff
Allen	156	Alb	Jonathan	507	Frd	Michael	100	Jff
Anne	567	Pre	Jos.	10	Hnr	Foulcher, William	55	Stf
Anthony	241	Aml	Joseph	753	Nwk	Foulding, George	461	Bdf
Archibald	818	Bck	Joseph	810	Nrf	James, Sr.	461	Bdf
Aron	498	Mnn	Joseph	830	Nrf	Foulerton, Jane	97	Jff
Asa	242	Aml	Joshua	157	Alb	Foulk, Jac.	497	Mnn
Barbary	214	Shn	Josiah	448	Mth	Foulkes, Daniel	566	Pre
Beauford	7	Knw	Josiah, Junr.	48	Chr	Jennings	565	Pre
Benjamin	680	Br	Josiah, Senr.	48	Chr	Josiah	565	Pre
Benjamin	567	Pre	Judiah	242	Aml	Nancy	566	Pre
Beverley	748	Brn	Julius S.	1	Rcm	Nathan	566	Pre
Booker	242	Aml	Larkin	242	Aml	Nathan	567	Pre
Booker	566	Pre	Ludson	48	Chr	Paschal	565	Pre
Daniel	214	Shn	Major	436	Flv	Sarah	566	Pre
Edmund	157	Alb	Martha	874	Sth	Thompson, Est.	566	Pre
Edmund	90	Spt	Mary	115	Hnr	William	565	Pre
Elizabeth	193	Alb	Mary	831	Wth	William	566	Pre
Elizabeth	748	Brn	Miles	587	Mnr	Fountain, Carter B.	522	Prw
Elizabeth	49	Chr	Nath	153	Sth	Jno.	454	Pra
Elizabeth	452	Mth	Nathaniel	7	Knw	Thos.	452	Pra
Elizabeth	567	Pre	Nimrod	6	Knw	Fouracres, Geo.	32	Clp
Elizabeth	502	Prw	Patridge	899	Nrf	Foushe, William	35	Hnr
Elizabeth	831	Wth	Peter	896	Hnv	Foushee, Chs.	30	Clp
Elizabh., R	447	Mth	Peter	898	Nrf	Danl.	33	Clp
Elizh., (Dd.)	448	Mth	Peter, Senr.	438	Mth	Geo.	32	Clp
Ezekiel	567	Pre	Peter R.	748	Brn	Philp.	33	Clp
Francis	157	Alb	Rachael	654	Glc	Sarah	30	Clp
Francis	929	Nrf	Richard	69	Chr	Thornton	30	Clp
Francs.	440	Mth	Richard	692	Nls	William	52	Stf
Frs.	898	Nrf	Richard	565	Pre	Wm.	116	Hnr
Geo., (SD)	12	Ntt	Richd.	242	Aml	Fout, Jno., Senr.	622	Btt
George	340	Lnn	Richd.	436	Mth	Lewis	860	Sth
George	563	Mnr	Robert	156	Alb	Fouthy, Eve	7	Wod
George, (Son Josiah)	48	Chr	Robert	340	Lnn	Fouts, Andrew	678	Br
George P.	565	Pre	Robert	167	Shn	Anne	678	Br
Gideon	48	Chr	Robt.	5	Ntt	David	678	Br
Grigsby	570	Mnr	Robt.	3	Rcm	Lemon	678	Br
Hayley	873	Sth	Ross	694	Br			

Foutt, Michael	799	Hmp	Fowlks, Jennings	341	Lnn	Thomas [2]	867	Cmp
Foutz, Jacob	461	Bdf	Fowls, James	156	Alb	William	857	Cmp
Fouy, Susannah	956	Hrr	Fowshee, Francis	407	Rch	William	867	Cmp
Fowcett, Priss	395	Rch	Fox, Adam	180	Shn	Fraizier, Caty	199	Kng
Fowe, Benjamin	193	Alb	Adam	232	Shn	Fralzer, William	91	Spt
Fowke, Thomas	199	Kng	Adam	739	Wsh	Fram, John	341	Lnn
Fowler, Aaron	268	Ldn	Ambrose	263	Ldn	Frame, Ann	54	Jff
Alex.	692	Gch	Amos	255	Frf	Benja.	541	Brk
Ann	54	Chs	Amos	244	Ldn	Matthew	56	Jff
Arthur	22	Isw	Ann	654	Glc	Saml.	338	Ags
Benja.	161	Sth	Anthoy.	34	Clp	see France		
Charles	151	Sth	Benja.	449	Grn	France, David	7	Knw
David	445	Bth	Bettey	357	Fqr	James	7	Knw
Edmond	46	Isw	Caleb	246	Ldn	James	13	Knw
Edmond	832	Wth	Charles	36	Rcm	James	978	Nrt
Elizabeth	124	Cmb	Chs.	253	Ldn	John	7	Knw
Enoch	675	Br	Elijah	257	Ldn	John	978	Nrt
Frances	62	Jff	Eliza.	163	Knq	John	405	Rch
Jacob	682	Brk	Enoch	381	Fqr	Joseph	10	Knw
Jacob	430	Flv	Ezra	257	Ldn	Thomas	7	Knw
James	852	Sth	Fred.	498	Mnn	Thomas, Jr.	978	Nrt
James	730	Wsh	Gabriel	255	Frf	Thomas, Sr.	978	Nrt
Jeremiah	58	Chs	Henry	655	Glc	William	978	Nrt
John	445	Bth	Henry	832	Wth	Frances, Ephraim	117	Spt
John	682	Br	Isaac	443	Bth	Fanney	887	Hnv
John	41	Isw	Jacob	831	Wth	John	753	Nwk
John	499	Mnn	James	752	Nwk	John	874	Sth
John	23	Rcm	James, f. negro	255	Frf	Mary	874	Sth
John	157	Sth	Jesse	245	Ldn	Samuel	875	Sth
John	852	Sth	Jno.	32	Clp	Francesco, Hannah	622	Btt
John	738	Wsh	John	414	Fqr	Michl.	622	Btt
John B.	779	Bck	John	514	Prw	Franceway, Jos.	515	Brk
Joseph	694	Br	John	872	Yrk	Francies, Henry	578	Mnr
Joseph	951	Chc	Joseph	693	Nls	John	580	Mnr
Joseph	411	Isw	Joseph	244	Ldn	Francis, ...h	257	Ldn
Joshua	10	Knw	Joseph	772	Wst	Abraham	678	Wrw
Levendor O.	567	Pre	Josephas	180	Alb	Abram	872	Yrk
Merine	253	Ldn	Margeret	254	Frf	Andrew	342	Fqr
Mills	34	Isw	Mary	242	Ldn	Calip	899	Hnv
Morris	252	Ldn	Mary	300	Ldn	Elizabeth	609	Mnt
N.	499	Mnn	Mathias	340	Ags	Henry	364	Fqr
Nancy	878	Cmp	Matthias	357	Fqr	Isaac	446	Bth
Partrick	893	Hnv	Michael	408	Fqr	Jacob	622	Btt
Resin	500	Mnn	Morris	254	Frf	John S.	678	Br
Richard	461	Bdf	Nathaniel	753	Nwk	Joseph	686	Br
Richard	694	Br	Nathaniel	58	Stf	Joseph	376	Fqr
Robert	728	Wsh	Peter	385	Mds	Joseph	131	Hnr
Thomas	42	Isw	Peter	831	Wth	Judith	132	Hnr
Thos.	623	Btt	Philladelphia	97	Spt	Mary	274	Ldn
Titus	875	Sth	Phillip	41	Stf	Nathl., f. negro	254	Frf
William	461	Bdf	Richard	883	Cmp	Natthaniel	795	Bck
William	675	Br	Richard	693	Nls	Patrick	393	Fqr
William	685	Br	Samuel	693	Nls	Rachel	129	Hnr
William	950	Chc	Sarah	883	Cmp	Rubin	955	Chc
William	255	Frf	Sebia	244	Ldn	Thomas	373	Fqr
William	2	Knw	Stophel	340	Ags	Thos.	232	Ldn
William	39	Rcm	Susanna	241	Ldn	William	129	Hnr
Wm.	59	Chs	Thomas	22	Acc	William	22	Oho
Wm.	124	Cmb	Thomas	858	Cmp	Wm.	340	Ags
Wm.	129	Sth	Thomas	210	Shn	Wm.	523	Brk
see F...wler			Thomas	42	Stf	Wm.	274	Ldn
Fowles, Ann	400	Rch	Thomas A.	449	Grn	Wm.	872	Yrk
Fowlkes, Archibald	49	Chr	Thos.	681	Wrw	Francisco, Chs. L.	450	Bth
Bass	341	Lnn	Thos. B.	654	Glc	Louis	622	Btt
Charles H.	11	Ntt	Toby	35	Stf	see Francesco		
Edward	49	Chr	Uriah	309	Ldn	Frane, John	39	Rcm
Gabriel	16	Ntt	Vincent	42	Stf	Frank, Anthony	803	Hmp
Hennery	341	Lnn	William	22	Acc	Boddington	199	Kng
Hennery, jr.	341	Lnn	William	449	Grn	Henry	60	Jff
Jane	11	Ntt	William	792	Hmp	James	199	Kng
Jno.	19	Ntt	Wm.	33	Clp	Jno., Senr.	199	Kng
John	341	Lnn	Wm.	655	Glc	Jno. Henry	622	Btt
Jos.	4	Ntt	Wm.	816	Nrf	John	461	Bdf
Jos. J.	1	Ntt	Foxwell, Jno.	654	Glc	John	772	Hmp
Josey	13	Ntt	Foxworthy, Sarah	512	Prw	John	835	Hmp
Judith	4	Ntt	Thomas	512	Prw	John, jr.	199	Kng
Molley	20	Ntt	Foy, Spry	898	Nrf	Joseph	449	Grn
Paschal	341	Lnn	Frail, Thos.	635	Mnt	Robert	199	Kng
Sterling	340	Lnn	Fraizer, Jonathan	82	Jff	Saml.	199	Kng
Wm.	10	Ntt	Micajah	867	Cmp	Wm.	199	Kng

116

Name	No.	Code
Wm.	720	Wsh
Franker, Catharine	338	Ags
Geo.	340	Ags
Frankeybarger, Saml.	621	Btt
Frankhauser, N.	499	Mnn
Franklin, Ann	22	Stf
Archer	461	Bdf
Aron	466	Frn
Benjamin	565	Pre
Bernard	193	Alb
Edmund	461	Bdf
Edmund	859	Cmp
Edward	48	Chr
Frances	452	Pra
Francis	621	Btt
George	54	Stf
Gilly	129	Hnr
Henry	454	Pra
James	283	Amh
James	623	Btt
James	124	Hnr
James	832	Wth
Jasper	466	Frn
Jeremiah	294	Amh
Jesse	242	Aml
Jesse	25	Hnr
Jno.	453	Pra
John	862	Cmp
John	869	Cmp
John	48	Chr
John	381	Fqr
John	518	Prw
John, Jr.	385	Fqr
Lewis	864	Cmp
Lewis	127	Hnr
Losson	461	Bdf
Mary	880	Hnv
Mary	19	Hnr
Miles	122	Hnr
Nathl.	622	Btt
Owen	460	Bdf
Peachey	269	Amh
Peter, Jur.	49	Chr
Peter, Senr.	49	Chr
Polley	126	Hnr
Reuben	466	Frn
Richard	193	Alb
Robert	68	Chr
Robert	692	Nls
Robt.	127	Hnr
Samuel	692	Nls
Susannah	258	Amh
Thomas	864	Cmp
Thomas	9	Hnr
Thomas	128	Hnr
Thomas	566	Pre
William	415	Fqr
William	341	Lnn
Zachariah	127	Hnr
see Frankling		
Frankling, John	869	Cmp
Robert	859	Cmp
Robert	877	Cmp
Stewart	772	Wst
William, Jur.	772	Wst
William, Senr.	772	Wst
see Franklin		
Franks, Henry	543	Frd
Henry	808	Hmp
John	802	Hmp
John	752	Nwk
William	589	Frd
Frankum, John	338	Ags
Frantz, Chrisley	623	Btt
Christn., Jr.	623	Btt
Danl.	623	Btt
David	623	Btt
Henry	623	Btt
Jacob	621	Btt
John	623	Btt
Michl., Jr.	623	Btt
Michl., (Younger)	623	Btt
Peter	623	Btt
Fraser, Alexr.	146	Dnw
James	339	Ags
James, jr.	339	Ags
James A.	340	Ags
Jno., jr.	146	Dnw
John, Senr.	145	Dnw
John W.	339	Ags
Mary	339	Ags
Nancy	332	Dnw
William	510	Frd
Wm.	339	Ags
Frasier, ---, Mrs.	430	Flv
John	712	Brn
John, dist.	711	Brn
Peter	325	Dnw
William	334	Dnw
Frasue, Robt.	668	Mnt
Frasur see Heldridth		
Frasure, Benj.	964	Hrr
Efrom	964	Hrr
Nimrod	964	Hrr
Presly	937	Hrr
Wm.	959	Hrr
Fravel, Henry	250	Shn
Jacob	239	Shn
Jacob	249	Shn
Fravell, George	247	Shn
Henry	203	Shn
Frawner, Betty	198	Kng
John	902	Crl
Joseph	902	Crl
William	902	Crl
Fray, Aron	385	Mds
Ephraham	385	Mds
John	385	Mds
John	758	Wsh
Moses	385	Mds
see Frayser		
Frayser, Beverley	753	Nwk
Elvira	752	Nwk
Hannah	691	Gch
Jackson	125	Hnr
Jesse	120	Hnr
John	102	Cmb
Robert	112	Cmb
William	126	Cmb
Wm.	126	Hnr
Frayzer, Billy	27	Hnr
Lucy	27	Hnr
Fraz..., Henry	445	Bth
Frazell see Feazell		
Frazer, Edward	92	Spt
Fredk.	33	Clp
Hugh	49	Chr
James	415	Bth
Jno.	854	Hnv
Jno.	295	Rck
John	764	Hmp
Polly	521	Frd
Reuben	103	Spt
Samuel	415	Bth
Samuel	427	Msn
Simon	64	Chs
Simon	65	Chs
see Fralzer		
Frazier, Daniel	460	Bdf
David	7	Oho
Frances	189	Elc
Hugh	461	Bdf
James	411	Fqr
John	460	Bdf
John	6	Oho
Johnn.	180	Elc
Joseph	6	Oho
Martha	397	Fqr
Noah	551	Frd
Samul	7	Oho
William	7	Oho
William	6	Rcm
Wm. E.	606	Srr
see Phreasure		
Frazierr, Saml.	26	Oho
Frecheh see Fucheh		
Fredd, Joseph	239	Ldn
Joseph	274	Ldn
Joshua	274	Ldn
Thomas	274	Ldn
Frederic, Jacob	461	Bdf
Frederick, Jacob	585	Frd
John	511	Frd
John	585	Frd
John	185	Shn
John	460	Bdf
Michael	460	Bdf
Free, Barney	509	Brk
George	580	Brk
Israel	497	Mnn
Freed, Jos.	249	Shn
Samuel	176	Shn
Freehold, William	42	Rcm
Freel, Charles	687	Br
Freeland, Abram	606	Srr
Archd.	67	Chs
Ben	499	Mnn
E.	498	Mnn
James	333	Dnw
James	23	Oho
Jno.	499	Mnn
Levi	498	Mnn
Mace	775	Bck
William J.	816	Bck
Freeman, Abm.	621	Btt
Alexr.	263	Ldn
Anna	34	Clp
Balaam	637	Sss
Ben	497	Mnn
Ceasar	426	Bth
Charles	637	Sss
David, (FB)	14	Ntt
Elizabeth	711	Brn
Elizabeth	637	Sss
Frank	853	Cmp
Frank, F. N.	636	Sss
Frederick	886	Hnv
Garriott	33	Clp
George	353	Fqr
Gerard	902	Crl
Harris	31	Clp
Henry C.	872	Yrk
Hezekiah	171	Shn
Hugh	188	Elc
Isaac	682	Br
Isaac	821	Bck
Isaac	845	Hnv
Jack, (FB)	17	Ntt
Jacob	591	Frd
James	31	Clp
James	654	Glc
James	637	Sss
James, Sr.	460	Bdf
Jane	30	Hnr
Jasper	654	Glc
Jno.	31	Clp
Jno.	32	Clp
Jno.	33	Clp
Jno.	654	Glc
Jno.	5	Ntt
Jno. H.	32	Clp
John	49	Chr
John	898	Nrf
John, (Free negro)	698	Wsh
Johnston	301	Rck
Jos.	899	Nrf
Joseph	606	Srr
Larken	832	Wth
Lucy	637	Sss
Mary	355	Fqr
Molly	340	Ags

Molly	637	Sss	William	794	Hmp	Geo.	281	Ldn
Morris	880	Cmp	William	20	Oho	John	37	Rcm
Nathan	691	Gch	William	13	Wod	Frizle, Henry	257	Shn
Nathl.	31	Clp	Wm.	623	Btt	Jno.	453	Pra
Orange	692	Gch	Wm.	655	Glc	Jona.	452	Pra
Rd.	254	Frf	see Carder			Joshua	452	Pra
Reubin	832	Wth	Frene, John	180	Shn	Mary	452	Pra
Richard	460	Bdf	Frensley, Elizabeth	902	Crl	Frizzle, Charles	764	Hmp
Ro.	654	Glc	James	902	Crl	John	815	Hmp
Robt., jr.	31	Clp	William	902	Crl	Thomas	547	Frd
Robt., Senr.	31	Clp	Freshaw, George	214	Pnd	William	255	Frf
Sally	753	Nwk	Jacob	214	Pnd	Froble, Jno. S.	254	Frf
Sally [2]	637	Sss	Freshwater, Archibald	690	Br	Froman, Hamlin	340	Lnn
Thomas	28	Hnr	Freshwaters, Frances	694	Br	Frost, Amos	533	Frd
Thos.	31	Clp	Reuben	694	Br	James	124	Hnr
Thos.	654	Glc	William	694	Br	Jos.	752	Wsh
William	386	Fqr	Fretwel, William	193	Alb	Joseph	899	Nrf
William, Jr.	414	Fqr	Fretwell, Alexander	156	Alb	Martha	293	Ldn
Willm.	621	Btt	Alexander	180	Alb	Stephen	22	Hnr
Wm.	31	Clp	Crenshaw	193	Alb	Frozzett, John	35	Stf
Wm.	805	Nrf	Jemma	156	Alb	Frum, Wm.	497	Mnn
Wm.	755	Wsh	John	193	Alb	Frumbo, George	216	Pnd
Wyatt	692	Gch	Wm.	407	Ags	Fruman, Betty	122	Hnr
Zachariah	435	Flv	Frew, Alexander	674	Br	John	124	Hnr
see ---, Freman, Fruman			Friar, Easter	852	Cmp	Mingo	130	Hnr
Freestone, Amos	917	Hrr	Elijah	523	Prw	Nat.	127	Hnr
Danl.	917	Hrr	John	523	Prw	Fry, Barbara	14	Rcm
Freeze, Danl.	13	Rcm	Tapley	526	Prw	Benjamin, E.J.	210	Shn
Jacob	10	Rcm	Friatt, John	511	Brk	Christr.	898	Nrf
John	8	Rcm	John, jr.	528	Brk	Daniel	59	Jff
Peter	29	Rcm	Fridale, John	757	Hmp	Daniel	214	Pnd
Freind, Thomas	126	Hnr	Fridey, George, (sen.)	26	Rcm	Daniel	209	Shn
Freman, Hennery	340	Lnn	Fridley, Charles	23	Rcm	Daniel	831	Wth
Jacob	161	Sth	George	23	Rcm	David	74	Jff
Peter	821	Bck	Henry	587	Frd	Elizabeth	572	Frd
Saml.	966	Hrr	Isaac	26	Rcm	Elizabeth	31	Rcm
Thrower	340	Lnn	Jacob	338	Ags	Elizabth.	898	Nrf
see Froman, Rease, Winn			see Fridey			Frederick	223	Shn
Fremon, M.	31	Hnr	Fridly, Elizabeth	514	Frd	George	119	Spt
French, Burgiss	393	Fqr	Friel, Manasses	831	Wth	George, Jur.	624	Gls
Daniel	391	Fqr	Friend, Andrew	417	Rnd	George, Sen.	624	Gls
David	624	Gls	Charles	562	Mnr	George M.	512	Frd
Geo.	557	Brk	George C.	48	Chr	Henry	624	Gls
Geo.	293	Ldn	Jacob	222	Pnd	Henry	314	Ldn
George	108	Spt	Jno., Est.	65	Chs	Henry	385	Mds
Henry	583	Brk	Joseph	424	Rnd	Henry	230	Shn
Henry	245	Shn	Joseph	425	Rnd	Henry	254	Shn
Hugh	5	Pwh	Joseph, Junr.	49	Chr	Henry, Jr.	385	Mds
Isaac	623	Gls	Joseph, Sen.	49	Chr	Isaac	239	Ldn
Jacob	549	Brk	Nathl.	328	Dnw	Jacob	571	Frd
James	624	Gls	Thomas	222	Pnd	Jacob	230	Shn
James	248	Ldn	Friends, Jos., Est.	5	Ntt	Jacob	248	Shn
Jno., Sr., (Dr.)	621	Btt	Frier, Susanna	196	Ess	Jno.	34	Clp
John	588	Brk	see Fiser, Fuaer			John	555	Brk
John	623	Gls	Frieze, David	604	Frd	John	790	Bck
John	833	Nrf	Martin	604	Frd	John	508	Frd
John	392	Rch	Michal	604	Frd	John	898	Nrf
John, Jr.	621	Btt	Frig, John	555	Brk	John	225	Shn
Lewis	253	Ldn	Frigg, Jereh.	510	Brk	John, Jnr.	66	Jff
Mary	146	Dnw	Frils, John	949	Hrr	John, Snr.	66	Jff
Mason	692	Gch	Fringer, Christopher	620	Btt	Joseph	369	Fqr
Mason	233	Ldn	Frisbey, Jos.	723	Wsh	Joseph	571	Frd
Mason	831	Wth	Nathaniel	832	Wth	Joseph	210	Shn
Mason, jr.	692	Gch	Frisinger, Peter	28	Rcm	Joshua	385	Mds
Matthew	624	Gls	Fristoe, Jack	510	Prw	Judah	555	Brk
Peter	621	Btt	John	178	Shn	Margaret	14	Isw
Polly	17	Rcm	Sarah	34	Clp	Mathias	621	Btt
Robert	830	Hmp	William, Junr.	179	Shn	Mathias	623	Btt
Robt.	692	Gch	William, Senr.	179	Shn	Matthias	555	Frd
Samuel	395	Fqr	Frith, Henry	242	Aml	Nathiel	28	Hnr
Samuel	55	Jff	Hurbert	461	Bdf	Nicholas	291	Ldn
Sarah	692	Gch	Mary	623	Gls	Peter	624	Gls
Shapleigh	544	Frd	Thomas	479	Frn	Peter	285	Ldn
Stephen	514	Prw	Wm.	59	Chs	Peter	210	Shn
Stephen	48	Stf	Frits, George	899	Nrf	Peter	751	Wsh
Stephen, ([his] Quar-			Fritter, Enoch	47	Stf	Philip	234	Ldn
ter)	419	Fqr	John	52	Stf	Philip	282	Ldn
Tho.	178	Elc	Moses	55	Stf	Thomas	87	Spt
William	145	Dnw	William	53	Stf	Thomas W.	385	Mds
William	624	Gls	Fritts, Conrod	832	Wth	Valentine	832	Wth

Name	Pg	Co	Name	Pg	Co	Name	Pg	Co
Wesley	385	Mds	Ezekill	5	Oho	John	601	Frd
Frye, Bengamin	769	Hmp	Jacob	262	Rck	John	4	Rcm
Enovina	85	Jff	James	722	Wsh	John	193	Shn
Henry	769	Hmp	Jas.	758	Wsh	John, Sen.	500	Mnn
John	769	Hmp	Jas., Jur.	758	Wsh	Joseph	13	Rcm
Fryer, John	59	Jff	Molly, (F.B.)	452	Pra	Michael	173	Shn
Richd.	898	Nrf	Northrup	641	Mnt	Peter	656	Mnt
Fryers, Samuel	390	Rch	Plumb, (FB)	453	Pra	Peter	171	Shn
Fryman, Jacob	243	Shn	Rosanna	216	Ess	Peter	195	Shn
Fuaer, Richd.	196	Ess	Sion	637	Sss	Philip	198	Shn
see Frier			Stephen, bound for a term			Saml.	621	Btt
Fucheh, Ezekiel	25	Oho	of years	447	Bth	Saml.	4	Rcm
Fuckwiler, Thomas	180	Shn	Thos., F.Blak	453	Pra	Funkhouser, Abraham	220	Shn
Fudge, Adam	734	Wsh	Fullgham, Allen	17	Isw	Barbary	219	Shn
Christn.	622	Btt	Charles	17	Isw	Chrisley	220	Shn
Coonrad	622	Btt	John	16	Isw	Daniel	211	Shn
Coonrod	734	Wsh	Joseph	33	Isw	Daniel	220	Shn
David	563	Mnr	Lemuel	27	Isw	David	199	Shn
John	734	Wsh	Mary	14	Isw	David	219	Shn
Fuel, Willis	199	Kng	Matthew	3	Isw	David	225	Shn
Fufler, Fanny	800	Nrf	Robert	29	Isw	Elizabeth	218	Shn
Fugale, Jeremiah	254	Frf	Willis	33	Isw	George	199	Shn
Fugate, Francis	355	Fqr	Fullheart, Henry	621	Btt	Isaac	340	Ags
Francis	831	Wth	Fullin, Charles	832	Wth	Isaac	225	Shn
Gerard	255	Frf	John	832	Wth	Jacob	199	Shn
Hannah	59	Stf	Fulmer, Jacob	2	Oho	Jacob	220	Shn
Randal	831	Wth	Fulmore, Joseph	254	Frf	John	219	Shn
William	355	Fqr	Fulse, Adam	22	Rcm	see Tunkhouser		
see Fugale			David	34	Rcm	Funston, Oliver	544	Frd
Fuggle, Larkin	567	Mnr	Jacob	34	Rcm	Oliver	595	Frd
Fugmore see Fuzmore			Philip	33	Rcm	Fuqua, ...y	69	Chs
Fuke, Joseph	790	Hmp	Reuben	33	Rcm	Aron	782	Bck
Fulcher, Elizabeth	303	Amh	Fulsher, James	258	Amh	Benjn.	115	Cmb
Flowery	10	Hnr	William	719	Wsh	Gabriel	778	Bck
Phil	115	Hnr	Fulston, Mark	34	Clp	Henry, Sr.	946	Chc
William	902	Crl	Fulton, Abe.	236	Ldn	Jno.	623	Btt
William	692	Gch	Alexander	124	Hnr	Jno.	59	Chs
William	10	Hnr	Andw.	339	Ags	John	442	Flv
Fulford, Asa	794	Nrf	David	232	Ldn	Joshua	948	Chc
Chas.	794	Nrf	David	626	Mnt	Moses	826	Bck
Chas., jr.	794	Nrf	Geo.	298	Ldn	Nathaniel	105	Cmb
Edan	794	Nrf	Hugh	340	Ags	Robert	829	Bck
Geo.	794	Nrf	Hugh, (Cpt.)	339	Ags	Saml.	64	Chs
Matthew	798	Nrf	James	340	Ags	Stephen	803	Bck
Fulgham, Henry	143	Sth	James	80	Jff	William	779	Bck
Jesse	825	Nrf	John	339	Ags	William	949	Chc
Jos.	898	Nrf	John	340	Ags	see Fewqua		
Fulghor, Henry	882	Sth	John	243	Ldn	Fuquay, Aaron	461	Bdf
Fulk, Christian	29	Rcm	Robert	56	Jff	Archibald	565	Pre
David	222	Pnd	Robert	240	Ldn	Caleb	461	Bdf
Henry	498	Mnn	Robt.	339	Ags	Elizabeth	49	Chr
John	29	Rcm	Robt.	297	Rck	F., Dr.	49	Chr
Fulkenson, Richd.	25	Rcm	Susan	291	Ldn	George M.	565	Pre
Fulkerson, Abram	755	Wsh	Thos.	340	Ags	Giles	566	Pre
Benjamin	197	Shn	William	255	Frf	Jacob	460	Bdf
Jac.	498	Mnn	Wm.	340	Ags	Jacob	462	Bdf
John	755	Wsh	Fults, Frederick	259	Amh	Joseph [2]	461	Bdf
Mary	744	Wsh	Leady	240	Shn	Joseph	567	Pre
Philip	241	Ldn	see Futts			Judith	461	Bdf
Richd.	754	Wsh	Fultz, Joseph	230	Shn	Moses	460	Bdf
Fulkes, Nicholes	728	Wsh	Joshua, Junr.	228	Shn	Peyton	566	Pre
Fulkeson, John	580	Frd	Martin	623	Btt	Ralph	461	Bdf
Fulkison, Benjamin	234	Shn	Peter	338	Ags	Samuel	48	Chr
Jonah	242	Ldn	Fulwider, Geo., Sr.	340	Ags	Temperance	49	Chr
Fulks, Charles	981	Nrt	Jacob	339	Ags	William	461	Bdf
David	606	Srr	John	339	Ags	William	462	Bdf
John	936	Hrr	Fulwiler, Abram	621	Btt	William	566	Pre
John	981	Nrt	Jacob	621	Btt	William, Sr.	461	Bdf
John B.	386	Mds	John	621	Btt	Furbush, Jessee	692	Gch
see Folks			Funk, Abram	341	Ags	Furby, Caleb	499	Mnn
Full, George	214	Pnd	Adam	240	Ldn	Geo.	499	Mnn
Lewis	221	Pnd	Christian	21	Rcm	Jno.	498	Mnn
Fullen, Alexr.	288	Rck	Danl.	339	Ags	Waterman	579	Frd
John	275	Rck	Frederick	392	Fqr	Wt.	498	Mnn
Wm.	733	Wsh	Henry	4	Rcm	Furgason, Francis	449	Grn
Fuller, Africa, F.B.	453	Pra	Isaac	220	Shn	Furgenson, Josiah	870	Sth
Barthollowmew	113	Spt	Jac.	499	Mnn	Furgerson, Archibald	461	Bdf
Brittan	500	Frn	Jacob	214	Shn	Caleb [?]	461	Bdf
Danl.	270	Rck	Jacob, Sen.	257	Shn	Francis	752	Nwk
Deana	802	Nrf	Jno.	499	Mnn	James S.	84	Jff

Jeremiah	461	Bdf	John	437	Bth	Galaspy, James	9	Wod
Jos.	328	Dnw	Gabrial, Peter	211	Shn	John	6	Wod
Rachael	463	Mdd	Gabriel, Augle	258	Frf	Galaway, Dav.	503	Mnn
see F...an			Salley	401	Ags	Galbraith, Jno., j.	303	Rck
Furgeson, Thomas	163	Knq	Gad, William	5	Oho	John	263	Rck
Furginson, Dixon	151	Sth	Gadberry, Prudence	117	Hnr	Galbreath, Thos.	346	Ags
Furgis, Francis	627	Mnt	Gadd, Ignatius	5	Oho	Wm.	264	Rck
Saml.	626	Mnt	Thos.	502	Mnn	Galden, Freeman	827	Bck
Furgison, Wm.	149	Sth	Gaddy, Jno. C.	893	Hnv	Judeth	158	Alb
Wm., Ra.	150	Sth	Joseph	872	Cmp	William	158	Alb
Zach.	149	Sth	Mary	463	Bdf	Gale, Alexander	7	Isw
Furguson, Jas. B.	692	Gch	Nancy	463	Bdf	Allen	3	Isw
Furgusson, Robert	242	Aml	William R.	14	Hnr	Andrew	7	Isw
Furley, Bowers	500	Mnn	Gaerrett, Danell	277	Ldn	George	794	Hmp
see Furby			Gagle see Gayle			Jethro	21	Isw
Furlong, Alexander	753	Nwk	Gaile, Margaret	165	Knq	John	21	Isw
Saml.	622	Btt	William	164	Knq	John B.	8	Isw
Furmard, John	72	Jff	Gain, John	946	Hrr	Jos.	326	Dnw
Furnace, Jno.	280	Ldn	Gaine, John	534	Frd	Joseph	20	Isw
Furr, Abraham	597	Frd	Gainer, Brian	429	Rnd	Rebecca	30	Isw
Enoch	400	Fqr	George	427	Rnd	Thomas, Jun.	8	Isw
Enoch	273	Ldn	John	21	Oho	Thos.	887	Hnv
Ephraim	262	Ldn	Sampson	580	Frd	Galehue, Jer	501	Mnn
John	597	Frd	Tho.	346	Lnc	Galespie, George	265	Amh
Jonas	272	Ldn	Gaines, Allen	35	Clp	Galespy, Henry	18	Wod
Mary	5	Rcm	Augustine	526	Prw	James	834	Wth
Minor	232	Ldn	Benja.	38	Clp	Richard	18	Wod
Minor	273	Ldn	Benja.	164	Knq	Galewood, John S.	127	Hnr
Thomas	773	Hmp	Collin	38	Clp	Galford, Thomas	420	Bth
Thompson	273	Ldn	Cornelius	512	Prw	William	420	Bth
William	397	Fqr	Edmund	49	Chr	Galispie, Roland	288	Amh
Wm.	263	Ldn	Elizabeth	165	Knq	Sherod M.	283	Amh
see Tarr			Francis	38	Clp	Gall, George	224	Pnd
Furrey, Daniel	746	Wsh	Harry	164	Knq	Jacob	217	Pnd
Danl.	23	Rcm	James	165	Knq	John	224	Pnd
Furror, Samuel	187	Shn	James	253	Ldn	see Gale		
see Forrer			John	391	Rch	Gallady, John	344	Ags
Furrow, Adam	630	Mnt	Nancy, (F. Negroe)	343	Fqr	Gallager, Peter	772	Wst
Charles	632	Mnt	Reuben	35	Clp	Gallaghan, Daniel	435	Bth
Jacob [2]	623	Btt	Richard W.	50	Chr	Gallagher, Benard	499	Prw
John	641	Mnt	Richd.	36	Clp	James	508	Prw
Matthias	641	Mnt	Robert B.	164	Knq	Robert	525	Frd
Furrur, Christeen	243	Shn	Thomas	49	Chr	Gallahar, John	695	Br
Furry, John	831	Wth	Thomas	164	Knq	Gallaher, James	589	Brk
Furtney, Jno.	498	Mnn	Thos.	36	Clp	John	592	Brk
Fussel, Benjamin	125	Hnr	Thos. L.	36	Clp	Polly	592	Brk
Betsy	122	Hnr	William	50	Chr	Rob.	594	Brk
Jane	132	Hnr	William	41	Stf	Gallavan, Frances	36	Hnr
Solomon	131	Hnr	Wm.	35	Clp	Gallaway, Harris	777	Bck
Thomas	131	Hnr	Wm.	38	Clp	Terry	798	Bck
Futts, George	225	Shn	see Games			William	120	Cmb
Joshua	224	Shn	Gains, A.	345	Ags	William	62	Jff
Fuzmore, Edwd.	691	Gch	Aaron	26	Rcm	Galle, Anby	326	Dnw
Isaac	692	Gch	Augustine	388	Mds	Gallego, Joseph	132	Hnr
Fye, John, (Jr.)	28	Rcm	Caty	116	Spt	Galleher, Wm.	261	Ldn
John, (Sen.)	28	Rcm	Edmond	388	Mds	Gallia..., Saml.	463	Bdf
			Edward	388	Mds	Gallian, Gilbert	904	Hrr
			Eliza.	347	Lnc	John	216	Pnd
--- G ---			Hannah	93	Spt	Galliher, David	265	Ldn
			Henry	856	Hnv	Samuel	251	Ldn
			Henry, & Daughter	387	Mds	Gallihorn, Robt.	731	Wsh
G..., ...	461	Bdf	Humphey	157	Alb	Gallim, Mitchell M.	873	Cmp
...	450	Frn	Jacob	946	Hrr	Gallimo, Joshua, (FN)	50	Chr
...	901	Nrf	John	93	Spt	Gallimore, George, (FN)	50	Chr
Henry	463	Bdf	Kemp	26	Rcm	William, (FN)	50	Chr
G...ham, Edwd.	266	Rck	Robert	20	Rcm	Galling, Samuel	753	Nwk
G...on, ...	463	Bdf	Sally	95	Spt	Samuel, junr.	754	Nwk
Ga..., Marmaduke	778	Bck	Thomas	946	Hrr	Gallinher, William	713	Wsh
Gaar, Abraham	386	Mds	Thomas	387	Mds	Gallion, Hosy	648	Mnt
Andrew	386	Mds	William	85	Spt	Gallogo, Joseph	7	Hnr
Aron	386	Mds	William	773	Wst	Gallohugh, Sary	387	Mds
Benjamin	386	Mds	William M.	388	Mds	Galloway, Benjn.	624	Btt
Margeret	386	Mds	Gairy, John	780	Bck	James	777	Hmp
Nicholas	386	Mds	Gaiter, Edward	8	Oho	John	13	Oho
Gab, William	487	Frn	Gaither, Catherine	591	Brk	John	513	Prw
Gabbart, Jacob	346	Ags	John	27	Rcm	Margarett	516	Frd
Jacob, Sr.	346	Ags	Ralph	823	Hmp	Richard L.	519	Frd
Peter	346	Ags	Galahan, John	9	Knw	Galobart see Gabohart		
Gabert, Henry	754	Wsh	Galahar, John	696	Br	Galt, Jno. E.	24	Hnr
Gabohart, John	416	Bth	Galasby, Theophilis	10	Knw	John	836	Nrf

John M.	607	Srr
Thos.	541	Prg
Wm.	21	Hnr
Galvan, Francis	36	Hnr
Jos.	753	Wsh
Galway, Samuel	684	Br
Gambel, Charlotte	159	Alb
James	689	Br
John	195	Alb
Josiah [2]	695	Br
Richard	157	Alb
Samuel	686	Br
William	157	Alb
Gambell, Henry J.	1	Rcm
John	341	Ags
Gamble, Adam	511	Frd
Catharine	4	Hnr
Edwd.	10	Hnr
George	700	Wsh
James	177	Elc
Joseph	508	Frd
Joseph	219	Pnd
Katy	900	Nrf
Margt.	264	Rck
Robt.	23	Hnr
Robt.	3	Oho
Wm.	501	Mnn
Gambo, Samuel	196	Alb
Gambol, Eliza.	679	Wrw
Gambriel, Edward	3	Wod
Gambrill, Ann	12	Wod
Gamdin, Benjn.	274	Rck
Gamer, Ely	200	Kng
Jacob	200	Kng
Jno., Junr.	200	Kng
John, Sr.	200	Kng
Games, Absalom	585	Frd
Basil	54	Jff
John	208	Ess
John	529	Frd
Robert	59	Jff
see Gamer, Ganies, Games		
Gamett see Garnett		
Gammon, Henry	799	Nrf
James	788	Nrf
Joel	455	Pra
John	693	Gch
Richd.	793	Nrf
Saml.	805	Nrf
Wm.	693	Gch
see Gannon, Gaumon		
Gamon, Rebecca	553	Brk
Ganaway, John	833	Wth
Thomas	834	Wth
William	833	Wth
Gander, George	191	Shn
Jacob	172	Shn
John	172	Shn
Gandy, Amos	503	Mnn
David	431	Rnd
Levy	502	Mnn
Reah	422	Msn
Saml.	503	Mnn
Ganeau, Mary	30	Hnr
Ganes, Barnard	799	Bck
Richard	194	Alb
William	538	Frd
Ganett see Garrett		
Gangware see Gongware		
Gania, Mathew	717	Wsh
Ganies, Francis	210	Ess
see Games		
Ganmon, Robert	799	Nrf
see Gammon		
Gannaway, John	793	Bck
Lucey	826	Bck
Robert	793	Bck
William	793	Bck
Woodson	780	Bck
see G...		

Gannawey, Robinson	741	Wsh
Ganno, Daniel	553	Brk
Stephen	553	Brk
Gannon, James	259	Frf
Smith	799	Nrf
see Ganmon		
Ganoe, Stephen	764	Hmp
Gant, Ambrose	259	Frf
Andw.	36	Clp
Edwd. S.	261	Frf
Erasmus	556	Brk
Henry	65	Jff
Jno.	259	Frf
John	345	Fqr
John	65	Jff
John, Senr.	530	Frd
Jos.	37	Clp
Joseph	259	Frf
Milly, f. negro	259	Frf
William	177	Shn
Willis	13	Oho
Gantum, Betsey	693	Gch
Garber, Abram	345	Ags
Danl.	37	Rcm
Henry	345	Ags
Jacob	233	Shn
Joseph	9	Rcm
M.	401	Ags
Martin	233	Shn
Michl.	342	Ags
Saml.	342	Ags
Saml.	6	Rcm
Saml.	32	Rcm
Solomon	341	Ags
Garbra, Eliza.	38	Clp
Garbret, Richd.	511	Brk
Gard, Jacob	519	Frd
John	519	Frd
John	12	Wod
John	13	Wod
Peggy	519	Frd
Samuel	775	Hmp
Garden, Catherine	50	Chr
Gardener, Comfort	97	Acc
Etheld.	156	Sth
John	96	Acc
Matt.	156	Sth
Rubin	860	Hnv
Gardiner, Henry	152	Sth
James	877	Sth
Loyd	697	Br
William	686	Br
Gardner, ---	895	Nrf
Absolam	530	Frd
Amos	161	Sth
Andrew	227	Pnd
Ann	463	Mdd
Ann [2]	878	Sth
Anthy.	164	Knq
Burwell	161	Sth
Eliza.	165	Knq
Eliza.	878	Sth
Francis	341	Ags
Francis	629	Mnt
George	463	Mdd
Henry	13	Pwh
Henry	139	Sth
Henry	879	Sth
Jacob	550	Frd
James	589	Brk
James	77	Jff
James	96	Jff
James	82	Spt
James I.	523	Frd
Jas., Jr.	629	Mnt
Jason	130	Sth
Jesse	878	Sth
Jno.	897	Hnv
John	196	Alb
John	58	Jff

John	866	Sth
John, Ju.	417	Bth
John, Ser.	417	Bth
Jor.	802	Nrf
Jos.	901	Nrf
Joseph	303	Ldn
Joshua	876	Sth
Js. C.	901	Nrf
Lewis	311	Ldn
Martha	853	Sth
Mary	417	Bth
Mary	259	Frf
Mary	77	Jff
Nancy	158	Alb
Peter	524	Brk
Robert	444	Bth
Saml.	343	Ags
Sylvia	154	Sth
Thompson	795	Bck
Thompson	797	Bck
Thos., [his] Plantation	83	Spt
William	260	Frf
William	65	Jff
William	93	Spt
Wim.	894	Hnv
Wm.	833	Nrf
Wm.	900	Nrf
Wm.	753	Wsh
Zachariah	260	Frf
Garett see Gasett		
Garland, Benja. N. [2]	390	Rch
Christopher	656	Glc
Christopher	795	Nrf
Clifton	180	Alb
Daniel	390	Rch
David	69	Chr
David, Amherst	696	Nls
David, jr.	343	Lnn
David, Sr.	342	Lnn
David S.	285	Amh
Edward	158	Alb
Elizabeth	158	Alb
Elizabeth	463	Mdd
Fanny	346	Lnc
George T.	396	Rch
Hudson M.	283	Amh
James	159	Alb
James P.	268	Amh
Jane	158	Alb
Jeremiah	394	Rch
Jno. B.	463	Mdd
John	395	Rch
Martha	69	Chr
Mary	391	Rch
Mary	404	Rch
Overton	158	Alb
Rice	159	Alb
Spotswood	695	Nls
Vincent	392	Rch
Garlick, George	746	Wsh
John	667	Mnt
Garlington, Lucy	981	Nrt
Nancy	981	Nrt
Garlow, Andw.	501	Mnn
Jno.	501	Mnn
Garmon, Jacob	646	Mnt
William	760	Hmp
Garmong, Christian	603	Frd
Garner, Andrew	293	Ldn
Ann	773	Wst
Arthur	268	Ldn
Daniel	772	Wst
Dianna	386	Fqr
Edmd.	36	Clp
Edward	97	Spt
Eliza	772	Wst
Elizabeth	579	Frd
Frances	500	Prw
G. G.	624	Btt
George	158	Alb

Name	Ref	Co
George	604	Frd
Hannah	773	Wst
James	304	Ldn
James, Sr.	654	Mnt
Jereh.	624	Btt
Jeremiah	239	Ldn
Jesse	36	Clp
Jesse	393	Rch
John	626	Btt
John	561	Frd
John	667	Mnt
Jonas	37	Clp
Jos.	312	Ldn
Joseph	285	Amh
Joseph	551	Brk
Joseph	37	Clp
Joshua	18	Oho
Lucy	393	Rch
Mahlon	279	Ldn
Presley	981	Nrt
Rachel	773	Wst
Richard	179	Alb
Samuel	982	Nrt
Samuel	215	Shn
Samuel	773	Wst
Samuel, Senr.	773	Wst
Tho., Jr.	347	Lnc
Thomas	370	Fqr
Thomas	834	Wth
Thophelus	37	Clp
Vincent	35	Clp
William	561	Frd
William	527	Prw
William	728	Wsh
William	772	Wst
Willis	772	Wst
Wm.	36	Clp
Wm.	502	Mnn
see Farner, Gamer		
Garnes, Joseph	624	Gls
Garnet, Armstead	823	Bck
James	787	Bck
James	754	Nwk
Jas.	34	Clp
John	50	Chr
Joseph	107	Spt
Lewis	823	Bck
Natthanl.	787	Bck
Phillip	89	Spt
Reuben	34	Clp
Robt.	34	Clp
Stephen	801	Bck
Thomas	786	Bck
William	813	Bck
Garnett, Frances	164	Knq
Grace, Mrs.	223	Ess
Grace ..., Miss	223	Ess
Henry	197	Ess
Henry	164	Knq
James	194	Alb
James	164	Knq
James ...	223	Ess
James J.	903	Crl
Jno. J.	163	Knq
John	387	Mds
John M.	223	Ess
M...	223	Ess
Majr. T.	10	Hnr
Martin	537	Frd
Musco, [his] estate	905	Crl
Reuben	218	Ess
Reuben M.	165	Knq
Robert	904	Crl
Robert	196	Ess
Susanna	500	Prw
Thomas	165	Knq
Thomas	34	Stf
Wm.	36	Clp
Wm.	196	Ess
see ...tt		
Garnhart, Henry	61	Jff
Garr see Gaar		
Garrat, Charles	779	Bck
Garratt, John	900	Nrf
Garret, Charles	24	Acc
Henry	233	Ldn
Sarrah	326	Dnw
Garrett, ...h [Isaiah?]	462	Bdf
Aaron	280	Ldn
Aaron	316	Ldn
Alexander	195	Alb
Allexander	124	Cmb
Benjamin	193	Shn
David	168	Shn
Elijah	869	Cmp
Elizabeth	554	Frd
Enos	314	Ldn
George	463	Mdd
Henry	715	Wsh
Isaac	165	Knq
Jacob	591	Frd
James	164	Knq
John	881	Cmp
John	464	Mdd
John	38	Rcm
John	872	Yrk
John C.	165	Knq
Joseph	276	Ldn
Laurence	537	Frd
Luke	591	Frd
Marry	463	Mdd
Patsy	904	Crl
Richd.	872	Yrk
Richd., Jr., (W)	872	Yrk
Richd. G.	163	Knq
Robert	512	Prw
Robert, Snr.	164	Knq
Sarah	277	Ldn
Silas	503	Frn
Stephen H.	211	Ess
Thomas	276	Ldn
Thos.	164	Knq
Thos.	747	Wsh
William	462	Bdf
William	903	Crl
William	14	Rcm
William, Snr.	163	Knq
Wm.	202	Ess
Wm., jr.	164	Knq
Wm. T. [?]	164	Knq
see Gaerrett		
Garriot, Keziah	456	Pra
Garriott, Ann	387	Mds
Jas.	35	Clp
Moses	386	Mds
Moses	418	Mds
Reuben	35	Clp
Robt.	37	Clp
Garrison, Aaron	43	Stf
Abel	25	Acc
Abram	624	Gls
Achillis	194	Alb
Bengamin	790	Hmp
Duannah	194	Alb
Edmond	455	Pra
Elijah	194	Alb
Elizabeth	25	Acc
Elizabeth	22	Stf
Ephraim	371	Fqr
George, jr.	43	Stf
George, Sr.	43	Stf
Henry	839	Nrf
Isiah	26	Acc
James	25	Acc
James	194	Alb
James	22	Stf
Jesse	23	Stf
Jno.	454	Pra
John	25	Acc
John	195	Alb
John	624	Gls
John	23	Stf
Mary	65	Jff
Molly	43	Stf
Moses	599	Frd
Moses	22	Stf
Nehemiah	372	Fqr
Patty	508	Prw
Robert	42	Stf
Samuel	194	Alb
Sarah	25	Acc
Seluda	195	Alb
William	24	Acc
William	194	Alb
William	624	Gls
Zachariah	194	Alb
Garriss, Thomas	449	Grn
Garritson, William M.	358	Fqr
Garrot, Alexander	837	Bck
Joshua	783	Bck
Thomas	783	Bck
Thomas, Jr.	802	Bck
William	782	Bck
see Garrat		
Garrott, Elizabeth	371	Fqr
Frances	50	Chr
Hannah	342	Lnn
James	343	Fqr
James	342	Lnn
John	241	Aml
John	109	Cmb
Mason	343	Lnn
Milley	343	Fqr
Richard	363	Fqr
Wm.	258	Frf
Garrow, John	900	Nrf
John	872	Yrk
Wm.	682	Wrw
Garst, Abm.	626	Btt
Fredk., Jr.	624	Btt
Fredk., Sr.	626	Btt
Jacob	626	Btt
Garten, Spencer	387	Mds
Garth, Elijah	179	Alb
Garland	195	Alb
Jessee	194	Alb
Thomas	194	Alb
Thomas	195	Alb
Gartin, Griffy	567	Mnr
Hugh	565	Mnr
Mary	573	Mnr
Nathl.	582	Mnr
Garton, Thomas	195	Alb
Garvel, Jacob	936	Hrr
Garven, Joseph	438	Bth
Garver, Arthur	462	Bdf
John	548	Brk
Garvin, James	24	Oho
Richard	257	Amh
Richard	277	Amh
Saml.	581	Mnr
Garvis, John	934	Hrr
Garwood, Josh.	625	Btt
Gary, --- [2]	329	Dnw
Benjamin	638	Sss
Daniel	904	Crl
Jack	330	Dnw
James	754	Nwk
Permelia	549	Prg
Richard	538	Prg
Sterling	547	Prg
Thomas E.	326	Dnw
Thos.	547	Prg
Gasett, Samuel	274	Ldn
Gaskin, John	19	Isw
Gaskings, Thomas	901	Nrf
Gaskins, Bartholomew	463	Bdf
David	395	Rch
Edward, jr.	981	Nrt
Edward, Sr.	981	Nrt

Geo. S.	455	Pra	Gathright, Absolom	128	Cmb	Susanna	33	Isw
Henry L.	982	Nrt	Jno.	879	Hnv	William	841	Bck
Isaac	40	Stf	Obediah	8	Hnr	William	35	Isw
Jas.	827	Nrf	Wm.	693	Gch	William	853	Sth
Jas.	454	Pra	Gathwright, Anselom	121	Hnr	Wm.	694	Gch
Jessee	501	Mnn	Ansolem	129	Hnr	Gayle, George	438	Mth
John H.	419	Fqr	Claiborne	128	Hnr	Hundley	446	Mth
Joseph	981	Nrt	Josiah	127	Hnr	Jno.	36	Clp
Mary	97	Acc	Judith	129	Hnr	Jno. T.	655	Glc
Milly	28	Isw	Robert	754	Nwk	John	903	Crl
Phillis	26	Acc	Saml.	121	Hnr	John	196	Ess
Ralph	595	Frd	Wm.	126	Hnr	John	440	Mth
Richard	981	Nrt	Gatnell, Simon	585	Brk	John	441	Mth
Spencer	981	Nrt	Gatrill, Stephen	22	Oho	John	872	Yrk
Thomas	981	Nrt	Gatwood, John	676	Br	Jos.	656	Glc
William	97	Acc	William	676	Br	Joshua, jr.	440	Mth
Gasquet, Francis	329	Dnw	Gaty, Jeremiah	624	Btt	Joshua, Sr.	446	Mth
Gass, Benjamin	696	Br	Gauden, John	195	Alb	Josiah	440	Mth
Henry	691	Br	Gauder, Samuel	593	Frd	Leaven	446	Mth
John	691	Br	Gaufhill, Benj.	26	Hnr	Mathew, Sr.	438	Mth
Gassaway, John	65	Jff	Gaugh, Adam	306	Ldn	Miles	437	Mth
Thomas	65	Jff	Thomas	192	Shn	Robert	49	Chr
Gaston, Andrew	953	Hrr	Gaughney, ---, Tem-			Thomas	50	Chr
John	940	Hrr	ple &	21	Hnr	Younger	892	Hnv
John	953	Hrr	Gaulding, Alexander	569	Pre	Gaylor, Edwd.	269	Rck
William	11	Oho	Jesse	567	Pre	John	269	Rck
Gates, Alex.	57	Chs	Jno.	883	Hnv	Nathl.	304	Rck
Charles	795	Hmp	John	567	Pre	Geanniny, Anthoney	157	Alb
Elias	15	Wod	John	569	Pre	Gear, Hosea	696	Br
Eppas	15	Pwh	Joseph	568	Pre	Gearen, Isaac	856	Hnv
James, jr.	53	Chs	Richard	568	Pre	Gearheart, Lenard	476	Frn
John	50	Chr	Gaulph, John	347	Fqr	Vallintine	450	Frn
John	52	Chs	Lucey	408	Fqr	Geddy, E., Mrs.	332	Dnw
Js., Senr.	57	Chs	Verlinda	408	Fqr	Robt.	9	Isw
Martin	624	Btt	Gault, Alexr., (W)	889	Yrk	William	753	Nwk
Rd.	57	Chs	Ann M.	25	Acc	Wm. W.	329	Dnw
Saml.	258	Frf	Gaumon, Betsy	800	Nrf	Gee, Bailey	146	Dnw
Thomas	257	Frf	see Gammon			Benjamin	749	Brn
Thomas	258	Frf	Gaunt, James, for Jno.			Benjamin	341	Lnn
Wm.	61	Chs	Gilliland	624	Btt	Benjamin	342	Lnn
Wm., sen.	62	Chs	John, Jr.	587	Frd	Catharine	342	Lnn
Gatewood, Andrew	438	Bth	Joseph	624	Btt	Charles	343	Lnn
Bartlett	903	Crl	Mary	35	Clp	Charles	537	Prg
Bartlett	904	Crl	Susanna	904	Crl	Drury	342	Lnn
Benja.	201	Ess	William	26	Stf	Ephraim	128	Sth
Bernard	95	Spt	Gauntz, George	601	Frd	George	342	Lnn
Chany	164	Knq	Gausney, Gabriel	294	Amh	Henery, jr.	343	Lnn
China	904	Crl	Richd.	35	Clp	Hennery	342	Lnn
Edmund	903	Crl	Gaw, John	246	Shn	Henry	638	Sss
Eliza.	221	Ess	Robert	246	Shn	James	342	Lnn
Elizabeth	904	Crl	Gawen, Alexander	772	Wst	James	860	Sth
Gabriel	204	Ess	Gawin, John	345	Ags	James S.	342	Lnn
Henry	68	Spt	see Guin			Jerry	342	Lnn
James	260	Amh	Gawthney, James	125	Hnr	Jessee, Sr.	342	Lnn
James	903	Crl	Gay, Charles	120	Hnr	John	712	Brn
James	223	Ess	Charles	125	Hnr	John	146	Dnw
John	903	Crl	Chloe	24	Isw	John	537	Prg
John	215	Shn	Edmond	638	Sss	Joshua	387	Mds
John, Senr.	904	Crl	Everett	196	Alb	Lucas	342	Lnn
Joseph	165	Knq	Henry	17	Isw	Nevil	342	Lnn
Joseph	68	Spt	Henry	46	Isw	Reubin	342	Lnn
Kemp	207	Ess	James	853	Sth	Robert	712	Brn
Lewis	219	Ess	Jerh.	853	Sth	Robert	146	Dnw
Philemon	900	Nrf	Jesse	46	Isw	Sarah S.	341	Lnn
Philip	905	Crl	Jno., esq.	296	Rck	Tabitha	749	Brn
Philip	221	Ess	Joseph, bound for a term			Thomas	343	Lnn
Philip	164	Knq	of years	448	Bth	Wilson	342	Lnn
Ransom	5	Knw	Joshua	46	Isw	Wm.	146	Dnw
Reubin	282	Amh	Mary	444	Bth	Geens, Josh.	933	Hrr
Richard	903	Crl	Mat [crossed out]	501	Mnn	Geer, ...as. [Chas. ?]	286	Rck
Robert	165	Knq	Mills	17	Isw	Geerhart, Henry	284	Rck
Salley	163	Knq	Nancy	638	Sss	Lewis	284	Rck
Sally	204	Ess	Robert	423	Bth	Geheagan, James	470	Frn
Thomas	220	Ess	Robert	295	Rck	Gehealer see Behealer		
Thos.	900	Nrf	Robt.	295	Rck	Gelbager, William	945	Chc
Travis	207	Ess	Saml.	3	Rcm	Gelbrith, Thomas	702	Wsh
William	438	Bth	Samuel	442	Bth	Gelding, John	900	Nrf
William	903	Crl	Samuel	47	Isw	Gelfellen, James	3	Oho
William, jr.	164	Knq	Sihon	638	Sss	Gellasby, Archelus	157	Alb
Wm., S. to J.	164	Knq	Simon	638	Sss	Gelleland, Nathan	422	Msn

Gellett, See.	32	Hnr	Richard	780	Hmp	Alexander [2]	462	Bdf
Gellum, Cornelieus	158	Alb	Sarah	19	Acc	Alexander	64	Chs
John	159	Alb	Sp.	346	Lnc	Aron	502	Mnn
Pleasant	157	Alb	Stephen	170	Shn	Charles	57	Jff
Gengrey, Tobias	626	Btt	Tho.	346	Lnc	Charles	387	Mds
Gennings, Sally	753	Nwk	Tho. M.	346	Lnc	China, (FB)	454	Pra
Genniny, Nicholass	157	Alb	Thomas	343	Lnn	Churchill	387	Mds
Gent, Jno.	247	Ldn	William	862	Cmp	David	463	Bdf
Gentry, Benajah	159	Alb	William	50	Chr	Edward	856	Cmp
Benjamin	164	Knq	William	384	Fqr	Elizabeth	62	Chs
Charles	894	Hnv	William	574	Frd	Frances	55	Jff
Christopher	194	Alb	William	464	Mdd	Francis	749	Brn
Clabon	158	Alb	William	981	Nrt	Gabriel	26	Isw
David	905	Crl	William	48	Stf	Gilbert	462	Bdf
David	895	Hnv	Wilmouth	379	Fqr	Henry	762	Yrk
Gadis	845	Hnv	Wm.	694	Gch	James	232	Ldn
Henry	848	Hnv	Wm.	503	Mnn	James	387	Mds
Jaik	895	Hnv	Wm., Junior	22	Oho	Jane	849	Cmp
James	158	Alb	Wm., (L.)	346	Lnc	Jno.	58	Chs
James	195	Alb	Wm., SM	347	Lnc	Jno.	64	Chs
Jas.	343	Ags	Wm. H.	347	Lnc	Jno.	655	Glc
Jno.	858	Hnv	Zamoth	347	Lnc	Jno. H.	258	Frf
John	194	Alb	see McGeorge			John	462	Bdf
Lucy	158	Alb	Gerald, Henry	829	Nrf	John	147	Dnw
Maryann	849	Hnv	Jonathan	241	Aml	John	10	Isw
Matthew	893	Hnv	Gerard, David	531	Brk	Luman	422	Msn
Nicholass	158	Alb	David	533	Brk	Matthew	62	Chs
Robert	857	Hnv	Matthew	534	Brk	Matthew	569	Pre
Wim.	895	Hnv	Gerden, Dunbar	955	Chc	Matthew, Botetourt	655	Glc
Wm.	114	Hnr	Gerhart, John	343	Ags	Michael	25	Rcm
George, Ann	900	Nrf	Germain, Lewis, (Y)	872	Yrk	Nancy	62	Chs
Bailey	382	Fqr	Peter	901	Nrf	Peter	856	Cmp
Bailey	346	Lnc	Gerrell, Francis	631	Mnt	Prymas	117	Spt
Benjamin	360	Fqr	Gershoa, Jonathan	542	Brk	Ralph	24	Isw
Benjamin	512	Prw	Gerstin see Gustin			Robert	462	Bdf
Betsey	982	Nrt	Gervese, Mary	681	Wrw	Robt.	13	Isw
Betsy, T.	347	Lnc	Gervin, James	457	Frn	Sally	712	Brn
Bidear	346	Lnc	Geslard, ---	901	Nrf	Stafford	50	Chr
Bird	126	Hnr	Gest see Gent			Thomas	34	Isw
Bird	754	Nwk	Getts, Barnet	232	Shn	William	241	Aml
Cathe.	626	Btt	Geurrant, Elizabeth	118	Cmb	William	462	Bdf
Charles D.	19	Ntt	Gevoden, John	838	Bck	William	463	Bdf
Cooper, F.N.	165	Knq	Joseph	808	Bck	William	26	Isw
Eliza L.	347	Lnc	Gew, Peggey	267	Amh	William, Jr.	463	Bdf
Eliza., D.	347	Lnc	Rosemery	267	Amh	Wm.	24	Hnr
Elizabeth	128	Hnr	Gewerant see Geurrant			Wm.	682	Wrw
Elizh.	284	Ldn	Ghant, Martin	8	Oho	Zachariah	387	Mds
Enoch	346	Lnc	Gheen, James	242	Ldn	Giberne, Mary	395	Rch
Fielding	384	Fqr	Thomas	242	Ldn	Gibron see Gibrons		
Foits.	347	Lnc	Thos.	318	Ldn	Gibrons, Jno., quarter	259	Frf
Geriemiah	749	Brn	Wm.	310	Ldn	Gibson, Abnor	301	Ldn
Harrison	347	Lnc	Ghent, Francis	146	Dnw	Amos	240	Ldn
Isaac	347	Lnc	Peter	146	Dnw	Charles	464	Mdd
James	780	Hmp	Thos., Senr.	146	Dnw	D.	342	Ags
Jesemine	97	Acc	Gholson, Jane	712	Brn	David	236	Ldn
Jesse	258	Ldn	Thomas	712	Brn	Dicey	571	Mnr
Jessee	431	Msn	Wm.	712	Brn	Elizabeth	107	Cmb
Jno.	38	Clp	Giar, John	246	Shn	Eubank	164	Knq
Jno.	346	Lnc	Gibans, Isaac	250	Shn	Francis	90	Jff
Jno.	284	Ldn	Gibb, David	833	Wth	Geo.	240	Ldn
Joe	26	Acc	George	25	Acc	George	26	Acc
John	387	Mds	James	833	Wth	George	6	Oho
John	22	Oho	William	26	Acc	George	16	Oho
John	638	Sss	Gibbens see Giberne			George	86	Spt
Joseph	330	Dnw	Gibbins, Abel	410	Ags	Hugh, Christiansburg	619	Mnt
Joseph	382	Fqr	Peter	568	Pre	James	688	Br
Lewis	903	Crl	Gibbon, Edmond	639	Sss	James	756	Hmp
Lewis	332	Dnw	James	5	Hnr	James	5	Wod
Lucy	147	Dnw	James	639	Sss	Jeduthon	753	Nwk
Marcus	328	Dnw	Jas.	502	Mnn	Jno.	342	Ags
Martin	345	Lnc	John	200	Kng	Jno.	346	Lnc
Martin, Jr.	347	Lnc	Gibbons, Cornelius	513	Frd	Joanna	476	Frn
Mary	387	Mds	Gilbert	54	Jff	John	425	Bth
Mat	501	Mnn	Jacob	546	Frd	John	539	Brk
Moses	346	Lnc	Lawe., (Y)	875	Yrk	John	207	Ess
Parker	97	Acc	Moses	76	Jff	John	369	Fqr
Patsey	463	Mdd	Ro., (Y)	875	Yrk	John	413	Fqr
Presley	384	Fqr	Stephen	293	Ldn	John	473	Frn
Reuben	547	Frd	Gibbs, Alexander	461	Bdf	John	610	Mnt
Reuben	570	Mnr				John	499	Prw

Name	No.	Co.	Name	No.	Co.	Name	No.	Co.
John	417	Rnd	Samuel	772	Wst	Presly	41	Stf
John	282	Rck	Stephen	502	Mnn	Rhody	62	Chs
John, Decd.	524	Prw	Thomas	196	Alb	Richard	513	Prw
John, J.	241	Ldn	William	772	Wst	Robert	6	Wod
Jonathan	395	Fqr	Zacha.	241	Aml	Sarah	981	Nrt
Levi	240	Ldn	Gilbirt, Saml.	729	Wsh	Susan	947	Chc
Levi	503	Mnn	Gilbort, John	535	Brk	Thomas	52	Stf
Lucy	889	Hnv	Gilchrist, Charles	881	Cmp	Thos.	525	Brk
Margaret	198	Ess	George	302	Rck	Vaden	55	Chs
Martha	569	Pre	Jack, (F.N.)	26	Isw	William	17	Oho
Mary	364	Fqr	Jno.	67	Chs	Winder	982	Nrt
Mary J.	655	Glc	Samuel	568	Pre	Wm.	55	Chs
Milly	86	Spt	Gilcoat, Roberson L.,			Gillam, Fanny	145	Sth
Moses	38	Clp	Doct.	423	Rnd	Martha	145	Sth
Moses	240	Ldn	Gilder, Daniel	270	Ldn	Wim.	869	Hnv
Mosses	439	Flv	Gilding see Eelding			Gillasby, Daniel	486	Frn
Nathan	888	Hnv	Giles, Benjamin	568	Pre	Evan	486	Frn
Patrick	280	Rck	Cannon	67	Chs	Gillaspie, Robt.	625	Btt
Phebe	240	Ldn	James	248	Ldn	Simon	625	Btt
Randolph	158	Alb	John	263	Amh	Gillaspy, Alexander	442	Bth
Randolph	159	Alb	John	345	Ags	David	447	Flv
Richard	164	Knq	Josiah	568	Pre	Jacob, Jur.	421	Bth
Rob	502	Mnn	Mary	676	Br	Jacob, Ser.	421	Bth
Robert	568	Pre	Sarah	67	Chs	John	444	Bth
Robert B.	107	Cmb	William	305	Amh	John	446	Bth
Robt.	901	Nrf	William	568	Pre	John [2]	447	Bth
Saml.	344	Ags	William B.	241	Aml	Nelly	418	Bth
Saml., jr.	344	Ags	Wm.	503	Mnn	Thomas	443	Bth
Sarah	514	Frd	see Jiles			William	194	Alb
Solomon	240	Ldn	Gilespee, Samuel	13	Knw	William	196	Alb
Stephen	344	Ags	Gilfin, John	773	Hmp	William	418	Bth
Thomas	677	Br	Gilham, Wm.	655	Mnt	William E.	195	Alb
Thomas	383	Fqr	Gilingwaters, Thomas	302	Amh	see Cillaspy		
Thos.	37	Clp	Gilkerson, David	344	Ags	Gillatt, James	98	Acc
Thos.	502	Mnn	David	401	Ags	William	25	Acc
William	402	Fqr	Francis	344	Ags	Gillchrist, Jack	334	Dnw
William	476	Frn	Henry	342	Ags	Gilleland, John	426	Bth
William, Jr.	413	Fqr	John	344	Ags	Gillenwaters, Elijah	752	Wsh
William, Sr.	413	Fqr	Wm.	344	Ags	John	718	Wsh
Willm.	636	Mnt	Gilkeson, John	542	Frd	Joshua	491	Frn
Wm.	347	Lnc	Gill, ---, Mrs.	334	Dnw	Gillespie, Andrew	16	Oho
Wm.	301	Rck	...	306	Rck	Daniel	16	Oho
Wm.	302	Rck	...y	305	Rck	Gillespy, John	677	Br
see Gisbon			Benja. [2]	55	Chs	Gillet, Hannah	889	Yrk
Giddens, Ishmael, (Y?)	875	Yrk	Betsey	328	Dnw	Gilliam, ---, Doctr.	141	Dnw
Rose	24	Acc	Charles	462	Bdf	Allen	50	Chr
Giddy, Nanny	326	Dnw	Daniel	239	Ldn	Ansalem	639	Sss
Peter	268	Ldn	Daniel	981	Nrt	Archerbald	271	Amh
Gideons, Kesiah	900	Nrf	Eli	982	Nrt	Burwell	638	Sss
Gidley, Jno.	501	Mnn	Elizabeth	940	Chc	Carter	639	Sss
Giffen, Danil	6	Oho	Ellis	981	Nrt	Charles	838	Bck
John	6	Oho	Erossum	358	Fqr	David	573	Frd
Robert	5	Oho	Ezekiah	981	Nrt	Eliza.	146	Sth
Giffin, William	554	Frd	George	981	Nrt	Elizabeth	638	Sss
Giffird, John	905	Hrr	George	392	Rch	Epaphroditus	754	Nwk
Gifford, John	924	Hrr	Good	55	Chs	Frances	754	Nwk
Giffy, Benjamin	679	Br	Harrison	461	Bdf	Heartwell	638	Sss
Giford, Benj.	967	Hrr	Hennery	341	Lnn	Henry R.	639	Sss
Gigle, Cristin	930	Hrr	Iham	62	Chs	Isham	784	Bck
Gilbert, Amos	12	Wod	Isaac	17	Hnr	James	852	Cmp
Aquilla	880	Cmp	Jacob	60	Chs	James	4	Pwh
Elizth.	901	Nrf	James	382	Fqr	James	856	Sth
Ezekiel	284	Amh	James	901	Nrf	James S.	330	Dnw
Ezekiel, jr.	304	Amh	James	517	Prw	Jarrett	265	Amh
Henry	291	Amh	James, Junr.	258	Frf	Jas. J.	549	Prg
Henry	60	Jff	James C.	981	Nrt	Jas. S.	20	Ntt
Humphrey	281	Amh	Jane	695	Nls	Jeffery	955	Chc
James	901	Nrf	Jeremiah	276	Ldn	Jno.	550	Prg
James	639	Sss	John	463	Bdf	John	265	Amh
Jos.	503	Mnn	John	367	Fqr	John	814	Bck
Joseph	500	Prw	John	63	Jff	John	50	Chr
Joseph	527	Prw	John	981	Nrt	John	186	Elc
Josias	538	Prg	John	982	Nrt	John	638	Sss
Kemuel	455	Frn	John	42	Stf	John, jr.	693	Gch
Mary	296	Amh	John	57	Stf	John, (S. Jno.)	780	Bck
Micheal	455	Frn	John, Jr.	367	Fqr	John, Senr.	693	Gch
Nancy	695	Nls	Lucy	950	Chc	John M.	50	Chr
Nathan	579	Frd	Mitchel	50	Chr	Merewether S.	147	Dnw
Natl.	342	Ags	Nathaniel	602	Frd	Patsy	639	Sss
Polly	695	Nls	Phillip	342	Lnn	Polly	639	Sss

Richard	803	Bck	Robt.	346	Lnc	Glaisbrook, James	754	Nwk
Richard C.	840	Bck	Robt.	289	Rck	James, junr.	754	Nwk
Richd.	176	Elc	Saml.	17	Rcm	Glascock, Chas.	501	Mnn
Robt.	129	Sth	Thomas	41	Rcm	Downing	241	Ldn
Ruben M.	548	Prg	William	12	Oho	Downing	263	Ldn
Samuel	712	Brn	Wm. G.	289	Rck	Eli	262	Ldn
Susanna	829	Bck	Gilock, John	247	Shn	Jno.	501	Mnn
Walter B.	548	Prg	Gilpin, Edward	823	Hmp	Mary	411	Rch
William	50	Chr	Frances	462	Bdf	Milton S.	400	Rch
William	606	Srr	James	402	Fqr	Richard M.	392	Rch
William	638	Sss	John	462	Bdf	Robert	407	Rch
William	639	Sss	William	462	Bdf	Thomas M.	407	Rch
Wm.	875	Yrk	William	78	Jff	Washington	397	Rch
see Harrup, McLemore			Gilron see Gibron			Wm.	241	Ldn
Gilliann, Kitty	548	Prg	Gilson, Wm.	747	Wsh	Glascow, Jos.	798	Nrf
Gilliat, John	342	Ags	Gimbo, James	80	Spt	Glasgoe, John	24	Oho
Gilliatt, Betsey	863	Hnv	Ginger, Lodowich	282	Rck	Glasgow, Arthur	268	Rck
Gillies, William	333	Dnw	Ginnatte, Thos.	852	Hnv	Joseph	833	Wth
Gillihand see Gilliland			Ginnewey, Money	740	Wsh	Glaspin, John	96	Acc
Gilliland, Davd.	715	Wsh	Ginnins, Frances	38	Clp	Glaspy, Nelly	956	Hrr
James	693	Wsh	Joseph	38	Clp	Glass, Charles	877	Cmp
Jas.	715	Wsh	Gint see Grist			David	694	Gch
Jas., Sr.	624	Btt	Gipson, John	780	Bck	David	754	Nwk
Jno.	624	Btt	John	742	Wsh	Elizabeth	98	Spt
Saml.	625	Btt	Labon	802	Bck	Esther	692	Brk
William	432	Msn	Miles	781	Bck	James	860	Cmp
William	568	Pre	Nicholas	911	Hrr	James	439	Flv
Gilliott, Martha	13	Hnr	P.	33	Hnr	James	547	Frd
Gillis, Wm.	958	Hrr	William	784	Bck	James	694	Nls
Gillison, John	357	Fqr	William	825	Bck	James	833	Wth
Sarah	414	Fqr	Girenger, David	581	Brk	John	435	Flv
Gillispie, George	567	Pre	Jacob	581	Brk	John	693	Gch
James	568	Pre	Gisbon, Joel	455	Pra	John	696	Nls
William, Est.	568	Pre	Gish, Abraham	624	Btt	Joseph	575	Frd
Gillium, Archellus	862	Cmp	David	626	Btt	Joseph	6	Wod
Mary	463	Bdf	George, Jr.	626	Btt	Js.	432	Flv
Gillman, Susanna	509	Prw	George, Sr.	626	Btt	Martin	693	Gch
Gillmore, Wm.	294	Ldn	Jacob, Jr.	626	Btt	Nancy	487	Frn
Gillock, Thomas	157	Alb	Jacob, Sr.	626	Btt	Robert	6	Oho
Thomas	158	Alb	John	626	Btt	Robert	23	Rcm
Gillrick see Gilluck			Gist, George	676	Br	Robert D.	574	Frd
Gills, Anderson	14	Ntt	James	677	Br	Samuel	574	Frd
Anthony	7	Ntt	Samuel	675	Br	Thom, Ju.	696	Nls
Eliza.	241	Aml	Given, Adam	414	Bth	Thomas	694	Nls
James	241	Aml	Henry	415	Bth	Thos.	894	Hnv
William	784	Bck	James	7	Knw	Thos.	827	Nrf
Gilluck, Robert	195	Alb	see Givens			Vincent	877	Cmp
Gillum, Elisha D.	195	Alb	Givens, Danl.	625	Btt	Vincent	37	Clp
Frederick	194	Alb	Elisha	625	Btt	William	864	Cmp
James	194	Alb	George	7	Knw	Wm., Sr.	436	Flv
James	568	Pre	Isiah	625	Gls	see Cluff		
James, Senr.	568	Pre	James	346	Ags	Glassburn, Davd., Jr.	625	Btt
Jno.	233	Ldn	Joseph	626	Btt	David, Sr.	625	Btt
John	195	Alb	Thos.	345	Ags	Glasscock, Agga	370	Fqr
John	568	Pre	William	8	Knw	Asa	396	Fqr
Rebecca	194	Alb	Willm.	624	Btt	Asa, (of Jno.)	397	Fqr
Gilmam, Edmund	857	Hnv	see Given			Benjamin	396	Fqr
Gilman, ...muel	168	Shn	Givins, John	345	Ags	Benjamin	599	Frd
Dickey	855	Hnv	Givon, Nancy	433	Bth	Charles	361	Fqr
Ezra	36	Clp	Robert	433	Bth	Daniel	396	Fqr
Jno.	899	Hnv	Samuel	433	Bth	Eli	36	Clp
Gilmer, George	196	Alb	see Gwin			Francis	551	Frd
Jac.	502	Mnn	Gl...well, Drury, overseer for			George	395	Fqr
John	182	Alb	H. Haxall	147	Dnw	George	773	Wst
Joseph	157	Alb	Gladden, Mildred	626	Btt	Gregory	396	Fqr
Gilmon, William	14	Hnr	Richd.	39	Rcm	Hezekiah, Jr.	395	Fqr
Gilmor, John	624	Btt	Saml.	297	Ldn	Hezekiah, Sr.	395	Fqr
Matw.	503	Mnn	Gladding, Geo	25	Acc	James	396	Fqr
Gilmore, Gad	41	Rcm	George	96	Acc	Jesse	394	Fqr
George	37	Rcm	Jesse	96	Acc	John, Jr.	366	Fqr
Henry	15	Rcm	Jesse	97	Acc	John, Senr.	395	Fqr
Hugh	425	Msn	John	96	Acc	Joseph	398	Fqr
James	124	Hnr	John	96	Acc	Moses	395	Fqr
James	269	Rck	Polly	97	Acc	Noah	397	Fqr
Jno. M.	346	Lnc	Rebecca	97	Acc	Peter	398	Fqr
John	269	Rck	Gladish, Benjamin	712	Brn	Peter	535	Frd
John	16	Rcm	Gladman, Molly [crossed			Thomas	388	Fqr
Joseph	273	Rck	out]	464	Mdd	Thomas, Sr.	389	Fqr
Richd., Mulo.	164	Knq	Gladstone, Arthur	408	Fqr	Uriel	397	Fqr
Ro., (free mulotto)	656	Glc	Gladwell, John	42	Rcm	William	388	Fqr

Name	No.	Abbr.	Name	No.	Abbr.	Name	No.	Abbr.
Glasscok, Silas	80	Jff	Gloyd, James	791	Hmp	Katharine	27	Isw
Glassell, Andrew	386	Mds	Samuel	783	Hmp	Nicholas P.	96	Acc
James	386	Mds	Gluver, John	965	Hrr	Patienc	825	Nrf
John	386	Mds	Glyn, Patrick	624	Btt	Robert	831	Nrf
Glassford, Alexander	93	Jff	Glynn, Cornelius	113	Hnr	Saml.	871	Sth
Glassgow, Henry	304	Ldn	Jno.	16	Hnr	Samuel	10	Isw
Glaudon, James	833	Wth	John	606	Mnt	Willis	831	Nrf
Glaze, Condrod	794	Hmp	Saml.	25	Rcm	see Counsil, Goodwin		
George	577	Frd	Go..., Fred	463	Bdf	Goe, Richard	13	Oho
George	226	Pnd	Goalder, Christopher	655	Glc	Thomas	6	Oho
Wandle	88	Jff	Goall, Jacob	545	Brk	Goee, John	462	Bdf
Glazebrook, Jno.	859	Hnv	Goar, Henry	625	Gls	Goff, Abram	625	Btt
Richard	859	Hnv	Robert	625	Gls	Allexander	429	Rnd
Gleanes see Gleaves			Goard, Abraham	462	Bdf	Archer	463	Bdf
Gleason, Robert	838	Nrf	Isam	649	Mnt	Byram	503	Mnn
Gleaves, William	833	Wth	James	649	Mnt	George	423	Rnd
Gleen, John	846	Hnv	Richard	462	Bdf	George E.	745	Wsh
Nathl.	860	Hnv	Goarman, John	527	Prw	Gobe	930	Hrr
William	847	Hnv	Goatier, Nicholas	809	Nrf	Hiriam	416	Rnd
Gleeson, James	901	Nrf	Gobble, Abram, Jur.	751	Wsh	Jas.	502	Mnn
Partrick	164	Knq	Abram, Senr.	751	Wsh	Jas., Jr.	502	Mnn
Susanna	895	Hnv	Christopher	751	Wsh	Jeremiah	462	Bdf
Glen, John	753	Nwk	George	752	Wsh	John	463	Bdf
Glendenning, George	359	Fqr	Isaac	751	Wsh	John	572	Frd
Glendy, Wm.	343	Ags	Isaac, Jur.	752	Wsh	John	752	Wsh
Glenn, Benj.	695	Wsh	Jacob	751	Wsh	John, Jr.	785	Bck
Daniel	569	Pre	John	752	Wsh	John S.	428	Rnd
Davd.	719	Wsh	John	225	Pnd	Josa.	503	Mnn
Edmund	26	Acc	Godby, Francis	620	Mnt	Joseph	462	Bdf
Gideon	568	Pre	John	667	Mnt	Megeher	463	Bdf
Hugh	342	Ags	Willm.	620	Mnt	Philip	67	Chs
James	26	Acc	Goddard, James	687	Br	Thomas	982	Nrt
James	114	Cmb	Goddin, Avery	754	Nwk	Thos.	503	Mnn
James	787	Hmp	Isham	127	Hnr	William	783	Bck
James	90	Jff	Godfree Abel	96	Acc	William, Jr.	802	Bck
James	592	Mnr	Joshua	98	Acc	Wm.	67	Chs
Jas., Sr.	625	Btt	Parker	26	Acc	Zackeriah	752	Wsh
John	401	Ags	Peter	95	Acc	see Goee		
John	114	Hnr	Spencer	98	Acc	Goffigon, Eliza	831	Nrf
Mary	719	Wsh	Godfrey, ---	754	Nwk	Goggin, Pleasant M.	462	Bdf
Matt.	901	Nrf	Alece	802	Nrf	Rachel	462	Bdf
Nathan	105	Cmb	Arthur	454	Pra	Stephen	462	Bdf
Peyton	569	Pre	Caleb	454	Pra	Goggins, Richard	881	Cmp
Robert	853	Hnv	Elizabth.	900	Nrf	Gohsline, James	9	Hnr
Thos.	901	Nrf	John	625	Btt	Gohun, John	624	Btt
William	49	Chr	Landon	503	Prw	Goin, David	904	Crl
William	106	Cmb	Levin	25	Acc	Going, Aaron	694	Nls
Glidewell, Anderson	146	Dnw	Mary	802	Nrf	Benjamin	195	Alb
Glisson, Thos.	501	Mnn	Mathew	455	Pra	David	195	Alb
Gloster, James	257	Frf	Molly	455	Pra	David	196	Alb
Glove, Rich.	278	Rck	Sally	13	Hnr	David	939	Chc
Glover, Amos	502	Mnn	Thos.	800	Nrf	Elizabeth [2]	196	Alb
Ben	502	Mnn	Wm.	811	Nrf	James	821	Bck
Cloe	257	Frf	Wm.	454	Pra	James	49	Chr
Daniel	749	Brn	Wm.	455	Pra	Jessee	196	Alb
Edmund	778	Bck	Wm., Pungo	813	Nrf	John	65	Chr
Elijah	126	Cmb	Wm., Sr.	813	Nrf	Jordan	821	Bck
James	61	Stf	Godfrig, John	905	Hrr	Joseph	256	Frf
Jesse	781	Bck	Godman, Betsey	595	Brk	Joshua	195	Alb
Jesse	149	Sth	Wm.	537	Brk	Phillip	694	Nls
John	775	Bck	Godsay, Wm.	746	Wsh	Sherrod	196	Alb
John	781	Bck	Godsey, Daniel	569	Pre	Thomas	50	Chr
John	833	Bck	Drusilla	98	Cmb	Goings, David	625	Gls
John	127	Cmb	Henry	61	Chs	George, f. negro	257	Frf
Mary	127	Cmb	Jno.	61	Chs	Joseph	292	Ldn
Nic.	501	Mnn	Joel	568	Pre	Luke	288	Ldn
Patrick	607	Srr	Joyce	816	Bck	Richd.	259	Frf
Richard	347	Fqr	Judith	815	Bck	Gold, Aaron	417	Rnd
Robert	35	Isw	Godwin, Anne	27	Isw	Ann	259	Frf
Samuel	779	Bck	Cornl.	274	Rck	Daniel	509	Frd
Thomas	779	Bck	Edmond	13	Isw	Daniel	909	Hrr
Thomas	67	Chs	Edmund	96	Acc	Ebenezer	417	Rnd
Thomas	260	Frf	Holland	26	Isw	Geo.	501	Mnn
Vincin	965	Hrr	James	624	Btt	James	417	Rnd
William	127	Cmb	James	10	Isw	James	262	Rck
William	256	Frf	Jenny	27	Isw	John	62	Jff
William	534	Prg	John	10	Hnr	John	691	Wsh
see Glove, Gluver			Joseph	463	Mdd	Rachl.	900	Nrf
Glovers, Robert	116	Cmb	Joseph, Jun.	30	Isw	Robert	264	Rck
Glovier, Jno.	39	Clp	Joseph, Sen.	26	Isw	Samuel	417	Rnd

Goldberry, John	78	Jff
Goldborough, Robert	832	Nrf
Golden, Charles	566	Brk
John	930	Hrr
Jonothan	17	Wod
Joseph	38	Clp
Michal	528	Frd
Warner	38	Clp
Wm.	36	Clp
Goldenburk, Frederick	2	Oho
Golder, Milly	334	Dnw
Golding, Daniel	900	Nrf
Easter	900	Nrf
James	132	Hnr
Thornton	412	Fqr
Vincent	412	Fqr
see Gelding		
Goldman, Danl.	131	Hnr
Lucy	123	Hnr
Polley	123	Hnr
see Parker		
Goldmon, Marthia	28	Hnr
Goldrick, Benjamin	260	Frf
Goldsberry, David	119	Spt
Edward	77	Jff
Robert	79	Jff
Goldsby, Effiah	278	Amh
Goldsmith, Benona	809	Hmp
John	348	Fqr
John	366	Fqr
Julia	773	Wst
see Chandlee		
Goler, Joseph	345	Ags
Golesby, Thomas	158	Alb
Goley, Jacob	251	Ldn
Goliah, Susannah	97	Acc
Golier, John T.	118	Spt
Golladay, Jacob	174	Shn
Jacob, Junr.	175	Shn
Joseph	174	Shn
see Golliday		
Gollady, David	345	Ags
Golleher, Joel	702	Wsh
John	702	Wsh
Golliday, Jacob, (of C)	174	Shn
Gollihorn, Catharine	60	Stf
Elizabeth	60	Stf
Sarah	56	Stf
Solomon	52	Stf
Solomon, U.	43	Stf
William	569	Pre
William	45	Stf
Golman, Asa	903	Crl
Golobed, Jno.	35	Clp
Gongware, George	6	Rcm
Joseph	5	Rcm
Magdalene	5	Rcm
Gonoe, John	568	Mnr
Gooch, Dabney C.	159	Alb
Francis	269	Amh
Lucy	158	Alb
Robt.	38	Clp
Sampson	157	Alb
William	241	Aml
Willm.	183	Elc
Wm., Senr.	3	Ntt
Goock, Thomas W.	159	Alb
Good, Abraham	813	Hmp
Abraham	231	Shn
Anderson	543	Frd
Ann	165	Knq
Casper	188	Shn
Daniel	386	Mds
Eliza	773	Wst
Francis	625	Btt
Francis P.	624	Btt
George	624	Btt
George	386	Mds
Henry	187	Shn
Henry, (Jr.)	4	Rcm

Henry, (Sen.)	4	Rcm
Jacob	343	Ags
Jacob	4	Rcm
Jacob	232	Shn
Jacob	249	Shn
John	626	Btt
John	265	Rck
John	6	Rcm
Jonas	188	Shn
Joseph	6	Rcm
Joseph	15	Rcm
Martin	626	Btt
Peter	17	Rcm
Peter	193	Shn
Phillip	799	Hmp
Phillis	570	Frd
Saml.	7	Rcm
Samuel	207	Shn
Ths.	27	Hnr
William	231	Shn
see Goud		
Goodal, John	572	Mnr
Goodall, John, (W)	889	Yrk
Jonathan	196	Alb
Parke	844	Hnv
Wm.	901	Nrf
Goodbar, John	270	Rck
Joseph	269	Rck
Goode, Benja.	56	Chs
Bennet	8	Pwh
Bennet, jr.	8	Pwh
Danl.	120	Hnr
David, Jr.	488	Frn
David, Sr.	478	Frn
Edmund	462	Bdf
Edmund	52	Chs
Edward	120	Hnr
Edward, (Est.)	50	Chr
Edwd.	56	Chs
Eliza.	260	Amh
Elizabeth	6	Pwh
Francis	8	Pwh
Hillery	50	Chr
James	463	Mdd
Jno.	65	Chs
John	50	Chr
John	464	Mdd
John	8	Pwh
John	567	Pre
John, Jr.	131	Hnr
John, jr.	7	Pwh
John, Snr.	120	Hnr
John C.	568	Pre
Jos.	57	Chs
Joseph	258	Amh
Joseph	797	Bck
Joseph	146	Dnw
Joseph	125	Hnr
Mac., Capt.	50	Chr
Mackness	241	Aml
Mark	56	Chs
Mary	120	Hnr
Phillip	50	Chr
Rd. B.	67	Chs
Richd.	900	Nrf
Robert	53	Chs
Robt.	57	Chs
Sally	569	Pre
Saml.	125	Hnr
Samuel	450	Frn
Tapley	52	Chs
Thomas	797	Bck
Thomas	50	Chr
Thomas	147	Dnw
Thos.	67	Chs
William	50	Chr
William	568	Pre
Wm.	56	Chs
Wm.	129	Hnr
Wm. E.	147	Dnw

Goodekoontz, Daniel	564	Frd
George	564	Frd
Gooden, John	80	Jff
Sam	501	Mnn
William	159	Alb
Goodhart, Jacob	286	Ldn
Goodin, Charles	512	Prw
Rebecca	212	Shn
William	512	Prw
Gooding, Frank	929	Hrr
John	914	Hrr
John	916	Hrr
Lucy	463	Bdf
Goodloe, Acquillo	903	Crl
Henry, jr.	70	Spt
Henry, Sr.	74	Spt
John	76	Spt
Robert	903	Crl
Sarah	86	Spt
Goodlow, James	268	Ldn
Goodman, Charles	196	Alb
David	463	Bdf
Edmd.	571	Brk
Elisabeth	754	Nwk
George	743	Wsh
George	834	Wth
Hasley	195	Alb
Jeremiah A.	194	Alb
John	463	Bdf
John	862	Cmp
John	441	Flv
Joseph	194	Alb
Joseph	122	Hnr
Joseph	131	Hnr
Nathan	159	Alb
Noton	104	Cmb
Philip	626	Btt
Phillip	626	Btt
Richard	847	Hnv
Roling	195	Alb
Saml.	275	Rck
Thomas	129	Hnr
Thos.	120	Cmb
William	15	Pwh
Zachariah	102	Cmb
see Godman, Gooman		
Goodmon, Jacob	744	Wsh
Goodnight, Chrisley	237	Shn
John	344	Ags
Samuel	567	Brk
Goodpasture, William	834	Wth
Goodrich, Abednego	607	Srr
Ann	748	Brn
Bell	639	Sss
Charles	35	Isw
Edmund	265	Amh
Fathy	47	Isw
George	16	Oho
James	607	Srr
Jno. B., Christians- burg	619	Mnt
Joseph	594	Frd
Mary	28	Isw
Meshack	607	Srr
Sally	47	Isw
Shadrach	607	Srr
Thomas	607	Srr
Thomas V.	270	Amh
Thos.	146	Dnw
Washington	449	Grn
Wilkins	450	Grn
William C.	639	Sss
Goodridge, Edward	26	Rcm
Lucy	196	Alb
Thads.	345	Lnc
William	981	Nrt
Goodrige, Elizabeth	196	Alb
William	196	Alb
Goodrum, John	450	Grn
Goodson, Henry	35	Isw

John	9	Isw	William	905	Crl	Samuel	551	Frd
John	703	Wsh	Goossman, Abrm.	501	Mnn	Samuel	35	Stf
Jordan	36	Isw	Gophenour, Isaac	238	Ldn	Sarah	663	Mnt
Josiah	36	Isw	Gorbie, Job	15	Oho	Susanna	217	Ess
Mourning	28	Isw	Gordan, Abner	342	Lnn	Susannah	395	Rch
Nicholas	6	Isw	Ann	547	Prg	Thomas	112	Cmb
Robt.	657	Mnt	Archibald	793	Bck	Thomas	17	Rcm
Thomas	27	Isw	Caleb	455	Pra	Thomas	773	Wst
Thos.	656	Mnt	Eliza	335	Dnw	Vincent	218	Ess
Thos., Sr.	657	Mnt	Elizabeth	548	Prg	William	981	Nrt
William	10	Isw	Geo.	297	Rck	William	568	Pre
William	607	Srr	John	462	Bdf	Wm.	558	Brk
Wilson	607	Srr	Gorden, Albin	695	Nls	Wm.	840	Nrf
Goodwin, Bird	274	Rck	Armisted	94	Spt	Wm.	291	Rck
Daniel	260	Frf	Chapman	853	Hnv	Gore, Isaac	197	Shn
David	314	Ldn	Geo.	401	Ags	Jacob	112	Spt
Edmd. C.	873	Hnv	James	256	Frf	James	462	Bdf
Edward	914	Hrr	Jno.	401	Ags	James	565	Mnr
Elizabeth	869	Hnv	Joseph	783	Bck	James	305	Rck
Francis	241	Aml	Nathaniel	106	Spt	Jno.	35	Clp
Francis	261	Amh	Samuel	787	Bck	Jonas	400	Fqr
George	861	Hnv	Samuel	111	Spt	Jos.	261	Ldn
George	32	Isw	William	107	Spt	Joseph	265	Ldn
Gideon	550	Frd	see Gordn			Joseph	289	Ldn
Henry	343	Ags	Gordin, Alexander	246	Shn	Joshua	557	Frd
James	241	Aml	Gording, James	163	Shn	Joshua	311	Ldn
James	858	Hnv	James	164	Shn	Nancy	271	Ldn
James	91	Spt	John	191	Shn	Polley	394	Fqr
Jno.	257	Frf	William	169	Shn	Sampson	97	Acc
John	343	Ags	Gordn, Alexr.	401	Ags	Solomon	569	Frd
John, Sr.	342	Lnn	Gordon, ---	327	Dnw	William	395	Fqr
Johr [John?]	342	Lnn	---	328	Dnw	Wm.	39	Clp
Joseph	343	Ags	---	336	Dnw	see Goee		
Joseph	10	Isw	Alexr.	37	Clp	Gorely, John	686	Br
Joseph	342	Lnn	Andrew	834	Wth	Gorher see Gortier		
Mathew	341	Lnn	Ann	5	Pwh	Gorley, John	518	Frd
Micajah	272	Amh	Bazil	34	Stf	William	58	Jff
Peter	872	Yrk	Betsey	594	Brk	Gorman, Patrick	690	Br
Peter, jr.	889	Yrk	Danl.	68	Chs	Thos.	625	Btt
Peterson	638	Sss	Elizabeth	118	Hnr	Gormley, Bryh.	901	Nrf
Rebecca	867	Hnv	Elizabeth	123	Hnr	Mary	900	Nrf
Reubin	869	Hnv	Elizth.	901	Nrf	Gormon, John	626	Btt
Salley	297	Amh	Francis	57	Chs	Gornto, Amy	454	Pra
Sarah E.	183	Elc	Francis	260	Frf	Arthur	455	Pra
Septimus	345	Ags	Francis	455	Pra	Jno.	454	Pra
Solomon	241	Aml	George	368	Fqr	Martha	455	Pra
Thomas	696	Nls	George	40	Rcm	Reuben	454	Pra
Thomas	111	Spt	Giles	626	Btt	Wm.	455	Pra
Thos.	626	Btt	James	118	Hnr	Wm., Jr.	455	Pra
Warner	299	Amh	James	123	Hnr	Gorrel, William	677	Br
William	256	Frf	James, (Overseer)	390	Fqr	Gorrell, Abraham	97	Jff
William	27	Isw	Jas.	38	Clp	Ralph	21	Oho
William B.	639	Sss	Jas., (Clerk for Col.			Robert	15	Oho
Wim. D.	869	Hnv	Jno. Tayloe)	625	Btt	Robert [2]	21	Oho
Wm.	19	Hnr	Jesse, (F.N.)	32	Isw	Thomas	21	Oho
Wm.	307	Ldn	Jno.	35	Clp	William	21	Oho
see Godwin, Goodson			John	565	Frd	Gorsel, Joseph	511	Brk
Goodwinn, Littleton	903	Crl	John	14	Hnr	Gorthrop, Thomas	944	Hrr
Goodwyn, Armsted	450	Grn	John	5	Pwh	Gortier, Frs.	900	Nrf
Braddock	147	Dnw	John	392	Rch	Gortner, John P.	463	Bdf
Collins	52	Chs	John	41	Rcm	Gortnor, Phillip	624	Btt
Esau	450	Grn	John, (A[?])	396	Rch	Gorum, Henson	254	Ldn
Frances	147	Dnw	John M.	852	Cmp	Goslin, Ezekiel	527	Prw
Joseph	147	Dnw	Jos.	835	Nrf	Gosling, Jesse	259	Frf
Judith	147	Dnw	Louis	900	Nrf	Gosnar see Goznar		
Peterson	147	Dnw	Margerett	366	Fqr	Goss, Amelia	689	Wsh
Peterson	450	Grn	Marshal	37	Clp	Frederick	546	Frd
Stephen	328	Dnw	Martha	626	Btt	George	833	Wth
Stephen, residing in			Nancy	253	Frf	Hammiton	943	Hrr
Petersburg	147	Dnw	Patrick	537	Frd	Henry	89	Spt
Susanna	147	Dnw	Phil	503	Mnn	Jacob	834	Wth
Gooles, Mary	180	Alb	Rachel	218	Ess	John	196	Alb
Gooll see Goall			Rachel	529	Frd	Joseph	96	Spt
Goolrick, John	100	Spt	Richard	118	Cmb	Gossage, David	16	Oho
Goolsberry, Alice	982	Nrt	Richd.	626	Btt	Nicholas	682	Br
Goolsby, Thos. F.	3	Ntt	Robert	900	Nrf	William	680	Br
William	157	Alb	Robt.	11	Hnr	Gossam, John	502	Prw
Gooman, John	739	Wsh	Robt.	122	Hnr	Thompson M.	524	Prw
Gooseman, John	596	Brk	Saml.	1	Oho	Gossel, Matthias	551	Brk
Goosley, Ludwell	875	Yrk	Samuel	386	Fqr	Gosset, Caty	477	Frn

John	477	Frn	Graday, Gregsley	257	Frf	Samuel	575	Mnr
Gossnell, Dawson	462	Frn	Gradey, Edwd.	275	Ldn	Samuel	833	Wth
Gossom, Thomas	257	Frf	Elizabeth	195	Alb	Sandy	511	Frd
Gothard, John	458	Frn	James	275	Ldn	Thomas	434	Bth
John	506	Prw	Jessee	195	Alb	Thos.	342	Ags
Gotobed see Golobed			Joshua	195	Alb	Walter	357	Fqr
Gouch, William	880	Hnv	Thomas	56	Jff	William	578	Mnr
Goud, Wm.	343	Ags	Grady, Ambrose	1	Rcm	William	513	Prw
Gougcher, William	5	Wod	Burrell	625	Btt	William	522	Prw
Gough, Fanny	330	Dnw	George	197	Shn	Wm.	607	Mnt
Rawleigh	37	Clp	John	2	Rcm	see G...ham, Greyham		
William	18	Oho	John	33	Rcm	Graley, Francis	158	Alb
Gouldin, Sally	200	Ess	Michl.	502	Mnn	Grammar, Burwell	19	Ntt
Goulding, Jessee	904	Crl	Nancy	49	Chr	Grammer, John	330	Dnw
John	903	Crl	Rebecca	905	Crl	John, jr.	537	Prg
John	904	Crl	Reuben	182	Alb	Gramner, Jno.	539	Prg
Philip	205	Ess	William	103	Spt	Joshua	539	Prg
Gouldman, Ann	199	Ess	Graffort, Jno.	260	Frf	Nathan	550	Prg
Danl.	203	Ess	Graftin, Phillip	195	Alb	William	539	Prg
Edmund	258	Amh	Grafton, Eliza.	165	Knq	Williamson	539	Prg
Francis	203	Ess	James	696	Br	Gramsil, Henry	165	Knq
Ralph, F n	164	Knq	Robert	696	Br	Gran, Salley	123	Hnr
Richard	200	Ess	William	904	Crl	Granberry, Lewis	834	Nrf
Thomas	200	Ess	William H.	695	Br	Granbery, John	900	Nrf
Gouldmond, Geo., Muto.	165	Knq	Gragg, William	221	Pnd	Grandle, Godfrey	27	Rcm
Gourley, David	900	Nrf	see Grogg			Grandling, Samuel	877	Hnv
Joseph	261	Ldn	Graham, Andw.	296	Rck	Grange, Des.	7	Hnr
Joseph	309	Ldn	Arthur	758	Hmp	Stephen	693	Gch
Goutier, ---, Mrs.	901	Nrf	Arthur	816	Hmp	Granger, Aaron	55	Chs
Govan, James	882	Hnv	Christopher	434	Bth	Aaron	147	Dnw
Gover, Samuel	308	Ldn	Dav.	502	Mnn	Patty	62	Chs
Gowan, John	329	Dnw	David	590	Mnr	Roger	416	Bth
Gowdy, Isaac	685	Br	Edmd.	596	Brk	Thomas	685	Br
Gowen, Ann	38	Clp	Elijah	258	Frf	Granier, Jos.	901	Nrf
Britten	386	Mds	Fras.	826	Nrf	Grannis, Edwd.	901	Nrf
Frances	656	Glc	George	258	Frf	Grant, Aaron	302	Ldn
James	196	Alb	George	526	Prw	Absolon	822	Nrf
James	655	Glc	George, jr.	275	Rck	Alex.	16	Hnr
James	850	Sth	George, Sr.	275	Rck	Ann	901	Nrf
Gower, Stanley P.	754	Nwk	Hugh	2	Knw	Chapman	946	Hrr
Gowin, David	834	Wth	Hugh	833	Wth	Chas.	840	Nrf
Wm.	661	Mnt	James	344	Ags	Daniel	512	Prw
Gowine, David	113	Hnr	James	851	Cmp	Daniel	638	Sss
Gowing, Benjamin	449	Grn	James	574	Mnr	Drewry	449	Grn
Henry	449	Grn	James	226	Pnd	Elisha	342	Lnn
James	449	Grn	James	524	Prw	George	365	Fqr
Gowings, Jason	55	Jff	James	833	Wth	George	166	Shn
Gowl, Adam	14	Rcm	Jane	444	Bth	Isaac	715	Wsh
William	14	Rcm	Jane	498	Prw	James	699	Wsh
Goznar, Henry	4	Oho	Jas.	503	Mnn	Jno.	502	Mnn
Grabill, Danl.	625	Btt	Jas.	815	Nrf	John	411	Fqr
Jacob	225	Pnd	Jno.	260	Frf	John	62	Jff
Jno., Jr.	625	Btt	Jno.	12	Hnr	John	812	Nrf
Jno., Sr.	625	Btt	Jno.	344	Ags	John	699	Wsh
Solomon	625	Btt	John	420	Bth	John, Jr.	405	Fqr
Grable, Abraham, Jr.	207	Shn	John	434	Bth	John, (Y)	872	Yrk
Chrisley	214	Shn	John	552	Brk	Jos.	745	Wsh
David	214	Shn	John	982	Nrt	Joseph	405	Fqr
George	194	Shn	John	503	Prw	Joseph	455	Pra
George	197	Shn	John	421	Rnd	Lewis	813	Nrf
Jacob	223	Shn	John	1	Rcm	Martha	693	Gch
John	197	Shn	John	38	Rcm	Mary	821	Nrf
John	214	Shn	John	696	Wsh	Mary	838	Nrf
John	223	Shn	John	833	Wth	Mary	715	Wsh
Jonas	215	Shn	John/	344	Ags	Mary	745	Wsh
Trancy	223	Shn	Joseph	574	Mnr	Peter	353	Fqr
Grace, ---, F.N.	165	Knq	Joseph	3	Rcm	Peter	694	Gch
...lip	760	Hmp	Keley	815	Nrf	Robert	294	Amh
Amie	41	Stf	Lante	296	Rck	Silas	838	Nrf
Daniel	724	Wsh	Leesan	462	Bdf	Susanah	745	Wsh
George	725	Wsh	Levi	35	Clp	William	830	Hmp
George	833	Wth	Mark	816	Hmp	William	512	Prw
Jacob	59	Jff	Michael	463	Bdf	Wm.	745	Wsh
John	833	Wth	Michael	2	Oho	Grantham, James	537	Prg
Rachel	53	Stf	Nancey	811	Bck	John	58	Jff
Thomas	53	Stf	Peter	391	Fqr	John	60	Jff
Unley	512	Prw	Robert	68	Chs	John	66	Jff
William	52	Stf	Robert	507	Prw	John, Jnr.	74	Jff
see Grass, Groce			Robert, Senr.	833	Wth	Joseph	66	Jff
Gracey, William	252	Shn	Robt.	344	Ags	Sampson	606	Srr

Name	No.	Loc
Uriah	327	Dnw
Wm.	562	Brk
Grantland, Jas.	888	Hnv
Grantlant, Wm.	438	Flv
Grantum, Philip	693	Gch
Grapes, David	792	Hmp
Sarah	550	Frd
Grason, Matilda	35	Stf
William	37	Stf
Grass, Calob	724	Wsh
Eml.	900	Nrf
Fred.	346	Ags
Jachob	158	Alb
Jacob	439	Bth
Jacob	9	Knw
John	158	Alb
John	708	Wsh
Peter	440	Bth
Solomon	16	Wod
see Grace		
Gratehous, Gabriel	935	Hrr
Sarah	961	Hrr
see Groateehouse		
Gratehouse, Herman	12	Oho
Isaac	3	Oho
Gratner, John	724	Wsh
Gratton, Robt.	39	Rcm
Gravatt, Ellis	904	Crl
Judith	905	Crl
Reuben	904	Crl
Grave, Eliza	26	Hnr
Graves, Acey	387	Mds
Ann	900	Nrf
Ann	901	Nrf
Arthur	241	Aml
Arthur	63	Chs
Benja.	60	Chs
Benjamin	387	Mds
Catharine	888	Hnv
Charles	63	Chs
Charles	330	Dnw
Charles	598	Frd
Charles H., Doctr.	606	Srr
Danl.	28	Rcm
Dangerfield	904	Crl
David	459	Frn
David	638	Sss
Edmond	31	Stf
Edmund	754	Nwk
Edward	387	Mds
Elijah	587	Frd
Euphon	902	Nrf
Fanney	304	Amh
Geo.	12	Hnr
Geo. [2]	22	Hnr
George	33	Rcm
Henry	543	Prg
Isaac	695	Nls
Isham	55	Chs
James	694	Gch
Jo.	889	Yrk
Joe	147	Dnw
Joel	387	Mds
John	158	Alb
John	904	Crl
John	450	Frn
John	588	Frd
John	655	Glc
John	164	Knq
John	387	Mds
John	695	Nls
John	33	Stf
John P.	694	Nls
Joseph	904	Crl
Joseph	80	Spt
Joseph	31	Stf
Joseph	50	Stf
Katy	804	Nrf
Leond.	36	Clp
Mary	6	Hnr
Nancy	260	Ldn
Phillip	387	Mds
Rhody	38	Stf
Rhuben	875	Yrk
Rice	694	Gch
Richard	880	Cmp
Richard	754	Nwk
Richd.	342	Ags
Robt.	900	Nrf
Rosey	331	Dnw
Snead [2]	695	Nls
Solomon	638	Sss
Spencer	218	Ess
Susanna	164	Knq
Tabitha	938	Chc
Thomas	165	Knq
Thomas	387	Mds
Thos.	60	Chs
Waller	387	Mds
William	50	Chr
William	450	Grn
William	14	Pwh
William	80	Spt
William	31	Stf
William	638	Sss
William, Ser.	50	Chr
William P.	33	Hnr
Wm.	655	Glc
Gravit, Stirling	14	Pwh
Gray, ---, Mrs.	334	Dnw
---, Mrs.	28	Hnr
Alexander	463	Bdf
Alxr.	823	Nrf
Archible	926	Hrr
Benja.	150	Sth
Bennedicter	376	Fqr
Betsey	96	Acc
Daniel	303	Ldn
Davey	257	Frf
David	107	Jff
Edward, Jr.	635	Mnt
Edward, Sr.	635	Mnt
Edwin	128	Sth
Edwin	638	Sss
Eliza.	679	Wrw
Elizabeth	831	Nrf
Elizh. A.	119	Hnr
Emmery	200	Kng
Forester, F.negro	258	Frf
Francis	851	Cmp
Frederick	147	Dnw
Frederick	607	Srr
Gabl.	35	Clp
Gabl., jr.	36	Clp
George	36	Isw
George, Sen.	47	Isw
Hanham	558	Frd
Henry	903	Crl
Henry	38	Isw
Henry, Sen.	606	Srr
Henry N.	126	Sth
Hugh	257	Frf
Isaac	696	Nls
Isaiah	835	Hmp
James	463	Bdf
James	507	Frd
James	6	Hnr
James	2	Isw
James	7	Oho
Jas.	693	Gch
Jas.	503	Mnn
Jno.	35	Clp
Jno., jr.	35	Clp
John	463	Bdf
John	535	Brk
John	904	Crl
John	521	Frd
John	558	Frd
John	578	Frd
John	37	Isw
John	58	Jff
John	597	Mnr
John	615	Mnt
John	900	Nrf
John	23	Oho
John [2]	25	Oho
John	702	Wsh
John C.	128	Sth
John G.	524	Prw
John H.	560	Frd
John P.	463	Bdf
Joseph	624	Btt
Joseph	625	Btt
Joseph	147	Dnw
Joseph	328	Dnw
Joseph	256	Frf
Joseph	693	Gch
Joseph	27	Isw
Joseph	149	Sth
Joseph	703	Wsh
Joseph, Jur.	703	Wsh
Josiah	26	Isw
Levin	25	Acc
Mary	393	Fqr
Mary	824	Nrf
Mary, ju.	570	Brk
Michl.	572	Brk
Morgan J.	904	Crl
Nathaniel	387	Fqr
Obadiah	199	Ess
Orrison	463	Bdf
Peggy	904	Crl
Phoebe	904	Crl
Rebe.	681	Wrw
Rebecca	36	Clp
Richd.	38	Clp
Robert	509	Frd
Robert	3	Rcm
Robinson	514	Prw
Rosey	201	Ess
Susan	540	Frd
Susanna	589	Frd
Thomas	97	Acc
Thomas	382	Fqr
Thomas	639	Sss
Thomas B. W.	207	Ess
Thos.	433	Flv
Thos.	693	Gch
Thos.	129	Sth
Uriah	260	Frf
William	462	Bdf
William	257	Frf
William	450	Frn
William	826	Hmp
William	37	Isw
William	516	Prw
William	254	Shn
William, Junr.	567	Pre
William, Senr.	568	Pre
William, Sr.	904	Crl
William F.	107	Spt
Willm.	625	Btt
Wm.	749	Brn
Wm.	693	Gch
Wm.	501	Mnn
Wm.	155	Sth
Wm.	702	Wsh
Wm. H.	693	Gch
Graybill, John	606	Mnt
Peter	834	Wth
Graydusan, Martha	833	Wth
see Grayson		
Grayham, Jacob	657	Mnt
Jno., Sr.	661	Mnt
John	71	Jff
John	641	Mnt
Jonathn.	641	Mnt
Matthew	70	Jff
Robert, Junr.	834	Wth
Robt.	660	Mnt

Name	No.	Abbr.
William	491	Frn
Willm.	648	Mnt
Grayson, Ambrose	812	Hmp
Ambrose	833	Wth
Benj.	261	Ldn
Chales	665	Mnt
David	498	Prw
Joel	386	Mds
Nice	120	Spt
Rachell	624	Mnt
Robert O.	509	Frd
William	386	Mds
Winney, (F.Negroe)	355	Fqr
see Graydusan		
Grean, Robt.	17	Hnr
Thos.	20	Hnr
Greaneals, Cornelius	923	Hrr
Grear, Levi	900	Nrf
Greathouse, Benjamin	696	Br
John	687	Br
John	421	Msn
Michl.	914	Hrr
William	696	Br
Wm.	502	Mnn
Greaver, John	409	Ags
Philip	343	Ags
Wm.	343	Ags
Greaves, Nathaniel	382	Fqr
Greear see Gruar		
Greegs, Harry	773	Wst
Greek see Greete		
Green, A.	3	Oho
Aaron	38	Clp
Abigail	694	Nls
Abraham	241	Aml
Alexander	147	Dnw
Alsey	32	Hnr
Andrew	520	Prw
Ann	26	Acc
Asher	14	Oho
Augustine	201	Shn
Balaam	638	Sss
Barnabas	4	Knw
Benkjah	7	Knw
Benjamin	712	Brn
Benjamin	50	Chr
Benjamin	17	Oho
Benjamin	639	Sss
Caleb	101	Cmb
Charles	392	Fqr
Charles	14	Oho
Charles	773	Wst
Cleman	45	Chr
Clement	749	Brn
Cloe	302	Ldn
Croxton	49	Chr
D. Carlos	554	Pre
Daniel	834	Wth
Delphi	50	Chr
Dolly	712	Brn
Edward	462	Bdf
Edward	624	Btt
Edward	754	Nwk
Edwd.	241	Aml
Elijah	505	Prw
Elijah	515	Prw
Elijah	735	Wsh
Elijah	745	Wsh
Elisebith	146	Dnw
Everet	849	Hnv
Fleming	898	Hnv
Fortunatus	13	Hnr
Fortunatus	49	Chr
Fortune	518	Prw
Frances	31	Hnr
Francis	546	Prg
Fred.	37	Clp
Fredk. L.	35	Clp
Gabl.	38	Clp
Geo.	682	Br
George		

Name	No.	Abbr.
George	903	Crl
George	527	Frd
George	773	Wst
Greenville	254	Ldn
Grusset	49	Chr
Henry	695	Nls
Henry	12	Rcm
Horatio	11	Isw
Isaac	35	Clp
Isaac	326	Dnw
Jacob	687	Br
James	49	Chr
James	342	Fqr
James	394	Fqr
James	343	Lnn
James	522	Prw
James	18	Rcm
James	57	Stf
James	607	Srr
James	639	Sss
Jas.	37	Clp
Jesse	583	Mnr
Jessee	519	Prw
Jno.	38	Clp
Jno.	502	Mnn
John	585	Brk
John	712	Brn
John	49	Chr
John	326	Dnw
John	403	Fqr
John	530	Frd
John	538	Frd
John	694	Gch
John [2]	783	Hmp
John	3	Knw
John	7	Knw
John	387	Mds
John	108	Spt
John	638	Sss
John	834	Wth
Joseph	513	Brk
Joseph	391	Fqr
Joseph	474	Frn
Joseph	298	Ldn
Joseph	834	Wth
Joshua, Mulo.	165	Knq
Kissiah	454	Frn
Lewis	694	Gch
Lucy	35	Clp
Luke	68	Jff
Margt.	292	Ldn
Mark	749	Brn
Martha	50	Chr
Mary Ann	903	Crl
Mastin	19	Ntt
Meacon	875	Hnv
Meacon	9	Hnr
Moses	35	Clp
Reuben	475	Frn
Reubin	607	Mnt
Richard	199	Ess
Richard	532	Frd
Richd.	271	Ldn
Richd.	901	Nrf
Robert	350	Fqr
Robt.	36	Clp
Robt.	17	Hnr
Robt.	440	Mth
Robt., (Son of Isa)	35	Clp
Rolly	521	Prw
Salley	383	Fqr
Saml.	344	Ags
Saml.	258	Frf
Saml.	200	Kng
Samuel, (Est.)	50	Chr
Samuel B.	532	Frd
Simon	655	Glc
Simon	656	Glc
Sterling	449	Grn
Sucky	334	Dnw

Name	No.	Abbr.
Susan	12	Hnr
Thomas	50	Chr
Thomas	415	Fqr
Thomas	692	Gch
Thomas	11	Isw
Thomas	569	Pre
Thomas	519	Prw
Thos.	655	Glc
Thos.	296	Ldn
Timothy	108	Spt
Whetzel	559	Frd
William	241	Aml
William	412	Bth
William	462	Bdf
William	50	Chr
William	349	Fqr
William	383	Fqr
William	258	Frf
William	549	Frd
William	34	Hnr
William	7	Isw
William	754	Nwk
William	521	Prw
William, Jr.	241	Aml
Wim.	897	Hnv
Wm.	518	Brk
Wm.	35	Clp
Wm.	37	Clp
Wm.	192	Elc
Wm.	656	Glc
Wm.	454	Mth
Wm.	456	Pra
see Grean, Gren		
Greenberry see Grimmet		
Greenbery, Thomas	585	Brk
Greene, Betsy	902	Nrf
Elizabeth	598	Frd
Francis	22	Stf
George, L.	54	Stf
George, (Upper)	49	Stf
Jesse	46	Stf
John	901	Nrf
John	21	Stf
William H.	833	Wth
Greener, J. D.	401	Ags
Greenfield, Gabriel	62	Jff
Greenhill, David	49	Chr
Wm.	10	Ntt
Greenhow, Geo.	20	Hnr
Jas.	11	Hnr
Robert	34	Hnr
Samul	8	Hnr
Greenlaw, William	773	Wst
Wm.	200	Kng
Greenleas, James	312	Ldn
Greenlee, ---, Widow	428	Msn
Davd.	283	Rck
Davd., jr.	288	Rck
David	532	Frd
Edward	428	Msn
Francis	615	Mnt
James	273	Rck
Jas.	289	Rck
John	585	Mnr
Saml.	272	Rck
William	10	Knw
Wm.	625	Btt
see Greenllee, Lee		
Greenllee, Aleexr.	421	Msn
John	420	Msn
Greenstreet, Jessee	220	Ess
John	204	Ess
John	220	Ess
Joseph	163	Knq
Thomas	903	Crl
Thomas	165	Knq
Greenville see Green		
Greenwald, Daniel	302	Ldn
Greenwalt, George	223	Pnd
George	226	Pnd

Name	Page	Co.
Greenway, George	647	Mnt
John	702	Wsh
Robt.	147	Dnw
Greenwell, Eligah	824	Hmp
Greenwood, Geo.	503	Mnn
Jas.	220	Ess
Jno.	257	Frf
Twyman	213	Ess
Wm.	625	Btt
Wm.	213	Ess
Greer, Alexr.	300	Rck
Charles	484	Frn
James	465	Frn
John	429	Msn
Joseph, Jr.	452	Frn
Joseph, Sr.	451	Frn
Joshua	15	Oho
Mary	466	Frn
Moses, Jr.	477	Frn
Moses, Sr.	478	Frn
Nathan	452	Frn
Robert	288	Rck
Greete, James	901	Nrf
Greever see Gruver		
Gregary, Isaac	423	Rnd
Gregery, Ch.	343	Ags
Gregg, Aaron	297	Ldn
Carrol	639	Sss
Elisha	291	Ldn
Geo.	297	Ldn
George	596	Frd
George	21	Oho
George, Jun.	21	Oho
Jno.	315	Ldn
Jno.	317	Ldn
John	590	Brk
Joseph	309	Ldn
Joshua	275	Ldn
Josiah	275	Ldn
Mahlon	271	Ldn
Mahlon	317	Ldn
Matthew	526	Prw
Naomi	21	Oho
Nathan	312	Ldn
Richard B.	639	Sss
Saml.	310	Ldn
Samuel	312	Ldn
Thomas	270	Ldn
Thomas	310	Ldn
Thomas	317	Ldn
Thomas	21	Oho
Thos.	275	Ldn
Thos., Capt.	322	Ldn
William	11	Oho
Wm.	297	Ldn
Greggs, James	450	Frn
John	15	Hnr
Thos.	501	Mnn
Gregory, ---, Doctr.	901	Nrf
Boswell	568	Pre
Charles	939	Chc
Edmund	806	Bck
Herbert	146	Dnw
Jacob	344	Ags
James	430	Bth
James	956	Chc
James	695	Nls
Janes	343	Lnn
Jno.	56	Chs
John	407	Ags
John	430	Bth
John	867	Cmp
John	957	Chc
John	921	Hrr
John	516	Prw
John, Jr.	868	Cmp
John, Junr.	772	Wst
John, Senr.	773	Wst
Joseph	413	Bth
Joseph	772	Wst
Joseph, Jur.	430	Bth
Joseph, Jur.	50	Chr
Joseph, Senr.	50	Chr
Josh.	38	Clp
Joshua	39	Rcm
Julia	905	Crl
Leanner	51	Stf
Mary	655	Glc
Nancy	280	Ldn
Nancy	773	Wst
Nanny	773	Wst
Philip	343	Ags
Presly	555	Frd
Richard	868	Cmp
Richard	368	Fqr
Richard C.	343	Lnn
Richd.	65	Chs
Richd.	111	Hnr
Robt.	594	Brk
Saml.	343	Ags
Samuel	431	Bth
Samuel	950	Chc
Thomas	463	Bdf
Thomas	905	Crl
Thomas	343	Lnn
Thomas, Junr.	772	Wst
Thomas, Senr.	773	Wst
Walker	949	Chc
Walter	110	Spt
William	284	Amh
William	793	Bck
William	754	Nwk
William	833	Wth
Wm.	597	Brk
see Grigory		
Greland, Alexander	931	Hrr
Gren, John	598	Brk
Gresham, Anthy.	163	Knq
Geo.	346	Lnc
Hannah	165	Knq
Henry	146	Dnw
Jno., jr.	163	Knq
James	164	Knq
John	396	Rch
John, Snr.	165	Knq
Ruth	165	Knq
Samuel	154	Knq
Samuel	184	Knq
Thomas	163	Knq
Thoms.	147	Dnw
William D.	165	Knq
Wm., Snr.	164	Knq
Greshan, William	860	Cmp
Gresset, John	773	Wst
Gressitt, James	665	Glc
Jno. D.	655	Glc
Lucy	656	Glc
Racheal	656	Glc
Thomas	655	Glc
Wm.	655	Glc
Wm.	656	Glc
Gressun, Ambros	343	Lnn
Gretter, C.F.	4	Hnr
Michal	22	Hnr
Grey, George	571	Brk
Jas., Sr.	625	Btt
John	43	Stf
John, (upper)	49	Stf
Joseph	455	Pra
William	624	Btt
Greyer, James	70	Jff
Greyham, Andrew	254	Lan
David	157	Alb
Hugh	254	Ldn
Reuben	261	Ldn
Thos.	268	Ldn
Greynies, Thos.	815	Nrf
Greyson, Jane		
John	158	Alb
William	158	Alb
Griast, Enoch	624	Btt
John, Sr.	624	Btt
Saml.	626	Btt
Gribble, Jno.	502	Mnn
Wm.	502	Mnn
Grice, George	193	Shn
Grider, Frederick	30	Rcm
Grier, Alexr.	806	Nrf
John	38	Rcm
Joseph	17	Rcm
Grifeth, Samuel	59	Jff
Griffee, Marshal	62	Jff
Griffen, Caty	388	Mds
Esther	428	Bth
Henry	916	Hrr
Jno.	544	Prg
William	446	Bth
William, Se.	446	Bth
see Giffen		
Griffeth, Archd.	342	Ags
Daniel	494	Frn
Owne	482	Frn
see Haynes		
Griffetth, John	416	Rnd
Griffey, David	180	Shn
Hannah	199	Shn
William	181	Shn
Griffie, Benjamin	848	Cmp
Griffin, Abner	431	Bth
Abnor	115	Hnr
Benjn.	153	Sth
Burgess	463	Bdf
Corbin, (Y)	875	Yrk
Daniel	430	Flv
David	118	Hnr
Dolley	326	Dnw
Edwd.	854	Sth
Elisha	904	Hrr
Elizabeth	257	Frf
Franky	456	Pra
George	552	Brk
George	13	Rcm
Harrisson	695	Nls
Helen	408	Fqr
Henry	35	Clp
Henry	301	Ldn
Henry	501	Mnn
Hezekh.	513	Brk
Horatio	200	Kng
Ichabod C.	6	Wod
James	114	Hnr
Jno.	455	Pra
John	205	Ess
John	538	Frd
John	694	Nls
John	47	Stf
John C.	624	Btt
Jones	9	Isw
Joseph	436	Flv
Josias	200	Kng
Josph	4	Oho
Leml.	158	Sth
Levi	429	Bth
Lindsy	696	Nls
Lott	41	Isw
Lucy	846	Sth
Mary	904	Crl
Mathias	455	Pra
Mich.	161	Sth
Mills	161	Sth
Nathl.	455	Pra
Obediah	118	Hnr
Orlando	437	Bth
Pearce	117	Hnr
Phebe	796	Nrf
Pleasant	695	Nls
Ralf	200	Kng
Richard	22	Stf
Richard	639	Sss
Rubin	959	Chc

Name	No.	Co.	Name	No.	Co.	Name	No.	Co.
S.S., (Y)	875	Yrk	Grigory, Jas.	589	Mnr	Danl.	36	Clp
Sam	398	Rch	Thos. D.	858	Hnv	Jno.	37	Clp
Saml.	462	Bdf	Grigsby, Aaron	385	Fqr	Nancy	258	Frf
Saml.	203	Ess	Daniel	43	Stf	Peyton R.	360	Fqr
Saml.	917	Hrr	Elisha	279	Rck	Philip	37	Clp
Sarah	901	Nrf	Enoch	368	Fqr	Robert	409	Fqr
Scarburgh	24	Acc	Etcherson	865	Cmp	William	409	Fqr
Shad.	878	Sth	Henry	36	Clp	Grimstead, Daniel	454	Pra
Thos.	655	Glc	Henry	37	Clp	James	454	Pra
Thos., (Y)	875	Yrk	Henry	592	Frd	Jona.	454	Pra
William	954	Chc	Jesse	188	Shn	Raughly	454	Pra
William, & Co.	332	Dnw	Jno.	37	Clp	Sylas	454	Pra
Wm.	656	Glc	John	200	Kng	Thos.	455	Pra
Wm.	303	Rck	John	22	Oho	Grinage, Sampson	47	Stf
Wright	712	Brn	John	166	Shn	Grindstaff, Adam [2]	15	Oho
Wright	6	Wod	Joseph	272	Rck	George	242	Shn
Zach.	36	Clp	Nathaniel	400	Fqr	George, (3d)	242	Shn
see Bishop, Giffin, Haynie			Nimrod	258	Frf	Jacob	14	Oho
Griffing, Ebenezer	15	Wod	Reuben	271	Rck	Lewis	15	Oho
Griffith, Abel	344	Ags	Taliaferro	363	Fqr	Griner, George	345	Ags
Abram	477	Frn	William	349	Fqr	John	341	Ags
Amey	952	Chc	William	592	Frd	Grines, Jacob	798	Nrf
Amos	502	Mnn	Wm.	283	Rck	Grinham, Sarah	343	Ags
Anne	686	Br	see Grrigsby			Grinnalds, Elijah	96	Acc
Benjamin	477	Frn	Grills, John	701	Wsh	Henry	96	Acc
David	534	Brk	Grim, Abraham	507	Frd	Richard	24	Acc
David	301	Ldn	Charles	506	Frd	Southey	96	Acc
Elijah	370	Fqr	Charles, Jr.	511	Frd	William	26	Acc
Isaac	286	Ldn	Christian	410	Ags	William, Jun.	24	Acc
James	684	Br	Dav.	503	Mnn	Grinnel, Nathaniel	3	Rcm
James	749	Brn	George	812	Hmp	Grinnen, Danl., jr.,		
Jno.	290	Ldn	Jacob	511	Frd	Este.	34	Clp
Jno.	297	Ldn	Jacob	529	Frd	Danl., Sen.	34	Clp
John	580	Frd	Jno.	297	Rck	Jno.	34	Clp
John	164	Knq	John	506	Frd	Grinnin, Daniel	113	Spt
John	1	Oho	John	224	Pnd	Grinnon, John	772	Wst
John	14	Wod	Peter	524	Frd	Grinshaw, Saml.	125	Hnr
Jonathan	477	Frn	Philip	343	Ags	Grinstead, Elizabeth	510	Prw
Jones	552	Brk	Philip	255	Shn	Francis	114	Cmb
Joseph	309	Ldn	see ... rim			James	118	Hnr
Nancy	307	Ldn	Grimes, Andrew	258	Ldn	John	194	Alb
Polley	165	Knq	Arther	423	Bth	John	981	Nrt
Robert	165	Knq	Besey	342	Ags	William	525	Prw
Samuel	529	Frd	Cary	789	Nrf	Wm.	693	Gch
Sarah	373	Fqr	Daniel	147	Dnw	Grinsted, Wm.	346	Ags
Thomas	165	Knq	Daniel	241	Ldn	Grinston, Jesse	944	Chc
Thomas	309	Ldn	Daniel	814	Nrf	Grisham, Asa	749	Brn
Thomas	833	Wth	Danl.	889	Yrk	Moses	342	Ags
William	956	Chc	Felix	425	Bth	Grishan, Isaac S.	859	Cmp
William	11	Knw	George	259	Frf	Grison, John	84	Jff
William	165	Knq	James	731	Wsh	Grissle, John H.	739	Wsh
Wm.	344	Ags	Jas.	798	Nrf	Grisso, Geo.	623	Btt
see Dickerson, Griffin			Jonathan	657	Mnt	Mathias	626	Btt
Griffitts, John	834	Wth	Jos.	789	Nrf	Grissom, Charles	264	Amh
Viney	834	Wth	Lewis	817	Nrf	Thomas	297	Amh
Griffy, Eligah	832	Hmp	Mark	421	Rnd	Grist, George	553	Frd
John	180	Shn	Mary	258	Frf	Grovenor	552	Brk
Griger, Gasper	180	Alb	Nace	258	Ldn	John	626	Btt
Grigg, Burwell	450	Grn	Peggy	889	Yrk	see Gryst		
Earrol	450	Grn	Rebecue	712	Brn	Griswit, James	878	Sth
Jesse	5	Ntt	Robert	594	Brk	Gritton, George	796	Hmp
Josiah	6	Ntt	Sarah	789	Nrf	Jacob	774	Hmp
Martha	450	Grn	Thomas	684	Br	John	763	Hmp
Mitchell	450	Grn	Thomas	836	Hmp	John	775	Hmp
Peter	17	Ntt	Thomas	567	Pre	John, Ser.	774	Hmp
Randolph	450	Grn	William	921	Hrr	William	774	Hmp
Wm.	749	Brn	William	510	Prw	Grizil, Jesse	735	Wsh
Griggs, Chas.	454	Pra	Wm.	342	Ags	Grizzard, Ambrose	146	Sth
Jacob	32	Hnr	Wm.	591	Brk	Henry	449	Grn
Jas.	10	Ntt	Wm.	502	Mnn	John	639	Sss
Jessee	215	Ess	see Grims			Mary	853	Sth
Joel	5	Ntt	Grimm, Joseph	427	Msn	Grizzle, Isaac	777	Bck
John	61	Jff	Grimmet, Greenberry	625	Gls	William	836	Bck
John	806	Nrf	Grimmit, John	493	Frn	Groatehouse see Gratehous		
Philip [2]	215	Ess	Nicholas	494	Frn	Groathouse, John	935	Hrr
Roger	23	Oho	Solomon	496	Frn	Groce, Charles	7	Isw
Thomas	57	Jff	Grims, James	689	Wsh	Jos.	655	Glc
Thomas	63	Jff	James	701	Wsh	Peter	608	Mnt
William	597	Frd	Robt.	731	Wsh	Willis	25	Isw
see Rigs			Grimsley, Barnett	387	Mds	Grodian, Christn.	625	Btt

Groes, George	253	Shn	John	7	Knw	Grul, Henry	626	Btt
Grogg, Philip	219	Pnd	Joseph	416	Fqr	Grumbecker, Peter	345	Ags
see Gragg, Groog			Joshua	296	Rck	Grumley, Thomas	692	Br
Groler, James	900	Nrf	Letty	47	Stf	Grumlie, John	8	Rcm
Gromoe, John	692	Br	Mary	343	Fqr	Grumsby, Wm.	38	Clp
Groog, John	225	Pnd	Mary	901	Nrf	Grundy, Molly	901	Nrf
see Grogg			Peter	571	Frd	Grunleass, George	944	Hrr
Groom, Jno.	164	Knq	Peter	768	Hmp	Grunlee see Greenlee		
Polley R.	164	Knq	Samuel	182	Shn	Gruver, Abraham	736	Wsh
Richard	435	Flv	Samuel	186	Shn	Phillip [2]	741	Wsh
Richd.	656	Glc	Susanna	183	Shn	Valentine	742	Wsh
Saml.	656	Glc	Thomas	351	Fqr	Grymes, Alexr.	792	Nrf
Saml.	164	Knq	Thomas	56	Stf	Benjn.	200	Kng
Thomas	463	Mdd	Thornton	411	Fqr	D. S.	124	Hnr
Groomes, John	62	Stf	William	411	Fqr	Edmund	904	Crl
Grooms, H. M.	407	Ags	William	543	Frd	Geo. N.	200	Kng
John	289	Amh	William	8	Oho	Israel	797	Nrf
Jonathan	463	Bdf	William	524	Prw	Jane	36	Clp
Grose, Samuel	217	Pnd	William, Jr.	341	Fqr	Jas.	817	Nrf
Gross, Adam	626	Btt	William, Jr.	347	Fqr	Judith	463	Mdd
Andrew	533	Brk	Grown, Hugh	830	Nrf	Martha	788	Nrf
Margaret	624	Btt	Grrigsby, Edmund	21	Oho	Mary	816	Nrf
Martin	834	Wth	Gruar, Mary	694	Wsh	Thomas	20	Oho
Philip	393	Fqr	Grub, Elizabeth	119	Spt	Thos.	817	Nrf
Grossclose, Adam	833	Wth	Jno.	501	Mnn	William	905	Crl
Elizabeth	833	Wth	Saml.	501	Mnn	Wm.	807	Nrf
Henry	833	Wth	Grubb, Adam	63	Jff	Wm. F.	200	Kng
Jacob	833	Wth	Adam	282	Ldn	Gryst, John	14	Oho
Grossman, Simon	554	Frd	Curtis	58	Jff	Gualding, Susannah	105	Cmb
Grots, Jacob	72	Spt	Danl.	19	Rcm	Gualing, Alexander	105	Cmb
Ground, George	626	Btt	Ebenr.	267	Ldn	Guartney, Michael	342	Lnn
Grove, Ab.	583	Brk	Edwd.	545	Brk	Guddes, Ann	23	Stf
Abraham	519	Frd	Elijah	462	Bdf	Guerney, Josh.	583	Brk
Benjn.	342	Ags	Elizabeth	20	Rcm	Guerrant, Charles	805	Bck
Benjn., jr.	345	Ags	Elizth.	900	Nrf	Daniel	693	Gch
Ch.	401	Ags	Francis	834	Wth	John	805	Bck
Charles B.	7	Hnr	Isaac	834	Wth	John	693	Gch
Daniel	520	Frd	Jacob	834	Wth	John, Minr.	723	Gch
David	345	Ags	Jesse	462	Bdf	John, Senr.	692	Gch
David	519	Frd	John	834	Wth	Peter, Sr.	830	Bck
David	38	Rcm	Joseph	503	Brk	Stephen	830	Bck
George	585	Brk	Joseph	266	Ldn	William	805	Bck
Jacob	84	Jff	Lewis	834	Wth	Guess, Sinrey [?]	574	Mnr
Jacob	238	Shn	Nancy	462	Bdf	Guest, Eliza.	246	Ldn
Jacob	834	Wth	Peter	19	Rcm	Eliza.	248	Ldn
John	521	Brk	Richard	268	Ldn	see Gest		
John	520	Frd	William	63	Jff	Guider, Peter	312	Ldn
John	79	Jff	Wm.	268	Ldn	Guilinge, George [crossed		
Joseph	14	Rcm	Grubbe, Nicholes	731	Wsh	out]	294	Rck
Leonard	285	Rck	Grubbs, Anderson	848	Hnv	George	300	Rck
Malaki	89	Jff	Benajah	37	Clp	Guill, Alexander	568	Pre
Martin	345	Ags	Charles	541	Frd	Josiah	568	Pre
Mary	9	Rcm	Danl.	37	Clp	Reuben	568	Pre
Michael	15	Wod	Darius	593	Frd	Guilliams, Richard	488	Frn
Peter	546	Brk	Darius, Jr.	594	Frd	William	487	Frn
Simon	342	Ags	Eddith	889	Hnv	Guillians, Robert	488	Frn
Windal	343	Ags	Edwd.	694	Gch	Guillim, Reason	543	Brk
Windal, jr.	343	Ags	Enoch	37	Clp	Guin, Elizabeth	268	Amh
Grover, Benj.	30	Hnr	Hensley	854	Hnv	Isaac	422	Bth
Ezra	556	Frd	Hickerson	712	Brn	James	345	Ags
John	516	Brk	Jesse	560	Frd	John	431	Bth
Groves, Adam	548	Frd	Jno.	859	Hnv	Joseph	345	Ags
Anne	342	Fqr	Jno.	889	Hnv	Leonard	431	Bth
Betsey	520	Frd	Jno., Jnr.	874	Hnv	Priscilla	431	Bth
Chrisley	186	Shn	John	749	Brn	Roger	431	Bth
David	183	Shn	Lewis	36	Clp	Thos.	345	Ags
Esther	186	Shn	Nathan	693	Gch	see Gawin		
Geo.	36	Clp	Nathan	37	Clp	Guines, Wm.	37	Clp
Henry	675	Br	Richard	854	Hnv	see Gaines		
Henry	556	Frd	Sebi	694	Gch	Guinn, Abiah	34	Clp
Henry	565	Frd	Stephen	561	Frd	Benja.	34	Clp
Jacob	556	Frd	Thomas	594	Frd	Ned, F.B.	11	Pwh
Jacob	771	Hmp	Thos.	146	Dnw	Guirrand, Peter	483	Frn
Jacob	596	Mnr	Thos.	858	Hnv	Gulatt, Charles	305	Ldn
Jacob	210	Shn	Wim.	850	Hnv	Gulick, Ferdinand	790	Hmp
Jno.	38	Clp	Wm.	38	Clp	Francis	10	Wod
John	681	Br	Gruber, Abbingal	74	Jff	Geo.	237	Ldn
John	351	Fqr	Abright	66	Jff	Leno	237	Ldn
John	555	Frd	Christian	66	Jff	Moses	234	Ldn
John	556	Frd	Grue see Greer			Gullet, William	563	Mnr

Willm.	580	Mnr	Gustine, Joel T.	509	Frd	Gwadkins, Charles	463	Bdf
Gulliford, Alley	625	Btt	Gutery, Jas.	501	Mnn	James	462	Bdf
Gullion, Barnabas	833	Wth	Gutherey, Henry	133	Cmb	Gwalding see Gualding, Gualing		
Duncan	834	Wth	William	111	Cmb	Gwaltney, Conny	606	Srr
Hugh	834	Wth	Guthery, Allexander	114	Cmb	James	9	Isw
John	834	Wth	James	1	Knw	James, jr.	607	Srr
William	834	Wth	John	106	Cmb	John	38	Isw
Gully, Polly	388	Mds	John	654	Mnt	Jordan	35	Isw
Gum, Abraham	217	Pnd	Richd.	640	Mnt	Lucrecia	28	Isw
Brida	224	Pnd	Guthre, George	218	Pnd	Ludwell	607	Srr
Isaac	224	Pnd	Guthrey, William	836	Bck	Richard	606	Srr
Jacob	225	Pnd	Guthrie, James	864	Cmp	Sampson	607	Srr
John	688	Wsh	Jas.	502	Mnn	Sarah	606	Srr
Val	501	Mnn	Jno.	656	Glc	Simmons	14	Isw
Gumart, Christian	107	Jff	John	342	Ags	Thomas P.	607	Srr
John	106	Jff	John, jr.	342	Ags	William	606	Srr
Gumby, John	562	Frd	John, Sr.	345	Ags	Willis	606	Srr
Rachel	595	Frd	Guthry, Richd.	164	Knq	Wm.	159	Sth
Gume, James	712	Brn	Robert	10	Knw	Gwathmey, Temple	165	Knq
Gumnell, William	257	Frf	William, Snr.	165	Knq	Gwatkins, Fanny	516	Prw
Gump, Michael	68	Jff	Wm.	164	Knq	Prudence	515	Prw
Gun, Sarah	875	Yrk	Gutrey, William	21	Oho	Gwens see Givens		
Gundry, Jno.	346	Lnc	Gutridge, Allen	347	Fqr	Gwin, Danl.	537	Brk
Gunn, Bidy	29	Hnr	Ed.	501	Mnn	David	435	Bth
Dudley	749	Brn	James	403	Rch	James	431	Bth
Gabriel	11	Ntt	Peter	363	Fqr	James	446	Mth
Griffin	2	Ntt	Reubin	344	Fqr	John	433	Bth
James	235	Ldn	Sally	24	Acc	John	435	Bth
James	342	Lnn	William	408	Fqr	Joseph	435	Bth
Jno.	10	Hnr	William	403	Rch	Robert	430	Bth
John	132	Hnr	Gutrie, William	905	Crl	Robert	435	Bth
John S.	126	Hnr	Guttery, David	293	Amh	Solomon	159	Sth
Reuben	326	Dnw	Edward	271	Amh	see Givon		
Saml.	12	Hnr	Francis	183	Shn	Gwinn, James	574	Mnr
Spencer	146	Dnw	Nathaniel	293	Amh	James, S.	587	Mnr
Willm.	647	Mnt	William	293	Amh	Moses	597	Mnr
Wm.	330	Dnw	Guttridge, John	772	Wst	Neal	22	Oho
see Gume			Molly	772	Wst	Robert	574	Mnr
Gunnell, Allen	260	Frf	Reuben	773	Wst	Saml.	593	Mnr
George	256	Frf	Thomas	772	Wst	Samuel	597	Mnr
Henry	257	Frf	Guy, Ann	905	Crl	Gwyn, Edwd.	693	Gch
Henry, Capt.	259	Frf	Archd.	342	Ags	Jno.	449	Mth
James	378	Fqr	Bailey	813	Nrf	Samuel	624	Gls
James S.	259	Frf	Benjamin	25	Stf	Wm.	799	Nrf
Ned, f. negro	260	Frf	Charles	27	Stf	Gwynn, Ann	656	Glc
Robert	260	Frf	Eilza	813	Nrf	Hugh	656	Glc
Robert, Jun.	260	Frf	Frances	903	Crl	Matthew W.	502	Prw
Wm., Esqr.	259	Frf	Geo.	455	Pra	Sally	527	Frd
Wm., Jun.	260	Frf	George	25	Acc			
see Gumnell			George	904	Crl			
Gunning, David	345	Ags	Henry	809	Nrf	--- H ---		
Guns see Guin			Henry	900	Nrf			
Gunter, Conrod	69	Jff	Isaac	344	Ags			
Edward	96	Acc	Israel	26	Acc	H..., ...	240	Aml
Famey	24	Acc	James	904	Crl	...	489	Bdf
James	292	Rck	James	27	Stf	Garland	466	Bdf
John	24	Acc	Jim, F.N.	639	Sss	Jera [?]	464	Bdf
John	620	Mnt	Jonathan	24	Acc	John	238	Aml
Joseph	24	Acc	John	24	Acc	Stephen	464	Bdf
Labon	25	Acc	John	345	Ags	William	464	Bdf
Stephen	24	Acc	John	865	Cmp	William	466	Bdf
Thomas	788	Bck	John	190	Elc	H...beth, Henry	854	Sth
Thomas	804	Bck	John	47	Stf	H...den, ..., sr.	465	Bdf
William P.	568	Pre	John, Jun.	190	Elc	H...dnal, ...	465	Bdf
Williamson	804	Bck	Joseph	344	Ags	H...er see H...		
Gunyon, William	353	Fqr	Joseph	20	Stf	H...ll, Berryman	148	Dnw
Gurd see Gard			Lewis	157	Alb	H...nes, Howel	150	Dnw
Gurley, Geo.	853	Sth	Rachel	24	Acc	H...on, William	468	Bdf
Geo.	864	Sth	Rachel	21	Stf	H...son, ...	241	Aml
Joseph	873	Sth	Robt.	343	Ags	H...y, Aron, (of S)	163	Shn
Gurs, Thomas	568	Pre	Sampson	238	Ldn	Aron, (of S)	164	Shn
Guseman, Abm.	502	Mnn	Samuel	872	Yrk	Ha..., ...n [?]	466	Bdf
Godfry	503	Mnn	Sarah	509	Prw	Edward	466	Bdf
Gusick, Jno.	502	Mnn	Thomas	508	Prw	George	466	Bdf
Peter	502	Mnn	Thos.	13	Hnr	Hampton	466	Bdf
Gussage, Abraham	97	Acc	Thos.	31	Hnr	Haas, Catharine	510	Frd
Guster, Daniel	26	Acc	William	24	Acc	Conrad	603	Frd
Gustin, Aberdee	575	Brk	William	26	Stf	Frederick	869	Cmp
Alpheus	575	Brk	Wm.	189	Elc	Haborne, Charles	393	Rch
Robert	575	Brk	see McGuy			Habron, James	774	Wst

William	774	Wst	Robert	695	Gch	Franky	52	Chr
Hachley see ---			William	465	Bdf	Holladay	450	Grn
Hack, George	30	Acc	Wm.	441	Flv	John	340	Fqr
Peter, Junr.	30	Acc	see H...den			John	218	Shn
Peter, Senr.	30	Acc	Hadley, Richd.	587	Brk	John	69	Spt
Peter, Sr.	632	Btt	Hadon, Jessee	161	Alb	Joseph	410	Fqr
Hacker, Alexr.	910	Hrr	Joseph	161	Alb	Peter	875	Yrk
John [2]	931	Hrr	Haegler, William	422	Rnd	Spencer	52	Chr
William	909	Hrr	Haferlin see Heferlin			Susanna	69	Chr
Hacket, Eliza	774	Wst	Haffey, Rodk.	333	Dnw	Hailman see Hoilman		
Jereh.	630	Btt	Haga, George	26	Rcm	Hailstock, Chs.	203	Kng
John	626	Gls	Hagan, Elizabeth	50	Stf	Joseph	119	Hnr
Peter	790	Bck	Enoch	464	Bdf	Hailstone, Lucy	35	Stf
Peter	869	Cmp	John [2]	684	Br	Haily, Dick.	876	Yrk
Thomas	630	Btt	John	546	Frd	Haimes see Haines		
Thomas	795	Bck	Hagans, Clary	838	Wth	Hain, John	189	Shn
Thomas	829	Bck	Hagarman, Benjamin	371	Fqr	Haines, Casper	19	Rcm
Hackett, Chiles	908	Crl	Hagel see Hazel			Christiana	24	Rcm
Durrett	905	Crl	Hageley, George	84	Jff	Daniel	390	Fqr
Garrett	906	Crl	Isaac	591	Frd	Daniel	64	Jff
Jereh.	629	Btt	Hagen see Hogar			Ezekiel	44	Clp
John	908	Crl	Hagens, Barnet	9	Oho	Frederick, (Jr.)	24	Rcm
Thomas	905	Crl	Hager, George	699	Nls	Frederick, (sen.)	24	Rcm
Thomas	908	Crl	John	698	Nls	Geo.	43	Clp
Thos., Jr.	629	Btt	John, Jnr.	698	Nls	Hannah	5	Rcm
Hackins, Wm.	2	Oho	William	259	Amh	Henry	56	Jff
Hackley, Ann	45	Clp	Hagerman, Aram	235	Ldn	Jacob	104	Jff
Jas.	42	Clp	Jos.	236	Ldn	John	53	Chr
John	29	Stf	Orion	235	Ldn	John	562	Frd
Joseph	560	Frd	Hagert, James	755	Wsh	John	63	Jff
Joseph, (free Negroe)	354	Fqr	Hagerty, George	906	Hrr	John	24	Rcm
Samuel	365	Fqr	John	401	Ags	John, (sen.)	24	Rcm
Walter	45	Clp	John	695	Wsh	Joseph	390	Fqr
William	15	Rcm	Haggaman, Mary A.	349	Lnc	Joseph	562	Frd
Hackney, Aaron	538	Frd	Haggard, Wm.	445	Flv	Mary	44	Clp
Benjamin	440	Flv	Haggins, Comfort	431	Bth	Nathan	63	Jff
Benjamin	464	Mdd	Hagin, Francis	263	Frf	Peter	55	Jff
Betsy	80	Spt	see Hggin			Simeon	560	Frd
Dolly	905	Crl	Hagins, Peter	631	Btt	Stacy	288	Ldn
George	261	Frf	Hagist, Federick	391	Mds	William	52	Chr
Jacky	331	Dnw	Hagle, John	940	Hrr	Hains, Henry	645	Mnt
James	581	Frd	Hagler, George	220	Pnd	Jacob	645	Mnt
James	464	Mdd	William	221	Pnd	John	755	Wsh
Joseph	581	Frd	Hagshead see Hogshead			Jos.	509	Mnn
Mildred	530	Prg	Hague, Amos	271	Ldn	Philip	351	Ags
Richard	440	Flv	Jno.	249	Ldn	Polly	681	Br
Samuel	594	Frd	Jonathan	45	Clp	Wm.	506	Mnn
Stephen	106	Spt	Joseph	773	Wst	Zacherah	756	Wsh
Thomas	159	Alb	Hagwad see Hogwod			Zacheriah	757	Wsh
Thomas	75	Spt	Hagy, Henry	692	Wsh	see Harris		
Hackworth, George	465	Bdf	Jacob	713	Wsh	Hair, Davd.	745	Wsh
Joseph	464	Bdf	John	520	Frd	James	536	Prg
Thomas	465	Bdf	Marton	713	Wsh	Joseph	626	Gls
William	464	Bdf	Michl.	750	Wsh	Wm.	306	Ldn
William, Sr.	464	Bdf	Haidy, Wm.	247	Ldn	Hairfield, Matthew	53	Chr
Hadaire, Thos.	904	Nrf	Haigler, Jacob	423	Rnd	Haistings, Peter	9	Ntt
Hadaway, Wm.	631	Btt	Hail, Benjamin	197	Alb	Haithcock, Reuben	159	Sth
Haddis, David	351	Ags	Catharine	131	Hnr	Hakiswilder, Jacob	685	Br
Mark	348	Ags	Elias	140	Sth	Hal..., Francis	984	Nrt
Haddix, Enoch	944	Hrr	George	197	Alb	Halbert, James	196	Ess
Wm.	945	Hrr	Leonard	701	Nls	John	198	Ess
Haddon, Abram	643	Sss	William	197	Alb	John	574	Frd
John	544	Prg	Haile, Benja.	209	Ess	Tho.	508	Mnn
Thomas	538	Prg	Jno. S.	267	Frf	William	522	Prw
Haddox, John	254	Shn	John, Sr.	208	Ess	Wm.	201	Ess
John, Jr.	591	Frd	Rd. T.	203	Ess	Wm.	508	Mnn
John, Senr.	591	Frd	Wheeler	167	Knq	Wm., jr.	200	Ess
Haddston, Samuel	13	Knw	Hailes, Benjn.	202	Kng	Halcom, Duriah	496	Frn
Haden, ...	464	Bdf	Benjn., Sr.	202	Kng	Haldane, Jno.	904	Nrf
Benjamin	856	Cmp	John	645	Sss	Haldeman, Jacob	352	Ags
George	447	Flv	Lucy	644	Sss	Halderman, John	925	Hrr
John	114	Cmb	Newton	203	Kng	Hale, Abm.	507	Mnn
John	696	Gch	Susan	644	Sss	Agness	666	Mnt
John	396	Rch	Wm.	202	Kng	And.	272	Rck
John M.	441	Flv	Hailey, Archibald	51	Chr	Benjamin	626	Gls
Joseph	464	Bdf	Benjamin	52	Chr	Benjamin	775	Wst
Joseph	432	Flv	Benjamin	28	Hnr	Edward	626	Gls
Richard	440	Bth	Daniel	340	Fqr	Francis	490	Frn
Richard D.	468	Bdf	Edmund	52	Chr	Jacob	666	Mnt
Richard P.	571	Pre	Eliza.	450	Grn	James	984	Nrt

Name	No.	Co.
James L.	451	Frn
Jehu	486	Frn
John	464	Bdf
John	466	Frn
John	485	Frn
Joseph	450	Frn
Joseph	420	Msn
Moses	984	Nrt
Thomas	465	Bdf
Thomas	486	Frn
Thomas	495	Frn
William	432	Msn
see Hal..., Hall		
Hales, Benjamin	463	Bdf
Catharine	509	Prw
William	695	Br
Haley, Ambrose	52	Chr
Chas.	350	Ags
David	404	Fqr
Humphrey	51	Chr
John	53	Chr
Joseph	53	Chr
Mary	906	Crl
Meriday	906	Crl
Pleasant	51	Chr
Pricilla	53	Chr
Thomas	53	Chr
Thomas	85	Jff
Halfacre, Michael	720	Wsh
Halkins, Thomas	13	Wod
Hall, Aaron	864	Hnv
Alexer.	351	Ags
Ambrus	198	Alb
Ananias	865	Hnv
Ann	658	Glc
Ann S.	404	Rch
Asa	505	Mnn
Asa	83	Spt
Asey	614	Mnt
Austin	986	Nrt
Barton	262	Frf
Barzilla	35	Rcm
Bazel	279	Ldn
Benjamin	148	Dnw
Benjamin	29	Stf
Benjamin H.	36	Stf
Benjn.	577	Mnr
Bennet	570	Frd
Betty	330	Dnw
Cary	658	Glc
Cary	799	Nrf
Charity	505	Mnn
Charles	625	Gls
Currel	458	Frn
Dabney	160	Alb
Daniel	984	Nrt
David	149	Dnw
David	625	Gls
David	912	Hrr
David	663	Mnt
David	827	Nrf
Dixon	100	Acc
Dudley	906	Crl
Ed.	509	Mnn
Edward	752	Brn
Edward	800	Bck
Edward	564	Frd
Edward	658	Mnt
Edward	791	Nrf
Eligah	955	Hrr
Eligal	940	Hrr
Elijah	242	Ldn
Elisha	465	Bdf
Elisha	409	Fqr
Elisha	113	Spt
Eliza	659	Glc
Eliza	19	Hnr
Eliza.	45	Clp
Elizabeth	465	Bdf
Elizabeth	906	Crl
Elizabeth	262	Frf
Elizabeth	537	Prg
Ezekiah	464	Bdf
Fracis.	806	Nrf
Frances	64	Chs
Frances	167	Knq
Francis	296	Amh
Francis	334	Dnw
Francis	547	Prg
Freeburn	624	Mnt
Geo. M.	833	Nrf
George	586	Frd
George	3	Isw
George T.	456	Pra
Gilbert	27	Acc
Hannah	97	Jff
Harriot	984	Nrt
Henny.	938	Hrr
Henry	658	Glc
Henry	659	Glc
Herbert	642	Sss
Instance	541	Prg
Isaac	17	Hnr
Isaac	773	Wst
Isham	874	Cmp
J...nce	240	Aml
Jac.	508	Mnn
Jacob	262	Frf
James [2]	198	Alb
James	410	Ags
James	64	Chs
James	341	Fqr
James	656	Glc
James	865	Hnv
James	4	Isw
James	9	Oho
James	569	Pre
James	305	Rck
James A.	106	Cmb
James D.	166	Knq
James., C	869	Hnv
Jams.	582	Mnr
Jeremh.	40	Clp
Jesse	907	Hrr
Jesse	915	Hrr
Jesse	614	Mnt
Jno.	41	Clp
Jno.	658	Glc
Jno.	864	Hnv
Jno.	348	Lnc
Jno.	903	Nrf
Jno.	904	Nrf
Jno., Snr.	865	Hnv
Jno. T.	864	Hnv
John	101	Acc
John	198	Alb
John	199	Alb
John	288	Amh
John	464	Bdf
John	906	Crl
John	150	Dnw
John	387	Fqr
John	480	Frn
John	450	Grn
John	912	Hrr
John	9	Isw
John	425	Msn
John	464	Mdd
John	582	Mnr
John	985	Nrt
John	10	Ntt
John	524	Prw
John	278	Rck
John	112	Spt
John	640	Sss
John, Sr.	644	Sss
John F.	288	Amh
Jonathan	606	Mnt
Jonathan	201	Shn
Jordan	504	Mnn
Jos.	658	Glc
Joseph	198	Alb
Joseph	912	Hrr
Joseph	963	Hrr
Joseph	431	Msn
Joseph	815	Nrf
Joshua	77	Jff
Josiah	294	Ldn
Laban	824	Nrf
Lancelot	983	Nrt
Leanard	628	Btt
Leonard	922	Hrr
Levi	102	Jff
Levi	301	Ldn
Lewis	657	Glc
Lewis	50	Stf
Lucretia	268	Rck
Martha	14	Isw
Martin	984	Nrt
Mary	804	Nrf
Maryland	535	Frd
Mathew	465	Bdf
Matthew	658	Glc
Mildred	658	Glc
Molly	100	Acc
Moses	291	Amh
Moses	6	Oho
Nancey	617	Mnt
Nancy	503	Brk
Nancy	543	Prg
Nancy	196	Shn
Nathan [2]	198	Alb
Nathan	282	Amh
Nathan	508	Mnn
Natl.	347	Ags
Overton	870	Hnv
Patrick	353	Ags
Peter	412	Rch
Philip	431	Msn
Rappee, f. negro	261	Frf
Randolp	658	Mnt
Reuben, f. negro	268	Frf
Rhoda	458	Frn
Richard	522	Frd
Richard	943	Hrr
Richard	756	Nwk
Richd.	715	Brn
Richd.	509	Mnn
Richd.	905	Nrf
Rihard	242	Ldn
Robert	98	Acc
Robert	456	Frn
Robin	526	Brk
Rodham	773	Wst
Roswell	839	Wth
Sally	333	Dnw
Sally	576	Frd
Sally	26	Isw
Saml.	921	Hrr
Saml.	935	Hrr
Saml.	226	Shn
Samuel	794	Bck
Samuel	785	Hmp
Sarah	865	Hnv
Sarah, Jnr.	865	Hnv
Severn	840	Nrf
Siclus H.	284	Amh
Squire	508	Mnn
Stephen	659	Glc
Susan	411	Rch
Susan.	406	Rch
Susanna	903	Nrf
Tho.	505	Mnn
Thomas	101	Acc
Thomas	790	Bck
Thomas	879	Cmp
Thomas	912	Hrr
Thomas	927	Hrr
Thomas	59	Jff
Thomas	97	Jff

Thomas	212	Shn
Thomas	104	Spt
Thomas, Sen.	26	Isw
Thos.	40	Clp
Thos.	334	Dnw
Thos. [2]	657	Glc
Thos.	505	Mnn
Thos.	799	Nrf
Thos., (Son of George)	4	Isw
Thos., (Son of James)	5	Isw
Timothy	862	Hnv
Trussel	773	Wst
W., Junr.	261	Frf
W., Senr.	261	Frf
Watlington	797	Nrf
Warner	658	Glc
William [2]	198	Alb
William	283	Amh
William	680	Br
William	786	Bck
William	790	Bck
William	879	Cmp
William	906	Crl
William	334	Dnw
William	336	Dnw
William	387	Fqr
William	456	Frn
William	64	Jff
William	68	Jff
William	429	Msn
William	6	Oho
William	11	Rcm
William	245	Shn
William, Junr.	773	Wst
William, Senr.	775	Wst
William H.	411	Rch
William W.	240	Aml
Williamson	161	Alb
Willis	800	Nrf
Wim.	864	Hnv
Wm.	353	Ags
Wm.	658	Glc
Wm.	659	Glc
Wm.	962	Hrr
Wm.	293	Ldn
Wm.	509	Mnn
Wm.	804	Nrf
Wm.	904	Nrf
Wm.	279	Rck
Wm., (snap)	658	Glc
see Hal..., Hale, Halls, Heill, Hull, Prince		
Hallaback, Abraham	821	Hmp
Daniel	822	Hmp
John	820	Hmp
see Hollaback		
Hallam, Charles	684	Br
Edward	8	Hnr
Nicholas	31	Hnr
Hallatt, John	28	Acc
Hallbrooks, John	773	Wst
Hallcomb, Richd.	129	Sth
Hallecomb, James	851	Sth
Haller, Jacob	627	Btt
Jacob	600	Frd
Jno. K.	36	Hnr
John	836	Wth
Halley, George	262	Frf
Henry H.	262	Frf
Henry S.	263	Frf
James	262	Frf
James	507	Prw
John	584	Brk
John	167	Shn
William	262	Frf
Halliday, ---	328	Dnw
Am [Ann?]	813	Nrf
Thos.	903	Nrf

Hallidy, John	464	Bdf
Hallon see Hatton		
Hallow, Augustine	241	Shn
Henry, (of P.)	241	Shn
Peter	241	Shn
see Hollow		
Hallowell, John	819	Nrf
John, jr.	820	Nrf
Halls, Robert, (est.)	645	Sss
Hallsbrooks, Sally	774	Wst
Hally, John	538	Frd
Halney, Sarah	29	Acc
Halsey, Isaac	757	Nwk
James	696	Gch
Jennett	903	Nrf
John	696	Gch
Halson, Geo.	177	Elc
Halstead, Chas.	804	Nrf
Elizabeth, (l)	797	Nrf
Henry	804	Nrf
Ivey	790	Nrf
Jas.	804	Nrf
John	808	Nrf
Matthias	793	Nrf
Matthias	808	Nrf
Nat.	799	Nrf
Richd.	797	Nrf
Sarah	799	Nrf
Simon	799	Nrf
Thos.	804	Nrf
Thos.	808	Nrf
Halsted, Simon, Sr.	809	Nrf
Halstine, Henry, Jr.	630	Btt
Henry, Sr.	630	Btt
Hugh	630	Btt
John	630	Btt
Mercy	630	Btt
Stephen, Jr.	630	Btt
Stephen, Sr.	630	Btt
Halterman, Henry	182	Shn
Haltermann, Christopher	22	Oho
Jacob	22	Oho
Haltimon, Jacob, Junr.	226	Shn
Jacob, Senr.	226	Shn
Halvey see Hulvey		
Haly, Mhony	935	Hrr
Halyburton, William	757	Nwk
Ham, ---	902	Nrf
Aggy	31	Hnr
Elijah	198	Alb
John	588	Mnr
Michael	84	Jff
Nancy	128	Hnr
Peter	512	Frd
Salley	9	Hnr
William	218	Pnd
Ham..., James	466	Bdf
Haman, Dannul	935	Hrr
Peter	262	Frf
Hambarger, John	446	Bth
Hambaugh, John	163	Shn
John	164	Shn
Hambelton, John	8	Hnr
Hamber see Humber		
Hamblen, Daniel	571	Pre
William	571	Pre
Hamblet, Rubin	29	Hnr
Thomas	703	Nls
Hambleton, Andrew	262	Amh
Elizabeth	569	Pre
Geo.	9	Hnr
James	467	Bdf
James	53	Chr
James	361	Fqr
James	702	Nls
Jno.	268	Frf
John	569	Pre
John, Junr.	569	Pre
John M.	104	Cmb
John W.	104	Cmb

Leonard	827	Bck
Mary	69	Chr
Mary	264	Frf
Morris	785	Bck
Robert	260	Amh
Robert	569	Pre
Salley, (F. Negroe)	369	Fqr
William	805	Bck
William	101	Cmb
see Hampliton		
Hamblin, Coleman	53	Chr
Thomas	53	Chr
William	240	Aml
Hambric, John	363	Fqr
Hambrick, Enoch	8	Knw
Jas.	629	Btt
Jno.	44	Clp
Joel	8	Knw
Joseph, Jr.	477	Frn
Joseph, Sr.	479	Frn
Peyton	45	Clp
Wm.	43	Clp
see Hambuck		
Hambrik, Josias	808	Hmp
Hambuck, Saml.	42	Clp
Hambury, Wm., (OM)	806	Nrf
Hameford, John	8	Knw
Hamentree, David	268	Frf
Hamer see Harner		
Hames, Wm.	4	Ntt
see Haines		
Hamett, Jno.	289	Ldn
Hamford see Hansford		
Hamige, Jacob	826	Nrf
Hamill, John	514	Prw
Hamilton, Abraham	41	Rcm
Alexr.	236	Ldn
Alexr.	690	Wsh
Andw.	627	Btt
Andw., Sr.	629	Btt
Arch	506	Mnn
Archibald	1	Oho
Ben	503	Mnn
Benjamin	6	Oho
Benjn.	82	Jff
Bradley	627	Btt
Charles	419	Bth
Charles	805	Hmp
David	353	Ags
Dido	793	Hmp
Elizabeth	78	Jff
Fergerson	60	Jff
George	41	Rcm
George	89	Spt
Gilbreath	835	Wth
Greeson	419	Bth
Hamilton H.	687	Br
Hen.	504	Mnn
Henry	837	Wth
James	352	Ags
James	353	Ags
James	419	Bth
James	538	Frd
James	304	Ldn
James	267	Rck
James, Ser.	419	Bth
Jane	306	Ldn
Jas.	508	Mnn
Jas.	835	Nrf
Jas., Sr.	627	Btt
Jno.	257	Ldn
Jno.	297	Ldn
Jno.	902	Nrf
Jno., Jr.	627	Btt
Jno., Sr.	629	Btt
John	351	Ags
John	352	Ags
John	353	Ags
John	419	Bth
John	687	Br

John	542	Frd	Bene.	411	Rch	Moses	125	Hnr
John	78	Jff	Elizabeth	602	Frd	Rowland	125	Hnr
John	7	Knw	Jacob	602	Frd	Sally	20	Isw
John	275	Rck	James	344	Lnn	Thomas	253	Shn
Js.	507	Mnn	John	781	Hmp	William, Jr.	348	Fqr
Osburn	419	Bth	John	400	Rch	William, Senr.	375	Fqr
Patienc	352	Ags	Nancy	602	Frd	Wm.	713	Brn
Rob.	507	Mnn	Thos.	631	Btt	Wm.	265	Frf
Robert	270	Ldn	William	344	Lnn	Wm.	125	Hnr
Robert	519	Prw	William	392	Rch	see Hampliton		
Robt.	271	Rck	Hammon, George	113	Spt	Hamrick, Benjamin	7	Knw
S... [Shad. ?]	281	Rck	Henry	588	Rck	Hams, John	708	Wsh
Saml.	516	Brk	John	774	Wst	Hamsor, Robt.	32	Hnr
Sarah, Mrs.	714	Wsh	Mary	632	Btt	Hamton, Ambrous S.	343	Lnn
Tho.	504	Mnn	Thimoty	918	Hrr	George	457	Frn
Thomas	674	Br	Wm.	713	Brn	Hanack, Martin	10	Knw
William	676	Br	Wm.	453	Mth	Hanan, Esham	632	Btt
William	826	Hmp	see Hamon			Hanback, Sarah	349	Fqr
William B.	774	Wst	Hammond, Absalom	794	Hmp	Hanberry, Willis	332	Dnw
Wm.	629	Btt	George	674	Br	Hanbury, Jas.	793	Nrf
Wm.	249	Ldn	George	23	Rcm	Jesse	793	Nrf
Wm.	305	Ldn	Jesse	348	Lnc	Job	796	Nrf
Wm.	286	Rck	Joel	328	Dnw	John, Sr.	793	Nrf
Wm.	301	Rck	John	676	Br	Thos., Sr.	793	Nrf
Wm., Jr.	630	Btt	Joshua	835	Wth	Wm.	793	Nrf
Wm., Sr.	630	Btt	Michl.	523	Brk	Hanby, Catrin	744	Wsh
see Hampliton			Molly	348	Lnc	Hance, Adam	626	Mnt
Hamlet, Burwell	755	Nwk	Nancy	349	Lnc	Henry	626	Mnt
Carter	715	Brn	Newman	773	Wst	Peter	626	Mnt
Elizabeth	715	Brn	Sarah	349	Lnc	Hancher, Nicholas	579	Frd
James	863	Cmp	Thomas	65	Jff	Thomas	579	Frd
John	148	Dnw	William	412	Rch	William	579	Frd
Stephen	345	Lnn	Hammondre, Rhoda	132	Cmb	Hancock, Abner	657	Mnt
William	700	Nls	Hammonds, Elizabeth	983	Nrt	Benjamin	453	Frn
see Hamlit			Nelly	878	Sth	Benjamin	490	Frn
Hamlett, Bedford	52	Chr	Hammons, Anna	49	Clp	Benjamin	163	Shn
David	572	Pre	Raleigh	344	Lnn	Benjamin	164	Shn
Elias	696	Nls	Robert	714	Brn	Francis	752	Brn
George	69	Chr	Thomas	344	Lnn	George	627	Btt
James, Jur.	52	Chr	William	344	Lnn	George	533	Frd
James, Snr.	53	Chr	William	645	Sss	George	177	Shn
Jessee	344	Lnn	Winnefred	114	Spt	Green	61	Chs
John	697	Nls	Hammontre, John	985	Nrt	James	31	Acc
William	52	Chr	Hammot, Nimrod	631	Btt	James	31	Isw
Hamlin, Hubard	3	Isw	Hammott, John	202	Kng	James	167	Shn
Jno.	547	Prg	Hamner, Agness	160	Alb	John	861	Cmp
John	149	Dnw	Charles M.	796	Bck	John	14	Isw
John	343	Lnn	Francis	159	Alb	John	171	Shn
Joseph	957	Chc	Henley	160	Alb	Joseph	848	Hnv
Martha	63	Chs	Henley	161	Alb	Lewis	458	Frn
Susan	533	Prg	Jerremiah	160	Alb	M.	11	Hnr
Thomas	343	Lnn	Morriss	51	Chr	Margaret	504	Prw
see Epps			Nicholas	160	Alb	Martin	69	Chr
Hamlit, George	940	Chc	Saml.	52	Chr	Samuel	466	Bdf
James	940	Chc	Samuel	833	Bck	Sarah	751	Brn
John	946	Chc	William	160	Alb	Simon	456	Pra
Thomas	940	Chc	William	696	Nls	Simon	490	Pra
Hamm, James	264	Amh	see Hhamner			Stephen	160	Sth
John T.	241	Aml	Hamney, Jacob	596	Brk	Thomas	102	Acc
Obedience	239	Aml	Hamon, Thomas	933	Hrr	Thomas	30	Isw
Stephen	280	Amh	Wm.	935	Hrr	William	99	Acc
Wm.	191	Elc	Hamond, James	589	Brk	William	19	Isw
Hammach, Lewes, Sr.	484	Frn	Hampliton, Robert	701	Nls	Wm.	265	Frf
Hammack, Lewis	482	Frn	see Hambleton			Wm.	143	Sth
Tollaver	453	Frn	Hampton, David	713	Brn	Hancocke, Elizabeth	641	Sss
Hamman, ---	328	Dnw	Elijah	20	Isw	James	641	Sss
Hammand, Merimond	67	Chs	Ephraim	11	Ntt	Jeremiah	640	Sss
Hammel, Littleton	27	Acc	Henry	513	Prw	Jesse	641	Sss
Hammer, George	223	Pnd	Jack	191	Elc	John	641	Sss
Henry	35	Rcm	Jacob	957	Chc	Zacheriah	642	Sss
John	24	Rcm	Jeremiah	713	Brn	Hand, Christn.	599	Mnr
Leonard	225	Pnd	Jeremiah	234	Ldn	George	599	Mnr
Palser	216	Pnd	Jno.	236	Ldn	Hannah	263	Ldn
Susanah	223	Pnd	Jno., Sr.	628	Btt	James	694	Wsh
Hammerly, Jno.	302	Ldn	John	464	Bdf	Jno.	264	Ldn
Hammersley, Francis	264	Frf	John	378	Fqr	Robert	593	Frd
Hammet, Geo.	303	Ldn	Joseph	265	Frf	Thos.	710	Wsh
Hammett, Robt.	627	Btt	Joseph	561	Frd	William	593	Frd
Hammilton, Crsl.	933	Hrr	Mary	371	Fqr	Wm.	263	Ldn
Hammock, Anna	344	Lnn	Mary	584	Frd	Handell, John	585	Frd

Name	No.	Place
Handen, John	547	Brk
Handey, Guina	238	Ldn
Wm. H.	237	Ldn
Handley, Archd.	583	Mnr
Daniel	309	Ldn
George	585	Mnr
Isaac	583	Mnr
James, Sr.	586	Mnr
John	577	Mnr
John	583	Mnr
Weir	303	Rck
William	626	Gls
William	602	Mnr
Zacha.	258	Ldn
Handlin, Philip	95	Jff
Handover, Charity	100	Acc
Lemuel	100	Acc
Handsford, ---, Doctr.	904	Nrf
see Hansford, Row		
Handy, John, Jr.	494	Frn
Haner, William	101	Spt
Hanery see Harvey		
Hanes, Benja.	915	Hrr
Curtis	570	Pre
Daniel	600	Frd
David	871	Hnv
David, Jnr.	866	Hnv
Dunston	900	Hnv
Gedeon	864	Hnv
George	802	Hmp
Henry	826	Hmp
Henry	9	Hnr
Isaac	778	Hmp
James	869	Hnv
John	778	Hmp
John	844	Hnv
Joseph	778	Hmp
Plesant	864	Hnv
see Hanies, Harris		
Haney, Edward	628	Btt
Eliz.	504	Mnn
Geo.	40	Clp
Jenkins	94	Spt
Peter	598	Mnr
Sarah	41	Clp
Thomas	94	Spt
Thos.	42	Clp
William	94	Spt
Hanger, David	352	Ags
Geo.	348	Ags
John	353	Ags
Martin	353	Ags
Peter	349	Ags
Peter, jr.	353	Ags
Hanies, Wm.	515	Brk
Hank, Caleb	572	Mnr
Wm.	582	Mnr
see Hawk		
Hankins, Daniel	51	Chr
Daniel	9	Knw
Prior	876	Yrk
Robert	51	Chr
Wm.	876	Yrk
Hanks, Hannah	344	Lnn
John	464	Mdd
Luke	395	Rch
Thos.	714	Brn
William	683	Br
Hanley, James	562	Mnr
William	695	Wsh
Hanlon, Walter	677	Br
Hanly, Isabala	698	Wsh
John	698	Wsh
Samuel	13	Knw
Hanmon, Pall	250	Shn
see Hommon		
Hanna, Andrew	831	Nrf
Isaac	347	Ags
Matthw	263	Rck
Nathan	8	Knw
Robt.	349	Ags
Thomas	8	Rcm
William	8	Rcm
Wm.	354	Ags
Hannah, Alexr.	627	Btt
David	428	Bth
George	51	Chr
Heny M.	22	Hnr
Hugh	578	Mnr
James	51	Chr
James, (NC[?])	51	Chr
Jan [e?]	221	Shn
Joseph	418	Rnd
Patterson	628	Btt
Rebeccah	51	Chr
Wallace	538	Brk
William	68	Chr
Hanner, George, (TB)	466	Bdf
see Harmer		
Hanners, Jesse	458	Pra
Wm.	458	Pra
Hanness, William	830	Hmp
Hanniford, Jno.	903	Nrf
Hannimel, Peter	4	Wod
Hannin, George	589	Brk
Michael	589	Brk
Hannison, Martha	579	Brk
Nancy	527	Brk
Wm.	579	Brk
Hannon, R.F.	328	Dnw
Richard F.	328	Dnw
Thomas	431	Msn
Hannum, Thomas	573	Frd
Hanover, Elizabeth	263	Frf
Thomas	263	Frf
Hansbarger, Adam	35	Rcm
Conrod	36	Rcm
Ephraim	15	Rcm
Robt.	352	Ags
Hansberry, John	801	Hmp
Hansbrough, Elijah	590	Frd
French	541	Frd
Jas.	39	Clp
John	201	Kng
Martha	699	Nls
Peter, jr.	39	Clp
Peter, ser.	39	Clp
Samuel	698	Nls
Wm., ser.	39	Clp
Hanse, Chrn.	348	Ags
Hansel, Charles	436	Bth
Jno.	505	Mnn
Hanserd, ---	332	Dnw
Hansford, Ben.	875	Yrk
Charles	678	Wrw
Edwd.	826	Nrf
Eliza.	678	Wrw
John	273	Amh
Lewis	875	Yrk
Theod.	202	Kng
Tho., (Y)	875	Yrk
William	838	Bck
see Handsford		
Hanshaw, Johm	431	Msn
Sarah	431	Msn
Hansil, Michael	98	Jff
Hansley, Eliza.	43	Clp
Hanson, Daniel	334	Dnw
Saml.	628	Btt
Thomas	580	Frd
Thomas	805	Hmp
Wm.	629	Btt
Hansucker, George	511	Frd
Jacob	531	Frd
Thomas	511	Frd
Hanvy, Patrick	522	Frd
Hanway, Rachl.	508	Mnn
Hanworth, Jno.	299	Rck
Hany, John	925	Hrr
Haok see Hook		
Happ, John	25	Rcm
see Hopp		
Happer, Marina	790	Nrf
Har..., James (...)	468	Bdf
John	468	Bdf
Harbarger, Jos.	261	Shn
Joseph	179	Shn
Harber, Edward	915	Hrr
John	946	Hrr
Samuel	946	Hrr
Thomas [2]	946	Hrr
Harberson, Anna	390	Mds
Harckins see Hankins		
Harcum, Charles	986	Nrt
James	986	Nrt
John	985	Nrt
Lee P.	985	Nrt
Philip J.	985	Nrt
Sarah C.	983	Nrt
William	983	Nrt
Hardacre, Benjamin	543	Frd
Hardaway, Benjamin	137	Dnw
Benjn.	147	Dnw
Daniel	239	Aml
Drury	882	Cmp
Grief	148	Dnw
John	147	Dnw
Markam	148	Dnw
Peter M.	148	Dnw
Standfield	148	Dnw
Thos. G.	149	Dnw
see Hardiway		
Hardbarger, Ab.	352	Ags
Harden, Elizabeth	250	Ldn
Daniel	923	Hrr
Edward	697	Nls
Frank	933	Hrr
Geo.	41	Clp
George	694	Gch
Jno.	304	Ldn
Heny	250	Ldn
Lewis	250	Ldn
Nancy	302	Ldn
Nathan	697	Nls
Nester	422	Rnd
Presly	249	Ldn
Richd.	583	Brk
Samuel	697	Nls
Thos.	807	Nrf
Harderson see Henderson		
Hardestie, Richard	16	Oho
Hardesty, Elijh.	508	Mnn
Jesse	4	Oho
Richard	66	Jff
Hardey, Geo.	292	Ldn
John	464	Mdd
Samuel	25	Isw
Thomas, Jun.	25	Isw
William	464	Mdd
Hardick, Joseph V	849	Cmp
Hardie, Clary	119	Spt
William	107	Spt
see Hendie		
Hardiman, Charles	781	Bck
Charles	833	Bck
John	841	Bck
Hardin, Benjamin	197	Alb
Charles	507	Prw
Daniel	197	Alb
Daniel	198	Alb
Edward	508	Prw
Edward	523	Prw
George	197	Alb
Hackey	442	Flv
Hal	350	Fqr
Isaac	197	Alb
Jesse	120	Hnr
John	266	Amh
Thomas	35	Isw
William	351	Fqr

Name	No.	Co.	Name	No.	Co.	Name	No.	Co.
William	502	Prw	Joseph	464	Mdd	Mary	160	Sth
William	512	Prw	Joshua	241	Ldn	Joseph	699	Nls
William	515	Prw	Josuewa	343	Lnn	Thomas	698	Nls
Harding, Clarka	48	Stf	Martin	829	Hmp	Hargus, John	27	Acc
Daniel	266	Frf	Mary [2]	149	Dnw	Levin	28	Acc
Elijah	44	Stf	Molley	149	Dnw	Harholt, Andrew	225	Pnd
Enoch	49	Stf	Robert	467	Bdf	John	220	Pnd
George	263	Frf	Rudolph	774	Hmp	Michal	223	Pnd
George	68	Jff	Solomon	466	Bdf	Haris, Benj.	35	Hnr
Henry	256	Shn	Solomon	295	Ldn	Joseph	10	Knw
Hopkins	983	Nrt	Solomon, Sr.	464	Bdf	Harisbarger, John	443	Bth
Job	265	Ldn	Thomas	463	Bdf	Harison, David	20	Hnr
Joel	24	Stf	Thomas, Sen.	11	Isw	Lidy	952	Hrr
John, of C.	42	Stf	Thos.	629	Btt	Hariston, George	51	Chr
John, Sr.	44	Stf	Vincent	344	Lnn	Harker, Christeeny	818	Hmp
Joseph	805	Nrf	William	266	Frf	Joseph	431	Msn
Josiah	539	Frd	Wm.	627	Btt	Harkerider, Benjamin	836	Wth
Lucy	43	Stf	Wm.	209	Ess	Benjamin	838	Wth
Mark	31	Stf	Wm.	657	Glc	Coonrod	838	Wth
Mary	335	Dnw	Wm.	904	Nrf	Isaac	836	Wth
Robert, jr.	334	Lnn	see Har...			Jacob	838	Wth
Robert, Sr.	344	Lnn	Hardyman, Francis	948	Chc	John	837	Wth
Samuel	985	Nrt	John	956	Chc	John	838	Wth
Tempe	830	Nrf	Tyler	954	Chc	Phillip	838	Wth
Thomas	345	Lnn	Hare, Adam	829	Hmp	Harkham, Peggy	10	Hnr
Thomas	982	Nrt	Alexander	132	Hnr	Harkrider, David	655	Mnt
Thomas	25	Stf	Eliza	821	Nrf	Jacob	467	Frn
Thos.	800	Nrf	Fred.	353	Ags	Salomon	476	Frn
William	982	Nrt	Isaac	695	Gch	Harlan, James	502	Brk
Hardison, Wm.	457	Pra	Jacob	963	Hrr	Harland, John	166	Knq
Hardister, Thomas	236	Ldn	Jno.	504	Mnn	Harle, Richard	466	Bdf
Hardisty, Henry	682	Br	John	821	Nrf	Harlen, Emor	325	Dnw
Hardivay, James H.	750	Brn	Jos.	23	Hnr	Geo.	549	Brk
Hardiway, Henry S.	752	Brn	Joseph	580	Frd	George	334	Dnw
Sarah	750	Brn	Richard	697	Nls	Joseph	161	Alb
Stith	21	Ntt	Saml.	821	Nrf	Harless, Abram	625	Gls
see Hardivay			Sarah	166	Knq	Daniel	625	Gls
Hardman, David	686	Br	Thomas	65	Chs	Fardanand	626	Gls
Henery	934	Hrr	Willm. B., City of			Isaac	626	Gls
Henry	934	Hrr	Richmond	702	Nls	Joseph	625	Gls
Jacob	953	Hrr	Hareder, Jno.	507	Mnn	Michael	626	Gls
John	910	Hrr	see Harreder			Philip	626	Gls
Peter	953	Hrr	Harell, George	13	Knw	Harley, George	265	Frf
Hardon, Isaac	162	Alb	Harford, Henry	400	Rch	James	726	Wsh
Thomas	242	Ldn	Jno.	43	Clp	Mildrerd	265	Frf
Hardway, Andrew	224	Pnd	Peter	831	Nrf	William	265	Frf
George	224	Pnd	Samuel	544	Frd	William	720	Wsh
Hardwick, Aaron	401	Rch	William	538	Frd	Harlin, Jesse	785	Hmp
Benjamin	819	Bck	Hargar, John	499	Frn	Jessee	159	Alb
George	8	Knw	Hargas, Thos.	721	Wsh	Silas	585	Brk
Jerremiah	570	Pre	Hargis, William	99	Acc	Thos.	607	Mnt
Joheph	345	Lnn	Hargo, Jean, (Color)	569	Mnr	Harlis, David	627	Mnt
John	773	Wst	Hargran see Hayran			Henry	642	Mnt
Lain	344	Lnn	Hargrave, Benjamin	608	Srr	Philip, Jr.	627	Mnt
Richard	273	Amh	George	640	Sss	Philip, Jr.	628	Mnt
Robert	567	Frd	Hamlin	640	Sss	Philip, Sr.	627	Mnt
Susanna	9	Ntt	Hannah	608	Srr	Saml.	627	Mnt
William	870	Cmp	Herman	608	Srr	Harlow, Brice	434	Flv
Hardy, Amey	100	Acc	James	148	Dnw	Cate	8	Hnr
Baptist	468	Bdf	Jno.	860	Hnv	Charles	161	Alb
Catharine	345	Lnn	Jno., jr.	872	Hnv	Christopher	433	Flv
Charles	346	Lnn	John	608	Srr	Edmund	160	Alb
Christopher	16	Ntt	Joseph	908	Crl	Geo.	697	Gch
Coventon	346	Lnn	Joseph	640	Sss	Jno.	631	Btt
Elizabeth	149	Dnw	Lucy	908	Crl	Joell	445	Flv
Elizabeth	344	Lnn	Nancy	645	Sss	John	161	Alb
Eve	784	Hmp	Pleasant	608	Srr	John	628	Btt
Frances	150	Dnw	Robert	640	Sss	John	112	Hnr
Hannah	54	Stf	Sally	608	Srr	John, Snr.	113	Hnr
Henry	627	Btt	Samuel	948	Chc	Mary	436	Flv
Joel	149	Dnw	Samuel	642	Sss	Molley	431	Flv
John	798	Bck	Wim.	869	Hnv	Nathaniel	443	Flv
John	829	Bck	Hargraves, Thomas	14	Isw	Nathaniel	700	Nls
John	570	Frd	Hargrove, Danl.	457	Pra	Nathaniel, Jnr.	699	Nls
John	784	Hmp	Elizabeth	907	Crl	P.	433	Flv
John	818	Nrf	Hezekiah	698	Nls	Selah	161	Alb
John	609	Srr	Hezikiah	698	Nls	Tandy	434	Flv
John C.	344	Lnn	Humphrey	906	Crl	Thomas	445	Flv
Joseph	467	Bdf	John	696	Nls	Thos. [2]	753	Wsh
Joseph	330	Dnw	John	149	Sth	Wm.	446	Flv

142

Name	No.	Co.	Name	No.	Co.	Name	No.	Co.
Wm. T.	112	Hnr	Anne	240	Aml	Harrier, Martin	85	Jff
Harlowe, Austin	160	Alb	Asa	397	Fqr	Harriff, Andw.	401	Ags
George	161	Alb	Asa	13	Ntt	Harriford, Robert	423	Msn
Larkins	198	Alb	Benjamin	570	Frd	Harring, Benja., f. negro	264	Frf
Nathaniel	162	Alb	Billups	7	Ntt	Harrington, Danl.	263	Frf
William	160	Alb	Casleton	160	Alb	Richd.	902	Nrf
Harly, John	718	Wsh	Catharine	167	Knq	Harris, ---, Mrs.	20	Hnr
Harman, Easter	30	Acc	Chs.	42	Clp	Abm.	507	Mnn
Elisabeth	755	Nwk	Claiborne	6	Ntt	Agness	900	Hnv
Emanuel	29	Acc	Daniel	220	Pnd	Amos	820	Hmp
Euphamy	102	Acc	Ealias	220	Pnd	Ams, Este.	902	Nrf
George	29	Acc	Elizth.	272	Rck	Anderson	781	Bck
George	627	Btt	Frances	6	Ntt	Anderson	794	Bck
Ithamar	755	Nwk	Hannah	400	Fqr	Ann	41	Clp
James	903	Nrf	Henry	657	Glc	Ann	879	Hnv
Jno.	629	Btt	Henry	702	Nls	Ann	131	Sth
John	28	Acc	Henry	217	Pnd	Anthony	589	Frd
John	101	Acc	Jacob [2]	220	Pnd	Anthony	867	Sth
John	102	Acc	James	262	Frf	Asa	504	Mnn
John	601	Frd	James	584	Mnr	Augustine	906	Crl
John	507	Mnn	James	273	Rck	Benja.	267	Frf
John	756	Nwk	James, Revd.	688	Wsh	Benjamin	159	Alb
John, jr.	756	Nwk	Jno.	263	Frf	Benjamin	799	Bck
John, Junr.	28	Acc	Jno.	268	Ldn	Benjamin	537	Frd
John, Senr.	28	Acc	Jno.	292	Ldn	Benjamin	697	Nls
Kendall	29	Acc	John	625	Gls	Benjamin	12	Pwh
Keziah	755	Nwk	John	166	Knq	Benjamin, Jr.	537	Frd
Margaret	29	Acc	John	241	Ldn	Betsey	15	Hnr
Matthias	601	Frd	John	839	Wth	Blake	197	Alb
Molly	102	Acc	John D.	166	Knq	Burwell	8	Isw
Scarburgh	101	Acc	Joseph	217	Ess	Chapman	608	Srr
Stephen	100	Acc	Joseph W.	148	Dnw	Charles	714	Brn
Thomas	29	Acc	Kennon	11	Ntt	Charles	595	Frd
William	27	Acc	Lavina	834	Nrf	Charles, (Y)	875	Yrk
William, Jun.	31	Acc	Leond., Junr.	263	Frf	Chavis	958	Chc
Harmanson, Matthew	27	Acc	Leond., Senr.	263	Frf	Christopher	752	Wsh
Pat	903	Nrf	Nancy	834	Nrf	Curthbert	261	Frf
Harmen, Elizt.	401	Ags	Nathaniel	714	Brn	Daniel	10	Oho
Geo. H.	352	Ags	Nicholas	268	Frf	David	33	Hnr
Henry	346	Ags	Nicholas	254	Ldn	David	100	Jff
Henry, jr.	346	Ags	Nicholas	216	Pnd	David	17	Wod
John	346	Ags	Nicholas	221	Pnd	David, Snr.	871	Hnv
Harmer, William	510	Frd	Philip [2]	220	Pnd	David, T	863	Hnv
Harmon, Catherine	610	Mnt	Richard	161	Alb	Dianna	861	Hnv
Henry	9	Knw	Robert	695	Br	Edward	959	Chc
Henry	10	Knw	Robert	210	Ess	Edward	700	Nls
Isaac	222	Pnd	Saml.	283	Rck	Egbert	9	Pwh
Jacob	651	Mnt	Samuel	570	Pre	Elijah, f. negro	265	Frf
Jeremiah	19	Hnr	Susanna	14	Ntt	Eliza	14	Hnr
John	10	Knw	Thomas	372	Fqr	Elizabeth	907	Crl
Reuben	220	Pnd	Thomas	241	Ldn	Elizabeth	697	Nls
Solomon	652	Mnt	Thos.	221	Ess	Elizabeth	702	Nls
Thomas	10	Knw	Wilkins	641	Sss	Fanney	160	Alb
Thos.	148	Dnw	William	101	Acc	Fanny	656	Mnt
Harmonds, Jno.	45	Clp	William	16	Hnr	Frances	9	Pwh
Harneck, Christ.	297	Rck	William	167	Knq	Francis	779	Bck
Harner, Danl.	346	Ags	William	36	Rcm	Francis	694	Gch
Elizt.	408	Ags	William R.	773	Wst	Francis, Dr.	6	Pwh
George	10	Rcm	Wm.	260	Ldn	George	537	Brk
Jacob	346	Ags	Wm.	288	Rck	George	56	Jff
John	346	Ags	Wm. W.	714	Brn	George	74	Jff
Phil.	507	Mnn	see Hearper			Hamlin	868	Sth
Harness, John	35	Rcm	Harpinding, Asbury	327	Dnw	Hannah	197	Alb
Michael	35	Rcm	Harpire, Jonathan	233	Shn	Hardy	608	Srr
Solomon	806	Hmp	Philip	233	Shn	Henry	197	Alb
Harnest, Jno.	295	Rck	Harpole, Catharine	31	Rcm	Henry	592	Frd
Harnett, James	420	Fqr	Daniel	940	Hrr	Henry T.	697	Nls
Harnige see Hamige			Michal	216	Pnd	Hezekiah	267	Frf
Harold, Ann	53	Stf	Nichs.	421	Msn	Hickman	537	Frd
Harp, Henry	571	Pre	Harpur, John	177	Elc	Holt	644	Sss
James	395	Fqr	Mary	177	Elc	Ignatious	462	Frn
see Tharp			Harras, Jno.	632	Btt	Isaac	631	Btt
Harper, Adam	220	Pnd	Harreder, Dan.	507	Mnn	Isaac	839	Bck
Adam	222	Pnd	see Hareder			Isaiah	872	Cmp
Adam	423	Rnd	Harreld, Nathan	429	Msn	James	197	Alb
Alexr.	559	Brk	Harrell, Elijah	847	Sth	James	354	Ags
Anderson	148	Dnw	Sarah	593	Frd	James	417	Bth
Andrew	277	Rck	Simon	167	Shn	James	467	Bdf
Ann	167	Knq	William	541	Frd	James	816	Bck
Ann D.	167	Knq	Harres see Hanes			James	906	Crl

Name	No.	Code	Name	No.	Code	Name	No.	Code
James	444	Flv	Nancy	550	Prg	Wm.	353	Ags
James	702	Nls	Nathan	197	Alb	Wm.	695	Gch
James	5	Oho	Nathan	696	Nls	Wm.	507	Mnn
James	6	Oho	Nathaniel	467	Bdf	Wm.	702	Nls
James	14	Pwh	Nathaniel	329	Dnw	Wm. Lee	702	Nls
James	139	Sth	Nathaniel	336	Dnw	Zephaniah	564	Mnr
James	850	Sth	Nathaniel	738	Wsh	see Hanes, Wilborn		
James, jr.	958	Chc	Nathl., fn.	266	Frf	Harrison, Alexa.	317	Ldn
James, Sr.	958	Chc	Newit	876	Sth	Alexander	944	Chc
James B.	608	Srr	Overton	198	Alb	Alexander	644	Sss
James E.	467	Bdf	Overton	900	Hnv	Alxr.	833	Nrf
Jane	859	Hnv	Overton, Jnr.	870	Hnv	Ann	543	Prg
Jane	304	Rck	Pamela.	904	Nrf	Ann	19	Rcm
Jane	775	Wst	Parke	901	Hnv	Battle	467	Bdf
Jas., Jr.	629	Btt	Patty	332	Dnw	Benja.	850	Sth
Jeromiah	77	Jff	Peter	505	Mnn	Benja. C.	609	Srr
Jesse	702	Nls	Plummer	872	Hnv	Benja. M.	609	Srr
Jessee	628	Btt	Rd.	43	Clp	Benjamin	713	Brn
Jno.	789	Bck	Rebeccah	15	Hnr	Benjamiin, (Jr.)	14	Rcm
Jno.	44	Clp	Reuben	697	Nls	Benjamin C.	645	Sss
Jno.	657	Glc	Reuben	17	Oho	Benjamin M.	334	Dnw
Jno.	141	Sth	Richard	695	Gch	Benjamn.	28	Acc
Jno.	680	Wrw	Richard	75	Spt	Benjm.	941	Chc
Jno., C.C.	850	Hnv	Richd.	65	Chs	Benjn.	14	Rcm
Jno., W.S.	847	Hnv	Richd.	509	Mnn	Berj. H.	540	Prg
Joel	197	Alb	Robert	29	Acc	Betsey	2	Rcm
John	159	Alb	Robert	160	Alb	Betty	457	Grn
John	160	Alb	Robert	197	Alb	Bey. [Benj. ?], (M)	549	Prg
John	161	Alb	Robert	862	Cmp	Bruditt	201	Kng
John	350	Ags	Robert	447	Flv	Burshaby	952	Chc
John	354	Ags	Robert	429	Msn	Caesar, (FN)	38	Rcm
John	466	Bdf	Sailey	859	Hnv	Catharine	500	Prw
John [2]	677	Br	Samel	943	Hrr	Charles	712	Brn
John	791	Bck	Saml.	697	Gch	Charles	644	Sss
John	834	Bck	Saml.	167	Knq	Chas.	203	Kng
John	905	Crl	Saml.	691	Wsh	Christopher	571	Pre
John	906	Crl	Samuel	198	Alb	Chs.	903	Nrf
John	849	Cmp	Samuel	862	Cmp	Con, (FN)	23	Rcm
John	958	Chc	Samuel	208	Ess	Cuddy	713	Brn
John	446	Flv	Samuel	782	Hmp	Custis	30	Acc
John	470	Frn	Samuel	85	Jff	Danl.	38	Rcm
John	119	Hnr	Samuel	8	Pwh	David	343	Lnn
John	629	Mnt	Sarah	5	Pwh	David	20	Rcm
John	698	Nls	Sarah	681	Wrw	Edward	148	Dnw
John	700	Nls	Simeon	430	Rnd	Elizab.	545	Prg
John	703	Nls	Sterling	714	Brn	Elizabeth	983	Nrt
John	2	Oho	Susannah	827	Bck	Elizabeth	43	Stf
John	146	Sth	Thomas	197	Alb	Ephraim	696	Br
John	866	Sth	Thomas	628	Btt	Evelin T.	540	Prg
John	744	Wsh	Thomas	871	Cmp	Ezekiel	4	Rcm
John	745	Wsh	Thomas	905	Crl	Gabriel	713	Brn
John	753	Wsh	Thomas	625	Gls	Geo. L.	265	Frf
John, (Captn.)	807	Bck	Thomas	124	Hnr	George	264	Frf
John, Jnr.	862	Hnv	Thomas	10	Pwh	George	836	Hmp
John, Majr.	9	Pwh	Thomas	536	Prg	George	390	Mds
John, Senr.	753	Wsh	Thomas	608	Srr	Hannah	14	Knw
John J.	812	Bck	Thomas	9	Wod	Henrietta M.	547	Prg
John L.	695	Gch	Thos.	354	Ags	Henry	752	Brn
John S.	797	Bck	Thos., B.C.	855	Hnv	Henry	127	Sth
John W.	698	Nls	Thos., C.R.	857	Hnv	Henry	146	Sth
Jona.	507	Mnn	Thos. H.	15	Hnr	Henry	640	Sss
Jordan	9	Pwh	Tyre	867	Hnv	Henry J.	640	Sss
Joseph	514	Brk	Wiley	348	Ags	Humphrey	162	Alb
Joseph	659	Mnt	William	197	Alb	Ishmael	642	Sss
Joshua	700	Nls	William	463	Bdf	Jacob	23	Hnr
Kenchen	752	Brn	William	794	Bck	James	29	Acc
Larkin	752	Brn	William	811	Bck	James	197	Alb
Lee W.	696	Nls	William	813	Bck	James	262	Amh
Lemuel	14	Oho	William	862	Cmp	James	549	Brk
Lewis	851	Sth	William	907	Crl	James	585	Brk
Lucy	908	Crl	William	413	Fqr	James	629	Btt
Lucy	874	Hnv	William [2]	696	Nls	James	944	Chc
Lucy, (W)	876	Yrk	William	697	Nls	James	264	Frf
Martha	714	Brn	William	698	Nls	James	345	Lnn
Mary	871	Hnv	William	219	Pnd	James	14	Rcm
Mary L.	607	Srr	William	417	Rnd	James	151	Sth
Matthew	700	Nls	William	16	Wod	James Q.	752	Brn
Matthew	702	Nls	William B.	699	Nls	Jane	391	Rch
Morris	939	Chc	Wim., L.	867	Hnv	Jas.	547	Prg
Moses	852	Hnv	Wim. O.	861	Hnv	Jas.	458	Pra

Name	No.	Loc	Name	No.	Loc	Name	No.	Loc
Jesse	21	Rcm	William	262	Frf	Samuel	774	Wst
John	514	Brk	William [2]	450	Grn	Wm.	876	Yrk
John	630	Btt	William	571	Pre	Harriway, Epaphroditus	878	Cmp
John	749	Brn	William	395	Rch	Harrod, Richd.	39	Rcm
John	390	Mds	William	14	Rcm	Harrold, Chrisley	419	Bth
John	505	Prw	William	20	Rcm	Susanna	419	Bth
John	395	Rch	William	640	Sss	Harrow, Anthoney	464	Mdd
John	27	Rcm	William	642	Sss	Jacob	926	Hrr
John, Jr.	390	Mds	William	704	Wsh	John	401	Ags
John, Mh.	751	Brn	William, Jr.	674	Sss	William	464	Mdd
John, Rs.	751	Brn	William, Jr. [2]	676	Sss	Harroway, Charles	52	Chr
John, S. M.	751	Brn	William, Sr.	642	Sss	Samuel	51	Chr
John S.	593	Brk	William A.	609	Srr	see Campbell		
Jos.	350	Ags	Willie	750	Brn	Harrup, Ann	643	Sss
Jos.	505	Mnn	Willoby	984	Nrt	Gilliam	640	Sss
Joseph	750	Brn	Wm.	750	Brn	Harry, Benjamin	515	Frd
Joseph	201	Kng	Wm., Sr.	540	Prg	George	624	Btt
Josiah	450	Frn	Wm. A.	546	Prg	James	511	Frd
Langford	201	Kng	Wm. B.	304	Ldn	Joseph	510	Frd
Lewis	390	Mds	Wm. H.	547	Prg	Martin	252	Shn
Lucey	393	Fqr	Zebulon	20	Rcm	Samuel	3	Rcm
Lucy	450	Grn	see Dance, English, George,			Harsel, Peter	822	Hmp
Mark	750	Brn	H...son, Hannison, Han-			Harsh, Fred.	508	Mnn
Mary	751	Brn	non, Hartwell, Hughes			Jacob	838	Wth
Mary	906	Crl	Harriss, Ann	572	Pre	Harsha, Thomas	547	Frd
Mary	381	Fqr	Benjamin	450	Grn	Harshaw, Beckey	352	Ags
Mary	571	Pre	Catharine	451	Grn	Harshbarger, Christn.	627	Btt
Mary	737	Wsh	David	918	Hrr	David	627	Btt
Mary Ann	750	Brn	David	618	Mnt	Jacob	354	Ags
Mason	543	Prg	Elizabeth	450	Grn	Saml.	628	Btt
Matthew	984	Nrt	Elizabeth	570	Pre	Saml., Jr.	628	Btt
Milly	467	Bdf	George	521	Prw	Harshey, Andrew	86	Jff
Moses	691	Br	Isaac	304	Ldn	**Harshman, Danl.**	**33**	**Rcm**
Nicholas	272	Amh	Jacob	428	Msn	Harston, Samuel	492	Frn
Obediah R.	334	Dnw	James	53	Chr	Hart, ...el	329	Dnw
Patience	770	Brn	James	410	Fqr	Abrm. D.	597	Mnr
Peachy	1	Rcm	Jerimiah	237	Ldn	Alden	167	Knq
Philip	499	Prw	Jno.	249	Ldn	Ann	645	Sss
Randolph	811	Bck	John	239	Aml	Ben.	306	Rck
Randolph	119	Cmb	John	51	Chr	Charles	143	Sth
Rebecca	547	Prg	John	150	Dnw	Charles	859	Sth
Reuben	25	Rcm	John	373	Fqr	Daniel [2]	416	Rnd
Reuben	40	Rcm	John	505	Prw	David	349	Ags
Reubin, Jr.	468	Frn	John, (PW)	52	Chr	Drewry	608	Srr
Reubin, Sr.	468	Frn	Joseph	52	Chr	Edward	416	Rnd
Richard	197	Alb	Joseph	103	Cmb	Edwin	130	Sth
Richard	272	Amh	Lucy	239	Aml	Elijah	755	Wsh
Richard	63	Chs	Mary	39	Isw	Eliza.	875	Sth
Richard	456	Pra	Nathaniel	410	Fqr	Ephraim	690	Br
Richd.	752	Brn	Rewben	751	Brn	Gregory	166	Knq
Richd.	505	Mnn	Richard	126	Cmb	Hannah	608	Srr
Richd.	162	Sth	Robert	714	Brn	Hartwell	607	Srr
Richd. J.	201	Kng	Robert	51	Chr	James	905	Crl
Robert	675	Br	Robert, Capt.	51	Chr	James	891	Hnv
Robert	390	Mds	Saml.	923	Hrr	James	306	Rck
Robert, Jr.	390	Mds	Samuel	127	Cmb	James B.	166	Knq
Robt.	547	Prg	Samuel	395	Fqr	James, jr.	166	Knq
S. H.	904	Nrf	Samuel	38	Isw	James, Snr.	167	Knq
Salley	750	Brn	Solaman	857	Hnv	Jane	143	Sth
Saml.	23	Rcm	Sterling	450	Grn	Jesse	141	Sth
Samuel J.	849	Cmp	Sterling	451	Grn	Job	349	Ags
Shadrach	533	Prg	Thomas	410	Fqr	John	100	Acc
Solo.	162	Sth	Thomas	434	Flv	John	332	Dnw
Spencer	907	Crl	Thomas	500	Prw	John	587	Frd
Susanna	984	Nrt	Thos., Dr.	857	Hnv	John	167	Knq
Theoderick	533	Prg	William	450	Grn	John	142	Sth
Thomas	685	Br	William	570	Pre	John	73	Spt
Thomas	241	Ldn	Wilson	751	Brn	John	608	Srr
Thomas	607	Mnt	Wim. E.	851	Hnv	John W.	416	Rnd
Thomas	512	Prw	Wingfield	861	Hnv	Jonathan	690	Br
Thomas	6	Rcm	Harrisson, Charles,			Josa.	505	Mnn
Thomas, Jr.	525	Prw	(F.N.)	37	Isw	Joseph	859	Sth
Thoms.	850	Sth	Daniel	773	Wst	Malcolm	67	Spt
Thornton	390	Mds	Edwd.	240	Aml	Malcolm, [his] Mill	82	Spt
Thos.	458	Pra	Henry	774	Wst	Miles	91	Jff
William	27	Acc	Judy	774	Wst	Moses	278	Rck
William	274	Amh	Lovell	773	Wst	Moses	845	Sth
William	849	Cmp	Nathl.	240	Aml	Nancy	859	Sth
William	908	Crl	Sam., (W)	875	Yrk	Peter	907	Crl
William	334	Dnw	Sampson	35	Isw	Rebecca	608	Srr

Reubin	402	Rch
Richard	102	Acc
Richd.	859	Sth
Robert	142	Sth
Robert	73	Spt
Salley	142	Sth
Sally	608	Srr
Samuel	328	Dnw
Thomas	83	Jff
Thomas	167	Knq
Thomas	274	Ldn
Thomas	70	Spt
Vincent	166	Knq
William	524	Prw
William	131	Sth
William C.	465	Bdf
Wm.	286	Rck
Zilpah	855	Sth
see Hurt		
Harte, Andrew	160	Alb
Harter, Adam	10	Wod
Francis	652	Mnt
Hartford, Matthew	698	Br
Robert	697	Br
Harthorn, Peter	714	Brn
Hartigan, Tim.	349	Ags
Hartinburg, Marha	903	Nrf
Hartless, Peter	288	Amh
Richard	284	Amh
William	298	Amh
Hartley, Ben	509	Mnn
Cathrine	641	Sss
Christopher	983	Nrt
Eliz.	506	Mnn
James	787	Hmp
John	787	Hmp
Jos.	506	Mnn
Hartly, Amos	506	Mnn
Chas.	458	Pra
Ed.	506	Mnn
Horatio	505	Mnn
Peter	306	Rck
Peter [crossed out]	311	Rck
Wm.	507	Mnn
Hartman, Christian	581	Brk
Daniel	509	Frd
Fredk.	627	Btt
Geo., (Waggon Maker)	628	Btt
Godlep	430	Bth
H.	347	Ags
Henry	762	Hmp
Henry	801	Hmp
Henry	226	Pnd
Henry, jr.	347	Ags
Jacob	800	Hmp
Jno.	507	Mnn
John	354	Ags
John	28	Rcm
M.	509	Mnn
Margret	227	Pnd
Martin	70	Jff
Murret	222	Pnd
Philip	18	Rcm
William	421	Bth
Hartmon, George	944	Hrr
Hartness, John	72	Jff
Hartshorne, William	261	Frf
Hartsock, Charles	704	Wsh
Daniel	746	Wsh
Saml.	746	Wsh
Hartsook, Geo.	657	Mnt
Jacob	350	Ags
Peter	350	Ags
Wm.	350	Ags
Hartsuck, Adam	388	Mds
John	388	Mds
Solomon	388	Mds
Hartwell, Armstead	752	Brn
Harrison	751	Brn

Littleberey S.	750	Brn
Paschal	148	Dnw
Richd.	749	Brn
see Hill		
Hartzell, Lewis	836	Wth
Harvel, Byrd	141	Sth
Harvell, Armistead	530	Prg
Martha	530	Prg
Leonard	532	Prg
Ransom	142	Sth
Richd.	530	Prg
Harvey, Alexander	198	Alb
Amos	280	Ldn
Ann	351	Ags
Benjamin	12	Oho
Benjamin, Jr.	11	Oho
Benjn.	576	Mnr
Celia	51	Chr
Eligah	798	Hmp
Elijah	391	Mds
Elizah.	628	Btt
Ellison	783	Bck
Henry	28	Acc
Henry	420	Msn
Henry	434	Msn
Hezekiah	797	Hmp
Isham	53	Chr
James	797	Hmp
James	774	Wst
Jesse	873	Cmp
John	800	Bck
John	52	Chr
John	565	Mnr
John	46	Stf
John	774	Wst
John, Snr.	68	Chr
John D.	51	Chr
Joshua	571	Mnr
Lewis	426	Msn
Mary	296	Ldn
Mattw.	627	Btt
Nat.	829	Nrf
Nathan	53	Chr
Nathen	703	Wsh
Nicholas	564	Mnr
Onesiphorus	982	Nrt
Reason	797	Hmp
Rebecca	984	Nrt
Richard	466	Bdf
Richard	413	Fqr
Robt.	627	Btt
Sukey	982	Nrt
Thomas	859	Cmp
Thomas	982	Nrt
Thomas, (BS)	51	Chr
Thomas, (BW)	53	Chr
Triford	712	Brn
William	867	Cmp
William	551	Frd
William	798	Hmp
William	576	Mnr
Wm., (48)	869	Cmp
Zachariah	797	Hmp
Harvie, Edwd. J.	1	Hnr
James	701	Nls
John	37	Rcm
Joseph	698	Nls
Mary	115	Hnr
Mary	699	Nls
Sarah	701	Nls
Harvill, Leath	532	Prg
Harvy, Bazle	937	Hrr
Bazle	956	Hrr
Harwell, Batty	147	Dnw
Elizabeth	645	Sss
Hartwell	150	Dnw
Isham	451	Grn
Ishmuel	713	Brn
John H.	713	Brn
Lucy	645	Sss

Lydia	640	Sss
Manson	713	Brn
Mary	451	Grn
Peyton	450	Grn
Robt.	150	Dnw
Sinor	713	Brn
Sterling	147	Dnw
Thomas	450	Grn
see Harvell		
Harwood, Ann	127	Hnr
Ann	644	Sss
Benjn.	678	Wrw
Celia	643	Sss
Christopher	465	Mdd
Daniel	644	Sss
Danl. P.	127	Hnr
Edward	941	Chc
Elizabeth	945	Chc
Frances	122	Hnr
Francis G.	470	Frn
George	128	Hnr
H. G.	658	Glc
Harlow	904	Nrf
Humphrey	679	Wrw
Jno. M.	658	Glc
Maria	902	Nrf
Martha.	681	Wrw
Milly	209	Ess
Pleasant	116	Hnr
Samuel	942	Chc
Thomas	166	Knq
Thomas	23	Stf
Thomas	644	Sss
Thos.	682	Wrw
Travis	336	Dnw
William	336	Dnw
Williamson	122	Hnr
Wm.	656	Glc
Wm.	682	Wrw
Hasbariger, Davd.	707	Wsh
Hasclip see Haselip		
Haselett, Moses	431	Msn
Haselgrove, Pleaseant	125	Cmb
Haselip, Henry	461	Frn
Henry	498	Frn
Spencer	461	Frn
Haselwood, Cliff	149	Dnw
Hasetell see Haselett		
Hasey see Harris		
Hashbarger, Christr.	627	Btt
Danl.	41	Rcm
Henry	25	Rcm
Henry	28	Rcm
Jacob	36	Rcm
John	39	Rcm
Hashberger, Abraham	235	Shn
John	837	Wth
Haskew, Frances	167	Knq
Joseph	240	Aml
see Heskew		
Haskins, Aaron	5	Pwh
Aaron, (Majr.)	65	Chs
Catharine	572	Pre
Creed	713	Brn
Creed	15	Pwh
Edward	3	Pwh
Elizabeth	713	Brn
Jep.	19	Oho
John	713	Brn
John	5	Pwh
R...	59	Chs
Richd.	920	Hrr
Robert	713	Brn
Robert	57	Chs
Sally	125	Cmb
Thomas	572	Pre
Thos.	696	Gch
William, (Est)	55	Chr
Haslegrove, John	756	Nwk
Mary	756	Nwk

Haslep, Abigail	262	Frf	Obed	63	Chs	Haughn, Hannah	203	Shn
Thomas	298	Rck	Prudence	312	Ldn	Henry	255	Shn
Hasler, George	187	Shn	Richard	464	Bdf	John	166	Shn
Haslerig, Archibald	838	Wth	Samuel	315	Ldn	Mary	166	Shn
Haslet, Andrew	276	Rck	Sarah	113	Cmb	Peter	164	Shn
James	294	Rck	Seth	7	Pwh	see Houghn		
Joseph	432	Msn	Tempy	467	Bdf	Haught, Jno.	504	Mnn
Robt.	350	Ags	Thomas	233	Ldn	Jno., Jr.	505	Mnn
Robt.	276	Rck	William	838	Bck	Peter	503	Mnn
Robt., jr.	350	Ags	Hatchett, Ab.	6	Ntt	Peter, Jr.	505	Mnn
Sam	507	Mnn	Archer	345	Lnn	see Hough		
see Haselett			Archibald	53	Chr	Haughten, Augustine,		
Haslett, John	505	Brk	Haney	345	Lnn	[crossed out]	791	Nrf
Robert	505	Brk	John, Junr.	52	Chr	Haughton, Affia	905	Nrf
Haslip, John S.	446	Flv	John, Senr.	52	Chr	Ann	678	Wrw
Robert	441	Flv	Thomas, Sen.	52	Chr	Patsey	806	Nrf
Haslop, John	29	Acc	William	344	Lnn	Walker	682	Wrw
Hass, George	55	Jff	William	571	Pre	Hauk, Jacob	253	Shn
Jacob	242	Shn	Wm.	5	Ntt	Hauling, Jemimah	279	Ldn
John	242	Shn	Hatchison, Geo.	351	Ags	Jno.	279	Ldn
Michael	250	Shn	Geo., jr.	351	Ags	Wm.	289	Ldn
Michael	704	Wsh	Hatchwell, Nelson	13	Isw	Haun, Michael	100	Jff
William	195	Shn	Hateway, Robert	930	Hrr	Haunt, James	100	Acc
Hasser, Jacob	681	Br	Hatfield, Diza	859	Sth	Hausbarger, Henry	39	Rcm
Hast, Phoeby	45	Clp	Edwd.	9	Rcm	Hause, Christian, (Jr.)	13	Rcm
Hastagan, Wm.	456	Pra	Mills	156	Sth	Christian, (sen.)	13	Rcm
Hastie, Clement	43	Clp	Wm.	507	Mnn	Israel	13	Rcm
John	902	Nrf	Hath, Daniel	657	Glc	Hauseworth, Abraham	198	Alb
Hastings, ---	925	Nrf	Hathaway, Eliza.	348	Lnc	Hausford see Hansford		
Jno.	509	Mnn	Ephm.	903	Nrf	Hausman, Chas.	507	Mnn
John	536	Frd	Francis	533	Frd	Hauston, Purnel	509	Mnn
Reece	507	Mnn	James	548	Frd	Havan, Elisah	946	Hrr
Robt.	545	Brk	Jno.	348	Lnc	Havely, Jacob	691	Wsh
William	239	Aml	John	566	Frd	William	557	Frd
William	565	Frd	Law.	347	Lnc	Haven, Charles	838	Wth
Haston, John	352	Ags	Lawson	371	Fqr	James	838	Wth
William	716	Wsh	Hathcock, Coleby	451	Grn	see Haver		
Hasty, Angelina	854	Sth	Francis	451	Grn	Havener, Adam	257	Ldn
Ann	847	Sth	Hathorn, Samuel	964	Hrr	Dominic	253	Ldn
Edwin	609	Srr	Hathway, Elijah	749	Wsh	Jacob	284	Ldn
Haswell see Harwell			Hatslend, Latimer	788	Nrf	Joseph	253	Ldn
Hatabough, Andrew	949	Hrr	Hatspiller, Abram	347	Ags	Havennell, John	565	Brk
Hatch, Jemmy	326	Dnw	Hattan, Rhode	30	Acc	Havenner, Jno.	254	Ldn
John	902	Nrf	Hatten, Francis	149	Dnw	Havens, Howard	753	Wsh
Mary	546	Prg	Goodrich	149	Dnw	John	612	Mnt
Nathl.	643	Mnt	Saml.	632	Btt	William	610	Mnt
Nicholas	536	Prg	Thomas	905	Crl	Haver, Richard	838	Wth
Hatch..., Henry	466	Bdf	Wm.	270	Rck	Haverty, Wm.	425	Rnd
Hatcher, Archer	64	Chs	Hatter, John	702	Nls	Havie, Thomas	702	Nls
Barnard	797	Bck	John	42	Rcm	Havwood, Polly	53	Stf
Benja.	68	Chs	Patty	516	Frd	Haw, Betsy	510	Prw
Benjn.	113	Cmb	Wm.	703	Nls	Jno.	895	Hnv
Branch	63	Chs	Hatthran, Robt.	294	Rck	John	393	Rch
Cecilia	464	Bdf	Hatton, Benjamin	99	Acc	Peter	349	Lnc
Danl.	64	Chs	Benjn.	902	Nrf	Haward, Mary	697	Nls
Doury	102	Cmb	Boling	266	Frf	Milly	329	Dnw
Drury	695	Gch	David	807	Hmp	Hawbert, George	194	Shn
Edmon	451	Frn	Elizabeth	19	Isw	Hawes, Aylet	42	Clp
Elijah	451	Frn	Elizabeth	817	Nrf	Eliza.	196	Ess
Hardaway	467	Bdf	Elizth.	904	Nrf	Richard	906	Crl
Henry	778	Bck	John	421	Bth	Thomas	393	Fqr
Henry	120	Cmb	Johannas	103	Acc	Walker	166	Knq
Isaac	310	Ldn	Joseph	421	Bth	Hawison, Stephen, Jr.	513	Prw
James	835	Bck	Judah	31	Acc	Hawk, Abraham	428	Bth
James	315	Ldn	Mary	902	Nrf	Abraham	802	Hmp
Jeremiah	466	Bdf	Richard	293	Amh	Andw.	707	Wsh
Jeremiah	467	Bdf	Rob.	681	Wrw	Elijah	372	Fqr
Jesse	467	Bdf	Robt.	903	Nrf	George	9	Rcm
Jesse	315	Ldn	Robt.	904	Nrf	Henry	802	Hmp
Jno.	265	Ldn	Samuel	814	Hmp	Isaac	428	Bth
John	467	Bdf	Sarah, f. negro	267	Frf	Jacob	426	Bth
John	122	Cmb	Thomas	572	Pre	John	348	Ags
Joseph	315	Ldn	Thos.	859	Hnv	John	428	Bth
Josiah	777	Bck	William	571	Pre	Mary	458	Frn
Josiah	63	Chs	Hattox, Abraham	506	Frd	Hawke, John	31	Rcm
Josiah	696	Gch	William	519	Frd	Hawker, Owen	509	Mnn
Julius	466	Bdf	Hauchins, Frank	352	Ags	Hawkes, Jno. B.	13	Ntt
Lucy [2]	63	Chs	Hauf, Eli	347	Ags	Jno. B.	20	Ntt
Lucy	696	Gch	Haugh, Gabriel	6	Knw	John	148	Dnw
Noah	316	Ldn	see Waugh			Joshua	20	Ntt

Joshua, jr.	21	Ntt	Uriah	750	Brn	Griffin	349	Lnc
Philip	13	Ntt	William	467	Bdf	Jessee	93	Spt
Priscilla	10	Ntt	William	904	Hrr	Jessee	101	Spt
Reubin	13	Ntt	William	424	Msn	Jessee, jr.	96	Spt
Richd.	13	Ntt	William	200	Elc	John, Jr.	982	Nrt
Hawkin, John L.	69	Jff	Willm.	182	Elc	John, Sr.	982	Nrt
Hawking, William	928	Hrr	Wm.	16	Hnr	Jud.	349	Lnc
Hawkings, John	941	Hrr	Wm.	504	Mnn	Lucy	348	Lnc
Hawkins, ---, & Alder	22	Hnr	Wm.	589	Mnr	Mary	101	Spt
Alice	418	Fqr	Wm. M.	166	Knq	Sarah	983	Nrt
Archd.	43	Clp	Young	304	Amh	Tho.	350	Lnc
Benjamin	571	Pre	see Hankins			Wm. O.	349	Lnc
Benjamin [2]	3	Rcm	Hawkit, Jonathan	650	Mnt	Haye, David	226	Pnd
Benjamin	200	Shn	Hawks, Abraham	869	Cmp	see Hoye		
Bracket	345	Lnn	C.	328	Dnw	Hayes, Ann	539	Frd
Bridet	278	Ldn	Henry	150	Dnw	Bennett	399	Fqr
Byrd	13	Rcm	Randal	150	Dnw	Catharine	702	Nls
Edward	715	Brn	Thomas	858	Cmp	Charles	702	Nls
Elijah	508	Mnn	Thomas	149	Dnw	David	815	Nrf
Elizabeth	677	Br	Thomas	836	Wth	Henry	19	Oho
Frederick	149	Dnw	Hawles, Peggy, f. negro	264	Frf	Jacob	399	Fqr
Gilliam	148	Dnw	Hawley, Abraham	197	Alb	James	23	Oho
Green	149	Dnw	Ams.	508	Mnn	Jeremiah	557	Frd
Grief B.	239	Aml	Barton D.	266	Frf	John	348	Fqr
Guardiner	148	Dnw	Jno.	316	Ldn	John	551	Frd
Hambleton	149	Dnw	John	244	Ldn	John	500	Prw
Isaah	344	Lnn	William	266	Frf	John G.	167	Knq
Isham	149	Dnw	Hawmaker, Danl.	346	Ags	Jos.	904	Nrf
Jacob	775	Hmp	Davied	347	Ags	Lemuel	807	Nrf
James	628	Btt	Hawood, James	166	Knq	Robert	822	Nrf
James	590	Mnr	Haword, Jane	15	Pwh	Robt.	836	Nrf
Jas.	43	Clp	John	15	Pwh	Saml.	217	Ess
Jno.	39	Clp	Haws, Daniel	854	Hnv	Thomas	703	Nls
Jno.	904	Nrf	Reuben	464	Bdf	William	420	Fqr
Jno. B.	40	Clp	Wim.	852	Hnv	William H.	500	Prw
Jno. J.	40	Clp	Hawthorn, Peter	344	Lnn	Wm.	656	Glc
Job	42	Clp	Robt.	509	Mnn	Haygood, Randolph	714	Brn
Joel	14	Ntt	Thos.	694	Gch	Richd.	714	Brn
John	467	Bdf	William	328	Dnw	Hayhurst, Dav.	506	Mnn
John	149	Dnw	William	344	Lnn	Jas.	505	Mnn
John	761	Hmp	Wm.	695	Gch	Hayley, William	27	Acc
John	836	Hmp	Hawthorne, Henry	642	Sss	Haylord, Will.	3	Hnr
John	63	Jff	Joshua	642	Sss	Haylter, Augustine	810	Nrf
John	343	Lnn	Mary	645	Sss	Haymaker, Adam	513	Frd
John	573	Mnr	Haxall, H.	147	Dnw	Adam	605	Frd
John	200	Shn	H.	332	Dnw	Henry	568	Frd
John	94	Spt	Joseph	328	Dnw	John	537	Frd
Jonatn.	629	Btt	Joseph	334	Dnw	Michal	510	Frd
Jos.	298	Ldn	W.	332	Dnw	Peter	631	Btt
Joseph	263	Amh	William	335	Dnw	Thomas	537	Frd
Joseph, Jur.	197	Shn	Haxhall, Philip	10	Hnr	Hayman, Robert	543	Frd
Joseph, Sen. ["Sen."			Haxton see Horton			Haymond, Calder	504	Mnn
crossed out]	197	Shn	Hay, Alexander	187	Shn	Ed.	508	Mnn
Joseph L.	81	Spt	Danl.	581	Brk	Jno.	506	Mnn
Judah	44	Clp	Edward	450	Grn	Jno.	508	Mnn
Laban	571	Pre	Eliz.	32	Hnr	John	951	Hrr
Lewis	149	Dnw	Enos	644	Sss	Stephen	4	Wod
Little B.	467	Bdf	Frances	56	Stf	Wilson	951	Hrr
Mathew	44	Clp	Frances	644	Sss	Wm.	504	Mnn
Mathew, jr.	42	Clp	George	122	Hnr	Haymore, Elizabeth	835	Wth
Moses	200	Shn	Gilbert	644	Sss	Hayner, ---, Widow	579	Frd
Nelly	774	Wst	John	560	Frd	Barbary	579	Frd
Nicholas	95	Spt	Peter	186	Shn	Haynes, Abraham	21	Oho
Noah	615	Mnt	Ruth	105	Jff	Andeson	464	Bdf
Obadiah	569	Pre	Susanna	907	Crl	Anthy.	214	Ess
Parker	27	Isw	William	450	Grn	Benjn.	630	Btt
Peggy	774	Wst	William	2	Hnr	Daniel	21	Oho
Peter	10	Hnr	William	23	Stf	David	919	Hrr
Peterson	467	Bdf	William	643	Sss	Eady	287	Amh
Philemon, jr.	148	Dnw	Hay..., William	466	Bdf	Elizabeth	457	Pra
Philemon, senr.	149	Dnw	Haybarger, Abram	349	Ags	Erasmus	456	Pra
Philip	818	Bck	Conrad	349	Ags	Frederick	659	Glc
Phillimon, Sr.	148	Dnw	Jacob	352	Ags	Francis	465	Bdf
Robert	467	Bdf	Haycock, Charles	533	Frd	Geo.	657	Glc
Robt.	147	Dnw	William	504	Brk	Griffeth	490	Frn
Samuel	200	Shn	Hayden, Jesse	593	Brk	Henry	464	Bdf
Smart	715	Brn	Haydon, Abner	94	Spt	Henry	451	Frn
Tho.	187	Elc	Charles, Jr.	983	Nrt	Henry	389	Mds
Thomas	699	Nls	Charles, Sr.	982	Nrt	Henry	589	Mnr
Thomas	92	Spt	George	982	Nrt	Isaac	631	Btt

Name	No.	Abbr.
Jacob	581	Mnr
Jas.	457	Pra
Jasper	10	Knw
Jno.	659	Glc
Jno., Jr.	456	Pra
Jno., Sr.	458	Pra
John	463	Bdf
John	467	Bdf
John	21	Oho
John, Sr.	493	Frn
Joseph	629	Btt
Joseph	589	Bdf
Js.	905	Nrf
Margte.	902	Nrf
Millner	465	Bdf
Nanny	656	Glc
Rd.	657	Glc
Saml.	827	Nrf
Samuel	835	Wth
Stephen	452	Frn
Susannah	659	Glc
Thomas	906	Crl
Thos. J.	902	Nrf
William	945	Chc
William	563	Mnr
William	835	Wth
Wm.	682	Wrw
Wm. H.	629	Btt
Wm. W.	838	Nrf
see Hagins, Hayner, Hughs, Hynes		
Hayney, Jesse	32	Stf
Haynie, Alexander	985	Nrt
Betsey	985	Nrt
Bridgar	983	Nrt
Catharine	561	Frd
Davenport	985	Nrt
David	983	Nrt
Griffin	523	Frd
Henry	985	Nrt
Holland	983	Nrt
Holland	985	Nrt
Isaac	985	Nrt
James	983	Nrt
Jesse	985	Nrt
John	526	Frd
Jourdon	985	Nrt
Lucy	986	Nrt
Maria	559	Frd
Maximilion	985	Nrt
Molley	985	Nrt
Nancy	984	Nrt
Presley	985	Nrt
Richard	986	Nrt
Rodham	983	Nrt
Sarah	986	Nrt
Stephen	983	Nrt
Stephen	985	Nrt
Thornton	986	Nrt
Wilalmira W.	413	Rch
William	393	Rch
Hayns, Sarah	459	Frn
Hayran, William	596	Frd
Hays, A.D.	33	Hnr
And.	263	Rck
Andrew	67	Jff
Curtis	504	Mnn
Geo.	31	Hnr
Hennery	963	Hrr
Isaac	507	Mnn
James	162	Alb
James	632	Btt
James	500	Prw
James	280	Rck
James	875	Yrk
Jerreniah	353	Ags
Jno., Jr.	632	Btt
Jno., Sr.	632	Btt
John	162	Alb
John	860	Cmp
John	83	Jff
John	14	Knw
John	983	Nrt
John	875	Yrk
Levy	632	Btt
Methias	236	Ldn
Micheal	16	Hnr
Millisent	986	Nrt
Patrick	349	Ags
Peter	693	Br
Polly	632	Btt
Saml.	349	Ags
Samuel	74	Jff
Thomas	983	Nrt
Thos.	632	Btt
William	102	Acc
William	162	Alb
William	860	Cmp
William	986	Nrt
William	741	Wsh
Wm.	506	Mnn
Wm., Jr.	506	Mnn
see Haye		
Hayse, Charles	835	Wth
James	835	Wth
John	935	Hrr
Tabner	837	Wth
William	835	Wth
William	836	Wth
Haystalk, Molly	198	Ess
Hayter, Esa	758	Wsh
see Hyter		
Hayton, George	725	Wsh
George Washington	725	Wsh
Isaah	725	Wsh
John	725	Wsh
Margret	738	Wsh
Sarah	725	Wsh
William	738	Wsh
Hayward see Haward		
Haywod, John	838	Nrf
Haywood, Alexr.	902	Nrf
J.D.	902	Nrf
Jas.	903	Nrf
Jno.	456	Pra
John	394	Rch
Will, (F.N.)	31	Isw
see Hawood		
Hayworth, Francis	219	Pnd
Hazalrig, Richd.	759	Wsh
Hazard, Alexr.	348	Lnc
Ann	398	Rch
Charles	774	Wst
Elias	348	Lnc
James	398	Rch
Joseph	397	Rch
Josiah	773	Wst
Rawligh	397	Rch
Thomas	407	Rch
William, Junr.	773	Wst
William, Senr.	773	Wst
Haze, Polly	631	Btt
Thos.	882	Hnv
William	419	Rnd
Wim.	894	Hnv
Wm.	631	Btt
Hazel, Elisha	41	Clp
Isaac	944	Hrr
Richd.	43	Clp
Hazelwood, Wm.	121	Hnr
see Bottom		
Hazle, James	17	Rcm
Hazlegrove, Elizabeth	100	Spt
James	859	Hnv
Salley	878	Hnv
Hazlewood, Benjamin	51	Chr
Cathe.	509	Brk
Danel, Sr.	345	Lnn
Daniel	345	Lnn
James	343	Lnn
Jesse	560	Brk
John	344	Lnn
Mary	345	Lnn
Nancy	69	Chr
Pleasant	464	Bdf
Richd.	631	Btt
Richd.	632	Btt
Richd., (W)	876	Yrk
Robert	506	Frd
Wyat S.	803	Bck
see Farish,		
Hazlwood, Reuben	346	Lnn
Hazwell see Harvell		
He..., Stephen	466	Bdf
Head, Gavin	755	Wsh
Geo.	304	Ldn
Geo., J.	304	Ldn
Isaac	774	Wst
Jas.	754	Wsh
John	629	Btt
Moriah	103	Spt
Uriah	8	Rcm
Wm.	746	Wsh
Headeshell, Adam	15	Rcm
Headey, William, Jr.	984	Nrt
Headington, Nicholas	689	Br
Headins, John	642	Mnt
Headley, Elizabeth	690	Br
Epaphroditus	983	Nrt
Griffen	984	Nrt
Henry	409	Rch
Henry W.	391	Rch
James	409	Rch
James	182	Shn
James, Jr.	984	Nrt
Lucey	349	Fqr
Richard	984	Nrt
Thomas	984	Nrt
William, Sr.	984	Nrt
Headly, William	594	Frd
Headrick, Pendleton	873	Cmp
Heagy, George	719	Wsh
John	719	Wsh
Michl.	760	Wsh
Heale, William	390	Fqr
Healy, Jane	464	Mdd
Thomas, Jr.	464	Mdd
Thomas, Senr.	464	Mdd
see Heuly		
Hearn, Ephram	657	Glc
Hearper, Jno.	263	Ldn
Heart, Jno.	657	Glc
Valentine	836	Wth
Hearter, Henry	484	Frn
Jacob	628	Btt
Heartman, Fredk.	629	Btt
George	632	Btt
John	632	Btt
Heartsell, Adam	475	Frn
George	475	Frn
Phillip	477	Frn
Hearty, John	25	Oho
Heaslop, Kendall	28	Acc
Heasten, Peter	180	Shn
Heastop, John	236	Shn
Heat, Abraham	239	Shn
Heaten, David	7	Knw
Heater, John	419	Rnd
John	31	Rcm
Polly	20	Rcm
Heath, Adam	530	Prg
Aggy	336	Dnw
Ambrous	849	Hnv
Andrew	244	Ldn
Augst.	541	Prg
Benjamin	861	Cmp
Chloe	984	Nrt
Coulson	615	Mnt
David	427	Msn
Edmund	450	Grn

Name	No.	Abbr.
Elle	532	Prg
Epes	532	Prg
Erasmus	791	Bck
Federick	530	Prg
Henry	150	Dnw
Henry G.	130	Hnr
Herbert, Sr.	538	Prg
James	11	Isw
Jas.	457	Pra
Jas., Jr.	458	Pra
Jesse	334	Dnw
Jessee	539	Prg
Jno.	12	Hnr
John	216	Ess
John	538	Prg
Jonas	73	Jff
Jones	538	Prg
Joseph	27	Acc
Joseph, Sr.	534	Prg
Joshua	530	Prg
Kennon	534	Prg
Leah	29	Acc
Lewis	325	Dnw
Lewis	330	Dnw
Major	29	Acc
Rachal	78	Jff
Richard	536	Prg
Robt.	12	Isw
Seller	334	Dnw
Seth	327	Dnw
Silvia	537	Prg
Susanna	536	Prg
Susannah	29	Acc
Thomas	864	Cmp
Thomas D.	641	Sss
Uriah C.	641	Sss
William	30	Acc
William	853	Cmp
William	858	Cmp
William	150	Dnw
William	537	Prg
Wm.	457	Pra
Wyatt	541	Prg
Zacariah	82	Jff
Zarababel	812	Nrf
Heatherly, James	427	Rnd
Heaton, Benja.	42	Clp
Catey	410	Fqr
James	316	Ldn
Jas.	45	Clp
Joseph	364	Fqr
Masey	835	Wth
Wm.	42	Clp
Heator, Philip	286	Ldn
Heatwell, John	455	Frn
Heavner, Chrisr.	622	Mnt
Patsey	637	Mnt
Heaydon see Haydon		
Hebant, Aaron	545	Brk
Hebarlin, John	533	Brk
Hebbs, Wm.	508	Mnn
Hebdin, Wm.	457	Pra
Hebunn, Jams	21	Oho
Heck, Jacob	632	Btt
Joseph	601	Frd
Justice	506	Mnn
Phebe	598	Brk
Simon	806	Nrf
Heckart, Peter	508	Mnn
Heckem, George	754	Wsh
Hecker see Huker		
Heckle, John	212	Shn
Heckler, James	435	Bth
Heckman, Jacob	274	Rck
Hecton, Margaret	56	Stf
Hederick, Cathne.	903	Nrf
Jacob	838	Wth
Peter	838	Wth
Hedge, Willm.	606	Mnt
Hedgeman, George	23	Stf
Hedger, Joseph	221	Pnd
Hedges, Aaron	12	Oho
Charles	679	Br
Elijah	10	Oho
Eliza.	577	Brk
Hiram	3	Oho
Ishem	511	Prw
John	578	Brk
John	532	Frd
John	10	Oho
Jonah	577	Brk
Jonas	548	Brk
Joseph [2]	679	Br
Joseph	532	Frd
Joshua	577	Brk
Robert	509	Prw
Sam, 2d.	548	Brk
Saml., jr.	577	Brk
Samuel	679	Br
Samuel, Sr.	549	Brk
Silas [2]	678	Br
Solomon	577	Brk
William	679	Br
Hedgpeth, Isaac	158	Sth
Hedly, Carrey	427	Rnd
Isaac	427	Rnd
Hedrick, Adam	223	Pnd
Charles	628	Btt
Charles	214	Pnd
Frederick	221	Pnd
Henry	223	Pnd
John	666	Mnt
John	220	Pnd
Nicholas	514	Frd
Heed, John	16	Rcm
Heerman, Mary	904	Nrf
Hees, John	532	Prg
Heese, Anderson	100	Cmb
Blackbun	100	Cmb
Thomas	113	Cmb
Heeth, Price	235	Ldn
Heett, James	12	Wod
see Hiett		
Heetwole, David	38	Rcm
Heferlin, John	548	Frd
Heffer, John	250	Shn
Peter	27	Hnr
Heffernan, Henry	465	Mdd
Hefflin, James	409	Fqr
John, Junr.	350	Fqr
John, Senr.	350	Fqr
Martin	354	Fqr
William, (Overseer)	356	Fqr
Heffling, William	364	Fqr
Heflin, Elizabeth	257	Shn
Hannah	49	Stf
James, B.	39	Stf
James, W.	50	Stf
William	44	Stf
Heft, Christopher	17	Wod
Peter	15	Wod
Hegginbotham, John	700	Nls
Hehair, Stephen	264	Frf
Hehn, John	75	Jff
Heifner, Henry	583	Mnr
Heiford, Lewis	984	Nrt
Heill, Ryner	504	Mnn
Heinzman, Henry	757	Hmp
Heirs, John	685	Br
Heise, Constant	956	Hrr
David	954	Hrr
Heishell, John	515	Frd
Heiskell, Adam	756	Hmp
Christopher	756	Hmp
Frederick	201	Shn
George	523	Frd
Isaac	759	Hmp
Jacob	756	Hmp
John	401	Ags
Peter	352	Ags
Peter	401	Ags
Heisler, Adam	257	Shn
Heissill, James	19	Oho
Heist, Thomas	508	Frd
Heistant, John	33	Rcm
Heister see Heisler		
Helaman, Jacob	84	Jff
Helbert, Michael	29	Rcm
Helbringer, Michal	532	Frd
Helderbrand, M.	508	Mnn
Heldrege, Reece	727	Wsh
Heldridth, Frasur	938	Hrr
Heldrith, William	836	Wth
Helen, P.Y.	903	Nrf
Helens, Barbara	591	Brk
Helfersley, John	598	Brk
Helfersly, Harry	598	Brk
Helfry, Christiana	27	Rcm
Helftine see Holstine		
Hellar, Benjn.	102	Jff
Hellen, Jas., Senr.	748	Wsh
Heller, George	207	Shn
see Hiller		
Hellim, Adam	632	Mnt
Hellums, Henry	25	Oho
Lewis	7	Oho
Hellyer, Thomas	779	Hmp
Helm, Charles	532	Frd
Eliza.	353	Fqr
Frances	549	Frd
George	636	Mnt
Jacob	635	Mnt
James	860	Cmp
James	877	Cmp
Jno. D.	666	Mnt
John	877	Cmp
John	532	Frd
Meredith	583	Frd
Philip	665	Mnt
Samuel	470	Frn
Thomas	483	Frn
William	877	Cmp
William	583	Frd
Helmendollar, Jacob	630	Btt
Michl.	630	Btt
Paulson	630	Btt
Helmiche, Philip	221	Pnd
Helmick, Adam	222	Pnd
Adam	430	Rnd
Dav.	505	Mnn
George	430	Rnd
Jacob	421	Rnd
John	423	Rnd
Helmik, John	354	Ags
Helmondollar, Wm.	629	Btt
Helms, Jno.	489	Bdf
Jno., Revd.	628	Btt
Leanard	631	Btt
Salley	351	Ags
Tabitha	21	Isw
Wm.	348	Ags
Helphinstine, William	511	Frd
Helprett, George	718	Wsh
Helsair see Hehair		
Helsey, Chas.	228	Shn
Jacob, Jr.	228	Shn
Peter	228	Shn
Helsick see Kelsick		
Helsy, Jacob, Junr.	228	Shn
Heltmaher see Keltmaher		
Helton, Archd.	651	Mnt
Betty	202	Kng
Edmund	650	Mnt
Elisha	650	Mnt
Elizabeth	650	Mnt
George	650	Mnt
James	650	Mnt
Jesse	652	Mnt
John	650	Mnt
John	72	Spt

Name	No.	Co.	Name	No.	Co.	Name	No.	Co.
Saml.	756	Wsh	John	644	Mnt	Hendricks, Dan	509	Mnn
William	201	Kng	John	697	Nls	Daniel	85	Jff
Helvey, Adam	838	Wth	John	699	Nls	George	696	Br
George	641	Sss	John	747	Wsh	James	90	Jff
John	611	Mnt	John	838	Wth	Jno.	260	Ldn
John	838	Wth	John G.	5	Wod	John	696	Br
Helvy, Adam	621	Mnt	Jonathan	837	Wth	John	86	Jff
Frederick	621	Mnt	Jones	644	Mnt	Rachel	692	Br
Peter, Jr.	621	Mnt	Joseph	347	Ags	Hendrickson, Jacob	905	Crl
Peter, Sr.	621	Mnt	Joseph	553	Brk	Zach.	630	Btt
Hembert, Frederick	515	Prw	Joseph	631	Mnt	Hendrid, Danl.	814	Nrf
Hemdon see Herndon			Judith	658	Glc	Hendrin, John	505	Brk
Hemey see Hewey			Judrith	809	Bck	Partrick	938	Chc
Heming, Andrew	963	Hrr	Lelborn L.	691	Wsh	Hendron, Saml.	264	Rck
Mary	963	Hrr	Mark	202	Kng	Henegar, Jacob	741	Wsh
Nathan	963	Hrr	Mary	629	Btt	Henergar, Henry	741	Wsh
Wm.	963	Hrr	Nathaniel	698	Nls	Heney, John	695	Br
Hemingway, John	166	Knq	Pattey	367	Fqr	Henfrey, Benjn.	631	Btt
Hemlin, Thomas	455	Frn	Polly	390	Mds	Heniger, Fred.	353	Ags
Hemmelwright, John	572	Frd	Richard	198	Alb	John	724	Wsh
Hemmings, Moze C.	791	Nrf	Richd.	303	Ldn	Henin, James	198	Alb
Robt.	31	Hnr	Rob.	508	Mnn	Hening, David	567	Frd
Hemn, Sarah	32	Hnr	Robert	688	Br	James	519	Frd
Hemnaway, Am	1	Hnr	Robert	387	Fqr	Robert	57	Stf
Hemp, John	349	Ags	Robert	700	Nls	Wm. W.	1	Hnr
Stophel	349	Ags	Robert	701	Nls	Henington, James	716	Wsh
Hemphill, Robt.	18	Rcm	Robert, Jn.	701	Nls	Henkens, Peter	505	Mnn
Saml.	8	Rcm	Robt.	352	Ags	Henkins, George	222	Shn
Hemter, Nelly	499	Prw	Robt.	645	Mnt	Henkle, Abraham	222	Pnd
Hen..., Benjamin	466	Bdf	Saml.	302	Ldn	Abraham, S.	222	Pnd
Hencely, Henry	609	Mnt	Sampson	792	Hmp	George	221	Pnd
Henckle, Justias	420	Rnd	Samuel	99	Acc	Isaac	221	Pnd
Henderleter, Michl.	631	Btt	Samuel	100	Acc	Jacob	214	Pnd
Henderlight, Joseph	467	Bdf	Samuel	926	Hrr	Jacob	222	Pnd
Henderson, Alexander	698	Nls	Samuel	930	Hrr	Jesse	223	Pnd
Alexander	499	Prw	Samuel	423	Msn	John	221	Pnd
Alexander	507	Prw	Shadrach	700	Nls	Leonard	222	Pnd
Alexander	10	Wod	Stephen	699	Nls	Michal	221	Pnd
Alexr.	627	Btt	Thomas	776	Hmp	Moses	223	Pnd
Alexr.	629	Btt	Thos.	347	Ags	William	221	Pnd
Ambrus	198	Alb	Thos.	628	Btt	Henley, Alexr.	630	Btt
Andw.	629	Btt	Thos.	858	Hnv	Chas.	458	Pra
Brittingham	99	Acc	Thos.	202	Kng	Cornelias	837	Nrf
Charles	266	Frf	V.	351	Ags	Elizh.	117	Hnr
Chs.	262	Frf	Westley	773	Hmp	Hez., Snr.	113	Hnr
Clabron	703	Nls	William	30	Acc	Hiz., Jr.	113	Hnr
Danl.	351	Ags	William	625	Gls	J., W. &	2	Hnr
David	346	Ags	William	390	Mds	Jas.	459	Pra
David	350	Ags	William	701	Nls	Jno.	458	Pra
David	829	Hmp	William	984	Nrt	Leonard	270	Amh
David	99	Spt	William	5	Oho	Leonard	117	Hnr
David	113	Spt	William	81	Spt	Patrick	239	Aml
Durkin, & Co.	327	Dnw	William H.	98	Acc	Thomas M.	206	Ess
Henry	235	Ldn	Willm.	201	Kng	Thos.	456	Pra
Hugh	395	Fqr	Wm.	267	Frf	Thos., Jr.	457	Pra
Isaac	28	Acc	Wm.	582	Mnr	Thos., (of Cors.)	458	Pra
James	240	Aml	see H...son			Turner R.	117	Hnr
James	346	Ags	Hendey, Patriarch	232	Shn	W., & J.	2	Hnr
James	352	Ags	Hendickson, Spencer	814	Hmp	see Hewey		
James	688	Br	Hendie, John	3	Oho	Henly, Charles	695	Gch
James	804	Bck	Hendle, Robert	268	Frf	John	837	Wth
James	166	Knq	Hendley, Hannah	413	Rch	Maryan	117	Hnr
James	564	Mnr	Hendrckson, Simn.	507	Mnn	Peter	837	Wth
James	4	Ntt	Hendren, John	172	Shn	Robert	902	Nrf
James	722	Wsh	Robert	398	Fqr	Robert	836	Wth
James	11	Wod	Hendrick, Daniel	53	Chr	William	837	Wth
James	14	Wod	Elijah H.	781	Bck	see Heuly		
James, (W)	875	Yrk	Esekiel	114	Cmb	Hennage, George	99	Spt
Jas.	505	Mnn	Garland	240	Aml	Hennecka, Fred	904	Nrf
Jesse	543	Frd	Goode	463	Bdf	Hennes, John	872	Cmp
John	161	Alb	Jarrot	831	Bck	Hennessy see Henssy		
John	422	Bth	Jesse	701	Nls	Henney, John	160	Alb
John	573	Brk	John D.	844	Hnv	Hennig, Henley	444	Bth
John	819	Bck	Lucy	240	Aml	Thos.	551	Brk
John	625	Gls	Martha	126	Cmb	Hennigar see Henegar, Henergar		
John	760	Hmp	Nancy	240	Aml	Henning, Jas.	627	Btt
John	836	Hmp	Obadiah	569	Pre	Jno.	265	Frf
John	81	Jff	William S.	105	Cmb	John [2]	27	Rcm
John	390	Mds	William	844	Hnv	Hennon, Mary	836	Wth
John	425	Msn	Zack	240	Aml	Henop see Henoss		

Name	No.	Co.	Name	No.	Co.	Name	No.	Co.
Henoss, Dl.	904	Nrf	Hensil, George	553	Frd	Herd, John	490	Frn
Jno.	904	Nrf	Hensington, John	501	Wsh	Herden, Edw.	348	Ags
Philip	902	Nrf	Hensley, Benjamin	799	Bck	Herdman, Jno.	17	Rcm
Henrey, Benjamin	466	Bdf	Elisebeth	746	Wsh	Samuel	685	Br
Wm.	566	Mnr	Enoch	42	Clp	Herdras, Leon	826	Nrf
Henrie, Sarah	12	Wod	Fielding	735	Wsh	Hereford, Francis	390	Fqr
Henry, Aron	503	Mnn	Henry	782	Bck	Margarett	390	Fqr
Aron	505	Mnn	Ithe	746	Wsh	Hereld, Jno.	61	Chs
Aron	172	Shn	James	34	Rcm	Herendon, John	376	Fqr
Caty	518	Brk	John	697	Nls	Heriford, Thomas	302	Ldn
Edmond	760	Wsh	Mary	34	Rcm	Herman, ---,[his]		
Edward	984	Nrt	Saml.	734	Wsh	(Plantn.)	457	Pra
Elisebeth	734	Wsh	Samuel	697	Nls	John	690	Br
Elizabeth	560	Frd	Sibba	159	Alb	Hermands, Wm.	44	Clp
Elizabeth	863	Hnv	William	467	Bdf	Hermon, Adam	838	Wth
Fayatte	873	Cmp	William	391	Mds	Jas., (F.B.)	458	Pra
Fran.	503	Mnn	William, Senr.	799	Bck	John	51	Chr
George	954	Hrr	Wm.	735	Wsh	Peter	595	Mnr
George	16	Oho	Henslow, Thos.	27	Hnr	Samuel	696	Br
George	6	Rcm	Hensly, Benjamin	465	Bdf	Hernden, Patric	20	Oho
George	774	Wst	Henson, Charles	810	Bck	Herndon, Benjamin	51	Chr
Harry	540	Frd	George	202	Kng	Dabney	118	Spt
Isaac	410	Fqr	James	798	Bck	Daniel	868	Cmp
Isaac	839	Nrf	James	910	Hrr	Edmund	859	Cmp
James	349	Ags	James	836	Wth	Edward	869	Cmp
James	674	Br	Jesse	201	Kng	Edward	92	Spt
James	588	Frd	John	260	Amh	Edward, & son	391	Mds
James	40	Rcm	John	790	Bck	Elizabeth	71	Spt
Jno.	632	Btt	John	239	Shn	Elliot	445	Bth
Jno.	13	Hnr	Murray	260	Amh	Geo.	437	Flv
Joel	40	Clp	Presley	774	Wst	George	366	Fqr
John	349	Ags	Shadrick	326	Dnw	George	384	Fqr
John	408	Ags	Henssy, Thos.	509	Mnn	George	391	Mds
John	682	Br	Henthorn, Hen.	507	Mnn	Jacob M.	103	Spt
John	463	Frn	James	7	Oho	Jessee	161	Alb
John	202	Kng	Jno.	507	Mnn	John	161	Alb
John	830	Nrf	Robert	7	Oho	John	51	Chr
Jos.	503	Mnn	Wm.	7	Oho	John	697	Gch
Lydia	296	Ldn	Wm., Jr.	7	Oho	John	391	Mds
Martin	569	Brk	Henton, Catharine	344	Lnn	John	70	Spt
Mary	167	Knq	James	345	Lnn	John L.	371	Fqr
Mary	17	Rcm	John	40	Rcm	Joseph, jr.	76	Spt
Moses	163	Shn	Joseph	17	Rcm	Joseph, Sr.	90	Spt
Moses	245	Shn	Silas	40	Rcm	Reuben	523	Prw
Nancy	281	Ldn	William	345	Lnn	Richard	283	Amh
Nathaniel	523	Frd	Hepburne, Wm.	262	Frf	Robt.	442	Flv
Nichos.	569	Brk	Hephner, Ander.	350	Ags	Sarah	373	Fqr
Otho	505	Mnn	Jacob	350	Ags	Tho.	508	Mnn
Patrick, (Est.)	52	Chr	Michl.	346	Ags	Thos.	697	Gch
Peter	569	Brk	Philip	348	Ags	William	91	Spt
Richard	552	Frd	Urbanus	347	Ags	William	110	Spt
Robert	486	Frn	Hepkins, Robert	774	Wst	Hernley, Nehemiah	160	Alb
Robert	734	Wsh	Samuel	774	Wst	Herod, Mildred	104	Spt
Robt., Sen.	761	Wsh	see Hopkins			Heron, Js.	904	Nrf
Rose	774	Wst	Hepler, George	627	Btt	Samuel	695	Br
Saml.	123	Hnr	John	595	Mnr	Heronomus, Pendleton	509	Frd
Saml.	472	Mdd	Hepner, Wm.	350	Ags	Herr, Isaac	938	Chc
Saml.	8	Rcm	Herbeirt, Max.	805	Nrf	Herrald, David	836	Wth
Samuel	679	Br	Herbert, Abram	775	Wst	Jacob	835	Wth
Samuel	931	Hrr	Ann	904	Nrf	John	835	Wth
Samuel	1	Knw	Anne	792	Nrf	John	838	Wth
Thomas	775	Wst	Anthony	755	Nwk	Reubin	838	Wth
William	632	Btt	Edward	792	Nrf	William	835	Wth
William	694	Br	James	791	Nrf	William	836	Wth
William	696	Br	Jno.	248	Ldn	Herramon, Jacob	261	Frf
Wm., Sr.	632	Btt	John	574	Brk	Herrell, Jno.	233	Ldn
see H...y, Hanvy, Henssy			John	176	Elc	Herren, Hanse	401	Ags
Hensetze, Peter	688	Wsh	John	599	Mnr	Walter	354	Ags
Hensey, Kinney	387	Fqr	John	902	Nrf	Herridon see Herndon		
Sarah	512	Prw	John C.	836	Nrf	Herriford, John	432	Msn
Thomas	511	Prw	Nancy	832	Nrf	Thos. A.	232	Ldn
Henshaw, Hiram	525	Brk	Peter	836	Nrf	Herrin, Ann	541	Prg
John, Qr.	390	Mds	Reuben	809	Nrf	Benjamin	199	Alb
Levi	525	Brk	Rheuben	902	Nrf	George	199	Alb
Philip	907	Crl	Thomas	836	Wth	Isaac, jr.	39	Clp
Samuel	390	Mds	Wm.	248	Ldn	John	838	Wth
Stephen	525	Brk	Wm.	599	Mnr	Jonathan	198	Alb
Uriah	525	Brk	Wm. B.	814	Nrf	Robert	269	Ldn
William	390	Mds	Herbich, John	536	Frd	Spencer	199	Alb
Henshew, Jacob	838	Wth	Herbison, James	837	Wth	see Herring		

Name	No.	Abbr.
Herring, Alexander	15	Rcm
Bethuel	38	Rcm
Cathen.	464	Mdd
Daniel	40	Isw
Elizabeth	38	Rcm
Hannah	39	Clp
Isac.	39	Clp
John	18	Isw
Natt, (F.N.)	40	Isw
Peter	805	Nrf
Stephen	345	Lnn
Thomas	1	Rcm
see Hening, Herrin		
Herrington, Danil	13	Oho
James	3	Oho
Nathan	7	Oho
Herron, James	694	Br
John	694	Br
Herseman, Abraham	825	Hmp
Christopher	825	Hmp
Hershberger, Henry	182	Shn
Isaac	191	Shn
Jacob	196	Shn
Samuel	185	Shn
Hervey, Jacob	567	Mnr
John	571	Mnr
John, Sr.	567	Mnr
William	683	Br
see Henrey		
Hervy, Albridgh.	156	Sth
David	964	Hrr
Heskett, Benj.	308	Ldn
Benjm.	81	Jff
James	236	Ldn
Jno.	275	Ldn
John	80	Jff
Heskew, Ann	166	Knq
Heslen, Abraham	160	Alb
Heslop, John G.	332	Dnw
Nathan	503	Prw
William	73	Spt
Hess, Abm.	507	Mnn
Abraham	584	Frd
Abraham	231	Shn
Benjn.	628	Mnt
Chris	353	Ags
Hezekiah	952	Hrr
Jacob	545	Brk
Jacob	631	Btt
Jeremiah	947	Hrr
Jno.	266	Ldn
Jno., J.	266	Ldn
Nicholas	541	Brk
P., Jr.	505	Mnn
Peter	544	Brk
Peter	505	Mnn
Philip	354	Ags
Philip	541	Brk
Hessee, Jno.	249	Ldn
Hesser, George	527	Frd
Hannah	309	Ldn
Jacob	195	Shn
Hessey, John	106	Jff
Hestant, David	99	Jff
Hesten see Heslen		
Hester, John	4	Knw
John	904	Nrf
Joseph	206	Ess
Robert	5	Knw
Hestings, Mary	742	Wsh
Heston, Silas	855	Cmp
Hestop, Thomas	231	Shn
Heter, John	947	Hrr
Heterick, Catharine	23	Rcm
Heth, Harry	66	Chs
Isaac	522	Prw
Hetherington, Christo-pher	626	Gls
Hetherling, Christo.	575	Brk
Hetherton, Andrew	15	Hnr
Hethorn, Robt.	695	Wsh
Saml.	694	Wsh
Hetson, Wm.	556	Brk
Hetterick, Charles	828	Hmp
Heuly, James, Jr.	465	Mdd
James, Senr.	465	Mdd
Heurtt, Kezia	798	Nrf
Hevally, John	216	Pnd
Heviner, Adam	217	Pnd
Catlip	215	Pnd
Freaderick, J.	217	Pnd
Freadericke, S.	215	Pnd
George	215	Pnd
Jacob	215	Pnd
Jacob	217	Pnd
John	215	Pnd
Lewis	215	Pnd
Nicholas	215	Pnd
Hewell, Wm.	656	Glc
Hewes see Huse		
Hewet, Peggy	14	Hnr
Hewett, John	83	Jff
Hewey, Helen	500	Prw
Hewise, Benjamin	1	Wod
Hewit, ...n	467	Bdf
Catharine	57	Stf
Edmund	465	Bdf
James	35	Stf
James, of W.O.	45	Stf
John	464	Bdf
John	57	Stf
John, (O)	465	Bdf
John, Sr.	465	Bdf
Molly	37	Stf
Rice	631	Btt
Thomas	467	Bdf
William	696	Br
William	57	Stf
Hewitt, Jno., Sr.	629	Btt
John	628	Btt
Kezia	810	Nrf
Susan	840	Nrf
William	357	Fqr
Wm.	795	Nrf
Hewlet, Henry	76	Spt
Miquiel	28	Hnr
Hewlett, Geo., free negro	70	Chs
Richd.	68	Chs
Sarah	908	Crl
Susan	908	Crl
William	16	Hnr
Hewlings, Jacob W.	570	Pre
Hews, Constant	294	Ldn
Hugh	314	Ldn
Isaac	237	Ldn
John	985	Nrt
Samuel	314	Ldn
Thos.	314	Ldn
William	984	Nrt
Heyburn, William	566	Frd
Heys, Henry	6	Knw
John	6	Knw
Heywood, Edmd. Hannah	658	Glc
Wm.	656	Glc
Wm.	657	Glc
Wm. V.	658	Glc
Hggin, Francis	263	Frf
Hhamner, John	160	Alb
Hi..., William	466	Bdf
Hiatt, Simmeon	459	Frn
Hibbet, James	696	Br
William	696	Br
William	698	Br
Hibble, Eliza. Geo.	658	Glc
Hibbons, Cyrus	659	Glc
William	72	Jff
Hibbs, Amos	67	Jff
	238	Ldn
John	807	Hmp
Valuntine	276	Ldn
Wm.	274	Ldn
Hibson, Margt.	269	Ldn
Hickam, John	755	Wsh
Jos.	758	Wsh
Hickee see Huker		
Hickembottem, Raph.	947	Hrr
Hickenbotom, Moses	715	Wsh
Hickenbottom, Thos.	581	Mnr
Hickerson, Chs.	43	Clp
Daniel	355	Fqr
Daniel	492	Frn
Frances	44	Clp
James	798	Bck
Joseph	352	Fqr
Nathaniel	357	Fqr
Rawleigh	386	Fqr
Walter	41	Clp
see Jachobs		
Hickey, Davd.	723	Wsh
Elizabeth	263	Frf
James	351	Ags
Wm.	747	Wsh
Hickle, Henry	775	Hmp
John	627	Btt
John	441	Flv
Samuel	565	Frd
Stephen	770	Hmp
Hicklen, George	413	Bth
Hickman, Adam	960	Hrr
Adam	281	Rck
Arthur	99	Acc
Benjn.	654	Mnt
Bridget	98	Acc
Coger L.	760	Wsh
Daniel	482	Frn
David	482	Frn
Elias	7	Wod
Elijah	99	Acc
Isaac, Cap.	103	Acc
Isaiah	98	Acc
Isham	799	Bck
Jacob	482	Frn
Jacob	512	Frd
James	419	Bth
James	539	Frd
John	30	Acc
John	281	Rck
John, Captn.	100	Acc
John, of B	102	Acc
John B.	99	Acc
Jonathan	45	Clp
Jos.	756	Wsh
Josa.	506	Mnn
Joseph	476	Frn
Kendall	99	Acc
Laney	98	Acc
Mary	522	Frd
Peggy	31	Acc
Peter	285	Ldn
Rachal	98	Acc
Rachel	28	Acc
Rachel	375	Fqr
Revel	98	Acc
Richard	99	Acc
Robert	103	Acc
Rodger	419	Bth
Saml.	191	Elc
Selby	98	Acc
Stephen	103	Acc
Thomas	28	Acc
Thomas	98	Acc
Thomas	906	Crl
Thomas, BS	27	Acc
Thos.	43	Clp
William	102	Acc
William	419	Bth
William	80	Jff
William	1	Pwh

Wm.	42	Clp	
Wm.	188	Elc	
Wm.	638	Mnt	
Zachariah	921	Hrr	
Hickmon, Cloey, F.B.	5	Pwh	
Michael	704	Wsh	
Peter	705	Wsh	
Hickok, Eben	699	Nls	
Ebenezer	699	Nls	
Samuel	699	Nls	
Hicks, Anderson	197	Alb	
Andrew	92	Spt	
Anthony	773	Bck	
Benjamin	33	Isw	
Bridget	2	Rcm	
Charles	197	Alb	
David	159	Alb	
David	176	Elc	
David	701	Nls	
Fanny, (M)	715	Brn	
Henry	848	Sth	
Isaac	714	Brn	
Isaiah	241	Ldn	
James	553	Brk	
James	751	Brn	
James	806	Bck	
James	371	Fqr	
Jesse	489	Bdf	
Jesse	332	Dnw	
Jessee	714	Brn	
Jno.	264	Frf	
Jno.	267	Frf	
John	535	Brk	
John	751	Brn	
John	874	Cmp	
John	596	Frd	
John	904	Nrf	
John	219	Pnd	
Jordan	714	Brn	
Joseph	2	Rcm	
Joseph	93	Spt	
Joshua	269	Rck	
Judith	750	Brn	
Kimble	399	Fqr	
Levi	533	Frd	
Lewis	750	Brn	
Nathaniel	53	Chr	
Paschal	749	Brn	
Peter	72	Spt	
R. P. Liggons [written in			
on photostats]	64	Chs	
Rebecca	882	Sth	
Rebeckah	749	Brn	
Reuben	714	Brn	
Reubin	838	Wth	
Richard W.	857	Cmp	
Robert	267	Frf	
Sabella	874	Cmp	
Solomon	160	Alb	
Stephen	264	Frf	
Thomas	69	Spt	
William	33	Isw	
William, Sr.	609	Srr	
Willm.	176	Elc	
Willm. C.	176	Elc	
Wm., Senr.	265	Frf	
see Hunt			
Hickson, John	571	Brk	
John	420	Rnd	
Robert	69	Jff	
William	420	Rnd	
Hicky, William	837	Wth	
Hicman, Abriham	933	Hrr	
Adam	934	Hrr	
Suel	936	Hrr	
Hida, Jacob	225	Pnd	
John, J.	225	Pnd	
John, S.	225	Pnd	
Hidd see Kidd			
Hide, George	431	Msn	

James	431	Msn	
Kitty	430	Msn	
Robt.	1	Hnr	
William	431	Msn	
Hidecker, Jacob	27	Rcm	
Hiden, Joshua	350	Ags	
Hieronomus, Conrad	556	Frd	
Henry	556	Frd	
Hieskel, Margaret	118	Spt	
Hiet, Daniel	838	Wth	
see Heett			
Hiett, Evan	784	Hmp	
James	85	Jff	
Jeremiah	784	Hmp	
John	530	Frd	
John	764	Hmp	
John	74	Jff	
John	12	Wod	
Jonathan	765	Hmp	
Joseph	783	Hmp	
Leonard	92	Jff	
Thomas	66	Jff	
William	74	Jff	
see Hite			
Higanbotham, David	182	Alb	
Higdon, Charles	201	Kng	
Higerty, Wm.	278	Ldn	
Higgason, John, Jnr.	845	Hnv	
Mary	857	Hnv	
Moses	862	Hnv	
Polley	857	Hnv	
Rachel	857	Hnv	
Richard	864	Hnv	
Higgenbottom, Jas.	506	Mnn	
Wm.	506	Mnn	
Wm., Jr.	506	Mnn	
see Hegginbotham, Hicken-			
botom, Higanbotham			
Higgens, Eugne.	904	Nrf	
Foster	756	Nwk	
John	17	Rcm	
Josiah	755	Nwk	
Robt.	18	Rcm	
Higginbotom, Jas.	734	Wsh	
Higgin see Highin			
Higginbotham, Absalem	296	Amh	
Benjamin	284	Amh	
Charles	295	Amh	
Daniel, & Co.	269	Amh	
James	294	Amh	
James S.	286	Amh	
John	299	Amh	
Joseph	298	Amh	
Joseph	467	Bdf	
Joseph, (SM)	286	Amh	
Nancy	300	Amh	
Thomas	850	Cmp	
Warner	274	Amh	
William	258	Amh	
Higginbottom, James	3	Knw	
Joseph	13	Knw	
see Higgenbottom			
Higgins, Cathne.	904	Nrf	
James	422	Bth	
James	833	Hmp	
Jerenh.	580	Brk	
John	766	Hmp	
John	831	Hmp	
John	423	Msn	
Joseph	828	Hmp	
Michel	27	Acc	
Thomas	548	Frd	
Thomas	421	Msn	
Wim.	880	Hnv	
Higgs, Noah	22	Rcm	
Parmenas	502	Prw	
Samuel	490	Frn	
High, ---	332	Dnw	
Frederick	802	Hmp	
Henry	802	Hmp	

Jacob	800	Hmp	
Jacob	19	Rcm	
John	803	Hmp	
John, sen.	802	Hmp	
Westmoland	52	Chr	
Higher, Leonard	922	Hrr	
Highin, Leonard	961	Hrr	
Highlander, John	304	Amh	
Robert	697	Nls	
Highly, John	552	Frd	
Hight, George	702	Nls	
Hartwell	874	Cmp	
Hightower, Joshua	21	Ntt	
Wood	18	Ntt	
Hights, Richard, (Est.)	52	Chr	
Highwarden, James	424	Rnd	
Higle, Hannah	954	Hrr	
Hilander, Jacob	41	Clp	
Hilbert, Conrod	248	Shn	
Hildrith, Jeffery	835	Wth	
Hile, Simon	244	Shn	
see Hill			
Hill, Abraham	904	Hrr	
Abraham	90	Jff	
Adrien	750	Brn	
Alexr. B.	353	Ags	
Ambo. Powell	389	Mds	
Andrew	567	Brk	
Andrew	458	Pra	
Armistead	64	Chs	
Barber	475	Frn	
Barberry	95	Jff	
Bayler, jr.	838	Nrf	
Ben.	504	Mnn	
Betsy	11	Knw	
Betty	876	Yrk	
Broadwater	99	Acc	
Charles	199	Alb	
Charles	715	Brn	
Charles	238	Ldn	
Charles	537	Prg	
Charles, (FN)	5	Isw	
Charles, Sen. (F.N.)	37	Isw	
Christian	104	Jff	
Clary	907	Crl	
Clary	204	Ess	
Costolo	482	Frn	
Dabney	278	Amh	
Daniel	2	Knw	
Daniel	7	Wod	
Davis	570	Pre	
Dick, (F.N.)	30	Isw	
Edward	166	Knq	
Edward G.	78	Spt	
Eli	695	Br	
Eliza.	349	Lnc	
Elizabeth	257	Amh	
Elizabeth	570	Pre	
Elizabeth	32	Stf	
Erasmus	513	Prw	
Fanny	35	Stf	
Francis	274	Amh	
Francis	497	Frn	
Francis	451	Grn	
G. B.	904	Nrf	
Gabriel	537	Prg	
George	567	Brk	
George	812	Hmp	
George	4	Knw	
George	166	Knq	
George	700	Nls	
Goodwin	959	Chc	
Harry	148	Dnw	
Hartwell	715	Brn	
Henry	198	Alb	
Henry	199	Alb	
Henry	854	Cmp	
Henry	4	Knw	
Henry	167	Knq	
Henry	389	Mds	

154

Henry	645	Sss	Pitman	357	Fqr	Hillary, William	344	Fqr
Henry, Jr.	389	Mds	Pleasant	239	Aml	Hilldrop, John	907	Crl
Herbert	715	Brn	Polly	628	Btt	Hiller, ...gal	263	Rck
Hugh	4	Hnr	Polly	4	Knw	Hillery, Clem	290	Ldn
Hull C.	126	Cmb	Rebecca	793	Nrf	Wm.	504	Mnn
Humphrey	907	Crl	Reuben	591	Mnr	Hilliard, Amos	27	Rcm
Humphrey	42	Clp	Reubin	837	Wth	Benskin	756	Nwk
Humpy.	204	Ess	Richard [2]	199	Alb	Benskin H.	756	Nwk
Isaac	643	Sss	Richard	427	Bth	Daniel	161	Sth
Jack, (M)	715	Brn	Richard	167	Knq	Isaac	657	Glc
Jacob	907	Hrr	Richard	642	Sss	Jacob	855	Sth
Jacob	10	Knw	Richd.	450	Grn	John	755	Nwk
Jacob	12	Rcm	Rob	504	Mnn	Mary	756	Nwk
Jacob	26	Rcm	Robert	102	Acc	Richard	756	Nwk
James	239	Aml	Robert	561	Brk	Thomas	757	Nwk
James	274	Amh	Robert	780	Bck	Hilliards, Jacob	550	Frd
James	464	Frn	Robert	204	Ess	Hilling, Nathaniel	588	Frd
James	896	Hnv	Robert	389	Mds	William	588	Frd
James	316	Ldn	Robert	570	Pre	Hillis, Hugh	408	Ags
James	700	Nls	Robert B.	167	Knq	see Hiller		
James	12	Pwh	Robt.	37	Rcm	Hillman, William	625	Gls
James	569	Pre	Robt., [his] est.	60	Chs	Hillory, James	345	Fqr
James [crossed out]	311	Rck	Roger	695	Br	Hillsman, James	240	Aml
James	608	Srr	Rose	148	Dnw	Jose	240	Aml
James, (C)	239	Aml	Russell	327	Dnw	Hilly, Freaderick	226	Pnd
James, jr.	282	Amh	Saml.	122	Hnr	Hillyard, Judith	774	Wst
James B.	401	Ags	Samuel	161	Alb	Hillyer, George	767	Hmp
Jas.	506	Mnn	Samuel	283	Amh	Robert	770	Hmp
Jemimah, (FB)	464	Bdf	Sarah	483	Frn	Hilman, Jacob	208	Shn
Jeremiah	428	Msn	Stophel	598	Brk	Nimrod	83	Spt
Jerry, free Negro	5	Knw	Swinfeild	484	Frn	Thomas	985	Nrt
Jesse	457	Pra	Terry	130	Hnr	William	67	Spt
Jesse	39	Stf	Thomas	427	Bth	Hilsey, Chistopher	228	Shn
Jessee	428	Msn	Thomas	685	Br	Hilt, Henry	299	Rck
Jimmy, (FB)	15	Ntt	Thomas	149	Dnw	Jacob	348	Ags
Jno.	348	Lnc	Thomas	204	Ess	see Hitt		
Joel	845	Hnv	Thomas	450	Frn	Hiltenberger, Daniel	838	Wth
John	100	Acc	Thomas	481	Frn	Hiltibrand, Henry	346	Ags
John	199	Alb	Thomas	482	Frn	Jacob	346	Ags
John	284	Amh	Thomas	483	Frn	Michl.	352	Ags
John	555	Brk	Thomas	57	Jff	Hilto..., John	466	Bdf
John	906	Crl	Thomas	166	Knq	Hilton, George	957	Hrr
John	908	Crl	Thomas	39	Stf	Jacob	837	Wth
John	106	Cmb	Thomas	774	Wst	Jno.	40	Clp
John	483	Frn	Thos.	904	Nrf	Matt, (FB)	15	Ntt
John [2]	780	Hmp	Valentine	820	Hmp	Matthew	106	Jff
John	844	Hnv	W.	508	Mnn	Molley, (FB)	15	Ntt
John	755	Nwk	Walter	720	Wsh	Sam, Persons of		
John	16	Oho	Walter	721	Wsh	Colour	106	Cmb
John	426	Rnd	Washington	280	Amh	Samuel	985	Nrt
John	570	Pre	Watt	696	Gch	William	465	Bdf
John	179	Shn	William	811	Bck	Wm.	965	Hrr
John	81	Spt	William	877	Cmp	see Hylton		
John	46	Stf	William	148	Dnw	Hilyard, James	719	Wsh
John	774	Wst	William	512	Frd	Jno.	285	Rck
John	17	Wod	William	812	Hmp	Mary	166	Knq
John, Junr.	570	Pre	William	464	Mdd	William	167	Knq
John, (Sp. creek)	570	Pre	William	44	Stf	Hilyer, ---	767	Hmp
John K.	116	Spt	William	5	Wod	Himes, And.	300	Rck
Jos.	509	Mnn	William, Jnr.	698	Nls	John	279	Rck
Joseph	829	Bck	William, Jnr.	700	Nls	Hinchey, Maurice	3	Rcm
Joseph	227	Pnd	William, (R.C.)	570	Pre	Hinchman, John	599	Mnr
Joseph	642	Sss	William, (S.M.)	570	Pre	William	574	Mnr
Josiah	3	Hnr	William, Senr.	570	Pre	Wm. [2]	585	Mnr
Josiah	14	Hnr	William E.	954	Chc	Hinckle, Thomas	422	Rnd
Julia	458	Pra	Wim. L.	878	Hnv	Hindal, Henry	241	Ldn
Lee	148	Dnw	Wm.	630	Btt	Hindell, John	417	Fqr
Leonard	44	Stf	Wm.	58	Chs	Hinderson see Henderson		
Leroy	812	Hmp	Wm.	348	Lnc	Hindman, John	8	Wod
Mary	877	Hnv	Wm.	508	Mnn	Hindrick, Jno.	264	Ldn
Mary	885	Hnv	Wm.	703	Nls	Hinds, Henry	572	Pre
Mary	908	Hrr	Wm.	275	Rck	Thomas	570	Pre
Mary	681	Wrw	Wm., jr.	44	Clp	Thomas	391	Rch
Matthew	886	Hnv	Wm., Senr.	42	Clp	William	571	Pre
Moses	837	Wth	Wm., (Tayr.)	40	Clp	William	716	Wsh
Nathaniel	836	Wth	see Carter, H...ll, Heill,			Hinemon, Henry	953	Hrr
Nathl.	848	Hnv	Hite, Hitt			Hiner, Abm.	631	Btt
Parkes	757	Nwk	Hillan, James	717	Wsh	Harmon	226	Pnd
Peter, F.N.	641	Sss	Hillard, John	941	Chc	Jacob	214	Pnd
Phil	508	Mnn	Joseph	950	Chc	Hines, Aleck	218	Pnd

Ann	857	Sth	Sarah	907	Crl	Jno.	41	Clp
Benja.	158	Sth	Sarah	214	Ess	Martin	346	Fqr
Calvin	643	Sss	see Pittman			Nathan	365	Fqr
Charles, f. negro	263	Frf	Hippert, John	21	Rcm	Reuben	412	Fqr
Donaldson	451	Grn	Hirly, Joshua	965	Hrr	Sarah	365	Fqr
Henry	51	Chr	Hirst, David	276	Ldn	Sarah	412	Fqr
Henry, (LE)	52	Chr	Jesse	315	Ldn	William	360	Fqr
Hugh	220	Shn	Richd.	317	Ldn	see Hill		
Isaac	646	Mnt	William	609	Mnt	Hitte, Josha., jr.	42	Clp
James	51	Chr	Hiser, Henry	214	Shn	Josha., Senr.	42	Clp
John	686	Br	Jacob	207	Shn	see Hitt, Hittle		
John	51	Chr	John	351	Ags	Hittelee, David	599	Brk
John	800	Hmp	Saml.	348	Ags	Hittle, Jacob	42	Clp
John	214	Shn	Saml., jr.	348	Ags	see Hitt, Hitte		
John, J.	217	Pnd	see Hisos			Hivally, Michal	220	Pnd
John, S.	218	Pnd	Hisey, Jacob	203	Shn	Hively, Jacob	630	Btt
Joseph	51	Chr	John	202	Shn	Hives, John	221	Pnd
Mellonton	343	Lnn	Hisia, Christian	242	Shn	Hix, Archibald	569	Pre
Patsy	68	Chr	Daniel	242	Shn	Blansford	273	Amh
Richd.	137	Sth	Danl.	243	Shn	Charles	643	Sss
Robert	643	Sss	Maria	243	Shn	David	12	Knw
Rudolph	686	Br	Hiskett, Joseph	696	Br	Edward	756	Nwk
Tarlton	695	Gch	Hisle, Benja.	43	Clp	Eliza.	272	Ldn
Temperance	857	Sth	Jno.	41	Clp	George	756	Nwk
Thomas	760	Hmp	Ro.	41	Clp	Israel	241	Ldn
Thos.	300	Rck	Hisletar, John	933	Hrr	James	277	Amh
William	516	Frd	Hisos, George	216	Pnd	James	464	Bdf
William	450	Grn	Hitapher, Jno.	235	Ldn	James	570	Pre
William	844	Hnv	Hitch, Aquilla	364	Fqr	Jeremiah	466	Bdf
William, Sr.	450	Grn	Nancey	406	Fqr	Jesse	570	Pre
Wm.	853	Sth	Robert	345	Fqr	Jno.	61	Chs
Wylie	641	Sss	Sarah	524	Prw	John [2]	697	Gch
see Himes			Tolman	344	Fqr	John	900	Hnv
Hiney, George	13	Rcm	Trueman	344	Fqr	John	757	Nwk
Hinkle, Adam	557	Frd	Hitchcock, Edmund	148	Dnw	Joseph	816	Bck
Henry	277	Rck	Hartwell	148	Dnw	Joseph	898	Hnv
John	72	Jff	John	149	Dnw	Josiah	3	Pwh
Pall	252	Shn	Ussery	148	Dnw	Meshac	697	Gch
Samuel	72	Jff	Wm.	918	Hrr	Nathaniel	756	Nwk
Sollomon	252	Shn	see Hickok			Rebecca	640	Sss
Hinkley, George	197	Shn	Hitchecock, Martha	166	Knq	Stephen	1	Pwh
Hinkston, William	675	Br	Hitchins, Ezekel	29	Acc	William	464	Bdf
Hinlin, George	751	Wsh	Hite, Alexander	256	Shn	William	2	Knw
Hinman, Major	98	Acc	Anthony	353	Ags	William	755	Nwk
Major, of M	101	Acc	Benjamine W.	343	Lnn	William, Sr.	464	Bdf
Thomas	101	Acc	Charnel	609	Srr	Wm.	694	Gch
William	98	Acc	Cordilla	12	Rcm	Wm.	696	Gch
William	101	Acc	Daniel	190	Shn	Hixon, John	488	Frn
Hinneger, Coorod	731	Wsh	Danl.	295	Rck	Hixson, Benj.	236	Ldn
Saml.	731	Wsh	Frederick	257	Shn	James	236	Ldn
Hinor, Anthony	631	Btt	Geo.	349	Ags	Mary	298	Ldn
Hinsley, Eliza.	45	Clp	Geo.	507	Mnn	Samuel	291	Ldn
see Hensley			George	57	Jff	Timothy	297	Ldn
Hinson, Ann	903	Nrf	Isaac	541	Frd	William	526	Prw
Eppa. J.	405	Rch	Jacob	281	Rck	Wm.	295	Ldn
James	408	Fqr	James	92	Jff	Hizer, Adam	99	Jff
James	399	Rch	John	936	Hrr	John	99	Jff
James [3]	402	Rch	John	539	Prg	John	100	Jff
Jonas	405	Rch	John, Je.	589	Brk	Hizey, Jacob	41	Rcm
Joshua	402	Rch	Joseph	93	Jff	Ho..., David	466	Bdf
Mary	403	Rch	Joseph, Jnr.	93	Jff	Hoages, Major	215	Ess
Robert	417	Fqr	Juceous	343	Lnn	Rachel	215	Ess
William	401	Rch	Mathias	947	Hrr	Hoard, Beckky	88	Spt
William	402	Rch	Matthew	703	Nls	Hiram	517	Prw
Hinton, Henry	348	Lnc	Matthias	546	Frd	James	52	Chr
James	450	Grn	Michael	241	Shn	James	359	Fqr
Jno. C.	348	Lnc	Nancy	641	Sss	James	94	Spt
John	333	Dnw	Nicholas	608	Srr	James	97	Spt
John, after	328	Dnw	Reuben	549	Frd	John	52	Chr
Nancy	348	Lnc	Saml.	292	Rck	Mary	33	Rcm
Peter	23	Rcm	Saml.	11	Rcm	Rhodin	97	Spt
Richd.	348	Lnc	Samuel	92	Jff	Susan	112	Spt
Samuel	332	Dnw	Simmons	334	Dnw	Hob, Mira	294	Ldn
Sp.	348	Lnc	William	11	Rcm	Hobb, Matthew	717	Wsh
Thomas	678	Br	see Hiett, Hill			Hobbs, Abram	872	Sth
Wm.	629	Btt	Hitehour, Elizabeth	346	Lnn	Ann	549	Prg
Hiphner, Gasper	347	Ags	William	345	Lnn	Benjamin	750	Brn
Hipingstall, Caleb	451	Frn	Hitt, Benjamin	392	Fqr	Edmund	535	Prg
Hipkin, Wm.	12	Hnr	Hannah	409	Fqr	Elisha	546	Prg
Hipkins, Elizabeth	907	Crl	Jno.	40	Clp	Elizabeth	641	Sss

Name	No.	Co.
Ezekiel	753	Wsh
Frederic	450	Grn
George	128	Sth
Gilliam	750	Brn
Hartwell H.	148	Dnw
Hinchey	643	Sss
Hubbard	714	Brn
James	465	Bdf
Jno.	714	Brn
Jno.	307	Ldn
Jno. P.	715	Brn
John	906	Hrr
John H.	450	Grn
Payton	609	Srr
Pleasants	148	Dnw
Richard	837	Wth
Sarah	751	Brn
Sarah	536	Prg
Sarah	545	Prg
Silas	867	Sth
Vinson	753	Wsh
William	450	Grn
William	642	Sss
Williamson	542	Prg
see Hobs		
Hobday, Howard	657	Glc
Lucy	902	Nrf
Rd.	656	Glc
Tho.	875	Yrk
Wm. A., Gloucester		
Town	657	Glc
Hobdy, ---, & Seaton	21	Hnr
George	444	Mth
Wm.	440	Mth
Hobker, John	585	Frd
Hobpson, Thomas S.	130	Cmb
Hobs, Barnaby	543	Prg
John [2]	948	Hrr
Nelly	962	Hrr
Hobson, Benjamin	465	Bdf
Benjn.	102	Cmb
Caleb	119	Cmb
John	122	Cmb
John	111	Hnr
John	10	Pwh
John, Jr.	810	Bck
John, M.	122	Cmb
Joseph	238	Aml
Josiah	68	Chs
Mary	128	Hnr
Matthew	467	Bdf
Matthew	792	Bck
Saml. L.	125	Hnr
Samuel	5	Pwh
Thomas	102	Cmb
Thomas C.H.	115	Cmb
Thos.	102	Cmb
William	104	Cmb
William	4	Pwh
Wm.	111	Hnr
see Hobpson		
Hocbetter, Henry	270	Rck
Hock, Jacob	903	Nrf
Martha	73	Jff
Peter, Jr.	631	Btt
Hockaday, Edmund W.	756	Nwk
Sally	756	Nwk
William	756	Nwk
Hockins, Moses	481	Frn
Hockman, Abraham	206	Shn
Abraham	215	Shn
Chrisley	214	Shn
Christian	221	Shn
George	214	Shn
George, (L. G.)	214	Shn
Henry	204	Shn
Henry	206	Shn
Henry	215	Shn
John	179	Shn
John	214	Shn
Hoddocks, Randolph	45	Clp
Hodge, Alexandria	774	Wst
George	625	Gls
Jno.	295	Rck
Mary	60	Jff
Moses	625	Gls
Robert	558	Frd
Robert R.	774	Wst
Thomas	907	Crl
William	828	Hmp
Wm.	347	Ags
Wm.	295	Rck
Hodges, Abednigo	456	Frn
Aron	453	Frn
Asa	456	Frn
Benjn.	438	Mth
Cabeb	829	Nrf
Caleb	793	Nrf
Charles	870	Cmp
Chas.	793	Nrf
Chas., (F.B.)	458	Pra
Daniel	806	Nrf
Danl., Sr.	793	Nrf
David	696	Gch
Edward	795	Nrf
Feriba	799	Nrf
Frances	467	Bdf
Francis	905	Crl
Galen	905	Crl
Isham	455	Frn
J.F.	905	Nrf
J...s.	788	Nrf
Jesse [2]	697	Gch
Jno.	902	Nrf
Jno., Dr.	903	Nrf
Joel	457	Frn
Joel	902	Nrf
John	457	Frn
John	458	Frn
John	219	Pnd
John, (F)	814	Nrf
John, (FP)	792	Nrf
John H.	806	Nrf
Johnson	697	Gch
Jos.	799	Nrf
Jos.	823	Nrf
Joseph	695	Gch
Joshua	458	Pra
Josiah	457	Frn
Josiah	793	Nrf
Lewis	458	Frn
Mary	657	Glc
Mary	547	Prg
Mattheus	823	Nrf
Molly	454	Mth
Nat.	814	Nrf
Peyton	458	Frn
Polly	789	Nrf
Polly, Sr.	789	Nrf
Priscilla	820	Nrf
Reuben	458	Frn
Richd.	443	Mth
Richd.	793	Nrf
Richd.	824	Nrf
Robert	453	Frn
Robert, Sr.	498	Frn
Roger	903	Nrf
Sam	793	Nrf
Sol.	829	Nrf
Squire	458	Frn
Stephen	793	Nrf
Stephen	814	Nrf
Thomas	695	Gch
Thos.	696	Gch
Thos.	805	Nrf
Thos., jr.	797	Nrf
Welcom	498	Frn
William, Jr.	458	Frn
William, Sr.	458	Frn
Wm. [2]	696	Gch
Wm.	444	Mth
Wm.	790	Nrf
Wm.	821	Nrf
see Hedges, Hoages		
Hodgeson, James	354	Ags
Hodgkin, Ralph	267	Frf
Hodgson, Abner	576	Frd
Robert	576	Frd
Hodnett, Matthew	831	Bck
Philip	792	Bck
Hodom, John	223	Pnd
Hodsden, Joseph	12	Isw
Hodson, John	510	Frd
John	568	Frd
Hofacre, Jacob	698	Wsh
see Holfacre		
Hoff, Amos	526	Prw
Benjamin	596	Frd
Cornelius	526	Prw
John	507	Frd
John	512	Frd
Lewis	508	Frd
Mathias	810	Hmp
Moo...	525	Prw
Philip	514	Frd
Hoffler, Thos.	827	Nrf
Wm.	816	Nrf
Hoffman, Andrew	99	Acc
Andrew	631	Btt
Anthony	201	Shn
Christn.	632	Btt
Christo	307	Rck
Henry	600	Frd
Henry	835	Wth
Jacob	506	Frd
Jacob	571	Frd
Jacob, Jr.	631	Btt
Jacob, Sr.	631	Btt
James	101	Acc
Jno., Jr.	631	Btt
Jno., of Jno.	631	Btt
Jno., Sr.	631	Btt
John	630	Btt
John	592	Frd
John	267	Rck
John	204	Shn
John, j.	307	Rck
John, jr.	573	Brk
Michal	593	Frd
Hoflin, William	906	Hrr
Hog, Jno.	887	Hnv
John	854	Sth
John, Snr.	844	Hnv
Mary	871	Hnv
Milly	121	Hnr
Salley	898	Hnv
Hogan, ...h	464	Bdf
Enoch	465	Bdf
Francis	87	Spt
George	984	Nrt
Hetha	489	Bdf
James	465	Bdf
James	57	Jff
Jeduthan	409	Rch
John	563	Brk
John	587	Frd
John	94	Jff
Margarett	583	Frd
Martin	563	Brk
Philip	630	Mnt
Thomas	812	Hmp
Thomas	409	Rch
Thomas, Jr.	409	Rch
Traverse	409	Rch
William	547	Frd
Hogar, John	290	Rck
Hogart, Jesse	756	Wsh
Hoge, Anna	786	Hmp
Daniel	626	Gls
James, Jr.	639	Mnt

Name	No.	Co.
James, Sr.	639	Mnt
John	665	Mnt
John	691	Wsh
Moses	771	Hmp
Moses	570	Pre
Solomon	563	Frd
Wm. F.	274	Rck
Hogg, Daniel	657	Glc
James	350	Ags
Jno. [2]	658	Glc
John	288	Amh
John	441	Flv
John	875	Yrk
John, Jr.	890	Yrk
Leah	658	Glc
Lewis	658	Glc
Lewis	875	Yrk
Mary	436	Flv
Peter	429	Msn
Polly, (Y)	875	Yrk
Randall	875	Yrk
Randolph	288	Amh
Reba.	890	Yrk
Samuel	266	Amh
Susan	890	Yrk
Thomas	424	Msn
Thos.	658	Glc
Wilbon	161	Alb
William	161	Alb
Wm.	657	Glc
Wm.	658	Glc
Hoggard, Thumer	456	Pra
Hoggins, Thos.	504	Mnn
Hogins, Susan	695	Gch
Hoglin, James	598	Brk
Hogshead, Chas.	352	Ags
David [2]	347	Ags
Gorden	347	Ags
James	346	Ags
Jas.	347	Ags
John	350	Ags
John	578	Mnr
Michl.	347	Ags
Sally	351	Ags
Thos.	347	Ags
Wm.	347	Ags
Hogshear, John	27	Acc
William	28	Acc
Hogston, James	723	Wsh
Hogue, James	278	Ldn
Jesse	311	Ldn
Joshua	395	Fqr
Saml.	311	Ldn
Sarah	306	Ldn
Solomon	311	Ldn
William	511	Frd
Wm.	311	Ldn
Hogwod, Jos.	815	Nrf
Hogwood, Benjamin [2]	644	Sss
Charles	150	Dnw
John	643	Sss
Ransom	643	Sss
Susanna	496	Frn
Thomas	643	Sss
William	645	Sss
Hoilman, Christopher	302	Rck
Henry	303	Rck
Philip	293	Rck
Salley	353	Ags
Simon	303	Rck
Hoine, P.	25	Hnr
Hoke, Andrew	21	Rcm
Catharine	591	Brk
Chrisley	587	Mnr
Christopher	576	Mnr
Henry	587	Mnr
Jacob	201	Shn
see Houke		
Hol..., Jacob	466	Bdf
Holand, John	963	Hrr

Name	No.	Co.
Holbart see Hebant		
Holbert, Aaron	424	Rnd
Elijah	101	Spt
John	567	Frd
John	247	Ldn
William	904	Hrr
Holbrook, Ezra	303	Rck
Holcomb, Jane	526	Prw
Ternelley	422	Bth
Timothy	429	Bth
Holcombe, John	876	Cmp
John	569	Pre
Phill	240	Aml
Thos. A.	240	Aml
Watthall	572	Pre
Holcumb, Samuel	700	Nls
Holdcropt, Edward	941	Chc
William	949	Chc
Holden, Abel	30	Acc
Abraham	102	Acc
Adam	30	Acc
Benjamin	100	Acc
Benjamin	31	Isw
James	305	Rck
James [crossed out]	311	Rck
Thos.	902	Nrf
Holder, Armisd.	45	Clp
Armistead, ([his] Quar')	413	Fqr
Benj.	939	Hrr
Davis	351	Fqr
Fielding, (Overseer)	417	Fqr
James	421	Rnd
John	422	Rnd
Thomas	422	Rnd
Holderby, John, jr.	167	Knq
John, Senr.	166	Knq
Holderfield, Hester	61	Chs
Holdeway, Charles	629	Btt
Henry	629	Btt
Holdoby, Joseph	750	Brn
Holdom, James	7	Hnr
Holdren, Bartholomew	463	Bdf
Carnelius	464	Bdf
Holdsworth, John	640	Sss
Luretta	953	Chc
Nancy	640	Sss
Robert	640	Sss
Robert, Sr.	642	Sss
Sarah	952	Chc
Hole, Jonah	465	Bdf
see Hob		
Holefield, Wm.	505	Mnn
Holeman, Dread	571	Pre
George	100	Cmb
Henry	696	Gch
James	696	Gch
John	14	Rcm
John, jr.	106	Cmb
John, Sr.	114	Cmb
Nathl.	852	Hnv
Susan.	697	Gch
Wm. M.	696	Gch
see Shoemaker		
Holemon, Jacob	235	Shn
Holensworth, John	533	Prg
Holesinger, David	27	Rcm
Michael	4	Rcm
Peter	4	Rcm
Holfacre, Henry	698	Wsh
see Hofacre, Holfare		
Holfare, Fredrck	698	Wsh
Holiday, Francis	985	Nrt
James	513	Prw
Holinger, Judy	208	Ess
Suckey	208	Ess
Holker see Hobker		
Holl..., Jiles	466	Bdf
Stephen	466	Bdf
Holla, Rawley	43	Stf

Name	No.	Co.
Hollaback, Margaret	821	Hmp
see Hallaback		
Holladay, Anne	29	Isw
James	81	Spt
Joseph	77	Spt
Lewis, jr.	77	Spt
Lewis, Sr.	82	Spt
Mills	28	Isw
Thomas, Jun.	10	Isw
Thomas, Sen.	24	Isw
Waller	83	Spt
Willis	139	Sth
Holladey, Joseph	4	Isw
Prudence	4	Isw
Hollady, William	106	Spt
William	7	Wod
Hollaman, Arthur	151	Sth
Jno.	138	Sth
Patsy	845	Sth
Rebecca	847	Sth
Thos.	142	Sth
Wm.	142	Sth
Hollamb, John	697	Br
Holland, Aaron	44	Isw
Ann	102	Acc
Benjamin	23	Isw
Brice	506	Mnn
Caple	506	Mnn
Charles	182	Elc
Charles	468	Frn
Chesley B.	5	Ntt
Christopher H.	572	Pre
Drury	464	Bdf
Edward	575	Frd
Elisha	23	Isw
Esther	102	Acc
Hardy	16	Isw
Henry	570	Pre
Hezekiah	434	Flv
Hudson	697	Gch
Isaac	102	Acc
Jac.	508	Mnn
Jac., Senr.	509	Mnn
Jacob	22	Isw
James	13	Isw
James	46	Isw
James	103	Spt
Jno.	41	Clp
Job	44	Isw
John	466	Bdf
John	440	Flv
John	237	Ldn
John M.	455	Frn
Joseph	45	Isw
Joseph J.	9	Isw
Major	437	Flv
Martha	184	Elc
Martha	696	Gch
Martha	570	Pre
Maston	470	Frn
Merridith, (of Jos.)	44	Isw
Merridith, Sen.	39	Isw
Mills	16	Isw
Nat.	696	Gch
Peter	455	Frn
Peter D.	456	Frn
Resen	506	Mnn
Richard	434	Flv
Richd.	239	Aml
Tho.	183	Elc
Thomas	470	Frn
Thomas, Sr.	471	Frn
Thos. S.	696	Gch
Usley	470	Frn
William	815	Bck
Wm.	445	Flv
see Holl..., Mcholland		
Hollarand, Wm.	578	Mnr
Hollaway, ---	332	Dnw
E. B.	332	Dnw

Name	No.	Co.	Name	No.	Co.	Name	No.	Co.
James	498	Frn	Jas.	694	Gch	Wm.	294	Ldn
Sarah	336	Dnw	Jesse	608	Srr	Wm.	830	Nrf
see Holl...			Jesse	641	Sss	Wm.	456	Pra
Hollawel, Gideon, (F.N.)	35	Isw	Jno.	849	Hnv	see Bushel, Smith		
Hollawell, Courtney	26	Isw	Jno., Jr.	630	Btt	Holmon, John	237	Shn
Holleman, Arthur	608	Srr	Jno., Sr.	630	Btt	Holms, Christian	96	Jff
George	608	Srr	Job	643	Sss	John	348	Ags
John	608	Srr	Joel	609	Srr	Joshua	622	Mnt
Hollenback, Heniritta	389	Mds	John	715	Brn	see Helms		
Hollensworth, William	702	Nls	John	908	Crl	Holsaple, George	743	Wsh
Holley, Davd.	726	Wsh	John	45	Stf	Jacob	743	Wsh
Francis	466	Bdf	John	608	Srr	Holsberry, John	422	Rnd
Francis, Sr.	466	Bdf	John	642	Sss	Holsey, Stephen	836	Wth
Gustavus	467	Bdf	Levi	596	Brk	Sylvester	837	Wth
Henry	28	Acc	Lewis	222	Pnd	Wm. A.	30	Hnr
Henry	628	Btt	M.	30	Hnr	Holsford, Elizabeth	18	Isw
James	852	Cmp	Mark	641	Sss	Holsople, Philip	576	Mnr
John	466	Bdf	Nathan	50	Stf	Holsted, Benjn.	566	Mnr
John	467	Bdf	Rachel	508	Frd	James	566	Mnr
Joshua	467	Bdf	Robt.	876	Yrk	John	581	Mnr
Sanford	466	Bdf	Samuel	466	Bdf	see Hosted		
Thomas	467	Bdf	Silas	608	Srr	Holstein, Benjamin	835	Wth
see Holl...			Thomas	276	Amh	Holstine, Cond.	508	Mnn
Holliday, Ellsworth	266	Frf	Thomas	25	Stf	Holston, Christon	745	Wsh
Geo.	525	Brk	Thomas	642	Sss	Elijah	639	Mnt
James	516	Frd	William	464	Bdf	James	27	Acc
James	33	Stf	William	405	Fqr	Thomas	162	Alb
John	55	Stf	William	609	Srr	William	162	Alb
Levi	659	Mnt	see ...oway			Holsworth, Elisabeth	755	Nwk
Richard	806	Hmp	Hollum, Bengamin	803	Hmp	Holt, Ann	875	Cmp
Robert	290	Rck	Holly, ...y	465	Bdf	Asa	875	Cmp
Samuel	55	Stf	Edward	13	Oho	Bird	837	Wth
Seth	56	Stf	Jacob	465	Bdf	Charles	641	Sss
William	510	Frd	Joseph	618	Mnt	David	239	Aml
William M.	529	Frd	Penelope	681	Br	David	571	Pre
Holligan, John	465	Bdf	Peter	630	Mnt	Edward S.	608	Srr
John	467	Bdf	William	610	Mnt	Elijah	503	Mnn
Partrick	465	Bdf	William, A Free			Elisha	504	Mnn
Holliman, Jesse	35	Isw	Molatto	11	Knw	Eliza. A.	607	Srr
John	13	Isw	Willm.	641	Mnt	Francis	608	Srr
Jonathan	3	Isw	Holman, Geo.	433	Flv	George	871	Cmp
Jordan	3	Isw	Henry	9	Pwh	Henry	903	Nrf
Josiah	2	Isw	Jessee	823	Bck	Herbert	642	Sss
Hollinger, Adam	241	Shn	Joseph	112	Hnr	James	238	Aml
Edmund	120	Spt	William	823	Bck	James	875	Cmp
Sally	208	Ess	Holmes, Alexander	404	Fqr	James	608	Srr
Hollingsworth, ---,			Alexander	835	Wth	Jeremiah	424	Rnd
Cooch &	99	Spt	Anne	388	Fqr	Jesse	145	Sth
George	531	Frd	Anthony	288	Rck	Jesse	148	Sth
George	835	Wth	Christ.	284	Rck	Jno.	504	Mnn
Hannah	605	Frd	Elizabeth T.	20	Ntt	Jno. E.	902	Nrf
Isaac	605	Frd	Hugh	517	Frd	John	103	Acc
John	314	Ldn	James	684	Br	John	875	Cmp
John W.	544	Frd	James	390	Mds	John	112	Cmb
Thomas	573	Frd	Jno.	291	Ldn	John	71	Jff
Hollins, Delphia	755	Nwk	Jno. [2]	457	Pra	John	569	Pre
Hollinsworth, Christo-			John	798	Bck	John	401	Rch
pher	1	Oho	John	804	Bck	John	643	Sss
William	699	Nls	John	404	Fqr	John	755	Wsh
Hollis, Caty	738	Wsh	John	590	Frd	Jos.	506	Mnn
Wm.	410	Ags	John	20	Oho	Josiah	875	Cmp
Holliway, Aaron	99	Acc	John	836	Wth	Judith	14	Ntt
Holloday, Ann	878	Hnv	John, Jr.	347	Fqr	Leonard	875	Cmp
Fielding	288	Amh	Joseph	311	Ldn	Mary	571	Pre
Jno.	878	Hnv	Joshua	457	Pra	Micajah	607	Srr
Holloman, Ann	645	Sss	Lewis	17	Oho	Mildred	608	Srr
Hollow, Henry, Sen.	241	Shn	Martha	280	Ldn	Nathaniel	643	Sss
Holloway, Aaron	26	Stf	Mary	828	Nrf	Phillip	132	Cmb
Charles	72	Spt	Nathaniel	351	Fqr	Polly	101	Acc
Daniel	752	Brn	Peter	386	Fqr	Ralph	506	Mnn
David	1	Hnr	Sally	458	Pra	Richard	345	Lnn
David	643	Sss	Samuel	551	Frd	Richard	571	Pre
Elizabeth	148	Dnw	Sarah Anne	351	Fqr	Richard	572	Pre
Fredrick	799	Nrf	Solomon	844	Sth	Richd.	352	Ags
George	405	Fqr	Thomas	689	Br	Robert	875	Cmp
Ira	642	Sss	Thomas	377	Fqr	Rowland	609	Srr
James	645	Sss	Thompson	27	Acc	Samuel	903	Nrf
James	875	Yrk	William	376	Fqr	Spratley	642	Sss
James, Junr.	875	Yrk	William	191	Shn	Thomas	51	Chr
James, Sr.	641	Sss	William	210	Shn	Thos.	239	Aml

Name	No.	Code
William	29	Acc
William	467	Bdf
William	875	Cmp
William	954	Chc
William	167	Knq
William	756	Nwk
William	571	Pre
William C.	794	Nrf
Wm.	458	Pra
Woodly	51	Chr
see H..., Harris, Richardson		
Holterman, Charles	224	Pnd
John	225	Pnd
Holton, Ths.	26	Hnr
Holtsclaw, Jacob	390	Mds
see Holtzclaw, Houltsclaw		
Holtworth, William	941	Chc
Holtzclaw, Charles	417	Fqr
Eli	407	Fqr
Elias	341	Fqr
Jacob	401	Fqr
John	380	Fqr
Josiah	365	Fqr
Holvers, Philip	194	Shn
Holwright, John	796	Bck
Holycross, Jno.	630	Btt
Wm.	147	Dnw
Holyday, Daniel	8	Knw
James	11	Oho
James	837	Wth
Hom, Henry	279	Rck
Homan, John	16	Rcm
John, (Sen.)	21	Rcm
Mark	465	Bdf
Matthew	465	Bdf
Michael	22	Rcm
Hombeck, William	421	Rnd
Home, Martin	349	Ags
Phillip	754	Wsh
Homer, Joshua	5	Knw
Philip	190	Shn
Homes, Edward	512	Prw
Fanny	33	Stf
Jno.	44	Clp
Joshua	54	Stf
Milly	572	Pre
Polley	19	Hnr
Rebecca	512	Prw
Richard	959	Chc
Samuel	6	Wod
Sarah A.	48	Stf
Susanna	1	Knw
Thomas	13	Oho
Thomas	513	Prw
Thomas	45	Stf
Valentine	3	Oho
William	836	Wth
Homick, Abraham	431	Rnd
Homman see Honman		
Hommon, Jacob	237	Shn
Jacob, Sen.	238	Shn
John	220	Shn
Mary	237	Shn
see Hanmon		
Honacer, Abraham	611	Mnt
Honaker, Fredk.	574	Mnr
Henry	835	Wth
Isaac	612	Mnt
Honell, James	282	Ldn
Honesty, Hannah	267	Frf
Jno.	267	Frf
Honey, George	56	Stf
Nancey	380	Fqr
Honeycut, William	425	Msn
Honeycutt see Wonycott		
Honeyman, Robert	897	Hnv
Honman, Stephen	517	Prw
Honn, Kerny	279	Rck
Honnel, James	299	Ldn
Honnell, Jacob	81	Jff

Name	No.	Code
Hontsbarger, John	227	Shn
Hoobaugh, Jacob	839	Wth
William	835	Wth
Hood, Abraham	149	Dnw
Allen	239	Aml
Chesley	148	Dnw
Dade	526	Prw
David	149	Dnw
Edward	391	Mds
Edwd.	239	Aml
Elias	9	Ntt
Frederick	346	Lnn
Frederick	571	Pre
Homon H.	502	Prw
James	7	Oho
James	9	Oho
Joel	345	Lnn
John	821	Bck
John	149	Dnw
John, Sr.	643	Sss
Jordan	148	Dnw
Lesica	270	Ldn
Lucretia	641	Sss
Mary S.	526	Prw
Natthaniel	819	Bck
Rhody	123	Hnr
Richard	345	Lnn
Robt. H.	526	Prw
Sally	13	Hnr
Solomon	239	Aml
Sterling	53	Chr
Susanna	15	Ntt
William [2]	345	Lnn
Wm. B.	16	Hnr
see Hooe		
Hoods see Hood		
Hooe, Abram B.	201	Kng
Alexander S.	201	Kng
Bernard, Sr.	518	Prw
Francis	38	Stf
Jane	385	Fqr
Jane	517	Prw
John	350	Fqr
Nathl. H.	201	Kng
Robert H.	33	Stf
William	201	Kng
Wm. H.	200	Kng
Hoof, Daniel	257	Shn
Fred.	350	Ags
George	22	Rcm
Henry	27	Rcm
Jacob	350	Ags
Lewis	348	Ags
see Houf		
Hoofager, Polly	632	Btt
Hoofman, Abm.	503	Mnn
Abraham	6	Rcm
Christian	6	Rcm
Conrod	25	Rcm
George	7	Rcm
Margaret	33	Rcm
Michael	31	Rcm
Reuben	28	Rcm
Solomon	7	Rcm
Hook, Hannah	628	Btt
James	347	Ags
Jeremiah	347	Ags
John	687	Br
Stepn., Jr.	629	Btt
Stepn., Sr.	629	Btt
Thomas	768	Hmp
William	768	Hmp
Hooke, Elijah	9	Rcm
George	9	Rcm
James	8	Rcm
James	9	Rcm
James	8	Rcm
William	853	Hnv
Hooker, Elizabeth	112	Hnr
George	112	Hnr
James	112	Hnr

Name	No.	Code
James	166	Knq
John	441	Flv
John	605	Frd
John	811	Hmp
Keziah	303	Amh
Lucy	114	Hnr
Patsey	853	Hnv
Sally	26	Hnr
William	303	Amh
William	584	Frd
Hoomes, Amos	757	Nwk
Armistead	906	Crl
Benja., Snr.	167	Knq
Benja. P.	166	Knq
Betsy	133	Hnr
John	906	Crl
Richard	908	Crl
Sarah	133	Hnr
William	906	Crl
Wm.	121	Hnr
Hoones see Homes		
Hoons, Henry	628	Btt
Jacob	631	Btt
Hooper, Benjamin	791	Bck
Benjamin	907	Crl
Daniel	844	Hnv
Edmund	883	Hnv
Eliza	24	Hnr
George	785	Bck
Jacob	594	Brk
James	16	Hnr
James	127	Hnr
James	166	Knq
Jane	177	Shn
Jarimiah	860	Hnv
Jerimiah, Snr.	881	Hnv
John	593	Brk
John	782	Bck
John	14	Rcm
Joseph	695	Gch
Joseph	391	Mds
Obadiah	859	Hnv
Perry	26	Hnr
Samuel	149	Dnw
Samuel	513	Frd
Stephen	794	Bck
Thomas	167	Knq
William	785	Bck
Wim.	872	Hnv
Hoops, David	552	Frd
Elisha	78	Jff
Evan	5	Rcm
Hoopwood, Jno.	268	Frf
Moses	266	Frf
Hoory, ---, & Sciesor	22	Hnr
Hooser, Michael	837	Wth
Hoot, Julius	509	Mnn
Hooten, Benjamin	114	Spt
Hooter, Christopher	428	Rnd
Hooton, Elijah	835	Wth
Ephraim P.	697	Gch
Samuel	181	Alb
Hooven, Jacob	628	Btt
see Hoons		
Hoover, Emanuel	14	Knw
George	220	Pnd
Harry	217	Pnd
Henry	528	Frd
Henry	548	Frd
Henry	506	Mnn
Henry	281	Rck
Henry	4	Rcm
Jacob	414	Bth
Jacob	769	Hmp
Jacob	827	Hmp
Jacob	226	Pnd
Jacob	4	Rcm
Jacob	23	Rcm
Jacob, S.	220	Pnd
Jno.	507	Mnn

John	15	Oho	Stephen	28	Acc	John	543	Brk
John	226	Pnd	Stephen A., Doc.	607	Srr	John	632	Btt
John	10	Rcm	Susanna	464	Mdd	Peter	465	Bdf
John	25	Rcm	Thomas	13	Rcm	Phillip	791	Hmp
Jonas	513	Brk	Thomas	1	Wod	Richard	645	Sss
Joseph	542	Brk	Warren	176	Elc	Shadrack	644	Sss
Mary	215	Pnd	William	161	Alb	Sherod	66	Spt
Michael	19	Rcm	William	463	Bdf	see Hora		
Michal	219	Pnd	William	22	Rcm	Hornbarger, George	659	Mnt
Michl.	353	Ags	William, Jur.	161	Alb	Peter	610	Mnt
Peter	86	Jff	William L.	36	Rcm	Hornbeck, Benjamin	420	Rnd
Peter	215	Pnd	Wm.	697	Gch	Horner, ---, Quarter		
Philip	512	Frd	Wm.	266	Rck	for	340	Fqr
Philip	528	Frd	Wm.	875	Yrk	Arthur	125	Cmb
Thomas	226	Pnd	Wm., & Mother	264	Frf	E.	65	Chs
William	575	Frd	Wm., jr.	43	Clp	Gustavus B.	421	Fqr
William	215	Pnd	see Hipkins			Isaac	505	Mnn
see ...oover			Hopp, Henry	353	Ags	Jno., jr.	44	Clp
Hop, Thomas	402	Fqr	John	351	Ags	Jno., Senr.	43	Clp
Hope, Christian	268	Ldn	Hopper, Elizabeth	268	Frf	Richard	89	Jff
Elijah	100	Acc	John	108	Cmb	Richd.	522	Brk
Geo., Jur.	181	Elc	John, for Creed			Saml.	41	Clp
Geo., Sr.	181	Elc	Taylor	108	Cmb	Sarah	178	Shn
George	102	Acc	Josa.	43	Clp	William	420	Fqr
George, Junr.	193	Elc	Joseph	357	Fqr	William, ([his]		
Giles	435	Flv	Mary Ann	44	Clp	Quarter)	419	Fqr
Henry	520	Prw	Wm.	43	Clp	Wm.	63	Chs
James	434	Flv	see Happer, Hoppis			Hornes see Homes		
James	696	Gch	Hoppies, John	625	Gls	Horns see Hoons		
James	716	Wsh	Hoppis, Henry	836	Wth	Hornsby, James	30	Acc
John	181	Elc	Hopson, Abram	876	Yrk	James	408	Rch
Jdhn	474	Frn	Charles	876	Yrk	John	29	Acc
John	858	Hnv	James	185	Elc	Susanh.	28	Acc
Lydia	336	Dnw	James	876	Yrk	Horse, Christian	795	Hmp
Margaret	522	Prw	Samuel	102	Cmb	George	782	Hmp
Rachel	410	Ags	Tho. E.	890	Yrk	Peter	795	Hmp
Richard	872	Hnv	Hopwood, Joshua	72	Jff	Horsely, A.	905	Nrf
William	520	Prw	Hora, Thomas	787	Hmp	Horseman, Isaias	247	Ldn
Hopes, Tinner	2	Hnr	Horbaugh, Adam	219	Shn	James	248	Ldn
Hopewell, Isaac	591	Frd	Isaac	212	Shn	Jesse	266	Frf
Joseph	166	Shn	Jacob	212	Shn	Jno.	267	Frf
Hopkins, Agnes	264	Rck	Peter, Jur.	212	Shn	Wm.	249	Ldn
Benja.	695	Gch	Peter, Ser.	212	Shn	Zachr.	267	Frf
Benskin	945	Chc	Hord, Alexander	41	Clp	Horsley, Belsey	659	Glc
Charles	264	Frf	Blocksome	905	Crl	Smith	658	Glc
Charles	465	Frn	Ezekiel	69	Spt	Thos.	658	Glc
Christopher	656	Glc	Jas.	506	Mnn	Horsman see Honman		
David	188	Elc	John	23	Stf	Hortenstine, Abram	743	Wsh
Elizabeth	695	Gch	Killis	28	Stf	Latron	743	Wsh
Henry	907	Crl	Mary	41	Clp	Horthem, Ursilla	544	Prg
James	191	Elc	Peggy	907	Crl	Horton, Absolum	356	Fqr
James	697	Gch	Peter	30	Stf	Baersheba	380	Fqr
James	876	Yrk	Rhodin	43	Stf	Catey	382	Fqr
Jno.	902	Nrf	Thomas	906	Crl	Corsom	46	Stf
Jno.	903	Nrf	Thomas	28	Stf	Craven	519	Prw
Jno., [his] (Plantan.)	456	Pra	see Herd, Hore			Elihu	509	Mnn
Joanna	12	Pwh	Hore, Elias	21	Stf	Enoch	355	Fqr
John	466	Bdf	Jennet S.	110	Spt	Jas.	43	Clp
John	586	Frd	Walter	20	Stf	John	413	Fqr
John	223	Pnd	William	20	Stf	John	625	Gls
John	13	Rcm	see Hord			Joseph	8	Knw
John	90	Spt	Hormel see Honnel			Levina	355	Fqr
Jona.	456	Pra	Horn, Allen	643	Sss	Robt.	41	Clp
Jos.	890	Yrk	Andrew	832	Hmp	William	23	Stf
Kiziah	457	Pra	Anthoney	753	Wsh	Horus see Hoons		
Lawrence	434	Bth	Charles	632	Btt	Hosacek, James	4	Oho
Lawson	88	Spt	Christopher	16	Oho	Hosack, David	9	Oho
Levy	425	Rnd	David	640	Sss	Margaret	10	Oho
Lundy	12	Pwh	Dived	837	Wth	Thomas	9	Oho
Margaret	264	Rck	Edwd.	273	Rck	Hosea, Jos.	805	Nrf
Mathew	451	Mth	Eliza. M.	349	Lnc	Saml.	792	Nrf
Molley	986	Nrt	Ephraim	644	Sss	Hoseley, John	701	Nls
Nancy	697	Gch	George	543	Brk	Joseph	701	Nls
Nelly	33	Hnr	George	765	Hmp	Nicholas	701	Nls
Phebe	15	Rcm	George, jr.	543	Brk	Robert	701	Nls
Philip	401	Ags	Henry	354	Ags	Hosely, John	701	Nls
Priscilla	755	Nwk	Henry	243	Shn	William	701	Nls
Rd.	656	Glc	Herbert	640	Sss	Hoser, Jeremiah	456	Pra
Rice	466	Bdf	Howell	644	Sss	Hosier, Robt.	457	Pra
Samuel	161	Alb	James	640	Sss	Hoskins, Andrew	808	Hmp

Name	No.	Co.	Name	No.	Co.	Name	No.	Co.
Barton	918	Hrr	Houf, Benjn.	350	Ags	Margaret	500	Prw
Benit	426	Rnd	see Hoof			Mary	317	Ldn
Benja.	167	Knq	Houff, Andrew	12	Rcm	Michl.	252	Ldn
Chs.	288	Ldn	Hough, Barnet	304	Ldn	Philip	252	Ldn
Elias	504	Mnn	Isaac	308	Ldn	Phillip	837	Wth
Elisha	782	Hmp	James	262	Ldn	Housewright, John	700	Nls
G., (of J)	507	Mnn	Jno.	299	Ldn	Housholder, M.	352	Ags
Geo.	507	Mnn	Jno.	506	Mnn	Housman, Christn.	631	Btt
John	93	Spt	Josiah	300	Ldn	George	190	Shn
John	100	Spt	Mahlon	307	Ldn	George, Jun.	190	Shn
John, Doctor	166	Knq	Saml. W.	296	Ldn	Martin	507	Brk
John, jr.	167	Knq	Samuel	307	Ldn	Peter	455	Frn
John, Senr.	167	Knq	Thomas	301	Ldn	Houston, Alexr.	279	Rck
Leo.	509	Mnn	Thos.	296	Ldn	Caleb	100	Acc
Ralph	426	Rnd	Thos.	313	Ldn	Catey	99	Acc
Robert	167	Knq	Wm.	300	Ldn	Elizh.	297	Rck
Spencer B.	166	Knq	Wm.	307	Ldn	James	907	Crl
Thomas	166	Knq	Wm.	310	Ldn	Math.	283	Rck
William	907	Crl	see Haught			Robert	906	Crl
Wm.	257	Ldn	Houghn, Jacob	207	Shn	Robert	276	Rck
see Heskew			Peter	163	Shn	Robert, junr.	907	Crl
Hoskinson, Geo.	504	Mnn	Houghton, Elijh.	43	Clp	S., Rev. [?]	284	Rck
Geo. B.	509	Mnn	Nat.	186	Elc	Thomas	307	Rck
Jerh.	505	Mnn	Saml.	166	Knq	William	100	Acc
Josh.	504	Mnn	Houk, George	256	Shn	William	905	Crl
Wm.	505	Mnn	Henry	19	Rcm	Wm.	271	Rck
Hosley, Henderson	463	Bdf	Houke, Jacob	589	Brk	see Hauston		
James	197	Alb	Richd.	589	Brk	Houswright, John	269	Amh
Roling	197	Alb	Sam	589	Brk	Joseph	285	Amh
William	460	Frn	see Hoke			Hout, Rudolph	87	Jff
Hospital, Andrew	295	Ldn	Houlder, Thomas	389	Mds	see Stout		
Hoss, Devol	284	Ldn	Houlken, Thos.	627	Btt	Houtchen, Jesse	224	Pnd
Hosseplook, Henry	207	Shn	Houltsclaw, Joseph	390	Mds	William	224	Pnd
Hosted, Enos	566	Mnr	see Holtsclaw			Houtt, William	942	Hrr
see Holsted			Houndshell, Andrew	836	Wth	Houtz, Jacob	627	Btt
Hosteler, Samuel	91	Jff	Andrew	837	Wth	Jno.	632	Btt
Hostetter, John	277	Rck	Andrew	838	Wth	Leanard	632	Btt
U...ich [Ulrich?]	276	Rck	John [2]	837	Wth	Hover, Frederick	222	Shn
Hostin, Nancy	52	Chr	John	838	Wth	John	203	Shn
Hosty, Daniel	16	Oho	Houre see House			see Ohover		
Hot, Lewis	123	Hnr	House, Ambrose	750	Brn	Hovus see Hoons		
Hoten, Edmund	465	Bdf	Charles	740	Wsh	How, Abner	412	Rch
Hoth see Heth			Claibourn	751	Brn	Ann	406	Rch
Hotherman, John	957	Hrr	Crawley	450	Grn	Christian	222	Pnd
Hotinger, Frederick	31	Rcm	Eliza	832	Nrf	Freaderick	220	Pnd
Henry	31	Rcm	Elizabeth	750	Brn	George	219	Pnd
John	31	Rcm	Elizabeth	9	Oho	Harvey	220	Pnd
Philip	31	Rcm	Green S.	714	Brn	Jacob	222	Pnd
Hotsenpeler, Jacob	576	Frd	Isaac	751	Brn	Wm.	286	Ldn
Joseph	572	Frd	Isaac T.	750	Brn	Howard, ---, & Lar-		
Stephen	593	Frd	James	787	Hmp	rence	37	Stf
Hotsepillar, Henry	16	Rcm	John	750	Brn	Abra.	281	Rck
Hott, Conrod	784	Hmp	John	752	Brn	Adam	19	Rcm
Danl.	348	Ags	John	818	Hmp	Allen	464	Mdd
Gworge	784	Hmp	John	922	Hrr	Anthony	577	Frd
John	578	Frd	Joseph	749	Brn	Benjamin	268	Amh
John	778	Hmp	Lackey	740	Wsh	Betsey	855	Hnv
John, senr.	830	Hmp	Lucy	450	Grn	David	465	Bdf
Saml.	348	Ags	Mathias	390	Mds	Edwin	450	Grn
Samuel	761	Hmp	Merritt	713	Brn	Elizabeth	584	Frd
Hotta, Christian	806	Hmp	Michael	389	Mds	Ezekiel	625	Mnt
Hotts, Conrod	21	Rcm	Moses	390	Mds	Frances, Miss	51	Chr
Henry	32	Rcm	Samuel	818	Hmp	Frank.	3	Hnr
Philip	18	Rcm	Wm.	713	Brn	George	101	Acc
Houchen, Jno.	702	Nls	Householder, Adam	297	Ldn	George	261	Amh
Moses	420	Bth	Danl.	282	Ldn	Henry	875	Yrk
Houchens, Charles	160	Alb	Fdk.	555	Brk	Henry, jr.	890	Yrk
Obed	160	Alb	John	571	Brk	Henry, Sr.	875	Yrk
William	162	Alb	Susann.	282	Ldn	Horton	2	Oho
Charles	697	Gch	Houseling, James	133	Hnr	Hyram	630	Mnt
James	697	Gch	Housely, Dines	237	Ldn	Jacob	598	Mnr
James	580	Mnr	Houseman, John	582	Frd	James	197	Alb
Jesse	349	Ags	Michal	568	Frd	James	560	Frd
John	696	Gch	Houser, Abram	278	Ldn	Jane	53	Stf
Joshua	696	Gch	Apalony	493	Frn	Jno.	629	Btt
Houck, Felty	467	Bdf	Charles D.	805	Hmp	Jno.	657	Glc
Houdeshell, Jacob	42	Rcm	Christ.	279	Ldn	Jno.	882	Hnv
Laurence	21	Rcm	Henry	278	Ldn	Jno.	550	Mnn
Michael	42	Rcm	Jacob	299	Ldn	Jno., Jr.	630	Btt
Michael, (Jr.)	22	Rcm	Jasper	493	Frn	John	101	Acc

John	627	Btt	Pleasant	787	Bck	Mary	755	Nwk
John	51	Chr	Robert	132	Hnr	Thomas	756	Nwk
John	443	Flv	Samuel	58	Jff	Howlett, Andrew	3	Oho
John	943	Hrr	Sarah	182	Alb	James	55	Chs
John [crossed out]	943	Hrr	Stephen	790	Bck	Nicholas	658	Glc
John	27	Hnr	Susanna	55	Jff	Thos.	65	Chs
John	24	Oho	William	425	Rnd	William	240	Aml
John	18	Rcm	Winny	68	Chr	Howry, Cathe.	631	Btt
John	192	Shn	Howell, ...	464	Bdf	Daniel, Christians-		
John	836	Wth	Abel	270	Ldn	burg	619	Mnt
John B.	452	Frn	Abner	465	Bdf	George	613	Mnt
John H.	609	Srr	Abnor	632	Btt	Jacob	628	Btt
Joseph	15	Pwh	Alfred	154	Sth	John	627	Btt
Katy	906	Crl	Amos	835	Wth	Michl.	658	Mnt
Lydia	847	Sth	Anne	240	Aml	Howsden, Judy	188	Shn
Martin	74	Jff	Benjamin	400	Fqr	Howsdon, James	188	Shn
Mary	36	Stf	Benjn.	653	Mnt	Howser, Frederick H.	563	Frd
Mathew	440	Bth	Butler	276	Ldn	Margaret	828	Nrf
Michael	19	Rcm	Daniel	653	Mnt	Howson, Jno.	7	Ntt
Michl.	285	Ldn	David	464	Bdf	Howton, Wm.	44	Clp
Nicholas	598	Brk	David	465	Bdf	Howze, John	16	Wod
Peter	658	Mnt	David	653	Mnt	Howzen, Ewell	775	Wst
Pleasant	467	Bdf	David, Jr.	655	Mnt	Molly	775	Wst
Polly	36	Stf	Elizah	18	Hnr	Hoxall see Haxall		
Rachl., (free)	628	Btt	Hezekiah	403	Fqr	Hoy, Thomas	486	Frn
Reason	792	Hmp	Hugh	508	Mnn	William	835	Wth
Reuben	852	Cmp	Jacob	330	Dnw	Zachariah	11	Rcm
Reuben	853	Cmp	Jeremiah	419	Rnd	Hoye, George	507	Frd
Rubin	882	Hnv	Jesse	465	Bdf	Sabut	199	Alb
Rubin	890	Hnv	Jesse	270	Ldn	William	197	Alb
Saml.	261	Frf	Jessee	632	Btt	Hoyer, Frs.	904	Nrf
Samul	24	Oho	Jno.	506	Mnn	Hoyle, Charles	279	Amh
Sarah	876	Yrk	John	466	Bdf	Charles	851	Cmp
Selby	464	Mdd	John	402	Fqr	Hozea, John	474	Frn
Sylvanus	466	Bdf	John	14	Hnr	Hu..., ...	466	Bdf
Thomas	447	Flv	John	25	Hnr	Elisha	466	Bdf
Thomas	75	Jff	John	570	Pre	Molly	467	Bdf
Thomas	167	Knq	Rebec.	184	Elc	Hub..., Stephen	466	Bdf
Thomas	12	Oho	Sampson	267	Frf	Hubard, Anne	14	Isw
Thomas	9	Pwh	Samuel	465	Bdf	George	955	Chc
Thos.	658	Glc	Samuel	265	Frf	Hubb, Joseph	8	Knw
Thos.	4	Hnr	Thomas	463	Bdf	Hubbard, Dc., Bucking-		
William	159	Alb	Thomas	465	Bdf	ham	700	Nls
William	198	Alb	Thomas	390	Mds	Geo.	697	Gch
William	269	Amh	Thos.	16	Hnr	Jabaz	349	Lnc
William	368	Fqr	William	464	Bdf	James	801	Nrf
William	74	Jff	William	401	Fqr	James T.	812	Bck
William	76	Jff	see Davis, Honell, Lewis			Jesse	579	Frd
Willm.	626	Mnt	Howenton, Harritage	279	Amh	Jesse	348	Lnc
Wm.	956	Hrr	Howerton, Anderson	113	Hnr	John	783	Bck
Wm.	875	Yrk	Catharine	220	Ess	John	866	Cmp
Wm., Sr.	640	Mnt	Charles	210	Ess	John	609	Srr
see Haward, Haword			Drury	715	Brn	Martha	572	Pre
Howards, James	8	Oho	George	869	Cmp	Mat., 2nd.	903	Nrf
Howatom, Harretage	861	Cmp	James	113	Hnr	Mattw.	902	Nrf
Howdershell, Jno.	258	Ldn	John	715	Brn	Moses	131	Cmb
Howdeshitt, Jno.	43	Clp	John	215	Ess	Nathar	818	Nrf
Howdishell, George	223	Shn	John	625	Mnt	Samuel	848	Cmp
Michael	223	Shn	Lewis	166	Knq	Samuel	869	Cmp
Howe, Danl.	639	Mnt	Obidiah	624	Mnt	Taliafo. G.	44	Clp
James	592	Frd	Thos.	113	Hnr	W.H.	23	Hnr
John	574	Frd	Thos.	648	Mnt	William	150	Dnw
Margarett	559	Frd	Wm.	215	Ess	see Hobbs		
Santee	837	Wth	Howington, Jno.	20	Hnr	Hubberd, Henry	876	Yrk
Wm.	40	Clp	Howisnard, L.J., Dr.	325	Dnw	James	876	Yrk
see Keith			Howison, Alexander	514	Prw	John, (W)	876	Yrk
Howel, Aaron	15	Oho	James	511	Prw	Matt.	681	Wrw
Abner	81	Jff	Stephen	506	Prw	Hubbert, Amos	982	Nrt
Bettey	167	Knq	Howisson, Samuel	116	Spt	Chs.	288	Ldn
Charles	695	Gch	Howl, Absalom	260	Amh	Hubble, Eliphelet	836	Wth
Gideon	778	Bck	Isaac	757	Nwk	Levi	741	Wsh
Isaac	810	Bck	James	641	Sss	Hubboard, Daniel	853	Hnv
Jacob	24	Rcm	Thomas	642	Sss	Samuel	886	Hnv
James	830	Bck	Howle, Charles	755	Nwk	Hubbord, Mathew	344	Lnn
Jane	797	Bck	Daniel	755	Nwk	Huber, George	499	Prw
John	799	Bck	Epaphroditus	868	Hnv	Joseph E.	500	Prw
John	694	Gch	Gideon	757	Nwk	Hubner, ---, Boher &	22	Hnr
Joseph	74	Jff	James	755	Nwk	Hubs, Elijah	4	Oho
Lucy	133	Hnr	John	755	Nwk	Hucherson, Wm.	13	Hnr
Peggy, (FN)	53	Chr	Lewis	755	Nwk	Huchings, Francis	774	Wst

Huckens, John	790	Bck	Nancy	452	Mth	Ezekl.	44	Clp
Huckstep, Charles	198	Alb	Wm.	438	Mth	Francis S.	202	Kng
David	198	Alb	see Hudjin			George	161	Alb
James	198	Alb	Hudgins, Anthony	445	Mth	George	304	Amh
John	161	Alb	Christopher	131	Cmb	George	349	Ags
Richard	286	Amh	Daniel	436	Mth	George	869	Cmp
Samuel	303	Amh	George	443	Mth	George	508	Frd
Hucle, Joseph	679	Br	George	451	Mth	Gregory	752	Brn
Mary	679	Br	Gregory	443	Mth	Henry	349	Lnc
Huddle, Andrew	243	Shn	Houlder	443	Mth	Irby	345	Lan
Chisp.	348	Ags	Hugh, jr.	444	Mth	Isaac	639	Mnt
Conrad	219	Shn	Keleb	448	Mth	Jacob	51	Chr
Daniel	204	Shn	Jesse	436	Mth	James	983	Nrt
Daniel	217	Shn	Jno.	443	Mth	James	13	Oho
Daniel	222	Shn	Jno.	448	Mth	Jane	663	Mnt
Danl.	206	Shn	Jno. L.	447	Mth	Jas.	44	Clp
David	202	Shn	John	680	Wrw	Jas.	827	Nrf
George	219	Shn	John, W.	125	Cmb	Jas. J.	39	Clp
George	241	Shn	John M.	121	Cmb	Jessee	627	Btt
Gideon	837	Wth	Joicy	452	Mth	Jno., [his] Est.	202	Kng
Henry	41	Rcm	Seymour	657	Glc	Joel	39	Clp
Henry	837	Wth	Thomas	436	Mth	John	161	Alb
Jacob	203	Shn	Thomas	26	Oho	John	257	Amh
Jacob, Jr.	205	Shn	Thos.	435	Mth	John	465	Bdf
Jacob, Senr.	205	Shn	Warner	449	Mth	John	908	Crl
Jacob	219	Shn	William, Urbanna	464	Mdd	John	104	Cmb
John	219	Shn	Wm.	657	Glc	John	2	Knw
John	837	Wth	Wm.	437	Mth	John	823	Nrf
Joseph	216	Shn	Wm.	450	Mth	John	984	Nrt
Margt.	627	Btt	Wm.	452	Mth	John	570	Pre
Solomon	202	Shn	Wm. H.	443	Mth	John [2]	571	Pre
Huddleston, Abraham	464	Bdf	see Hudgeins			Joshua	569	Pre
Daniel	6	Knw	Hudjin, Houlder, Jur.	186	Elc	Larking	791	Bck
George	464	Bdf	Hudlin, Joseph	6	Knw	Leven	42	Isw
Henry	463	Bdf	William	6	Knw	Lewellin	52	Chs
Henry	778	Hmp	Hudlow, Andw.	10	Rcm	Lucy	297	Amh
Job	6	Knw	John	9	Rcm	Mary	265	Frf
Joel	463	Bdf	Hudnal Richard	465	Bdf	Mary	202	Kng
John	6	Knw	Thomas S.	465	Bdf	Mary	829	Nrf
John, Junr.	6	Knw	William	467	Bdf	Maurice	13	Knw
Joseph	467	Bdf	Hudnall Ann	986	Nrt	Meridith	390	Rch
Nathan	778	Hmp	Daniel G.	656	Glc	Milly	9	Ntt
Nathan	3	Knw	James	984	Nrt	Nelly	203	Kng
Nathan	6	Knw	John	340	Fqr	Peter	345	Lan
Solomon	9	Knw	John	983	Nrt	Peter	837	Wth
Thomas	468	Bdf	Joseph	361	Fqr	Philip	906	Crl
Thomas	794	Bck	Lawson	703	Nls	Reubn.	39	Clp
Thos.	240	Aml	Richard	986	Nrt	Richard	908	Crl
William	8	Knw	Thomas	361	Fqr	Richard C.	52	Chs
William, Ser.	6	Knw	Thomas	984	Nrt	Richd.	354	Ags
see Haddston			Warner	979	Nrt	Richd.	9	Ntt
Hudgeins, James	123	Cmb	William	986	Nrt	Richd.	229	Shn
John	116	Cmb	Hudson, Abner	39	Clp	Robert	715	Brn
Hudgell, Thos.	513	Brk	Alexander	465	Bdf	Robert	774	Wst
Hudgen, Jas.	456	Pra	Alexr.	42	Clp	Robt.	43	Clp
Philip	198	Ess	Andrew	11	Knw	Rodham	774	Wst
Robt.	458	Pra	Ans.	504	Mnn	Rush	298	Amh
Thos.	457	Pra	Benjamin	52	Chr	Rush	405	Fqr
Wm.	456	Pra	Bennett	282	Amh	Rush, jr.	257	Amh
Hudgens, Burwell	2	Ntt	Catharine	216	Ess	Samuel	12	Knw
Carter	2	Ntt	Charles	51	Chr	Samuel	984	Nrt
Mitcham	128	Hnr	Chas.	349	Ags	Samuel	11	Pwh
Rebecca	3	Ntt	Christopher	161	Alb	Samuel	513	Prw
Thomas	4	Pwh	Daniel	52	Chr	Samuel	53	Stf
Hudgeon, John	390	Mds	Daniel, (Est)	53	Chr	Sarah	281	Amh
Hudgin, Antho.	451	Mth	Davd., jr.	39	Clp	Simon	464	Bdf
Archa.	454	Mth	Davd., Senr.	39	Clp	Thomas	678	Br
Baily	451	Mth	David	11	Knw	Thomas	103	Cmb
Dorathy	454	Mth	David	344	Lan	Thomas	345	Lan
Gabrl.	438	Mth	David	39	Stf	Thomas	983	Nrt
Hdr.	439	Mth	Delphia	6	Ntt	Thomas	984	Nrt
Holder	656	Glc	Dennis	374	Fqr	Thomas	231	Shn
Holloway	113	Cmb	Drury	715	Brn	Thos.	631	Btt
Isack	452	Mth	Edmund	281	Amh	Thos.	903	Nrf
James	451	Mth	Edwd.	902	Nrf	Vincent	657	Glc
Jno.	454	Mth	Elijah	630	Btt	Walter	44	Clp
Johanna	451	Mth	Elijah	571	Pre	William	796	Bck
Lewis	452	Mth	Eliza.	240	Aml	William	103	Cmb
Martha	464	Mdd	Elizabeth	363	Fqr	William	795	Hmp
Mary [2]	450	Mth	Elizabeth	32	Stf			

Name	Pg	Co.	Name	Pg	Co.	Name	Pg	Co.	Name	Pg	Co.
William	167	Knq	Molley	384	Fqr	Jesse	431	Flv	Hughett, John	649	Mnt
Wm.	202	Kng	Moses	758	Wsh	Jesse	443	Flv	Willm.	649	Mnt
see Davis, Holland, Lyall,			Nathaniel	389	Mds	Jessee	422	Msn	Hughey see Hueye		
Morris			Nimrod	388	Mds	Jno.	657	Glc	Hughland, Andw.	26	Rcm
Hueston, Saml.	253	Shn	Peter	255	Shn	John	240	Aml	Hughlett, Augt.	349	Lnc
Huey, Thomas	835	Wth	Philip	255	Shn	John	466	Bdf	Elizabeth	983	Nrt
Hueye, John	12	Oho	Rickus	388	Mds	John	685	Br	Elizabeth	985	Nrt
Huff, Anthoney	429	Rnd	Robt. S.	40	Clp	John	786	Bck	Eph.	348	Lnc
Francis	401	Ags	Saml.	42	Clp	John	806	Bck	Ephraim	982	Nrt
Geo.	273	Ldn	Sampson	389	Mds	John	868	Cmp	Esther	984	Nrt
Henry	287	Ldn	Samuel	389	Mds	John	698	Nls	John	983	Nrt
James	752	Brn	Tillman	40	Clp	John	13	Oho	Martin	349	Lnc
Jno.	289	Ldn	Tilman	389	Mds	John	680	Wrw	Molley	983	Nrt
Jno.	302	Ldn	William	415	Fqr	John, Jr.	239	Aml	Roger W.	982	Nrt
John	348	Ags	William, Qr.	389	Mds	John, Junr.	52	Chr	Samuel	985	Nrt
John	484	Frn	Zachariah	389	Mds	John, Snr.	52	Chr	Thomas W.	982	Nrt
John	949	Hrr	see Huffmand			John H.	790	Nrf	William	983	Nrt
John	653	Mnt	Huffmand, Chaty	250	Shn	Judith	1	Pwh	Hughs, ...	467	Bdf
John	741	Wsh	Huffmon, Jos.	721	Wsh	Leander	789	Bck	Aaron	788	Hmp
Jonathan	265	Frf	Moses	721	Wsh	Littleberry	806	Bck	Ann	268	Frf
Joseph	651	Mnt	Hufford, Henry	351	Ags	Luke, (F. Mo.)	40	Clp	Aschelus	5	Hnr
Lewis	752	Brn	Henry	836	Wth	Luke, jr. (Mo.)	40	Clp			
Lowry	262	Ldn	Jacob	351	Ags	Mary	443	Flv			
Lydia	282	Ldn	Rudolph	684	Br	Mary	7	Hnr			
Mary	651	Mnt	Hufman, Benjamin	680	Br	Mathew	41	Clp			
Philip	634	Mnt	Christian	224	Pnd	Melburn	414	Bth			
Sally	263	Rck	David	87	Jff	Moses	419	Bth			
Saml.	668	Mnt	Eve	226	Pnd	Moses	703	Nls			
Theophelus	43	Clp	Henry	219	Pnd	Nimrod	732	Wsh			
William	426	Rnd	John	243	Ldn	Powel	817	Bck			
Wm.	751	Brn	Michal	220	Pnd	Reuben	467	Bdf			
see Mahon			Moses	962	Hrr	Reuben, jr.	439	Flv			
Hufferd, George	11	Oho	Robert	87	Jff	Reubin, Sr.	438	Flv			
Huffman, Aaron	801	Hmp	Hugeley, Abraham	268	Frf	Rice, (stanton)	465	Bdf			
Abraham	388	Mds	Charles	261	Frf	Richd.	30	Rcm			
Abrm.	515	Brk	James	268	Frf	Robert	159	Alb			
Absalem	195	Shn	Hugely, Job	268	Frf	Saml., (F.N.)	13	Rcm			
Adam	782	Hmp	John	254	Ldn	Samuel	678	Br			
Andrew	183	Shn	Huges, Gabriel	436	Mth	Sarah	162	Alb			
Benjamin	389	Mds	Thos.	531	Brk	Sarah	52	Chr			
Chrisley	186	Shn	Huggart, Moses	269	Rck	Sirbey	117	Hnr			
Chrisley	202	Shn	Huggins, Eliza, Christians-			Stephen	162	Alb			
Chs.	40	Clp	burg	619	Mnt	Thomas	344	Fqr			
Conrod	801	Hmp	Hugh, Martha	149	Dnw	Thomas, Snr.	430	Msn			
Daniel	189	Shn	Hughart, Elizabeth	446	Bth	Thomes, jr.	430	Msn			
David	787	Hmp	James	443	Bth	Thos.	42	Clp			
David	188	Shn	Hughbanks, John	699	Nls	William	159	Alb			
Elijah	388	Mds	Hughes, ...	238	Aml	William	286	Amh			
Elisha	389	Mds	Anthy.	41	Clp	William	149	Dnw			
Enock	388	Mds	Benja.	694	Gch	William	421	Msn			
Ephraham	388	Mds	Benjamin	880	Cmp	Wm.	42	Clp			
Frederick	186	Shn	Benjamin	700	Nls	Wm.	44	Clp			
Geo.	504	Mnn	Benjamin	11	Pwh	Wm.	694	Gch			
George	189	Shn	Blackburn	240	Aml	Wm., jr.	432	Flv			
Harbert	201	Shn	Charles	852	Hnv	Wm., Sr.	440	Flv			
Harmon	389	Mds	Daniel	740	Wsh	Wm. B.	657	Glc			
Harn.	40	Clp	Edward	160	Alb	Wm. H.	29	Hnr			
Henry, jr.	40	Clp	Edward	149	Dnw	see Aughes, Haynes, Huges,					
Heny.	40	Clp	Edward	7	Knw	Hugs, Huse					
Isaac	256	Shn	Elisabeth	756	Nwk						
Jacob	284	Ldn	Emmory	464	Bdf						
Jacob	666	Mds	Frs.	902	Nrf						
Jas.	40	Clp	George	464	Bdf						
Jeremiah	188	Shn	George	907	Crl						
Jesse	353	Fqr	George	876	Yrk						
Jno.	40	Clp	Harrison	291	Amh						
Jno.	508	Mnn	Harrison	467	Bdf						
John	550	Brk	Henry	332	Dnw						
John	356	Fqr	Henry	657	Glc						
John	87	Jff	Hudson	438	Bth						
John	101	Jff	Hugh	447	Mth						
John	234	Shn	Isaac	733	Wsh						
John	733	Wsh	Israel	438	Bth						
Joseph	781	Hmp	Jacob	430	Msn						
Joseph	389	Mds	James	695	Gch						
Josh.	40	Clp	James	697	Gch						
Lewis	216	Shn	James	699	Nls						
Lydia	358	Fqr	James	10	Oho						
Mary	185	Shn	James	740	Wsh						
Michael	388	Mds	Jasper	656	Glc						

Charles	574	Frd	Humber, Elizabeth	695	Gch	[his] Est.	201	Kng		
David	879	Cmp	Danl.	348	Ags	Charles	201	Kng		
Eliza	20	Hnr	Jacob	348	Ags	Charles	39	Stf		
Elizabeth	953	Chc	see Hunber			George	985	Nrt		
George	451	Frn	Humble, Michal	536	Frd	Jas.	458	Pra		
George	626	Gls	Humbles, Dick	821	Bck	Jesse	458	Pra		
Henry	625	Gls	Samuel	821	Bck	Jno.	264	Ldn		
Ismael	917	Hrr	Hume, Armistead	39	Clp	Jno., jr.	203	Kng		
Jacob	152	Sth	Charles	391	Mds	Jno., Sr.	201	Kng		
James	57	Jff	Charles, Sr.	391	Mds	John	794	Nrf		
Jane	463	Frn	Christopher	25	Oho	John, Jr.	985	Nrt		
Jno.	889	Hnv	Edwd.	41	Clp	John, Sr.	985	Nrt		
John	351	Ags	Francis	39	Clp	Joseph	985	Nrt		
John	943	Chc	George	360	Fqr	Margt.	630	Btt		
John	292	Rck	Humphrey	44	Clp	Nelson	465	Mdd		
John	118	Spt	Jas., Senr.	39	Clp	Rawley	29	Stf		
Leander	5	Hnr	John	384	Fqr	Sarah	630	Btt		
Moses, Jnr.	699	Nls	John	391	Mds	Seaton	464	Mdd		
Peter	351	Ags	John	25	Oho	Staige	464	Mdd		
Rice	893	Hnv	Joseph	391	Mds	Susana.	248	Ldn		
Richd.	20	Hnr	Joseph	25	Oho	Thomas	847	Cmp		
Richd.	187	Shn	Moriah	107	Spt	Thos.	40	Clp		
Robt. H.	128	Hnr	Robt.	45	Clp	Thos.	458	Pra		
Rubin	891	Hnv	Thomas	384	Fqr	Wm.	630	Btt		
Salley	888	Hnv	Thos.	903	Nrf	Wm.	202	Kng		
Simon	570	Pre	William	391	Mds	Humphrise, George	76	Spt		
Tho.	349	Lnc	Humes, Ann	170	Shn	John	75	Spt		
Thomas	918	Hrr	Asa	344	Fqr	John	102	Spt		
Thomas	411	Rch	George, (Marsh)	417	Fqr	Letticy	75	Spt		
Thos.	26	Hnr	Hubert	564	Brk	Humphry, Abnor	274	Ldn		
William	120	Spt	John	71	Jff	Bartlett	443	Flv		
Wim.	884	Hnv	Nancy	793	Hmp	Randolph	467	Bdf		
Wm.	629	Btt	Thomas	4	Hnr	Humphy, Mary	774	Wst		
see Hews, Hughes, Hugs			Hummel, Valentine	5	Rcm	Humpston, John	366	Fqr		
Hughson, John	694	Gch	Hummer, Wm., Sr.	249	Ldn	Thomas	365	Fqr		
Hugins, Ruth	533	Brk	Humner, Wm.	249	Ldn	Humstead, Mary	43	Clp		
Hugs, David	626	Gls	Humphers, Saml.	602	Mnr	Hunber, Wm.	695	Gch		
Huirr see Stuirr			Humperys, David	349	Ags	see Humber				
Huker, Richard	14	Oho	Humphey, Robert	12	Oho	Hundleton, Edwd.	264	Frf		
Hukman, Arter	936	Hrr	Humpheys, Mary	401	Ags	Wm.	264	Frf		
Stud	936	Hrr	Humphlet, Edward	986	Nrt	Hundley, Ambrose	221	Ess		
Hulch, Elizabeth	436	Bth	Humphres, Samuel	602	Mnr	Amos	470	Frn		
Hulett, Mary	868	Hnv	Humphrey, Chs.	269	Ldn	Ann	465	Mdd		
Rhewben	701	Nls	David	162	Alb	Asa	6	Ntt		
William	408	Fqr	David	467	Bdf	Benja.	211	Ess		
Hulit, Martin	949	Chc	Edmond	436	Flv	David	810	Bck		
William	947	Chc	Elijah	440	Flv	Edward	848	Hnv		
Hulitt, Charles	512	Frd	Fountain	443	Flv	Elizabeth	7	Ntt		
Hull, Adam	225	Pnd	Isaah	197	Alb	James	799	Bck		
Barthnw.	737	Wsh	Jacob	264	Ldn	James R. H.	440	Mth		
Bengamin	811	Hmp	Jesse	436	Flv	Jno. B.	441	Mth		
Brandie S.	101	Spt	Jesse	260	Ldn	John	879	Cmp		
Danl.	353	Ags	Jno.	44	Clp	John	53	Chr		
George	438	Bth	John	431	Flv	John	213	Ess		
Green	344	Lnn	Jonathan	905	Hrr	John	391	Mds		
Henry	563	Mnr	Joseph	11	Oho	John	570	Pre		
Henry	225	Pnd	Lewis	467	Bdf	John P.	166	Knq		
Jacob	214	Pnd	Lewis	434	Flv	Joshua	239	Aml		
James	737	Wsh	Mark	271	Ldn	Josiah	16	Ntt		
Jerry	296	Rck	Mary	895	Hnv	Keleb	439	Mth		
Jno.	44	Clp	Robert	11	Oho	Mary	441	Mth		
John	354	Ags	Susannah	431	Flv	Mary	157	Sth		
John	679	Br	Thomas	270	Ldn	Matthew	905	Crl		
John	985	Nrt	William	905	Hrr	Nehemiah	449	Mth		
Moses	17	Oho	Wm.	433	Flv	Ransom	53	Chr		
Norton	710	Wsh	see Harrison			Richd.	441	Mth		
Peter	303	Rck	Humphreys, Benja.	42	Clp	Robt.	438	Mth		
Peter, S.	217	Pnd	David	58	Jff	Sarah	907	Crl		
Philip	297	Rck	James	580	Mnr	Sarah	439	Mth		
Thomas G.	127	Hnr	Jesse	42	Clp	Thomas	211	Ess		
Wm.	904	Nrf	John	54	Jff	Wim.	871	Hnv		
see Hall, Hill, Steele			John	579	Mnr	Wm.	7	Ntt		
Hulls, George	261	Frf	John, J.	579	Mnr	Wm. B.	7	Ntt		
John	277	Ldn	Roger	70	Jff	Hundly, Nehemiah	451	Frn		
Hults, John	353	Ags	Saml.	564	Mnr	Richd.	448	Mth		
William	690	Br	Saml.	579	Mnr	Hungate, Wm.	658	Mnt		
Hulver, John	232	Shn	Wm.	579	Mnr	Hungerford, John	774	Wst		
Hulvey, Conrod	6	Rcm	see Humphers, Humphrise,			John P.	774	Wst		
George	31	Rcm	Umphris			Thos.	201	Kng		
George	37	Rcm	Humphries, Anderson,			Hunicutt, Ephram	549	Prg		

Thos.	547	Prg	Saml.	569	Mnr	Thomas	198	Alb
Hunley, Eliza	17	Hnr	Samuel	3	Isw	Thomas	379	Fqr
Hunly see Henly			Sarah	159	Alb	Thomas	982	Nrt
Hunnel, Moses	727	Wsh	Sarah	876	Yrk	William	379	Fqr
Nancey	727	Wsh	Sarah, Mrs.	51	Chr	William W.	365	Fqr
Hunnicut, Joshua	14	Pwh	Stephen	465	Bdf	Wim.	862	Hnv
Mary	149	Dnw	Thomas	641	Sss	Huntsburg, Conrad	549	Frd
Daniel	534	Prg	Thomas, Jr.	640	Sss	Huntsman, Carrington	51	Chr
Edward	535	Prg	Thomas, Sr.	645	Sss	James	52	Chr
Glaister	642	Sss	Wilkins J.	644	Sss	Peggy	352	Ags
Hartwell	607	Srr	William	52	Chr	Peter	464	Bdf
James	148	Dnw	William	377	Fqr	Richd.	646	Mnt
John	538	Prg	William	511	Prw	Huntsucker, Abram	735	Wsh
John, Sr.	607	Srr	Hunter, Alexander	877	Cmp	Huntzberry, Henry	96	Jff
Lemuel	535	Prg	Alexander	53	Chr	Hup, Henry	18	Oho
Pleasant	642	Sss	Andw.	351	Ags	Martin	248	Shn
Rebecca	695	Gch	Ann	599	Brk	Philip	18	Oho
Robert, Sr.	607	Srr	Austin	695	Gch	see ...p		
Robert B.	607	Srr	Benjamin	867	Cmp	Hupman, Gasper	349	Ags
Samuel	536	Prg	Blandana	458	Pra	John	348	Ags
Thomas	609	Srr	David	701	Nls	Hupp, Abraham	197	Shn
William	534	Prg	Elijah	249	Ldn	Balser	196	Shn
William	607	Srr	Elizabeth	457	Pra	Samuel	193	Shn
Hunniman, Charles	801	Hmp	Forrest	697	Gch	Hurd, Calvin	457	Pra
Hunsecker, Peter	61	Jff	Fowler	903	Nrf	Charles	653	Mnt
Hunsicker, Jacob	405	Fqr	Francis	466	Bdf	Hurdick, Edmond	855	Cmp
Hunsman, William	37	Stf	Geo. W.	268	Frf	Hurford, Rachel	575	Frd
Hunspaker, Abram, Jur.	744	Wsh	Jacob	456	Pra	Hurle, William	556	Frd
Hunston, Edward	561	Frd	James	351	Ags	Hurley, Caleb	504	Mnn
Hunsucker, Abram, Jur.	753	Wsh	James	693	Br	Henry	32	Rcm
John	754	Wsh	James	223	Ess	Mary, (Mo.)	41	Clp
Peter	754	Wsh	James	34	Isw	Ruth, (Mo.)	41	Clp
see Hunsicker, Hunspaker,			James	579	Mnr	Hurlock, John	465	Frn
Huntsucker			James	902	Nrf	Hurly, Sim.	505	Mnn
Hunt, ...mas	167	Shn	Jno.	267	Frf	see Hirly, Hurley		
Caty	328	Dnw	Jno.	457	Pra	Hurndon, Reuben	199	Alb
Charles	445	Flv	Jno. C.	263	Frf	Hurry, Isabella	794	Hmp
Charlott	332	Dnw	John	349	Ags	Jas.	506	Mnn
Charlotte	583	Mnr	John	352	Ags	Hursh, Hannah	847	Sth
Chrispin	749	Wsh	John	574	Brk	Hurst, Aaron	389	Fqr
Crispin C.	440	Flv	John	877	Cmp	Absalom	836	Wth
Christopher	52	Chr	John	69	Chr	Ashan	580	Frd
Curtis	875	Yrk	John	489	Frn	Benja.	262	Frf
Daniel	499	Frn	John	773	Wst	Christr.	627	Btt
David	461	Frn	Jona.	456	Pra	Daniel	263	Frf
Dick	478	Frn	Jonah W.	788	Nrf	Drew	150	Sth
Elizabeth	833	Nrf	Joseph	181	Alb	Edward	389	Fqr
Elizabeth	505	Prw	Josiah W.	456	Pra	Edwd.	454	Mth
Elizabeth	645	Sss	Juana	500	Prw	Isaac	982	Nrt
Geo.	40	Clp	Mathew	350	Ags	James	92	Jff
George, F.N.	644	Sss	Moses	636	Mnt	James	982	Nrt
Gerard	261	Frf	Muscoe G.	201	Ess	Jane	982	Nrt
Hicks, & Co.	327	Dnw	Peter	467	Bdf	Jeremiah	835	Wth
Jacob	465	Bdf	Peter, Sr.	466	Bdf	Jno.	450	Mth
Jacob	247	Shn	Pleasant	41	Clp	John	92	Jff
James	870	Cmp	Richard	822	Hmp	John	983	Nrt
James	264	Frf	Robert	865	Cmp	John [2]	836	Wth
James	3	Oho	Robert	625	Gls	John	838	Wth
James, Senr.	52	Chr	Robert, Jur.	626	Gls	John, Senr.	263	Frf
Jas.	508	Mnn	Robt.	350	Ags	Martha	280	Ldn
Jno.	280	Ldn	Sally	904	Nrf	Olive	161	Sth
John	463	Bdf	Saml.	350	Ags	Rich.	178	Elc
John	499	Frn	Saml., sr.	349	Ags	Samuel	871	Sth
John	450	Grn	Samuel	535	Brk	Solomon	143	Sth
John	347	Lnc	Samuel	774	Wst	Solomon	150	Sth
John	983	Nrt	Taleaferro	207	Ess	Solomon	845	Sth
John	875	Yrk	Thomas	254	Ldn	Thomas	393	Fqr
Joseph	306	Ldn	Thos.	457	Pra	Thomas	982	Nrt
Julius	44	Clp	William	871	Cmp	William	535	Frd
Lucy	25	Hnr	William	489	Frn	William	982	Nrt
Major	294	Ldn	William	551	Frd	William	836	Wth
Mary	310	Ldn	Willie	152	Sth	Wm.	444	Mth
Mary	390	Mds	Wm.	903	Nrf	Hurt, Absolum	346	Lnn
Mims	149	Sth	see Hemter, Hunber			Ann	907	Crl
Nancy	505	Prw	Huntley, Jno.	903	Nrf	Anson	239	Aml
Obadiah	465	Bdf	Hunton, Alexander	390	Mds	Benjamin	906	Crl
Owen	499	Frn	Charles	198	Alb	Eliza.	39	Clp
Patt	871	Sth	Eppa	375	Fqr	Elizabeth	835	Wth
Philip	315	Ldn	James	386	Fqr	Francis	569	Pre
Robert	420	Rnd	Robert	417	Fqr	Henry	464	Bdf

Name			Name			Name		
James	463	Bdf	Davd.	263	Rck	Hutchuson see Hutcherson		
James	389	Mds	Elizabeth	265	Frf	Hutsler, Jacob	578	Frd
James	24	Oho	Ely	265	Frf	Hutson, Abrm.	283	Rck
James	571	Pre	John	166	Knq	Betsey	101	Acc
James, Sr.	464	Bdf	Joshua	266	Frf	Joel	484	Frn
Jas.	13	Hnr	Mordecai	391	Mds	John	149	Dnw
Jno.	1	Ntt	Nancy	30	Acc	John	935	Hrr
John	464	Bdf	Richd.	27	Acc	John	126	Hnr
John	570	Pre	Robert	626	Gls	John	391	Mds
Josiah	572	Pre	Saml.	266	Frf	Polly	812	Nrf
Lew	346	Lnn	Samuel	626	Gls	Rebecca	94	Jff
Macon	343	Lnn	Stephen	803	Bck	Robert	98	Acc
Mary	464	Bdf	Thomas	264	Frf	Thomas	692	Br
Meriwether	346	Lnn	Vincent	261	Frf	William	101	Acc
Mourning	39	Clp	William	30	Acc	William	868	Cmp
Nancey	629	Mnt	William	797	Bck	Hutt, Benjamin	556	Frd
Obadiah	571	Pre	William	166	Knq	Gerard	774	Wst
Pleasant	836	Wth	Wm.	266	Frf	John	202	Kng
Ruth	464	Bdf	Zerubl.	27	Acc	Joseph	202	Kng
Stephen	466	Bdf	Hutchings, Benjamin	644	Sss	Maria	774	Wst
West	166	Knq	Jno.	347	Lnc	Thomas	330	Dnw
William	908	Crl	John	150	Dnw	Walker	202	Kng
William	389	Mds	Littleton	643	Sss	Huttan, Jonathan	419	Rnd
Wm., Jr.	389	Mds	Richd.	347	Lnc	Hutton, Catharin	24	Hnr
Zachariah	836	Wth	Turner	132	Hnr	Dixon	731	Wsh
see Heurtt			Wm.	147	Dnw	Edward	731	Wsh
Hurte, Jno.	904	Nrf	see Huchings			James	731	Wsh
Hurtt, Jane	160	Alb	Balam	145	Sth	Jas., Senr.	701	Wsh
William	160	Alb	Carter	145	Sth	John	731	Wsh
Husan, Nancy	331	Dnw	Francis	585	Frd	Joseph	429	Msn
Husbands, James	594	Brk	John	902	Nrf	Leonard, Jur.	700	Wsh
Huse, Anthony	116	Cmb	Joseph	596	Frd	Leonard, Sen.	701	Wsh
Crafford	343	Lnn	Joshua	902	Nrf	Moses	700	Wsh
John	939	Hrr	Peyton	145	Sth	Rachal	77	Jff
Sarah C.A.	541	Prg	Thos.	353	Ags	Hutts, Lenard	465	Frn
William	344	Lnn	Wm.	456	Pra	Micheal	464	Frn
see Heese, Heise			Hutchinson, Jno.	904	Nrf	William	465	Frn
Husher, George	14	Wod	John	908	Crl	see Hults		
Hushour, Henry	229	Shn	John	557	Frd	Hutzell, George	838	Wth
Husk, Mashae	937	Hrr	John	796	Nrf	John [3]	838	Wth
Thomas	99	Acc	Levi	907	Crl	Huzelrig, William	12	Wod
Huskey, James	751	Brn	Mons [crossed out]	796	Nrf	Huzza, George	347	Fqr
Huson, Molly	876	Yrk	William	906	Crl	Hyatt, Esther	681	Br
Hussill see Heissill			William	84	Spt	Ezekiel	681	Br
Hustead, James	914	Hrr	Hutchison, Alexdr.	599	Mnr	John	685	Br
John	914	Hrr	Andrew	244	Ldn	Thomas	470	Frn
Moses	914	Hrr	Andrew	246	Ldn	Hyde, Daniel	92	Spt
Hustin, Jane	20	Hnr	Andw.	576	Mnr	John	8	Oho
Thomas	34	Hnr	David	571	Mnr	Richd.	13	Ntt
Hustley, John H.	28	Acc	David	645	Mnt	William	148	Dnw
Huston, Benjamin	835	Wth	Eli	248	Ldn	Hyder, Adam	757	Hmp
George	11	Rcm	Geo.	248	Ldn	Hyer, Jacob [2]	909	Hrr
John	10	Rcm	Isaac	563	Mnr	John [2]	909	Hrr
John	702	Wsh	James	246	Ldn	Hyle, John	238	Ldn
Joseph	410	Ags	James	247	Ldn	Nicholas	238	Ldn
Robert	694	Wsh	James	5	Pwh	Hyler see Hyter		
Robert	714	Wsh	Jeremiah	244	Ldn	Hyley, James	478	Frn
Thomas	476	Frn	Jdhn	958	Mnr	John	479	Frn
see Haston			J hn	244	Ldn	Thomas	479	Frn
Hutchenson, Bennet	482	Frn	Jöhn	562	Mnr	Hyllard, Christopher	837	Wth
Isaac	10	Wod	John	594	Mnr	Hylor, Jno.	250	Ldn
Matthew	459	Frn	John	603	Mnr	Wm.	250	Ldn
Oliver	11	Wod	Jdhn	523	Prw	Hylton, Danl. L.	9	Hnr
William	500	Frn	Joseph	244	Ldn	Danl. L.	121	Hnr
Wm.	117	Hnr	Joseph	246	Ldn	George	698	Nls
Hutcherson, Archibald	7	Knw	Lewis	244	Ldn	John	757	Nwk
Collier	51	Chr	Margt.	569	Mnr	Vallentine	698	Nls
D.C.	3	Hnr	Mary	247	Ldn	Hyman, Henry	287	Rck
David	53	Chr	Nathan	245	Ldn	Hymes, Abram	631	Btt
Fanny	349	Lnc	Robert M.	625	Gls	David	631	Btt
George	201	Shn	Rueben	243	Ldn	Hyndman, James	694	Br
Jacob	7	Knw	Sampson	246	Ldn	John	694	Br
James	34	Hnr	William	836	Bck	Samuel	694	Br
John	295	Amh	William	565	Mnr	Hynes, Jno.	299	Ldn
John	122	Cmb	William	510	Prw	Lewis	23	Isw
Mary	865	Cmp	Wm.	437	Flv	Susanna	835	Wth
Samuel	8	Knw	Wm.	244	Ldn	see Haynes		
Sarah	239	Aml	Zach.	572	Mnr	Hypes, Henry	628	Btt
Hutcheson, Anderson	264	Rck	see Hatchison			John	628	Btt
Benja.	266	Frf	Hutchon, Joseph	781	Hmp	Peter	628	Btt

Hyres, Saml. 287 Rck
Hysel, Strother 389 Mds
Hyter, Abram 731 Wsh
Abram 758 Wsh
Abram, Senr. 758 Wsh
Iseral 758 Wsh
John T. 758 Wsh
see Hayter

--- I ---

Iberla, Geo. 905 Nrf
Icanberry see Ikenbury
Icbull, Frederick 426 Msn
Ice, Abm. 510 Mnn
Adam 511 Mnn
Andw. 511 Mnn
Jno. 510 Mnn
Tho. 511 Mnn
Wm. 509 Mnn
Wm. 510 Mnn
Icener, Henry 430 Rnd
Thomas 420 Rnd
Icenhower, Jacob 288 Rck
Jacob 290 Rck
Michl. 274 Rck
Iddings, Henry 632 Mnt
James 633 Mnt
see Idings
Iden, Jacob 377 Fqr
Jonah 556 Frd
Iding, John 580 Brk
Idings, Calib 21 Hnr
Idle, Henry 634 Btt
Jno. 633 Btt
Martin 634 Btt
Idon, John 238 Ldn
Jonah 259 Ldn
Jont. 258 Ldn
Saml. 315 Ldn
Samul 235 Ldn
Ihinger, Christopher 26 Rcm
Ikenbury, John 477 Frn
Iler, John 632 Btt
Iliff, Stephen 829 Hmp
Imber, Louis 906 Nrf
Immal, Peter 5 Rcm
Impoden, Fred. 408 Ags
Impotin, Catharine 355 Ags
Jacob 356 Ags
Impswiler, Philip 518 Frd
Imswiler, Jacob 240 Shn
Inbody, John 62 Jff
Inchminger, Jonn. 633 Btt
Inge, Claiborne 573 Pre
James 54 Chr
Jane 573 Pre
John 349 Lnn
Paton 789 Bck
Vincent 346 Lnn
Vincent, Sr. 349 Lnn
Wm. 876 Yrk
Ingle, Isaac 793 Hmp
Wm. 503 Brk
Jo... 967 Hrr
Ingles, John 328 Dnw
John 606 Mnt
William 327 Dnw
Inglesh, George 8 Oho
Inglish, Jesse 16 Isw
John 22 Isw
Nancy 21 Isw
Ingmire, Robert 800 Hmp
Ingraham, Benjamin 753 Brn
Ingram, Aron 626 Mnt
Abraham 420 Rnd
Abram 917 Hrr
Barthw. 150 Dnw

Catharine 753 Brn
Chas. 350 Lnc
Elexander 489 Frn
Fanny 202 Ess
George 908 Crl
Jno. 906 Nrf
John 451 Grn
John 82 Jff
John 986 Nrt
Joseph B. 55 Chr
Margarett 201 Ess
Mary 350 Lnc
Moore 201 Ess
Polly 621 Mnt
Robn. 906 Nrf
Samuel 348 Lnn
Sarah 906 Nrf
Silvanus 348 Lnn
Thomas 386 Fqr
Thomas 920 Hrr
Thomas 986 Nrt
Uriah 918 Hrr
William 197 Ess
William 451 Grn
William 424 Rnd
William G. 758 Nwk
Wm. 609 Srr
Ingrar, Josias 986 Nrt
Ingred, Wm. 356 Ags
Ingyard, Lewis 10 Oho
Inkeep, James 67 Chs
Inloe, Henry 4 Oho
Inman, Henry 853 Sth
Isham 609 Srr
Innes, Burwell 500 Frn
Edmund 908 Crl
James 908 Crl
Robert 481 Frn
Susanna 908 Crl
Innis, Alexr. 270 Rck
Susan 905 Nrf
William 50 Stf
Wm. 934 Hrr
Insco, Jessee 11 Knw
Inscoe, Edward 205 Kng
Robert 17 Oho
Thomas 205 Kng
Insell, James 830 Nrf
N...l...n 827 Nrf
Nicholas 806 Nrf
Inshwiler, John 229 Shn
Inskeep, --- 46 Clp
Joel 46 Clp
see Inkeep
Inskip, James 810 Hmp
John 763 Hmp
Joseph 795 Hmp
William 763 Hmp
Insley, Abraham 660 Glc
Cumfort 876 Yrk
Matthias 876 Yrk
Insminger, George 947 Hrr
Intsminger, Anthy. 592 Mnr
Ipling, Isaac 627 Gls
Irbey, Robert 955 Chc
Irby, Douglas 634 Btt
Edmd. 13 Ntt
Edmund 451 Grn
Francis 948 Chc
Jacob 331 Dnw
Jacob 130 Hnr
Littlebery 954 Chc
Pheoby 130 Hnr
Wm., jr. 16 Ntt
Wm., (S) 7 Ntt
Ireland, Alexander 932 Hrr
James 563 Frd
Jane 2 Rcm
John 938 Chc
John 160 Sth

Mary 328 Dnw
Wm. 633 Btt
Irenes, Mary 828 Nrf
Ireson see Irson, Jacson
Irey, Jno. 311 Ldn
Irick, Geo. 355 Ags
John 665 Mnt
Julia Ann 16 Rcm
Michael 16 Rcm
Iridale, John 360 Fqr
Ironmonger, George 31 Acc
James 32 Acc
Wm. 809 Nrf
Irons, John 738 Wsh
Thos. 578 Mnr
Irson, William 706 Wsh
Irven, William 347 Lnn
Irvin, Eliz. 32 Hnr
Elizabeth 163 Alb
James 697 Br
John 469 Bdf
John 510 Frd
Jonas 469 Bdf
Joseph 469 Bdf
Saml. 634 Btt
Samuel 163 Alb
Thomas 513 Frd
William 469 Bdf
Irvine, Andrew 38 Rcm
Benjamin, (Jr.) 38 Rcm
Benjn., (Sen.) 38 Rcm
Clemments 38 Rcm
Hugh 277 Rck
Jane [2] 39 Rcm
John 263 Rck
John, Junr. 875 Cmp
John, Sr. 870 Cmp
John H. 854 Cmp
Joseph 876 Cmp
Mathew T. 870 Cmp
Robert 289 Rck
Robt. C. 633 Btt
Saml. 38 Rcm
Samuel 854 Cmp
William 881 Cmp
Irving, Ann 811 Bck
Charles 795 Bck
Geo. N. 442 Flv
Robert 833 Bck
Robert 429 Flv
Irwin, Alexander 4 Oho
David 2 Oho
Francis 46 Clp
James 451 Grn
Thomas 13 Knw
Wm. 46 Clp
Wm. 1 Oho
Isaac see Isacc
Isaacks, David 179 Alb
Isaacs, Molly 699 Gch
Tobias 127 Hnr
Isaac's, Isaac 103 Acc
Isacc, Tobias 704 Nls
Isahower, Saml. 633 Btt
Isam, Charles 756 Wsh
Isbell, Benja. 698 Gch
Christopher 280 Amh
George 908 Crl
Henry 698 Gch
James 99 Cmb
John 99 Cmb
Lewis 99 Cmb
William 105 Cmb
Wm. 698 Gch
Zachariah 294 Amh
Isenbarger, Jacob 634 Btt
Iseral, Isaac 934 Hrr
Ish, Jacob 242 Ldn
Ishams, James 805 Bck

Isler, Catharina	532	Frd	Abel	444	Bth	Jno.	10	Hnr
Henry, Jur.	56	Jff	Aggy	332	Dnw	Jno.	281	Ldn
Henry, Snr.	56	Jff	Anna	465	Mdd	Jno.	705	Nls
Ison, George	168	Knq	Arnold	573	Pre	Jno., Junr.	271	Frf
Lucy	168	Knq	Arthur	14	Ntt	Jno., Senr., Do. [ditto] as		
Israel, Elianer	46	Clp	Bailey	518	Prw	admo. of Wiggnt.	271	Frf
see Iseral			Benona	19	Hnr	Jno. C.	8	Hnr
Isral, Jacob	966	Hrr	Bernard	515	Frd	Jno. E., [his] Est.	18	Ntt
Itson, Rebecca	397	Fqr	Betsey, (FB)	469	Bdf	Jno. R.	327	Dnw
Ivans, John	440	Mth	Bettey, F.N.	168	Knq	Joel	573	Pre
Josiah	437	Mth	Billey	370	Fqr	John	163	Alb
Josiah	451	Mth	Burwell	705	Nls	John	355	Ags
Thos.	440	Mth	Cain	54	Chr	John	913	Hrr
Wm., jr.	440	Mth	Capt.	544	Prg	John	84	Jff
Wm., Sr.	440	Mth	Charles	17	Ntt	John	105	Jff
Ivers, William	5	Oho	Charles	876	Yrk	John	203	Kng
Iverson, George	443	Mth	Claiborne	237	Aml	John	465	Mdd
James, jr.	836	Bck	Coleman	752	Brn	John	511	Mnn
John	798	Bck	Coleman	151	Dnw	John	610	Mnt
Richd.	440	Mth	Curtis	573	Pre	John	519	Prw
Ives, Bartlet	459	Pra	Dan	510	Mnn	John	759	Wsh
David	818	Nrf	Daniel	848	Cmp	John [2]	839	Wth
James	717	Brn	Daniel	400	Rch	John, & Sons	393	Mds
Jesse	459	Pra	David	717	Brn	John, Junr.	54	Chr
Saml.	818	Nrf	David	34	Hnr	John, (little)	54	Chr
Sol.	820	Nrf	David	242	Ldn	John F.	238	Aml
Theopilus	818	Nrf	Davis	237	Aml	John R.	329	Dnw
Thos. Old	459	Pra	Edwd.	699	Gch	Jordan	347	Lnn
see Ivy			Edwd.	927	Nrf	Jordan	21	Ntt
Iveson, Edwards	659	Glc	Elizabeth	946	Chc	Jordan	23	Ntt
see Lewis			Elizabeth	347	Lnn	Jordan	132	Sth
Ivey, Bridget	537	Prg	Elizabeth	349	Lnn	Joseph	372	Fqr
David, F.N.	648	Sss	Elizabeth	117	Spt	Joseph	9	Hnr
Elizabeth	648	Sss	Ephraim	717	Brn	Joseph	626	Mnt
Geo.	811	Nrf	Ephraim	752	Brn	Joseph	521	Prw
Henry	648	Sss	Francis	238	Aml	Joseph	839	Wth
Hugh	646	Sss	Francis	54	Chr	Josiah	53	Chr
Jesse	646	Sss	Francis	15	Ntt	Josiah	539	Frd
Joel	869	Sth	Francis	41	Stf	Kindred	874	Sth
Jos.	798	Nrf	Francis	647	Sss	Leonard	465	Mdd
Joshua	536	Prg	Geo.	11	Ntt	Lewis	451	Grn
Littleberry	645	Sss	Geo., (W)	876	Yrk	Littlebury	150	Dnw
Nelly	905	Nrf	George	567	Frd	Luke	391	Rch
Sally	868	Sth	George	79	Jff	Martha	465	Mdd
Ivie, Anslin	717	Brn	George	465	Mdd	Martha	137	Sth
Hardeman S.	717	Brn	George	527	Prw	Martha, F.N.	647	Sss
Ivins, John	346	Lnn	George	32	Stf	Mary	54	Chr
Robert	346	Lnn	Gordon	11	Rcm	Mary	151	Dnw
Ivy, David	851	Sth	Green	717	Brn	Mary	334	Dnw
George [2]	866	Sth	Hannah	440	Bth	Mary	132	Sth
John	753	Brn	Hark	155	Sth	Mary	32	Stf
Lucy	851	Sth	Henry	836	Bck	Michl.	295	Rck
Wyatt	847	Sth	Henry	518	Frd	Mingo	9	Hnr
see Ives, Ivie			Henry	13	Pwh	Mingo	35	Hnr
			Henry	4	Wod	Moses	237	Aml
			Hezekiah	574	Pre	Nancy	151	Dnw
--- J ---			Holley, free negro	70	Chs	Nathaniel	585	Frd
			Hugh	706	Wsh	Nathaniel	572	Pre
			Hy., Jr.	906	Nrf	Ned, (FB)	14	Ntt
J..., ...	237	Aml	Hy., Sr.	906	Nrf	Newman	775	Wst
J...ll see Insell			Isaac	426	Msn	Peter	67	Jff
J...mes, Ann	52	Stf	Isaac, (FN)	68	Chr	Peter	347	Lnn
Jabler see Vabler			J...n [John?]	878	Cmp	Primus	906	Nrf
Jachobs, Hickerson	163	Alb	Jacob	421	Fqr	Priscilla	295	Rck
Jack, Andrew	205	Shn	James	633	Btt	Ralph	53	Chr
James	634	Btt	James	834	Bck	Randolph	752	Brn
James	942	Hrr	James	151	Dnw	Rd.	48	Clp
James	13	Oho	James	532	Frd	Rd., quarter	271	Frf
Jereh.	589	Brk	James	80	Jff	Rebeccah	9	Hnr
John	205	Shn	James	392	Mds	Reuben	648	Sss
Robert	589	Brk	James	465	Mdd	Reubin	124	Hnr
see Jacke			James	906	Nrf	Richard R.	775	Wst
Jack..., John	756	Hmp	James	4	Oho	Richd.	753	Brn
Jacke, John	218	Pnd	James	573	Pre	Richd.	512	Mnn
Jackman, Geo.	659	Glc	James	138	Sth	Richd.	876	Yrk
Thos.	659	Glc	James	114	Spt	Robert	686	Br
William	697	Br	Jas.	805	Nrf	Robert	717	Brn
Jackson, Aaron	758	Nwk	Jas.	16	Ntt	Robert	271	Frf
Abbey	884	Hnv	Jeremiah	465	Mdd	Robert	218	Pnd
Abel	237	Aml	Jno.	46	Clp	Ruth	553	Frd

Name	No.	Dist.
Salley	9	Hnr
Sally	122	Hnr
Sally	648	Sss
Saml.	355	Ags
Saml.	634	Mnt
Samuel	565	Frd
Samuel	232	Ldn
Samuel	516	Prw
Samuel	400	Rch
Samuel	208	Shn
Samuel	2	Wod
Simon C.	2	Ntt
Spencer	271	Frf
Stephen	717	Brn
Stuart	573	Pre
Susan	906	Nrf
Susan	927	Nrf
Susanah	945	Chc
Thomas	163	Alb
Thomas	54	Chr
Thomas	471	Frn
Thomas	587	Frd
Thomas	393	Mds
Thomas	775	Wst
Thomas	839	Wth
Thos.	410	Ags
Thos.	204	Kng
Tobias	179	Alb
W...ll..., (FB)	469	Bdf
William	151	Dnw
William	326	Dnw
William	390	Fqr
William	394	Fqr
William	795	Hmp
William	97	Jff
William	758	Nwk
William [2]	572	Pre
William	573	Pre
William	72	Spt
William	105	Spt
William	113	Spt
Wily	237	Aml
Wm.	717	Brn
Wm.	49	Clp
Wm.	150	Dnw
Wm.	6	Ntt
Wm.	278	Rck
Wm., (JC)	17	Ntt
Wm., jr.	150	Dnw
Wm., Senr.	150	Dnw
Wm., (W)	876	Yrk
Wood	151	Dnw
see Jacson		
Jackston, Zacariah	953	Chc
Jaco, Joseph	951	Hrr
Reuben	512	Mnn
Tho.	512	Mnn
Wm.	512	Mnn
Jacob, Gabriel	11	Oho
Jacob	206	Shn
Jos.	21	Hnr
Thomas	31	Acc
Jacobs, Ben	510	Mnn
Benjamin	908	Crl
Benjamin	465	Mdd
Cathne.	905	Nrf
Cealey	627	Gls
Clabourne	872	Cmp
Dav.	511	Mnn
David	427	Bth
David	950	Hrr
David	704	Nls
Dossy	289	Ldn
Edward	269	Frf
Elijah	278	Ldn
Elisha	706	Nls
George	204	Kng
Greenberry	806	Hmp
J.	905	Nrf
Jacob	313	Ldn

Name	No.	Dist.
Jno.	706	Nls
John	351	Fqr
John	523	Frd
John	73	Jff
John	284	Rck
John, Jnr.	706	Nls
John J.	796	Hmp
Jona.	511	Mnn
Jonathan	950	Hrr
Joseph	270	Frf
Joseph	813	Hmp
Perter	704	Nls
Polley	354	Fqr
Price	260	Ldn
Rowley	629	Mnt
Thomas	302	Ldn
Thos., jr.	47	Clp
William	270	Frf
William	705	Nls
William	40	Stf
Wm., jr.	46	Clp
Wm., Senr.	46	Clp
Wm. B.	707	Nls
see Jachobs		
Jacobus, Eml.	905	Nrf
Jacson, David	962	Hrr
Edward	932	Hrr
John G.	954	Hrr
Polly	521	Brk
Samuel	966	Hrr
Stephen	937	Hrr
Wm.	931	Hrr
Jakes, James	495	Frn
John	495	Frn
James, Abel	245	Ldn
Ann	660	Glc
Ann	244	Ldn
Ann	758	Nwk
Ann	848	Sth
Bart	350	Lnc
Benj.	245	Ldn
Betty	459	Pra
Billey	131	Hnr
Braxton	490	Frn
Cary	753	Brn
Chas.	350	Lnc
Chloe	468	Bdf
D...niel	468	Bdf
Daniel	382	Fqr
Daniel	543	Frd
Daniel	392	Mds
Danl.	634	Btt
Danl., Jr.	632	Btt
David	104	Acc
David	237	Ldn
David	818	Nrf
David, J.	316	Ldn
Edward	769	Brn
Edward, Sr.	459	Pra
Edwd.	459	Pra
Edwd., (of Wm.)	459	Pra
Edy	698	Gch
Eliza	838	Nrf
Elizabeth	460	Pra
Enoch	923	Hrr
Ezekiel	839	Wth
Foster	845	Hnv
Francis	365	Fqr
Francis J.	115	Cmb
Frank	810	Bck
Frederick	105	Cmb
Geo.	46	Clp
Henry	459	Pra
Henry, (of Chs.)	459	Pra
Isaac	414	Bth
Isaac	468	Bdf
Isaac	808	Hmp
Isaac	610	Srr
Isaac	104	Acc
James	468	Bdf

Name	No.	Dist.
James	811	Bck
James	825	Bck
James	854	Cmp
James	839	Wth
Jedithan	986	Nrt
Jeremiah	610	Srr
Jesse	4	Ntt
Jessee	8	Knw
Jno.	350	Lnc
Jno., Jr.	459	Pra
John	514	Brk
John	633	Btt
John	698	Gch
John [example]	436	Mth
John	970	Nrt
John	572	Pre
John	129	Sth
John	109	Spt
John, & Mother	392	Mds
John P.	753	Brn
Johnson	468	Bdf
Jonathan	468	Bdf
Jont.	316	Ldn
Joseph	910	Crl
Joseph	382	Fqr
Joseph	392	Mds
Joshua	459	Pra
Levi	308	Ldn
Lydia	32	Acc
Mary	698	Gch
Mat.	350	Lnc
Molly	905	Nrf
Nelly	890	Yrk
Nicholas	485	Frn
Nicholas	492	Frn
Patience	31	Acc
Philip	910	Crl
Poley	853	Cmp
Polley	160	Sth
Polly	334	Dnw
Robert	148	Sth
Robert S.	810	Bck
Robt.	769	Brn
Robt.	351	Lnc
Salley	861	Hnv
Sally	32	Acc
Sally	775	Wst
Samuel	419	Bth
Sarah	28	Stf
Sherad	839	Wth
Sherrod	775	Wst
Silviah	610	Srr
Simon, F.N.	646	Sss
Spencer	494	Frn
Susanna	909	Crl
Susanna	845	Hnv
Tho.	350	Lnc
Thomas	634	Btt
Thomas	104	Jff
Thomas	66	Spt
Thomas	839	Wth
Thos.	270	Ldn
Thos.	445	Mth
Thos.	459	Pra
William	124	Cmb
William	346	Fqr
William	474	Frn
William	484	Frn
William	523	Frd
William	126	Hnr
William	107	Spt
Wm.	660	Glc
Wm.	244	Ldn
Wm.	245	Ldn
Wm.	512	Mnn
Wm., jr.	753	Brn
Wm., Jr.	459	Pra
Wm., Sr.	753	Brn
Wm., Sr.	459	Pra
Wm. M.	459	Pra
	350	Lnc

York	131	Hnr
see J...mes, Jones		
Jameson, Alexander	186	Shn
Alexander	42	Stf
Andw.	354	Ags
Clem. R., Dr.	54	Chr
Daniel	531	Prg
Davd.	46	Clp
David	909	Crl
Edmund	53	Chr
Enoch	351	Fqr
John	354	Ags
John	16	Oho
John	49	Stf
Margaret	199	Alb
Peggy	32	Stf
Robt.	296	Rck
Thomas	179	Alb
Thos.	750	Wsh
Wm.	295	Rck
see Jamison		
Jamieson, Thomas, Urbanna	465	Mdd
Jamison, Banjamin	512	Prw
David	514	Prw
Issabella	682	Br
James	355	Ags
Jno.	46	Clp
John	633	Btt
John	787	Bck
John	816	Bck
John	741	Wsh
Margaret	13	Wod
Martha	355	Ags
Mary	686	Br
Nathan	163	Alb
Robert	678	Br
William	514	Prw
see Jameson		
Jandrell, Thos.	905	Nrf
Jane, William	162	Alb
William	948	Chc
Janes, Henry	597	Frd
Henry	739	Wsh
William	217	Pnd
Janey, Joseph	211	Ess
Jankins, Milta	103	Acc
Janners, Abiel	299	Ldn
Janney, Abijah	310	Ldn
Amos	282	Ldn
Aron	491	Frn
Blexton	315	Ldn
David	315	Ldn
Eli	312	Ldn
Elisha	301	Ldn
Geo.	309	Ldn
Hannah	491	Frn
Israel	315	Ldn
Jacob	501	Prw
Jonas	309	Ldn
Jonathan	311	Ldn
Joseph	308	Ldn
Joseph	315	Ldn
Mahlon	298	Ldn
Mahlon	308	Ldn
Mahlon	312	Ldn
Moses	491	Frn
Moses	307	Ldn
Stacey	314	Ldn
Stephen	308	Ldn
Jaques, Thomas	986	Nrt
Jaquish, Rachal	105	Acc
Jardan, Jno.	307	Rck
Jarden, Mills	22	Isw
Jarman, William	163	Alb
Jarmon, James	347	Fqr
Jarrad, Israel	468	Bdf
James B.	646	Sss
John	646	Sss
Joseph	646	Sss
Margaret	646	Sss
Nicholas	646	Sss
Nicholas	647	Sss
Squire	3	Knw
William	647	Sss
see Jarred		
Jarrard, William	348	Lnn
Jarratt, David	753	Brn
Martha	151	Dnw
Richard	327	Dnw
Jarred, David	2	Knw
Jonathan	3	Knw
see Jarrad		
Jarrel, Elijah	567	Mnr
James	71	Spt
Lemuel	565	Mnr
Mary	567	Mnr
Solomon	582	Mnr
William	200	Alb
Jarrell, Elizebeth	392	Mds
Jeremiah	392	Mds
John	392	Mds
Mary	868	Sth
Richard	392	Mds
Sary	392	Mds
Jarret, George	5	Knw
Jarrett, Addey	460	Frn
Allin	500	Frn
Ann	699	Gch
Ben	511	Mnn
David	8	Knw
Devereaux	699	Gch
Jacob	8	Knw
Jesse	6	Knw
John	9	Knw
Justice	510	Mnn
Wm.	511	Mnn
Wm. N.	511	Mnn
Jarrott, Molly	648	Sss
Jarvas, Ann	439	Mth
Frances	450	Mth
James	442	Mth
Jno.	454	Mth
Jno. B.	447	Mth
Jno. D.	437	Mth
Jarvis, ---, & Williamson	2	Hnr
Caty	906	Hrr
Charles	909	Crl
Charles	874	Hnv
Elizabeth	206	Ess
Field	596	Mnr
John	828	Nrf
Joseph	258	Amh
Mildred	659	Gcl
Raymd.	906	Nrf
Susan	876	Yrk
Wm.	807	Nrf
Wm.	927	Nrf
Wm.	876	Yrk
Jasper, Antony	890	Yrk
Archer, free negro	70	Chs
Henry, free negro	70	Chs
Jno.	905	Nrf
Wiley, free negro	70	Chs
Javins, George	269	Frf
James	269	Frf
Jno.	269	Frf
Jno.	270	Frf
Joseph	269	Frf
Javis, Elizabeth	808	Nrf
Jeanes, Jos.	512	Mnn
Jeans, Edward	217	Pnd
John	512	Mnn
John	217	Pnd
Jefers, John	429	Msn
Jefferies, Eliza	5	Hnr
James	813	Bck
John	10	Knw
Mary	813	Bck
Opie	986	Nrt
William	986	Nrt
see Jofres		
Jefferries, James	200	Alb
Jeffers, Henry	451	Grn
John	427	Msn
Jefferson, Benja.	269	Frf
Feild	459	Frn
Field	827	Bck
Hamilton	57	Jff
Henry	367	Fqr
James	465	Mdd
Jeremiah	269	Frf
Jno.	465	Mdd
John	118	Cmb
John	18	Oho
John G.	238	Aml
Peler	347	Lnn
Phabe	831	Nrf
Randolph	785	Bck
Randolph, jr.	811	Bck
Robert L.	827	Bck
Samuel	9	Isw
Samuel	346	Lnn
Thomas, Jur.	162	Alb
Thomas, President of the United States 1801-1805	163	Alb
William	417	Fqr
Wm.	653	Mnt
Jeffery, Rd., Doctr.	906	Nrf
Jeffes, Ephraim	936	Hrr
Jeffreis see Jeffries		
Jeffres, Colman	348	Lnn
George	107	Cmb
James	348	Lnn
John	347	Lnn
Moses	330	Dnw
Richard	347	Lnn
Thomas	347	Lnn
Thomas H.	348	Lnn
Jeffress, Elisha	11	Ntt
Jeffrey, Benjamin	11	Oho
John	485	Frn
John	4	Oho
John	12	Oho
Jeffries, Alexander	346	Fqr
Alexander, (Overseer)	340	Fqr
Alice	168	Knq
Anderson	213	Ess
Ben [2]	511	Mnn
Brian	598	Frd
Den	511	Mnn
Edmond X. [R. ?]	408	Rch
Edward	168	Knq
Elizabeth	168	Knq
Enoch	387	Fqr
Ewell	343	Fqr
George	388	Fqr
James	342	Fqr
James	378	Fqr
Jno., Senr.	48	Clp
Jno. M.	451	Grn
John, Junr.	48	Clp
John, (Overseer)	416	Fqr
Joseph	394	Fqr
Lewis	67	Chs
Margarett	387	Fqr
Moses	47	Clp
Naniel	168	Knq
Pleasant	368	Fqr
Reub.	48	Clp
Richd.	45	Clp
Robert	168	Knq
Thomas	168	Knq
Thomas, BL	168	Knq
Thos.	45	Clp
William	910	Crl
William	342	Fqr

Name	Ref		Name	Ref		Name	Ref	
William S.	444	Grn	Levi	259	Ldn	Jesse, Snr.	112	Hnr
William S.	451	Grn	Littleberry	573	Pre	John	355	Ags
Willis	367	Fqr	Margt.	511	Mnn	John	699	Gch
Wm.	47	Clp	Mary	511	Mnn	John	98	Spt
Wm.	203	Ess	Nancey	272	Frf	Jonathen	21	Oho
Jeffriess, Jeremiah	775	Wst	Obadiah	574	Pre	Laban	647	Sss
Nelly	776	Wst	Prescilla	394	Rch	Langly B.	19	Ntt
Sarah	776	Wst	Priscillai	270	Frf	Lewis	393	Mds
Jeffriss, William	775	Wst	Quire	105	Spt	Littleberry	646	Sss
Jeffry, John B.	168	Knq	Richard	210	Shn	Mary	177	Elc
Jeikie, James	200	Alb	Robert	103	Acc	Mary	11	Ntt
Jeleott, Jos.	821	Nrf	Robert	869	Cmp	Micajah	8	Ntt
Jemm, Ann J.	610	Srr	Robert	403	Rch	Moody	129	Hnr
Jemson, Doctor	124	Hnr	Rosey	183	Elc	Nancy	113	Hnr
Jenings, Edmd.	281	Ldn	Saml.	271	Frf	Nancy	572	Pre
Hazle	62	Stf	Saml.	249	Ldn	Nathan	53	Chr
Mary	49	Clp	Samuel	406	Fqr	Paschal	869	Cmp
Jenkens, Richd.	831	Nrf	Silas	47	Clp	Polly, (W)	877	Yrk
Jenkims, Isham	811	Bck	Simon	254	Ldn	R. C.	905	Nrf
Jenkins, Abraham	468	Bdf	Smith	776	Wst	Robert	303	Amh
Amos	626	Gls	Stephen	563	Frd	Sally	116	Hnr
Ann	882	Sth	Sylvester	272	Frf	Saml., Jr.	112	Hnr
Anthony	572	Pre	Th.	510	Mnn	Samuel K.	848	Cmp
Ben	510	Mnn	Tho.	511	Mnn	Stephen	848	Cmp
Benj.	274	Ldn	Thomas	583	Frd	Thomas	114	Hnr
Benjamin	83	Spt	Thomas	600	Frd	Thomas O.	420	Fqr
Daniel	404	Rch	Thomas	253	Ldn	Thos.	177	Elc
Danl.	269	Frf	Thomas	403	Rch	Thos.	906	Nrf
Dav.	510	Mnn	Thomas	88	Spt	Thos.	927	Nrf
Davd., (Mo.)	47	Clp	Thos.	14	Knw	Tyree	877	Cmp
David	585	Frd	Thos.	204	Kng	William	163	Shn
David	308	Ldn	William	596	Frd	William	164	Shn
David D.	440	Bth	William	626	Gls	Willm.	180	Elc
Dolly	35	Stf	Winfred	775	Wst	see Maupin		
Edward	545	Frd	Winney	776	Wst	Jennkings, Joseph	128	Hnr
Edward, Jr.	545	Frd	Wm.	267	Ldn	Jenny, Daniel	798	Hmp
Edwd.	515	Brk	Wm.	286	Ldn	Free	839	Wth
Elias	295	Ldn	Wm.	272	Rck	Lightfood	126	Hnr
Elisha	524	Prw	see Haney, Jankins, Jinkens,			Jent, Jno.	5	Ntt
Eliz	511	Mnn	Jinkins, Junkons			Jentry, James	891	Hnv
Ephraim	205	Kng	Jenner, Jone	18	Hnr	P. H.	112	Hnr
Ephraim	183	Shn	Jennet, James	39	Rcm	Jephs, Jas.	510	Mnn
Evan	509	Mnn	Jennett, Susanah	118	Hnr	Jerard, Joseph	688	Br
Fanny	253	Ldn	Jenney, Jesse	809	Hmp	Samuel	691	Br
Frank	104	Acc	Ruth	63	Jff	Thomas	698	Br
Gibson	85	Spt	William	798	Hmp	Jerdan, Edward	717	Brn
Hannah	401	Rch	Jenning, Lucy	119	Spt	Freeman	716	Brn
Hanson	270	Frf	Thos.	905	Nrf	John M.	717	Brn
Henry	278	Ldn	Jennings, Alexander W.	349	Lnn	Jerden, ---	952	Chc
Henry	288	Ldn	Allen	573	Pre	Anderson	949	Chc
Herman	403	Rch	Anderson	54	Chr	Edwd.	660	Glc
Jacob	568	Frd	Ann	13	Ntt	Jeredian, L. H.	133	Hnr
Jacob	761	Hmp	Anne	21	Ntt	Jerman, James	199	Alb
James	271	Frf	Augustine	414	Fqr	Pleasant C.	199	Alb
James	392	Rch	Benjn.	12	Pwh	Jerro, Peter	905	Nrf
James	183	Shn	Burwell	647	Sss	Jerrome, Elias	3	Oho
James H.	402	Rch	Chas.	176	Elc	Jerry, Elijah	647	Sss
Jane	508	Frd	Clem A.	54	Chr	Mary	647	Sss
Jerimiah	271	Ldn	Daniel	568	Frd	William	646	Sss
Jesse	920	Hrr	Daniel	12	Pwh	Jervis, Amos	355	Ags
Jno.	47	Clp	David	113	Hnr	Jesper, Danl.	49	Clp
Jno.	271	Frf	Dickenson	54	Chr	George	399	Rch
Jno.	262	Ldn	Edmund	469	Bdf	Jno.	47	Clp
Joel	14	Knw	Edwd.	698	Gch	Peter, (FB)	459	Pra
John	633	Btt	Eliz.	178	Elc	Richard	391	Rch
John	634	Btt	Eliza.	399	Rch	Robt.	47	Clp
John	797	Bck	Elsy	573	Pre	Jesse, Jno.	53	Chs
John	836	Hmp	Fanney	833	Bck	John	184	Shn
John	248	Ldn	George	533	Brk	John, Jr.	465	Mdd
John	511	Mnn	George	53	Chr	John, Senr.	465	Mdd
John	2	Rcm	Henry	8	Ntt	Thomas	574	Pre
John	25	Rcm	Hezh.	112	Hnr	William	574	Pre
John	185	Shn	Isham	112	Hnr	Jessee, Betsy	54	Chr
John	142	Sth	James	54	Chr	John	908	Crl
John, Jur.	626	Gls	James	112	Cmb	Phillip	634	Btt
Jona	511	Mnn	James	123	Cmb	Thomas	119	Cmb
Jos.	512	Mnn	James	522	Prw	Thos.	659	Glc
Joseph	183	Shn	Jamima	821	Bck	Jester, Ader	32	Acc
Judith	699	Gch	Jesse	573	Pre	David	684	Br
Leroy	88	Spt	Jesse	722	Wsh	James	105	Acc

John, Jun. 104 Acc
John, Senr. 105 Acc
Thomas E. 54 Chr
Jestice, Ann 890 Yrk
Swin 24 Hnr
Jeter, Allen 237 Aml
Anderson 237 Aml
Armstead 347 Lnn
Henry 469 Bdf
Henry 633 Btt
Horatio 909 Crl
John 238 Aml
John 451 Grn
John 347 Lnn
Joseph 348 Lnn
Lovereign 469 Bdf
Mary 238 Aml
Pleasant 633 Btt
Rodophil 238 Aml
Tilmon E. 238 Aml
Jett, Anthoney 58 Jff
Bailey 775 Wst
Barsheba 46 Stf
Burkett 909 Crl
Buskett 364 Fqr
Dan 510 Mnn
Francis 715 Brn
Francis 343 Fqr
Franics 60 Stf
George 409 Fqr
George 61 Stf
Gilson 203 Kng
J. 188 Kng
James 203 Kng
James 28 Stf
Jas. 46 Clp
Jas. 753 Wsh
Jessee 98 Spt
Jessee 775 Wst
Jno. [2] 47 Clp
John 923 Hrr
John 205 Kng
John 61 Stf
Mary 363 Fqr
Mathias 47 Clp
Mildred 47 Clp
Mildred 522 Frd
Newton 203 Kng
Patty 775 Wst
Peter 269 Frf
Peter 403 Fqr
Peter 69 Jff
S. 225 Kng
Stephen 204 Kng
Stephen 753 Wsh
Susan 775 Wst
Susanna 47 Clp
Thomas 986 Nrt
Thornton 753 Brn
Washington 71 Jff
William 402 Rch
William 31 Stf
William 775 Wst
William, Jr. 345 Fqr
William, Senr. 363 Fqr
William D. 369 Fqr
William S. 775 Wst
Wm. 48 Clp
Wm. S. 204 Kng
Jew, Zeakle 225 Pnd
Jewel, Jane 4 Rcm
Thos. 662 Mnt
Jewell, Alexander 299 Amh
George 48 Stf
John 776 Wst
Presly 41 Stf
Seth 519 Prw
Thomas 299 Amh
William 775 Wst
Zachariah 588 Frd

Jewry, Lewis 275 Ldn
Mary 275 Ldn
Owen 263 Ldn
Rice 49 Clp
Silas 271 Ldn
Jilcott see Jeleott
Jiles, John 5 Isw
Jiller see Tiller
Jimason, John 476 Frn
Samuel 496 Frn
Jinens, William 724 Wsh
Jinkens, John 839 Wth
Joseph H. 111 Cmb
Mary 839 Wth
Jinkins, Abraham 48 Clp
Abraham 392 Mds
Absolam 875 Hnv
Absolam 892 Hnv
Ambs. 49 Clp
Anthy. 48 Clp
Avy 660 Glc
Benja. 49 Clp
Benja. 660 Glc
Benjamin 874 Hnv
Bennett 267 Amh
Bob, (FB) 15 Ntt
Caleb 660 Glc
Catey 660 Glc
David 898 Hnv
Elijah 644 Mnt
Eliza. 49 Clp
Evin 49 Clp
Ezekiel 644 Mnt
Filding 660 Glc
Isaac 6 Knw
Jacob 660 Glc
James 660 Glc
Jerrimiah 293 Amh
Jno. 49 Clp
Jno. 660 Glc
Jno., Jnr. 895 Hnv
Jno., Snr. 895 Hnv
John 260 Amh
John 706 Nls
John, Senr. 626 Gls
Joseph 936 Hrr
Lewis 660 Glc
Liander 77 Jff
Lucy 105 Cmb
Nathan 392 Mds
Nimrod 392 Mds
Obediah 660 Glc
Osburn 936 Hrr
Patsey 326 Dnw
Polley 704 Nls
Randolph 660 Glc
Rd. 48 Clp
Reuben 48 Clp
Richard 127 Cmb
Richard 392 Mds
Rolin 49 Clp
Salley 875 Hnv
Saml. 660 Glc
Solomon 660 Glc
Stephen 392 Mds
Timothy 48 Clp
Thomas 73 Jff
Valentine 2 Isw
Wilie 23 Isw
William 28 Isw
William 91 Jff
Wm. 355 Ags
Wm. [2] 48 Clp
Wm. 103 Cmb
Wm. 660 Glc
Wm. 49 Clp
Zach. 17 Hnr
Jinks, James
Jirkins see Jinkins
Jiter, John 468 Bdf
Jitt see Jett

Jno. Son, Jeremiah 197 Ess
Joans, Henry 431 Bth
Joarden, John 163 Alb
Job, Charity 529 Brk
Henry 594 Brk
Jacob 355 Ags
Jobe, Sarah 183 Shn
Thomas 182 Shn
Zachariah 177 Shn
Jober, Wm. 510 Mnn
Joblin, Daniel 162 Alb
James, Jur. 162 Alb
James, Senr. 162 Alb
Jobson, Kiziah 459 Pra
Joey see Ivey
Joff, Molley 5 Hnr
Jofres, Haekey 986 Nrt
John, Benjamin 590 Frd
Daniel 403 Fqr
Dav. 511 Mnn
Free 238 Aml
Griffith 646 Mnt
Isaac 709 Wsh
Janney, (F.Negroe) 356 Fqr
Jessee, Jr. 14 Oho
Leml. 512 Mnn
Lewis 510 Mnn
Sarah 331 Dnw
Thomas 403 Fqr
Thomas 828 Hmp
Wm. 510 Mnn
Johns, Amos 876 Yrk
Anthony, Dr. 54 Chr
Betsey 327 Dnw
Charles, (FB) 469 Bdf
Daniel 813 Bck
Davy 546 Prg
Edmund 860 Cmp
Glover 826 Bck
James 282 Amh
James 219 Pnd
Jerimiah 219 Pnd
Jesse, (FB) 468 Bdf
Joel 347 Lnn
John 778 Bck
John 826 Bck
John A. 348 Lnn
Joseph 108 Cmb
Joshua 533 Prg
Lyndsey 849 Cmp
Mallory 286 Amh
Maza 546 Prg
Patterson, (FB) 469 Bdf
Phillip 120 Cmb
Rheubin 113 Cmb
Robt. 654 Mnt
Samuel 783 Bck
Samuel 826 Bck
Sarah 219 Pnd
Stephen 699 Gch
Thomas 284 Amh
Thomas 54 Chr
Thomas 108 Cmb
William 271 Amh
William 778 Bck
Johnson, --- 332 Dnw
---, & Reat 20 Hnr
... 335 Dnw
..., for Andrew
Lewis 478 Frn
...ph 469 Bdf
Abell 42 Isw
Abice 820 Nrf
Abraham 163 Alb
Abraham 200 Alb
Abraham 644 Mnt
Abrm. 529 Brk
Abrm. 137 Sth
Absolam 716 Brn
Absolam 704 Nls

Name	Pg	Co	Name	Pg	Co	Name	Pg	Co
Absolum	199	Alb	Dennis	269	Frf	Jane	237	Ldn
Adam	17	Oho	Draden	272	Frf	Jas.	15	Hnr
Alexr.	280	Rck	Edward	451	Grn	Jere	838	Nrf
Allen	237	Aml	Elijah	9	Isw	Jere.	866	Sth
Allison	504	Prw	Elijah	858	Sth	Jeremiah	52	Chs
Amos	32	Acc	Eliz.	512	Mnn	Jesse	347	Lnn
Amos	302	Ldn	Eliza.	49	Clp	Jesse	573	Pre
Anderson	716	Brn	Elizabeth	508	Prw	Jessee	55	Chr
Andrew	238	Aml	Elizh.	117	Hnr	Jno.	270	Frf
Andrew	573	Pre	Elley	326	Dnw	Jno.	659	Glc
Ann	213	Ess	Ephraim	628	Mnt	Jno.	859	Hnv
Ann	216	Ess	Ezra	4	Oho	Jno.	883	Hnv
Ann	346	Lnn	Frances	508	Prw	Jno.	235	Ldn
Ann	906	Nrf	Francis	775	Wst	Jno.	274	Ldn
Ansolum	469	Bdf	Frans.	326	Dnw	Jno.	290	Ldn
Archabald	168	Knq	General	703	Nls	Jno.	510	Mnn
Archd.	126	Hnr	Geo.	905	Nrf	Jno.	704	Nls
Archibald	524	Prw	George	58	Jff	Jno.	155	Sth
Aron	841	Nrf	George	705	Nls	Jno.	853	Sth
Asa	347	Lnn	George	775	Wst	Jno., Sr.	653	Mnt
Austin	131	Hnr	Gerrard	882	Cmp	Jno. B.	887	Hnv
Baley	2	Wod	Gerrard, Sr.	862	Cmp	Jno. M.	510	Mnn
Bars.	511	Mnn	Gideon	332	Dnw	Joel	716	Brn
Bazel	291	Ldn	Gregory	151	Dnw	Joel	869	Sth
Benj.	31	Hnr	Guy	776	Wst	John	354	Ags
Benj.	704	Nls	Hanah	859	Sth	John	355	Ags
Benj., Jr.	704	Nls	Henrietta	309	Ldn	John	571	Brk
Benja.	48	Clp	Henry	716	Brn	John	581	Brk
Benja.	698	Gch	Henry	132	Hnr	John	633	Btt
Benja.	699	Gch	Henson	254	Ldn	Jo hn	799	Bck
Benja.	160	Sth	Hezekiah	831	Bck	John	873	Cmp
Benja. W.	850	Sth	Hezriah	104	Acc	John [2]	272	Frf
Benjaman	100	Jff	Hugh	238	Ldn	John	474	Frn
Benjamin	163	Alb	Isaac [2]	633	Btt	John	498	Frn
Benjamin	181	Alb	Isaac	330	Dnw	John	699	Gch
Benjamin	199	Alb	Isaac	168	Knq	John	24	Hnr
Benjamin	200	Alb	Isaac	11	Rcm	John	10	Knw
Benjamin	469	Bdf	Isaack	128	Cmb	John	346	Lnn
Benjamin	129	Hnr	Isaah	876	Yrk	John	511	Mnn
Benjamin	8	Knw	Isabella	906	Nrf	John	587	Mnr
Benjamin	706	Nls	Isabella	927	Nrf	John	706	Nls
Benjamin, jr.	716	Brn	Isaiah	103	Acc	John	906	Nrf
Benjamin, Se.	716	Brn	Isaiah	478	Frn	John	573	Pre
Bennett	270	Frf	Isham	286	Amh	John	15	Wod
Betsey	326	Dnw	Isham	355	Ags	John, (Cpl.)	442	Flv
Betsey	8	Hnr	Isham	451	Grn	John, jr.	468	Bdf
Betsy	130	Hnr	Jacob	185	Elc	John, Jr.	868	Cmp
Bicket G.	45	Clp	Jacob	627	Gls	John, (Jr.)	430	Flv
Britain	844	Sth	Jacob	698	Gch	John, jr.	348	Lnn
C.	355	Ags	Jacob	43	Isw	John, Jun.	22	Isw
C.	402	Ags	Jacob	607	Mnt	John, Sen.	22	Isw
Caleb	103	Acc	Jacob	704	Nls	John, Sen.	43	Isw
Casper	276	Ldn	Jacob	20	Oho	John, Senr.	573	Pre
Charles	854	Cmp	James	104	Acc	John, Sr.	468	Bdf
Charles	881	Cmp	James [2]	238	Aml	John, Sr.	348	Lnn
Charles	699	Gch	James	355	Ags	John, (W)	445	Flv
Cholle.	905	Nrf	James	414	Bth	John H.	55	Chr
Chrisey	776	Wst	James	468	Bdf	Jonathan	881	Cmp
Christopher	788	Bck	James	579	Brk	Jordan	155	Sth
Clabron	706	Nls	James [2]	633	Btt	Jos.	837	Nrf
Clary	203	Ess	James	831	Bck	Joseph, Jun.	44	Isw
Clary	123	Hnr	James	861	Cmp	Joseph, Sen.	42	Isw
Constantia	124	Hnr	James	862	Cmp	Joshua	199	Alb
Cornelious	347	Lnn	James	54	Chr	Joshua	334	Dnw
Councel	156	Sth	James	221	Ess	Joshua	349	Lnn
Curtes	162	Alb	James	451	Grn	Joshua	152	Sth
Daniel	61	Chs	James	9	Isw	Josseph	930	Hrr
Daniel	69	Jff	James	41	Isw	Js., Capt.	906	Nrf
Danl.	698	Gch	James	704	Nls	Julious	346	Lnn
Davd.	48	Clp	James	705	Nls	Kate, Jun. (F.N.)	43	Isw
David	468	Bdf	James [2]	906	Nrf	Kate, Sen. (F.N.)	40	Isw
David	507	Brk	James	927	Nrf	Kiddey, (F.N.)	43	Isw
David	451	Grn	James	12	Oho	Kidey, (F.N.)	9	Isw
David	853	Hnv	James	24	Oho	Kinchen	22	Isw
David	80	Jff	James, Jun.	4	Isw	Laban	43	Isw
David	757	Nwk	James, Junr.	775	Wst	Lemma	105	Acc
David	504	Prw	James, Senr.	776	Wst	Lemuel	469	Bdf
David	610	Srr	James, Sr.	864	Cmp	Lemuel	42	Isw
David, Sr.	452	Grn	James, Younger	775	Wst	Levi	905	Nrf
David L.	848	Hnv	James, B.H.	439	Mth	Levy	609	Srr

Name	No.	Co.
Lewis	200	Alb
Lewis	753	Brn
Lewis	804	Bck
Lewis	17	Isw
Lewis	3	Oho
Littleberry	333	Dnw
Lively	705	Nls
Lucetia	775	Wst
Lucey	872	Sth
Lucy	716	Brn
Lucy	2	Hnr
Major	130	Hnr
Margaret	354	Ags
Margeret	413	Rch
Martin	199	Alb
Mary	354	Ags
Mary	213	Ess
Mary	659	Glc
Mary	452	Grn
Mary	698	Gch
Mary	117	Hnr
Mary	609	Srr
Matthew	17	Isw
Michael	426	Bth
Michal	349	Lnn
Micheal	480	Frn
Molly, of Joseh.	104	Acc
Moorman	856	Cmp
Moses	349	Lnn
Moses	142	Sth
Moses	610	Srr
Nace	776	Wst
Nancey	34	Rcm
Nancy	115	Cmb
Nancy	334	Dnw
Nancy	698	Gch
Nancy	27	Hnr
Nancy	123	Hnr
Nancy	47	Isw
Nancy	703	Nls
Nancy	515	Prw
Nancy, etc.	270	Frf
Nat	510	Mnn
Nathan	481	Frn
Nathan	139	Sth
Nathl.	355	Ags
Naum	69	Chr
Newby	872	Cmp
Nicholas	469	Bdf
Nicholas	887	Hnv
Obadiah	117	Cmb
Obediah	163	Alb
Obediah	487	Frn
Oliver	54	Chr
Orsmus	614	Mnt
Patty	776	Wst
Peggy	775	Wst
Perter	705	Nls
Peter	905	Nrf
Peter	573	Pre
Peter	610	Srr
Philip	293	Amh
Philip	817	Bck
Philip	208	Ess
Philip	238	Ldn
Philip	572	Pre
Phillip	451	Grn
Pitway	156	Sth
Pleasant	856	Cmp
Polly	104	Acc
Polly, FN	104	Acc
Primis	776	Wst
Prince	775	Wst
Prince, Jnr.	776	Wst
Pumphrey	442	Flv
Rachel	2	Oho
Randolph	610	Srr
Rebecca	54	Chr
Reuben	347	Lnn
Reubin, Junr.	54	Chr
Reubin, Snr.	54	Chr
Richard	162	Alb
Richard	163	Alb
Richard	182	Alb
Richard	468	Bdf
Richard	774	Bck
Richard	852	Hnv
Richard	88	Jff
Richard	610	Srr
Richard	776	Wst
Richd.	238	Aml
Richd.	213	Ess
Richd.	698	Gch
Richd.	512	Mnn
Richd.	599	Mnr
Richd.	131	Sth
Richd.	857	Sth
Robert	866	Cmp
Robert	54	Chr
Robert	55	Chr
Robert	42	Isw
Robert	586	Mnr
Robert	705	Nls
Robt.	579	Brk
Robt.	23	Hnr
Robt.	132	Hnr
Roger	927	Nrf
Rutland, Jr.	527	Prw
Rutland, Sr.	527	Prw
S. H.	119	Hnr
Saml.	183	Elc
Saml.	209	Ess
Saml.	699	Gch
Saml.	32	Hnr
Saml.	499	Prw
Saml., jr.	210	Ess
Samuel	103	Acc
Samuel	418	Bth
Samuel	858	Cmp
Samuel	878	Cmp
Samuel	269	Frf
Samuel	8	Hnr
Samuel	705	Nls
Sarah	162	Alb
Sarah	270	Frf
Sarah	8	Rcm
Sarah	610	Srr
Shedrick	910	Hrr
Sius, (Est)	55	Chr
Spencer	163	Alb
Stanhope	443	Flv
Stephen	355	Ags
Stephen	699	Gch
Stephen	706	Nls
Stephen	157	Sth
Stutton	272	Frf
Susanna	150	Dnw
Susannah	706	Nls
Sylvanus	632	Btt
Tabby	328	Dnw
Thomas	200	Alb
Thomas	468	Bdf
Thomas	469	Bdf
Thomas	830	Bck
Thomas	854	Cmp
Thomas	873	Cmp
Thomas	98	Cmb
Thomas	150	Dnw
Thomas	114	Hnr
Thomas	47	Isw
Thomas	80	Jff
Thomas	168	Knq
Thomas	576	Mnr
Thomas	1	Oho
Thomas	572	Pre
Thomas	9	Pwh
Thomas	129	Sth
Thomas	776	Wst
Thomas	4	Wod
Thomas	5	Wod
Thomas, Junr.	775	Wst
Thomas, SS	104	Acc
Thomas, Senr.	775	Wst
Thomas B.	704	Nls
Thos.	517	Brk
Thos.	646	Btt
Thos.	47	Clp
Thos.	86	Jff
Thos.	289	Ldn
Thos.	292	Ldn
Thos.	628	Mnt
Thos.	905	Nrf
Thos., (W)	876	Yrk
Thos. M.	659	Glc
Walter	435	Flv
Watkins	573	Pre
William	31	Acc
William	104	Acc
William	199	Alb
William	468	Bdf
William	830	Bck
William	850	Cmp
William	881	Cmp
William [2]	54	Chr
William	326	Dnw
William	332	Dnw
William	269	Frf
William	627	Gls
William	22	Isw
William	347	Lnn
William	758	Nwk
William	573	Pre
William	173	Shn
William	181	Shn
William	775	Wst
William, Jr.	816	Bck
William, (Son Naum)	54	Chr
William E.	704	Nls
William T.	12	Pwh
Willis	875	Sth
Wim.	877	Hnv
Wm.	579	Brk
Wm.	634	Btt
Wm.	46	Clp
Wm.	48	Clp
Wm. [2]	271	Frf
Wm.	437	Flv
Wm. [2]	698	Gch
Wm.	699	Gch
Wm.	273	Ldn
Wm.	275	Ldn
Wm.	439	Mth
Wm.	599	Mnr
Wm.	703	Nls
Wm.	705	Nls
Wm.	706	Nls
Wm.	821	Nrf
Wm.	832	Nrf
Wm. [2]	906	Nrf
Wm.	542	Prg
Wm., Jr.	716	Brn
Wm., jr.	717	Brn
Wm., jr.	47	Clp
Wm., (Y)	876	Yrk
Wm. B.	204	Kng
Wm. G.	46	Clp
Wm. L.	434	Flv
Wm. M.	716	Brn
Wm. W.	634	Btt
Younger	203	Kng
Zach.	633	Btt
Zachariah	42	Isw
Zadock	105	Acc
see Ballard, Hodges, Jno. Son, Johrson, Keeton, Mallory, Martin, Pearson, Philips		
Johnsons, James	799	Bck
Johnsten, Jehu	227	Pnd
John	227	Pnd
Joss...h	224	Pnd

Samuel	223	Pnd	John	788	Hmp	William	627	Gls
Johnston, Abel	693	Br	John [2]	827	Hmp	William	787	Hmp
Abraham	927	Hrr	John	927	Hrr	William	827	Hmp
Adam	627	Gls	John	8	Knw	William	393	Mds
Agness	69	Spt	John	429	Msn	William	421	Msn
Allen	910	Crl	John	613	Mnt	William	713	Wsh
Alloner	703	Wsh	John	811	Nrf	William	839	Wth
Amos	684	Br	John	82	Spt	William, (F. Negroe)	420	Fqr
Amos	570	Frd	John	729	Wsh	Williamson	740	Wsh
Andrew	627	Gls	John [2]	839	Wth	Willis	417	Fqr
Ann	114	Spt	John, Jur.	729	Wsh	Wm.	303	Ldn
Anne	8	Knw	John S.	68	Spt	Wm.	296	Rck
Anthony P.	951	Chc	Jonathan	104	Spt	Wm., Jr.	205	Kng
Armstrong	601	Frd	Joseph	557	Frd	Wm., Sr.	203	Kng
Atwell	572	Frd	Joseph	569	Frd	Yelles	417	Fqr
Aylce	114	Spt	Joseph	766	Hmp	Young J.	451	Grn
Bailey, Senr.	344	Fqr	Joseph	788	Hmp	Zach.	299	Rck
Barnabas	839	Wth	Joseph	393	Mds	Johnstone, Barton	46	Stf
Beede	410	Fqr	Joseph, (Overseer)	397	Fqr	Elizabeth	30	Isw
Bengamin	780	Hmp	Larkin	840	Wth	George	26	Stf
Benjamin	421	Msn	Larkins	204	Kng	James	40	Isw
Benjamin	66	Spt	Launcelot	543	Frd	John	40	Stf
Catharine	822	Hmp	Levina	590	Frd	Johrson, John, (R)	443	Flv
Celia	648	Sss	Mary	813	Nrf	Joiner, Absalom	158	Sth
Charles	410	Fqr	Mary	839	Wth	Dolly	332	Dnw
Charles	568	Frd	Matthew	222	Pnd	Eli	152	Sth
Charles L.	909	Crl	Mildred	76	Spt	Elisha	158	Sth
Chilton	364	Fqr	Moses	419	Fqr	Jere.	152	Sth
Collins	648	Sss	Moses	451	Grn	John	150	Dnw
Daniel	418	Fqr	Murty	585	Frd	John	156	Sth
David	569	Frd	Nancy	787	Hmp	John	881	Sth
David	627	Gls	Nimrod	369	Fqr	Jordan	138	Sth
David	289	Ldn	Okey	822	Hmp	Joseph	155	Sth
Dennis	507	Frd	Okey	824	Hmp	Joseph	158	Sth
Drusilla	205	Kng	Peter	927	Hrr	Joseph	881	Sth
Edmond	646	Sss	Phebe	595	Frd	Joshua [2]	158	Sth
Eleanor	766	Hmp	Philip	910	Crl	Kinchen	847	Sth
Elisebeth	732	Wsh	Philip	541	Frd	Lemuel	867	Sth
Elizabeth	537	Frd	Philip, Senr.	541	Frd	Matt	158	Sth
Elizabeth	646	Sss	Rebeca	596	Frd	Michl.	156	Sth
Epham	705	Wsh	Rebecca	451	Grn	Milley	867	Cmp
Esther	839	Wth	Reuben	909	Crl	Nancy	325	Dnw
Fauntley	909	Crl	Reuben	627	Gls	Polly	330	Dnw
Frederick	595	Frd	Richard	85	Spt	Sarah	161	Sth
George	344	Fqr	Richard	86	Spt	Sinclair	157	Sth
George	585	Frd	Richard	93	Spt	Thomas	334	Dnw
George [2]	595	Frd	Richard	108	Spt	William	870	Cmp
Gideon	420	Fqr	Richard L.	114	Spt	Willie	161	Sth
Hugh	627	Gls	Robert	548	Frd	Wm. B. ["B" crossed		
Hugh	839	Wth	Robert	204	Kng	out]	154	Sth
Isaac	441	Bth	Robert	646	Sss	see Joyner		
Isaac	796	Hmp	Robert	648	Sss	Joins see Jones		
Isaac	806	Hmp	Robert	720	Wsh	Joliff, John	510	Mnn
Isaac	426	Rnd	Roswell	663	Mnt	Wm.	511	Mnn
Israel	396	Fqr	Salley	352	Fqr	Wm., Senr.	510	Mnn
Jacob	704	Wsh	Saml.	705	Wsh	Joliffe, Mary	818	Nrf
Jacob, (FB)	15	Ntt	Saml.	747	Wsh	Jollet, John	580	Brk
James	150	Dnw	Saml.	752	Wsh	Jolley, Colwell	150	Dnw
James	544	Frd	Samuel	585	Frd	Edward	150	Dnw
James	626	Gls	Smith	402	Fqr	Elizabeth	573	Pre
James	451	Grn	Stephen	561	Frd	Jacob	397	Fqr
James	761	Hmp	Susan	598	Frd	Robt.	125	Hnr
James	800	Hmp	Susan	118	Spt	Wm.	132	Hnr
James	278	Rck	Susanna	513	Frd	Jollif, James	947	Hrr
James	306	Rck	Susanna	117	Spt	Thomas	947	Hrr
James	70	Spt	Suzanna	827	Hmp	Jolliff, Scasebrooke	38	Isw
James	109	Spt	Thomas	423	Bth	Jolliffe, John	537	Frd
James, Jur.	627	Gls	Thomas	697	Br	Jolly, Benjamin	557	Frd
Jas.	800	Nrf	Thomas	950	Chc	John, Jun.	4	Isw
Jemima	417	Fqr	Thomas	387	Fqr	Lewis	647	Sss
Jeremiah	415	Fqr	Thomas	767	Hmp	Nancy	272	Frf
Jno.	459	Pra	Thomas	108	Spt	Jolsen, Samuel	589	Brk
Jno. J.	13	Hnr	Thos.	307	Rck	Jonas, Isaac	465	Mdd
John	425	Bth	Thos.	714	Wsh	John	565	Frd
John	691	Br	Wilford	338	Fqr	Jonathan, Abram	610	Srr
John	530	Frd	William	908	Crl	Ben., a free mulotto	987	Nrt
John	596	Frd	William	909	Crl	Moses	131	Hnr
John	773	Hmp	William	352	Fqr	Jones, ---, Morriss &	16	Ntt
John	775	Hmp	William	522	Frd	Abednege, (M)	718	Brn
John	787	Hmp	William	575	Frd	Abraham	829	Bck

Name	No.	Abbr.	Name	No.	Abbr.	Name	No.	Abbr.
Abraham	38	Isw	Creden	944	Hrr	Flem.	510	Mnn
Abraham	19	Oho	Dabny	14	Knw	Francis	634	Btt
Abraham	232	Shn	Danl.	582	Mnr	Francis	97	Jff
Abram	485	Frn	Daniel	698	Br	Frans.	20	Ntt
Abram	646	Sss	Daniel	358	Fqr	Fras. S.	46	Clp
Absolam	875	Hnv	Daniel	758	Nwk	Fred	326	Dnw
Agness	200	Alb	Daniel	573	Pre	Fred	547	Prg
Allen	633	Btt	Daniel	28	Stf	Frederic	451	Grn
Allen	23	Isw	Danl.	297	Rck	Frederick	128	Cmb
Allen	126	Sth	Darnall	384	Fqr	Gabriel	469	Bdf
Allen	47	Stf	Davd.	709	Wsh	Gabriel	659	Glc
Allen	678	Wrw	Davey, f. negro	270	Frf	Gabriel	874	Hnv
Ambe, Sr.	633	Btt	David	469	Bdf	Gabriel	8	Knw
Ambrose	469	Bdf	David	632	Btt	Gabriel	51	Stf
Ambrose	909	Crl	David	858	Cmp	Gabriel, Estate	465	Mdd
Ambrose	392	Mds	David	53	Chr	Geo.	430	Flv
America	328	Dnw	David	55	Chr	Geo.	318	Ldn
Amey	633	Btt	David	151	Dnw	Geo.	6	Ntt
Ann [2]	168	Knq	David	445	Flv	Geo. M.	204	Kng
Anne	238	Aml	David	698	Gch	George	104	Acc
Ansalom	451	Grn	David	346	Lnn	George	237	Aml
Anthony	777	Bck	David, Jnr.	846	Hnv	George	437	Bth
Anthony, (N)	718	Brn	David, jr.	445	Flv	George	567	Brk
Anthony D.	802	Bck	David, jr.	204	Kng	George	676	Br
Archer	238	Aml	David, (Otter)	469	Bdf	George	373	Fqr
Archer	11	Ntt	David, Snr.	846	Hnv	George	918	Hrr
Argyle	927	Nrf	David, Sr.	203	Kng	George	933	Hrr
Armstead	346	Lnn	David C.	238	Aml	George	85	Jff
Arthur	807	Bck	Davidson	827	Bck	George	204	Kng
Arthur	16	Isw	Davis	327	Dnw	George	986	Nrt
Barbara	573	Frd	Demsey	835	Nrf	George	573	Pre
Barbara O.	896	Hnv	Dennis	280	Ldn	George	410	Rch
Barbary	240	Shn	Dudley	878	Cmp	George	178	Shn
Bayley	29	Stf	Dudley	54	Chr	George	24	Stf
Ben	510	Mnn	Dudley	294	Rck	George	647	Sss
Ben	512	Mnn	Edmd.	204	Ess	George, of C.	40	Stf
Benedict	270	Frf	Edmon	497	Frn	George C.	130	Cmb
Benja.	698	Gch	Edmund	909	Crl	George H.	716	Brn
Benja.	451	Grn	Edmund	3	Knw	Gipson	34	Hnr
Benja.	168	Knq	Edvard	796	Nrf	Godfry, Snr.	53	Chr
Benja.	866	Sth	Edward	468	Bdf	Gray	646	Sss
Benjamin	716	Brn	Edward	774	Bck	Hall	151	Dnw
Benjamin	214	Ess	Edward	374	Fqr	Hannah	350	Lnc
Benjamin	451	Grn	Edward	758	Nwk	Hannah, a free mu-		
Benjamin	120	Hnr	Edward	7	Ntt	latto	986	Nrt
Benjamin	36	Isw	Edward	97	Spt	Hardy	9	Isw
Benjamin	204	Kng	Edward B.	531	Frd	Harrison	698	Gch
Benjamin	89	Spt	Edwd.	221	Ess	Harrison, D.	122	Cmb
Benjamin, Sr.	882	Cmp	Edwd. H.	151	Dnw	Harry	248	Ldn
Billey [?]	132	Hnr	Elias	813	Hmp	Henry	414	Bth
Branch	347	Lnn	Elis	697	Br	Henry	49	Clp
Cadwallender	54	Chr	Elisabeth	757	Nwk	Henry	3	Isw
Cadwallender, Senr.	54	Chr	Eliza. [2]	49	Clp	Henry	572	Pre
Catesby	373	Fqr	Eliza.	205	Ess	Henry	879	Sth
Catesby	986	Nrt	Eliza.	211	Ess	Henry	61	Stf
Cesar	184	Elc	Eliza.	217	Ess	Henry	648	Sss
Chalmers, & Co.	332	Dnw	Eliza.	679	Wrw	Henry	712	Wsh
Chamberlain	237	Aml	Elizabeth	162	Alb	Henry, (E. fd.)	45	Clp
Charles	163	Alb	Elizabeth	716	Brn	Henry B.	868	Hnv
Charles	468	Bdf	Elizabeth	805	Bck	Henry H.	858	Hnv
Charles	676	Br	Elizabeth	758	Hmp	Henry Winn	5	Ntt
Charles	805	Bck	Elizabeth	29	Isw	Herbert	38	Isw
Charles	838	Bck	Elizabeth	504	Prw	Hopkins	432	Bth
Charles	542	Frd	Elizabeth	610	Srr	Howell	451	Grn
Charles	2	Knw	Elizabeth	647	Sss	Howell	647	Sss
Charles	204	Kng	Elliot	199	Alb	Hugh	205	Kng
Charles	704	Nls	Ely	580	Mnr	Ignatius	269	Frf
Charles	758	Nwk	Emanuel	660	Glc	Irby	609	Srr
Charles	112	Spt	Emanuel	882	Sth	Isaac	684	Br
Charles, jr.	29	Stf	Enoch	354	Ags	Isaac	595	Frd
Charles, Sr.	29	Stf	Enoch	509	Mnn	Isaac	32	Isw
Chesley	758	Nwk	Enus, (M)	718	Brn	Isaac	708	Wsh
Chestator	579	Mnr	Eppa	398	Rch	Isacc	111	Spt
Christopher	716	Brn	Erasmus	875	Cmp	Isaiah	354	Ags
Christopher T.	331	Dnw	Erasmus	205	Ess	J.R.	21	Hnr
Churchill	60	Stf	Esther	812	Hmp	J.W.	292	Ldn
Churchill, Qre.	392	Mds	Ezekial	839	Wth	J..., (Upper)	28	Stf
Cillar	757	Nwk	Ezekiel	9	Hnr	Jacob	633	Btt
Clarissa	390	Fqr	Fanny	909	Crl	Jacob	873	Cmp
Colvert	203	Kng	Flamstead	782	Bck	Jacob	512	Mnn

Name	No.	Loc.
Jacob, Jur.	512	Mnn
James	105	Acc
James	469	Bdf
James	634	Btt
James	849	Cmp
James	866	Cmp
James [2]	909	Crl
James	910	Crl
James	48	Clp
James	331	Dnw
James	332	Dnw
James	380	Fqr
James	464	Frn
James	659	Glc
James	4	Hnr
James	35	Hnr
James	113	Hnr
James	119	Hnr
James	350	Lnc
James	346	Lnn
James	576	Mnr
James	580	Mnr
James	706	Nls
James	217	Pnd
James	162	Sth
James [2]	857	Sth
James	112	Spt
James	28	Stf
James	609	Srr
James [2]	839	Wth
James, (M)	717	Brn
James, not Taken	33	Hnr
James, Snr.	168	Knq
James E.	396	Rch
James S.	869	Cmp
Jane	910	Crl
Jane	47	Clp
Jane	401	Fqr
Jane	880	Hnv
Jane	506	Prw
Jared	647	Sss
Jas.	47	Clp
Jas.	510	Mnn
Jeremiah	627	Gls
Jeremiah	402	Rch
Jesse	281	Amh
Jesse	468	Bdf
Jesse	563	Brk
Jesse	49	Clp
Jesse	395	Fqr
Jessee	909	Crl
Jessee	910	Crl
Jinney	417	Bth
Jno.	46	Clp
Jno.	49	Clp
Jno.	867	Hnv
Jno.	890	Hnv
Jno.	235	Ldn
Jno.	264	Ldn
Jno., S.G.	887	Hnv
Jno. L.	898	Hnv
Jo	929	Hrr
Joanna	681	Wrw
Joel	47	Clp
Joel	848	Hnv
John	163	Alb
John	179	Alb
John	439	Bth
John	510	Brk
John	716	Brn
John	836	Bck
John	862	Cmp
John	877	Cmp
John [3]	910	Crl
John	54	Chr
John	150	Dnw
John	151	Dnw
John	204	Ess
John	371	Fqr
John	373	Fqr
John	444	Flv
John	532	Frd
John	539	Frd
John	552	Frd
John	626	Gls
John	627	Gls
John	790	Hmp
John	13	Isw
John	89	Jff
John	9	Knw
John	168	Knq
John	392	Mds
John	512	Mnn
John	576	Mnr
John	579	Mnr
John	585	Mnr
John	791	Nrf
John	3	Ntt
John	19	Oho
John	24	Oho
John	215	Pnd
John	219	Pnd
John	392	Rch
John	405	Rch
John	409	Rch
John	273	Rck
John	165	Shn
John	89	Spt
John	94	Spt
John	647	Sss
John	679	Wrw
John	708	Wsh
John	839	Wth
John, F.N.	34	Isw
John, F.N.	647	Sss
John, Jr.	237	Aml
John, jr.	150	Dnw
John, jr.	205	Kng
John, Jun.	105	Acc
John, Jur.	680	Wrw
John, Jur.	708	Wsh
John, of W.C.	27	Stf
John, (S of B)	219	Ess
John, (S of E)	204	Ess
John, Sen.	105	Acc
John, Senr.	205	Kng
John, Sr.	237	Aml
John A.	841	Bck
John C.	716	Brn
John C.	827	Bck
John H.	102	Cmb
John S.	866	Cmp
Jonathan	909	Crl
Jonathan	11	Knw
Jonathn.	576	Brk
Jonathun	4	Hnr
Josa.	511	Mnn
Joseph	634	Btt
Joseph	151	Dnw
Joseph	217	Ess
Joseph	353	Fqr
Joseph	35	Isw
Joseph	168	Knq
Joseph	205	Kng
Joseph	568	Mnr
Joseph	986	Nrt
Joseph	1	Oho
Joseph	224	Pnd
Joseph	34	Rcm
Joseph	60	Stf
Joseph	328	Dnw
Joseph	328	Dnw
Joseph	544	Frd
Joseph, Genl.	45	Clp
Joseph, Jr.	46	Clp
Joseph H.	818	Hmp
Josh.	392	Mds
Joshua	649	Mnt
Joshua	706	Nls
Joshua	219	Shn
Josias	841	Bck
Judy	392	Mds
Kary	150	Dnw
Kennon	753	Brn
Kennon	150	Dnw
Kim	876	Yrk
L. P.	24	Hnr
Landy	117	Hnr
Laney	896	Hnv
Langston	118	Hnr
Lee	48	Clp
Lemuel	346	Lnn
Leven	775	Wst
Levi	9	Knw
Lew	348	Lnn
Lewallen	781	Bck
Lewellin, residg in Nottoway	151	Dnw
Lewin	270	Frf
Lewis	151	Dnw
Lewis	704	Nls
Lewis	52	Stf
Lewis	839	Wth
Lewton	131	Sth
Littlebury H.	633	Btt
Lizzy	910	Crl
Loving	7	Hnr
Loyd	272	Frf
Lucy	26	Hnr
Lucy	34	Hnr
Lucy	119	Hnr
Lucy	407	Rch
Luellin, (ME)	54	Chr
Lydda	510	Prw
Mark	816	Nrf
Martha	238	Aml
Mary	47	Clp
Mary	208	Ess
Mary	659	Glc
Mary	880	Hnv
Mary	963	Hrr
Mary	38	Isw
Mary	13	Ntt
Mary	548	Prg
Mary	509	Prw
Mary	877	Sth
Mary	13	Wod
Mary, (FB)	459	Pra
Mary Ann	203	Ess
Maryann	875	Hnv
Melanthe	906	Nrf
Michael	787	Bck
Michael	891	Hnv
Milly	350	Lnc
Mishall	48	Clp
Moreland	647	Sss
Morgan	8	Oho
Morgan	26	Oho
Morris	986	Nrt
Moses	568	Brk
Moses	910	Crl
Moses	270	Frf
Moses	809	Hmp
Moses, (M)	718	Brn
Nancy	376	Fqr
Nancy	355	Ags
Nancy	753	Brn
Nancy	151	Dnw
Nancy	333	Dnw
Nancy	580	Frd
Nancy	25	Hnr
Nancy	119	Hnr
Nancy	757	Nwk
Nancy	758	Nwk
Nathan	491	Frn
Nathan	568	Frd
Nathan	609	Srr
Ned, (M)	717	Brn
Nelson	150	Dnw
Nelson	595	Frd

Name	#	Abbr	Name	#	Abbr	Name	#	Abbr
Nelson	758	Nwk	Saml.	204	Kng	Thomas D.	393	Rch
Nicholas	9	Knw	Saml.	512	Mnn	Thos. [2]	47	Clp
Nicholas	266	Rck	Saml., Jr.	238	Aml	Thos.	45	Clp
Nicholes	94	Spt	Saml., Sr.	238	Aml	Thos.	659	Glc
Noah	16	Hnr	Samuel	575	Frd	Thos.	797	Nrf
Norman	46	Clp	Samuel	900	Hnv	Thos.	927	Nrf
Notley	271	Frf	Samuel	906	Hrr	Thos.	153	Sth
Owen	468	Bdf	Samuel	963	Hrr	Thos.	746	Wsh
Owen	7	Oho	Samuel	33	Hnr	Thos., Senr.	659	Glc
Partrick	6	Ntt	Samuel	583	Mnr	Tilbury	580	Frd
Paschal	18	Ntt	Samuel	14	Pwh	Timothy	46	Clp
Patsey	900	Hnv	Samuel	846	Sth	Topsall, (M)	718	Brn
Patty, (F.N.)	38	Isw	Samuel	115	Spt	Valentine	578	Mnr
Paul G.G.	10	Hnr	Samuel, (Captn.)	801	Bck	Vincent	397	Rch
Peggy	118	Hnr	Samuel, (M)	718	Brn	Walker	330	Dnw
Peter	355	Ags	Sanford	394	Rch	Walter	125	Cmb
Peter	557	Brk	Sar...	757	Hmp	Walter	986	Nrt
Peter	790	Hmp	Sarah	910	Crl	Watts	204	Kng
Peter	204	Kng	Sarah	188	Elc	Wenny	351	Lnc
Peter	3	Ntt	Sarah	85	Jff	Wiley	5	Ntt
Peter	535	Prg	Sarah	264	Ldn	William	105	Acc
Peter, (D)	238	Aml	Scerv.	681	Wrw	William	293	Amh
Peter, jr.	347	Lnn	Sely	549	Prg	William	442	Bth
Peter, Sr.	347	Lnn	Shedrick	633	Btt	William	444	Bth
Peter B.	1	Ntt	Short	54	Chr	William	909	Crl
Philip P.	46	Clp	Simpson	839	Wth	William	910	Crl
Phillip	53	Chr	Stanfield	909	Crl	William	328	Dnw
Plesant	889	Hnv	Stanfield	910	Crl	William	352	Fqr
Polly	104	Acc	Stephen	468	Bdf	William	481	Frn
Precia	882	Sth	Stephen	48	Clp	William	491	Frn
Precilla	277	Ldn	Stephen	346	Lnn	William	494	Frn
Prudance	237	Aml	Susanah	113	Hnr	William	507	Frd
Publeus	857	Cmp	Susanna	909	Crl	William	523	Frd
Rebecca	459	Pra	Susanna	645	Sss	William	539	Frd
Rebecca	857	Sth	Tabner	392	Mds	William	626	Gls
Reps	18	Ntt	Theoderick	348	Lnn	William	813	Hmp
Reubin	118	Hnr	Tho.	179	Elc	William	9	Knw
Richard	293	Amh	Tho.	350	Lnc	William	347	Lnn
Richard	682	Br	Thomas	103	Acc	William	348	Lnn
Richard	909	Crl	Thomas	199	Alb	William	392	Mds
Richard	55	Chr	Thomas	468	Bdf	William [2]	758	Nwk
Richard	150	Dnw	Thomas	716	Brn	William	987	Nrt
Richard	35	Isw	Thomas	882	Cmp	William	574	Pre
Richd.	212	Ess	Thomas	909	Crl	William	33	Rcm
Richd.	219	Ess	Thomas	271	Frf	William	94	Spt
Richd.	659	Glc	Thomas	372	Fqr	William	100	Spt
Richd.	919	Hrr	Thomas	485	Frn	William	106	Spt
Richd.	112	Hnr	Thomas	559	Frd	William	45	Stf
Richd.	168	Knq	Thomas	582	Frd	William	57	Stf
Richd., Est.	237	Aml	Thomas	813	Hmp	William	609	Srr
Richd. C.	659	Glc	Thomas	846	Hnv	William	690	Wsh
Richd. M.	237	Aml	Thomas	945	Hrr	William, (C)	792	Bck
Rihd.	1	Ntt	Thomas	3	Isw	William, (C. Spring)	355	Fqr
Robert	716	Brn	Thomas	78	Jff	William, (F.N.)	34	Isw
Robert	55	Chr	Thomas	7	Knw	William, jr.	758	Nwk
Robert	358	Fqr	Thomas	9	Knw	William, (O.A)	833	Bck
Robert	484	Frn	Thomas	168	Knq	William, (S.Ro.)	784	Bck
Robert	813	Hmp	Thomas	275	Ldn	William, Sr.	469	Bdf
Robert	757	Nwk	Thomas	348	Lnn	William L.	282	Amh
Robert	126	Sth	Thomas	706	Nls	William P.	276	Amh
Robert	610	Srr	Thomas	906	Nrf	William R.	468	Bdf
Robert	646	Sss	Thomas [2]	21	Oho	William S.	541	Frd
Robert, (M)	718	Brn	Thomas	227	Pnd	Willie	856	Sth
Robert, (Senr.)	783	Bck	Thomas	165	Shn	Willis	716	Brn
Robert, Sr.	648	Sss	Thomas	245	Shn	Willis	986	Nrt
Robert E.	758	Nwk	Thomas	71	Spt	Willis	610	Srr
Robert S.	168	Knq	Thomas	103	Spt	Willm.	580	Mnr
Robt.	355	Ags	Thomas	106	Spt	Willm.	620	Mnt
Robt.	48	Clp	Thomas	44	Stf	Wills	756	Wsh
Robt.	328	Dnw	Thomas	610	Srr	Wim.	899	Hnv
Robt., [his] Est.	13	Ntt	Thomas	646	Sss	Winfield	646	Sss
Roger	6	Hnr	Thomas, C.P.	874	Cmp	Wm.	557	Brk
Roger	118	Hnr	Thomas, F.N.	647	Sss	Wm.	46	Clp
Russel	199	Alb	Thomas, Jr.	869	Cmp	Wm.	445	Flv
Salley	355	Ags	Thomas, (of Ba [?])	207	Ess	Wm. [2]	660	Glc
Salley	987	Nrt	Thomas, (S of B)	222	Ess	Wm.	262	Ldn
Sally	119	Hnr	Thomas, Senr.	399	Rch	Wm.	510	Mnn
Sally	350	Lnc	Thomas, Sr.	468	Bdf	Wm.	512	Mnn
Sally	821	Nrf	Thomas, Sr.	860	Cmp	Wm.	576	Mnr
Sally	857	Sth	Thomas B.	877	Cmp	Wm.	14	Ntt

Name	Pg	Co	Name	Pg	Co	Name	Pg	Co
Wm.	682	Wrw	John	867	Sth	Mary	47	Clp
Wm., f. negro	270	Frf	John, Jun.	5	Isw	Mary	49	Clp
Wm., (N.F.)	46	Clp	John, Jun.	32	Isw	Mathew	876	Cmp
Wm., Senr.	48	Clp	John, Sen.	10	Isw	Nancy	512	Prw
Wm., Senr.	204	Kng	John, Sr.	347	Lnn	Rachel	47	Clp
Wm. A.G.	204	Kng	Joseph	21	Stf	Samuel	864	Cmp
Wm. D., (FB)	20	Ntt	Josiah M.	530	Prg	Samuel	876	Cmp
Wm. S.	203	Ess	Keziah	660	Glc	Thos.	49	Clp
Wm. S.	205	Kng	Laborn	347	Lnn	William	269	Frf
WmSon. P.	350	Lnc	Leroy	468	Bdf	Wm.	48	Clp
Eyllie	468	Bdf	Margaret	168	Knq	Wm.	289	Ldn
Younger	70	Spt	Mary	126	Hnr	Wm.	309	Ldn
Zachariah	522	Frd	Mary	20	Isw	see Jarden, Jerdan, Jorden,		
Zachariah	56	Stf	Matthew	9	Isw	Jordin, Jourdan		
see Allen, Browder, Chris-			Matthias	7	Isw	Joseph, Abraham	14	Rcm
tian, Heath, Janes, Joans,			Miles	348	Lnn	Jerh.	510	Mnn
Jomes, Osborne, Stephens,			Molly	124	Hnr	John	402	Ags
Tyre			Moses	801	Nrf	John	24	Hnr
Joness, Jacob	839	Wth	Nikolas	6	Isw	John	428	Rnd
Jonster, Frances	429	Rnd	Noble	111	Hnr	Joseph	428	Rnd
see Jonston			Peg of, (F.N.)	28	Isw	L.	23	Hnr
Jonston, Benn.	881	Sth	Polly	2	Rcm	Nathen	959	Hrr
Edward	423	Rnd	Rachel, (FN)	5	Isw	Wm.	509	Mnn
Garret	429	Rnd	Reuben	530	Frd	Wm. F.	117	Cmb
John	430	Rnd	Reuben	698	Gch	Josephs, Moses	437	Bth
Levy	430	Rnd	Robert	168	Knq	Jossling, James	469	Bdf
Robert	429	Rnd	Robert, Jun.	8	Isw	Thomas	468	Bdf
Sally	880	Sth	Robert, Sen.	32	Isw	Jourdan, Elijah	54	Chr
see Jonster			Sally	909	Crl	John	206	Shn
Jopes see Jofres			Sally	20	Isw	Joseph	573	Pre
Jopling, Edward	11	Knw	Saml.	811	Nrf	Matthew	69	Chr
Holeman	703	Nls	Samuel	348	Lnn	Rieves	54	Chr
Jesse	706	Nls	Samuel, Jun.	13	Isw	Jourden, Jacob	106	Jff
John	831	Bck	Samuel, Sen.	6	Isw	Jourdon, John	246	Shn
John	704	Nls	Sarah	634	Btt	Michl., Christians-		
Ralph	3	Knw	Simmeon	5	Isw	burg	618	Mnt
Ralph	703	Nls	Tashwell	468	Bdf	Journey, William	572	Pre
Ralph	705	Nls	Thomas	632	Btt	Joy, John	513	Brk
Thomas	826	Bck	Thomas	678	Br	Joseph	394	Rch
Thomas	3	Knw	Thomas	410	Fqr	Mat	510	Mnn
Thomas	705	Nls	Thomas	27	Isw	Richard	132	Hnr
William	270	Amh	Thomas, jr.	348	Lnn	Joyce, Jas.	45	Clp
see Jossling			Thomas, Sr.	348	Lnn	Joyner, Amos	874	Sth
Jordan, ---, and Doug-			Thos.	6	Ntt	Back, (F.N.)	39	Isw
las	757	Nwk	Upshaw	451	Grn	Baker	132	Sth
Absolom	468	Bdf	Vinson	468	Bdf	Daniel	30	Isw
Alexr.	905	Nrf	William	468	Bdf	Dick, (F.N.)	39	Isw
Alexr.	264	Rck	William, Jun.	6	Isw	Edgenton	126	Sth
Annis	348	Lnn	William, (of Jno.)	13	Isw	Henry	7	Isw
Banester	349	Lnn	William, Sen.	8	Isw	Ja... [Joseph?]	853	Sth
Baxter	346	Lnn	Willoug. T.	876	Yrk	John	15	Isw
Ben, (F.N.)	10	Isw	Woodson	468	Bdf	John	869	Sth
Benja.	451	Grn	see Brewer, Goodson, Gor-			Laurence	858	Sth
Benja.	131	Sth	don, Gwaltney, Jackson,			Martha	858	Sth
Charles	373	Fqr	Jurdon, Taylor			Mathew	858	Sth
Clem	348	Lnn	Jorden, Andrew	218	Pnd	Priscilla	867	Sth
Covey	468	Bdf	Bennett	4	Oho	Priscilla	869	Sth
David	203	Shn	James	218	Pnd	Reuben	854	Sth
Edmund	909	Crl	Jno.	49	Clp	Robert	137	Sth
Edward	346	Lnn	John	219	Pnd	Sally	39	Isw
Freeman	6	Ntt	John	221	Pnd	Tabetha	867	Sth
Frs.	905	Nrf	Saml., Given in by Thomis-			Thomas, Jun.	25	Isw
George	131	Sth	son Overseer	633	Btt	Thomas, Sen.	31	Isw
Hazekiah	262	Rck	Thomas	705	Nls	Thos., (of Thos.)	25	Isw
Henry	206	Shn	William	219	Pnd	see Joiner		
Henry	890	Yrk	Wm.	27	Hnr	Joynes, Ann	31	Acc
Hezekiah	451	Grn	Wm.	705	Nls	Elias	31	Acc
Hiram	468	Bdf	see Jerden			John G.	31	Acc
Isham	9	Isw	Jordin, Absolem	49	Clp	Levin	31	Acc
Jacob	161	Sth	John	428	Bth	Peggy	32	Acc
James	633	Btt	Jordine, Robert S.	392	Mds	William	31	Acc
James	451	Grn	Jordon, Ann	248	Ldn	William, BS	31	Acc
James	348	Lnn	Ann	252	Ldn	Jube, ---	633	Btt
Jeremiah	468	Bdf	Geo., free negro	70	Chs	Jubody see Subody		
Jerremiah	21	Stf	George	10	Oho	Judah, Abriham	214	Ess
Jesse	30	Stf	Henry	522	Prw	B.H.	11	Hnr
Jno., Captn.	633	Btt	Jno.	275	Ldn	Diannah	9	Hnr
John	124	Hnr	John	123	Cmb	Emanuel	22	Hnr
John	348	Lnn	John	505	Prw	Isaac H.	9	Hnr
John	14	Pwh	Joseph	504	Prw	Moses H.	28	Hnr

Judd, John	717	Brn
Pearson	180	Shn
Sally	29	Stf
Thomas	717	Brn
Jude, George	876	Cmp
Federick	117	Hnr
Judkins, Amos	610	Srr
Eliza.	609	Srr
Frederick J.	647	Sss
George	609	Srr
James	39	Isw
James, Sr.	610	Srr
Jesse	609	Srr
John	609	Srr
John	647	Sss
John H.	609	Srr
Joseph	610	Srr
Nathl.	609	Srr
Sally	610	Srr
Samuel	609	Srr
Samuel	646	Sss
Sylvia, F.N.	646	Sss
Thomas	29	Isw
William	610	Srr
William	648	Sss
Judy, Abraham	190	Shn
Frederick	295	Rck
Henry	221	Pnd
Jacob	221	Pnd
Jacob	302	Rck
Margret	214	Pnd
Martin	221	Pnd
Julian, Charles	37	Stf
James	106	Spt
Julianne, And.	328	Dnw
Jumper, Atler, (FN)	54	Chr
Junkons, Bengamin	798	Hmp
Junor, Hugh	125	Cmb
Jurden, Pleasant R.	877	Hnv
Jurdon, Moses	713	Wsh
Moses	716	Wsh
Jury, David	397	Fqr
Jusco see Imsco		
Justice, Bob	32	Acc
Isaiah	105	Acc
James	491	Frn
John	451	Grn
Leah	32	Acc
Ratram	752	Brn
Rebecca	752	Brn
Richard	103	Acc
Robert	104	Acc
Thomas	103	Acc
Thomas, BS	104	Acc
William, of R	105	Acc
William, Senr.	103	Acc
Zachariah	12	Ntt
Justis, Daniel	348	Lnn
William	346	Lnn
Justiss, Ann	610	Srr
John	610	Srr
Justus, Moses	512	Mnn

--- K ---

Kabler, Danl.	51	Clp
Enoch	50	Clp
Wm.	50	Clp
Kackley, Abraham	772	Hmp
Elias	536	Frd
see Keckley		
Kain, Hannah	165	Shn
Henry, f. negro	275	Frf
James	638	Mnt
Joshua, Junr.	163	Shn
Joshua, Junr.	165	Shn
Joshua, Senr.	167	Shn
William	166	Shn

Kaipe, Lanslot	840	Wth
Kalas, James	598	Mnr
Kale, Davd., j.	294	Rck
George	775	Hmp
Henry	514	Mnn
John	357	Ags
Peter	356	Ags
Peter, jr.	357	Ags
Wm.	356	Ags
Kaler, Andrew	833	Hmp
Charles	707	Nls
Kalnute, Jane	623	Mnt
John	623	Mnt
Kamp, Peter	907	Nrf
Kamper, Jno.	50	Clp
Josh.	50	Clp
Martin	50	Clp
Peter	50	Clp
Kanada, Joseph	277	Amh
Kanady, Reuben	393	Mds
Kanauvashew, John	809	Hmp
Kanawha, Wm.	707	Nls
Kancind, James	470	Bdf
Kane, Patk.	907	Nrf
Richd.	807	Nrf
Thomas	776	Wst
Karler, George	416	Rnd
Karr, Issibal	628	Gls
James	627	Gls
James	703	Wsh
John	627	Gls
John	699	Wsh
John R.	164	Alb
Robert	627	Gls
Wm.	703	Wsh
Kash, Henry	229	Shn
Kates, Henry	718	Brn
Katron, Christon	758	Wsh
Kattson, Felty	756	Wsh
Kauffmam, Humphrey, F.N.	169	Knq
Kauffman, Richard see Watts	169	Knq
Kay, Ann	199	Ess
Charles	517	Prw
Christopher	168	Knq
Delphia	198	Ess
Gabl.	50	Clp
Jas.	50	Clp
Jesse	830	Nrf
John	827	Nrf
Jonathan	830	Nrf
Robt.	50	Clp
Kaylor, Jno.	51	Clp
Kays, Daniel	461	Pra
Edwd.	461	Pra
Wm.	461	Pra
Kayser, Joseph D.	357	Ags
Keacys, John	557	Brk
Kealing, Jas.	637	Mnt
Kean, Ann	507	Frd
David	595	Mnr
Marcus	601	Frd
Mary	597	Frd
Moses	4	Knw
Nathaniel	510	Frd
Keaner, Elizabeth	250	Shn
Eve	203	Shn
Kearling, Jacob	232	Shn
Kearns, Barney	776	Hmp
Catharine	758	Hmp
Daniel	360	Fqr
Elizabeth	357	Fqr
Henry	44	Stf
Jacob	349	Fqr
Jacob	772	Hmp
Jacob	206	Shn
John	383	Fqr
John	771	Hmp
Joseph	772	Hmp

Levy	188	Shn
Mary	4	Knw
Mary	205	Shn
Samuel, (Barbadoes)	214	Shn
Samuel, (R)	215	Shn
Thomas	416	Fqr
William	358	Fqr
Kearsley, John	110	Jff
Kearton, Fanny	367	Fqr
Keath, Catherine, Christiansburg	619	Mnt
Keatley, James	566	Mnr
Keatly, Francies	565	Mnr
Keaton, Priscilla	661	Glc
Keayes, Jas.	510	Brk
Keblinger, Catharine	36	Rcm
Keckley, Elias, Jr.	536	Frd
George	571	Frd
Jacob	536	Frd
John	571	Frd
Joseph	221	Shn
Margarett	571	Frd
Samuel	571	Frd
see Kackley		
Kedick, John	567	Brk
Kednedy, Edwd.	547	Brk
Kee, ARon	227	Pnd
George	423	Bth
James	216	Pnd
James	610	Srr
John, (free)	349	Lnn
Robert	910	Crl
Robert	610	Srr
William B.	611	Srr
Keeble, Anderson	385	Fqr
Ephraim	377	Fqr
Richard	364	Fqr
Keeblimger, Adam	200	Alb
Keech, Charles	519	Prw
Keeding, Peter	519	Frd
Keef, James, Jr.	651	Mnt
James, (Son of Cage [?])	651	Mnt
James, Sr.	651	Mnt
John, Jr.	651	Mnt
Joshua	652	Mnt
Keefavor, Peter	636	Btt
Keefer, William	7	Oho
Keefers, George	828	Hmp
Keeland, Susannah	36	Rcm
Keele, Robert	906	Nrf
Keeler, William	16	Rcm
Keeling, ---, Widow	906	Nrf
Alexr.	828	Nrf
Amy	907	Nrf
Edwd.	55	Chr
Eliza	907	Nrf
Elizabeth	460	Pra
Henry	460	Pra
Henry, (Parson)	461	Pra
Isaac	460	Pra
Jacob	460	Pra
Jno.	460	Pra
Jno. T.	460	Pra
Martha	55	Chr
Molly	460	Pra
Peggy	460	Pra
Thos., Jr.	460	Pra
Thos., Sr.	460	Pra
William	574	Pre
Wm.	351	Lnc
Wm.	460	Pra
Wm., Sr.	460	Pra
Wm. T.	460	Pra
Keen, John	164	Alb
John	452	Frn
Keenan, Cavan	5	Oho
Edward	573	Mnr
James	13	Oho
Jas.	833	Nrf

John	829	Nrf	Kellam, Argyl, Junr.	33	Acc	John	179	Alb
Michael	1	Knw	Arrabella	35	Acc	John	423	Bth
Patrick	563	Mnr	Cathne.	907	Nrf	John	688	Br
Wm.	5	Oho	Ezekel	105	Acc	John	719	Brn
Keene, Elisha	459	Frn	Leah	106	Acc	John	352	Fqr
Francis	274	Frf	Rachel	34	Acc	John	483	Frn
Geo.	273	Ldn	Samuel	907	Nrf	John	116	Hnr
Leven	776	Wst	Samuel	460	Pra	John	574	Pre
Richd.	251	Ldn	Severn	907	Nrf	John	2	Rcm
Wm.	273	Frf	see Kellen			John	698	Wsh
see Keine			Kellar, Francis	9	Wod	John	727	Wsh
Keener, Geo.	514	Mnn	Philip	573	Mnr	Joseph	718	Brn
S., Jr.	514	Mnn	Kellen, Yost	566	Frd	Joseph	561	Frd
Sam	514	Mnn	Kellenberger, Michal	528	Frd	Lewis	718	Brn
Ulry	514	Mnn	Keller, Adam	15	Oho	Martha	754	Brn
Keenon, Charles	594	Mnr	Conrad	573	Mnr	Milley	152	Dnw
Keenum, Richard	469	Bdf	Daniel	744	Wsh	Moris	678	Br
Keer, Dabney	120	Cmb	David	15	Oho	Nathaniel	574	Pre
Kees, Amos	205	Shn	Fred	358	Ags	Nelly	437	Bth
Keesee, George	130	Hnr	Frederick	840	Wth	Patrick	417	Fqr
John	911	Crl	Geo.	358	Ags	Peter	253	Ldn
Rachel	196	Ess	Geo.	514	Mnn	Polley	328	Dnw
Keeser, James	987	Nrt	George	561	Brk	Robin, free negro	70	Chs
Keesling, Coonrod	840	Wth	George	211	Shn	Saml.	697	Wsh
George	840	Wth	George	213	Shn	Sarah	686	Br
Jacob	840	Wth	George	229	Shn	Scarburgh	107	Acc
John	219	Pnd	Henry	219	Shn	Thomas	107	Acc
Keetch, Elisha	678	Br	Jacob	548	Frd	Thomas	718	Brn
Keeth, Smith	302	Ldn	Jacob	424	Rnd	Thos.	50	Clp
Keeton, Garret	120	Spt	Jacob	174	Shn	William	34	Acc
James	200	Alb	Jacob [2]	840	Wth	William	106	Acc
James	563	Mnr	John	358	Ags	William	432	Bth
Jno.	661	Glc	John	548	Frd	William	475	Frn
John	87	Spt	John	15	Oho	William	987	Nrt
Johnson	600	Mnr	John	222	Pnd	Wm.	718	Brn
Larken	200	Alb	John	754	Wsh	Kelliam, Arabella	34	Acc
Warner	349	Lnn	Joseph	211	Shn	Argyl, Sen.	32	Acc
Wm.	600	Mnr	Lewis	8	Rcm	Charity	34	Acc
Keezle, Henry	12	Rcm	Martin [2]	15	Oho	Custis, Carpr.	33	Acc
Margaret	11	Rcm	Michl.	274	Frf	Custis, Taylr.	34	Acc
Keffer, Abraham	250	Shn	Nancy	759	Hnrp	Edward	106	Acc
Jacob	628	Gls	Peter	546	Frd	Elizabeth	106	Acc
Martin	250	Shn	Peter	18	Rcm	Fredrick	33	Acc
Mary	241	Shn	Philip	9	Rcm	George	33	Acc
Kegley, Christian	841	Wth	Sam	514	Mnn	Heward	32	Acc
George, Junr.	841	Wth	Samuel	164	Alb	Housham	33	Acc
George, Senr.	841	Wth	Kelley, Anderson	733	Wsh	Hutcheson	33	Acc
John	841	Wth	Andw. E.	698	Wsh	John	33	Acc
Lewis	841	Wth	Austin	114	Hnr	John, WM	34	Acc
Martain	841	Wth	Benj.	726	Wsh	Molly	33	Acc
Kehoe, Peter	3	Oho	Charles	16	Hnr	Nathaniel	33	Acc
Kehoon, John	221	Pnd	Daniel	869	Cmp	Peggy	32	Acc
Keichs see Keriho			Daniel	574	Pre	Revel	34	Acc
Keifer, George	26	Rcm	David	754	Brn	Robert	33	Acc
Keinan see Kernan			Dennis	106	Acc	Sarah	33	Acc
Keine, Jeremiah	866	Cmp	Dennis	865	Cmp	Severn	32	Acc
Keiningham, Benja.	661	Glc	Doniphan	366	Fqr	Spencer	33	Acc
Benjamin	759	Nwk	Edmunds	718	Brn	Susanna	34	Acc
Jno.	661	Glc	Edwd.	250	Ldn	Thomas	33	Acc
Samuel	759	Nwk	Elizabeth	915	Hrr	Zerobl.	33	Acc
see Kiningham			Elizabeth	574	Pre	see Kellam		
Keirdle, Elias	34	Rcm	Elizh.	274	Frf	Kellie, Isaac	5	Oho
Keister, Freadericke,			Ezekiel	732	Wsh	John	5	Oho
Jr.	215	Pnd	George	898	Hnv	Kellinger, George	738	Wsh
Fredericke, S.	215	Pnd	George	427	Msn	John	243	Shn
George	215	Pnd	Greenberry	725	Wsh	Kello, John	559	Frd
James	215	Pnd	Henry	719	Brn	Richd.	876	Sth
Keith, Alexanour	407	Fqr	Isaiah	33	Acc	Saml.	161	Sth
Howe	70	Jff	Israel	627	Gls	Kellom, John	987	Nrt
Isham	273	Frf	Jacob	106	Acc	William	987	Nrt
James	950	Hrr	James	106	Acc	Kellow, Ridley	879	Sth
James	262	Rck	James	437	Bth	Kellum, Bowden	806	Nrf
James, quarter	275	Frf	James	469	Bdf	Kellune, Major	840	Nrf
John	443	Bth	James	718	Brn	Kelly, Abel W.	423	Rnd
John	390	Fqr	James	733	Wsh	Aroon	6	Knw
John	951	Hrr	Jesse	107	Acc	Benjamin	9	Knw
Judah	354	Fqr	Jesse	429	Msn	Charles	34	Acc
Peyton	275	Amh	Jessee	754	Brn	Cornelius	592	Brk
Vincent	390	Fqr	Jno.	50	Clp	Ebenezer	427	Rnd
Kelgore, Gideon	811	Nrf	John	106	Acc	Eliza	776	Wst

Elizabeth 100 Acc
Elizabeth 205 Kng
Elizabeth 51 Stf
Elizbh. 290 Rck
George 907 Nrf
Hannah 188 Shn
Henry 594 Mnr
Henry 805 Nrf
Hugh 825 Nrf
Jacob 8 Knw
James 910 Crl
James 9 Knw
James 5 Oho
James 33 Stf
Jas. 351 Lnc
Jas. 512 Mnn
Jno. 513 Mnn
Jno., Sen. 513 Mnn
Jno., Senr. 636 Btt
John 34 Acc
John 957 Hrr
John 5 Knw
John 606 Mnt
John 834 Nrf
John 403 Rch
John 166 Shn
John 840 Wth
Mary 460 Pra
Michael 812 Hmp
Milly 334 Dnw
Molly 399 Rch
Moses 14 Knw
Nancy 34 Acc
Pat. 513 Mnn
Patrick 801 Hmp
Patrick 840 Wth
Polly 27 Hnr
Richard 34 Acc
Richd. 816 Nrf
Samuel 840 Wth
Thomas 636 Btt
Thomas 911 Crl
Timothy 34 Acc
William 910 Crl
William 423 Rnd
William 166 Shn
William, Senr. 910 Crl
Willm. 205 Kng
Willm. 641 Mnt
Wm. 50 Clp
Wm. 513 Mnn
see Kellie
Kellyhon, James 249 Ldn
Kelmer, David 543 Brk
Kelrick, James 176 Elc
Kelsay, Smith 778 Hmp
Kelsey, Andrew 611 Srr
Daniel 624 Mnt
Henry 228 Shn
Thomas 624 Mnt
Kelsick, Richd. 836 Nrf
Samuel B. 390 Rch
Kelso, Eliz. 514 Mnn
Hugh 514 Mnn
Hugh 293 Rck
James 442 Bth
James 770 Hmp
John 109 Cmb
Joseph 294 Rck
Robert 574 Pre
Keltmaher, Lewis 297 Rck
Keltner, Michael 841 Wth
Kem, William 840 Wth
Kemer, Philip 445 Bth
Kemmer, Jac. 514 Mnn
Jno., Jr. 514 Mnn
John 514 Mnn
Kemp, Ann 169 Knq
James 620 Mnt
Jas. 461 Pra

Jesse 540 Frd
Jno. 351 Lnc
John 347 Fqr
John 168 Knq
Lewis 55 Chr
Matthew 661 Glc
Peter 661 Glc
Peter, jr. 661 Glc
Peter, Senr. 661 Glc
Ro. 661 Glc
Ro., Senr. 661 Glc
Thomas 169 Knq
Thos. [2] 661 Glc
William 181 Shn
Wm. 660 Glc
Willo. 460 Pra
Kempe, Jno. 461 Pra
Kemper, Charles, Jr. 406 Fqr
Charles, Senr. 413 Fqr
Elias 413 Fqr
George 351 Fqr
Jacob 50 Clp
John 418 Fqr
John, Senr. 413 Fqr
Joshua 362 Fqr
Moses 361 Fqr
Thomas 362 Fqr
William 362 Fqr
William 393 Mds
Kemplin, William 482 Frn
Kempten, Betsy 824 Nrf
Kems, Joshua 206 Kng
Kenaday, Hugh 840 Wth
Kenady, And. 299 Rck
Andw. 357 Ags
James 490 Frn
John 357 Ags
John 402 Ags
Stuart 402 Ags
William 490 Frn
Kenard, James 432 Bth
Michael 432 Bth
Kenchloe, Daniel 6 Wod
Raber 10 Wod
Kendal, George 508 Prw
Kendall, Aaron 25 Stf
Alexander 56 Stf
Benjamin 172 Shn
Braxton B. 23 Stf
Charles 48 Stf
Daniel 27 Stf
Gearly [?] 27 Stf
James 177 Shn
Jesse 45 Stf
James 49 Stf
John 589 Frd
Joshua 24 Stf
Js. 513 Mnn
Lucy 62 Stf
Moses 24 Stf
Peter 19 Ntt
Rachel 55 Stf
Ransom 541 Frd
Sam 513 Mnn
Sam, Ser. 513 Mnn
Thos. 51 Clp
William 589 Frd
Zebedee 589 Frd
Kendel, Jack 206 Kng
Toney 206 Kng
Wm. 205 Kng
Kendell, Enock 344 Fqr
George 344 Fqr
Kendrick, Benja. 593 Frd
Danl. 51 Clp
Elisebeth 753 Wsh
John 567 Brk
John 718 Wsh
Mary 249 Shn
Robt. 113 Hnr

Robt. 115 Hnr
Thornton 566 Brk
Thos. 753 Wsh
Kenedy, Hugh 513 Mnn
Hugh 297 Rck
James 299 Rck
Jane 719 Brn
Jessee 719 Brn
John 559 Brk
Joseph 299 Rck
Robert 719 Brn
Sam. 512 Mnn
Wm. 513 Mnn
Wm. 300 Rck
Wm., jr. 719 Brn
Wm., Ser. 719 Brn
Kener, John 952 Hrr
Kenester, Hannah 513 Frd
John 512 Frd
Kengerry, John 194 Shn
see Kingury
Kenidy, Benjamin 469 Bdf
Kening, Lawrence 695 Br
Keniviard, Joseph 5 Wod
Kennard, Davd., jr. 51 Clp
Geo. 51 Clp
Joshua 374 Fqr
Wm. 51 Clp
Kennedie, John 7 Oho
Kennedy, Aaron 547 Brk
Alexr. 595 Brk
Benjamin 46 Stf
George 35 Stf
Henry 35 Stf
Jacob 822 Hmp
John 353 Fqr
Joseph 713 Wsh
Levi 756 Wsh
Mark 754 Wsh
Mathew 760 Hmp
Reuben 747 Wsh
Saml. 558 Brk
Saml. 756 Wsh
William 692 Wsh
William 707 Wsh
Wm. 356 Ags
see Kednedy
Kenner, John B., Jr. 988 Nrt
John B., Sr. 987 Nrt
John D. 987 Nrt
Martha 382 Fqr
Robt. 50 Clp
Rodham 910 Crl
Rodham 51 Clp
Sarah 987 Nrt
Wendey 419 Fqr
Kennerley, Saml. 635 Btt
Kennerly, James 357 Ags
Joseph 293 Amh
Reuben 358 Ags
Kennester, Freadericke 216 Pnd
Kennet, Nehemiah 881 Cmp
Peter 462 Frn
Zachariah 452 Frn
Kennett, John 469 Bdf
Joseph B. 469 Bdf
Kenney, Abraham 680 Br
Andrew 383 Fqr
James 358 Ags
William 95 Jff
see Kinney
Kennier, Ailsey 100 Jff
Kenniford, Henry 512 Frd
Kennison, Charles 423 Bth
Kennon, Geo. 819 Nrf
Thomas 534 Frd
Kenny, James 634 Btt
Jno., Sr. 635 Btt
Joseph 524 Frd
Mildred 117 Spt

Name	No.	Co.	Name	No.	Co.	Name	No.	Co.
Moses	272	Frf	Kerfoot see Kerfott			Thos.	848	Hnv
William	594	Frd	Kerfott, John	544	Frd	Kersh, Jacob	24	Rcm
see Kerney			Samuel	546	Frd	Matthias	24	Rcm
Kennyhorn, John	34	Acc	William	535	Frd	Kersley, John	105	Jff
William	32	Acc	William	546	Frd	Jonathan	72	Jff
Kensey, Wm.	12	Hnr	William, Jr.	545	Frd	Kertley, Philip	275	Frf
Kent, Abm.	440	Flv	Kerian, Patrick	426	Bth	Keryser see Kayser		
Beasley, & Co.	328	Dnw	Kerick, Walter	315	Ldn	Kesecker, Andw.	585	Brk
Benj.	263	Ldn	Keriho, Christopher	9	Rcm	Conrod	585	Brk
Charles, Jr.	987	Nrt	Kerin, Timothy	571	Frd	John	578	Brk
Charles, Sr.	987	Nrt	Kerk, Wm.	304	Ldn	Mary	585	Brk
Danl.	351	Lnc	Kerlin, Robert	516	Frd	Matthias	587	Brk
Elias	264	Ldn	Kermer, Robert	575	Frd	Kesee, Avery	879	Cmp
Elijah	506	Prw	Kern, Burgess	351	Lnc	Kesinger, John	587	Brk
Gideon	1	Oho	Caty	351	Lnc	Mathias	580	Mnr
Isaac	469	Bdf	Geo.	514	Mnn	Michl.	580	Mnr
Isaac	264	Ldn	George	636	Btt	see Kisenger		
Isaac	306	Ldn	Jno.	513	Mnn	Keslar, Danl.	635	Btt
Jacob	614	Mnt	M.	514	Mnn	Kesleng, Jacob	416	Rnd
John	469	Bdf	M., Jr.	513	Mnn	Kesler, Abm.	636	Btt
John	867	Cmp	Richd.	351	Lnc	Benjn.	635	Btt
John	617	Mnt	William	605	Frd	Christn.	636	Btt
John	987	Nrt	Kernan, Patrick	586	Mnr	David	636	Btt
John, Sr.	440	Flv	Kernberglin, Jas.	635	Btt	Geo., Jr.	636	Btt
John T.	434	Flv	see Kimberlin			Geo., Sr.	636	Btt
Joseph	840	Wth	Kerney, Alley	98	Jff	Henry	358	Ags
Rad.	351	Lnc	Anthoney	97	Jff	Jacob	636	Btt
Robert	886	Hnv	Hannah	635	Btt	Jno.	635	Btt
Robt.	439	Flv	James	97	Jff	Jno.	645	Mnt
Smith	882	Cmp	Robt.	543	Brk	Jo., Jr.	634	Btt
Tho.	351	Lnc	Susan	599	Brk	Loderrick	476	Frn
Thomas	264	Ldn	Wm.	511	Brk	Peter	635	Btt
Thomas	759	Nwk	Kerns, Adam	528	Frd	Peter	477	Frn
Thomas	987	Nrt	George	470	Bdf	Kesner, Adam	223	Pnd
William	759	Nwk	George	554	Frd	John	223	Pnd
William	507	Prw	Jacob	592	Brk	Kesrick, Hugh	410	Fqr
William, Jr.	987	Nrt	Jacob	554	Frd	Kessler, Andw.	8	Rcm
William, Sr.	987	Nrt	Jacob, Sr.	597	Brk	John	32	Rcm
William B.	987	Nrt	Jonathan	7	Wod	Kester, Peter	608	Mnt
Wm.	434	Flv	Michael	594	Brk	Philip	608	Mnt
see McKent			Michael, Sr.	470	Bdf	Kesterson, Benjamin	707	Nls
Kenter, Jacob	590	Brk	Moses	470	Bdf	Francis	987	Nrt
Kenup, John	248	Shn	Nathan	554	Frd	Huzzard	356	Ags
Kenyon, Elizabeth	5	Pwh	Nicholas	528	Frd	Jas.	351	Lnc
Keough, Jane	516	Prw	Pat	513	Mnn	John S.	987	Nrt
Keorn, Aron	598	Mnr	Reuben	469	Bdf	Silvester	357	Ags
Kephart, Bernard	523	Brk	Wm.	50	Clp	W.	408	Ags
Henry	41	Rcm	see Kirnes			William	987	Nrt
Thos.	288	Ldn	Kerr, Abner	4	Pwh	Kesther, John	200	Alb
Kepler, Mary	295	Rck	Alexa.	358	Ags	Kestler see Kesner		
Keplinger, Peter	358	Ags	Alexander	68	Chs	Kettering, Adam	841	Wth
Ker, And.	288	Rck	Daniel	421	Bth	Jacob	840	Wth
Danl.	282	Rck	Francis	169	Knq	Jacob	841	Wth
Davd.	303	Rck	Henry	107	Acc	Laurance	841	Wth
David C.	77	Spt	Hezekiah	61	Chs	Michael	841	Wth
Pamelia	179	Elc	James	179	Alb	Susanna	840	Wth
Thomas	278	Rck	James	356	Ags	Ketterman, George	221	Pnd
see Kerr, Kers			James, (W)	877	Yrk	Kettle, Abraham	422	Rnd
Kerbman, Peter, Jr.	635	Btt	Job	105	Acc	Isaac	421	Rnd
Peter, Sr.	635	Btt	John	358	Ags	Richard	421	Rnd
Kerby, Bengamin	798	Hmp	John	55	Chr	see Kittle		
Elisha	894	Hnv	Levin	34	Acc	Kettille, Jacob	422	Rnd
Eliz.	179	Elc	Nancy	326	Dnw	Kettner, Henry	610	Mnt
Elizabeth	164	Alb	Robt.	303	Rck	Jacob	31	Rcm
James	643	Mnt	Samuel	163	Alb	Ketts, Philip	21	Rcm
Jehue	618	Mnt	Sarah	417	Fqr	Keve, Thomas	987	Nrt
Jno.	890	Hnv	see Elam			Key, George	451	Frn
Kitty	636	Mnt	Kerrell, Jemima	20	Oho	Jacob	875	Cmp
Larkin	164	Alb	Kerrick, Thomas	294	Ldn	Jessee B.	200	Alb
Susannah	164	Alb	see Kesrick			Jno.	287	Rck
William	164	Alb	Kerrs, Jacob	558	Brk	John	200	Alb
William	81	Jff	Kers, Richard A.	74	Spt	John	686	Br
Wm.	640	Mnt	see Ker			John	55	Chr
Zachariah	273	Frf	Kersey, Agathy	146	Sth	John	328	Dnw
see Ker, Kirby			Betsey	895	Hnv	John	184	Elc
Kerchaval, Benjn.	75	Jff	Edmon	484	Frn	John	648	Sss
Kercheval, Elijah	550	Frd	Elizabeth	55	Chr	Joshua	200	Alb
Rd.	661	Glc	Jno.	874	Hnv	Martin	469	Bdf
Samuel	521	Frd	John	484	Frn	Martin	699	Gch
Kerchwall, John	168	Knq	Thomas	146	Sth	Robert	574	Pre

Susannah	707	Nls	Kidd, Absolum	829	Bck	Marshall P.	274	Frf
Thandy	163	Alb	Andrew	835	Nrf	Thomas	268	Ldn
Thomas	470	Bdf	Arnold	292	Amh	Walter	13	Wod
Walter	200	Alb	Bartholomew	169	Knq	Wm. [2]	50	Clp
William	881	Cmp	Benjamin	910	Crl	Wm.	275	Frf
William	820	Hmp	Benjamin	168	Knq	Zedekiah	273	Frf
Keyes, Arm P	764	Hmp	Benjamin	465	Mdd	Kiekley, Isaac	771	Hmp
Catharine	767	Hmp	Benjn.	430	Flv	Kiesinger, Mathias	572	Mnr
Elizabeth	510	Prw	Burgess	465	Mdd	see Kisenger		
Francis	742	Wsh	Catharine	466	Mdd	Kiest, Peter	283	Ldn
George	802	Hmp	Charles	540	Brk	Philip	284	Ldn
Jno.	661	Glc	David	18	Hnr	Kiestley, Jamima	50	Clp
William	800	Hmp	Delphia	852	Cmp	Kiger, Amelia	598	Frd
William	511	Prw	Elizabeth	910	Crl	Andrew	506	Frd
Wm.	661	Glc	George	237	Aml	Andrew	511	Frd
Keyhs, Thos.	690	Wsh	George	459	Frn	Anthony	214	Pnd
see Keyto			Godwick	465	Mdd	Geo.	358	Ags
Keykendall, Isaac	763	Hmp	Henry	829	Bck	Geo.	561	Brk
Keyloe see Hylor			Henry	437	Flv	George	508	Frd
Keys, Barbara	432	Bth	James	12	Hnr	George	810	Hmp
Briner	117	Spt	James, (Colo.)	466	Mdd	George	34	Stf
Elisabeth	699	Wsh	James, Jun.	465	Mdd	George, jr.	561	Brk
Frances	776	Wst	Jas.	22	Hnr	Henry	268	Rck
George	511	Prw	Jasper	237	Aml	Jacob	508	Frd
Gersham	68	Jff	Jesse	438	Flv	Jacob	515	Frd
Harvey	731	Wsh	Jm. [?]	707	Nls	John	561	Brk
Humphrey	593	Mnr	Joel	223	Ess	John	511	Frd
James	487	Frn	John	259	Amh	Peter	559	Brk
James	511	Prw	John	852	Cmp	Philip	952	Hrr
James	715	Wsh	John	436	Flv	Solomon	233	Shn
Jno.	442	Mth	John	501	Frn	Kiggin, John	102	Spt
Jdhn	511	Prw	John, jr.	168	Knq	Kight, David	931	Hrr
John	693	Wsh	John, Snr.	169	Knq	Kilbey, Jos.	50	Clp
Jdhn	749	Wsh	Joseph	719	Brn	Kilbreath, Joseph	911	Hrr
Mary	432	Bth	Joseph	707	Nls	Kilburne, Isaac	584	Mnr
Peterson	151	Dnw	Juriah	707	Nls	Kilby, Armend.	51	Clp
Polly	119	Spt	Lewis B.	851	Cmp	Jas.	51	Clp
Roger	699	Wsh	Lodwick	151	Dnw	Jno.	877	Hnv
Rolly	511	Prw	Mary	169	Knq	John T.	759	Nwk
Salina	163	Alb	Pleasant	707	Nls	see Kelley		
Sally	38	Stf	Richard	548	Frd	Kilden, Michl.	540	Brk
Saml.	51	Clp	Richard	605	Frd	Kile, Abraham	238	Shn
Samuel	72	Jff	Richd.	22	Hnr	Ann	550	Frd
Thomas	151	Dnw	Richd.	115	Hnr	Henry	230	Shn
Thomas	497	Frn	Saml.	430	Flv	Jacob	356	Ags
Thomas	68	Jff	Samuel	810	Bck	John	238	Shn
Thornton	110	Spt	Samuel	907	Nrf	Peter	238	Shn
Wesley	475	Frn	Shadrack	829	Bck	Kiles, Robert, Jur.	816	Hmp
William	364	Fqr	Thomas	466	Mdd	Robert, Sen.	816	Hmp
William	510	Prw	William	300	Amh	William	94	Jff
see Keayes, Key, Keyhs			William	805	Bck	Kiley, James	304	Rck
Keyser, William	412	Bth	William	707	Nls	Kilgore, Jno.	460	Pra
Keysor, Casa	292	Ldn	William, jr.	304	Amh	William	547	Frd
Keyto, Mary	690	Wsh	William, Junr.	466	Mdd	see Kelgore		
see Keyhs			William, Senr.	465	Mdd	Kilgrove, James	907	Nrf
Keyton, Bernerd	262	Rck	William N.	466	Mdd	Killey, William	112	Hnr
Keywod, Stephen	720	Wsh	Willis	910	Crl	Wm.	245	Ldn
Keywood, Benj.	720	Wsh	Wm.	18	Hnr	see Kelley		
Lucey	720	Wsh	see Marquis			Killgore, Geo.	249	Ldn
Thos.	720	Wsh	Kiddle, William	409	Fqr	Killinger, George, Jur.	740	Wsh
Kezer, Jacob	578	Frd	Kiddy, Jacob	306	Rck	Killingworth, Richard	218	Pnd
Kibbins, James, Jr.	51	Clp	Jasper	306	Rck	Killman, Betty	106	Acc
Jas.	51	Clp	Kider, Nancey	5	Hnr	Charles	106	Acc
Kibble, Anderson	518	Prw	Kidweler, Michael	85	Jff	Comfort	106	Acc
James	573	Mnr	Kidwell, Alexa.	273	Frf	Edward	105	Acc
Kibler, Adam	179	Shn	Barton	274	Frf	Ezekel	33	Acc
John	519	Brk	Benj.	296	Ldn	Ezekil	106	Acc
John	179	Shn	Courtney	274	Frf	Thomas [2]	106	Acc
John	203	Shn	Elender	88	Jff	Killy, Caty	118	Hnr
Martin	179	Shn	Gibson	51	Clp	Fanny	118	Hnr
Philip	180	Shn	Hezekiah	272	Frf	Kilmor, George	634	Btt
William	242	Shn	Hezikiah	274	Frf	Kilpatrick, Benjamin	416	Bth
Kiblinger, John	184	Shn	James	272	Frf	Jas.	580	Mnr
Kichen, Jacob	555	Brk	James	273	Frf	John	358	Ags
Kick, Daniel	803	Hmp	James	376	Fqr	Nancy	416	Bth
Kid, Agness	881	Hnv	Jane	168	Shn	Samuel	416	Bth
Fras.	351	Lnc	Jeston	272	Frf	Thomas	416	Bth
Jessee	699	Gch	John	826	Hmp	Kilpest, Margaret	252	Shn
Jonathan	373	Fqr	Joshua	274	Frf	Kilwell, Robert	819	Hmp
Patsey	163	Alb	Josiah	58	Jff	William	840	Wth

Kimberlin, Adam	428	Msn	And., Sr.	301	Rck	Jno.	661	Glc
Jacob	635	Btt	John	293	Rck	Jno.	512	Mnn
Jacob	428	Msn	Kines, William	405	Fqr	Jno., Jnr.	871	Hnv
Jno.	635	Btt	Kinhead see Kinkead			Jno., Snr.	896	Hnv
Michl.	635	Btt	King, Abraham	469	Bdf	Jno. S.	152	Dnw
Nancy	428	Msn	Alexander	820	Hmp	John	635	Btt
see Kernberlin			Andrew	754	Wsh	John	718	Brn
Kimberling, George	841	Wth	Andrew.	592	Mnr	John	273	Frf
Jacob	840	Wth	Anthony	662	Mnt	John	443	Flv
John	840	Wth	Antony	877	Yrk	John	586	Frd
Kimble, Benj.	23	Hnr	Aquilla	540	Frd	John	11	Hnr
Caty	579	Frd	Arnall	818	Nrf	John	27	Isw
John	245	Ldn	Bazil	515	Prw	John	513	Mnn
Wim.	928	Hrr	Benja.	326	Dnw	John	223	Pnd
Kimbler, Henry	840	Wth	Benjamin	753	Brn	John	523	Prw
Kimbral, John	32	Isw	Benjamin	519	Prw	John	400	Rch
Kimbrough, James	899	Hnv	Berryman	910	Crl	John	691	Wsh
Jno., Jnr.	854	Hnv	Bolling	649	Sss	John	841	Wth
Richard	900	Hnv	Briant	855	Cmp	John, jr.	435	Flv
Wim.	874	Hnv	Caroline	99	Spt	John, Jr.	638	Mnt
Kimbrought, Jno., Snr.	847	Hnv	Catey	412	Fqr	John, (Overseer)	376	Fqr
Kime, Henry	99	Jff	Charles	635	Btt	John, Sr.	633	Mnt
Jacob	74	Jff	Charles	676	Br	Jos.	820	Nrf
Kimes, Abraham	412	Bth	Charles	696	Br	Josehp, Christians-		
Jno.	513	Mnn	Charles	753	Brn	burg	618	Mnt
Kimler, Moses	520	Prw	Charles	573	Frd	Joseph	151	Dnw
Kimmey, John	176	Elc	Charles	628	Gls	Joseph	152	Dnw
Kinbead, William	442	Bth	Charles W.	6	Knw	Joseph	435	Flv
Kincaid, Andrew	414	Bth	Charlotte	718	Brn	Joseph	2	Oho
Ann	440	Bth	Christian	841	Wth	Joshua	924	Hrr
Charles	436	Bth	Corneals	430	Msn	Joshua	293	Ldn
David	436	Bth	Cors.	514	Mnn	Julius	151	Dnw
Ferdinand	436	Bth	Daniel	384	Fqr	Lawrance	3	Wod
Isaiah	275	Rck	Daniel	525	Prw	Lighty	490	Frn
John	414	Bth	David	437	Flv	Lucy	611	Srr
John	436	Bth	Edward	349	Lnn	Machach	25	Oho
John	445	Bth	Edwd.	273	Frf	Martin	469	Bdf
Robert	440	Bth	Elias	753	Brn	Martin	445	Flv
Robert	707	Nls	Elias	540	Frd	Mary	718	Brn
Thomas	433	Bth	Elias	513	Prw	Mary	25	Hnr
William	420	Fqr	Eligah	952	Hrr	Mary, Mrs.	690	Wsh
see Kinkead			Elijah	516	Prw	Mason	331	Dnw
Kincaide, Thomas	225	Pnd	Elisha	151	Dnw	Matthew	205	Kng
Kincannon, Andrew	840	Wth	Evan	840	Wth	Michael	187	Elc
Davd.	692	Wsh	Fanny	661	Glc	Michael, jr.	470	Bdf
Jas.	708	Wsh	Frances	953	Hrr	Miles	718	Brn
Jno., Jur.	709	Wsh	Frank	86	Spt	Miles	187	Elc
Mathew	709	Wsh	Gedion	844	Hnv	Miles	453	Mth
Kincanon, Francis	692	Wsh	Geo.	277	Ldn	Miles, Jr.	906	Nrf
Kincel, Jacob	841	Wth	Geo.	289	Ldn	Miles, Sr.	906	Nrf
see Kinsel			Geo.	820	Nrf	Milly	331	Dnw
Kincey, Solo.	460	Pra	George	939	Chc	Mord...cai	519	Prw
Wm.	460	Pra	George	349	Fqr	Nathaniel	349	Lnn
Kincheloe, Alexander	526	Prw	George	799	Hmp	Nathaniel	776	Wst
Cornelius	274	Frf	George	592	Mnr	Philip	611	Srr
Heetor	274	Frf	George	574	Pre	Phillip	55	Chr
James	389	Fqr	George	5	Rcm	Polly	330	Dnw
Jesse	274	Frf	George	841	Wth	Polly	646	Mnt
John	526	Prw	Gillum	470	Bdf	Rebecca	611	Srr
Mildred	526	Prw	Hannah	330	Dnw	Reuben	29	Rcm
Wildmam	2	Wod	Hargess	274	Frf	Rhody	330	Dnw
Kindal, Adam	282	Ldn	Harman	470	Bdf	Richd.	356	Ags
Kindall, Frs.	51	Clp	Henry	358	Ags	Robert	151	Dnw
see Kendall			Henry	151	Dnw	Robert	886	Hnv
Kindell, Chilton	402	Fqr	Henry, (Overseer)	376	Fqr	Robert	46	Stf
Kinden, Benjamin	814	Nrf	Isaac	853	Cmp	Robert	757	Wsh
Kinder, Christian	841	Wth	Isaac	661	Glc	Robt.	662	Mnt
George	840	Wth	Jacob	892	Hnv	Robt.	820	Nrf
George [2]	841	Wth	Jacob	223	Pnd	Rodham	510	Prw
Jacob	739	Wsh	James	58	Jff	Sabrid	200	Alb
Jacob	840	Wth	James	607	Mnt	Sackville	864	Cmp
Jacob [2]	841	Wth	James	611	Mnt	Salley	152	Dnw
John	9	Knw	James	502	Prw	Sally	820	Nrf
Peter	636	Btt	James	79	Spt	Sam	661	Glc
Peter	840	Wth	James	776	Wst	Saml.	502	Prw
Peter	841	Wth	James, jr.	78	Spt	Sampson	274	Frf
Kindle, Henry	87	Jff	Jas.	513	Mnn	Samuel	93	Jff
Kindred, Thomas	200	Alb	Jesse	610	Srr	Samuel	513	Prw
Kindrick, Nathan	859	Hnv	Jno.	50	Clp	Samuel	776	Wst
Kinear, And., jr.	301	Rck	Jno.	273	Frf	Sarah	518	Prw

Sarah, Mrs.	688	Wsh
Shadrach	25	Oho
Smith	776	Wst
Solomen	2	Oho
Stephen	489	Frn
Stephen	519	Prw
Stephen	3	Wod
Tho.	513	Mnn
Thomas	152	Dnw
Thomas	47	Isw
Thomas	42	Rcm
Thomas	776	Wst
Thos.	820	Nrf
Tobias, (FM)	51	Clp
Val.	514	Mnn
Walter	525	Prw
William	870	Cmp
William	336	Dnw
William	826	Hmp
William	503	Prw
William [2]	841	Wth
William, Junr.	776	Wst
William, Senr.	776	Wst
William H.	553	Frd
Willm.	179	Elc
Willm.	664	Mnt
Willm., Sr.	616	Mnt
Wim., Jnr.	849	Hnv
Wim., Snr.	860	Hnv
Wm.	357	Ags
Wm.	402	Ags
Wm.	718	Brn
Wm.	277	Ldn
Wm.	513	Mnn
Wm.	820	Nrf
Wm.	835	Nrf
Wm., (BC)	357	Ags
Wm. B.	503	Brk
see Kring		
Kingery, Abrm.	423	Msn
Kingree see Kingury		
Kingrey, Peter	4	Knw
Kingry, Christian	483	Frn
Henry	476	Frn
Peter, Jr.	483	Frn
Peter, Sr.	483	Frn
Kingsolver, George W.	164	Alb
Kingsworthy, Thos.	635	Btt
Kingury, Solomon	193	Shn
Kinhard, W., Jur.	514	Mnn
Kiningham, Baylor	661	Glc
Nancy	661	Glc
see Keiningham		
Kinkaid, Jas.	513	Mnn
Kinkead, Archd.	357	Ags
Robt.	357	Ags
Thanks	694	Br
Thomas	357	Ags
Wm.	356	Ags
Wm.	357	Ags
Wm., Sr.	357	Ags
Kinker see Skinker		
Kinlin, William	537	Frd
Kinnaird see Keniviard		
Kinnard, Davd. [2]	51	Clp
Lucy	51	Clp
Kinnemon, Richd.	711	Wsh
Kinner, Judith	408	Ags
William	775	Bck
Kinneson, David	414	Bth
Jacob	414	Bth
Kinney, Abm.	636	Btt
Chesley	357	Ags
Chesley	402	Ags
Christn., Jr.	636	Btt
Jacob	356	Ags
John	23	Rcm
Matthias	593	Brk
Robt.	356	Ags
Wm.	356	Ags

see Kenney		
Kinniard, John A.	13	Wod
Kinnison, Amos	426	Bth
Charles	426	Bth
Charles, Ju.	426	Bth
Mark	426	Bth
William	424	Bth
Kinsale, Michael	372	Fqr
Kinsbrough see Kimbrough		
Kinsel, Anna	840	Wth
see Kincel		
Kinser, Anna	841	Wth
Frederick	840	Wth
George	840	Wth
Michael	841	Wth
Michl.	666	Mnt
Peter	840	Wth
Peter	841	Wth
Kinsey, Absolem	51	Clp
Christn., Sr.	636	Btt
Danl.	636	Btt
Drury, (Est)	55	Chr
Jacob	636	Btt
Kinsie, Jacob	19	Oho
Kinsil, Jacob	107	Jff
Kinsley, Christian	6	Rcm
Kinsolving, James	164	Alb
Kinsy, ...	306	Rck
Kinter, Phillip	636	Btt
Kintzer, Adam	469	Bdf
Kinzer, Christian	5	Rcm
Kiphart, Linea	303	Ldn
Kipling, Jacob	24	Rcm
Kiplinger, John	639	Mnt
Kips, George	252	Shn
Jacob	197	Shn
Kirbey, John	275	Frf
Kirby, Ann	128	Sth
Ann	877	Yrk
Ann R.	152	Dnw
Benjamin	164	Alb
Hawkins	810	Bck
James	164	Alb
James	767	Hmp
James	66	Spt
James	877	Yrk
Jerre	357	Ags
John	151	Dnw
Nancy	857	Sth
Nathan	773	Hmp
Noel	164	Alb
Sarah	164	Alb
Silas	868	Sth
Thomas	273	Frf
see Kerby, Kirley		
Kirder, Joseph	831	Nrf
Kirk, Eliaz	776	Wst
Felix	906	Nrf
Hezekiah	205	Kng
James	358	Ags
Jerremiah	51	Stf
Jno.	514	Mnn
John	356	Ags
John	627	Gls
John	987	Nrt
John	10	Oho
Joseph	627	Gls
Joseph	10	Oho
Michael	691	Br
Nimrod	634	Btt
Radal	987	Nrt
Randell	776	Wst
Reuben	273	Frf
Sampson	905	Hrr
Sarah A.	408	Rch
Theophilas	691	Br
Thomas	756	Hmp
Thomas, Jur.	627	Gls
Thomas, Ser.	627	Gls
William	691	Br

Wm.	351	Lnc
Kirkard, Jos.	514	Mnn
Wm.	514	Mnn
Kirker, George	299	Rck
Kirkham, Jacob	151	Dnw
John	987	Nrt
Thomas	987	Nrt
William	987	Nrt
Kirkhart, Ant.	514	Mnn
Elizabeth	97	Jff
Kirkindall, Jacob	221	Pnd
John	220	Pnd
Kirkland, Bartlin	536	Prg
David	719	Brn
David	8	Oho
Hartwell	532	Prg
John	719	Brn
John, (l)	719	Brn
Stephen	719	Brn
Wm.	719	Brn
Kirkley, James	987	Nrt
Kirkmann, Ann	23	Oho
Kirkmyer, Frederick	987	Nrt
Kirkpatrick, Andw.	634	Btt
Ben.	282	Rck
Charles [crossed out]	286	Rck
Chas.	267	Rck
Jno., Ser.	286	Rck
John	10	Knw
John	427	Msn
John	286	Rck
John, Jr.	527	Prw
John, Sr.	527	Prw
Michl.	302	Rck
Robert	413	Bth
Robt.	303	Rck
Thos.	635	Btt
William	373	Fqr
Kirks, Charles	151	Dnw
Kirkwood, Sarah	284	Rck
Kirley, Asa	906	Hrr
Robert	906	Hrr
Kirnes, Jacob	469	Bdf
Kirtland, John	151	Dnw
Mildred	544	Prg
Susanna	151	Dnw
Kirtley, St. Clair	24	Rcm
Kirtly, Abraham	393	Mds
Francis	393	Mds
Kisbey, Peggy	290	Ldn
Richd.	288	Ldn
Kise, Jacob	402	Ags
Kisenger, Michael	572	Mnr
see Kesinger, Kiesinger, Kissenger		
Kiser, Andrew	191	Shn
Benjn.	357	Ags
Danl.	356	Ags
George	917	Hrr
Henry	302	Rck
Jacob	914	Hrr
Joseph	191	Shn
Noah	191	Shn
Val.	267	Rck
Wm.	634	Btt
see Kiger		
Kisner, Frederick	514	Frd
Jacob	536	Frd
Kissenger, Andrew	628	Gls
John	628	Gls
Michael	628	Gls
Kissin, John	6	Oho
Kister, Henry	569	Brk
Kitchen, Alexdr.	585	Mnr
Bohannah	833	Bck
Caleb	466	Frn
Danl.	275	Frf
Dixon	855	Sth
Drury	648	Sss

Enos	648	Sss	Isaac	585	Frd	Jacob	247	Shn
Frederick	648	Sss	Klugh, Ephraham	393	Mds	Knisely, Henry	249	Shn
James	273	Frf	Michael	393	Mds	Knoble, Jacob	553	Brk
John	866	Sth	Klymer, George	300	Rck	Knocks, Nehemiah	55	Chr
John	648	Sss	Knafe, Michael	589	Brk	Knot, Richard	349	Lnn
Joseph	553	Brk	Knap, George	503	Brk	Richard, jr.	349	Lnn
Lucy	855	Sth	Moses	428	Msn	Knott, John	819	Nrf
Maryam	273	Frf	Valentine	503	Brk	Saml.	690	Wsh
Nat.	872	Sth	Knave, George	841	Wth	William	987	Nrt
Robert	907	Nrf	Henry	357	Ags	Knotts, Absm.	514	Mnn
Samuel	140	Sth	Martin	357	Ags	Ed.	514	Mnn
Thomas	845	Sth	Michael	740	Wsh	Rob.	514	Mnn
Thompson	273	Frf	Michael	841	Wth	Tho.	514	Mnn
William	274	Frf	Knelms, John	143	Sth	Knotty, John	356	Ags
William	867	Sth	Knick, Wm.	64	Chs	Knowles, James	408	Ags
Wm.	140	Sth	Knight, Augusta	933	Hrr	Wm.	357	Ags
Wm.	854	Sth	Benjamin	114	Spt	Knowls, John	493	Frn
Kite, Benjamin	33	Rcm	Bennett	205	Kng	Knowlton, A.J.	907	Nrf
Christian	33	Rcm	Betty	34	Acc	Knox, Dan	512	Mnn
Danl.	33	Rcm	Catharine	292	Amh	Elisha, Jr.	635	Btt
Henry	34	Rcm	Catharine	446	Bth	Elisha, Sr.	635	Btt
John	33	Rcm	Charles, jr.	16	Ntt	George	1	Oho
John	3	Wod	Charles, Senr.	16	Ntt	Isaac M.	159	Sth
Martin	33	Rcm	Coleman	16	Ntt	James	635	Btt
Noah	804	Nrf	Elijah	102	Spt	John	441	Bth
Olive	804	Nrf	Elijah	22	Stf	John	597	Mnr
Philip	34	Rcm	Eliza	5	Hnr	Nickolas	106	Acc
Samuel	814	Hmp	Elizabeth	649	Sss	Sarah	635	Btt
William	814	Hmp	Ephraim	443	Flv	Susannah	36	Stf
see Kile			Ephraim	648	Sss	Thos.	50	Clp
Kiter, George	771	Hmp	George	289	Amh	Washington	513	Mnn
Kits, George	224	Pnd	James	50	Stf	William	413	Bth
Kitsmiller, Martin	306	Ldn	Jerremiah	25	Stf	William	332	Dnw
Kitterman, John	656	Mnt	Jerremiah, G	45	Stf	William	575	Mnr
Peter	497	Frn	Jno.	448	Mth	Wm.	635	Btt
Kittinger, Jacob	636	Btt	Jno.	513	Mnn	Knoxville, Ann	54	Stf
Rudolph	636	Btt	Jo.	447	Mth	Knup, David	22	Rcm
Wm.	636	Btt	John	292	Amh	Peter [2]	27	Rcm
Kittirman, Henry	498	Frn	John	349	Lnn	Philip	4	Rcm
Kittle, Abraham	421	Rnd	John, jr.	53	Stf	Koats, Joseph	191	Shn
Abraham, Ju.	426	Rnd	John, Sr.	53	Stf	Kollingsworth, Solomon	540	Frd
Daniel	1	Wod	Josiah	10	Hnr	Konekum, Thomas	229	Shn
George	18	Wod	Judith	649	Sss	Kook, Henry	840	Wth
Hezekiah	427	Rnd	Kinchey	648	Sss	Peter, (F.Negro)	52	Clp
John	422	Rnd	Lewis	130	Sth	Winney, (FN)	51	Clp
see Kettle			Nathaniel	649	Sss	Kooksey, Charles	349	Lnn
Kitts, Christopher	23	Oho	Orson	272	Amh	Koon, Henry	472	Frn
Nicholas	25	Oho	Peggy	587	Frd	Michael	516	Prw
Kizer, Joseph, Dr.	627	Gls	Peter	925	Hrr	Koons, Jacob	576	Brk
Molly	399	Rch	Peter	574	Pre	Koonts, Adam	283	Ldn
Kleet, Christain	476	Frn	Samuel	349	Lnn	George	623	Mnt
Klien, Jacob	906	Nrf	Silas	452	Grn	Koontz, Adam	19	Rcm
Klimer, John	510	Brk	Tarlton W.	349	Lnn	Christiana	19	Rcm
Kline, Abraham	781	Hmp	Tho., Jnr.	513	Mnn	George	171	Shn
Adam	768	Hmp	Tho., Sen.	513	Mnn	George	246	Shn
Anthony	520	Frd	Thomas	583	Frd	Jacob	186	Shn
Anthony	603	Frd	Thos.	907	Nrf	John	6	Rcm
Casper	521	Frd	Uriah, jr.	47	Stf	John	12	Rcm
Donrod	7	Rcm	Uriah, Sr.	45	Stf	John	26	Rcm
Elizabeth	543	Frd	William	268	Amh	John	186	Shn
Frederick	21	Rcm	William	290	Amh	John	188	Shn
Henry	588	Frd	William	547	Frd	Joseph	189	Shn
Henry	31	Rcm	William	925	Hrr	Peter	515	Frd
Inglehart	524	Frd	William	759	Nwk	Peter	12	Rcm
Jacob	523	Frd	William	105	Spt	Peter	26	Rcm
Jacob	603	Frd	William	53	Stf	Philip	19	Rcm
John	802	Hmp	William	649	Sss	Philip, (Sen.)	27	Rcm
John	7	Rcm	Wm.	513	Mnn	Phillip	422	Rnd
Joseph	358	Ags	Woodson	349	Lnn	Rebecca	199	Shn
Michal	542	Frd	Woodson	6	Ntt	Kounts, Henry	5	Knw
Michl.	356	Ags	Knighten, Thos.	50	Clp	Kountz, George	594	Mnr
Peter	356	Ags	Knip, George	841	Wth	Henry	594	Mnr
Phillip	768	Hmp	John	840	Wth	John	422	Msn
Phillip	802	Hmp	Verner	840	Wth	Michal	426	Msn
Saml.	21	Rcm	Knipe, Henry	519	Frn	Michl.	356	Ags
William	588	Frd	Knipple, Frederick	27	Rcm	Philip	183	Shn
Klinebell, Geo.	356	Ags	Kniseley, George	174	Shn	Kout, Peter	356	Ags
Klingingpeel, Jacob	357	Ags	George C.	250	Shn	Krantz, Jacob	469	Bdf
Klipstine, Philip	508	Frd	Henry	172	Shn	Mary	469	Bdf
Klotz, Abraham	564	Frd				Michael	469	Bdf

Thomas	469	Bdf
William	469	Bdf
Kratzer, John	16	Rcm
Josep, (Jr.)	16	Rcm
Joseph, (Sen.)	16	Rcm
Kreamer, Adam	501	Prw
Kremer, Conrad	512	Frd
Kreps, John	72	Jff
Maryann	71	Jff
Krest, Andw.	4	Rcm
Krick, Jacob	59	Jff
Krider, Frederick	302	Ldn
Krim, John, (Jr.)	26	Rcm
John, (Sen.)	26	Rcm
Peter	509	Brk
Peter, (Jr.)	25	Rcm
Peter, (Sen.)	25	Rcm
Peter, Sr.	509	Brk
Kring, Frederick	16	Rcm
George	253	Shn
Joshua	253	Shn
Krizer, Leah	592	Frd
Kroan, Adam	664	Mnt
Krouse, Jacob, Sr.	635	Btt
John	559	Frd
Krusen, Wm.	586	Brk
Kugall, Ben	513	Mnn
Kuhn, Henry	68	Chs
Kunum see Keenum		
Kurtz, Adam	514	Frd
Anthony	509	Frd
Frederick	506	Frd
Jacob	402	Ags
Kuth see Keith		
Kwall, Abram	746	Wsh
Kybert, Danl.	636	Btt
Kyger, Christian, (Jr.)	10	Rcm
Christian, (Sen.)	12	Rcm
Fielding	512	Mnn
Frederick	12	Rcm
Jac.	514	Mnn
Jacob	37	Rcm
John	12	Rcm
see Kyzer		
Kyle, Barclay	635	Btt
Barclay	788	Bck
David	775	Bck
David	1	Rcm
Duget	636	Btt
James	2	Rcm
Jeremiah	1	Rcm
John	526	Brk
Mathew	393	Mds
Robt., Jr.	634	Btt
Robt., Sr.	634	Btt
William	481	Frn
Wm., Sr.	634	Btt
Kynes, John	363	Fqr
Kyser, John	591	Brk
Wm.	635	Btt
see Kyzer		
Kyzer, Abraham	6	Rcm
Henry	635	Btt
Isaac	4	Rcm
Jacob	39	Rcm
John	19	Rcm
John	33	Rcm
see Kyger, Kyser		
--- L ---		
L..., ...	236	Aml
...	237	Aml
Horatio [crossed out]	802	Nrf
L...h, John	237	Aml
La..., John	237	Aml
Labaierrere, Jno.	61	Chs
Labbin, James, Jnr.	710	Nls

Labby, Mary	124	Hnr
Laboo, Michael	58	Jff
Labsue, Peter	908	Nrf
Lacard, Aron	932	Hrr
Lacey, Aron	394	Mds
David	295	Ldn
Elias	302	Ldn
Israel	243	Ldn
James	406	Fqr
Joseph	413	Fqr
Josiah	60	Chs
Malon	364	Fqr
Manuel	406	Fqr
Mary	313	Ldn
Meshech	301	Ldn
Metilda	242	Ldn
Michl.	907	Nrf
Thomas	214	Shn
Thomas	777	Wst
Lacher, Fanney	291	Ldn
Lachey, John	284	Amh
Lacker, Jacob	689	Wsh
Lackett, Jacob	236	Aml
Lackey, Hugh	14	Oho
Mary	592	Brk
Mary	989	Nrt
William	394	Mds
Lackland, Zadock	785	Bck
Lacklin, John	647	Mnt
Lacky, James	637	Btt
Lacy, Archibald	760	Nwk
Bacon	760	Nwk
Benjamin	164	Alb
Carles	165	Alb
Danl.	14	Knw
David	12	Pwh
Drury	575	Pre
Edwd.	25	Hnr
John	236	Aml
John	263	Amh
Lucy	699	Gch
Mary	759	Nwk
Matthew	700	Gch
Philemon	759	Nwk
Stephen	164	Alb
Stephen	759	Nwk
Susan	700	Gch
William	760	Nwk
Ladd, Benjm. W.	955	Chc
David	760	Nwk
James	201	Alb
James	759	Nwk
James	611	Srr
James D.	940	Chc
Jessee	956	Chc
John	938	Chc
John	701	Gch
John	759	Nwk
Joseph	954	Chc
Peter	954	Chc
Robert	955	Chc
Samuel	954	Chc
Thomas	6	Hnr
William	760	Nwk
Wm.	4	Hnr
Laer, Margt.	580	Brk
Lafawn, John	629	Gls
Lafferty, George	94	Jff
Thomas	90	Jff
William	565	Mnr
Laffoon, Daniel	350	Lnn
Jeremiah	350	Lnn
Jesse	350	Lnn
John	350	Lnn
Mathew	350	Lnn
Wm.	721	Brn
see Laffson		
Laffson, Nathaniel	461	Frn
Laflet, Peter	4	Ntt

Lafoe, Daniel	911	Crl
Nicholas	911	Crl
Lafon, Francis	169	Knq
Thomas	63	Chs
Lafong, George	911	Crl
Lag see Lay		
Lager, Adam	225	Shn
Laidley, Tho.	515	Mnn
Lain, Pattey	710	Nls
Samuel P.	709	Nls
Laine, Margt.	26	Hnr
Lainer, Edmond	709	Nls
Lair, Andw.	40	Rcm
Ferdinand	215	Pnd
Laird, David	12	Rcm
James	422	Bth
James	307	Rck
John	280	Rck
Laissaint, Frs.	907	Nrf
Lake, Geo.	517	Mnn
James	395	Fqr
Jerh.	517	Mnn
Jonathan	585	Brk
Mary	637	Btt
Nicholas	592	Mnr
Susanna	392	Fqr
Vincent	53	Clp
William	388	Fqr
William	927	Hrr
William, Jur.	928	Hrr
Lakenan, James ["John"		
crossed out]	3	Hnr
John	1	Hnr
William	421	Fqr
Laknan, Daniel	7	Hnr
Lall, Elizabeth	802	Hmp
Lalor, Jno.	1	Ntt
Lam, Christopher	248	Ldn
Henry	286	Ldn
Michal	226	Pnd
Lamantonge, P. A.	909	Nrf
Lamasters, Benjamin	8	Knw
Lamb, ---, (FB)	463	Pra
Abram	359	Ags
Adam	23	Rcm
Agness	650	Sss
Daniel	336	Dnw
George	488	Frn
Henry	4	Rcm
Isham	153	Dnw
Jacob	359	Ags
John	236	Aml
John	360	Ags
John	421	Bth
John	949	Chc
John	152	Dnw
John, jr.	359	Ags
John C.	650	Sss
Manson	858	Cmp
Nancy	882	Cmp
Nicholas	29	Rcm
Philip	34	Rcm
Robert	153	Dnw
Samuel	192	Shn
Theok.	153	Dnw
W. B.	908	Nrf
William	429	Bth
William	11	Hnr
William	34	Rcm
Lambden, John	107	Acc
Lambdon, John	36	Acc
Lambert, Abraham	248	Shn
Abram	360	Ags
Adam	359	Ags
Adam, jr.	360	Ags
Benjami	754	Brn
Benjamin	842	Wth
Charles	471	Bdf
Christley	362	Ags
Danl.	264	Rck

Name	No.	Co.
David	359	Ags
David	33	Hnr
Elizabeth	853	Hnv
Francis	362	Ags
Garret	842	Wth
George	471	Bdf
George	221	Pnd
George	843	Wth
Henry	172	Shn
Henry	842	Wth
Jacob	256	Shn
James	397	Rch
Jeremiah	350	Lnn
Jesse	908	Nrf
Jessee	908	Nrf
Jno.	867	Hnv
John	359	Ags
John	376	Fqr
John	939	Hrr
John [2]	842	Wth
Jos.	516	Mnn
Jos.	813	Nrf
Joseph	677	Br
Josiah	18	Hnr
Leroy	56	Chr
Lewis	721	Brn
Mary	29	Rcm
Michael	843	Wth
Milley	350	Lnn
Nancy	221	Pnd
Patrick	37	Rcm
Perminius	300	Ldn
Sally	841	Nrf
Saml.	628	Gls
Sarah	721	Brn
Thomas	278	Frf
Thomas	842	Wth
Thos.	811	Nrf
Thos.	812	Nrf
Tobias	296	Rck
see Flours		
Lambertson, Jeremiah	192	Shn
Lambeth, Bornard	197	Ess
Francis	848	Cmp
George	848	Cmp
John	169	Knq
Meredith	848	Cmp
Washington	853	Cmp
William	784	Bck
Wm.	662	Glc
Lambs, Antoney	943	Chc
Lamburt, Lewis	350	Lnn
Lamden, William	683	Br
Lamemon, Henry	218	Shn
John	218	Shn
Lamey, Andw.	727	Wsh
Lamkin, Benedict	777	Wst
Fleet	777	Wst
Griffin	637	Btt
Jane	350	Lnn
John	348	Fqr
Peter	348	Fqr
Samuel	777	Wst
Lamkins, James	290	Ldn
Lamoin, ---, Mrs.	329	Dnw
K., Mrs.	336	Dnw
Lamp, George	568	Frd
Lampet, Jacob	852	Cmp
Lamphen, Richd.	169	Knq
Lamphin, Anthony	236	Aml
Lampkin, James	56	Chr
Jane	988	Nrt
Jno.	54	Clp
Jno., jr.	52	Clp
Lewis, Jr.	989	Nrt
Lewis, Sr.	988	Nrt
Matthew	988	Nrt
Morgan	53	Clp
Nancy	54	Clp
Rebecca	988	Nrt
Thos.	53	Clp
Lampton, Samuel	176	Shn
Lampy, William	843	Wth
Lanah, George	39	Rcm
Lanays, ---, Mrs.	907	Nrf
Lancaster, Aaron	814	Nrf
Courtny	818	Nrf
Elizabeth	584	Frd
Elizabeth	817	Nrf
John	110	Cmb
Joseph	116	Hnr
Margaret	16	Hnr
Robert	471	Bdf
Robert	576	Pre
Ursula	118	Hnr
William	402	Rch
Wm.	515	Mnn
see Lankester		
Lance, George	217	Pnd
Joseph	216	Pnd
Peter	284	Rck
see Cance, Lanier		
Lancely, Charlotte	67	Spt
Lanchaster, Joseph	85	Jff
Lancy see La...		
Land, Batson	464	Pra
Batson, (of B)	461	Pra
Batson, (of Hosa.)	461	Pra
Caleb	462	Pra
Chas.	463	Pra
Curtis	650	Sss
David	463	Pra
Edwin	574	Pre
Elizabeth	462	Pra
Elizabeth	651	Sss
Enoch	462	Pra
Francis M.	461	Pra
Henry, Sr.	462	Pra
Hillary	464	Pra
Isaac	461	Pra
James	828	Bck
James	575	Pre
James	461	Pra
Jeremiah	839	Nrf
Jno.	462	Pra
John	575	Pre
John W.	649	Sss
Joshua	463	Pra
Langley	462	Pra
Lewellin	651	Sss
Lititia	462	Pra
Molly	462	Pra
Nathl.	452	Grn
Robert	462	Pra
Robert W.	452	Grn
Peter	462	Pra
Ree	462	Pra
Reuben	463	Pra
Richd.	463	Pra
Simon	461	Pra
Tully	462	Pra
William	651	Sss
Wm.	463	Pra
Wm., (of Nat.)	463	Pra
see Sand		
Landcraff, Nathaniel	180	Alb
Lander, Frederick	825	Hmp
Landers, ---, Mrs.	30	Hnr
John	360	Ags
Landing, Michel	109	Acc
William	847	Sth
Landis, Peter, Jr.	639	Btt
Peter, Sr.	638	Btt
Landman, Vincent	413	Rch
Landmon, Newman	54	Clp
Landon see Carter		
Landram, Thomas	256	Amh
Landres, Meridith	710	Nls
Landrum, James	350	Lnn
Lucy	184	Elc
Lunsford	350	Lnn
Reuben	90	Spt
Rheubin	124	Cmb
Thomas	777	Wst
Will.	186	Elc
William	350	Lnn
William	91	Spt
Landsdown, John	512	Prw
Landus, Peter	868	Cmp
Lane, Barthw.	590	Mnr
Batts	611	Srr
Benjamin	108	Acc
Benjn. W.	13	Pwh
Carr W.	278	Frf
Catharine	238	Ldn
Charles	275	Frf
Daniel	788	Hmp
Daniel	105	Spt
David	278	Frf
Drury, Jr.	650	Sss
Drury, Sr.	649	Sss
Edward	201	Alb
Elisha	440	Flv
Eliza.	452	Grn
Frs.	909	Nrf
George	49	Stf
Henry	287	Amh
Henry	611	Srr
James	201	Alb
James	557	Frd
James	427	Msn
James D.	278	Frf
James S.	106	Jff
James S.	611	Srr
Jasper	849	Hnv
Jeremiah	462	Pra
Jeremiah, Jr.	463	Pra
Jno.	463	Pra
Joel	611	Srr
John	461	Frn
John	575	Pre
John	611	Srr
John	649	Sss
John, (son Jo.)	611	Srr
Jonathan	7	Oho
Joseph	201	Alb
Joseph	139	Sth
Keziah	885	Hnv
Larance	431	Msn
Lovy	462	Pra
Lucy	611	Srr
Martha	56	Chr
Mary	201	Alb
Micajah	754	Brn
Peter	649	Sss
Philo R.	275	Frf
Powell	830	Hmp
Rd.	277	Frf
Rebecca	611	Srr
Richard	85	Spt
Robert	649	Sss
Sally	611	Srr
Samuel	855	Sth
Sarah	278	Frf
Simon	755	Brn
Solo.	463	Pra
Thomas	266	Amh
Thomas	539	Frd
Thomas	296	Ldn
Thomas, Sen.	611	Srr
Ths.	4	Hnr
Unity	436	Flv
William	848	Sth
William	649	Sss
Willoughby W.	54	Jff
Wm.	278	Frf
Wm.	453	Mth
Wm. A.	53	Clp
Wm. S.	441	Flv
Woodson	3	Knw

see La...
Laney, Dixon 24 Hnr
Lanford, Francis 8 Wod
Lang, Alexander 109 Acc
  Elixander 108 Acc
  Geo., (W) 877 Yrk
  George 904 Hrr
  James 67 Chs
  James 586 Frd
  James 54 Stf
  John 372 Fqr
  John 917 Hrr
  John 81 Jff
  John H. 700 Gch
  Lewis 171 Shn
  Robert 206 Kng
  Stanbury 904 Hrr
  William 163 Shn
  William 164 Shn
  see ... ang, Long
Langdon, Henry 618 Mnt
Lange, Abraham 359 Ags
  Ann 908 Nrf
Langfair, Wm. 516 Mnn
Langfilt, Philip 516 Prw
Langfitt, Fulsome 21 Stf
  John 34 Stf
Langford, Charles 201 Alb
  Jacob 359 Ags
  John 115 Hnr
  Jonthn. 756 Wsh
  Parks 165 Alb
  Philip 521 Prw
  Selby 108 Acc
  Thomas 201 Alb
  West 165 Alb
  William 165 Alb
  Zachariah 118 Hnr
Langfort, Stephen 157 Sth
  Jesse 156 Sth
Langham, Edmond 169 Knq
Langhorn, Henry 800 Bck
  Maurice 794 Bck
  Maurice 112 Cmb
Langhorne, Maurc. 681 Wrw
  Wm. 682 Wrw
Langley, --- 908 Nrf
  Alexr. 305 Ldn
  Ann 812 Nrf
  Benjamin 524 Frd
  Billy 330 Dnw
  Curtis 581 Frd
  David 168 Shn
  Elizabeth 907 Nrf
  Elizabeth 462 Pra
  Henry B. 760 Nwk
  John 812 Nrf
  John 833 Nrf
  John W. 760 Nwk
  Jos., jr. 838 Nrf
  Joseph 524 Frd
  Martha 629 Gls
  Mary 812 Nrf
  Robert 830 Nrf
  Walter 235 Ldn
  William 760 Nwk
  Wm., jr. 812 Nrf
  see Longley
Langlin, Saml. 618 Mnt
Langly, J.B. 908 Nrf
Langsdon, Benjn. 11 Pwh
  John 11 Pwh
  Phobe 11 Pwh
  William 11 Pwh
Langyher, Jacob 518 Prw
Lanham, Amasa 598 Frd
  Arch. 517 Mnn
  Ben Dd. 708 Nls
  Coleman 262 Ldn
  Dennis 597 Frd

  Francis 935 Hrr
  Henry 177 Shn
  Henry, Jr. 599 Frd
  Henry, Senr. 599 Frd
  Jacob 528 Frd
  Jeremiah 599 Frd
  John 708 Nls
  Lucy 516 Mnn
  Moses 599 Frd
  Peggy 599 Frd
  Robert 244 Ldn
  Samuel 597 Frd
  Sarah 708 Nls
  Thomas 170 Shn
  Walter 232 Ldn
  Wm. 515 Mnn
  Wm. 708 Nls
Lanier, Abner 452 Grn
  Allen 754 Brn
  Benjamin 720 Brn
  Benjamin 649 Sss
  Buckner 649 Sss
  David, Sr. 720 Brn
  Druly 719 Brn
  Edwin 750 Sss
  Francis 152 Dnw
  Frederick 755 Brn
  James 452 Grn
  John 720 Brn
  John 821 Nrf
  Lewis 152 Dnw
  Littleton 649 Sss
  Nicholas 719 Brn
  Robert 720 Brn
  Robert 755 Brn
  Robert 326 Dnw
  Sarah 755 Brn
  Sterling 720 Brn
  Tabitha 452 Grn
  Thomas 452 Grn
  Thos. 719 Brn
  Thos., jr. 720 Brn
  William 452 Grn
  Wm. 720 Brn
  see Lawer
Lankester, James 470 Bdf
  John 470 Bdf
  Lewis 470 Bdf
  Nancy 470 Bdf
Lankford, Chr. 709 Nls
  Eliza 662 Glc
  Henry 895 Hnv
  Hiram 661 Glc
  Isabella 661 Glc
  James 892 Hnv
  John 782 Bck
  John 169 Knq
  Matthew 708 Nls
  Mildred 169 Knq
  Stephen 880 Sth
  Winnifred 40 Isw
  Wm. 710 Nls
Lann see Larue
Lannan, Jno. 54 Clp
Lannon, Cathaline 165 Alb
Lannum, Edwd. 277 Frf
  Lecttous 277 Frf
  Loyd 279 Frf
Lansdel, Benjamin, Jr. 988 Nrt
  Benjamin, Sr. 988 Nrt
  John 989 Nrt
Lansdown, Saml. 508 Prw
  Sarah 54 Clp
  William 470 Bdf
Lansford see Launceford
Lantenmann, William 17 Oho
Lanthorp, John 651 Sss
Lanthrope, Elizabeth 539 Prg
  Jesse 531 Prg
Ledbetter 531 Prg

  Mary 539 Prg
  Rebecca 531 Prg
  Wm. 544 Prg
Lanton, Ebby 911 Crl
Lantrip, John 153 Dnw
  Martha 153 Dnw
Lantz, Hen. 517 Mnn
  Jacob 30 Rcm
  Jacob 240 Shn
  John 513 Frd
  Peter 637 Btt
Laperouse, Jno. 908 Nrf
Lapington, Thos. 717 Wsh
Laporte, Abm. 908 Nrf
  Peter 402 Ags
Lapp, Abraham 40 Rcm
  John 516 Mnn
Laprade, Jno. 61 Chs
  Susan. 700 Gch
Larau, Jeremiah 25 Oho
  see Larue
Lard, Andrew 165 Alb
Lare, Barbary 295 Rck
Larence, Bilcey, a free woman
  of couler 721 Wsh
Larew, Benjn. 362 Ags
  Jacob 362 Ags
  Joseph 362 Ags
Largent, Abraham 766 Hmp
  James 773 Hmp
  John 834 Hmp
  John, Jur. 763 Hmp
  John, Ser. 766 Hmp
  Lewis 762 Hmp
  Lewis 834 Hmp
  Thomas 761 Hmp
Larience, John 574 Mnr
Larimore, James 788 Hmp
  John 763 Hmp
  Joseph 788 Hmp
  William 788 Hmp
Lark, Edward 8 Hnr
Larke, John 638 Btt
  John 127 Hnr
  Tennisson 877 Yrk
Larkey, James 758 Wsh
  John 758 Wsh
Larkin, Hugh 638 Btt
  James 573 Mnr
  Thomas 524 Prw
Larkins, John 759 Hmp
  Patrick 988 Nrt
Laroo, Isaac 312 Ldn
  Richd. 270 Ldn
Larrence, Absolem 130 Hnr
  James 118 Hnr
  John 119 Hnr
  John 130 Hnr
  Nancy 130 Hnr
Larrick, Caleb 4 Rcm
  Caspar 571 Frd
  Frederick 569 Frd
  George 602 Frd
  Henry 570 Frd
  Jacob 571 Frd
  John 570 Frd
  Margarett 602 Frd
Larrimer, John 692 Wsh
  John, Jur. 715 Wsh
Larrius, Adam 637 Btt
  Jacob 637 Btt
Larry, John 175 Shn
Larue, Cornelius 766 Hmp
  Ed. 516 Mnn
  Hanah 766 Hmp
  Isaac 20 Oho
  Jabez 534 Frd
  Jacob 766 Hmp
  Jacob 20 Oho
  Michael 8 Oho

Noah	773	Hmp	John	748	Wsh	Sherwd.	442	Flv
Peter	784	Hmp	Laughlin, James	911	Crl	Thomas	9	Knw
Peter	580	Mnr	Lauk, Phillip	111	Spt	William	279	Amh
Samuel	534	Frd	Lauman, John	636	Btt	Lawler, James	377	Fqr
see Larau, Laroo			Launce, Geo.	516	Mnn	Joseph	346	Fqr
Lary, William	520	Prw	Jno.	515	Mnn	Nicholas	346	Fqr
Lasey, Agness	113	Hnr	Launceford, Wm.	291	Rck	Lawless, John	699	Wsh
John	459	Frn	Launtis, Benjn.	359	Ags	Richard	262	Amh
John	113	Hnr	Christby	360	Ags	William	278	Amh
Lash, Jehue	962	Hrr	Danl.	359	Ags	Wm.	515	Mnn
Thomas	757	Hmp	John	359	Ags	Lawlor, Jno.	14	Hnr
Lashbough, Martin	402	Ags	John, jr.	359	Ags	Michael	53	Clp
Lashorn, John	528	Brk	Laurance, Thomas	608	Mnt	Lawman, Elizabeth	471	Bdf
Lassen, John	908	Nrf	Wm.	607	Mnt	James	585	Brk
Lasure, Hyatt	7	Wod	Laurence, ---, Howard			see Lowman		
Laswell, Andw.	730	Wsh	&	37	Stf	Lawns, Thomas	332	Dnw
John	723	Wsh	Edward	532	Frd	William	328	Dnw
Lasy, Wenny	118	Hnr	Hardy	157	Shn	Lawrance, Edward	165	Shn
Latane, Wm.	222	Ess	James	568	Frd	Fanny	327	Dnw
Latcha, Solomon	267	Rck	James	207	Kng	John	701	Gch
Latchem, George	38	Acc	Jane	777	Mnn	John	169	Shn
Latham, Charles	204	Ess	Jno.	881	Sth	Kendall	37	Acc
Geo., (Son of Anthy.)	353	Fqr	John	358	Ags	Lewis	170	Shn
Francis	353	Fqr	John	360	Fqr	William	36	Acc
Franklin	380	Fqr	Mason	344	Fqr	William	222	Pnd
George, (of Geo.)	383	Fqr	Phillip	880	Sth	William	170	Shn
James	373	Fqr	Rhodham	381	Fqr	Lawrence, Benja.	878	Sth
James	408	Fqr	Sterling, (M)	721	Brn	David	26	Hnr
John	353	Fqr	Timothy	806	Nrf	Jacob	922	Hrr
John	561	Frd	William	777	Wst	Jno., Jr.	641	Mnt
John	36	Stf	Wim.	850	Hnv	Jno., Sr.	641	Mnt
John, U.	39	Stf	Wm.	583	Mnr	John	179	Elc
Philip	52	Clp	Wm.	152	Sth	John	908	Nrf
Richard	398	Fqr	Wood, (PN)	69	Chr	John, Jun.	40	Isw
Robert	523	Prw	Laurene, Thos.	888	Hnv	John, Sen.	11	Isw
Robt.	52	Clp	Laurey, George	408	Fqr	Joseph	463	Pra
Sally	30	Stf	Laurge, Wm.	529	Brk	Joshua	190	Elc
Sarah	908	Nrf	Laurison, Robert	3	Oho	Joshua	463	Pra
Thomas	407	Fqr	Lauter, John	843	Wth	Millicent	33	Isw
Travis	914	Hrr	William	843	Wth	Mills	41	Isw
William	30	Stf	Lave see Lowe			Peter	53	Clp
Wm.	52	Clp	Lavender, George	637	Btt	Rd.	53	Clp
Lathey, William	362	Fqr	George	709	Nls	Robert, Jun.	33	Isw
Lathim, Edward	716	Wsh	Jessee	639	Btt	Saml.	817	Nrf
John	706	Wsh	John	488	Frn	Sammuel	855	Hnv
Moses	706	Wsh	Robert	478	Frn	Samuel	911	Crl
Lathom, Mary B.	471	Bdf	Thos.	637	Btt	Walter	53	Clp
Latimer, Geo.	192	Elc	Thos.	639	Btt	William	9	Knw
James	191	Elc	Law, Burwell	459	Frn	Willis	53	Clp
John	179	Elc	Cheadle	455	Frn	see Larience		
Roe	191	Elc	Daniel	452	Frn	Lawrey, Gillis	52	Clp
Susan	189	Elc	David	452	Frn	Jno.	52	Clp
Tho.	178	Elc	Edward	639	Btt	Richd.	31	Hnr
Tho.	188	Elc	Henry	453	Frn	Lawright see Lewright		
Latouche, J.W.	330	Dnw	Henry	454	Frn	Lawry see Laurey		
Latour, Frs.	908	Nrf	Henry	455	Frn	Laws, Amine	352	Lnc
Latshaw, Betsey	361	Ags	James	8	Oho	Criss	352	Lnc
Isaac	646	Mnt	Jas.	515	Mnn	Fabious	236	Aml
Lattimer, Thomas	278	Frf	Jesse	453	Frn	John	107	Acc
William	30	Isw	Jno.	515	Mnn	John	394	Fqr
Wm., Junr.	278	Frf	John	1	Wod	Sally	109	Acc
see Lattinner			John, Sr.	455	Frn	Tubman	831	Nrf
Lattimore, Betsey	988	Nrt	Nathaniel	459	Frn	William	397	Fqr
Polly	908	Nrf	Samuel	453	Frn	Lawson, Alexander	806	Hmp
William	989	Nrt	Thomas	693	Br	Andrew	912	Crl
Lattinner, W., Senr.	279	Frf	Thomas	455	Frn	Antho ny	464	Pra
Laubinger, George M.	759	Hmp	Thomas	962	Hrr	Ben	516	Mnn
Lauchry, Patrick	929	Hrr	William	462	Frn	Benjamin	56	Chr
Lauck, Abraham	506	Frd	William P.	932	Hrr	Boswell	912	Crl
George	551	Frd	see Low			Catlett	912	Crl
Peter	540	Frd				Charles	662	Glc
Simon	506	Frd	Lawer, George	589	Brk	Charles	894	Hnv
Laud, Nelly	912	Crl	Lawfer, Fredk.	501	Brk	Charles	296	Ldn
Laudridge, Thos.	638	Btt	Lawharn, Isham	470	Bdf	Chs., jr.	662	Glc
Laugh, Jno.	515	Mnn	Lawhorn, Benjamin	437	Flv	Dan.	877	Yrk
Laugheny, Pad.	948	Hrr	Daniel	470	Bdf	Daniel	400	Rch
Laughern, Thomas	843	Wth	George	296	Amh	Daniel, Jr.	395	Rch
Laugherty, Wm.	424	Rnd	Henry	295	Amh	Davd., jr.	270	Rck
Laughlan, Hugh	262	Rck	Henry, jr.	296	Amh	David	270	Rck
Laughland, Alexr.	734	Wsh	John	296	Amh	Eleanor	663	Glc

Elizabeth	912	Crl	see Lyne			Leake, Fanny	699	Gch
Ellen	236	Aml	Layr, Cornode	223	Shn	John	700	Gch
George	70	Chr	Lays, Sarah	224	Pnd	Josiah	700	Gch
George	37	Stf	Layton, Braxton	466	Mdd	Samuel	165	Alb
Hanna	629	Gls	Geo. W.	466	Mdd	Selah	201	Alb
Henry C.	352	Lnc	James	290	Rck	Thomas	906	Hrr
Hillery	277	Frf	James	27	Rcm	William	165	Alb
Isaac, Sr.	304	Rck	John	22	Rcm	Leaman, Jno.	539	Mnn
Ishua	628	Gls	John, j.	466	Mdd	Leanard, Joseph	831	Nrf
James	389	Fqr	John, Senr.	466	Mdd	Leaper, George	69	Jff
Janus	270	Rck	Obadiah	27	Rcm	Lear, Abraham	813	Hmp
Jno.	663	Glc	Richard	394	Mds	Andrew	637	Btt
John	592	Frd	Robert	93	Spt	Jno.	52	Clp
John	794	Hmp	Robert	95	Spt	John	110	Spt
John	500	Prw	Thomas	466	Mdd	William	346	Fqr
John	507	Prw	Laywell, Abraham	11	Knw	see Laer		
John	34	Rcm	Mary	842	Wth	Leary, Abednego	17	Rcm
Lotty	912	Crl	Lazenby, Robert, Sr.	471	Bdf	Edith	127	Sth
Mary	352	Lnc	Lazer, Jerome	681	Br	Lease, Jacob	402	Ags
Michael	708	Nls	Jesse	678	Br	Nancy	263	Rck
Nancy	520	Prw	Joseph	681	Br	Leason, Michael	876	Cmp
Philip	700	Gch	Lazier, Zephaniah	511	Frd	Leaster, Saml.	361	Ags
Polly	89	Spt	Zephaniah	556	Frd	Leasure, Jonathan	18	Wod
Richd.	461	Pra	Lazwell, Andw.	722	Wsh	Leatch, George	131	Hnr
Robert	270	Rck	Wm.	740	Wsh	James	179	Alb
Robt.	300	Rck	Lazzle, Tho.	515	Mnn	Samuel	179	Alb
Thos.	360	Ags	Tho., Jr.	515	Mnn	Leath, ...	236	Aml
Thos.	53	Clp	LBottom, Samuel	452	Grn	Abraham	327	Dnw
Thos.	908	Nrf	Lea, Augustine	443	Flv	James	153	Dnw
William	760	Nwk	Gideon, Junr.	852	Cmp	Jno.	21	Ntt
Wm.	277	Frf	Gideon, Senr.	872	Cmp	John	20	Oho
Wm.	662	Glc	John	443	Flv	Lewis	236	Aml
Zachariah	56	Chr	see Sea			Mary	239	Ldn
Lawton, Thomas	869	Cmp	Leach, Absalom	588	Mnr	Richd.	720	Brn
W.B.	908	Nrf	Andrew	47	Stf	Stephen	152	Dnw
Lawwell, Saml.	276	Frf	Bartlet	4	Wod	Stephen	537	Prg
Lawyer, Caty	545	Frd	Benjamin	58	Stf	Wm.	238	Ldn
Eve	545	Frd	Betsey	374	Fqr	Leathe..., Joseph	254	Shn
John	545	Frd	Charles	594	Frd	Leatherberry, Charles	35	Acc
Lawyers, James	12	Knw	Elijah	401	Fqr	Gilbert	36	Acc
Lay, Conrad	553	Frd	Elisha	518	Mnn	John, Junr.	36	Acc
Jacob	105	Jff	Esam	569	Mnr	John, Senr.	35	Acc
Jemima	275	Frf	George	541	Frd	Peter	37	Acc
Margeret	278	Frf	George	1	Wod	Thomas	36	Acc
Marmaduke	520	Prw	Hugh B.	562	Frd	Leatherman, Abraham	824	Hmp
Michal	586	Frd	James	152	Dnw	Daniel	824	Hmp
Laycock, Saml.	279	Ldn	James	153	Dnw	John	824	Hmp
Layfayette, James	759	Nwk	James	568	Frd	Lewis	824	Hmp
Layfield, George	35	Acc	James	24	Stf	Nicholas	824	Hmp
Wm.	960	Hrr	John	153	Dnw	Peter	824	Hmp
Layler, Betcy	37	Isw	John	395	Mds	Leathers, George	395	Mds
Luke	37	Isw	John	219	Pnd	Nicholas	395	Mds
Laylor, Arthur	37	Acc	Joshua	581	Mnr	Leathty, William	11	Wod
Nicholas	611	Srr	Samuel	5	Hnr	Leavel, Burwell	71	Spt
Patience	35	Acc	Susannah	599	Mnr	Leavell, Benja.	52	Clp
Layne, Anthony	700	Gch	Rebecca	403	Fqr	Jos.	52	Clp
Archibald	819	Bck	Thomas	373	Fqr	Jos.	53	Clp
Betsey	700	Gch	Valentine	589	Frd	Leavit, Charles	877	Yrk
Claibourne	701	Gch	William	989	Nrt	Leavitt, Wm.	662	Glc
David	818	Bck	William	524	Prw	Leay, A.B.	729	Nls
David	820	Bck	Wm.	600	Mnr	Leazer, Joseph	219	Pnd
David	832	Bck	Leachman, John	524	Prw	LeBailey, Frs.	908	Nrf
David	701	Gch	Leonard	370	Fqr	Leban, Wolly	920	Hrr
Faris	471	Bdf	Nancy	516	Prw	Lebe, John, Jun.	185	Elc
Fredrick	701	Gch	Thomas	1	Wod	John, Sr.	185	Elc
Gabriel	783	Bck	Wm.	258	Ldn	Molly	183	Elc
Harris	170	Knq	Leack, Thomas	262	Ldn	Lebee, James	877	Yrk
Henry	470	Bdf	Leader, Richard	989	Nrt	Lebevrodus, Francis	2	Hnr
Henry	700	Gch	Samuel	989	Nrt	Lebrell, Nicholas	849	Sth
James	822	Bck	Leadley, James G.	16	Wod	Lecatoe, Elizabeth	35	Acc
Jesse	819	Bck	Leagan, Elizabeth	708	Nls	Jane	36	Acc
Jessee	700	Gch	Frances	710	Nls	Littleton	36	Acc
Mary	700	Gch	Polley	710	Nls	Major	36	Acc
Matthew	700	Gch	League, James	236	Aml	Shadrach	37	Acc
Richd.	700	Gch	James	575	Pre	Lechaize, E.V.	22	Hnr
Samuel	820	Bck	Milly	236	Aml	Lechman, George	525	Prw
William	820	Bck	Leak, Elias	53	Clp	Leckeis, Alexr.	835	Nrf
Wm.	699	Gch	Isaac	238	Ldn	Leckey, James	304	Rck
Wm.	700	Gch	Mask	165	Alb	Thomas, jr.	269	Rck
Woodson	700	Gch	Rd.	53	Clp	Thomas, Senr.	284	Rck

Name	Pg	Co	Name	Pg	Co	Name	Pg	Co
Thos.	302	Rck	James	650	Sss	Susanna, Senr.	196	Ess
Lecrow see Leeson			James Green	200	Oho	Tho.	352	Lnc
Lecky, Isaac	302	Rck	Jeremiah	524	Prw	Thomas	59	Chr
Ledbetter, Coleman	575	Pre	Jesse	9	Wod	Thomas	100	Jff
Edmund	535	Prg	Jno.	2	Hnr	Thomas	9	Oho
Guardiner	152	Dnw	Joel	530	Prg	Thos.	537	Brk
Hanslen	755	Brn	John	537	Brk	Thos.	908	Nrf
Hubbard	755	Brn	John	867	Cmp	Thurza	504	Prw
Isaac	754	Brn	John	879	Cmp	William	37	Acc
James	754	Brn	John	55	Chr	William	278	Amh
Josh.	637	Btt	John	152	Dnw	William	693	Br
Osbern	755	Brn	John	485	Frn	William	65	Jff
Richd.	153	Dnw	John	85	Jff	William	207	Kng
Wm.	152	Dnw	John	5	Knw	William	523	Prw
Ledford, John	988	Nrt	John	828	Nrf	William	575	Pre
William	988	Nrt	John	907	Nrf	William, Jr.	806	Bck
Ledgerwood, Wm.	647	Mnt	John	9	Oho	Willis	414	Fqr
Ledgwick, John	115	Hnr	John	879	Sth	Willis, Senr.	369	Fqr
Ledley, William	692	Br	John	680	Wrw	Wm.	430	Flv
Ledwidge, William	102	Spt	John	877	Yrk	Wm.	877	Yrk
Lee, Abraham	329	Dnw	John P.	207	Ess	Wm. H.	682	Wrw
Adam	535	Prg	John S.	701	Gch	Wm. W.	683	Wrw
Adam	549	Prg	Jonathan	638	Btt	Wm. W.	684	Wrw
Adam	418	Rnd	Joseph	874	Cmp	Wyatt	152	Dnw
Alexander	470	Bdf	Joseph	907	Hrr	Yong	729	Wsh
Alexander	523	Prw	Joseph	516	Prw	Zach.	638	Btt
Alexander	532	Prg	Joseph D.	98	Cmb	see Harris, See		
Ammon	538	Prg	Joshua	675	Br	Leebrich see Lubrich		
Ann	466	Mdd	Joshua	251	Ldn	Leech, Davd.	287	Rck
Anthoney	537	Brk	Kendal	439	Flv	Henry	516	Mnn
Anthoney	20	Hnr	Kendal	988	Nrt	James	272	Rck
Archer	733	Wsh	Lance Lot, Jnr.	62	Jff	James [crossed out]	311	Rck
Arthur	842	Nrf	Lancelot	62	Jff	James, j.	305	Rck
Arthur	907	Nrf	Le...i	866	Cmp	Jer.	517	Mnn
Asell	519	Prw	Lewis	911	Crl	Jno., jr.	287	Rck
Baldwin M.	777	Wst	Lewis	466	Mdd	John	276	Rck
Barnet	570	Brk	Linsey	385	Fqr	John, (Sen.)	275	Rck
Benjamin D.	840	Bck	Littleberry	530	Prg	Jonathan	730	Wsh
Betsey	328	Dnw	Lucy	118	Spt	Sarah	243	Ldn
Beverley	470	Bdf	Ludwell	254	Ldn	Sarah	908	Nrf
Burwell	879	Cmp	Margaret	523	Prw	Thomas	282	Rck
Charles	100	Cmb	Martha	152	Dnw	Leeds, William	7	Isw
Charles	466	Mdd	Mary	530	Prg	Leedy, John	842	Wth
Charles	648	Mnt	Mary	531	Prg	John	843	Wth
Charles	514	Prw	Matthew	524	Prw	Jonathan	842	Wth
Charles H.	552	Frd	Micheal	419	Rnd	Joseph	843	Wth
Dan	516	Mnn	Milley	466	Mdd	Saml.	360	Ags
Daniel	675	Br	Nancy	13	Hnr	Saml.	6	Rcm
Daniel	517	Frd	Nathan	530	Prg	Leek, John	757	Wsh
Danl.	919	Hrr	Nathan	35	Rcm	Mark	291	Rck
David	7	Wod	Nathaniel	326	Dnw	Leeker, John	55	Chr
Edward	56	Chr	Nathl.	543	Prg	Leep, Geo.	516	Mnn
Edward	330	Dnw	Phillis	336	Dnw	Henry	942	Hrr
Edward	333	Dnw	Polley	326	Dnw	James	689	Br
Edwd.	700	Gch	Polley	399	Fqr	Leese, Andrew	822	Hmp
Edwin	908	Nrf	Polly	334	Dnw	Jacob	821	Hmp
Eliza.	678	Wrw	Polly	632	Mnt	John	822	Hmp
Elizabeth	517	Prw	R. H.	906	Nrf	William	792	Hmp
Fanny	254	Ldn	Rd. B.	279	Frf	Leeson, John	55	Chr
Francis L.	470	Bdf	Reubin	369	Fqr	Js.	515	Mnn
Garnet	470	Bdf	Richard	471	Bdf	R.	515	Mnn
Geo. W.	223	Ess	Richard	199	Ess	Ricd.	517	Mnn
George	530	Frd	Richard	988	Nrt	Thos.	561	Brk
George	988	Nrt	Richard	508	Prw	Leet, Jepthah	13	Pwh
George M.	194	Ess	Richard	9	Wod	Leeth, George	176	Shn
Green	651	Sss	Richard	10	Wod	Leezanee, Elizabeth	462	Frn
Gresham	821	Bck	Richd.	810	Nrf	Lefever, Henry	586	Brk
Guy	807	Bck	Richd.	877	Yrk	Henry	254	Ldn
Hancock	277	Frf	Richd. E.	810	Nrf	Honour	278	Ldn
Hancock	414	Fqr	Ro.	877	Yrk	Wm.	278	Ldn
Henry, Junr.	777	Wst	Rob.	681	Wrw	Lefevre, John	546	Frd
Henry, Senr.	777	Wst	Robert	521	Prw	Leffell, Jno.	638	Btt
Herbert	536	Prg	Rody	619	Mnt	Sam.	638	Btt
Hump.	877	Yrk	Salley	988	Nrt	Leffew, Elias	479	Frn
Isaac	536	Prg	Sally	549	Prg	Leffingwall, Saml.	830	Nrf
James	293	Amh	Samuel	675	Br	Lefle, Abegail	541	Brk
James	693	Br	Sarah	726	Wsh	Leflee, Sarah	19	Hnr
James	152	Dnw	Shelley	863	Cmp	Leforest, A.	11	Hnr
James	207	Kng	Stephen	721	Wsh	Leforge, Jno.	282	Rck
James	629	Mnt	Sucky	330	Dnw	Lefoy, John	470	Bdf

Name	No.	Co.	Name	No.	Co.	Name	No.	Co.
Leftwich, ...l...mus	470	Bdf	Lehew, John	167	Shn	William	486	Frn
Austin, jr.	470	Bdf	Moses	178	Shn	Lemoine, Feriol	352	Lnc
Austin, sr.	470	Bdf	Nancy	592	Frd	Peter	710	Nls
Jabez	470	Bdf	Spencer	592	Frd	Lemon, Abraham	19	Rcm
Jacky	471	Bdf	William	842	Wth	Abram	360	Ags
James	471	Bdf	William	843	Wth	Alexr.	512	Brk
James, (RH)	470	Bdf	Leib, Henry	28	Rcm	Christn.	637	Btt
Jesse	470	Bdf	Matthias	35	Rcm	Edwd.	662	Glc
Joel	471	Bdf	Nicholas	11	Rcm	Eliza	663	Glc
John [2]	470	Bdf	Leigh, Ann	165	Alb	Geo.	534	Brk
John, (Otter)	471	Bdf	Bach. G.	236	Aml	Geo.	307	Ldn
John A.	471	Bdf	Benja. W.	331	Dnw	George	636	Btt
Little B.	471	Bdf	David G.	350	Lnn	Haily	662	Glc
Mary	843	Wth	Elizabeth	574	Pre	Jno. [2]	663	Glc
Peyton	470	Bdf	Ferd.	301	Rck	John	662	Glc
Thomas	471	Bdf	Francis	662	Glc	John	23	Rcm
Uriah, Sr.	470	Bdf	John	791	Hmp	Lewis	662	Glc
Valentine	470	Bdf	John	351	Lnn	Lewis	23	Rcm
William, jr.	470	Bdf	John T.	236	Aml	Lewis, (Jr.)	26	Rcm
William, (RR)	470	Bdf	Paschal G.	574	Pre	Mary	661	Glc
William, Sr.	471	Bdf	Richard	710	Nls	Molly	662	Glc
Wm., (WH)	470	Bdf	Stephen	763	Hmp	Mord.	662	Glc
Lefuer, David	616	Mnt	Wm.	662	Glc	Nancy	169	Knq
Jacob	616	Mnt	Wm. H.	708	Nls	Peter	13	Hnr
John	616	Mnt	see L...h			Richard	507	Frd
Joseph	616	Mnt	Leighlider, Coonrod	86	Jff	Richd.	662	Glc
Leg, G., (MG)	517	Mnn	Leighliker, George	816	Hmp	Richd.	663	Glc
Thos.	52	Clp	Leightliter, John	816	Hmp	Ro.	662	Glc
Legaar, John	35	Acc	Peter	819	Hmp	William	20	Rcm
Legan, Richd.	130	Hnr	Leinkell, Peter	267	Ldn	Wm.	526	Brk
Legate, James	359	Ags	Leiper, ppp, Mrs.	26	Hnr	Lemons, Andrew	438	Bth
Lege, Andw.	361	Ags	Leipley, John	774	Hmp	John	579	Mnr
Leget, Hannah	843	Wth	Leishills, James	862	Cmp	Lemont, John	470	Bdf
Issabella	843	Wth	Leister, Andrew	44	Isw	Lemore, Jno.	68	Chs
Joseph	843	Wth	William	44	Isw	Lemount, Henry	463	Pra
Thomas	843	Wth	Leith, James	827	Hmp	Jas.	464	Pra
William	843	Wth	Leland, Baldwin M.	989	Nrt	Joshua	463	Pra
Legeth, Peter	246	Shn	Charles	989	Nrt	Lempson, Richd.	839	Nrf
Legg, Davenport	589	Mnr	Ellis	989	Nrt	Lenagen, Isaac	628	Gls
Edmund	571	Mnr	Lelleston, George	107	Acc	Lenahan, Dennis	1	Rcm
Eli	521	Prw	Lelley, Edmond	445	Flv	Lenair, Robert	326	Dnw
Elijah	247	Ldn	Eliz.	434	Flv	Lenard, Garner	517	Mnn
Eliza.	588	Mnr	John	434	Flv	John	420	Rnd
Eliza.	589	Mnr	Robt.	432	Flv	Samuel	952	Chc
Eliza., Jr.	589	Mnr	Lelman, Conrod	573	Brk	Lender, George	752	Wsh
Eloener	599	Mnr	Leman, Robert	15	Pwh	Lendrum, Jas.	52	Clp
Fielding	247	Ldn	Lemans, Js.	518	Mnn	Mark	53	Clp
Geo.	517	Mnn	Lemaskus, Thomas	962	Hrr	Leneave, Mary Ann	576	Pre
Gibson	594	Mnr	Lemaster, Isaac	429	Msn	Lenham, John	82	Jff
James	521	Prw	Thomas	427	Msn	Lenney, Henderson	447	Flv
John	570	Mnr	Lemasters, R.	516	Mnn	Lenow, Henry	138	Sth
John	521	Prw	Lemay, David	701	Gch	Lenox, James	760	Hmp
Lewis	278	Ldn	Saml.	701	Gch	Michael	506	Prw
Thos.	580	Mnr	Samuel	899	Hnv	Nathan	533	Brk
Thos.	588	Mnr	Lembrick, Joh...	39	Stf	Thomas	760	Hmp
Walter	418	Fqr	Lemerick, Jonathan	394	Mds	Lenton, John	502	Prw
William	350	Fqr	Lemessinier see Lemessurier			Lenty see Lurty		
Willis	246	Ldn	Lemessurier, John	326	Dnw	Lenxas, J.B.	22	Hnr
Zeph.	257	Ldn	John	336	Dnw	Leomard, Lewis	400	Fqr
Leggan, Frank	121	Hnr	Leming, John	515	Mnn	Leonard, ...s	236	Aml
Peggy	132	Hnr	Lemly, George	519	Frd	Adam	843	Wth
Roothy	128	Hnr	Michal	519	Frd	Christena	94	Jff
Saml.	128	Hnr	Sam	515	Mnn	Daniel S.	859	Cmp
Thos.	121	Hnr	Lemmon, Cooonrod	638	Btt	Frederick	11	Ntt
Wm.	121	Hnr	Daniel	462	Frn	Fredrick	704	Wsh
Legget, Evan	464	Pra	Fredk.	638	Btt	Geo.	362	Ags
Henry	462	Pra	George [2]	638	Btt	George	22	Rcm
Jas.	515	Mnn	Jacob	638	Btt	George	842	Wth
Jas.	464	Pra	Jane	97	Jff	Jacob	521	Frd
Jno.	515	Mnn	John	55	Jff	James	585	Mnr
Robt. J.	464	Pra	John	659	Mnt	John	22	Rcm
Leggitt, ---, Matthews &	34	Stf	Mersey	97	Jff	Mary	332	Dnw
Legon, Nancy	9	Hnr	Peter	638	Btt	Peter	17	Rcm
Legrand, Alexander	575	Pre	Peter	5	Hnr	Peter	719	Wsh
Alexander, Jr.	575	Pre	Robert	95	Jff	Reuphis	666	Mnt
Baker	575	Pre	Thomas	75	Jff	Richie	278	Frf
Isaiah	55	Chr	William	97	Jff	Sasfield	531	Prg
Josiah	575	Pre	Lemmons, Danl.	638	Btt	Vand	540	Prg
Nash, Revd.	56	Chr	Isaac	487	Frn	William	373	Fqr
Leguire, Joseph	814	Nrf	Isles	830	Nrf	see Leomard		

196

Leopard, Adam	579	Brk	John	754	Brn	Betsey	5	Hnr
Michael	503	Brk	Robert	13	Knw	Bettey	169	Knq
Philip	361	Ags	Lettelier, J.B.	909	Nrf	Britain	358	Fqr
Lepage, ---, Mrs.	908	Nrf	Lettellier, Thos.	5	Hnr	Burnett	760	Nwk
Lepford, John	350	Lnn	Letteral, Richd.	639	Btt	Carban	471	Bdf
Lephap, James	439	Bth	Vincent	639	Btt	Catey	759	Nwk
Leplace see Lephap			see Litteral			Caty	394	Mds
Leppard, William	55	Chr	Lettin, Willm.	668	Mnt	Charles	424	Bth
Leprad, Nancy	236	Aml	Letuz, Henry G.	777	Wst	Charles	680	Br
Leps, George	506	Frd	Leuesque, George	182	Shn	Charles	912	Crl
Lepscomb, John	516	Frd	Levell, Edwd.	53	Clp	Charles	700	Gch
Le Rue, Benjn.	638	Btt	John	69	Spt	Charles	232	Ldn
Lesieave, William	236	Aml	Levellee, Jne.	908	Nrf	Charles	246	Ldn
Lesley, Andrew	470	Bdf	Levergall, Adam	358	Ags	Charles	29	Rcm
Jno.	12	Hnr	Henry	360	Ags	Charles	106	Spt
Saml.	360	Ags	Philip	360	Ags	Charles	28	Stf
Leslie, Geo.	829	Nrf	Leveton, Mary	37	Acc	Charles, Sr.	631	Mnt
Jno.	306	Rck	Levey, Marcus	29	Hnr	Charles A.L.	197	Ess
John	908	Nrf	Levi, John	615	Mnt	Charles E.	68	Chs
Thomas	269	Ldn	Levingston, Jno.	908	Nrf	Charles G.	629	Mnt
see Leslire			Margte.	909	Nrf	Charles W.	583	Mnr
Leslire, Jonathan	282	Rck	Leviston, Andrew	967	Hrr	Chris. T.	442	Mth
Lesneur see Lesueur			Jno.	464	Pra	Coleman	278	Frf
Lessenberry, David	650	Sss	Levit, Rachal	106	Jff	Cornelius	463	Pra
Francis	335	Dnw	Levy, Betsey	206	Kng	Custis	35	Acc
Peter	542	Prg	Ezekiel	412	Rch	Dangerfield	206	Kng
Sarah	650	Sss	Henry	206	Kng	Daniel	36	Acc
William	650	Sss	Jacob	206	Kng	Daniel	778	Hmp
Lessinger, George	568	Frd	Moses	622	Mnt	Daniel	29	Hnr
Lessley, John	843	Wth	William	206	Kng	Daniel	9	Knw
Lesslie, Benjamin	754	Brn	Willm. H.	206	Kng	Daniel	35	Stf
Lessuer, John L.	55	Chr	Lewallen, Charles	865	Cmp	Danl.	276	Frf
Lester, Alexander	350	Lnn	Lewark, John	751	Wsh	David	152	Dnw
Archd.	8	Ntt	Lewcas, Reubin	53	Clp	David	248	Ldn
Benjamin	901	Hnv	Lewell, Elisha	254	Ldn	David	662	Mnt
Briant	55	Chr	Lewellen, ---, Dr.	516	Mnn	David	842	Wth
Bryant, jr.	350	Lnn	Abe	810	Nrf	David J.	201	Alb
Bryant, Sr.	350	Lnn	James	857	Cmp	Dick	25	Hnr
Claiborne	721	Brn	Jno.	516	Mnn	E.	18	Oho
Edmun W.	350	Lnn	Sam	516	Mnn	Edgcomb S.	55	Chr
George	53	Chs	Saml.	517	Mnn	Edmund	18	Oho
Hennery	350	Lnn	T., Jr.	517	Mnn	Edward	649	Sss
Henry	628	Gls	Tho.	517	Mnn	Edward	650	Sss
Isham	350	Lnn	Lewellin, Catharine	662	Glc	Edward D.	989	Nrt
Jeremiah	58	Chs	Mary	575	Pre	Elam	56	Chr
Jerman	792	Bck	Lewelling, Abel	908	Nrf	Elisha	162	Sth
Jerman	808	Bck	James	681	Wrw	Elizabeth	201	Alb
Jno.	461	Pra	Joseph	833	Nrf	Elizabeth	152	Dnw
John	806	Bck	Lewes, A.	458	Frn	Elizabeth	521	Frd
John	349	Lnn	Lewi, Mason	720	Brn	Elizabeth	988	Nrt
Jdhn, Jr.	660	Mnt	Lewin, Chas.	352	Lnc	Erny	26	Hnr
John, Sr.	350	Lnn	Molly	352	Lnc	Evan	471	Bdf
John, Sr.	660	Mnt	Samuel	168	Shn	Evan	579	Frd
Lewis	56	Chr	Lewis, Abigal	36	Acc	Exum	880	Sth
Morgan	350	Lnn	Abigal	107	Acc	Fank	26	Hnr
Nathl.	897	Hnv	Abraham	581	Frd	Fanny	117	Spt
Parker	56	Chr	Abraham	394	Mds	Feilding	948	Chc
Saml.	661	Mnt	Abraham, Jr.	394	Mds	Francis, Capt.	13	Pwh
Thos.	908	Nrf	Abram	638	Btt	Frank	26	Hnr
William	628	Gls	Absolam, Jr.	109	Acc	George	109	Acc
Willm.	660	Mnt	Absolem, sr.	108	Acc	George	206	Kng
Lestor, Miles	862	Cmp	Alice	988	Nrt	George	424	Msn
Lesueur, Chastain	831	Bck	Andrew	478	Frn	George	443	Mth
James	777	Bck	Andrew	427	Msn	George	20	Oho
Paton	800	Bck	Andrew	429	Msn	George	393	Rch
Lesure, Fell	471	Bdf	Andrew	607	Mnt	George, (F.B.)	463	Pra
John	471	Bdf	Andw., Jr.	637	Btt	Ghent	152	Dnw
Letbetter, William	530	Prg	Andw., Sr., by Jno.			Gilley	129	Cmb
Letcher, Mary	269	Rck	Martin Clk	639	Btt	Griffin	988	Nrt
Letchfield, Susan	25	Hnr	Ann	662	Glc	Hannah	988	Nrt
Letchford, Arthur	869	Cmp	Ann	24	Hnr	Harding	802	Bck
Letellier, Jno.	2	Hnr	Anne	93	Spt	Hen.	516	Mnn
see LeTellier, Lettellier			Archaleus	52	Clp	Hen., Jr.	517	Mnn
LeTellier, Jno.	462	Pra	Ash.	954	Hrr	Henry	450	Bth
Leterson, Charles	227	Pnd	Austin	76	Spt	Henry	662	Glc
Lethcow, James	843	Wth	Benja.	130	Sth	Henry	463	Pra
Letler, Abraham	177	Shn	Benjamin	720	Brn	Herbert	452	Grn
Le toney, Pierre	807	Nrf	Benjamin	55	Chr	Howel	56	Chr
Lett, Charles	78	Jff	Benjamin	9	Rcm	Howell	165	Alb
Daniel	244	Shn	Benjn., Sar.	424	Msn	Howell	52	Clp

Name	No	Place
Isaac	424	Msn
Iveson	169	Knq
Jacob	791	Hmp
Jacob	240	Ldn
Jacob	1	Oho
Jacob	8	Oho
James	36	Acc
James	108	Acc
James	179	Alb
James	201	Alb
James	425	Bth
James	831	Bck
James	152	Dnw
James	247	Ldn
James	292	Ldn
James	908	Nrf
James	394	Rch
Jas.	461	Pra
Jenkin	273	Ldn
Jeremiah	410	Rch
Jesse	37	Acc
Jessee	165	Alb
Jessee	720	Brn
Jessee	105	Cmb
Jno.	52	Clp
Jno.	662	Glc
Jno.	246	Ldn
Jno.	517	Mnn
Jno.	463	Pra
Jno. F.	662	Glc
Joanna	233	Ldn
Job	680	Br
Joel	471	Bdf
John	108	Acc
John	109	Acc
John	417	Bth
John	507	Brk
John	810	Bck
John	327	Dnw
John	179	Elc
John	190	Elc
John	222	Ess
John	277	Frf
John	701	Gch
John	247	Ldn
John	466	Mdd
John	594	Mnr
John [2]	988	Nrt
John	266	Rck
John	93	Spt
John	109	Spt
John	724	Wsh
John	744	Wsh
John, Jur.	417	Bth
John, of S	107	Acc
John, Sr.	989	Nrt
John T.	909	Hrr
John W.	181	Alb
Jonas	17	Wod
Joseph	441	Bth
Joseph	240	Ldn
Joseph	246	Ldn
Joseph	394	Mds
Joseph	820	Nrf
Joseph	836	Nrf
Joseph	218	Pnd
Joseph	574	Pre
Joseph, F. N.	649	Sss
Joshua	591	Mnr
Joyce	815	Hmp
Ked	27	Hnr
Labon	36	Acc
Lawrence	277	Frf
Levy	275	Frf
Lewis	263	Ldn
Louisa	132	Hnr
Lucy	86	Spt
Luver	128	Hnr
Margaret	418	Bth
Mary	507	Brk
Mary	662	Glc
Mary	393	Rch
Mat	329	Dnw
Matilda	115	Spt
Milly	911	Crl
Molly	201	Alb
Mordichi	842	Wth
Nancy	115	Spt
Nanney	109	Acc
Nathaniel	707	Wsh
Nelly	907	Nrf
Nicholas	5	Oho
Nicholas	214	Pnd
Nicholas E.	720	Brn
Phil	517	Mnn
Pleasant	574	Pre
Polley	153	Dnw
Rachel	108	Acc
Raymond	108	Acc
Reese	362	Ags
Revell	109	Acc
Richard	37	Acc
Richmond	93	Spt
Robert	55	Chr
Robert	9	Knw
Robert	575	Pre
Robert	82	Spt
Robert	60	Stf
Roger	759	Nwk
Ruel	720	Brn
Sally	236	Aml
Sam.	190	Elc
Saml.	569	Mnr
Saml., Sr.	591	Mnr
Samuel	572	Frd
Samuel	258	Shn
Samuel	777	Wst
Sandal	720	Brn
Sarah	37	Acc
Sarah	165	Alb
Sarah	988	Nrt
Sary	394	Mds
Scarburgh	108	Acc
Sinah	408	Rch
Sophia	38	Acc
Spencer	107	Acc
Susan M.	13	Hnr
Susanah	125	Hnr
Susanna	207	Ess
Thomas	35	Acc
Thomas	107	Acc
Thomas	416	Bth
Thomas	109	Cmb
Thomas	152	Dnw
Thomas	574	Frd
Thomas	232	Ldn
Thomas	534	Prg
Thomas	97	Spt
Thomas, of Richd.	37	Acc
Thos.	334	Dnw
Thos.	113	Hnr
Thos., (ST)	153	Dnw
Tuerman	91	Spt
Vicy	330	Dnw
Vincent	988	Nrt
Waller	79	Spt
Walter	25	Oho
Warner	701	Gch
Willard	2	Oho
William	37	Acc
William	108	Acc
William	784	Bck
William	817	Bck
William	334	Dnw
William	208	Ess
William	452	Grn
William	956	Hrr
William	988	Nrt
William	989	Nrt
William	7	Pwh
William	499	Prw
William	398	Rch
William	408	Rch
William	32	Rcm
William	116	Spt
William	118	Spt
William	2	Wod
William	12	Wod
William, (Overseer)	375	Fqr
William F.	777	Wst
William J.	880	Cmp
Willian	827	Bck
Willis	101	Spt
Winnifred	988	Nrt
Wm.	585	Brk
Wm.	637	Btt
Wm.	52	Clp
Wm.	191	Elc
Wm.	701	Gch
Wm., (Hatter)	152	Dnw
Wm., jr.	720	Brn
Wm., senr.	153	Dnw
Wm., Sr.	720	Brn
Wm. L.	246	Ldn
Zachariah	164	Alb
Zachh.	232	Ldn
Zadock	38	Acc
Zebulon	849	Sth
see Lewes, Lewi		
Lewright, Robert	565	Frd
Leyburn, John	262	Rck
Leycock, Daniel	776	Wst
Jeremiah	776	Wst
Leymour, Richd.	838	Nrf
Leynard, Mary	942	Chc
Liberty, George	162	Sth
Lichmutt, Wm. D.	22	Oho
Lickey, Jno. C.	276	Ldn
Lickhart, Bernard	555	Frd
Lickins, Andrew	8	Knw
John	8	Knw
Peter	5	Knw
Licklighter, Peter	626	Mnt
Lickliter, Adam	174	Shn
Jacob	173	Shn
Jacob, Junr.	175	Shn
John	174	Shn
Lidebotham, Joseph	516	Frd
Life, Anny	217	Pnd
Christian	217	Pnd
John	217	Pnd
Martin	908	Hrr
see Lipe		
Ligate, Stephen	698	Br
Liggen, John	430	Flv
Ligget, Jacob	3	Rcm
Liggins, Winey, free negro	70	Chs
Liggit, James, Jr.	105	Jff
Liggon, Betty, persons of colour	103	Cmb
Elijah	116	Cmb
James	55	Chr
Samuel	351	Lnn
William	115	Cmb
Liggons see Hicks		
Light, Frederick	555	Frd
Henry	555	Frd
Henry	632	Mnt
Jacob	521	Brk
James	632	Mnt
John	521	Brk
John	23	Rcm
John	728	Wsh
Joseph	521	Brk
Peter	555	Frd
Peter	577	Frd
Peter, jr.	589	Brk
Peter, Sr.	521	Brk
Saml.	521	Brk

Name	No.	Co.
Samuel	728	Wsh
Lightburn, Robt.	437	Mth
Wm.	352	Lnc
Lightfoot, Barth.	7	Isw
Daniel	442	Flv
Elinon	452	Grn
Francis	650	Sss
Goodrick	395	Mds
Harry	429	Msn
Issaba., (W)	877	Yrk
John	755	Brn
Philip	912	Crl
Philip	52	Clp
Philip, Est.	777	Wst
Sally	7	Isw
Saml.	276	Frf
Samuel	575	Pre
Thomas	413	Rch
Wm.	276	Frf
Wm.	446	Flv
Lighthizer, Nathan	79	Jff
Lightle, William	470	Bdf
Lightner, Adam	419	Bth
Hannah	419	Bth
John	38	Rcm
Peter	419	Bth
William	419	Bth
Liging, Wim.	851	Hnv
Ligon, Henry	575	Pre
Janett	13	Pwh
John	13	Pwh
John T.	576	Pre
Joseph	236	Aml
Nancy	576	Pre
Pabe, F.B.	10	Pwh
Richd.	9	Ntt
Robert	236	Aml
Thomas	576	Pre
Thomas, Senr.	576	Pre
Thomas D.	576	Pre
William [2]	574	Pre
William B.	236	Aml
Like, Bernard	17	Rcm
Likens, James	102	Jff
Jane	102	Jff
Mary	551	Frd
Rebecca	551	Frd
Thomas	57	Jff
Likes, John	129	Hnr
Liland, LeRoy P.	352	Lnc
Liler see Siler		
Liliston, David	188	Elc
Lillard, Absalom	54	Clp
Benj., Jr.	394	Mds
Benja.	53	Clp
Benjamin	394	Mds
Dennis	394	Mds
Frances	394	Mds
Franky	394	Mds
Henry	394	Mds
Jno.	53	Clp
John	394	Mds
Thos.	54	Clp
Liller, George	801	Hmp
Henry	812	Hmp
Lilleston, Edmund	35	Acc
Geo. W.	38	Acc
George	36	Acc
John	38	Acc
Nanny	38	Acc
Sarah	37	Acc
Selby	38	Acc
Tully	35	Acc
William	38	Acc
Lilley, Edmond	628	Gls
Hardy	752	Wsh
John	362	Ags
Lindsey	361	Ags
Natha.	754	Brn
Patty	575	Pre
Richd.	449	Mth
Thos.	449	Mth
William	628	Gls
William	24	Rcm
William A.	575	Pre
Wm.	710	Nls
Lilly, David	6	Knw
Elizabeth	124	Cmb
Frederick	650	Sss
John	649	Sss
Robert	628	Gls
Robert	4	Knw
Thomas	628	Gls
William	6	Knw
Lily, Joseph	777	Wst
Limbrick, George	46	Stf
John	58	Stf
William	59	Stf
William, jr.	59	Stf
Limes, William	580	Frd
Limrick, James	340	Fqr
Thomas	384	Fqr
Linch, Aden	754	Brn
Isaac	947	Hrr
John	360	Ags
Levy	961	Hrr
Mary	358	Ags
Peter	940	Hrr
Peter	941	Hrr
Robt.	362	Ags
Syon	754	Brn
Syrach	754	Brn
Wm.	754	Brn
Lincoln, Jacob	16	Rcm
Jesse	4	Rcm
John	4	Rcm
Lincus, Henry	667	Mnt
Jacob	667	Mnt
John	667	Mnt
Lind, George	211	Shn
Lindamood, Andrew, Junr.	230	Shn
Andrew, Snr.	230	Shn
Michael	230	Shn
Stuffle	230	Shn
Lindamoood, Michael, (of S)	230	Shn
Lindemood, George	704	Wsh
Michael	705	Wsh
Michl.	704	Wsh
Lindenberger, John L.	842	Wth
Linder, John	752	Wsh
Wm.	751	Wsh
Lindsay, Adam	810	Nrf
Adam	907	Nrf
Alexander	73	Spt
Anne	276	Frf
Caleb	70	Spt
Edwd., (W)	877	Yrk
Geo.	909	Nrf
Katharine	70	Spt
Matty.	908	Nrf
Opie	276	Frf
Reuben	201	Alb
Robert	275	Frf
Samuel	312	Ldn
Sarah	55	Chr
Sarah	277	Frf
Thomas	279	Frf
Wm.	275	Frf
see Linsey, Linzey, Lyndsay		
Lindsey, Aaron	576	Pre
Abraham	533	Frd
Alexander	107	Jff
Elizt.	361	Ags
Jacob	531	Frd
James	587	Frd
James	394	Mds
James	268	Rck
John	531	Frd
John	70	Jff
John	394	Mds
John	759	Nwk
Larken	394	Mds
Mary	531	Frd
Mathew	842	Wth
Moses	126	Hnr
Robert	266	Rck
Thomas	36	Acc
Thomas	531	Frd
William	575	Pre
Lindsy, John	131	Hnr
Lindwiler see Linksweiler		
Line, Henry	101	Jff
John	100	Jff
Lineback, Jos.	825	Nrf
Linebaugh, Saml.	499	Prw
Linelsee, Barbara	597	Brk
Lineoweaver, Jacob	217	Shn
Linerick see Limrick		
Lines, Mary	96	Jff
Lingenfelter, Mary	585	Brk
Linger, Nicholas	952	Hrr
Lingle, Jacob	24	Rcm
Jacob, (Sen.)	24	Rcm
Paul	37	Rcm
Lingo, Archabald	164	Alb
John	37	Acc
William	37	Acc
Link, Adam	358	Ags
Adam	85	Jff
Gasper	628	Gls
Geo.	362	Ags
John	359	Ags
John	224	Shn
Mathias	359	Ags
Mathias, jr.	361	Ags
Nicholas	362	Ags
Peter	359	Ags
Philip	362	Ags
Wm.	361	Ags
Linkenhoger, Elias, Jr.	638	Btt
Elias, Sr.	638	Btt
Geo.	638	Btt
Jno.	638	Btt
Josh.	638	Btt
Mary	638	Btt
see Linkinhoker		
Linkhart, Andrew	76	Jff
Barney	75	Jff
Linkinhoker, Josh.	637	Btt
Linksweiler, Adam	302	Rck
Linn, Adam	361	Ags
Daniel	508	Frd
Eleanor	5	Rcm
Henry	402	Ags
Jacob	301	Rck
John	508	Frd
Robt.	5	Rcm
Saml.	5	Rcm
William	581	Frd
Linney see Caldwell		
Linsay, Jno.	463	Pra
Linsey, Isaac	693	Wsh
James	748	Wsh
Slies	693	Wsh
William	936	Hrr
Linsley, Andrew	24	Oho
Linssy, Hennery	932	Hrr
Linsy, Walter	935	Hrr
Lint, Patrick	471	Bdf
Linter, Henry	711	Wsh
Linthacum, Nathan	102	Jff
Linthicum, Archibald	782	Hmp
Hezkiah	766	Hmp
Linticum, Edmund	258	Amh
Linton, Bennett	788	Nrf
Elijah	451	Mth
Isaac	681	Br
Jno.	306	Ldn

John	498	Prw	Catharine	279	Frf	Livesay, Amos	536	Prg
John	507	Prw	Chs.	276	Frf	Andrew	499	Frn
Mary	499	Prw	David	638	Btt	Hubbard	534	Prg
Nathan, Junr.	109	Acc	David	70	Jff	Joel	536	Prg
Nathan, Senr.	109	Acc	David	282	Ldn	Peter	499	Frn
William	596	Mnr	Eleanard	54	Clp	Thomas, jr.	538	Prg
see Lynton			Elsey	516	Mnn	Livesey, Anm	542	Prg
Linvelle, Benjamin	18	Rcm	George	831	Hmp	Burwill	539	Prg
Linvill, John	915	Hrr	George	71	Jff	Clemont	540	Prg
Linzey, William	473	Frn	Jacob	545	Frd	Herbert	540	Prg
Lion, Andrew	518	Prw	James	510	Frd	Jamima	539	Prg
Sarah	36	Acc	James	258	Shn	Jno.	539	Prg
Lionback, John	186	Shn	Jesse, jr.	611	Srr	Randolph	539	Prg
see Lyonback			John	545	Frd	Thos.	539	Prg
Lionergam, John	256	Amh	John	611	Srr	Thos.	540	Prg
Lions, John	931	Hrr	Joseph	302	Rck	William	539	Prg
Lipcom, Ambros	425	Rnd	Micajah	612	Srr	Livesie, Claiborne	13	Ntt
Lipe, Moses	639	Btt	Peter	360	Ags	Green	13	Ntt
Lipencut, Samuel	108	Acc	Robert H.	522	Prw	Livick, John	360	Ags
Lipford, Amos	575	Pre	Samuel	650	Sss	Livingston, James	571	Frd
Henry	123	Cmb	Sarah	53	Clp	Peter	754	Wsh
Lipp, Jacob	395	Mds	Thomas	628	Gls	Sarah	852	Cmp
Lipscomb, Ambs.	517	Mnn	Thomas	908	Hrr	see Leviston, Lovingston		
Elizabeth	884	Hnv	William	79	Jff	Livley, Charles	165	Alb
Henry	104	Cmb	William	842	Wth	Elizabeth	164	Alb
Henry	889	Hnv	William, (Carter's			William	165	Alb
James	56	Chr	run)	346	Fqr	Livly, Charles	164	Alb
John	32	Hnr	Wm.	637	Btt	Llewellin, Richard	64	Jff
John	78	Spt	Wm. [2]	516	Mnn	Lloyd, Evan	370	Fqr
John, F. B.	5	Pwh	Wm.	280	Rck	George	394	Fqr
Nathl. C.	898	Hnv	Wm., Jr.	637	Btt	Joseph	398	Fqr
Phillip	112	Spt	Wm., Sr.	638	Btt	Samuel	584	Frd
Richd. G.	56	Chr	Zackh.	53	Clp	Thomas	397	Fqr
Spotwood	1	Hnr	see Sittle			Thomas	550	Frd
Thomas	85	Spt	Littlejohn, Jno.	288	Ldn	William	201	Alb
Wm.	518	Mnn	Joseph	558	Frd	William	394	Fqr
see Lipcom, Lipsicomb			Wm.	556	Brk	William	599	Frd
Lipscombe, Henry C.	8	Ntt	LittleJohn, James	351	Lnn	Wilson	15	Rcm
Spotswood	129	Hnr	Littlepage, Jno. C.	873	Hnv	see Gloyd, Loydd		
Temple	9	Ntt	Samuel B.	2	Knw	Loah, David	18	Rcm
Uriah	11	Ntt	William L.	412	Bth	William	18	Rcm
Lipsicomb, Anderson	792	Bck	Wm.	871	Hnv	Loak, Michael	250	Shn
Hezekiah	824	Bck	Littler, Elijah	537	Frd	Loaman, Ephm.	581	Brk
John	794	Bck	John	537	Frd	Loana, Betsey	14	Hnr
Liptrop, Isaac	361	Ags	Nathan	537	Frd	Loar, Michael	25	Rcm
Lisley, Joseph	466	Mdd	Littleton, Charles	274	Ldn	Peter	25	Rcm
Lissey, William	452	Grn	Jno.	292	Ldn	Lobbin, Jesse	708	Nls
List, John	5	Oho	Sampson	270	Ldn	John	165	Alb
Lister, George	55	Chr	Solomon	299	Ldn	John	710	Nls
Levi	698	Wsh	Thomas	600	Frd	Wm.	710	Nls
Sally	546	Frd	see Evans, Hammel, Lecatoe,			Locas, Billy	133	Hnr
Wm.	698	Wsh	Nock, Savage, Trader,			George	133	Hnr
Liston, Lotty	109	Acc	Walker			Loche, Thomas	152	Dnw
Litchfeild, Jas.	806	Nrf	Littrel, William	31	Stf	Lochet, Thomas	709	Nls
Litchfield, Bridget	108	Acc	Littrell, John	543	Brk	Lochhead, ---	332	Dnw
Francs.	439	Mth	Litz, Leonard	842	Wth	Lock, Alexander	60	Jff
Jno.	517	Mnn	William	843	Wth	George	56	Chr
Southey	108	Acc	Liveley, James	273	Amh	George, Jr.	530	Frd
Lite, John	420	Rnd	Mary	304	Amh	James	721	Brn
Litefoot, John	453	Grn	Matthew	273	Amh	John	350	Lnn
Lithgow, Alexander	508	Prw	Lively, Benjn.	567	Mnr	John	17	Rcm
Lithletter, Cornod	246	Shn	Chilion	74	Spt	John	748	Wsh
Litler, Nathan	761	Hmp	Cotrell	577	Mnr	John, Jur.	62	Jff
Litner, Saml.	361	Ags	David	74	Spt	John, Snr.	63	Jff
Litt, Francis	481	Frn	Eliza., Gloucester			Neal	553	Frd
Litten, Abram	359	Ags	Town	662	Glc	Richd.	721	Brn
John	758	Wsh	Garland	79	Spt	Thos.	596	Brk
Samuel	693	Br	James	709	Nls	William	553	Frd
Litteral, Hannah	988	Nrt	James	877	Yrk	Wm.	748	Wsh
Samuel	460	Frn	Jno.	866	Hnv	Lockard, Daniel	843	Wth
Thomas	988	Nrt	John	360	Ags	Wm.	710	Nls
Thos.	637	Btt	Joseph	587	Mnr	Lockart, Isaac	589	Brk
Thos.	639	Btt	Mark	708	Nls	John	7	Hnr
see Letteral, Littrel			Robt.	176	Elc	John	793	Nrf
Litterel, Rhody	31	Stf	Saml.	184	Elc	John	17	Wod
Litterill, George	633	Mnt	Wm.	708	Nls	see Lockhart		
Thomas	633	Mnt	Wm.	877	Yrk	Locke, Jos.	352	Lnc
Littick, Polly	292	Rck	Liverpool, Fanny	702	Gch	Solomon	290	Rck
Little, Adam	545	Frd	James	114	Spt	Locker, Thomas	275	Frf
Anne	18	Isw	Livers, Hercules	680	Br	Walter	278	Frf

William	409	Fqr	
Lockerd, Walter	470	Bdf	
Locket, Obediah	12	Pwh	
Stephen	14	Pwh	
Lockett, Chas.	61	Chs	
David	470	Bdf	
Edith	60	Chs	
Edmond	576	Pre	
Elam	59	Chs	
Francis, jr.	60	Chs	
Henry W.	236	Aml	
James	236	Aml	
Jeremiah	471	Bdf	
Jesse	471	Bdf	
J hn	236	Aml	
Jʃ.	57	Chs	
Lucy, (FB)	471	Bdf	
Magdaline	60	Chs	
Osborne	576	Pre	
Samuel L.	575	Pre	
Walthall	56	Chs	
Lockhart, Alex.	518	Mnn	
James	636	Btt	
Jas.	793	Nrf	
John	452	Grn	
Robert	569	Frd	
Samuel	760	Nwk	
William	760	Hmp	
see Lockart, Lockheart			
Lockheart, David	177	Shn	
John	171	Shn	
Lockie, William	882	Cmp	
Locklin, Elisha	637	Btt	
Locknane, Miles B.	846	Hnv	
Lockridge, Ann	360	Ags	
Lanly	422	Bth	
Robert	418	Bth	
Saml.	360	Ags	
Locks, William	55	Chr	
Locksman, Christley	4	Rcm	
Lockson, George	395	Mds	
Rachel, (FN)	27	Rcm	
Lodge, Wm.	318	Ldn	
Loe, David	677	Br	
John	677	Br	
John	691	Br	
Loffland, Dorman	6	Rcm	
Lofftus, James	360	Ags	
Loftan, Keziah	848	Sth	
Loftin, Augustin	650	Sss	
Elizabeth	650	Sss	
James	649	Sss	
Martha	452	Grn	
Loftis, Wash.	954	Hrr	
Loga, Alexander	355	Fqr	
Logan, Alexander	276	Amh	
Andrew	690	Br	
Anthony	285	Amh	
David	22	Hnr	
Easther	701	Gch	
Eddy	848	Cmp	
Frank, (FB)	1	Pwh	
Henry	276	Frf	
Irvine	269	Rck	
James	280	Amh	
James	612	Srr	
James	269	Rck	
James	732	Wsh	
Jas., Jr.	637	Btt	
Jas., Junr.	733	Wsh	
John	107	Acc	
John	361	Ags	
John	241	Ldn	
John, jr.	361	Ags	
Kitty	19	Hnr	
Robert	700	Gch	
Robert	733	Wsh	
Robt.	636	Btt	
Tarlton	126	Hnr	
Thomas	40	Rcm	

Loggins, Martin	56	Chr	
Loghagen, Wm.	529	Brk	
Login, Mary	278	Frf	
Logsden, Bennet	18	Oho	
Logwood, Burwell	471	Bdf	
Edmund	471	Bdf	
Thomas	471	Bdf	
Thomas	789	Bck	
Thomas G.	471	Bdf	
Loister, David	590	Brk	
Hannah	590	Brk	
Lokadoo, Wm.	64	Chs	
see Lookadoo			
Lokey, James	27	Rcm	
John	22	Rcm	
Margaret	27	Rcm	
Sarah	25	Rcm	
William	25	Rcm	
Lolhmiller, Jacob	211	Shn	
Loller, Js.	517	Mnn	
Willis	517	Mnn	
Lollis, Ann	44	Stf	
Lomax, John	382	Fqr	
John T.	397	Rch	
Joseph	38	Stf	
Margarett	405	Fqr	
Stephen	276	Frf	
Thomas	912	Crl	
Lombard, Patience	38	Acc	
Lomboard, Stephen	38	Acc	
Stephen	109	Acc	
Lon, Henry	181	Shn	
Lonas, Leynard	227	Shn	
Lonaz, George	226	Shn	
London, James	293	Amh	
Jane	709	Nls	
John	276	Amh	
Larkin	295	Amh	
Loney, Daniel	883	Hnv	
Fanny	122	Hnr	
John	15	Hnr	
Patsey	883	Hnv	
Long, Abner	5	Knw	
Adam	7	Rcm	
Amey	912	Crl	
Amey	651	Sss	
Andrew	103	Jff	
Armisd.	52	Clp	
Benjamin	911	Crl	
Betsy	73	Spt	
Brumfield	54	Clp	
Catharine	911	Crl	
Charles	637	Btt	
Charles	651	Sss	
Christiana	28	Rcm	
Christn. C.	638	Btt	
Conrad	577	Frd	
Daniel	906	Hrr	
David	359	Ags	
David	34	Rcm	
David	611	Srr	
David, Jun.	813	Hmp	
David, Sen.	813	Hmp	
Elias	515	Mnn	
Ellis	637	Btt	
Ellis	519	Frd	
Eml.	359	Ags	
Frances	69	Spt	
Francis	87	Spt	
Frederick	239	Shn	
Frederick	240	Shn	
Gabl.	52	Clp	
Geo.	360	Ags	
Geo.	267	Ldn	
George	419	Rnd	
George	28	Rcm	
Gideon	426	Msn	
Hannah	611	Srr	
Henry	402	Ags	

Henry	297	Ldn	
Henry	34	Rcm	
Henry	229	Shn	
Isaac	40	Rcm	
Jacob	360	Ags	
Jacob	793	Hmp	
Jacob	821	Hmp	
Jacob	104	Jff	
Jacob	283	Ldn	
Jacob	691	Wsh	
James	912	Crl	
James	5	Knw	
James	69	Spt	
James	651	Sss	
Jesse	650	Sss	
Jno.	267	Ldn	
Jno.	286	Ldn	
Jno.	300	Rck	
John	179	Alb	
John	359	Ags	
John	911	Crl	
John	600	Frd	
John	793	Hmp	
John	466	Mdd	
John	634	Mnt	
John	34	Rcm	
John	87	Spt	
John, Jr.	520	Frd	
John, Jr.	643	Mnt	
Jonas	425	Msn	
Joseph	361	Ags	
Joshua	68	Spt	
Kitty	667	Mnt	
Lazarus	651	Sss	
Leonard	395	Mds	
Letty	336	Dnw	
Levi	37	Acc	
Levy	516	Mnn	
Levy	651	Sss	
Liel	516	Mnn	
Lucy	146	Sth	
Martin	9	Knw	
Mary	912	Crl	
Matthias	34	Rcm	
Milly	9	Knw	
Nicols	7	Hnr	
Peter	359	Ags	
Peter	691	Wsh	
Philip	911	Crl	
Philip	262	Ldn	
Philip	426	Msn	
Philip	188	Shn	
Polly	854	Cmp	
Rebecca	612	Srr	
Reuben	637	Btt	
Reuben	911	Crl	
Reuben	912	Crl	
Reuben	189	Shn	
Robert	466	Mdd	
Robert	776	Wst	
Saml.	358	Ags	
Thomas	564	Frd	
Ware	5	Knw	
William	471	Bdf	
William	595	Brk	
William	911	Crl	
William	611	Srr	
William	695	Wsh	
William, Senr.	912	Crl	
Willis	611	Srr	
Willm.	637	Btt	
Willm., & Oversr.	395	Mds	
Wm.	31	Hnr	
Wm.	518	Mnn	
Wm., Junr.	695	Wsh	
see Lang			
Longacre, Elizabeth	575	Frd	
John	575	Frd	
Joseph	567	Frd	
Longacrie, Saml.	306	Rck	

Longbottom, Booling	755	Brn	Hannah	55	Jff	Lovegrove, William	471	Bdf
John	754	Brn	John	518	Mnn	Loveing, Gabriel	117	Cmb
LongBottom, Harwood	452	Grn	Mishach	548	Frd	Loveitt, Rueben	490	Pra
see LBottom			Lotts, Geo.	361	Ags	Lovejoy, Josiah	418	Bth
Longbrake, Jacob	85	Jff	Geo., Sr.	362	Ags	Rebecca	438	Bth
Longerbane, Abraham	584	Frd	John	361	Ags	see Lovjoy		
Catharine	598	Frd	Louas, John	569	Brk	Lovel, Jas.	516	Mnn
George	584	Frd	Louch, John	236	Shn	Steven	949	Hrr
Longest, Carter	169	Knq	Louden, Samuel	55	Jff	Loveless, Archibald	277	Frf
Daniel	169	Knq	William	193	Shn	Luke	279	Frf
Frances	200	Ess	Louderback, David	183	Shn	Philip	279	Frf
James	170	Knq	Joseph	188	Shn	Lovell, Wm.	52	Clp
John	130	Hnr	Magdalene	188	Shn	Lovely, Randolph	8	Knw
John	170	Knq	Philip	188	Shn	Lovengood, Jacob	952	Hrr
Lindsey	170	Knq	Loudermilik, M.	358	Ags	Lovern, Moses	575	Pre
Richard	169	Knq	Loudermilk, Geo.	360	Ags	Lovesey, Isham	331	Dnw
Sally	203	Ess	Jacob	21	Rcm	John P.	330	Dnw
Tabby	116	Hnr	Loudon, Phebe, f.negro	276	Frf	Lovet, Elizabeth	85	Spt
William	169	Knq	Lough, Adam	216	Pnd	Lovett, Adam	462	Pra
Longhorn, William B.	108	Cmb	Adam	220	Pnd	Adam, Jr.	463	Pra
Longinaker, Jacob	248	Shn	Conrod	226	Pnd	Daniel	294	Ldn
Longler, Peter	760	Wsh	George	223	Pnd	Edmd.	276	Ldn
see Longley			John	216	Pnd	Jno.	462	Pra
Longley, Benj.	760	Wsh	John	226	Pnd	Jno., Jr.	461	Pra
Geo.	277	Ldn	Jos.	515	Mnn	Jno., Sr.	464	Pra
Jas.	689	Wsh	Sam	516	Mnn	Jno. S.	461	Pra
Joseph	232	Ldn	Loughead, James	698	Br	John	806	Nrf
Joseph	240	Ldn	Loughridge, John	327	Dnw	Jonathan	569	Frd
see Langley, Longler			Loum, John	217	Shn	Jos.	261	Ldn
Longshores, Thos.	317	Ldn	Loury, Edward	912	Crl	Lancaster	462	Pra
Longston, Clotilda	12	Hnr	Nelson	912	Crl	Molly	462	Pra
Longwell, James	21	Oho	Richard	912	Crl	Randolph	462	Pra
Mathew	713	Wsh	Louthain, George	842	Wth	Reuben, Jr.	461	Pra
Longwith, Burgess	777	Wst	John	842	Wth	Reuben, Sr.	461	Pra
George	777	Wst	Louthan, Henry	546	Frd	Wm.	463	Pra
Jno.	352	Lnc	Lucy	583	Frd	see Loveitt		
Longworth, Burges	401	Rch	Louther, Elias	933	Hrr	Lovewell, Lucy	496	Frn
William	401	Rch	Jesse	937	Hrr	William	490	Frn
Lonner, Jacob	257	Shn	Thomas	938	Hrr	William	494	Frn
Lonsford, Isaac	697	Wsh	Wm.	939	Hrr	Lovice, Mary	821	Nrf
Looden, James	476	Frn	Wm.	963	Hrr	Lovin, Adam	55	Chr
Lookadoo, Jno.	61	Chs	Love, ---	332	Dnw	Loving, Abram	434	Flv
see Lokadoo			Alexander	23	Oho	Christopher	911	Crl
Looman, Barton	22	Oho	Alexr.	816	Nrf	George	709	Nls
Loomer, Fancy	826	Nrf	Allen	754	Brn	James	708	Nls
Looney, Jno.	637	Btt	Augustine	237	Ldn	James, Jnr.	709	Nls
Jno., Jr.	638	Btt	Chappell	350	Lnn	John	433	Flv
Jontn.	638	Btt	Charles	251	Ldn	John	169	Knq
Josh.	638	Btt	Chs. J.	276	Frf	Joseph	709	Nls
Robt.	637	Btt	David	13	Oho	Larkin	170	Knq
Loontz, Henry	213	Shn	Elias	131	Sth	Lewis	169	Knq
Loop, Chris.	361	Ags	Elizabeth	251	Shn	Lunsford	708	Nls
Philip	361	Ags	George	391	Fqr	Martha	446	Flv
Simon	361	Ags	Hannah	316	Ldn	Neomy	709	Nls
Looseley, Jonathan	23	Oho	Henry	161	Sth	Pittman	912	Crl
Loot, Mary	216	Shn	James	754	Brn	Richard	113	Hnr
Loots, Henry	236	Shn	James	314	Ldn	Samuel	709	Nls
Loper, Bnjn.	933	Hrr	James	19	Oho	Sarah	433	Flv
Lorain, Thomas	334	Dnw	Jno.	316	Ldn	Thomas	912	Crl
Lord, Gerrard	206	Kng	Jno. S.	279	Frf	William	169	Knq
Robinson	113	Hnr	John	518	Prw	Wm.	433	Flv
Lore, Peter	360	Ags	John	842	Wth	Wm.	709	Nls
Lorer, ---, Mr.	908	Nrf	Joseph	736	Wsh	Lovingston, Margaret	828	Nrf
Lorey see Sorey			Mary	29	Hnr	Lovjoy, Joseph	586	Mnr
Lorimer, J.H.T.	466	Mdd	Mary	161	Sth	Low, Benjamin	10	Knw
Lorn see Law			Philip	522	Prw	Crutz	962	Hrr
Lorrain, Lewis	909	Nrf	Robert	350	Lnn	Dav.	515	Mnn
Lorrel, Hannah	133	Hnr	Robert	424	Msn	David	575	Pre
Lorton, Sarah	629	Mnt	Samuel	316	Ldn	Geo.	515	Mnn
Thos.	629	Mnt	Thomas	452	Grn	Harry	243	Ldn
Losch, Elizabeth	303	Ldn	Thomas	428	Msn	Henry	714	Wsh
Jane	304	Ldn	Thos.	316	Ldn	John	561	Brk
Losh, Adam	19	Rcm	Thos.	156	Sth	Jos.	515	Mnn
Adam, (Jr.)	26	Rcm	William	141	Sth	Rhewben	710	Nls
Danl.	12	Rcm	William	718	Wsh	Thomas	277	Ldn
Stephen	6	Rcm	Winferd	910	Hrr	see Law		
Losier, Nicholas	842	Wth	Wm., Majr.	736	Wsh	Lowair, John	697	Wsh
Lossin, Wm. L.	709	Nls	see Lowe			Joshua	697	Wsh
Lott, Benjamin	548	Frd	Loveall, Sollomon	940	Hrr	Lowden, Robert	936	Hrr
Geo.	516	Mnn	Lovecy, Drury	153	Dnw	Lowder, Frederick	59	Jff

Name	Pg	Co
James	728	Wsh
John	639	Mnt
Joseph	697	Wsh
Lowderback, Thomas L. [?]	19	Oho
Lowdin, John	956	Hrr
Lowdon, William	922	Hrr
Lowe, Benjamin	277	Frf
Edward	21	Stf
Elizabeth	942	Hrr
Fredrick	326	Dnw
Jesse	360	Fqr
Jno.	161	Sth
John	586	Mnr
John	499	Prw
John	881	Sth
Joshua	578	Mnr
Judith	367	Fqr
Ledbetter	161	Sth
Lemuel	881	Sth
Levey	577	Mnr
Micajah	882	Sth
Nathan	586	Mnr
Nehemiah	586	Mnr
Sally	882	Sth
Saml., Sr.	207	Kng
Samuel	586	Mnr
Sanford	988	Nrt
Thomas	586	Mnr
Walter	277	Frf
Zach.	586	Mnr
Zaddock	586	Mnr
see Love		
Lowen, John	801	Hmp
Mary	52	Clp
Lower, Christian	696	Br
Henry	609	Mnt
Lowery, Aron	432	Flv
Charles	988	Nrt
James	22	Stf
James, Sr.	61	Stf
Jeremiah	276	Frf
John	629	Gls
Joseph	954	Hrr
Nathan	430	Flv
Robert	54	Stf
William	989	Nrt
Lowgest see Longest		
Lowman, Abram	410	Ags
Barnerd	410	Ags
Jacob	410	Ags
Jno.	298	Rck
John	361	Ags
Joseph	361	Ags
Moses	516	Mnn
Wm.	361	Ags
Lown, John	579	Brk
Lownds, Charles	93	Jff
James	907	Nrf
Jno.	908	Nrf
Lowns, Jas.	31	Hnr
Lowny, George	386	Fqr
Lowrey, ---, Mrs.	27	Hnr
Darkis	699	Wsh
Davd.	749	Wsh
Davd., Jur.	749	Wsh
James	700	Wsh
John	907	Nrf
John	1	Oho
John	759	Wsh
Oveton	165	Alb
Lowry, Absalem	201	Alb
Albert	200	Alb
Anne	793	Nrf
Cathn.	187	Elc
Clabourn	898	Hnv
Daniel	548	Frd
Danl.	18	Rcm
Eliz.	178	Elc
Elizabeth	701	Gch

Name	Pg	Co
Frances	178	Elc
James	563	Brk
James	637	Btt
James	867	Hnv
James	639	Mnt
James	699	Wsh
Jno.	662	Glc
Jno.	351	Lnc
Joel	701	Gch
John	471	Bdf
John	103	Jff
John	639	Mnt
Joseph	639	Btt
Matthew	701	Gch
Matthias	521	Prw
Moses	639	Btt
Nancy	631	Mnt
Nelson	200	Alb
Overton	869	Hnv
Polley	701	Gch
Rob.	187	Elc
Soloman, Jnr.	867	Hnv
Soloman, Snr.	868	Hnv
Solomon	362	Ags
Thornton	701	Gch
Thos.	596	Mnr
William	430	Bth
William	470	Bdf
Wm.	701	Gch
Lowther, James, Junr.	843	Wth
James, Senr.	843	Wth
John	842	Wth
William	692	Br
Lowyres, Thomas	574	Mnr
Loy, Adam	765	Hmp
Adam	297	Ldn
Daniel	828	Hmp
Jacob	835	Hmp
John	761	Hmp
John, Junr.	831	Hmp
William	764	Hmp
Loyal, James	201	Ess
Loyals, ---	918	Nrf
Loyd, Benjamin	482	Frn
Elisha	17	Wod
Elizabeth	827	Bck
George	152	Dnw
Henry	470	Bdf
Henry	277	Frf
Henry	395	Mds
Henry, Jr.	470	Bdf
Hugh	277	Frf
Isaac	215	Shn
John	152	Dnw
John	489	Frn
John	394	Mds
Lewis	394	Mds
Mary	255	Shn
Mary	755	Wsh
Maryanne	516	Prw
Neal	468	Frn
Rd.	278	Frf
Robert	489	Frn
Talton	490	Frn
Thomas	153	Dnw
Thomas	394	Mds
Thomas	11	Wod
William	793	Bck
William	505	Prw
Wm.	727	Wsh
Loy'd, Stephen	721	Brn
Loydd, Wm.	701	Gch
Loyde, Catharine	196	Ess
George	206	Ess
Polly	200	Ess
Sarah	203	Ess
Lubrich, Daniel	711	Nls
Lucado, Isaac	442	Flv
Lucas, Aaron	113	Hnr
Ant.	258	Ldn

Name	Pg	Co
Basil	551	Brk
Caley, (F.Negroe)	379	Fqr
Charles	721	Brn
Charles	523	Prw
Charles	118	Spt
Daniel	107	Acc
David	628	Gls
David	206	Kng
Edmund	452	Grn
Edward	629	Gls
Eliza	4	Hnr
Elliott	109	Acc
Ephraim	680	Br
Esau	628	Gls
Fielding	111	Spt
Francis, f.negro	276	Frf
George	200	Shn
George	255	Shn
Happy	54	Clp
James	523	Prw
Jno.	53	Clp
John	629	Gls
John	113	Hnr
John	640	Mnt
Joseph	124	Hnr
Luke	109	Acc
Mary	611	Srr
Molly	121	Hnr
Parker	108	Acc
Parker	629	Gls
Philip	206	Kng
Philip	503	Prw
Phillip	676	Br
Polly	109	Acc
Prudence	628	Gls
Ralph	629	Gls
Randolp	628	Gls
Rebecca	524	Prw
Robert	92	Jff
Saml.	113	Hnr
Saml.	643	Mnt
Saml.	518	Prw
Samuel	912	Crl
Samuel	258	Ldn
Sarah	417	Fqr
Sarah	628	Gls
Simeon	24	Rcm
Solomon	121	Hnr
Southey	108	Acc
Stephen	611	Srr
Thomas	629	Gls
Thomas	201	Shn
William	523	Prw
William, Jur.	629	Gls
William, Ser.	629	Gls
William L.	107	Acc
Wilson	113	Hnr
Wm.	662	Glc
Zachariah	111	Spt
see Locas		
Luck, Austin	104	Spt
Fanny	104	Spt
George	79	Spt
George, Senr.	911	Crl
George P.	892	Hnv
John B.	911	Crl
Larkin	76	Spt
Marshall	912	Crl
Mary	182	Alb
Nathan	911	Crl
Nathaniel	868	Cmp
Richard	77	Spt
Robert	76	Spt
Samuel	911	Crl
Samuel	866	Hnv
Luckett, Ignatius	382	Fqr
Levin	322	Ldn
Liven	236	Ldn
Richard	382	Fqr
Saml.	290	Ldn

Thomas	420	Fqr	Thomas	169	Knq	Fielding	557	Frd
William	176	Shn	Thos.	897	Hnv	Robert	557	Frd
Luckey, Thomas	330	Dnw	Lumpkins, Reuben	395	Mds	Winnifred	557	Frd
Luckhane, Wm.	352	Lnc	Dudley	463	Frn	Luty, John	842	Wth
Lucky, Joseph	574	Frd	Lumsden, Thos.	907	Nrf	Luzardar, An.	517	Mnn
Lucis, Charity	29	Hnr	Lumsdon, Henry	84	Spt	Luzarder, An., Jr.	517	Mnn
Lucus, Ambrose	288	Amh	Lunceford, Baldwin	360	Fqr	Lyall, Hudson	396	Rch
Barbary	777	Wst	James, jr.	153	Dnw	Samuel	391	Rch
Bazle	955	Hrr	James, Senr.	153	Dnw	Lybrook, Henry	629	Gls
Burdit	777	Wst	Joseph	152	Dnw	John	628	Gls
Frances	874	Cmp	Joseph, Senr.	152	Dnw	Lyder, Lewis	317	Ldn
Gideon	861	Cmp	Leroy	153	Dnw	Lyell, Dozier	777	Wst
Isham	112	Hnr	Wm.	152	Dnw	John	777	Wst
James	281	Amh	Lunderman, John	574	Pre	Wm.	663	Glc
John	906	Hrr	John, Junr.	574	Pre	Lyford, Wm. G.	402	Ags
John	34	Stf	William	56	Chr	Lynch, Jessy	35	Hnr
Margeret	777	Wst	Lundie, Elizabeth	720	Brn	Lykins, Jonis	632	Mnt
Milly	777	Wst	Leroy	720	Brn	Marcus	632	Mnt
Nancy	20	Hnr	Lundy, James	666	Mnt	Lyle, Archd.	272	Rck
Nathaniel	36	Stf	James, Jr.	650	Sss	Danl.	301	Rck
Nathaniel	777	Wst	James, Sr.	650	Sss	Ibby	538	Brk
Peggy	35	Stf	Jno. H.	146	Sth	James	67	Chs
Polly	35	Stf	Joshua C.	452	Grn	James	293	Rck
Spencer	777	Wst	Lansfort	126	Sth	Jane	885	Hnv
William	861	Cmp	Mary	146	Sth	Jno.	442	Mth
William	777	Wst	Luney, Peter	481	Frn	John	129	Hnr
see Lewcas, Luires			Lunley, Polly	851	Sth	John	301	Rck
Lucy, Ann	938	Chc	Lunsford, Epas	352	Lnc	Margaret	402	Ags
Edward	687	Br	Jane	696	Wsh	Matthew	576	Pre
Frederick	721	Brn	Jno.	351	Lnc	Saml.	300	Rck
Jessee	721	Brn	John	420	Bth	Sarah	760	Hmp
Joshua	721	Brn	John	392	Rch	Sarah	282	Rck
Polly	336	Dnw	Lenton	353	Lnc	Wm.	272	Rck
Rachal	721	Brn	Moses	352	Lnc	Wm., esq.	293	Rck
Robert	721	Brn	Moses	697	Wsh	Wm., jr.	293	Rck
see Lacy			Nicholas	9	Oho	Lyles, George	470	Bdf
Ludrick, Catharine	804	Hmp	Richard	988	Nrt	John	650	Sss
Daniel	825	Hmp	Rcd.	352	Lnc	Joseph	276	Frf
Jacob	804	Hmp	Rod, [his] Est.	353	Lnc	W.	276	Frf
Ludson, Dianah	957	Hrr	Starling	988	Nrt	Lylor, Philip	280	Rck
Ludwick, John	102	Jff	Swanson	788	Hmp	Lyman, Jac.	515	Mnn
see Luidwick			Thadeus	611	Srr	Lyn, Robert	16	Oho
Lufman, Wm.	461	Pra	William	368	Fqr	Lynaugh, Philip	387	Fqr
Lufmyre, Nancy	67	Chs	William	37	Stf	Lynch, Anslem	872	Cmp
Lugar, Adam	629	Gls	see Landrum, Lonsford,			Catrin	689	Wsh
George	629	Gls	Lunceford, Luntzford			Christopher	849	Cmp
Lugg, Macon	839	Nrf	Luntz, Nancy	516	Prw	Dafny	326	Dnw
Peter, Capt.	908	Nrf	Luntzford, Lewis	3	Rcm	Edmond	853	Cmp
Luidwick, Felix	32	Rcm	Lupton, David, Jr.	582	Frd	Edward	854	Cmp
Jacob	32	Rcm	David, Senr.	581	Frd	Edward	759	Wsh
Luires, John	302	Amh	Isaac	582	Frd	Elijah	867	Cmp
see Lucus			Isaac	780	Hmp	Francis	332	Dnw
Luke, Faithfull	482	Frn	Jesse	779	Hmp	Geo.	273	Ldn
Jacob	533	Frd	John	575	Frd	James	55	Chs
James	591	Frd	Joseph	582	Frd	Jas.	14	Hnr
Jno.	250	Ldn	Joshua	575	Frd	Jas. H.	14	Hnr
John	591	Frd	Samuel	582	Frd	Jno.	515	Mnn
Paul D.	192	Elc	William	780	Hmp	John	683	Br
Thomas	579	Frd	Lurton see Leveton			John	389	Fqr
Vincent	927	Hrr	Lurty, Moore	206	Kng	John	20	Hnr
Wim.	870	Hnv	Lusey, John	522	Brk	John	593	Mnr
Wm.	829	Nrf	Lusher, Jacob	427	Rnd	John, (Capt.)	854	Cmp
Lukens, Jonathan	567	Frd	Lusk, ...	288	Rck	John, Senr.	854	Cmp
Lum, Jno.	311	Ldn	John	279	Rck	Mattw.	637	Btt
Lumber, Wm.	516	Mnn	Luster, Abner	657	Mnt	Mattw	639	Btt
Lumkin, Robert	941	Chc	William	860	Cmp	Peyton	328	Dnw
Lumm, Jesse	258	Ldn	Jonathan	867	Sth	Richard	899	Hnv
Lumpkin, Anderson	575	Pre	see Suter			Robert	701	Gch
Coleman	662	Glc	Luterwick, George	230	Shn	Saml.	626	Mnt
Harry, Snr.	169	Knq	Lutewick, Jos.	230	Shn	Sol.	788	Nrf
Henry, jr.	169	Knq	Philip	230	Shn	Stephen	788	Nrf
Jacob	170	Knq	Lutholts, George	220	Shn	Tatem	788	Nrf
Jno.	206	Kng	Lutrall, John	391	Rch	Thos.	701	Gch
John	219	Ess	Leroy	410	Rch	Willm.	589	Mnr
Moore	574	Pre	Lutrell, Mary	380	Fqr	Wm.	516	Mnn
Robert	894	Hnv	Rd.	52	Clp	see Lyinch		
Salley C.	169	Knq	Lutterell, Robert	515	Prw	Lyndsay, James, jr.	873	Cmp
Sarah	911	Crl	William	777	Wst	James, Sr.	856	Cmp
Spencer	170	Knq	Luttrell, Burrel	54	Clp	Robert	856	Cmp
Thomas	471	Bdf				Robert	865	Cmp

Edward	169	Knq
Robert	244	Ldn
William	169	Knq
Wm.	244	Ldn
see Layne		
Lyneweaver, John	42	Rcm
see Lineoweaver		
Lynn, Benson	515	Prw
Charles	650	Sss
Curtis	650	Sss
Elizabeth	511	Prw
Fielding	237	Ldn
Francis	389	Fqr
George	637	Btt
George	519	Frd
Isabel	517	Mnn
Jno.	517	Mnn
John	510	Prw
Joseph	352	Fqr
Joseph	511	Prw
Lewis	389	Fqr
Martha	15	Oho
Moses	511	Prw
Nehemiah	511	Prw
Olivia	510	Prw
Stephen	870	Hnv
Thompson	390	Fqr
William	514	Prw
Lynton, Jno.	250	Ldn
Lyoe see Syoe		
Lyon, Daniel	757	Hmp
Eligah	815	Hmp
Elijah	455	Frn
Elisha	815	Hmp
Elizabeth	911	Crl
Ephraim	665	Mnt
Jacob	722	Wsh
James	710	Nls
James	724	Wsh
John	16	Oho
Judah	260	Amh
Lawrence	685	Br
Lewis	37	Rcm
Peter	451	Frn
Peter	708	Nls
Richard	834	Hmp
Stephen	724	Wsh
Thomas	335	Dnw
Thos.	53	Clp
William	760	Nwk
William	718	Wsh
Wm.	710	Nls
Lyonback, David	186	Shn
Peter	186	Shn
Lyons, Abel	909	Hrr
Daniel	877	Yrk
Jacob	21	Hnr
James	598	Frd
James	35	Hnr
Jno.	872	Hnv
John	371	Fqr
John	815	Hmp
John	820	Hmp
John	65	Jff
John	207	Kng
John	235	Ldn
John	254	Ldn
Mary	569	Frd
Nancy	14	Hnr
Paul	637	Btt
Thomas	206	Kng
Wm.	362	Ags
Lysoot, Wim.	894	Hnv

--- M ---

M..., ... [2]	476	Bdf
M...d, ...	235	Aml
M...ers, Elijah	313	Ldn
M...y..., Joseph [crossed out]	437	Bth
Maben, ---	332	Dnw
Mathew	328	Dnw
Mabens, ---	328	Dnw
Mabin, David	331	Dnw
Mabnary, George	17	Wod
Mabnory, William	18	Wod
Mabray, Gray	755	Brn
Jno.	284	Frf
Mabrey see Malrey		
Mabry, Edward	452	Grn
Hinchia	452	Grn
Lewis	329	Dnw
Mary	654	Sss
Richd.	161	Sth
Thomas	452	Grn
Mabury, William	8	Wod
Macandrea, Eliza.	665	Glc
Macatee, Bedicter	506	Prw
Macaulister, Susanna	499	Prw
Macbride, John	7	Hnr
MacCall see Call		
Maccaulay, Lizah., (Y)	878	Yrk
Mace, Ebenezer	419	Rnd
Hennery	961	Hrr
Henry	37	Brn
Henry, Jur.	417	Rnd
Isaac	417	Rnd
Jacob	952	Hrr
James	952	Hrr
Jeremiah	417	Rnd
John	952	Hrr
Macentine, Samuel	965	Hrr
Macfarland, James	351	Lnn
Machoniche, Jas. R.	56	Clp
Macitee, Colly	247	Ldn
Mack, Richard	511	Prw
Macker, John	255	Shn
Mackey, James	42	Rcm
John	277	Rck
Mary	301	Rck
Ruth	594	Brk
Wm.	593	Brk
Mackie, Eliza.	465	Pra
Geo.	818	Nrf
Henry	465	Pra
Jno.	464	Pra
Macklen, Sally	133	Hnr
Macklin, Patty	878	Yrk
Macky, Henry	277	Rck
James	278	Rck
John	542	Frd
John [2]	928	Hrr
Robert	517	Frd
Robert	540	Frd
Robert	113	Spt
Thomas	58	Chr
Maclean, James	6	Oho
John	4	Oho
John	26	Oho
Maclin, Augustin	721	Brn
Elizabeth	757	Brn
Frederick	722	Brn
Henry	722	Brn
Henry	452	Grn
James	452	Grn
John D.	453	Grn
Joseph	722	Brn
Thos.	721	Brn
William	453	Grn
Macom, James	219	Pnd
Joseph	219	Pnd
William	219	Pnd
Macon, ---, Estate	99	Cmb
Sally	125	Cmb
Thomas	397	Mds
William H.	762	Nwk
Wim.	882	Hnv
Macons, ---, Estate	105	Cmb
Macreery, James	15	Oho
Wm.	15	Oho
Macshan, Nehemiah	116	Cmb
Madaris, Henry	8	Hnr
Madcaff, James	11	Knw
Madcalf, Masham	89	Jff
Maddan, Sam	931	Hrr
Madden, Dennis	282	Frf
Henry	7	Oho
Jane	587	Frd
Jno.	283	Ldn
John	817	Hmp
John	910	Nrf
Mabra	546	Frd
Michl.	910	Nrf
Polly, Jr.	56	Clp
Samuel	818	Hmp
Sarah, Jr.	56	Clp
Sarah, Ser.	56	Clp
Theely	817	Hmp
Thomas	281	Frf
William	587	Frd
Maddera, Lucy	612	Srr
Thomas	612	Srr
Maddison, Coasar, (F. Negroe)	349	Fqr
John	365	Fqr
Maddox, Agnes	808	Bck
Bennett	60	Clp
David	793	Bck
Equilia	2	Wod
Hezekiah	79	Jff
James	813	Bck
James	816	Bck
Jessee	705	Gch
Jno.	58	Clp
Jno. W.	847	Hnv
John	303	Amh
John	114	Acc
John	57	Chr
John	123	Hnr
Michael	813	Bck
Molly	702	Gch
Notley	58	Clp
Notley, jr.	60	Clp
Rosel	10	Wod
Saml.	58	Clp
Sarah	614	Mnt
Wilfred	351	Lnn
Wim. G.	847	Hnv
Wm.	702	Gch
Maddrey, Richard	36	Isw
Maddux, Allison	511	Prw
Babah	358	Fqr
Bennet	517	Prw
Bennet	524	Prw
Craven	392	Fqr
Elizabeth	368	Fqr
Godwin	171	Shn
Hannah	376	Fqr
Hendly	520	Prw
Henry	520	Prw
Henry	171	Shn
John	367	Fqr
John	519	Prw
Lawson	509	Prw
Lazarus	512	Prw
Noah	511	Prw
Notley	167	Shn
Patty	509	Prw
Thomas B.	369	Fqr
Thomas M.	513	Prw
Thornton	360	Fqr
Walter	519	Prw
Walter	525	Prw
Maddy, Henry	577	Mnr
James	564	Mnr
John	583	Mnr
Madera, Chrisn.	518	Mnn

N. B.	518	Mnn
Nic.	518	Mnn
Madery, Danl.	246	Shn
John T.	471	Bdf
Madey, Mathw.	581	Mnr
Madieras, James	467	Mdd
Madill, Alexr.	453	Grn
Madin, Benj.	746	Wsh
Madison, Catlett	395	Mds
Gregory	116	Hnr
Henry, Jur.	57	Chr
Henry, Senr.	57	Chr
James	202	Alb
James, [his] Qr.	395	Mds
John	915	Crl
Mary	913	Crl
Mary	898	Hnv
Saml.	706	Wsh
Susan	395	Mds
Susanna	643	Btt
William	913	Crl
William	395	Mds
Madling, Fred	472	Bdf
Madon, James	757	Wsh
Madox, Mical	948	Chc
Michael	57	Chr
Madra, James	154	Dnw
Madson, Thomas, (FB)	472	Bdf
Maellery, John	9	Oho
Maffitt, Whl., Revd.	284	Frf
Mafics, John	223	Shn
Mafris, Adam	222	Shn
George	222	Shn
Maganet, George	23	Rcm
Magann, John	262	Amh
Joseph	260	Amh
Maganos, ---, Madm.	910	Nrf
Magart, John	277	Rck
Magee, Alexander	97	Spt
Amey	653	Sss
Andrew	328	Dnw
Cary	652	Sss
Cathe.	640	Btt
Drewry	453	Grn
Forten	653	Sss
George	326	Dnw
Gilliam	138	Sth
Henry	653	Sss
Jno.	138	Sth
John	652	Sss
Michael, [his] (est.)	654	Sss
Samuel	96	Spt
Thomas	91	Spt
Thomas	97	Spt
William	70	Spt
Wily	115	Spt
Magers, Joseph	542	Frd
Maget, Priscilla	612	Srr
Magett, James	160	Sth
Nicholas	872	Sth
Saml.	872	Sth
Maggart, Davd.	296	Rck
Maggert, John	36	Rcm
Maggeson, Thos.	912	Nrf
Maggot, Christian	190	Shn
John	190	Shn
Maghert, David	595	Mnr
Magill, Archibald	509	Frd
Charles	517	Frd
Charles	520	Frd
Charles	540	Frd
James	38	Rcm
Robt.	39	Rcm
Magnert, Henry	597	Mnr
Magoveem, Eleanor	249	Shn
Magret, Henry	591	Mnr
Magruda, James	684	Br
Magruder, Daniel	539	Frd
Elias	520	Mnn
George A.	589	Frd
John B.	436	Flv
Ninian	600	Frd
Presley	58	Clp
Thomas	914	Crl
Maguier, Bernard	833	Nrf
George	588	Mnr
Mahaffey, James	18	Oho
Mahan, Chs.	912	Nrf
Mahanes, Lewis	203	Alb
Mary	354	Lnc
Samuel	203	Alb
Mahaney, Jerry	191	Shn
Maharra see Mahon		
Maheoren see Mahwren		
Maher, John	515	Brk
Patrick	300	Rck
Pattrick	420	Rnd
Maherry, James	5	Oho
Mahew, Alexander	539	Frd
William	587	Frd
Mahin, Brian	533	Brk
Mahoeney, Austin	170	Shn
Mahomey, Dennis, jr.	208	Kng
Dennis, Sr.	207	Kng
George	209	Kng
Hethe	210	Kng
Mahon, Benja.	170	Knq
James	170	Knq
James Elijah ["Huff" ? crossed out]	19	Oho
John	581	Mnr
John, jr.	584	Mnr
Thomas	171	Knq
William	171	Knq
Mahone, Daniel	300	Amh
James	612	Srr
John	291	Amh
Richard	761	Nwk
William	32	Isw
Mahoney, Dennis	412	Bth
James	82	Jff
John	181	Shn
Mahony, Henry	41	Rcm
James	17	Rcm
Mahood, Alexander	845	Wth
Mahorney, Margarett	405	Fqr
Stephen	208	Shn
Mahu, John	515	Brk
Richard	204	Alb
Mahue, Perry	531	Brk
Mahundro, John O.	447	Flv
Thos. O.	436	Flv
Mahunny, Caty	206	Ess
Mahurine, Caleb	584	Mnr
Isaac	584	Mnr
Mahwren, Seth	5	Knw
Maiden, James	36	Rcm
Nancy	413	Rch
Sally	412	Rch
Maidlin, Elizabeth	154	Dnw
Jane	154	Dnw
Joel	154	Dnw
Michael	724	Brn
Maigne, J.C.	912	Nrf
Mail, Js.	522	Mnn
Wm.	522	Mnn
Mails, Jno.	644	Btt
Maiming, Thos.	756	Brn
Main, Hanah	712	Wsh
John	132	Sth
Seb...	709	Wsh
Thimothy	736	Wsh
Mainard, Ed. C. [L. ?]	546	Prg
Mains, Joannah	750	Wsh
Maires, Stephen	528	Brk
Mairs, Benjn.	654	Mnt
Cathn.	190	Elc
Maisters, James	716	Nls
James	717	Nls
Jno.	717	Nls
Maitin, Plesant	883	Hnv
Maitland, Alexander	653	Sss
R.	332	Dnw
Richd.	452	Grn
Robt.	911	Nrf
Maiton, Desire	723	Brn
Maize, Ann	911	Nrf
James	631	Gls
Major, Babel	43	Acc
Bernard	612	Srr
Charles	396	Mds
Edward	952	Chc
George	44	Acc
Josiah	170	Knq
Martha	939	Chc
Mathew	467	Mdd
Patiance	957	Chc
Rd.	58	Clp
Rosary	42	Acc
Saml. H.	234	Aml
Samuel	154	Dnw
William	44	Acc
Majors, John	474	Bdf
John	693	Br
Samuel	352	Lnn
Wm.	54	Clp
Makeall, Benjmin	687	Br
Makee, George	508	Prw
Maker see Mahu		
Makern, Samuel	21	Oho
Malbon, Chas.	468	Pra
Darkis	468	Pra
David	465	Pra
Francis	467	Pra
Jas.	467	Pra
Jno.	468	Pra
Lemuul	468	Pra
Peter	464	Pra
Philip	465	Pra
see Molbon		
Malbone, Danl.	910	Nrf
Thos.	912	Nrf
Malcom, Alexn.	365	Ags
James, Ser.	774	Hmp
Jane	425	Bth
John	365	Ags
Joseph	579	Mnr
Mathew	366	Ags
Nancy	424	Bth
Peter	774	Hmp
Saml.	579	Mnr
William	424	Bth
William	774	Hmp
Male, Wilmore	826	Hmp
Malery, James	848	Cmp
Malett, Henry	674	Br
Maley, Agness	9	Wod
John	990	Nrt
Samuel	410	Rch
William	18	Wod
Winnifred	990	Nrt
Malhafey, Hugh	715	Wsh
Malhorn, Robert	944	Hrr
Malick, ...lip	833	Hmp
John	765	Hmp
Malin, Frances	207	Kng
William	69	Jff
Mallery, Aggy	32	Hnr
Henry	640	Btt
Roger	724	Brn
Mallicote, Geo.	679	Wrw
John	612	Srr
Patsey	681	Wrw
Thos., Jur.	681	Wrw
Thos., Ser.	681	Wrw
Wm.	682	Wrw
Malling, James	644	Btt
see Mulling		
Mallory, Anna	900	Hnv
Anne	411	Fqr

Name	No.	Code	Name	No.	Code	Name	No.	Code
Billey	854	Hnv	James	850	Hnv	Joel	567	Pre
Chas. K.	181	Elc	John	525	Mnn	John	413	Bth
David	876	Hnv	Rachel	199	Ess	John	216	Ess
Edw.	178	Elc	Thomas	844	Hnv	John	510	Frd
Edward	540	Frd	Wm., Jr.	525	Mnn	John	170	Knq
Eliz. M.	177	Elc	Manancour, M.S.	910	Nrf	John	564	Mnr
Eliza.	326	Dnw	Manard, Crawley	947	Chc	John	579	Pre
George	872	Hnv	Manbell, Laurenc	827	Nrf	Joseph	170	Knq
James	362	Fqr	Manble, John	948	Hrr	Josiah	234	Aml
James	34	Rcm	Mancar see Manear			Lucy	874	Cmp
Jno.	847	Hnv	Manchy, George	277	Rck	Lucy	578	Pre
Johnson	813	Nrf	Mandly, Jesse	569	Frd	Mary	642	Btt
Johnson	912	Nrf	Mane, Sabeus	520	Mnn	Mary	171	Knq
Mary	854	Hnv	Manear, David	425	Rnd	Mary Ann	62	Chs
Minor	13	Ntt	Manacey	425	Rnd	Mary F.	233	Aml
Overton	853	Hnv	Maneffee, George	495	Frn	Moses	413	Bth
Philip, Senr.	366	Fqr	Maneley, Jesse	163	Shn	Peter	62	Chs
Robert	855	Hnv	Jesse	164	Shn	Philip	213	Ess
Roger	332	Dnw	Manes, Peter	583	Brk	Phoeby	64	Chs
Roger	13	Rcm	Maney, Alexa.	185	Elc	Rebecca	910	Nrf
Susan	855	Hnv	Manford, Wm.	541	Brk	Richard	877	Cmp
Thilman	855	Hnv	Mang, George	548	Brk	Saml.	234	Aml
Thomas, Jnr.	847	Hnv	see Mong			Thomas	216	Ess
Thos., Snr.	866	Hnv	Mangos, Jno., Jr.	641	Btt	William	233	Aml
Urial	397	Mds	Jno., Sr.	641	Btt	William	235	Aml
William	28	Isw	Mangrum, Isham	453	Grn	William	413	Bth
William	397	Mds	Mangum, Samuel	652	Sss	William	35	Hnr
Willm. S.	186	Elc	William	652	Sss	William	172	Knq
Wim.	856	Hnv	Manier, Dav.	524	Mnn	William, (F. Negroe)	366	Fqr
see Maellery			Jno.	524	Mnn	William, not Taken	33	Hnr
Mallow, George	223	Pnd	Moses	524	Mnn	William F., jr.	130	Cmb
George	10	Rcm	Sam	525	Mnn	William F., Sr.	122	Cmb
Henry	226	Pnd	Wm.	524	Mnn	Willm.	642	Btt
Jacob	640	Btt	Manin, Ann	38	Stf	Worsham	54	Chs
Jacob	221	Pnd	Maning, David	484	Frn	Mannay, Chas.	798	Nrf
Michal	642	Btt	John	494	Frn	Manner, Eliza.	197	Ess
Mallox see Mattox			John	97	Spt	Jane	201	Ess
Malon, James	905	Hrr	William	97	Spt	Nancy	201	Ess
Malone, Benjn.	154	Dnw	Maniply, Nathaniel	257	Amh	Manners, Stophle	642	Btt
Daniel	654	Sss	Manker see Marker			Mannin, Armistead	763	Nwk
Danl.	154	Dnw	Mankin, Benjamin	504	Prw	Jacob H.	83	Jff
Fred.	598	Brk	William	3	Wod	Richard	763	Nwk
George	756	Brn	Mankins, Wm.	235	Ldn	Richardson	762	Nwk
George	154	Dnw	Manley, John	814	Nrf	William	762	Nwk
George	654	Sss	Richd.	18	Ntt	see Manin		
Harper	154	Dnw	Rose	246	Ldn	Manning, Benjamin	6	Oho
James	756	Brn	Manlove, Christopr.	154	Dnw	Benjamin, Jr.	6	Oho
John	914	Crl	John	154	Dnw	Creadle	801	Nrf
John	155	Dnw	Robt.	154	Dnw	Henry K.	465	Pra
John	65	Jff	see Medford			Jas.	819	Nrf
John	30	Rcm	Manly, ---, Miss	330	Dnw	John	629	Gls
John	651	Sss	Charles	154	Dnw	Jos.	809	Nrf
John P.	757	Brn	David	153	Dnw	Matthew	822	Nrf
Jordan	756	Brn	see Mandly			Nathaniel	300	Ldn
Lucy	756	Brn	Manlyer, Peter	145	Sth	Robert	820	Nrf
Robert	155	Dnw	Mann, Abner	234	Aml	William	629	Gls
Thomas	452	Grn	Adam	564	Mnr	Willis	820	Nrf
Thomas, Jr.	652	Sss	Adam, Jr.	600	Mnr	Wm.	757	Brn
Thomas, Sr.	652	Sss	Archd.	1	Ntt	see Mannay		
Thos.	640	Btt	Archer	57	Chs	Manoggin, Sam.	665	Glc
William	915	Crl	Barnet	241	Ldn	Manon, Henry	10	Knw
William	654	Sss	Branch	60	Chs	Manor, Benjn.	551	Brk
William, Jr.	652	Sss	Cain	235	Aml	Joseph	516	Brk
Wm.	154	Dnw	Cain	55	Chs	Saml.	536	Brk
Wm., jr.	154	Dnw	Charles	789	Bck	Manry, William	652	Sss
Maloney, Danl.	529	Brk	Daniel	234	Aml	Mansfeild, Jas.	804	Nrf
James	529	Brk	David	234	Aml	John	794	Nrf
James	859	Cmp	Fiel	234	Aml	Mansfied, Malachi	804	Nrf
Malory, George	69	Jff	Field	578	Pre	Mansfield, Iaac	587	Mnr
Grace	89	Jff	George	394	Fqr	John	473	Bdf
Mary	69	Jff	Hezekiah	58	Chr	Joseph	445	Flv
William	70	Jff	Jacob, jr.	564	Mnr	Julia	804	Nrf
Maloy, Thomas	714	Nls	Jacob, S.	564	Mnr	Matthias	466	Pra
Malrey, Garland	166	Alb	James	876	Cmp	Reubin	166	Alb
Malsby, John	933	Hrr	James	202	Ess	Richd.	806	Nrf
Malt, James	916	Crl	James	575	Mnr	Willoughby	804	Nrf
Malvin, Anne, (F. Negroe)	408	Fqr	Jessee	58	Chr	Wm.	444	Flv
Man, Dolley	19	Hnr	Jno.	65	Chs	see Manspield		
George	860	Hnv	Jno.	284	Ldn	Manson, Hardaway	154	Dnw
			Joel	234	Aml	John	723	Brn

John	832	Nrf	Mariner, Dolly	114	Acc
Nathaniel J.	271	Amh	George	113	Acc
Nathl.	153	Dnw	Hanson	520	Mnn
Peter	153	Dnw	Mark, Henry	532	Frd
Peter	330	Dnw	John	107	Spt
Ths. P.	25	Hnr	Markee, Benjamin	38	Rcm
Manspield, Michl.	640	Btt	Marker, Catharine	287	Ldn
Thos.	639	Btt	Jacob	502	Brk
Mantelow, David	892	Hnv	Jacob	565	Brk
Mantilow, Jno.	877	Hnv	John	572	Frd
Mantor, Jephet	505	Brk	Travis	955	Hrr
Manuel, Ezekiel	516	Prw	Markes, James	399	Rch
Fortunatus	385	Fqr	Joel	529	Prg
Fotune	518	Prw	Vincent	714	Nls
Francis	385	Fqr	Markey, Leanard	645	Btt
William	517	Prw	Nichs.	644	Btt
William	163	Shn	Wm.	272	Rck
William	164	Shn	Markham, Allen W.	27	Stf
Manvell, Patrick	1	Oho	Jas.	640	Btt
Manyfee see Maneffee			Jas. L.	56	Clp
Manzey see Masezey			Jno.	639	Btt
Mapings, Elizabeth	95	Jff	John	474	Bdf
Marable, Benjamin	653	Sss	John	703	Gch
Benjm.	944	Chc	John	27	Stf
Edward	126	Hnr	Nl.	640	Btt
Edward	653	Sss	Thomas	474	Bdf
Marcey see Maxey			Markley, John	697	Br
March, Betsey	663	Glc	Marks, Abel	271	Ldn
David	256	Shn	Abner	546	Prg
Ellis	256	Shn	Alexander	675	Br
Henry	22	Rcm	Charles H.	533	Prg
Jacob	22	Rcm	David	938	Hrr
Jno.	280	Frf	Edward	432	Flv
Jno.	313	Ldn	Edward	612	Srr
John	26	Rcm	Edward, jr.	549	Prg
Martin	24	Rcm	Edward, Senr.	536	Prg
Mary	273	Ldn	Geo.	264	Ldn
Michael	11	Rcm	Harrison	531	Prg
Michal	506	Frd	Heman	26	Hnr
Peter	22	Rcm	Isaiah	275	Ldn
Saml.	22	Rcm	Jacob	194	Shn
Sebastian	22	Rcm	James	170	Shn
Spencer	957	Hrr	Jno.	275	Ldn
Marchand, ---, Dr.	912	Nrf	Jno.	318	Ldn
John	567	Brk	Joel	530	Prg
Reuben	9	Oho	Joel [crossed out]	550	Prg
Marchant, Abm.	507	Brk	Joel	551	Prg
Aden	76	Jff	John	334	Dnw
Gideon	809	Nrf	John	210	Kng
Isaac	506	Brk	John	538	Prg
Jordan	805	Nrf	John	612	Srr
Jordan	909	Nrf	Jos.	23	Hnr
Philip	909	Nrf	Joseph	876	Sth
Wm.	507	Brk	Lucy	202	Alb
see Merchant			Martha	531	Prg
Marck see Mauk			Mary	170	Shn
Marckl, Charles	475	Bdf	Mordica	15	Hnr
Marckle, John	475	Bdf	Nathan	139	Sth
Marcom, James	492	Frn	Nathaniel	533	Prg
Marcum, Mary	58	Chr	Reuben	779	Wst
Marcus, Isaac	524	Mnn	Sarah	275	Ldn
Zachariah	550	Frd	Solomon	911	Nrf
Marcy, Peter	57	Clp	Thomas [2]	921	Hrr
Marders, Eliza.	210	Kng	Thomas	170	Shn
James, jr.	209	Kng	Thos.	314	Ldn
Jno., jr.	207	Kng	William	574	Frd
Jno., Senr.	209	Kng	William	921	Hrr
Js., Senr.	207	Kng	William, jr.	532	Prg
Stephen	209	Kng	William, Senr.	531	Prg
Mares, Alexr.	637	Mnt	see ---, Markes, Marx		
Archibd.	631	Gls	Markwell, Ally	927	Hrr
Isreal	755	Brn	Markwod, Jacob	370	Ags
Margaret, ---, Madm.	912	Nrf	Markwood, John	61	Jff
Margrave, Mary	264	Rck	Marley, William	419	Bth
Maria, Holdy	17	Hnr	Marlin, Peggy	334	Dnw
Marible, John	352	Lnn	Marling, Jacob	328	Dnw
Mathew	352	Lnn	John	10	Oho
Tabitha	352	Lnn	John, Jr.	10	Oho
Marica, Catherine	101	Jff	Marlow, Betty	217	Ess
Marick, Geo.	503	Brk	Edwd.	287	Ldn

James	367	Fqr
James	170	Shn
John	216	Ess
John	386	Fqr
John	9	Oho
Nancey	413	Fqr
Sarah	237	Ldn
William	591	Frd
Wm. W.	60	Clp
see Morlow		
Marmadke, Mary	308	Ldn
Marmaduke, Jno. A.	301	Ldn
Joseph	778	Wst
Meredith M.	779	Wst
Presley	104	Jff
Sarah	525	Prw
Vincent	778	Wst
William, Jur.	778	Wst
Marman, John	170	Knq
Marmeduke, Daniel	400	Rch
Marner, James	910	Nrf
Marnex, Benj., Gloucester		
Town	663	Glc
Marney, James	399	Fqr
Sarah	540	Frd
Marno, James	465	Pra
Maron, Elizabeth	500	Prw
Marple, Benjamin	577	Frd
David	568	Frd
Ezekiel	568	Frd
Enoch	577	Frd
George	804	Hmp
John	570	Frd
Sarah	577	Frd
Thomas	570	Frd
Marpol, Thos.	505	Brk
Marquess, Mathew	396	Mds
Miles	396	Mds
Samuel	111	Spt
Marquis, Elijah	10	Hnr
Fielding	262	Ldn
Jno.	4	Hnr
Kidd	596	Frd
Sarah	209	Kng
Marquiss, Anthony	38	Stf
Marquort, Nicholas	595	Brk
Marquot, Phillip	641	Btt
Marr, Alexander	716	Nls
Andw.	912	Nrf
Daniel	415	Fqr
George	166	Alb
James	296	Amh
John	714	Nls
John	838	Nrf
Nancy, F.N.	56	Clp
Marrable, Benjanin	757	Brn
Marrass, Jno.	911	Nrf
Marriott, Ann	612	Srr
Marris, Daniel	404	Rch
Marrow, ---, Mr.	912	Nrf
Daniel	678	Wrw
Rob.	187	Elc
Marrs, Abram	564	Mnr
Harcules	474	Frn
Marsden, Frs.	912	Nrf
Mary	909	Nrf
Marsh, Aaron	56	Chs
Alexr.	354	Lnc
Benjn.	423	Rnd
Charles	989	Nrt
Cuthbert	990	Nrt
Eaney	466	Pra
Edward	585	Frd
Epaphroditus	990	Nrt
Gideon	989	Nrt
Holland	990	Nrt
James	259	Ldn
James	19	Wod
John	472	Bdf
Leanna	989	Nrt

Name	No.	Co.
Peter R.	472	Bdf
Richard	539	Frd
Robert	989	Nrt
Royal M.	58	Chr
Saml.	912	Nrt
Thomas	989	Nrt
Wm.	466	Pra
Zopher	578	Pre
Marshal, Aaron	690	Br
Aaron	691	Br
Benajah	577	Pre
Benjamin	56	Chr
David	365	Ags
Eli	520	Mnn
Elizabeth	69	Chr
Geo.	366	Ags
Henry	204	Alb
Horace	120	Spt
Jacob	250	Ldn
James	363	Ags
James	683	Br
James	698	Br
James H.	572	Mnr
John	368	Ags
John	264	Rck
John H.	56	Chr
Joshua	314	Ldn
Lindsey	363	Ags
Mary	204	Alb
Robert	698	Br
Samuel	683	Br
Sarah	56	Clp
Thomas [2]	204	Alb
Thomas	688	Br
Thomas	689	Br
Thos.	363	Ags
William [3]	204	Alb
William	35	Rcm
Marshalhead, George	204	Alb
Marshall, ---	342	Fqr
Alexander	64	Chs
Alexr.	577	Pre
Almarine	845	Wth
Benjamin	112	Acc
Benjamin	524	Prw
Benjamin, Sen.	113	Acc
Carter	913	Crl
Daniel G.	110	Acc
Danl.	6	Ntt
David	796	Hmp
Francis	283	Frf
George	382	Fqr
George	8	Oho
George, of Isma	115	Acc
Hannah	13	Pwh
Henry	112	Acc
Hez.	520	Mnn
Isaac	113	Acc
Jacob	251	Ldn
James	112	Acc
James	914	Crl
James	284	Frf
James	588	Frd
James M.	593	Frd
Jno.	54	Clp
Jno.	282	Frf
Jno.	284	Frf
Jno.	248	Ldn
Jno.	275	Ldn
John	110	Acc
John [2]	112	Acc
John	233	Aml
John	530	Brk
John	757	Brn
John	881	Cmp
John	370	Fqr
John	561	Frd
John	822	Hmp
John	30	Hnr
John	127	Hnr
John	171	Knq
John	816	Nrf
John, of Wm.	111	Acc
Lewis	909	Nrf
Lucey	420	Fqr
Mumford	355	Fqr
Peggy	114	Acc
Polly	210	Ess
Rd.	284	Frf
Reuben	914	Crl
Richard	171	Knq
Richard	579	Pre
Richd. L.	207	Kng
Robert	349	Fqr
Robert P.	210	Kng
Robt.	8	Isw
Robt., Est.	233	Aml
Saml.	208	Kng
Sampson	112	Acc
Samuel	112	Acc
Samuel	12	Pwh
Solomon	878	Yrk
T.	30	Hnr
Tabitha, SS	115	Acc
Thomas	112	Acc
Thomas	913	Crl
William	473	Bdf
William	913	Crl
William	8	Hnr
Wm.	512	Brk
Wm.	531	Brk
Wm.	756	Brn
Marshel, Delpha	397	Mds
Henry	397	Mds
Marshell, Jane	728	Wsh
Marshon, Joseph	244	Ldn
Thomas	244	Ldn
Marstella, Nicholas	422	Rnd
Marston, Joshua	779	Wst
Susanna	612	Srr
Mart, Nathan	631	Gls
Martaen, Henry	428	Rnd
Martain, John	721	Brn
Marteney, Wm.	422	Rnd
Marter see Martin		
Marthena, John	736	Wsh
Martial, Archibal	352	Lnn
John	352	Lnn
Robert	352	Lnn
Thomas	352	Lnn
Martiall, Robt.	650	Mnt
Martin, Abner	20	Oho
Abram	300	Amh
Alice	762	Nwk
Allen	520	Mnn
Andrew	238	Ldn
Andrew	12	Oho
Andw.	909	Nrf
Angus	911	Nrf
Ann	467	Mdd
Anne	803	Nrf
Anne	811	Nrf
Anne Frances	849	Cmp
Austin	127	Cmb
Barbara	166	Alb
Barbary	666	Mnt
Bartlett	644	Btt
Benja.	54	Clp
Benjamin	166	Alb
Benjamin	716	Nls
Benjamin	102	Spt
Blackley	165	Shn
Briman	543	Frd
Cafry	616	Mnt
Caleb	760	Nwk
Carter	890	Hnv
Cary	166	Alb
Caveleer	92	Jff
Charles	872	Cmp
Charles	415	Fqr
Charles	209	Kng
Charls	965	Hrr
Chrisley	365	Ags
Chs.	58	Clp
Conrad	583	Frd
Dabney	166	Alb
Dan	523	Mnn
Dandridge	761	Nwk
Daniel	631	Gls
Daniel	20	Oho
Daniel	32	Stf
David	166	Alb
David	364	Ags
David	645	Btt
David	869	Cmp
David	7	Hnr
David	295	Ldn
Edward	40	Acc
Edward	112	Acc
Edwd.	43	Acc
Elias	374	Fqr
Elisabeth	761	Nwk
Elisha	166	Alb
Elizabeth	884	Hnv
Ellyson	762	Nwk
Ely	930	Hrr
Ephraim	20	Oho
Francis	415	Fqr
Francis	165	Shn
Francis T.	524	Frd
Frederick	14	Rcm
Geo.	521	Mnn
Geo.	878	Yrk
George	869	Cmp
George	415	Fqr
George	171	Knq
George	613	Mnt
George	715	Nls
Gidian	630	Gls
Glopath	890	Hnv
Golder	76	Spt
Hannah	962	Hrr
Hannah	521	Mnn
Henry	104	Cmb
Henry	105	Cmb
Henry	447	Flv
Henry [2]	521	Mnn
Henry	2	Rcm
Henry	37	Rcm
Henry	878	Yrk
Hezekiah	417	Fqr
Hezekiah	713	Nls
Hudson	711	Nls
Hudson	716	Nls
Hudson, Jnr.	716	Nls
Ingle	12	Rcm
Isriah	715	Nls
J. P.	909	Nrf
Jacob	204	Alb
Jacob	506	Brk
Jacob	705	Gch
Jacob	962	Hrr
Jacob	963	Hrr
James	112	Acc
James	367	Ags
James	836	Bck
James	847	Cmp
James	914	Crl
James	282	Frf
James	408	Fqr
James	468	Frn
James	489	Frn
James	493	Frn
James	795	Hmp
James	820	Hmp
James	888	Hnv
James	714	Nls
James	715	Nls
James	763	Nwk
James	910	Nrf

James, jr.	299	Amh	Li...in H., Negroes of Co-			Thomas E. [C?]	171	Knq
James, (SM)	300	Amh	lour [Live in? H.			Thos.	368	Ags
James, Senr.	299	Amh	Martin]	685	Nls	Thos.	58	Clp
James L.	526	Frd	Lucy	53	Chs	Tilman	351	Fqr
Jane	15	Pwh	Lucy	332	Dnw	William	203	Alb
Jas.	59	Clp	Luther	795	Hmp	William	234	Aml
Jefrey	166	Alb	Margaret	211	Shn	William	300	Amh
Jeptha	514	Brk	Mary	581	Frd	William	473	Bdf
Jeremiah	20	Oho	Mary	889	Hnv	William	876	Cmp
Jesse	489	Frn	Mary	8	Knw	William	916	Crl
Jesse A.	26	Hnr	Mary	711	Nls	William	367	Fqr
Jno.	56	Clp	Mary	6	Oho	William	468	Frn
Jno.	24	Hnr	Matthew	713	Nls	William	490	Frn
Jno.	285	Ldn	Meridith	715	Nls	William	496	Frn
Jno.	525	Mnn	Morris	283	Rck	William	548	Frd
Jno. [2]	716	Nls	Moses	105	Cmb	William	600	Frd
Jno., Clk	639	Btt	Moses	301	Rck	William	921	Hrr
Jno., free negro	70	Chs	Nancy	166	Alb	William	965	Hrr
Job	6	Knw	Nelly	104	Spt	William	763	Nwk
Joel	910	Hrr	Noah	282	Frf	William	171	Shn
John [2]	166	Alb	Obadia	170	Knq	William	27	Stf
John	441	Bth	Patsy	913	Crl	William, jr.	256	Amh
John	575	Brk	Peggy	330	Dnw	William B.	761	Nwk
John	869	Cmp	Peter	643	Btt	William P.	882	Cmp
John [2]	913	Crl	Peter	119	Hnr	Willis	60	Clp
John	914	Crl	Peter	92	Jff	Willis	171	Knq
John	915	Crl	Peter	910	Nrf	Wm.	640	Btt
John	127	Cmb	Phil.	524	Mnn	Wm. [2]	61	Clp
John	416	Fqr	Philip, Jr.	613	Mnt	Wm.	945	Hrr
John	461	Frn	Philip, Sr.	613	Mnt	Wm.	354	Lnc
John	493	Frn	Phillip	641	Btt	Wm.	238	Ldn
John	549	Frd	Pleasant	475	Bdf	Wm.	711	Nls
John	631	Gls	Poley	715	Nls	Wm.	714	Nls
John	702	Gch	Presly	522	Mnn	Wm.	716	Nls
John	704	Gch	Rachel	280	Ldn	Wm., free negro	70	Chs
John	763	Hmp	Rawley	518	Mnn	Younger	914	Crl
John	780	Hmp	Rebecca	538	Frd	Zach	332	Dnw
John	812	Hmp	Reubin	166	Alb	Zachariah	154	Dnw
John	209	Kng	Richard	587	Frd	Zebedee	910	Nrf
John	238	Ldn	Roadham	846	Wth	Zeph.	521	Mnn
John	586	Mnr	Robert	42	Acc	see Maitin, Mastin, Mortin		
John	763	Nwk	Robert	203	Alb	Martiny see Marteney		
John	17	Oho	Robert	469	Frn	Marton, Benjn.	708	Wsh
John	20	Oho	Robert	703	Gch	Davd.	710	Wsh
John	578	Pre	Robert	889	Hnv	Jesse	736	Wsh
John	66	Spt	Robert	588	Mnr	John	710	Wsh
John, Jr.	366	Fqr	Robert	579	Pre	Sarah	747	Wsh
John, Jr.	497	Frn	Robert	846	Wth	Tarlton	725	Wsh
John, jr.	170	Knq	Robt.	622	Mnt	Welcom	694	Wsh
John, Jr.	21	Oho	Rose	465	Pra	Marts, George	428	Rnd
John, Jun.	780	Hmp	Saml.	702	Gch	Richard	428	Rnd
John, Snr.	171	Knq	Saml.	705	Gch	Wm.	428	Rnd
John, Sr.	497	Frn	Sampson	282	Frf	Marx, Joseph	126	Hnr
John J.	270	Amh	Samuel [2]	877	Cmp	Solomon	115	Hnr
John S.	760	Nwk	Samuel	535	Prg	Mary, Elizabeth	949	Chc
Johnson	644	Btt	Saul	283	Frf	Peter	912	Nrf
Jonathan	632	Gls	Sherod	715	Nls	see Merry		
Jos.	523	Mnn	Sibbeous	493	Frn	Marye, William S.	187	Shn
Jos.	910	Nrf	Smith	39	Acc	Masa, Lewis	294	Ldn
Joseph	202	Alb	Snowden	548	Frd	Masbarger, Joseph	630	Gls
Joseph	533	Brk	Sophia	716	Nls	Masezey, Peter	384	Fqr
Joseph	6	Knw	Spaks	711	Nls	Mash, Elijh.	937	Hrr
Joseph	715	Nls	Spencer	947	Hrr	Wilson	749	Wsh
Joseph	20	Oho	Stephen	474	Bdf	Masin see Maxen		
Joseph W.	256	Amh	Stephen	784	Bck	Masincup, Jacob	715	Nls
Joshua	943	Hrr	Stephen	922	Hrr	see Messincup		
Joshua	762	Nwk	Sucky	334	Dnw	Maskell, Sally	207	Kng
Joshua	763	Nwk	Susanah	577	Pre	Maslin, Wm.	533	Brk
Josiah	258	Amh	Susannah	43	Acc	Mason, A.B.T.	290	Ldn
Josiah	642	Btt	Tabith	42	Acc	A.F.	292	Ldn
Josiah	170	Knq	Tho.	520	Mnn	Adam	43	Acc
Julius	760	Nwk	Tho.	524	Mnn	Adam	394	Fqr
Julius, jr.	761	Nwk	Thomas	44	Acc	Alexr.	517	Brk
Leonard	209	Kng	Thomas	166	Alb	Andrew	555	Frd
Levi	98	Jff	Thomas	280	Amh	Anthony	652	Sss
Levi	305	Rck	Thomas	439	Bth	Ayres	110	Acc
Levy	488	Frn	Thomas	208	Kng	Bable	38	Acc
Levy	943	Hrr	Thomas	615	Mnt	Bailey	55	Clp
Lewis	260	Amh	Thomas, Jr.	864	Cmp	Bartlett	51	Stf
Lewis G.	24	Stf	Thomas C.	579	Pre	Benjamin	75	Spt

Name	No.	Abbr	Name	No.	Abbr	Name	No.	Abbr
Benson	55	Clp	Lawrence	796	Bck	William	654	Sss
Betsey	990	Nrt	Lewis	474	Bdf	Massey, Alexander	565	Mnr
Betsey	37	Rcm	Lewis	44	Stf	Ann	93	Jff
Bingley	555	Frd	Littleton	850	Sth	Asa	411	Fqr
Catharine	579	Pre	Major	39	Acc	Avent	453	Grn
Celia	60	Clp	Major	111	Acc	Barbary	778	Wst
Charles	58	Chr	Margaret	115	Acc	Caleb	110	Acc
Charles	653	Sss	Margaret	42	Stf	Chas., Senr.	208	Kng
Chloe, a free mulatto	989	Nrt	Mary	111	Acc	Dade	88	Spt
Christr.	911	Nrf	Mary	880	Cmp	Dolley	364	Fqr
Colvert	387	Fqr	Mary	293	Ldn	Elizabeth	111	Acc
Daniel	27	Stf	Mary	840	Nrf	Elizabeth	56	Jff
Danl.	644	Btt	Nancey	352	Fqr	Frances	103	Spt
David	589	Frd	Nancy	43	Acc	Henry	563	Mnr
David	653	Sss	Nathan	497	Frn	Henry	597	Mnr
Edmunds	452	Grn	Nathaiel	723	Brn	James D.	208	Kng
Edwd.	519	Brk	Nathaniel	914	Crl	Jeptha	597	Mnr
Edwd.	878	Yrk	Nelson	55	Clp	John	113	Acc
Eli	990	Nrt	Nelson	49	Stf	John	453	Grn
Elisebeth	751	Wsh	Overton	913	Crl	John S.	208	Kng
Eliza.	664	Glc	Penelope	351	Lnn	Lee	285	Frf
Elizabeth	756	Brn	Peter	869	Cmp	Mary	210	Kng
Elizabeth	375	Fqr	Peter	523	Mnn	Mildred	207	Kng
Elizabeth	703	Gch	Peter	989	Nrt	Pettypool	453	Grn
Elizabeth	75	Spt	Peter, Senr.	57	Chr	Reuben	209	Kng
Elizabeth	652	Sss	Peyton	534	Prg	Reuben	566	Mnr
Enoch	55	Clp	Peyton	653	Sss	Reuben	104	Spt
Enoch	45	Stf	Philip	864	Cmp	Ro.	663	Glc
Evandor	42	Acc	Philip	875	Cmp	Ro.	664	Glc
Ewell	204	Alb	Rachel	39	Acc	Sally	210	Kng
Fanny	79	Spt	Rane	786	Bck	Samuel	81	Jff
Frances	875	Cmp	Rebecca	654	Sss	Samuel	93	Jff
Frederick	654	Sss	Rezin	556	Frd	Sarah	664	Glc
Geo.	59	Clp	Richard	653	Sss	Sherwood	577	Pre
George	41	Acc	Richd.	612	Srr	Thomas	411	Fqr
George	43	Acc	Sarah	42	Acc	Thomas	209	Kng
George	913	Crl	Sarah	913	Crl	Thomas	565	Mnr
George	328	Dnw	Sarah	395	Fqr	Thomas C.	90	Spt
George	283	Frf	Sarah B.	504	Prw	Warner P.	209	Kng
George	857	Hnv	Seth	651	Sss	William	365	Fqr
George	850	Sth	Smith	914	Crl	William	453	Grn
Henry	44	Acc	Tho.	354	Lnc	William	208	Kng
Henry	57	Clp	Thomas	41	Acc	William, (Overseer)	394	Fqr
Isham B.	56	Clp	Thomas	57	Chr	Winifred	209	Kng
Jacob	44	Acc	Thomas	928	Hrr	Massie, Anne	763	Nwk
Jacob	406	Fqr	Thomas	654	Sss	Charles	704	Gch
James	114	Acc	Thompson	283	Frf	Charles, Jur.	166	Alb
James	519	Brk	Thos.	663	Glc	Charles, Senr.	166	Alb
James	521	Brk	Val M.	264	Rck	Edmund	257	Amh
James	757	Brn	W. T.	289	Ldn	Francess	704	Gch
James	654	Sss	Walter	387	Fqr	Gideon	704	Gch
Jeremiah	114	Acc	William	43	Acc	Hugh	763	Nwk
Jesse	857	Cmp	William	863	Cmp	James	202	Alb
Jessee [3]	203	Alb	William	105	Cmb	John	166	Alb
Jno.	57	Clp	William	283	Frf	John	763	Nwk
Jno.	60	Clp	William	452	Grn	John	19	Oho
Jno.	353	Lnc	William	351	Lnn	John T.	166	Alb
Jno. F.	306	Ldn	William	396	Mds	Jonathan	4	Knw
Joel	913	Crl	William	31	Rcm	Josiah	510	Frd
Joel	46	Stf	William, Jr.	378	Fqr	Moses	4	Knw
John	723	Brn	William, Senr.	374	Fqr	Robert	4	Knw
John	769	Brn	William, Sr.	874	Cmp	Robt.	116	Hnr
John	798	Bck	Wim.	869	Hnv	Susannah	257	Amh
John	840	Bck	Wm.	866	Cmp	The	114	Hnr
John	863	Cmp	Wm.	55	Clp	Thomas	166	Alb
John	913	Crl	Wm.	523	Mnn	Thomas	717	Nls
John	915	Crl	Wm., Sr.	757	Brn	William	257	Amh
John	466	Mdd	see Maron, Moore, Moson			William	761	Nwk
John	523	Mnn	Masowell, David	932	Hrr	see Masezey		
John	761	Nwk	Mass, John	848	Cmp	Massingbery, Wm.	910	Nrf
John, junr.	914	Crl	Peter	853	Cmp	Massingham, Js.	910	Nrf
John R.	612	Srr	Massay, James	113	Acc	Massy, Benjamin	92	Spt
John R.	654	Sss	Massen, Peter	911	Nrf	Masten, Charles	341	Fqr
Jonathan	558	Frd	Massenberg, Peter	909	Nrf	Samuel	473	Bdf
Jonatn.	644	Btt	Massenbird, George	426	Bth	Master, John	965	Hrr
Joseph	58	Chr	Massenburg, Geo.	176	Elc	Masters, Henry	8	Oho
Joseph	652	Sss	John, Sr.	655	Sss	Jerrard	11	Wod
Josh., (free Negro)	642	Btt	John, Sr.	653	Sss	Lot	23	Oho
Judith	757	Brn	Mary	654	Sss	Nathen	23	Oho
Judith	869	Hnv	Thos.	663	Glc	Rebecca	352	Lnn

Stephen	525	Mnn	Sampson	448	Bth	Joshua	110	Acc
Thomas	52	Stf	Sampson [3]	450	Bth	Judith	198	Ess
Masterson, Wm.	367	Ags	Samuel	869	Cmp	Levin	114	Acc
Mastin, Abram	489	Frn	Samuel	874	Cmp	Lucy	755	Brn
Mordecai	111	Spt	Thomas	2	Knw	Luke, (N)	724	Brn
Peter	475	Bdf	Thos.	909	Nrf	Martha	129	Cmb
see Martin			Thos., (M)	724	Brn	Mary	207	Kng
Maston, James	850	Cmp	William	203	Alb	Matthew	723	Brn
Richd.	728	Wsh	William	856	Cmp	Molly	121	Hnr
Mat, Toney	154	Dnw	William	466	Mdd	Nancy	57	Chr
Matchet, Wm.	307	Rck	Wm.	582	Mnr	Nancy	702	Gch
Matchett, Richard	715	Nls	see ---, Matheos, Matthws			Nathaniel	576	Pre
Mathany, Daniel	778	Wst	Mathewson, David	332	Dnw	Nelley, (M)	724	Brn
Nat., Jr.	521	Mnn	James	203	Alb	Newman	524	Prw
Thomas	778	Wst	Mathias, Ann	808	Nrf	Peggy	910	Nrf
Matheney, John	81	Jff	Mathies, Rich.	808	Nrf	Peggy	51	Stf
Jonas	81	Jff	Mathis, James	700	Wsh	Philip	578	Pre
Matheny, Abm.	524	Mnn	Mathony, Archibald	414	Bth	Plesant	867	Hnv
Dan	520	Mnn	Mathuny, Frederick	811	Hmp	Polly	909	Nrf
David	430	Bth	Mathus, Anderson	737	Wsh	Priscilla, (Y)	878	Yrk
Epm.	523	Mnn	Sherwood	737	Wsh	Rains	474	Bdf
Jno.	518	Mnn	Matley, Francis	284	Frf	Rebecca	912	Nrf
Jos.	523	Mnn	Matleys, Rebecca	951	Chc	Reuben	121	Hnr
Js.	523	Mnn	Matlock, Hester	56	Clp	Saley	714	Nls
Nat, Sen.	521	Mnn	Jos.	61	Clp	Sally	39	Acc
Nathan	522	Mnn	Matocks, Wm.	291	Ldn	Sally	207	Kng
Noah	520	Mnn	Matson, Benjamin	514	Frd	Samuel	723	Brn
Reub.	518	Mnn	John	531	Brk	Sarah	576	Pre
Stephen	15	Rcm	John	560	Frd	Solomon	713	Nls
William	15	Rcm	John	563	Frd	Solomon	37	Rcm
Matheos, Jas. S.	832	Nrf	Matthew, Caley	378	Fqr	Tarlton	577	Pre
Mathers, Benjamin	526	Prw	Elias	518	Prw	Thomas	166	Alb
see Masters			Jesse	378	Fqr	Thomas, of S	113	Acc
Mathes, James	702	Wsh	Simon	361	Fqr	Thos.	702	Gch
Matheus, Nancy	816	Nrf	Matthewis, Drury	353	Lnn	Thos.	704	Gch
Mathewis, John	351	Lnn	Jeremia...	353	Lnn	Thos.	25	Hnr
Susannah	351	Lnn	Robert	352	Lnn	Washburn	113	Acc
Mathews, Ben.	524	Mnn	William	352	Lnn	William	42	Acc
Benja., jr.	55	Clp	Matthews, ---, &			William	110	Acc
Benja., ser.	55	Clp	Leggitt	34	Stf	William	111	Acc
Benjamin	202	Alb	...hard [Richard?]	596	Frd	William	4	Isw
Bradly	95	Spt	Abraham	171	Shn	William	5	Oho
Catharine	403	Ags	Agnes	40	Rcm	William, of Wm.	114	Acc
Catharine	418	Bth	Ailsey	704	Gch	Willis	39	Isw
Danl., (Mo.)	55	Clp	Anthony	39	Acc	Wim.	890	Hnv
Deborah	268	Ldn	Betsey	704	Gch	Wm.	705	Gch
Ed.	518	Mnn	Betsey	890	Hnv	Wm.	121	Hnr
Francis	363	Ags	Betsy	909	Nrf	Wm.	208	Kng
Gregory	5	Pwh	Candis	44	Acc	Wm.	2	Ntt
Hannah	203	Alb	Daniel	612	Srr	Zachariah	7	Isw
Isaac	642	Btt	Danl.	5	Rcm	Zachariah	39	Isw
Isaac	524	Mnn	Drury	755	Brn	Zachariah, Sen.	20	Isw
James	784	Hmp	Edwd.	704	Gch	Matthias, David	464	Pra
Jas.	54	Clp	Elias	114	Acc	Elizabeth	464	Pra
Jas., Sr.	642	Btt	Eliza., of W	113	Acc	Isaac	465	Pra
Jno.	642	Btt	Enoch	527	Brk	Jno.	912	Nrf
Jno.	316	Ldn	George	111	Acc	Jno., (B.B.)	468	Pra
Jno., Est.	55	Clp	George	114	Acc	John	549	Frd
John	365	Ags	George	5	Oho	Lucy	911	Nrf
John	595	Brk	George, BM	113	Acc	Wm.	912	Nrf
John	784	Hmp	George, SS	115	Acc	Wm., Sr.	466	Pra
John	820	Nrf	Griffin	524	Prw	Matthws, Abel	820	Nrf
John	844	Wth	Hutchings	576	Pre	Mattingley, John	505	Prw
Jonathan	597	Mnr	Jacob	111	Acc	Mattix, Mathew	915	Hrr
Jont.	267	Ldn	James	129	Cmb	Mattocks, Thomas	915	Crl
Jos.	524	Mnn	James	868	Hnv	Matton, Thomas	913	Crl
Joseph	365	Ags	James	121	Hnr	Mattox, Bazil	24	Stf
Luke	875	Cmp	Jesse	11	Isw	Collin	18	Ntt
Mary	61	Clp	Jno.	664	Glc	Gabriel	453	Frn
Mary	437	Mth	John	113	Acc	John	537	Prg
Mary	118	Spt	John	458	Frn	John Q.	107	Cmb
Moses	467	Mdd	John	130	Hnr	Josiah	120	Cmb
Nat	524	Mnn	John	34	Isw	Matthew	959	Hrr
Nathan	815	Nrf	John	711	Nls	Median	296	Ldn
Nathan, bound for a term			John	16	Oho	Nathan	455	Frn
of years	447	Bth	John	511	Prw	Robert	564	Frd
Richard	844	Wth	John, Jnr.	711	Nls	Thomas	123	Cmb
Richd.	272	Ldn	John W.	704	Gch	Thos.	530	Prg
Rochel	275	Rck	Joseph	33	Isw	William	533	Prg
Sampson	447	Bth	Joseph	712	Nls	Mauck, Frederick	550	Frd

Michal	563	Frd	William	797	Bck	Warean	229	Shn
Mauk, David	182	Shn	Maxfield, Billy	133	Hnr	see M...y..., Moyer		
David	190	Shn	Hez.	526	Mnn	Mayers see Moyers		
Frederick	214	Shn	Jos.	26	Hnr	Mayes, Chr.	712	Nls
John	216	Shn	Judith	897	Hnv	Drury	155	Dnw
Joseph	190	Shn	Richard	897	Hnv	Edward	12	Ntt
Peter	206	Shn	Salley	844	Hnv	Elijah	712	Nls
Robert	186	Shn	Thomas	845	Hnv	Frederick	153	Dnw
Maule, Ths.	25	Hnr	Maxi, Elizabeth	630	Gls	Fredk.	2	Ntt
Mauley, Barnabas	244	Shn	Maxwel, John	689	Br	Henry	409	Fqr
Maulty, Philip	950	Hrr	Samuel	692	Br	James	713	Nls
Maultyman, George	951	Hrr	Maxwell, ---, Mrs.			James, Jr.	713	Nls
Maund, Harriott L.	780	Wst	[crossed out]	3	Hnr	Judith	234	Aml
Marcun	801	Nrf	---, Mrs.	33	Hnr	Lewis	713	Nls
Noah	791	Nrf	Abner	949	Hrr	Polly	235	Aml
Maupin, Amos	203	Alb	Alexr.	530	Brk	Robert	712	Nls
Blan	202	Alb	Bezaleel	166	Alb	Salley	155	Dnw
Chapman W.	204	Alb	David	934	Hrr	Susannah	713	Nls
Cornelius	165	Alb	David	621	Mnt	see Mays, Mayse, Mazes		
Daniel [2]	202	Alb	Elizabeth	621	Mnt	Mayfield, Abm.	519	Mnn
Daniel	203	Alb	Hugh	563	Brk	Abm., Jr.	521	Mnn
David	202	Alb	James	166	Alb	Henry	370	Ags
Gabriel	204	Alb	James	576	Brk	Jane	644	Mnt
Geo. W.	827	Nrf	James	595	Brk	Jas.	522	Mnn
Jennings	202	Alb	James	720	Wsh	Js.	521	Mnn
John	201	Alb	Jane	948	Hrr	Mayhew, Peyton	284	Frf
John	202	Alb	Jas.	824	Nrf	Reason	472	Bdf
John	204	Alb	Jno.	912	Nrf	Wm.	284	Frf
Matthew	204	Alb	John	563	Frd	Mayhon, Richard	874	Hnv
Pleasant	203	Alb	John	9	Oho	Mayhue, Moses	472	Bdf
Robert	204	Alb	John	12	Oho	Maynard, Edward, Sr.	612	Srr
Thomas	203	Alb	Mary	166	Alb	Robert C.	612	Srr
Thomas	802	Bck	Mary	533	Brk	Stith	850	Cmp
Thomas	12	Knw	Nathaniel	747	Wsh	William	612	Srr
William [2]	202	Alb	Polly	621	Mnt	Mayo, Abra.	17	Hnr
Wm. C.	717	Nls	Thos.	703	Gch	Anity	124	Hnr
Zachariah	202	Alb	Thos.	748	Wsh	Bob	133	Hnr
Maurice, Elisha	34	Rcm	William	6	Oho	Cato, Persons of		
Ester	912	Nrf	Wm.	642	Btt	Colour	132	Cmb
Js.	910	Nrf	Wm.	748	Wsh	Daniel	115	Cmb
Nathan	23	Rcm	see Manbell			Daniel	14	Pwh
Thomas	35	Rcm	Maxwill, Robert	426	Rnd	Dylsy, Persons of		
Mausey, Michl.	366	Ags	May, Adam	7	Rcm	Colour		
Mauzey, Anne	281	Frf	Allen	654	Sss	Edward, Dr.	7	Pwh
John	772	Hmp	Daniel	238	Shn	Graycey	123	Hnr
Peter	772	Hmp	Eliza	13	Hnr	Henry	441	Flv
Thomas	23	Rcm	Frank	286	Ldn	Jacob	429	Flv
Mauzy, Joseph	11	Rcm	George	396	Mds	James [2]	166	Alb
Maves, Andrew	16	Oho	George	20	Rcm	John	166	Alb
Mavries, David	218	Shn	George	30	Rcm	John	122	Hnr
Maxcey, Feby	454	Frn	George	845	Wth	Joseph	816	Bck
Maxcy, James	464	Frn	Henry	522	Mnn	Joseph	444	Flv
Maxen, Elijah	523	Mnn	Henry	18	Rcm	Joseph, Majr.	11	Pwh
George	958	Hrr	James	235	Shn	Joseph H.	125	Hnr
Nat	526	Mnn	James	653	Sss	Joseph T.	436	Flv
Simion	966	Hrr	Jno.	640	Btt	Lewis	442	Flv
Thomas	956	Hrr	John	431	Bth	Lucy	17	Hnr
Wm.	523	Mnn	John	549	Frd	Peter	688	Wsh
Zebean	959	Hrr	John	197	Shn	Peter, F.B.	9	Pwh
Maxey, Benjamin	779	Bck	John F.	330	Dnw	Peter, (Free N)	20	Rcm
Charles	774	Bck	Joseph	790	Bck	Reubin	729	Wsh
Charles	832	Bck	Molly	118	Spt	Rhoda	777	Bck
Clabon	790	Bck	Moses	916	Crl	Richard	441	Flv
David	7	Pwh	Nancy	119	Spt	Stephen	440	Flv
Edward	780	Bck	Peter	845	Wth	T. A.	403	Ags
Edward	795	Bck	Robt.	132	Hnr	Valentine	444	Flv
Edward	827	Bck	Rosanna	513	Frd	William	117	Cmb
Elisha	12	Pwh	Samuel	170	Knq	Wm.	125	Hnr
Elizabeth	790	Bck	Thomas	782	Bck	Mayor, Wm.	723	Brn
Elizabeth	795	Bck	Thomas	171	Knq	Mayree, Elizabeth	100	Spt
Jacob	774	Bck	William	430	Bth	Mays, Charles	282	Amh
James	809	Bck	William	431	Bth	Charles, jr.	292	Amh
James	870	Cmp	William	806	Bck	Darkis, free negro	70	Chs
James	882	Cmp	Wm.	439	Flv	Elijah	472	Bdf
John	12	Pwh	Wm.	522	Mnn	George	260	Amh
John, Senr.	11	Pwh	Mayberry, Elizabeth	238	Shn	Hannah	452	Grn
John	790	Bck	Maycal, Jane	36	Rcm	Irwin B.	453	Grn
Priscilla	11	Pwh	Mayer, Lewis	105	Jff	James	472	Bdf
Turbyfield	807	Bck	Martin	592	Brk	James	643	Btt
William	791	Bck	Phillip	114	Spt	Jesse, free negro	70	Chs

Jessee	296	Rck	James	434	Bth	John	748	Wsh
John	286	Amh	Robert	434	Bth	Thos.	748	Wsh
John	301	Rck	McBane, Jesse	364	Fqr	McCallion, James	534	Prg
Joseph	291	Amh	John	345	Fqr	McCallister, Chris.	593	Brk
Joseph	851	Cmp	William	417	Rnd	Mccallty, John	932	Hrr
Joseph, jr.	286	Amh	McBarber, Peter	14	Oho	McCallum, Dan	523	Mnn
Lucy	100	Cmb	McBee, Hannah	343	Fqr	McCally, Addison	779	Hmp
Mary	473	Bdf	Sarah	587	Brk	George	779	Hmp
Mattw.	643	Btt	Thos.	539	Brk	see Mecally		
Molley, free negro	70	Chs	William	416	Fqr	McCalpin, Robt.	274	Rck
Patience, free negro	70	Chs	McBeeth, Thos.	747	Wsh	Wm.	274	Rck
Pearce W.	259	Amh	McBray, Moses	532	Brk	McCamar, John	234	Aml
Philis, free negro[2]	70	Chs	McBride, Alexander	763	Hmp	McCamey, Wm.	370	Ags
Rachl.	644	Btt	Alexander	829	Hmp	McCammant, James	12	Oho
Rebeca, free negro	70	Chs	Ann	705	Gch	McCammin, Jno.	285	Rck
Richard	300	Amh	James	395	Fqr	McCammont, James	697	Br
Richard	472	Bdf	James	831	Hmp	McCampbell, Anna	845	Wth
Susannah	259	Amh	James, Ser.	766	Hmp	Davd.	267	Rck
Thomas T.	281	Amh	Jane	703	Gch	Jno.	263	Rck
William	257	Amh	Jno.	250	Ldn	Jno.	268	Rck
William	445	Bth	John	294	Amh	John	303	Rck
William	58	Chr	John	582	Brk	Robt., Sr.	270	Rck
William	190	Shn	John	779	Hmp	Robt., Sr.	270	Rck
see Mayo			John	821	Hmp	Wm.	272	Rck
Mayse, Isaac	446	Bth	John	293	Rck	see ...ampbell, Campbell		
James	439	Bth	Mary	14	Hnr	McCamy, James	365	Ags
Joseph	415	Bth	Minor	705	Gch	John	365	Ags
Joseph, bound for a term			Patsey	702	Gch	Mccan, Patric	940	Hrr
of years	448	Bth	Robert	830	Hmp	McCan, Daniel	475	Bdf
Phebe	446	Bth	Robert	845	Wth	John	631	Gls
Richard	446	Bth	Robt.	705	Gch	Larry	966	Hrr
William	426	Bth	Sally	702	Gch	Mary	95	Jff
William	442	Bth	Thomas	829	Hmp	McCanahan, Charles	16	Oho
Maze, Ebenr.	643	Btt	Thomas	830	Hmp	McCance, James	132	Hnr
Mazes, Isaac	422	Msn	Thomas	834	Hmp	Thomas	72	Jff
Mblaughlin see MClaughlin			Wm.	519	Mnn	McCandless, Robert	605	Frd
MBride, Joseph	429	Msn	see MBride			McCane, Willis	703	Gch
Mc...tt, Wm.	266	Rck	McBroom, Isaac	731	Wsh	McCann, Daniel	944	Hrr
McAdam, John	368	Ags	James	536	Prg	Jno.	16	Ntt
McAexander, Samuel	165	Alb	Rober	676	Br	see Mchan		
McAlester, Robt.	61	Clp	William, Jnr.	845	Wth	McCarey, Daniel	202	Alb
McAlexander, Alexander	676	Nls	William, Senr.	845	Wth	John	201	Alb
James	676	Nls	McC... see McCammin,	Taylor		McCargo, David	871	Cmp
John	676	Nls	McCabe, Ann	464	Pra	David	58	Chr
see McAexander			Hugh	265	Amh	Hezekiah	57	Chr
McAlferson, Polly	32	Hnr	James	346	Fqr	James	57	Chr
Mcalister, Daniel	305	Ldn	John	472	Bdf	John	58	Chr
McAlister, John	600	Frd	Wm.	22	Hnr	John, Junr.	58	Chr
Richard	12	Knw	McCador, Catharine	581	Frd	Robert	58	Chr
McAllester, George	870	Cmp	Mccafry, Baily	238	Ldn	Thomas	57	Chr
John	871	Cmp	James	233	Ldn	McCarmick, Mary	499	Prw
MCallester, Garrett	425	Msn	Jno.	238	Ldn	McCarr, Thos.	545	Prg
McAllison, William	780	Wst	Mccaib, Jane	305	Ldn	McCarrol, Thos.	641	Btt
McAllister, David	911	Nrf	McCakle, James	614	Mnt	McCarte, Jno.	11	Hnr
Elizth.	910	Nrf	McCale, Elizabeth	437	Bth	McCarter, Thomas	868	Cmp
Jas.	702	Gch	McCaleb, Aneas	290	Rck	McCartey, Danl.	57	Clp
McAlpine, Jas., (Doctr.)	465	Pra	Arch.	522	Mnn	Wm.	58	Clp
McAlster, Jenny	116	Hnr	McCalee see McCabe			see Mecartey		
McALster, John	132	Hnr	McCalep, William	683	Nls	McCartney, Andrew	432	Bth
McAndlish, Thos.	910	Nrf	McCaleste, Ben	267	Rck	Andw.	642	Btt
Wm.	912	Nrf	McCalf see McCay			Jno.	639	Btt
McAnnally, Thomas	95	Jff	McCalister, Betsey	591	Brk	John	958	Hrr
McArdle, Colin	21	Oho	John	595	Mnr	Joseph	56	Jff
Mcartor, James	299	Ldn	McCall, Agness	694	Wsh	Thomas	793	Hmp
Jonathan	301	Ldn	Barny	917	Hrr	Mccarty, Dennis	235	Ldn
Moses	280	Ldn	James	694	Wsh	Thadius	235	Ldn
Mcarty, Chs.	281	Ldn	John	730	Wsh	Washington	235	Ldn
Cornelius	245	Ldn	Michl.	640	Btt	Wm.	235	Ldn
Danl.	254	Ldn	Nathl.	27	Rcm	McCarty, Bartho.	391	Rch
Dennis	242	Ldn	Robert	918	Hrr	Benj.	727	Wsh
Timothy	279	Ldn	William	456	Frn	Betsey	209	Kng
McAtee, Charity	284	Frf	William	24	Rcm	Daniel	426	Bth
Henry	2	Rcm	McCallahan, William	778	Wst	Daniel, Est.	779	Wst
Jno.	279	Frf	McCallester, Benjamin	204	Alb	Daniel L.	395	Rch
Thomas	543	Frd	Garland	640	Btt	David	369	Ags
Wm.	283	Frf	Nathan	203	Alb	Edward	810	Hmp
McAtlee see McAttee			William	203	Alb	Eliza.	412	Rch
McAttee, Wm.	582	Brk	see MCallester			Enoch	729	Wsh
McAut, Jno.	278	Rck	McCalley, George	674	Br	Frances	209	Kng
McAvoy, Franky	434	Bth	James	944	Hrr	James	552	Frd

214

Jno.	300	Rck	Mordaica	472	Bdf	McClentec, Alexander	339	Bth
John	413	Bth	Thos.	760	Wsh	William	439	Bth
John	208	Kng	McClallen, John	839	Nrf	McCleven, Thomas	429	Bth
John	224	Pnd	McClanaham, Andrew	388	Fqr	McClewer, Samuel	13	Knw
John	391	Rch	Andrew	400	Fqr	McCley see MCley		
Judith G.	407	Rch	David	388	Fqr	McClintick, Saml.	367	Ags
Jus.	57	Clp	David, Jr.	389	Fqr	McClintoch, Robert	674	Br
Katy	910	Nrf	Gerrard	388	Fqr	McClintock, James	593	Mnr
Loudon	762	Nwk	Hugh	389	Fqr	William	474	Bdf
Patrick	281	Frf	James	380	Fqr	McCllanee, Peter	743	Wsh
Peggy	61	Clp	James, Jr.	389	Fqr	Mccloud, Wm.	253	Ldn
Peter	514	Frd	James, Sr.	389	Fqr	McCloud, Anguies	280	Amh
Richd.	58	Clp	John	522	Prw	Daniel [2]	695	Br
Sarah	283	Frf	Lettice	379	Fqr	Isam	750	Wsh
Sydnor	390	Rch	Peter	375	Fqr	Jno.	283	Frf
Thos.	585	Mnr	Rachael	388	Fqr	Jno.	518	Mnn
Timothy	447	Bth	Thomas	391	Fqr	John	204	Alb
see Fitzhugh, Mcarty			William	379	Fqr	Patcey	709	Wsh
McCary, Daniel	684	Nls	McClanahan, Elijah	641	Btt	Richard	90	Spt
Martha	702	Gch	Elizabeth	990	Nrt	see MCloud		
Peter	61	Chs	Green	643	Btt	McCloy, Alexr.	75	Jff
McCashlin, Oliver	591	Frd	Henry	909	Nrf	James	61	Jff
McCaslin, Benja.	58	Clp	Jas.	641	Btt	McCluer, Alexander	166	Alb
John	413	Bth	Jno.	644	Btt	Alexr.	307	Rck
McCason, David	363	Ags	Peter G.	990	Nrt	Arthur	280	Rck
McCaul, Jno.	849	Hnv	Reheubn.	911	Nrf	Jno.	306	Rck
Richd.	702	Gch	Robert	166	Shn	Jno., j.	307	Rck
Stokes	703	Gch	Thomas	62	Jff	John	166	Alb
McCauley, Camel	613	Mnt	Thomas	169	Shn	John	279	Rck
Daniel	573	Frd	Will	644	Btt	John [crossed out]	311	Rck
Eliza.	679	Wrw	William J.	989	Nrt	Michl.	266	Rck
James	574	Frd	McClanathan, Wm.	639	Btt	Michl. [crossed out]	281	Rck
John	574	Frd	McClane, Isaac	280	Frf	Robert	273	Rck
John	808	Hmp	see MClane			see McCleer, McClure		
Peter	202	Alb	McClannahan, John	778	Wst	McCluney, William	684	Br
see McColley			Kiszer	778	Wst	William	698	Br
McCauly, Cornelius	808	Hmp	McClard, Daniel	475	Frn	McClung, Archd.	641	Btt
John	38	Stf	Samuel	492	Frn	Henry	263	Rck
McCausland, Andrew	412	Bth	Seth	483	Frn	Jame	293	Rck
James	5	Rcm	McClary, Joseph	474	Bdf	James	364	Ags
John, & C.	13	Rcm	McClasky, Jas.	640	Btt	James	274	Rck
McCauslin, Wm.	592	Brk	McClaugherty, James	631	Gls	James	279	Rck
McCautry, James	60	Jff	James, Jr.	630	Gls	James	291	Rck
William	56	Jff	McClaxner, John	805	Nrf	James, jr.	302	Rck
McCave, John	990	Nrt	McClay, John	524	Frd	Jno.	293	Rck
James	32	Hnr	see MClay			John	292	Rck
McCawlin, Henry	11	Knw	McClearey, Jno.	494	Brk	Robert	439	Bth
McCay, Jno.	280	Rck	John	599	Brk	Robt.	366	Ags
John	541	Brk	McCleary, John	501	Brk	Wm.	266	Rck
Thomas	280	Rck	McCleave, Robert	602	Frd	McClunn, Hannah	528	Frd
Wm.	22	Hnr	McCleer, Halbert	301	Rck	Jonathan	519	Frd
Wm.	275	Rck	McCleery, Thomas	682	Br	Thomas	565	Frd
Wm., Sr.	275	Rck	see MCleery			Thomas	602	Frd
see McCoy			McClelan, Billy	467	Pra	McCluny see McClenry		
McChann, Richd.	537	Prg	Cason	466	Pra	McClure, Alexander	602	Frd
McCherney, Robt.	294	Rck	David	551	Frd	Alexh.	911	Nrf
McChesney, Adam	368	Ags	Jas., (of Joab)	466	Pra	Andrew	688	Br
James	368	Ags	Jere.	467	Pra	Andrew	689	Br
Robert	798	Hmp	Jno.	467	Pra	Andw.	370	Ags
Robt.	368	Ags	Jno., (NC)	468	Pra	David	370	Ags
Thos.	748	Wsh	Joshua	467	Pra	Elizt.	370	Ags
see McChisney			Moses, Jr.	467	Pra	Halbert	366	Ags
McChisney, John	364	Ags	Moses, Sr.	467	Pra	Isaac	370	Ags
see McChesney			Sinah	468	Pra	James	25	Hnr
McCiery, Andw.	369	Ags	Thos.	467	Pra	Jno.	643	Btt
McCisten, Francis	366	Ags	Wm.	465	Pra	John	370	Ags
McClaim, Jennifer	87	Acc	Wm., Sr.	467	Pra	John	538	Brk
McClain, A.F.	391	Rch	McCleland, Thomas S.	854	Cmp	John	688	Br
Abner	418	Rnd	McClelland, Andw.	2	Rcm	John	549	Frd
Henry [2]	684	Nls	Jno.	263	Rck	John	227	Pnd
Henry, Jur.	684	Nls	John	689	Wsh	John	709	Wsh
James	472	Bdf	Saml.	267	Rck	Josiah	370	Ags
James	418	Rnd	McClellen, Wm.	364	Ags	Richard	698	Br
James, Jr.	418	Rnd	McClellin, Saml.	299	Rck	Richard	1	Oho
Jno.	523	Mnn	McClenahan, David	647	Mnt	Richd.	642	Btt
John	472	Bdf	McClennen, William	58	Jff	Robert	677	Br
John	300	Rck	McClenny, Henchy	161	Sth	Saml.	370	Ags
John, jr.	473	Bdf	Thomas	16	Isw	Saml.	2	Oho
John, Sr.	473	Bdf	Thomas	43	Isw	Sarah	13	Oho
Jonathan	125	Hnr	McClenry, John	438	Bth	William	475	Bdf

Wm.	711	Wsh	McCord, Alexr.	737	Wsh	James	280	Rck
see McLure			Benjn.	699	Wsh	Jno.	269	Rck
McClurg, Jas.	31	Hnr	Davd.	748	Wsh	Malcom	13	Knw
McCluskey, James	777	Wst	George	513	Frd	Mathew	13	Knw
Thomas	778	Wst	James	7	Oho	Patrick	416	Bth
McCoach, James	592	Brk	John	201	Alb	Saml.	282	Rck
McCoid, James	408	Ags	Samuel	201	Alb	see MCown		
McCollam, Samuel	579	Frd	Sarah	166	Alb	Mccoy, Benj.	295	Ldn
McCollester, Daniel	396	Mds	William	201	Alb	McCoy, ...	476	Bdf
Eve	396	Mds	see Brady, MCord			Adam	25	Isw
James	396	Mds	McCordle, Peter	26	Oho	Alexander	14	Oho
Jerry	396	Mds	McCorell see McCouell			Alxander	16	Oho
McColley, Daniel	202	Alb	McCorkle, John, esq.	276	Rck	Arthur	281	Rck
David	202	Alb	Joseph	10	Oho	Benjamin	218	Pnd
David	203	Alb	Patrick	283	Rck	Daniel	683	Nls
Juonias	203	Alb	Robert	12	Knw	Danl.	703	Gch
Mary	203	Alb	Saml.	266	Rck	David	7	Knw
McCollister, Ezekiel	33	Rcm	Saml.	282	Rck	Elizabeth	27	Stf
George	495	Frn	Wm.	275	Rck	George	612	Mnt
James	441	Bth	McCormac, Anderson	471	Bdf	George	2	Rcm
Joab	33	Rcm	Dennis	472	Bdf	Hezekiah	381	Fqr
John	440	Bth	James	476	Bdf	James	16	Oho
Thomas	440	Bth	Jesse	471	Bdf	James	98	Spt
William	440	Bth	John	476	Bdf	John	202	Alb
McCollock, Cad	155	Dnw	John, Jr.	362	Fqr	John	14	Oho
Francis	155	Dnw	John, Jr.	415	Fqr	John	21	Oho
John	155	Dnw	John, Sr.	408	Fqr	Joseph	912	Hrr
Martha	155	Dnw	Micajah	471	Bdf	Moses	20	Oho
McCollom, David	426	Bth	Richard	471	Bdf	Olliver	222	Pnd
William	423	Bth	Stephen	380	Fqr	Robert	9	Oho
McColluch, Thomas	202	Alb	William	408	Fqr	Samuel	26	Isw
McCollum, James	271	Rck	Wm.	527	Brk	Thomas	475	Bdf
McColly, Charles	74	Spt	see MCormac			Thos.	640	Btt
James	73	Spt	McCormach, Anderson	466	Frn	Walter	411	Fqr
McComack, Henry	293	Rck	John	467	Frn	Wilcum	23	Oho
McComb, James	366	Ags	William	467	Frn	William	475	Bdf
James	436	Bth	McCormack, Claiborn	689	Wsh	William	528	Brk
James	694	Br	David	782	Bck	William	14	Oho
John	697	Br	David	794	Bck	William [2]	20	Oho
Martha	302	Rck	David	832	Bck	William	227	Pnd
McCombs, Manuel	632	Gls	Duke	832	Bck	William	44	Stf
Polley	464	Frn	James	63	Jff	William, of R.	31	Stf
Sheldrak	631	Gls	John	688	Wsh	Willm.	612	Mnt
McComick, Ann	25	Hnr	John	752	Wsh	Wim.	852	Hnv
McComus, James	9	Oho	Mary	809	Bck	Wm.	466	Pra
McCon, Mary	911	Nrf	Micajah	700	Wsh	see McCay, McCory, MCoy,		
Thomas	16	Oho	Moses	64	Jff	Mccoy		
McConaha, James	403	Fqr	Rachal	774	Bck	McCrabb, John	706	Wsh
John	472	Bdf	Robt.	298	Rck	McCracken, Freedom	795	Hmp
Saml.	472	Bdf	Saml.	815	Bck	John	694	Wsh
Samuel	403	Fqr	Saml.	689	Wsh	Mary	794	Hmp
McConchie, Alexander	351	Fqr	Samuel	774	Bck	Virgil	786	Hmp
Mary Ann	351	Fqr	Stroud	780	Bck	Mccrady, James	246	Ldn
McConkey, Jacob	947	Hrr	McCormic, Cornelius	525	Brk	McCrady, Stephen	86	Acc
Jno.	265	Rck	McCormick, David	367	Ags	William	86	Acc
John	705	Wsh	George	545	Frd	Wm.	741	Wsh
Saml.	705	Wsh	George	10	Oho	McCrae see Crae, MCrae		
Saml., Jur.	705	Wsh	Hadson	679	Br	McCraken, Lydia	674	Br
McConnathy, Antony	8	Oho	James	679	Br	McCrakin, John	693	Wsh
McConnel, Abm.	525	Brk	James	586	Frd	McCrasky, Geo.	640	Btt
Abram	748	Wsh	James	799	Hmp	McCravey, Ele [?]	726	Wsh
Elizabeth	693	Br	Jno.	304	Ldn	Margrat	727	Wsh
Jessee	643	Btt	John	674	Br	McCraw, Dancy	875	Cmp
Jno.	643	Btt	John	699	Br	Edward	473	Bdf
Joseph	685	Br	John	587	Frd	Francis	786	Bck
Michael	235	Aml	Province	531	Frd	Hugh	473	Bdf
Moses	639	Btt	Samuel	545	Frd	James	475	Bdf
William	697	Br	Thomas	531	Frd	John	454	Frn
McConnell, Alexander	10	Oho	William	531	Frd	Saml.	1	Hnr
Jas., Sr.	640	Btt	Wm.	364	Ags	Stephen	58	Chr
John	14	Oho	Wm.	367	Ags	William	56	Chr
Samiel	4	Oho	Mccortny, Thomas	951	Hrr	McCray, Jane	615	Mnt
Wm.	1	Oho	McCouell, Jno., Este.	54	Clp	John	514	Prw
McConnico, Andw.	909	Nrf	McCoul, Ann	113	Spt	Robert	436	Bth
McConnol, James	757	Hmp	Neil	703	Gch	Robert	219	Pnd
McCook see McCool			McCoult, Elizt.	403	Ags	Stephin	614	Mnt
McCool, James	577	Frd	McCowen, Danl.	705	Gch	Thomas	787	Bck
James D.	582	Frd	John	705	Gch	Mccrea, James	294	Ldn
John, Senr.	576	Frd	Mccowett, Agness	304	Ldn	McCrea, Charles	530	Frd
Neal	900	Hnv	McCown, James	1	Knw	Jane	296	Rck

John	299	Rck
Jos.	294	Rck
Joseph	274	Rck
Wm.	521	Mnn
McCreary, Hugh	272	Rck
John	333	Dnw
McCreasey see Creasey		
McCredia, Nancy	31	Hnr
McCredie, Eliza., free		
negro	70	Chs
McCreery, Thomas	683	Br
William	682	Br
McCrery, James	641	Btt
Jas., Sr.	640	Btt
Saml.	365	Ags
McCrory, Jas.	291	Rck
Saml.	262	Rck
Wm.	291	Rck
McCroskey, James	24	Oho
Jas.	734	Wsh
John	631	Gls
Joseph	302	Rck
McCrosky, Elizh., (W)	878	Yrk
McCroy see MCroy		
McCrumly see Crumly		
McCue, Charles	642	Btt
Charles	684	Nls
David	7	Knw
James	364	Ags
John	369	Ags
Moses	366	Ags
Moses	403	Ags
see McCure		
McCuen, Mary	506	Prw
Patrick	502	Prw
Thomas	502	Prw
McCulach, Jane	366	Ags
McCullach, George	13	Oho
McCulley, Charles	693	Br
James	9	Oho
James	23	Oho
McCulloch, Abraham	13	Oho
Jno.	290	Rck
John	202	Alb
John	7	Oho
John	284	Rck
Robert [2]	201	Alb
Roderick	271	Amh
see McCulloch		
McCullock, Peter	326	Dnw
Thomas	42	Rcm
McCulloh, Robert	317	Ldn
McCullough, John	720	Wsh
Robt.	732	Wsh
Wm.	757	Wsh
McCullum, Archd.	641	Btt
McCully, Jas.	177	Shn
Joseph	198	Shn
McCuloch, James	403	Ags
Jane	403	Ags
McCulough, Wm. F.	757	Wsh
McCune, Archd.	369	Ags
Isaac	694	Wsh
Isaac	750	Wsh
James	370	Ags
John	370	Ags
John	694	Wsh
Robert	576	Pre
Saml.	369	Ags
Saml., jr.	370	Ags
see McCure, MCune		
McCurdey, Samuel	990	Nrt
McCurdy, And.	294	Rck
McCure, Andw.	369	Ags
see McCune		
McCutchean, Robert	295	Rck
Robt.	296	Rck
McCutchen, Downey	368	Ags
Elenor	368	Ags
James	367	Ags
John	365	Ags
John	367	Ags
Jonas	438	Bth
Joseph	365	Ags
Saml.	364	Ags
Saml.	368	Ags
Saml., (C. P.)	365	Ags
Saml., (Capt.)	368	Ags
Wm.	364	Ags
Wm.	367	Ags
McCutchin, Hugh	9	Oho
McCuthen, John	365	Ags
McCuthing, David	473	Bdf
Mcdade, John	408	Ags
McDade see MDade		
McDaid, Stephen	526	Mnn
McDaneld, William	718	Wsh
McDanell, Edward	316	Ldn
Martin N.	316	Ldn
Mcdaniel, Mary	493	Frn
McDaniel, Alexander	201	Alb
Ambrose	56	Clp
Bawldy	474	Bdf
Daniel	406	Fqr
Daniel	508	Prw
Duncan	579	Pre
Edward	630	Gls
Eliza	780	Wst
Eliza.	60	Clp
Fantley	415	Fqr
George	849	Cmp
George, jr.	279	Amh
Gustavus	394	Fqr
Henry [2]	566	Mnr
James	58	Chr
James	583	Frd
James	905	Hrr
James	208	Kng
James	566	Mnr
Jas.	307	Rck
Jeremiah	397	Mds
Jesse	277	Ldn
Joel	60	Clp
John	273	Amh
John	944	Hrr
Joseph	695	Br
Lott	55	Clp
Lucy	915	Crl
Mary	61	Clp
Michl.	526	Mnn
Osborn	55	Clp
Patrick	397	Mds
Polly	48	Stf
Robert	507	Brk
Salley	351	Fqr
Sally	210	Kng
Thos., & Father	55	Clp
William	305	Amh
William	508	Prw
William	780	Wst
William, (Mercht.)	359	Fqr
William, Sr.	351	Fqr
Wm.	566	Mnr
see McDanld, McDanue		
McDanill, Daniel	525	Brk
McDanld, Alexander	474	Bdf
McDannel see MDannel		
McDanold, Elizabeth	35	Rcm
McDanue, George	264	Amh
McDarmet see MDarmet		
McDarmit, Wm.	643	Btt
McDavid see McDaniel		
McDavit see MDavit		
McDeaney see McDenney		
McDearman, Jas.	705	Gch
Thomas, Sr.	58	Chr
McDearmon, Bryant	578	Pre
Joseph	577	Pre
Richard	578	Pre
McDearmott, Nancy	95	Spt
McDenney, Ann	535	Frd
McDent, Lewis	573	Brk
McDivid, Michl.	757	Wsh
McDogle, Jane	887	Hnv
Jno.	880	Hnv
Richard	888	Hnv
Thos.	887	Hnv
McDonald, Alexander	364	Fqr
Alexr.	562	Brk
Ann	16	Hnr
Anna	580	Frd
Archibald	506	Frd
Aron	525	Mnn
Bengamin	833	Hmp
Benja.	554	Frd
Benjamn.	606	Mnt
Brian	567	Brk
Charles	579	Frd
Charles	674	Hmp
Collin	153	Dnw
Daniel	504	Brk
Daniel	538	Frd
Edward	635	Mnt
Edwd.	641	Btt
Elinor	398	Fqr
Fredk.	646	Mnt
George	630	Mnt
Girrard	399	Fqr
Hannah	507	Prw
Hugh	64	Jff
James	154	Dnw
James	856	Hnv
James	80	Jff
Jas.	539	Brk
Jesse	589	Frd
Jno.	14	Hnr
John	537	Brk
John	541	Frd
John	818	Hmp
John	92	Jff
John	6	Oho
John	23	Oho
John	286	Rck
Jonas	607	Mnt
Margaret	834	Hmp
Mary	332	Dnw
Mary	665	Mnt
Matthew	286	Rck
Moses	531	Brk
Nancy	774	Hmp
Nancy	286	Rck
Robert	281	Frf
Robert	6	Oho
Samuel	541	Frd
Sarah	774	Hmp
Thomas	599	Frd
Thomas	630	Gls
Volinda	283	Frf
William [2]	398	Fqr
Wm.	525	Mnn
Wm.	286	Rck
Wm. G.	210	Kng
see McDanld, McDonlald, McDornald		
McDoniel, Jno.	466	Pra
McDonlald, Wm.	643	Btt
McDonnald, Archibald	14	Oho
Asa	192	Shn
Hugh	412	Bth
John	443	Bth
John	181	Shn
Margaret	445	Bth
Samuel	438	Bth
McDonnaw see McDonnun		
McDonnell, Joseph	914	Hrr
McDonnough see MDonnough		
McDonnun, James	7	Oho
McDonold, Columbus	846	Wth
Mary	958	Hrr
Solomon	846	Wth

McDonough, James	18	Oho	McFarling, John W.	179	Shn	Mat	524	Mnn
McDormant, David	85	Spt	Ralph	171	Shn	McGiuer, John	944	Hrr
McDornald, Daniel	687	Nls	see McFan...y			McGivan, Nancy	208	Ess
McDougal, Benja.	58	Clp	McFarren, Martin	639	Btt	McGlamer, Andw.	580	Mnr
McDougle, Jno.	519	Mnn	Saml.	641	Btt	McGlamery, John	366	Ags
McDougul, Martha	910	Nrf	McFatridge, Malcolm	846	Wth	see MGlamery		
McDowall, Amelia	911	Nrf	Mcfearson, Stephen	472	Bdf	McGlasgo, Thomas	453	Grn
Dd.	911	Nrf	McFee, John	30	Stf	McGlasson, ...	235	Aml
Hy.	911	Nrf	McFeeley, Isaac	582	Brk	James W.	577	Pre
McDowel, James	862	Hnv	McFerran, Thos.	639	Btt	John	473	Bdf
Robert .	9	Oho	Mcferson, Benjamin	203	Alb	John	787	Bck
McDowell, Archd.	581	Mnr	Stephen	273	Ldn	Thomas W.	577	Pre
Elsey	403	Ags	Stephen	276	Ldn	William	234	Aml
James	591	Mnr	Wm.	273	Ldn	William	473	Bdf
James	293	Rck	McFerson, Edmond	2	Wod	William	804	Bck
John	234	Aml	Robt.	301	Rck	McGlaughlan, Jane	295	Rck
John	366	Ags	McFirson, James	936	Hrr	McGlaughlin, Amos	79	Jff
John	403	Ags	McG..., James	562	Mnr	Betsey	403	Ags
John	439	Bth	Mcgaha, Benj.	295	Ldn	Daniel	91	Jff
Robt.	366	Ags	Patrick	292	Ldn	Ely	846	Wth
Thos.	642	Btt	McGahey, Tobias	11	Rcm	James	367	Ags
William	398	Fqr	McGallim see Gallim			John	14	Wod
Wm.	284	Frf	McGarrey, John	91	Jff	McGlauglan, Chas.	285	Rck
Wm.	637	Mnt	McGarrice, James	24	Oho	McGlauglor, Wm.	289	Rck
see ...well, Anderson			McGary, Duke	57	Chs	McGlemre, John	868	Sth
McDuff, John	439	Bth	McGath, Thomas	19	Oho	McGlochland, Aaron	432	Msn
McDugell, James	823	Hmp	see MGath			Mcgloclin, Henry	933	Hrr
McDunnahaw, James	780	Wst	McGavack, Patrick	300	Ldn	McGloghlan, Wm.	734	Wsh
Mcean, Thomas	925	Hrr	McGavock, Hugh	844	Wth	McGlothlin, Richard	192	Shn
Thomas	931	Hrr	James, Junr.	844	Wth	McGloughlin, Daniel	412	Bth
McEldowney, Robert	19	Oho	James, Senr.	844	Wth	Hugh	433	Bth
McElhenny, Mary	304	Rck	McGaw, James	851	Hnv	James	442	Bth
McElrie, John	247	Shn	William	695	Nls	Jane	416	Bth
McElroy, Adam C.	577	Pre	Mcgeath, Jno.	307	Ldn	John	432	Bth
Patric	23	Oho	McGeath, Gabriel	259	Ldn	John	442	Bth
Tho.	525	Mnn	James	242	Ldn	William	442	Bth
William	103	Jff	Mary	242	Ldn	McGluthom, John	472	Bdf
McElvany, Christopher	912	Hrr	Mcgee, Jno.	519	Mnn	McGomery, Thomas	100	Jff
McElwain, Jno.	642	Btt	McGee, Auston	738	Wsh	McGongall, James	403	Ags
McElwee, Bridget	447	Bth	James	63	Chs	McGoudond, John	595	Mnr
McEndree, John	73	Jff	Polly	579	Brk	McGovern, Mark	687	Br
William	81	Jff	Robert	855	Sth	McGovran, Philip	594	Brk
McEntire, Hugh	571	Mnr	Thompson	739	Wsh	McGowan, Jno.	912	Nrf
Robert	680	Br	Will.	866	Sth	Paul	642	Btt
McEntosh, Geo. G.	403	Ags	Wm.	692	Wsh	William	681	Br
MCetiton, Nancy	965	Hrr	Mcgehee, John	495	Frn	McGowen, John	54	Jff
McEwen, Clement	16	Oho	McGehee, Abraham	577	Pre	McGown, Henry	346	Fqr
McFadden, Francis	782	Bck	David B.	577	Pre	Mcgraw, Thomas	776	Hmp
James	367	Ags	Francis	166	Alb	McGraw, Barnwell	11	Wod
John	364	Ags	Gracey	579	Pre	Martin	575	Mnr
William	784	Bck	Jacob	579	Pre	Molly	912	Crl
Wm.	410	Ags	Jno.	881	Hnv	Robert	442	Bth
Mcfaden, Patrick	292	Ldn	John	571	Mnr	Sally	569	Frd
McFaden, John	544	Frd	John	579	Pre	McGready see MGready		
John	258	Shn	Joseph	915	Crl	McGregary, Walter	477	Frn
Mcfairland, ---	332	Dnw	Joseph	881	Hnv	McGreggor, Allen	5	Oho
McFalin, Nancy	527	Brk	Saml.	473	Bdf	John	5	Oho
McFall, Cornelieus	166	Alb	Sarah	579	Pre	McGrew, Pat	522	Mnn
Jno., Jr.	641	Btt	see McGhee			see MGrew		
Jno., Sr.	639	Btt	McGenniss, Roger	1	Oho	McGriffin, Richd.	265	Rck
McFan...y, Obadiah	163	Shn	McGeorge, Jas.	661	Mnt	see McGuffin		
Obadiah	165	Shn	John	375	Fqr	McGrigger, John	763	Nwk
Mcfarland, Ezekiel	804	Hmp	Thos.	661	Mnt	McGrigor, Jas.	896	Hnv
Mary	521	Mnn	William	472	Bdf	Mary	872	Hnv
McFarland, Asa	591	Frd	see M.George			McGrudah, William	12	Pwh
Ezekiel	8	Wod	McGhee, Benjamin	166	Alb	McGruder, Ninean	398	Fqr
James	307	Rck	Joseph	166	Alb	Zac	113	Hnr
John [2]	566	Frd	Lively	572	Mnr	Zepheniah	66	Chs
John	272	Rck	William	167	Alb	MCgruder, Normond	4	Wod
Levin	570	Frd	see McGehee			Mcguffin, William	482	Frn
Sarah	331	Dnw	McGill, Cathne.	522	Mnn	McGuffin, Betsy	414	Bth
McFarlane, Mary	911	Nrf	Chas.	525	Mnn	Hugh	292	Rck
Mcfarlin, W,lliam	227	Pnd	Chs., Jr.	526	Mnn	James	414	Bth
McFarlin, James	217	Ess	Henry	369	Ags	Saml.	362	Ags
Jas.	58	Clp	James	708	Wsh	Thomas	362	Ags
Mcfarling, James	246	Ldn	Job	525	Mnn	Thos.	364	Ags
Robert	290	Ldn	Nat.	910	Nrf	McGuinice, Samuel	400	Rch
Sarah	210	Kng	see MGill			McGuinis see McGinnis		
Stephen	207	Kng	McGinnis, Archd.	699	Wsh	McGuire, Amelia	780	Wst
Wm.	273	Ldn	Hiram	695	Nls	Danl.	41	Rcm

Name	Pg	Co	Name	Pg	Co	Name	Pg	Co
Edmd.	810	Nrf	Lahlare	285	Frf	Presley, Jur.	779	Wst
Edward	509	Frd	Loyd	285	Frf	Presley, Senr.	780	Wst
Francis	674	Br	Msry	498	Prw	Roberson	859	Cmp
Hugh	5	Oho	Robert, jr.	612	Srr	Stephen	917	Hrr
James	686	Br	Robert, Sr.	612	Srr	William	870	Cmp
John	480	Frn	Saml.	681	Wrw	William	779	Wst
John	778	Wst	Thomas	281	Frf	Wm.	529	Brk
Millecent	512	Frd	Walter	285	Frf	Wm.	722	Brn
Robert	674	Br	Wm.	55	Clp	see McKinney		
Samuel	422	Bth	McInturf, Daniel	175	Shn	McKennis, Davd.	278	Rck
Thomas	58	Stf	David	173	Shn	McKennon, Lathland	652	Sss
Travese	780	Wst	Frederick	175	Shn	McKenny, Charles	758	Br
William	14	Oho	Henry	173	Shn	Charles	953	Chc
William	779	Wst	McIntyre, Chs.	280	Frf	Cornelias	406	Rch
see McGiuer			David	9	Oho	Elizabeth	914	Crl
Mcgumery, George	949	Hrr	Michael	235	Ldn	Gerard	778	Wst
McGureman, Elizabeth	607	Srr	Patrick	303	Ldn	James	406	Rch
James	607	Srr	Wm.	288	Ldn	Jane	526	Mnn
McGuy, Malinda	208	Ess	see McTyre			Jarret	108	Spt
McGwinn, Mary	600	Frd	McItee, Harrison	252	Ldn	John [2]	406	Rch
McGwire, Josiah	8	Oho	McIver, Daniel	871	Cmp	John	74	Spt
Thomas	877	Cmp	Jno.	280	Frf	John	31	Stf
McHaffy, Andrew	628	Mnt	McIvers, Jno.	642	Btt	Mathew	61	Clp
Mchan, Elijah	218	Ess	McJitton, John	262	Rck	Michl.	929	Hrr
McHaney, Terry	867	Cmp	McJusty, William	197	Shn	Reubin	406	Rch
Mchanney, James	261	Ldn	McKae, Colin	67	Chs	Thomas	519	Prw
McHarely, Henry	873	Cmp	McKaha, Andw.	644	Btt	Thomas	74	Spt
McHarry, Js.	526	Mnn	McKain, John	198	Shn	McKenry, Alexr.	268	Rck
McHenderson, John	791	Bck	Mckan, Lucy	468	Mdd	James	270	Rck
McHenry, Andw.	756	Wsh	Mary	467	Mdd	Jno.	288	Rck
James	23	Oho	McKay, Asa	562	Frd	Jno., j.	268	Rck
John	31	Hnr	Daniel	691	Br	John, Sr.	268	Rck
John	13	Oho	Donald	154	Dnw	Thomas	268	Rck
John	26	Oho	Enos	182	Shn	see Kinsy, McKiney		
Laur.	525	Mnn	Isaac	176	Shn	McKensey, Wm.	18	Hnr
Nancy	517	Frd	Jacob, Jr.	560	Frd	McKent, James	106	Spt
Saml.	428	Rnd	Jacob, Senr.	560	Frd	McKenzie, Donald	334	Dnw
Thos.	607	Mnt	Jeremiah	176	Shn	Mary	396	Mds
Wm.	22	Hnr	Jesse	562	Frd	Sally	207	Kng
Wm.	722	Wsh	John	586	Frd	Saml.	209	Kng
see McKenry			John	604	Frd	see Beverley		
McHollams, John	42	Acc	Joseph	21	Rcm	McKerel, Salley	398	Fqr
William	30	Acc	Moses	560	Frd	Mckever, John	770	Hmp
William	43	Acc	William	235	Aml	Paul	768	Hmp
Mcholland, Allen	182	Elc	Wm.	60	Clp	Paul, Sen.	768	Hmp
Jno.	912	Nrf	Mckee, John	503	Brk	McKever, Peter	270	Rck
McHorney, Susan	780	Wst	McKee, Andrew	124	Hnr	McKewan, Isaac	535	Brk
Winney	780	Wst	Andrew	698	Wsh	Michael	596	Brk
MCHorney, Benjn.	643	Mnt	Barton	554	Frd	Thomas	517	Frd
McIlhaney, Hannah	280	Ldn	James	443	Bth	McKewen, Isaac	532	Brk
McIlhany, Margt.	281	Ldn	James	79	Jff	McKewn, Gilbert	535	Brk
see McCllanee			James	304	Rck	John	535	Brk
McIlheny, Robert	270	Rck	John	645	Btt	Samuel	535	Brk
McIllwee, Geo.	370	Ags	John	553	Frd	Mckey, Andrew	179	Alb
McIlvoy, John	410	Ags	John	270	Rck	Mckibbin, William	771	Hmp
McIner, James	856	Cmp	Robert	554	Frd	McKibbin, David	684	Br
Mcintire, Joseph	958	Hrr	Robt.	294	Rck	Mckie, James	18	Oho
McIntire, ---	368	Ags	William	554	Frd	McKildoe, William	778	Wst
Andrew	915	Hrr	Wm.	368	Ags	McKillup, Hugh	54	Clp
Charles	557	Frd	Wm.	300	Rck	Mckim, James	313	Ldn
Charles	906	Hrr	Wm.	690	Wsh	Alex.	12	Hnr
Charles	915	Hrr	see MKee			Eliza	30	Hnr
Geo.	180	Elc	McKeehan, Samuel	10	Oho	Robt.	12	Hnr
Henry	44	Stf	McKeel, James	909	Nrf	Wm.	3	Hnr
John	599	Brk	see Bonwell			McKinder, James	911	Nrf
Prudence	106	Jff	McKeever, Angus	556	Brk	McKindrie, James	453	Grn
Saml.	369	Ags	McKemy see McKenry			Mckine, James	244	Ldn
Sarah	48	Stf	McKenly, Tho.	518	Mnn	McKiney, James	275	Rck
Thomas	557	Frd	McKenney, Ann	780	Wst	Joseph	429	Rnd
William	916	Hrr	Armstrong	778	Wst	Larrence	428	Rnd
William	44	Stf	Geo.	59	Clp	Mary	527	Brk
see Macentine			George	392	Fqr	see McKenry		
MCintire, Jams	956	Hrr	Gerrard, Senr.	779	Wst	Mckinley, Eleanor	794	Hmp
McIntosh, Alex	524	Mnn	Henry	866	Cmp	McKinley, Ebenezer	7	Oho
Catherine	521	Prw	James	723	Brn	Nicholas	573	Frd
Geo.	910	Nrf	Jessee	780	Wst	McKinly, Wm.	3	Oho
Geo., [his] (Plantan.)	466	Pra	John	93	Jff	McKinna, Jas.	60	Clp
James	510	Prw	Letty	780	Wst	Mckinney, Francis	282	Ldn
Jno.	281	Frf	Mary	93	Jff	James	239	Ldn
Josh.	55	Clp	Newman	779	Wst	Jno.	233	Ldn

John	244	Shn
Joseph	630	Gls
McKinney, George	429	Rnd
Salley	871	Cmp
Thomas	75	Jff
Thomas	93	Jff
Wm.	12	Hnr
see McKenney, McRinney		
McKinnie, Rebecca	537	Prg
McKinny, Charles	56	Chr
James	642	Btt
Jno.	643	Btt
William	69	Chr
McKinsey, Henry	282	Frf
John	367	Ags
McKinzey, James	450	Frn
Thomas	476	Frn
see Talbert		
Mckinzie, Isaac	632	Gls
Isaac	644	Gls
Mordock	631	Gls
McKinzie, Eliza.	60	Clp
Thomas	21	Rcm
Wm.	123	Hnr
McKirgen, Thos.	410	Ags
McKitrich, Alexander	676	Br
McKnay, Mark	909	Nrf
McKnight, Ann	525	Brk
Geo.	640	Btt
Harmon	60	Jff
James	365	Ags
Jno.	640	Btt
John	60	Jff
Tim.	365	Ags
McKown, Alexander	326	Dnw
McKoy, Bennett	780	Wst
Cabeb	808	Nrf
George	780	Wst
Gerard	780	Wst
James	778	Wst
Jonah [Josiah?]	808	Nrf
Margrt.	809	Nrf
Martha	800	Nrf
Melachi	791	Nrf
Nathan, jr.	796	Nrf
Rodham	778	Wst
McLain, L.	26	Hnr
Samuel	302	Amh
Mclakin, Jesse	712	Nls
Mclamore, Jno.	873	Sth
MClane, Hugh	18	Wod
James	426	Msn
James	429	Msn
McLane, Alexander	348	Fqr
Danl.	421	Rnd
John L.	14	Oho
McLarin, Archibald	343	Fqr
Daniel	416	Fqr
McLaughlin, Daniel	795	Hmp
James	923	Hrr
John	916	Crl
Joseph	587	Frd
MClaughlin, James	352	Lnn
Stephen	352	Lnn
McLauglin, James	580	Frd
McLaurie, John	235	Aml
McLaurine, James	4	Pwh
William	4	Pwh
MClay, Jacob	421	Msn
John	428	Msn
Soloman	424	Msn
McLean, Duncan	333	Dnw
John	581	Frd
MCleery, Wm.	518	Mnn
McLeland, Thomas S.	841	Bck
McLemore, Gilliam	653	Sss
Harrison	146	Sth
James	651	Sss
Joel	146	Sth
McLeod, Jno.	68	Chs
William	519	Frd
MCley, John	424	Msn
McLin, James	259	Ldn
McLoan, Hugh	801	Hmp
McLocklin, Denis	23	Hnr
MCloud, Henry	246	Shn
James	845	Wth
McLoughland, John	21	Rcm
McLoy, James	793	Hmp
McLure, John	1	Oho
McMahan, Benjamin	14	Oho
James	18	Oho
John	424	Bth
Patric	9	Oho
William	431	Bth
McMahon, James	16	Oho
James	20	Oho
James	39	Rcm
William	818	Hmp
William	1	Rcm
MCmahon, Mariam	17	Wod
McMakin, John, Jnr.	65	Jff
John, Snr.	65	Jff
William	64	Jff
Mcmanamy, James	294	Ldn
McManamy, ...	303	Rck
McManany, James	279	Rck
McManen, John	329	Dnw
McManis, Luke	583	Brk
McMaster, James	110	Acc
Jno.	296	Rck
McMasters, Jno.	522	Mnn
John	92	Jff
Tho.	522	Mnn
McMath, Mary	115	Acc
McMechan, Richd.	587	Brk
McMekins, Nancy	704	Gch
McMellan, Archd.	235	Aml
McMial, Jacob	161	Sth
McMials, Frederick	873	Sth
Mary	873	Sth
McMichael, John	58	Chr
McMichaels, John	53	Chs
McMicken, Alexr.	279	Ldn
McMillen, Hugh	675	Br
James	682	Br
John	692	Br
McMillion, John	512	Prw
McMime, William	518	Frd
McMorris, David	397	Fqr
McMullan, James	195	Shn
Jane	444	Bth
see McMullar		
McMullar, Hugh	443	Bth
McMullen, Alexander	506	Frd
Jno.	262	Rck
Matthew, Sr.	474	Bdf
Robert	567	Frd
Saml.	630	Gls
see MMullen		
McMullin, Alexander	58	Jff
Alexn.	363	Ags
Alexr.	242	Ldn
Daniel	242	Ldn
Geo.	540	Brk
James	363	Ags
Jno.	881	Hnv
John	666	Mnt
Matthew, jr.	473	Bdf
Michael	714	Nls
Rob.	524	Mnn
Robert	589	Brk
Sampson	396	Fqr
Samuel	465	Frn
Thomas	716	Nls
Wm.	666	Mnt
see Mullin		
McMullon, Jno.	884	Hnv
McMunn, Elizabeth	508	Frd
McMurdo, Chs. J.	11	Hnr
Chs. J.	30	Hnr
McMurran, Joseph	86	Jff
McMurray, Peter	532	Frd
McMurrey, Saml.	755	Wsh
McNab, Alexr.	305	Rck
James	258	Ldn
Jno.	305	Rck
Wm.	236	Ldn
McNamara, Tim.	353	Lnc
McNarey, John	825	Hmp
Mcnaughton, Danl., Ur-banna	467	Mdd
McNeal, Abraham	429	Bth
Alex.	871	Sth
Charles	787	Bck
Danl.	643	Btt
Enoch	423	Bth
Gabriel	412	Bth
Gabriel	424	Bth
Isaac	429	Bth
Jacob	480	Frn
Jno.	640	Btt
Jno.	55	Clp
John	429	Bth
John, Jur.	423	Bth
Jonathan	424	Bth
Martha	641	Btt
Rebecca	423	Bth
William	425	Bth
McNeale, John R.	778	Wst
Mary	779	Wst
McNealley, George	501	Frn
McNear, Elizt.	363	Ags
James	581	Mnr
Richard	564	Mnr
McNeary, William	689	Br
McNeel, James	577	Pre
Johnson	576	Pre
Neel	721	Wsh
see Neel		
McNeeladge, Jas.	739	Wsh
McNeeley, John	578	Brk
McNeely, George	14	Knw
Rebecca	617	Msn
McNeil, Susanna	245	Ldn
McNeill, Hector	328	Dnw
Sarah	816	Hmp
McNeilla, Sarah	245	Ldn
McNeir, Jno.	11	Hnr
McNeley, John	165	Shn
McNelogy, James	306	Ldn
McNemar, Phillip	807	Hmp
McNerlan, John	696	Br
McNess see Rowlett		
McNew, Catharin	732	Wsh
Edward	758	Wsh
George	721	Wsh
John	720	Wsh
Wm.	721	Wsh
see McNeel		
McNight, Anthoney	751	Wsh
Deborah	318	Ldn
Eli	317	Ldn
James	274	Rck
James	291	Rck
Jesse	317	Ldn
Jno.	317	Ldn
Jno.	718	Nls
John	694	Br
Uriah	317	Ldn
see McKnight, McNite		
McNite, Thos.	754	Wsh
McNutt, James	368	Ags
John	599	Mnr
see Mc...tt, Nutt		
McNutte, Joseph	7	Knw
McOboy, Benjamin	371	Fqr
MCord, John	247	Shn
MCormac, George	16	Wod
MCown, Isaac	426	Msn

John	844	Wth	William	93	Jff	James	631	Gls
MCoy, John	422	Msn	McSpadon, Moses	715	Wsh	Joab	630	Gls
John	426	Msn	Thos.	700	Wsh	John	630	Gls
William	424	Msn	McTyre, Chas. L.	353	Lnc	Josiah	630	Gls
McPeak, Wm.	650	Mnt	Henry	467	Mdd	Wm.	593	Mnr
McPhael, John	910	Nrf	Joseph	467	Mdd	Meadow, Ann	469	Frn
McPheeters, James	367	Ags	Sally	354	Lnc	Anne	235	Aml
Jane	367	Ags	Wm. C.	353	Lnc	Benjamin	472	Bdf
Rachel	362	Ags	MCulloch, John	423	Msn	Benjamin	466	Frn
Mcpherson, Alexander	632	Gls	MCune, James	14	Wod	Eliza.	235	Aml
Daniel	62	Jff	McVeigh, Jeremiah	372	Fqr	Hesekiah	471	Bdf
Isaac	632	Gls	Joice	23	Rcm	James	471	Frn
Jacob	632	Gls	Jonathan	372	Fqr	Jehu	469	Frn
Job	315	Ldn	Mcvey, Jesse	301	Ldn	Jeremiah	472	Bdf
John	62	Jff	McVey, ---	253	Aml	Jeremiah, jr.	472	Bdf
William	62	Jff	Evan	695	Br	Jesse	467	Frn
McPherson, Andrew	796	Nrf	George	475	Frn	Job	470	Frn
Cloe	789	Nrf	James	475	Frn	John	473	Bdf
Delilah	910	Nrf	Ely	845	Wth	John	470	Frn
Dunn.	910	Nrf	McVicar, Jas.	518	Mnn	Joseph	471	Frn
Elizabeth	804	Nrf	McVickar, Barbara	580	Frd	Leroy	468	Frn
Geo.	796	Nrf	McVicker, Archibald	768	Hmp	Lucy	235	Aml
Jeremiah	797	Nrf	Duncan	770	Hmp	Obadiah	472	Bdf
Jno.	21	Hnr	James	770	Hmp	Richard	472	Bdf
John	399	Fqr	William	770	Hmp	Susanna	471	Frn
John	235	Ldn	McVickers, Archd.	249	Ldn	Thomas	471	Bdf
Joseph	233	Ldn	Mcwharter, Hennery	932	Hrr	Thomas	468	Frn
Mons [crossed out]	796	Nrf	McWhartin, Dabny	10	Pwh	William	472	Bdf
Moses	790	Nrf	Mcwherter, Francis	784	Hmp	see Turner		
Peter	590	Frd	McWherton, James	443	Bth	Meadows, Jacob	35	Rcm
Polly	505	Prw	McWhirt, John	66	Spt	James	35	Rcm
Robt.	796	Nrf	McWhorter, Alexander	568	Frd	James, (Jr.)	35	Rcm
Saml.	789	Nrf	David	437	Bth	Jesse	630	Gls
Samuel	559	Frd	Thomas	437	Bth	John	576	Pre
Sebastin	284	Frf	Walter	953	Hrr	John	36	Rcm
Thomas	238	Ldn	Mcwicher, John	929	Hrr	John A.	578	Pre
Willoughby	789	Nrf	McWilliams, Anderson	114	Spt	Matthias	4	Knw
McPhetrdge, Wm.	731	Wsh	David	369	Ags	Nancy	578	Pre
Mcphilin, Hugh	63	Jff	Go...	1	Rcm	Nathaniel	576	Pre
McPike, John	29	Rcm	James	231	Shn	Sally	578	Pre
McPurdy, Jno.	521	Mnn	Jenny	34	Isw	Susana	4	Knw
McQeen, Alex.	54	Clp	John	363	Ags	William	576	Pre
McQuade, Catharine	18	Ntt	Mary	114	Spt	Meads, John	878	Yrk
McQuain, Ealexander	223	Pnd	Robert	65	Jff	Milley	33	Hnr
Mcqueen, Jno.	548	Prg	Saml.	23	Rcm	Meak, Hugh	254	Shn
McQueen, Saml.	60	Clp	William	64	Jff	Meakes, Wm.	714	Nls
see McQeen			MDade, James	431	Msn	Meakins, Jane	26	Hnr
McQuerry, Absalem	166	Alb	MDannel, Jeremiah	431	Msn	Meaks, Richard	713	Nls
Mcquiggen, Wm.	243	Ldn	MDarmet, Sally	425	Msn	Mealey, Daniel	777	Wst
Mcquilkin, Thomas	97	Jff	MDavit, Uriah	520	Mnn	Meana see Moana		
McQuiller, Robt.	290	Rck	MDonnough, Edwd. H.	426	Msn	Meanley, Richd.	755	Brn
McQuillon, Hugh	909	Nrf	Meacham, Jeremiah	655	Sss	Meanly, Archd.	124	Hnr
McQuin, Ann	909	Nrf	Meachum, John	584	Frd	Elisabeth	762	Nwk
Mary	409	Fqr	Meacons, Milly	15	Hnr	James	724	Brn
McQuire, John	396	Mds	Mead, Danl.	21	Hnr	John	330	Dnw
McQuown, Moses	307	Rck	Jno.	315	Ldn	Robert	942	Chc
McQwiter, Thomas	943	Hrr	Milley	13	Hnr	Means, Archd.	295	Ldn
McRae, F.	519	Mnn	Nicholas	474	Bdf	Hugh	643	Btt
John	704	Gch	Sam	522	Mnn	Isaac, Jur.	804	Hmp
MCrae, Daniel	845	Wth	Samuel	315	Ldn	Isaac, Sen.	804	Hmp
McRalep, Thomas	712	Nls	Stith	850	Cmp	John	40	Rcm
McRea, Pemela	5	Pwh	Wm.	279	Ldn	Robert	804	Hmp
McRennolds, Joseph	863	Cmp	Meade, D.	15	Pwh	Robt.	525	Mnn
Oliver	866	Cmp	David	722	Brn	Wm.	295	Ldn
McReonalds, James P.	791	Bck	David	1	Pwh	Mearns, Jno.	912	Nrf
McRinney, James	716	Wsh	Mary	233	Aml	Mears, Abel	41	Acc
McRobert, Ebenezer	578	Pre	Richard K.	560	Frd	Armstead	43	Acc
Theodorick B.	579	Pre	Ricd. K.	722	Brn	Arthur	39	Acc
McRobertson, James	40	Stf	Richd. E.	235	Aml	Bartholomew	111	Acc
McRoy, Nathan	788	Nrf	William	559	Frd	Betty	43	Acc
MCroy, David	844	Wth	Meador, Banistor	24	Isw	Hillary	42	Acc
McRynals, Jas.	733	Wsh	Jessee	113	Cmb	James	44	Acc
Jos.	733	Wsh	Jessee	122	Cmb	John	41	Acc
Robert	733	Wsh	Jessee	130	Cmb	John, BN	43	Acc
McRynels, Saml.	733	Wsh	Spencer	221	Ess	John, of L.	41	Acc
McRynols, John	700	Wsh	Thomas	170	Knq	John F.	42	Acc
Mcshane, Rob.	523	Mnn	Vincent	170	Knq	Jonathan	111	Acc
McShane, Nehemiah	805	Bck	William	112	Cmb	Levin	44	Acc
see Mshane			Meadors, Elijah	593	Mnr	Meshack	115	Acc
McSherry, William	59	Jff	Emun	630	Gls	Milly	41	Acc

Nathaniel	465	Pra	James	788	Hmp	John	104	Cmb
Ned, (F.N.)	32	Isw	Joseph	775	Hmp	John	440	Flv
Polly	111	Acc	Joseph	761	Nwk	Joseph	430	Flv
Richard	39	Acc	Ned	760	Nwk	Joseph	890	Hnv
Richard	43	Acc	Meeks, Elizabeth	573	Brk	Pierce W.	436	Flv
Richard, SS	41	Acc	Isaac	513	Prw	Roda	166	Alb
Richd., of Ricd.	44	Acc	Jacob	678	Br	Samuel	130	Cmb
Robert	41	Acc	Mary	831	Nrf	Thomas	711	Nls
Shadrach	114	Acc	Moses	572	Brk	Thos.	750	Wsh
Susannah	114	Acc	Polly	910	Nrf	Wm.	430	Flv
Thomas W.	39	Acc	Thos.	525	Mnn	Wm.	250	Ldn
William, M'ss	42	Acc	Wm.	644	Btt	Wm.	715	Nls
William, of E	39	Acc	Meelisa, Adam	23	Rcm	Melvin, Benjn.	83	Jff
William, of Jno.	40	Acc	Meem, Gilbert	254	Shn	Hezekiah A.	631	Gls
William, of Jno.	41	Acc	Meemly see Meanly			James	114	Acc
Wm.	816	Nrf	Meese, Peter	453	Frn	James W.	115	Acc
Meary, Henry	838	Nrf	Meete see Micle			John	86	Jff
Mecally, Jams	930	Hrr	Mefford, Abraham	19	Rcm	Mary	577	Pre
see Mecully			Benjamin	36	Rcm	Samuel	86	Jff
Mecan see Mccan			Mary	8	Rcm	Silas	83	Jff
Mecartey, Jno.	664	Glc	Megarity, Andrew	312	Ldn	Thomas	83	Jff
Thos.	663	Glc	Megehe, Charles	474	Bdf	W.B.	283	Frf
Mechesney, Hugh	706	Wsh	Meggenson, Joseph C.	840	Bck	Mendenall, Amos	509	Brk
Mechum, Harry	705	Gch	Meggs, Fanny	801	Nrf	Jacob	530	Brk
Robt.	705	Gch	Jas., (free negro)	665	Glc	Saml.	532	Brk
Meckle, Elijah	694	Wsh	Joel	132	Cmb	Mendinhall, Samuel	66	Jff
Jacob	694	Wsh	Ro., (free negro)	665	Glc	Mendum, Robert	5	Pwh
Mecom, Rebecca	156	Sth	Robert	801	Nrf	Menfee, John	732	Wsh
Mecow, Richard	915	Crl	Willoughby	801	Nrf	Menfee, John	453	Grn
Richard S.	914	Crl	Meginnis, Daniel	312	Ldn	Meng, Charles	520	Prw
Mecoy, Geo.	663	Glc	Megloclin, Michal	225	Pnd	Menginni, Josephi	508	Brk
Mecully, George	935	Hrr	Meguineas, Josie	124	Cmb	Meniar, Isaac	945	Hrr
Rachil	935	Hrr	Mehauney, Clemence	267	Ldn	Menifee, Henry [2]	59	Clp
Medab, Levin	38	Acc	Meickle, William	325	Dnw	Jas.	59	Clp
Peter	44	Acc	Melcher, Philip	19	Rcm	Jno., jr.	58	Clp
Stephen	44	Acc	Melker, Adam	1	Wod	Jno., Senr.	58	Clp
see Meedab			Mellan, Allan	563	Brk	Jno. M.	60	Clp
Medad, William	110	Acc	Meller, David	505	Brk	Jonas	60	Clp
Medcalf see Madcaff			Henry	523	Brk	Lewis	58	Clp
Mede, William	846	Wth	Mary	584	Brk	Lucy	59	Clp
see Meede			Mellet, Arth.	521	Mnn	Wm.	57	Clp
Medearis, Iververson	56	Clp	Jesse	521	Mnn	see Maneffee, Menefee		
Wilson	179	Alb	Mellon, Patrick	363	Ags	Meniger, Henry	57	Clp
Meder, Roderick	822	Nrf	Melmic, Jacob	944	Hrr	Menitree, Isom	679	Wrw
Meders, Henry	759	Wsh	Melon, John	704	Wsh	Mennis, Mary	878	Yrk
Joel	734	Wsh	John	746	Wsh	Menny, Cal...	475	Bdf
Mederwell see Moderwell			Melony, John	115	Acc	Mensor, Conrad	826	Hmp
Medford, Manlove	641	Btt	John	505	Brk	Menton, Joseph	112	Hnr
Mediton, Ann	19	Hnr	Melorin, James	126	Cmb	Meommack, Pleasant	120	Cmb
Medlecott, Saml.	664	Glc	Joseph	114	Cmb	Mercer, Chas. F.	325	Ldn
Medler, Sebastian	67	Jff	Melson, Charles	472	Bdf	Elisabeth	763	Nwk
Medley, Frances	396	Mds	Edmund	111	Acc	Henry	264	Ldn
George	473	Bdf	George	40	Acc	Hugh	109	Spt
Jacob	396	Mds	George	111	Acc	James	18	Isw
Job	371	Fqr	George, M	112	Acc	Jesse	301	Ldn
Reuben	396	Mds	Isaac	41	Acc	Job	549	Frd
Rezen	3	Knw	James	115	Acc	Joseph	577	Frd
Wm.	20	Oho	Jeremian	112	Acc	Levi	424	Msn
Medly, John	2	Knw	John	38	Acc	Rob.	520	Mnn
Medoniel, John	927	Hrr	John M.	44	Acc	Robert	142	Sth
Medsher, Dan.	526	Mnn	Joseph	40	Acc	Merchant, Jacob	500	Prw
Mee, John	185	Elc	Joseph	110	Acc	John	499	Prw
Meeckes see Meakes			Middleton	878	Yrk	Justes	507	Brk
Meedab, Betty	44	Acc	Nancy	38	Acc	Richd.	507	Brk
Meede, Thomas	846	Wth	Noah	38	Acc	Sally	178	Elc
see Mede			Robert	39	Acc	Thoms.	285	Frf
Meek, Charles	731	Wsh	Robinson	40	Acc	Thos.	446	Mth
Elizt.	365	Ags	Seymour	40	Acc	William	499	Prw
Elizt., (N.M)	367	Ags	Seymour	110	Acc	see Marchant, Merchat.		
James	678	Br	Smith	40	Acc	Merchat., Abram	446	Mth
James	731	Wsh	Melstead, Peter	269	Amh	Ambrose	438	Mth
Jesse	731	Wsh	Meltaire, Jeremiah	809	Nrf	Merchunt, William, (FB)	474	Bdf
Joseph	731	Wsh	Melton, Absalom	890	Hnv	Meredeth, Pleasant	115	Hnr
Saml.	701	Wsh	Charles	803	Bck	Meredith, Abm.	520	Mnn
Samuel	696	Br	Elisha	166	Alb	Caty	354	Lnc
Stephen	731	Wsh	Elizabeth	467	Frn	Dav.	521	Mnn
Thos.	365	Ags	George	713	Nls	David	522	Mnn
Meekins, Christmas	761	Nwk	Isham	796	Bck	Francis	153	Dnw
David	761	Nwk	James	848	Sth	Hugh	628	Mnt
Isaac	762	Nwk	Jno.	882	Hnv	Lewis	153	Dnw

Nancy	13	Hnr
Pet.	524	Mnn
Tho.	521	Mnn
Wm. A.	153	Dnw
Mereweather, William	235	Aml
Merewether, Francis T.	474	Bdf
William	203	Alb
Merideth, Edwin D.	91	Spt
Meridith, Ann L.	892	Hnv
David	722	Brn
David, jr.	722	Brn
Frederick, (M)	724	Brn
George	171	Knq
James	881	Hnv
Jane	275	Amh
Richard	713	Nls
Robert	885	Hnv
Thos.	722	Brn
Wm.	722	Brn
Meridoth, David	234	Aml
Merifield, Jos.	523	Mnn
Polly	526	Mnn
Merikey, Christopher,		
(Jr.)	34	Rcm
Christopher, (sen)	34	Rcm
Conrod	34	Rcm
John	33	Rcm
Meriman, Allen	715	Nls
Presley	915	Crl
Williamson	499	Frn
Merimon, Pleasant	102	Cmb
Merimun, Edward	102	Cmb
Jessee	105	Cmb
John T.	121	Cmb
Thomas	119	Cmb
Meriner, John	913	Crl
Merit, Jno. M.	22	Hnr
S. M.	30	Hnr
Thomas	874	Cmp
Meritt, Ann	14	Hnr
Meriwether, Elizabeth	915	Crl
Merkal, Daniel	103	Jff
Merrack, John	12	Oho
Merrel, Jno.	519	Mnn
Jos.	522	Mnn
Merret, Major	472	Bdf
Saml.	640	Btt
Wruford	474	Bdf
Merrett, John [2]	802	Hmp
Merriack, William	11	Oho
Merridith, James	837	Bck
see Meridith		
Merrill, Josiah	400	Fqr
Merriman, Wm.	56	Clp
Merrimon, Ralph	577	Pre
Merrin, Jessee	703	Gch
Merrit, Nicholass	166	Alb
Wm.	363	Ags
Merritt, Charles	769	Brn
Dick, (M)	724	Brn
Henry	723	Br
James	769	Br
John	291	Amh
John, jr.	290	Amh
John F.	303	Amh
Toby, (N)	724	Brn
Merriweather, Robt.	705	Gch
Merry, John	957	Chc
Philip	414	Fqr
Prettyman	805	Bck
see Mary		
Merryfield, John	426	Msn
Merryman, Milly	354	Lnc
Nicholas	696	Br
Thomas	763	Nwk
see Tucker		
Merrymoon, Jesse	154	Dnw
Nicholas	154	Dnw
Mershon, Benja.	56	Clp
Mersy, Simon	24	Oho
Mertins, John L.	325	Dnw
Meryfield, Jno.	519	Mnn
Sam.	519	Mnn
Meserley, Solomon	233	Shn
Mesingo, George	747	Wsh
John	752	Wsh
Mesmer, Nicholas	515	Frd
Messenger, Ab.	520	Mnn
Messer, Ann	63	Jff
Edward	578	Frd
Joshua	547	Frd
Joshua	555	Frd
William	578	Frd
Messerly, Jno.	17	Rcm
Messersmith, Barnabas	845	Wth
Barnabas	846	Wth
Godfrey	846	Wth
John	664	Mnt
Peter	846	Wth
Messey, Thos.	815	Nrf
Messicin see Missicen		
Messick, Elihu	14	Rcm
George	14	Rcm
James	5	Rcm
John	3	Rcm
John	777	Wst
Zadock	878	Yrk
Messincup, Jno.	714	Nls
see Masincup		
Metcalf, Anty.	910	Nrf
Isaac	453	Grn
John	40	Acc
see Madcaff, Metecalf		
Metcalfe, Asa	372	Fqr
Betsey	373	Fqr
Metcalf, Vernon	294	Amh
Meteer, Samuel	282	Rck
see Metter		
Methias, Jno.	303	Ldn
Method, Marry	33	Hnr
Metsel, Henry	955	Hrr
Mettard, Mary	27	Hnr
Mettauer, Joseph	579	Pre
Metter, Wm.	282	Rck
see Meteer		
Metton, David	111	Hnr
George	113	Hnr
Mary	473	Bdf
Saml.	115	Hnr
Metts, George	70	Jff
Elizabeth	192	Shn
Jacob	522	Mnn
Leo.	521	Mnn
Peter	192	Shn
see Mitts		
Meuller, John	810	Nrf
see Mullen		
Meux, Hubbard R.	762	Nwk
Thomas	762	Nwk
William	914	Crl
Mewkes see Meakes		
Mewman, George	603	Frd
Mews, Thomas	254	Ldn
Meyers, Peter, jr.	578	Brk
see Moyers		
Mezel, Thos.	736	Wsh
Mezengo, Thomas	780	Wst
Mezingo, John	397	Rch
Penny	780	Wst
William	779	Wst
Mgan, Pleasant	473	Bdf
MGath, Jessee	427	Msn
MGee, Ths.	524	Mnn
Wm.	524	Mnn
M. George, Lawrence	472	Bdf
MGill, Adam	522	Mnn
MGlamery, Matth.	582	Mnr
MGready, Mary	431	Msn
MGrew, Js.	522	Mnn
M'guire, Samuel	756	Hmp
MGuire, Hugh	432	Msn
John, jr.	421	Msn
John, Sr.	425	Msn
Mianty see Meanly		
Miars, Christian	58	Chr
Michael, Adam	23	Rcm
Andrew	570	Brk
Conrad	582	Brk
Dan	520	Mnn
Dav.	519	Mnn
Elizabeth	781	Hmp
Frederck.	273	Rck
Frederick	781	Hmp
Geo.	364	Ags
George	781	Hmp
Henry	760	Hmp
Jacob	571	Brk
James	950	Hrr
Jas.	521	Mnn
John	364	Ags
Jonas	364	Ags
Michael	570	Brk
Paul	950	Hrr
Peter	573	Brk
Phillip	781	Hmp
William	24	Rcm
Wilm.	11	Rcm
Wm.	520	Mnn
Wm.	522	Mnn
see Mickael, Micle		
Michaels, Daniel	368	Fqr
Jacob	274	Rck
Michal, Charles	223	Pnd
Michalls, Isaac	17	Hnr
Michaux, Daniel W.	12	Pwh
Jacob	7	Pwh
Jacob	577	Pre
Jesse	579	Pre
John	126	Cmb
Joseph	125	Cmb
Richard	4	Pwh
Jesse	936	Hrr
Michell, Adam	282	Frf
Charter	725	Wsh
John, & Jno. Craig		
& Co.	707	Wsh
Robert	720	Wsh
Saml.	644	Btt
William	722	Wsh
Michem, Ann	447	Mth
Banks	579	Pre
Jno.	447	Mth
Richd.	448	Mth
Michia, David	204	Alb
Francis	203	Alb
Michie, John	203	Alb
John	705	Gch
William	204	Alb
Mick, George B.	249	Shn
Peter	691	Br
Polly	691	Br
Mickael, Peter	573	Brk
Mickel, Samuel	99	Jff
Mickelborough, Henry	467	Mdd
Lewis	466	Mdd
Mickey, Robert	848	Hnv
Mickle, James	577	Pre
William	880	Cmp
Micle, Hannah	946	Hrr
Philip	948	Hrr
Micon, James R.	207	Ess
John	198	Ess
John B.	204	Ess
Paul	198	Ess
Micow, Henry	209	Kng
Middelton, Ben	523	Mnn
Middeton, Studley	234	Ldn
Middins, Timothy	444	Flv
Middlebrook, John	914	Crl

Name	No.	Abbr.
Middlecauff, Jno.	639	Btt
Middlekauff, David	640	Btt
Middleswath, Anthony	691	Br
Middleton, Bethewel	553	Brk
Geo.	911	Nrf
George	40	Acc
Hutchingson	87	Jff
Keziah	372	Fqr
Jeremiah	778	Wst
John	909	Hrr
John	989	Nrt
John	224	Shn
Mary	644	Btt
Robert F.	72	Jff
Smallwood C.	254	Ldn
Tabia.	190	Elc
Thomas	110	Acc
Thomas	40	Acc
Thos.	553	Brk
William	39	Acc
William	528	Frd
Middows, Thos.	644	Btt
Midelton, John	935	Hrr
Miell, Geo.	282	Ldn
Mienk, Joseph	153	Dnw
Miers, Joshua	72	Spt
Miffing, Terence	131	Hnr
Miffleton, Burditt	210	Kng
Chas.	208	Kng
Henry	208	Kng
Miflin, Charles	48	Stf
Migget, James	643	Btt
Mightenger, Reynard	257	Ldn
Milam, John	474	Bdf
Micajah	474	Bdf
Sarah	474	Bdf
Simeon	14	Knw
Zacheriah	474	Bdf
see Milum		
Milbey, Henry	170	Knq
John	171	Knq
Richd.	171	Knq
Milbourne, Isaac	565	Mnr
Sarah W.	565	Mnr
Milburn, Elizabeth	277	Ldn
Euphamy	113	Acc
John	550	Frd
Levi	275	Ldn
Samuel W.	112	Acc
Thomas	113	Acc
William	112	Acc
Milburne, David	3	Knw
Milby, Susan	663	Glc
William	31	Isw
William	170	Knq
Mildred, Carlton	159	Knq
Milen, Hugh	11	Hnr
Miler, Matthew	473	Bdf
Thomas	473	Bdf
Thomas	474	Bdf
Miles, ...am [Isham?]		
J.	473	Bdf
Ann	103	Jff
Benjamin	272	Amh
Chs., Sen.	54	Clp
Comfort	114	Acc
David	113	Acc
Edward	959	Chc
Edward	154	Dnw
Eliza.	57	Chs
Elizabeth	155	Dnw
Ephraim	154	Dnw
George	110	Acc
George	605	Frd
George	400	Rch
Isaac	940	Chc
Isaac	959	Chc
James	256	Amh
Jesse	115	Acc
Joab E.	154	Dnw
John	405	Fqr
John	774	Hmp
John	102	Jff
John A.	466	Mdd
Joseph	473	Bdf
Josiah	761	Hmp
Lloyd	515	Brk
Peter	325	Dnw
Rachel	110	Acc
Richard	953	Chc
Ruth	774	Hmp
Susanna	155	Dnw
Tabby	56	Clp
Thadeus	301	Amh
Thomas	279	Amh
Thomas	781	Bck
William	115	Acc
William	474	Bdf
William	587	Brk
William	467	Mdd
Wm.	56	Clp
see Miler, Mills		
Milestone, Jno.	886	Hnv
Miley, Abm.	520	Mnn
Chris.	262	Ldn
Henry	25	Rcm
Jacob	262	Ldn
Jno.	262	Ldn
John	218	Shn
Martin	218	Shn
Walter	297	Rck
Milhado, David	910	Nrf
Milher, Winkle	226	Shn
Milhollen, Mary	296	Ldn
Patrick	296	Ldn
Milirons, David	631	Gls
Milison, Henry	268	Rck
Mill..., Nathaniel	343	Fqr
Millagan, John	114	Acc
Millan, Jno.	281	Frf
Thomas	279	Frf
Wm.	285	Frf
Millar, James	876	Sth
Nancy	654	Sss
Robert	874	Sth
Millaway, Isaac	201	Alb
Millay, Isabella	507	Frd
Millburn, Elias	553	Frd
Robert	551	Frd
Stephen	414	Fqr
Millegan, John	4	Oho
Millen, Jos.	826	Nrf
Joseph	934	Hrr
Millenor, Anna	123	Hnr
Millephant, Sarah	644	Btt
Miller, ...imon	55	Clp
Abigail	825	Hmp
Abraham	367	Ags
Abraham	216	Pnd
Abraham	39	Rcm
Abraham	202	Shn
Abrm.	606	Mnt
Adam	367	Ags
Adam	522	Frd
Adam	267	Ldn
Adam	397	Mds
Adam	643	Mnt
Adam	5	Rcm
Adam	846	Wth
Alexander	434	Bth
Alexander	582	Frd
Alexander	844	Wth
Amenadab	116	Hnr
And.	290	Rck
Anderson	19	Hnr
Anderson P.	578	Pre
Andrew	427	Rnd
Andw.	588	Mnr
Andw., & Father	55	Clp
Ann	474	Bdf
Anthony	5	Rcm
Armistead	4	Ntt
Armistead	577	Pre
Ben	824	Nrf
Ben.	801	Nrf
Benjamin	723	Brn
Brice	579	Frd
Brice	591	Mnr
Butler	802	Nrf
Casper	557	Frd
Casper	188	Shn
Catharine	283	Ldn
Catharine	36	Rcm
Catherine	814	Hmp
Cathr.	291	Rck
Charles	677	Br
Charles	216	Pnd
Chas.	801	Nrf
Chas.	802	Nrf
Chrisley	191	Shn
Chrisley	203	Shn
Chrisn.	565	Brk
Christian	589	Brk
Christian	26	Rcm
Christian	36	Rcm
Christn.	911	Nrf
Christo.	570	Brk
Christopher	762	Nwk
Chrs.	266	Ldn
Compton	521	Mnn
Conrod	565	Brk
Conrod	811	Hmp
Conrod	223	Pnd
Corbett	914	Crl
Corneales	428	Msn
Dabney A.	467	Mdd
Daniel	281	Ldn
Daniel	622	Mnt
Daniel	221	Pnd
Danl.	643	Btt
Danl.	30	Rcm
Danl.	37	Rcm
Danl.	233	Shn
Davd.	59	Clp
Davd.	589	Mnr
Davd.	735	Wsh
David	369	Ags
David	428	Bth
David	688	Br
David	4	Rcm
David	26	Rcm
David	252	Shn
Dobney	234	Aml
Edward	804	Nrf
Elisabeth	715	Wsh
Elisebeth	734	Wsh
Elisha	273	Ldn
Elizabeth	685	Br
Elizabeth	4	Pwh
Elizabeth	264	Rck
Esther	538	Brk
Eve	222	Shn
Fanny	369	Ags
Frances	913	Crl
Francis	202	Alb
Francis	434	Brn
Francis	882	Cmp
Frederick	439	Bth
Frederick	220	Shn
Fredk.	508	Brk
Fredk.	641	Btt
Fredk.	645	Btt
Gabriel, Jr.	452	Mth
Gabrl.	440	Mth
Geo.	523	Brk
Geo.	254	Ldn
Geo.	266	Ldn
Geo.	278	Ldn
Geo.	801	Nrf
Geo.	909	Nrf

Geo. W.	803 Nrf	Jacob, (C.A.T.)	250 Shn	John	202 Shn
George	806 Bck	Jacob, (C.C)	363 Ags	John	715 Wsh
George	334 Dnw	Jacob, (Hatter	249 Shn	John	722 Wsh
George	914 Hrr	Jacob, jr.	581 Brk	John	735 Wsh
George	99 Jff	Jacob, (LM)	367 Ags	John	743 Wsh
George	571 Mnr	Jacob, Sr.	598 Mnr	John [2]	844 Wth
George	572 Mnr	James	364 Ags	John	845 Wth
George	1 Oho	James	434 Bth	John	846 Wth
George	220 Pnd	James	473 Bdf	John, (BS)	54 Jff
George	226 Pnd	James	509 Brk	John, (H.C.)	184 Shn
George [2]	32 Rcm	James	866 Cmp	John, jr.	572 Mnr
George, Jun.	241 Shn	James	663 Glc	John, junr.	915 Crl
George, Junr.	224 Shn	James	8 Knw	John, Junr.	846 Wth
George, Sen.	241 Shn	James	637 Mnt	John, (L George	222 Shn
George, Senr.	224 Shn	James	662 Mnt	John, (S.R)	369 Ags
Godfry	225 Shn	James	289 Rck	John, Senr.	915 Crl
Hanna	364 Ags	James	778 Wst	John, Senr.	844 Wth
Hannah	542 Brk	James	844 Wth	John, (Taylor)	54 Jff
Hannah	300 Ldn	Jane	167 Alb	John W.	509 Frd
Hannah	298 Rck	Jane	796 Nrf	Joseph	537 Brk
Hen.	523 Mnn	Jas.	55 Clp	Joseph	566 Frd
Henry	364 Ags	Jas.	518 Mnn	Joseph	570 Mnr
Henry	367 Ags	Jesse	794 Nrf	Joseph	589 Mnr
Henry	523 Brk	Jesse	795 Nrf	Joseph	730 Wsh
Henry	58 Clp	Jesse	802 Nrf	Joseph	844 Wth
Henry	516 Frd	Jessee	99 Cmb	Joseph, jr.	439 Mth
Henry	803 Hmp	Jno.	644 Btt	Joseph, Sr.	439 Mth
Henry	83 Jff	Jno.	57 Clp	Josiah	803 Nrf
Henry	522 Mnn	Jno. [2]	59 Clp	Josias	519 Prw
Henry	526 Mnn	Jno.	21 Hnr	Js.	519 Mnn
Henry	668 Mnt	Jno.	519 Mnn	Keath I.	704 Gch
Henry	800 Nrf	Jno.	520 Mnn	Margaret	19 Hnr
Henry	285 Rck	Jno.	524 Mnn	Margaret	100 Jff
Henry	4 Rcm	Jno.	525 Mnn	Martaen	424 Rnd
Henry	12 Rcm	Jno.	526 Mnn	Martha	115 Hnr
Henry	15 Rcm	Jno.	550 Prg	Martin	644 Btt
Henry	23 Rcm	Jno.	263 Rck	Martin	40 Rcm
Henry	36 Rcm	Jno.	267 Rck	Martin	846 Wth
Henry	187 Shn	Jno.	276 Rck	Marx	207 Shn
Henry	202 Shn	Jno., Jr.	522 Mnn	Mary	185 Shn
Henry	844 Wth	Jno., Ser.	58 Clp	Mary	198 Shn
Henry, jr.	555 Brk	Jno. J.	59 Clp	Mary Ann	507 Frd
Hugh	155 Dnw	Joab	803 Nrf	Matthias	32 Rcm
Hugh	719 Wsh	Joel	802 Nrf	Max.	794 Nrf
Hugh M.	68 Chs	John	369 Ags	Meson	801 Nrf
Isaac	554 Frd	John	501 Brk	Michael	420 Msn
Isaac	801 Hmp	John	559 Brk	Michael	572 Mnr
Isaac	819 Hmp	John	565 Brk	Michael	14 Rcm
Isaac	638 Mnt	John	581 Brk	Michael	40 Rcm
Isaac	215 Pnd	John	583 Brk	Michal	221 Pnd
Isaac	6 Rcm	John	597 Brk	Molly	583 Brk
Isaac	167 Shn	John	688 Br	Morris	130 Hnr
Isaah N.	803 Nrf	John	803 Bck	Moses	473 Bdf
Isham	466 Mdd	John	852 Cmp	Moses [2]	282 Ldn
Jac.	522 Mnn	John	915 Crl	Natt	801 Nrf
Jac.	525 Mnn	John	56 Chr	Nicholas	57 Chr
Jac.	526 Mnn	John	457 Frn	Nicholas	800 Nrf
Jacob	362 Ags	John	507 Frd	Patrick	436 Bth
Jacob	472 Bdf	John	803 Hmp	Paul	647 Mnt
Jacob	515 Brk	John	835 Hmp	Peter	577 Brk
Jacob	576 Brk	John	113 Hnr	Peter	642 Btt
Jacob	581 Brk	John [2]	117 Hnr	Peter	643 Btt
Jacob	585 Brk	John	100 Jff	Peter	560 Frd
Jacob	589 Brk	John	397 Mds	Peter	281 Ldn
Jacob [2]	644 Btt	John	466 Mdd	Peter	282 Ldn
Jacob	723 Brn	John	570 Mnr	Peter	521 Mnn
Jacob	824 Hmp	John	572 Mnr	Peter	567 Mnr
Jacob	79 Jff	John	643 Mnt	Peter	570 Mnr
Jacob	282 Ldn	John	2 Oho	Peter	10 Rcm
Jacob	572 Mnr	John	16 Oho	Peter, Jun.	242 Shn
Jacob	18 Rcm	John	214 Pnd	Peter, Sen.	242 Shn
Jacob [2]	32 Rcm	John	215 Pnd	Peter ...	353 Lnc
Jacob	204 Shn	John	3 Pwh	Philip	576 Frd
Jaocb	207 Shn	John	418 Rnd	Philip	23 Rcm
Jacob	225 Shn	John	425 Rnd	Philip	26 Rcm
Jacob	236 Shn	John	4 Rcm	Philip	208 Shn
Jacob	715 Wsh	John	5 Rcm	Philip	247 Shn
Jacob	749 Wsh	John	20 Rcm	Polley	17 Hnr
Jacob	844 Wth	John	24 Rcm	Polly	596 Brk
Jacob	846 Wth	John	180 Shn	Rachal	215 Pnd

Randolph	792	Nrf	Millington, Saml.	613	Srr	see Bracey, Mill...		
Reddeck	802	Nrf	Million, Cuthbert	42	Stf	Milltin, William	514	Prw
Richard	214	Ess	Jos.	910	Nrf	Milly, Archd.	612	Srr
Richard	73	Jff	Millirons, Henry	473	Bdf	Milnen see Milom		
Richd.	113	Hnr	Millison, Bengamin	777	Hmp	Milrose, Archabold	2	Wod
Rob.	520	Mnn	Jas.	815	Nrf	John	5	Wod
Robert	914	Crl	John, Jur.	777	Hmp	Milslagle, Andrew	783	Hmp
Robert	16	Oho	John, Ser.	777	Hmp	Andrew	791	Hmp
Robert	844	Wth	Millner, Jno.	475	Bdf	Catherine	105	Jff
Ruth	573	Mnr	Richard	474	Bdf	George	765	Hmp
Sally	568	Mnr	Thomas	474	Bdf	George	831	Hmp
Sam H.	271	Rck	William	474	Bdf	Jacob	761	Hmp
Saml.	364	Ags	William, Sr.	474	Bdf	Milson, Wm.	911	Nrf
Saml.	803	Nrf	Williamson	474	Bdf	Milstead, Isaac	511	Prw
Saml.	269	Rck	Millon, Eli	259	Ldn	John	516	Prw
Saml.	289	Rck	Mills, Alexander	540	Frd	Joseph	287	Amh
Saml.	41	Rcm	Alexander, Sr.	590	Frd	Joseph	103	Spt
Saml.	735	Wsh	Anne	280	Frf	Noah	527	Prw
Saml., (MT)	369	Ags	Arthr.	911	Nrf	Miltabarger, John	9	Rcm
Saml., (sen)	17	Rcm	Arthur	472	Frn	Milton, Alexander	533	Frd
Samuel	677	Br	Benjamin	13	Oho	Elijah	533	Frd
Samuel	305	Ldn	Benjamin	72	Spt	James	74	Jff
Sarah	674	Br	Charles, Snr.	863	Hnv	James	396	Mds
Simon	223	Ess	Cillis	98	Spt	John	587	Frd
Sophy	367	Ags	Danl.	279	Frf	Randolph	146	Sth
Stuffle	223	Shn	Dizon	503	Prw	Thos.	719	Wsh
Tho.	354	Lnc	Edmund	114	Spt	William	520	Prw
Tho.	519	Mnn	Edwd.	703	Gch	see Metton		
Thomas	537	Brk	Elizabeth	915	Crl	Milum, Rush	641	Btt
Thomas	915	Crl	Elizabeth	279	Frf	Milwin see Milum		
Thomas	482	Frn	Elizabeth	72	Spt	Mily, Martin	203	Shn
Thomas	127	Hnr	Elizabeth	114	Spt	Mimms, Thomas	57	Chr
Thomas	989	Nrt	Fanny	363	Ags	Mims, Duguid	703	Gch
Thomas	4	Pwh	Fanny, F.N.	171	Knq	Elizabeth	703	Gch
Thomas, Capt.	4	Pwh	Francis	474	Bdf	Elizabeth	705	Gch
Thompson	112	Hnr	Francis	10	Hnr	Martin	365	Ags
Thos.	703	Gch	George	5	Oho	Randolph	431	Flv
Thos.	598	Mnr	George	514	Prw	Robt. [2]	703	Gch
Thos., [his] Plantation	80	Spt	Henry	202	Alb	see Mines		
Tobias	954	Hrr	Jacob	404	Fqr	Mincan, Thos.	912	Nrf
Ulrick	247	Shn	Jacob, (X Keys)	363	Ags	Minchy, Dyonetius	844	Wth
Valentine	368	Ags	James	204	Alb	Richard	845	Wth
Valentine	266	Ldn	James	912	Crl	Mine see ---		
Valentine	581	Mnr	James	403	Fqr	Miner, Burket	524	Mnn
Valentine	3	Rcm	James	806	Nrf	Coleman	197	Ess
Valintine	403	Ags	Jas.	465	Pra	Sam	520	Mnn
W.	21	Hnr	Jno.	20	Ntt	William	92	Jff
William	472	Bdf	Jno.	465	Pra	Mines, David	367	Ags
William	788	Hmp	John	763	Nwk	Isaac	39	Rcm
William	810	Hmp	John	506	Prw	Jno.	306	Ldn
William	4	Pwh	John	112	Spt	Lewis	365	Ags
William	257	Shn	John	32	Stf	Peter	365	Ags
William A.	791	Bck	Joseph	202	Alb	Saml.	296	Rck
Wm.	369	Ags	Mary	888	Hnv	Minetree, Nancy	336	Dnw
Wm.	55	Clp	Menan	167	Alb	John	336	Dnw
Wm.	59	Clp	Nancy	351	Lnn	Mineyard, Edward	850	Hnv
Wm.	702	Gch	Nathan	202	Alb	Ming, Hester	56	Clp
Wm.	519	Mnn	Nathl.	847	Hnv	Samuel	798	Bck
Wm.	520	Mnn	Nicholas	68	Chs	Samuel	826	Bck
Wm.	525	Mnn	Nicholas	876	Hnv	Minga, Ann	155	Dnw
Wm.	801	Nrf	Robert	474	Bdf	Charles	155	Dnw
Wm.	285	Rck	Robert	857	Hnv	Minge, Jesse	531	Prg
Wm., jr.	802	Nrf	Robt.	363	Ags	Peter	536	Prg
Wm. H.	705	Gch	Saml.	629	Gls	Rumford	328	Dnw
Zach.	523	Brk	Saml.	236	Ldn	Minger, Henry	368	Ags
Zach.	559	Brk	Samuel	576	Pre	Peter	368	Ags
see Meder, Meller, Mill...,			Sarah	202	Alb	Minges, John	943	Chc
Millen			Sarah	171	Knq	Mingle, Betsey	599	Brk
Millers, Patsy	809	Nrf	Thomas	341	Fqr	Jane	846	Wth
Milleson, Jacob	802	Nrf	Toney	17	Oho	Mingo, Billy	548	Prg
Millet, Thos.	824	Nrf	Wiat	99	Spt	William	856	Sth
Millett, Thos.	909	Nrf	William	472	Frn	see Jackson		
Milley, James	612	Srr	William	802	Hmp	Minic, Saml.	288	Rck
see Miley			William	577	Pre	see Mires		
Millhorn, Henry	172	Shn	William	51	Stf	Minich, Betsey	366	Ags
Peter	568	Frd	Wm.	281	Frf	K.	366	Ags
Millicar, Martha	286	Rck	Wm.	283	Frf	Minick, Adam	761	Wsh
Robert	286	Rck	Wm.	264	Ldn	Benjn.	640	Btt
Milliner, Eliza	452	Grn	Wm.	751	Wsh	Eliza.	294	Ldn
Smith	41	Acc	Zachariah	204	Alb	George	31	Rcm

Henry, Jur.	751	Wsh
Henry, Sen.	750	Wsh
John	25	Rcm
John	32	Rcm
John	748	Wsh
Mary	846	Wth
Matthias	4	Rcm
Peter	735	Wsh
Minigar, Jno. C.	252	Ldn
Mink, Lawrence	285	Ldn
Mary	710	Wsh
Peter	710	Wsh
Minkey, Henry	645	Btt
Minnes, Robert	221	Pnd
Minnick, Cathe.	645	Btt
Jacob	663	Mnt
John	645	Btt
John, Wagon Maker	643	Btt
Phillip	640	Btt
Phillip	645	Btt
see Minic, Minick		
Minning, Peter	691	Wsh
Minnis, Carrol, (FN)	70	Chr
Peggy	210	Kng
Minnix, Charles	482	Frn
Minnor, John	581	Mnr
Minny, Dan	526	Mnn
Minor, Aarmsted	474	Bdf
Dabney	203	Alb
Dudly	101	Cmb
Edwd.	911	Nrf
Elizabeth	913	Crl
Elizabeth	915	Crl
Frances	663	Glc
Garret	116	Spt
George	280	Frf
James	203	Alb
James	18	Hnr
John	664	Glc
John	99	Spt
John, for Mary Page	115	Spt
John, Senr.	170	Knq
Jonathan	117	Spt
Josha.	60	Clp
Kiszer	778	Wst
Mary	769	Hmp
Mary	579	Pre
Mildred	280	Frf
Peter	203	Alb
Rebecca	579	Frd
Reuben	170	Knq
Ro.	663	Glc
Thomas	277	Ldn
Thomas	87	Spt
Thomas, jr.	71	Spt
Thomas, Sr.	71	Spt
Threes	473	Bdf
Turnor, Botetourt	663	Glc
William	474	Bdf
William	207	Kng
Wim.	898	Hnv
Wm.	663	Glc
Wm.	291	Ldn
Minson, Geo.	190	Elc
Tho.	189	Elc
Willm.	177	Elc
Minston, John	948	Chc
Minter, Anthony	454	Mth
Anthony	7	Pwh
Barker	218	Ess
Edward	418	Fqr
James [2]	450	Mth
Jesse	268	Amh
Jno.	447	Mth
Johanoh	454	Mth
John	122	Cmb
John	220	Ess
John	398	Rch
Joseph	379	Fqr
Josiah	445	Mth

Micajer	130	Cmb
Tho.	445	Mth
Thomas	212	Ess
Thomas	220	Ess
William	473	Bdf
William	379	Fqr
Mintle, Henry	683	Br
Valentine [2]	683	Br
Minton, Abenezer	698	Wsh
Jesse	483	Frn
John	5	Isw
John	782	Bck
John	17	Wod
Phillipe	708	Wsh
Simon H.	56	Chr
see Marton		
Mintor, Adam	644	Btt
Mathias	644	Btt
Mintz, Drury	4	Isw
Miranda, Chn.	911	Nrf
Mires, Gideon	298	Rck
Jacob	97	Jff
John	107	Jff
Ludwick	102	Jff
Mirphy, John	960	Hrr
Joice	960	Hrr
Saml.	960	Hrr
Wm.	960	Hrr
Mirrick see Minick		
Mise, John	351	Lnn
Lilver	351	Lnn
Miser, Fred.	368	Ags
John B.	362	Ags
see Mires		
Mishler, Caty	477	Frn
Miskel, Henry	153	Dnw
Miskell, Austin	585	Frd
George	391	Rch
Henry	390	Rch
John	351	Lnn
Samuel	391	Rch
Misner, Peter	10	Wod
Misnor, Absolom	8	Wod
Miss, Barne	934	Hrr
Missersmith see Messersmith		
Missicen, Nicholas	24	Oho
Mister, Benjamin	40	Acc
Isaac	40	Acc
James	41	Acc
Thomas	326	Dnw
William	39	Acc
William	112	Acc
William, BS	41	Acc
Mitch..., Benj.	472	Bdf
Mitchal, George	220	Pnd
Marry	215	Pnd
Mitcham, Elijah	632	Mnt
Mitchan, Henry	547	Prg
Thos.	548	Prg
Mitchel, Alexr.	302	Rck
And.	275	Rck
Andrew	91	Spt
Archabald	500	Frn
Arche.	704	Gch
Archer M.	58	Chr
Benja.	115	Hnr
Charles	644	Btt
David	704	Gch
Dianna	722	Brn
Edward	832	Bck
Edwd.	641	Btt
Garland	858	Hnv
Geo.	403	Ags
George	910	Hrr
Henry	500	Frn
Hickman	201	Ess
James	362	Ags
James	370	Ags
James	500	Frn
James	429	Msn

James	421	Rnd
James	845	Wth
James L.	18	Wod
Jno.	883	Hnv
Jno.	714	Nls
John	787	Hmp
John	941	Hrr
John	945	Hrr
Joshua	572	Mnr
Mathew	304	Ldn
Nathaniel	473	Frn
Oliver	776	Bck
Peggy	199	Ess
Peggy	201	Ess
Reuben	93	Spt
Rheuben T.	711	Nls
Richard	500	Frn
Robert	58	Chr
Robert	153	Dnw
Robert	714	Nls
Robt.	115	Hnr
Sally	584	Brk
Solomon	945	Hrr
Thomas	58	Chr
Thos.	370	Ags
Walter	57	Chr
William	56	Chr
William	990	Nrt
Wm.	368	Ags
Wm.	703	Gch
see Michel, Mitchell		
Mitchell, Adam	259	Amh
Agnus	911	Nrf
Ala...	329	Dnw
Alexander	4	Oho
Amy	839	Nrf
Andrew	474	Bdf
Andrew	1	Oho
Andw.	910	Nrf
Ann	56	Clp
Ann	722	Brn
Archelus	266	Amh
Archelus	289	Amh
Archilus, Christians-		
burg	618	Mnt
Banister	453	Grn
Benja.	284	Frf
Benjamin	531	Frd
Blanks	652	Sss
Bowling	262	Amh
Branch	653	Sss
Caleb	914	Crl
Carter	411	Rch
Cary	120	Cmb
Catharine	392	Fqr
Chaney [2]	453	Grn
Charles	652	Sss
Daniel	473	Bdf
Danl. P.	353	Lnc
David	594	Frd
Drewry	453	Grn
Drewry, Jr.	453	Grn
Elijah	474	Bdf
Eliza.	613	Srr
Elizabeth	578	Pre
Enos	473	Bdf
Geo.	176	Elc
Geo. M.	353	Lnc
Henry	353	Lnc
Ignatius	472	Bdf
Isaac	651	Sss
Isaac M.	153	Dnw
Jacob	652	Sss
James	473	Bdf
James	476	Bdf
James	882	Cmp
James	562	Frd
James	171	Knq
James	577	Pre
James	578	Pre

Name	No.	Co.	Name	No.	Co.	Name	No.	Co.
James	501	Prw	Mitcheller, Thomas	415	Bth	Jno.	444	Mth
James	26	Stf	Mitchelltre, George	12	Oho	Mohorn, John	352	Lnn
Janes	330	Dnw	Mitchill, Hugh	4	Oho	Richard	352	Lnn
Jas.	353	Lnc	Samuel	9	Oho	Moiers, Frederick	603	Frd
Jessee	722	Brn	Mitchner, Jno.	523	Mnn	Henry	601	Frd
Jno.	664	Glc	Mitchum, Collin	189	Shn	Michal	602	Frd
John	235	Aml	Jesse	354	Lnc	Moires, William	602	Frd
John	262	Amh	John	92	Spt	Molair, Maryanne	515	Prw
John	473	Bdf	Mitts, Jacob	184	Shn	Moland, Enos	286	Frf
John	879	Cmp	Jacob	191	Shn	James	283	Frf
John	155	Dnw	Peter	184	Shn	Jno.	283	Frf
John	547	Frd	Peter, Junr.	184	Shn	John	285	Frf
John	565	Frd	see Metts			Mary	473	Bdf
John	598	Frd	Mitz see Mitts			Molar, Sarah	77	Jff
John	171	Knq	Mixwell, George	655	Mnt	Molbon, Abslom	468	Pra
John	240	Ldn	Peter	655	Mnt	see Malbon		
John	734	Wsh	Mize, Dennis	722	Brn	Molen, William	914	Crl
John	779	Wst	Eady	758	Brn	Moler, Adam	84	Jff
Joseph	474	Bdf	Henry B.	758	Brn	Frederick	87	Jff
Joseph	453	Grn	Jeremiah	756	Brn	Fredk.	268	Rck
Joseph C.	837	Nrf	John	755	Brn	Jane	82	Jff
Joshua	757	Brn	Lucy	758	Brn	Martin	231	Shn
Js.	910	Nrf	Mizick, James	72	Acc	Mary	87	Jff
Lewis	15	Hnr	MKee, Robert	434	Msn	Michael	87	Jff
Loveless	396	Mds	William	426	Msn	Moles, George	631	Gls
Lucy	722	Brn	Mllaughlin see MClaughlin			Jeremiah	631	Gls
Martha	525	Prw	MMullen, Joseph	429	Msn	Zachy.	595	Brk
Mary	779	Wst	Mo..., James	302	Rck	Molin, James	71	Jff
Nancy	545	Frd	Moana, David	535	Brk	Rebecca	83	Jff
Paul	652	Sss	Moands, William	523	Brk	Mollahan, John	418	Rnd
Perry	524	Frd	Mobberly, John G.	524	Prw	Samuel	418	Rnd
Peterson	538	Prg	Mobbley, Thompson	732	Wsh	Mollehorne, Sarah	283	Frf
Polly	56	Clp	Mobbly, William	732	Wsh	Moller, Peter	741	Wsh
Randolph	757	Brn	Mobbs, Lewis	34	Rcm	Molley see Motley		
Reuben	850	Cmp	Mobley, Edward	685	Br	Moloham, George	3	Knw
Reuben	55	Wsh	John	719	Wsh	Molohan, George	7	Knw
Richard	170	Knq	Mocaboy, Thomas	520	Prw	Moltimer, Winnifred	990	Nrt
Richd., Jr.	354	Lnc	Mock, Abraham	39	Rcm	Moma, David	182	Shn
Richd., Snr.	353	Lnc	Frederick	629	Gls	Moman, Clarke	862	Hnv
Richd., yr.	353	Lnc	George	227	Shn	Robert	166	Alb
Robert	475	Bdf	Henry	298	Ldn	Monahon, Catherine	55	Jff
Robert	722	Brn	Jacob	313	Ldn	Monan, Francis	421	Msn
Robert	171	Knq	Peter	631	Gls	Monceau, ---, Doctr.	909	Nrf
Robert	537	Prg	Moderwell, Robt.	639	Btt	Moncure, Edwin C.	20	Stf
Robert B.	411	Rch	Modeset, Brooksy	945	Hrr	John	23	Stf
Robt.	25	Hnr	Modisett, Uriah	916	Hrr	Wm.	32	Hnr
Robt.	794	Nrf	Zachaus	917	Hrr	Monday, Abraham	203	Alb
Saml.	621	Mnt	Modnia, Francis	203	Alb	Charles	257	Amh
Samuel	301	Amh	Modock, William	175	Shn	Clem	793	Hmp
Samuel	473	Bdf	Mody, Elizabeth	948	Chc	Cretia	137	Sth
Sarah	453	Grn	Moewboy, Mary	503	Prw	James	914	Crl
Sarah	578	Pre	Moffat, Henrietta	909	Nrf	John	293	Amh
Sarah	13	Rcm	Moffatt, John	533	Frd	Jonathan	203	Alb
Stephen E.	476	Bdf	Wm.	909	Nrf	Rachael	913	Crl
Susanna	652	Sss	Moffett, Anderson	22	Rcm	Samuel	203	Alb
Tarples	267	Amh	David	304	Ldn	Mondy, Marth.	32	Hnr
Thads.	353	Lnc	Geo.	363	Ags	Monen, John	273	Rck
Thomas	263	Amh	James	364	Ags	Moner, Adam	944	Hrr
Thomas	604	Frd	James	367	Ags	Money, James	585	Frd
Thomas	171	Knq	James, (C.C.)	366	Ags	Nicholas	282	Frf
Thomas	172	Knq	Jesse	386	Fqr	Perry	285	Frf
Thomas	577	Pre	Jno.	252	Ldn	Samuel	249	Ldn
Thomas	395	Rch	John	368	Ags	Thomas	504	Prw
Thomas	651	Sss	John	419	Fqr	Money Maker, John	367	Ags
Thos.	722	Brn	Josiah [2]	278	Ldn	Moneypenny, Wm.	948	Hrr
Thos.	614	Mnt	Margt.	252	Ldn	Mong, George	962	Hrr
William	474	Bdf	William	40	Rcm	John	545	Brk
William	544	Frd	Wm.	368	Ags	see Mang		
William	171	Knq	Moffit, Charles	811	Bck	Mongald, John	630	Gls
William	578	Pre	Moffitt, John	747	Wsh	Monger, Cornelius	40	Acc
William	502	Prw	Thomas	51	Stf	John	41	Acc
William	779	Wst	Thos.	714	Wsh	John	836	Hmp
William, Jr.	578	Pre	see Maffit			Levin	41	Acc
Willm.	622	Mnt	Moffott, Wm.	827	Nrf	Mongold, Jacob	225	Pnd
Wm.	639	Btt	Mogan, Dennis	5	Oho	Volentine	221	Pnd
Wm.	54	Clp	Jno., jr.	284	Rck	Mongomery, ---, Mrs.	16	Hnr
Wm.	56	Clp	see Morgan			Benjm.	351	Lnn
Wm.	280	Frf	Moheen, Sarah	841	Nrf	John	429	Rnd
Wm.	25	Hnr	Mohler, John	366	Ags	Moniger, Henry	266	Ldn
see Michell, Mitch...			Mohone, George	438	Mth	Monley, Tully	813	Nrf

Monnett, Joseph, (Y)	878	Yrk	Richd.	693	Wsh	see Moorman		
Monroe, Andw.	197	Ess	Robert	551	Frd	Moon, Abner H.	353	Lnn
Christein	433	Bth	Robert	285	Rck	Christopher	761	Nwk
Daniel	433	Bth	Robert	707	Wsh	Jachob	166	Alb
Daniel	30	Stf	Robt.	287	Rck	James	541	Brk
Daniel, Jr.	434	Bth	Robt.	750	Wsh	Jane	538	Brk
David	779	Wst	Saml.	2	Oho	John	274	Amh
Eliza	780	Wst	Tho.	523	Mnn	John	60	Chr
Eliza.	401	Rch	Thomas	600	Frd	John J.	990	Nrt
Elizabeth	590	Frd	Thos.	750	Wsh	Jos.	2	Ntt
Jacob	434	Bth	William	105	Cmb	Josiah P.	869	Cmp
James	166	Alb	William	600	Frd	Littleberry	166	Alb
James	860	Cmp	William	5	Rcm	Littleberry	795	Bck
James	777	Hmp	William	844	Wth	Pleasant	351	Lnn
Jas.	55	Clp	Wm.	370	Ags	Richard [2]	166	Alb
Jesse	826	Hmp	Wm.	274	Rck	Semon	539	Brk
Jno.	642	Btt	see Mongomery, Mountgomary,			Thomas	541	Brk
John	783	Hmp	Mtgomery.			William	166	Alb
John	713	Nls	Montgomonry, Hugh	37	Isw	William	272	Amh
Nelson	717	Nls	Montjoy, Edward	416	Fqr	William	990	Nrt
Patty	780	Wst	Mony, James	362	Fqr	William, Senr.	166	Alb
Richard	780	Wst	Mood, John	840	Nrf	William C.	57	Chr
Robert	865	Cmp	Moodey, Beverly	7	Isw	Moone, Benjn.	19	Ntt
Sally	30	Stf	Christian	39	Isw	Mooney, John	5	Oho
Sarah	273	Amh	Isaac	13	Isw	Kesiah	281	Frf
Sulivan	600	Mnr	Ishmael	2	Isw	Martin	202	Alb
William	590	Frd	Joseph	25	Isw	Nicholas	385	Fqr
William	779	Wst	William B.	25	Isw	Peter	682	Br
see Munrowe			Moodie, Henry H.	58	Clp	Richard	204	Alb
Monroney, William	361	Fqr	Jas.	59	Clp	Moor, Barnett	154	Dnw
Monrow, Marth.	32	Hnr	Moody, Andw.	369	Ags	Benjamin	486	Frn
Monster, Lydia	243	Ldn	Archer	180	Elc	Bury	353	Lnn
Monsy, Jesse	924	Hrr	Benja.	334	Dnw	Catherine	39	Acc
Montague, Abraham	212	Ess	Blanks	328	Dnw	Elisha	351	Lnn
Ann	467	Mdd	Blanks	612	Srr	Jacob	484	Frn
Catharine	467	Mdd	Briant	5	Knw	James	500	Frn
James	212	Ess	Burges S.	353	Lnc	John	485	Frn
John	212	Ess	Carter	218	Ess	John	5	Knw
John	8	Pwh	Carter	703	Gch	John, jr.	154	Dnw
Mickleborough	4	Pwh	David	153	Dnw	John, Junr.	40	Acc
Peter	115	Cmb	David	155	Dnw	Joseph	466	Frn
Philip	467	Mdd	Elijah	221	Ess	Joseph C.	2	Knw
Philip T.	212	Ess	Henry	543	Prg	Laban	111	Acc
Rice D.	119	Cmb	Henry	654	Sss	Levi	41	Acc
Saml., (Est.)	212	Ess	Hundly	220	Ess	Mason, E.	353	Lnn
Saml., Este.	467	Mdd	James	57	Chs	Polly	44	Acc
Thomas	115	Cmb	James	114	Hnr	Stephen	39	Acc
Thomas T.	467	Mdd	James	59	Jff	Thomas	43	Acc
William	126	Cmb	James	12	Rcm	William	495	Frn
William	467	Mdd	James, jr.	56	Chs	William W.	579	Pre
Wm.	212	Ess	Jeremiah	7	Pwh	William T.	40	Acc
Wm. L.	467	Mdd	Jno.	280	Frf	Moore, ---	332	Dnw
Monteith, Enos	58	Stf	Jno.	548	Prg	---, Oden &	18	Hnr
Lea	58	Stf	John	632	Gls	Abel	55	Chs
Montford, Wade	22	Isw	John	702	Gch	Abner	366	Ags
William	22	Isw	John	11	Hnr	Absolem	664	Glc
Montgomery, Andrew	779	Wst	John	14	Knw	Aggatha	171	Knq
Chs.	523	Mnn	John	171	Knq	Alexander	54	Chs
Claton	716	Nls	John	352	Lnn	Alexr., sen.	298	Rck
Cynthia	845	Wth	Kitty	14	Hnr	Amos	702	Gch
Francis	526	Prw	Lewis	222	Ess	Andrew	336	Dnw
Henry	13	Knw	Molly	222	Ess	Andrw, esq.	279	Rck
Henry	699	Wsh	Peggy	548	Mnn	Andw.	842	Nrf
Isiah	369	Ags	Rob.	524	Mnn	Ann C.	702	Gch
James	717	Nls	Robt.	547	Prg	Aron	423	Bth
James	778	Wst	Sally	704	Gch	Aron	198	Shn
Jane	909	Nrf	Samuel	492	Frn	Arthur	703	Wsh
Jas.	522	Mnn	Samuel	864	Hnv	Asa	307	Ldn
Jas.	742	Wsh	Spencer	171	Knq	Aug., Sr.	186	Elc
John	365	Ags	Tho.	546	Prg	Baker	66	Jff
John	499	Prw	Thomas	761	Nwk	Barham	652	Sss
John	693	Wsh	Wm.	69	Chs	Bengamin	785	Hmp
John	716	Wsh	Wm.	153	Dnw	Benjamin	166	Alb
John	760	Wsh	Wm.	287	Rck	Benjamin	474	Bdf
John	844	Wth	Mooman, Christn.	643	Btt	Benjamin	773	Bck
Joseph	716	Nls	Eliza.	643	Btt	Benjamin	14	Pwh
Joseph	844	Wth	Jno., Jr.	643	Btt	Benjamin, Senr.	166	Alb
Joseph	845	Wth	Jno., Sr.	643	Btt	Berjanin	723	Brn
Mathew	757	Hmp	Nancy	472	Bdf	Berjanin, Ov.	723	Brn
Mupl. [?]	688	Wsh	Phillip	642	Btt			

Name	No.	Co.	Name	No.	Co.	Name	No.	Co.
Bernad	761	Nwk	James	313	Ldn	Jonathan, Senr.	179	Shn
Caleb	466	Pra	James	351	Lnn	Jonethan C.	54	Chs
Caturah	166	Alb	James	717	Nls	Joseph [2]	166	Alb
Caty	170	Knq	James	990	Nrt	Joseph	599	Brk
Charles	301	Amh	James	542	Prg	Joseph	242	Ldn
Charles	773	Bck	James	424	Rnd	Joseph	198	Shn
Charles	23	Rcm	James	286	Rck	Joseph	233	Shn
Charles	193	Shn	James	278	Rck	Joseph	654	Sss
Charles	651	Sss	James	844	Wth	Joshua	912	Nrf
Charles	678	Wrw	James	846	Wth	Josiah	813	Hmp
Christian	873	Cmp	James, esq [?]	307	Rck	Judith	664	Glc
Cyrus	990	Nrt	James, Senr.	286	Rck	Kedar	464	Pra
Daniel	810	Hmp	James G.	412	Rch	Levi, Jur.	423	Bth
Daniel	430	Rnd	James L.	870	Cmp	Lewis	58	Clp
Davd.	286	Rck	James V.	183	Elc	Lewis	199	Shn
David	851	Cmp	Jane	402	Fqr	Lodowick	171	Knq
David	330	Dnw	Jane	95	Jff	Lucy	57	Chr
David	90	Jff	Jas.	811	Nrf	Lucy, F. N.	171	Knq
David	654	Mnt	Jas.	817	Nrf	Lydia	464	Pra
David	194	Shn	Jas., (DN)	467	Pra	Mae.	364	Ags
David	197	Shn	Jas., Jr.	642	Btt	Malachi	466	Pra
Dunford [2]	664	Glc	Jas., (of Cason	467	Pra	Margaret	613	Srr
Early	203	Alb	Jas., Sr.	640	Btt	Margte.	912	Nrf
Eddins	352	Lnn	Jeditham	990	Nrt	Marry	166	Alb
Eden B.	248	Ldn	Jepha. F.	727	Wsh	Martha	154	Dnw
Eden B.	274	Ldn	Jeremh.	281	Frf	Martha	627	Mnt
Edith	52	Chs	Jerry	852	Cmp	Martha	292	Rck
Edward	453	Grn	Jesse	78	Jff	Martin	165	Alb
Eleanor	24	Rcm	Jesse	352	Lnn	Marton	717	Wsh
Eli	807	Hmp	Jesse	635	Mnt	Mary	690	Br
Eli	523	Mnn	Jesse	612	Srr	Mary	664	Glc
Elija	990	Nrt	Jno.	282	Frf	Mary	534	Prg
Elijah	352	Lnn	Jno.	286	Frf	Mary	296	Rck
Elijah	253	Shn	Jno. [2]	664	Glc	Mary, Jr.	465	Pra
Elisha	282	Frf	Jno.	524	Mnn	Mary A.	401	Rch
Eliza.	854	Sth	Jno.	911	Nrf	Mason	351	Lnn
Elizabeth	913	Crl	Jno.	539	Prg	Mathew	858	Cmp
Elizabeth	6	Pwh	Jno.	542	Prg	Mchl.	518	Mnn
Elizabeth	466	Pra	Jno.	468	Pra	Micl., Jr.	518	Mnn
Enoch	467	Pra	Jno.	271	Rck	Millington	331	Dnw
Evans	612	Srr	Jno.	153	Sth	Molly	578	Pre
Fanney	366	Ags	Jno. [?]	280	Rck	Molly P.	391	Rch
Frances	878	Yrk	Jno., (B. Smith)	465	Pra	Mordicai	913	Crl
Francis	453	Grn	Joel	351	Lnn	Morris	263	Ldn
Francis	744	Wsh	John	110	Acc	Moses	294	Rck
Francis	777	Wst	John [2]	166	Alb	Nancy [2]	989	Nrt
Frederick	915	Crl	John	363	Ags	Nancy	990	Nrt
Frederick	18	Oho	John	364	Ags	Nathaniel	990	Nrt
Garland	91	Jff	John	403	Ags	Olive	867	Cmp
Geo. H.	54	Chs	John	425	Bth	Oliver	435	Flv
George	915	Hrr	John	473	Bdf	Patcey	723	Wsh
George	467	Mdd	John	639	Btt	Peter	369	Ags
George	579	Mnr	John	697	Br	Peter	990	Nrt
Gersham	822	Nrf	John	870	Cmp	Peter	878	Sth
Hannah	780	Wst	John	914	Crl	Phebe	27	Rcm
Henry	642	Btt	John	154	Dnw	Phil.	518	Mnn
Henry	774	Bck	John	282	Frf	Philip	181	Alb
Henry	507	Frd	John	813	Hmp	Pleasant	879	Hnv
Henry	775	Hmp	John	13	Hnr	Polley	58	Chs
Henry	467	Pra	John	74	Jff	Precilla	653	Sss
Henry	755	Wsh	John	821	Nrf	Predie	862	Cmp
Hillary	464	Pra	John	990	Nrt	Presley	415	Bth
Horatio	830	Nrf	John	276	Rck	Presly	598	Frd
Hugh	277	Rck	John	292	Rck	Rachael	342	Fqr
Isaac	368	Ags	John	22	Rcm	Reub.	55	Clp
Isaac	414	Bth	John	193	Shn	Richard	915	Crl
Isham	57	Chr	John	655	Sss	Richard	897	Hnv
Ja...es	877	Cmp	John	680	Wrw	Richd.	758	Brn
Jac.	518	Mnn	John	878	Yrk	Richd.	171	Knq
Jacob	369	Ags	John, (DJ)	237	Shn	Richd.	541	Prg
Jacob	13	Rcm	John, (Jr.)	23	Rcm	Robert	422	Bth
James	643	Btt	John, (sen.)	23	Rcm	Robert	472	Bdf
James	861	Cmp	John, Ser.	429	Bth	Robert	774	Bck
James	866	Cmp	John, Sr.	757	Brn	Robert	577	Frd
James	341	Fqr	John A.	763	Nwk	Robert	713	Nls
James	522	Frd	John W.	689	Wsh	Robert, Maj.	57	Chr
James	537	Frd	Johnston	582	Brk	Robert T.	697	Br
James	452	Grn	Jonathan	529	Frd	Saml.	292	Rck
James	781	Hmp	Jonathan	114	Hnr	Samuel	68	Chr
James	116	Hnr	Jonathan, (M)	178	Shn	Samuel	402	Fqr

Name	No.	Code	Name	No.	Code	Name	No.	Code
Samuel	420	Fqr	Moorland, John	489	Bdf	Morell, ---, Monsr.	912	Nrf
Samuel	813	Hmp	Moorman, Abraham	878	Cmp	Elisebeth	750	Wsh
Samuel	273	Ldn	Achilles	872	Cmp	Moren, Edward	15	Rcm
Samuel	181	Shn	Charles	473	Bdf	Morens, Henry, & Co.	328	Dnw
Samul	14	Oho	David H.	882	Cmp	Moreton, William	915	Crl
Sarah, (wd. Jas.)	467	Pra	Henry	856	Cmp	Morey see Mony		
Stephen	166	Alb	Jacob	472	Bdf	Morgan, Abel	57	Clp
Stephen	642	Btt	James C.	855	Cmp	Abel	397	Fqr
Stephen, f.n.	283	Frf	Jas. C.	883	Cmp	Abraham	98	Jff
Sterling	756	Brn	John A.	474	Bdf	Abram	630	Gls
Sygnal	3	Ntt	Mecoyah	864	Cmp	Andrew	98	Jff
Tempce.	874	Sth	Reuben	861	Cmp	Andrew	712	Nls
Thomas	263	Amh	Samuel	881	Cmp	Andrew M.	862	Cmp
Thomas	693	Br	Thomas	856	Cmp	Benj.	743	Wsh
Thomas	856	Cmp	Thomas	878	Cmp	Benjn.	584	Mnr
Thomas	873	Cmp	Wm.	640	Btt	Charles	493	Frn
Thomas	58	Chr	see Johnson, Mooman, Morgan			Chs.	286	Ldn
Thomas	154	Dnw	Moorriss, Henry	755	Brn	Daniel	98	Jff
Thomas	170	Knq	Mooser, A.	307	Ags	Daniel	5	Oho
Thomas	12	Ntt	Mopp, George T.	42	Acc	Daniel	244	Shn
Thomas	277	Rck	Houston	39	Acc	Danl.	274	Rck
Thomas	25	Rcm	John	42	Acc	Dav.	521	Mnn
Thomas, (Jr.)	22	Rcm	Robert	44	Acc	Dav.	524	Mnn
Thos.	642	Btt	Samuel	114	Acc	David	630	Gls
Thos.	4	Hnr	Moppin, George	724	Wsh	Dennis D.	57	Chr
Thos., jr.	17	Ntt	Mopping, Gabrel	630	Gls	Dick, (F B)	15	Ntt
Tully, (of Tully	468	Pra	Morain, Blare	11	Oho	Edward	949	Chc
Thos., S D	756	Brn	Gilliam	803	Bck	Edward	511	Frd
Turner	758	Brn	Elijah	717	Nls	Edward	631	Gls
Vincent	94	Jff	James	911	Nrf	Elizabeth	412	Fqr
Vincent, Jr.	990	Nrt	Jno. M.	252	Ldn	Elizabeth	98	Jff
Vincent, Sr.	990	Nrt	Saml.	300	Ldn	Enoch	57	Clp
W. C.	911	Nrf	William	166	Alb	Enoch	59	Clp
William	166	Alb	Winneford	717	Nls	Evan	525	Mnn
William	278	Amh	Wm.	252	Ldn	George	336	Dnw
William	774	Bck	Wm.	258	Ldn	George	960	Hrr
William	859	Cmp	Morau see Moran			Gilbert	208	Kng
William	860	Cmp	Morcherson, John	863	Cmp	Gilbert	170	Shn
William	863	Cmp	Mordock, Jesse	1	Wod	Hiram	448	Mth
William	328	Dnw	More, Abram.	57	Clp	Horatio	519	Mnn
William	782	Hmp	Alexander	104	Spt	Hugh	865	Cmp
William	807	Hmp	Anthonia	942	Hrr	Hugh	524	Mnn
William	397	Mds	David	98	Spt	Isaac	525	Mnn
William	761	Nwk	David	101	Spt	Jacob	579	Pre
William	20	Oho	Dinah	37	Stf	James	343	Fqr
William	535	Prg	Elizabeth	96	Spt	James	947	Hrr
William	516	Prw	Enoch	956	Hrr	James	789	Nrf
William	198	Shn	Gawin	96	Spt	James	577	Pre
William	695	Wsh	George	956	Chc	James B.	579	Pre
William	778	Wst	George	57	Chr	Jane	761	Nwk
William H.	554	Frd	Gilmer	517	Brk	Jane	23	Oho
Willm.	186	Elc	James	91	Spt	Jas.	521	Mnn
Wilson	352	Lnn	James	98	Spt	Jas.	525	Mnn
Wm.	640	Btt	James	27	Stf	Jesse	352	Lnn
Wm.	723	Brn	John	98	Spt	Jno.	444	Mth
Wm.	664	Glc	Phobe	12	Pwh	Jno.	15	Ntt
Wm.	4	Hnr	Rich.	950	Hrr	Jno. L.	61	Chs
Wm.	273	Ldn	Richard	937	Hrr	John	234	Aml
Wm.	826	Nrf	Richard	949	Hrr	John	781	Bck
Wm.	911	Nrf	Thomas	101	Cmb	John	881	Cmp
Wm.	17	Ntt	William	105	Spt	John	913	Crl
Wm., esqr.	292	Rck	Morecock, John	952	Chc	John	56	Chr
Wm., (of Do. [Ditto for Cason?])	467	Pra	Nancy	952	Chc	John	57	Chr
Wm., (of Tully)	465	Pra	Thomas	954	Chc	John	377	Fqr
Wm., Sr.	757	Brn	Moredock, Godfrey	59	Clp	John	584	Frd
Wm. D.	57	Chs	John	525	Prw	John	587	Frd
Zadok	799	Hmp	Morehead, Alexander	383	Fqr	John	704	Gch
Zebe	654	Mnt	Chs.	60	Clp	John	630	Mnt
see Barrock, Brockenbrough, Moon, More, Morr, Scott			Geo.	920	Hrr	John	1	Oho
Moorhead, Andrew	689	Br	George	341	Fqr	John	5	Oho
Eli	622	Mnt	John, Jr.	343	Fqr	John	6	Pwh
Jno.	264	Rck	John, Sr.	343	Fqr	John	283	Rck
Jos., Jr.	622	Mnt	Nathaniel	374	Fqr	John	198	Shn
Jos., Sr.	623	Mnt	Presley	374	Fqr	John, Jr.	5	Oho
Margaret	688	Br	Turner	348	Fqr	John, Sr.	636	Mnt
Robert	690	Br	Moreland, John	599	Frd	John N.	452	Grn
Wm.	622	Mnt	John	878	Yrk	Jonas	244	Shn
Moorisan, John	292	Rck	Philip	269	Ldn	Jos.	521	Mnn
			Richard	761	Hmp	Joseph	350	Fqr
			William	169	Shn	Joseph	557	Frd

Name	No.	Co.
Joseph	5	Oho
Joseph H.	576	Pre
Joshua	439	Mth
Joshua	417	Rnd
Js., Cap.	519	Mnn
Levina	845	Wth
Levy	521	Mnn
Lewis	471	Bdf
Mark	442	Mth
Mark	446	Mth
Martha	529	Frd
Mary	530	Brk
Moorman	869	Cmp
Mordaica	473	Bdf
Mordecai	6	Oho
Morgan	472	Bdf
Morgan	473	Bdf
Morgan	530	Brk
Morgan	521	Mnn
Morgan	525	Mnn
Morgan	22	Oho
Noah	57	Clp
Peggy	92	Jff
Peggy	641	Mnt
Peter	395	Rch
Rawleigh	87	Jff
Rebecca	544	Prg
Reece	474	Bdf
Reese	472	Bdf
Reuben	247	Ldn
Reubin	351	Lnn
Richard	90	Jff
Richd.	641	Btt
Richd.	446	Mth
Robert	58	Chr
Robert	576	Pre
Rufis	688	Wsh
Rufus	845	Wth
Saml.	630	Gls
Saml.	5	Ntt
Saml.	12	Ntt
Saml.	15	Ntt
Saml., (C)	12	Ntt
Samuel	471	Bdf
Samuel	57	Chr
Samuel	116	Cmb
Samuel B.	352	Lnn
Sarah, (Y)	878	Yrk
Sdck. [?]	22	Oho
Simon	234	Aml
Simon	914	Crl
Steph.	520	Mnn
Stephen	351	Lnn
Stepn.	524	Mnn
Terril	58	Chr
Thomas	473	Bdf
Thomas	577	Pre
Thomas, jr.	352	Lnn
Thomas, Sr.	352	Lnn
Thos.	208	Kng
Umphrey	786	Hmp
Uriah	519	Mnn
William	851	Cmp
William	75	Jff
William	98	Jff
William	397	Mds
William	576	Pre
William	390	Rch
William, Senr.	845	Wth
Willis	509	Frd
Willoughby	396	Rch
Winefred	665	Glc
Wm.	12	Ntt
Zadakiah	417	Rnd
Zac.	520	Mnn
see Mgan, Mogan, Mozingo		
Morgen, Sarah	926	Hrr
Morgin, Ganaway	948	Chc
Morice, Leonard	9	Knw
Moricle, Jno.	651	Mnt

Name	No.	Co.
Morill, John	720	Wsh
Moring, Robert	612	Srr
William	612	Srr
Moris, Betsey	7	Hnr
John	8	Knw
Martha	12	Hnr
Simson	35	Hnr
Morison, ---	332	Dnw
Alexander	940	Hrr
Andrew	10	Knw
Jno., Jnr.	712	Nls
John	12	Knw
Robt.	301	Rck
Morland, Alexander	10	Oho
Bazil	765	Hmp
David	763	Hmp
William	775	Hmp
William	792	Hmp
Morlat, Abm.	513	Brk
Abm.	515	Brk
Leah	512	Brk
Peter	512	Brk
Morlatt, Abm.	512	Brk
Morlow, Thomas	24	Oho
see Marlow		
Morman see Mooman		
Morninstar, Philip	10	Oho
Moro, Lucy	909	Nrf
Morolee, Thomas	303	Ldn
Morr, Abel	233	Aml
Thomas	204	Alb
Morral, Sameul	216	Pnd
Morran, Elijah	714	Nls
Morrel, Edward	697	Br
Morress, George	265	Amh
Thomas	270	Amh
Morric, Danniel	964	Hrr
Morrier, George	179	Shn
Morrington, John	563	Brk
Morris, Alexr.	363	Ags
Ambrose	472	Bdf
Anderson	472	Bdf
Ann	192	Elc
Anna	468	Pra
Antony [2]	878	Yrk
Archibald	413	Bth
Arnold	508	Brk
Austin	856	Hnv
Batts	763	Nwk
Benjamin	472	Bdf
Benjamin	814	Bck
Benjamin	9	Knw
Betsy	14	Hnr
Bettey	328	Dnw
C.	403	Ags
Carrol	6	Knw
Catharine	5	Knw
Claybourn	643	Mnt
Cornelias	332	Dnw
Daniel	761	Nwk
Daniel	12	Oho
Daniel	130	Sth
David	468	Pra
David	277	Rck
Edmund	12	Knw
Edward	414	Bth
Edwd.	705	Gch
Elijah	25	Oho
Eliza.	663	Glc
Enoch	513	Frd
Ephram	754	Wsh
Floyd	643	Btt
Geo.	664	Glc
Geo.	878	Yrk
George	413	Bth
Gilbert	111	Acc
Henry	1	Knw
Hudson	802	Bck
Hudson	406	Rch
Hugh R.	167	Alb

Name	No.	Co.
Isaac	939	Hrr
Isaac	6	Oho
Isaac	5	Wod
Israel	473	Bdf
Jacob	42	Acc
Jacob	474	Bdf
Jacob	59	Clp
James	957	Chc
James	664	Glc
James	20	Oho
James	737	Wsh
Jane	167	Alb
Jane	440	Bth
Jesse	880	Cmp
Jesse	826	Nrf
Jesse	466	Pra
Jno.	285	Frf
Jno.	290	Ldn
Jno.	519	Mnn
Jno.	716	Nls
Jno.	680	Wrw
Joel	468	Pra
John	42	Acc
John	115	Acc
John	473	Bdf
John	778	Bck
John	862	Cmp
John	864	Cmp
John	942	Chc
John	330	Dnw
John	550	Frn
John	5	Knw
John	8	Knw
John	526	Mnn
John	762	Nwk
John	25	Oho
John	402	Rch
John	271	Rck
John	131	Sth
John	780	Wst
John C.	763	Nwk
Joseph	940	Hrr
Joseph	11	Knw
Josh.	56	Clp
Joshua	1	Knw
Js.	520	Mnn
Larkin	80	Spt
Leonard	4	Knw
Levi	9	Knw
Levy	519	Mnn
Mahlon	266	Ldn
Mark	276	Rck
Mark, j.	304	Rck
Martha	19	Hnr
Mary	352	Fqr
Mary	663	Glc
Natthaniel	814	Bck
Natthaniel, Jr.	783	Bck
Nehemh.	280	Frf
Noah	520	Mnn
Polly	664	Glc
Powel	165	Alb
Rice	403	Ags
Richard	28	Hnr
Richard, Jnr.	847	Hnv
Richd.	272	Ldn
Richd.	519	Mnn
Richd.	522	Mnn
Robert	439	Bth
Robt.	704	Gch
Robt.	112	Hnr
Rosanna, F.B.	5	Pwh
Ruth	468	Pra
Sally	130	Hnr
Samuel	534	Frd
Seth	664	Glc
Thomas	760	Nwk
Thomas	7	Oho
Thomas	276	Rck
Thos.	54	Clp

Name	Pg	Dist	Name	Pg	Dist	Name	Pg	Dist
Thos.	664	Glc	Eliza.	59	Chs	James	579	Pre
Thos., jr.	57	Clp	Eliza.	453	Grn	Jno., Capt.	56	Chr
Uriah	395	Fqr	George	905	Hrr	John	298	Amh
Vincent	472	Bdf	George, jr.	288	Amh	John	832	Bck
William	182	Alb	Guthree	435	Flv	John	820	Hmp
William	154	Dnw	Henry	517	Brk	John	576	Pre
William	332	Dnw	Henry	724	Brn	John, (Son little Joe)	57	Chr
William	6	Knw	Henry	664	Glc	John C.	579	Pre
William	171	Knq	Isaac	234	Aml	Jonn, & Company	70	Chr
William	25	Oho	Isaac	9	Ntt	Joseph, (Son Will)	57	Chr
William	404	Rch	James	67	Chs	Mary	807	Nrf
William	102	Spt	Jno.	56	Chs	Mary	579	Pre
William	104	Spt	Jno.	59	Chs	Mary Ann, (Widow		
William	779	Wst	Joel	234	Aml	Qui)	57	Chr
William	7	Wod	John	235	Aml	Nathaniel	578	Pre
William, Jr.	405	Rch	Lucy	453	Grn	Prosiller	28	Hnr
Willm.	617	Mnt	Meriweather	439	Flv	Richard	56	Chr
Wim.	858	Hnv	Nathaniel	723	Brn	Robert	56	Chr
Wm.	664	Glc	Nicholas	652	Sss	Robert	16	Oho
Wm.	258	Ldn	Phebean	396	Mds	Sarah	114	Spt
Wm.	518	Mnn	Robert	723	Brn	Thog. [Frog. ?]	7	Hnr
Wm.	520	Mnn	Robert	851	Cmp	Thomas	57	Chr
Wm.	271	Rck	Robert	452	Grn	Thomas A.	579	Pre
York	44	Acc	Sabra	58	Chr	Will. L., Capt.	56	Chr
Youel	103	Spt	Sarah	234	Aml	William	577	Pre
Zadk.	519	Mnn	Sarah	19	Ntt	William, Col.	57	Chr
see David			Sherod	724	Brn	William B., Capt.	58	Chr
Morrison, Aaron H.	714	Nls	Susannah	235	Aml	Wm.	523	Mnn
Alexander	20	Oho	Williamson	453	Grn	Wm., Este.	55	Clp
Alexandr.	39	Acc	Wm.	56	Chs	see Mourton		
Archabald	949	Hrr	Wm. A.	4	Ntt	Mosbey, Armstead	403	Ags
Archd.	281	Ldn	Zack	235	Aml	Ezekiah	6	Hnr
David	507	Brk	Morrissett, Jno.	465	Pra	Joseph	899	Hnv
Edward	407	Fqr	Jona.	468	Pra	Sammuel	847	Hnv
Elizabeth	716	Nls	Morrisson, James	3	Isw	Mosby, Benja.	131	Hnr
Gabl.	59	Clp	Sally	26	Isw	Benjamin	3	Pwh
Hambleton	1	Wod	Morrow, Adam	689	Br	Benjn.	740	Nls
James	427	Bth	Adam	24	Oho	Benjn.	676	Nls
James	392	Fqr	Alexander	690	Br	Daniel	713	Nls
James	922	Hrr	Eliza.	679	Wrw	Hezekiah	4	Pwh
Jas.	354	Lnc	John	694	Br	John	14	Hnr
Jesse	508	Brk	John	121	Cmb	John	123	Hnr
Jno.	58	Clp	John	104	Jff	John	711	Nls
Jno.	60	Clp	John	760	Wsh	Joseph	853	Cmp
Jno.	712	Nls	Mary	681	Wrw	Josiah	129	Hnr
Jno.	714	Nls	Matthew	10	Oho	Laneston	705	Gch
John	543	Brk	Ralph	905	Hrr	Littlebery, Genl.	4	Pwh
John	351	Lnn	William	55	Jff	Micajah	776	Bck
Jonathan	512	Brk	Wm.	703	Gch	Robert	6	Pwh
Joseph	989	Nrt	see Mowrow			Sally	1	Pwh
Markhm.	702	Gch	Morse, Ann	166	Alb	Saml.	4	Hnr
Mary	59	Clp	Biddy	911	Nrf	Susannah	1	Pwh
Patrick	524	Frd	David	468	Pra	Thomas	133	Cmb
Richard	990	Nrt	Ebernezer	778	Wst	Tillar	114	Hnr
Richd.	508	Brk	Jas.	468	Pra	Wade	3	Pwh
Robert	166	Alb	Joel	468	Pra	Wm. H.	715	Nls
Robert	689	Br	John	166	Alb	see Mosley, Pulliam		
Samuel	576	Pre	Joseph	778	Wst	Moseby, Mordicai	487	Frn
Tarpley	60	Clp	Mary T.	779	Wst	Moseley, Amy	13	Pwh
Thankful	507	Brk	Nancy	779	Wst	Amy	466	Pra
Thomas	407	Fqr	Nathan	468	Pra	Arthur	780	Bck
Thomas	715	Nls	Oliff	794	Nrf	Arthur	785	Bck
William	573	Frd	Tanny	778	Wst	Arthur	13	Pwh
William	13	Wod	Thos.	723	Brn	Benjamin	800	Bck
William, Jr.	990	Nrt	Thos.	804	Nrf	Cary	654	Sss
William, Sr.	989	Nrt	Morson, Alexander	58	Stf	Charles	781	Bck
Wm.	366	Ags	Morten, Jacob	302	Rck	Christr.	464	Pra
Wm.	518	Brk	Mortimer, John	537	Brk	Daniel	793	Bck
Wm.	12	Oho	John	109	Spt	Daniel	802	Bck
see Moorisan			Mortimore, ---, Dr.	912	Nrf	Daniel, S.J	812	Bck
Morriss, ---, & Jones	16	Ntt	Mortin, John	949	Hrr	E.H.	490	Pra
Allison	288	Amh	William	854	Cmp	Edward, Majr.	14	Pwh
Ambrose	878	Yrk	Morton, Ann	3	Hnr	Edw. H.	466	Pra
Anne	37	Isw	Ann, Mrs.	57	Chr	Francis	791	Bck
Benjamin	446	Flv	Ben	522	Mnn	Francis	352	Lnn
Chs., free negro	70	Chs	Celia	57	Chr	George	7	Pwh
Dabny	16	Ntt	Eliza	57	Chr	Heartwell	651	Sss
Daniel	756	Brn	Hanah	522	Mnn	Jane	756	Brn
Edward J.	723	Brn	Hezekiah	578	Pre	Jas., (Dctr.)	464	Pra
Eliza.	234	Aml	Jacob, Maj.	56	Chr	Jessee	756	Brn

Jimny	325	Dnw	Elijah	8	Wod	George	778	Wst
Levy	757	Brn	Elisha	60	Clp	Jas. H.	779	Wst
Magdalen	802	Bck	Elizabeth	809	Bck	Jas. S.	779	Wst
Mary	757	Brn	Elizabeth	834	Bck	John	402	Rch
Nathan	757	Brn	Fanney	833	Bck	John, Junr.	780	Wst
Patsey	787	Bck	Francis	475	Frn	John, Senr.	778	Wst
Peter	62	Chs	Francis	578	Pre	Nathaniel	778	Wst
Rebeca	756	Brn	George	761	Nwk	Nathl.	404	Rch
Richard	13	Pwh	George	36	Rcm	Peggy	778	Wst
Robert	800	Bck	Gideon	846	Wth	Richd.	777	Wst
Robert	824	Bck	Henry	652	Sss	Samuel	779	Wst
Robert	14	Pwh	Henry P.	652	Sss	William	778	Wst
Spotsford	13	Pwh	Howell	453	Grn	Motley, Elizabeth	170	Knq
Tabitha	756	Brn	Isham	807	Bck	Henry	913	Crl
Tully	465	Pra	Jacob	366	Ags	John	14	Ntt
William	781	Bck	James	777	Bck	Thomas	912	Crl
William	802	Bck	James	835	Bck	William	60	Stf
William	827	Bck	James	578	Mnr	Moton, Edmond	30	Stf
William	14	Pwh	James	578	Pre	Richard	26	Stf
Winney	757	Brn	James	878	Yrk	Ursilla	26	Stf
Wm.	466	Pra	Jane	724	Brn	Mots, Jacob, S.	225	Pnd
Wm.	490	Pra	Jesse	118	Hnr	see Motes		
see Mossley			Jno.	281	Frf	Mott, Elizabth.	910	Nrf
Mosely, Eleanor	910	Nrf	John	641	Btt	Isaac	240	Ldn
Hilly.	909	Nrf	John	30	Hnr	Joseph	989	Nrt
James	810	Hmp	John	225	Pnd	Sylvester	813	Hmp
Saml.	909	Nrf	John	577	Pre	William	418	Fqr
Moser, Adam	223	Pnd	John	578	Pre	Motter, John	107	Jff
Christopher	83	Jff	John	651	Sss	Joseph	23	Rcm
Jacob	74	Jff	John	878	Yrk	Mottley, John, Sr.	233	Aml
Michael	83	Jff	Judith	762	Nwk	Joseph	235	Aml
Moses, Aaron	307	Ldn	Julius	762	Nwk	William	234	Aml
Anna	467	Pra	Kendell	208	Kng	Motts, David	190	Shn
Mark	111	Acc	Mary	756	Brn	Moubray, Andrew	397	Mds
Peter	790	Bck	Matildia	7	Hnr	Joseph	397	Mds
Peter, Jr.	790	Bck	Meridith	756	Brn	Moudy, Adam	59	Jff
Samuel	715	Nls	Moses	577	Mnr	Geo.	641	Btt
Samuel F.	57	Chr	Moses	518	Prw	Moughon, Ann	663	Glc
Tully	466	Pra	Patty, free negro	70	Chs	Moul, Philip	292	Ldn
Wm.	715	Nls	Polly	32	Hnr	Moulding, Wm.	251	Ldn
Mosey, John S.	16	Hnr	Presly	518	Prw	Mouls, John	641	Btt
Moslander, John	17	Oho	Rd., free negro [3]	70	Chs	Polly	641	Btt
Mosley, Benjamin	855	Cmp	Richd., (FB)	474	Bdf	Thos.	641	Btt
Bennet	639	Btt	Robert	282	Frf	Moulson, Geo.	828	Nrf
Blackman	234	Aml	Saml.	704	Gch	Mouner, Humphry	916	Hrr
Edwd.	58	Chr	Samuel	762	Nwk	Zekiel	916	Hrr
Edwd.	66	Chs	Samuel, junr.	762	Nwk	Mount, Ezekl.	237	Ldn
Edwd., Jur.	59	Chr	Sarah	835	Bck	Thomas	370	Fqr
Hillery, Capt.	57	Chr	Sarah	515	Prw	William	334	Dnw
Jacob	58	Chr	Silvey	702	Gch	William	525	Prw
James	166	Alb	Step.	241	Ldn	Mountague, Wm.	128	Hnr
John	58	Chr	Thomas	834	Bck	Mountain, John B.	467	Mdd
John	578	Pre	Thomas	326	Dnw	Mountcastle, Benjm.	947	Chc
Josiah	57	Chr	Thomas	284	Frf	Christian	948	Chc
Keziah	853	Hnv	Thomas	278	Ldn	Daniel	284	Amh
Matthew	235	Aml	Thomas	405	Rch	Elizabeth	946	Chc
Peter	10	Hnr	Thos.	58	Clp	Jas.	325	Dnw
Robert	57	Chr	Vincent	395	Fqr	John	275	Amh
Robert	578	Pre	William	786	Bck	Joseph	956	Chc
Thomas	56	Chr	William	838	Bck	Robert	330	Dnw
William	58	Chr	William	282	Frf	Mountcastles, William	577	Pre
William F.	57	Chr	William	452	Grn	Mountford, Lucy	40	Isw
see Mottley			William	761	Nwk	Sally	38	Isw
Moson, John	452	Frn	William	762	Nwk	Mountfortt, Wade	682	Wrw
Moss, Aggy	118	Hnr	Wm.	724	Brn	Mountgomary, Samuel	476	Frn
Alexander	712	Nls	Wm.	704	Gch	Mountgomery, Jno.	260	Ldn
Alfred	653	Sss	Wm.	878	Yrk	Mountjoy, Francis	23	Stf
Anderson	279	Amh	Wm., jr.	878	Yrk	George	166	Alb
Anne	835	Bck	see Armistead			John	510	Prw
Anne	282	Frf	Mosses, Peter, F.N.	653	Sss	Nancy	502	Prw
Billy	118	Hnr	Mossey, Meshack	32	Stf	Thomas	54	Stf
Biorrel, (FN)	68	Chr	Mossley, Samuel	756	Brn	William	373	Fqr
Charlotte	298	Amh	Motes, Adam	226	Pnd	William	26	Stf
Diley, (M)	724	Brn	George	225	Pnd	Mountz, Providence	10	Oho
Drewry	712	Nls	Jacob, J.	225	Pnd	Mouren see Mourier		
Edmon	475	Frn	Michal	225	Pnd	Mourier, George	201	Shn
Edmund	654	Sss	see Mots			see Mowrier		
Edward, (FB)	473	Bdf	Motherset, Brooks	265	Rck	Mouring, Tho.	182	Elc
Edwd.	187	Elc	Mothershead, Charles C.	411	Rch	Mourman, Hannah	704	Gch
Edwd.	878	Yrk	Daniel	779	Wst	Mourning, Jno.	865	Hnv

Thomas	914	Crl	Henry	845	Wth	Muller, Benjamin	473	Bdf
William	913	Crl	Isaac	236	Shn	Casper	823	Nrf
Wm.	664	Glc	Jacob	222	Pnd	Mary	836	Nrf
Wyatt	6	Ntt	Jacob	16	Rcm	Mulligan, Benjamin	8	Oho
Mourton, Edward	219	Pnd	Jacob	17	Rcm	Jane	306	Ldn
John	659	Mnt	John	18	Rcm	Mullin, Abraham	171	Knq
Mouse, Daniel	220	Pnd	John	844	Wth	Charles	915	Crl
Danl.	423	Rnd	John D.	183	Shn	James	620	Mnt
Mouser, Abraham	192	Shn	Lewis	222	Pnd	James, jr.	915	Crl
Chs.	526	Mnn	Lewis	181	Shn	James, Senr.	915	Crl
Frederick	192	Shn	Martin	218	Pnd	John	171	Knq
George	67	Jff	Michael	30	Rcm	John [written over		
Henry	182	Shn	Michael	845	Wth	"Thomas"?]	760	Nwk
John	67	Jff	Michal	215	Pnd	Joseph	170	Knq
John	192	Shn	Peggy	166	Alb	Mosely M.	88	Spt
William	184	Shn	Peter	6	Rcm	Nancy	759	Wsh
Mouton, J.F.	328	Dnw	Peter	846	Wth	Saml.	171	Knq
Mouts, Deval	945	Hrr	Philip	224	Pnd	William	915	Crl
Movetee, William	487	Frn	Philip	12	Wod	William	171	Knq
Moway, Jno.	3	Ntt	Saml.	40	Rcm	Wm.	626	Mnt
Mowde, Michael [2]	745	Wsh	see Meyers			Mullinax, Abraham	221	Pnd
Mower, John	127	Hnr	Moyler, John	654	Sss	James	217	Pnd
Mowers, Henry	87	Jff	Thomas K.	651	Sss	Samuel	224	Pnd
Mowery, Jacob	243	Shn	Moyres, Danl.	366	Ags	Mulling, Danl.	644	Btt
Mowrey, Abram	369	Ags	Moyrs, John	75	Jff	see Malling		
Henry	366	Ags	John	666	Mnt	Mullings, John	778	Wst
Lewis	369	Ags	Saml.	646	Mnt	Spencer	779	Wst
Leynard	243	Shn	Moyur, George	234	Shn	Mullins, Anthony	166	Alb
Mowrier, John	242	Shn	Mozen, Francis	631	Gls	Archibald	211	Ess
see Mourier			Mozenette, John	6	Oho	Betsey	703	Gch
Mowrow, George	218	Pnd	Mozingo, Benja.	57	Clp	Bowker	489	Frn
George, J.	220	Pnd	Chas.	57	Clp	Coleman	56	Chr
Philip	218	Pnd	Edward	406	Rch	Conley	705	Gch
Mowry, Frederick	565	Frd	Geo.	57	Clp	Edmund	56	Chr
Henry	417	Bth	Geo.	59	Clp	George	57	Chr
John	667	Mnt	James F.	406	Rch	Giles C.	56	Chr
Lewis, jr.	369	Ags	Jno.	57	Clp	James, (ME)	56	Chr
Michael	28	Rcm	Milly	61	Clp	James, (Sadler)	57	Chr
Mowston see Mourton			Morgan	57	Clp	Jesse	488	Frn
Moxley, Ann	780	Wst	Reubin B.	400	Rch	Jessee	59	Chr
Christopher	778	Wst	Wm.	61	Clp	Joannah	57	Chr
Daniel	989	Nrt	Mozley, James	472	Bdf	Joel	58	Chr
Daniel	777	Wst	John	475	Bdf	John	201	Alb
Elizabeth	417	Fqr	Josiah	474	Bdf	John	630	Gls
Gilbert	519	Prw	Pamale	474	Bdf	John	703	Gch
Jack	239	Ldn	Mshane, Fran.	523	Mnn	Nehemiah	488	Frn
James	54	Chs	Mtgomery., Wm.	178	Elc	Rutha	467	Mdd
James	247	Ldn	Muck, Daniel	564	Frd	Thos.	444	Mth
Jno.	284	Frf	George	652	Mnt	William	489	Frn
Job	285	Frf	Ruscena	257	Shn	Wm.	758	Wsh
John	356	Fqr	Muckelwane, Thomas	478	Frn	see Mullis		
John	247	Ldn	Muckklewain, Antony	220	Pnd	Mullis, Ambris	758	Wsh
Jos.	258	Ldn	Mucklehang, Saml.	644	Btt	Ann	705	Gch
Jos.	305	Ldn	Mucklewain, Jno.	643	Btt	Multon, Wm.	820	Nrf
Js.	59	Chs	Mucklewane, John	611	Mnt	Muma, David	231	Shn
Mary	89	Spt	Mudd, Jno.	310	Ldn	Mumford, Edward	5	Pwn
Rodham	779	Wst	Ned	237	Ldn	Eliza.	210	Kng
Spencer	285	Frf	Muh see Micle			George	215	Pnd
Wm.	284	Frf	Muire, Catharine	172	Knq	Jacob, J.	215	Pnd
see Mosley, Moxly			James	170	Knq	Jacob, S.	215	Pnd
Moxly, Samuel	104	Spt	John	170	Knq	James	847	Sth
Moyan, Aaron	19	Oho	Richd., Snr.	170	Knq	Joseph	17	Rcm
Moyer, George	229	Shn	Wm.	664	Glc	Mathw.	153	Sth
George	846	Wth	Mulenix, Henry	59	Jff	Minor	334	Dnw
Jacob	712	Nls	Mulhall, Ians	598	Brk	Mumfort, Sally	879	Sth
Jacob	32	Rcm	Mulholland see Mcholland			Mummy, Christopher	677	Br
Jno.	526	Mnn	Mulinax, John	75	Jff	Mumpowar, Peter	704	Wsh
John	846	Wth	Mull, David	283	Ldn	Henry	704	Wsh
Michael	174	Shn	Wm.	439	Mth	Peter, Jur.	754	Wsh
Peter	846	Wth	Mullady, Thomas	756	Hmp	Muncas, Francis	855	Hnv
see Mayer			Mullen, Daniel	305	Ldn	Muncey, Holten	631	Gls
Moyers, Casper	16	Rcm	Isaac	226	Pnd	Jeremiah	630	Gls
Chrisley	208	Shn	John	911	Nrf	Luke	617	Mnt
Christian	200	Shn	John	216	Pnd	Tunas	631	Gls
Christiana	33	Rcm	John O.	810	Nrf	Willm.	617	Mnt
Christian	236	Shn	Joseph	709	Wsh	Zachariah	630	Gls
Conerod	166	Alb	Pheeby	216	Pnd	Muncy, Jesse	937	Hrr
Francis	844	Wth	Sarah	209	Kng	John	674	Br
Henry	33	Rcm	Thomas	523	Frd	Mundall, John	128	Sth
Henry	199	Shn	see Meuller			Joseph	874	Sth

Munday, Aaron	527	Prw	Murfee, Simon	875	Sth	Richd.	126	Sth
B.H.	202	Ess	Murfey, Bazel	761	Wsh	Samuel	511	Frd
Francis	197	Ess	John	473	Bdf	Thomas	680	Br
George	521	Prw	John, Sr.	472	Bdf	Thos.	643	Btt
Izabel	60	Clp	Larkin	519	Prw	Thos.	519	Mnn
James	203	Ess	Murkia, Jno.	15	Hnr	Thos.	831	Nrf
James	517	Prw	Murphee, Wills	140	Sth	Walter	783	Hmp
John	517	Prw	Murphey, Aaron	16	Rcm	William	793	Bck
Micajah	204	Ess	Anthy.	467	Pra	Wm.	509	Brk
Robert	517	Prw	Bayley	56	Clp	Wm.	562	Brk
William	526	Prw	Butler	475	Frn	Wm.	305	Rck
Wm. L.	59	Clp	Charles	396	Mds	Wm. [crossed out]	311	Rck
Munden, Anne	802	Nrf	Eleanor	410	Fqr	see Douglas, Mirphy, Muphy,		
James	468	Pra	Eliza	57	Clp	Murfey, Murpy		
Jno.	465	Pra	Hedgeman	41	Stf	Murpy, John	740	Wsh
John	802	Nrf	James	599	Mnr	Murrain, John	825	Bck
Nathan	468	Pra	James	713	Nls	Murray, Abraham	60	Clp
see Mundis, Murden			Jno. B.	58	Clp	Benjamin	914	Crl
Mundis, Betsey	25	Rcm	John	347	Fqr	Benjamin	11	Oho
Mundle, Michael	811	Hmp	John	220	Pnd	Charles	280	Frf
Munds, Elizabeth	653	Sss	Jonathan	58	Jff	David	190	Elc
Munford, Jas. H.	15	Ntt	Margaret	59	Clp	David S.	464	Pra
Wm.	5	Hnr	Miles	396	Mds	Elizabeth	524	Frd
Mungar, Henry	28	Rcm	Patrick	7	Knw	Fredk.	639	Btt
Henry, (Jr.)	35	Rcm	Thomas	232	Ldn	Geo.	912	Nrf
Henry, (sen.)	35	Rcm	Thomas	272	Ldn	George	467	Mdd
Mungle, Jacob	718	Wsh	Thos.	7	Knw	Isaac	466	Pra
Muniep, Peter	238	Shn	Tonly	272	Ldn	James	914	Crl
Munk, Thos.	59	Clp	Warren	653	Sss	James	60	Clp
Munles, William	3	Oho	William	629	Gls	James	242	Ldn
Munn, James	209	Shn	William	7	Knw	James	501	Prw
Munnett, Jeremiah	818	Hmp	Wm.	59	Clp	Jas.	641	Btt
Munns, Jas.	912	Nrf	Wm.	468	Pra	Jno. [2]	280	Frf
Munoe, George	281	Frf	Murphrey, Demsey	20	Isw	Jno.	295	Ldn
Munro, John	20	Oho	George	25	Isw	John	560	Frd
Munroe, ---	328	Dnw	Lemuel	20	Isw	John	467	Mdd
Andw.	285	Frf	Mary, Jun.	20	Isw	Johns	51	Stf
Jane	692	Br	Mary, Sen.	20	Isw	Lucy	15	Pwh
Jane	280	Frf	Michael	32	Isw	Mary	391	Fqr
Jno.	264	Ldn	Murphy, ---, & Crimp	22	Hnr	Mary	9	Rcm
John	281	Frf	Ann	912	Nrf	Matthew	203	Alb
Nancy	285	Frf	Burwell	126	Sth	Ralph	391	Fqr
Sarah	285	Frf	Catha.	563	Brk	Reuben	386	Fqr
Solomon	683	Br	Charlotte	818	Hmp	Saml. A.	442	Flv
Spence	281	Frf	Daniel	577	Frd	Samuel	302	Ldn
see Munoe			Danl.	1	Hnr	Thomas	515	Prw
Munrowe, George	406	Fqr	Dav.	525	Mnn	William	235	Aml
Hugh	342	Fqr	Edward	5	Oho	William	914	Crl
Munsel, Levi	429	Msn	Edwd. N.	826	Nrf	William	421	Fqr
Muntz, Jacob	15	Rcm	Elijah	306	Rck	Zach.	562	Brk
Muphy, Nat., 2nd	910	Nrf	Eliz.	526	Mnn	Murrel, Stephen	702	Gch
Murchead, George	926	Hrr	Ephrm	563	Brk	Murrell, James	873	Cmp
Murchland, James	694	Br	Harris	85	Spt	John	851	Cmp
John	698	Br	Horatio	580	Frd	Robert	874	Sth
William	694	Br	Hugh [2]	525	Mnn	Thomas	873	Cmp
Murdaugh, Josiah	128	Sth	James	911	Nrf	Thos., Jr.	873	Cmp
Murden, Adam	465	Pra	Jno.	640	Btt	William M.	946	Chc
Ann	909	Nrf	Jno.	911	Nrf	Murren, Daniel	804	Nrf
Daniel	467	Pra	Jno., Jr.	1	Hnr	Parker	829	Nrf
Henry	467	Pra	John	796	Hmp	Murrey, Edward	707	Wsh
James	466	Pra	John	819	Hmp	Richd.	370	Ags
Jeremiah	467	Pra	John	208	Kng	Robert	202	Alb
John	798	Nrf	John	271	Rck	Samuel	322	Ldn
John	803	Nrf	John	779	Wst	Murril, James	58	Chr
Jos.	798	Nrf	John, Ser.	1	Hnr	Murrill, Chr.	711	Nls
Malachi	465	Pra	Js.	524	Mnn	Jane	712	Nls
Malachi, (B.W.)	466	Pra	Levi	533	Frd	Thomas	712	Nls
Mary	466	Pra	Martin	521	Mnn	Wm.	755	Brn
Robert	798	Nrf	Mary	558	Brk	Wm.	711	Nls
Simon	464	Pra	Mary	795	Hmp	Murry, ---, Tompkins &	20	Hnr
Thos.	803	Nrf	Michael	474	Bdf	Abraham	396	Mds
Wm.	466	Pra	Michael	41	Rcm	Archd.	614	Mnt
see Munden			Milly	40	Stf	Chas.	519	Mnn
Murdoch, William	779	Wst	Murdoch	779	Wst	Henry	396	Mds
Murdock, Elijah	472	Bdf	Nancy	597	Frd	James	11	Isw
James	577	Mnr	Nat.	909	Nrf	James	33	Rcm
John	718	Wsh	Nixon	641	Btt	John	116	Cmb
Joseph	328	Dnw	Peter	208	Kng	John	643	Mnt
Mure, Sally	43	Acc	Philip	562	Brk	Leonard	845	Wth
Murehead, Andrew	627	Mnt	Richard	801	Bck	Mathew	326	Dnw

Name	Page	Loc
Nicholas	692	Br
Patrick	192	Shn
Peggy	34	Isw
Peggy	779	Wst
Reubin	166	Alb
Reubin	353	Lnc
Richard	95	Spt
Saml.	123	Hnr
Susanna	845	Wth
Thos.	891	Hnv
William	762	Nwk
Wilson	30	Isw
Murston, Robert N.	952	Chc
Murtle, Wm.	57	Clp
Muschett, Catharine	499	Prw
James	498	Prw
Muse, Alex P.	172	Knq
Charles	779	Wst
Elizabeth	467	Mdd
Elliott	279	Frf
Elliott	467	Mdd
James	207	Ess
James	210	Kng
James, Junr.	779	Wst
James, Senr.	779	Wst
Jessee A.	780	Wst
John	644	Btt
John	598	Frd
Lawrence	207	Ess
Lewis	825	Nrf
Margarett	66	Jff
Robert	598	Frd
Saml.	222	Ess
Thomas, Junr.	780	Wst
Thomas, Senr.	778	Wst
Thomas, Urbanna	467	Mdd
Thos., Younger	780	Wst
Walker	778	Wst
William	291	Amh
William, jr.	291	Amh
Museler, John	553	Brk
Musgrave, Dav., 2d.	521	Mnn
Musgrove, Benjamin	473	Bdf
Dav.	521	Mnn
Henry	650	Mnt
Henry, sr.	650	Mnt
Job	520	Mnn
Thos.	651	Mnt
Wm.	301	Ldn
see Muskrove		
Mushler, Jacob	557	Frd
Mushrow, Avarilla	831	Nrf
Musick, John	754	Wsh
Muskrove, James	14	Oho
Muslet, Adam	427	Rnd
Muslewhee, John	722	Wsh
Muslewhite, Worley	722	Wsh
Muss, George	595	Mnr
Mussell, William	879	Cmp
Musselman, Elizabeth	32	Stf
Henry	52	Stf
Mussen, James	441	Bth
Musser, Adam	739	Wsh
Adam	845	Wth
George	739	Wsh
Jacob	846	Wth
John	844	Wth
Peter	846	Wth
Musseter, Christian	597	Brk
Mussleman, David	184	Shn
John	184	Shn
Musslewhite, John	730	Wsh
Mustard, James	629	Gls
Muster, Anthony	444	Bth
Dorothy	444	Bth
Mustin, Henry	208	Kng
John	598	Frd
John	841	Nrf
Leonard	209	Kng
William	598	Frd
Mustlewhite, Mary	530	Prg
Musy see Mersy		
Muter, ---, & Stewart	2	Hnr
Mutherfar, George	286	Rck
Muthersfar, Philip	286	Rck
Muthersfrau see Mutherfar		
Mutlow, Zacheriah	762	Nwk
Mutter, Tho.	878	Yrk
Myars, Charles	416	Rnd
Henry	419	Rnd
John	430	Rnd
Peter	647	Mnt
Myeres, Andrew	430	Bth
Robert	417	Bth
William	417	Bth
Myers, ---, & Sons	911	Nrf
Adam	584	Brk
Adam	643	Btt
Ann	523	Mnn
Betsy	132	Hnr
Catharine	518	Frd
Charles	96	Spt
Coonrod	642	Btt
Elizabeth	305	Ldn
Francis	275	Rck
Fred.	520	Mnn
Geo.	568	Brk
Geo.	826	Nrf
George	642	Btt
George, Junr.	826	Hmp
George, Senr.	826	Hmp
Henry	522	Brk
Henry	586	Brk
Henry	639	Btt
Henry	694	Br
Henry	779	Hmp
Henry	907	Hrr
Isaac	311	Ldn
J.A.	33	Hnr
Jacob	585	Brk
Jacob	640	Btt
Jacob	705	Gch
Jacob	279	Ldn
Jacob	423	Msn
Jno. [2]	519	Mnn
Jno.	523	Mnn
Jno., Jr.	641	Btt
Jno., Sr.	641	Btt
Jno. H.	639	Btt
John	363	Ags
John	515	Brk
John	531	Brk
John	569	Brk
John	644	Btt
John	697	Br
John	326	Dnw
John	402	Fqr
John	482	Frn
John	506	Frd
John	564	Frd
John	566	Frd
John	907	Hrr
John, jr.	522	Brk
John, sr.	518	Brk
Jos.	518	Mnn
Jos.	819	Nrf
Joseph	310	Ldn
Joseph A.	35	Hnr
Joshua	518	Frd
Josiah	520	Frd
Judiah	24	Hnr
Lambert	300	Ldn
Mahlon	296	Ldn
Martin	772	Hmp
Mary	525	Mnn
Matthew [erased]	318	Ldn
Moses M.	23	Hnr
Peter	515	Frd
Peter	285	Ldn
Peter, Sr.	577	Brk
Saml.	23	Hnr
Solomon	509	Frd
Stephen	520	Frd
Tho.	353	Lnc
Thos.	815	Nrf
William	765	Hmp
Wm.	641	Btt
see M...ers, Myres		
Myes, Isaac	669	Mnt
Mynes see Myeres		
Myres, Geo.	403	Ags
M.A.	14	Hnr
Myrick, David	162	Sth
John	132	Sth
John	852	Sth
Lucy	654	Sss
Matthew	757	Brn
Owen	852	Sth
William	152	Sth
Myrill, George	110	Acc
Joseph	113	Acc
Myrrah, Sally	705	Gch
Myrs, Abram	934	Hrr
Barnett	963	Hrr
Myse, James	648	Mnt
Mysick, James	113	Acc
Lucy	848	Sth
Mytinger, Daniel	519	Frd
Isaac	518	Frd

--- N ---

Name	Page	Loc
N..., ...	475	Bdf
...	476	Bdf
James	839	Bck
N...ance, Thomas	156	Dnw
N...ew, William	156	Dnw
N...ps, Andrew	209	Shn
Nabone, Matt.	913	Nrf
Nace, Jacob	645	Btt
Jacob	102	Jff
Jno.	645	Btt
Mary	87	Jff
Peter	274	Rck
Nadenboush, Philip	596	Brk
Nadenbush, Henry	523	Brk
Nadler, Andrew	526	Brk
Nafe, George	545	Brk
Nail, John	218	Pnd
Michael	951	Hrr
Nicholas	243	Shn
Peter	179	Shn
Philip	181	Shn
William	179	Shn
Nailer, Benjamin	205	Alb
Edward	204	Alb
Thomas	204	Alb
Naimeson, James	581	Brk
Naler, Thompson	287	Frf
Naley, Jno.	718	Nls
Nalle, Francis	62	Clp
Jesse	62	Clp
Judah	61	Clp
Larkin G.	61	Clp
Martin	61	Clp
Wm.	62	Clp
Nalley, Aaron	286	Frf
Bennett	718	Nls
Elkannah	286	Frf
Hezekiah	393	Frf
Jesse	400	Fqr
Moses	167	Alb
William	167	Alb
Nalls, Elizabeth	378	Fqr
William	374	Fqr
Nally, Sarah	518	Prw
Nance, Ann	945	Chc
Cambel	59	Chr

Isham	453	Grn	Christley	31	Rcm	see Wears		
James	947	Chc	David	474	Frn	Nease, George	238	Shn
Mary	475	Bdf	Isaac	477	Frn	Jacob	236	Shn
Nathl.	155	Dnw	Jacob	474	Frn	Joseph	236	Shn
Rissy	951	Chc	John	646	Btt	Neasom, Eppa. L.	392	Rch
Tavner	353	Lnn	John	23	Rcm	William	392	Rch
Thomas	453	Grn	Matthias	31	Rcm	Neathers, Jno.	62	Clp
Zacariah	946	Chc	Michael	21	Rcm	Nebeker, William	916	Crl
see N...ance			Navell, Henry	547	Frd	Nedley, Js.	527	Mnn
Nann, Moses	172	Knq	Nawsworthy, Jos.	155	Dnw	Needes, Nat	526	Mnn
Nanney, Abel	758	Brn	Nay, Benj.	965	Hrr	Needham, Caleb	301	Ldn
Drury	758	Brn	Jacob	956	Hrr	John	188	Elc
Tabitha	758	Brn	Jacob	965	Hrr	Needler, George	770	Hmp
Wyatt	758	Brn	John	963	Hrr	Needley, Jacob	510	Brk
Nanno, Jno.	913	Nrf	Vincent	62	Clp	Needlins, Peter	509	Brk
Naper, Archer	494	Frn	William	965	Hrr	Neeise, Jacob	718	Nls
Ashford	461	Frn	Naylor, Richd.	27	Hnr	Neel, Daniel	715	Wsh
Elizabeth	455	Frn	William	757	Hmp	J.	929	Hrr
John	491	Frn	Nazlerad, Freadericke	215	Pnd	Rebecca	62	Jff
Talton	455	Frn	Neagley, George	223	Pnd	Saml.	750	Wsh
Thomas	455	Frn	Neail, Joseph	35	Hnr	Walter	958	Hrr
Napier, Benjamin W.	443	Flv	Neake, Adam	194	Shn	Wm.	721	Wsh
Elizabeth [2]	438	Flv	Neal, Archer, jr.	233	Aml	see McNeel, Neal, Neely,		
John	439	Flv	Archer, Sr.	233	Aml	Neil, Neill, Neille		
Mary	632	Gls	Charles	14	Knw	Neeley, John	632	Gls
Patrick	632	Gls	Darlus	966	Hrr	Neely, Charles	715	Wsh
Rena	706	Gch	Geo.	258	Ldn	Hugh	700	Wsh
William P.	916	Crl	George	15	Wod	John	632	Gls
Napper, Archd.	652	Mnt	Henry	105	Spt	Robert	700	Wsh
Charles, (F Black)	475	Bdf	Jacob	475	Bdf	William M.	4	Knw
Fortunatus	167	Alb	James	243	Ldn	see Neel		
Mary	167	Alb	James	991	Nrt	Neer, Henry	6	Rcm
Nappier, James	167	Alb	James	1	Wod	James	70	Jff
Narsworthy, Ellis	5	Isw	John	233	Aml	John	41	Rcm
Joseph	30	Isw	John	928	Hrr	Martin, (Jr.)	6	Rcm
Thompson	30	Isw	John	6	Knw	Martin, (sen.)	6	Rcm
Narvill, Peyton	499	Prw	John	353	Lnn	Samuel	79	Jff
Nash, ---	328	Dnw	John	16	Wod	Neet see Neer		
Abner	580	Prw	John L.	916	Crl	Neetar, James	961	Hrr
Abner, Jr.	580	Pre	Kenneth	665	Glc	John	961	Hrr
Benjamin	129	Hnr	Laban	580	Pre	Neff, Abraham, Junr.	194	Shn
Betsey	717	Nls	Mary	692	Br	Abraham, Senr.	194	Shn
Cabeb	809	Nrf	Mary Ann	59	Chr	Chrisley	194	Shn
Chas.	808	Nrf	Matthew	991	Nrt	Christian	10	Oho
Cornelius	791	Nrf	Richard	3	Wod	David	194	Shn
Daniel	717	Nls	Rodham	991	Nrt	Francis	537	Frd
Emly	332	Dnw	Samuel	8	Knw	Francis	194	Shn
Fanny	408	Rch	Sarah	1	Hnr	George	820	Hmp
Geo.	268	Ldn	Thomas	991	Nrt	Henry	10	Oho
George	780	Wst	Thomas, New Port	16	Wod	Henry	194	Shn
James	59	Chr	Thos.	758	Brn	Jacob	194	Shn
James	406	Rch	W.S.	296	Ldn	James	600	Frd
James	780	Wst	Walter	680	Br	John	557	Frd
James	781	Wst	Wm.	335	Dnw	John	10	Oho
Jno.	61	Chs	Wm.	290	Ldn	John	30	Rcm
John	833	Nrf	Wm.	15	Ntt	John	194	Shn
John	991	Nrt	Wm., Jr.	645	Btt	John	196	Shn
John	580	Pre	see Neail, Neale, Neel, Veal			Martin	539	Frd
John	500	Prw	Neale, Daniel	286	Frf	Negar, Michael	854	Cmp
John	37	Stf	James	359	Fqr	Negley, Harry	123	Hnr
John	781	Wst	John	363	Fqr	Jacob	131	Hnr
John T.	353	Lnn	John	781	Wst	Neighberger, Jacob	256	Shn
Nancy	397	Rch	Joseph	394	Fqr	Neighbors, Abraham	807	Bck
Paul	328	Dnw	Joseph	402	Fqr	Isaac	775	Bck
Robert	875	Cmp	Matthew	374	Fqr	Jas.	646	Btt
Rubin	851	Hnv	Presley	780	Wst	John	817	Bck
Soloman	851	Hnv	Rodham	781	Wst	Nathan	817	Bck
Thomas	58	Chr	Neallie, Loranna	7	Oho	Neighbours, Dorratha	475	Bdf
Thomas	103	Cmb	Nealy, James	526	Mnn	John	59	Chr
Thomas	717	Nls	Neams, William	275	Amh	William	59	Chr
Thos., Jr.	808	Nrf	Near, Cunrod	266	Ldn	William	580	Pre
Traverse	379	Fqr	Cunrod, J.	266	Ldn	William, Snr.	59	Chr
William	781	Wst	David	265	Ldn	Wm.	408	Ags
Wim.	863	Hnv	David	266	Ldn	Neigt, Jacob	582	Brk
Wm., jr.	791	Nrf	David	267	Ldn	Neil, Bartholomew	715	Wsh
Wm., Sr.	822	Nrf	Henry	266	Ldn	John	573	Mnr
Nasler, Boston	632	Gls	Jno. [2]	265	Ldn	Mary	304	Rck
Natt, Daniel	45	Acc	Jno.	266	Ldn	Stothard	268	Rck
Natts, Edmund	45	Acc	Nathaiel	266	Ldn	Neile, William	596	Mnr
Nave, Adam	21	Rcm	Wm.	268	Rck	Wm.	578	Mnr

Name	No.	Co.	Name	No.	Co.	Name	No.	Co.
Neiley, William	786	Hmp	Matthias	572	Frd	Benjm.	957	Chc
Neill, Abraham	521	Frd	Mycajah	958	Chc	Bolling	655	Sss
Ann	512	Frd	Nancy	45	Acc	George C.	172	Knq
Charles	590	Mnr	Nathaniel	682	Br	Henry	811	Hmp
Jacob	555	Frd	Nathl., Botetourt	665	Glc	James	233	Aml
John	586	Mnr	Peter	897	Hnv	James W.	951	Chc
Lewis	532	Frd	Philip	559	Frd	Jesse	947	Chc
Lewis	537	Frd	Polly	548	Prg	John	371	Ags
Lewis, 1st.	551	Frd	Ralph	773	Hmp	John	122	Hnr
Owen	583	Mnr	Reason	736	Wsh	Joseph	128	Hnr
Richd.	594	Mnr	Rebecca	913	Nrf	Mary	944	Chc
Robert	577	Mnr	Robert	80	Jff	William	944	Chc
Thomas	537	Frd	Robt.	130	Hnr	William	464	Frn
Thomas	550	Frd	Ruth	806	Hmp	see N...ew		
Thomas	822	Hmp	Saml.	706	Gch	Newal, Hibert	422	Rnd
Thomas, 3rd.	63	Jff	Thomas	10	Ntt	Newall, Amos	212	Ess
Walter	590	Mnr	Thomas, Senr.	380	Fqr	Thos.	645	Btt
Winfried	599	Mnr	Thos.	371	Ags	Newbanks, James	761	Hmp
Neille, Wm.	584	Mnr	Thos.	898	Hnv	John	771	Hmp
Neillis, Thomas	5	Oho	Thos.	4	Hnr	John	779	Hmp
Neilson, Job	5	Pwh	William	117	Acc	Moses	570	Frd
John	5	Oho	William	286	Frf	John	761	Hmp
John, Jr.	5	Oho	William	510	Prw	Newbell, Grace	353	Lnn
Neil	14	Hnr	William	781	Wst	Hennery	353	Lnn
Robt.	21	Hnr	William V.	117	Acc	Nathanl.	213	Ess
Thomas, & Co.	332	Dnw	Wim.	898	Hnv	Wm.	214	Ess
Neimon, A. Hanna	408	Ags	Wim. R.	893	Hnv	Newberry, John	568	Brk
Neley, John	942	Hrr	York, of Color	585	Mnr	Samuel	847	Wth
Nelly, fch	913	Nrf	Nelums, Charles	476	Bdf	Newbey, John	5	Isw
Nelms, Aaron	991	Nrt	Neman, Solomon	5	Isw	Newbill, Jno., jr.	172	Knq
Edwin	991	Nrt	Nemme, Joseph	791	Nrf	John, Senr.	172	Knq
Harris	469	Pra	Nemned, Gersham	811	Nrf	John G.	452	Frn
Peter	990	Nrt	Nemore, Robert	167	Alb	Mary	172	Knq
William	991	Nrt	Nemric, John	5	Rcm	Nathaniel	452	Frn
William B.	991	Nrt	Nephews, John	293	Rck	Peter	211	Ess
see Knelms			Nepton, Henry	526	Mnn	Thomas	172	Knq
Nelson, Alexr.	370	Ags	Nergmier, Nathl.	913	Nrf	Newbrough, Jno.	526	Mnn
Alexr.	302	Rck	Nesbet see Nizbitt			Jos.	526	Mnn
Alexr., Esqr.	371	Ags	Nesbit, Jane	419	Bth	Joshua	512	Frd
Amelia	510	Prw	Margt.	295	Rck	William	539	Frd
Andrew	99	Cmb	Neseley, Jacob	243	Shn	Newburn, Fanny	133	Hnr
Ann	613	Srr	Nesewander, Abram	632	Gls	Thos.	665	Glc
Benjamin	33	Isw	Jacob	632	Gls	Newbury, William	490	Frn
Betsey	45	Acc	see Neswander			Newby, Betsy	355	Lnc
Catherine	80	Jff	Nesley, Jacob	743	Wsh	Cyrus	354	Lnc
David	469	Pra	George	935	Hrr	David	74	Spt
Edward	869	Hnv	Nesselroad, John	430	Msn	Edwd.	62	Clp
Eleanor	513	Prw	Nestell, ---, Dr.	913	Nrf	Elisha	59	Chs
Eza	369	Fqr	Nester, Frederick	625	Mnt	Jacob, F.N.	656	Sss
Ezekiel	847	Wth	George	429	Rnd	James	110	Spt
Frances, (Y)	879	Yrk	Jacob	648	Mnt	Jesse	233	Aml
Francis	876	Nrf	Jacob	428	Rnd	Jno.	355	Lnc
Frank	29	Hnr	Nestor, Geo.	913	Nrf	Joseph, (F.N.)	20	Isw
George	116	Acc	Neswander, David	632	Gls	Joseph, F.N.	656	Sss
George	117	Acc	see Nesewander			Levy	63	Chs
George	362	Fqr	Netherland, Jane	6	Pwh	Nathl.	56	Chs
Henry	580	Pre	Littleby.	5	Pwh	Peter	855	Sth
Hugh	205	Alb	Richard	5	Pwh	Pritchard, & Co.	62	Clp
Isaac	221	Pnd	Nettle, Abraham	569	Mnr	William	573	Frd
James	344	Fqr	Nettles, Vecaries	187	Elc	Wm.	59	Chs
James	772	Hmp	Wm.	119	Hnr	Wm.	354	Lnc
James	591	Mnr	Neuchum, Lance	167	Alb	Newchum, Hannah	204	Alb
James, Junr.	772	Hmp	Neucummer, Jacob	296	Rck	John	204	Alb
Jno.	287	Frf	Neuley see Niceley			see Neuchum		
John	45	Acc	Neuton, James	288	Rck	Newchurch, John	847	Wth
John	645	Btt	Nevel, Lewis	797	Bck	Newcomb, Ann	172	Knq
John	407	Fqr	Nevell, Willis	4	Isw	Benja.	172	Knq
John	30	Isw	Nevil, Jas.	645	Btt	Bowden	665	Glc
John	71	Spt	Neiley	718	Nls	Elisha	550	Prg
John	31	Stf	Zachariah	718	Nls	Francis	468	Mdd
John G.	421	Msn	see Navell, Nvel			Mary	172	Knq
Jonas	578	Frd	Nevill, Thomas	259	Amh	James	59	Chr
Joseph	67	Spt	Nevils, George	59	Chr	Jesse	810	Nrf
Judith	7	Hnr	Nevison, Jno.	913	Nrf	Jno.	172	Knq
Judith	472	Mdd	Jno., [his] (Plantn.)	469	Pra	John, Junr.	59	Chr
Lucy, (Y)	879	Yrk	Nevitt, Isaac	552	Frd	John, Snr.	59	Chr
Mary	683	Br	James	12	Oho	Joseph	172	Knq
Mary	131	Cmb	James, Jr.	12	Oho	Usley	68	Chr
Mary	359	Fqr	New, Armstead	946	Chc	William	172	Knq
Mary	781	Wst	Benjamin	122	Hnr	Wm.	665	Glc

Newcombs, Elisha	781	Wst	James	286	Frf	Charles	128	Cmb
Margaret	991	Nrt	James	523	Prw	Charles	140	Sth
Newcomer, Jacob	99	Jff	James	781	Wst	Geo.	913	Nrf
Newcumer, Jno.	264	Rck	Jas., & Son	646	Btt	Henry	916	Crl
Newel, Joseph	964	Hrr	Jenny	118	Hnr	Henry	96	Spt
Newell, ---, Mrs.	332	Dnw	Jesse	289	Ldn	Henry, jr.	96	Spt
Benja.	532	Prg	Jno.	645	Btt	Hosea	850	Sth
Catharine	834	Nrf	Jno.	61	Clp	Isaac	916	Crl
Isham	328	Dnw	Jno.	286	Frf	Isaac	411	Rch
James	418	Bth	John	590	Frd	Isaac	60	Stf
James	538	Prg	John	595	Frd	Jas., Sr.	645	Btt
James, Junr.	847	Wth	John	11	Isw	Jessee	916	Crl
James, Senr.	847	Wth	John	626	Mnt	Jno.	665	Glc
Jas.	469	Pra	John	781	Wst	Jno.	305	Ldn
Robert	221	Shn	Jonan., Jr.	645	Btt	Jo., Jr.	645	Btt
Samuel	209	Shn	Jonathan	612	Btt	John	809	Bck
Thomas	221	Shn	Joseph	286	Frf	John	127	Cmb
Thomas, Jr.	208	Shn	Joshua	818	Hmp	Joseph	804	Bck
Thomas, Sr.	531	Prg	Martha, (Y)	879	Yrk	Joseph	288	Ldn
Thos., jr.	531	Prg	Mary	803	Nrf	Judith	303	Ldn
William	532	Prg	Musco	398	Mds	Martha	913	Nrf
Newgant, William	537	Prg	Rachel	254	Shn	Mary	87	Spt
Newgen, John	3	Knw	Reuben	2	Rcm	Richard	486	Frn
Polley	475	Bdf	Reuben	196	Shn	Robert	295	Ldn
Newgent, Rawligh	408	Rch	Richard	522	Prw	Shad.	850	Sth
Sally	334	Dnw	Robert	504	Brk	Thomas	676	Br
Tho.	354	Lnc	Robt.	6	Isw	Thomas	60	Stf
Newham, James	519	Frd	Samuel	197	Shn	Thos.	820	Nrf
Newhouse, Anne	378	Fqr	Stacey	289	Ldn	Thos.	913	Nrf
Benjamin	680	Br	Thomas	12	Isw	Thos., jr.	809	Nrf
Henry	2	Knw	Thomas	523	Prw	William	779	Bck
Isaac	704	Wsh	Thomas	781	Wst	Willoughby	780	Wst
James	684	Br	Thomas, Jr.	522	Prw	Wm.	62	Clp
James	752	Wsh	Thomas J.	523	Prw	Wm.	820	Nrf
James	759	Wsh	Walter	420	Msn	Wm.	139	Sth
John	751	Wsh	Walter	196	Shn	see Cox, Newlon, Newlor		
Jonathan	301	Ldn	Walter	847	Wth	Nibblet, Frances	656	Sss
Michael	3	Knw	Wm.	370	Ags	Polly	655	Sss
William	682	Br	Wm.	288	Ldn	William H.	655	Sss
Ziba	369	Fqr	Wm. H.	398	Mds	Niberger, Chrsn.	526	Mnn
Newkirk, George	550	Brk	Newmans, ---, Messrs.	434	Msn	Nible, Jacob	42	Rcm
Newland, Isaac	11	Oho	Newonger see Neswander, Ni-			John	42	Rcm
John	556	Frd	wonger			Niblet, Nathaniel	10	Ntt
John	200	Shn	Newsam, Barham	724	Brn	Thomas	461	Frn
John	847	Wth	Baxter	724	Brn	William	461	Frn
Mark	2	Rcm	Robert	334	Dnw	Niblett, Janes	353	Lnn
Newley, Wm., Christians-			Newsom, Aaron	769	Brn	Martha	533	Prg
burg	618	Mnt	Anthony	873	Sth	Sterling	353	Lnn
Newlin, Geo.	273	Ldn	David	126	Sth	Nice, Jacob	645	Btt
James	273	Ldn	David	153	Sth	Niceley, Anthony	301	Amh
John	239	Ldn	Isham	150	Sth	Saml.	301	Amh
Nicholas	776	Hmp	James	150	Sth	Nicely, Anthony	17	Rcm
Wm.	945	Hrr	Joel	153	Sth	Barbara	17	Rcm
Wm.	261	Ldn	John [2]	149	Sth	David	17	Rcm
Newlon, John	475	Bdf	Nathl.	850	Sth	George	646	Btt
William	397	Fqr	Randolph	875	Sth	Henry	646	Btt
Newlor, Lige	929	Hrr	Sally	868	Sth	Henry	98	Jff
Tham	929	Hrr	Thomas	148	Sth	Jacob	17	Rcm
Newman, Abner	559	Frd	Turner	150	Sth	Jacob, Jr.	646	Btt
Adam	475	Bdf	William	849	Sth	Jacob, Sr.	645	Btt
Alexander	398	Mds	William, Ra.	148	Sth	Michl.	646	Btt
Alexander	15	Rcm	Wm.	870	Sth	Nicewander, Henry	22	Rcm
Andrew	15	Rcm	see Newsam, Newsum			Isaac	19	Rcm
Arthur	475	Bdf	Newson see Newsom			Nicewanger, Christian ["g" may be		
Benjamin	196	Shn	Newstep, Rachel, (W)	879	Yrk	written over a "d"]	38	Rcm
Catharine	118	Hnr	Newsum, Benjamin	613	Srr	Nicewonger, Jacob	688	Br
Dannis	781	Wst	Caty	613	Srr	Nicholas, Francis	225	Pnd
Dorothy	758	Brn	Charles	655	Sss	George	423	Rnd
Edwd.	913	Nrf	Charles S.	655	Sss	Henry	224	Pnd
Eligah	793	Hmp	David [2]	655	Sss	Jacob	10	Rcm
Eliza.	233	Aml	Jack	327	Dnw	John	45	Acc
Francis	781	Wst	Jack	330	Dnw	John	204	Alb
Geo.	286	Frf	Joel	613	Srr	John	758	Brn
George	398	Mds	Littleberry	613	Srr	John, Senr.	155	Dnw
George	398	Rch	Sarah	655	Sss	Leven	417	Rnd
George	847	Wth	William	326	Dnw	Martha	837	Bck
Hannah	595	Frd	William	172	Knq	Michael	62	Clp
Henry	475	Bdf	Wm.	469	Pra	N.	32	Hnr
Henry	246	Ldn	Newton, Benjamin	60	Stf	Nathl.	469	Pra
James	916	Crl	Charles	119	Cmb	Peter	36	Rcm

Ransom	847	Wth	Brid.	355	Lnc	Nimms, Jno.	469	Pra
Scipio A.	30	Stf	John, a free mulatto	990	Nrt	John	475	Bdf
Wilson C.	807	Bck	Richd.	355	Lnc	Robert	476	Bdf
Nicholass, Lewis	167	Alb	Nickens, James, Jr.,			Robert, Sr.	475	Bdf
Wilson C.	167	Alb	(F. Negroe)	368	Fqr	Nine, Chrisn.	527	Mnn
Nicholes, James	6	Knw	James, Sr. (F. Ne-			Nininger, Christn.	645	Btt
John	12	Knw	groe)	368	Fqr	Nisbet, Robt.	21	Hnr
Leonard	12	Knw	Nickes, David	596	Frd	Nise, George	25	Oho
Soph.	8	Knw	Nickey, Saml.	371	Ags	Phillp	24	Oho
Nicholls, Zach.	822	Nrf	Nicking, Abraham	408	Rch	Nisewander see Nesewander		
Nichols, ...	475	Bdf	Suckey	408	Rch	Nisewanger, Jacob	223	Shn
Alexr.	801	Nrf	Nickins, Benjamin	506	Prw	John	233	Shn
Amos	521	Brk	Daniel	506	Prw	Niswander, Abraham	564	Frd
Archer	475	Bdf	James	507	Prw	John	603	Frd
Elisha	475	Bdf	Wm.	198	Ess	Niswanger, Catharine	265	Ldn
Evan	276	Ldn	Nickle, Andrew	575	Mnr	Jno.	646	Btt
Frances	793	Nrf	Andrew	591	Mnr	Jno.	265	Ldn
Geo.	271	Ldn	Andrew, jr.	596	Mnr	Nives, Daniel	655	Sss
Humphry	710	Wsh	Francies	587	Mnr	Niwonger, Chris.	232	Ldn
Isaac [2]	276	Ldn	George	599	Mnr	Nixon, Benj.	960	Hrr
Isaac	314	Ldn	Isaac	597	Mnr	George	779	Hmp
Jacob	260	Ldn	James	591	Mnr	Hugh	23	Oho
James	475	Bdf	John	586	Mnr	Hughe	790	Bck
James	270	Ldn	John [2]	591	Mnr	James	27	Hnr
James B.	286	Frf	John	598	Mnr	John	787	Hmp
Jesse	475	Bdf	Robert	576	Mnr	Jonathan	810	Hmp
Jesse	829	Nrf	Nickles, John	371	Ags	Jonathan	279	Ldn
John	521	Brk	Nicklin, Jno.	526	Mnn	Letty	549	Prg
John	166	Shn	Jos.	62	Clp	Margte	913	Nrf
John	174	Shn	Martha	538	Frd	Randolph	778	Bck
John, Sr.	475	Bdf	Nickodemus, Henry	222	Shn	Rhoda	18	Oho
John, Sr.	792	Nrf	Nickols, Aron	398	Mds	Royal	811	Bck
John W.	792	Nrf	Benjamin	398	Mds	Samuel	536	Prg
Joshua	806	Nrf	Edwin	398	Mds	Thos.	836	Nrf
Josiah	799	Nrf	Elijah	527	Mnn	William	780	Bck
Levan	425	Bth	John	398	Mds	William	775	Hmp
Mary	396	Fqr	Phil.	527	Mnn	Williem	23	Oho
Mathias	710	Wsh	Shadrach	398	Mds	Nixson, Geo.	279	Ldn
Matthias	8	Oho	Thomas	398	Mds	George	907	Hrr
Nathan	270	Ldn	William	398	Mds	Isaac	288	Ldn
Nathan	272	Ldn	Nickolson, John	132	Hnr	James	281	Ldn
Pamelia	694	Br	Nicks, Jos.	839	Nrf	Jesse	907	Hrr
Philpot	475	Bdf	Nickson, James	102	Jff	Jno.	293	Ldn
Rebecca	4	Oho	Nicol, Michael	61	Clp	Joel	294	Ldn
Saml.	276	Ldn	Nicolan, James	377	Fqr	Robert	908	Hrr
Saml.	799	Nrf	Nicols, John	955	Hrr	Sanco	307	Ldn
Saml.	913	Nrf	Richard	14	Wod	Sarah	908	Hrr
Samuel	259	Ldn	Thomas	14	Wod	Wm.	281	Ldn
Sanl.	276	Ldn	Nicolson, ---, Mrs.	34	Hnr	Nizbitt, James	504	Prw
Sevithin	276	Ldn	Eliza., (Y)	879	Yrk	Noakes, Gilbert	514	Frd
Stephen, Sr.	801	Nrf	Geo. D., Urbanna	468	Mdd	Priscilla	507	Frd
Thos.	269	Ldn	John	17	Hnr	Thomas	516	Frd
William	441	Bth	Margt.	25	Hnr	Noble, Alexander	725	Brn
William	684	Br	Nidey, Adam	632	Gls	Cisseah	759	Wsh
William, jr.	475	Bdf	David	632	Gls	Geo.	262	Ldn
William, Sr.	475	Bdf	Peter	632	Gls	James	370	Ags
Wm.	14	Knw	Niedy, Abraham	645	Btt	James	210	Shn
Wm.	316	Ldn	George	646	Btt	John	233	Aml
Nicholson, Buckner	655	Sss	John	646	Btt	Joseph	233	Aml
Chas.	138	Sth	Niell see Null			Joseph	526	Frd
Cheas.	152	Sth	Niesley, John	687	Br	Josiah	14	Ntt
Eliza.	188	Elc	Nigh, Benjamin	1	Rcm	Mary Ann	586	Frd
Geo.	912	Nrf	Nighburt, Thos.	645	Btt	Thomas	513	Prw
Howell	129	Sth	Night, Baly	915	Hrr	Thomas	522	Prw
Howell	655	Sss	Christopher	949	Hrr	William	126	Hnr
John	129	Sth	George	609	Mnt	Nobles, Joshua	475	Bdf
John	655	Sss	John	646	Btt	Mark	63	Chs
Joseph	287	Frf	William	287	Frf	Noblet, J.M.	913	Nrf
Lydia	655	Sss	see Neigt			Noblin, Saml.	681	Wrw
Robt.	12	Isw	Nighten, Peggy	916	Crl	Nock, Benjamin	116	Acc
Robt.	876	Sth	Nightingal, James	991	Nrt	Betsey, of R	45	Acc
Stith	138	Sth	Nihiser, Chrisley	205	Shn	Charles	117	Acc
Tho. L.	189	Elc	Nikle, Mathias	725	Wsh	Edward	45	Acc
Thomas	836	Hmp	Niler, Eleanor	14	Knw	Elijah	116	Acc
Thos.	791	Nrf	Nimmo, Gershm.	912	Nrf	George	45	Acc
Wm.	838	Nrf	James	580	Pre	James	45	Acc
Nick, Wm.	277	Rck	Js.	912	Nrf	John	45	Acc
Nickel, Jacob	69	Jff	Wm. J.	469	Pra	John, shif.	116	Acc
Nicken, Amos, a free			Wm. T.	469	Pra	Littleton [2]	116	Acc
mulatto	990	Nrt	see Nemned			Samuel	45	Acc

Soloman	45	Acc
Spencer	117	Acc
William, Junr.	116	Acc
William, Senr.	117	Acc
Noe, Nancy	96	Spt
Noel, Alfred	105	Spt
Alick	200	Ess
Barbary	302	Amh
Betty	196	Ess
Caleb	196	Ess
Carnelius, Sr.	475	Bdf
Cornelius, jr.	475	Bdf
Edwin	203	Ess
Frederick	468	Mdd
James	475	Bdf
Jesse	475	Bdf
John	916	Crl
John	276	Rck
Oswald	196	Ess
Philip	172	Knq
Reuben	196	Ess
Simon M.	475	Bdf
Spencer	201	Ess
Talbert	267	Amh
Theodk.	204	Ess
Thomas	475	Bdf
Thomas	378	Fqr
Thompson	268	Amh
William	267	Amh
Wm., jr.	201	Ess
Wm., Sr.	197	Ess
Noell, Edmond	446	Flv
John	446	Flv
Poindexter	444	Flv
Robt.	444	Flv
Saml.	439	Flv
Noftsinger, David	645	Btt
Jacob	646	Btt
Josh.	646	Btt
Peter	646	Btt
Saml.	645	Btt
Nokes, Elisebeth	759	Wsh
see Noakes		
Nolan, Thomas	916	Crl
Noland, Charles, Jr.	287	Frf
Charles, Senr.	286	Frf
Gregory	239	Ldn
Henry	542	Frd
James	514	Prw
James	24	Rcm
Jno.	527	Mnn
Mima	368	Fqr
Nancy	520	Frd
Obed	555	Brk
Philip	555	Brk
Philip	521	Prw
Pierce	556	Frd
Thos.	555	Brk
Thos.	291	Ldn
William	555	Brk
William	520	Frd
Wm.	291	Ldn
Wm.	325	Ldn
Nolley, Josiah	724	Brn
Nehemiah	724	Brn
Thos.	724	Brn
Nolnor, Henry	328	Dnw
Nonnan see Norman		
Nooc, Zephaniah	61	Clp
Noomar see Novmar		
Noor, John B.	398	Mds
Noose see Nuse		
Nopsinger, Thomas	103	Jff
Norbourn, Mary	26	Hnr
Norcut, Ellen	816	Nrf
Norcutt, Daniel	301	Amh
Nordich, Barnigah	744	Wsh
Norfleet, Aaron	850	Sth
Norfolk, Ellender	578	Frd
Thomas	578	Frd
Norford, Joseph	19	Rcm
Noris, John	933	Hrr
Norma, Clemment	939	Hrr
Normam, Delpha, Mulo.	172	Knq
Norman, Absolom	62	Clp
Baly	939	Hrr
Bazil	569	Frd
Betty	575	Frd
Charles	862	Hnv
Courtney	61	Clp
Edward	511	Prw
Edward	22	Stf
Elizabeth	515	Prw
Elizabeth	54	Stf
Isaac	61	Clp
Isaac	291	Rck
James	770	Hmp
James	429	Rnd
Jno.	62	Clp
Jno.	172	Knq
John B.	34	Stf
Joseph	62	Clp
Mary	62	Clp
Matthew	22	Stf
Thomas	991	Nrt
Thos.	61	Clp
William	511	Prw
Wm.	62	Clp
Norment, John	916	Crl
Joseph	916	Crl
Nancy	916	Crl
Nathaniel	916	Crl
Normin, Jams	966	Hrr
Normon, John, [his]		
Est.	210	Kng
Norrel, James	646	Btt
Thos.	706	Gch
Norrell, John	353	Lnn
Thos.	11	Hnr
Young	646	Btt
Norris, Amy	469	Pra
Ann	355	Lnc
Benj.	17	Hnr
Bernard	290	Ldn
Beverly	414	Bth
Daniel	439	Flv
Dav.	527	Mnn
David	172	Knq
Eliza.	355	Lnc
Elizabeth	418	Fqr
Epa.	354	Lnc
Geo.	527	Mnn
Geo.	469	Pra
George H.	587	Frd
Ignatius	303	Ldn
Jas.	354	Lnc
Jas.	469	Pra
Jas., Jr.	354	Lnc
Jno.	913	Nrf
Joseph	418	Fqr
Joseph	540	Frd
Lucinda J.	286	Frf
Luke	613	Srr
Richard	680	Br
Richard	123	Hnr
Richd.	61	Clp
Samuel	387	Fqr
Samuel	428	Rnd
Sowell	469	Pra
Thaddeus	421	Fqr
Thaddeus, ([his] Quarter)	419	Fqr
Thomas	172	Knq
William	204	Alb
William	991	Nrt
Wm.	527	Mnn
Wm.	469	Pra
Norriss, Joseph	904	Hrr
Thomas	128	Cmb
Norstedler, Adam S.	326	Dnw
Norsworthy, John	845	Sth
North, Abraham	156	Dnw
Anthony	817	Bck
Anthony	106	Cmb
Anthony	155	Dnw
Anthony, Jur.	59	Chr
Anthony, Senr.	70	Chr
David	475	Bdf
Edward	405	Fqr
George	56	Jff
Jno.	10	Ntt
John	475	Bdf
John	155	Dnw
John	3	Hnr
Margaret	371	Ags
Peter	776	Bck
Rd.	67	Chs
Richard	780	Bck
Richard	58	Chr
Sarah	156	Dnw
Thomas	58	Chr
Thomas	105	Cmb
William	475	Bdf
William	106	Cmb
William	580	Pre
Northam, Custis	116	Acc
Jacob	116	Acc
Rebeca	116	Acc
Southey	117	Acc
William, Junr.	116	Acc
William, Sen.	116	Acc
Northcraft, Edward	171	Shn
Northcross, Frederick	655	Sss
Thomas	655	Sss
William	655	Sss
Northen, Edmond	393	Rch
Edward J.	391	Rch
James	394	Rch
Peter	411	Rch
William	398	Rch
Northern, Edwd.	913	Nrf
Geo.	833	Nrf
Jonathan	591	Frd
Minty	540	Frd
William	591	Frd
Norton, Alexr.	273	Ldn
George	756	Wsh
George, Senr.	757	Wsh
Jane	665	Glc
Jno.	665	Glc
Nancy	330	Dnw
Nat.	238	Ldn
Sarah	335	Dnw
William	468	Mdd
Nortow, Billey	326	Dnw
Norvel, Jno.	860	Hnv
Wim.	848	Hnv
Norvell, William	824	Bck
Norville, Thos.	646	Btt
Norway, Jno., f. negro	287	Frf
Norwood, George	108	Spt
John, Junr.	780	Wst
Richd.	307	Ldn
Nosay, Keziah	789	Nrf
Ruth	789	Nrf
Nosman see Norman		
Nosseman, John	568	Mnr
John, j.	568	Mnr
Nossett, Joseph	528	Frd
William	575	Frd
Notherlin, Nancy	864	Hnv
Nottingham, Jacob	420	Bth
Jos. B.	807	Nrf
Susanna	420	Bth
William	420	Bth
Notts, Wm.	879	Yrk
Novell, Wingfield	718	Nls
Noviel see Norrel		
Novmar, Moses	421	Bth
Nowel, Charles	58	Chr

Frances	848	Hnv	Obadih.	155	Dnw	Maniard	63	Clp
Garnet	454	Frn	Obediah	11	Ntt	Oakum, Nathan	469	Pra
Geman C. [written over			Spencer	55	Chs	Oakwood, Henry	326	Dnw
in photostats]	859	Cmp	Thos.	155	Dnw	Oaler, William	33	Rcm
John	554	Frd	Wm.	155	Dnw	Oar, Thomas	288	Frf
Perrin G.	58	Chr	Wm.	9	Ntt	Oarbough, Abraham	32	Rcm
Stven	105	Cmb	see Nummelay			Adam	23	Rcm
Nowell, George	167	Alb	Nunnelly, Absalom	580	Pre	Andw.	32	Rcm
Henry	847	Cmp	Benjamin	580	Pre	Christian	32	Rcm
Hugh	277	Amh	Ephraim	580	Pre	William	25	Rcm
James [2]	167	Alb	Littleberry	580	Pre	Oard, Jessee	523	Prw
John	167	Alb	Mary	233	Aml	Joseph	523	Prw
Maryanne	167	Alb	Peter	580	Pre	William	927	Hrr
Reuben	273	Amh	Peter, Jr.	580	Pre	Oast, Gideon	840	Nrf
Spencer	274	Amh	Nunnery, Nathl.	544	Prg	see Oess		
William	847	Cmp	Nuse, Jac.	527	Mnn	Oats, Jacob, Jur.	760	Hmp
see Norcutt, Spencer			Micl.	527	Mnn	Jacob, Senr.	772	Hmp
Nowlan, Golesby	667	Mnt	Nut, Rody	955	Hrr	William, a free		
Nowland, Danl.	229	Shn	Nutt, Alex. M.	279	Rck	mulatto	991	Nrt
Nowlin, Abraham	789	Bck	Edward	532	Frd	Oatts, John	215	Shn
John	494	Frn	James	577	Frd	OBanian, Elias	518	Prw
Samuel	817	Bck	John	577	Frd	OBannon, Anne	393	Fqr
Susannah	287	Amh	John	584	Frd	Benjamin	369	Fqr
Nowline, James	852	Hnv	Jos.	355	Lnc	Enoch	347	Fqr
Nowling, Stephen	706	Gch	Joseph	267	Ldn	George	389	Fqr
Nox, Jas.	550	Prg	Richard	371	Fqr	Isham	366	Fqr
Jos.	303	Ldn	Richard	991	Nrt	James	374	Fqr
Wm.	293	Ldn	Sarah	991	Nrt	John	376	Fqr
Noyell, Thos.	913	Nrf	Walter	991	Nrt	John	93	Jff
Noyes, Isaac	2	Knw	William	990	Nrt	Joseph	369	Fqr
Nozworthy, John	656	Sss	Nuttall, Geo.	665	Glc	Samuel	369	Fqr
Nubill, Wm.	7	Ntt	Henry L.	665	Glc	Thomas	348	Fqr
Nuckles, Nathaniel	847	Wth	Jas.	665	Glc	William	366	Fqr
Nuckolds, Charles	706	Gch	Jno.	665	Glc	Obeer, Ann	991	Nrt
Pouncey	706	Gch	Nutten, James	936	Hrr	Obeirn, Danl.	547	Brk
Saml.	706	Gch	Nutter, Christ.	939	Hrr	see Oburn		
Thos.	706	Gch	Christopher	913	Hrr	Oberry, Bailey	871	Sth
Wm.	706	Gch	David	580	Mnr	Henry	129	Sth
Nuckolls, Andrew	844	Hnv	Elizabeth	920	Hrr	Jordan	154	Sth
John	847	Hnv	John	913	Hrr	OBrady see Bradly		
Nathl., Jnr.	847	Hnv	John	916	Hrr	Obrian, Ann	55	Stf
Thomas	844	Hnv	Margaret	912	Hrr	Matthias	476	Bdf
William	847	Hnv	Martha	948	Hrr	William	476	Bdf
Nuckols, Roses	305	Amh	Thomas	920	Hrr	OBrian, Jne.	913	Nrf
William	304	Amh	Wm.	948	Hrr	OBrians, Thos.	662	Mnt
Nuckools, Rubin	847	Hnv	Zadock	646	Btt	O Briant, Adam	955	Hrr
Nuell, William	563	Mnr	see Webb			John	736	Wsh
Nughbours, Franhey	260	Amh	Nuttle, Thos.	29	Hnr	Thos.	587	Brk
Null, Jacob	4	Knw	Nuzam, Geo.	527	Mnn	OBrien, Daniel	513	Prw
Leonard	34	Rcm	Jas.	527	Mnn	Obryan, Johanah	6	Wod
Peter, Charleston	14	Knw	Tho.	527	Mnn	O. Bryant, Glenn	792	Bck
Philip	12	Knw	Wm.	527	Mnn	OBryant, Mark	838	Bck
William, Cabin Creek	4	Knw	Nuzan, Jno.	527	Mnn	Patrick	804	Bck
Nulton, John	511	Frd	Nvel, Eli	718	Nls	OBryen, Charles	362	Fqr
Nummelay, Charles [written in			Nye, John P.	847	Wth	Oburn, Danl.	549	Brk
on photostats]	66	Chs	Nyswonggerin, Jno.	718	Nls	see Obeirn		
Nunely, John	725	Brn				OCain, Henry	371	Ags
Nunemaker, George	70	Jff				O'Canner, Bryan	63	Clp
Nunn, Elisha	847	Wth	--- O ---			Ochabundro, James	59	Chr
John	847	Wth				Oche, Abram	408	Ags
Michle	937	Hrr				Ocheltre, Thos.	285	Rck
Nancy	179	Shn	O..., ...	476	Bdf	Ockerman, Daniel	205	Alb
Nancy	847	Wth	Mary A.	562	Mnr	John	172	Shn
Thomas	172	Knq	O...t..., Moses	233	Aml	Ockletree, Michael	371	Ags
Thomas	847	Wth	Oaden, Thomas	966	Hrr	OConnelly, Cornelius	349	Fqr
Whaton	847	Wth	see Vaden			OConner, Jeremiah	584	Frd
William	177	Shn	Oagan see Organ			John	371	Ags
Nunnally, ...	66	Chs	Oakes, Ann	173	Knq	OConnor, James	914	Nrf
Aaron	155	Dnw	Thomas	172	Knq	OConson, Thomas	863	Cmp
Arthur	782	Bck	William	172	Knq	Odell, Edward	187	Shn
Barnard	797	Bck	Oakley, Daniel	820	Nrf	Jeremiah	177	Shn
Danl.	155	Dnw	Erasmus	105	Cmb	John	177	Shn
David	55	Chs	George, Junr.	170	Shn	Samuel	177	Shn
Edwd.	58	Chs	James	764	Nwk	see Adell		
Elizabh.	155	Dnw	John	793	Nrf	Oden, ---, & Moore	18	Hnr
Jeremiah	57	Chs	Shedrack	121	Cmb	Hezk.	243	Ldn
Joel	155	Dnw	Wm.	62	Clp	John	59	Chr
John	155	Dnw	Oaks, Henry	168	Alb	Martha	244	Ldn
John, Majr.	5	Pwh	Major	783	Bck	Solomon	257	Ldn
Josiah	787	Bck	Major, jr.	807	Bck	Odeon, Richd.	791	Nrf

Name	Pg	Co	Name	Pg	Co	Name	Pg	Co
Wm.	792	Nrf	Oglevie, David	65	Jff	Thomas	781	Wst
Oder, Elwood	63	Clp	Ogmoore, Richd.	759	Brn	Oliver, ... [J...h...?]	329	Dnw
Joel	63	Clp	Oharrow, Kizziah	412	Rch	Ambrose	665	Glc
Smith	63	Clp	Ohaver, John	221	Shn	Ann	468	Mdd
Susanna	354	Fqr	OHaydon see Haydon			Benjamin	59	Chr
Odle, Jacob	847	Wth	Ohover, George	781	Hmp	Benjamin, Jnr.	886	Hnv
Jeremiah	7	Knw	Henry	579	Mnr	Benjamin, Snr.	882	Hnv
Joshua	959	Hrr	Peter	582	Mnr	Betty	201	Ess
Sylvanus	6	Knw	Okeley, John	10	Rcm	Charles	10	Ntt
ODobson see Dobson			John, Snr.	126	Hnr	Daniel	275	Amh
O'Donala, John	127	Sth	Phil	120	Hnr	Daniel	428	Msn
O'Donnala, Benja.	139	Sth	Okey, Betty	117	Acc	David	874	Hnv
Odor, Gabl.	62	Clp	OLarrow see Oharrow			Elizabeth	469	Pra
Hester	63	Clp	Old, Abijah	168	Alb	Geo. P.	355	Lnc
Wm.	62	Clp	Baxter	2	Ntt	Gravely	666	Glc
Ody, John	398	Mds	Clement	156	Dnw	Gulidath	909	Hrr
Oens, John	4	Wod	Delphae	156	Dnw	Harmon	811	Bck
Willis	8	Wod	Edward	647	Btt	Isaac	156	Dnw
Oess, Hiram	15	Rcm	Elizabeth	156	Dnw	Isaac	882	Hnv
Oferral, Ignatius	525	Brk	Frederick	469	Pra	Isac	353	Lnn
O Ferral, James	575	Brk	Kedar	794	Nrf	James	589	Frd
Offet, Solomon	524	Brk	James	168	Alb	James	666	Glc
Offett, Hamilton	253	Ldn	James	793	Nrf	James	266	Rck
Nathanniel	719	Nls	William	168	Alb	Jas.	913	Nrf
Offord, John	774	Hmp	Oldacre, Henry	425	Msn	Jas., (free negro)	665	Glc
Offutt, Charles	288	Frf	Isaac	422	Msn	Jesse D.	468	Mdd
James	784	Hmp	John	422	Msn	Jno.	666	Glc
Joseph	81	Jff	John, Sn.	428	Msn	Jno.	882	Hnv
Reezen	288	Frf	William	425	Msn	Jno.	11	Ntt
Samuel	57	Jff	Oldacres, Hister	404	Fqr	Jno., jr.	173	Knq
William	287	Frf	Oldaire, Abram	936	Hrr	John	783	Bck
William M.	288	Frf	Oldam see Oldaire			John [2]	916	Crl
Oflighter, George	719	Nls	Oldham, Ann	355	Lnc	John	913	Nrf
Ogborne, Elizabeth	656	Sss	Bishop	725	Brn	John	509	Prw
Mary	656	Sss	Charles	725	Brn	John, jun.	917	Crl
Ogbourn, Edward	725	Brn	Edward	399	Rch	John, Snr.	173	Knq
Benjamin	725	Brn	Elizabeth	991	Nrt	Judith	10	Ntt
Henry W.	725	Brn	George	991	Nrt	Marshall	916	Crl
Winney	725	Brn	Isaac	725	Brn	Marshall	917	Crl
Ogburn, John	353	Lnn	Isaac	16	Oho	Martha	916	Crl
Ogden, Chs.	250	Ldn	Jane	428	Bth	Mary	156	Dnw
Cloe	288	Frf	Jerry	991	Nrt	Mary	914	Nrf
Nancy	947	Hrr	Joseph	428	Bth	Nathan	517	Prw
Robert	300	Ldn	Nathaniel	781	Wst	Nelly	470	Pra
Thomas	287	Frf	Richd., by Thos.			Richd., [his] Est.	16	Ntt
Thoms., Senr.	288	Frf	Johnson	646	Btt	Samuel	909	Hrr
William R.	957	Hrr	Thomas, Jr.	991	Nrt	Tho., [his] Este.	355	Lnc
Ogdin, Mary	7	Wod	Thomas, Sr.	991	Nrt	Thomas	916	Crl
Ogdon, Andrew	316	Ldn	William	428	Bth	Thomas	59	Chr
Benjamin	271	Amh	Oldner, Malai.	914	Nrf	Thomas	423	Msn
Charles	84	Jff	Oldridge, John	440	Bth	Thomas, Junr.	59	Chr
Henry	295	Amh	William	425	Bth	Thomas C.	59	Chr
John	277	Amh	Olds, ...	232	Aml	Thos.	25	Hnr
John	61	Jff	Josiah	67	Chs	Thos.	29	Hnr
Phenias	575	Brk	Olebaugh, Peter	584	Brk	Thruston	850	Hnv
Plyah	287	Frf	Olebough, Christian	14	Rcm	Vincant	116	Hnr
Thos., of Cloe	287	Frf	John	31	Rcm	William	295	Amh
William	287	Frf	Oleriger see Oterger			William	446	Bth
Ogelby, Judith	232	Aml	Olever, Thomas	285	Amh	William	916	Crl
Ogelin, Nathon	957	Hrr	Olford, George	189	Shn	William	172	Knq
Ogesby, Jesse	719	Nls	Thos.	647	Btt	William	781	Wst
OGlass, Jas.	913	Nrf	Oliffe, George	403	Rch	Wm.	665	Glc
Ogle, James	24	Oho	James	403	Rch	Wm.	355	Lnc
Mary	6	Oho	William	403	Rch	see Ohover, Olliver		
Rosanah	760	Wsh	Oliger, David	235	Shn	Oliveria, ---, & Sons	913	Nrf
Oglebe, Ann	173	Knq	Olinger, Abm.	647	Btt	Olivia, Louisa	914	Nrf
Ogleby, Humphrey	317	Ldn	Jacob	847	Wth	Olivier, Augustine	666	Glc
Louis	914	Nrf	Mary	647	Btt	Ollebaugh, Katy	597	Brk
William	476	Bdf	Peter	415	Fqr	Oller, Peter	518	Brk
Oglesbey, Daniel	858	Cmp	see Otinger			Ollive, Thomas	66	Spt
David	869	Cmp	Oliphant, John	916	Crl	Oliver, Asa	656	Sss
Jacob	850	Cmp	John	917	Crl	Benjamin	580	Pre
Peter	850	Cmp	Robert	913	Nrf	Caty	98	Spt
William	870	Cmp	Olive, Charles	781	Wst	Ely	288	Frf
Oglesby, Federick	958	Chc	George	781	Wst	Henry	97	Spt
Jacob	205	Alb	John D.	781	Wst	Hezekiah	366	Fqr
Pleasant	205	Alb	Joseph	211	Kng	John	97	Spt
William	916	Crl	Reuben D.	781	Wst	Josiah	356	Fqr
see Ogesby			Stephen			Leonard	424	Msn
Oglesvie, Esaias	601	Frd				Leonard, Jr.	359	Fqr

Name	Pg	Loc	Name	Pg	Loc	Name	Pg	Loc
Leonard, Senr.	383	Fqr	William A.	105	Cmb	Robert	172	Knq
Leven	360	Fqr	Orbison, John	266	Rck	Orrison, David	298	Ldn
Leven, Senr.	384	Fqr	Thos.	294	Rck	Saml.	297	Ldn
Lewis	288	Frf	Orchard, Nancy	756	Hmp	Ort, Gasper	527	Mnn
Rhoda	383	Fqr	Sukey	371	Ags	Margret	724	Wsh
Saml.	934	Hrr	Ordirs, John	453	Grn	Orton, John	819	Nrf
Samuel	416	Fqr	Ore, Wm.	371	Ags	Mary	818	Nrf
Thomas	356	Fqr	Orear, Enoch, ([his]			Thos. K.	819	Nrf
Thomas	580	Pre	Quarter)	383	Fqr	Orum, Henry	270	Ldn
Walter	360	Fqr	Jesse, Senr.	588	Frd	Orvick, David	194	Shn
William	288	Frf	ORear, Benjamin	588	Frd	Osbern, Joseph	923	Hrr
William	357	Fqr	Enoch	512	Prw	Osborn, Abigail	913	Nrf
Olmerod, Fredrick	746	Wsh	Jesse, Jr.	587	Frd	Jno.	914	Nrf
OLougholin, Catharine	526	Prw	Orebaugh, Peter	371	Ags	Osborne, Aquilla	597	Frd
Olover, Augustin	200	Ess	Orendorf, Philip	212	Shn	Benja.	52	Chs
Olpin, Charles	942	Chc	Philip, Sr.	212	Shn	Branch	1	Ntt
Olver, Charles	880	Cmp	Orendorff, Henry	266	Amh	Claiborne	59	Chr
Geo.	63	Clp	Orenduff, James	706	Wsh	Daniel	59	Chr
Olves, Charles	871	Cmp	Jeremiah	691	Wsh	David	511	Frd
Olvis, Rhody	132	Hnr	Lewis	743	Wsh	Eliza.	232	Aml
Omara, Frs.	913	Nrf	Orgain, Littleberey	725	Brn	Elizabeth	481	Frn
Michael	287	Frf	Polly	725	Brn	Francis	52	Chs
Thos.	913	Nrf	Wm.	725	Brn	John H.	581	Pre
Omell see Ornell			Wm. D.	725	Brn	John	333	Dnw
Omensetser, Pall	248	Shn	Organ, Eliza	538	Prg	Jones, (Est.)	59	Chr
Omohundro, Alen	168	Alb	Enos	858	Cmp	Peter	566	Frd
John	781	Wst	John	857	Cmp	Phillip	59	Chr
Richard	168	Alb	Thomas	353	Lnn	Raps	59	Chr
Richard	580	Pre	Orid..., ...hl., free			Squire	764	Nwk
Richard	781	Wst	negro	70	Chs	Osbourn see Ausbourn		
Thomas	781	Wst	Oringduff, Henry	98	Jff	Osbun, Peter	527	Mnn
William	782	Bck	Orison, Andrew	258	Ldn	Osburn, Craven	270	Ldn
William	798	Bck	Arthur	238	Ldn	David [2]	90	Jff
William	825	Bck	John	239	Ldn	Hannah	269	Ldn
William	781	Wst	Orkerman, David	718	Nls	Jno.	270	Ldn
see Mahundro			Orm, Jno.	527	Mnn	Joel	270	Ldn
Oneal, Con	276	Ldn	Orme, Margt.	62	Clp	John	457	Frn
Daniel	237	Ldn	Zach.	62	Clp	Jonathan	101	Jff
Danl.	63	Clp	Ormond, Larence	286	Ldn	Joseph	533	Brk
Ferdenando	263	Ldn	Ormsby, Ellen	913	Nrf	Joseph	101	Jff
Hugh	488	Frn	Ornbum, Henry	298	Rck	Joseph	238	Shn
John	541	Brk	Ornburn, Lewis	292	Rck	Joshua	270	Ldn
John	237	Ldn	Orndorf, Benjamin	536	Frd	Mary	437	Bth
John	252	Shn	John	571	Frd	Morris	270	Ldn
Jos.	527	Mnn	Jonathan	571	Frd	Nicholas	271	Ldn
Judah	63	Clp	Samuel	536	Frd	Richd.	269	Ldn
Robert	264	Ldn	William	536	Frd	Robert	347	Fqr
ONeal, Hugh	693	Wsh	Orndorff, Jesse	476	Bdf	Thomas	788	Bck
Michel	916	Hrr	Ornduff, Saml.	269	Rck	Thomas	91	Jff
O. Neal, Johnson	18	Oho	Su...	304	Rck	Thos.	269	Ldn
ONeale, Charles	499	Prw	Ornell, John	237	Shn	William	90	Jff
Thomas L.	392	Rch	Oronduff, David	769	Hmp	Zarah	428	Rnd
ONeel, John	100	Jff	Orr, Alexander	633	Gls	Osgood, L. [S. ?]	34	Hnr
Oneil, Elizth.	914	Nrf	Alexr.	827	Nrf	Oslin, James	942	Chc
ONeil, Thomas	945	Hrr	Arthur	700	Wsh	Osman, Saml.	514	Brk
O. Neil, Constantine	26	Oho	Arthur	712	Wsh	Osmore, John	156	Dnw
O'Neil, Darius	282	Rck	Arthur, Senr.	700	Wsh	Ostean, Cornelius	470	Pra
Felix	646	Btt	James	697	Wsh	Osten, Jno.	527	Mnn
Oney, Ben	872	Sth	John	698	Br	Oster, Citizen	914	Nrf
David	632	Gls	John	533	Frd	OSuttan see Suttan		
John	144	Sth	John	527	Mnn	Oswald, Martha	305	Ldn
John	845	Sth	John, Junr.	700	Wsh	see Aswald		
Joseph	632	Gls	John, Senr.	712	Wsh	Oterger, Adam	240	Shn
William	872	Sth	John D.	535	Frd	Oterwall, Georg	648	Mnt
Onions, Raynor	117	Acc	Thomas	786	Hmp	Otey, Armstead	476	Bdf
William	117	Acc	Thomas	9	Oho	Elisabeth	764	Nwk
Only, Francis	46	Acc	William	686	Br	Frazier	476	Bdf
Mildred	548	Prg	William	632	Gls	Isaac	764	Nwk
Nancy	117	Acc	William	847	Wth	James	764	Nwk
Onroe, Jacob	299	Rck	Wm.	541	Brk	John, Sr.	476	Bdf
see Ovior			see Oar			John H.	476	Bdf
Onvick see Orvick			Orrell, Charles	879	Yrk	Mary Anne [Anne		
Operfield, Frederick	507	Frd	John, (W)	879	Yrk	Mary?]	764	Nwk
Opie, Hiram	991	Nrt	Mary	879	Yrk	Thomas	131	Hnr
Opoher, Jacob	297	Rck	Minutree	879	Yrk	Walter	476	Bdf
Oram, Moses	81	Jff	Orrick, Charles	549	Brk	William	489	Bdf
Peter	677	Br	George	516	Frd	Otinger, Jacob	647	Btt
Orange, Elizabeth	123	Hnr	Nicholas	574	Brk	see Olinger		
Josuah	112	Cmb	Orrill, Daniel	172	Knq	Otis, Asa	23	Hnr
Thomas	945	Chc	Frances	173	Knq	Hy.	914	Nrf

Name	Pg	Co	Name	Pg	Co	Name	Pg	Co
Otley, Covington	469	Pra	Overly, Henry	12	Rcm	Nathaiel	726	Brn
Otnett, Christian	234	Shn	Thos.	725	Brn	Phillip	758	Brn
Otrong, John	767	Hmp	Overman, John	841	Nrf	Reed	666	Glc
Ott, Geo.	913	Nrf	John	913	Nrf	Robert	475	Bdf
George	247	Shn	Mary	841	Nrf	Robert	725	Brn
Henry	642	Mnt	Overpeck, Jacob	163	Shn	Samuel	656	Sss
Henry	204	Shn	Salome	163	Shn	Sarah	847	Wth
Jacob	250	Shn	Salome	164	Shn	Sterling	726	Brn
John	371	Ags	Oversham, Wm.	622	Btt	Thos.	759	Brn
John	68	Jff	Overshiner, John	371	Ags	Tolliaffero	476	Bdf
John, Junr.	202	Shn	Overstreet, Benjn.	233	Aml	William	476	Bdf
John, Senr.	202	Shn	Charles	205	Alb	William	580	Pre
Mary	250	Shn	James	476	Bdf	William	161	Sth
Michael	246	Shn	John	476	Bdf	William	656	Sss
Philip	61	Jff	John	811	Nrf	William	656	Sss
Polley	68	Jff	Jno.	7	Ntt	Winney	468	Mdd
Otter, John G.	764	Nwk	John, jr.	476	Bdf	William	764	Nwk
Otterson, Jane	469	Pra	John, (Otter)	476	Bdf	Wm.	706	Gch
Joseph	470	Pra	John, Sr.	476	Bdf	Wm., Sr.	758	Brn
Tully	470	Pra	John H.	580	Pre	Owens, Aaron	211	Kng
Ottey, Susan	285	Rck	Thomas	476	Bdf	Abm.	527	Mnn
Otty, Thomas	283	Rck	Thomas, Jr.	475	Bdf	Barnett	616	Mnt
Thos., jr.	285	Rck	William	476	Bdf	Benjn.	437	Mth
Oty, Isaac	476	Bdf	William	59	Chr	Catey	173	Knq
Otyneal, Thomas	476	Bdf	see Wyatt			Charles	379	Fqr
Oul, David	2	Wod	Overton, Elizabeth	19	Ntt	Edwd.	441	Mth
Jacob	12	Wod	Lewis	398	Mds	Elias	645	Mnt
Oun see Orn			Marg	233	Aml	Elizabeth	499	Prw
Ourdam, Jeremiah	282	Ldn	Moses	1	Ntt	Elzebeth	824	Nrf
Oury, Christopher	847	Wth	Penelope	580	Pre	Frances	520	Prw
George	847	Wth	Richard	167	Alb	George	355	Fqr
John	847	Wth	Richd.	3	Ntt	George	436	Mth
Thomas	847	Wth	Saml.	13	Hnr	George	439	Mth
Outland, Edward	22	Isw	Thos.	11	Ntt	Harrison	419	Fqr
Elisha	37	Isw	William	69	Chr	James	211	Knq
Thomas	16	Isw	Willis	103	Spt	James	89	Spt
Outten, Betsey [2]	46	Acc	see O...t..., Pettus			Jeremiah	561	Frd
Daniel	46	Acc	Ovior, Adam	301	Rck	Jno., Sr.	447	Mth
Ephraim	46	Acc	see Onroe			John	117	Acc
George	117	Acc	Owans, Davd.	696	Wsh	John	833	Nrf
Isaac	46	Acc	Margeret	425	Msn	John	518	Prw
Matthias	46	Acc	William	420	Msn	John C.	581	Pre
Purnell	46	Acc	Owden, Jessee	504	Prw	Joseph	287	Frf
William D.	46	Acc	Owen, Abner	725	Brn	Joshua	368	Fqr
Oval, Daniel	428	Rnd	Ann	580	Pre	Levi	718	Nls
Ovenchain, Danl.	646	Btt	Anthony	847	Wth	Mary	205	Alb
George	646	Btt	Assa	693	Br	Meroma	211	Kng
Phillip	646	Btt	Balaam	656	Sss	Moses	518	Prw
Rindhalt	646	Btt	Barnett	295	Amh	Owen	851	Cmp
Sam	646	Btt	Bernard	475	Bdf	Owen	958	Hrr
Oventon, John	791	Nrf	Booling	758	Brn	Peter	375	Fqr
Overacro, Thomas	476	Bdf	Chambliss	656	Sss	Reuben, jr.	211	Kng
Overaker, Daniel	508	Frd	Christopher	468	Mdd	Reuben, Sr.	211	Kng
Overall, Isaac	176	Shn	Christopher	474	Mdd	Robert	290	Ldn
John	499	Prw	David	656	Sss	Robt.	647	Btt
John	176	Shn	Drury	656	Sss	Samuel	111	Spt
Overby, Bastley	874	Cmp	Eley	42	Isw	Sarah	205	Alb
Buckner	758	Brn	Elisha	8	Pwh	Susan	828	Nrf
Frederick B.	156	Dnw	Elisha	580	Pre	Taylor	117	Acc
George	353	Lnn	Ephraim	656	Sss	William	851	Cmp
John	156	Dnw	George	6	Pwh	William	211	Kng
John R.	156	Dnw	George	580	Pre	Yonell	211	Kng
Sally	156	Dnw	Hughes	6	Pwh	Zachariah	288	Frf
Sterling	156	Dnw	James	476	Bdf	Zachariah	824	Nrf
Susannah	353	Lnn	Jesse	580	Pre	see Oens, Owen, Owings		
Overdorf, John	238	Shn	Jesse	656	Sss	Owers, Nicholas	416	Rnd
Overfelt, Charles	477	Frn	Jno.	666	Glc	OWilliams, Thomas	416	Rnd
Matthias	477	Frn	Jno.	296	Rck	Owin, William	233	Aml
Michael	476	Bdf	Joel	8	Pwh	Owings, Feilding	781	Wst
Overfield, Benj.	275	Ldn	John	476	Bdf	Owins, Thomas	615	Mnt
Martin	275	Ldn	John	758	Brn	Ownby, Powell	476	Bdf
Peter	920	Hrr	John	21	Oho	William	476	Bdf
Saml.	919	Hrr	John	656	Sss	Ox, George	102	Jff
see Operfield			John, Senr.	468	Mdd	Oxenbridge, Richd.	665	Glc
Overhall, Robert	49	Stf	Joshua	656	Sss	Oxleef, ...nkins	476	Bdf
Overhalts, Abm.	647	Btt	Kinchen	19	Isw	Oxley, Aaron	292	Ldn
Overholt, David	473	Frn	Lewis	656	Sss	Everet	289	Ldn
Overholtz, Mark	26	Rcm	M.H.	119	Hnr	Jane	292	Ldn
Overhotz, Christian	633	Gls	Mary	468	Mdd	Jno.	62	Clp
Overhultz, Peter, 1st	236	Shn	Meacham	468	Mdd	Oyler, Fred.	289	Rck

Name	Pg	Co	Name	Pg	Co	Name	Pg	Co
Frederick	456	Frn	Edward	722	Nls	Martin	506	Brk
Henry	289	Rck	Eliza	24	Hnr	Oris	31	Hnr
Jacob	289	Rck	Elizabeth	478	Bdf	Rice	515	Prw
Jane	720	Wsh	Francis	284	Amh	Richd.	177	Elc
John	469	Frn	Gabriel	294	Amh	Richd.	12	Rcm
Vallintine	465	Frn	George	878	Cmp	Thomas	510	Prw
Vallintine, Sr.	466	Frn	George	364	Fqr	Thomas	12	Rcm
Ozborne see Ogborne			George, Campbell	719	Nls	Thos.	571	Brk
			Gwynn	523	Prw	William	587	Brk
			James	296	Amh	William	510	Prw
--- P ---			James	478	Bdf	Wm.	65	Clp
			James	832	Bck	Wm.	270	Ldn
P..., John	919	Crl	Jesse	443	Flv	see Pai...		
P...plin, John	355	Lnn	Jessee	709	Gch	Painten, John	791	Nrf
P...yne, James	476	Bdf	Jno.	892	Hnv	Painter, Abraham	32	Rcm
Pa...ton, Wm.	301	Rck	John	917	Crl	Adam	239	Shn
Pace, Benjamin	169	Alb	John	110	Cmb	Alexr.	32	Rcm
Bignal	158	Dnw	John	604	Frd	Conrad	184	Shn
Edward	169	Alb	John	123	Hnr	Conrod	648	Btt
Geo. S.	468	Mdd	John	632	Mnt	David	240	Shn
George	169	Alb	John	740	Wsh	Edwd.	267	Ldn
Jessee, jr.	709	Gch	Joseph	918	Crl	Frederick	298	Amh
Jessee, senr.	709	Gch	Leonard	708	Gch	George	543	Brk
John	445	Flv	Leticia	13	Hnr	George	239	Shn
Joseph	839	Bck	Lettitia	621	Mnt	George, jr.	503	Brk
Joseph	710	Gch	Lewis	710	Gch	George, (L. G.)	240	Shn
Nancy	444	Flv	Mama	668	Glc	Henry	373	Ags
Newsum	17	Ntt	Mann	897	Hnv	Henry	648	Btt
Robert	709	Gch	Margarett	667	Glc	Henry	193	Shn
Stephen	327	Dnw	Maria L.	16	Hnr	Ithael	880	Hnv
Talton	444	Flv	Mary	115	Spt	Jacob	372	Ags
William	329	Dnw	Matthew	583	Frd	Jacob	503	Brk
William	333	Dnw	Mordecai	861	Hnv	Jacob	543	Brk
Wm.	447	Flv	Nath.	18	Hnr	Jacob	547	Brk
Wm.	710	Gch	Nathanl.	512	Brk	Jacob	649	Btt
Pack, George	633	Gls	Nicholas	169	Alb	Jacob, jr.	503	Brk
James	35	Stf	Reuben	710	Gch	Japeth	881	Hnv
John	566	Mnr	Robert	169	Alb	Jno.	647	Btt
Matthew	633	Gls	Robert	426	Bth	Jno.	649	Btt
Molly	35	Stf	Robert	561	Frd	John	601	Frd
Samuel	578	Mnr	Robert	632	Mnt	John	73	Jff
see Packs			Robert	5	Wod	John	723	Nls
Packer, Henry	549	Brk	Samuel	721	Nls	John	226	Pnd
Packet, William	992	Nrt	Thomas	478	Bdf	John	230	Shn
Packett, Henry	395	Rch	Thomas T.	504	Prw	Joseph	184	Shn
John	61	Jff	William [2]	169	Alb	Mathias	240	Shn
William R.	391	Rch	William	292	Frf	Matthias	849	Wth
Packs, Samuel	578	Mnr	William	173	Knq	Philip	239	Shn
Packson, Thos.	647	Btt	William	429	Msn	Philip, (L. P.)	240	Shn
Packston, Joseph	634	Gls	William B.	332	Dnw	Robert	601	Frd
Paden, Francis, Jr.	641	Mnt	William B.	534	Frd	Sarah	601	Frd
Jno., Sr.	658	Mnt	Wm.	707	Gch	William	805	Hmp
Padget, Abram	112	Hnr	Wm.	708	Gch	William	82	Jff
Padgett, Mildred	668	Glc	Wm. [3]	709	Gch	Wm.	800	Nrf
Rd.	666	Glc	Pagett, Edmund	544	Frd	Paints, Joseph	404	Ags
Reubin	282	Amh	Timothy	244	Ldn	Pair, Marcus	658	Sss
Richard	274	Amh	Pai..., ...	527	Prw	Robert	454	Grn
Willian.	289	Frf	Paichard see Prichard			see Pai..., Pain		
Abner	283	Amh	Pain, David	568	Pnr	Paisley, John	12	Rcm
Benja.	289	Frf	Francis	666	Glc	Paisons, Betty	540	Prg
Beverley	301	Amh	James	453	Grn	Palf, John	515	Brk
Edmund	259	Amh	John	66	Jff	Pall, Caty	173	Knq
Ephrain.	256	Amh	Michl.	555	Brk	Pallen, Solomon	173	Knq
Fred	477	Bdf	Raphiel	76	Jff	Pallerson see Patterson		
Henry	289	Frf	Walter	453	Grn	Pallett, Jno.	470	Pra
John, jr	259	Amh	see Pair			Matthew	470	Pra
John, Senr	305	Amh	Paine, Abraham	24	Rcm	Wm.	916	Nrf
Pagan, Alexander	680	Br	Easter	506	Prw	Palman, Watson	114	Hnr
Andrew	680	Br	Gabriel	10	Rcm	Palmer, Abel	264	Ldn
David	469	Frn	George	506	Brk	Adam	372	Ags
Page, ---, Mrs.	35	Hnr	George, jr.	506	Brk	Armd. J.	355	Lnc
Archilus	616	Mnt	Henry [2]	506	Brk	Ben.	356	Lnc
Benja. [2]	711	Gch	Henry	518	Prw	Benj.	17	Hnr
Carter	111	Cmb	Isaac	526	Frd	Benj.	308	Ldn
Carter B.	23	Hnr	Jesse	506	Brk	Benjamin	811	Bck
Dabney A.	707	Gch	John	372	Ags	Benjamin	838	Bck
David	634	Gls	John	177	Elc	Catharine	245	Ldn
Edmond	777	Bck	Jonathan	596	Frd	Charles	290	Amh
Edward	205	Alb	Joseph	526	Prw	Charles	173	Knq
			Laurence	36	Rcm	Daniel	243	Ldn

Danl.	65	Clp	William	722	Nls	Samuel	723	Nls
David	81	Jff	Panter, Joshua	281	Rck	Sherard	708	Gch
David	468	Mdd	Thos.	732	Wsh	Sherrard	708	Gch
Elihu	8	Oho	Paradise, John	119	Acc	Thomas F.	61	Chr
Geo.	374	Ags	Lucy L.	613	Srr	Turner	710	Gch
Halcoat	60	Chr	Lucy L., (W)	880	Yrk	William	633	Gls
Isaac	829	Bck	Parker	118	Acc	William	3	Knw
Isham	803	Bck	Patience	119	Acc	William	766	Nwk
Jacob	374	Ags	Paramore, Isaac	118	Acc	Wm.	191	Elc
James	271	Ldn	John	119	Acc	Wm.	708	Gch
Jas.	64	Clp	William, Jur.	49	Acc	Park, Amos	763	Hmp
Jno.	313	Ldn	William, Senr. [2]	50	Acc	Amos, Ser.	779	Hmp
Jno.	914	Nrf	Parbury, Ann	500	Frn	Andw.	529	Mnn
Job	916	Nrf	Parcil, Richard	498	Frn	George	763	Hmp
John	372	Ags	Pare, Ann	918	Crl	John	834	Hmp
John	478	Bdf	Richard	918	Crl	John, Jun.	791	Hmp
John	579	Brk	Robert	919	Crl	Robert	684	Br
John	785	Bck	Thomas	917	Crl	Robert	688	Br
John	826	Bck	see P...			Sally	783	Wst
John	598	Frd	Parham, Abram	658	Sss	Samuel	763	Hmp
John	992	Nrt	Booth	659	Sss	Samuel, Ser.	763	Hmp
John R.	598	Frd	Caesar, F.N.	660	Sss	Solomon	762	Hmp
Joseph	992	Nrt	Gelley	157	Dnw	Parke, Benjamin	109	Spt
Joseph	2	Oho	James	454	Grn	Edmund	764	Nwk
Liny	29	Stf	Jno.	2	Ntt	Parken, George	14	Oho
Lot	356	Lnc	John	657	Sss	Parker, ---	327	Dnw
Luke	60	Chr	John, (S.[G.?]	658	Sss	Alexander	73	Spt
Mary	239	Ldn	Leonard H.	659	Sss	Alexander	95	Spt
Philip	245	Ldn	Lewis	726	Brn	Alexander	782	Wst
Raw.	356	Lnc	Lewis	658	Sss	Andrew	237	Ldn
Robert	407	Rch	Lewis A.	760	Brn	Ann	67	Clp
Robt.	63	Clp	Nathaniel, F.N.	657	Sss	Ann Saml.	200	Ess
Robt. D.	355	Lnc	Nathl.	726	Brn	Archibald	414	Fqr
Roger	173	Knq	Nicholas	158	Dnw	Archibald	658	Sss
Salley	788	Bck	Sally	659	Sss	Barbara	590	Brk
Sally	822	Bck	Simon	537	Prg	Bengamin	804	Hmp
Saml.	317	Ldn	Smith	657	Sss	Benjm.	956	Chc
Stophel	374	Ags	Thomas	157	Dnw	Billy	48	Acc
Thomas	60	Chr	Thomas	658	Sss	Bob	50	Acc
Thomas	291	Frf	Thomas	659	Sss	Charles	359	Fqr
Ths.	63	Clp	Thomas, Sr.	657	Sss	Clem.	186	Elc
William	407	Rch	Thos.	726	Brn	Copeld.	914	Nrf
William, Junr.	391	Rch	William	454	Grn	Elijah	173	Knq
Wm.	372	Ags	William (G.[S.?]	657	Sss	Eliza	783	Wst
Wm.	728	Brn	William, (M.	657	Sss	Elizabeth	46	Acc
Wm.	668	Glc	William R.	657	Sss	Ezra	477	Bdf
Wm.	264	Ldn	Wm.	726	Brn	Geo.	679	Wrw
Wm., [his] (planta-			Parimer, Davd.	693	Wsh	George	451	Frn
tion)	468	Mdd	William	760	Wsh	Goldman	174	Knq
Palmore, Benjamin	478	Bdf	Paris, Elizabeth	581	Pre	Grace	835	Hmp
Branch	60	Chr	James	581	Pre	Hannah	47	Acc
Colemon	60	Chr	John	409	Fqr	Henry	46	Acc
Flemming	118	Cmb	Obadiah	582	Pre	Henry	474	Frn
Jane	132	Cmb	Parish, Aaron	708	Gch	Henry	659	Sss
John P.	106	Cmb	Allen	708	Gch	Hugh	440	Bth
Salley	832	Bck	Booker	710	Gch	Jacob	804	Hmp
Thomas	582	Pre	David M.	708	Gch	James	49	Acc
Palsgrove see Pulsgrove			Ed.	528	Mnn	James	440	Bth
Palsley, Jac.	529	Mnn	Fredric	453	Grn	James	477	Bdf
Pamplet, William	874	Cmp	Gwo.	708	Gch	James	186	Elc
Pamplin, Armstead	875	Cmp	Geo. W.	708	Gch	James	201	Ess
Henry, Est.	61	Chr	Goodwin	727	Brn	James	344	Fqr
Leonard	59	Chr	Henry	727	Brn	James	823	Hmp
Rachel	721	Nls	Humphry	708	Gch	James	468	Mdd
see P...plin, Phamplin			James	708	Gch	Jephthah	120	Hnr
Pancake, Elizabeth	793	Hmp	James B.	760	Brn	Jessee	122	Cmb
Isaac	792	Hmp	John	156	Dnw	Jno.	872	Hnv
Pancoast, Jno.	309	Ldn	John	708	Gch	Jno.	529	Mnn
Pane, Henry	427	Rnd	John	766	Nwk	John	678	Br
Pangle, Henry	566	Frd	John, jr.	728	Brn	John	458	Frn
Joseph	567	Frd	John, Sr.	727	Brn	John	922	Hrr
Pankey, Keziah	775	Bck	Joseph	554	Frd	John	120	Hnr
Martha	13	Pwh	Mark	179	Elc	John	173	Knq
Thomas	129	Cmb	Meridith	256	Amh	John	243	Ldn
Pankos, Simeon	2	Oho	Nat.	183	Elc	John	354	Lnn
Pannel, Benjn.	648	Btt	Patsey	709	Gch	John	815	Nrf
Jesse	372	Ags	Richard	924	Hrr	John	680	Wrw
Luke	648	Btt	Robt.	709	Gch	John H.	122	Cmb
Pannell, George	1	Oho	Robt.	1	Hnr	John S.	182	Elc
Samuel	873	Cmp	Saml.	915	Nrf	Jonathan	804	Hmp

Name	No.	Code
Joseph	359	Fqr
Joseph	236	Ldn
Joseph	592	Mnr
Joseph	258	Shn
Joseph, Jr.	382	Fqr
Lemuel	803	Nrf
Levi	920	Crl
Lewis, (F.N.)	10	Isw
Martin	414	Fqr
Martin P.	60	Chr
Mildred	866	Sth
Moses	477	Bdf
Nancy	726	Brn
Nancy	31	Hnr
Nathaniel	478	Bdf
Peggy	49	Acc
Peter	793	Hmp
Precilla	332	Dnw
Reuben	478	Bdf
Richard	47	Acc
Richard	22	Oho
Richard	581	Pre
Richard	783	Wst
Richard, Jr.	385	Fqr
Richard, Senr.	385	Fqr
Rives	454	Grn
Robert	918	Crl
Robert	200	Ess
Robert	788	Hmp
Robert L.	918	Crl
Samuel	400	Brn
Samuel	105	Spt
Sarah	50	Acc
Simon	48	Acc
Solomon	762	Hmp
Sterling	760	Brn
Temperance	849	Sth
Thomas	48	Acc
Thomas	200	Ess
Thomas	385	Fqr
Thomas	582	Frd
Thomas	416	Rnd
Thos. H.	914	Nrf
Watts	918	Crl
William	467	Frn
William	782	Wst
Wm.	200	Ess
Wm.	124	Hnr
Wm.	613	Srr
Wyatt	200	Ess
see Davis, Fogg, Packer, Taylor, Wills		
Parkerson, Jacob	19	Isw
Nancy	16	Isw
William	24	Isw
Parkes, Elijah	118	Acc
Joseph	118	Acc
Joseph	371	Ags
Parkill, ---, Bryson &	11	Hnr
Parkins, Abraham	48	Acc
Easther	70	Acc
Hannah	48	Acc
Isaac, Senr.	575	Frd
John	605	Frd
Parkinson, Major	47	Acc
Richard	47	Acc
William	765	Nwk
Parkison, Elisabeth [2]	765	Nwk
James	28	Hnr
Joseph	765	Nwk
Joshua	765	Nwk
Margaret	697	Br
Parks, Andrew	430	Msn
Andw.	529	Mnn
Betty	174	Knq
Charles	115	Hnr
David	5	Oho
Edmund	118	Acc
Ezekiel	454	Grn
Gabl.	66	Clp
Jacob	193	Shn
James	24	Hnr
James	185	Shn
John	118	Acc
John	532	Brk
John	17	Hnr
John	429	Rnd
John, Junr.	118	Acc
John, Senr.	118	Acc
Martin	267	Amh
Raymond	119	Acc
Rd.	66	Clp
Robert	945	Hrr
Sacker	118	Acc
Soloman	118	Acc
William	5	Knw
William	186	Shn
William	697	Wsh
see Langford, Purks		
Parmel see Pannel		
Parmelion, Wm.	582	Brk
Parmer, Abner	363	Fqr
Isaac	362	Fqr
John	409	Fqr
John, Senr.	359	Fqr
Joseph	15	Hnr
Sarah	126	Hnr
William	781	Wst
Wm.	585	Brk
Parnal, John	16	Isw
Joseph	33	Isw
Willis	6	Isw
Parnell, Jno.	65	Clp
Parr, Caleb	471	Pra
James	340	Fqr
Jas., jr.	64	Clp
John	2	Isw
Jordan	9	Isw
Richard	614	Srr
Will.	373	Ags
William	34	Isw
William	93	Spt
Parrack, John	722	Nls
see Parrock		
Parrel, Joseph, Jr.	549	Frd
Joseph, Senr.	549	Frd
Parrell, John	549	Frd
Parret, Saml.	372	Ags
Parris, Andw.	373	Ags
Daniel	252	Ldn
Geo.	373	Ags
John	372	Ags
Parrish, Anderson	435	Flv
Charles	942	Chc
Collin	649	Btt
David	439	Flv
David	354	Lnn
Edward	333	Dnw
Francis	841	Bck
Isham	852	Hnv
James	956	Chc
Joel	441	Flv
Joel	354	Lnn
John	946	Chc
John	354	Lnn
Lucretia	354	Lnn
Mor. E.	328	Dnw
Robert	354	Lnn
Saml.	649	Btt
William	772	Hmp
William	354	Lnn
Parrock, George	723	Nls
see Parrack		
Parron, William	468	Mdd
see Parrow		
Parrot, Christopher	808	Hmp
Robert	119	Spt
Parrott, Augustin	442	Mth
Augustin	443	Mth
Frederick	213	Shn
George	21	Rcm
Henry	13	Rcm
Isaac	10	Rcm
Jacob	213	Shn
Jno.	449	Mth
John	213	Shn
Peter	517	Frd
Rachel	581	Frd
Richard	19	Oho
Saml.	13	Rcm
Saml., (Jr.)	21	Rcm
William	354	Lnn
Parrow, William B.	59	Chr
see Parron		
Parrt, William	88	Jff
Parry, James	282	Rck
Parsels, Enoch	555	Brk
Parsins, James	241	Ldn
John	531	Mnn
Parsley, Eliza	10	Hnr
Mary	845	Hnv
Robert	804	Bck
Solomon	111	Hnr
Solomon, Snr.	114	Hnr
Wim.	885	Hnv
Parson, Saml.	13	Hnr
Tandy	719	Nls
see Parsons		
Parsones, George	423	Rnd
Parsons, Absolem	442	Mth
Anthony	961	Hrr
Armagr.	879	Yrk
Benjamin	17	Oho
Charles	168	Alb
Charles	881	Hnv
Charles	4	Hnr
Chas.	804	Nrf
David	800	Hmp
David	188	Shn
Davis	633	Gls
Elizabeth	296	Amh
Francis	291	Frf
Fredrick	796	Nrf
Geo. M.	66	Clp
Hopewell	764	Nwk
Horatio	471	Pra
Isaac	424	Rnd
James	826	Hmp
James	424	Rnd
John	477	Bdf
John	404	Fqr
John	278	Rck
John	37	Rcm
Joseph	334	Dnw
Joseph	340	Fqr
Joseph	658	Sss
Jury	330	Dnw
Kisiah	6	Hnr
Lucy	65	Clp
Mary	899	Hnv
Mary	452	Mth
Nancey	798	Bck
Nancy	15	Hnr
Richard	169	Alb
Richd.	284	Rck
Robert	659	Sss
Roscow	186	Elc
Salley	158	Dnw
Saml. P.	113	Hnr
Samuel	477	Bdf
Stephen	25	Hnr
Sterling	157	Dnw
Tabby	118	Hnr
Thomas	292	Frf
Thomas	793	Hmp
Thos.	158	Dnw
Thos.	879	Hnv
Wiley	157	Dnw
William	68	Chr
William	341	Fqr

William	658	Sss
Wm.	801	Nrf
Wm.	471	Pra
Wm.	424	Rnd
see Pasins, Passons		
Parson's, Eliza.	471	Pra
John, [his] Est.	211	Kng
Parsott, Henry	718	Wsh
Partin, James	54	Chs
Jno.	62	Chs
Pleasants	25	Hnr
Robert	62	Chs
Susan	27	Hnr
Wm. C.	613	Srr
Partloe, Benja.	66	Clp
Elisha	66	Clp
Partlon see Partlow		
Partlow, Benja.	67	Clp
Elijah	67	Spt
John	103	Spt
Lewis	79	Spt
Partrick, John	168	Alb
Partridge Littleberry	657	Sss
Pascal, John	563	Frd
Pascel David	777	Hmp
Paschall, Isaac	592	Brk
Pash, Jno.	290	Frf
Jno., Senr.	292	Frf
William	526	Frd
Pasins, Joseph	961	Hrr
see Parsons		
Paskar, Peter	916	Nrf
Paskett, William A.	397	Rch
Paskill, John	560	Frd
Pasley, James	724	Wsh
Moses	724	Wsh
Wm.	724	Wsh
Pasmer, Mary	582	Brk
Pasons see Paisons		
Pass, Saml.	454	Grn
Passley, Robert	464	Frn
Passons, Edward	961	Hrr
see Parsons		
Pastell, George	193	Shn
Jacob	238	Shn
Pastuer, Wm.	441	Flv
Pasture, Susan	177	Elc
Pastures, Solomon	6	Isw
Patch, John	168	Shn
Pate, Absolum	855	Hnv
Adam	624	Mnt
Austin	864	Hnv
Daniel, Jr	625	Mnt
Danl., Sr.	606	Mnt
Edmund	476	Bdf
Edwd.	599	Mnr
Henry	624	Mnt
Jacob	608	Mnt
Jeremiah, Jr.	624	Mnt
Jeremiah, Jr.Jr.	625	Mnt
Jeremiah, Sr.	625	Mnt
Jno.	647	Btt
Jno.	884	Hnv
John	473	Frn
John	659	Sss
Jordan	659	Sss
Minor	649	Btt
Sally	659	Sss
Thomas	659	Sss
William	476	Bdf
William	625	Mnt
William	659	Sss
see Peite		
Paterson, David	168	Alb
John	168	Alb
Peggy	5	Hnr
William	168	Alb
Pates, Catharine	26	Stf
Lewis	58	Stf
Patience, Juday, (F.		
Negroe)	420	Fqr
Patillo, James	759	Brn
Patisole, Jacob	650	Btt
Patitte see Patillo		
Patman, Wm.	739	Wsh
Paton, Richard	252	Shn
Patram, Danl.	58	Chs
Francis, jun.	59	Chs
Francis, Senr.	58	Chs
Jno., est.	59	Chs
Polley	59	Chs
Patrick, C.S.	373	Ags
Edmd.	880	Yrk
Edmd., jr.	880	Yrk
Edmund	59	Chr
Hezekiah	848	Wth
Isaac	768	Hmp
John	61	Chr
John	879	Yrk
Levi	14	Knw
Mary	880	Yrk
Merritt C.	186	Elc
Pel.	529	Mnn
Ro.	880	Yrk
Tho.	880	Yrk
Walker	682	Wrw
Willm.	186	Elc
Wm.	373	Ags
see Partrick		
Patridge, Matthew	61	Jff
Patsbarger, Abraham	220	Pnd
Patson, ---, Wilson &	264	Rck
Pattan, Wm. [2]	288	Rck
Patte, Wm. S.	542	Prg
Patteison, John	548	Brk
Patten, Nathan	306	Rck
Pattern, George	549	Frd
Vincent	860	Cmp
Patterson, Aaron	552	Frd
Abijh.	233	Ldn
Abnor	239	Ldn
Adam	372	Ags
Alexr., S.	291	Rck
Andrew	460	Frn
Ann	701	Wsh
Catharine	510	Prw
Charles	478	Bdf
Charles	721	Nls
Charles, Est.	721	Nls
Charles C.	722	Nls
David	859	Cmp
David R.	722	Nls
Dolly	914	Nrf
Fanny	594	Frd
Flemon	307	Ldn
George	372	Ags
George	550	Prg
Hezekiah	39	Stf
Hugh	545	Brk
James	680	Br
James	864	Cmp
James	462	Frn
James	829	Hmp
James	868	Hnv
James	239	Ldn
James	294	Rck
James, jr.	373	Ags
Jas.	529	Mnn
Jesse	765	Nwk
Jessee	504	Prw
Jessee	510	Prw
Joel	12	Oho
John	372	Ags
John	477	Bdf
John	478	Bdf
John	520	Brk
John	674	Br
John	332	Dnw
John	776	Hmp
John	111	Hnr
John	291	Rck
John	107	Spt
John	58	Stf
John	848	Wth
John	880	Yrk
Jonathan	456	Frn
Kitty	646	Mnt
Landis	861	Cmp
Littleberry	860	Cmp
Mary	372	Ags
Mary	173	Knq
Mary	292	Ldn
Mary	723	Nls
Molly	594	Frd
Nancy	133	Hnr
Perry	91	Spt
Phil	531	Mnn
Posey	507	Prw
Rob.	530	Mnn
Robert	693	Br
Robert	11	Oho
Salley	14	Hnr
Sam	530	Mnn
Saml.	293	Rck
Samuel	680	Br
Samuel	919	Crl
Thomas	96	Jff
Thomas	722	Nls
Thomas	16	Oho
Thomas	303	Rck
Thomas	28	Stf
Thos.	64	Clp
William	290	Frf
William	552	Frd
William	505	Prw
Wm.	649	Btt
Wm.	7	Oho
Wm.	298	Rck
Wm.	299	Rck
see ...atterson, Hannah, Wright		
Patteson, David	66	Chs
Pattey, ---	766	Nwk
John	348	Fqr
William	420	Fqr
Pattillo, John	760	Brn
Littleton	759	Brn
Robert	728	Brn
see Patillo		
Pattin, Andrew	926	Hrr
Isibal	930	Hrr
Robert	926	Hrr
Ruth	926	Hrr
Pattison, Addison	815	Bck
Alexander	815	Bck
Ben.	815	Bck
David	841	Bck
Edward	839	Bck
Elizabeth	821	Bck
George	815	Bck
James, Jr.	808	Bck
James, Senr.	789	Bck
John	788	Bck
John	816	Bck
John	839	Bck
John	10	Oho
John, (S)	825	Bck
Nancey	815	Bck
Nancey	838	Bck
Samuel	796	Bck
Sarah	815	Bck
Squire	815	Bck
Thomas	819	Bck
William	780	Bck
William, Sr.	801	Bck
Pattman, Thomas	811	Bck
Patton, Ann	53	Stf
George	39	Stf
Henry, Jr.	606	Mnt
Henry, Sr.	667	Mnt
Isaac	637	Mnt

Name	No.	Co.	Name	No.	Co.	Name	No.	Co.
James	542	Brk	John	12	Knw	James	593	Mnr
James	291	Frf	Joseph	11	Knw	James	48	Stf
James	593	Frd	L. A.	373	Ags	James, (son to Richd.)	351	Fqr
James	283	Ldn	Paup, Betty, (M)	728	Brn	Jesse	345	Fqr
James	1	Oho	Thos.	726	Brn	Jesse	444	Flv
James	298	Rck	Pavey, John	263	Rck	Jesse	32	Stf
James	25	Stf	Paxon, Wm.	307	Ldn	Jno.	303	Ldn
Jane	300	Rck	Paxton, Hugh	274	Rck	Joanna, (F. Negroe)	375	Fqr
Jno.	550	Prg	James	266	Rck	John	868	Cmp
Jno.	306	Rck	John	722	Nls	John	447	Flv
John	682	Br	John	273	Rck	John	563	Frd
John	382	Fqr	John	290	Rck	John	720	Nls
John	602	Frd	Jonathan	288	Rck	John	37	Stf
John	929	Hrr	Joseph	303	Rck	John, Jr.	345	Fqr
John	933	Hrr	Joseph, esq.	274	Rck	John, Jr.	468	Frn
John	590	Mnr	Reubin	648	Btt	John, Junr.	782	Wst
John	637	Mnt	Saml.	372	Ags	John, Senr.	368	Fqr
Joseph	286	Rck	Saml.	275	Rck	John, Senr.	783	Wst
Nimrod	612	Mnt	Saml.	279	Rck	John, Sr.	468	Frn
Rachel	39	Stf	Saml.	292	Rck	John W.	710	Gch
Richard	54	Stf	Samuel	284	Amh	John W.	26	Stf
Robert	290	Frf	Thomas	513	Prw	Johnatn. S.	710	Gch
Robert	635	Gls	Thomas	290	Rck	Joseph	444	Bth
Robert	573	Mnr	Wm.	271	Rck	Joseph	467	Frn
Robert	99	Spt	Wm. [2]	273	Rck	Josiah	447	Flv
Robert	111	Spt	Wm.	290	Rck	Josiah, jr.	444	Flv
Robt., Este.	64	Clp	Wm., (Capt.)	274	Rck	Josiah, (younr.[?])	444	Flv
Saml.	620	Mnt	see Pa...ton, Panter			Kelly	49	Stf
Sampson	636	Mnt	Paydon, Chas.	471	Pra	Laurance, jr.	212	Kng
Thomas	825	Bck	Obadiah	14	Oho	Lewis	441	Bth
Thomas	634	Gls	Obadiah, Jr.	19	Oho	Ludd	40	Stf
Thos.	66	Clp	Paylor, Davis	10	Ntt	Mary	40	Stf
Thos.	636	Mnt	Richd.	60	Chr	Mer.	355	Lnc
Tristram	590	Mnr	William	69	Chr	Moses	475	Bdf
William	297	Rck	Payne, Alex. S.	708	Gch	Philip	869	Cmp
William	849	Wth	Ann	915	Nrf	Pollard	477	Bdf
Wm., jer.	286	Rck	Ann	782	Wst	Polly	117	Spt
see Patson, Patten			Anthony	20	Isw	Presley	345	Fqr
Pauff, Charles	848	Wth	Archer	708	Gch	Rachal	36	Stf
Paugh, John	810	Hmp	Augustine	345	Fqr	Rachel, U.	32	Stf
Joseph	921	Hrr	Barnet	468	Frn	Rd.	63	Clp
Michael	810	Hmp	Barrett G.	438	Flv	Richard H.	900	Hnv
Nicholas	814	Hmp	Benjamin	381	Fqr	Richd.	356	Lnc
William	798	Hmp	Benjamin	720	Nls	Richd. B.	436	Flv
Paukey, Saml.	708	Gch	Caty	522	Frd	Robt. B.	439	Flv
Paul, ---, Campell &	21	Hnr	Daniel	429	Flv	Rodrick	707	Gch
Agnes	42	Rcm	Daniel, of Jno.	342	Fqr	Saml.	15	Hnr
Andw.	546	Brk	Daniel, (of Wm.)	412	Fqr	Sanford	292	Frf
Andw.	294	Rck	Dubel [written in on photo-			Smith	784	Bck
Babel	49	Acc	stats p. 476]	475	Bdf	Tarltan	710	Gch
Daniel	12	Knw	Edward	841	Nrf	Theodosious	33	Stf
George	12	Knw	Edwd.	355	Lnc	Thomas	477	Bdf
Hugh	374	Ags	Eleander	64	Clp	Thomas	26	Stf
Hugh	12	Knw	Elijah	57	Stf	Thomas	57	Stf
Iaac	597	Mnr	Eliza.	471	Pra	Thomas, Jr.	388	Fqr
Jacob	530	Mnn	Elizabeth	709	Gch	Thomas, Jr.	467	Frn
James	372	Ags	Elizabeth	100	Spt	Thomas, Senr.	344	Fqr
James	7	Hnr	Elizabeth	40	Stf	Thomas, Sr.	467	Frn
Jenny	128	Hnr	Elizabeth	57	Stf	William	468	Frn
John, Junr.	12	Knw	Flayl	452	Frn	William	563	Frd
John, Seigr.	12	Knw	Flowerrie	344	Fqr	William	589	Frd
Peter	14	Rcm	Fosaria [? written over			William	57	Stf
Robert	9	Oho	"John"]	37	Stf	William, (Clifton)	390	Fqr
Robt.	65	Clp	Francis, Jr.	344	Fqr	William, (Son of Fs.)	361	Fqr
Salley	7	Hnr	Francis, Senr.	368	Fqr	William, (of Jno.)	366	Fqr
Sapina	451	Mth	Frans.	64	Clp	William, (Waggoner)	367	Fqr
Wm.	502	Brk	Geo.	63	Clp	Wm.	292	Frf
Paulet, Richard	866	Cmp	Geo.	3	Clp	Wm.	446	Flv
Richard	583	Pre	Geo. W.	711	Gch	Wm.	357	Lnc
Paulett, Elizabeth	60	Chr	George	443	Bth	Wm., (Colo.)	289	Frf
Halcomb	60	Chr	George	467	Frn	see P...yne		
Harvey	60	Chr	George	710	Gch	Payntar, Nathl.	470	Pra
Thomas, Jur.	60	Chr	George	782	Wst	Payson, William	437	Bth
Paulis, Adam	373	Ags	George H.	418	Fqr	Payton, Garnet	662	Mnt
Paulley, Jonathan	633	Gls	Hancock	291	Frf	Garnet	848	Wth
Joseph, Jr.	633	Gls	Harrison	442	Bth	Isaiah	65	Clp
Joseph, Senr.	633	Gls	James	360	Fqr	Jno.	66	Clp
Thomas	633	Gls	James	446	Flv	Peggy	610	Mnt
Paulsin, John	836	Nrf	James	468	Frn	Peace, Grace	57	Jff
Pauly, Henry	11	Knw	James	563	Frd	Jno.	879	Hnv

John	354	Lnn	Jane	60	Chr	Rebecca	102	Jff
Joseph	354	Lnn	Jane	516	Prw	Richard	583	Pre
Samuel, jr.	354	Lnn	John	759	Brn	Saml.	921	Hrr
Samuel, Sr.	354	Lnn	John	512	Prw	Simmons	581	Pre
Wim.	881	Hnv	John B.	919	Crl	William	7	Pwh
Peacemaker, John	556	Frd	Johnson	760	Brn	Zadok	531	Frd
Peach, Daniel	375	Fqr	Joseph	8	Knw	Peckings, Thompson	431	Msn
Nancey	394	Fqr	Littleton	759	Brn	Peckler, John	219	Shn
Peacham, J. B.	914	Nrf	Morriss	759	Brn	see Pockle		
Peachy, Mary M.	881	Yrk	Northumberland	511	Prw	Peckles, Rebecca	206	Ess
Peacock, Hizekiah	300	Ldn	Thomas	476	Bdf	Pectol, Jacob	571	Brk
Jno.	281	Ldn	William	503	Prw	see Pechtall, Pechtol		
Richard	108	Spt	William	110	Spt	Pedeler, Abraham	203	Shn
Saml.	282	Ldn	Wm.	759	Brn	Ulrich	186	Shn
Wm.	299	Ldn	Wm.	531	Mnn	Peden, Benjn.	636	Mnt
Pead, Elice	782	Wst	see Sincox			Mary	813	Nrf
James	782	Wst	Pearsons, Adam	430	Msn	Pedero, James	634	Mnt
John	782	Wst	George	420	Msn	Pedin, Edmond	12	Isw
Peade, Leml.	470	Pra	John	421	Msn	Peebles, Allen G.	727	Brn
Peagram, Edward	727	Brn	Joseph	430	Msn	Anne	454	Grn
Peah see Peat			William	420	Msn	Benja.	454	Grn
Peake, Abner	11	Wod	see Persons			Frederick	727	Brn
Elizabeth	291	Frf	Peas, T.	644	Btt	Hartwell	534	Prg
Hannah	807	Bck	Peasey, John	478	Bdf	James	156	Dnw
Henry	514	Prw	see Pearsey			Jane	727	Brn
Humphrey, (Quarter)	384	Fqr	Peasly, Gabriel	116	Cmb	Jessee	727	Brn
Humpy.	290	Frf	Peat, Mary	849	Sth	Josiah	549	Prg
James	515	Prw	Thos.	849	Sth	Mary	727	Brn
John	178	Elc	Peatross, Ann	918	Crl	Michaja	549	Prg
John	782	Wst	Ann	919	Crl	Mordaic	549	Prg
Richard	832	Bck	Henry	918	Crl	Nathaniel	454	Grn
Thomas	290	Frf	Richard	918	Crl	Nathaniel	658	Sss
William	919	Crl	Thomas	918	Crl	Rebecca	534	Prg
Peal, Hunter	477	Bdf	Thomas	919	Crl	Sarah	657	Sss
James	649	Btt	Peatt, Benjn.	372	Ags	Stephens	535	Prg
Richd.	649	Btt	Elizabeth	801	Hmp	Thomas E.	658	Sss
Peale, James	799	Hmp	William	801	Hmp	Willie	454	Grn
Pearce, Beverly	174	Knq	Pebsworth, Wm. J.	470	Pra	Peecher, Jesse	539	Brk
Dan	529	Mnn	Pebworth, Frs.	915	Nrf	Peed, Behethleon	212	Kng
Eliz.	528	Mnn	Jno. L.	470	Pra	James	212	Kng
Francis	125	Hnr	Sarah	470	Pra	Nat.	828	Nrf
Geo.	530	Mnn	Sarah	866	Sth	Peede, James	439	Mth
Isaac	528	Mnn	Wm.	470	Pra	Robert	829	Nrf
Jacob	423	Rnd	see Pebsworth, Petworth			Wm.	454	Mth
Jacob, jr.	277	Amh	Pecatt, John	475	Frn	Peek see Peck		
Jacob G.	294	Amh	William	478	Frn	Peel, ...n.	305	Rck
John R.	125	Hnr	Pechtall, Barbara	580	Brk	Barnet	254	Shn
Joseph	13	Oho	Pechtol, John	569	Brk	Peeling, John	649	Btt
Mable	528	Mnn	Pecious, Wm.	915	Nrf	Peer, Daniel [David]	211	Shn
Martin	581	Pre	Peck, Adam	633	Gls	John	211	Shn
Michl.	917	Hrr	Andw.	373	Ags	Margarett	212	Shn
Peter	281	Amh	Benjain, Ser.	634	Gls	Matthias	211	Shn
Rebecca	334	Dnw	Benjamin, Jr.	634	Gls	Philip	211	Shn
Robert	274	Amh	Charles	581	Pre	Peerman, Elisha	331	Dnw
Sam	530	Mnn	Danl.	373	Ags	James	849	Wth
Samuel	808	Bck	Elisha	16	Hnr	John, (W)	880	Yrk
Samuel	332	Dnw	Esther	583	Pre	Michl.	304	Rck
Wm.	124	Hnr	Garret	217	Pnd	Thomas	765	Nwk
Wm.	126	Hnr	Jacob	373	Ags	Peers, Elizabeth	713	Gch
see Griffin			Jacob	404	Ags	Nicholas	302	Ldn
Pearcy, Richard	727	Brn	Jacob	569	Mnr	Thos.	706	Gch
Peares, George, Jun.	633	Gls	Jacob	640	Mnt	Peery, Andrew	606	Mnt
George, Sen.	634	Gls	Jacob	217	Pnd	Peesley see Pusley		
Pearey, Isam	693	Wsh	Jacob	224	Pnd	Peeters see Puters		
Pearl, Samuel	389	Fqr	Jacob	739	Wsh	Pefley, David	648	Btt
Pearse, Arthur	13	Oho	Jacob, jr.	374	Ags	Henry	650	Btt
Rice B.	131	Sth	Jno., Sr.	647	Btt	Saml.	650	Btt
Spencer	131	Sth	John	634	Gls	Peg, Eliza	782	Wst
Wm.	878	Sth	John	217	Pnd	Thomas	781	Wst
Pearsey, Charles	478	Bdf	John	581	Pre	Pegg, Catharine	245	Ldn
James	467	Frn	John	400	Rch	Pegott, Ralph	832	Nrf
see Peasey			John	782	Wst	Pegram, Baker	157	Dnw
Pearson, Aecy	515	Prw	Joseph	647	Btt	Daniel	477	Bdf
Classey	501	Frn	Joseph	633	Gls	Edward	477	Bdf
Cumberland	516	Prw	Joseph	923	Hrr	Edward	326	Dnw
David	7	Oho	Joshua	111	Hnr	Edward	657	Sss
Drury	760	Brn	Josiah	920	Hrr	Edward, after	328	Dnw
Edmund B.	854	Hnv	Letitin	531	Frd	Edwd., Senr.	157	Dnw
George	503	Prw	Margret	216	Pnd	Elizabeth	158	Dnw
James	581	Frd	Peter	430	Msn	Geo. S.	156	Dnw

Name	Page	Co.
George	157	Dnw
George	330	Dnw
John, jr.	156	Dnw
John, Senr.	156	Dnw
Rebecca	157	Dnw
Robt.	157	Dnw
Wm. B.	156	Dnw
Peirce, Anne	40	Isw
Arthur	18	Isw
Henry	10	Rcm
John	106	Jff
John	56	Stf
John	782	Wst
Randell	782	Wst
Susanna	18	Isw
Thomas, Sen.	32	Isw
Thomas, Jun.	18	Isw
William	19	Isw
William, (of Anne)	40	Isw
Wm.	815	Nrf
see Pence, Perry		
Peirey, Joseph	373	Ags
Peirman, Collier	956	Chc
Fenley	948	Chc
Harwood	950	Chc
John	956	Chc
Peite, Benjamin	658	Sss
Pelham, Frances	333	Dnw
Pompy	728	Brn
Pell, Rd.	290	Frf
Pellway, John	453	Grn
Pelly, James	676	Br
Nathan	676	Br
Pelteir, Anthy.	326	Dnw
Pelter, Peter	473	Frn
Peltis see Pettis		
Pemberton, Aggy	918	Crl
Hanah	10	Pwh
Henry	169	Alb
Henry	494	Frn
James	872	Cmp
John	174	Knq
John	10	Pwh
Joseph	879	Cmp
Larkin	63	Clp
Staunton	748	Wsh
Thomas	168	Alb
Thomas	173	Knq
Thos.	710	Gch
William G.	919	Crl
Wm.	131	Hnr
Wm.	748	Wsh
Penall, Richd.	64	Clp
Penam, Andrew	681	Br
Pence, Abraham	188	Shn
Adam	11	Rcm
Charles	20	Rcm
David	28	Rcm
Frederick	187	Btt
Geo.	648	Btt
George, (Jr.)	12	Rcm
George, (Sen.)	12	Rcm
Henry	12	Rcm
Henry, (Sen.)	12	Rcm
Jacob	609	Mnt
Jacob	6	Rcm
Jacob	201	Shn
Jacob, (B.T.)	187	Shn
Jacob, (Cooper)	187	Shn
Jacob, jr.	664	Mnt
John	1	Rcm
John	9	Rcm
John	34	Rcm
Lewis	179	Shn
Nicholas	201	Shn
Peter	648	Btt
Philip	236	Shn
William, (Jr.)	37	Rcm
William, (Sen.)	28	Rcm
see Peirce, Perce		
Pendale, Gebl.	301	Rck
Pendall, Jac.	529	Mnn
Tho.	529	Mnn
Pendell, Jac.	528	Mnn
Pender, Benjn.	915	Nrf
Pendergrass, Vinct.	915	Nrf
Pendleton, Benjamin	68	Spt
Benjn.	586	Brk
Catlet	63	Clp
Edmd.	64	Clp
Edmund	917	Crl
Edmund, jun.	885	Crl
Edmund, jun.	887	Crl
Edmund, jur.	935	Crl
Edmund, sr.	917	Crl
George	352	Fqr
Henry	63	Clp
Henry	86	Spt
James	280	Amh
James	839	Bck
James	856	Hnv
James	849	Wth
James, Docr.	173	Knq
James, Senr.	173	Knq
John	917	Crl
John	104	Spt
Mary Ann	174	Knq
Micajuh	721	Nls
Nathanial	227	Pnd
Philip	478	Bdf
Phillip	78	Spt
Reubin	263	Amh
Richard	264	Amh
Robert	92	Spt
Robert	30	Stf
Sarah	917	Crl
Sarah	850	Hnv
Thos.	63	Clp
William	275	Amh
Wm.	549	Brk
Wm.	63	Clp
Wm. G.	18	Hnr
see Hendrick, Heronomus		
Pendred, Jno., 2nd.	915	Nrf
John	915	Nrf
Penetent, John	614	Mnt
Penham, Wm.	743	Wsh
Penick, Agness	581	Pre
Edwd.	11	Ntt
John	354	Lnn
John	582	Pre
Josiah	581	Pre
Nathan	582	Pre
Thomas	582	Pre
Thompson	5	Ntt
Thompson	582	Pre
William [2]	582	Pre
Penington, John	697	Br
Peniston, Jno. G.	330	Dnw
Samuel	329	Dnw
Penistone, Anthy.	539	Prg
Penler, Francis	509	Prw
John	509	Prw
William	509	Prw
Penn, ... R.	477	Bdf
Alexander	279	Amh
Benjn.	915	Nrf
Edmund	97	Spt
Elizabeth	727	Brn
George	276	Amh
George	79	Spt
James	869	Cmp
Jessee	60	Chr
Jno.	292	Frf
John	272	Amh
John	283	Amh
John	727	Brn
John	334	Dnw
John	914	Nrf
John	79	Spt
Martha	815	Bck
Sarah	283	Amh
Thomas	721	Nls
Thomas	101	Spt
Walter	290	Frf
William	281	Amh
William	66	Spt
see Pinn		
Pennal, Francis	633	Gls
Pennel, Edward	552	Frd
Pennell see Purnell		
Penner, Christian	627	Mnt
John	612	Mnt
Pennery, Richd.	588	Brk
Pennigar, Henry, J.	216	Pnd
Henry, S.	216	Pnd
John	225	Pnd
Pennington, Abraham	787	Hmp
Eligah	768	Hmp
James	657	Sss
James	674	Sss
John	659	Sss
Marcus	659	Sss
Nancy	659	Sss
Richard	221	Pnd
Richard	222	Pnd
Sarah	659	Sss
Thos.	699	Wsh
Wheeler	567	Mnr
Wm.	727	Brn
Wm.	567	Mnr
Wm., Jr.	567	Mnr
Pennock, Wm.	915	Nrf
Penny, James	920	Hrr
James	545	Prg
John	92	Spt
Lincefield S.	69	Spt
Pennybacker, Abraham	195	Shn
Benjamin	195	Shn
Hannah	195	Shn
John	194	Shn
Pennybaker, Jacob	559	Frd
William	559	Frd
Pennywel see Pennywit		
Pennywit, Jacob	199	Shn
John	198	Shn
Penock, William	456	Frn
Penquite, William	375	Fqr
Penrose, Abm.	529	Mnn
Ben	529	Mnn
Jesse	529	Mnn
Pentecost, John	59	Chr
Richard	60	Chr
Scarborough, (Es)	60	Chr
Thos.	158	Dnw
William	61	Chr
Penticost, Wm.	728	Brn
Pentoney, Luke	596	Brk
Peoples, Hance	127	Hnr
James	404	Ags
James	18	Rcm
Peors see Pevis		
Peper, Geore	932	Hrr
James	289	Frf
Pepher, Samuel	548	Brk
Peppen, John	529	Brk
Mary	529	Brk
Arabella	546	Frd
James	627	Mnt
Jeremiah	401	Fqr
Jesse	634	Gls
John	764	Hmp
John	619	Mnt
John, Ser.	765	Hmp
William	119	Acc
William	510	Frd
William	920	Hrr
William, Jr.	630	Mnt
Wm., Sr.	668	Mnt

Name	Page	County
Pepperly, Geo.	374	Ags
Perce, Conrode	235	Shn
John	235	Shn
John	241	Shn
see Pence		
Percefield, Michael	849	Wth
Percell, Peter	142	Sth
see Perscell		
Percivall, Joseph	726	Brn
Perdue, Daniel	480	Frn
Elizabeth	57	Chs
Francis	859	Cmp
Happy	480	Frn
Isham	18	Ntt
James	634	Gls
Jno., jun.	60	Chs
Jno., senr.	66	Chs
Meshack	480	Frn
Molley	60	Chs
Nancy	21	Ntt
Peter	60	Chs
Richard	54	Chs
Shadrack	59	Chs
Thomas	634	Gls
Thos.	59	Chs
William	455	Frn
Zacharias	634	Gls
Zackariah	472	Frn
see Pordue		
Peregen, Job	703	Wsh
Perfater, Philip	71	Jff
Perfect, Rob.	529	Mnn
Perfects, Robert	303	Ldn
Perge, Jacob	764	Nwk
Perke, Isaac	117	Hnr
Perkens, Adam	820	Nrf
Perkenton, Willm.	176	Elc
Perkes, Edmund	116	Hnr
Perkin see Purkus		
Perkins, Ann	158	Dnw
Archelaus	710	Gch
Baker, Senr.	158	Dnw
Benjamin	849	Cmp
Benjamin	354	Lnn
Benjn.	158	Dnw
Bernard	158	Dnw
Edward	158	Dnw
Elizabeth	800	Bck
Elizabeth	434	Flv
Geo.	706	Gch
Geore	114	Cmb
Gidion	728	Brn
Grief	710	Gch
Hardin	825	Bck
Hute	157	Dnw
James	543	Prg
Jno.	849	Hnv
John	435	Bth
John	773	Bck
John	850	Cmp
John	453	Frn
John [?]	820	Nrf
John, (B)	158	Dnw
John, jr.	157	Dnw
John, Senr.	158	Dnw
Joseph	264	Amh
Joseph	823	Bck
Joshua	157	Dnw
Joshua, jr.	158	Dnw
Nancy	158	Dnw
Nat.	709	Gch
Polley	157	Dnw
Price	825	Bck
Robert	765	Nwk
Saml.	541	Prg
Sarah	796	Bck
Sarah	825	Bck
Temple	869	Cmp
Thomas	292	Frf
Travers W.	445	Bth
Whitney	440	Mth
William	11	Isw
William, (T)	784	Bck
Willis	157	Dnw
Wim.	876	Hnv
Wm.	710	Gch
Young D.	727	Brn
see Purkins		
Perkinson, Daniel	231	Aml
Ezekiel	54	Chs
Henry	231	Aml
Herbert	61	Chr
Jackmon	61	Chr
Jno.	54	Chs
Jno.	69	Chs
John	232	Aml
John	54	Chs
Jos.	55	Chs
Munford	55	Chs
Noel	157	Dnw
Sarah	54	Chs
Thos.	232	Aml
Travis	532	Prg
see Purkinson		
Perks, Coleman	919	Crl
Samuel	918	Crl
Perlin, Jacob	544	Frd
Perrey, Joseph	290	Ldn
Robert	246	Ldn
Robert	252	Ldn
Perrigo, Henry	675	Br
Perril, John	106	Jff
Joseph	60	Jff
Perrill, Edward	764	Hmp
John	768	Hmp
William	770	Hmp
Perriman, Philip	174	Knq
Richd.	174	Knq
Perrin, Bevon	872	Hnv
Henry	872	Hnv
Isaac	232	Aml
Isaac	860	Hnv
John	581	Pre
John	680	Wrw
Joseph	849	Hnv
Peter	914	Nrf
Piere	915	Nrf
Wm. K.	667	Glc
Perrine, Wm.	1	Oho
Perron, Charles	777	Bck
Guerrant	777	Bck
John	798	Bck
Perrow, Charles	722	Nls
Daniel	721	Nls
Daniel B.	862	Cmp
Stephen	862	Cmp
Perrum, Lewis	355	Lnn
Perry, Ann	110	Spt
Caleb	848	Wth
Collin M.	810	Bck
Dinah	915	Nrf
Fewell	519	Prw
George	205	Alb
George	68	Spt
Henry	18	Oho
Hezekiah	523	Prw
James	105	Spt
Jno. S.	292	Frf
John	205	Alb
John	852	Cmp
John	591	Frd
John	787	Hmp
John	82	Jff
John	107	Jff
John	575	Mnr
John	578	Mnr
John	599	Mnr
John, Sr.	73	Spt
Jonathan	917	Crl
Joseph	563	Mnr
Joseph	440	Mth
Judy	5	Isw
Mary	436	Bth
Mary	685	Br
Moses	92	Spt
Nelson	433	Flv
Peirce	64	Clp
Peter	15	Ntt
Peter, a free man of couler	749	Wsh
Pierce	64	Clp
Robert	4	Knw
Rolin	787	Hmp
Saml.	8	Ntt
Sarah	5	Hnr
Sarah	723	Nls
Simon	919	Crl
Thomas	169	Alb
Thomas	168	Shn
Thos.	55	Jff
William	168	Alb
William	73	Spt
Wm.	212	Ess
Wm.	707	Gch
see Pervy		
Perryman, Anthony	60	Chr
Polly	548	Prg
Perrymon, John	582	Pre
Perscell, James	17	Oho
see Percell		
Persey, Ann	914	Nrf
Persinger, Andw.	648	Btt
Barbary	648	Btt
Henry	649	Btt
Jacb., (Younger)	648	Btt
Jacob	13	Knw
Jacob, Jr.	648	Btt
Jacob, Sr.	649	Btt
Jno.	650	Btt
Jno., Sr.	648	Btt
John	13	Knw
Luke	10	Knw
Moses	648	Btt
Moses	649	Btt
Persise, Saml.	12	Ntt
Wm.	658	Mnt
Persival, Elijah	356	Lnc
Person, Mary	454	Grn
Thomas	476	Frn
see Purson, Turner, Wmson		
Persons, Charles	420	Msn
Ches., Snr.	420	Msn
George	430	Msn
George	285	Rck
Henry	613	Srr
John	240	Shn
Mary	613	Srr
William	614	Srr
see Pearsons		
Pervin, Isaac	638	Mnt
Pervy, William	722	Nls
Pescud, Edward	328	Dnw
Ro.	879	Yrk
Thos.	681	Wrw
Thos., of Warwick County has Slaves in York County	880	Yrk
Pestrage, Hettie	212	Kng
Sarah	212	Kng
Wm.	213	Kng
Peteer, Saml.	301	Rck
Peter, Antony	880	Yrk
Isaiah	21	Oho
John	270	Amh
John	614	Srr
Joseph	914	Hrr
Moza	274	Amh
Sarah	541	Prg
Thomas	613	Srr
William	265	Amh

see Piles		
Peterfish, Jacob	28	Rcm
John	28	Rcm
Mary	28	Rcm
Peterman, Benjamin	917	Crl
Danl.	647	Btt
Danl.	640	Mnt
George	647	Btt
Jacob	649	Btt
John	596	Brk
Michl.	641	Mnt
Petero, Henry	423	Rnd
Peters, Abm.	647	Btt
Abraham	25	Rcm
Abrm.	303	Rck
Armstead	614	Srr
Benj.	749	Wsh
Betty	857	Hnv
Christian	568	Mnr
Conrad	569	Mnr
Daniel	198	Shn
Elisha	721	Nls
Godfrey	919	Hrr
Henry	454	Grn
Isaac	11	Rcm
Jacob	648	Btt
Jacob	649	Btt
James	765	Hmp
James	834	Hmp
John	454	Grn
John	789	Hmp
John	790	Hmp
Jdhn	25	Rcm
John	27	Rcm
John, Junr.	633	Gls
John, Senr.	634	Gls
Joshua	764	Hmp
Joshua, (Feb)	3	Rcm
Judith	182	Alb
Lucy	333	Dnw
Lucy	116	Spt
Martha	454	Grn
Mary	528	Frd
Matt.	681	Wrw
Micheal, Jr.	479	Frn
Micheal, Sr.	479	Frn
Milner	916	Nrf
Molley, a free mulatto	992	Nrt
Peter	173	Shn
Philip	634	Gls
Philip	25	Rcm
Phillip	765	Hmp
Phillip, Jur.	765	Hmp
Rebeciah	8	Hnr
Robert	927	Hrr
Sally	880	Yrk
Samuel	830	Hmp
Stephin	653	Mnt
Tunis	830	Hmp
Warner	372	Ags
William	593	Frd
William	258	Shn
William	657	Sss
Zackariah	492	Frn
see Petero, Puters		
Petersan, Peter	559	Brk
Peterson, Daniel	17	Oho
Doratha	157	Dnw
Eli, Jr.	610	Mnt
Eli, Sr.	613	Mnt
Ezekiel	953	Hrr
Fred.	548	Prg
Geo.	372	Ags
Isaac	570	Brk
Isaac	258	Shn
Izarel	258	Shn
Jessee	727	Brn
Jno.	916	Nrf
John	911	Hrr
John	608	Mnt
John H.	530	Prg
Kinchen	454	Grn
Mor.	325	Dnw
Mortin	608	Mnt
Peter	698	Br
Peter	939	Chc
Peter	454	Grn
Sally	543	Prg
Soloman	214	Pnd
Thomas	690	Br
William	922	Hrr
see Goodwyn		
Petery, Alexr.	712	Wsh
John	712	Wsh
Pethal, John	781	Hmp
Peticolas see Pettecoals		
Peticrew, Jno.	285	Rck
Robt.	284	Rck
Wm.	283	Rck
Petijohn, James	420	Bth
Petiss, James	383	Fqr
Petit, John	832	Nrf
Steward	182	Elc
Petitt, Alexander	7	Oho
James	5	Oho
Petree, Eliza	811	Nrf
Petrie, Geo.	914	Nrf
Petser, Andrew	425	Rnd
Pettecoals, Philip A.	32	Hnr
Pettejohn, William	290	Amh
Pettenhelser, Barbara	207	Shn
Petter, Sampson	292	Frf
Pettery, John	662	Mnt
Pettet, Labin	471	Pra
Pettett, Andrew	294	Ldn
Jacob	294	Ldn
Thomas	789	Hmp
Pettey, John	169	Alb
Pettigrew see Peticrew		
Pettillo see Pattillo		
Pettis, Beverley	917	Crl
David	354	Lnn
Delilah	848	Wth
Isaac	848	Wth
John	917	Crl
John	355	Lnn
Molley	917	Crl
Samuel	354	Lnn
Stephen	355	Lnn
see Thacher		
Pettit, George	613	Srr
Hugh	168	Alb
Irea	206	Alb
Isaac	67	Clp
James	264	Amh
Jno.	65	Clp
Mary	38	Stf
Saml.	430	Flv
William	290	Frf
see Pittit		
Pettitt, Elizabeth	119	Acc
Jno.	289	Frf
Jonathan	180	Shn
Thomas	118	Acc
Thomas	407	Fqr
Wm.	291	Frf
Pettrey, James	633	Gls
Martin	633	Gls
Pettus, Freeman	59	Chr
John	436	Flv
John	583	Pre
John, (Cocram)	61	Chr
Overton	61	Chr
Susannah	60	Chr
Thomas	582	Pre
Thomas, Capt.	60	Chr
William	61	Chr
Pettway, Edwin	658	Sss
Eliza.	613	Srr
Robert	658	Sss
William	658	Sss
Petty, Abner	650	Btt
Anne	516	Prw
Dudley	2	Wod
Edwd.	470	Pra
Foushee	66	Clp
Francis	470	Pra
George	61	Chr
Henry	31	Hnr
Henry	470	Pra
James	470	Pra
James	2	Wod
Jane	291	Frf
Jno.	67	Clp
Jno.	470	Pra
John	399	Mds
John	519	Prw
John, Senr.	59	Chr
Larkin	66	Clp
Mary	470	Pra
Mashall	64	Clp
Rodham	64	Clp
Rolley, Sen.	64	Clp
Rolly, jr.	64	Clp
Thomas	61	Chr
Traverse	518	Prw
William	800	Bck
William	520	Prw
Wm.	650	Btt
see Pelly		
Pettyford, Thornton	336	Dnw
Wm.	335	Dnw
Pettypool, Anderson	454	Grn
Henry	453	Grn
see Massey, Pool		
Petway, Herbert	530	Prg
Petworth, Henry	866	Sth
see Pebworth		
Petzer, Jno.	529	Mnn
Peuch see Peach		
Pevis, Thos.	114	Hnr
Pew, David	261	Ldn
Elijah	720	Nls
John	303	Amh
Josiah	445	Mth
Josiah	454	Mth
Lot	866	Cmp
Sally	454	Mth
Saml.	372	Ags
Samuel	260	Ldn
Samuel	274	Ldn
Spencer [?]	274	Ldn
Wm.	915	Nrf
see ...w, Pugh		
Pewett, John	355	Lnn
Pewsey, Joshua	296	Ldn
Stephen	47	Acc
William	47	Acc
Wm. S.	437	Flv
Peydon, Mary	916	Nrf
Peyton, Ann	67	Clp
Ann	43	Stf
Antoney	782	Wst
Chandler	408	Fqr
Charles	60	Stf
Craven	169	Alb
Francis	236	Ldn
Francis	302	Ldn
Franis	289	Frf
George	76	Spt
H.J.	404	Ags
Henry, Jr.	365	Fqr
Henry, (Marsh)	359	Fqr
Henry, Senr.	376	Fqr
Isaac	67	Clp
James	58	Stf
Jeremh.	66	Clp
John	666	Glc
John	28	Stf
John	782	Wst

Name	Page	Co.	Name	Page	Co.	Name	Page	Co.
John H.	373	Ags	John	860	Cmp	John	468	Frn
John H.	403	Ags	John	869	Cmp	John	123	Hnr
John H.	54	Stf	John	349	Fqr	John	124	Hnr
Molly	782	Wst	John	629	Mnt	John	25	Isw
Nancy	65	Clp	John	720	Nls	John	429	Rnd
Samuel	48	Stf	John	534	Prg	John, Junr.	49	Acc
Sibbella	502	Prw	John	27	Rcm	John, Senr.	47	Acc
Susan	508	Frd	Johnson	304	Amh	Jonathan	49	Acc
Townshead	235	Ldn	Jonas	191	Shn	Joseph	429	Rnd
Valentine	44	Stf	Jonathan	192	Shn	Keteley	471	Pra
William	596	Frd	Joseph	256	Amh	Larkin	114	Hnr
Pflanigan, Robert	226	Pnd	Joseph	719	Nls	Levin	47	Acc
Pfleger, Michl.	647	Btt	Joshua	719	Nls	Lucy	231	Aml
Phamplin, James	721	Nls	Julius	764	Nwk	Mary	438	Bth
John	721	Nls	Margte.	916	Nrf	Mary	614	Srr
see Pamplin			Mary	257	Amh	Matthias	47	Acc
Pharas, John	720	Nls	Mary	596	Frd	Matthias, Senr.	47	Acc
Robert	422	Rnd	Mary	992	Nrt	Moaning	114	Hnr
Phares, John	687	Br	Mingo	132	Sth	Moser	421	Rnd
Pharis, Ealija	221	Pnd	Moses	258	Amh	Nancy	760	Brn
John	217	Pnd	Moses	67	Clp	Newton	53	Stf
Soloman	221	Pnd	Nelson	719	Nls	Phillip	205	Alb
Pharish, Jno.	852	Hnv	Richard	867	Hnv	Plunkett	827	Hmp
Phaup, William	60	Chr	Richard	721	Nls	Robert	948	Chc
Phefae, Mary	332	Dnw	Samuel	477	Bdf	Sam., Sr.	649	Btt
Phelps, Abingdon	754	Wsh	Samuel	478	Bdf	Samuel	120	Spt
Alexander	776	Bck	Squire	799	Bck	Sarah	485	Frn
Charles, (Captn.)	817	Bck	Thomas	477	Bdf	Stephen	849	Wth
Elijah	18	Wod	Thomas	307	Ldn	Thomas	46	Acc
Elisha	521	Frd	Thompson	259	Amh	Thomas	5	Isw
Hugh	10	Wod	Tully	471	Pra	Thomas, Senr.	47	Acc
James	773	Bck	William	864	Cmp	Thos.	760	Brn
James	818	Bck	William	516	Frd	Thos.	880	Yrk
John	3	Wod	William	582	Pre	William	47	Acc
Randolph	477	Bdf	William	41	Rcm	William	953	Chc
Richard	477	Bdf	William	242	Shn	William	689	Br
Robert	818	Bck	Wm.	649	Mnt	Wm.	156	Dnw
Saml.	751	Wsh	Wm., (F.N.)	66	Clp	Wm.	739	Wsh
Valentine	743	Wsh	Zach.	598	Mnr	Wm.	879	Yrk
William C.	2	Knw	Zach., Jr.	598	Mnr	Younger	782	Wst
see Philps			Zariah	719	Nls	Zachariah	36	Isw
Phenix, Wm.	726	Brn	Philipson, Philip	311	Ldn	see Fellips, Fillips, Phelps		
Phibbs, John	695	Br	Phill, ---, F.N.	174	Knq	Philpert, Mary	82	Jff
Philbates, Edward	765	Nwk	Phillippi, Christian	849	Wth	Philpot, Benjamin	36	Rcm
John	946	Chc	Christopher [2]	849	Wth	Philpott, Jno.	292	Frf
John	129	Hnr	John	849	Wth	Philpotts, Jno.	667	Glc
Mary	940	Chc	Phillips, Abel	49	Acc	Jno., jr.	667	Glc
Philip, Thos.	373	Ags	Anthony	59	Chr	John	711	Gch
Philips, Abraham	22	Rcm	Archibald	849	Wth	Lucy	666	Glc
Anderson	54	Chs	Benj.	880	Yrk	Okley	22	Hnr
Ann	174	Knq	Benja.	188	Elc	Paul	667	Glc
Anne	381	Fqr	Betsey	48	Acc	Philps, John	754	Wsh
Asa	908	Hrr	Betsy	84	Spt	Philson, Mary	686	Br
Benj.	272	Ldn	Charles	918	Crl	Phip see Phup		
Catharin	211	Ess	Chas.	188	Elc	Phipp, Jesse	731	Wsh
Charles	173	Knq	Celia	5	Isw	Matthew	731	Wsh
Charles	212	Kng	Edward	47	Acc	Phipps, Benjamin	760	Brn
Cornelous	720	Nls	Edwin	31	Isw	Gasper	739	Wsh
Daniel	554	Frd	Eliza	19	Hnr	John	568	Mnr
David	295	Ldn	Elizabeth	205	Alb	Mary	744	Wsh
Elizabeth	582	Pre	Elizabeth	48	Stf	Phips, Elisebith	756	Wsh
Frederick	61	Chs	Ephram	427	Rnd	Isaac	848	Wth
Gabriel	174	Knq	Geo.	540	Prg	James	848	Wth
Geo.	372	Ags	George	650	Btt	William	848	Wth
Geo., jr.	373	Ags	George	917	Crl	see Fips		
George	525	Frd	George	227	Pnd	Phreasure, James	252	Ldn
Henry	22	Rcm	Henry	954	Chc	Phup, John	689	Wsh
Henry	141	Sth	Henry	429	Rnd	Piatt, James	373	Ags
Isaac	597	Frd	Henry T.	120	Spt	Piatte, Francis	24	Hnr
Israel	272	Ldn	Isaac	114	Hnr	Picardat, Lewis C.	917	Crl
Jacob	264	Amh	Isaac	430	Rnd	Pichler, Michael	182	Shn
Jacob	603	Frd	James	48	Acc	Pickels, John	174	Knq
James	584	Frd	James	59	Chr	Mildred	174	Knq
James	173	Knq	James	468	Frn	Pickenpaw, Adm.	528	Mnn
James	16	Oho	James	4	Knw	Geo.	528	Mnn
Jinkin	362	Fqr	Jas.	29	Hnr	Js.	528	Mnn
Jno.	312	Ldn	Jessee	540	Prg	Pickens, Alexr.	922	Hrr
Jno.	7	Ntt	Jno.	140	Sth	David	570	Frd
John	259	Amh	John	759	Brn	Ealexandrew	219	Pnd
John	281	Amh	John	949	Chc	Pickerell, Levi	499	Prw

Name	No.	Abbr.	Name	No.	Abbr.	Name	No.	Abbr.
Thomas	505	Prw	Nathanl.	151	Sth	Pill, Henry	531	Prg
Thos.	67	Clp	Paul	583	Frd	Piller, John	582	Pre
Pickerill, Jonathan	544	Frd	Peter	152	Sth	William	582	Pre
Pickerin, Danl. [2]	373	Ags	Rebe.	681	Wrw	Willis	232	Aml
Jonathan	373	Ags	Reubn.	63	Clp	Pillsbury, George	174	Knq
Pickering, Barbara	37	Rcm	Richard	613	Srr	Sally	782	Wst
Danl.	37	Rcm	Richd.	640	Mnt	Pilsher, Charles	71	Spt
Jacob	11	Rcm	Saml.	629	Mnt	Pin, Mary, Jr.	357	Lnc
John	580	Frd	Saml.	914	Nrf	Mary, Senr.	356	Lnc
John	22	Rcm	Staunton	848	Wth	Minor, (F.Negroe)	380	Fqr
Picket, Mace	205	Alb	Warwick	848	Wth	Molly	357	Lnc
Pickett, Abm.	190	Elc	Wm.	268	Ldn	Nanny	357	Lnc
Ashby	848	Wth	see Pierca, Pine, Purce			Peggy, (F.Negroe)	418	Fqr
Geo.	31	Hnr	Pierceall, John	820	Hmp	Robt.	357	Lnc
George	212	Kng	Piere, Abm.	647	Btt	Pinalton, Jos.	721	Wsh
George B., (Quarr.)	418	Fqr	Phil	647	Btt	Pincham, Nancy	582	Pre
James	390	Fqr	Pierpoint, John	530	Mnn	Wm.	4	Ntt
John	48	Acc	Lark.	530	Mnn	Pinchard, Jas.	63	Clp
Martha	390	Fqr	Obadiah	312	Ldn	Spencer	63	Clp
Nancy	211	Kng	Samuel	307	Ldn	Thomas	67	Clp
Reubin	14	Hnr	Zac	530	Mnn	Pinchback, Jno.	53	Chs
Sandford	371	Fqr	see Preipoint			Pinckard, Cyrus	992	Nrt
William	581	Pre	Pierpont, Joseph	559	Frd	Elizabeth	991	Nrt
William, jr.	917	Crl	Pierson, Adderson	454	Grn	Elizabeth	992	Nrt
William, Jr.	346	Fqr	William	992	Nrt	Thomas	781	Wst
William, Senr.	918	Crl	William	36	Rcm	Pinder, John	215	Shn
William, Senr.	346	Fqr	see Purson			Pindle, Jams	964	Hrr
Wm.	12	Hnr	Pieruall see Pierceall			Pine, George	649	Btt
see Puckett			Pifer, Henry	603	Frd	George W.	8	Oho
Pickilsimer, Solomon	496	Frn	Peter	31	Rcm	Lazarus	526	Frd
Pickle, Henry	849	Wth	Pigeon, Jno.	916	Nrf	Robert	588	Mnr
Henry, Jur.	849	Wth	Pigg, Salley	59	Chs	Pinel, Adam	301	Ldn
Henry, Senr.	849	Wth	William	582	Pre	Pines, William	635	Gls
Jacob	693	Wsh	Wm.	880	Yrk	Pineter, Levin	528	Mnn
Jones	849	Wth	Pigget, Mary	906	Hrr	Wm.	528	Mnn
Lenard	955	Hrr	Piggott, Ebenezar	315	Ldn	see Pinters		
Tobias	849	Wth	Jno.	315	Ldn	Pinhorne, John	35	Isw
Pickles, Michl.	635	Mnt	Wm.	315	Ldn	William	9	Isw
see Peckles			Pigitt, Jesse	938	Hrr	Pinick, Nathaniel	108	Cmb
Pickleshimer, Abm.	636	Mnt	Pike, John C.	334	Dnw	Pinkard, Baley	492	Frn
Jacob	636	Mnt	Nancy	26	Isw	Charles	417	Fqr
Pickrell, H.	30	Hnr	Pilcher, Ann	58	Stf	Edwd.	356	Lnc
Pickrill, Eleanor	402	Fqr	Charles	88	Spt	Elias	498	Frn
John	403	Fqr	Daniel	27	Stf	George	212	Kng
Pickron, Lucy	993	Nrt	Frederick	109	Spt	John	492	Frn
Mott	993	Nrt	James	576	Frd	Molley	492	Frn
Presley	992	Nrt	James	35	Stf	Pinkerton, Robt.	560	Brk
William	992	Nrt	Jessee	510	Prw	Pinkly, Elizabeth	596	Mnr
Picot, Giles	7	Hnr	John	399	Mds	Pinkstaff, Leonard	396	Fqr
Pidgeon, Isaac	854	Cmp	Joshua	576	Frd	Molley	396	Fqr
Piemont, Ann	915	Nrf	Lewis	919	Crl	Pinkstone, Frances	377	Fqr
Thomas	764	Nwk	Moses	25	Stf	Pinn, James	302	Amh
Pierault see Pierceall			Moses	1	Wod	Johnston, (F.Negroe)	378	Fqr
Pierca, Lydia	547	Frd	Peter	381	Fqr	Turner	302	Amh
Pierce, Aaron	849	Wth	Stephen	505	Prw	Pinnell, Jno., jr.	65	Clp
Amos	241	Ldn	Thomas	33	Stf	Wm.	67	Clp
Ann	89	Spt	see Pilsher			Wm. R.	65	Clp
Benjamin, (F.Negroe)	412	Fqr	Pile, Amos	924	Hrr	Pinner, Benja.	148	Sth
Copelin	63	Clp	John	904	Hrr	Dixon	2	Isw
Daniel	766	Hmp	Piles, Christian	289	Frf	Pinnor, Mary	825	Nrf
Daniel	849	Wth	Dav.	528	Mnn	Pinters, John	528	Mnn
David	914	Nrf	Elijah	529	Mnn	see Pineter		
David	849	Wth	Elizabeth	250	Ldn	Piper, Abraham	520	Frd
Dianna	678	Wrw	Francis	422	Bth	Betsey	118	Acc
Ezekiel	766	Hmp	Hunter	530	Mnn	Cary, f. negro	289	Frf
Frances	188	Elc	Jacob	634	Gls	David	221	Shn
Frank	100	Spt	John	587	Brk	Dualey C.	718	Wsh
Goodsom	36	Hnr	Nathan, (F.Negroe)	369	Fqr	Eml.	530	Mnn
Jane	343	Fqr	Robert	76	Jff	Jacob	72	Jff
Jessee	849	Wth	Samuel	69	Jff	Jacob	221	Shn
Joathum	640	Mnt	Williamson	19	Ntt	James	718	Wsh
Joel	848	Wth	Wm.	528	Mnn	John	168	Alb
Jno.	65	Clp	Zac.	528	Mnn	John	575	Frd
John	810	Hmp	Zachariah	250	Ldn	John	759	Hmp
John	232	Ldn	Pilkenton, Joel	158	Dnw	John	212	Shn
John	67	Spt	Parmenas	200	Ess	Mary	221	Shn
Joseph, Jr.	546	Frd	Pilkilton, Salley	53	Chs	William	168	Alb
Joseph, Senr.	546	Frd	Pilkington, David	727	Brn	William	62	Jff
Michal	544	Frd	Willis	726	Brn	Pipher, Danl.	404	Ags
Mildred	707	Gch	Pilkinton, Larkin	4	Pwh	Pippel, William	827	Hmp

Name	No.	Co.	Name	No.	Co.	Name	No.	Co.
Pippenger, John	691	Br	James [2]	919	Crl	Pletcher, Henry	284	Ldn
Pippin, Wm.	667	Glc	John	49	Acc	Plomey, John	438	Bth
Pirchetts, ---	332	Dnw	John	26	Rcm	Robert	418	Bth
Pirkey, Catharine	9	Rcm	Leven	919	Crl	Plotner, Danl.	581	Brk
Elizabeth	9	Rcm	Litea	48	Acc	Morris	582	Brk
Henry	9	Rcm	Magarett	176	Knq	Plott, Henry	649	Btt
Henry, (Jr.)	9	Rcm	Mary	26	Rcm	Ploughy, John	241	Shn
Henry, (Sen.)	9	Rcm	Mary G.	919	Crl	Plum, Abraham	770	Hmp
Jacob	9	Rcm	Musco	918	Crl	Plumb, Abraham	803	Hmp
John	9	Rcm	Obediah	917	Crl	Conrod	11	Rcm
Solomon	9	Rcm	Oby	919	Crl	John, Jur.	803	Hmp
Pirkins, Flamsted	410	Ags	Philip	204	Ess	John, Sen.	803	Hmp
Pirnill, James	720	Wsh	Phillis	119	Acc	Sylvester	336	Dnw
Pitchford, John	232	Aml	Purnell	829	Nrf	Plume, ---, & Co.	915	Nrf
Peter	232	Aml	Richd.	668	Glc	Jacob	253	Shn
Pitcock, John	572	Frd	Sally	204	Ess	Plumer, Eli	681	Br
Stephen	573	Frd	William	49	Acc	Lucy	68	Chs
Pitman, Andrew	518	Frd	Pittzel, George	8	Knw	Plummer, Asa	853	Cmp
Asa	53	Chs	Pitzer, Abm.	648	Btt	Cassander	681	Br
Augt.	356	Lnc	Bernard	648	Btt	Jeremiah	471	Pra
Cyrus	992	Nrt	Fredk.	647	Btt	Joel	914	Hrr
Dicey	855	Sth	George	648	Btt	John	797	Nrf
Elija	992	Nrt	Jno., Jr.	647	Btt	Obadiah	817	Hmp
Elismon	992	Nrt	Jno., Sr.	647	Btt	Robt.	915	Hrr
Emmanuel	219	Shn	Pixket, Frances	449	Mth	Thomas	782	Wst
Fortunatus	992	Nrt	Pixler, Sam	531	Mnn	Thos.	914	Nrf
Geo.	356	Lnc	Place, Abm.	565	Brk	see Prummer		
James	112	Cmb	Neheh.	585	Brk	Plunkart, Adam	417	Fqr
Jesse	993	Nrt	Plaher, John	37	Rcm	Plunket, Ambrose	864	Cmp
John	520	Frd	Plan see Place			Benjamin	864	Cmp
Jonathan	221	Shn	Plankinship see Blankinship			Thomas	266	Rck
Joseph	426	Rnd	Plant, James	582	Pre	Reuben	917	Crl
Lawrance	201	Shn	see Plaut			Ply, Barbara	684	Br
Philip	220	Shn	Planter, James	48	Acc	Plyborne, Rebecka	464	Frn
Reubin	633	Gls	Plaster, Conrad	655	Mnt	Plymer, Amy	477	Bdf
Ruth	157	Dnw	Henry	260	Ldn	Plymon, Anthony	634	Gls
Tho.	356	Lnc	Platcher, James	56	Chs	Poage, George	416	Bth
Tho., Jr.	357	Lnc	Platenburgh, George	685	Br	George	648	Btt
William	518	Frd	Plaut, Peter	621	Mnt	James	373	Ags
William	992	Nrt	Pleasant, Beauford	658	Sss	James	648	Btt
Wm.	356	Lnc	Burwell	614	Srr	Jane	648	Btt
Pitmon, Williamson H.	16	Ntt	Faithy	658	Sss	Jno.	650	Btt
Pitmond see Fidler			Richard	169	Alb	John	371	Ags
Pitser, Conrod	539	Brk	William	659	Sss	John	277	Rck
John	539	Brk	Pleasants, Anthoney	848	Cmp	Martha	301	Rck
John, 2d.	539	Brk	Archebald	707	Gch	William	424	Bth
Matthias	539	Brk	Charles	568	Frd	Wm.	372	Ags
Michael [2]	539	Brk	Cuffy	131	Hnr	Wm.	650	Btt
Pitt, Dearis	819	Nrf	Cupid	865	Cmp	Poague, Peggy	298	Rck
Elizabeth	11	Isw	Dick	28	Hnr	Poak, Thomas	4	Oho
Henry	10	Isw	Frances	125	Hnr	Pock, Michael	950	Hrr
James	329	Dnw	Isaac W.	707	Gch	Pockle, Jacob	218	Shn
James	330	Dnw	James	182	Alb	see Peckler		
John	4	Isw	James	707	Gch	Pocsel see Poisel		
Joseph, Sen.	11	Isw	Jincy	334	Dnw	Poe, Fras.	66	Clp
Lewit	22	Oho	John	15	Pwh	Jacob	508	Frd
Riddick	10	Isw	John T.	8	Pwh	Jno.	66	Clp
Thomas	4	Isw	John W.	115	Hnr	Saml.	66	Clp
Thomas	22	Oho	Joseph	707	Gch	Stephen	530	Mnn
Wm.	64	Clp	Joseph	119	Hnr	Thomas	126	Hnr
Pittenger, Eliza.	64	Clp	Mariah	708	Gch	William	409	Fqr
Pittit, Wm.	442	Flv	Philip	707	Gch	Wm.	880	Yrk
Pittman, Hipkins	919	Crl	Richard	168	Alb	Poff, George	633	Mnt
James	919	Crl	Robert	168	Alb	Henry	746	Wsh
James	34	Isw	Robt.	707	Gch	John	634	Mnt
John	784	Bck	Robt. L.	707	Gch	Peter	634	Mnt
John	919	Crl	Saml.	23	Hnr	Poffenbarger, M.	404	Ags
Jordan	30	Isw	Saml.	124	Hnr	Pogue, Stephen	15	Oho
Robert	918	Crl	Samuel	8	Pwh	Poindexter, C.B.	915	Nrf
Samuel	29	Isw	Tarlton	707	Gch	James	10	Pwh
Thomas	38	Isw	Thomas E.	781	Bck	James	8	Rcm
Pitts, Ambrose	919	Crl	Thos., Estate	130	Hnr	John	456	Frn
Benja.	173	Knq	Plece, Jno. D.	439	Mth	John, Jr.	857	Cmp
Benjn.	915	Nrf	Pledge, Archer	707	Gch	John L.	766	Nwk
Coleman	212	Kng	Nancy	707	Gch	Joseph, Jr.	860	Cmp
Elijah	745	Wsh	Wm. [2]	708	Gch	Joseph, Sr.	858	Cmp
Elisah	745	Wsh	Plesants, ---, Ralston &	23	Hnr	Judith	765	Nwk
George	48	Acc	Jno. S.	29	Hnr	Lightfoot	764	Nwk
Henry	918	Crl	Talton	863	Hnv	Lydia	805	Nrf
Ismaiah	32	Isw	Plessing, Jacob	848	Wth	Polley	765	Nwk

Name	No.	Code
Polly	764	Nwk
Reuben	863	Cmp
Richard A.	918	Crl
Saml.	477	Bdf
Sarah	873	Cmp
Susan	3	Hnr
Susan	765	Nwk
Poindextur, William	206	Alb
Pointer, Dian.	184	Elc
Eliza.	666	Glc
Honora	915	Nrf
Jno.	542	Prg
John	849	Cmp
John	354	Lnn
Michael	666	Glc
Rebecca	9	Pwh
Saml.	667	Glc
Sanl.	837	Nrf
Thos.	666	Glc
Wm.	666	Glc
Pointter, William	953	Chc
Poisal, Boston	598	Brk
Poisel, Jacob	501	Brk
John	597	Brk
Peter	501	Brk
Poit...x, Michal	12	Hnr
Poitiaux see Poit...x		
Pok, John	11	Oho
John, Jr.	11	Oho
Poke, Adam	225	Shn
Polacy, Laer O. [?]	791	Nrf
Poland, Amos	790	Hmp
Jno.	292	Frf
John	790	Hmp
John, Jur.	791	Hmp
Martin	907	Hrr
Price	156	Dnw
Robert	790	Hmp
Samuel	806	Hmp
Samuel	908	Hrr
Samuel	82	Jff
Thomas	157	Dnw
Polcel, Peter	13	Rcm
Polk, Josh., Jr.	649	Btt
Josh., Sr.	649	Btt
Mary	108	Spt
Willm.	649	Btt
Pollack, Mayer	709	Gch
Polland, Mark	427	Rnd
Martaen	427	Rnd
Martaen [2]	429	Rnd
Peter	429	Rnd
Ricd.	429	Rnd
Richard C.	722	Nls
Roger	426	Rnd
Samuel	426	Rnd
Samuel	427	Rnd
William	426	Rnd
Pollard, Abner	388	Fqr
Ambrose	231	Aml
Anne	765	Nwk
Benja.	915	Nrf
Benjamin	896	Hnv
Edmd.	64	Clp
Fielding	764	Nwk
Francis	60	Chr
Francis	1	Ntt
George	232	Aml
George	60	Chr
George	454	Grn
Henry	35	Hnr
Henry, for Skinker	350	Fqr
Hunsford	477	Bdf
John	231	Aml
John	477	Bdf
John	332	Dnw
John	565	Frd
John	764	Nwk
Joseph	232	Aml
Joseph	477	Bdf
Joseph	706	Gch
Joseph	173	Knq
Joseph	74	Spt
Joseph	108	Spt
Joseph, Sr.	232	Aml
Leah	231	Aml
Lindsey	211	Kng
Lucy	356	Lnc
Martha	108	Spt
Mary	357	Lnc
Milldred	353	Fqr
Nancy	544	Frd
Pleasant	765	Nwk
Rebecca	336	Dnw
Richard	869	Cmp
Robert	887	Hnv
Robert	173	Knq
Robert	765	Nwk
Robert, [his] planta- tion	174	Knq
Robert Y.	173	Knq
Robt.	31	Hnr
Sally	914	Nrf
Saml.	667	Glc
Samuel	60	Chr
Sarah	849	Cmp
Thomas	477	Bdf
Thomas	211	Kng
Thos.	232	Aml
Thos.	874	Hnv
Thos., Sr.	232	Aml
W. P.	914	Nrf
William	399	Mds
Wim.	872	Hnv
Wm.	668	Glc
Wm.	356	Lnc
Wm.	245	Ldn
Pollett, John	917	Crl
Pollick, John	821	Nrf
Pollock, A.	20	Hnr
Alexander	198	Shn
David	693	Br
Epraim	24	Dnw
John	60	Chr
London	157	Dnw
Robt.	20	Hnr
William	3	Pwh
Pollok, Robert	328	Dnw
Pollove, Samuel	966	Hrr
Poltney, John N.	353	Lnn
Pomeroy, Richard	173	Shn
Pomfrey, John	10	Oho
Mildred	764	Nwk
Pleasant	766	Nwk
Silas	11	Oho
Spotswood	108	Spt
William	765	Nwk
Pompey, Beckey	770	Brn
Betsey	770	Brn
Jacob	47	Stf
Mary	770	Brn
Wm.	769	Brn
Pon, Caty	178	Shn
Ponce, Jacob	440	Bth
Poncomby see Ponsonby		
Pond, Daniel	130	Sth
James	161	Sth
John	956	Chc
John H.	152	Sth
Lemuel	139	Sth
Mary	614	Srr
Patrick	152	Sth
William	953	Chc
William	20	Stf
Pongrove, Elijah	966	Hrr
Ponn, Elizabeth	157	Dnw
Ponner, Hartwell	335	Dnw
Ponsonby, Ann	157	Dnw
David	9	Isw
Richard	614	Srr
Ponteruff, Catharine	441	Bth
Ponton, Elizabeth	14	Ntt
Jael	720	Nls
John	232	Aml
Peter	326	Dnw
see Procton		
Pool, Dennis	291	Frf
Edmd.	293	Frf
Edward P.	581	Pre
Esther	774	Hmp
Israel	280	Ldn
Israel	316	Ldn
Jno. P.	157	Dnw
John	634	Gls
John, Jun.	192	Elc
John C.	519	Frd
Joseph	531	Prg
Peter	569	Frd
Phebe	555	Frd
Price	183	Shn
Richard	12	Wod
Robt. P.	157	Dnw
Stephen P.	157	Dnw
Susanah	700	Wsh
Wm.	61	Chs
Wm. P.	157	Dnw
Poole, Geo.	915	Nrf
John	176	Elc
John H.	806	Nrf
Mary Anne	371	Fqr
Richd.	189	Elc
Sarah	292	Frf
William, (F.N.)	30	Isw
Winney	916	Nrf
Pooll, William	788	Hmp
Pools, Benjamin	693	Br
Poor, ---, Webster &	21	Hnr
Edwd.	709	Gch
James	709	Gch
Judith	709	Gch
Robert	5	Knw
Thomas	709	Gch
Thomas	710	Gch
Thomas	782	Wst
Poore, John	168	Alb
Pope, Andrew	160	Sth
Ann	155	Sth
Anne	870	Sth
Augustus	155	Sth
Daniel	23	Isw
Edwin	160	Sth
Eliza.	155	Sth
Eliza.	871	Sth
Evzns	160	Sth
Francis	992	Nrt
George H.	408	Rch
Hannah	783	Wst
Henson	155	Sth
Howell	849	Sth
Humphrey	411	Rch
Isaac	160	Sth
Jacob	871	Sth
John	140	Sth
John	154	Sth
John, Sen.	3	Isw
Jonas	152	Sth
Joseph	23	Isw
Joseph	155	Sth
Kinchen	155	Sth
Martha	20	Isw
Martha	160	Sth
Mary	837	Nrf
Mills	7	Isw
Molly	782	Wst
Nancy	991	Nrt
Nathan	131	Sth
Nathan	161	Sth
Nathan	869	Sth
Nathan	849	Wth
Patience	161	Sth

Peneliper	782	Wst	Peter	10	Pwh	Poteet, James	463	Frn	
Polley	859	Hnv	Philip	546	Frd	William	463	Frn	
Reuben	153	Sth	Phillip	766	Hmp	Poterfield, Robt.	373	Ags	
Richard	821	Bck	Reason	168	Alb	Potes, Hannah	47	Stf	
Richd.	7	Isw	Reizen	581	Pre	William	211	Kng	
Robt.	7	Isw	Richd.	528	Mnn	Potram, Julius	11	Rcm	
Sampson	874	Sth	Robert	443	Bth	Pots, Isaiah	65	Clp	
Susanna	132	Sth	Robert	576	Brk	Pottenfeild, Jacob	284	Ldn	
Thadecas	396	Rch	Robert	849	Wth	Potter, Aggy	326	Dnw	
Thomas	849	Sth	Saml.	649	Btt	Alexr.	302	Rck	
Thos.	707	Gch	Saml.	814	Nrf	Cathe.	290	Frf	
Thos.	709	Gch	Samuel	377	Fqr	David	297	Rck	
Thos. S.	14	Hnr	Samuel	399	Mds	James	290	Frf	
William	350	Fqr	Samuel	848	Wth	James	782	Wst	
William	1	Pwh	Sarah	766	Hmp	Jno.	304	Ldn	
William	115	Spt	Thomas	677	Br	Joseph	831	Nrf	
Willm.	176	Elc	Thomas	365	Fqr	Joseph	11	Oho	
Winnifred	993	Nrt	Thomas	9	Pwh	Lewis	453	Frn	
see Claxton			Thomas	38	Rcm	Philip	302	Rck	
Popejoy, Nancey	398	Fqr	Thomas	27	Stf	Rebecca	289	Frf	
Popham, Ann	67	Clp	Thos.	529	Mnn	Reuben	289	Frf	
Popkins, Jno.	233	Ldn	Thos.	915	Nrf	Richd.	915	Nrf	
Popler, James	291	Frf	Thos.	129	Sth	Robert	854	Hnv	
Poppan, Jno.	647	Btt	Trijall	770	Brn	Robert	8	Hnr	
Porch, Esom	31	Stf	William	477	Bdf	Shadrach	614	Srr	
Isebella	759	Brn	William	399	Mds	Solomon	757	Wsh	
James	157	Dnw	William	111	Spt	Wallon	31	Hnr	
James	533	Prg	William	782	Wst	William, Jur.	290	Frf	
James	657	Sss	William, SM	399	Mds	Wm., Senr.	291	Frf	
Mary	660	Sss	Wm.	66	Clp	Potterfield, Henry	287	Ldn	
Thomas	659	Sss	Wm.	128	Hnr	Jno.	284	Ldn	
Pordue, Bartholomew	53	Chs	Wm.	269	Rck	Potts, Benjamin	433	Bth	
Pore, Elisha	822	Bck	Wm. M.	1	Ntt	David	83	Jff	
Elisha	828	Bck	Porterfield, Betsey	586	Brk	Edwd.	270	Ldn	
Robert	788	Bck	Charles	586	Brk	Eliza	269	Ldn	
Soloman	823	Bck	Geo.	549	Brk	Elizabeth	269	Ldn	
Porear, Jessee	872	Hnv	John	502	Brk	Enoch	992	Nrt	
Thos.	854	Hnv	John	730	Wsh	Enos	309	Ldn	
Porkapice, John	258	Shn	Josiah	633	Gls	Ephraim	60	Chr	
Porlan, Alexr.	586	Brk	Robert	740	Wsh	Francis	841	Nrf	
Porte, Andw.	915	Nrf	Wm.	586	Brk	George C.	211	Kng	
Porter, Abrm.	878	Sth	Portis, Gideon	859	Sth	Grace	354	Lnn	
Adam	443	Bth	Portlet, John	915	Nrf	Isaiah	311	Ldn	
Adam, jr.	443	Bth	Portlock, Baldy	792	Nrf	Jno.	266	Ldn	
Allen	614	Srr	Jno.	915	Nrf	Jno.	915	Nrf	
Andrew	581	Pre	Lemuel	792	Nrf	Joana	587	Brk	
Andrew	849	Wth	Reuben	807	Nrf	John	397	Fqr	
Benjamin W.	867	Cmp	Simon	807	Nrf	John	15	Hnr	
Charity	40	Stf	Thos.	808	Nrf	John	354	Lnn	
Daniel	398	Fqr	Wm.	914	Nrf	John	657	Sss	
Daniel	658	Sss	Wm., Jr.	807	Nrf	Jonas	269	Ldn	
Edward	782	Wst	Wm., Sr.	807	Nrf	Jonas	270	Ldn	
Eli	417	Fqr	Portwood, Loyd	61	Chr	Joseph	848	Wth	
Elizabeth	828	Nrf	Thomas	61	Chr	Joshua	549	Frd	
Elizabeth	118	Spt	Posey, Benja.	292	Frf	Joshua	269	Ldn	
Elliott	782	Wst	Richard	505	Prw	Nathan	354	Lnn	
Eppa	365	Fqr	Thomas	12	Wod	Nathaniel	943	Hrr	
Harrison	65	Clp	Posh, George	605	Frd	Nathen	924	Hrr	
Henry	128	Sth	Poshe, Lewis	214	Pnd	Presly	357	Lnc	
Jacob	873	Sth	Post, Isaac	416	Rnd	Richard, senr.	212	Kng	
James	438	Flv	Jacob	910	Hrr	Richd., jr.	212	Kng	
James	765	Nwk	Martin	913	Hrr	Samuel	5	Oho	
Jno.	58	Chs	Sally	201	Ess	Soloman	354	Lnn	
John	435	Bth	Posten, J. W.	530	Mnn	Temperance	266	Ldn	
John	593	Brk	Postle, Nancy	529	Mnn	Thomas	199	Ess	
John	821	Bck	Richd.	530	Mnn	Thomas	992	Nrt	
John	866	Cmp	Sam	530	Mnn	Thomas	657	Sss	
John	427	Msn	Wm.	528	Mnn	Timothy	115	Spt	
John	764	Nwk	Poston, Alexander	783	Hmp	Unice	269	Ldn	
John	581	Pre	Elias	722	Wsh	Wm., (Y)	880	Yrk	
John	278	Rck	Esiballa	725	Wsh	see Potes			
John	253	Shn	Jos.	299	Ldn	Pouge, George, Jur.	429	Bth	
Joseph	269	Rck	Richard	783	Hmp	Pough, Levy	960	Hrr	
Joseph, & son in law	399	Mds	Samuel	829	Hmp	Poulson, Abigal	50	Acc	
Lewis	66	Clp	Sarah	723	Wsh	Ann	48	Acc	
Martin	413	Fqr	William	783	Hmp	Derastus	118	Acc	
Molly	783	Wst	William	725	Wsh	James	49	Acc	
Nancy	959	Hrr	Wilsey	232	Ldn	John	49	Acc	
Nicholas	284	Rck	Posy, Edw.	957	Hrr	Sarah, of Wm.	49	Acc	
Peter	168	Alb	Vurlender	966	Hrr	William	47	Acc	

Name	Page	Co.
Zadock	49	Acc
Poulston, Jasper	314	Ldn
Jno.	314	Ldn
Poulter, Jane	66	Clp
Poulton, Jno.	271	Ldn
Martha	271	Ldn
Thos.	316	Ldn
Pound, Reuben	64	Clp
Richard	95	Spt
Wm.	64	Clp
Pours, Wm.	940	Hrr
Pourtney, William	104	Spt
Povall, Charles	3	Pwh
Francis B., Capt.	9	Pwh
John	10	Pwh
see Carter		
Pow, Henry	698	Wsh
Powal, Grass	730	Wsh
Powe, Samuel	582	Pre
Powel, Abner	245	Shn
Benjamin J.	205	Alb
Elisha	64	Clp
Fedk.	113	Hnr
George	88	Jff
George	355	Lnn
Griff.	530	Mnn
Henry	120	Cmb
Henry	777	Hmp
Honorias	35	Rcm
Isaas	528	Mnn
Jas.	64	Clp
Jos.	530	Mnn
Matthew	35	Rcm
Peyton	5	Pwh
Robert	355	Lnn
Robert, Jr.	451	Frn
Robert, Sr.	451	Frn
Silas	529	Mnn
Sophia	873	Sth
Stephen	927	Hrr
Susannah	848	Cmp
Susannah	571	Mnr
Thomas	88	Jff
Thos.	470	Pra
William	452	Frn
William	927	Hrr
William	847	Sth
Wm., jr.	707	Gch
Wm., senr.	707	Gch
see Morris		
Powell, Aaron	477	Bdf
Abraham	232	Aml
Alfred H.	517	Frd
Ann	667	Glc
Bayley	253	Ldn
Benj., (W)	880	Yrk
Benja.	916	Hrr
Benjamin	399	Mds
Benjamin	721	Nls
Benjamin, Jun.	33	Isw
Benjamin, Sen.	21	Isw
Burr	234	Ldn
Charles	47	Isw
Cornelius	269	Amh
Dade	239	Ldn
Edward	759	Brn
Edward	326	Dnw
Edward	288	Frf
Edward	399	Mds
Elijah	399	Mds
Eliza.	668	Glc
Feilding	399	Mds
Gasper	169	Alb
George	297	Amh
Isham	454	Grn
James	269	Amh
James	759	Brn
James	453	Grn
James	777	Hmp
James	291	Ldn
James	399	Mds
James	10	Oho
James	155	Sth
James	97	Spt
Jas.	815	Nrf
Jeremiah	468	Mdd
Jesse	478	Bdf
Jethro	21	Isw
Jno.	292	Frf
Jno.	17	Ntt
Jno., jr.	17	Ntt
Jno., Sr.	442	Mth
John	168	Alb
John	551	Brk
John	819	Nrf
John	879	Yrk
John	880	Yrk
John, Botetourt	666	Glc
John, S.J.	759	Brn
John, (3	817	Nrf
John S.	759	Brn
Joseph	50	Acc
Joseph	288	Frf
Joseph	21	Isw
Joseph	253	Ldn
Joseph	848	Wth
Leml.	818	Nrf
Leven [?]	234	Ldn
Leven	314	Ldn
Ludwell	728	Brn
Martin	849	Wth
Mary	634	Gls
Mary	723	Nls
Matthew	5	Isw
Matthew	21	Isw
Micajah	47	Isw
Nancy	667	Glc
Nathaniel	47	Acc
Nathaniel	721	Nls
Nehemiah	848	Wth
Peter, (W)	880	Yrk
Phillis	155	Sth
Pricilla	48	Acc
Prosser	263	Amh
Ptolemy	84	Spt
Rd.	290	Frf
Reuben	424	Bth
Richard	263	Amh
Richd.	232	Aml
Richd.	818	Nrf
Richd., jr.	814	Nrf
Richd., Sr.	797	Nrf
Robert	551	Brk
Robert	657	Sss
Robert M.	239	Ldn
Sally	818	Nrf
Saml.	819	Nrf
Samuel	168	Alb
Sarah	65	Clp
Sarah	454	Grn
Sarah	18	Isw
Sarah	262	Ldn
Sarah	158	Sth
Semore	454	Grn
Semr., (Y)	880	Yrk
Seymour [2]	668	Glc
Solomon	186	Elc
Thad.	162	Sth
Thomas	263	Amh
Thomas	477	Bdf
Thomas	453	Grn
Thos.	232	Aml
Thos.	759	Brn
Thos.	818	Nrf
Thos.	545	Prg
Thos., (L)	817	Nrf
Thos. G.	838	Nrf
Wiatt	296	Amh
William	47	Acc
William	119	Acc
William	232	Aml
William	424	Bth
William	477	Bdf
William	21	Isw
William	520	Prw
William	98	Spt
William	103	Spt
William H.	453	Grn
William H.	658	Sss
Wm.	67	Clp
Wm.	291	Frf
Wm.	233	Ldn
Wm.	246	Ldn
Wm.	273	Ldn
Wm.	275	Ldn
Wm.	583	Mnr
Wm.	880	Yrk
see Hill, Ziglar		
Powelson, Cornelius	805	Hmp
Henry	761	Hmp
John	761	Hmp
Lewis	790	Hmp
Powener, John, Jur.	790	Hmp
Power, Henry F.	759	Brn
John, (W)	880	Yrk
Michael	848	Wth
Robert	389	Fqr
Valentine	849	Wth
Walter	276	Ldn
Powers, Charles P.	60	Chr
David	918	Crl
Edward	515	Frd
Edward	771	Hmp
Elizabeth	917	Crl
James	544	Frd
James	993	Nrt
Jas.	666	Glc
Jno.	649	Btt
Jno., Jr.	647	Btt
John	706	Gch
John	942	Hrr
John	530	Mnn
John	782	Wst
John	17	Wod
John W.	707	Gch
Joseph	470	Pra
Julius	117	Cmb
Kisiah	706	Gch
Lewis	708	Gch
Madison	706	Gch
Major	706	Gch
Michael	720	Nls
Molley	992	Nrt
Moses	372	Ags
Nehh.	529	Mnn
Norman	205	Alb
Reubin	667	Glc
Ridley	144	Sth
Ridley	854	Sth
Saml.	161	Sth
Samuel	354	Lnn
Samuel, jr.	354	Lnn
Stephen	771	Hmp
Stephen	832	Hmp
Vollentine	417	Rnd
William	992	Nrt
Wm.	530	Mnn
Powlison, Charles	789	Hmp
Powner, Elisha	789	Hmp
George	789	Hmp
Isaac	787	Hmp
John	790	Hmp
Jonathan	787	Hmp
Jonathan	790	Hmp
Joshua	789	Hmp
Samuel, F.B.	11	Pwh
Thomas	787	Hmp
see Powener		
Poyner, John	788	Nrf
Jos.	795	Nrf
Robt.	824	Nrf

Poythress, Betey	542	Prg	Thomas	614	Srr	Edward	853	Cmp
Mary	844	Sth	Thomas L.	657	Sss	Edward	8	Knw
William	534	Prg	Wm.	879	Yrk	Elizabeth	710	Gch
Praast, Mary	354	Lnn	Preston, Billey	20	Hnr	Elizabeth	614	Srr
Pradan, John	206	Alb	Bowker	469	Frn	Elizabeth, jr.	212	Kng
Prager, Frederick	868	Hnv	Celia	416	Fqr	Elizabeth, sr.	212	Kng
Prat, James	943	Hrr	Francis	758	Wsh	Evan	5	Knw
Prater, Jonathan	477	Bdf	James	141	Sth	Frederick	276	Amh
Silas	834	Hmp	James P.	664	Mnt	George	484	Frn
Prather, Charles	685	Br	Jeremiah	359	Fqr	Henry	635	Gls
Henry	684	Br	Jno.	649	Btt	Henry D.	667	Mnt
Prathor, Thomas	871	Cmp	Jno., (Genl.)	648	Btt	Ignatius	757	Hmp
Prator, Thos.	720	Wsh	Joel	477	Bdf	Isaa	528	Mnn
Pratross, James	478	Bdf	John	477	Bdf	Jacob	667	Mnt
Pratt, Benjamin	399	Mds	John	878	Cmp	Jacob	582	Pre
Bernerd	707	Wsh	John	627	Mnt	James	581	Pre
Elizabeth	653	Mnt	John	703	Wsh	Jas.	751	Wsh
Fulden	727	Wsh	John, Colo.	703	Wsh	Jno.	883	Hnv
Henry	708	Wsh	John, jr.	477	Bdf	Jno. F.	9	Hnr
Isaiah	66	Clp	Joshua	759	Brn	John	205	Alb
James	441	Mth	Moses	469	Frn	John	683	Br
James	654	Mnt	Nancy	760	Brn	John	918	Crl
James	663	Mnt	Peggy	359	Fqr	John	107	Cmb
Jno.	67	Clp	Robert	291	Frf	John	126	Cmb
John	918	Crl	Robert	702	Wsh	John	514	Frd
John	654	Mnt	Robert	703	Wsh	John	825	Hmp
John	220	Shn	Robert, (FN)	60	Chr	John	127	Hnr
John	58	Stf	Robt.	647	Btt	John	581	Pre
John	782	Wst	Saml.	695	Wsh	John, Snr.	117	Hnr
John, Estate	198	Ess	Stephen	477	Bdf	John F.	30	Hnr
Jonathan	399	Mds	Susannah	664	Mnt	John F.	133	Hnr
Jonathan, SM	399	Mds	Thornton	388	Fqr	Joseph	169	Alb
Joseph	399	Mds	Thos.	263	Rck	Joseph	127	Cmb
Oliver	716	Wsh	William	477	Bdf	Joseph	483	Frn
Polly	663	Mnt	William	583	Pre	Joseph F.	861	Hnv
Rachel	49	Acc	William	848	Wth	Levi	596	Brk
Stephen	477	Bdf	Pretlow, Bridgt.	915	Nrf	Lewis	666	Mnt
Thos., jr.	65	Clp	Samuel	657	Sss	Lucy	1	Hnr
Thos., Senr.	65	Clp	Pretty, Thomas	205	Alb	Majr.	28	Hnr
William	480	Frn	Prettyman, ... R.	8	Oho	Marian	19	Hnr
Pratter, Wm.	733	Wsh	Preuett, Uriah	666	Glc	Mary	38	Stf
Pray, John	914	Nrf	Prewet, Joseph	60	Chr	Mary, Est.	582	Pre
Prayle, John	375	Fqr	Obed	425	Msn	Matthias	471	Pra
Prayter, Newman	650	Mnt	Prewett, Richard	173	Knq	Michl.	529	Mnn
Preacher see Peecher			Tunstall	173	Knq	Michl.	627	Mnt
Preachet, Thomas	783	Wst	Walker	173	Knq	Nat W.	118	Hnr
Zebelon	782	Wst	Prewit, Samuel	882	Cmp	Nathan	818	Hmp
Preble, John	869	Cmp	Prewitt, George, Junr.	46	Acc	Nathaniel	582	Pre
Martin	879	Cmp	George, Junr.	118	Acc	Pugh W.	583	Pre
Precious, Mary	915	Nrf	Pribble, Thomas	14	Wod	Randolph	760	Brn
Predmore, Benjamin	526	Prw	Price, ---, Revd.	914	Nrf	Richard	182	Alb
Preipoint, Fran	531	Mnn	Abm.	433	Flv	Richd.	529	Mnn
Prencehorn, Henry	572	Brk	Abraham	169	Alb	Richd.	531	Mnn
Prentice, Henry	3	Wod	Adam	28	Rcm	Robert	477	Bdf
Jonathan	4	Wod	Alexander	477	Bdf	Robert	816	Bck
Joshua	914	Nrf	Alexander	608	Mnt	Robt.	127	Hnr
Stanton	3	Wod	Argalon	811	Hmp	Sally	15	Hnr
Prentis, Moses	586	Mnr	Argalon	821	Hmp	Sally	114	Hnr
Wm.	326	Dnw	Banoni	289	Frf	Samuel	397	Fqr
Prescot, Henry	914	Nrf	Benj.	291	Ldn	Samuel	57	Jff
Prescott, James	914	Nrf	Benjamin	683	Br	Samuel	614	Srr
Presgraves, Geo.	251	Ldn	Benjamin H.	581	Pre	Sarah	481	Frn
Jno.	248	Ldn	Bennett	211	Kng	Sarah	13	Hnr
Richd.	248	Ldn	Bohonnon	924	Hrr	Sarah	188	Shn
Presley see Marmaduke, Priesley			Caleb	528	Mnn	Silas	758	Hmp
Preson, Frances	180	Elc	Catharine	635	Gls	Stephen	821	Nrf
John	176	Elc	Charles	477	Bdf	Susanah W.	114	Hnr
Presscott, Caty	119	Acc	Charles	381	Fqr	Thomas	4	Knw
George	119	Acc	Charles	13	Knw	Thomas	212	Kng
Pressey, Anne	8	Isw	Charles	4	Wod	Thomas	613	Srr
Pressgraves, Wm.	247	Ldn	Dan	529	Mnn	Thomas J.	830	Bck
Presson, Avarilla	613	Srr	David	464	Frn	Thorn	483	Frn
Elizh.	880	Yrk	David	483	Frn	Thos.	372	Ags
James	880	Yrk	David	634	Gls	Thos.	649	Btt
James, jr.	880	Yrk	David	1	Hnr	Thos., Jnr.	897	Hnv
John	880	Yrk	David	30	Hnr	Thos., Snr.	860	Hnv
Nicholas	657	Sss	David	31	Rcm	Thos. D.	860	Sth
Richard	657	Sss	David	613	Srr	Tobias	613	Srr
Ro.	880	Yrk	Edmund	2	Knw	William	232	Aml
Tho.	880	Yrk	Edmund	3	Knw	William	410	Fqr

Name	No.	Co.
William	33	Hnr
William	583	Pre
William	188	Shn
William, Jr.	581	Pre
William, (ME)	59	Chr
William N.	410	Fqr
Wilshor	127	Hnr
Wilson	117	Hnr
Wm.	907	Hrr
Wm.	433	Flv
Wm.	530	Mnn
Wm. G.	793	Nrf
see Stiglar, Underwood		
Prichard, Benjamin	44	Stf
Elijah	401	Fqr
John	694	Br
John	454	Grn
Nathaniel	406	Fqr
Tho.	530	Mnn
William	21	Hnr
Wm.	122	Hnr
Prichart, Ed	529	Mnn
Prichet, Bird	206	Alb
George	949	Hrr
James	206	Alb
John	206	Alb
Prichett, Henry	828	Nrf
Wm.	827	Nrf
Pricht, Rebecah	728	Wsh
Pricket, Isaah	529	Mnn
Jac.	528	Mnn
Jno.	528	Mnn
Job	529	Mnn
Thos.	528	Mnn
Prickly, Eliza.	587	Mnr
Priddy, Ann	876	Hnv
Henry	850	Cmp
Robert	443	Flv
Robt.	3	Hnr
Sammuel	856	Hnv
Susanna	876	Hnv
Thomas	445	Flv
Wim.	859	Hnv
Wm.	404	Ags
Pride, Eliza.	231	Aml
Francis	231	Aml
Hen.	528	Mnn
James	65	Chs
Jno.	530	Mnn
Peter, jr.	156	Dnw
Peter, Senr.	156	Dnw
Polly	336	Dnw
Thomas D.	354	Lnn
Thos.	232	Aml
Pridham, Chrstopher	783	Wst
Priesley, Wm.	714	Wsh
Priest, Elizabeth	478	Bdf
Geo.	67	Clp
Henry	675	Br
Jas.	66	Clp
Jno., Jr.	65	Clp
Jno., Senr.	66	Clp
John	345	Fqr
Joseph	478	Bdf
Lewis	604	Frd
Mason	345	Fqr
Peter	67	Clp
Stephen	683	Br
Stephen	697	Br
Thomas	478	Bdf
Thomas	391	Fqr
William	406	Fqr
Wm.	65	Clp
see Pruet		
Priestly, Samuel	10	Knw
Prigmore, William	290	Frf
Prince, William, Snr.	174	Knq
Prill, Mich.	563	Brk
Saml.	313	Ldn
Prillimin, Daniel	488	Frn

Name	No.	Co.
Dennis	450	Frn
Jacob	487	Frn
Jacob	488	Frn
John	483	Frn
John	488	Frn
Prim, John	357	Fqr
Thos.	374	Ags
William	507	Frd
Winfieal	352	Fqr
Primace, Free	453	Mth
Primm, Susanna	507	Prw
William	512	Prw
William, jr.	30	Stf
William, Sr.	25	Stf
Prin, Laureat	915	Nrf
Prince, Abraham	184	Shn
David	185	Shn
Elizabeth	659	Sss
George	184	Shn
Godfrey	650	Btt
Hall	174	Knq
Henry	184	Shn
Hubbert	10	Wod
James	173	Knq
James	174	Knq
James S.	832	Nrf
Jas.	173	Knq
Jno.	634	Gls
John	184	Shn
John	187	Shn
John	128	Sth
Joseph	659	Sss
Levi	266	Ldn
Noah	3	Pwh
Peter	184	Shn
Philip	185	Shn
Ro.	173	Knq
Robert, Snr.	174	Knq
Roudon	267	Ldn
Stephen R.	286	Rck
William	634	Gls
William	4	Wod
see Priince		
Prine, Antony	221	Pnd
Pring, Richd.	281	Rck
Pringle, John	910	Hrr
Saml.	911	Hrr
William	908	Hrr
Printy, Samuel	967	Hrr
Printz, Henry	512	Frd
Michal	550	Frd
Peter	506	Frd
Prior, Allyn	426	Msn
Ben	285	Rck
Braz. W.	177	Elc
Elizabeth	365	Fqr
Joseph	9	Knw
Luke	3	Knw
Nicholas	9	Knw
William	477	Bdf
Priscat, Leonard	326	Dnw
Prise, Henry	399	Mds
Pritchard, Abram	114	Hnr
Benjn.	212	Kng
Francis	288	Frf
Howson	574	Frd
John	777	Hmp
John	807	Hmp
Rees, Jur.	836	Hmp
Rees, Senr.	836	Hmp
Stephen	542	Frd
Travis	288	Frf
Pritchet, Ann	102	Spt
Edward	119	Spt
Gabriel S.	992	Nrt
John	818	Bck
William	818	Bck
William	91	Spt
Pritchett, Benja.	66	Clp

Name	No.	Co.
Caleb	158	Dnw
Daniel	726	Brn
Dolly	330	Dnw
Edmund	726	Brn
James	726	Brn
Jane	826	Nrf
Jeremh.	158	Dnw
John	354	Lnn
Joshua	726	Brn
Moses	726	Brn
Peter	157	Dnw
Peter	833	Nrf
Rodham	391	Rch
Susannah	156	Dnw
Wm.	66	Clp
Wm.	158	Dnw
Wm., jr.	726	Brn
Wm., SM	726	Brn
see Prichet, Prtchett		
Pritlaw, Joseph	328	Dnw
Pritlow, Jenny, (F.N.)	40	Isw
Joshua	860	Sth
Thos. [2]	860	Sth
Pritt, Edward	433	Bth
Elijah	581	Mnr
James	433	Bth
John	417	Bth
Margaret	434	Bth
Robert	433	Bth
William [2]	433	Bth
Probasco, Samuel	773	Hmp
Proby, ---, & Saunders	914	Nrf
Mary	178	Elc
Wm.	915	Nrf
Prockler, John	191	Shn
Procter, Charles	96	Spt
Drury A.	540	Prg
Elizabeth	205	Alb
John	68	Spt
John	88	Spt
Richd.	246	Shn
see Porter, Prockler		
Procton, George	723	Nls
William	722	Nls
see Ponton		
Proctor, Christopher	666	Glc
Christopher	667	Glc
Christopher	537	Prg
Eliza.	393	Rch
John	6	Knw
Mildred	667	Glc
Ricd.	66	Clp
Saml.	814	Nrf
William	28	Isw
William	6	Knw
William	102	Spt
Wm.	666	Glc
Proffett, Jessee	720	Nls
John	720	Nls
Profit, Conrod	31	Rcm
George	709	Gch
Sally	709	Gch
Samuel	709	Gch
Wm.	709	Gch
Prondfit, Jno.	915	Nrf
Prophet, Betsey	491	Frn
Washington	795	Bck
Props, Adam	220	Pnd
Christian	216	Pnd
Daniel	223	Pnd
George	220	Pnd
George	225	Pnd
Henry	216	Pnd
Henry	225	Pnd
Jacob	220	Pnd
John [2]	215	Pnd
Leonard	225	Pnd
Michal	225	Pnd
Michal, J.	220	Pnd
Propst see Props, Propts		

Name	Page	Code
Propts, Henry	10	Rcm
Michael	33	Rcm
Prosser, Daniel	687	Br
James	666	Glc
John	215	Ess
John	522	Prw
Jonathan	698	Br
Mary	32	Hnr
Samuel	992	Nrt
Thos. H.	111	Hnr
William	687	Br
William	992	Nrt
Wm.	130	Hnr
Prothery, Thomas	486	Frn
Protsman, Nathl.	2	Rcm
Prouce, John	252	Shn
Proudfoot, John	911	Hrr
see Prondfit		
Provins, Elizabeth	34	Isw
Provoo, Dawson	190	Elc
Joanah, (Y)	880	Yrk
Proyer, James	71	Jff
Prtchett, Wm., Sr.	726	Brn
Pru, Thomas	783	Wst
Pruddy, John	481	Frn
Pruden, Nathl.	11	Isw
Prudhomme see Prencehorn		
Pruet, Obh.	648	Btt
Richard	77	Spt
Pruett, Charles	918	Crl
Edmund	917	Crl
Elijah	918	Crl
Molly	48	Acc
Moses	918	Crl
Thaddeus	918	Crl
see Preuett		
Pruit, David	460	Frn
Prummer, John	797	Nrf
Pruner, George M.	848	Wth
Michael	849	Wth
Prunk, Jacob	648	Btt
Jno.	648	Btt
Prunty, David	928	Hrr
Isaac	934	Hrr
Jesse	456	Frn
Jesse	929	Hrr
John	926	Hrr
Josep	929	Hrr
Robert	459	Frn
Thomas	633	Gls
Prupecker, Abram	474	Frn
Henry	478	Frn
John	478	Frn
Prutsmon, Lawrance	5	Wod
Prye, Wintle	806	Hmp
Pryor, David	289	Amh
Edm...nd	829	Nrf
Jno. C.	666	Glc
John	710	Gch
John C.	267	Amh
Langston	786	Bck
Luke	728	Brn
Nicholas	286	Amh
Phillip	728	Brn
Richard	157	Dnw
Saml.	710	Gch
Samuel	6	Hnr
Susanna	786	Bck
Susanna	10	Hnr
Tabathy	852	Hnv
William, jr.	289	Amh
William, Senr.	269	Amh
Wm.	710	Gch
Zane	785	Bck
Psalter, Old	510	Prw
Ptomey see Plomey		
Ptomy, Jno.	295	Rck
Pucket, Abel	157	Dnw
Haley	10	Pwh
Jacob	719	Nls
Jeramiah	469	Frn
John	91	Spt
Peter	77	Spt
Samuel	719	Nls
Starkey	157	Dnw
William	104	Spt
Puckett, Aggy	336	Dnw
Archd.	56	Chs
Claiborne	57	Chs
Jacob	60	Chr
Jacob	720	Nls
Lawson	13	Hnr
Lewis	52	Chs
Lizey	335	Dnw
Pascall	13	Hnr
Paskil	20	Hnr
Pleasant	231	Aml
see Pickett		
Puffenberry, George	226	Pnd
see Puppenberry		
Pugh, Abraham	60	Chr
Abraham	833	Hmp
Azariah	767	Hmp
Bengamin	832	Hmp
Benjamin	538	Frd
Brina	61	Chr
Elizabeth	563	Frd
Elizabeth	722	Nls
Evan	14	Wod
Ezekial	60	Chr
Hugh	691	Br
Jacob	777	Hmp
James	60	Chr
James	722	Nls
James	14	Wod
Jas.	530	Mnn
Jasper	841	Nrf
Jesse	832	Hmp
Jesse	530	Mnn
Jesse	193	Shn
Job	570	Frd
John	60	Chr
John	582	Frd
John	530	Mnn
John	720	Nls
John	722	Nls
John	12	Wod
Joha, Jur.	720	Nls
John M.	61	Chr
Jonathan	833	Hmp
Jonothan	863	Cmp
Joseph	773	Hmp
Joseph	722	Nls
Lewis	919	Crl
Mishael	767	Hmp
Moses	692	Br
Peter	691	Br
Richard	462	Frn
Robert	767	Hmp
Samuel	6	Wod
Samuel	14	Wod
Theos.	530	Mnn
Thomas	721	Nls
Willoughby	919	Crl
Young	60	Chr
Pulers see Puters		
Puliam, Betsy	67	Clp
Pullam, Joseph	69	Chr
Pullem, Loghes	418	Bth
Pullen, ...	306	Rck
...h [Joseph?]	306	Rck
Andrew	404	Rch
Everard	405	Rch
Fras.	357	Lnc
James	410	Rch
James	90	Spt
Jesse	405	Rch
Jno.	356	Lnc
John	835	Nrf
Jud.	356	Lnc

Page	Code	Name	Page	Code
469	Frn	Lindsy	356	Lnc
91	Spt	Simon	829	Nrf
77	Spt	Thomas	90	Spt
719	Nls	Wm.	355	Lnc
157	Dnw	Pullens, Elizabeth	435	Bth
104	Spt	Jonathan	435	Bth
336	Dnw	Samuel	435	Bth
56	Chs	Thomas	435	Bth
57	Chs	Puller, Jno.	64	Clp
60	Chr	Jno.	667	Glc
720	Nls	Joseph	277	Ldn
13	Hnr	Lester	398	Fqr
52	Chs	Mary	666	Glc
335	Dnw	Thos.	667	Glc
13	Hnr	Pulley, John	944	Chc
20	Hnr	William	355	Lnn
231	Aml	Pulliam, James	104	Spt
		John	67	Spt
226	Pnd	John	73	Spt
		Joseph	68	Spt
60	Chr	Mosby	113	Hnr
833	Hmp	Rawlings	87	Spt
767	Hmp	Richard	70	Spt
832	Hmp	Robert	858	Hnv
538	Frd	Robert	65	Clp
61	Chr	Salley	858	Hnv
563	Frd	Thos.	66	Clp
722	Nls	William	846	Hnv
14	Wod	Pullin, Archer	477	Bdf
60	Chr	Jno.	647	Btt
691	Br	Joseph, jr.	305	Rck
777	Hmp	Leroy	992	Nrt
60	Chr	Richard	993	Nrt
722	Nls	Thomas	477	Bdf
14	Wod	Pulling, Thos.	16	Hnr
530	Mnn	Pullon, Jas.	818	Nrf
841	Nrf	Pullum, Fanny	582	Pre
832	Hmp	George W.	581	Pre
530	Mnn	Hermon	126	Cmb
193	Shn	Pully, Lewis	613	Srr
570	Frd	Pulse, Geo.	503	Brk
60	Chr	Michael	508	Brk
582	Frd	Pulsgrove, Henry	593	Brk
530	Mnn	Pultz, David	66	Jff
720	Nls	George	60	Jff
722	Nls	Jacob	76	Jff
12	Wod	John	555	Brk
720	Nls	Pumfrey, Nathan	32	Rcm
61	Chr	Pummel, Francy	258	Shn
833	Hmp	Pumoroy, Jno. L.	291	Frf
863	Cmp	Truman	291	Frf
773	Hmp	Pumory, Francis D.	290	Frf
722	Nls	Pumphrey, Beal	681	Br
919	Crl	Nicholas	680	Br
767	Hmp	Reason	680	Br
692	Br	Reason	697	Br
691	Br	Pumroy, James	782	Wst
462	Frn	Punch, James	211	Kng
767	Hmp	Pund, Jno.	4	Hnr
6	Wod	Pupp, Peter	215	Pnd
14	Wod	Puppenberry, Henry	220	Pnd
530	Mnn	Purce, Juse	817	Nrf
721	Nls	Purcel, Jno. [2]	310	Ldn
919	Crl	Joseph	281	Ldn
60	Chr	Samuel [2]	280	Ldn
		Purcell, Charles	516	Prw
67	Clp	James	582	Pre
69	Chr	James	526	Prw
418	Bth	Lydia	280	Ldn
306	Rck	Samuel	517	Prw
306	Rck	Purchase, Townshd.	212	Kng
404	Rch	Purdam, Benj.	307	Ldn
405	Rch	Purdie, Geo.	880	Yrk
357	Lnc	John	15	Isw
410	Rch	Jonathan	3	Oho
90	Spt	Thomas	15	Isw
405	Rch	Thos., has slaves in		
356	Lnc	York County	880	Yrk
835	Nrf	Purdue, Laben	528	Mnn
356	Lnc	Thos.	232	Aml

Purdul, Bennet	477	Bdf	Putman, Ernestus	68	Jff	James	553	Brk
Jemimah	477	Bdf	Jacob	816	Hmp	Jno.	300	Ldn
Purdy, Leonard	728	Brn	John	437	Bth	John	169	Alb
Purgett, Frederick	803	Hmp	John	5	Knw	John	554	Frd
Henry	803	Hmp	Peter	815	Hmp	John	471	Pra
Henry	815	Hmp	Joseph D.	386	Fqr	Martin	553	Frd
Purgram, Susanna	485	Frn	Putney, Benja.	454	Grn	Tunis	234	Shn
Purkapile, Elizabeth	185	Shn	Ellis	837	Bck	William	23	Rcm
Purkenson, Branch	157	Dnw	John	614	Srr	Quickle, Adam, Jr.	650	Btt
Purkepile, John	10	Rcm	Samuel	837	Bck	Adam, Sr.	650	Btt
Purkey, Chrisley	848	Wth	Putt, Soloman	722	Nls	Elizabeth	447	Bth
Daniel	848	Wth	Putty, Billy	115	Hnr	John	440	Bth
Purkins, Elisha	477	Bdf	Pyland, Eliza.	613	Srr	Quicksell see Qucksell		
Gabl.	220	Ess	John	613	Srr	Quigg, Henry	859	Cmp
Richard	477	Bdf	Obediah	613	Srr	Quiggen, Susanna	766	Nwk
Samuel	720	Nls	Sarah	613	Srr	Quigley, Charles	650	Btt
Stephen	433	Flv	Thomas P.	613	Srr	James	272	Rck
Thomas	614	Srr	Pyle, George	114	Cmb	Jno. M.	531	Mnn
Purkinson, John	582	Pre	Pyles, Ann	24	Oho	Sarah	476	Frn
Josiah	582	Pre	Pynes, Benja.	173	Knq	Quincy, Robert	355	Lnn
Powell	327	Dnw	Caty	174	Knq	Quinn, H.	408	Ags
Rowlett	582	Pre	Eliza.	174	Knq	James	15	Rcm
Purks, John	468	Mdd	Robert	173	Knq	Quisenberry, Edward S.	353	Fqr
Purkus, Thomas	289	Frf	Pyott, Jno.	279	Ldn	Elijah	82	Spt
Purler see Penler						Elizabeth	415	Fqr
Purley, Sally	4	Hnr				Quishenbury, James	858	Cmp
see Pusley			--- Q ---			Qween, John	777	Hmp
Purnal, Jesse	78	Jff				Patrick	822	Hmp
Purnell, John	583	Pre						
William	514	Prw	Quade, Ignt.	547	Brk			
Purrington, James	836	Nrf	Quails, Gabriel	849	Wth	--- R ---		
Purse, Baker	782	Wst	Quaintance, Jno.	67	Clp			
Pursel, George	407	Fqr	Quall see Kwall					
see Perscell, Purcell			Qualls, Elizbth.	639	Mnt	R, Michael	174	Shn
Pursell, Chs.	27	Hnr	Judith	621	Mnt	R..., ...	479	Bdf
Clary	666	Glc	Quan, Edwd.	292	Rck	Ann	917	Nrf
Edwd. M.	668	Glc	Quarles, Catharine	728	Brn	R...b...m, ...	917	Nrf
George	7	Oho	Francis W.	210	Ess	R...olph, ...	230	Aml
George	391	Rch	Henry	210	Ess	R...re, ---, Madm.	917	Nrf
Jas.	667	Glc	James	728	Brn	Rabb, Geo.	404	Ags
Jas. B.	666	Glc	James	432	Flv	John	374	Ags
Jno.	666	Glc	Jno.	728	Brn	Raber, Chr., Jr.	531	Mnn
Lucy	667	Glc	John	478	Bdf	Chrisr.	531	Mnn
Mary	667	Glc	John	436	Flv	Wm.	531	Mnn
Morgan	667	Glc	John	468	Mdd	see Robes		
Reubin	395	Rch	John	83	Spt	Raby, Jacob	955	Hrr
Ro.	667	Glc	John S.	231	Aml	Race, Pheby	70	Clp
Sarah	394	Rch	Minors	920	Crl	Rachal, Frank	730	Brn
Tobias	411	Rch	Nathl.	67	Chs	Rachell, Jarrott	661	Sss
Wm. R.	667	Glc	Robt.	3	Hnr	Racherty, William, Est.	62	Chr
Pursley, George, Sr.	412	Fqr	Samuel	478	Bdf	Radebaugh, Geo.	534	Mnn
James	212	Kng	Sarah	880	Cmp	Rader, Adam	5	Rcm
Jessee	647	Btt	Susanna	17	Ntt	Casper	850	Wth
John	783	Wst	Thomas	478	Bdf	Coonrod	852	Wth
Thomas	212	Kng	William	920	Crl	George, (Jr.)	31	Rcm
Purson, James	454	Grn	Wm.	728	Brn	George, (Sen.)	31	Rcm
Purssell, Jeremiah	782	Wst	Quarls, Judith	823	Bck	Henry	15	Rcm
John	782	Wst	Susannah	830	Bck	Henry	722	Wsh
Molly	782	Wst	William	830	Bck	Jacob	98	Spt
Purtlebough, George	577	Frd	Quarrier, Elex.	12	Hnr	John	4	Rcm
Purvis, Charles	720	Nls	Quary, Elijah	650	Btt	John	20	Rcm
George	721	Nls	Quash, Cloa	206	Alb	Sebastian	41	Rcm
James	531	Frd	Qucksell, Jonathan	115	Hnr	Radford, Benjamin	779	Bck
John	92	Spt	Qudy see Judy			George	471	Frn
Wm.	719	Nls	Quearry, Vallentine	116	Hnr	George	7	Pwh
Puryear, ---	332	Dnw	Queen, Abram	911	Hrr	James	783	Bck
Ann	710	Gch	Carnelius	923	Hrr	James	490	Frn
Ellis	706	Gch	Charles	923	Hrr	James	356	Lnn
Ezekiah	29	Hnr	Derry	923	Hrr	John	786	Bck
John	115	Hnr	John	939	Hrr	John	175	Knq
Reuben	802	Bck	see Qween			John	7	Pwh
Pusapager, Jacob	218	Shn	Queensbury, John	583	Pre	Reuben	782	Bck
Pusey, Algernon	60	Stf	Querry, Charles	851	Hnv	William	779	Bck
Janot	52	Stf	Quesenberry, James	468	Mdd	William	855	Cmp
see Persey			Quesenbury, Eliza	783	Wst	Radibough, Henry	635	Gls
Pusley, James	27	Stf	George	783	Wst	Radiffer, John	4	Oho
Stuard	992	Nrt	Nicolas	783	Wst	Radish, John	921	Crl
William	277	Amh	William	783	Wst	Radisom, Elizabeth	3	Oho
Puter, Mary	12	Wod	Queto, Rachl.	916	Nrf	Radlif, John	921	Hrr
Puters, John	755	Wsh	Quick, Geo.	531	Mnn	Jonathan	923	Hrr

Name	No	Code
Rador, Conrod	17	Rcm
Rady, Daniel	395	Rch
Patrick	378	Ags
Rae, May	615	Srr
William	615	Srr
Ragan, Jno.	296	Frf
Robert	920	Crl
William	102	Jff
Ragen, Barthw.	378	Ags
Rager, Jacob	255	Shn
John	255	Shn
Sarah	255	Shn
Ragin, Danl.	20	Rcm
John	14	Rcm
Mary Ann	2	Rcm
Richd.	14	Rcm
William	295	Frf
Raglan, Dudly	712	Gch
Finch	712	Gch
Joel	712	Gch
Ragland, Absolam	873	Hnv
Dick	766	Nwk
Fendall	871	Hnv
George	766	Nwk
James	207	Alb
James	831	Bck
John	807	Bck
John	435	Flv
Mary	876	Hnv
Nathaniel	207	Alb
Patsey	478	Bdf
Reuben	478	Bdf
Reuben, Sr.	479	Bdf
Shelton	861	Hnv
Wim.	858	Hnv
Ragsdale, ...amin	335	Dnw
Baxter	356	Lnn
Drury	355	Lnn
Elizabeth	357	Lnn
Fred.	546	Prg
Hennery	356	Lnn
John	355	Lnn
John	356	Lnn
Joshua	356	Lnn
Nimrod	728	Brn
William	356	Lnn
see Bagsdale		
Ragsdall, Harrison	851	Wth
Rahouser, Jacob	796	Hmp
Rai..., James	52	Chs
Raiborn, George	115	Hnr
Raider, John	664	Mnt
Nicholas	664	Mnt
Railey, Martin	171	Alb
Raimey, Joshua	403	Rch
Rainbow, Ned	766	Nwk
Raincock, Geo.	918	Nrf
Raine, Charles	61	Chr
Jacob	587	Brk
Thomas	62	Chr
Raines, Ann	922	Crl
Anthony	584	Pre
Charles	661	Sss
Dorothy	921	Crl
James	922	Crl
James	561	Frd
Jessee	920	Crl
Mary	561	Frd
Nathaniel	662	Sss
Robert	571	Mnr
Wm.	14	Ntt
Rainey, Alexander	662	Sss
Daniel	761	Brn
Isham	662	Sss
John	557	Brk
Judith	761	Brn
Peter	660	Sss
Thomas	63	Chr
William	660	Sss
Rainie, George	527	Prw
Rains, Adam	40	Stf
Anthony	294	Frf
Elizabeth	87	Spt
Hannah	72	Spt
James	230	Aml
James	2	Rcm
James	34	Rcm
John	760	Brn
John	635	Gls
Larkin	10	Rcm
Meredith	662	Mnt
Nancy	100	Spt
Nathl.	543	Prg
Presley	724	Nls
Raw	358	Lnc
Rebecca	761	Brn
Richard	635	Gls
Richd.	542	Prg
Sarah	35	Rcm
William	10	Rcm
Wm.	573	Mnr
see Ranes		
Rainy, Jno.	549	Prg
Raisner, Leonard	268	Ldn
Rakes, David	803	Bck
Elisha	494	Frn
Henry	490	Frn
William	807	Bck
Rakestrae, Joseph	406	Fqr
Rakestraw, Jno.	70	Clp
Raleigh see Rayleigh		
Raley, Thomas	383	Fqr
see Roby		
Ralford, Aggy	18	Hnr
Ralfsnider, Aaron	543	Brk
Raligh, Wm.	271	Rck
Ralls, Caleb	281	Amh
Kenner	359	Fqr
Ralph, Jno.	274	Ldn
Thomas	545	Frd
Thos.	375	Ags
see Relph		
Ralphford, Philip	846	Sth
Ralston, ---, & Plesants	23	Hnr
Agness	375	Ags
Archabald	14	Wod
Benjamin	14	Wod
James	563	Mnr
James	2	Oho
Joseph	698	Br
Mary	13	Wod
Michael	851	Wth
Peter	4	Hnr
Sam	533	Mnn
Samuel	698	Br
William	851	Wth
Wm.	375	Ags
Rambaut, Richard	330	Dnw
Rambo, Ezekiel	693	Wst
Rambottom, James	400	Mds
William	400	Mds
Rambough, Jacob	421	Bth
Ramer, Daniel	253	Shn
Ramey, Abraham	588	Frd
Arch	167	Shn
Benjamin	601	Frd
Caleb	562	Frd
Elijah	179	Shn
Isaac	597	Frd
Jacob	68	Clp
Jas.	67	Clp
John	593	Frd
John	165	Shn
Levi	399	Fqr
Lewis	179	Shn
Rody	165	Shn
Samuel	562	Frd
Sanford	300	Ldn
Ramifold, John	597	Brk
Ramison see Siamison		
Ramley, Samuel	87	Jff
Rams see Rains		
Ramsay, Andrew	921	Crl
Elizth.	917	Nrf
Henry	920	Crl
James	18	Oho
Jno.	305	Ldn
Jno.	531	Mnn
John	532	Mnn
John J.	61	Chr
Joseph	62	Chr
Sarah	301	Rck
William	61	Chr
Wm.	531	Mnn
Ramsey, Andrew	525	Prw
Andw.	375	Ags
Anne E.	872	Cmp
Bartw.	572	Mnr
Benj.	692	Wsh
Benjamin	479	Bdf
Charles	13	Knw
Daniel	692	Wsh
George	636	Gls
James	375	Ags
James	730	Brn
James	471	Frn
James	725	Nls
James	13	Oho
James, Ju.	725	Nls
Jams	375	Ags
Jane	378	Ags
Joel	725	Nls
John	170	Alb
John	375	Ags
John	493	Frn
John	725	Nls
John	693	Wsh
Joseph	692	Wsh
Joseph	850	Wth
Joshua	525	Brk
Mary	159	Dnw
Mary	714	Wsh
Noden	493	Frn
Richd.	590	Mnr
Saml.	378	Ags
Saml.	303	Rck
Samuel	694	Br
Thomas	459	Frn
Thomas	500	Frn
Thomas, Jr.	460	Frn
Vinct.	211	Ess
William	170	Alb
William	496	Frn
William	725	Nls
Wm.	376	Ags
Woodson	496	Frn
see Romsey		
Ramsy, James	874	Sth
Ramy, Butler	25	Stf
Ranck, Geo., Sr.	651	Btt
Randal, Abram [2]	936	Hrr
Richard	55	Stf
Sarah	55	Stf
William, sr.	56	Stf
Randall, Augustus	386	Fqr
James	822	Hmp
John	343	Fqr
Js.	534	Mnn
Mason	513	Frd
Richard	343	Fqr
Robt.	917	Nrf
Sylvia	916	Nrf
Thompson	515	Prw
Thos.	802	Nrf
see Randol		
Randalph, Ann	15	Pwh
Randle, John	679	Wrw
Rebecca	97	Jff
Roger	515	Brk

Name	No.	Co.
Randol, John	783	Wst
Jos.	263	Ldn
Joseph	315	Ldn
Norman	962	Hrr
Robert	784	Wst
William	928	Hrr
Randolly, Wm.	126	Hnr
Randolp, Brett	69	Clp
Randolph, ...	231	Aml
Abraham	946	Hrr
Adam	791	Nrf
Archibald	559	Frd
Beverley	480	Bdf
Brett	3	Pwh
Edmond	31	Hnr
Edward	697	Br
Edward	728	Brn
Edward	945	Chc
Frs.	918	Nrf
Geo.	177	Elc
Grief	850	Wth
Guy	4	Hnr
Henry	119	Hnr
Isham	374	Ags
Isham	4	Pwh
James	660	Sss
Jediah	712	Gch
John	170	Alb
John	62	Chr
John, jr.	7	Pwh
Judeth	119	Hnr
Judith	584	Pre
Lindy	332	Dnw
Mariah	334	Dnw
Martha	101	Cmb
Mary	14	Hnr
Mary	54	Stf
Peter	21	Ntt
Peyton	54	Chs
Peyton	31	Hnr
Peyton	16	Isw
Peyton	583	Pre
Richard K.	583	Pre
Richd.	130	Hnr
Robert	365	Fqr
Robert B.	290	Rck
Robt.	825	Nrf
Ryland	6	Hnr
Sally	12	Hnr
Saml.	712	Gch
Thomas E.	170	Alb
Thomas M.	207	Alb
William	101	Cmb
William	20	Hnr
William, Jr.	47	Stf
Willm.	177	Elc
Wm.	126	Hnr
Wm.	472	Pra
Wm.	615	Srr
see R...olph, Ranolph		
Rane, John	109	Cmb
Ranes, Ephram	542	Prg
see Rains		
Raney, Berjanin	730	Brn
Buckner	158	Dnw
Enock	472	Pra
Francis	158	Dnw
Henry	158	Dnw
Jane	472	Pra
Jas.	472	Pra
John	158	Dnw
Mary	472	Pra
Peter	159	Dnw
Wm.	471	Pra
Wm., jr.	730	Brn
Wm., Sr.	730	Brn
Ranger, Joe.	185	Elc
Solomon	508	Prw
Rank, Jacob	651	Btt
Rankin, James	651	Btt
James	5	Rcm
Jas.	376	Ags
Joseph	376	Ags
Matthew	568	Frd
Richd.	376	Ags
Robt.	376	Ags
Saml.	571	Brk
Thos.	376	Ags
Saml.	376	Ags
William B.	694	Br
Wm.	571	Brk
Rankins, James	627	Mnt
John	816	Hmp
John	9	Knw
Milly	851	Wth
Robert	852	Wth
William	530	Frd
Rann, Mary	161	Sth
Rannels, Sarah	513	Brk
Ranol see Randol		
Ranolph, Judith	108	Cmb
Ransbarger, Benjn.	378	Ags
Philip	376	Ags
Ransdell, Susanna	350	Fqr
Ranshaw, Jas.	713	Wsh
Ransom, Elizabeth	792	Bck
John F.	792	Bck
William	792	Bck
see Kendall		
Ransome, Henry	109	Cmb
Ranson, Edward	66	Jff
Matthew	58	Jff
Ransone, Anne	668	Glc
Elizabeth	120	Cmb
Elliott	437	Mth
Henry	438	Mth
Peter	515	Frd
Rd.	668	Glc
Richd.	547	Brk
Robert	122	Cmb
Robert, Botetourt	668	Glc
Tho., jr.	449	Mth
Thos.	669	Glc
Thos., Sr.	446	Mth
William	119	Cmb
Wm.	668	Glc
Rantin, Hugh	918	Nrf
Rany, Jesse	730	Brn
Peler	356	Lnn
Rap, John	268	Rck
Matthias	271	Rck
see Ruf		
Rape, Daddy	233	Shn
Raphell, Solo.	21	Hnr
Raposs, Daniel	851	Wth
Frederick	851	Wth
John	851	Wth
see Repass		
Rasberry, Betsy	3	Oho
Rase, John	296	Frf
John	800	Hmp
William	832	Hmp
Rasey, John	769	Hmp
Luke	772	Hmp
Thomas	767	Hmp
William	767	Hmp
Rash, John	356	Lnn
Robert	355	Lnn
William	356	Lnn
Rass, James, Estate	171	Alb
Ratchford, William	4	Rcm
Ratcliff, Benja.	909	Hrr
James	921	Hrr
Jeremiah	648	Mnt
John	15	Wod
Moses, Sr.	658	Mnt
Ralph	659	Mnt
Rebeccah	659	Mnt
Richd.	659	Mnt
Ratcliffe, Burdett	26	Stf
Chas.	810	Nrf
Giddeon, (W)	882	Yrk
John	294	Frf
John	882	Yrk
John A.	21	Stf
Quinton	501	Prw
Rd.	294	Frf
Richard	40	Stf
Richard, L.	54	Stf
Robert	293	Frf
Saml.	293	Frf
Shadrach	519	Prw
Thomas	766	Nwk
William	766	Nwk
William	767	Nwk
Zephaniah	501	Prw
Ratee, Jno. B.	285	Ldn
Ratekin, John	866	Cmp
John, Jr.	865	Cmp
Rathbone, Elisha	10	Wod
Rather, Brightwell	5	Ntt
Rayleigh	479	Bdf
Samuel	478	Bdf
Ratherford, Philip	942	Hrr
Ratliff, Isaac	955	Chc
Jams, (Overseer)	407	Fqr
Jeremiah	625	Mnt
Nathin, Sr.	625	Mnt
Virginia	12	Hnr
William	7	Wod
Wm.	625	Mnt
Rattekin, Laurence	861	Cmp
Rattray, David	14	Pwh
Raulings, Daniel	297	Ldn
Ravencroft, Saml.	1	Oho
Ravens, Wm.	124	Hnr
Ravenscroft, Charles	812	Hmp
Francis	812	Hmp
John [2]	811	Hmp
John S.	357	Lnn
Rawden, John	504	Prw
Rawdon, Mary	24	Oho
Rawles, James	330	Dnw
Rawlett, Elijah	214	Kng
Margt.	214	Kng
William	329	Dnw
Rawley, Elizabeth	206	Alb
Reuben	41	Rcm
William	20	Rcm
Wm.	5	Hnr
Rawling, Betsy	78	Spt
David	576	Brk
Rawlings, Bartholomew	662	Sss
Benjanin	729	Brn
Daniel	729	Brn
Henry	662	Sss
James	730	Brn
Littleberry	729	Brn
Lucy	328	Dnw
Lucy	114	Spt
Mary	161	Sth
Randolph	729	Brn
Reese	158	Dnw
Richd.	299	Ldn
Robt.	161	Sth
Sarah	729	Brn
Susanna	660	Sss
Rawlins, Alexander	922	Crl
Anthony	922	Crl
Benjamin	921	Crl
Jeremiah	920	Crl
John	922	Crl
Margarett	921	Crl
Rawls, Aaron	16	Rcm
John	870	Sth
Rawson, James	170	Alb
Ray, Adly	534	Mnn
Barton	653	Btt
Elijah	653	Btt
Elijah	584	Pre

Name	No.	Co.	Name	No.	Co.	Name	No.	Co.
Isaac	942	Hrr	John	839	Nrf	Rebel, Christopher	628	Mnt
James	879	Cmp	John	44	Stf	Rebeneck, Chas.	597	Brk
James	334	Dnw	John, Bkr.	51	Acc	Reck, George	431	Rnd
Jesse	41	Rcm	John B.	328	Dnw	Recoust see Ricourt		
Jesse, (Jr.)	10	Rcm	John B.	332	Dnw	Rector, Bennett	729	Wsh
John	378	Ags	Julaner	68	Clp	Braxton	356	Fqr
John	479	Bdf	Lewis	892	Hnv	Burrell	353	Fqr
John	635	Gls	Luther	52	Acc	Catharine	395	Fqr
John	756	Hmp	Michal	121	Acc	Charles	377	Fqr
John B.	867	Cmp	Milly	933	Hrr	Charles	394	Fqr
Luke	267	Amh	Polly	832	Nrf	Conoway	795	Hmp
Luke	480	Bdf	Rachel	53	Acc	Elias	356	Fqr
Mary	378	Ags	Richard	52	Acc	Elizabeth	395	Fqr
Mary	109	Cmb	Robt.	70	Clp	Henry	377	Fqr
Salley	328	Dnw	Robt. C.	69	Clp	Jesse	928	Hrr
Saml.	516	Brk	Sally	336	Dnw	Joel	340	Fqr
Samuel, jur.	515	Brk	Sarah	52	Acc	John	342	Fqr
Sweringen	517	Brk	Stephen	213	Kng	John, Junr.	356	Fqr
Thomas	479	Bdf	Susan	806	Nrf	John, Senr.	356	Fqr
Thomas	8	Knw	Theophilus	68	Clp	Ludwill	348	Fqr
William	479	Bdf	Thomas	872	Cmp	Thomas, Jr.	394	Fqr
William	118	Cmb	Thomas, Dr.	61	Chr	Thomas, Sr.	406	Fqr
Wm.	960	Hrr	Thomas, Jr., Colo.	62	Chr	William	394	Fqr
Rayan, William	529	Frd	Thomas, Ser., Colo.	61	Chr	William	503	Prw
William	760	Hmp	William	50	Acc	Red, Jessee	711	Gch
Rayborne, Eliza.	231	Aml	William	530	Frd	Joseph	384	Fqr
Raybourn see Reabourn			Wm.	935	Hrr	Mary	711	Gch
Rayburn see Reyburn			Reade, Caty	175	Knq	Susanna	384	Fqr
Rayfield, Custis	53	Acc	Edmund	468	Mdd	Wim.	897	Hnv
Levi	120	Acc	Jno.	471	Pra	Redcross, John	260	Amh
Major	51	Acc	Lovey	472	Pra	John	882	Yrk
William	51	Acc	Robert R.	2	Isw	John, jr.	882	Yrk
Rayford, Mildred	859	Sth	Robt. R.	2	Isw	Redd, Andrew	564	Frd
Rayhill, Esther	595	Mnr	Reader, Adam	423	Msn	Benjamin	175	Knq
Mathius	595	Mnr	George	8	Knw	George	921	Crl
Rayleigh, Charles	479	Bdf	Jacob	239	Ldn	George	567	Frd
Isaac	479	Bdf	James	420	Msn	George	584	Pre
Philip	479	Bdf	Michael	420	Msn	James	175	Knq
see Rather			Michael	112	Spt	John	63	Chr
Raymond, Betsey	328	Dnw	Richard	18	Wod	John	568	Frd
Raynolds, Henry	216	Shn	Wm.	239	Ldn	John	174	Knq
Raynor, John [2]	207	Alb	Reador, John	945	Nrf	John	584	Pre
William	207	Alb	Reads, Daniel	26	Stf	Joseph	114	Cmb
Raze see Rase			Mehethelom	48	Stf	Joseph	583	Pre
Razer, George	401	Mds	Ready, Isaac	446	Bth	Lucy	921	Crl
Razor, Daniel	851	Wth	James	345	Fqr	Philip	920	Crl
Jacob	401	Mds	Reagon, Nicholes	720	Wsh	Phillip D.	89	Spt
Jno.	290	Ldn	Nicholes	729	Wsh	Saml.	916	Nrf
Mary	290	Ldn	Nicholes, Jur.	729	Wsh	Samuel	920	Crl
Rea, Danl.	302	Rck	Wm.	740	Wsh	Thomas	584	Pre
Eligah	945	Hrr	Realy, Polly	877	Sth	William	920	Crl
Jane	292	Rck	Ream, Andrew	653	Btt	Reddick, John	852	Wth
Joseph	280	Rck	Reamey, Jas.	738	Wsh	Redding, Benja.	591	Frd
Robert	206	Alb	Jeremiah	755	Wsh	Ezeki	479	Bdf
Samuel	509	Frd	Reams, Claiborne	158	Dnw	James	421	Bth
Thomas	206	Alb	Simeon	159	Dnw	James	765	Hmp
Reab, Jno.	297	Rck	William	159	Dnw	Martha	537	Prg
Reabourn, Charl.	580	Mnr	Wood	159	Dnw	Thomas	281	Rck
Reabourne, John	586	Mnr	Reamy, Bearriman	783	Wst	Wm.	829	Nrf
Reace, James	730	Brn	William	783	Wst	Reddinger, Michl.	652	Btt
Read, Casper	543	Frd	Rearden, John	300	Rck	Reddis, James	851	Wth
Clem	62	Chr	Reardon, Elizth.	917	Nrf	Reddish, Aaron	851	Wth
Clement	158	Dnw	Jno.	294	Frf	Burdett	402	Mds
Cordall	873	Sth	Letitia	600	Frd	James	402	Mds
Dorothy, Gloucester Town	668	Glc	Rease, Freman	355	Lnn	Reddy, Fanny	651	Btt
Edmund	51	Acc	Jacob	234	Shn	Redenan see Riderson		
Francis	468	Mdd	Josiah	356	Lnn	Reder, Benj.	938	Hrr
Frank	956	Hrr	Marsh	949	Hrr	Redfarn, Saml.	595	Brk
George	121	Acc	Reason, Robert	575	Frd	Redford, Andrew	126	Hnr
George	299	Rck	Reasons, Wm.	67	Clp	Edward	125	Cmb
Griffin	68	Clp	Reasor see Resoor			Edwd.	21	Ntt
Helen	918	Nrf	Reat, ---, Johnson &	20	Hnr	Ellis	117	Hnr
Isaac	62	Chr	Reaveley, Ann	69	Spt	Francis	712	Gch
Jane, Mrs.	61	Chr	George	870	Cmp	John	107	Cmb
Jas.	69	Clp	Reaves, Elisha	9	Knw	John	125	Hnr
Jno.	68	Clp	Ephraim	219	Shn	John M.	117	Hnr
John	121	Acc	Richard	159	Dnw	Joseph	125	Hnr
John	871	Cmp	see Rives			Mary	121	Hnr
John	949	Hrr	Reavs, Jno., Jnr.	539	Prg	Mary	129	Hnr
			Nancy	730	Brn	Milner	126	Hnr

Perrin	126	Hnr	Danl.	268	Rck	Sally	873	Sth
Richard	711	Gch	Davd.	279	Rck	Samuel	274	Ldn
Richd.	711	Gch	Elizabeth	316	Ldn	Samuel	280	Ldn
Robt.	711	Gch	Emanuel	297	Rck	Sanders A.	10	Rcm
Sally	711	Gch	Frederick	302	Rck	Sarah	309	Ldn
Ursula	126	Hnr	Fredk.	652	Btt	Stephen	921	Hrr
Ware	126	Hnr	Geo.	533	Mnn	Stephen	275	Ldn
William	126	Hnr	Geo., (Son of Andw.)	660	Mnt	Stephin	634	Mnt
Wm.	711	Gch	Geo., (Son of Hupy.)	660	Mnt	Thomas	55	Jff
Redgway, Robert	290	Amh	George	515	Frd	Thomas	262	Ldn
Redifer, Conrod	21	Rcm	George	566	Frd	Thomas	314	Ldn
William	31	Rcm	George	661	Mnt	Thomas	301	Rck
Wm.	377	Ags	Humphrey	660	Mnt	Thomas	168	Shn
Reding, Henry	242	Shn	Humphrey, Jr.	661	Mnt	Thos.	650	Btt
William	289	Amh	Isaac	532	Mnn	William	599	Brk
Redman, Bude	343	Fqr	Isaac	534	Mnn	William	858	Cmp
Caleb	994	Nrt	Jacob	374	Ags	William	866	Cmp
Collier	63	Chr	Jacob	651	Btt	William	393	Fqr
Daniel	584	Frd	James	527	Brk	William	540	Frd
Elizabeth	343	Fqr	James	296	Frf	William	920	Hrr
George	63	Chr	James	566	Frd	William	69	Jff
George	345	Fqr	James	784	Hmp	Willm.	660	Mnt
Harmn.	916	Nrf	James	260	Ldn	Wm.	651	Btt
Jno. D.	213	Kng	James	300	Ldn	Wm.	534	Mnn
John	651	Btt	James	313	Ldn	Wm.	268	Rck
John	783	Wst	James	612	Mnt	see Peed, Peede, Reeed		
John, Junr.	390	Rch	James	182	Shn	Reede, Geo.	916	Nrf
John, Senr.	390	Rch	James	700	Wsh	Reeder, Benjamin	170	Shn
Joseph, Senr.	397	Rch	James, Sr.	615	Mnt	Benjamin Franklin	478	Mnn
Leticia	63	Chr	Jas., J.	260	Ldn	Benjamin Franklin	558	Mnn
Margret	219	Pnd	Jeremiah, Jur.	770	Hmp	Henry	205	Shn
Nelly	71	Clp	Jeremiah, Senr.	770	Hmp	Jacob	850	Wth
Reuben	9	Oho	Jesse	385	Fqr	Jno.	533	Mnn
Richard L.	537	Frd	Jesse	916	Hrr	John	778	Hmp
Samuel	217	Pnd	Jno.	650	Btt	Mary	850	Wth
Soloman	783	Wst	Jno.	270	Ldn	Samuel	851	Wth
Thomas	192	Shn	Jno.	534	Mnn	William	778	Hmp
William	63	Chr	Jno., Jr.	534	Mnn	see Ruder		
see Davis			John	376	Ags	Reeding, Chales	479	Bdf
Redmon, Jeremiah	245	Shn	John	404	Ags	Reeds, ...	479	Bdf
Redmond, Benj.	245	Ldn	John	651	Btt	Reedy, Augustine	204	Shn
George	295	Amh	John	688	Br	Philip	218	Shn
Henry	480	Bdf	John	294	Frf	Reeed, Geo.	826	Nrf
Nancy	245	Ldn	John	383	Fqr	Reel, Andrew	488	Frn
Redmons, Jesse	245	Shn	John	509	Frd	Micheal	486	Frn
Thomas	245	Shn	John	589	Frd	Peter	513	Brk
Redpath, James	642	Mnt	John	775	Hmp	Reely see Ruly		
Redwell, James	401	Mds	John	696	Wsh	Reem, Tobs.	533	Mnn
Redwick, Richard	346	Fqr	John	850	Wth	Rees, Daniel	237	Ldn
Redwood, John	766	Nwk	John D.	70	Jff	Danl.	535	Brk
see Ridwood			Jonathan	920	Hrr	Davd.	720	Wsh
Ree see Kee			Jonathan	633	Mnt	David	579	Frd
Reece, Abraham	424	Rnd	Jont.	272	Ldn	Evan	37	Rcm
David	479	Bdf	Joseph	444	Bth	Even	529	Brk
David	918	Nrf	Joseph	691	Br	Jacob	530	Brk
Edwin	868	Sth	Joseph	275	Ldn	Jacob	581	Frd
Geo.	534	Mnn	Joseph	784	Wst	John	870	Cmp
George	737	Wsh	Joseph, fn.	295	Frf	John	595	Mnr
Herod	862	Cmp	Js.	916	Nrf	Silas	237	Ldn
Hugh	61	Chr	Junes	561	Brk	Thos.	529	Brk
Jacob	30	Rcm	Letty	784	Wst	Thos., jr.	529	Brk
John	296	Frf	Lydia	275	Ldn	see Bennett		
Jordan	478	Bdf	Margaret	404	Ags	Reese, Christ.	298	Ldn
Jos.	534	Mnn	Martin	476	Frn	Christ.	301	Ldn
Joseph	866	Sth	Mary	375	Fqr	David	312	Ldn
Lewis	868	Sth	Michl.	296	Rck	Edwd.	241	Ldn
Mary	480	Bdf	Nancy	294	Frf	Elizabeth	533	Prg
Sally	868	Sth	Obediah	868	Cmp	Esther	215	Shn
William	478	Bdf	Pattey	343	Fqr	Francis	159	Dnw
see Reed, Reese, Reice			Pattey	344	Fqr	Frederick	159	Dnw
Reed, Abraham	37	Rcm	Paul, Jur.	874	Cmp	Henry	159	Dnw
Alexander	436	Bth	Peter	920	Hrr	Herbert, jr.	159	Dnw
Alexer.	376	Ags	Peter	661	Mnt	Herbert, Senr.	159	Dnw
Allen	254	Ldn	Philip	377	Ags	Jno.	299	Ldn
Andw., Sr.	660	Mnt	Philip	297	Rck	Jno.	849	Sth
Ann	295	Frf	Philip	13	Wod	John	375	Ags
Archibd.	652	Btt	Richard	784	Wst	Jordan	159	Dnw
Ben	534	Mnn	Robert	376	Ags	Joseph	155	Sth
Charles	802	Hmp	Robert	295	Frf	Lucy	533	Prg
Cornelious	634	Mnt	Robert	72	Jff	Maurice	67	Clp

Michael	297	Ldn
Nancy	159	Dnw
Sterling	13	Ntt
Thomas	823	Hmp
Thomas	824	Hmp
William	821	Bck
William	824	Hmp
William	533	Prg
Wm.	533	Mnn
see Reser		
Reessee, Danl.	358	Lnc
Reetz, Charles	99	Jff
Reeve, Jos.	917	Nrf
Reeves, Eve	37	Rcm
Frederick	458	Frn
Hezekiah	514	Prw
James	294	Frf
John	503	Prw
Jonathan	519	Prw
Josiah	697	Br
Margaret	37	Rcm
Mary	115	Spt
Robert	917	Nrf
Regan, ---, Doctr.	918	Nrf
Regg, Sarah	294	Frf
Reggon, John	357	Lnn
Reice, David	290	Amh
John [written in on photostats]	478	Bdf
Reichter see Riechter		
Reid, An, jr.	336	Dnw
Andrew	266	Rck
Benjn.	575	Mnr
Clement	16	Oho
Edmund	480	Bdf
Ellis	23	Hnr
Francis	479	Bdf
Geo.	839	Nrf
H.C.	11	Hnr
James	480	Bdf
James	761	Brn
James	11	Oho
James	16	Oho
James	501	Prw
Jesse	730	Brn
John	589	Mnr
John	6	Oho
John	15	Oho
John	518	Prw
John T.U.	480	Bdf
Joseph	503	Prw
Nancy	730	Brn
Oney	760	Brn
Ralph	7	Oho
Ralph	16	Oho
Robert	170	Alb
Robert	589	Mnr
Saml.	374	Ags
Saml.	27	Hnr
Samuel	480	Bdf
Susanna	730	Brn
Tabitha	760	Brn
see Ried		
Reihart see Richart		
Reily, Margaret	374	Ags
Rein, Wm.	945	Hrr
Reince see Prince		
Reinhard, Matthew	230	Aml
Reins, James	951	Hrr
James	222	Pnd
Robert	221	Pnd
William	993	Nrt
Reisor, Daniel	206	Alb
Relph, William	564	Frd
Remore, Richard	20	Hnr
Renack see Revark		
Renchael, Thomas	425	Rnd
Renden, Lewis	400	Mds
Rengyl, Jacob	217	Pnd
Renick, John	2	Oho
Renn, Wm.	32	Hnr
Rennier, William	503	Brk
Rennin, George	421	Rnd
Renno, John	216	Ess
Rennolds, Eliza.	199	Ess
Isaac	881	Cmp
Lindsay	199	Ess
Philip	201	Ess
Richard	199	Ess
Sthieshly	205	Ess
Renoe, Bayless	516	Prw
Charles	515	Prw
David	519	Prw
Eli	519	Prw
Enoch	511	Prw
Frances	515	Prw
Francis	515	Prw
George	350	Fqr
Maddin	515	Prw
Page, (F.Negroe)	340	Fqr
Peter	572	Frd
Scarlet	515	Prw
William	524	Prw
Renolds, Hesekiah	14	Ntt
Renshaw, Js.	532	Mnn
Rentfro, John	651	Mnt
Joseph	631	Mnt
Rentis, T.D.	2	Hnr
Reonalds, David	823	Bck
David	832	Bck
William	788	Bck
see McReonalds		
Repass, Frederick	850	Wth
Samuel	850	Wth
see Raposs		
Repetoe, James	725	Nls
Peter	725	Nls
William	725	Nls
Repiton, Jos., (W)	881	Yrk
Replogle, Jacob	266	Rck
Repperto, Anna	207	Alb
John	207	Alb
Reser, Chrisley	203	Shn
John	189	Shn
Resign, Nicholas	565	Brk
Resoor, John	70	Clp
Respass, Elizabeth	444	Mth
Resser, Jacob	802	Hmp
Restall, George	70	Clp
Retson see Ritson		
Reuark, Alice	394	Rch
Reun, Jno.	651	Btt
Revaland, L.M.	32	Hnr
Reveal, William	597	Frd
Reveer, Bushrod	358	Lnc
Jas., Jr.	357	Lnc
Jas., Senr.	357	Lnc
Jno. W.	358	Lnc
Tho.	357	Lnc
Reveir, Isaac	468	Mdd
Reveley see Reaveley		
Revell, Elizabeth	51	Acc
Holladay	150	Sth
Humphrey	19	Isw
Revells, James	295	Frf
Reven see Reveir		
Reville, Geo.	189	Elc
Rew, Reuben	121	Acc
Rews, Robert	839	Nrf
Rewtrough, Thos.	658	Mnt
Rexrode, George	216	Pnd
George	219	Pnd
Henry	217	Pnd
Jacob	216	Pnd
John	218	Pnd
Leonard	217	Pnd
Zachariah	216	Pnd
Reyburn, Henry	428	Msn
Henry, jr.	428	Msn
James	429	Msn
James	663	Mnt
Jno.	645	Mnt
Joseph	639	Mnt
Thos.	645	Mnt
Wm.	663	Mnt
Reymal see Rymal		
Reymer, William	218	Pnd
Reynalds, Danl.	652	Btt
Michl.	276	Rck
Saml.	282	Rck
Reynals, Archelus	291	Amh
Charles	290	Amh
Reynard, George	200	Shn
Reynels, John	931	Hrr
Reynolds, Alexander	479	Bdf
Benj.	917	Nrf
Benja.	412	Rch
Benja., Jr.	392	Rch
Benjamin	81	Spt
Benjn.	215	Kng
Bernard	113	Hnr
Betsy	128	Hnr
Catharine	921	Crl
Charles	480	Bdf
Cornelius	922	Crl
Cornelius	214	Kng
Cornilus	918	Hrr
David	826	Nrf
David	584	Pre
Dinah	128	Hnr
Edward	479	Bdf
Elcanah	584	Pre
Francis	840	Nrf
Geo.	882	Yrk
George	87	Jff
H.B.	14	Oho
Henry	6	Isw
Isaac	480	Bdf
Jacob	920	Crl
James	61	Chr
James	712	Gch
James	390	Rch
Jane	535	Frd
Jerimiah	64	Jff
Jesse	479	Bdf
Jno.	69	Clp
Jno., Sr.	652	Btt
John	478	Bdf
John	479	Bdf
John	480	Bdf
John	920	Crl
John	62	Chr
John	636	Gls
John	9	Hnr
John	1	Knw
John	213	Kng
John	584	Pre
John J.	120	Cmb
Jonas	479	Bdf
Josh.	652	Btt
Larkin	651	Btt
Lewis	479	Bdf
Martha	27	Isw
Mary	840	Nrf
Maures	423	Msn
Nat	128	Hnr
Nathiel	479	Bdf
Obadiah	480	Bdf
Obadiah	132	Cmb
Philip	479	Bdf
Randal	7	Isw
Reuben	783	Wst
Richard	214	Kng
Richard	412	Rch
Richd.	6	Isw
Robert	793	Hmp
Robert	390	Rch
Samuel	110	Cmb
Sarah	214	Kng
Silas	14	Knw

Sophia	6	Isw	Isaac	994	Nrt	Ambrose	400	Mds
Thomas	921	Crl	Isham	583	Pre	Ann	209	Ess
Thomas	556	Frd	Isham	584	Pre	Ann	399	Rch
Thomas	20	Oho	Jac.	532	Mnn	Bazel	702	Wsh
Thos.	590	Mnr	Jac., Jr.	532	Mnn	Benjamin	207	Alb
Vincent, Senr.	390	Rch	James	729	Brn	Benjamin	485	Frn
William	922	Crl	James	296	Ldn	Benjamin, Jr.	486	Frn
William	784	Wst	James	718	Wsh	Boswell	584	Pre
Wm.	652	Btt	James	784	Wst	Brice	714	Wsh
Wm.	653	Btt	James B.	604	Frd	Christian	608	Mnt
Wm., Sr.	643	Mnt	Jane	584	Pre	Edmon	499	Frn
see Reonalds, Ronolds			Jese	312	Ldn	Edward	498	Frn
Rhea, Archd.	292	Rck	Jessee	864	Hnv	Frs.	917	Nrf
Edward	9	Oho	Jno.	358	Lnc	George, Snr.	232	Shn
John	717	Wsh	Jno.	532	Mnn	George, (TA)	232	Shn
Jos.	696	Wsh	Jno. H., Revd.	51	Chr	Godfrey	758	Hmp
Jos.	706	Wsh	John	878	Cmp	Henry	293	Frf
Patrick	3	Oho	John	579	Frd	Henry	537	Frd
Rezen	759	Wsh	John	398	Rch	Henry	233	Shn
Robert	423	Bth	John	20	Rcm	Isaac	486	Frn
Thomas	443	Bth	John, Jr.	994	Nrt	Isaac	934	Hrr
Thomas	682	Br	John, Sr.	993	Nrt	Isaac	274	Ldn
Thomas	12	Oho	John B.	729	Brn	Isaac	662	Mnt
Wm.	706	Wsh	Joseph	993	Nrt	James	549	Brk
Rhert, Jacob	8	Rcm	Joseph	21	Oho	James	92	Spt
Rhodehiffer, David	439	Bth	Luke	41	Rcm	James	113	Spt
Rhoderick, Frederik	207	Alb	Martha	129	Hnr	Jane	505	Brk
Rhodes, Abraham	564	Frd	Matthew H.	435	Flv	Jeremiah	659	Mnt
Danl.	834	Nrf	Peter	993	Nrt	Jesse	549	Brk
Geo.	295	Ldn	Presley	738	Wsh	Jno.	240	Ldn
J.R.	917	Nrf	Rachael	668	Glc	John	478	Bdf
Jacob	524	Frd	Richard	993	Nrt	John	832	Bck
Jacob	540	Frd	Richd.	761	Brn	John	159	Dnw
Jacob	564	Frd	Samuel	479	Bdf	John	174	Elc
James	23	Isw	Samuel	62	Chr	John	406	Fqr
Jno.	270	Ldn	Sarian	993	Nrt	John	537	Frd
Jno.	916	Nrf	Shadk.	533	Mnn	John	712	Gch
John	183	Shn	Tarlton	440	Flv	John	175	Knq
Joseph	184	Shn	Thomas	479	Bdf	John	584	Pre
Lewis	602	Frd	Thomas [2]	583	Pre	John	19	Wod
Michael	206	Shn	Thomas	8	Rcm	John, Jr.	362	Fqr
Phoely	730	Brn	William	479	Bdf	Jonathan	614	Srr
Randolph	240	Ldn	William	872	Cmp	Joseph	676	Br
Samell	234	Ldn	William	62	Chr	Laopol	170	Alb
Tholomiah	275	Ldn	William	401	Mds	Lucy	711	Clp
see Roads, Rohodes			William	584	Pre	Mark	35	Hnr
Rhopp, Nicholas	265	Ldn	William	390	Rch	Mary	635	Gls
Simon	266	Ldn	William	41	Rcm	Merit	584	Pre
Rhymus, William	508	Prw	William	784	Wst	Prasilla	725	Wsh
Rhyne, Christopher	358	Fqr	William, Senr.	784	Wst	Richd.	569	Brk
Martin	417	Bth	Wm.	652	Btt	Richd.	261	Ldn
Riadon, Sarah	96	Spt	Wm.	590	Mnr	Saml.	261	Ldn
Riale, Mary, a free woman			Wm.	825	Nrf	Sampson	287	Ldn
of coler	691	Wsh	Wm., Sr.	729	Brn	Shaderick	499	Frn
Rian, John	572	Brk	Zacheriah	583	Pre	Thomas	400	Mds
Ribel, Jonas	666	Mnt	Ziphanias	863	Hnv	Thomas	8	Oho
Rice, Abner	918	Hrr	see Garland, Jewry, Morris,			Thos.	557	Brk
Amos	918	Hrr	Price, Rue, Vass			Thos., Est.	68	Clp
Baley	5	Wod	Rich, Armstead	413	Rch	W., Senr.	293	Frf
Benajah	401	Mds	Betty [2]	407	Rch	Waitman	498	Frn
Benjamin, (Jr.)	479	Bdf	Charles	819	Bck	William	478	Bdf
Benjamin, Sr.	479	Bdf	Criss	407	Rch	William	293	Frf
Bohannon	918	Hrr	David	407	Rch	William	240	Ldn
Charles	784	Wst	David, a free negro	994	Nrt	William	517	Prw
Charles, Jr.	993	Nrt	Geo.	532	Mnn	William	33	Stf
Charles, Sr.	993	Nrt	George	407	Rch	Wm.	68	Clp
Chs.	532	Mnn	George	413	Rch	Wm.	712	Gch
Davd.	652	Btt	Jno.	532	Mnn	Wm.	949	Hrr
David	61	Chr	Mary	407	Rch	Wm.	658	Mnt
David	863	Hnv	Robert	198	Ess	Richardson, Amy	9	Ntt
Dudley W.	435	Flv	Robert	407	Rch	Ann	993	Nrt
Elijah	401	Mds	Wilmouth	408	Rch	Ann	105	Spt
Elijah	532	Mnn	Winney	407	Rch	Archibald	661	Sss
Ellinor	583	Pre	Richard, Daniel	534	Frd	Arthur	761	Brn
Francis	583	Pre	Henry	536	Frd	Aylsey	467	Frn
Francis, Junr.	583	Pre	Matthew	706	Wsh	Barnett	615	Mnt
George	550	Frd	Michael	103	Jff	Ben	783	Wst
George	993	Nrt	see George, Prichard			Benjamin	467	Frn
Holman	227	Lee	Richards, Aaron	714	Wsh	Bernard	126	Cmb
Isaac	531	Mnn	Alexander	33	Stf	Betty	662	Sss

Name	No.	Code	Name	No.	Code	Name	No.	Code
Bowker	464	Frn	Samuel	874	Hnv	William	635	Gls
Charles	326	Dnw	Samuel	244	Shn	William	760	Hmp
Clary	202	Ess	Severn	52	Acc	Richner, Danl.	533	Mnn
Daniel	50	Acc	Skelton	465	Frn	Richwine, Jacob	4	Rcm
David	170	Alb	Susan	916	Nrf	Rickerd, Ernest	378	Ags
David	654	Mnt	Thomas	478	Bdf	Rickets, Elisa.	70	Clp
Dudley	443	Flv	Thomas	335	Dnw	Ignatious	426	Rnd
Edmon	466	Frn	Thos.	582	Brk	Ricketts, Jno. J. [T.?]	293	Frf
Edmund	766	Nwk	Thos.	761	Brn	Matthew	292	Amh
Edward	819	Nrf	Thos.	711	Gch	Rickey, Joseph	851	Wth
Eliza	18	Hnr	Thos.	712	Gch	William	801	Hmp
Elizabeth	856	Hnv	Thos.	887	Hnv	Rickhart, Adam	422	Msn
Geo.	437	Flv	Turner	767	Nwk	Ricks, Arnold	152	Sth
Harriot	994	Nrt	Will	653	Btt	Davy	148	Sth
Holt	767	Nwk	William	51	Acc	Eliza.	151	Sth
Isaac	727	Wsh	William	478	Bdf	Jack	161	Sth
Isham	61	Chr	William	479	Bdf	Jno.	532	Mnn
James	571	Brk	William	62	Chr	Johanna	872	Sth
James	809	Bck	William	341	Fqr	Nicholas	170	Alb
James	61	Chr	William	474	Frn	Patience	871	Sth
James	604	Frd	William	455	Grn	Rebecca	871	Sth
James	74	Spt	William	100	Jff	Richd.	130	Sth
James	660	Sss	William	766	Nwk	Robert	877	Sth
Jas.	546	Prg	William	526	Prw	Tony	871	Sth
Jesse	478	Bdf	William	222	Shn	Rickter, John	532	Mnn
Jesse	850	Wth	William	37	Stf	Ricourt, Peter	393	Fqr
Jessee	784	Wst	William, F.N.	660	Sss	Roctor, Jas.	744	Wsh
Jno.	853	Hnv	William, Junr.	850	Wth	Warrint	744	Wsh
Jno.	292	Ldn	William, Senr.	850	Wth	Ricus, Powen	809	Nrf
Jno. A.	891	Hnv	William P.	62	Chr	Riddle, Andw.	652	Btt
Jno. D.	61	Chr	Wim.	859	Hnv	Benjamin	424	Rnd
Joel	652	Btt	Wim.	887	Hnv	George	653	Btt
John	52	Acc	Wm.	652	Btt	George	202	Shn
John	413	Bth	Wm.	22	Hnr	Isaac	202	Shn
John	479	Bdf	Wm.	23	Hnr	James	734	Wsh
John	110	Cmb	Wm.	276	Ldn	John	711	Gch
John	196	Ess	Wm.	436	Mth	John	425	Rnd
John	432	Flv	Wm.	633	Mnt	John	285	Rck
John	950	Hrr	Wm., Sr.	822	Nrf	Patsey	838	Bck
John	767	Nwk	Wm. M.	712	Gch	Richard	921	Crl
John	810	Nrf	see Brown, Curle, Darby,			Robert	711	Gch
John	821	Nrf	Richdardson, Taylor,			Stephen	378	Ags
John	917	Nrf	Tiller			Thomas	921	Crl
John	162	Sth	Richarson, Frances	28	Hnr	Vaughan	175	Knq
John, (BH)	62	Chr	Richart, Benjamin	12	Rcm	William	596	Brk
John, (MH)	62	Chr	Richarts, Sarah, (Y)	881	Yrk	William	920	Crl
John P.	61	Chr	Richdardson, Richd.	545	Prg	Wm.	69	Clp
Jonathan	456	Frn	Riche, Robt.	650	Btt	Riddlebarger, Jno., Jr.	652	Btt
Jordan	760	Brn	Richerdson, Jane	713	Wsh	Jno., Sr.	651	Btt
Jordan	454	Grn	William	702	Wsh	Saml.	652	Btt
Jordan	661	Sss	Richerick, Philip	81	Jff	Riddlehurst, Francis	942	Chc
Leray	546	Prg	Thomas	81	Jff	Riddlemoyer, Martin	237	Shn
Lewis	455	Frn	Richerson, Elisha	230	Aml	Riddlesberger, Samuel	850	Wth
Lewis	660	Sss	Elizabeth	356	Lnn	Rideinger, Stephen	696	Br
Lucy	467	Frn	John	854	Cmp	Ridenaur, Jac.	533	Mnn
Martha	434	Flv	John	615	Mnt	Martin	533	Mnn
Martha	859	Hnv	Richeson, Elizabeth	175	Knq	Ridenbaugh, Margt.	283	Ldn
Mary	662	Sss	Giles	256	Amh	Ridenger, Saml.	658	Mnt
Matthew	689	Br	James, jr.	175	Knq	Ridenhour, Christopher	77	Jff
Mourning	784	Wst	James, Snr.	175	Knq	Ridenour, Adam	215	Shn
Nancy	51	Acc	Jesse	279	Amh	Adam	173	Shn
Nancy	120	Acc	John	285	Amh	Adam	174	Shn
Nancy	358	Lnc	John	175	Knq	George	173	Shn
Neicey	53	Acc	Mary	266	Amh	Henry [2]	173	Shn
Polly	662	Sss	Thomas	920	Crl	Jacob	173	Shn
Precilla	850	Wth	Thomas	921	Crl	Ridens, Jno.	901	Hnv
Ralph	121	Acc	William, jr.	174	Knq	Rideout, Elijah	158	Dnw
Randolph	661	Sss	William C.	175	Knq	Giles	729	Brn
Richard	170	Alb	Wm., Senr.	175	Knq	John	729	Brn
Richard	62	Chr	Richet, Thomas	270	Rck	Wm., jr.	729	Brn
Richard	122	Cmb	Richey, James	290	Rck	Wm., Sr.	729	Brn
Richard	341	Fqr	Jno.	289	Rck	Rider, Abraham	669	Glc
Richard	467	Frn	Mary	376	Ags	Aeabed	254	Shn
Richard, Ser.	829	Bck	Michl.	284	Ldn	Alexander	400	Mds
Robert	872	Cmp	Saml.	284	Ldn	Christeen	227	Shn
Robert	117	Cmb	Richie, Philip, (Jr.)	29	Rcm	Hezekiah	882	Yrk
Robt.	652	Btt	see Ritchie			Jacob	227	Shn
Saml.	295	Frf	Richmond, Jacob	635	Gls	James	430	Bth
Saml.	441	Flv	James	836	Hmp	James	882	Yrk
Samuel	63	Chr	Mary	635	Gls	Jno.	669	Glc

John	430	Bth	Rigging, Willm.	882	Sth	Margt.	246	Ldn
John	479	Bdf	Riggle, George	603	Frd	Mary	73	Jff
Jos.	669	Glc	George, Jr.	545	Frd	Mary M.	295	Frf
Peter	227	Shn	George, Senr.	545	Frd	Matson	9	Wod
Solomon	669	Glc	Joseph	545	Frd	Michal	508	Frd
Thomas	430	Bth	see Rigle			Nancy	179	Alb
Thomas	836	Hmp	Riggleman, John	30	Rcm	Nathaniel	399	Fqr
William	430	Bth	Riggor, Jno.	303	Ldn	Richd.	301	Ldn
William	2	Knw	Riggs, Alex	531	Mnn	Samuel	681	Br
Wm.	881	Yrk	Aron	534	Mnn	Thomas	387	Fqr
Riderson, Elizabeth	567	Brk	Bazil	20	Oho	Thos.	505	Brk
Ridges, Jas.	22	Hnr	Benjamin	18	Wod	Thos.	517	Brk
Ridgeway, Joseph	478	Bdf	Cyrus	533	Mnn	William	586	Frd
Rebecca	64	Jff	David	472	Pra	William	72	Jff
see Redgway			George	121	Acc	William	255	Shn
Ridgley, Perigrine	6	Oho	Jno.	532	Mnn	William, of Stepn.	121	Acc
see Rigley			Joseph	121	Acc	Zacariah	77	Jff
Ridgway, Bazil	294	Frf	Leah	121	Acc	see Ryley		
Cath.	533	Mnn	Philip	431	Msn	Rimmon, John	227	Shn
Charity	530	Frd	Samuel	14	Oho	Rince see Riner		
David	552	Frd	Townley	488	Frn	Rineberg, Henry	517	Brk
Noah	531	Mnn	see Rigs			Rineburg, Geo.	539	Brk
William	575	Frd	Righ, Joseph	529	Brk	Rinecker, Henry	28	Rcm
Riding, George T.	214	Kng	Righstine, William	106	Jff	Rinehart, Abraham	761	Hmp
Ridings, Peter	525	Frd	Right, Ab.	7	Ntt	Abraham	779	Hmp
Ridisell, Thomas	317	Ldn	Anne	525	Prw	Andw.	377	Ags
Ridley, Eliza.	678	Wrw	Ester	62	Chr	Elizabeth	28	Rcm
Frances	679	Wrw	Jno.	532	Mnn	George	822	Hmp
Peter	681	Wrw	John	207	Alb	Jacob	34	Rcm
Sally	802	Nrf	John	15	Hnr	John	824	Hmp
Thomas	127	Sth	John	516	Prw	John	20	Rcm
Thomas	867	Sth	Saml.	532	Mnn	Jomiah	424	Rnd
William	116	Spt	Sarah	509	Prw	Katy	377	Ags
Ridman see Redman			Seaymore	110	Cmb	Michael	28	Rcm
Ridshaw, Jos.	695	Wsh	Seaymore, jr.	107	Cmb	Rineheart, Adam	197	Shn
Jos., Jur.	695	Wsh	Stark	207	Alb	Adam	234	Shn
Ridwood, John	328	Dnw	William	119	Cmb	Francis	650	Btt
Riechter, Geo.	289	Ldn	William	514	Prw	Jacob	478	Frn
Ried, Joseph	480	Bdf	Rightnour, Henry	70	Clp	Jacob	479	Frn
see Reid			Rights, Green	104	Cmb	Lewis, Jun.	235	Shn
Rieff, Andw.	404	Ags	Rigle, Michl.	667	Mnt	Mary	239	Shn
Riegal, John	851	Wth	Rigley, Absolom	3	Oho	Matthias	191	Shn
Simon	851	Wth	Rigney, Charles	495	Frn	Owen	652	Btt
Rieley, Samuel	799	Hmp	Isam	655	Mnt	Peter	653	Btt
Riely, James	792	Hmp	Rigs, Isaac	533	Mnn	see Beneheart		
Thomas	758	Hmp	John	23	Oho	Rinehearte, John	239	Shn
Rien, Thomas	926	Hrr	Rile, George	256	Shn	Michael	239	Shn
Rife, Conrod	545	Brk	Rilee, Frances	669	Glc	Riner, Adam	557	Brk
David	651	Btt	Jno.	668	Glc	Henry	557	Brk
Jacob	21	Rcm	Thos.	669	Glc	Jacob	563	Brk
John	170	Alb	Riles, Stephen	77	Jff	John	542	Brk
John	374	Ags	Riley, ...hn	168	Shn	Peter	543	Brk
John	252	Shn	Alexander	294	Frf	Ringer, Geo.	532	Mnn
Joseph	16	Rcm	Alexr.	61	Jff	Ringlesby, Christopher	9	Wod
Peter	612	Mnt	Charles	408	Fqr	Ringley, John	744	Wsh
Riffe, Henry	588	Mnr	Charles, Jr.	411	Fqr	John, Senr.	746	Wsh
Riffee, George	652	Btt	Elizabeth	507	Frd	Joseph	209	Shn
Jno.	651	Btt	Frederick	72	Jff	Samuel	209	Shn
Riffey, Mary, (SF)	223	Shn	Garrett	510	Brk	Rinker, Absalom	227	Shn
Riffie, Jacob	70	Clp	George	370	Fqr	Christeen	227	Shn
Riffle, Frances	952	Hrr	George	588	Frd	Edwd.	304	Ldn
George	951	Hrr	George	91	Jff	Edwd.	306	Ldn
George	429	Msn	James	507	Brk	George, 3d.	229	Shn
Isaac	419	Rnd	James	409	Fqr	Henry	229	Shn
Jacob	951	Hrr	James	509	Frd	Jacob	580	Frd
Jacob	419	Rnd	James	93	Jff	Jacob	227	Shn
Mathias	423	Msn	James	270	Rck	Jacob	247	Shn
Rigby, Matilda	515	Frd	James F.	414	Bth	Jacob, 3d.	230	Shn
Riger, Abram	909	Hrr	Jas.	68	Clp	John	802	Hmp
Isaac	912	Hrr	Jesse	376	Ags	John	804	Hmp
Jacob	910	Hrr	Jesse	346	Fqr	Samuel	805	Hmp
John	912	Hrr	Jesse	925	Hrr	Rinor, Daniel	402	Mds
Philip	911	Hrr	John	514	Frd	John	401	Mds
Susana	911	Hrr	John	68	Jff	Rinqu see Resign		
Riggan, John	614	Srr	John	520	Prw	Rion, John	428	Rnd
Rachel	614	Srr	John, Junr.	368	Fqr	see Wilson		
Susanna	614	Srr	John, Sr.	367	Fqr	Ripley, Jacob	573	Brk
William, Sr.	614	Srr	Joseph	3	Wod	Jno.	285	Rck
Riggen, Stephen	119	Acc	Joshua	304	Ldn	John	437	Mth
Thomas	568	Mnr	Joshua	518	Prw	Lemuel	7	Isw

Lewis	22	Oho
Mathias	289	Rck
Richd.	436	Mth
Ripnin, Wilson	170	Alb
Ripple, Peter	86	Jff
Philip	84	Jff
Rippy, David	540	Brk
Matthew	532	Brk
Saml.	532	Brk
Rire, Thomas	224	Shn
Risbey, Thos.	259	Ldn
Wm.	307	Ldn
Rise, William	824	Bck
see Rice		
Riser, John	584	Brk
Matthias	502	Brk
Matthias	565	Brk
see Reser		
Risher, Saml.	668	Glc
Rising, Delia	526	Prw
James	505	Prw
James	525	Prw
Peter	505	Prw
Peter	525	Prw
William	509	Prw
Risk, John	377	Ags
Wm.	377	Ags
Rison, Ellery	230	Aml
John	52	Chs
Peter	231	Aml
Rispess, Christopher	614	Srr
John	614	Srr
Risque, Betsy	292	Rck
James	650	Btt
Ritacre, Amasa	242	Ldn
Elijah	242	Ldn
Mary	242	Ldn
Ritche, James	3	Hnr
Ritchie, Alexander	584	Pre
Archd.	218	Ess
Isaac	29	Rcm
Jacob	29	Rcm
John	207	Ess
John	356	Lnn
John	16	Oho
John	31	Rcm
John E.	583	Pre
Philip	30	Rcm
Robert	328	Dnw
Thos.	3	Hnr
see Richie		
Ritchison, John	2	Oho
Ritenour, George	520	Frd
Michal	543	Frd
Riter, John	938	Hrr
Peter	905	Hrr
Ritson, G. B.	917	Nrf
Jnon.	918	Nrf
Rittenhause, Henry	725	Nls
Saml.	169	Alb
see Writtenhouse		
Ritter, Daniel	851	Wth
Henry	427	Bth
Jacob	13	Rcm
Michael	15	Rcm
Michael	36	Rcm
Sarah	851	Wth
Rittor, Thomas	142	Sth
Rival, John	917	Nrf
Rivers, Christopher	687	Br
Joshua	307	Ldn
Nancy	851	Sth
Robert	300	Amh
Robt.	10	Ntt
Sarah	306	Ldn
William	159	Dnw
William	454	Grn
see Rives		
Rives, ---, Sturdevant &	333	Dnw
Anne	536	Prg
Anthony	159	Dnw
Charles B.	159	Dnw
Chirstopher	159	Dnw
George	662	Sss
Green	159	Dnw
Henry	105	Cmb
James	532	Prg
John	454	Grn
John, jr.	530	Prg
Jos.	819	Nrf
Martha	159	Dnw
Nathaniel	454	Grn
Peyton	532	Prg
Rebecca	661	Sss
Richd.	819	Nrf
Robert	726	Nls
Thomas	158	Dnw
Thomas E.	662	Sss
Timothy	530	Prg
William, Senr.	535	Prg
William D.	455	Grn
William E.	532	Prg
see Parker, Reaves, Rivers		
Rix, Jane, F.N.	661	Sss
Jim	549	Prg
Jos.	838	Nrf
Mike, F.N.	661	Sss
Robert	838	Nrf
Rixey, Chs.	68	Clp
Jno.	68	Clp
Presley	411	Fqr
Samuel	342	Fqr
Wm., & Mother	68	Clp
see Roxey		
Ro...l, Wm.	159	Dnw
Ro...ling, Jo...n	883	Cmp
Roach, Ashcraft	271	Amh
Charles	651	Btt
Cornelius	266	Amh
Davd.	593	Mnr
Elija	939	Chc
Elijah	593	Mnr
Elisha	63	Chr
Eliza	230	Aml
George	271	Amh
George	353	Fqr
George	526	Prw
Henry	261	Amh
Jacob	792	Nrf
James	576	Brk
James	281	Ldn
James	748	Wsh
Jeremiah	593	Mnr
Jno. S.	895	Hnv
John	544	Brk
John	379	Fqr
John	538	Frd
John, Jur.	62	Chr
John, Senr.	61	Chr
Jonathan	593	Mnr
Joshua	875	Cmp
Luke	855	Hnv
Mahlon	301	Ldn
Maridith	953	Chc
Martha	230	Aml
Mary	953	Chc
Mickleberry	593	Mnr
Price	295	Frf
Reuben	593	Mnr
Richd.	375	Ags
Sarah	922	Crl
Thomas	949	Chc
Thomas	378	Fqr
Thos.	793	Nrf
William	271	Amh
William	875	Cmp
William	565	Frd
Wm.	69	Clp
Wm.	70	Clp
see Roush		
Roache, Absolam	35	Rcm
Jacob	35	Rcm
Jacob, (FN)	42	Rcm
Saml.	36	Rcm
Roadcap, Chrisley	295	Rck
Emanuel	29	Rcm
John	14	Rcm
Peter	29	Rcm
Roads, Christian	32	Rcm
Christor.	273	Rck
Christr.	651	Btt
Elizt.	404	Ags
Frederick	7	Rcm
Fredk.	597	Brk
George	267	Rck
George	273	Rck
Henry	20	Rcm
Henry	41	Rcm
Jacob	22	Rcm
Jno.	293	Frf
Jno.	531	Mnn
Jno.	533	Mnn
Jno., 3d.	532	Mnn
John	228	Shn
John, (jr. [?])	223	Shn
Philip	27	Rcm
Robert	478	Bdf
Valentine	223	Shn
Roan, Daniel	53	Acc
Elizh.	881	Yrk
James	374	Ags
James	940	Chc
Stephen	52	Acc
Roane, Ann	922	Crl
Charles	175	Knq
Jane	300	Rck
John	469	Mdd
John, [his] est.	175	Knq
John M.	175	Knq
Marg	175	Knq
Mary E. M.	174	Knq
Spencer	887	Hnv
Thos.	669	Glc
Warner	469	Mdd
William	175	Knq
Wm.	669	Glc
Roarer, Henry	18	Rcm
Roark, Philemon	27	Rcm
Roathwell, Clabon	170	Alb
Robb, Jas.	358	Lnc
Lucy	921	Crl
Robert G.	784	Wst
Robbens, Job	583	Brk
Robbey, Acquilla	419	Rnd
Robbin, Augustis	52	Acc
Robbins, Elijah D.	77	Spt
Isaac	52	Acc
John	71	Spt
Kate	8	Acc
Michel	119	Acc
Thomas	53	Acc
Robbinson, David	861	Hnv
Joseph	993	Nrt
Robenet, Nathan	635	Gls
Stephen	635	Gls
Robenson, David	457	Frn
George	481	Frn
Nicholas	451	Frn
Robeon see Robuo		
Roberdett, James	64	Jff
Roberds, Elizabeth	170	Alb
Robers, J.S.	533	Mnn
Roberson, Aachibald	207	Alb
Archabald	207	Alb
Barnett B.	8	Hnr
Benjamin	207	Alb
David	726	Nls
James	170	Alb
James	206	Alb
James	723	Nls

John	169	Alb	John	724	Nls	Thos.	624	Mnt
John	207	Alb	John	23	Oho	William	442	Bth
John	724	Nls	John	530	Prg	William	678	Br
John	424	Rnd	John	3	Rcm	William	693	Br
John, Jn.	724	Nls	John	689	Wsh	William	795	Bck
John, Jnr.	169	Alb	John	725	Wsh	William	491	Frn
Leroy	725	Nls	John	726	Wsh	William	806	Hmp
Levi	170	Alb	John	727	Wsh	William	425	Msn
Peter	724	Nls	John	881	Yrk	William	12	Oho
Thomas	724	Nls	John, (B.S.)	63	Chr	William, Jnr.	96	Jff
William	169	Alb	John, jr.	300	Amh	William, Snr.	96	Jff
William	170	Alb	John, jr.	478	Bdf	William J.	118	Spt
William	206	Alb	John, Jur.	62	Chr	William S.	50	Acc
Wm.	175	Knq	John, (of John	42	Isw	Williet	661	Sss
Robertnet, Edward	220	Pnd	John, (Otter	478	Bdf	Willis	40	Isw
Roberts, Abel	445	Bth	John, Sen.	17	Isw	Wilson	206	Alb
Alexander	723	Nls	John, Sr.	478	Bdf	Wm.	532	Brk
Alexr.	231	Aml	John W.	16	Isw	Wm.	58	Chs
Amos	532	Mnn	Johnathan	505	Brk	Wm.	444	Flv
Archibald	532	Prg	Jona.	531	Mnn	Wm.	295	Ldn
Arthur	52	Acc	Jos.	69	Clp	Wm.	532	Mnn
Bartholomew	62	Chr	Joseph	880	Cmp	Wm.	810	Nrf
Barwell	921	Crl	Joseph	62	Jff	Wm.	917	Nrf
Bazel	726	Wsh	Joseph	724	Nls	Wm., Estate	70	Clp
Benjamin	400	Mds	Joseph	813	Nrf	Wylie	68	Chr
Boyd	505	Brk	Joseph C.	724	Nls	Zachariah	723	Nls
Chastain	230	Aml	Lamuel	543	Brk	Zorababel	815	Nrf
Daniel	478	Bdf	Lemuel	916	Nrf	Robertson, ...	229	Aml
Daniel	679	Br	Leonard	479	Bdf	...	230	Aml
Dolly	53	Acc	Lewis	63	Chr	Abraham	478	Bdf
Edward	822	Nrf	Lina	68	Clp	Alexe.	70	Clp
Edwin, (F.N.)	38	Isw	Mack, (for Watts			Alexr.	375	Ags
Eliza.	62	Chs	Estate)	652	Btt	Alexr.	69	Clp
Eliza.	358	Lnc	Margaret	375	Ags	Amos	296	Ldn
Eliza.	472	Pra	Margaret	678	Br	Andw.	358	Lnc
Elizabeth	570	Mnr	Mary	875	Cmp	Ann	358	Lnc
Elizabeth	723	Nls	Mary	513	Frd	Archer	230	Aml
Enos	592	Frd	Mary	400	Mds	Archer	21	Ntt
Fanny	724	Nls	Mary	584	Pre	Arthur	491	Frn
Francis	52	Acc	Mimy	215	Shn	Benjamin	296	Amh
Francis	63	Chr	Molley	770	Brn	Betsy, Mrs.	62	Chr
Gaias	23	Oho	Morris	860	Cmp	Charles	857	Hnv
Geo.	69	Clp	Nancey	373	Fqr	Charles C.	920	Crl
Geo.	828	Nrf	Nancey	406	Fqr	Christopher	63	Chr
George	853	Cmp	Nancy	882	Yrk	Christopher	105	Cmb
George	636	Gls	Nat.	845	Sth	Clark	662	Sss
George	12	Oho	Nathan	527	Brk	Cole	786	Bck
Godfrey	881	Yrk	Nathan	18	Oho	David	332	Dnw
Gersham	807	Hmp	Oliver	61	Chs	David	489	Frn
Harry	880	Cmp	Peter	422	Msn	David, residig Peters-		
Henry	250	Ldn	Phs.	71	Clp	burg	159	Dnw
Henry	584	Pre	Pleasant	584	Pre	Edward	729	Brn
Henry, Senr.	63	Chr	Reuben	14	Oho	Edward	474	Frn
Isaac	11	Knw	Richard	478	Bdf	Elijah	70	Clp
Jacob	231	Aml	Richard	690	Br	Eliza.	231	Aml
James	170	Alb	Richard	695	Br	Feild	122	Cmb
James	434	Bth	Richard	18	Oho	Feild	131	Cmb
James	533	Brk	Richard	22	Oho	Francis	327	Lnn
James	852	Cmp	Richd.	726	Wsh	Francis	355	Lnn
James	507	Frd	Richd.	881	Yrk	Francis	371	Lnn
James	766	Nwk	Roberts	268	Ldn	Fred.	149	Sth
James	717	Wsh	Robt.	725	Wsh	George	231	Aml
James	881	Yrk	Samuel	679	Br	George	59	Stf
Jesse	17	Isw	Samuel	246	Ldn	Giles	70	Clp
Jno.	69	Clp	Samuel, F.N.	661	Sss	Gross	122	Cmb
Jno.	917	Nrf	Sarah	418	Bth	Henry	729	Brn
Jno.	1	Ntt	Sarah	661	Sss	Henry	334	Dnw
Jno. B.	443	Mth	Simon	745	Wsh	Henry	493	Frn
Joel	472	Frn	Stephen	268	Ldn	Henry W.	231	Aml
John	52	Acc	Susana	68	Clp	Hupet	258	Ldn
John	231	Aml	Tabitha [2]	120	Acc	Isaac	792	Bck
John	300	Amh	Thomas	479	Bdf	Isaac	831	Bck
John	374	Ags	Thomas	810	Bck	Isaac	69	Chr
John	434	Bth	Thomas	62	Chr	James	378	Ags
John	865	Cmp	Thomas	63	Chr	James	413	Bth
John	880	Cmp	Thomas	159	Dnw	James	783	Bck
John	921	Crl	Thomas	489	Frn	James	790	Bck
John	485	Frn	Thomas	531	Frd	James	866	Cmp
John	96	Jff	Thomas	356	Lnn	James	869	Cmp
John	400	Mds	Thos.	58	Chs	James	553	Frd

Name	No.	Abbr.	Name	No.	Abbr.	Name	No.	Abbr.
James	357	Lnn	Wm.	21	Ntt	David	454	Grn
James	850	Wth	Wm., jr.	375	Ags	David	938	Hrr
James, (GJ)	230	Aml	see Ryland			David	644	Mnt
James, jr.	230	Aml	Robertts see Robsitts			Dixon	385	Fqr
James, Sr.	230	Aml	Robes, Rob	531	Mnn	Elijah	694	Br
Jane	375	Ags	see Raber			Eliza	784	Wst
Jeffery	129	Cmb	Robeson, Agnes	531	Mnn	Eliza.	185	Elc
Jeffery, Sr.	129	Cmb	Jas.	531	Mnn	Elizabet	934	Hrr
Jennings	3	Ntt	Jno.	534	Mnn	Elizabeth	906	Hrr
Jesse	583	Pre	Mat.	533	Mnn	Elizabeth	469	Mdd
Jno.	56	Chs	Tho.	534	Mnn	Ellender	97	Spt
Jno.	297	Ldn	Wm.	534	Mnn	Everd.	881	Yrk
Jno.	872	Sth	Robey, Richard	111	Spt	Fields	120	Hnr
Jno., Dr.	10	Ntt	Sally	422	Bth	Francis	783	Wst
Jno., jr.	10	Ntt	Thomas	224	Pnd	Garey	593	Frd
Jno., Senr.	9	Ntt	Vincent	803	Hmp	Gartrude	644	Mnt
Jno. A.	11	Ntt	Robinet, Daniel	850	Wth	Geo.	558	Brk
Jno. F.	67	Chs	James	681	Brk	Geo.	358	Lnc
John	230	Aml	Michael	850	Wth	Geo.	469	Mdd
John	231	Aml	Robinette, Jesse	445	Flv	George	921	Crl
John	729	Brn	Robinison, Francis	294	Frf	George	922	Crl
John	798	Bck	James	296	Frf	George	517	Prw
John	69	Chr	Sarah	296	Frf	George	784	Wst
John	54	Chs	Robins, ---, & Enderson	11	Hnr	Hannah	295	Frf
John	469	Frn	Abraham	770	Brn	Henry	651	Btt
John	559	Frd	Adam	770	Brn	Henry	872	Cmp
John	355	Lnn	Armistead	668	Glc	Henry	867	Hnv
John	356	Lnn	George	479	Bdf	Isaac	651	Btt
John	660	Sss	James	91	Spt	Isaac	711	Gch
John, (BH)	231	Aml	Jesse	358	Lnc	Isaac	420	Msn
John, (RS)	61	Chr	Jno.	669	Glc	Israel	559	Brk
John, Snr.	123	Cmb	Jno.	916	Nrf	James	548	Brk
Jonas	53	Chs	John	798	Nrf	James	559	Brk
Joseph	400	Mds	Martha	668	Glc	James	577	Brk
Js.	57	Chs	Mary	832	Nrf	James	653	Btt
Lewis	583	Pre	Mary F.	723	Wsh	James	674	Br
Louis	916	Nrf	Rose	52	Acc	James	881	Cmp
Lucy	292	Amh	Thos.	668	Glc	James	587	Frd
Mathew	376	Ags	William	175	Knq	James	596	Frd
Maximilian	69	Clp	Wm.	668	Glc	James	120	Hnr
Michl.	150	Sth	Robinson, Aaron	674	Br	James	7	Knw
Mitchel	62	Chr	Abby	918	Nrf	James	10	Oho
Mitchell	177	Shn	Abraham	877	Cmp	James	520	Prw
Molly	729	Brn	Abrm.	563	Brk	James	702	Wsh
Nancey	824	Bck	Adam	472	Pra	James	710	Wsh
Nicholas	793	Bck	Alexr.	585	Brk	James	783	Wst
Paschal	63	Chr	Alexr.	699	Wsh	James, Senr.	742	Wsh
Patience	150	Sth	Alexr.	709	Wsh	James, Sr.	615	Mnt
Patsey	827	Bck	Alexr. H.	615	Mnt	Jams	924	Hrr
Peter	159	Dnw	Alexr. M.	697	Wsh	Jane	374	Fqr
Presilla	59	Stf	Allen	69	Clp	Jas.	358	Lnc
Richard	61	Chr	Alsey	3	Hnr	Jas.	471	Pra
Richward	453	Frn	Andrew	553	Frd	Jas.	760	Wsh
Robert	305	Ldn	Andrew	4	Oho	Jas., (B. fork)	649	Mnt
Robert	767	Nwk	Ann	469	Mdd	Jas., Colo.	471	Pra
Robt.	916	Nrf	Ann	918	Nrf	Jas., Jr.	358	Lnc
Robt. M.	357	Lnc	Archabald	849	Cmp	Jas., Jr.	644	Mnt
Roger	69	Clp	Archabold	18	Wod	Jas., M. Creek	648	Mnt
Simeon	303	Amh	Archibald	553	Frd	Jas., (of A)	472	Pra
Simeon	479	Bdf	Archer	18	Hnr	Jeffery	479	Bdf
Susanna	159	Dnw	Azuriah	3	Oho	Jeremiah	994	Nrt
Susanna	660	Sss	Bengamin	760	Hmp	Jno.	651	Btt
Susannah	122	Cmb	Benj.	938	Hrr	Jno.	12	Hnr
Tho. G.	357	Lnc	Benja.	905	Hrr	Jno.	267	Rck
Thomas	462	Frn	Benjamin	479	Bdf	Jno.	297	Rck
Thomas	196	Shn	Benjamin	921	Crl	Jno., Jr.	651	Btt
Walthall	11	Pwh	Benjamin	131	Hnr	Jno., Revd.	61	Chr
Warner P.	356	Lnn	Benjamin	83	Spt	Jno., Sr.	651	Btt
William	230	Aml	Betsy	119	Spt	Job	906	Hrr
William	291	Amh	Beverley	480	Bdf	Joe	651	Btt
William	332	Dnw	Braxton	454	Grn	John	479	Bdf
William	465	Frn	Brown	784	Wst	John	593	Brk
William	14	Pwh	Catharine	22	Rcm	John	692	Br
William	189	Shn	Charles	420	Fqr	John	851	Cmp
William	660	Sss	Charles	469	Mdd	John	864	Cmp
Winnifred	660	Sss	Charles	472	Pra	John	873	Cmp
Wm.	376	Ags	Chle.	918	Nrf	John	922	Crl
Wm.	56	Chs	Christopher	873	Cmp	John	180	Elc
Wm.	68	Clp	Davd.	712	Wsh	John	386	Fqr
Wm.	248	Ldn	David	920	Crl	John	446	Flv

John	478	Frn	Susan	29	Hnr	Andw.	531	Mnn
John	454	Grn	Susanna	378	Fqr	Elizabeth	636	Gls
John	771	Hmp	Thomas	921	Crl	George	653	Btt
John	779	Hmp	Thomas	325	Dnw	James	19	Hnr
John	127	Hnr	Thomas	511	Frd	John	948	Chc
John	131	Hnr	Thomas	594	Frd	John	993	Nrt
John	106	Jff	Thomas	569	Mnr	John	243	Shn
John	569	Mnr	Thomas	471	Pra	Judith	993	Nrt
John	577	Mnr	Thos.	557	Brk	Margret	956	Chc
John	579	Mnr	William	683	Br	Thomas	636	Gls
John	584	Mnr	William [2]	921	Crl	Thomas	993	Nrt
John	665	Mnt	William [2]	293	Frf	William	956	Chc
John	994	Nrt	William	346	Fqr	William	993	Nrt
John	7	Oho	William	454	Grn	Rockenbaugh, Jacob	96	Jff
John	16	Oho	William	914	Hrr	Jacob	105	Jff
John	266	Rck	William	3	Hnr	John	68	Jff
John	41	Rcm	William	469	Mdd	Rockhold, Charles	7	Wod
John	117	Spt	William	3	Oho	Mary	9	Wod
John	712	Wsh	William	24	Oho	Rockwell, Jesse	581	Brk
John, Jr.	878	Cmp	William	513	Prw	Roday, Jas.	581	Brk
John, jr.	469	Mdd	William	527	Prw	Roddish, Joel	44	Stf
John, Senr.	882	Cmp	William	8	Rcm	Roddy, Samuel	97	Spt
John, Senr.	469	Mdd	William	21	Rcm	Rodecap, Abraham	190	Shn
Jonathan, Jun.	44	Isw	William	783	Wst	David	180	Shn
Jonathan, Sen.	44	Isw	William	784	Wst	George, Jun.	190	Shn
Jos.	668	Glc	William, Jr.	406	Fqr	George, Sen.	190	Shn
Joseph	90	Jff	William P.	71	Spt	Joseph	190	Shn
Joshua	471	Pra	Winney	783	Wst	Roder, Simon	957	Hrr
Js.	532	Mnn	Winnifred	454	Grn	Rodes,...hoditus ["Ephrditus"		
Judith	993	Nrt	Wm.	69	Clp	crossed out]	207	Alb
Larkin	920	Crl	Wm.	949	Hrr	Charles	724	Nls
Lava.	916	Nrf	Wm.	22	Hnr	Clifton	170	Alb
Lewis	674	Br	Wm.	120	Hnr	David	724	Nls
Littleberry	454	Grn	Wm.	918	Nrf	George	444	Flv
Lot O.	959	Hrr	Wm.	271	Rck	Henry	446	Flv
Margaret B.	71	Spt	Wyatt	760	Brn	Henry	612	Mnt
Mark	696	Wsh	see Bobinson, Gray, Robini-			Hezekiah	207	Alb
Martin	712	Gch	son, Savage			James	446	Flv
Mary	454	Grn	Robison, Andw.	377	Ags	Joel	533	Mnn
Mary	905	Hrr	B.	375	Ags	John	170	Alb
Mary	577	Mnr	Charles	1	Oho	John	206	Alb
Mary	818	Nrf	Jno.	271	Rck	John	207	Alb
Maryan	120	Hnr	Martha	374	Ags	Matthew	206	Alb
Merit	918	Nrf	Mathew	374	Ags	Neomy	724	Nls
Michael	101	Spt	Peter	22	Oho	Reuben	207	Alb
Micheal			Saml.	377	Ags	Wm.	534	Mnn
Mima	784	Wst	Samuel	5	Oho	Zac.	533	Mnn
Moaning	131	Hnr	Robs see Roles			Rodgers, Andrew	24	Oho
Moses	357	Lnc	Robsitts, Nancy	36	Hnr	Benjamin	295	Frf
Nancy	29	Hnr	Robson, Jno.	68	Clp	Edw.	375	Ags
Nat	132	Hnr	Robuo, Thomas F.	133	Cmb	Ezekiel	11	Oho
Nat.	120	Hnr	Roby, Elijah	360	Fqr	Jacob	422	Bth
Olley	590	Frd	Elisha	296	Frf	James	425	Bth
Parker	860	Hnv	Elizabeth	367	Fqr	John	51	Acc
Peggy	471	Pra	Elkany	950	Hrr	John	951	Chc
Peter	926	Hrr	Ely	62	Chr	Joseph	376	Ags
Peter	17	Hnr	Hezh.	296	Frf	Leonand	14	Oho
Peter	469	Mdd	James	62	Chr	Levin	50	Acc
Peter	7	Ntt	Jeremiah	966	Hrr	Luke	53	Acc
Randol	117	Hnr	John	360	Fqr	Major	53	Acc
Richard	779	Hmp	Michl.	294	Frf	Mary	11	Oho
Richard	512	Prw	Michl. H., Senr.	296	Frf	Nathaniel	53	Acc
Robert	296	Frf	Patrick	905	Hrr	Peggy	53	Acc
Sally	13	Hnr	Sarah	503	Prw	Peggy, And John		
Sally	525	Prw	Thomas	905	Hrr	Tatham	65	Acc
Sally	783	Wst	William	73	Jff	Peter	51	Acc
Saml.	295	Frf	William B.	501	Prw	Richard	52	Acc
Saml.	445	Flv	see Raley, Rooby			Richard	120	Acc
Saml.	712	Gch	Rocembaugh, George	374	Fqr	Robert	51	Acc
Saml.	472	Pra	Rochas, Eleanor	917	Nrf	Robert	5	Knw
Saml.	696	Wsh	Rochell, Charles	662	Sss	Wm.	376	Ags
Saml.	710	Wsh	Henry	660	Sss	Rodhiffer, Samuel	232	Shn
Sampson	597	Frd	Hinchey	660	Sss	Rodiffer, Philip	15	Oho
Sampson	454	Grn	Jemima	662	Sss	Rodihaver, Jno.	533	Mnn
Samuel	85	Spt	John	149	Sth	Rodiheffer, Elizabeth	222	Shn
Sarah	379	Fqr	Judith	156	Sth	Flora	223	Shn
Sarah	232	Ldn	Levy	661	Sss	George	248	Shn
Sarah	13	Rcm	Rochelle, Levy	145	Sth	Jacob	223	Shn
Solomon	793	Hmp	Rochester, Jeremiah	784	Wst	Samuel	222	Shn
Starky	881	Yrk	Rock, Alexander	993	Nrt	Rodman, Alexr.	38	Rcm

Joseph	833	Nrf
Roe, Bernard	420	Fqr
James	828	Hmp
James, Jur.	635	Gls
James, Sen.	636	Gls
James B.	213	Kng
John	635	Gls
Lewis	929	Hrr
Sally	58	Stf
Solomon	636	Gls
Stephen	635	Gls
Thomas	635	Gls
William	661	Sss
William, Jr.	661	Sss
see Wroe		
Roebuck, Rolly	401	Mds
William	401	Mds
Roger, Michael	564	Frd
see Ragen		
Rogers, ...obert	167	Shn
Aaron	919	Hrr
Aaron	918	Nrf
Abraham	676	Br
Achellis	206	Alb
Ann	206	Alb
Ann	357	Lnc
Arthur	529	Frd
Benjamin	277	Amh
Benjamin	213	Kng
Benjamin	614	Srr
Bowlin	618	Mnt
Charles	206	Alb
Charles	215	Kng
Charls	940	Hrr
Chs.	916	Nrf
Edward	945	Hrr
Edward	994	Nrt
Edwin	615	Srr
Elizabeth	34	Stf
Elizh.	882	Yrk
George	650	Btt
George	728	Brn
George	379	Fqr
George	214	Kng
Gordon	20	Rcm
Gusty	213	Kng
Hamilton	311	Ldn
Henry	343	Fqr
Hosea	214	Kng
Hugh	235	Ldn
Jacob	909	Hrr
James	14	Rcm
James	661	Sss
James	851	Wth
James	852	Wth
Jane	917	Nrf
Jane, jr.	213	Kng
Jane, Sr.	213	Kng
Jno.	651	Btt
Jno.	68	Clp
Jno.	357	Lnc
Jno.	532	Mnn
Jno.	300	Rck
Joanna	388	Fqr
John	206	Alb
John [2]	207	Alb
John	698	Br
John	728	Brn
John	177	Elc
John	576	Frd
John	930	Hrr
John	942	Hrr
John	214	Kng
John	523	Prw
John	100	Spt
John	851	Wth
John, (Y)	881	Yrk
John A.	881	Yrk
Jonn.	916	Nrf
Joseph	400	Mds

Joseph	993	Nrt
Joseph	852	Wth
Josiah	487	Frn
Jud	358	Lnc
Kirtland	68	Chs
Lewis	929	Hrr
Martha	128	Cmb
Mary	343	Fqr
Micajah	615	Srr
Owen	780	Hmp
Owen, Senr.	833	Hmp
Parmenius	206	Alb
Philip	711	Gch
Reuben	356	Lnn
Rhoda	529	Frd
Rice	215	Kng
Richard	661	Sss
Robert	764	Hmp
Robert	929	Hrr
Robert	850	Wth
Rodam	947	Hrr
Rodeam	937	Hrr
Sally	52	Stf
Samuel	600	Frd
Samuel	927	Hrr
Sandford	523	Prw
Stephen	661	Sss
Susan	918	Nrf
Susan	57	Stf
Thomas	920	Crl
Thomas	158	Dnw
Thomas	524	Frd
Thomas	829	Hmp
Thomas	523	Prw
Thomas	106	Spt
Thomas, Senr.	525	Frd
William	206	Alb
William	230	Aml
William	603	Frd
William	994	Nrt
William	24	Oho
William	523	Prw
William	96	Spt
William	615	Srr
William	784	Wst
William	852	Wth
W., ...	916	Nrf
Wm., jr.	215	Kng
Wm., 2nd.	917	Nrf
Wm., senr.	213	Kng
Wm., 3d.	917	Nrf
Wm., (yr.)	213	Kng
Wm. A.	668	Glc
Wm. A.	931	Hrr
Zadok	582	Frd
see Royers		
Roggers, Ann	95	Spt
Rohdieffer, John	246	Shn
Rohodes, Augustin	69	Clp
Rohr, Jacob	263	Rck
Jacob	2	Rcm
Philip	851	Cmp
Roin, John	377	Fqr
Rolacan see Rolasan		
Roland, Elizabeth	532	Frd
Martin	542	Frd
Samuel	530	Frd
Rolasan, Aaron	283	Rck
Wm.	285	Rck
Rolason, Nathnl.	285	Rck
Roleman, Christian	219	Pnd
Christian, J.	219	Pnd
Rolen, Jeremiah	159	Dnw
Roler, Conrod	440	Bth
Peter	18	Rcm
Susannah	7	Rcm
Roles, Joseph E.	248	Ldn
Roley, Sarah	293	Frf
see Roby		
Rolin, Geo.	376	Ags

John	376	Ags
Rolins, Hinchia	454	Grn
Rolinson, Thos., Dr.	328	Dnw
Roller, Paul	376	Ags
Rolley, William	35	Hnr
Rolling, Wm., [his] Est.	215	Kng
Rollings, Charlott	334	Dnw
John	169	Shn
Joseph R.	215	Kng
Rollins, Aaron, (Over-seer)	390	Fqr
Bengamin	805	Hmp
Benjamin	198	Ess
Benjamin	214	Kng
Eligah	823	Hmp
Elijah	416	Rnd
Eliza.	215	Kng
Henry	215	Kng
James	388	Fqr
James	215	Kng
Jno.	70	Clp
John	519	Prw
John R.	214	Kng
Jos.	881	Yrk
Jos., Est.	213	Kng
Moses, (PM)	187	Shn
Rhoda	236	Ldn
Richmond	538	Prg
Saml.	214	Kng
Saml., Senr.	213	Kng
Thomas	393	Fqr
Wm.	70	Clp
Wm.	214	Kng
Zachariah	905	Hrr
Rolls, James	784	Wst
Jesse	45	Stf
John	507	Prw
Sally	507	Prw
Thomas	507	Prw
William	364	Fqr
Rolsenberry, John	772	Hmp
Rolstone, David	42	Rcm
Roman, Eman	916	Nrf
Romans, Joshua	738	Wsh
Thomas	558	Frd
Romick, Michael	238	Shn
Romine, Christopher	12	Rcm
Hannah	567	Frd
Isaac	597	Frd
Isaac	533	Mnn
Jacob	935	Hrr
James	921	Hrr
James	948	Hrr
Johanna	601	Frd
John	913	Hrr
Joseph	909	Hrr
Peter	957	Hrr
Peter	274	Ldn
Rachel	954	Hrr
Rebecca	275	Ldn
Reuben	588	Frd
Samuel	957	Hrr
William	178	Shn
see Romme		
Romines, Zachariah	620	Mnt
Romm, Mary	943	Hrr
Romme, Peter	942	Hrr
Romons, Mary	738	Wsh
Romsey, Elisabeth	578	Brk
Ronald, Andrew	480	Bdf
George W.	850	Cmp
Ronalds, John	650	Mnt
Sarah	651	Mnt
Wm. S., Christiansburg	619	Mnt
Roney, Michl.	573	Brk
Rebecah	158	Dnw
Ronimus, Andrew	75	Jff
Conrod	85	Jff
George	95	Jff

Lewis	85	Jff	James	406	Rch	Ross, ---	42	Rcm
Ronnis, Robin	955	Hrr	James E.	513	Prw	Adam	176	Shn
Ronolds, Wm.	445	Flv	Jesse	62	Stf	Alexander	207	Alb
Roobey, Wheeler	295	Frf	Jno.	292	Ldn	Alexander	925	Hrr
Roof, George	38	Rcm	Jno.	533	Mnn	Andrew	39	Stf
Jacob	27	Rcm	Job	245	Ldn	Armstrong	279	Ldn
Jacob	195	Shn	Joel S.	784	Wst	Catharine	552	Frd
John	27	Rcm	John	921	Crl	Daniel	488	Frn
Rooker, Wm.	761	Brn	John	41	Isw	Danl.	68	Clp
Rooks, Thomas	120	Acc	John	245	Ldn	David	653	Btt
Rookwood, Sarah	371	Fqr	John	471	Pra	David	882	Cmp
Rooles, Michael	15	Rcm	John	30	Rcm	David	434	Flv
Roop, Henry	233	Shn	John, jr.	215	Kng	David	13	Hnr
Michael	15	Rcm	John M.	795	Bck	David	257	Ldn
Rooper, John	237	Shn	John N.	294	Amh	David	175	Shn
Root, Jacob	218	Pnd	John P.	215	Kng	David R.	29	Hnr
Jno.	849	Hnv	Joseph	684	Br	Eliz. M.	439	Flv
Rootes, Abraham	15	Rcm	Joseph	636	Gls	Elizabeth	446	Bth
Thomas R., jr.	109	Spt	Lacy	215	Kng	Elizabeth, Jr.	643	Mnt
Roots, George	200	Shn	Margeret	784	Wst	Elizabeth, Sr.	662	Mnt
Thomas R.	99	Spt	Mary	214	Kng	Enos	551	Frd
Roper, Benjm.	940	Chc	Mary	819	Nrf	George	920	Crl
Charles	105	Cmb	Milton, & Co.	327	Dnw	Henry	532	Mnn
Charles	159	Dnw	Obediah	636	Gls	Jacob	281	Ldn
Eldridge	767	Nwk	Patrick	812	Bck	James	51	Acc
Eliza	19	Hnr	Patrick	725	Nls	James	377	Ags
Elizabeth	132	Hnr	Peter, Jr.	795	Bck	James	446	Bth
James	105	Cmb	Peyton R.	662	Sss	James	636	Gls
John	332	Dnw	Reuben	920	Crl	James	111	Spt
John	125	Hnr	Richard	661	Sss	James, Urbanna	469	Mdd
John	767	Nwk	Richd.	245	Ldn	Jane	635	Gls
Lucy	159	Dnw	Robert	367	Fqr	Jane	766	Nwk
Nancy	159	Dnw	Sally	812	Nrf	Jno.	895	Hnv
Nicholas	67	Jff	Sally	816	Nrf	Jno.	533	Mnn
Peter	10	Hnr	Sally	841	Nrf	John	121	Acc
William	766	Nwk	Saml.	818	Nrf	John	438	Bth
Wm.	131	Hnr	Sarah	735	Wsh	John [2]	533	Frd
Ropp, George	101	Jff	Silas	250	Ldn	John	925	Hrr
Sollomon	89	Jff	Thomas	920	Crl	John	645	Mnt
Rorabough, Anthony	913	Hrr	Thomas	541	Frd	John	13	Oho
Catharine	921	Hrr	Thomas	215	Kng	Jonathan	1	Knw
Rori see Row			Thompson	245	Ldn	Joseph	207	Alb
Rorick, Timothy	234	Shn	Thos.	19	Hnr	Joseph	279	Ldn
Roroek see Rosock			Walter	213	Kng	Joshua	293	Ldn
Ros..., John	689	Wsh	Washington	247	Ldn	Julian	837	Bck
Rosanville, Jno.	918	Nrf	William	864	Cmp	Lydia	917	Nrf
Rosary, Lidea	52	Acc	William	332	Dnw	Mary [2]	446	Bth
Rosbam, George	692	Wsh	William	636	Gls	Mary	39	Stf
Rose, ---	241	Ldn	William	11	Hnr	Mashac	925	Hrr
Adah	471	Pra	William	37	Stf	Nathan	551	Brk
Alexander B.	726	Nls	Wm.	517	Brk	Peter	434	Flv
Archd.	917	Nrf	Wm.	730	Brn	Randolp	628	Mnt
Bennett	784	Wst	Wm.	16	Hnr	Reuben, (F. Mo.)	68	Clp
Catharine	253	Ldn	Wm.	244	Ldn	Robt.	652	Btt
Christopher	250	Ldn	Wm., Junr.	214	Kng	Sally	446	Bth
Chs.	532	Mnn	Wm., Senr.	213	Kng	Samuel	438	Bth
Daniel	513	Prw	Wm., (yr.)	214	Kng	Tho.	185	Elc
Dicy	214	Ess	Wm. N.	214	Kng	Valentine	738	Wsh
Elan	916	Nrf	Rosebam, John	692	Wsh	William	53	Acc
Elias [bound for a term			Roseberry, Anthony	507	Brk	William	121	Acc
of years]	448	Bth	see Rolsenberry			William	159	Dnw
Elijah	159	Dnw	Rosebough, Adam	285	Ldn	William	767	Nwk
Elizabeth	730	Brn	Rosebrough, John	519	Frd	William	850	Wth
Elizabeth	636	Gls	Rosenberger, Frederick	76	Jff	Wm.	378	Ags
Enoch	213	Kng	Jacob	566	Frd	Rosser, Burwell	329	Dnw
Ephraim	653	Btt	John	538	Frd	James N.	400	Mds
Fielding	660	Sss	Michal	559	Frd	Jamimah	536	Prg
Gabl.	617	Mnt	Rudolph	220	Shn	Joel	327	Dnw
Geo.	245	Ldn	Rosenbom, Adam	851	Wth	John	412	Fqr
Gustavas A.	855	Cmp	Elizabeth	851	Wth	John	455	Grn
Henry	730	Brn	George	851	Wth	Joseph	660	Sss
Henry	922	Crl	Rosenburgh, Ossa	726	Nls	Kinchian	544	Prg
Henry	214	Kng	Roser, Wm.	917	Nrf	Michael	159	Dnw
Hopkins	532	Mnn	Roserlear, Wm.	918	Nrf	Pleasant	863	Cmp
Isaac	441	Bth	Rosey see Rasey			Pleasant	872	Cmp
Isaac	68	Clp	Rosinbarger, George	186	Shn	Priscilla	412	Fqr
Isaac	16	Hnr	Henry	221	Shn	Thomas	881	Cmp
Isriel	618	Mnt	John	186	Shn	Thos.	327	Dnw
James	441	Bth	Rosinberry, Abraham	225	Shn	William	412	Fqr
James	513	Prw	Rosock, Barney	509	Brk	Wm.	864	Cmp

Rossin, David	11	Wod	John, jr. (N)	201	Ess	Thomas	660	Sss
Rosson, Bartlett	400	Mds	John, Jr.	400	Mds	Thos.	650	Btt
Gabl.	68	Clp	John, Sr.	196	Ess	Thos.	689	Wsh
Larkin	69	Clp	see Rouse			Willm.	182	Elc
Reub.	68	Clp	Row, Benj.	712	Wsh	Wm.	741	Wsh
Wm.	68	Clp	Edmon	702	Wsh	Wm., Jr.	652	Btt
Rosster see Ryster			Geo.	284	Ldn	Rowler, Cunrod	283	Ldn
Roszel, Step. C.	318	Ldn	Handsford	175	Knq	John	233	Shn
Step. C.	322	Ldn	James G.	175	Knq	Rowles, Joseph, quarter	294	Frf
Step. C.	325	Ldn	James H.	174	Knq	Rowlet, Edith	584	Pre
Stephen C.	320	Ldn	John	478	Frn	John	357	Lnn
Stephen Chilton	232	Ldn	John	937	Hrr	Mathew J.	357	Lnn
Stephen W.	310	Ldn	John	697	Wsh	Rowlett, Abner	62	Chr
see Rozel			Lucy	175	Knq	Benjamin	357	Lnn
Roteruck, Daniel	825	Hmp	Mary	175	Knq	Danl.	58	Chs
Rotherbough, John	908	Hrr	Stuffle	561	Brk	Jesse	584	Pre
Rothlone see Rathbone			Wilson	175	Knq	Jno., jun.	58	Chs
Rothrock, George	108	Spt	Rowan, Charles	593	Mnr	Jno., senr.	58	Chs
Rothwel, John	206	Alb	Jas.	688	Wsh	John	55	Chs
Rothwell, John	207	Alb	John	421	Rnd	John	584	Pre
Thomas	170	Alb	Manus	213	Kng	Mac.	62	Chr
see Roathwell			Rowand, John	783	Wst	McNeas	584	Pre
Rottenberry, John	455	Grn	Thomas	783	Wst	Nathan	62	Chr
Roudebush, George	7	Rcm	Rowark, David	851	Wth	Peter	53	Chs
Jacob	18	Rcm	Rowe, Anderson	182	Alb	Richard	62	Chr
Rouderbush, Eml.	374	Ags	Ann	669	Glc	Thos.	230	Aml
Rouf, Jno.	918	Nrf	Ann	879	Hnv	William	230	Aml
Rough, Geo.	377	Ags	Benja.	669	Glc	William	62	Chr
Henry	240	Shn	Benjamin	401	Mds	Wm.	55	Chs
John	377	Ags	Dobson	669	Glc	Wm.	59	Chs
Peter	377	Ags	Edmond	669	Glc	Wm.	17	Hnr
Peter, jr.	377	Ags	Edward	669	Glc	Zach.	59	Chs
Rouk, Jno.	652	Btt	James	411	Fqr	Rowley, Archibald, Sr.	46	Stf
Roundtree, Eliz., (W)	881	Yrk	James	669	Glc	James	121	Acc
Saml.	711	Gch	Jas.	653	Btt	Joel	346	Fqr
Thos.	711	Gch	Jasper C.	669	Glc	Major	215	Kng
Rountree, James	128	Hnr	Jere.	158	Sth	Maryann	213	Kng
Wm.	70	Clp	John	669	Glc	Rowlins, Neffy	63	Chr
Wm.	113	Hnr	John	670	Glc	Rowlison, Mathias, Chris-		
Rour, Henry	219	Shn	John	915	Hrr	tiansburg	619	Mnt
Rourk, Peter	918	Nrf	John	130	Sth	Rowllings, Elizabeth	416	Rnd
Rourke, Jno.	917	Nrf	Johnson	183	Alb	Rowls, Nancey	566	Mnr
Rous, Lucy	853	Cmp	Leml.	159	Sth	Rowly, Archibald, jr.	24	Stf
Rousay, Edward T.	870	Hnv	Saml.	536	Brk	Rowntree, Judith	2	Hnr
Rousch, Daniel	423	Msn	Sarah	922	Crl	Rowsey, Archer	288	Amh
John	423	Msn	Setty	328	Dnw	Edward	590	Frd
Rouse, Adam	400	Mds	Susanna	921	Crl	Michael	16	Hnr
Agness	755	Wsh	Thos.	881	Yrk	Reuben	600	Frd
Ephraham	400	Mds	William	401	Mds	Rowton, Nancy	190	Elc
Henry	200	Ess	William, Jr.	401	Mds	William	61	Chr
Jacob	736	Wsh	Zacheriah	669	Glc	Rowzie, William	10	Pwh
John	709	Wsh	Rowel, William	2	Wod	Rowzy, William	244	Shn
John	851	Wsh	Rowell, Eliza.	455	Grn	Roxey, Richard	387	Fqr
Joseph	400	Mds	Elizabeth	227	Shn	Roy, Beverley	368	Fqr
Philip	708	Wsh	James	614	Srr	Beverly	175	Knq
Polser	696	Wsh	Robert	614	Srr	Elijah	176	Shn
Polser	708	Wsh	Samuel	614	Srr	Hugh	70	Spt
Rufis	697	Wsh	Susan	455	Grn	James	199	Ess
Wm.	196	Ess	Thomas	615	Srr	James	171	Shn
see Rouzee			Rowen, Jno.	534	Mnn	James H.	443	Mth
Rousey, Ruiben	243	Ldn	Rowhoof, Peter	10	Rcm	Jno. C.	174	Knq
Thos.	374	Ags	Rowland, Abraham	3	Oho	John	197	Ess
Roush, Nichos.	543	Brk	Elizabeth	662	Sss	John	584	Pre
Nichos., jr.	526	Brk	Geo.	251	Ldn	John	171	Shn
Rout, Daniel	569	Frd	Geo.	916	Nrf	Joseph	431	Rnd
Elizabeth	414	Fqr	George	170	Shn	Mungo	921	Crl
James	414	Fqr	Jacob	3	Oho	Walker	197	Ess
James	959	Hrr	James	650	Btt	Wiley	417	Fqr
John	540	Frd	James	660	Sss	Wiley, Doctor	175	Knq
Peter, Junr.	414	Fqr	Jas.	583	Mnr	Royal, Joseph	98	Cmb
Peter, Senr.	414	Fqr	John	155	Sth	William	596	Mnr
Richard	993	Nrt	John	709	Wsh	see Ro...l		
William	993	Nrt	Jonathan	636	Gls	Royall, Elizabeth	11	Pwh
Routon, James	825	Bck	Joseph	662	Sss	Jno.	10	Ntt
Jesse	828	Bck	Nathaniel	662	Sss	Jno. D.	1	Ntt
William	584	Pre	Rachel	901	Hnv	John	949	Chc
Routsong, Christiana	652	Btt	Rezen	169	Shn	Jos., Est.	230	Aml
Rouzee, Edwd.	197	Ess	Rich.	178	Elc	Littleberry	13	Ntt
John	400	Mds	Simion	129	Hnr	William	231	Aml
John, jr.	198	Ess	Thomas	295	Frf	William	955	Chc

Name	No.	Co.	Name	No.	Co.	Name	No.	Co.
William, Sr.	955	Chc	Sally	230	Aml	Rebecca	547	Prg
Royalty, Daniel	289	Amh	Thomas	479	Bdf	Susan	614	Srr
Royan, Solomon	421	Rnd	Tinsley	276	Amh	Thos.	856	Sth
Royce, Aron	533	Mnn	William	479	Bdf	Ruffman, Samuel	24	Oho
Edward	766	Hmp	William	401	Mds	Ruffner, Abraham	3	Knw
Moses	534	Mnn	see Rusher			Daniel	2	Knw
Sarah	767	Hmp	Ruckman, David	430	Bth	David	2	Knw
Royer, Christian	24	Rcm	Jacob	791	Hmp	Emanuel	14	Knw
Hunter, (W)	882	Yrk	John	778	Hmp	Jonas	187	Shn
John	811	Hmp	Joseph	831	Hmp	Joseph	3	Knw
John	8	Rcm	Peter	791	Hmp	Joshua	187	Shn
John	24	Rcm	Richard	790	Hmp	Peter	187	Shn
Peter	24	Rcm	Samuel	430	Bth	Samuel	10	Knw
Philip	10	Rcm	Samuel	790	Hmp	Tobias	14	Knw
see Boyers			Samuel	791	Hmp	Ruick, Js.	70	Clp
Royers, Daniel	581	Frd	Thomas	431	Bth	Rule, Geo., Jr.	652	Btt
see Rogers			Rucks, Jabez	57	Chs	Geo., Sr.	652	Btt
Royle, Elizabeth	256	Shn	John	356	Lnn	Jacob	652	Btt
Royson, Elijah	179	Alb	Keron	356	Lnn	Jno.	652	Btt
Royster, Agness	712	Gch	Rudaciller, Jacob	170	Shn	Ruley see Ruby		
David	955	Chc	Rudasilla, Jno.	69	Clp	Ruly, George	275	Amh
Jas. H.	21	Hnr	Philip	69	Clp	Rumbo, Wm.	563	Brk
Jno.	3	Hnr	Wm.	69	Clp	Wm., jr.	556	Brk
John	712	Gch	Rudd, Edw.	178	Elc	Rumburgh, Thos.	610	Mnt
Littlebury	127	Hnr	Edwd.	191	Elc	Rumickhouser, Jacob	225	Shn
Prudence	711	Gch	Elijah	53	Chs	John	225	Shn
Royston, Conguest	174	Knq	Elizabeth	357	Lnn	Runan, Susannah	932	Hrr
Rhody	922	Crl	Frederick	57	Chs	Runion, Elijah	913	Hrr
Robert	922	Crl	Jno.	57	Chs	Richd.	612	Mnt
Thomas	920	Crl	Jno.	14	Ntt	Runkel, Lewis	70	Clp
Thomas B.	174	Knq	John	583	Pre	Runkle, Chrisley	377	Ags
Thos.	669	Glc	Joseph	357	Lnn	Geo.	377	Ags
William	920	Crl	Kizzey	59	Chs	Jacob	377	Ags
Roystor, Saml.	669	Glc	Nancy	184	Elc	John	33	Rcm
see Royston			Phoebe	66	Chs	Peter	28	Rcm
Rozekroontz, Hezekiah	420	Rnd	Sarah	191	Elc	Runnels, Charles [2]	170	Alb
Rozel, Stephen C.	321	Ldn	Thomas	61	Chr	Henry	723	Wsh
Stephen C.	323	Ldn	Thomas	357	Lnn	James	170	Alb
see Roszel			Rudder, Alexander	355	Lnn	James	577	Brk
Rozell, Jno.	68	Chs	Benjamin	355	Lnn	Josh.	577	Brk
Rubel, Jac.	532	Mnn	Charles	356	Lnn	Nathaniel	729	Wsh
Jacob	913	Hrr	Charles	792	Nrf	Shaderick	170	Alb
John	555	Frd	Edward	355	Lnn	William	170	Alb
Rubil, Owen	486	Frn	Jno.	471	Pra	see Rannels		
Ruble, Adam	2	Wod	Ruddle, John	29	Rcm	Runner, Hen	534	Mnn
Balser	10	Wod	Ruder, Abel	912	Hrr	Lews	533	Mnn
George	9	Wod	Adam	650	Btt	Runnion, Anderson	31	Rcm
George	15	Wod	Benjamin	407	Fqr	Jacob	31	Rcm
Jac.	533	Mnn	Isaac	917	Hrr	John, (Jr.)	31	Rcm
John	586	Mnr	Joseph	912	Hrr	John, (Sen.)	23	Rcm
Ruby, Dennis	447	Flv	Thomas	912	Hr.	Saml.	913	Hrr
Henry	239	Shn	Rudesilla, Jacob	70	Clp	Runnolds, Ann	401	Mds
John	239	Shn	Rudicil, Jacob	724	Nls	Henry	401	Mds
Ruckberry, Reuben	293	Frf	Rudisell, Jacob	650	Btt	Robert	401	Mds
Rucker, Absalom	275	Amh	Rudolph, Elizabeth	536	Frd	Runyan, Isaac	850	Wth
Ambrose	264	Amh	George	211	Shn	Joseph	850	Wth
Ambrose	479	Bdf	Jacob	211	Shn	Rupe, Henry	641	Mnt
Angus	400	Mds	Rudy, George	850	Wth	John	464	Frn
Anthony	291	Amh	John	714	Wsh	Rupert, Michael	348	Fqr
Armestead	290	Amh	Rue, Abijah	534	Mnn	Ruple, Martin	377	Ags
Augustine	401	Mds	Charles	119	Acc	Thomas	540	Brk
Benjamin	273	Amh	John	119	Acc	Ruse see Reese		
Benjamin	400	Mds	Oney	120	Acc	Rusell, James	265	Ldn
Bennett	273	Amh	see Rice			James	289	Ldn
Bernard	479	Bdf	Ruf, Joseph	264	Rck	Rusels, Samuel	574	Brk
Clabourn	4	Knw	see Rap			Rush, Benjamin	402	Mds
George	479	Bdf	Rufess, Machen C.	535	Frd	Crafford	402	Mds
Gideon	293	Amh	Ruff, Britton	881	Cmp	Elizebeth	402	Mds
Isaac	284	Amh	John	492	Frn	Ephraim	69	Clp
Jarvis	401	Mds	John	263	Rck	Jacob	513	Brk
John	263	Amh	Jos., (F. Black)	480	Bdf	Jacob	24	Oho
John	401	Mds	Ruffin, Ann	614	Srr	Jacob	10	Rcm
John	723	Nls	Diley	16	Hnr	Jeremiah	24	Oho
Jonathan	479	Bdf	Francis	535	Prg	Jeremiah	759	Wsh
Lemuel	230	Aml	George, [his](est.	661	Sss	John	424	Rnd
Margaret	401	Mds	Joe.	29	Hnr	John	10	Rcm
Moses	271	Amh	Monikey, a free woman			John	718	Wsh
Reubin	230	Aml	of couler	729	Wsh	Jonathan	207	Alb
Reubin	292	Amh	Nancy	19	Hnr	Peter	377	Ags
Richard	272	Amh	Polly	25	Hnr	Thomas	817	Hmp

Wm.	519	Brk	Marcus	383	Fqr	Jas.	5	Ntt
see Rai..., Rust			Maria	825	Nrf	Peter	6	Ntt
Rusher, Andrew	479	Bdf	Michael	723	Wsh	Richard	63	Chr
James	479	Bdf	Molly	917	Nrf	William	454	Frn
see Rucker			Moses	572	Frd	William	6	Oho
Rusk, Samul	237	Ldn	Pennell	918	Nrf	see Rutlidg		
Rusmisel, Adam	375	Ags	Peter F.	63	Chs	Rutlege, Deborah	377	Ags
Christn.	375	Ags	Philip	356	Lnn	Geo.	376	Ags
Fred.	375	Ags	Polley	59	Chs	James	376	Ags
John	375	Ags	Rebec.	187	Elc	Rutler see Rutter		
Russcau, James	250	Ldn	Rob.	187	Elc	Rutlidg, Joseph	357	Lnn
Russel, Abel	120	Acc	Robert	550	Frd	Rutlidge, Edward	644	Mnt
Adam	378	Ags	Robert	104	Jff	George	644	Mnt
Andrew	120	Acc	Robert	273	Ldn	James	644	Mnt
Andw.	378	Ags	Robt.	632	Mnt	John	644	Mnt
Ann, Mrs.	62	Chr	Samuel	785	Hmp	William	18	Rcm
Armistead	766	Nwk	Samuel	57	Jff	Rutliff, Martin	446	Bth
Benjamin	120	Acc	Sarah	356	Lnn	Rutroke, Abraham	804	Hmp
Benjamin	4	Pwh	Sarah	881	Yrk	Ruttedge, John	678	Br
Betty	120	Acc	Tho.	881	Yrk	Rutter, Hannah	605	Frd
David	675	Br	Thos.	239	Ldn	Henry	548	Frd
David	244	Shn	William	834	Hmp	James	547	Frd
Elijah	651	Btt	William	356	Lnn	Jas.	830	Nrf
Henry	378	Ags	William	501	Prw	John	545	Frd
Henry	651	Btt	Wm.	280	Ldn	John	401	Mds
Hessey	120	Acc	Wm., (W)	881	Yrk	J hn	830	Nrf
Hezekiah	62	Chr	Russle, James	531	Brk	J$_0$nathan	592	Frd
Isaiah	375	Ags	Russmisel, Adam, jr.	375	Ags	William	36	Stf
James	869	Cmp	Russull, William	111	Cmb	Ruttor, Jeremiah	823	Nrf
Jno.	235	Ldn	Rust, Abraham	269	Rck	Ry...n, Rachal	263	Amh
John	120	Acc	Alice	399	Rch	Ryal, James	432	Flv
John	377	Ags	Ann	413	Rch	Ryall, James	122	Hnr
John	683	Br	Benedict	567	Frd	Ryalls, Samuel	392	Rch
John	132	Hnr	Benedict, Jr.	544	Frd	Ryan, Cathrean	419	Rnd
John	256	Shn	Benjamin	392	Fqr	Cornelius	691	Br
Joshua	376	Ags	Eliza	784	Wst	Danl.	374	Ags
Mary	120	Acc	Geo.	232	Ldn	David	62	Chr
Mary	62	Chr	George	872	Cmp	Derby	576	Frd
Milby	51	Acc	George	783	Wst	Elizabeth	712	Gch
Mosses	378	Ags	James B.	392	Fqr	Francis	62	Chr
Richard	62	Chr	Jeremiah	534	Frd	James	711	Gch
Robert	121	Acc	John	379	Fqr	James	13	Oho
Robert	266	Ldn	John	544	Frd	Jesse	586	Frd
Samuel	50	Acc	John	395	Rch	John	534	Mnn
Sarah	309	Ldn	John S.	293	Fqr	John	18	Oho
Soloman	50	Acc	Mary	392	Fqr	John, (Jr.)	12	Rcm
Susan, Mrs.	334	Dnw	Mary	302	Rck	John, (Sen.)	12	Rcm
Thomas	61	Chr	Mathew	236	Ldn	Lazarus	18	Oho
Thomas	233	Ldn	Mathias	295	Rck	Major	712	Gch
William	62	Chr	Molly	560	Frd	Mary	404	Ags
William	767	Nwk	Peter	232	Ldn	Patk.	917	Nrf
Wm.	531	Mnn	Peter	783	Wst	Randal	63	Chr
see Bussel			Rebecca	398	Fqr	Rebecca	296	Frf
Russell, ---, & Wallace	21	Hnr	Thomas	566	Frd	T.R.	332	Dnw
Andw.	690	Wsh	Valt.	296	Rck	Thomas	565	Frd
Arther	100	Jff	see Rhert			William	691	Br
Barnabas	850	Wth	Ruth, Jonathan	635	Gls	William	838	Bck
Charles	540	Prg	Joseph	594	Mnr	William	586	Frd
Daniel	377	Fqr	Rutherford, Archd.	519	Brk	William, Ser.	62	Chr
David	510	Frd	Archd.	3	Rcm	see Ry...n, Rayan, Rion		
Elizabeth	294	Frf	Barberry	103	Jff	Ryborn, John	696	Wsh
Elizth.	917	Nrf	Drusillar	77	Jff	John, Jur.	696	Wsh
George, Sen.	120	Acc	Elliot	2	Rcm	Mathew	730	Wsh
Hinde	679	Wrw	Finney	850	Wth	William	696	Wsh
James	537	Frd	Howard	650	Btt	Ryder, Jno.	70	Clp
James	585	Frd	James	851	Wth	Rye, David	293	Frf
Jane	69	Clp	John	594	Frd	Gustavus	46	Stf
Jane	12	Knw	John A.H.	61	Chr	John W.	120	Cmb
John	288	Amh	Mary	651	Btt	Sarah	55	Stf
John	478	Bdf	Randolph	851	Wth	Susan	584	Pre
John	187	Elc	Robert	850	Wth	Ryer, Jacob	5	Oho
John	572	Frd	Robt.	2	Rcm	Ryerson, Elizabeth	418	Bth
John	68	Jff	Saml.	712	Gch	Ryfe, Daniel	2	Oho
John	99	Jff	Thos.	5	Hnr	Ryherz, James	568	Mnr
John	356	Lnn	Van	88	Jff	Ryland, Joseph	202	Ess
John	753	Wsh	Van	110	Jff	Josiah	175	Knq
Jos.	825	Nrf	William	850	Wth	Leverson	760	Brn
Joseph	583	Pre	Wm. [2]	712	Gch	Richd.	219	Ess
Joseph	754	Wsh	Rutlard, Benj.	696	Wsh	Robertson	355	Lnn
Lewis	2	Hnr	Rutledge, David	63	Chr	Thomas	355	Lnn

Thos. M.	668	Glc	Nancy	713	Gch	Samuel	269	Amh
Ryley, ---	917	Nrf	Richd.	448	Mth	Samuel	82	Spt
Elisebeth	723	Wsh	Robert	228	Aml	Thomas	482	Bdf
Elizabeth	70	Clp	Robt.	436	Mth	William	290	Amh
James	43	Stf	Robt.	447	Mth	William	924	Crl
John	623	Mnt	Saml.	229	Aml	William, Senr.	926	Crl
Letty	247	Ldn	Thomas	63	Chs	Wm. J.	203	Ess
Michael	305	Ldn	Thomas	585	Pre	Sales, Alexander	848	Cmp
Thomas Rea	51	Acc	Thos.	433	Flv	Lucy	824	Nrf
William	119	Acc	Thos.	445	Mth	Salesberry, Thomas	637	Gls
William	17	Oho	William	228	Aml	Salesbery, Mary	637	Gls
William	43	Stf	William B.	228	Aml	Saley, Mary	69	Jff
Wm.	70	Clp	Saere see Sacre			Sallard, Charles	17	Ntt
see Rilee			Saffarons, George	653	Btt	George	395	Rch
Rylie, John G.	174	Knq	Saffer, George	303	Frf	Sallards, Alce	183	Shn
Rymal, Barbara	21	Rcm	John	574	Mnr	Salle, ---	327	Dnw
Ryne, Abraham	851	Wth	Jonas	75	Clp	Isaac	61	Chs
Jos. B.	27	Hnr	Saffert, Adam	655	Btt	Sallee, Isaac	780	Bck
William	27	Hnr	Saffield, Isaac	360	Fqr	Judith	779	Bck
Ryon, ...	479	Bdf	Obed	375	Fqr	Salley, ---, F.N.	178	Knq
Elizabeth	725	Nls	Saffle, Isaac	69	Jff	Salliers, John	165	Shn
Jams	940	Hrr	Jessee	255	Shn	Sally, Henry	268	Rck
Milley	725	Nls	Saffley, Catharine	7	Rcm	Peter	274	Rck
Nancy	725	Nls	George	7	Rcm	Salman, George	125	Hnr
Phillips	726	Nls	Safley, Henry	655	Btt	Salmon, James	183	Alb
Samuel	724	Nls	Safly, Willm.	646	Mnt	John D.	208	Alb
William	724	Nls	Safron, John	218	Pnd	Thomas	208	Alb
Ryster, David	853	Hnv	Sagarly, Peter	513	Brk	Salmons, Charity	715	Gch
Mary	853	Hnv	Sager, Chrisley	237	Shn	Jas.	473	Pra
			Gabriel	213	Shn	John	714	Gch
--- S ---			Henry	16	Rcm	John C.	715	Gch
			Jno.	285	Ldn	Richd.	476	Pra
S..., ...	227	Aml	Peter	226	Shn	Wm. [2]	715	Gch
...	921	Nrf	Philip	199	Shn	Salree see Sabree		
..., Dr.	919	Nrf	Philip	231	Shn	Salter, WmH., (Y)	883	Yrk
Daniel	227	Aml	Sagle, Henry	73	Jff	see Saulter		
John	420	Msn	Saigh, Jacob	9	Rcm	Salusbuary, Jno. S.	473	Pra
John	1	Pwh	Sainclair, Thomas	243	Ldn	Salvage, Benjamin	16	Rcm
Robert	228	Aml	Saing see Iding			Samford, James	361	Lnn
S...es, Allen	162	Dnw	Sainsentaffer, Jacob	659	Btt	Saml., Michael	214	Ess
S...ilman, James	56	Stf	St. Clair, John	229	Aml	Sammerville, John	937	Hrr
Sa...on, Reuben	522	Prw	Robt. B.	405	Ags	Sammons, Allen	665	Sss
Sab, Betsey	12	Hnr	Wm.	540	Mnn	Hardy	664	Sss
Sabastin, Wm.	216	Kng	see Waugh			Mary	3	Ntt
Sabins, Thomas	626	Mnt	St. George, John M.	615	Srr	Samuel	455	Grn
Sablong, Charles	123	Hnr	see Tucker			Sarah	360	Lnn
Sabree, Robert	260	Amh	St. John, Ann	214	Ess	William	477	Frn
Sacket, Lewis, Senr.	10	Knw	Isaac	70	Chr	Sample, Ader	60	Acc
see Backet			Jacob	64	Chr	Betty	60	Acc
Sackett see Tackett			John	214	Ess	Daniel	60	Acc
Sackrider, D.W.	25	Hnr	John	544	Frd	Eletia	59	Acc
Sacray, John	218	Kng	John	8	Hnr	Jno.	316	Ldn
Rebecca	218	Kng	William	854	Wth	Jno.	543	Mnn
Sukey	218	Kng	Wm.	469	Mdd	John	462	Frn
Thomas	218	Kng	see Dixon, Santejan			Joseph	605	Frd
Sacre, Charles	80	Spt	St. Leger see Carter			Samuel	548	Frd
Jno.	898	Hnv	Sairls, Lemuel	802	Nrf	Scarburgh	61	Acc
Nelly	80	Spt	Sakenan, Daniel	51	Stf	Smith	59	Acc
Rubin	898	Hnv	Sala, Jacob	3	Rcm	Tinney	61	Acc
Sabra	868	Hnv	Peter	2	Rcm	Samples, Bethuel	2	Rcm
Saddler, Fratherstone	733	Brn	Salanave, ---, Mr.	920	Nrf	James	224	Pnd
Henry	733	Brn	Sale, Benjamin	261	Amh	Robert	599	Mnr
John	733	Brn	Benjamin S.	925	Crl	Sampsell, John	520	Frd
John B.	837	Bck	Caleb	924	Crl	Nicholas	603	Frd
Mildred	178	Knq	George	923	Crl	Sampson, Elizabeth	6	Pwh
Sadler, Absolem	448	Mth	Humphrey	927	Crl	George	995	Nrt
Benja. [2]	713	Gch	James	202	Ess	James	786	Wst
Edwd.	449	Mth	Jane	925	Crl	Jessee	506	Prw
Elizabeth	306	Ldn	Jane	449	Mth	Jno.	360	Lnc
Henry	437	Mth	John	258	Amh	John	404	Mds
James	229	Aml	John	925	Crl	John, M.	404	Mds
John	228	Aml	John	197	Ess	Martin	359	Lnc
John	437	Flv	Joseph	541	Frd	Mary	404	Mds
John	586	Pre	Leonard	223	Ess	Mary H.	714	Gch
John	845	Sth	Nancy	204	Ess	Richard	208	Alb
Leahan	228	Aml	Owney	177	Knq	Richmond	330	Dnw
Marthey	210	Ess	Reuben	204	Ess	Robert	713	Gch
Michl.	443	Mth	Richard, jr.	923	Crl	Samuel	427	Bth
			Richard, Senr.	923	Crl	Sarah	444	Mth
			Robert	924	Crl	see ...amp...on		

Sampsons, Lydda, &			John L.	513	Prw	Sandum, Molly	673	Glc
Daughters	406	Mds	John S.	348	Fqr	Sandy, John	406	Rch
Samptom see ... amp... on			Js.	74	Clp	Mary	899	Hnv
Sams, Jonathan	11	Wod	Leonard	518	Prw	Nancy	406	Rch
Saml.	592	Mnr	Lewis	419	Fqr	Thomas	391	Rch
Samser, Marthia	34	Hnr	Martin	75	Clp	Uriah	412	Rch
Samson, Jacob	546	Brk	Natl.	75	Clp	William	800	Hmp
Joseph	527	Brk	Nimrod	5	Wod	William	40	Rcm
Nicholas	598	Brk	Philip	283	Rck	Saneer, Claiborne	850	Sth
Samuel, Andrew	925	Crl	Presley	414	Fqr	Sanester, John	714	Gch
Ann	177	Knq	Robert	610	Mnt	Sanford, Daniel	397	Rch
Anthony	924	Crl	Robert	498	Prw	Edward	305	Frf
Fielding	406	Mds	Robert, Jur.	854	Wth	Elizabeth	995	Nrt
Gray	924	Crl	Robert, Snr.	854	Wth	James	587	Pre
Henry	176	Knq	Samuel	800	Bck	James	397	Rch
Henry, jr.	177	Knq	Samuel	824	Bck	Jeremiah	265	Ldn
James [2]	923	Crl	Stephen	781	Bck	Jno.	74	Clp
James, jr.	923	Crl	Stephen	161	Dnw	Joseph	72	Clp
Leonard	924	Crl	Stephen	854	Wth	Joshua	405	Rch
Micajah	196	Ess	Stephen, Senr.	854	Wth	Leah	123	Acc
Moses	71	Clp	Thomas	839	Bck	Milley	731	Brn
Nicholas	923	Crl	Thomas	378	Fqr	Nancy, bound for a term		
Philipe	925	Crl	Thos.	718	Wsh	of years	447	Bth
Presley	923	Crl	William	160	Dnw	Reuben	406	Mds
Reuben	71	Clp	William	857	Wth	Reubin	404	Rch
Richard	923	Crl	Wm.	75	Clp	Robert	296	Ldn
Robert	77	Spt	Sanderson, Dorothy	117	Cmb	Robt.	384	Ags
Sarah	924	Crl	John	129	Cmb	Steward	406	Mds
Sarah	72	Clp	Robert	111	Cmb	Vincent	265	Ldn
Thomas, Senr.	926	Crl	Wm.	21	Hnr	William	399	Rch
Thos.	229	Aml	Sandford, Alexarer	243	Shn	Sangster, James	297	Frf
Ths.	73	Clp	Augustin	787	Wst	Jno.	301	Frf
William	923	Crl	Caty	786	Wst	Margeret	301	Frf
William	177	Knq	Charles	785	Wst	see Sanester		
see Parker, Saml.			Daniel	920	Nrf	Sanks, George	66	Jff
Samuels, Greenbury	2	Knw	Diann	785	Wst	Tho.	454	Mth
Isaac	201	Shn	Edward	785	Wst	Sanner, Anna	406	Mds
Joseph	34	Rcm	Elisha	785	Wst	Sansom, Wim.	893	Hnv
Shadrack	11	Knw	Elizabeth	378	Fqr	Santee see Howe		
Sand, Jesse	802	Nrf	Francis	786	Wst	Santejan, J.B.	920	Nrf
Sandafer, Joshua	160	Dnw	George	785	Wst	Santmire, ...acob	168	Shn
Wm.	160	Dnw	Laurence	32	Stf	Sap, Elias	925	Hrr
Sandage, Dillard	208	Alb	Nancey	387	Fqr	John	925	Hrr
John	208	Alb	Peggy	786	Wst	Sapington, Thomas	89	Jff
John	209	Alb	Richd., Jur.	785	Wst	Sapp, Jos.	539	Mnn
Joshua	208	Alb	Richd., Senr.	786	Wst	Sappington, Jno.	308	Ldn
Nathan	173	Alb	Robert	786	Wst	Sarence, Philip	24	Hnr
Polley	713	Gch	Spence	787	Wst	Sargant, Wm. H.	546	Prg
Reuben	208	Alb	Thomas	524	Prw	Sargeant, Dav.	541	Mnn
William	209	Alb	Thomas R.	786	Wst	Edward	529	Frd
Wm.	713	Gch	Washington	831	Nrf	Sarience see Larience		
Sandbower, Jno.	284	Ldn	William	785	Wst	Sarl, Jep	928	Hrr
Sandeford, James	160	Sth	William S.	786	Wst	Sarr, Benjamin	18	Wod
Sandege, James	278	Amh	Sandidge, Anne	67	Spt	Sarry see Larry		
Pulliam	295	Amh	Martin	874	Hnv	Sartain, James	502	Prw
William	282	Amh	Zachariah	77	Spt	Sartin, Elijah	638	Gls
Sanders, Adam	853	Wth	Sandifer, John, (Est)	64	Chr	Joel	638	Gls
Almon	414	Fqr	Sandiforth, Eliz.	184	Elc	John	638	Gls
Britton	522	Prw	Mary	184	Elc	Thomas	639	Gls
Daniel	297	Frf	Sandige, Benjamin	294	Amh	Sarver, Henry [2]	658	Btt
Edward	812	Bck	Beverly	127	Cmb	Jasper	658	Btt
Elijah	375	Fqr	John	127	Cmb	Saml.	658	Btt
Francis	792	Bck	Walter	297	Amh	Sasley, John	863	Cmp
Fredrick	754	Wsh	Sandridge, Augustine	67	Spt	Satchel, Bridget	58	Acc
George	300	Frf	see Sandidge, Sandige			Christopher	59	Acc
George	900	Hnv	Sands, Abijah	294	Ldn	George	122	Acc
George	177	Knq	Ann	182	Elc	John	55	Acc
James	814	Bck	Garrett	286	Amh	Sirus	57	Acc
James	513	Prw	Jacob	297	Ldn	Satchell, ---, Foster &	23	Hnr
James, Junr.	374	Fqr	Jonas	314	Ldn	Sattawhite, John	713	Gch
James, Senr.	375	Fqr	Margaret	64	Chr	Satterfield, Ben	540	Mnn
Jannes	781	Bck	Mary	161	Dnw	Sarah	542	Mnn
Jno.	74	Clp	Mary	297	Ldn	Satterwhite, J.	2	Hnr
Jno.	304	Frf	Thomas	286	Amh	James	9	Pwh
John	793	Bck	Thomas	309	Ldn	Mildred	926	Crl
John	814	Bck	Thos., (W)	883	Yrk	Polly	198	Ess
John	348	Fqr	Sandsberry, Thomas	73	Jff	Richard	926	Crl
John	536	Mnn	William	73	Jff	Robert	925	Crl
John	857	Wth	Sandsburg, Eleonor	245	Shn	Saul, John	481	Frn
John, (son of Wm.)	374	Fqr	Zwelock	245	Shn	Mary	853	Wth

Samuel, Jr.	481	Frn	John	469	Frn	George	128	Hnr
Samuel, Sn.	481	Frn	John [2]	713	Gch	George S.	54	Acc
William	854	Wth	John	115	Hnr	Jacob	56	Acc
Saulmire see Santmire			John	30	Isw	Jacob	289	Ldn
Saulsbury, John	427	Bth	John	80	Jff	Jacob	253	Shn
Nathan	54	Acc	John	470	Mdd	Jacob, Sen.	61	Acc
Robert	56	Acc	John	726	Nls	James	445	Bth
Thomas	57	Acc	John	768	Nwk	James	376	Fqr
Thomas	427	Bth	John	405	Rch	James	762	Hmp
Saulter, Ann	845	Sth	John	844	Sth	James	502	Prw
Saulters, James	23	Oho	John, Jun.	18	Isw	Jessee	729	Nls
Saum, Adam	198	Shn	John, Sen.	15	Isw	John	126	Acc
Saunders, ---, & Cun-			John H.	6	Pwh	John	304	Amh
ningham	920	Nrf	John H., The Revd.	1	Pwh	John	729	Nls
---, Proby &	914	Nrf	Joseph	732	Brn	John, of Wm.	56	Acc
Aaron	259	Ldn	Joseph	16	Isw	John T.	176	Elc
Aaron	289	Ldn	Judith	925	Crl	Joseph	546	Frd
Abner	926	Crl	Julius	482	Bdf	Kendall	54	Acc
Alexander	786	Wst	Julius	767	Nwk	Littleton	61	Acc
Almond	923	Crl	Julius, Sr.	489	Bdf	Mary	58	Acc
Amy	786	Wst	Lewis	695	Br	Moses	58	Acc
Benj.	311	Ldn	Lucy	670	Glc	Nancy, of Wm.	126	Acc
Benja.	714	Gch	Lucy	672	Glc	Patrick	797	Hmp
Benjamin	688	Br	Margt.	282	Ldn	Peggy	58	Acc
Betsey	204	Ess	Mary	826	Bck	Peggy	59	Acc
Betty	125	Acc	Patey	15	Isw	Rigial	55	Acc
Billy	404	Rch	Patty	405	Rch	Robbin	123	Acc
C.H.	20	Hnr	Peter	282	Ldn	Robert	57	Acc
Caty	405	Rch	Peter	726	Nls	Robert	377	Fqr
Charles	925	Crl	Peter, Jr.	492	Frn	Robinson	58	Acc
Charles	211	Ess	Peter, Sr.	490	Frn	Sally	59	Acc
Christopher	879	Cmp	Philip	277	Ldn	Severn	55	Acc
Clayborne	471	Frn	Phillemon	451	Frn	Southy	768	Nwk
Cyrus	77	Jff	Pleasant	471	Frn	William	128	Hnr
Daniel	482	Bdf	Pres.	359	Lnc	William F.	54	Acc
Daniel	404	Rch	Presly	259	Ldn	see Broadwater, Corban,		
Daniel J.	857	Cmp	Prisly	293	Ldn	Crippin		
David	481	Bdf	Putterman	726	Nls	Savedge, Ann	615	Srr
David	714	Gch	Reuben	926	Crl	David	616	Srr
Ebin	732	Brn	Reuben	714	Gch	Doiley	616	Srr
Edward	688	Br	Richard	923	Crl	Hartwell	616	Srr
Edward	412	Rch	Richard	926	Crl	Hezekiah	616	Srr
Edwd.	269	Ldn	Ro., (W)	883	Yrk	Joel	616	Srr
Elias	15	Isw	Robert	492	Frn	Michl.	615	Srr
Eliza.	673	Glc	Robert	360	Lnn	Savely, Christh.	557	Brk
Elizabeth	925	Crl	Robt. H.	713	Gch	Savey, John	226	Shn
Elizh.	882	Sth	S.S.	67	Chs	Savier, Bartw.	535	Mnn
Everett	305	Ldn	Sam	474	Frn	Jas.	538	Mnn
Fanny	883	Yrk	Samuel	15	Pwh	Mary	538	Mnn
Fleming	457	Frn	Tarlton	67	Chs	Saville, Abra.	305	Rck
George	480	Bdf	Thomas	270	Ldn	Robt.	286	Rck
George	482	Bdf	Thomas	280	Ldn	Savils, Absolam	792	Nrf
George	762	Brn	Thomas	304	Ldn	Elizabeth	791	Nrf
George	926	Crl	Thomas	403	Rch	Saml.	798	Nrf
George	467	Frn	Thos.	762	Brn	Tho.	791	Nrf
George	472	Frn	Thos.	714	Gch	Savin, Jno.	474	Pra
George	768	Nwk	Vincent	219	Kng	Savina, ---, Madm.	918	Nrf
George W.	482	Bdf	William	482	Bdf	Saward see Soward		
Henry	293	Ldn	William	926	Crl	Sawrey see Saurey		
Henry	126	Sth	William	400	Rch	Sawyer, David	381	Ags
Hide	360	Lnn	William	786	Wst	Sawyers, George	657	Btt
Hundley	398	Rch	Winney	205	Ess	Sampson	654	Btt
Isaac	603	Frd	Wm.	732	Brn	Saxon, Benajor	734	Brn
Isaac	767	Nwk	Wm.	713	Gch	Saxton, Joseph	856	Wth
James	482	Bdf	Wm.	714	Gch	Magaret	405	Ags
James	187	Elc	Wm.	273	Rck	Phoeby	853	Wth
James	311	Ldn	Wm.	882	Yrk	Say, Martin	256	Shn
James	403	Rch	Wm. B.	80	Jff	Sayben, David	10	Oho
Jerry	879	Cmp	Saunderson, John E.	481	Bdf	Sayer, Chas.	473	Pra
Jesse	732	Brn	Saurey, Peter	829	Nrf	Sayers, Abner	853	Wth
Jesse	443	Flv	Sautesau see Santejan			David, Junr.	853	Wth
Jesse	452	Frn	Savage, Abram	254	Shn	David, Senr.	853	Wth
Jno.	289	Ldn	Arthur	58	Acc	Hartwell	707	Wsh
Jno.	541	Mnn	Charles, Senr.	55	Acc	John T.	853	Wth
Jno.	920	Nrf	Chars., Junr.	55	Acc	Robert	856	Wth
John	505	Brk	Fed	535	Prg	Saylor, Jacob	6	Rcm
John	925	Crl	Francis	58	Acc	John	38	Rcm
John	98	Cmb	Geo.	278	Ldn	Palser	30	Rcm
John	191	Elc	Geo.	281	Ldn	Ulrick, (jr.)	7	Rcm
John	460	Frn	George	382	Ags	Ulrick, (sen.)	7	Rcm

see Taylor			Thomas, Snr.	177	Knq	Cromuell, (F.N.)	46	Isw
Saylors, Martin	585	Pre	Uriah	177	Knq	Cuthbert	348	Fqr
Sayre, Ben	537	Mnn	Wm.	203	Ess	Daniel	727	Nls
Dan	535	Mnn	Schoonover, John	786	Wst	Danl.	4	Hnr
Jes	928	Hrr	Schrech see Shraach			Dav. [2]	539	Mnn
Jos.	535	Mnn	Schrimsure, Charity	400	Rch	Dav., 3rd.	540	Mnn
Selea	538	Mnn	Thomas J.	398	Rch	David	330	Dnw
Sylice	229	Aml	William	397	Rch	David W.	303	Frf
Scaddon, Thomas	824	Hmp	Schultz, John	229	Aml	Day	92	Spt
Scaff, Jas.	473	Pra	Schwartz, Elizabeth	18	Ntt	Drucilla	779	Bck
Scaggs, John	578	Mnr	Sciesor, ---, Hoory &	22	Hnr	Drury, a man of col-		
Joseph	661	Mnt	R. M.	24	Hnr	ler	707	Wsh
Scales, Richard	405	Mds	Sciple, Conrad	383	Ags	Dully	217	Kng
Scammell, James	665	Sss	Scisson, Barnell	785	Wst	Edia	9	Hnr
Thomas	615	Srr	Lewis	297	Frf	Edward	160	Dnw
William	615	Srr	Robert	300	Frf	Edward	893	Hnv
Scandland, John	925	Crl	Sarah	297	Frf	Edward	9	Pwh
Milly	926	Crl	Sclater, Richard	442	Flv	Edward	586	Pre
Scanland, Benjn.	655	Btt	Wm. S.	883	Yrk	Elisebeth	711	Wsh
Cain	658	Btt	Wm. S., jr.	882	Yrk	Elizabeth	727	Nls
Jo., Jr.	657	Btt	Scofeild, John	830	Nrf	Elizebith	736	Wsh
Jo., Sr.	657	Btt	Elisha	210	Shn	Ellis	671	Glc
Scantling, Elizabth.	921	Nrf	John	243	Ldn	Esther	277	Rck
Reuben	3	Rcm	see Schofield			Felix	540	Mnn
Scarboro, Howel	140	Sth	Scoggan, John	366	Fqr	Francis	160	Dnw
Scarborough, Collin	665	Sss	Scoggin, Benja.	538	Prg	Francis	638	Gls
Elijah	873	Sth	Celia	662	Sss	Francis, Jr.	39	Chr
Jane	734	Brn	Jeremiah	538	Prg	Francis, Junr.	64	Chr
Jno.	153	Sth	Robert	538	Prg	Francis, Junr.	71	Chr
John	637	Gls	Scoggins, Gordner	733	Brn	Francis, Major	63	Chr
Robert	499	Frn	Henry	733	Brn	Francis, Senr.	160	Dnw
Wm.	734	Brn	John	733	Brn	Geo.	261	Ldn
see Pentecost, Scarborough			Scogings, Eliza	786	Wst	George	55	Acc
Scarbrough, James	533	Prg	Scoolcraft, Jacob	926	Hrr	George	229	Aml
Robt.	594	Mnr	Scoonoren, Henry	951	Hrr	George	948	Hrr
Sterling	358	Lnn	Scoot, Joseph	36	Hnr	George	406	Mds
Scarburgh, Americus	57	Acc	Salley	6	Hnr	George	3	Oho
Geo.	55	Acc	Scorelock, Milly	785	Wst	George	732	Wsh
Polly	59	Acc	Scot, James	292	Rck	George	758	Wsh
Thomas	57	Acc	James	19	Wod	Gusts. H.	303	Frf
William	54	Acc	Nancy	119	Spt	Harriott	329	Dnw
see Harman, Kelley,	Lewis,		Robert	292	Rck	Henry	78	Clp
Tunnel, Wood			Scotland, Benjamin	472	Mdd	Henry E.	63	Chr
Scarff, James	582	Frd	Mary	126	Hnr	Hugh	732	Wsh
John	563	Frd	Scott, Aaron	124	Hnr	Isaac	283	Amh
Nicholas	539	Frd	Absolem	657	Btt	Isaac	330	Dnw
Scasebrooke see Jolliff			Aggy	328	Dnw	Isaac	558	Frd
Scates, Elijah	405	Rch	Alexander	695	Br	Isaac	472	Pra
Joseph	402	Rch	Alexander	348	Fqr	J.	306	Ldn
Scaxting, Fieldlg.	77	Clp	And., sen.	293	Rck	Jack	121	Hnr
Scay see Seay			Anderson, jr.	177	Knq	Jacob	285	Amh
Sceisor see Sciesor			Anderson, Snr.	177	Knq	Jacob	8	Rcm
Schaffer, Christopher	22	Oho	Andr., jr.	292	Rck	James	208	Alb
Schewmake, Stephen	68	Jff	Ann	848	Sth	James	227	Aml
Schofield, Betsy	360	Lnc	Anne	501	Prw	James	229	Aml
Henry	360	Lnc	Arthar	854	Wth	James	480	Bdf
Joseph	995	Nrt	B.	11	Hnr	James	482	Bdf
Salley	996	Nrt	Belly, Senr.	57	Acc	James	68	Chs
Tho.	360	Lnc	Ben	860	Sth	James	302	Frf
Schoolcraft, Michl.	728	Wsh	Benjamin	835	Bck	James	304	Frf
see Scoolcraft			Benjamin, (M)	835	Bck	James	581	Frd
Schooler, Abner	33	Stf	Betsey	14	Hnr	James	714	Gch
Issabella	82	Spt	Betty	55	Acc	James	590	Mnr
Samuel	66	Spt	Betty, & Ovr.	406	Mds	James	585	Pre
Thomas	38	Stf	Billy	120	Hnr	James	854	Wth
Schooley, Isaac	315	Ldn	Billy	121	Hnr	James	855	Wth
Jno.	296	Ldn	Billy [Betty?]	872	Sth	James, jr.	160	Dnw
Jno.	297	Ldn	Carey	874	Sth	James, Senr.	160	Dnw
Mahlon	313	Ldn	Cath.	539	Mnn	James B.	468	Frn
Wm.	296	Ldn	Catharine	854	Wth	Jane	178	Knq
Schoolfield, Aron	880	Cmp	Celia	876	Sth	Jane	57	Stf
Benjamin	851	Cmp	Charity	919	Nrf	Janett	867	Cmp
Enoch	759	Wsh	Charles	120	Hnr	Jarrald	160	Dnw
John	851	Cmp	Charles	611	Mnt	Jas.	11	Hnr
Samuel	851	Cmp	Charles	17	Oho	Jas. [2]	540	Mnn
Schoolley, Reuben	296	Ldn	Charles	724	Wsh	Jenny	810	Bck
Schools, Elijah	176	Knq	Charles A.	836	Bck	Jessee	179	Alb
George	176	Knq	Charles R.	419	Fqr	Jno.	77	Clp
James	176	Knq	Christian	330	Dnw	Jno.	671	Glc
Thomas	176	Knq	Clark	850	Cmp	Jno.	12	Hnr

Jno.	534	Mnn	Rawley	543	Mnn	Scruggs, Allen	805	Bck
Jno.	921	Nrf	Rd. M.	298	Frf	Archibald	805	Bck
Jno. G.	455	Grn	Reba.	919	Nrf	David	895	Hnv
Jo.	644	Gls	Rebecah	160	Dnw	Drury	824	Bck
John	229	Aml	Rebeccah	19	Hnr	Edward	110	Cmb
John	379	Ags	Ritter	124	Hnr	Edward	126	Cmb
John	480	Bdf	Rob.	540	Mnn	Finch	834	Bck
John	690	Br	Robert	926	Crl	Finch, (E)	836	Bck
John	923	Crl	Robert	359	Lnn	Isham	836	Bck
John	850	Cmp	Robert	586	Pre	Isham	837	Bck
John	72	Clp	Robt.	379	Ags	James	714	Gch
John	305	Frf	Ryal	714	Gch	James	856	Wth
John	420	Fqr	Sam	883	Yrk	Jemima	805	Bck
John	129	Hnr	Saml.	229	Aml	John	776	Bck
John	35	Isw	Saml.	304	Frf	John	824	Bck
John	567	Mnr	Saml.	20	Ntt	John	837	Bck
John	801	Nrf	Saml.	701	Wsh	John	727	Nls
John	8	Oho	Samuel	818	Bck	John	730	Nls
John	15	Oho	Samuel	867	Cmp	Micajah	805	Bck
John	533	Prg	Samuel	882	Cmp	Oglesby	830	Bck
John	281	Rck	Samuel	19	Oho	Richd.	715	Gch
John	68	Spt	Samuel	585	Pre	Robert	112	Cmb
John	113	Spt	Sarah	181	Alb	Samuel	727	Nls
John	854	Wth	Silas	779	Bck	Samuel S.	727	Nls
John, F.N.	666	Sss	Silvy	715	Gch	Timothy	728	Nls
John, (Quarter)	418	Fqr	Sol.	837	Nrf	William	833	Bck
John J., jr.	160	Dnw	Spencer	72	Clp	Scrugham, Rebeckah	95	Spt
Johnson	171	Alb	Squi... [Squire?]	276	Rck	Scutt, Charles, Junr.	784	Wst
Johnson	836	Bck	Stephen	313	Ldn	Charles, Senr.	785	Wst
Jos.	761	Wsh	Susanna	171	Alb	Elizabeth	31	Stf
Joseph	228	Aml	Tent.	823	Nrf	Fanny	787	Wst
Joseph	253	Aml	Theos.	145	Sth	Scypher, John	853	Wth
Joseph	874	Cmp	Thomas	874	Cmp	Sea, ---, Mrs.	430	Flv
Joseph	883	Cmp	Thomas	358	Lnn	Jacob	11	Ntt
Joseph	639	Gls	Thomas	636	Mnt	Matthew	443	Flv
Joseph	715	Gch	Thomas	10	Pwh	see Lea		
Joseph	323	Ldn	Thomas	586	Pre	Seaborne, Howell	664	Sss
Joseph	325	Ldn	Thomas	423	Rnd	Seabrook, John	6	Hnr
Joseph	371	Lnn	Thomas	271	Rck	Seaburn, Isaac	681	Wrw
Joseph	228	Pnd	Thomas	1	Rcm	Nathl.	681	Wrw
Joseph	721	Wsh	Thomas, (BS)	69	Chr	Seacat, Charles	654	Btt
Joseph	855	Wth	Thomas C.	308	Ldn	Phillip	660	Btt
Joseph, Esq.	967	Hrr	Thomas T.	585	Pre	Seacatt, George	653	Btt
Joseph, Esqr.	494	Brk	Thompson	228	Aml	Seachrist, Henry	13	Rcm
Joseph, Esqr.	699	Br	Thos.	227	Aml	Melcher	13	Rcm
Joseph, Esqr.	603	Mnr	Thos.	535	Mnn	Seagar, William	14	Isw
Joseph, Marshall of			Thos.	826	Nrf	Seagler, Jacob	460	Frn
Virginia	184	Knq	Tom	326	Dnw	John	459	Frn
Joseph, Mr.	980	Nrt	William	298	Amh	William	460	Frn
Joshua	715	Gch	William	688	Br	Seal, Bennett	924	Crl
Keely	61	Acc	William	869	Cmp	David	923	Crl
Levina	57	Acc	William	874	Cmp	Fielding	654	Btt
Lewis	823	Bck	William	160	Dnw	John, & Sons	404	Mds
Lewis	713	Gch	William	453	Frn	Peter	290	Rck
Lucy	9	Hnr	William	358	Lnn	Reuben	516	Frd
Magaret	380	Ags	William	359	Lnn	Thornton	922	Crl
Margaret	172	Alb	William	15	Oho	Sealock, William	363	Fqr
Mary	638	Mnt	William	19	Oho	Seaman, Dav.	538	Mnn
Matthew	635	Mnt	William	8	Pwh	Jas.	536	Mnn
Meriam	876	Sth	William	1	Rcm	Jonah	5	Oho
Milly	20	Hnr	William	88	Spt	Thos.	920	Nrf
Mimy	332	Dnw	William, (Bry.)	587	Pre	Seamans, Simon	19	Oho
Molly	473	Pra	William, (S. R)	585	Pre	Seamon, Ann	523	Brk
Moore	76	Clp	William C.	586	Pre	Jonas	526	Brk
Moser	779	Bck	Winnifd.	72	Clp	Jonathan	524	Brk
Moses	532	Frd	Wm.	76	Clp	Seamor, William	516	Frd
Moses	262	Rck	Wm.	824	Nrf	Seamore, Claiborne	160	Dnw
Moses	296	Rck	Wm. H.	287	Rck	Wm.	734	Brn
Moses, (F.N.)	44	Isw	see Bowis, Slott			Seargent, Abel. M.	432	Msn
Nancy	296	Amh	Scrange, Henry	218	Kng	Searight, John	382	Ags
Nancy	727	Nls	Scrarborough, Alexd.	543	Prg	Searing, John	232	Shn
Nathan	661	Btt	Scratton see Seratton			Sears, Henry	673	Glc
Nicholas	161	Dnw	Screws, John	156	Sth	Henry	470	Mdd
Nicholas	616	Srr	Scribner, Samuel	208	Alb	Hezekiah	313	Ldn
Patty	876	Sth	Scritchfield, Joseph	816	Hmp	Hiram	524	Prw
Peggy	60	Acc	Joseph	855	Wth	Hizekiah	296	Ldn
Peter	130	Hnr	Scrivener, James	217	Kng	Jno.	673	Glc
Peter	725	Wsh	John	218	Kng	John	801	Bck
Pleasant	481	Bdf	Vincent	575	Frd	Paul	549	Prg
Polly	852	Sth	Scroggin, James	566	Frd	Philip P.	177	Knq

Robert	236	Ldn	George C.	379	Fqr	Henry	503	Prw
Robert, J.	249	Ldn	Sedwick, Benja.	77	Clp	Thomas	504	Prw
Thomas, jr.	176	Knq	Benjn.	218	Kng	William	501	Prw
Thomas, Snr.	177	Knq	Zadock	76	Clp	Selecruan see Selecman		
Thos.	673	Glc	See, Eliza	419	Bth	Self, Francis	177	Knq
William G.	73	Spt	George	852	Cmp	Francis	784	Wst
Wm.	299	Frf	Margaret	295	Rck	Job	784	Wst
Wm. B.	301	Frf	Mary	438	Bth	John	593	Frd
see Seay			Michael	424	Msn	John	35	Rcm
Searugg, John	635	Mnt	see Lee			John, Senr.	924	Crl
Seates, Nancy	64	Chr	Seecrist, Frederick	768	Hmp	John C.	786	Wst
Seaton, ---, Hobdy &	21	Hnr	Henry	769	Hmp	Larkin	6	Pwh
George	114	Hnr	Jno.	653	Btt	Mosses	787	Wst
Hiram	233	Ldn	Seegle, Jacob	853	Wth	Robert	794	Bck
James	382	Fqr	Seek, Adam	852	Wth	Samuel	401	Rch
James	391	Fqr	George	852	Wth	Thomas	995	Nrt
Seaver, Casper	550	Frd	Layton	76	Clp	Walter	785	Wst
Eliza. S.	615	Srr	Paul	386	Ags	William	995	Nrt
George	550	Frd	see Sick, Sisk			Selfoos, Mary	23	Rcm
Seavers, Henry	550	Frd	Seekfrit, John	28	Rcm	Sell, Thos.	659	Btt
Seavill, Jas. S.	673	Glc	Seelser, James	24	Rcm	Sellars, Adam	11	Rcm
Seawell, Frances	670	Glc	Seemones, William	450	Frn	Andw.	20	Rcm
John B., (W)	883	Yrk	Seever, Jacob	757	Wsh	Conrod	26	Rcm
Jos.	671	Glc	John	30	Rcm	Danl.	28	Rcm
Sterling	671	Glc	Seevily, Joseph	7	Rcm	Henry	24	Rcm
Seay, Abner	780	Bck	Seevy, Matthias	13	Rcm	James	14	Rcm
Abraham	727	Nls	Seford, Peter	658	Btt	John	28	Rcm
Agness	228	Aml	Segar, John	177	Knq	Michael	19	Rcm
Austin	228	Aml	Richd. M.	470	Mdd	Peter	11	Rcm
Dudly	229	Aml	Segen, Jno.	538	Mnn	Sellers, Henry	82	Jff
James	229	Aml	Seglan, Thos.	250	Ldn	Paul	570	Frd
James	729	Nls	Segler, Sam	539	Mnn	Philip	570	Frd
Jas.	870	Hnv	Segull, Thomas	809	Hmp	Selley, James	529	Brk
Joab	715	Gch	Sehorn, John L.	819	Hmp	see Lelley		
John	228	Aml	Seibert, Jacob	426	Bth	Selman, Joseph	78	Clp
John	133	Cmb	Seiblet, Mathew	873	Cmp	Wm. A.	300	Frf
John	729	Nls	Seiford see Syford			Selock, John	371	Fqr
Luke	870	Hnv	Seigle, Michael	198	Shn	Robert	405	Fqr
Moses	228	Aml	Seiler, Jacob	386	Ags	Samuel	405	Fqr
Reuben	786	Bck	Seilser see Seelser			Thomas	405	Fqr
Thomas	871	Cmp	Seirs, James	597	Mnr	Thomas, Senr.	405	Fqr
Thos.	715	Gch	Seizer, John	276	Rck	Selser, Henry	252	Shn
William	585	Pre	Selater see Sclater			Selsson, John	785	Wst
Wim.	870	Hnv	Selbay, Ebenezer	404	Rch	Selter, Sarah	18	Hnr
Sebastian, Joseph	926	Crl	Joseph T.	404	Rch	Selvey, John	184	Shn
Sebastion, Benja.	301	Frf	Selbe, Charles	654	Btt	Selvy, Saml.	958	Hrr
Nichs.	301	Frf	Charles	586	Pre	Semones, Isaac	460	Frn
Sebert, Jacob	584	Brk	John	586	Pre	John	460	Frn
see Sibert			Samuel	586	Pre	Semple, ---	334	Dnw
Sebrea, James	208	Alb	Selbey, William	994	Nrt	James, has Slaves in		
Sebree, Jno.	359	Lnc	Selby, Henry	124	Acc	York County	883	Yrk
Nichs.	359	Lnc	James J.	325	Dnw	Wm.	282	Rck
Sebrell, Benja.	129	Sth	John	782	Hmp	Semry, Abel	545	Brk
David	615	Srr	John	182	Shn	Sence, Henry	223	Pnd
David	621	Srr	Magruder	538	Mnn	Seneca, Frances	476	Pra
James	128	Sth	Nathan	766	Hmp	James	475	Pra
Nathl.	615	Srr	Nathan	782	Hmp	Jesse	476	Pra
Sebrey, James	996	Nrt	Peter	124	Acc	Malachi	475	Pra
John	995	Nrt	Southey	124	Acc	Richard	8	Oho
Tapley [2]	994	Nrt	Walter B.	106	Jff	Wm.	476	Pra
William	994	Nrt	William, Esqr.	124	Acc	Sensabaugh, Jacob	103	Jff
William	995	Nrt	Zadock	54	Acc	Sense, Adam	468	Frn
William	996	Nrt	Selden, Cary	56	Stf	Senseney, John	564	Frd
Sebring, John	762	Hmp	Jacob, (FB)	489	Bdf	Mary	510	Frd
Sebure, Peter	512	Brk	Jno. W.	8	Ntt	Sensibaugh, Fred.	381	Ags
Seburn, Danl.	554	Brk	Miles	662	Sss	John	381	Ags
Secefuce, Catherine	225	Pnd	Richd.	359	Lnc	Wm.	380	Ags
Elisa	225	Pnd	Robt.	178	Elc	Sentz, Jacob	653	Btt
Sechafoos, John	70	Jff	Susan.	189	Elc	Seranage, William	368	Fqr
Sechman, Philip	508	Brk	Seldomridge, B.	379	Ags	Serart, Arch.	404	Ags
Sechrist, Michael	427	Msn	Seldon, ---	918	Nrf	Seratton, Jas.	24	Hnr
Seck, Jacob	18	Rcm	Elizabeth	959	Chc	Serbers, Henry	658	Btt
Secrist, Andrew	571	Frd	Miles	541	Prg	Josh.	658	Btt
George	571	Frd	Miles, Jr.	130	Hnr	Sergeant, William	552	Frd
Jacob	571	Frd	Miles, Snr.	126	Hnr	Sergent, Jeremiah	9	Wod
Seddens, John	685	Br	Nat.	127	Hnr	Serrel, Edward, a free		
Seddon, John	61	Stf	Robert	878	Hnv	mulatto	996	Nrt
Thomas, jr.	34	Stf	W.B.	921	Nrf	James, a free mulatto	996	Nrt
Thomas, sr.	55	Stf	W.C.	289	Ldn	Jesse, a free mulatto	996	Nrt
Sedgwick, Fs.	541	Mnn	Selecman, George	501	Prw	Serrick, Adam	30	Rcm

Seruggs see Scruggs		
Servant, Rich.	178	Elc
Seslar, Nancy	659	Btt
Sesler, Thomas	655	Btt
Seth, Fran.	537	Mnn
Setleff, Abraham	809	Bck
Setliff, John	778	Bck
Setser, Catharine	222	Shn
Settle, Francis	481	Bdf
Francis	73	Clp
George	408	Fqr
John	541	Frd
John	591	Frd
Larkin	561	Frd
Lewis	481	Bdf
Newman	482	Bdf
Reuben	785	Wst
Vincent	541	Frd
William	480	Bdf
William	502	Prw
William	390	Rch
Settlemire, Casper	552	Frd
Settler, Barbara	600	Frd
Daniel	513	Frd
Joseph	600	Frd
Settles, Joel	218	Kng
Reuben	218	Kng
Settleton, John	218	Pnd
Setzer, Martin	208	Shn
see Seelser		
Seul, J. M.	921	Nrf
Sevant, Geo.	286	Ldn
Sevart, James	250	Ldn
James, J.	250	Ldn
see Swart		
Seveno, ---	901	Nrf
Sevent see Swent		
Severns, Elizabeth	32	Rcm
Severson, Benjamin	681	Br
Sevice see Lovice		
Sevick, Ant.	259	Ldn
Sevrance, Edmund	558	Frd
Sewall, Wm.	653	Btt
Seward, Albridgton	616	Srr
Ann	470	Mdd
Benjanine	177	Knq
Carter	616	Srr
Cary	616	Srr
Cofield	533	Prg
Edward	470	Mdd
James	176	Knq
John	734	Brn
John	176	Knq
John	358	Lnc
William	178	Knq
William	664	Sss
see Soward		
Sewards, Benjamin	469	Mdd
John	469	Mdd
Zach.	469	Mdd
Sewel, Jno.	541	Prg
Sewell, James	654	Btt
Joseph	304	Frf
Thomas	654	Btt
Thomas	302	Frf
Sewter, Henry	867	Sth
Sexsmith, Simon	116	Spt
Sexton, Gerard	563	Frd
Thomas	567	Frd
Seybert, George	224	Pnd
Henry	225	Pnd
Jacob	217	Pnd
James	224	Pnd
John	15	Oho
Seymore, Edwd.	472	Pra
Seymour, Ephraim	57	Acc
Rachel	180	Elc
Robt.	187	Elc
Thos.	920	Nrf
William	57	Acc

Seypherd, Methias	285	Ldn
Seypole, John	666	Mnt
Seyre, Daniel, Snr.	426	Msn
Danil, jr.	426	Msn
Sh...lin, John	481	Bdf
Shaak, John	380	Ags
Shabbinett, Peter	918	Nrf
Shack, Henry	7	Knw
Shackelford, Abraham	670	Glc
Alex	178	Knq
Bannister	387	Fqr
Benja.	671	Glc
Benja.	672	Glc
Benja.	176	Knq
Benjamin	305	Amh
Benjamin	67	Spt
Cher.	178	Knq
Chs.	672	Glc
Geo.	670	Glc
Geo. D.	176	Knq
Harry	670	Glc
James, jr.	178	Knq
James, Snr.	176	Knq
Jane	176	Knq
Jno.	671	Glc
Jno. R.	176	Knq
John	212	Ess
John	559	Frd
John	80	Spt
John M. C.	178	Knq
Joseph	561	Frd
Leonard	177	Knq
Mary	178	Knq
Polley	176	Knq
Rachel	176	Knq
Richard	172	Alb
Richd.	214	Ess
Richd.	532	Prg
Roger	214	Ess
Samuel J.	561	Frd
Soloman	351	Fqr
Zach.	214	Ess
Shackelton, Richard L.	585	Pre
Shacklefoot, Benja.	73	Clp
Caelea	74	Clp
Chs.	76	Clp
Danl.	73	Clp
Jno., Aty.	73	Clp
Jno., N Fd.	73	Clp
John, BB	74	Clp
Mallory	74	Clp
Mary	74	Clp
Shackleford, Banister	12	Ntt
Clement	396	Rch
Dudley	77	Clp
Elisabeth	78	Clp
James	77	Spt
John	399	Rch
Jos.	537	Mnn
Vincent	396	Rch
Warner	523	Prw
William	469	Mdd
William	394	Rch
Wm. D.	469	Mdd
Zach., (Y)	883	Yrk
Zachariah	21	Rcm
Shackleton, Wm.	132	Hnr
Shacklett, Benj.	13	Hnr
Edward	342	Fqr
Hezekiah, Jr.	398	Fqr
Hezekiah, Sr.	395	Fqr
John	398	Fqr
Samuel	399	Fqr
William	21	Stf
Shacktel, Edwd., Jr.	79	Clp
Shadacre, Sarah	268	Ldn
Shaddock, William	926	Crl
Shade, Geo.	517	Brk
Jacob	558	Frd
Richd.	579	Brk

Shadle, John	699	Wsh
Shadock, James	197	Ess
Shadows, John	626	Mnt
Shaer see Shaw		
Shaever, Jacob	427	Msn
Shafer, Henry	593	Brk
Peter	554	Brk
Peter	595	Brk
Shaffer, Jacob	527	Brk
Martin	587	Brk
Michael	637	Gls
Shaffleberger, Abram	854	Wth
Shafner, Casper	573	Brk
Shafstal, Isaac	545	Brk
Shagleford, Zachariah	208	Alb
Shahan, Frdk.	579	Brk
Shail, Martin	385	Ags
Shalcupp, Wm.	731	Wsh
Shalft, Polly	27	Hnr
Shall, Anny	222	Pnd
Peter	941	Hrr
see Shull		
Shamboch, Daniel	602	Frd
Jacob	602	Frd
John	592	Frd
Philip	601	Frd
Shan see Shaw		
Shands, Augustin	663	Sss
John	543	Prg
Thomas	665	Sss
William	665	Sss
Shane, James	509	Brk
see McShane		
Shaner, George	103	Jff
Shank, Adam	38	Rcm
Christian	575	Brk
George	791	Hmp
Henry	20	Rcm
Jacob	5	Rcm
Jacob	18	Rcm
John	385	Ags
Joseph	791	Hmp
Martin	5	Rcm
Michael	391	Fqr
Shanklin, Absolm.	657	Btt
Andrew	3	Rcm
Isaac	501	Prw
Jno.	654	Btt
Linny	218	Kng
Richard	562	Mnr
Robert	592	Mnr
Robert	11	Wod
Robert S.	419	Rnd
Saml.	607	Mnt
Wm.	657	Btt
Wm.	592	Mnr
see Sh...lin		
Shanks, Christian	573	Brk
Christn.	658	Btt
David	653	Btt
Wm.	573	Brk
Wm.	192	Elc
Shannon, ---	902	Nrf
Henry	571	Mnr
James	872	Cmp
James	637	Gls
John	386	Ags
John	729	Wsh
Joseph	109	Spt
Patrick	387	Ags
Thomas	637	Gls
Thomas	760	Hmp
Shapardson, Francis	114	Hnr
M.	113	Hnr
Wm.	111	Hnr
Share see Shaw		
Sharer, Rob.	541	Mnn
Sharetts, John	857	Wth
Sharff, George	826	Hmp
Shark, Thos.	555	Brk

Sharkey, Nics.	657	Btt	Shats, Daniel	554	Frd	Jane	408	Fqr		
Patk.	659	Btt	George	554	Frd	Janes	167	Shn		
Sharks, Dorothy	828	Nrf	Shatter, Solomon	234	Shn	Jervis	507	Prw		
Sharky, Jno.	655	Btt	Shattz, Jachob	180	Alb	Jervis	517	Prw		
Sharot, Daniel	435	Bth	Shaum, Henry	198	Shn	Jno.	72	Clp		
Sharp, ...lins	303	Rck	Shaun, John	289	Rck	Jno.	305	Ldn		
Aron	847	Sth	Shauver, George	656	Btt	John	678	Br		
Abram	130	Hnr	see Shawver			John	836	Nrf		
Andrew	441	Bth	Shaver, Abm.	655	Btt	John	501	Prw		
Ann	126	Hnr	Abm., Sr.	658	Btt	Joseph	8	Oho		
Aron	966	Hrr	Abram	233	Shn	Js.	73	Clp		
Barvel	125	Hnr	Adam	285	Ldn	Keziah	15	Wod		
Benjamin	414	Fqr	Adam	536	Mnn	Margaret	811	Nrf		
D. W.	111	Hnr	Andw., Jr.	660	Btt	Matthew	291	Rck		
Daniel	423	Bth	Andw., Sr.	660	Btt	Nelly	73	Clp		
Edmund	350	Fqr	Catherine	950	Hrr	Ralph	169	Shn		
Elizabith	132	Cmb	Charles	592	Mnr	Robert	807	Bck		
Frances	350	Fqr	Chas.	380	Ags	Robt.	10	Hnr		
Francis	99	Cmb	Chaty	249	Shn	Robt.	22	Hnr		
George	536	Brk	Chrisr.	543	Mnn	Sam	535	Mnn		
Isaac	779	Bck	Christian	224	Pnd	Samuel	941	Hrr		
Isaac	130	Hnr	Conrod	286	Ldn	Stephen	537	Brk		
Jacob	333	Dnw	Cunrod	286	Ldn	Thomas	116	Hnr		
James, jr.	425	Bth	Daniel	854	Wth	William	481	Bdf		
James, ser.	422	Bth	Danl.	378	Ags	William	533	Frd		
Jas. H.	864	Hnv	David	383	Ags	William	522	Prw		
John	423	Bth	David	776	Hmp	Wm.	537	Mnn		
John	432	Bth	Eve	180	Shn	Zachariah	167	Shn		
John	793	Bck	George	224	Pnd	see Show				
John	914	Hrr	George	13	Rcm	Shawen, Cornelius	298	Ldn		
John	924	Hrr	George	20	Rcm	Shawhan, David	599	Brk		
John	120	Hnr	George	205	Shn	Shawl, Gasper	171	Shn		
John, jr.	483	Bdf	George	236	Shn	George	74	Jff		
John, Ser.	425	Bth	George	746	Wsh	Jacob	76	Jff		
John, Sr.	483	Bdf	Henry	381	Ags	Michael	76	Jff		
John G.	616	Srr	Henry	538	Mnn	Michael	171	Shn		
Joseph	381	Ags	Henry	236	Shn	Nicholass	76	Jff		
Josiah	208	Alb	Isaac	30	Rcm	Shawn see Shawhan				
Josiah	587	Pre	Jacob	659	Btt	Shawver, Christian	596	Mnr		
Lewis	73	Clp	Jacob	388	Fqr	George	657	Btt		
Mary	657	Btt	Jacob	961	Hrr	Jacob	596	Mnr		
Richard	208	Alb	Jacob	5	Knw	Sebastin	596	Mnr		
Richard	108	Cmb	Jacob	578	Mnr	see Shauver, Showver				
Richd., a man of			Jacob	278	Rck	Shay, Eli	125	Acc		
couler	759	Wsh	Jacob	42	Rcm	Nathaniel	126	Acc		
Robert	864	Hnv	Jacob	233	Shn	Stephen	303	Frf		
Robert	2	Oho	Jacob	235	Shn	Teackle [2]	125	Acc		
Samson	483	Bdf	Jno.	283	Ldn	see Shuy				
Sarah	328	Dnw	Jno.	284	Ldn	Shayer, John	591	Brk		
Spencer	585	Pre	Jno.	285	Ldn	Shealor, Danl., Sr.	654	Mnt		
Susanna	25	Hnr	Jno.	300	Ldn	George	658	Mnt		
Thos.	381	Ags	John	565	Frd	see Shelor				
Turner	68	Chs	John	215	Pnd	Sheals, David	820	Hmp		
William	209	Alb	John	21	Rcm	Sheaman, Conrad	384	Ags		
William	424	Bth	John	745	Wsh	Shean, John	305	Rck		
William	330	Dnw	Martin	776	Hmp	Joseph	275	Rck		
William	414	Fqr	Michael	285	Ldn	Robt.	271	Rck		
William, se	423	Bth	Michl.	690	Wsh	Mary	304	Rck		
William, Ser.	422	Bth	Modelene	21	Rcm	see Spear				
Wm.	750	Wsh	Molly	383	Ags	Sheardson, William	180	Alb		
see Balltrip			Moses	203	Shn	Shearer, Andrew	866	Cmp		
Sharpe, William	32	Stf	Palser	30	Rcm	Archd.	590	Brk		
Sharper, Jonathan	310	Ldn	Peter	32	Rcm	James	869	Cmp		
Sharpless, Betsey	359	Fqr	Philip	36	Rcm	Philip	506	Frd		
Sharpley, Henry	125	Acc	Philip	180	Shn	Thos.	590	Brk		
John	126	Acc	Philip	233	Shn	William	865	Cmp		
William	125	Acc	Samuel	788	Hmp	Shearing, Mattias	204	Shn		
Zadock	125	Acc	Subinah	172	Alb	Shearman, Adam	173	Shn		
Sharply, Thomas	126	Acc	Wm.	924	Hrr	Ezl. G.	360	Lnc		
Sharpp, Spencer	14	Wod	Wm.	285	Ldn	Henry	482	Bdf		
Sharps, Jesse	800	Hmp	see Shover, Shrawer, Shrever			John C. [?]	638	Mnt		
Sharret, Catherine	224	Pnd	Shavers, Bartlett, (FB)	480	Bdf	Jos.	359	Lnc		
Sharrets, Daniel	853	Wth	Shaw, Archibald	361	Fqr	Martin	359	Lnc		
Sharricks, William B.	495	Frn	Ben	536	Mnn	Robert	561	Frd		
Sharrod, Hilary	124	Acc	Charles	945	Hrr	Sam. M.	368	Lnc		
Margaret	55	Acc	Charles	518	Prw	Sam. M.	369	Lnc		
Thomas	56	Acc	Charles	167	Shn	Saml. M.	359	Lnc		
Sharrow, ---, Mrs.	29	Hnr	Davd.	301	Rck	Tho.	359	Lnc		
Shastead, James	265	Amh	George	441	Bth	Thomas	540	Frd		
Shasteen, Robt.	281	Rck	George	590	Frd	Shearock, Robert	875	Hnv		

Name	No.	Loc.	Name	No.	Loc.	Name	No.	Loc.
Shearwood, Ann	215	Ess	Susan	49	Stf	Shep, George	11	Rcm
Ann	548	Prg	Shell, Edmunds	733	Brn	John	11	Rcm
Fanny	222	Ess	Elizabeth	761	Brn	Shepard, Ephraim	210	Ess
John	220	Ess	Fanny	768	Nwk	Farney	250	Shn
John	775	Hmp	Henry	693	Wsh	Frederck.	611	Mnt
Richd.	218	Ess	Jacob	668	Mnt	Jacob	520	Brk
Thomas	218	Ess	James	637	Mnt	Nathiel	33	Hnr
Shebblin, ---, Mr.	918	Nrf	John	733	Brn	Reuben	213	Ess
Sheckles, Richd.	257	Ldn	John	637	Mnt	Wm.	211	Ess
Sheely, Jno.	656	Btt	Linman	733	Brn	Wm., (BB)	474	Pra
Sheers, John	584	Mnr	Simon	32	Rcm	see Shipard		
Thomas	590	Mnr	Stephen	938	Chc	Shepear, Saml. B.	473	Pra
Thos.	584	Mnr	Wm.	761	Brn	Shephard, Jonathan	1	Wod
Sheets, Conrad	536	Mnn	Shelleson, Wm.	757	Wsh	Shepheard, John	112	Spt
George	32	Rcm	Shelley, Elizabeth	162	Dnw	Shephed, John	811	Nrf
Henry	19	Rcm	John	733	Brn	Shepherd, Abraham	89	Jff
Henry	205	Shn	Phillip	162	Dnw	Abram	445	Flv
Henry, Jun.	242	Shn	Thomas	616	Srr	Alexe.	72	Clp
Henry, Sen.	242	Shn	Shellon, Thomas	172	Alb	Anthony	171	Alb
Jacob	656	Btt	Shelly, Adam	743	Wsh	Augustin	729	Nls
Jacob	242	Shn	Benjamin	664	Sss	Benjamin	587	Pre
John	956	Hrr	Christa.	384	Ags	Christopher	435	Flv
John	958	Hrr	John	384	Ags	David	105	Cmb
John	202	Shn	John	743	Wsh	David	435	Flv
John	226	Shn	Moses	110	Spt	David	585	Frd
John, (Steward & C.)	11	Rcm	Shelmon, John	728	Nls	Drewrey	171	Alb
Sheetz, Ann	758	Hmp	Shelor, Danl., Jr.	657	Mnt	Eliza	921	Nrf
Frederick	758	Hmp	William	619	Mnt	Elizabeth	587	Pre
Henry	16	Wod	see Shealor			Eunice B.	469	Mdd
Jacob	104	Jff	Shelter, Molburn	808	Nrf	Frank	2	Hnr
Jacob	16	Wod	Sheltman, Felix	18	Rcm	George	60	Acc
John	405	Ags	John	20	Rcm	Jacob	480	Bdf
John [3]	16	Wod	Shelton, ---, White &	23	Hnr	Jacob	75	Jff
Michael	72	Jff	Clough	729	Nls	James	430	Flv
Michael [2]	16	Wod	Diana	841	Nrf	James	714	Gch
Oth...	758	Hmp	Frederic	455	Grn	James	21	Hnr
see Shutz			James	190	Elc	James	290	Ldn
Shefey see Sherfey			James	713	Gch	James	3	Rcm
Sheffield, Colin	535	Prg	James	455	Grn	John	59	Acc
Hardman	616	Srr	Jeremiah	455	Grn	John	681	Br
Henry	616	Srr	John	264	Amh	John	72	Clp
James	535	Prg	John	29	Stf	John	302	Frf
James	615	Srr	John, & Co.	125	Hnr	John	445	Flv
Jno.	4	Ntt	John, jr.	713	Gch	John	23	Hnr
Jos.	3	Ntt	Joseph	714	Gch	John	176	Knq
Leonard	19	Ntt	Joseph	728	Nls	John	921	Nrf
Peter	535	Prg	Joshua	263	Amh	John M.	112	Spt
Susanna	3	Ntt	Lucy	207	Alb	Joseph	535	Frd
Sheffle, Abram	705	Wsh	Lydia	10	Hnr	Lewis	380	Ags
Christinia	704	Wsh	Reuben	832	Bck	M.A.	921	Nrf
Jacob	704	Wsh	Richard	263	Amh	Margaret	177	Knq
Sheffly, Henry L.	857	Wth	Richard	810	Bck	Mary	178	Knq
Sheffy, Daniel	857	Wth	Richard	96	Spt	Mary	470	Mdd
Shehen, Geo.	537	Mnn	Samuel	171	Alb	Mercer	552	Frd
Jno.	537	Mnn	Stephen	358	Lnn	Moses	551	Frd
William	555	Frd	Thomas	96	Spt	Philip	379	Ags
Shehon, John	398	Rch	Walter	124	Hnr	Polly	48	Stf
Shehorn, John	455	Grn	Weatherston	173	Alb	Rebec.	192	Elc
Wilson	455	Grn	William	173	Alb	Rebeckah	89	Spt
Sheild, John	822	Nrf	William	263	Amh	Richard	587	Pre
Ro.	890	Yrk	William	96	Spt	Saml.	18	Hnr
Sam.	882	Yrk	William	45	Stf	Samuel	780	Bck
Saml., jr.	883	Yrk	William	58	Stf	Samuel	6	Isw
Sheilds, David	125	Cmb	William H.	726	Nls	Samuel	587	Pre
James	729	Nls	Wilson	20	Stf	Samuel	856	Wth
John	730	Nls	see Shilton			Thomas	541	Frd
Margaret	730	Nls	Shem see Shaw			Thomas	99	Jff
Mary	729	Nls	Shen, Samuel	421	Msn	Thomas	586	Pre
Samul	10	Oho	Shenk, Elizabeth	181	Shn	William	208	Alb
Robert	728	Nls	Henry	181	Shn	William	261	Amh
William	729	Nls	Jacob	181	Shn	William	779	Bck
Sheit see Streit			John	178	Shn	William	105	Cmb
Shekel, Cephas	172	Alb	John, (of M)	180	Shn	William	299	Frf
Shelborn, James	357	Lnn	Shenott, Partrick	101	Cmb	William	551	Frd
Semuen	357	Lnn	Partrick	105	Cmb	William	22	Hnr
Thomas	360	Lnn	Shens, William	481	Bdf	William	177	Knq
Shelby, Saml.	703	Wsh	Shenton, Charles	88	Jff	Winny	588	Frd
Shelds, David	15	Wod	Zadock	88	Jff	Wm.	713	Gch
Sheliday, Andrew	481	Bdf	Sheoff, George	246	Shn	Wm.	290	Ldn
Shelkit, John	20	Stf	Sheon, Richard	482	Bdf	Shepherdson, David	730	Nls

Nathan	730	Nls	Jno.	660	Btt	Thomas	403	Mds
Nathaniel	586	Pre	see Shewa, Shoealter			Shingletor, William	930	Hrr
see Shapardson			Shewbridge, Catherine	73	Jff	Shinholtzer, Jacob	764	Hmp
Sheppard, Benja.	116	Hnr	John	68	Jff	John	779	Hmp
Benja., Snr.	122	Hnr	Shewmake, Daniel	460	Frn	Peter	779	Hmp
Dubartus	654	Btt	Shewmaker, Isaac	481	Frn	Peter	784	Hmp
Elizh.	113	Hnr	Jacob	702	Wsh	Shinley, Richard	522	Prw
Frances	893	Hnv	Joshua	722	Wsh	Shinn, Clement	957	Hrr
Jas.	672	Glc	Shewman, Andrew	591	Brk	Daniel	956	Hrr
Jno. M.	901	Hnv	Shews see Shens			Jonathen	957	Hrr
John	786	Hmp	Shewster, Jacob	920	Nrf	Joseph	956	Hrr
Mosby	113	Hnr	Geo.	920	Nrf	Mosis.	957	Hrr
Moses	8	Oho	Shick, Michael	29	Rcm	Samuel	937	Hrr
Nat.	115	Hnr	see Shuh			Soloman	915	Hrr
Philip	874	Hnv	Shickler, Christian	380	Ags	Walter	957	Hrr
Reuben	116	Hnr	Shicle, John	553	Brk	see Shen, Shum		
William, Jr.	9	Oho	Shider, John	431	Rnd	Ship, Alice	205	Ess
Wm.	660	Btt	Shidmor, Isaac	223	Pnd	Caty	120	Spt
Sheppart, Adam	591	Brk	Shidmore, Andrew	223	Pnd	Godfrey	816	Hmp
Shepperd, Abm.	637	Mnt	Ealizabeth	220	Pnd	Jas.	431	Flv
George	607	Mnt	Magdelen	223	Pnd	John	534	Frd
Godphrey	66	Jff	see Skidmor, Skidmore			Mary	604	Frd
Jas.	583	Brk	Shield, Aser	55	Acc	Richard	925	Crl
Shepperson, Charles	887	Hnv	John	182	Elc	Thomas	924	Crl
Elisha	887	Hnv	John	143	Sth	Wm.	715	Gch
Marget	162	Dnw	Nancy	61	Acc	Shipard, James	395	Rch
Sheppert, Robert	944	Hrr	Patty	58	Acc	Shipe, Adam	385	Ags
Shepton, Robt.	379	Ags	Samuel	58	Acc	Christian	174	Shn
Shepwash, Mason	806	Nrf	Wm.	556	Brk	Henry	412	Bth
Sally	826	Nrf	Shields, Adam	379	Ags	Henry	14	Knw
Sherad, Thos.	654	Btt	Alexr.	262	Rck	Nancy	522	Frd
Sheradan, Abraham	811	Hmp	Chas.	541	Mnn	Shipler, George	564	Frd
Sherard, Wm.	535	Brk	David	559	Brk	George, Jr.	565	Frd
Sherboch, Jacob	555	Frd	James V., (W)	883	Yrk	Shipley, Joseph	450	Mth
Sherd, John	305	Frf	Jno.	541	Mnn	Shipman, Isaiah	41	Rcm
Sherer, John	563	Brk	John	404	Ags	Jonathan	41	Rcm
Sherfey, Abraham	231	Shn	John	559	Brk	Shipp, Bartlet	472	Pra
Benjamin	232	Shn	John	637	Gls	Batson	472	Pra
Sheridan, John	15	Rcm	John	574	Mnr	Jas.	473	Pra
Thos.	9	Oho	Joseph	315	Ldn	Jno.	475	Pra
Sheriff, William	557	Frd	M. W.	681	Wrw	Peggy	475	Pra
Sherinn, William	454	Frn	Nancy	286	Amh	Reuben	475	Pra
Sheriyah, Gilion	16	Rcm	Otwey	3	Hnr	Wm.	723	Wsh
Sherley, Elizabeth	482	Bdf	Peter	116	Spt	Shippy, David	16	Hnr
Elizabeth	850	Hnv	Rachel	379	Ags	Ships, William	364	Fqr
Wim.	850	Hnv	Rachel	290	Rck	Shipwash, Fany	806	Nrf
Sherlock, Robert, (free)	893	Hnv	Robert	905	Hrr	see Shepwash		
Thos.	838	Nrf	Saml., Christians-			Shireman, Peter	212	Shn
Sherly, Judith	404	Mds	burg	618	Mnt	Shiremon, Barnheart	228	Shn
Thos.	404	Mds	William	916	Hrr	Shirey, Jacob	6	Rcm
Zachary	404	Mds	Willm.	611	Mnt	Shirich, Philip	386	Ags
Sherman, Ballard	767	Nwk	Wm.	386	Ags	Shirkey, James	8	Knw
Edmund	655	Btt	Wm.	559	Brk	Shirley, Bahathaland	995	Nrt
Michael	769	Nwk	Wm., jr.	386	Ags	Eliza	787	Wst
Thomas	994	Nrt	Wm., (T.)	379	Ags	Ephriam	57	Jff
Shero, John	383	Ags	see Shelds			George	995	Nrt
Sherrard, Robert	771	Hmp	Shifflett, Stephen	35	Rcm	Gervas	79	Jff
Sherrer see Shmer			Thomas	36	Rcm	James	75	Jff
Sherriff, Bengamin	821	Hmp	William	35	Rcm	John	75	Jff
Sherrington, John	185	Elc	Shiflit, Joel	172	Alb	John, (Lab)	79	Jff
Sherront see Shevront			Lewis	208	Alb	Peter	395	Rch
Sherwood, Adaech	710	Wsh	Micajah	209	Alb	Robert	79	Jff
Caleb	474	Pra	Richard [2]	209	Alb	Sarah	372	Fqr
Elisha	474	Pra	Sarah	208	Alb	Susanna	352	Fqr
Gerard	300	Frf	Thomas	209	Alb	Valintine	384	Ags
Hillary	473	Pra	Shilling, John	625	Mnt	Walter	77	Jff
Isaac	473	Pra	John	5	Oho	William	57	Jff
John	189	Elc	Rosannah	633	Mnt	William	995	Nrt
Thomas	304	Frf	Shilton, Edward	28	Stf	Shirly, Jonathan	380	Ags
see Shearwood			Shin, David, Jur.	772	Hmp	Shirry, John	293	Rck
Shery see Shuy			David, Sen.	772	Hmp	Shirtliff, Richard	586	Frd
Shettles, Notly	932	Hrr	Elizabeth	915	Hrr	Shiry, Henry	385	Ags
Shetzer, Philn., & Fa-			Francis	79	Clp	John	384	Ags
ther	661	Btt	George	915	Hrr	Lewis	387	Ags
Shevront, Aron	939	Hrr	Isaac	915	Hrr	Michl.	383	Ags
Shew, Augustine	256	Shn	Shinalt, William	299	Amh	see Shirly		
Joseph	219	Shn	Shineberger, Michael	89	Jff	Shisher, Jno.	539	Mnn
Shewa, Jno.	660	Btt	Shingler, Conrod	103	Jff	Shisler, Nichs.	542	Mnn
Shewalter, Henry	660	Btt	Richard	76	Jff	Shittenbury, William	798	Hmp
Isaac	74	Jff	Shingleton, Absalom	790	Hmp	Shiveley, Jacob	586	Frd

John	491	Frn	Lander	759	Hmp	Jacob	89	Jff
Shively, Geo.	247	Ldn	Richard	599	Frd	Showalter, Chrisley	30	Rcm
Jacob	298	Ldn	Soloman	58	Acc	Danl.	21	Rcm
Jno.	539	Mnn	Thomas	559	Frd	Jacob	563	Frd
Phil	539	Mnn	Thomas	799	Hmp	Jacob	4	Rcm
Shivers, George	6	Isw	Thos., jr.	442	Flv	Jacob	7	Rcm
John	6	Isw	William	599	Frd	John	6	Rcm
Sally	6	Isw	Shorewater, Abraham	480	Bdf	Joseph	13	Rcm
Slaughter	47	Isw	see Shurewaters			see Shurewaters		
Wilson	6	Isw	Shornberg, Hezekiah	9	Oho	Showen, Andrw.	574	Mnr
Shmer, John	545	Frd	Short, Adam	282	Rck	Showers, Erquenund	526	Brk
Shoals, Philip	297	Frf	Anderson	732	Brn	Joshua	60	Jff
Shoan, Jno. [crossed			Archd.	61	Chs	Samuel	80	Jff
out]	311	Rck	Armstead	732	Brn	Showls, Jacob	879	Cmp
Shobe, John	223	Pnd	Benjamin	585	Pre	Showman, Michael	92	Jff
Shober, John	599	Brk	David	661	Btt	Showmore, Stephen	229	Shn
Shockey, Jacob	564	Brk	Edmund	732	Brn	Showver, Fredrick	598	Mnr
John	633	Mnt	Edy	333	Dnw	Jacob	598	Mnr
Joseph	794	Hmp	Elisebeth	714	Wsh	John	590	Mnr
Shockley, Dav.	539	Mnn	Eliza.	360	Lnc	see Shawver		
Shocky, Rachael	564	Brk	Elizabeth	732	Brn	Shraach, Christian	576	Frd
Shoealter, Henry, Sr.	660	Btt	Frances	218	Kng	Conrad	549	Frd
Shoemake, Lewis	11	Rcm	George	786	Wst	Henry	549	Frd
Shoemaker, Barbary	282	Ldn	Griffin	732	Brn	Shrader, Daniel	272	Amh
Christley	29	Rcm	Henry	284	Ldn	George	283	Amh
Daniel	282	Ldn	Henry	298	Ldn	Jacob	225	Pnd
Danl.	282	Ldn	Isaac	774	Hmp	Martin	200	Shn
Elizabeth	29	Rcm	James	83	Jff	Shradrick, John	501	Brk
Geo.	282	Ldn	James	616	Srr	Shrawer, Jno.	283	Ldn
George	29	Rcm	James	854	Wth	Shreeve, Benj.	279	Ldn
George	241	Shn	Jas.	734	Wsh	Elias	123	Acc
Henry, (Jr.)	22	Rcm	Jeremiah	786	Wst	Shreeves, William	419	Rnd
Henry, (sen.)	22	Rcm	Jno.	66	Chs	Shrekengost, Dan	10	Rcm
Holeman	713	Gch	Jno., Senr.	66	Chs	Shreoch, Adam	425	Msn
Jeremiah	289	Amh	John	402	Fqr	Shreve, Benjamin	994	Nrt
Jeremiah	483	Bdf	John, Sr.	732	Brn	Shrever see Shaver		
Jerimiah	846	Hnv	John C.	732	Brn	Shreves, Abm.	542	Mnn
John	589	Mnr	John C.	216	Kng	Ben	542	Mnn
John	29	Rcm	Judith	36	Stf	John	214	Pnd
Jonathan	208	Alb	Major	733	Brn	Shrewsberry, Nancy	665	Sss
Judith	713	Gch	Nancy	660	Btt	Shrewsbury, Elijah	480	Frn
Paul	23	Rcm	Nathan	589	Brk	Joel	460	Frn
Peter	803	Hmp	Polly	196	Ess	John, Sr.	5	Knw
Simon [2]	282	Ldn	Reuben	494	Frn	Samuel	5	Knw
Thos.	111	Hnr	Richard	774	Hmp	Shride, Charity	769	Hmp
William	262	Amh	Saml.	33	Rcm	Shrigley, Enoch	299	Ldn
Wm.	661	Btt	Susannah	752	Wsh	Joseph	299	Ldn
Zedekiah	261	Amh	Thomas	586	Frd	Shrimplin, William	684	Br
see Schewmake, Shewmaker,			Thomas	216	Kng	Shriock, Jacob	201	Shn
Shomaker			William	796	Hmp	Shriver, Abm.	541	Mnn
Shoemate, Baabs	560	Frd	William	33	Rcm	Adam	540	Mnn
Peyton	409	Ags	Willie	732	Brn	Henry	579	Brk
Shoernove, John	252	Shn	Wm.	409	Ags	Jacob	919	Nrf
see Shoremon			Wm.	732	Brn	Stopkle	267	Ldn
Shoewalter see Shewalter			Shorte, F.P.	34	Hnr	Shrock, William	756	Hmp
Shofetal, David	547	Brk	Shorter, Jeremiah	63	Chr	see Shryoch		
Shokey, Lewis	565	Brk	Robert	64	Chr	Shrode, Solomon	535	Brk
Sholp, John	209	Alb	Shortness, Thomas	293	Ldn	Shroder, Solomon	509	Brk
Shomaker, Wm.	729	Wsh	Shorttoe, George	25	Oho	Shroff, Adam	247	Shn
Shonaberry, Jacob	217	Pnd	Shortzer, Phillip	655	Btt	Shropshire, John	217	Kng
Shooks, Frederick	298	Frf	Shot, Long	66	Chs	see Sopshire		
Shooler, Conrad	570	Frd	Shotner, Nancy	383	Ags	Shrowder, Jacob	616	Mnt
Shooltzman, Peter	768	Hmp	Shott, Richd.	387	Ags	Jacob	634	Mnt
Shooner, Jinny	196	Ess	Shottle, Michl.	383	Ags	Michl.	617	Mnt
Shoop, John	855	Wth	Shoub, Henry	13	Rcm	Shroyer, George	18	Rcm
Peter	855	Wth	Shoulderman, Henry	9	Rcm	Jacob	383	Ags
Shoot, John	829	Hmp	Shoulders, Jacob	221	Pnd	Jno.	537	Mnn
Shootman, Nicholas	616	Mnt	Uriah	222	Pnd	John	39	Rcm
Nics.	655	Btt	Shoultz, Henry, Jr.	567	Frd	Shrum, John	42	Rcm
Shop, Peter, & Sam	399	Mds	Henry, Senr.	567	Frd	Shryoch, Geo.	257	Ldn
Sam, Peter &	399	Mds	Shouman, Jacob	24	Rcm	Michl.	257	Ldn
Shopart, Nicholas	594	Brk	Shove, John	803	Hmp	Shuff, Solo.	539	Mnn
Shope, Elizabeth	54	Jff	John	817	Hmp	Shuffield, Saml.	545	Prg
Shore, Henry S.	8	Hnr	Shover, Frederick	39	Rcm	Stephen	228	Aml
Jno.	21	Ntt	Simon	283	Ldn	Shugart, Michael	707	Wsh
John	334	Dnw	see Shaver			Zacheriah	749	Wsh
Thomas	328	Dnw	Shoves, Michael	922	Hrr	Shuger see S...		
Shoremon, Anthony	252	Shn	Shovidine, Richd.	841	Nrf	Shuh, Jacob	99	Jff
see Shoernove			Shovler, Frances	29	Hnr	Shuk, Jno.	286	Ldn
Shores, John	599	Frd	Show, Henry	87	Jff	Shular, Michael	29	Rcm

293

Shule, Jacob	380	Ags	Jacob	219	Shn	George	386	Ags
Shull, Geo.	386	Ags	Jacob, jr.	551	Brk	Jaspir	382	Ags
Henry	209	Shn	John	543	Brk	Wm.	382	Ags
Jacob	383	Ags	John	215	Shn	Sillivan, Dennis	996	Nrt
John	526	Brk	John	219	Shn	Sills, Andw.	705	Wsh
Jonathan	565	Frd	Moses	175	Shn	John	455	Grn
Joseph	572	Frd	Susan	531	Brk	John	705	Wsh
Joshua	590	Frd	see Sybert			Richd.	455	Grn
Lewis	383	Ags	Sibley, Benson	470	Mdd	Solomen	705	Wsh
Love	548	Frd	David	469	Mdd	Silman, Mager	930	Hrr
Michael	209	Shn	John	469	Mdd	Zachariah	401	Fqr
Peggy	101	Jff	Leonard	586	Pre	Silva, Susan	55	Stf
see Sull			Robt.	443	Mth	Silver, Chrsth.	543	Brk
Shuller, Jacob	743	Wsh	Sicafoos see Secefuce, Sechafoos			Silvers, Aron	619	Mnt
Shullers, John	747	Wsh	Sick, John	232	Shn	Francis	525	Brk
Shult see Shutt			Sickle, Adam	235	Shn	James	562	Frd
Shultice, John	109	Spt	Andrew, Junr.	235	Shn	John	408	Ags
Shults, Christina	380	Ags	Andrew, Snr.	235	Shn	Silverthorn, Geo.	823	Nrf
John	684	Br	Anthoney V.	424	Msn	Henry	691	Br
Susanna	387	Ags	Ginge	235	Shn	John	122	Acc
Valintine	385	Ags	John	235	Shn	Kendall	123	Acc
Shultz, Adam	16	Rcm	Lewis, Jun.	235	Shn	Southey	123	Acc
Benjamin	363	Rcm	Michael	235	Shn	Silvery, Abraham	786	Wst
Christiana	37	Rcm	Zack V.	425	Msn	Silvie, William	209	Alb
David	378	Ags	Siddons, Ezekiel	900	Hnv	Silvy, Moses	406	Mds
John	516	Frd	Sidebottom, Nancy	516	Prw	Simamon, Peter	235	Shn
Shultzer, Adam	805	Hmp	Thomas	376	Fqr	Simbley, Andrew	24	Oho
Shum, George	121	Hnr	William	54	Stf	Simco, James	406	Mds
Shuman, Hen.	540	Mnn	Sider, Solomon	276	Rck	Simcoe, Henry	671	Glc
Jno.	542	Mnn	see Siders, Syders			Reubin	212	Ess
Phil	541	Mnn	Siders, Fred.	268	Rck	Simers, John H.	574	Frd
Shumate, Bailey	171	Alb	George	275	Rck	Simkins, Joshua	448	Mth
Berryman	382	Fqr	Jesse	582	Frd	William	638	Gls
Daniel	568	Mnr	Michl.	277	Rck	Simmerell, Ruth	882	Sth
Danl., j.	567	Mnr	Sidner, John	179	Shn	Simmerman, Areheart	852	Wth
George	358	Fqr	Sidnor, John	160	Dnw	Christopher [2]	853	Wth
Hardin	568	Mnr	Sidwell, Hugh	536	Mnn	David	598	Brk
John	380	Fqr	Sarah	580	Frd	David	852	Wth
John	568	Mnr	Sifford, Adam, Sr.	659	Btt	George	852	Wth
Joseph	357	Fqr	Christn.	657	Btt	Michl.	571	Brk
Lewis	355	Fqr	Harmon	665	Mnt	Simmers see Simers		
Silas	568	Mnr	Sigafoos, John	512	Frd	Simmes, Margaret	18	Oho
Taliaferro	358	Fqr	Siggler, Jacob	28	Rcm	Simmington, Wm.	918	Nrf
Thomas	358	Fqr	John	33	Rcm	Simmoman, Andw.	656	Btt
Tolison	568	Mnr	Siggs, Jemney	126	Acc	Wm.	656	Btt
see Shoemate			Sigler, Wm.	537	Mnn	Simmon, Ephraim	657	Btt
Shunk, Simon	95	Jff	Sigman, John	486	Frn	Eve	226	Pnd
Shurewaters, John	472	Frn	Peter	496	Frn	George	225	Pnd
Shurldes, Ann	670	Glc	Sikes, Barnaba	535	Prg	Henry	100	Jff
Wm.	670	Glc	Chloe	31	Isw	Henry	216	Pnd
Shurley, Daniel	473	Pra	Dick	129	Hnr	Henry	218	Pnd
Richard	793	Nrf	Jessee	546	Prg	Jacob	656	Btt
Shutt, Philip	104	Jff	John	31	Isw	John	655	Btt
Shutter, Henry	744	Wsh	Joseph	3	Isw	John	222	Pnd
see Shuller, Shullers			Simon	476	Pra	John	226	Pnd
Shuttle, John	745	Wsh	World	538	Prg	Jonatn.	656	Btt
Shuttleworth, Phil	542	Mnn	Silas, Philip, sen.	288	Rck	Joseph	220	Pnd
Shutz, Andw.	382	Ags	Silcott, Abram	315	Ldn	Leonard	216	Pnd
Danl.	382	Ags	Jacob	239	Ldn	Leonard	219	Pnd
George	386	Ags	Jesse	317	Ldn	Michael, J.	218	Pnd
Henry	382	Ags	Wm.	310	Ldn	Michal	226	Pnd
Jacob	383	Ags	Siler, Eliza.	557	Brk	Phil	653	Btt
Jacob, jr.	387	Ags	George	565	Brk	Simmonds, ...	919	Nrf
John	387	Ags	Jacob	548	Brk	Chas.	360	Lnc
Joseph	380	Ags	Jacob	785	Hmp	Jno.	360	Lnc
Leonard	386	Ags	John	548	Brk	Mills	920	Nrf
Peter	382	Ags	Margaret	587	Brk	Wm.	360	Lnc
Philip	382	Ags	Philip	557	Brk	Simmons, Anthony	472	Frn
Shuy, Adam	381	Ags	Susan	579	Brk	Benja.	304	Frf
John	381	Ags	see Piles, Silas			Benjamin	360	Lnn
John	386	Ags	Siles, Christian	21	Rcm	Benjamin	292	Amh
Siamison, Mary	428	Bth	Silfrese, William	235	Shn	Bernett	209	Alb
Sibble, Burkheart	855	Wth	Abraham	234	Shn	Charles	468	Frn
Sibert, Adam	173	Shn	Silket, Joel	5	Knw	Charles	776	Hmp
Adam	197	Shn	Silkniter, Geo.	383	Ags	Charles	660	Mnt
Franey	252	Shn	Sill, Abram	705	Wsh	Charles	161	Sth
George	430	Msn	Sillinger, Gaspur	658	Btt	Coleman	534	Prg
George	175	Shn	Sillings, Abraham	386	Ags	Daniel	326	Dnw
Henry	519	Brk	Andw.	386	Ags	David	543	Frd
Henry	176	Shn	David	382	Ags	Elizabeth	481	Bdf

Elizabeth	298	Frf	Simonds, ...oy [written over			Thomas	765	Hmp
Epharim	570	Mnr	"Robt." ?]	269	Rck	Thomas	292	Rck
Ephraim	209	Alb	Richd.	270	Rck	William	173	Alb
Franky	198	Ess	Simons, Asa	533	Brk	William	404	Mds
George	483	Bdf	Barnett	594	Frd	William	216	Pnd
George	467	Frn	Chas. H.	804	Nrf	William	527	Prw
Henry	534	Prg	Jacob	506	Prw	William	245	Shn
Henry	475	Pra	Jacob	416	Rnd	William	94	Spt
Jacob	657	Btt	Joshua	301	Frf	William, jr.	94	Spt
Jehu	587	Pre	Lanard	926	Hrr	Willm.	610	Mnt
Jeremh.	304	Frf	Mason	539	Prg	Wm.	298	Frf
Jno.	475	Pra	Simpkins, Chas.	540	Mnn	Wm.	301	Frf
Jno., (B.W.)	475	Pra	James	626	Mnt	Wm.	302	Frf
Jno., (Pungo)	476	Pra	Reubin	672	Glc	Wm., Jr.	404	Mds
Joab	570	Mnr	Robt.	302	Rck	see Lempson		
Joel	570	Mnr	Robt., Jr.	648	Mnt	Sims, ---, Revd.	918	Nrf
Joel	586	Pre	Robt., Sr.	612	Mnt	Abner	75	Clp
John	811	Nrf	Young	178	Knq	Alexander	941	Chc
John	1	Oho	Simple, Robert B.	177	Knq	Austin	116	Cmb
John	866	Sth	Simeon	177	Knq	Bartholemew	590	Mnr
John	867	Sth	Simpson, Aaron	95	Spt	Benjamin	785	Wst
John, jr.	813	Nrf	Abraham	95	Spt	Bernard	105	Cmb
Jonan.	656	Btt	Alexander	405	Mds	Chloe	995	Nrt
Joseph	467	Frn	Alexander	856	Wth	David	876	Hnv
Joseph	665	Sss	Allin	633	Mnt	Edmd.	77	Clp
Joseph	855	Wth	Ann	531	Frd	Edward	953	Hrr
Lucy	868	Sth	Anne	305	Frf	Edward	3	Knw
Micajoh	855	Wth	Anne	357	Fqr	Edward	14	Pwh
Peggy	198	Ess	Azel	405	Mds	Elizabeth	381	Fqr
Peter	851	Sth	Daniel	95	Spt	Henry	78	Clp
Rebecca	857	Sth	David	828	Hmp	Hezekiah	953	Hrr
Sally	874	Sth	Ebenezer	792	Hmp	Isaac	209	Alb
Simon	303	Frf	Ed. W.	299	Frf	James	57	Chs
Stephen	106	Jff	F. T.	919	Nrf	James, J.	219	Pnd
Tho.	857	Sth	Fanny	122	Acc	James, S.	219	Pnd
Thomas	161	Dnw	Francis	507	Prw	Jeromh.	75	Clp
Thomas	467	Frn	George	123	Acc	Jno.	57	Chs
Thos.	731	Brn	George	299	Frf	John	75	Clp
Thos.	161	Dnw	George	303	Frf	John	965	Hrr
Valentine	853	Sth	George	57	Jff	Joseph T.	74	Clp
William	579	Frd	Hancock, Pr. Neo.	56	Acc	Js.	71	Clp
William	794	Nrf	Isaac	856	Wth	Js., Jr.	75	Clp
William	504	Prw	James	547	Frd	Martha	64	Chr
Williamson	358	Lnn	James	615	Srr	Mary	78	Clp
Willis	808	Nrf	James	856	Wth	Matthew	881	Hnv
Wm.	198	Ess	James	589	Frd	Oliver	77	Clp
Wm.	858	Sth	Jane	93	Spt	Reuben	823	Bck
Wm., (Pungo)	476	Pra	Jessee	71	Spt	Reuben	77	Clp
see Drake, Hite, Sinmons,			Jessee	112	Spt	Richard, (Est.)	64	Chr
Timmons			Jno.	300	Frf	Samuel	597	Mnr
Simms, Betty	404	Mds	Jno.	476	Pra	Susan	785	Wst
Charles	303	Frf	John	445	Bth	William	424	Bth
Clabourne	13	Oho	John	839	Bck	William	480	Bdf
Edward	404	Mds	John	298	Frf	William	855	Cmp
George	404	Mds	John	535	Frd	William	877	Cmp
Humpy., Negro	301	Frf	John	405	Mds	William	996	Nrt
James	298	Frf	John	727	Nls	William D.	78	Clp
James	8	Knw	John	921	Nrf	William S.	103	Cmb
James	404	Mds	John	225	Pnd	Wim.	865	Hnv
James	54	Stf	John	785	Wst	Wim., S of F.	866	Hnv
Jo...ter	13	Oho	Joseph	301	Frf	Wm.	384	Ags
John	304	Frf	Joseph	302	Frf	Wm.	940	Hrr
Larken	404	Mds	Josiah	298	Frf	Wm.	361	Lnc
Lee, f. negro	299	Frf	Julia	334	Dnw	see Sirms, Vaiden		
Maria	25	Oho	Leroy	404	Mds	Simson, Eliah	539	Mnn
Martin	8	Knw	Margt.	655	Btt	Jno.	539	Mnn
Presly	42	Stf	Mary	546	Frd	Richard	105	Cmb
Richard	4	Oho	Mary	276	Ldn	Robert	8	Wod
Richard, jr.	24	Stf	Maryan	300	Frf	Sincell, Elijah	406	Fqr
Richard, sr.	42	Stf	Moses	302	Frf	John	412	Fqr
Samuel	18	Oho	Presley	298	Frf	Sinck, Abram	479	Frn
William	8	Knw	Revel	123	Acc	Daniel	463	Frn
William	404	Mds	Richd.	298	Frf	David	463	Frn
Wm.	304	Frf	Robert	686	Br	Henry	463	Frn
see Sirms, Timms			Robert	943	Hrr	Stephen	463	Frn
Simon, Benja.	912	Hrr	Rodham	524	Prw	Sinclair, Archibald	370	Fqr
N.	920	Nrf	Solomon	653	Btt	Arthr.	921	Nrf
Nics.	810	Nrf	Susanah	246	Shn	David	919	Nrf
Sherad	653	Btt	Thomas	303	Frf	Edith	290	Ldn
see Simmon			Thomas	355	Fqr	Geo.	291	Ldn

295

Geo.	313	Ldn	Sipe, David	11	Rcm	Skelton, Edward	9	Wod
Isaac	371	Fqr	Emanuel	208	Alb	John	620	Mnt
James	359	Fqr	George	10	Rcm	John	178	Shn
James	591	Frd	Henry	11	Rcm	Mary	926	Crl
John	380	Fqr	John	23	Rcm	Meriweather	178	Knq
John	670	Glc	Siple, Hannah	239	Shn	Mildred	177	Knq
John	62	Jff	Sirls, James	611	Mnt	Rachel	178	Knq
John	236	Ldn	Polly	925	Crl	William	64	Chr
John	7	Oho	Polly	611	Mnt	William	177	Knq
Robert	799	Hmp	Vincent	924	Crl	William	178	Shn
Seth	290	Ldn	Sirms, Howel	734	Brn	William E., Dr.	14	Pwh
Thomas	14	Isw	see Siroms			see Shelton		
William	416	Fqr	Siroms, Richd.	762	Brn	Skenk, Rebecca	179	Alb
Wm.	713	Gch	Siscoe, Absm.	541	Mnn	Skete, James	592	Frd
Sinclare, James	12	Wod	Sisk, Allen	77	Clp	Skidmore, Abraham	417	Rnd
John	918	Hrr	Benja.	76	Clp	Abraham	418	Rnd
Nathan	918	Hrr	Benja.	78	Clp	Andrew	421	Rnd
Thomas	918	Hrr	Chs.	76	Clp	Andrew	422	Rnd
William	4	Wod	Timothy	77	Clp	Elija	223	Pnd
Sincler, Thomas	298	Frf	Timothy	724	Wsh	James	224	Pnd
Sincox, John	511	Prw	see Seek			James	430	Rnd
Pearson	506	Prw	Sisson, Abner	654	Btt	John	417	Rnd
Thomas	506	Prw	George	351	Fqr	John	56	Stf
Sindall, William	926	Crl	Henry	419	Fqr	Joshua	61	Stf
Sine, Adam	224	Shn	Henry	390	Rch	Levi	418	Rnd
John	224	Shn	Henry	402	Rch	Nancy	223	Pnd
Peter	230	Shn	Jas.	659	Btt	Randel	654	Btt
Siner, James	480	Bdf	Martin	410	Rch	Sarah	216	Kng
see Sinor			Mary S.	410	Rch	Suffrend	832	Nrf
Singan, George	740	Wsh	Stanley	660	Btt	Thomas	430	Rnd
Singener see Surgener			Wm.	74	Clp	William	61	Stf
Singer, Chs.	276	Ldn	Sites, George	2	Rcm	see Shidmore		
John	360	Fqr	George, (Jr.)	20	Rcm	Skiles, Henry	383	Ags
Ostin	949	Hrr	Henry	655	Btt	Jane, Charleston	10	Knw
Peggy	384	Fqr	John	653	Btt	Skillern, Wm. P.	654	Btt
Thomas	552	Brk	John	11	Rcm	Skillman, Abram	259	Ldn
Singers, John	580	Frd	William	40	Rcm	Skillmor, Ann	654	Btt
Singhause, Christian	600	Frd	Sitlingler, Robert	417	Bth	Skilmon, Isaac	481	Bdf
Christian, Jr.	605	Frd	Sitlington, Elizabeth	445	Bth	Skimp, John	569	Brk
Single, Coonrod	67	Jff	W. [2]	450	Bth	Skiner, Wm.	289	Rck
Singleton, Benjamin	373	Fqr	Sittle, Abraham	76	Clp	Skinker, ---	350	Fqr
Charles	734	Brn	Chs.	76	Clp	John, [his] Est.	216	Kng
Esther	61	Acc	Chs.	78	Clp	Martin	47	Stf
James	576	Frd	Colvert	74	Clp	Samuel	39	Stf
Jas.	472	Pra	Edward	413	Fqr	William	354	Fqr
Jno.	918	Nrf	Elijah	76	Clp	Skinklen, David, f.		
John	590	Frd	Enoch	78	Clp	Negro	301	Frf
John	825	Hmp	Frans.	76	Clp	Skinmer, John	299	Frf
Joshua	370	Fqr	Henry, Sr.	74	Clp	Skinner, Amos	250	Ldn
Joshua	670	Glc	Isaac	398	Fqr	Anthony	513	Prw
Mary	839	Nrf	James, (Overseer)	374	Fqr	Cornelius	250	Ldn
Minor	406	Fqr	John M.	413	Fqr	Cornelius	521	Prw
Randolph	761	Brn	Joseph	79	Clp	Daniel	6	Oho
Rd.	670	Glc	Merryman	76	Clp	Elijah	402	Mds
Ro.	670	Glc	Obediah	77	Clp	Elisha	217	Kng
Robert	714	Gch	Strother	76	Clp	Ezekiel	49	Stf
Saml.	921	Nrf	William, (Green)	367	Fqr	Hugh	78	Clp
Samuel	364	Fqr	William, Jr.	414	Fqr	Isaac	402	Mds
Samuel	233	Ldn	Wm.	77	Clp	Jacob	281	Ldn
William	358	Lnn	Wm., Jr.	78	Clp	Jno.	75	Clp
Wm.	670	Glc	Siva, George	218	Pnd	John	924	Crl
Wm.	714	Gch	Sivick, Adam	241	Shn	John	183	Elc
Zebulon	358	Lnn	Sivil, Bengamin	776	Hmp	John	360	Lnn
Sink, Laurance	172	Shn	Joseph	776	Hmp	John	361	Lnn
Philip	172	Shn	Oliver	776	Hmp	John	402	Mds
Sinkhorn, Jno.	657	Btt	Six, George	808	Hmp	Judith	681	Wrw
Sinkler, Edward	483	Bdf	Isaac	228	Shn	Nathun	243	Ldn
George	483	Bdf	John	19	Wod	Ned	334	Dnw
Isaac	483	Bdf	Phillip	799	Hmp	Peter	242	Ldn
John	480	Bdf	William	857	Wth	Phineas	521	Prw
John [2]	481	Bdf	Sizer, Bartlet	8	Pwh	Price	299	Frf
Robert	483	Bdf	George	922	Crl	Reuben	359	Lnn
Robert, jr.	483	Bdf	John	922	Crl	Samuel	234	Ldn
Weymon	480	Bdf	Samuel	10	Pwh	Samuel	361	Lnn
Sinmons, Eliza	809	Nrf	William, F. Mulo.	76	Clp	Stead	74	Clp
Sinnet, Henry	220	Pnd	Skaggs, Henry	54	Jff	Tho.	191	Elc
Partrick	225	Pnd	Skates, James	785	Wst	Thomas	296	Frf
Sinor, John	480	Bdf	Skean see Shean			Vincent	359	Lnn
see Siner			Skeen, James	198	Shn	Walter	6	Oho
Sinurs see Smurr			Skelten, Moses	383	Ags	William	922	Crl

William	923	Crl
William	358	Lnn
Willm.	183	Elc
Wm.	305	Frf
see Collins, Skinker, Skinmer		
Skipwith, Eliza.	326	Dnw
Geo. N.	229	Aml
George	100	Cmb
Henry, (W)	883	Yrk
Letty	328	Dnw
Polley	10	Hnr
Wm.	101	Cmb
Skogings, Wm.	79	Clp
Skoonover, Benjn.	422	Rnd
Danl.	430	Rnd
Skuller, Elizabeth	130	Hnr
Slack, Enoch	277	Ldn
Henry	789	Hmp
James	778	Hmp
James	14	Knw
Jeremiah	251	Ldn
John	482	Bdf
John	2	Knw
John	17	Oho
Josiah W. [U.?]	472	Pra
Lott	480	Bdf
Nat, f. negro	299	Frf
Samuel	14	Knw
see Leack		
Slackton see Stackton		
Slacum, George	297	Frf
Slade, Clemmy	616	Srr
Jesse	615	Srr
John, junr.	616	Srr
John, senr.	615	Srr
Joshua	853	Sth
Samuel	854	Sth
Thomas	616	Srr
William	456	Grn
William, junr.	616	Srr
William, Senr.	616	Srr
Sladyen, Daniel	714	Gch
John	714	Gch
Slaghter, Lucy	856	Hnv
Slagle, Geo.	385	Ags
Hannah	818	Hmp
John	515	Frd
John	747	Wsh
Joseph	515	Frd
William	704	Wsh
Slain, Thomas	777	Hmp
Slaits, Federick	283	Ldn
Slaitser, Jacob [2]	287	Ldn
Jno.	297	Ldn
Slane, Bengamin	835	Hmp
Elias	835	Hmp
Hugh	761	Hmp
James	834	Hmp
John	835	Hmp
Slankack, Peler	359	Lnn
Slarling, Ely [Elij?]	538	Mnn
Slarn see Slane, Starn		
Slater, Abm., Sr.	660	Btt
Daniel	768	Nwk
Edward	512	Frd
Henly	768	Nwk
Jacob	660	Btt
Jacob	29	Rcm
James	113	Spt
James	857	Wth
Mary	768	Nwk
William	768	Nwk
William	244	Shn
see Stater		
Slatham, Thomas	727	Nls
Slatlemen, Dewault	572	Brk
Slator, Richard	957	Hrr
Slatzer, Martin	704	Wsh
Slaughter, Charles	859	Cmp
Elias	884	Hnv

Elizabeth	360	Lnn
Ezekiel	4	Ntt
Francis	728	Nls
Geo.	162	Dnw
George W.	923	Crl
Goodrich	14	Knw
Hennery	360	Lnn
Henry	404	Fqr
James	404	Mds
James	890	Yrk
Jno. S.	77	Clp
John	360	Lnn
John	883	Yrk
John P.	857	Cmp
Joseph	481	Bdf
Joseph	404	Fqr
Milly	527	Brk
Munncy	361	Lnn
Philip	71	Clp
Reuben	482	Bdf
Reuber	14	Knw
Richard	482	Bdf
Robert	289	Amh
Robt.	71	Clp
Saml.	71	Clp
Samuel	889	Hnv
Sina	360	Lnn
Smith	66	Jff
Staunton	71	Clp
Susanna	101	Spt
Susanna	399	Fqr
Thomas	923	Crl
Wm.	75	Clp
Wm.	162	Dnw
Slaven, Henry	420	Bth
John	224	Pnd
Stuart	431	Bth
Slaves, Ben	123	Hnr
Nathl.	901	Hnv
Slaw, Gab	538	Mnn
Slawter, Judith	879	Hnv
Slaylor, Andw.	79	Clp
Slayton, Sarah	897	Hnv
Isaac	208	Alb
Sleagle, Jacob	235	Shn
Sleatt, David	943	Hrr
Sled, John	305	Amh
John	10	Pwh
Thos.	715	Gch
William	289	Amh
Sledge, Amos	616	Srr
Augustin	663	Sss
Charles	664	Sss
Henry	874	Sth
Herbert	663	Sss
Javous	664	Sss
Javous	665	Sss
John	481	Bdf
Lemuel C.	615	Srr
Molly	665	Sss
Noah	664	Sss
Parrott	664	Sss
Raimond	664	Sss
Richard	665	Sss
Sleed, Ann	918	Nrf
R. E.	920	Nrf
Sleess see Sluss		
Sleet see Steel		
Sleigh, Henry	84	Jff
Mathias	84	Jff
Slemons, Thomas	528	Frd
Slenup, Nicholas	234	Shn
Sleppy, Frederick	85	Jff
Sless, John	230	Shn
Slider, Susin	6	Hnr
Slimp, Frederick	855	Wth
John	855	Wth
Slitt, William	10	Knw
see Still		
Sloan, Andw.	386	Ags

David	852	Wth
Henry	796	Hmp
James	553	Brk
Nancy	660	Btt
Richard	762	Hmp
Sloane, Jno.	76	Clp
Jno.	263	Rck
Macl.	76	Clp
Slocum, Robert	765	Hmp
see Slacum		
Slocumb, William	54	Acc
William, Sen.	122	Acc
Slokem, John	925	Hrr
Slonaker, Christian	772	Hmp
Slone, Clifford	472	Frn
James	462	Frn
Patrick	462	Frn
Salley	480	Frn
Samuel	687	Br
Thomas	462	Frn
Sloneking, Jas.	542	Mnn
Sloser, George	67	Jff
Sloss, Robert	280	Rck
Slote, Barbara	507	Frd
Slott, Peggy	61	Acc
Slotts, John	726	Wsh
Slough, John	274	Rck
Slover, Christian	248	Shn
Slovis, Jervas	119	Hnr
Slower, Jane	438	Bth
Slusher, Christopher, Jr.	655	Mnt
Christopher, Sr.	655	Mnt
Conrad	381	Ags
George	564	Frd
George	603	Frd
George	297	Rck
Jacob	36	Rcm
Jno.	7	Rcm
John	646	Mnt
John	608	Mnt
Slushour, Peter	229	Shn
Sluss, David	853	Wth
Frederick	856	Wth
Henry	853	Wth
John	853	Wth
John	857	Wth
Sly, Jacob	378	Ags
Slye, Abrm.	281	Rck
Smails, Thos.	385	Ags
Small, Daniel	4	Oho
Henry	577	Brk
Jacob	577	Brk
James	591	Brk
James	596	Brk
John	585	Brk
John	730	Nls
Levi	125	Acc
Richard	6	Oho
William	730	Nls
Wm.	920	Nrf
Smalley, Daniel	26	Oho
Wm.	73	Clp
Wm.	246	Ldn
Smallwood, Bean	267	Ldn
Charles	68	Spt
Elijah	598	Frd
Gabriel	73	Jff
George	91	Jff
Hebron	599	Frd
Hezekiah	511	Prw
James	599	Frd
Leven	307	Ldn
Rachel	628	Mnt
Soloman	125	Acc
Thomas	56	Jff
Van	399	Fqr
see Middleton, Swallwood		
Smalts, George	10	Rcm
Smalwood, Zadock	711	Wsh

Name	No.	Co.	Name	No.	Co.	Name	No.	Co.
Smar..., John	161	Dnw	Alice G., (Y)	883	Yrk	Chas., K.V.	472	Pra
Smarr, Andrew	302	Ldn	Allen	585	Pre	Chesley	803	Bck
Charles	392	Fqr	Allen	664	Sss	Chesley	823	Bck
Robert	391	Fqr	Ambrose	178	Knq	Chrilders	727	Nls
Smart, Edmund	865	Cmp	Ambrose	75	Spt	Christeen	174	Shn
Elisha C.	862	Cmp	Ambrose	79	Spt	Christian	558	Frd
Henry	123	Acc	Andrew	473	Pra	Christian	571	Frd
John	866	Cmp	Ann	335	Dnw	Christian	636	Gls
Thomas	542	Frd	Ann	919	Nrf	Christn.	659	Btt
Zacariah	65	Jff	Ann	760	Wsh	Christopher	924	Crl
Smedley, William	590	Frd	Anne	367	Fqr	Christopher	673	Glc
Smelcer, Abraham	483	Bdf	Anne [2]	455	Grn	Chs.	298	Frf
Jesse	483	Bdf	Anne	767	Nwk	Clarke	9	Pwh
John	483	Bdf	Anny	75	Clp	Clem	361	Lnn
Smell, Jac.	537	Mnn	Antho.	542	Mnn	Clement	762	Brn
Micl.	537	Mnn	Anthony	715	Gch	Conrad	382	Ags
Phil	537	Mnn	Anthy.	672	Glc	Conrad	172	Shn
Smelly, Thomas, Jun.	21	Isw	Aron	960	Hrr	Conrad	230	Shn
Thomas, Sen.	7	Isw	Auge. J.	299	Frf	Conrod	771	Hmp
Smelser, Jacob	15	Rcm	Augustin	730	Nls	Coonrod	14	Knw
Smelt, David	187	Elc	Augustine	533	Frd	Cudbith	762	Brn
James	186	Elc	Augustine	176	Knq	Dabny	14	Hnr
Johnson	182	Elc	Augustine, Jr.	376	Fqr	Daniel	490	Frn
Miles	474	Pra	Augustine, Senr.	383	Fqr	Daniel	520	Frd
Willm.	182	Elc	Austin	482	Bdf	Daniel	81	Jff
Wm.	682	Wrw	Austin	75	Clp	Daniel	403	Mds
Smerr, Charles	589	Brk	Austin	217	Kng	Daniel	218	Pnd
see Smurr			Bailey	186	Elc	Daniel	747	Wsh
Smether, Edmd.	204	Ess	Ballard	410	Ags	Daniel, persons of		
John	204	Ess	Barnet	98	Spt	colour	105	Cmb
Wm.	197	Ess	Barnett	208	Alb	Danisen	657	Btt
Smidny, Jesse	616	Mnt	Barns	960	Hrr	Danl.	73	Clp
Reubin	616	Mnt	Barshaba	448	Mth	Danl.	288	Ldn
Robert	616	Mnt	Bartholomew	531	Frd	Danl.	296	Ldn
Smiley, ...ert	168	Shn	Bengamin	809	Hmp	Danl.	5	Rcm
Alexander	291	Rck	Benj.	744	Wsh	Danl.	38	Rcm
Andw.	280	Rck	Benja.	326	Dnw	Darnall	358	Fqr
Danl.	658	Btt	Benja.	455	Grn	Dav.	541	Mnn
George	291	Rck	Benja.	917	Hrr	Davd,	729	Wsh
James	656	Btt	Benjamin	63	Chr	David	653	Btt
James	3	Rcm	Benjamin	119	Cmb	David	455	Grn
James	728	Wsh	Benjamin	406	Fqr	David	940	Hrr
John	727	Wsh	Benjamin	453	Frn	David	631	Mnt
Nancy	658	Btt	Benjamin	11	Knw	David	3	Ntt
Nancy	727	Wsh	Benjamin	17	Rcm	David	12	Rcm
Wm.	659	Btt	Benjamin O.	995	Nrt	Delphia	270	Amh
Smilie, Archd.	380	Ags	Benjamin P.	785	Wst	Diana	28	Rcm
John	385	Ags	Benjm.	939	Chc	Dianah	822	Bck
John	24	Oho	Benjn.	654	Btt	Dorathy	11	Rcm
Smith, ---	332	Dnw	Bescoe	75	Clp	Dorcas	803	Nrf
---, Mrs.	661	Btt	Bethia	807	Nrf	Downing	403	Mds
...am [William?]	515	Prw	Betsey	61	Acc	Dulany	345	Fqr
...uel	481	Bdf	Betsey	501	Brk	Edmond	177	Knq
Aaron	944	Hrr	Betsey	804	Nrf	Edward	939	Chc
Aaron	15	Hnr	Betty, free negro	70	Chs	Edward	330	Dnw
Abner	170	Shn	Bew D.	671	Glc	Edward	303	Frf
Abraham	761	Brn	Billey	161	Dnw	Edward	605	Frd
Abraham	328	Dnw	Bolling	762	Brn	Edward	663	Sss
Abraham	336	Dnw	Bowling	172	Alb	Edward J.	606	Frd
Abraham	644	Mnt	Burwell	10	Ntt	Edy	732	Brn
Abraham	39	Rcm	Caesar, (FN)	16	Rcm	Edy	590	Frd
Absolem, Sr.	655	Btt	Caleb	77	Clp	Elias	801	Hmp
Absolum	620	Mnt	Caleb	216	Kng	Elijah	126	Acc
Acey	403	Mds	Caleb, (Y)	883	Yrk	Elijah	190	Elc
Adam	532	Brk	Calip	223	Pnd	Elijah	373	Fqr
Adam	940	Hrr	Cathrine	597	Mnr	Elijah	406	Fqr
Adam	4	Pwh	Cathrine	412	Rch	Elijah	645	Mnt
Adam	183	Shn	Caty	206	Ess	Elijah	793	Nrf
Adam	196	Shn	Charles	833	Bck	Elijah	745	Wsh
Agga	9	Ntt	Charles	557	Frd	Elijah, (FB)	475	Pra
Agness, Persons of			Charles	829	Hmp	Elijah, Jr.	647	Mnt
Coulour	108	Cmb	Charles	242	Ldn	Elisa.	730	Nls
Alexander	64	Chs	Charles	360	Lnn	Elisha	868	Cmp
Alexander	577	Frd	Charles	729	Nls	Elisha	64	Chr
Alexander	854	Wth	Charles	769	Nwk	Elisha	945	Hrr
Alexander	855	Wth	Charles	794	Nrf	Eliz.	183	Elc
Alexr.	713	Wsh	Charles	407	Rch	Eliza	455	Grn
Alexr.	747	Wsh	Chas.	799	Nrf	Eliza.	247	Ldn
Alexr.	755	Wsh	Chas.	814	Nrf	Elizabeth	262	Amh
Alexr. H.	693	Wsh	Chas.	476	Pra	Elizabeth	924	Crl

Name	No.	Co.	Name	No.	Co.	Name	No.	Co.
Elizabeth	78	Clp	George	13	Wod	Jacob	563	Mnr
Elizabeth	79	Clp	George, Junr.	57	Acc	Jacob	596	Mnr
Elizabeth	364	Fqr	George, Senr.	61	Acc	Jacob	633	Mnt
Elizabeth	375	Fqr	George B.	785	Wst	Jacob	426	Rnd
Elizabeth	393	Fqr	George N.	584	Frd	Jacob	34	Rcm
Elizabeth	714	Gch	George R.	871	Hnv	Jacob	173	Shn
Elizabeth	869	Hnv	Gidian	490	Frn	Jacob	184	Shn
Elizabeth	8	Isw	Granvell	667	Mnt	Jacob	705	Wsh
Elizabeth	178	Knq	Granville	713	Gch	Jacob	719	Wsh
Elizabeth	361	Lnn	Gulielemus	81	Spt	Jacob	856	Wth
Elizabeth	586	Pre	Hannah	605	Frd	Jacob, W	639	Gls
Elizabeth	503	Prw	Hannah	290	Ldn	Jael	729	Nls
Elizh.	112	Hnr	Hannah	645	Mnt	James	282	Amh
Elizt.	384	Ags	Hannah [2]	616	Srr	James	482	Bdf
Enoch	476	Pra	Hannah	785	Wst	James	519	Brk
Ephram	704	Wsh	Hedgman	77	Clp	James	686	Br
Ervin	484	Frn	Hen.	540	Mnn	James	694	Br
Essabier [?]	751	Wsh	Henry	588	Brk	James	731	Brn
Ethreld.	851	Sth	Henry	659	Btt	James	763	Brn
Ezekel	60	Acc	Henry	454	Frn	James	794	Bck
Ezekiel	636	Gls	Henry	462	Frn	James	862	Cmp
Ezekiel	472	Pra	Henry	809	Hmp	James	74	Clp
Ezekiel, (of Jno.)	475	Pra	Henry	867	Hnv	James	160	Dnw
Featherston C.	228	Aml	Henry	59	Jff	James	331	Dnw
Feild	727	Nls	Henry	215	Kng	James	390	Fqr
Fielding	403	Mds	Henry	280	Ldn	James	405	Fqr
Fleet	303	Ldn	Henry	540	Mnn	James	479	Frn
Francis	275	Amh	Henry	572	Mnr	James	551	Frd
Francis	480	Bdf	Henry	727	Nls	James	597	Frd
Francis	925	Crl	Henry	802	Nrf	James	714	Gch
Francis	161	Dnw	Henry	4	Oho	James	455	Grn
Francis	209	Ess	Henry	219	Pnd	James	783	Hmp
Francis	178	Knq	Henry	473	Pra	James	906	Hrr
Francis	358	Lnn	Henry	424	Rnd	James	126	Hnr
Francis	649	Mnt	Henry [2]	42	Rcm	James	10	Isw
Francis	587	Pre	Henry	38	Rcm	James	77	Jff
Francis	740	Wsh	Henry	851	Sth	James	449	Mth
Frank	869	Cmp	Henry	665	Sss	James	562	Mnr
Frank	879	Cmp	Henry, Jr.	639	Mnt	James	578	Mnr
Fred	535	Mnn	Henry, Jr.	646	Mnt	James	623	Mnt
Frederick	731	Brn	Henry, Senr.	178	Knq	James	11	Oho
Frederick	67	Jff	Henry, Sr.	608	Mnt	James	16	Oho
Frederick	30	Rcm	Henry M.	383	Ags	James	21	Oho
Frederick, jr.	732	Brn	Hezekiah	302	Frf	James	503	Prw
Fredrick	798	Nrf	Hiram	854	Wth	James	509	Prw
Frs.	921	Nrf	Holmes B.	533	Prg	James	280	Rck
Gabriel	403	Mds	Humphrey	822	Bck	James	296	Rck
Garnet	856	Wth	Humphrey	632	Mnt	James	36	Rcm
Gasper	652	Mnt	Hy.	919	Nrf	James	70	Spt
Geo.	386	Ags	Isaac	56	Acc	James	75	Spt
Geo.	715	Gch	Isaac	123	Acc	James	77	Spt
Geo.	265	Ldn	Isaac	172	Alb	James	90	Spt
Geo.	283	Ldn	Isaac	379	Ags	James	709	Wsh
Geo.	538	Mnn	Isaac	64	Chr	James	712	Wsh
Geo.	539	Mnn	Isaac	538	Frd	James	751	Wsh
Geo.	822	Nrf	Isaac	630	Mnt	James	755	Wsh
Geo.	919	Nrf	Isaac	225	Pnd	James, (B)	358	Lnn
Geo.	474	Pra	Isaac	476	Pra	James, (C)	358	Lnn
Geo., (FB)	475	Pra	Isaac	855	Wth	James, Capt.	996	Nrt
Geo. S.	715	Gch	Isaac	689	Wsh	James, jr.	176	Knq
Geo. W.	18	Hnr	Isaac, Junr.	63	Chr	James, Jr.	995	Nrt
George	124	Acc	Isariel	453	Mth	James, jr.	70	Spt
George	173	Alb	Isham, FN	68	Chr	James, Sr.	64	Chs
George	482	Bdf	J.Wm. [?]	300	Rck	James, Sr.	995	Nrt
George	732	Brn	Jabez	558	Frd	James, (W)	704	Wsh
George	808	Bck	Jac.	536	Mnn	Jamima	81	Spt
George	79	Clp	Jac.	539	Mnn	Jane	182	Alb
George	162	Dnw	Jack	121	Hnr	Jane	761	Brn
George	530	Frd	Jacob	386	Ags	Jane	165	Shn
George	568	Frd	Jacob	523	Brk	Jas.	672	Glc
George	797	Hmp	Jacob [2]	658	Btt	Jas.	11	Hnr
George	924	Hrr	Jacob	822	Bck	Jas.	746	Wsh
George	14	Knw	Jacob	367	Fqr	Jas., (of Diff)	475	Pra
George	575	Mnr	Jacob	636	Gls	Jemay [?]	591	Mnr
George	501	Prw	Jacob	794	Hmp	Jeremiah	5	Hnr
George	307	Rck	Jacob	112	Hnr	Jeremiah	784	Wst
George	13	Rcm	Jacob	276	Ldn	Jermh.	919	Nrf
George	749	Wsh	Jacob	425	Msn	Jerusa	78	Clp
George	759	Wsh	Jacob	429	Msn	Jesse	161	Dn·v
George	784	Wst	Jacob	538	Mnn	Jesse	118	Hnr

Name	No.	Co.	Name	No.	Co.	Name	No.	Co.
Jesse	309	Ldn	John	585	Pre	Jos.	535	Mnn
Jessee	9	Knw	John	513	Prw	Joseph	404	Ags
Jessy	35	Hnr	John	525	Prw	Joseph	416	Bth
Jno.	654	Btt	John	281	Rck	Joseph	161	Dnw
Jno.	77	Clp	John [2]	3	Rcm	Joseph	297	Frf
Jno.	673	Glc	John	39	Rcm	Joseph	371	Fqr
Jno.	883	Hnv	John	163	Shn	Joseph	589	Frd
Jno.	286	Ldn	John	164	Shn	Joseph	941	Hrr
Jno.	288	Ldn	John	165	Shn	Joseph	130	Hnr
Jno.	536	Mnn	John	231	Shn	Joseph	8	Knw
Jno.	539	Mnn	John	243	Shn	Joseph	299	Ldn
Jno.	540	Mnn	John	248	Shn	Joseph	726	Nls
Jno.	473	Pra	John	71	Spt	Joseph	223	Pnd
Jno.	285	Rck	John	91	Spt	Joseph	585	Pre
Jno.	287	Rck	John	111	Spt	Joseph	586	Pre
Jno., (Carptr.)	472	Pra	John	117	Spt	Joseph	525	Prw
Jno., (& Const.)	64	Chs	John	31	Stf	Joseph	853	Sth
Jno., (Const.)	56	Chs	John	663	Sss	Joseph, (D. run)	355	Fqr
Jno., (Cove)	655	Btt	John	696	Wsh	Joseph, (Dison)	342	Fqr
Jno., Jr.	472	Pra	John	708	Wsh	Joseph A.	163	Shn
Jno., (L)	64	Chs	John	742	Wsh	Joseph A.	164	Shn
Jno., (of Diff)	475	Pra	John	754	Wsh	Joseph D.	383	Fqr
Jno., of Faurq. & his Overseer	76	Clp	John	760	Wsh	Joseph Y.	66	Spt
Jno., (of Geo.)	476	Pra	John	785	Wst	Joshua	678	Br
Jno., (of J)	534	Mnn	John	7	Wod	Joshua	160	Dnw
Jno. M.	358	Lnc	John	852	Wth	Joshua	915	Hrr
Jno. M.	281	Rck	John [2]	855	Wth	Joshua	357	Lnn
Jno. P.	869	Hnv	John	882	Yrk	Joshua	438	Mth
Jno. W.	15	Hnr	John, a man of coler	742	Wsh	Josiah	3	Pwh
Job	13	Rcm	John, B. J.	763	Brn	Js.	60	Chs
Joel	172	Alb	John, (Bumby.)	344	Fqr	Js.	919	Nrf
Joel	77	Clp	John, (FN)	64	Chr	Js. C.	919	Nrf
John	59	Acc	John, jr.	160	Dnw	Judith	715	Gch
John	172	Alb	John, jr.	177	Knq	Judith	663	Sss
John [2]	173	Alb	John, Jr.	661	Mnt	Jury	924	Crl
John	207	Alb	John, Jr.	667	Mnt	Jury	456	Frn
John	275	Amh	John, (Jr.)	8	Rcm	Kezia	793	Nrf
John	383	Ags	John, Jur.	428	Bth	Kidd	537	Mnn
John	412	Bth	John, Jur.	637	Gls	Lane	300	Frf
John	571	Brk	John, Jur.	786	Wst	Larkin	177	Knq
John	574	Brk	John, (Manor)	344	Fqr	Larkin	536	Prg
John	599	Brk	John, Mercht.	63	Chr	Larkn.	920	Nrf
John	677	Br	John, (Overseer)	416	Fqr	Lawrence	123	Cmb
John	686	Br	John, (PS)	172	Shn	Leonard, Est.	64	Chs
John	697	Br	John, RM.	403	Mds	Leroy	11	Pwh
John	160	Dnw	John, (RO)	162	Dnw	Levi	538	Frd
John	213	Ess	John, S. of A	762	Brn	Levi	915	Hrr
John	451	Frn	John, (S. R.)	587	Pre	Levin	883	Yrk
John	455	Frn	John, Sen.	177	Knq	Lewis	386	Ags
John	486	Frn	John, Senr.	56	Acc	Lewis	560	Frd
John	557	Frd	John, Senr.	161	Dnw	Lewis	455	Grn
John	562	Frd	John, Senr.	586	Pre	Lewis	74	Jff
John	575	Frd	John, Senr.	786	Wst	Lewis	177	Knq
John	606	Frd	John, Ser.	428	Bth	Lewis	243	Ldn
John	715	Gch	John, Ser.	639	Gls	Lewis	166	Shn
John	775	Hmp	John, (Son of Jos.)	349	Fqr	Lewis	740	Wsh
John	794	Hmp	John, Sr.	486	Frn	Loucretia	334	Dnw
John	809	Hmp	John, Sr.	625	Mnt	Lucetia	786	Wst
John	905	Hrr	John, (Tay)	161	Dnw	Lucetta	217	Kng
John	906	Hrr	John, (Taylor)	3	Rcm	Lucretia	161	Dnw
John	949	Hrr	John A.	421	Fqr	Lucy	454	Frn
John	954	Hrr	John A.	432	Flv	Lucy	5	Rcm
John	962	Hrr	John H., (W)	883	Yrk	Lucy, (W)	883	Yrk
John	60	Jff	John P.	520	Prw	Luther	921	Nrf
John	97	Jff	John S.	403	Mds	Maget	615	Srr
John	359	Lnn	John S.	525	Prw	Margaret	645	Mnt
John	563	Mnr	John T.	189	Elc	Margaret	189	Shn
John	572	Mnr	Johnac	221	Pnd	Margeret	302	Frf
John	610	Mnt	Johnson	382	Ags	Maria	11	Hnr
John	666	Mnt	Joice	114	Spt	Mark	908	Hrr
John	730	Nls	Jona	535	Mnn	Martha	172	Alb
John	769	Nwk	Jonas	760	Wsh	Martha	161	Dnw
John	804	Nrf	Jonathan	654	Btt	Martha	114	Hnr
John	806	Nrf	Jonathan	690	Br	Martha	32	Isw
John	14	Ntt	Jonathan	569	Frd	Martha	537	Prg
John	17	Oho	Jonathan	691	Wsh	Martin	382	Ags
John	214	Pnd	Jonathan	729	Wsh	Martin	114	Cmb
John	223	Pnd	Jonathn	419	Rnd	Martin	593	Frd
John	226	Pnd	Jonn.	473	Pra	Martin	586	Pre
			Jos.	582	Brk	Mary	173	Alb

Name	No.	Co.
Mary	379	Ags
Mary	162	Dnw
Mary	208	Ess
Mary	453	Frn
Mary	516	Frd
Mary	783	Hmp
Mary	801	Hmp
Mary	359	Lnn
Mary	454	Mth
Mary	810	Nrf
Mary	825	Nrf
Mary	221	Pnd
Mary	6	Pwh
Mary	11	Pwh
Mary	586	Pre
Mary	498	Prw
Mary	473	Pra
Mary	195	Shn
Mary D.	616	Srr
Mathias	704	Wsh
Maths.	658	Btt
Mexhec	659	Btt
Micajah	64	Chs
Michael	672	Glc
Michael jr.	673	Glc
Michal	531	Frd
Miles	160	Dnw
Milley	60	Chs
Milly	726	Nls
Mitchell	792	Nrf
Molley	15	Ntt
Moses	403	Mds
Mourning	212	Ess
Mourning	31	Stf
Nancy	595	Brk
Nancy	548	Prg
Nanncy	415	Fqr
Nat.	715	Gch
Nathan	834	Bck
Nathan	593	Frd
Nathen	747	Wsh
Neal	795	Nrf
Nelly	340	Fqr
Nicholas	598	Brk
Nicholas	786	Hmp
Nicholas	12	Knw
Nicholas	427	Rnd
Nimrod	637	Gls
Owen	586	Pre
P. F.	67	Chs
Paley	124	Hnr
Parritt	646	Mnt
Patric	16	Oho
Patrick, Jr.	575	Frd
Payton	360	Lnn
Peggy	330	Dnw
Peggy	368	Fqr
Peggy	785	Wst
Peleg	795	Nrf
Pemberton	585	Pre
Perrin	450	Mth
Peter	385	Ags
Peter	658	Btt
Peter	761	Hmp
Peter	3	Hnr
Peter	633	Mnt
Peter	223	Pnd
Peter	302	Rck
Peter	256	Shn
Peter	787	Wst
Peter, Jr.	659	Btt
Peter, Jr.	996	Nrt
Peter, Sr.	659	Btt
Peter, Sr.	995	Nrt
Peter P.	78	Clp
Peyton, (Y)	883	Yrk
Phebe	19	Ntt
Philip	519	Brk
Philip	74	Clp
Philip	796	Nrf
Philip	256	Shn
Phillemon	477	Frn
Phillip	81	Spt
Pleasant	761	Brn
Pleasant	957	Chc
Pleasant	959	Chc
Polley	490	Frn
Polley	3	Hnr
Polley	12	Hnr
Polley	18	Ntt
Presley	304	Rck
Rachel	12	Hnr
Ralph	123	Acc
Ralph	14	Oho
Ralph	22	Oho
Randolph	919	Hrr
Rebecca	615	Srr
Rebekah	904	Hrr
Reuben	9	Knw
Reubin	64	Chr
Richard	269	Amh
Richard	833	Bck
Richard	926	Crl
Richard	827	Hmp
Richard	852	Hnv
Richard	852	Wth
Richard	855	Wth
Richd.	65	Chs
Richd.	161	Dnw
Richd.	182	Elc
Richd.	713	Gch
Richd.	535	Mnn
Richd.	538	Mnn
Richd.	540	Mnn
Richd. S.	761	Brn
Rice	922	Crl
Robert	429	Bth
Robert	812	Bck
Robert	857	Cmp
Robert	105	Cmb
Robert	637	Gls
Robert	176	Knq
Robert	359	Lnn
Robert	16	Oho
Robert	587	Pre
Robert	747	Wsh
Robert, free negro	70	Chs
Robert, (HC)	64	Chr
Robert, Jr.	570	Frd
Robert, Senr.	570	Frd
Robert, (TC)	64	Chr
Robt.	71	Clp
Robt.	271	Rck
Robt. P.	122	Hnr
Rody, (FB)	475	Pra
Roseener	255	Shn
Rowley	163	Shn
Rowley	164	Shn
Rozell	300	Frf
S. R.	335	Dnw
Sally	763	Brn
Sally	531	Prg
Sally	851	Sth
Sam	535	Mnn
Sam.	883	Yrk
Saml.	659	Btt
Saml.	778	Bck
Saml.	303	Frf
Saml.	264	Rck
Saml.	293	Rck
Saml., jr.	293	Rck
Samuel	839	Bck
Samuel	867	Cmp
Samuel	515	Frd
Samuel	239	Ldn
Samuel	272	Ldn
Samuel	403	Mds
Samuel	78	Spt
Samuel	403	Mds
Samuel, Jr.	403	Mds
Samuel, Ovsr.	403	Mds
Sarah	64	Chs
Sarah	455	Grn
Sarah	257	Ldn
Sarah	6	Rcm
Sarah	730	Wsh
Seth	75	Jff
Shadrack	822	Bck
Shadrick	585	Pre
Sherod	763	Brn
Silla	330	Dnw
Simms	473	Pra
Solomon	561	Brk
Sophia	297	Frf
Stephen	762	Brn
Stephen	205	Ess
Stephen	452	Frn
Stephen	466	Frn
Stephen	672	Glc
Stephen	113	Hnr
Stephen	8	Isw
Stephen	2	Knw
Stephen	884	Yrk
Sterling	119	Hnr
Sterling	585	Pre
Sterling W.	762	Brn
Stirling, F. B.	8	Pwh
Susan	333	Dnw
Susan	5	Hnr
Susan	284	Ldn
Susan	403	Mds
Susan	919	Nrf
Susan, [her] (Plantn)	473	Pra
Susanah	403	Mds
Susanna	172	Alb
Susanna	220	Ess
Susanna	347	Fqr
Susanna	920	Nrf
Temple	304	Frf
Theos.	580	Mnr
Tho. G.	176	Knq
Thomas	56	Acc
Thomas	209	Alb
Thomas	435	Bth
Thomas [2]	480	Bdf
Thomas	64	Chr
Thomas	74	Clp
Thomas	302	Frf
Thomas	395	Fqr
Thomas	592	Frd
Thomas	600	Frd
Thomas	904	Hrr
Thomas	945	Hrr
Thomas	6	Knw
Thomas	235	Ldn
Thomas	240	Ldn
Thomas	317	Ldn
Thomas	359	Lnn
Thomas	403	Mds
Thomas	629	Mnt
Thomas	1	Pwh
Thomas	509	Prw
Thomas	31	Stf
Thomas	663	Sss
Thomas	712	Wsh
Thomas, Jr.	403	Mds
Thomas, Botetourt	671	Glc
Thomas, (CC)	69	Chr
Thomas, SS	59	Acc
Thomas C.	599	Brk
Thompson	360	Fqr
Thos.	381	Ags
Thos.	730	Brn
Thos.	219	Ess
Thos.	672	Glc
Thos.	715	Gch
Thos.	869	Hnv
Thos.	813	Nrf
Thos.	919	Nrf
Thos.	736	Wsh
Thos.	747	Wsh

Thos., Jr.	649	Mnt	William T.	587	Pre	Smithson, Cement	64	Chr
Thos., Jur.	755	Wsh	William W.	56	Acc	Charles	359	Lnn
Thos., N.T.	726	Wsh	William W.	786	Wst	Christopher T.	358	Lnn
Timothy	782	Hmp	Williamson	665	Sss	David	732	Brn
Tobias	25	Rcm	Willis	208	Alb	Drummond	863	Cmp
Tobias	730	Wsh	Willis	411	Fqr	John	171	Alb
Tobias	760	Wsh	Willm., Sr.	635	Mnt	John	360	Lnn
Townley	41	Stf	Wim.	848	Hnv	Manoah	361	Lnn
Tully	474	Pra	Wim.	869	Hnv	Martha	361	Lnn
Uriah	780	Bck	Wim.	886	Hnv	Nathaniel	358	Lnn
Walter	953	Hrr	Wim.	895	Hnv	Nicholas	358	Lnn
Walter A.	374	Fqr	Wm.	382	Ags	Richard	361	Lnn
Weeden	73	Clp	Wm.	523	Brk	Samuel	208	Alb
Wiett	735	Wsh	Wm.	550	Brk	Samuel	864	Cmp
Wilkins	531	Prg	Wm.	580	Brk	Samuel	406	Mds
William	59	Acc	Wm.	658	Btt	William	359	Lnn
William	122	Acc	Wm.	660	Btt	Smithy, Casander	768	Nwk
William	173	Alb	Wm.	732	Brn	Polly	768	Nwk
William	208	Alb	Wm.	72	Clp	Robert, Sinr.	178	Knq
William	227	Aml	Wm.	78	Clp	Smitley, Adam	283	Ldn
William	285	Amh	Wm.	670	Glc	Geo.	283	Ldn
William	413	Bth	Wm.	672	Glc	Smitly, Methias	283	Ldn
William	676	Br	Wm.	24	Hnr	Smitsen, Chesley	48	Stf
William	822	Bck	Wm.	113	Hnr	Smitson, Thos.	585	Mnr
William	834	Bck	Wm.	360	Lnc	Smock, Esma	128	Hnr
William	64	Chr	Wm.	312	Ldn	Esme	11	Hnr
William	102	Cmb	Wm.	538	Mnn	James	107	Spt
William	116	Cmb	Wm.	539	Mnn	James	736	Wsh
William	374	Fqr	Wm.	595	Mnr	Matthias	559	Brk
William	383	Fqr	Wm.	645	Mnt	Peter	113	Spt
William	462	Frn	Wm.	798	Nrf	William	107	Spt
William [2]	469	Frn	Wm.	812	Nrf	Smoker, Jacob	218	Shn
William	475	Frn	Wm.	827	Nrf	Nicholas	218	Shn
William	491	Frn	Wm.	836	Nrf	Peter	218	Shn
William	535	Frd	Wm.	919	Nrf	Smooker, Ferdinand	206	Shn
William	557	Frd	Wm.	475	Pra	Smool, Benja.	116	Hnr
William	581	Frd	Wm.	421	Rnd	Smoot, Barton	116	Hnr
William	592	Frd	Wm.	430	Rnd	Benja.	79	Clp
William	636	Gls	Wm.	682	Wrw	George	524	Prw
William	455	Grn	Wm.	734	Wsh	Henry	171	Shn
William	762	Hmp	Wm.	883	Yrk	Jane	575	Brk
William	801	Hmp	Wm., (T.G.)	75	Clp	John	406	Mds
William	926	Hrr	Wm. H.	806	Nrf	Jonah	112	Hnr
William	17	Hnr	Yearmon	36	Hnr	Lewis	596	Frd
William	9	Knw	Yearmon, not Taken	34	Hnr	Noly	728	Nls
William	13	Knw	Yost	853	Wth	Ths.	74	Clp
William	178	Knq	see ---, Beasley, Blackburn,			Thomas	516	Prw
William	359	Lnn	Blankenship, Bunting,			Wm.	78	Clp
William	726	Nls	Bunton, Caldwell, Car-			see Smool, Smott		
William	729	Nls	mine, Ellis, Horsley,			Smoote, Barton	371	Fqr
William	730	Nls	Keeth, Kelsay, Kent, Mar-			Edward	410	Fqr
William	767	Nwk	tin, Mason, Melson, Mil-			John	410	Fqr
William	9	Oho	liner, Parham, S...,			Leonard	410	Fqr
William [2]	218	Pnd	Sample, Slaughter, Smuth,			Thomasin	409	Fqr
William	223	Pnd	Snith, Thomson, Topping,			William	410	Fqr
William	4	Pwh	Web, Wheelton, Wyatt			Smoots, Abraham	218	Shn
William	536	Prg	Smithee, Mary	498	Prw	see Smottz		
William	500	Prw	Smither, Gabl.	79	Clp	Smoott, Barton	778	Hmp
William	509	Prw	Geo.	360	Lnc	Joshua	779	Hmp
William	390	Rch	George	996	Nrt	Josias	804	Hmp
William	412	Rch	Jno.	77	Clp	Sarah	776	Hmp
William	21	Rcm	Joseph	78	Clp	Smotherman, Saml.	300	Frf
William	34	Rcm	Leonard, jr.	176	Knq	Smothers, David	20	Oho
William	210	Shn	Leonard, Senr.	176	Knq	Smott, James	237	Ldn
William	245	Shn	Robert	176	Knq	Jno.	74	Clp
William	30	Stf	Saml.	228	Aml	Smotts, Abraham	216	Shn
William	712	Wsh	Sarah	409	Rch	Smottz, Matthias	218	Shn
William	727	Wsh	William	176	Knq	see Smoots		
William	785	Wst	William	995	Nrt	Smullen, William	122	Acc
William	853	Wth	Wm.	360	Lnc	Smurr, Andrew	101	Jff
William, (CC)	63	Chr	see Smithey			Ann	597	Brk
William, (D. run)	357	Fqr	Smithers, Jas. S.	21	Hnr	Jacob	101	Jff
William, OH	124	Acc	Michl.	644	Mnt	see Smerr, Smyrr		
William B.	785	Wst	Sally	277	Rck	Smuth, Mary	798	Nrf
William C.	392	Rch	Smithey, George	96	Jff	Smyrr, Peter	105	Jff
William D.	403	Mds	John M.	228	Aml	see Smurr		
William H.	403	Mds	Joshua	228	Aml	Smyth, Ebenezer	852	Wth
William R.	387	Fqr	Mary	229	Aml	Samuel	852	Wth
William S.	727	Nls	Moses	95	Jff	Smyther, Jno.	75	Clp
William T.	63	Chr	see Smither			Smythers, Pleasant	129	Hnr

Snail, Cristopher	810 Nrf	Js.	60 Chs	Davd.	700 Wsh
Hillary	473 Pra	Snelon, Charles	195 Shn	Davd.	731 Wsh
Mary	813 Nrf	Snelson, Bartlett	865 Hnv	Davd., (Forks)	702 Wsh
Sarah	476 Pra	Jno.	671 Glc	Davd., Jur.	700 Wsh
Snape, Nathaniel	97 Spt	Nathanl.	334 Dnw	Elisha	542 Mnn
Snapp, Adam	570 Frd	Nathl., & Co.	328 Dnw	Henry	656 Btt
George	536 Frd	Robert	229 Aml	Henry	657 Btt
Jacob	573 Frd	Snevely, Jacob	852 Wth	Hugh	701 Wsh
Jacob	215 Shn	Snickers, William	587 Frd	Isaac	630 Mnt
John, (Jr.)	10 Rcm	Snidaw, Christian, Jr.	639 Gls	James	620 Mnt
John, (Sen.)	9 Rcm	Christian, Sr.	639 Gls	Jane	543 Mnn
Joseph	386 Ags	Jacob	638 Gls	Jas.	695 Wsh
Mary	207 Shn	John	639 Gls	Jas., Majr.	695 Wsh
Philip	220 Shn	Snidegar, Garret [2]	697 Br	Jno.	657 Btt
Snare, Henry	216 Shn	Snider, Abraham	602 Frd	Jno., Jur.	735 Wsh
Jacob	216 Shn	Abraham	86 Jff	John	638 Gls
Snavely, Samuel	105 Jff	Abrm.	559 Brk	John	7 Oho
Snavly, John	622 Mnt	Adam	220 Pnd	John	700 Wsh
Snead, Agnes	899 Hnv	Andw.	379 Ags	John	735 Wsh
Anney	899 Hnv	Boston	739 Wsh	Jos.	541 Mnn
Benjamin	873 Hnv	Catherine	226 Pnd	Jos., Senr.	735 Wsh
Charles	54 Acc	Christian	94 Jff	Joseph	636 Gls
George W.R.	54 Acc	Christn.	660 Btt	Joseph	700 Wsh
Harmon	3 Hnr	Daniel	660 Btt	Josh.	655 Btt
Henry	68 Chr	Daniel	220 Pnd	Josh.	658 Btt
Isaac	55 Acc	Daniel	187 Shn	Mary	658 Btt
Israel	854 Cmp	David	659 Btt	Mary	7 Oho
James, 3	56 Acc	David	660 Btt	Rob., Sr.	548 Brk
Jno.	920 Nrf	Frederick	557 Frd	Robert	639 Gls
John	54 Acc	Fredk.	549 Brk	Robt.	541 Brk
John	191 Elc	George	541 Frd	Robt.	713 Wsh
John	431 Flv	George	54 Jff	Stephen	550 Brk
John H.	122 Acc	George	219 Pnd	William	695 Wsh
Joseph	405 Mds	George W.	252 Shn	Wm.	557 Brk
Mary	113 Hnr	Henry	405 Ags	Wm.	541 Mnn
Patsy	127 Hnr	Henry	655 Btt	Wm., Jnr.	542 Mnn
Philip	357 Lnn	Henry	660 Btt	see Forks	
Randolph	302 Amh	Henry	628 Mnt	Snodgross, Saml.	286 Rck
Rebecka	854 Cmp	Henry	6 Rcm	Snody, Robert	866 Cmp
Richard	412 Bth	Jacob	654 Btt	Snoots, Henry	287 Ldn
Robert	125 Acc	Jacob	601 Frd	Snow, Betsey	994 Nrt
Robert	846 Hnv	Jacob	217 Pnd	Daniel	869 Cmp
Robt.	114 Hnr	Jacob, Sr.	659 Btt	James	575 Brk
Samuel	357 Lnn	Jno.	653 Btt	John B.	994 Nrt
Sarah	359 Lnn	Jno.	660 Btt	Richard	208 Alb
Thomas	54 Acc	John	656 Btt	Sylas	994 Nrt
Thomas	57 Acc	John	661 Btt	Wm.	654 Btt
Tully	54 Acc	John	462 Frn	Snowdagall see Snowdall	
William	256 Amh	John	472 Frn	Snowdal, Peter	549 Brk
William	797 Bck	John	939 Hrr	Snowden, John	691 Br
William	856 Cmp	John	90 Jff	William	691 Br
William, of P.	58 Acc	John	94 Jff	Snuffer, George	644 Mnt
Wm.	113 Hnr	John	665 Mnt	Jacob	634 Mnt
Snebly, Henry	856 Wth	Margaret	936 Hrr	Snyder, Aam	403 Mds
see Sneebly		Martin	380 Ags	Agatha	481 Bdf
Sneebly, Adam	855 Wth	Martin	509 Brk	Barksdale	482 Bdf
Jacob, Junr.	856 Wth	Mathias	655 Btt	Betsey	584 Brk
Jacob, Senr.	856 Wth	Peter [2]	659 Btt	Christian	259 Ldn
John	855 Wth	Peter	200 Shn	Daniel	507 Brk
Peter	855 Wth	Phillip	659 Btt	Dav.	540 Mnn
see Snebly		Thos.	739 Wsh	David	693 Br
Sneed, Alexr.	5 Ntt	Valentine	28 Rcm	David	402 Mds
Archer	429 Flv	Snidow, Abraham	667 Mnt	E.	540 Mnn
Benjamin	586 Pre	Henry	667 Mnt	Eliz.	542 Mnn
Claiborn	447 Flv	Snipe, Robert	40 Stf	Geo.	536 Mnn
Evan	482 Bdf	Snipp, Joseph	572 Frd	Geo.	539 Mnn
John	923 Crl	Smith, Mary	809 Nrf	Henry	481 Bdf
John	489 Frn	Snivley, Henry	249 Shn	Henry	537 Mnn
Sally	768 Nwk	Snodden, George	38 Rcm	Jac.	536 Mnn
William	208 Alb	Snoddy, Cary	830 Bck	Jacob	598 Brk
Sneider, Frederick	269 Rck	Daniel	272 Amh	Jerh.	539 Mnn
Isaac	304 Rck	David	482 Bdf	Jessee	537 Mnn
John	269 Rck	James, Jr.	834 Bck	Jno.	537 Mnn
Snell, Jacob	15 Rcm	James, senr.	834 Bck	Jno.	538 Mnn
John	172 Alb	Samuel	809 Bck	Jno.	539 Mnn
Snellin, Catharine	60 Stf	Snodgras, John	23 Oho	Jno., Jr.	540 Mnn
Snelling, Samuel	350 Fqr	William	23 Oho	John	584 Brk
see Wilkinson		Snodgrass, Alexr.	659 Btt	John	525 Frd
Snellings, Alexander	58 Chs	Alexr.	647 Mnt	John	756 Hmp
George	61 Chs	Barbara	543 Mnn	John	727 Nls

John	855	Wth	Peter	662	Mnt	John	857	Wth
John	856	Wth	see Stonger			William	857	Wth
John, jr.	584	Brk	Sonner, Anthony	250	Shn	see Southren		
Jos.	542	Mnn	John	215	Shn	Southgale, R.	32	Hnr
Lau [?]	537	Mnn	Philip P.	220	Shn	Southgate, Charles	12	Hnr
Margte.	918	Nrf	Sonns, Bryan	759	Hmp	Jno.	920	Nrf
Martin	24	Rcm	Sonscney, Peter	522	Frd	John	176	Knq
Matthias	31	Rcm	Sonserville see Somerville			Southmard, Charles	663	Sss
Michael, P.W.	403	Mds	Soper, John	441	Mth	Southren, Jessee	857	Wth
Michael, R.	402	Mds	Sophes, Wm.	281	Ldn	Southwick, Mary	920	Nrf
Michael, RM.	402	Mds	Sophire, Semoir	729	Nls	Southwirth, Jos.	536	Mnn
Nimrod	537	Mnn	Sorcy see Sorey			Southwood, Edwd.	511	Brk
Peter	252	Ldn	Sorey, Ivy	474	Pra	Wim.	901	Hnv
Peter	42	Rcm	Joab	474	Pra	Southworth, John	924	Crl
Peter	853	Wth	Kedar	797	Nrf	Reuben	923	Crl
Phillip	402	Mds	Philip	475	Pra	Reuben	926	Crl
Robert	402	Mds	Tatem	794	Nrf	Richard	924	Crl
Samuel	402	Mds	Wm., Jr.	474	Pra	Thomas	923	Crl
Simon	28	Rcm	Wm., Sr.	474	Pra	William	924	Crl
Susanna	857	Wth	Sorrel, Ashmond	73	Spt	Souvener see Scrivener		
Wm.	538	Mnn	Joseph	290	Rck	Sovain, Henry	638	Gls
Soary see Sorey			Philip	786	Wst	Soverns, Dan	535	Mnn
Sockman, ---, Revd.	299	Ldn	Thomas	104	Spt	Dan	538	Mnn
Henry	1	Oho	Sorrell, Beverley	924	Crl	Jno.	536	Mnn
John	2	Oho	John	923	Crl	Jos.	535	Mnn
John	8	Oho	John	96	Spt	Soward, Benjamin	761	Brn
Peter	1	Oho	Sally	924	Crl	Isaac	637	Gls
Solais, Thomas	799	Hmp	Thomas A.	784	Wst	John, jr.	763	Brn
Solard, Gab	534	Mnn	William	926	Crl	John, Sr.	762	Brn
Sole, Sally	768	Nwk	William, junr.	926	Crl	Joseph	762	Brn
Soleleather, Mary	208	Ess	Sorrels, Lewis	384	Ags	Samuel	762	Brn
Philip	208	Ess	Sorsbury, Nathan	480	Bdf	Silvy	770	Brn
Soles, Dawson	670	Glc	Sorsby see Sowby			Sowby, Rebecca	615	Srr
Jno.	670	Glc	Sot...can, Samel	943	Hrr	Sowden, John	508	Prw
Jno.	673	Glc	Soule, Rufis	690	Wsh	Sowder, Jacob	286	Ldn
Wm.	673	Glc	Sound, ---	908	Nrf	Philip	286	Ldn
Solestine, Joseph	206	Shn	Soundalet, Peter	920	Nrf	Sowel, George	63	Chr
Solf, John	923	Crl	Sourbeer, Anthony	3	Rcm	Owney	63	Chr
Solliday, John	833	Hmp	Sourwine, Peter	32	Rcm	Sarah	210	Ess
Sollis, James	628	Mnt	South, Hardy	176	Knq	William	64	Chr
Sollomon, Nancy	927	Crl	Southall, Charles	176	Knq	Sowell, Benjamin	171	Alb
Soloman, Thomas	914	Hrr	Elizabeth	132	Cmb	Elijah	171	Alb
Solomon, Aaron	38	Rcm	Furnea	941	Chc	Elisha	171	Alb
Elizabeth	254	Ldn	George	129	Cmb	John	171	Alb
Solovo, Lewis	2	Hnr	Henry H.	228	Aml	John, [his] Est.	217	Kng
Somers, Adam	281	Rck	Henry H.	941	Chc	Philip	299	Amh
Horsey	126	Acc	James	131	Cmb	Sowells, Jesse	479	Frn
Somersall, Jno. W.	93	Clp	James B.	14	Isw	Sowers, Balser	184	Shn
Somervail, Alexandr.	202	Ess	Jesse	228	Aml	Daniel, Jr.	559	Frd
Somervill, Alexander	948	Hrr	John	228	Aml	Daniel, Senr.	547	Frd
Thomas	963	Hrr	John	955	Chc	Fielding	547	Frd
Wm.	262	Rck	John	120	Cmb	Frederick	184	Shn
Somerville, ---	328	Dnw	Js.	58	Chs	George	657	Mnt
Frances	829	Hmp	Nancy	132	Cmb	Henry	657	Mnt
James	5	Rcm	Peyton, (Y)	883	Yrk	Jacob	534	Frd
Js.	72	Clp	Philip	961	Chc	Jacob	658	Mnt
William	509	Frd	Phillip	957	Chc	James	559	Frd
Sommer, Andrew	206	Shn	Sarah	941	Chc	John	382	Ags
see Sonner			Stephen B.	16	Ntt	John	545	Frd
Sommerell, Sterord [?]	881	Sth	Turner	941	Chc	John	601	Frd
see Simmerell, Sommerll			Southard, Allen	61	Stf	Sowther, Stophel	104	Jff
Sommerll, Asa	882	Sth	Fielding	404	Mds	Sowyres see Lowyres		
Sommers, Barbary	249	Shn	Henry	56	Stf	Sp..., Isaac	480	Bdf
Christeen	237	Shn	James	61	Stf	Sp...le, Peter	1	Rcm
Joshua	185	Shn	John	381	Ags	Space, Wm.	567	Brk
Mathias	248	Shn	Joseph	404	Mds	Spacey, Ursula	356	Fqr
Philip, Junr.	185	Shn	Moses	404	Mds	Spade, Frederick	768	Hmp
Philip, Senr.	185	Shn	Saml. L.	217	Kng	George	768	Hmp
Sommerson, Mary	925	Crl	Travers	34	Rcm	John	768	Hmp
Sommervill, James	341	Hrr	William	995	Nrt	John	600	Mnr
Thomas	948	Hrr	William	80	Spt	Spadee, Jesse	833	Nrf
Sommerville, Wm.	595	Brk	William	61	Stf	Spader, Jacob	9	Rcm
Sompawe, Jno.	921	Nrf	see Suthard			see McSpadon		
Sonafrank, Agnes	30	Rcm	Souther, Michael	404	Mds	Spagane, Isaac	697	Wsh
George	30	Rcm	Southerland, ---	299	Frf	Spahr, John	5	Oho
Sonely, George	413	Bth	see Sutherland			Spain, Abraham, jr.	162	Dnw
Songer, Abraham	37	Rcm	Southerlin, Phillemon	452	Frn	Absalem	664	Sss
Christian	856	Wth	Ransom	452	Frn	Daniel	160	Dnw
George	666	Mnt	Southerling see ...therling			Daniel	665	Sss
Jacob, Jr.	622	Mnt	Southern, John	176	Knq	Danl., Senr.	161	Dnw

Danl., (son)	161	Dnw
Elizabeth	666	Sss
Eppes	162	Dnw
Frances	3	Ntt
Henry	162	Dnw
Jno., (SH)	162	Dnw
John	160	Dnw
John	874	Sth
John, (SA)	161	Dnw
Joshua	15	Ntt
Martha	162	Dnw
Peter	326	Dnw
Richd.	161	Dnw
Stephen	160	Dnw
Stephen F.	161	Dnw
Thomas	665	Sss
William	160	Dnw
William, Sr.	665	Sss
William H.	665	Sss
Wm.	762	Brn
Wm.	2	Ntt
Wm., junr.	161	Dnw
Wm., Senr.	18	Ntt
Spakes, Nicholes	715	Wsh
Spalding, John, Gloucester		
Town	670	Glc
Spalee see Spadee		
Span see Sparr		
Spangle, Vance	210	Shn
Spangler, Charles	639	Gls
Danl., Jr.	657	Mnt
Danl., Sr.	657	Mnt
Frederick	1	Rcm
Geo.	657	Mnt
George	68	Jff
George	855	Wth
Jacob	857	Wth
John	54	Jff
John	8	Knw
John	853	Wth
Peter	854	Wth
Spann, Anne	127	Sth
Daniel	672	Glc
Francis	476	Pra
Rd.	672	Glc
Thomas	470	Mdd
Thos.	474	Pra
Zephaniah	476	Pra
see Spunn		
Spark, Ephram	721	Wsh
Reubin H.	690	Wsh
Solomon	682	Br
Sparkes, Thomas	244	Ldn
Sparks, Davd.	748	Wsh
Elizebeth	405	Mds
Henry	405	Mds
James	7	Knw
Jasper	405	Mds
Pheba	405	Mds
Thomas	405	Mds
William	926	Crl
Sparr, Fred	535	Mnn
George	586	Mnr
John	579	Mnr
John, j.	587	Mnr
Sparrow, Anthy., (FB)	474	Pra
Billy, (FB)	474	Pra
Bridget, (FB)	474	Pra
Geo., (FB)	474	Pra
George	522	Brk
Henry	473	Pra
Jacob	123	Acc
John	728	Nls
Nancy	125	Acc
Nanny, (FB)	474	Pra
Richard	125	Acc
Richd.	792	Nrf
Spartle, Jacob	543	Brk
Spates, Benj.	306	Ldn
Spaulding, John	587	Pre

Speak, Geo.	919	Nrf
Speake, Lucreatia	301	Frf
Patty	302	Frf
Speakes, William	73	Jff
Speakman, Ebenez	483	Bdf
Jesse	483	Bdf
Spealman, Elizabeth	36	Rcm
Spear, Jacob	291	Rck
James	54	Jff
Joseph	854	Wth
William	695	Br
see Sphear, Spher		
Spearman, Mary	926	Crl
Spears, James	172	Alb
James	841	Bck
James J.	762	Brn
Jane	172	Alb
Jesse	3	Pwh
John	171	Alb
John	172	Alb
John	53	Chs
John	128	Cmb
John	726	Nls
Robert	128	Cmb
Saml.	637	Mnt
Sarrah	118	Cmb
William	2	Hnr
Wm., the Estate of	128	Cmb
Specht, Charles	380	Ags
Speck, Henry	408	Ags
Lewis	583	Brk
Martin	41	Rcm
Peter	547	Brk
Speece, Conrade	878	Cmp
George	868	Cmp
Peter	868	Cmp
Speed, Henry	883	Yrk
Jno.	672	Glc
Susan	883	Yrk
Speekaugle see Spukaugle		
Speer, Anthony	911	Hrr
Speers see Peers		
Speight, Josiah	55	Acc
Speigle, Lawrance	197	Shn
Michael	204	Shn
Peter	204	Shn
Speirwood, Thomas	499	Frn
Spellman, John	417	Rnd
Spelman, John, Jur.	418	Rnd
Spen see Spew		
Spence, Catrin	711	Wsh
Edward	785	Wst
Jane	527	Brk
Jno.	295	Ldn
John	540	Frd
John	455	Grn
John	498	Prw
John	280	Rck
Nathl.	657	Btt
Thomas	785	Wst
Thomas, Jun.	785	Wst
William	2	Wod
William	854	Wth
Spencer, Ann	880	Hnv
Ann T.	176	Knq
Charles	208	Alb
Charles	63	Chr
David	883	Yrk
Edward	348	Fqr
Eliza.	671	Glc
Elizabeth	171	Alb
Elizabth.	919	Nrf
Elizebeth	16	Isw
Ellender	300	Frf
Elliott	455	Grn
Ezekiel	132	Sth
Fras.	672	Glc
Fras., Senr.	672	Glc
Gideon	64	Chr
Henry	63	Chr

Henry	11	Wod
Jasper	298	Frf
Jno.	309	Ldn
John	799	Bck
John	105	Cmb
John	302	Frf
John	455	Grn
John	176	Knq
John	728	Nls
John	8	Wod
Joseph	6	Wod
Lucy, Mrs.	64	Chr
Magehe	15	Hnr
Mary	799	Bck
Mary	455	Grn
Moses	787	Bck
Nowill	281	Amh
Rebeccah	302	Ldn
Robert	455	Grn
Salley	57	Chs
Samuel	79	Jff
Samuel	728	Nls
Samuel	585	Pre
Samuel F., Maj.	64	Chr
Seth	109	Spt
Sharp, Senr.	585	Pre
Sion	63	Chr
Thomas	64	Chr
Thomas	455	Grn
Thomas H.	64	Chr
William	774	Bck
William	802	Bck
William	300	Frf
William	728	Nls
William, Jr.	799	Bck
see Spercer		
Spenglar, Anthony	222	Shn
Spengler, Philip	255	Shn
Spenny, Benja.	75	Clp
Js., Jr.	79	Clp
Js., Sr.	79	Clp
Spenser, James	815	Hmp
Jane	172	Alb
John	814	Hmp
Thomas	771	Hmp
Wm.	155	Sth
Spercer, David	10	Wod
Sperrer, John	728	Wsh
Sperry, John	405	Ags
Nichs.	79	Clp
Thomas, Christians-		
burg	619	Mnt
Spery, Elizabeth	513	Frd
Ephraim	857	Sth
Jacob	541	Frd
John	508	Frd
Nicholas	516	Frd
Speser, Michl.	656	Btt
Spew, Nicholas	571	Brk
Sphar, Henry	746	Wsh
Sphear, James	694	Wsh
John	713	Wsh
Spher, William	694	Wsh
Spicely, James	160	Dnw
Spicer, Benja.	79	Clp
Benjamin	869	Hnv
David	870	Hnv
Jno.	308	Ldn
Moses	75	Clp
Randolph	76	Clp
Thomas	764	Hmp
William	765	Hmp
William, Junr.	369	Fqr
William, Senr.	369	Fqr
Wim.	869	Hnv
Spickard, George	576	Mnr
George	579	Mnr
Henry	653	Btt
Mary	655	Btt
Phillip	655	Btt

Spicklemire, Abraham	652	Mnt
Leonard	652	Mnt
Spicknal, Leonard	67	Jff
Spigg, John	910	Hrr
Spignal, Bazil	553	Frd
Clement	539	Frd
Spikard, Thomas	638	Gls
Spiker, Samuel	220	Shn
Spilkey, Godfrey	28	Rcm
Spiller, Ann	360	Lnc
Elizabeth	385	Fqr
George	822	Bck
George	832	Bck
Joseph	185	Shn
Philip	296	Frf
Philip	517	Prw
Spillman, Elizabeth	796	Hmp
Susanna	525	Prw
William	794	Hmp
Williams	796	Hmp
Spilman, Alce	71	Clp
Henry	71	Clp
Jacob	573	Frd
Jno., Captn.	71	Clp
Jno., Jr.	72	Clp
Jno., Sen.	71	Clp
Jno. R.	74	Clp
John	217	Kng
Merriman	46	Stf
Php.	72	Clp
Robt.	77	Clp
Ths.	71	Clp
Wm.	360	Lnc
see Spitman		
Spindle, Adam	381	Ags
Barbee	199	Ess
John	104	Spt
Letticy	90	Spt
Lewis	925	Crl
Mordecai	197	Ess
Philip	927	Crl
Ths.	72	Clp
William	90	Spt
Spindler, ---, & Crozel	2	Hnr
Spinker, Elizabeth	925	Crl
Spinkley, Henry	226	Shn
Spinks, Chandler	297	Frf
Gerard	525	Prw
Rolly	504	Prw
Spinner, Jesse	302	Amh
John	229	Aml
John	420	Rnd
Richard	173	Alb
Spinny see Spenny		
Spires, Adam	663	Sss
Ann M.	70	Acc
Anne	532	Prg
Charles	663	Sss
Charles	665	Sss
Henry	663	Sss
John	663	Sss
John, Sr.	663	Sss
Patience	56	Acc
Tabitha	55	Acc
Spirlock, Judy	920	Nrf
Spitfatham, John	257	Amh
Spitler, Abraham	190	Shn
Danl.	657	Btt
Jacob	384	Ags
Jacob	656	Btt
Jacob, jr.	384	Ags
John	381	Ags
Joseph	656	Btt
Josh.	656	Btt
Michl.	657	Btt
Spitman, Geo.	360	Lnc
see Spilman		
Spitser, Andre	254	Shn
Henry	254	Shn
Spitter, John, Junr.	224	Shn

John, Senr.	224	Shn
Mathias	224	Shn
Spittle, Richard	527	Prw
Spitzer, Andrew	37	Rcm
Andw.	2	Rcm
Danl.	24	Rcm
Henry, (Jr.)	27	Rcm
Henry, (Sen.)	27	Rcm
Philip	10	Rcm
Spivey, Britain	856	Sth
Jacob	23	Isw
John [2]	690	Br
Stephen	21	Isw
Thomas	23	Isw
William	855	Sth
Sponcelor, Daniel	852	Wth
Spoon, John	468	Frn
Peter	570	Frd
Spooner, George W.	98	Spt
George W. B.	120	Spt
Mary	159	Sth
Sporr, Dolly	569	Brk
Henry	569	Brk
Spots, Andrew	97	Jff
Spotswood, Alexander	88	Spt
Elliott	73	Clp
George W.	88	Spt
Spott, Wm.	247	Ldn
see Shott		
Spotts, George	854	Wth
Jacob	385	Ags
Jacob, jr.	378	Ags
John	385	Ags
Spottswood, D.	328	Dnw
N.	328	Dnw
Robt.	161	Dnw
Spraach see Shraach		
Spradlin, Edward	461	Frn
John	172	Alb
Richard	172	Alb
Spradling, Abner	481	Bdf
Benjamin	481	Bdf
Lucy	728	Nls
Nathan	208	Alb
Susanna	728	Nls
William	481	Bdf
Sprag, Mary	302	Frf
Spraggins, John	943	Chc
Mary	768	Nwk
Nathaniel	953	Chc
Rebecca	19	Ntt
Thomas	943	Chc
William	950	Chc
Spraker, Charles	41	Rcm
Sprales, John	735	Wsh
Spratla, Richd.	921	Nrf
Spratley, Jenny, (F.N.)	38	Isw
John	615	Srr
Walter, junr.	616	Srr
Walter, Senr.	616	Srr
William	615	Srr
Spratt, Henry	474	Pra
Isaac	729	Wsh
John	853	Wth
Spreker, Christopher	857	Wth
George	857	Wth
Spriddle, Betty, a free mulatto	994	Nrt
Nancy, a free mulatto	996	Nrt
Sprig, William	534	Frd
Sprigg, Corbin	178	Elc
Osburn	796	Hmp
Zachariah	2	Oho
Sprigs, Eli	132	Hnr
Epm.	359	Lnc
Nancy	995	Nrt
Nathan	359	Lnc
Thos.	597	Brk
Spring, Adam	287	Ldn
Frederick	292	Ldn

Fridk.	291	Ldn
Gasper	287	Ldn
Jacob	287	Ldn
Nicholas	300	Rck
Springer, Jno.	540	Mnn
Springle, Anthoney	106	Jff
Springston, Jacob	421	Rnd
Sprinkle, Henry	852	Wth
Jacob	852	Wth
William	2	Rcm
Wm.	737	Wsh
Sprint, Patrick	54	Jff
Spriss see Sprigg		
Spritsman, Fred.	541	Mnn
Sproles, James	744	Wsh
John	744	Wsh
Mary	752	Wsh
Saml.	734	Wsh
see Sprales		
Sprouce, Benjamin	173	Alb
John	173	Alb
John, Jnr.	173	Alb
Mary	173	Alb
Peter	172	Alb
Tandy	171	Alb
Zachariah	172	Alb
Sproul, John	381	Ags
Wm.	380	Ags
Wm.	293	Rck
Sproule, Wm.	532	Brk
Sprout, Jane	510	Frd
Sprowel, James	590	Mnr
Sprowl, Elizabeth	854	Wth
Hazlet	854	Wth
James	440	Bth
John	432	Bth
Margaret	440	Bth
Robert	854	Wth
Spry, Jas.	796	Nrf
Spukaugle, Jacob	269	Ldn
Spunn, Jos.	810	Nrf
Spunogle see Spukaugle		
Spurgen, Jas.	535	Mnn
Jessee	535	Mnn
Jno.	535	Mnn
Jona.	535	Mnn
Mary	536	Mnn
Spurgin, William	726	Wsh
Spurling, Elisha	786	Wst
James	785	Wst
Jesse	919	Hrr
Reuben	786	Wst
William	304	Frf
William	786	Wst
Spurr, William	19	Hnr
Spyker, Benj.	720	Wsh
Davd.	760	Wsh
Squaire, Isabella	172	Alb
Squires, Acy	951	Hrr
Elizabeth	392	Fqr
John [2]	480	Bdf
John	482	Bdf
Levi	480	Bdf
Martin	391	Fqr
Micajah	391	Fqr
Neh.	536	Mnn
Rubin	542	Mnn
Thomas	480	Bdf
Uriah	482	Bdf
Srader, Peter	853	Wth
Phillip	853	Wth
Srawbaugh, David	283	Ldn
Srey see Sorey		
Sriem, George	246	Shn
Srieves, Goseph	934	Hrr
Sriver, Jno.	539	Mnn
Srusbury, William	481	Bdf
St...ngton, William	443	Bth
St...rd, Armsted.	450	Mth
Staats, Jessee	536	Mnn

Stackey, Isaac	259	Ldn	Isaac	420	Rnd	see Standley		
Jos.	259	Ldn	Jacob	416	Rnd	Stanly, Abel	649	Mnt
Stackhouse, Hazwell	540	Prg	Jacob	423	Rnd	Abraham	649	Mnt
John	917	Hrr	John	416	Rnd	Archelaus	553	Brk
Stackton, Aaron	14	Knw	John, of ...	422	Rnd	George	481	Bdf
Stacy, Jane	664	Sss	Velt	422	Rnd	Harris	6	Knw
Ro. D.	671	Glc	Wm.	428	Rnd	Jacob	941	Hrr
Stadler, Jacob	383	Fqr	Stalp, Henry	23	Rcm	Jonathan	953	Hrr
John	512	Prw	John	23	Rcm	Thomas	953	Hrr
Stadly, Frdk.	552	Brk	Jonas	23	Rcm	Wm.	953	Hrr
see Stedly			Staltman, Peleg	961	Hrr	Stannard, Elizabeth H.	116	Spt
Stafard, Levi	742	Wsh	Staly, Jacob	964	Hrr	Larkin	67	Spt
Stafford, Edward	637	Gls	Stalzer, Phillip	417	Rnd	Stanners, William	359	Fqr
George	638	Gls	Stamback, Litty. E.,			Stannins, George	331	Dnw
James, SR	638	Gls	& Co.	328	Dnw	Stansbery, Fran	542	Mnn
James, Jur.	636	Gls	Michl.	660	Btt	Stant, James	62	Acc
Jno.	536	Mnn	Phillip	660	Btt	Stanton, Andrew	585	Pre
Jno., Jr.	538	Mnn	Stamp, Samuel	21	Isw	Champ	404	Mds
John, Sen.	637	Gls	Stamper, Catharine	470	Mdd	James	160	Dnw
James, Sen.	638	Gls	John	469	Mdd	James	664	Sss
John, Ed	638	Gls	Nelson	470	Mdd	John	162	Dnw
John, H	638	Gls	Saml., Urbanna	470	Mdd	John, jr.	162	Dnw
John, Jur.	638	Gls	Samuel	474	Mdd	Thos.	2	Hnr
Jos.	536	Mnn	Stanard, James	470	Mdd	William	38	Rcm
Joseph	817	Hmp	Stanback, Geo. H.	21	Hnr	Stanworth, Tho.	179	Elc
Richard	817	Hmp	Stanberry see Stansbery			Stapels, John	34	Hnr
Seth	536	Mnn	Standafer, Luke	487	Frn	Staples, Beverly A.	796	Bck
Tho.	538	Mnn	Standard, Rebecca	178	Knq	Charles	789	Bck
Thomas	637	Gls	Standfield, John	162	Dnw	David	807	Bck
Thomas	638	Gls	Standiford, John	678	Br	Eli	359	Lnn
Thos.	821	Nrf	Skelton	678	Br	Henry	217	Kng
Thos., Sr.	821	Nrf	Standish, John	64	Chr	Mary	277	Amh
Wm. [?]	799	Nrf	Standleg, John	926	Crl	Nath.	12	Hnr
Stag, Thomas	948	Chc	Standley, Joseph	637	Gls	Saml.	118	Hnr
Stagg, John	130	Hnr	Joshua	357	Lnn	Samuel	277	Amh
Stags, George	805	Hmp	Moses	922	Crl	Samuel	729	Nls
Stainback, Becky	330	Dnw	Obadiah	862	Hnv	Thomas	360	Lnn
Nicholas	542	Prg	Solomon	862	Hnv	William	278	Amh
Robertson	733	Brn	Strangman	862	Hnv	William	118	Hnr
Tabitha	548	Prg	Thomas	822	Bck	William, Jr.	118	Hnr
William	325	Dnw	Thomas	489	Frn	Wm.	217	Kng
Wm.	733	Brn	Thos.	154	Sth	Stapleton, James	617	Mnt
Wm. H.	540	Prg	William, Jr.	492	Frn	see Crutchfield		
Stainpove, Ann	873	Sth	William, Sr.	489	Frn	Star, Anthony	115	Spt
Stair, Henry, Sr.	656	Btt	see Stanley			Benjamin	561	Brk
Stakes, Elijah	882	Yrk	Standoff, Henry	278	Rck	Starick, John	17	Oho
William	58	Acc	John	277	Rck	Stark, Ann	21	Hnr
Wm.	189	Elc	Stanford, John	16	Wod	Belfield	455	Grn
Stalcopp, John	729	Wsh	Joseph	77	Jff	Benj.	702	Wsh
Stalcup, Israel	816	Hmp	Stanforth, Richd.	228	Shn	Daingerfield	472	Pra
Stalcupp, Peter	742	Wsh	Stanger, Jacob	665	Mnt	Daniel	72	Spt
Staley, Abram	466	Frn	Stanhope, Jno.	303	Frf	Edwin	920	Nrf
Andw.	654	Btt	William	77	Jff	James	382	Fqr
Barbara	518	Frd	Wm.	920	Nrf	Mary	5	Knw
Daniel	107	Jff	Stankack see Slankack			Thomas	422	Msn
Jacob	89	Jff	Stanlese, Wm.	944	Hrr	Thos.	381	Ags
Jacob	90	Jff	Stanley, Ann	637	Gls	William	501	Brk
James	545	Brk	Charles	862	Hnv	Starke, Elizabeth	882	Hnv
John	107	Jff	Ferebee	475	Pra	James	511	Prw
Peter	89	Jff	Isaac	863	Hnv	John	844	Hnv
Peter, Jr.	654	Btt	James	17	Wod	John	1	Knw
Stepen	104	Jff	John	551	Brk	John	41	Stf
Stephen	89	Jff	John	87	Spt	Joseph	20	Stf
see Stayley			John	17	Wod	Lewis	731	Brn
Stalker, Henry	673	Glc	Jonathan	441	Flv	Margaret	506	Prw
Stall, Jesse	92	Jff	Joseph	551	Brk	Richard	897	Hnv
John	527	Brk	Joshua	847	Hnv	Thos.	873	Hnv
Stallard, Davd.	73	Clp	Michael	862	Hnv	William	384	Fqr
Randolph	73	Clp	Moses	27	Hnr	William	47	Stf
Ths.	73	Clp	Pleast.	659	Btt	Wm.	162	Dnw
Stallings, Abraham	575	Frd	Poemcy	116	Hnr	Starkey, Elijah	464	Frn
Benja.	554	Frd	Rebecca	863	Hnv	Jonathan	464	Frn
James	37	Isw	Sabra	68	Chs	Joshua	465	Frn
Newman	600	Frd	Thomas	18	Wod	William	105	Cmb
Stallions, Hutcha	254	Shn	Thos.	857	Hnv	William	482	Frn
Stalman, Lewis	951	Hrr	Thos., Jnr.	862	Hnv	Starks, James	946	Hrr
Stalnaker, Andrew	420	Rnd	Thos., S.J.	864	Hnv	Robert	946	Hrr
Bostan	418	Rnd	Ursula	864	Hnv	Wm.	431	Flv
Bostan	422	Rnd	William	74	Spt	Starky, Edward	780	Hmp
George	422	Rnd	Wim.	862	Hnv	Frederick	763	Hmp

George	780	Hmp	William	71	Jff	Steenbergen, Peter	193	Shn
John	114	Cmb	William	85	Jff	William	193	Shn
Joseph	854	Wth	Steagall, Thos.	762	Brn	Steep, Jacob	191	Shn
William	788	Hmp	Steagale, Bottom	731	Brn	John	189	Shn
Starling, Aaron	60	Acc	Steal, Jno.	542	Mnn	Steer, Benj.	300	Ldn
Andw.	535	Mnn	Steale, Cloe	305	Frf	Isaac [2]	291	Ldn
Henry	124	Acc	Stealy, Jno.	541	Mnn	Isaac	300	Ldn
James	171	Alb	Steams, Henry	222	Shn	Isaac	313	Ldn
John	56	Acc	Stearman, Wm.	654	Mnt	James	553	Frd
John	122	Acc	Stears, John	102	Spt	Jno.	284	Ldn
Josius	123	Acc	Stearts, Abraham	208	Shn	Jno., J.	284	Ldn
Polly	60	Acc	Steatt see Sleatt			Joseph	300	Ldn
Samuel	125	Acc	Stedly, John	552	Brk	Steerman, John	809	Hmp
Samuel	126	Acc	see Stadly			see Sturman		
see Slarling			Stedman, John	882	Yrk	Steffey, John	855	Wth
Starn, John	762	Hmp	Steed, Ann	761	Brn	Philip	26	Rcm
Joseph	829	Hmp	Henry	2	Wod	Steffy, Abraham	856	Wth
Starner, George	819	Hmp	Jesse	172	Shn	Henry, Junr.	856	Wth
Starnes, Adam	742	Wsh	John	18	Oho	Henry, Senr.	856	Wth
Saml.	729	Wsh	Mark	762	Brn	Joseph	856	Wth
Starpless, Jnn.	919	Nrf	Mary	537	Frd	Michael	856	Wth
Starr, Elizabeth	913	Hrr	Thomas	530	Frd	Peter	857	Wth
Fredk.	522	Brk	Steel, Alexander	877	Cmp	Stegall, Aaron	358	Lnn
John	913	Hrr	Ebenezar	517	Brk	Allen	358	Lnn
Richard	491	Frn	Edith	413	Bth	John	358	Lnn
Starratt, Jno.	542	Mnn	Edmond	856	Wth	Mastin	650	Mnt
Starry, Daniel	561	Brk	Elizabeth	869	Cmp	Randolph	358	Lnn
Nicholas	56	Jff	George	656	Btt	Stegar, Hance	586	Pre
Startsen, John	952	Hrr	George	877	Cmp	M., Mrs.	330	Dnw
State, John	734	Brn	James	74	Clp	Samuel	824	Bck
Randolph	731	Brn	James	565	Frd	Thos.	229	Aml
Staten, Thomas	291	Rck	James	856	Wth	Steger, Francis	4	Pwh
Stater, Joseph	402	Mds	Jas.	540	Mnn	Hanse	4	Pwh
Statham, James	789	Bck	Jas.	542	Mnn	Isham	4	Pwh
Wm. D.	447	Flv	John	596	Frd	Peyton	4	Pwh
see Slatham			John	603	Frd	Samuel	4	Pwh
Statia, Laurence	733	Brn	John	10	Knw	Samuel, jr.	4	Pwh
Statler, Abm., Jr.	660	Btt	John	226	Pnd	Skip	128	Cmb
Jno.	281	Ldn	John	699	Wsh	Thos. H.	116	Cmb
Jno.	541	Mnn	Margt.	551	Brk	William	824	Bck
Statom, Charles	859	Cmp	Maudoves	251	Ldn	William	99	Cmb
Richmond	865	Cmp	Richard	217	Kng	William	12	Pwh
Staton, Andrew M.	274	Amh	Robert	514	Frd	Stegletter, George	12	Rcm
Archibald	796	Bck	Robert	856	Wth	Steivens, Lucey	881	Sth
Ayres	125	Acc	Robt.	658	Btt	Steivenson, Nathl.	847	Sth
Benjamin	780	Bck	Samuel	552	Frd	Samul.	882	Sth
Charles	796	Bck	Tho.	542	Mnn	Steivinson, Mary	859	Sth
Cornelius	798	Bck	Thomas	565	Frd	Stell, Dennis	160	Dnw
Elijah	728	Nls	Thos.	537	Mnn	George	160	Dnw
George	122	Acc	William	699	Wsh	Godfry	541	Mnn
Isaac	799	Bck	Wm.	129	Hnr	Jereh.	162	Dnw
James	122	Acc	Zeah	426	Msn	John	162	Dnw
James, Senr.	797	Bck	Steele, Agness	280	Rck	Jos.	162	Dnw
John	126	Acc	Danl.	307	Rck	Shadrach	162	Dnw
Rane	796	Bck	David	385	Ags	Geo. W.	162	Dnw
Warrington, Jun.	124	Acc	George	591	Mnr	Stelwell, Stephen	568	Brk
William	124	Acc	Gerard	297	Frf	Stembridg, John	360	Lnn
William	304	Amh	James	385	Ags	Stemple, Dav.	536	Mnn
William, of G	124	Acc	James	591	Mnr	John	536	Mnn
see Slatham			John	379	Ags	Martin	536	Mnn
Statson, Elizth.	919	Nrf	John	10	Oho	Stenson, Mary	750	Wsh
Staunton, Bevely	383	Ags	John	785	Wst	Step, Fanny	541	Brk
Mary	857	Sth	Jonathan	502	Prw	Joseph	877	Cmp
Thos.	381	Ags	Mary	379	Ags	see Stipe		
see Slaughter			Robt.	385	Ags	Stepe, Anthony	70	Jff
Staves, George	891	Hnv	Saml.	379	Ags	Stephans, Anna	334	Dnw
see Slaves			Saml., jr.	387	Ags	Robert	173	Alb
Stavins, Coonrod	689	Wsh	Samuel	379	Fqr	William	208	Alb
Staws, Geo. F.	20	Hnr	Thomas	573	Mnr	Stephason, Andrew	35	Hnr
Stayar, Jacob	110	Spt	Wm. [2]	410	Ags	Stephen, Albert	545	Brk
Stayley, Jacob	654	Btt	Wm.	302	Frf	Alexr.	523	Brk
Peter, Sr.	656	Btt	Wm., (MR)	381	Ags	Wm.	385	Ags
see Staley			Steely, Abraham	856	Wth	Stephens, Abraham	171	Alb
Ste..., Henry	562	Mnr	Jacob	856	Wth	Alex	326	Dnw
Steadman, James	69	Jff	John	857	Wth	Amos	689	Br
James	71	Jff	Martin	857	Wth	Augustine	541	Prg
James	73	Jff	Valentine	854	Wth	Benjamin	463	Frn
John	73	Jff	see Sheely			Benjn.	546	Prg
Mary	681	Wrw	Steembock, Martin	181	Shn	Brian	603	Frd
Thomas	73	Jff	Steen, William	850	Cmp	Celia	518	Frd

Charles	23	Isw	George	564	Mnr	Sters, Rachel	115	Spt
D...d., ...	713	Wsh	George	587	Mnr	Stetman, Jacob	107	Jff
David	569	Frd	George	868	Sth	Stetson, Benj.	20	Hnr
David	770	Hmp	Harrison	143	Sth	Steuart, W., Jr.	541	Mnn
David	540	Prg	James	57	Jff	see Stuart		
Dennis	102	Jff	James	224	Pnd	Stevard, Charles	245	Ldn
Ezra	681	Br	James	211	Shn	Charles, J.	245	Ldn
George	846	Hnv	Jas.	535	Brk	Stevart, Wm.	261	Ldn
George	421	Msn	Jere.	879	Sth	Stevens, ---, Widow	921	Nrf
George	423	Msn	Jesse	152	Sth	Absm.	919	Nrf
George	596	Mnr	Jdhn	533	Brk	Absm., 2nd.	921	Nrf
Giles	598	Brk	John	13	Knw	Ann	178	Knq
Henry	566	Frd	John	211	Shn	Bowler	470	Mdd
Henry	854	Wth	John	845	Sth	Edmund	469	Mdd
Isaac	689	Br	John	663	Sss	Edwd.	73	Clp
James	799	Bck	John	5	Wod	Ephraim	388	Fqr
James	99	Jff	John	852	Wth	George M.	93	Spt
James	786	Wst	Joseph	686	Br	Henry	482	Bdf
Jas.	473	Pra	Joseph	558	Frd	Henry	290	Ldn
Jas.	752	Wsh	Joseph	666	Sss	James	405	Mds
Jeremiah	995	Nrt	Josiah	143	Sth	James	729	Nls
Jeremy	786	Wst	Leml.	155	Sth	James	23	Oho
Jno.	536	Mnn	Leml.	845	Sth	James	85	Spt
Jno.	542	Prg	Levie	11	Wod	James	87	Spt
Jno., Ser.	547	Prg	Lucy	157	Sth	James, Ju.	729	Nls
John	56	Acc	Lucy	879	Sth	Jno.	74	Clp
John	775	Bck	Margret	219	Pnd	Jno.	671	Glc
John	98	Jff	Martin	852	Sth	Jno.	314	Ldn
John	562	Mnr	Michal	547	Frd	John	922	Crl
John	585	Pre	Michl.	867	Sth	John	727	Nls
John	17	Wod	Mills	6	Isw	John	86	Spt
John, Sen.	41	Isw	Robert	124	Acc	John	87	Spt
Jones	532	Prg	Salley	143	Sth	John	733	Wsh
Joseph	533	Prg	Sally	144	Sth	Leven	272	Ldn
Josiah	474	Pra	Thomas	682	Br	Magaret	109	Spt
Julias	850	Hnv	Thomas A.	63	Chr	Mary	922	Crl
Laurance	853	Wth	William	60	Jff	Mary B.	74	Spt
Lewis	541	Frd	William	80	Jff	Matt.	883	Yrk
Lewis	565	Frd	William	222	Shn	Nathaniel	87	Spt
Lewis	26	Rcm	Willis	664	Sss	Richard	23	Stf
Lois	681	Br	Wm.	579	Mnr	Sally	105	Spt
Mary	57	Acc	Wm.	150	Sth	Samuel	328	Dnw
Mary	405	Ags	Stephins, David	631	Mnt	Sarah	924	Crl
Mary	518	Frd	John	656	Mnt	Thomas	355	Fqr
Mary	218	Kng	Peter	631	Mnt	Thomas	177	Knq
Molley	995	Nrt	Thomas	101	Jff	Vincen	405	Mds
Nancy	122	Acc	Stephison, Daniel	905	Hrr	Warrington	807	Nrf
Nathl.	847	Hnv	Stepinger, John	226	Shn	William	481	Bdf
Peter	578	Frd	Stepleton, Sarah	618	Mnt	William	355	Fqr
Rebecca	546	Prg	Steps, Frederick	442	Bth	William	99	Spt
Richd.	359	Lnc	Stepter, William	10	Knw	Wm.	74	Clp
Robert	501	Brk	Steptoe, Elizabeth	470	Mdd	Wm.	919	Nrf
Robert	713	Gch	James	864	Cmp	Wm. R.	671	Glc
Robert	104	Jff	James, Est. in Bed-			see Stavins, Steivens		
Ruth	533	Prg	ford	483	Bdf	Stevenson, Andw.	304	Frf
Susannah	59	Acc	James, jr.	483	Bdf	Benjamin	403	Fqr
Thomas	59	Acc	Sterling, Joseph	119	Spt	Carter L.	112	Spt
Thomas	34	Hnr	see Corr, Fowlkes, Niblett,			David	12	Knw
Thomas	218	Kng	Starling			James	403	Fqr
Thomas	314	Ldn	Sterm, Nicholas	429	Rnd	James	112	Spt
Thomas	17	Wod	Stermbough, John	429	Bth	John	433	Bth
Thomas	854	Wth	Stern, David	926	Crl	Robt.	11	Hnr
Thomas, Jr.	775	Bck	Elizabeth	925	Crl	Turner	920	Nrf
Thos.	660	Btt	George	257	Shn	see Steivenson, Steivinson		
Waltr.	921	Nrf	James	192	Shn	Stever, Geo., Sr.	655	Btt
William	682	Br	Peter	859	Cmp	Michl.	655	Btt
William	775	Bck	William	926	Crl	Stevins, Edward	388	Fqr
William, Jr.	18	Isw	Yelverton	926	Crl	George	600	Mnt
William, Sen.	17	Isw	Sterne, Francis	162	Dnw	Robert	173	Alb
Wm.	654	Btt	John	27	Stf	Sirly	117	Hnr
Wm.	734	Wsh	Lidia	62	Stf	Stevison, James	163	Shn
see Stephins			Sterns see Kerns			Steward, ---, & C.	11	Rcm
Stephenson, Amos	149	Sth	Sterret, Fanny	504	Brk	Allen	380	Fqr
Andw.	303	Frf	James	504	Brk	Andrew	54	Acc
Ann	783	Hmp	Sterrett, Alexa.	381	Ags	Ann	218	Kng
Charles	149	Sth	Henry	384	Ags	Ann	919	Nrf
Chls.	846	Sth	John	384	Ags	Archabald	79	Jff
David	385	Ags	Robt.	379	Ags	Armstead	445	Mth
Elizabeth	5	Wod	William	427	Msn	Asa	161	Dnw
George	698	Br	Wm.	384	Ags	Charles	408	Fqr

Name	Pg	Co
Chs.	311	Ldn
James	56	Acc
James	178	Knq
James	261	Ldn
James, of A.	55	Acc
Jno., free negro	70	Chs
John	61	Acc
John	64	Chr
John	63	Jff
John	768	Nwk
John, (FB)	1	Pwh
Joseph, jr.	79	Clp
Lucy	768	Nwk
Robert	8	Hnr
Saml.	660	Btt
Samuel	69	Chr
Thomas	768	Nwk
Thomas E.	768	Nwk
William	177	Knq
William, Jr.	380	Fqr
William, Senr.	386	Fqr
Wm.	213	Ess
see St...rd, Stweard		
Stewart, ---, Muter &	2	Hnr
Alexr.	798	Nrf
Benjamin	687	Br
Benjamin	90	Spt
Betsy	331	Dnw
Betsy	333	Dnw
Betsy	334	Dnw
Brice	499	Frn
Caleb	733	Brn
Catharine	133	Cmb
Charles	482	Bdf
Charles	215	Ess
Charles	575	Frd
Charles	120	Spt
Charles	663	Sss
Charles, jr.	22	Stf
Charles, Sr.	25	Stf
Chas.	797	Nrf
Chs.	72	Clp
Constantine	481	Bdf
Daniel	378	Fqr
David	687	Br
David	500	Frn
David	7	Knw
Dempsey	770	Brn
Edmund	455	Grn
Edward	406	Mds
Ezekiel	331	Dnw
George	958	Hrr
George	90	Spt
George	747	Wsh
Henry	792	Nrf
Henry, (F.Black)	482	Bdf
Hugh	14	Oho
James	678	Br
James	852	Cmp
James	498	Frn
James	14	Oho
James	208	Shn
James	701	Wsh
James, (F.Black)	483	Bdf
James, Jr.	498	Frn
James, of A. [of T.?]	26	Stf
James, Sr., of C. L.	54	Stf
James N.	23	Stf
Jas.	815	Nrf
Jesse	615	Srr
Jessee	481	Bdf
Jno.	72	Clp
John	775	Bck
John	791	Bck
John	832	Bck
John	326	Dnw
John	330	Dnw
John	336	Dnw
John	494	Frn
John	455	Grn
John	816	Hmp
John	2	Oho
John	20	Oho
John	81	Spt
John [2]	90	Spt
John	112	Spt
John	716	Wsh
John	742	Wsh
John	786	Wst
John, Senr.	835	Bck
John, (W)	818	Bck
John B.	616	Srr
John L.	728	Nls
John M.	257	Amh
Joseph [2]	71	Spt
Joseph	736	Wsh
Joseph	10	Wod
Joseph, Sr.	75	Clp
Joshua	330	Dnw
Josiah	57	Chs
Lazarus	597	Brk
Luke	854	Cmp
Mary	327	Dnw
Mary	880	Hnv
Mary	921	Nrf
Maryanne	504	Prw
Mathew	960	Hrr
Max.	792	Nrf
Moses	69	Spt
Nurcy	689	Wsh
Nancy	330	Dnw
Nancy	331	Dnw
Nathaniel	482	Bdf
Natl.	75	Clp
Peney, a woman of coler	707	Wsh
Peter	161	Dnw
Pheoby	328	Dnw
Pressy	334	Dnw
Richard	455	Grn
Richard	786	Wst
Rob.	539	Mnn
Robert	332	Dnw
Robert	464	Frn
Robert	522	Frd
Robert	4	Oho
Robert	6	Oho
Robert	15	Oho
Robt.	834	Nrf
Robt.	701	Wsh
Saml.	526	Prw
Saml.	687	Br
Samuel	615	Srr
Stephen	688	Br
Susannah	480	Bdf
Thomas	687	Br
Thomas	791	Bck
Thomas	851	Cmp
Thomas	331	Dnw
Thomas	586	Frd
Thomas	586	Pre
Thomas, jr.	482	Bdf
William	328	Dnw
William	464	Frn
William	525	Frd
William	804	Hmp
William	6	Oho
William	72	Spt
William	96	Spt
William	663	Sss
William	701	Wsh
William B.	86	Spt
Wm.	770	Brn
Wm.	960	Hrr
Wm.	4	Hnr
Wm.	798	Nrf
Wm.	730	Wsh
see Stuwrod, Stweart		
Stewert, Chs.	538	Mnn
Sthreshley, John	925	Crl
Robert	925	Crl
William	927	Crl
Stibbin, Benjamin	684	Br
Sticher, Wiliam	34	Hnr
Stickle, Geo.	262	Ldn
Jacob	384	Ags
Stickleman, John	384	Ags
Philip	656	Mnt
Stickley, Abraham	564	Frd
John	211	Shn
Joseph	208	Shn
Tobias	208	Shn
Stiers, William	420	Rnd
Stierwall, Peter	25	Hnr
Stife, Christian	590	Frd
Stiff, Hannah	437	Bth
Jacob	483	Bdf
James	481	Bdf
James	483	Bdf
James	469	Mdd
John	437	Bth
John, Jun.	483	Bdf
John B.	437	Bth
Susanna	469	Mdd
Thomas	470	Mdd
Thomas	505	Prw
William	499	Prw
Wm. N.	505	Prw
Stifle, Frederick	286	Ldn
John	286	Ldn
Margaret	728	Nls
Stifler, Jno.	352	Fqr
Jno., Ser.	403	Fqr
Stiger, John	354	Fqr
Price	216	Kng
William	590	Frd
William	351	Fqr
Stigler, David	590	Frd
James	574	Brk
John	1	Hnr
Stiles, Catherine	10	Ntt
Geo. A.	328	Dnw
Jas.	616	Srr
John	541	Mnn
Jdhn, Senr.	541	Mnn
Stephen	927	Crl
Wm.	326	Dnw
Still, Allen	2	Knw
Dennis	832	Bck
George	880	Cmp
Isham	2	Knw
Jacob	13	Knw
James	858	Cmp
James	785	Wst
John		
Thomas		
see Slitt		
Stillwell, Obadiah	4	Oho
Stilwel, Stephen, Sr.	557	Brk
Stimmell, Hannah	802	Hmp
Stimson, Wm.	74	Clp
Stinebough, Jno.	536	Mnn
Stinnett, Benjamin	296	Amh
Charles	296	Amh
William	296	Amh
Stinson, Archibald	781	Bck
Cary	791	Bck
Cary, Jr.	793	Bck
David	835	Bck
Isaac	652	Mnt
Jacob	637	Gls
James	812	Bck
James	164	Shn
James, Sr.	546	Brk
Jas.	557	Brk
John	834	Bck
John, ...	835	Bck
Jonathan	124	Acc

Wm.	538	Mnn	German Y.	358	Lnn	Josias	512	Prw
Wm.	652	Mnt	Hennery	360	Lnn	Kindsey	209	Alb
see Stevison			Henry	586	Pre	Lemuel	475	Pra
Stioud see Stroud			James R.	10	Pwh	Lewes	488	Frn
Stip, George	562	Frd	Jas.	805	Nrf	Lewis	707	Wsh
Stipe, David	548	Frd	John	883	Yrk	Manoah	520	Prw
George	545	Frd	Jonathan	805	Nrf	Martha	860	Cmp
Henry	543	Frd	Jonathan, Jr.	805	Nrf	Martha	787	Wst
Stipp, John, Jnr.	88	Jff	Josiah	64	Chr	Mathew	849	Hnv
Susanna	90	Jff	Mary	809	Nrf	Menoah	481	Bdf
Stith, Andrew	731	Brn	Moses	664	Sss	Micajah	480	Bdf
Arianna	731	Brn	Nancy	665	Sss	Moses, (Overseer for		
Davi... B.	701	Brn	Peter	360	Lnn	Ed. Watts)	655	Btt
David B.	772	Brn	Richard	203	Ess	Peter	734	Brn
Drury	731	Brn	Thomas	360	Lnn	Peter	281	Ldn
Fanny	731	Brn	Thos.	805	Nrf	Peter	219	Pnd
Griffin	731	Brn	William [2]	360	Lnn	Peter, J.	220	Pnd
Griffin	156	Sth	Wm.	805	Nrf	Philip	59	Jff
Jaro, (M)	734	Brn	Young	64	Chr	Purssel	786	Wst
John	731	Brn	see McCaul, Tunstill			Rebeca	406	Mds
John	215	Kng	Stokesberry, Davd.	72	Clp	Richard	359	Lnn
Laurence	218	Kng	Jacob	72	Clp	Richard	20	Stf
Lucy	731	Brn	Wm.	72	Clp	Richd.	733	Brn
Nancy	731	Brn	Stoll see Stott			Richd.	475	Pra
Obadiah	731	Brn	Stone, Admire	482	Bdf	Robert, Snr.	177	Knq
Richd.	731	Brn	Affire	481	Bdf	Salley	177	Knq
Thomas	299	Rck	Alexander H.S.	20	Stf	Saml., Jr.	76	Clp
Thos.	731	Brn	Ann	359	Lnn	Saml., Sr.	76	Clp
Wm.	537	Mnn	Ann	60	Stf	Samuel	926	Crl
Stitzer, William	38	Rcm	Anthony	850	Hnv	Simon	473	Pra
Stivers, Peter	84	Spt	Asher	359	Lnn	Thomas	209	Alb
Stoakes, Christopher	671	Glc	Barton	24	Stf	Thomas	54	Chs
Francis	672	Glc	Benammie	283	Amh	Thomas	444	Flv
Lewis	672	Glc	Benjm.	360	Lnn	Thomas	359	Lnn
Thos.	672	Glc	Caleb	302	Frf	Thomas	475	Pra
Stoaks, Lucey	28	Hnr	Charles	41	Stf	Thomas	786	Wst
Stoback, Abm.	612	Mnt	Christian	226	Pnd	W. T.	919	Nrf
Stoball, Landis P.	101	Cmb	Daniel	300	Frf	William	480	Bdf
Stobaugh see Stobo			Daniel	443	Flv	William	880	Cmp
Stoblair, Alexa.	404	Ags	Daniel	176	Knq	William	352	Fqr
Stobo, Sarah	826	Nrf	Daniel	307	Ldn	William	178	Knq
Stock, Catharine	298	Ldn	Danl.	301	Frf	William	26	Stf
Stockdell, John	405	Mds	Danl., est.	60	Chs	William	759	Wsh
Nancey	405	Mds	Edwd.	301	Frf	William G.	112	Spt
Polly	405	Mds	Edwd.	313	Ldn	William S.	113	Spt
Stockdill, Robt.	379	Ags	Elijah	406	Mds	Wm.	439	Flv
Stockley, Hannah	122	Acc	Elizabeth	20	Stf	Wm.	541	Mnn
Stockly, Hannah	54	Acc	Fauntleroy	357	Fqr	see Stong		
Henry	122	Acc	Francis	301	Frf	Stoneaugel, Palser	217	Pnd
Levin	58	Acc	Francis	279	Ldn	Stoneburner, Andrew	29	Rcm
Levina	61	Acc	Geo.	78	Clp	Daniel	286	Ldn
Nathaniel	124	Acc	George	481	Bdf	Godfrey	242	Ldn
Nelly	123	Acc	Hen.	540	Mnn	Frederick	284	Ldn
Peggy	57	Acc	Henry	209	Alb	Jacob	242	Ldn
Spencer	59	Acc	Henry	817	Hmp	Jacob	287	Ldn
Stocks, William	210	Shn	Hezekiah	441	Flv	Jno.	286	Ldn
Stockton, Richard	460	Frn	Isaac	71	Clp	John	229	Shn
Stockwell, Jno.	537	Mnn	James	482	Bdf	Peter	287	Ldn
Stocus, Armisted	115	Spt	James	176	Knq	Philip	29	Rcm
Stoddart, Solo.	442	Flv	Jane	380	Fqr	Stoneham, Mary	728	Nls
Stodghill, Joel	571	Mnr	Jas.	474	Pra	Stoneking see Sloneking		
John	572	Mnr	Jathan	734	Brn	Stoneman, John	857	Wth
Stoenedvorth, Isaac	509	Brk	Jesse	60	Stf	Stoner, Abraham	14	Rcm
Stoers see Slovis			Jno.	921	Nrf	Danl.	659	Btt
Stogdale, James	856	Wth	Jno., Jr.	657	Btt	Henry	298	Rck
Stogdon, Phillip	208	Alb	Jno., (of Jno.)	476	Pra	Jacob	653	Btt
Stogel, James	850	Hnv	Jno., (of Richd.)	475	Pra	Michl.	689	Wsh
Stoggell, Susannah	440	Flv	Jno., [his] (Plantan.)	474	Pra	Saml.	31	Rcm
Stogton, Newbury	483	Bdf	Jno., (Pungo)	476	Pra	William	220	Shn
Stokeley, John	5	Wod	Jno., Sr.	654	Btt	Stonestreet, Basel	248	Ldn
Stokely, Thomas	1	Oho	John	209	Alb	Butler	415	Bth
Stoker, Jno.	541	Mnn	John	734	Brn	Edward	600	Frd
John	774	Hmp	John	358	Lnn	Stong, Jacob	511	Brk
William	774	Hmp	John	514	Prw	Stonger, John	857	Wth
Stokes, Ann	360	Lnn	John	721	Wsh	see Songer		
Bartlet	360	Lnn	John S.	503	Prw	Stonnel, Sally	505	Prw
Benja.	203	Ess	Johnson	474	Pra	Stonnell, James	113	Spt
Edmd.	205	Ess	Joseph	832	Hmp	Stonsiffer, Henry	405	Mds
Edward	325	Dnw	Joseph	304	Ldn	Stonstreet, Thomas	246	Ldn
Eliza	25	Hnr	Joshua	393	Rch	Stonum, George N.	397	Rch

311

Name	No.	Co.	Name	No.	Co.	Name	No.	Co.
Susannah	391	Rch	Thomas	930	Hrr	Mary	878	Cmp
William	408	Rch	Stoutemire, Bernard	28	Rcm	Mary	284	Rck
Stony, Harrass	481	Bdf	Casper	25	Rcm	Michael	893	Hnv
Stookey, Jacob	550	Brk	Dorathy	25	Rcm	Robert	481	Bdf
Stoop, Abraham	33	Rcm	Jacob	24	Rcm	Wm. C.	444	Flv
Elias	856	Wth	John	383	Ags	Stras, Wm.	128	Hnr
Stoops, Philip	303	Rck	Stoutsaberger, Jno.	287	Ldn	Stratner see Shotner		
Stoors, Wm.	189	Elc	Stovall, Elizabeth	863	Cmp	Stratten, Thos.	715	Gch
Stooter, Philip	7	Rcm	George	863	Cmp	Stratton, Archer	480	Bdf
Stoots, Elijah	10	Wod	John	878	Cmp	Edward	3	Pwh
Isaac	7	Wod	Stove, Chresley	256	Shn	Edward	6	Pwh
Stootzman, John	777	Hmp	Stoven, Chs.	252	Ldn	James	125	Cmb
Storer, Edward	873	Cmp	Stover, Abraham	204	Shn	James	14	Pwh
Godleb	410	Ags	Christian	256	Shn	Jno.	69	Chs
Storey, James	78	Clp	Daniel	824	Hmp	Jno.	921	Nrf
Wm.	77	Clp	Daniel	182	Shn	John	857	Cmp
Storie, Jacob	530	Frd	Danl.	661	Btt	John	445	Flv
Storke, Bailey W.	216	Kng	Davd.	75	Clp	John H.	615	Mnt
John	514	Prw	David	384	Ags	Joseph	860	Cmp
John	786	Wst	David	206	Shn	Mary	3	Pwh
Thomas	26	Stf	George	481	Bdf	Peter	228	Aml
William	786	Wst	Jacob	382	Ags	Peter	836	Bck
Wm.	216	Kng	Jacob	660	Btt	Robert	127	Cmb
Storrs, Benj.	189	Elc	Jacob	5	Knw	Thomas	480	Bdf
Storth, George	678	Br	Jacob	215	Shn	Thomas	69	Chs
Storts, Dinah	299	Frf	Jno.	661	Btt	William	480	Bdf
Story, Archibald	803	Bck	John	472	Frn	William	115	Cmb
Charles	150	Sth	John, (N.R.)	202	Shn	William	3	Pwh
Francis	5	Knw	Joseph	241	Shn	William, Capt.	3	Pwh
James	870	Sth	M.	379	Ags	Straughan, John C.	995	Nrt
John	150	Sth	Mary	202	Shn	Richard	995	Nrt
Lewis	128	Sth	Mathias	240	Shn	Thos.	473	Pra
Mary	406	Mds	Michael	240	Shn	Wm.	475	Pra
Pleasant	482	Bdf	Michl.	660	Btt	Straughder, Adam	786	Wst
Samuel	132	Sth	Obediah	489	Frn	Samuel L.	410	Rch
William	9	Knw	Paul	382	Ags	Thomas	101	Spt
Zacheus	129	Sth	Samuel	182	Shn	Straw, John	71	Jff
Stotler, Jacob	819	Hmp	Simon	382	Ags	Leonard	855	Wth
John	566	Brk	Wm.	660	Btt	Peter	853	Wth
John, Sr.	566	Brk	see Stove			see Strain		
Peter	566	Brk	Stow, Herbert	54	Chs	Strawder, Anthony	806	Hmp
Stott, Ebenezer	334	Dnw	John	63	Chr	John	806	Hmp
Eliza.	409	Rch	Peter	229	Aml	Strayer, Adam	512	Brk
Eppa.	408	Rch	William	68	Chr	Adam	227	Pnd
James	398	Rch	Stowe, Joel	161	Dnw	Cathl.	547	Brk
James	408	Rch	John, Senr.	161	Dnw	Jacob	199	Shn
John	29	Isw	Wiley	160	Dnw	John	253	Shn
John	407	Rch	Stowers, Adam	406	Mds	Streach, John	482	Bdf
Margerett	408	Rch	Coleman	366	Fqr	Stream, Henry	286	Ldn
Oliver	395	Rch	Lewis, free Molatto	5	Knw	Michael	283	Ldn
Rawley	824	Bck	Thomas	784	Wst	Street, Anthony	454	Frn
Thomas	30	Isw	Travis	637	Gls	Anthony	876	Hnv
Wm.	359	Lnc	Strachan, ...	331	Dnw	Brooks	578	Brk
see Slott, Stoll			Alex.	330	Dnw	Daniel	522	Prw
Stotts, Jacob	421	Msn	Alexd. G.	548	Prg	David	359	Lnn
Jacob	726	Wsh	Strader, John	924	Hrr	Dudley	112	Cmb
Joshua	853	Wth	Stradford, Thomas	817	Hmp	George	877	Hnv
Stottz, Abraham	421	Msn	Straghan, James	638	Gls	Henry	210	Ess
Stoug see Stong			Strahan, Wm.	535	Mnn	James	328	Dnw
Stouker, Peter	919	Nrf	Straight, Jacob	12	Oho	John	714	Gch
Stout, Amos	906	Hrr	Jno.	542	Mnn	John	469	Mdd
Cath	929	Hrr	Peter	542	Mnn	John	11	Pwh
Daniel	951	Hrr	Wm.	542	Mnn	John T.	357	Lnn
Davd.	688	Wsh	Straily, George	952	Hrr	Lucy	359	Lnc
Elizabeth	71	Clp	Strain, Agnes	299	Rck	Martha	920	Nrf
Hezekiah	936	Hrr	David	380	Ags	Mary	358	Lnn
Hezekiah [2]	948	Hrr	John	693	Br	Parke	876	Hnv
Isaiah	172	Alb	William	692	Br	Richard	395	Rch
Jacob	71	Clp	Strair, John	23	Oho	Waddy	357	Lnn
Jacob	949	Hrr	Straith, Alexr.	61	Jff	William	11	Pwh
John H.	357	Lnn	Christian	685	Br	Wm.	14	Hnr
Joseph	932	Hrr	Straley, Andrew	638	Gls	Streets see Sheets		
Js.	71	Clp	Christian	910	Hrr	Streetton, Rebeccah	636	Gls
Michl.	517	Brk	Jacob	638	Gls	Streit, Christian	513	Frd
Moses	717	Wsh	Stran, William	122	Acc	Stribling, E.	404	Ags
Noah	959	Hrr	Strange, A. A.	438	Flv	Francis	605	Frd
Peter	577	Brk	Benjamin	733	Brn	Sarah	526	Frd
Rebecca	200	Shn	David	171	Alb	Thomas	574	Frd
Sarah	961	Hrr	Geo. A.	444	Flv	William	36	Stf
Thomas	906	Hrr	John A.	438	Flv	Strichberry, Elizabeth	193	Shn

Name	No.	Code
William	192	Shn
Stricker, George	17	Oho
Samuel	15	Oho
Strickhiser, Geo.	408	Ags
Strickland, John	275	Rck
Strickle, John	554	Frd
Stricklend, Abigail	730	Nls
Abill	730	Nls
Samuel	729	Nls
Strickler, Abraham	189	Shn
Barbary	189	Shn
Daniel	183	Shn
Danl.	269	Rck
David	189	Shn
David	196	Shn
Isaac	189	Shn
Jacob	190	Shn
Joseph	33	Rcm
Joseph	195	Shn
Martin	33	Rcm
Samuel	196	Shn
Solomon	14	Knw
see Stickler		
Stricklin, Levy	657	Btt
Stricter, Lewis	597	Mnr
Strider, Christianna	83	Jff
Elizabeth	59	Jff
Henry	78	Jff
Isaac	96	Jff
Jacob	83	Jff
Strine, Jonas	40	Rcm
Stringer, Daniel	53	Chs
Daniel	932	Hrr
Jacob	59	Acc
James	228	Aml
Josiah	54	Chs
Nancy	60	Acc
Polly	57	Acc
see S...		
Stringfeild, Benj., Jun.	24	Isw
Fanny	25	Isw
Joseph	37	Isw
Martin	37	Isw
Womble	27	Isw
Stringfeller, Benj.	273	Ldn
Stringfellow, George	585	Frd
Henry	76	Clp
James	355	Fqr
Robert	353	Fqr
Susan	72	Clp
William	34	Stf
Stringfield, Wm.	140	Sth
Strinss, Hilary	816	Nrf
Stripes, Eustice	476	Pra
Striplin, Nancy	219	Kng
Stritter, Henry	549	Frd
Strobia, J.H.	24	Hnr
Strock, Joshua	16	Rcm
Strode, Jno.	73	Clp
Ths.	72	Clp
William	550	Brk
Stroder, Frances	223	Pnd
Stroep, Henry	26	Oho
John	17	Oho
Strole, Christian	29	Rcm
Strong, David	64	Chr
James	380	Ags
John	786	Bck
John	793	Nrf
Martin	850	Hnv
Nancy	819	Nrf
Nathan	715	Gch
Richd.	538	Mnn
Richd.	920	Nrf
Samuel	681	Brk
Stroop, Sarah	22	Rcm
Stroope, Jane	538	Frd
William	538	Frd
Strosnider, Michael	211	Shn
Strother, Athony	90	Jff
Benjamin	506	Prw
Catharine	438	Flv
Danl. F.	73	Clp
French	392	Fqr
George	217	Kng
George	60	Stf
George F.	73	Clp
Hannah	207	Shn
Isaac	416	Rnd
James	377	Fqr
James	588	Frd
Jeremiah	386	Fqr
Jeruneah	77	Clp
Jno., Jr.	76	Clp
Jno., Sr.	77	Clp
John	386	Fqr
Joseph	77	Jff
Lewis	347	Fqr
Mary	399	Fqr
Reubin	392	Fqr
Thomas	954	Hrr
William	374	Mds
William	406	Mds
William	418	Mds
William	929	Hrr
Stroud, Benj.	882	Yrk
James	882	Yrk
Jno.	919	Nrf
Thos.	734	Brn
Strough, Jacob	660	Btt
Stroup, John P.	857	Wth
Strouse, Leond.	583	Brk
Strow, Henry	656	Btt
Henry	659	Btt
Wilhelms	656	Btt
Wm.	659	Btt
Struggs, Peggy	13	Hnr
Strupe, William	187	Shn
Struthers, Wm.	272	Rck
Struts see Sheets		
Strutton, Franky	96	Spt
John	97	Spt
Stuart, Alexa.	384	Ags
Alexander	567	Mnr
Am.	541	Mnn
And.	271	Rck
And.	303	Rck
Archd.	379	Ags
Archd.	384	Ags
Calwell	855	Wth
Charles	17	Oho
Charles	855	Wth
Charles H.	664	Sss
Chas.	542	Mnn
Chas., Est.	217	Kng
Daniel	854	Wth
David	305	Frf
David	216	Kng
David	855	Wth
David, ([his] Quarter)	379	Fqr
Donald	1	Ntt
Edward	435	Bth
Geo.	542	Mnn
Hance	963	Hrr
Henry	443	Bth
Henry	588	Mnr
Hugh	304	Frf
Hugh	293	Rck
Jacob W.	217	Kng
James	435	Bth
James	444	Bth
Jane	405	Ags
Jno., j.	294	Rck
John	435	Bth
John	589	Brk
John	925	Crl
John	958	Chc
John	14	Oho
John	294	Rck
John G.	216	Kng
Margret	218	Pnd
Mary	216	Kng
Rachel	19	Ntt
Rachel	855	Wth
Ralph	637	Gls
Richard	216	Kng
Rob.	540	Mnn
Robert	444	Bth
Robert	927	Hrr
Robert	9	Oho
Robin, f. negro	297	Frf
Robt.	387	Ags
Robt.	409	Ags
Robt.	526	Brk
Robt.	538	Mnn
Robt.	294	Rck
Sally K.	216	Kng
Sam	541	Mnn
Saml.	538	Brk
Thomas	207	Ess
William	435	Bth
William	958	Chc
William	385	Fqr
William	628	Mnt
William	663	Sss
William	856	Wth
Wm.	547	Brk
Wm.	540	Mnn
Wm.	541	Mnn
Wm.	5	Ntt
Wm.	270	Rck
see Steuart, Stwart		
Stubblefeild, John S.	941	Chc
Stubblefield, Henry	586	Frd
Henry	78	Spt
James	70	Jff
Jams., f. n.	304	Frf
Jno.	670	Glc
John	65	Jff
Js., Estate	73	Clp
Mary	671	Glc
Priscilla	534	Frd
Ro.	671	Glc
Simon	670	Glc
Wm.	671	Glc
Stubbs, Chs., (free negro)	672	Glc
Eliza.	672	Glc
Francis	672	Glc
Jas. C.	670	Glc
Jas. N.	671	Glc
Jno.	671	Glc
John S.	128	Hnr
Laurence	672	Glc
Saml.	670	Glc
Sarah	670	Glc
Susanna	898	Hnv
Thom	128	Hnr
Wm.	671	Glc
Stuck, Peter	285	Ldn
Stuckey, Molly	409	Rch
Studdy, John	118	Spt
Studivant see Sturdivant		
Stuff, Saml.	660	Btt
Stuirr, Catha.	555	Brk
Stukey see Stookey		
Stull, Danl.	658	Btt
Geo., Jr.	658	Btt
Geo., Sr.	658	Btt
Jacob	657	Btt
Jno.	657	Btt
see Steel		
Stults, Danl.	521	Brk
Stultz, Jacob	827	Hmp
Philip	30	Rcm
Stumbaugh, Eve	8	Rcm
Peter	426	Rnd
Stump, Bengamin	775	Hmp
Daniel	562	Frd
David	592	Frd

John	563	Frd	Martha	9	Pwh	Martin, jr.	217	Kng
John	600	Frd	Peter	13	Pwh	Martin, Sr.	217	Kng
John	775	Hmp	William	12	Pwh	Mary	118	Spt
Joseph	775	Hmp	see Seiblet			Molly	204	Ess
Lewis	602	Frd	Sublett, Peter D.	229	Aml	Mortho	312	Ldn
Micle	947	Hrr	William	63	Chr	Owin	372	Fqr
Mikel	943	Hrr	William, Jur.	68	Chr	Richard	209	Alb
Nelsa	283	Ldn	Subody, Nicholas	524	Brk	Susan	59	Stf
Peter	775	Hmp	see Surbody			Thomas	3	Rcm
Philip	580	Brk	Succede, Frs.	921	Nrf	Thomas	59	Stf
Thomas	482	Bdf	Sudbury, Frances	9	Ntt	Thos.	219	Kng
Stunbridge see Stembridg			John	229	Aml	Ulissies	202	Ess
Stunkard, Hanna	383	Ags	William	585	Pre	William	208	Alb
Sturdavant, Wm.	734	Brn	Suddarth, James	172	Alb	Wm.	655	Btt
Sturdevant, ---, & Rives	333	Dnw	Jarrott	171	Alb	Wm.	200	Ess
Edward	358	Lnn	Tandy	171	Alb	Wm.	218	Kng
Hennery	358	Lnn	William	173	Alb	see Sillivan		
John	358	Lnn	Suddeth, James D.	301	Frf	Sullivant, Joel	64	Chr
Sturdeven, Anthoney	749	Wsh	Lewis	298	Frf	Woodson	359	Lnn
Sturdivant, Ann	663	Sss	Wm.	536	Mnn	Sully, Chester	918	Nrf
Dal.	21	Ntt	Suddgrass, Robt., jr.	579	Brk	Sulser, Henry	36	Rcm
Elizath.	160	Dnw	Suddoth, Baylor	78	Clp	see Seelser		
James	161	Dnw	Benja.	77	Clp	Sult, Peter	857	Wth
James, jr.	531	Prg	Benjamin, (O)	412	Fqr	Sumerfield, Joseph	430	Rnd
Jas., senr.	531	Prg	Benjamin, Sr.	361	Fqr	Sumerlle, Samuel	341	Hrr
Joel	160	Dnw	Elias	349	Fqr	Sumers, Andw.	380	Ags
Joel	550	Prg	Isaac	349	Fqr	David	380	Ags
John, jr.	531	Prg	John	391	Fqr	Jacob	380	Ags
John, sr.	535	Prg	John	397	Fqr	Sumhot, Peter	508	Brk
Lucas	762	Brn	John, Jr.	349	Fqr	Summerell, Dicy	141	Sth
Mary	550	Prg	John, (Marsh)	416	Fqr	Eliza.	846	Sth
Matthew	665	Sss	John, Senr.	361	Fqr	George	845	Sth
Richd.	530	Prg	Levi	416	Fqr	Thos.	844	Sth
Robert	665	Sss	Mary	78	Clp	see Sommerell		
Sally	334	Dnw	William	391	Fqr	Summerfield, Jno.	656	Btt
Susannah	763	Brn	Sudduth, Wm.	310	Ldn	Richd.	656	Btt
Thomas	663	Sss	Sudsberry, Caty	832	Bck	Saml.	656	Btt
Washington	664	Sss	David	793	Bck	Thos.	431	Rnd
William	455	Grn	Sudsbury, Ezekiel	13	Ntt	see Sumerfield		
Wm.	162	Dnw	Sudwards, William	729	Nls	Summerle, Elk	933	Hrr
Sturges, Babel	60	Acc	Sue, Jacob	386	Ags	Summerlin, Silas	137	Sth
John, Junr.	60	Acc	Joseph	380	Ags	Summers, Alex	538	Mnn
John, Senr.	60	Acc	Sufferance, John	2	Rcm	Andrew	782	Hmp
Thomas	58	Acc	Sugars, Benjamin	254	Shn	Danl.	5	Rcm
Zerobabel	16	Acc	Suggs, Geo.	920	Nrf	David	638	Mnt
Sturgin, Saml.	730	Wsh	George	474	Pra	Geo., Jr.	303	Frf
Sturign, James	559	Brk	Suit, Augustin	664	Sss	George	300	Frf
Sturk see Stark			Milley	162	Dnw	George	638	Mnt
Sturling see Starling			Sulavan, Samuel	454	Frn	Henry	660	Btt
Sturman, Foxhall	785	Wst	Sulivan, Jno.	540	Mnn	Henry	249	Ldn
Sturms, Jacob	956	Hrr	Owen	785	Wst	Hez.	539	Mnn
Sturnbaugh, Frederick	5	Rcm	Pat	539	Mnn	James	219	Pnd
Stutler, John	941	Hrr	Sull, Frederick	572	Frd	John	296	Frf
Stutslager, Daniel	257	Shn	see Shull			John	638	Mnt
Stutson see Hutson			Sullars, Wm.	444	Mth	John, Jun.	298	Frf
Stutzer, Marton	742	Wsh	Sullenbarger, Michl.	385	Ags	Michael	37	Rcm
Stuvard see Steward			Saml.	36	Rcm	Paul	218	Pnd
Stuwrod, Cornelius	8	Oho	Sullivan, Cors.	359	Lnc	Richard	123	Acc
Daniel	8	Oho	Daniel	60	Stf	Saml.	297	Frf
Stwart, Alex	541	Mnn	Danl.	806	Nrf	Saml.	282	Rck
see Stuart			Dennis	384	Ags	Susanna	247	Ldn
Stweard, Armistead	161	Dnw	Derby	209	Alb	Thomas	297	Frf
Thomas, Est.	161	Dnw	Eleanor	55	Stf	Walter	782	Hmp
see Steward			Eliza.	205	Ess	Wm.	572	Brk
Stweart, Charles	162	Dnw	Eliza.	288	Ldn	Wm.	297	Frf
Charles	585	Mnr	Enoch	336	Dnw	Summersett, Thos.	9	Oho
Elizabeth	162	Dnw	Francis	85	Spt	Summervill, Samiel	423	Msn
Styers, Cornelius	301	Ldn	Gabriel	45	Stf	see Sommervill, Sumerlle		
Stygers, Henry	527	Frd	Henry	574	Frd	Summovill, Joseph	954	Hrr
Styles, William F.	13	Knw	Hiram	994	Nrt	Summs, Francis	954	Hrr
Styron, Henry	472	Pra	James	55	Stf	Sumner, Daniel	17	Isw
Hillary	475	Pra	Jno.	79	Clp	Hezekiah, Sr.	659	Mnt
Malachi	475	Pra	John	200	Ess	Sumners, Philip	268	Rck
Robert	476	Pra	John	372	Fqr	Winney	239	Ldn
Smith	474	Pra	John	994	Nrt	Sumproal, Jacob	505	Brk
Subarty, Martin	549	Frd	John	502	Prw	Sumpter, Andrea	63	Chr
Suber, John	534	Brk	John	55	Stf	Edmund	655	Mnt
Peter	531	Brk	Jonas	56	Stf	George	656	Mnt
Sublet, Arthur	11	Pwh	Joseph	995	Nrt	Henry	67	Chs
Benjamin	13	Pwh	Lucretia	996	Nrt	John	64	Chr

Nancy	64	Chr	Emos	719	Wsh	Swanson, Dennis	42	Rcm
Thomas	64	Chr	Enoch	17	Oho	Gabriel	473	Frn
Sumption, Thomas	594	Frd	Fanny	406	Rch	John	256	Amh
Suner, Saml.	755	Wsh	Hanna	421	Bth	John	761	Brn
Supinger, Catharine	221	Shn	Henry	25	Oho	Joseph	278	Amh
Jacob	172	Shn	James	994	Nrt	Judith	994	Nrt
Jacob	221	Shn	James	785	Wst	Levi	587	Mnr
John	221	Shn	James, Junr.	787	Wst	see Lunsford		
Surber, Adam	712	Wsh	Jas.	359	Lnc	Swart, Barnett	378	Fqr
Adam, Jur.	708	Wsh	Jeremiah	787	Wst	Swartz, Conrad	549	Frd
Henry	442	Bth	John	420	Bth	Gilbert	592	Frd
Jacob	712	Wsh	John	924	Crl	see Swatz		
John	444	Bth	John	967	Hrr	Swartzley, John	386	Ags
John	694	Wsh	John	55	Jff	Swatts, Christian	17	Rcm
John	747	Wsh	John, jr.	923	Crl	Phineas	15	Rcm
Joseph	416	Bth	John, Junr.	376	Fqr	Samuel	14	Rcm
Surbine, Lydia	665	Mnt	John, Senr.	924	Crl	Swatz, John	550	Frd
Surbody, Matthias	524	Brk	John, Senr.	376	Fqr	Sweaney, Hannah	55	Jff
see Subody			Jos.	540	Mnn	John	586	Pre
Surewaters see Shurewaters			Joseph	426	Bth	William	586	Pre
Surface, George	607	Mnt	Joseph	924	Crl	Swearengin, Hezekiah	89	Jff
Henry	607	Mnt	Joseph	787	Wst	Joseph	98	Jff
John	607	Mnt	Reuben	785	Wst	Van	87	Jff
John	664	Mnt	Richard	995	Nrt	Swearingem, John	2	Knw
Martin	666	Mnt	Sarah	920	Nrf	Swearingen, Eli	586	Frd
Michl.	666	Mnt	Thomas	787	Wst	Swearinger, Clementeas	443	Bth
Surgener, James	527	Frd	William	420	Bth	Van	444	Bth
Surpes, Christopher	299	Rck	William	25	Oho	Swearingin, Daniel	689	Br
Surrils, Willm.	628	Mnt	William	787	Wst	George	694	Br
Surtherington, Winding	163	Shn	William, Senr.	785	Wst	George D.	686	Br
see ...therling			Wm.	360	Lnc	John	689	Br
Survine see Surbine			Zaphariah	829	Hmp	Thomas	686	Br
Suryer see Sweyer			Swadger, Lewes	428	Rnd	Sweatman, Neri	73	Clp
Susong, Andw.	705	Wsh	Swadley, George	220	Pnd	Sweeney, George	381	Fqr
Andw., Senr.	705	Wsh	Henry	226	Pnd	Jonathan	768	Nwk
Jacob	705	Wsh	Henry, J.	220	Pnd	see Swiney		
Suster, John	869	Cmp	Swagely, Mathias	84	Jff	Sweeny, Jacob	806	Bck
Suter, James	405	Fqr	Swain, Charles	661	Btt	Malachi	838	Bck
John	590	Frd	George	482	Bdf	Phelix	921	Nrf
see Teeter			Jeremiah	480	Bdf	Simon	302	Ldn
Sutfin, Henry	651	Mnt	John	654	Btt	Sweet, John	748	Wsh
John	418	Fqr	Mary	681	Wrw	Leonard	386	Ags
William	481	Bdf	Rebecca	67	Jff	Wm.	380	Ags
Suthard, John	384	Fqr	Samuel	67	Jff	Sweetnan, John	32	Stf
Owen	381	Ags	Swaine, Thomas	212	Shn	Sweit, Molley	655	Btt
Suthards, Thomas	8	Hnr	Swaker, Daniel	231	Shn	Sweker, Windle	854	Wth
Sutharland, Joseph	171	Alb	Nathanl.	228	Shn	Sweney, Elisabeth	768	Nwk
Judah	172	Alb	Swallow, Elizabeth	299	Frf	Swenney, Joel	359	Lnn
Sutherland, Alex.	305	Ldn	Wm.	299	Frf	Swent, Adam	536	Mnn
David	25	Oho	Zachariah	370	Fqr	Sweny, Morgan	107	Spt
Fendall C.	161	Dnw	Swallwood, James	311	Ldn	Swerangen, Van	585	Mnr
Fendall T.	161	Dnw	Swam see Swann			Swerengin, Saml.	537	Mnn
George	443	Flv	Swamey, John	527	Brk	Sweringen, Isaac	505	Brk
John	605	Frd	Swan, Henry	25	Oho	Sweringer, Thos.	515	Brk
John	3	Wod	James	90	Jff	Sweringin, John V.	692	Br
Sanders	446	Flv	Richard	994	Nrt	Swesy, Amos	680	Brk
Suttan, James	419	Rnd	Robert	33	Stf	Swetman, William	405	Mds
John	417	Rnd	Thos.	293	Ldn	Swetnan, Levina	219	Kng
Nathaniel	481	Bdf	Walter	326	Dnw	Sweyer, George	70	Jff
Sutten, Jonas	224	Pnd	Swane, Charles	457	Frn	Swift, Ann	865	Hnv
Suttle, Austin	216	Kng	Swaney, Abner	4	Rcm	Charles	865	Hnv
Benjamin, jr.	216	Kng	Swank, Jacob	9	Rcm	Elizabeth	994	Nrt
Benjn., Senr.	216	Kng	Philip	285	Ldn	Martha	516	Brk
Daniel	244	Ldn	Swanks, Jno.	919	Nrf	Samuel	994	Nrt
Henry	243	Ldn	Swann, Alexander	587	Pre	William	995	Nrt
John	28	Stf	Charles	363	Fqr	Swiger, Christopher	905	Hrr
John P.	217	Kng	Charles	397	Rch	Jacob	905	Hrr
Joseph	217	Kng	Jane	1	Pwh	John	925	Hrr
Newman	244	Ldn	Jno. T.	859	Hnv	Mary	946	Hrr
Reuben	245	Ldn	John	1	Pwh	Solomon	905	Hrr
William	218	Kng	Joshua	927	Crl	Swillingbarger, ---,		
William	173	Shn	Leven C.	9	Knw	Mrs.	623	Btt
Wm. B.	218	Kng	Mary	14	Pwh	Josh.	661	Btt
Suttler, Winney	728	Nls	Samuel A.	924	Crl	Sarah	661	Btt
Suttles, William	729	Nls	Thomas	925	Crl	Swim, Matthias	569	Brk
Sutton, Benjamin	26	Oho	Thomas	9	Knw	Swimley, Jacob	505	Brk
Cyrus	995	Nrt	Thomas T. [F. ?]	14	Pwh	Swindal, Clayton	78	Clp
David	25	Oho	Thos.	921	Nrf	Swindel, Joseph	405	Mds
Edward	787	Wst	Willis	4	Pwh	Swinder, Clayton	537	Mnn
Elijah	575	Brk	Wilson	922	Crl	Dav.	537	Mnn

Swindler, Henry	75	Clp	Sydnor, Ann	896	Hnv	Jno.	922	Nrf
Jno.	75	Clp	Anthony	160	Dnw	Jno. Y.	165	Dnw
Js.	73	Clp	Anthony	994	Nrt	Joe	187	Elc
Swineheart, George	688	Br	Edward G.	872	Hnv	John Y.	164	Dnw
Swiney, Delaney	639	Gls	Fortunatus	482	Bdf	Langhorne	814	Nrf
Swingland, John	8	Rcm	James D.	407	Rch	Mary A.	227	Aml
Swingle, Michael	706	Wsh	John	396	Rch	Philip	674	Glc
Swink, George	208	Alb	John, Jun.	401	Rch	Ro.	884	Yrk
Henry	385	Ags	Thomas	394	Rch	Robert	95	Jff
Jno.	303	Frf	Wm.	18	Ntt	Sarah, Gloucester		
Mathias	385	Ags	WmSon.	361	Lnc	Town	673	Glc
Wm.	299	Frf	see Bayley, Belfild			Sarah, of Gloucester		
Swinney, Benjamin	486	Frn	Syford, Coonrod	657	Btt	County has Slaves in		
James	565	Mnr	M.	404	Ags	York County	884	Yrk
James	728	Nls	Sykes, Alexr.	801	Nrf	Thos.	595	Brk
John P.	271	Amh	Amy	920	Nrf	Thos.	453	Mth
William	859	Cmp	Arthur	801	Nrf	William	599	Brk
William	566	Mnr	Benja.	455	Grn	Wm.	884	Yrk
Swinny, John	481	Bdf	Betsy	800	Nrf	Tabbott, Kedar	811	Nrf
Swinton, Phoebe	922	Crl	Caleb	806	Nrf	Thos.	811	Nrf
Swires, Jacob	777	Hmp	Cary	799	Nrf	Taber, Arch.	620	Mnt
Swisher, Christophe	938	Hrr	Ely	334	Dnw	James	612	Mnt
Christopher	940	Hrr	Fredrck	803	Nrf	Tabern, Abel	28	Hnr
Fred.	539	Mnn	Isabella	793	Nrf	Tabler, George	519	Brk
Jac.	543	Mnn	James	794	Nrf	Henry	519	Brk
Jacob	379	Ags	Jas.	788	Nrf	Wm.	523	Brk
Jacob	546	Brk	John	800	Nrf	see Vabler		
Jacob	912	Hrr	Joseph, jr.	792	Nrf	Tachet, Lydia	537	Prg
Jacob	938	Hrr	Josiah	803	Nrf	Tachett, Ann	544	Prg
Jas.	542	Mnn	Katy	789	Nrf	Tackel, Nimrod	574	Mnr
John	382	Ags	Lemuel	793	Nrf	Tacket, Sally	164	Dnw
Joseph	938	Hrr	Michael	801	Nrf	Tackett, Archd.	81	Clp
Maths.	659	Btt	Polly	334	Dnw	Bayless	350	Fqr
Peter	953	Hrr	Rob.	540	Mnn	George	350	Fqr
Peter	537	Mnn	Sarah	803	Nrf	John	2	Knw
Switer, Hezekiah	79	Clp	Waltr	795	Nrf	Lewis	3	Knw
Switezer, Sarah	35	Rcm	William	455	Grn	Samuel	12	Knw
Switzer, Henry	579	Brk	Willis	824	Nrf	William	350	Fqr
Jno.	654	Btt	Syles, John	560	Brk	Tade, John	858	Wth
John, Jur.	781	Hmp	Sylvester, John	795	Nrf	Taff, Jno.	362	Lnc
John, Sen.	780	Hmp	Syme, Andw.	332	Dnw	Peter	471	Mdd
Josh.	654	Btt	Nicholas	887	Hnv	Travis	212	Ess
Margaret	257	Shn	Sarah	859	Hnv	Tafflinger, Jacob	13	Rcm
Nathan	654	Btt	Symington, Robt.	920	Nrf	John	13	Rcm
Thos.	656	Btt	Symmons, William	172	Alb	Taffolet, George	918	Hrr
Valentine	769	Hmp	Syms, Elisha	715	Gch	Tager, Elizabeth	9	Rcm
Wm., Jr.	656	Btt	John	129	Hnr	Tagert, John	595	Mnr
Wm., Sr.	656	Btt	Synes, Hen., Jr.	535	Mnn	Robt.	742	Wsh
Swiver, Jacob	729	Nls	Henry	534	Mnn	Taggart, John	762	Hmp
Swoards, John	598	Mnr	Wm.	535	Mnn	Martin	587	Pre
Swoke, Nicholas	224	Shn	Synor, Jenny	405	Mds	Taggert, James	273	Rck
Swol, Joseph	547	Frd	Synot, Thom.	954	Hrr	Taggle, John	822	Bck
Swoop, George	297	Rck	Syoe, Abel V.	18	Oho	Tailor, Benj.	950	Hrr
Swoope, Henry	384	Ags	Sypher, Andw.	728	Wsh	William	867	Cmp
Jacob	379	Ags	Syphert, Philip	577	Frd	see Taylor		
Peter, (Jr.)	41	Rcm	Syphor, Joseph	299	Ldn	Tait, Caleb	855	Cmp
Peter, (Sen.)	41	Rcm	Syphret, George	546	Frd	William	362	Fqr
George	430	Msn	Sypolt, Chrisr.	535	Mnn	Taite, Jesse	395	Rch
James	592	Mnr	Geo.	535	Mnn	Talbert, George	306	Frf
Jonathan	587	Mnr	Geo., Jr.	535	Mnn	John	396	Fqr
Joseph	571	Mnr	Nat.	535	Mnn	Mary	169	Shn
Joseph	578	Mnr	Syrus, Bartholomew	860	Cmp	McKinzey	307	Frf
Joseph, S.	588	Mnr	Nicholas	860	Cmp	Pleasant	857	Cmp
Swords, Ewdw.	387	Ags	Solomon	862	Cmp	Richd.	911	Hrr
Geo.	404	Ags				Thomas	306	Frf
Swyers, George	581	Frd				Walter	307	Frf
Sybert, Christian, Junr.	852	Wth	--- T ---			Wm., Junr.	307	Frf
Christian, Senr.	852	Wth				Wm., Senr.	307	Frf
Frdk.	542	Brk				see Tolbert		
George	574	Mnr	T..., ...	226	Aml	Talbot, Richard	447	Bth
Jacob, jr.	502	Brk	T...iford, Obedh.	923	Nrf	Samuel	858	Wth
Jacob F.	507	Brk	T...ker see Tucker			Talbott, Bazel	712	Wsh
John	852	Wth	T...ler, Clarisa	163	Dnw	Benja.	309	Frf
Mary	852	Wth	T...on, Chs.	923	Nrf	Charles	858	Cmp
Peggy	542	Brk	Tabb, Edwd.	546	Brk	Edward	582	Frd
see Sibert			Edwd., jr.	520	Brk	Elisha	697	Brk
Sybold, Henry	260	Ldn	Francis	227	Aml	James	240	Ldn
Sycote, Abnen	19	Oho	George	549	Brk	John	862	Cmp
Syders, Solomon, Sr.	268	Rck	Henry	187	Elc	John	521	Frd
see Sider			Henry	828	Nrf	Jos.	307	Ldn

Mary	305 Frf	
Williston	862 Cmp	
Wm.	58 Chs	
Talbut, John	77 Jff	
see Talbert		
Taleferro, Roderick	848 Cmp	
Taley, James	5 Hnr	
James	16 Wod	
William	65 Chr	
Taliaferio, Wm.	447 Flv	
Taliafero, Francis	175 Alb	
Taliaferro, Ann	179 Alb	
Ann	930 Crl	
Benjamin	276 Amh	
Burton	927 Crl	
Charles	276 Amh	
Charles	833 Bck	
Charles C.	930 Crl	
Charles P.	269 Amh	
Elizabeth	269 Amh	
James B.	179 Knq	
James G.	219 Kng	
Jane	931 Crl	
John	325 Dnw	
John	219 Kng	
Jdn, jr.	221 Kng	
Meriwether	220 Kng	
Norborne	927 Crl	
Philip	928 Crl	
Richard	928 Crl	
Richd.	179 Knq	
Roderick	290 Amh	
Sarah	179 Knq	
William	930 Crl	
William	931 Crl	
Wm.	673 Glc	
Taliaffero, Elth.	80 Clp	
Hay	80 Clp	
Henry	80 Clp	
Tall, Magnus	528 Brk	
Tallbert, Levi	6 Rcm	
Tallent, Christr.	220 Kng	
Wm.	220 Kng	
Talley, Bittey	894 Hnv	
Charles	778 Bck	
Charles, Jnr.	888 Hnv	
Charles, Snr.	885 Hnv	
Dibdel	888 Hnv	
Elcanah	872 Hnv	
Jas.	875 Hnv	
Jno.	889 Hnv	
John	130 Cmb	
Joseph	890 Hnv	
Mary	885 Hnv	
Mary	888 Hnv	
Mary, Snr.	889 Hnv	
Moses	997 Nrt	
Nathl.	873 Hnv	
William, Sr.	115 Cmb	
William P.	113 Cmb	
Wim.	882 Hnv	
Talliaferro, Champ T.	88 Spt	
Francis	89 Spt	
John	107 Spt	
Lewis	86 Spt	
William W.	88 Spt	
Tallman, Benjamin	27 Rcm	
John	769 Nwk	
Talloss see Tulloss		
Tallough, Eady	46 Isw	
James	46 Isw	
Tally, Abner	226 Aml	
Champ.	362 Lnc	
Ebenezar	269 Ldn	
Fleming C.	770 Nwk	
Geo.	362 Lnc	
Grieve	736 Brn	
Jas.	362 Lnc	
Jno., Jr.	361 Lnc	
Jno., Senr.	362 Lnc	

Martha	164 Dnw	
Nicholas	770 Nwk	
Obedience	226 Aml	
Susanna	268 Ldn	
Tho. J.	361 Lnc	
Talmage, E.	5 Hnr	
Talman, James	420 Bth	
Talmash, William	26 Stf	
Talmon, Austin	125 Hnr	
Talten, Methias	314 Ldn	
Tambling, Saml.	795 Nrf	
Tamplen, William	69 Spt	
Tamplin, Ann	930 Crl	
Edward H.	930 Crl	
Tanahill, Martha	82 Clp	
Tancell, John D.	412 Fqr	
William	382 Fqr	
Tanchell, Saml.	545 Mnn	
Wm.	545 Mnn	
Tandy, Elisabeth	770 Nwk	
John	770 Nwk	
Ralph	102 Spt	
Roger	83 Spt	
Tanguary, James	581 Frd	
Walter	560 Frd	
Tank, George	65 Acc	
Tankersley, Charles	930 Crl	
Fountain	20 Ntt	
George	930 Crl	
Nathaniel	928 Crl	
Obh.	662 Btt	
Reuben	662 Btt	
Richard	289 Amh	
Richd.	368 Lnc	
Tankersly, Dauathy	759 Wsh	
John	65 Chr	
Peter	361 Lnc	
Tankesley, Edmund	300 Rck	
Richd.	387 Ags	
Tann, Thomas	617 Srr	
Tanner, ... [Geo. ?]	227 Aml	
Abraham	408 Mds	
Benjamin	870 Cmp	
Branch	876 Cmp	
Christopher	408 Mds	
Federick	408 Mds	
Geo.	388 Ags	
Isel	876 Cmp	
Jacob	408 Mds	
John	388 Ags	
Jdn	870 Cmp	
John	408 Mds	
John G.	408 Mds	
Joseph, (FB)	485 Bdf	
Leonard	390 Ags	
Michael	408 Mds	
Michl.	661 Btt	
Nathan	869 Cmp	
Reuben	408 Mds	
Richd.	764 Brn	
Robert	227 Aml	
Saml.	422 Msn	
Solomon	388 Ags	
Susanna	188 Shn	
Thomas	14 Ntt	
Tobias	388 Ags	
William	227 Aml	
Tansel, William	507 Prw	
Tansell, John	515 Prw	
William	511 Prw	
see Tanchell		
Tanstall, Richd. G.	178 Knq	
Taper, Francis, a free		
negro	996 Nrt	
Tapp, Elijah	80 Clp	
James	81 Clp	
John	562 Frd	
Lewis	565 Frd	
Nimrod	80 Clp	
Samuel	545 Frd	

Vincent	405 Ags	
Vintcent	80 Clp	
Wm.	80 Clp	
Tappy, William	29 Rcm	
Tapscott, C.	361 Lnc	
C.	367 Lnc	
Chichester	336 Lnc	
Chichester	368 Lnc	
Chichester	369 Lnc	
Henry	362 Lnc	
Henry	787 Wst	
James	662 Btt	
James	785 Bck	
John S.	787 Wst	
Mary	362 Lnc	
Raw	361 Lnc	
Rawley	781 Bck	
Robt. H.	275 Rck	
William	796 Bck	
Wm.	509 Brk	
Tarbill, Homes	6 Oho	
Tardy, John	824 Nrf	
John	277 Rck	
O. [D. ?]	282 Rck	
S.	282 Rck	
Tarely, William	850 Cmp	
Tarflinger, Jacob	601 Frd	
Philip	601 Frd	
Tarkleson, Tarkle	362 Lnc	
Tarlton see Hines		
Tarman, Benjamin	385 Fqr	
William	385 Fqr	
Tarpley, Edward J.	736 Brn	
Elizabeth	736 Brn	
John	736 Brn	
Martha	736 Brn	
Oldham	65 Chr	
Robert	65 Chr	
Thomas	393 Rch	
Tarply, Wm.	736 Brn	
Tarr, Conrod	226 Pnd	
George	131 Acc	
Peter	685 Br	
Thomas	265 Ldn	
Tarrant, Carter	922 Nrf	
Francis [crossed out]	791 Nrf	
Francis	810 Nrf	
Lucy	177 Elc	
Richard	928 Crl	
Tarrence see Tarrant		
Tarrent, Thomas	179 Knq	
Tart, Jonathan	817 Nrf	
Robt.	822 Nrf	
Saml.	824 Nrf	
Thos.	817 Nrf	
see Tait, Tant		
Tarver, Andrew	764 Brn	
Tary, Nathaniel	733 Nls	
Tascar, George	798 Hmp	
Tase, Saml.	700 Wsh	
Tast, John L.	35 Hnr	
Taswe, James	364 Fqr	
Tate, ..., for Calaway &		
Earleys Exs.	481 Frn	
Benj.	30 Hnr	
Caleb	481 Frn	
Charles	727 Wsh	
David	662 Btt	
Edmond	882 Cmp	
Henry	484 Bdf	
Hugh	580 Frd	
James	388 Ags	
James	434 Bth	
Jane	388 Ags	
Jane	37 Stf	
Jno.	662 Btt	
John	484 Bdf	
John	39 Rcm	
John	725 Wsh	
John, jr.	535 Brk	

John, sr.	535	Brk	Joseph	314	Ldn	Christopher	178	Knq
Jos.	279	Rck	Richd.	314	Ldn	Clemons	770	Nwk
Joshua	104	Spt	Tavinor, Thomas	4	Wod	Conrad	554	Frd
Levi	276	Ldn	Tavner see Nance			Creed	108	Cmb
Mary	98	Jff	Tawney, Daniel	640	Gls	Creed	133	Cmb
Matthew	11	Rcm	John	640	Gls	Creed [crossed out]	3	Hnr
Michill	691	Wsh	Tawny, George	859	Wth	Creed	33	Hnr
Nancy	483	Bdf	Tawrance, John	764	Hmp	Daniel	66	Chs
Obadiah	483	Bdf	Taws, Andrew	63	Jff	Daniel	307	Frf
Peter	541	Frd	Taybour, John	623	Mnt	Daniel	822	Hmp
Rhody	11	Rcm	Nelly	623	Mnt	Daniel, jr.	735	Brn
Robt.	388	Ags	Tayburn, Mourning	335	Dnw	Daniel, Sr.	735	Brn
Saml.	535	Brk	Tayler, Alexander	415	Bth	Davd.	272	Rck
Samuel	588	Pre	Charles	439	Bth	Davd.	278	Rck
Stermen	952	Hrr	John	305	Frf	David	735	Brn
Tham	954	Hrr	Martha	163	Dnw	David	581	Frd
Thos.	727	Wsh	Richd. F., residing in			David	859	Wth
William	929	Crl	Petersburg	164	Dnw	Dick	150	Sth
William	54	Jff	Sam, Jr.	546	Mnn	Duke	401	Fqr
William, Genl.	726	Wsh	Sarah	439	Bth	Eben	533	Frd
Wm.	959	Hrr	William	413	Bth	Edmand	900	Hnv
Zacheriah	484	Bdf	Tayloe, Daniel W.	267	Amh	Edmond	179	Knq
Tatem, James	792	Nrf	Jno., Col. [2]	620	Btt	Edmond	407	Mds
Jas., (P)	824	Nrf	Jno., Col.	625	Btt	Edmund	483	Bdf
Jas., Sr.	807	Nrf	John	219	Kng	Edmund	484	Bdf
John	807	Nrf	John	504	Prw	Edmund	929	Crl
Js.	922	Nrf	John	396	Rch	Edmund	7	Pwh
Mary	807	Nrf	see Taylor			Edmund	36	Rcm
Nathaniel	792	Nrf	Taylon, Absolum	361	Lnn	Edmund F.	362	Lnn
Sarah	833	Nrf	Daniel	361	Lnn	Edward	804	Hmp
Tates, Beverly	409	Mds	John, (L)	361	Lnn	Edward	16	Oho
John	409	Mds	Molley	361	Lnn	Edward	25	Oho
Wm. [2]	409	Mds	Richard	362	Lnn	Edward	120	Spt
Tatham, Ayres	130	Acc	William	361	Lnn	Edward, Senr.	268	Amh
John	62	Acc	see Taylor			Eleazer	546	Frd
John	65	Acc	Taylor, ---, Kerby			Eli	7	Knw
Record	63	Acc	Drake & [?]	11	Hnr	Elisabeth	82	Clp
William	130	Acc	---, Mrs. (Widow)	219	Ess	Elizabeth	735	Brn
Tatom, Isham	408	Mds	...us	168	Shn	Elizabeth	929	Crl
Nathaniel	408	Mds	Aaron	617	Srr	Elizabeth	221	Kng
Tatum, Amie	536	Prg	Abraham	551	Frd	Elizabeth	279	Ldn
Batt	736	Brn	Adam	640	Gls	Elizabeth	815	Nrf
Benjamin	65	Chr	Alexa.	310	Frf	Elizebeth	408	Mds
Benjm. G.	362	Lnn	Alexander	484	Bdf	Elon	483	Bdf
Betsey	537	Prg	Alexander	334	Dnw	Esther	130	Acc
Charles	536	Prg	Alexander	72	Jff	Ezekel	128	Acc
David	666	Sss	Allen	661	Btt	Ezekiel	357	Fqr
Edward	666	Sss	Also	362	Lnn	F.S.	921	Nrf
Gravot	65	Chr	Alsop	485	Bdf	Fanny	408	Mds
Henry	52	Chs	Ambrose	604	Frd	Forguson	15	Pwh
James	65	Chr	Ann	62	Acc	Frances	99	Spt
John	363	Lnn	Ann	117	Spt	Francis	268	Amh
Littleberry E.	542	Prg	Ann	62	Stf	Francis	15	Hnr
Mary	81	Clp	Anthoney	484	Bdf	Francis	179	Knq
Obedience	52	Chs	Archd.	120	Hnr	Francis	519	Prw
Peter	531	Prg	Archerbald	123	Cmb	Francis, of E	130	Acc
Reubin	65	Chr	Arthr.	922	Nrf	Geo.	389	Ags
Richard	537	Prg	Arthur, [his] (Plantn)	476	Pra	Geo. K.	542	Prg
Robert	335	Dnw	Bagwell	127	Acc	George	210	Alb
Thomas	65	Chr	Bartholemew	928	Crl	George	298	Amh
William	811	Bck	Barton	151	Sth	George	198	Ess
William	363	Lnn	Benj.	3	Hnr	George	310	Frf
see Fatum			Benj.	276	Ldn	George	405	Fqr
Taugham, Michl.	543	Mnn	Benjamin	736	Brn	George	550	Frd
Taughman, Jno.	543	Mnn	Benjamin	379	Fqr	George	565	Frd
Taughtman, Chrsr.	544	Mnn	Benjamin	526	Frd	George	912	Hrr
George	544	Mnn	Benjamin	730	Nls	George	9	Pwh
Jno.	544	Mnn	Bennett	65	Jff	George	69	Spt
Micl.	544	Mnn	Bernard	315	Ldn	George, Jr.	609	Mnt
Teter	544	Mnn	Betsy	816	Nrf	George, Sr.	609	Mnt
Taugue, John	240	Shn	Betty	128	Acc	George B.	955	Chc
Taulman, James	28	Hnr	Blagrave	10	Pwh	George K.	334	Dnw
Tauman, Thomas	65	Chr	Brocking	179	Knq	George W.	293	Amh
Taunt, James	501	Prw	Brockman	210	Alb	Greenbury	484	Bdf
Taurance, William	836	Hmp	Bushrod	534	Frd	Griffin	534	Frd
Tavener, Geo.	315	Ldn	Caleb	179	Knq	Hannah	62	Stf
James	411	Fqr	Carter	407	Mds	Henry	309	Frf
Tavenner, Geo.	314	Ldn	Charles	930	Crl	Henry	287	Ldn
Isaac	315	Ldn	Charles	407	Mds	Henry	629	Mnt
Jonah	314	Ldn	Charles	631	Mnt	Henry, I	130	Acc

Hezekiah	731	Nls	John	801	Nrf	Peter	17	Rcm
Jaby	128	Acc	John	810	Nrf	Phil.	161	Sth
Jacob	661	Btt	John	18	Oho	Philip	278	Ldn
Jacob	676	Br	John	10	Pwh	Pleasant	61	Chs
Jacob	577	Frd	John	526	Prw	Polley	485	Bdf
Jacob	640	Gls	John	270	Rck	Polly	674	Glc
James	62	Acc	John	38	Rcm	Polly	546	Mnn
James	210	Alb	John	116	Spt	Prince	197	Ess
James	265	Amh	John	11	Wod	Purnell	127	Acc
James	484	Bdf	John, & Brothers	8	Rcm	R. B.	922	Nrf
James	814	Bck	John, 1st.	63	Acc	R. L. [2]	922	Nrf
James	819	Bck	John, jr.	820	Nrf	Rachel	128	Acc
James	869	Cmp	John, jr.	822	Nrf	Rachel	759	Hmp
James	871	Cmp	John, Jr.	18	Oho	Raymond	128	Acc
James	930	Crl	John, of S	65	Acc	Reuben	930	Crl
James	128	Cmb	John, (S)	362	Lnn	Richard	127	Cmb
James	34	Hnr	John, SS	65	Acc	Richard	833	Hmp
James	566	Mnr	John, Sr.	484	Bdf	Richard	29	Hnr
James	575	Mnr	John, Sr.	822	Nrf	Richard	89	Jff
James	769	Nwk	John W.	588	Pre	Richard, of R	129	Acc
James	18	Oho	Jones	736	Brn	Richard F.	334	Dnw
James	588	Pre	Jordan	27	Isw	Richardson	771	Nwk
James, of Jas.	128	Acc	Jos.	316	Ldn	Richd.	64	Chs
James, of S	127	Acc	Joseph	126	Acc	Richd.	814	Nrf
James, SM	127	Acc	Joseph	409	Ags	Richd.	922	Nrf
James, 3 thumbs	407	Mds	Joseph	483	Bdf	Richd. F.	2	Ntt
James, (W)	884	Yrk	Joseph	763	Brn	Ro. H.	484	Bdf
Jams	926	Hrr	Joseph	128	Cmb	Robert	484	Bdf
Jane	795	Nrf	Joseph	199	Ess	Robert	15	Pwh
Jane	809	Nrf	Joseph	640	Gls	Robert	44	Stf
Jas., Majr.	726	Wsh	Joseph	202	Shn	Robt.	735	Brn
Jeremh.	82	Clp	Joshua	64	Acc	Robt.	815	Nrf
Jeremiah	129	Acc	Joshua	485	Bdf	Robt.	922	Nrf
Jeremiah	260	Amh	Joshua	788	Bck	Salley	900	Hnv
Jesse	66	Chs	Joshua	306	Ldn	Salley	3	Hnr
Jesse	566	Frd	Js., Jr.	922	Nrf	Sally	179	Knq
Jesse	603	Frd	Langhorn	220	Kng	Sally	769	Nwk
Jesse	795	Nrf	Lettic	283	Rck	Sally	839	Nrf
Jesse	819	Nrf	Levi	86	Jff	Saml.	516	Brk
Jessee	202	Ess	Levina	128	Acc	Saml.	814	Bck
Jno.	662	Btt	Lewis B.	763	Brn	Samuel	67	Chs
Jno.	310	Frf	Lucy	64	Acc	Samuel	486	Frn
Jno.	32	Hnr	Lucy	220	Ess	Samuel	526	Frd
Jno.	252	Ldn	Lyttleton	407	Mds	Sarah	485	Bdf
Jno.	544	Mnn	Mahlon	316	Ldn	Sarah	16	Hnr
Jno.	627	Mnt	Majar	922	Nrf	Sarah	232	Ldn
Jno.	923	Nrf	Major	63	Acc	Sarah	509	Prw
Jno., Dr.	921	Nrf	Major	127	Acc	Selvy	811	Nrf
Jno. McC.	627	Mnt	Major	931	Crl	Septimus	796	Hmp
John	174	Alb	Mandly	560	Frd	Shadrach	129	Acc
John	302	Amh	Mark	267	Rck	Simion	722	Wsh
John	305	Amh	Mary	929	Crl	Simon	794	Hmp
John [2]	389	Ags	Mary	309	Frf	Skelton	466	Frn
John	484	Bdf	Mary	550	Frd	Sophia	64	Acc
John [2]	485	Bdf	Mary	250	Ldn	Southey	128	Acc
John	565	Brk	Mary	278	Ldn	Stacey	316	Ldn
John	576	Brk	Mary	593	Mnr	Stanton	62	Acc
John	736	Brn	Mary	642	Mnt	Stanton	408	Mds
John	763	Brn	Mary	770	Nwk	Stephen	604	Frd
John	814	Bck	Mary	132	Sth	Stephen	722	Wsh
John	930	Crl	Mathew	13	Pwh	Susanna	204	Ess
John	332	Dnw	Miles	119	Hnr	Tabitha, of W.	129	Acc
John	213	Ess	Mordecai	580	Frd	Talsey	771	Nwk
John	305	Frf	Moses	298	Amh	Teackle	129	Acc
John	306	Frf	Nancy	37	Isw	Tho.	361	Lnc
John	385	Fqr	Nancy	117	Spt	Thomas	265	Amh
John	390	Fqr	Nancy	52	Stf	Thomas	794	Bck
John	539	Frd	Nath.	25	Hnr	Thomas	929	Crl
John	456	Grn	Nathaniel	260	Ldn	Thomas	309	Frf
John	846	Hnv	Natt, (Y)	884	Yrk	Thomas	390	Fqr
John	909	Hrr	Natten [Nathn?]	730	Wsh	Thomas	797	Hmp
John	950	Hrr	Ned.	884	Yrk	Thomas	800	Hmp
John	27	Hnr	Nehemiah	127	Acc	Thomas	249	Ldn
John	132	Hnr	Nicholas	372	Fqr	Thomas	362	Lnn
John	60	Jff	Nimrod	359	Fqr	Thomas	407	Mds
John	220	Kng	Parker	130	Acc	Thomas	119	Spt
John	246	Ldn	Paschal	681	Br	Thomas A.	64	Chs
John	362	Lnn	Paul	552	Brk	Thomas T.	65	Acc
John	407	Mds	Peggy	126	Acc	Thomas W.	485	Bdf
John	423	Msn	Peggy	369	Fqr	Thos.	735	Brn

Thos.	335	Dnw	John	64	Acc	Epes	537	Prg
Thos.	868	Hnv	Thomas	126	Acc	Frances	537	Prg
Thos.	3	Hnr	see Shay			Herbert	538	Prg
Thos.	807	Nrf	Teaford, Geo.	390	Ags	Humphrey, est	179	Knq
Thos.	819	Nrf	Henry	388	Ags	John	203	Ess
Thos.	722	Wsh	Teagle, Edwd., (W)	884	Yrk	Joseph, jr.	179	Knq
Thos., jr.	220	Kng	Richard	354	Fqr	Joseph, Senr.	178	Knq
Thos., jr.	809	Nrf	Teagles, John	388	Ags	Joshua, jr.	537	Prg
Thos., Senr.	220	Kng	Teague see Tigue			Joshua, Sr.	537	Prg
Timothy	276	Ldn	Teal, Jacob	243	Ldn	Nancy	543	Prg
Vincent	306	Frf	Teany, Danl.	390	Ags	Randolph	543	Prg
Vincent	349	Fqr	Teas, John	869	Cmp	Sabastian	388	Ags
Wat	871	Cmp	Thomas	869	Cmp	Samuel	538	Prg
William	174	Alb	Teays, William	732	Nls	Thos.	544	Prg
William	261	Amh	Tebbs, Anne	499	Prw	William	22	Hnr
William	484	Bdf	Elizabeth	500	Prw	William	179	Knq
William	485	Bdf	Fowshee G.	391	Rch	see Semple		
William	805	Bck	W. P.	670	Btt	Templeman, Ann	788	Wst
William	814	Bck	W. P.	671	Btt	Edward	50	Stf
William	871	Cmp	William	506	Prw	Ephraim	39	Stf
William	882	Cmp	Wm. P.	602	Btt	Feilding	345	Fqr
William	929	Crl	Wm. P.	661	Btt	James	28	Stf
William	941	Chc	Tebo, Conrad	564	Frd	Lewis	50	Stf
William	101	Cmb	Conrad	603	Frd	Moses	30	Stf
William	216	Ess	George	603	Frd	Samuel	787	Wst
William	534	Frd	Tecter, Peter	388	Ags	William	192	Shn
William	565	Frd	Peter, jr.	387	Ags	Templer, James	294	Ldn
William	762	Hmp	Tedd, William K.	439	Bth	Jno.	311	Ldn
William	833	Hmp	Tedric, John	581	Brk	Stacey	293	Ldn
William	86	Jff	Peter	581	Brk	Wm.	307	Ldn
William	219	Kng	Tedrick, Christo.	581	Brk	Templeton, Davd.	307	Rck
William	407	Mds	Geo.	581	Brk	James	307	Rck
William	575	Mnr	Tedrow, Jona	544	Mnn	Jno.	298	Rck
William	769	Nwk	Teel, George	472	Frn	William	697	Br
William	771	Nwk	Henry	220	Kng	William	9	Oho
William	996	Nrt	Peter	477	Frn	Ten... see Ter...		
William	519	Prw	Teelan, Elenor	690	Br	Tenant, Jno.	543	Mnn
William	5	Rcm	William	690	Br	Jos.	543	Mnn
William	69	Spt	Teeny, John	11	Rcm	Peter	543	Mnn
William, jr.	484	Bdf	Teet, Ann	787	Wst	Richd.	543	Mnn
William, junr.	929	Crl	Campbell	787	Wst	Richd., Jr.	543	Mnn
William, of E	62	Acc	James, Junr.	787	Wst	William	298	Amh
William, Senr.	929	Crl	James, Senr.	787	Wst	Wm.	543	Mnn
William D.	179	Knq	Joseph	787	Wst	Tench, James	535	Prg
William L.	179	Knq	Peggy	787	Wst	William	534	Prg
William R.	128	Acc	Samuel	788	Wst	Tender, Benjamin	20	Rcm
William R.	770	Nwk	William	787	Wst	Tennable, Elizth.	922	Nrf
William T.	391	Fqr	Teeter, ...	222	Pnd	Tennain, Peter	30	Hnr
Wim.	900	Hnv	George	221	Pnd	Tennel, George	523	Prw
Wm.	662	Btt	Jacob	422	Rnd	Tennent, George W.	929	Crl
Wm.	736	Brn	Jacob	425	Rnd	John	929	Crl
Wm.	207	Ess	Joel	221	Pnd	Sarah	929	Crl
Wm.	9	Hnr	Paul	221	Pnd	Tennerson, Henry	271	Amh
Wm.	120	Hnr	Philip	222	Pnd	Tennis, Aaron	884	Yrk
Wm.	263	Ldn	Reuben	222	Pnd	Abram	190	Elc
Wm.	295	Ldn	Teetor, Sameul	220	Pnd	Jessee	884	Yrk
Wm.	597	Mnr	Teets, Adam	546	Mnn	John	884	Yrk
Wm.	793	Nrf	Henry	545	Mnn	Sarah	190	Elc
Wm.	819	Nrf	Jacob	545	Mnn	Tennison, Joshua	83	Clp
Wm.	270	Rck	Tegarding, John	1	Oho	Shadrach	484	Bdf
Wm.	279	Rck	Tegnall, Wm.	813	Nrf	see Tinnisoa		
Wm.	873	Sth	Tellar, Henry	456	Grn	Tenser, Joseph	884	Yrk
Wm.	726	Wsh	James	456	Grn	Tensley, Anthoney G.	485	Bdf
Wm., (G)	819	Nrf	Tellcart, Christian	36	Rcm	John	26	Hnr
Wm., Jr.	407	Mds	Philip	36	Rcm	Wm.	859	Hnv
Wm., jr.	820	Nrf	Teller see Tiller			Tepence, David	6	Hnr
Wm. Clerk	690	Wsh	Telles, David	485	Bdf	Tepling, Erasms.	922	Nrf
Zachariah	112	Cmb	Tellis, Rodham	997	Nrt	Tepton, Wm.	168	Shn
Zachary	407	Mds	Tellus, David	769	Hmp	Terdale see Tisdale		
Zingo	291	Ldn	Tembrook, John	778	Hmp	Ternan, James	127	Hnr
see Saylor, Tailor, Taylon,			Temery, Jno.	265	Ldn	Terpin, Alexander	129	Hnr
Toler, Toylon, Traylor			Peter	266	Ldn	John	126	Hnr
Tazewell, Wm., (W)	884	Yrk	Temple, ---, & Gaugh-			Miles	129	Hnr
Tazwell, Littleton W.,			ney	21	Hnr	Obediah	304	Amh
[his] (Plantn.)			Allen	532	Prg	Strabbo, Persons of		
Wm.	63	Chs	Anne	537	Prg	Coulour	124	Cmb
Teachner, Aron	544	Mnn	Armistead	530	Prg	William	118	Cmb
Jona.	544	Mnn	David	536	Prg	Terr..., Jas.	546	Prg
Moses	544	Mnn	Drury	536	Prg	Terrel, Chiles	210	Alb
Teackle, Exer	65	Acc	Emanuel	537	Prg	Joel	210	Alb

John	174	Alb	Tetchnal, Step	545	Mnn	Mary	758	Hmp
Keeling	111	Spt	Teter see Peter, Teeter			Milly	362	Lnc
Mat	545	Mnn	Teterel, F., (W)	884	Yrk	Stephen	272	Ldn
Nathan	868	Hnv	Tetrah, Philip	15	Rcm	Ths.	82	Clp
William	769	Nwk	Tetric, Amy	965	Hrr	Wm.	316	Ldn
see Terril			John	965	Hrr	Thaxton, Benjamin	588	Pre
Terrell, Ann	408	Mds	Joseph	965	Hrr	David	588	Pre
Catharine	930	Crl	see Fetro			James	588	Pre
Charles	930	Crl	Tetrick, Henry	950	Hrr	John	588	Pre
Charles L.	867	Cmp	Jacob	545	Mnn	Nathaniel	588	Pre
Christopher	928	Crl	see Tedric			Sarah	588	Pre
Daniel	6	Oho	Tettell see Tillett			William	588	Pre
Edward	869	Cmp	Tevalt, Peter	573	Frd	Thayer, Seeva	325	Dnw
Eli	13	Oho	Tevault, Andrew	781	Hmp	William	370	Fqr
Fleming	928	Crl	Tewalt, Jacob	544	Mnn	Thed, George	82	Clp
George	931	Crl	John, Jr.	536	Frd	Nathl.	83	Clp
Henrietta	522	Prw	John, Senr.	536	Frd	William	83	Clp
Jessee	928	Crl	Tewell, Wm.	309	Frf	Thimpson, Precilla	221	Kng
Jonathan	929	Crl	Tewmond, Eliza	179	Knq	Third, George	133	Hnr
Joseph	929	Crl	George	179	Knq	Harry	288	Ldn
Mary	408	Mds	Teys see Feys			Thockmorton, Jos.	555	Brk
Micajah	83	Clp	Thacher, Ally	437	Bth	Thoiston, William	930	Crl
Robert	928	Crl	Pettis	297	Amh	Thom, Reuben	111	Spt
Robert	408	Mds	Philip	927	Crl	see Thorn		
Samuel	930	Crl	Sackville	927	Crl	Thomas, A.J.	35	Hnr
Timothey	861	Cmp	William	927	Crl	Aaron	13	Rcm
see Ferrell, Tennel			Thacker, Austin	878	Hnv	Abel	275	Rck
Terrett, George	306	Frf	D.H.	112	Hnr	Abijah	710	Wsh
Wm. H.	306	Frf	Danel	174	Alb	Absolam	864	Hnv
Terrey, Champ	492	Frn	David	163	Dnw	Adam	575	Mnr
Terrie, Tumothy	942	Hrr	David	717	Gch	Adam	21	Oho
Terriel, James	439	Mth	Edmund	866	Hnv	Allen	262	Amh
Terrier, Francis	442	Mth	Elisha	390	Ags	Allen	763	Brn
Jno.	454	Mth	Ezekial	174	Alb	Allen	928	Crl
Phillip	109	Spt	Holt	883	Hnv	Amos	275	Rck
Terril, Charles	869	Hnv	James	866	Hnv	Amy, a free mulatto	997	Nrt
David	866	Hnv	Jas.	854	Hnv	Ann	210	Alb
Edmund	864	Hnv	Jno.	899	Hnv	Ann	132	Cmb
Elizabeth	876	Hnv	Joel	456	Grn	Ann, Este.	922	Nrf
Jno.	866	Hnv	John	735	Brn	Aquila	94	Jff
John	739	Wsh	Martin	174	Alb	Archd.	273	Rck
Pleasant	861	Hnv	Martin	175	Alb	Atha.	4	Ntt
Richmond	864	Hnv	Meridith	847	Hnv	Athainatius	210	Alb
Roger	876	Hnv	Nathan	878	Hnv	B.A.	30	Hnr
Salley	862	Hnv	Randolph	899	Hnv	Beckum	788	Wst
Wim.	876	Hnv	Reuben	718	Gch	Ben	546	Mnn
Wim., Jnr.	862	Hnv	Reubin	639	Gls	Benjamin	686	Br
see Terrel			Robert	850	Hnv	Benjamin	407	Mds
Terrill, Abner	24	Oho	Thomas	175	Alb	Benjamin	35	Stf
Daniel	26	Oho	William	174	Alb	Benjamin	666	Sss
George	667	Mnt	Wim.	866	Hnv	Benjn.	661	Btt
Terry, Dabney	65	Chr	Wm.	735	Brn	Biscow	177	Elc
Dennis	178	Knq	Wyatt	716	Gch	Buck, (FB)	20	Ntt
Elijah	658	Mnt	Zerish	717	Gch	Camp	858	Wth
Elijah	872	Sth	see Thacher			Catherine	86	Jff
Enoch W.	484	Bdf	Tharman, Nancy, (FN)	36	Rcm	Catlett	929	Crl
Francis, Mrs.	65	Chr	Tharp, Amos	219	Pnd	Charles	484	Bdf
James	930	Crl	Danl.	15	Rcm	Charles	307	Frf
Jane	642	Mnt	David	274	Ldn	Charles	997	Nrt
Jesper	658	Mnt	George	386	Fqr	Charles	22	Oho
Jno.	898	Hnv	James	695	Wsh	Charles	280	Rck
John	18	Rcm	Jesse	408	Fqr	Christopher J.	716	Gch
Jonathan	636	Mnt	John	408	Fqr	Clabourn	5	Hnr
Josiah	659	Mnt	John	830	Hmp	Cloud H.	14	Hnr
Mills	846	Hnv	Nathanl.	556	Brk	Cornelius	83	Clp
Obadiah	84	Spt	Thomas	408	Fqr	Daniel	778	Bck
Polly	613	Mnt	William	361	Fqr	Daniel	241	Ldn
Rowland	930	Crl	William, bound for a term of years	447	Bth	Daniel W.	512	Frd
Stephen	273	Rck	William, Jr.	365	Fqr	David	485	Bdf
Thomas	305	Amh	Wm.	556	Brk	David	763	Brn
Thomas	64	Chr	see Sharp			David	163	Dnw
William	287	Amh	Tharpe, Benjamin	601	Frd	David	332	Dnw
William	485	Bdf	John, sr.	49	Stf	David	444	Flv
William	408	Mds	Thomas, jr.	50	Stf	David	526	Frd
Wm.	717	Gch	Thomas, sr.	50	Stf	David	272	Ldn
Wm.	613	Mnt	Thatcher, Elisha	118	Spt	David	129	Sth
Wm., Sr.	636	Mnt	Jonah	271	Ldn	David	8	Wod
Wm. M.	717	Gch	Jonathan	546	Brk	David, jr.	7	Ntt
Tert, Jno.	546	Mnn	Mary	553	Brk	David, Senr.	7	Ntt
Tester, George	216	Shn				Ebenezer	332	Dnw

Name	No.	Co.
Edward	174	Alb
Edward	123	Hnr
Edward G.	996	Nrt
Elias E.	559	Brk
Elisha	858	Wth
Eliza.	674	Glc
Elizabeth	489	Bdf
Elizabeth	508	Prw
Elizabeth	412	Rch
Ellen	997	Nrt
Elliot	840	Bck
Ellis	19	Oho
Evan	18	Rcm
Even	943	Hrr
Ezekiel	19	Rcm
Francis	661	Btt
Frederic	21	Oho
Gasper	266	Rck
Geo.	232	Ldn
George [2]	484	Bdf
George	662	Btt
George	855	Hnv
George	943	Hrr
George	407	Mds
George	996	Nrt
George D.	127	Acc
Giles	646	Mnt
Grace	499	Prw
Griffith	701	Wsh
Gustavus	517	Prw
Henry	22	Oho
Henry	148	Sth
Isaac [2]	485	Bdf
Isaac	701	Wsh
Isham	836	Bck
Jacob	308	Ldn
Jacob	545	Mnn
Jacob	4	Rcm
James	174	Alb
James	210	Alb
James	817	Bck
James	928	Crl
James	177	Elc
James	197	Ess
James	370	Fqr
James	716	Gch
James	882	Hnv
James	118	Hnr
James	101	Jff
James	12	Knw
James	254	Ldn
James	454	Mth
James	574	Mnr
James	732	Nls
James	399	Rch
James	666	Sss
James, Jun.	787	Wst
James, Senr.	788	Wst
James, Sr.	437	Mth
Jas.	546	Mnn
Jason	82	Clp
Jesse	443	Bth
Jesse	437	Mth
Jessee	174	Alb
Jno.	308	Ldn
Jno.	544	Mnn
Jno.	922	Nrf
Job H.	119	Cmb
John [3]	174	Alb
John	210	Alb
John	388	Ags
John	484	Bdf
John	485	Bdf
John	800	Bck
John	808	Bck
John	65	Chr
John	309	Frf
John	398	Fqr
John	446	Flv
John	535	Frd
John	639	Gls
John	772	Hmp
John	908	Hrr
John	74	Jff
John	14	Knw
John	470	Mdd
John	733	Nls
John	997	Nrt
John	169	Shn
John	148	Sth
John	71	Spt
John	708	Wsh
John	710	Wsh
John	717	Wsh
John	858	Wth
John, jr.	388	Ags
John, Sr.	445	Flv
John L.	118	Hnr
Jos.	545	Mnn
Joseph [2]	818	Bck
Joseph	128	Cmb
Joseph	56	Jff
Joseph	12	Knw
Joseph	272	Ldn
Joshua	126	Acc
Joshua	485	Bdf
Joshua	4	Ntt
Josiah	178	Knq
Jowel	438	Mth
Leonard	67	Jff
Levy	191	Elc
Lewis [2]	175	Alb
Lewis	11	Knw
Lewis	667	Sss
Lewis	694	Wsh
Lindsey	2	Knw
Lukey, a free mulatto	997	Nrt
Margaret	997	Nrt
Margarett	197	Ess
Martha	272	Ldn
Martha	617	Srr
Mary	388	Ags
Mary	82	Clp
Mary	201	Ess
Mary	305	Frf
Mary	716	Gch
Mary	30	Isw
Mary	220	Kng
Mary	305	Ldn
Mary	84	Spt
Massey	220	Kng
Matthew	617	Srr
Michael	173	Alb
Michael	174	Alb
Moses	661	Btt
Moses	309	Frf
Moses	807	Hmp
Nancy	293	Ldn
Nancy	527	Prw
Nathan	446	Flv
Nathaniel	997	Nrt
Nelley	392	Fqr
Norborne	732	Nls
Obediah	730	Nls
Olive	124	Hnr
Opie	996	Nrt
Pwen	359	Fqr
Oziah	21	Oho
Peter	37	Rcm
Peter	858	Wth
Phenias	274	Ldn
Philip	203	Ess
Philip	271	Ldn
Price	869	Hnv
Price	787	Wst
Prudence	174	Alb
Rachel	222	Shn
Ralph	173	Alb
Ralph	174	Alb
Ralph	328	Dnw
Ralph, (F. Negroe)	370	Fqr
Raughlen, a free mulatto	997	Nrt
Rebecca	823	Bck
Rebecca	552	Frd
Reuben	174	Alb
Reuben	407	Mds
Reuben	701	Wsh
Richard	616	Srr
Richd.	717	Gch
Richd.	22	Rcm
Robert	197	Ess
Robert	716	Gch
Robert	407	Mds
Robert	418	Mds
Robert, Jr.	308	Frf
Robert, Sr.	308	Frf
Rod.	361	Lnc
Rodes	210	Alb
Rosa	829	Nrf
Rubin	959	Chc
Rufus	485	Bdf
Saml.	66	Jff
Saml.	545	Mnn
Saml.	681	Wrw
Sampson	307	Rck
Samuel	817	Bck
Samuel	825	Hmp
Samuel, (F. Negroe)	370	Fqr
Sarah	793	Hmp
Sarah	18	Ntt
Sarah	708	Wsh
Spencer	996	Nrt
Spencer, a free mulatto	997	Nrt
Spencer, Jr.	996	Nrt
Sucky	332	Dnw
Susan	65	Chr
Thomas	779	Bck
Thomas	819	Bck
Thomas	710	Wsh
Thos.	312	Ldn
Thos.	546	Mnn
Thos.	586	Mnr
Thos., (W)	884	Yrk
Throuston	897	Hnv
William [2]	485	Bdf
William	865	Cmp
William	392	Fqr
William	816	Hmp
William	118	Hnr
William	93	Jff
William	21	Oho
William	169	Shn
William	617	Srr
William	666	Sss
William	858	Wth
William, Jr.	400	Rch
William, Sen.	404	Rch
Wm.	81	Clp
Wm.	306	Frf
Wm.	441	Flv
Wm.	437	Mth
Wm.	743	Wsh
Wright	412	Bth
Younger	595	Mnr
Thomason, Geo.	388	Ags
James	470	Frn
Jane	587	Pre
Jesse	587	Pre
John	483	Bdf
John	113	Hnr
John	83	Spt
Wm.	432	Flv
Thomasson, Mary	851	Hnv
Thomilson, Hamilton	886	Hnv
Thomison, Jno., Jr.	662	Btt
Thomisson, ---, Overseer	633	Btt
Banister	736	Brn

Name	No.	Abbr.	Name	No.	Abbr.	Name	No.	Abbr.
Thomkins, John	484	Bdf	James	13	Knw	Moses	737	Wsh
Thomley, Aaron	220	Kng	James	731	Nls	Nancy	640	Mnt
Berry B.	220	Kng	James	733	Nls	Nancy	527	Prw
Willm.	220	Kng	James	508	Prw	Nathaniel	209	Alb
Thomnton, John	299	Rck	James	277	Rck	Nathl.	847	Hnv
Thompson, Aaron	432	Msn	James	713	Wsh	Nathl.	651	Mnt
Absalom	858	Wth	James, (R. Oak)	353	Fqr	Nathl.	617	Srr
Adam	650	Mnt	James, Revd.	388	Fqr	Nathl., Jnr.	873	Hnv
Aga	595	Frd	James M.	362	Lnn	Nimrod	918	Hrr
Alexander	858	Wth	Jane	527	Prw	Patsy	40	Stf
Amas	858	Wth	Jane	277	Rck	Polly	330	Dnw
Amos	544	Mnn	Jas.	544	Mnn	Rd.	306	Frf
Andrew	819	Bck	Jas., Sr.	653	Mnt	Rd.	310	Frf
Andrew	856	Cmp	Jas., Sr.	659	Mnt	Rd., Jr.	306	Frf
Andrew	878	Cmp	Jason	403	Fqr	Rebecah	638	Mnt
Andrew	377	Fqr	Jno.	310	Frf	Rebecca	617	Srr
Andrew	316	Ldn	Jno.	893	Hnv	Rob.	545	Mnn
Andrew [2]	858	Wth	Jno.	362	Lnc	Robert	764	Brn
Andw.	544	Mnn	Jno.	446	Mth	Robert	716	Gch
Anne	309	Frf	Jno.	544	Mnn	Robert	788	Wst
Ant.	310	Ldn	Jno.	263	Rck	Robt.	827	Nrf
Avey	4	Knw	Jno. W.	543	Mnn	Roger	209	Alb
B.	11	Hnr	John	416	Bth	Rubin	943	Chc
Benj.	239	Ldn	John	822	Bck	Sally	617	Srr
Benjamin [2]	10	Rcm	John	856	Cmp	Saml.	309	Frf
Benjamin	858	Wth	John	859	Cmp	Saml.	640	Mnt
Bennett	788	Wst	John	864	Cmp	Samuel	869	Cmp
Bob	533	Prg	John	931	Crl	Samuel	810	Hmp
Broothers	444	Mth	John	945	Chc	Samuel	72	Jff
Cathrin	303	Rck	John	958	Chc	Samuel	617	Srr
Charles	731	Nls	John	64	Chr	Samuel	788	Wst
Charles	732	Nls	John	164	Dnw	Sarah	307	Ldn
Charles, Jr.	866	Hnv	John	373	Fqr	Stith	163	Dnw
Charles, Snr.	861	Hnv	John	405	Fqr	Susan	864	Hnv
Charles X. [R. ?]	398	Rch	John	526	Frd	Susanna	859	Wth
Cloe	39	Stf	John	552	Frd	Tabitha	64	Acc
Craven	300	Ldn	John	581	Frd	Thomas	918	Hrr
Dan	544	Mnn	John	763	Hmp	Thomas	56	Jff
Daniel	364	Fqr	John	782	Hmp	Thomas	269	Rck
Daniel	262	Ldn	John	796	Hmp	Thomas	304	Rck
Darvill	736	Brn	John	17	Hnr	Thos.	226	Aml
David	862	Cmp	John	84	Jff	Thos.	258	Ldn
David	655	Mnt	John	220	Kng	Thos.	839	Nrf
David	41	Rcm	John	640	Mnt	Vincent	308	Frf
Ed.	308	Frf	John	731	Nls	W. H.	922	Nrf
Edmund	845	Hnv	John	732	Nls	William	175	Alb
Eleanor	785	Hmp	John	733	Nls	William	414	Bth
Eli	404	Fqr	John	770	Nwk	William	778	Bck
Elisebith	738	Wsh	John	835	Nrf	William	859	Cmp
Elisha	782	Hmp	John	221	Pnd	William	352	Fqr
Eliza	788	Wst	John	525	Prw	William	363	Fqr
Elizabeth	396	Fqr	John	404	Rch	William	916	Hrr
Elizabeth	402	Fqr	John	247	Shn	William	362	Lnn
Elizabeth	32	Rcm	John	737	Wsh	William	105	Spt
Elswick	661	Mnt	John	788	Wst	William	107	Spt
Even	713	Wsh	John	858	Wth	William	60	Stf
Evin	731	Wsh	John, Senr.	737	Wsh	William	617	Srr
Francis	858	Wth	Jos.	823	Nrf	William	719	Wsh
George	940	Chc	Joseph	174	Alb	William	738	Wsh
George	65	Chr	Joseph	403	Fqr	William	787	Wst
George	340	Fqr	Joseph	782	Hmp	William	858	Wth
George	5	Pwh	Joseph	911	Hrr	William Edloe	617	Srr
Harey	5	Hnr	Joseph	25	Hnr	Willis	617	Srr
Henry	661	Btt	Joseph	732	Nls	Willoughby	788	Wst
Henry	911	Hrr	Joseph	511	Prw	Wm.	309	Frf
Henry	814	Nrf	Josha.	327	Dnw	Wm.	674	Glc
Henry	617	Srr	Js.	922	Nrf	Wm.	716	Gch
Horatio	310	Frf	Larkin	640	Mnt	Wm.	269	Ldn
Hugh	674	Glc	Lucy	14	Hnr	Wm.	828	Nrf
Hugh	269	Ldn	Lydia	103	Jff	Wm.	922	Nrf
Isaac	9	Rcm	M.	81	Clp	Wm., Sr.	654	Mnt
Israel	613	Mnt	Margaret	83	Jff	Wm. B.	163	Dnw
James	929	Crl	Mark	722	Wsh	Em. Evans	617	Srr
James	305	Frf	Martha	172	Shn	see Furr, Gardner, Gossam,		
James	421	Fqr	Mary	210	Alb	Holmes, McGee, Mobbley,		
James	531	Frd	Mary	821	Hmp	Randall, Rose, Wilbon		
James	595	Frd	Mary R.	845	Hnv	Thomson, Alexa.	389	Ags
James	639	Gls	Mathew	877	Cmp	Alexr.	389	Ags
James	782	Hmp	Matthew	790	Bck	Anderson	485	Bdf
James	31	Hnr	Moore	788	Wst	Andw.	388	Ags

Archibald	997	Nrt
Benjamin	439	Bth
Bennet	558	Brk
Betsy	74	Spt
Catharine	405	Ags
Cicely	540	Brk
Cornl.	518	Brk
Davd.	570	Mnr
David [2]	362	Lnn
David, Sr.	362	Lnn
Elias	561	Brk
Eliza.	456	Grn
Henry	188	Elc
Huldy	942	Hrr
James	558	Brk
James	570	Mnr
James	596	Mnr
James	770	Nwk
John	387	Ags
John	389	Ags
John	390	Ags
John	485	Bdf
John	571	Brk
John	361	Lnn
John	570	Mnr
John, jr.	390	Ags
John, Jr.	570	Mnr
John, (L. M.)	390	Ags
Joseph	389	Ags
Joseph	508	Brk
Mary	390	Ags
Moses	2	Oho
Nelly	943	Hrr
Paterson	389	Ags
Pleasant	485	Bdf
Polly	770	Nwk
Randolph	361	Lnn
Robert	577	Mnr
Robt.	389	Ags
Sally	103	Cmb
Saml.	570	Mnr
Samuel	478	Frn
Sarah	362	Lnn
Smith	405	Ags
Thomas	479	Frn
Waddy	485	Bdf
William	485	Bdf
William	479	Frn
William	493	Frn
William [2]	362	Lnn
Wm.	389	Ags
Wm.	390	Ags
Wm.	570	Mnr
Wm., Sr.	390	Ags
Thomton, Francis	220	Kng
Jno.	219	Kng
Wm., [his] Est.	219	Kng
Thonhill, William	483	Bdf
Thonton, Mordcai	390	Ags
Thopson, W. M.	35	Hnr
Thorborn, Js.	922	Nrf
Thorborne, Andrew	547	Prg
Thorbourn, Obed.	191	Hrr
Thorn, Ben [2]	543	Mnn
Dolly	82	Clp
Euphamey	127	Acc
George	81	Clp
Jno.	80	Clp
Jno.	544	Mnn
John	515	Prw
John	303	Rck
John, Sr.	503	Prw
Joshua	544	Mnn
Peregrin	82	Clp
Sarah	82	Clp
Tho.	546	Mnn
William	503	Prw
William	855	Sth
Wm.	544	Mnn
Thornberry, William	385	Fqr
Thornburg, Daniel	546	Frd
Drusilla	86	Jff
John	89	Jff
Thos.	521	Brk
William	507	Frd
Wm.	571	Brk
Thornbury, Henry	519	Prw
Thorne, William	83	Clp
Thornel, Thomas	775	Bck
Thornell, Absolum	775	Bck
Jessee	775	Bck
William	775	Bck
Thornhill, Charles	380	Fqr
Elijah	421	Fqr
Henry	36	Rcm
Reuben	22	Rcm
Ths.	81	Clp
William	378	Fqr
Wm.	939	Hrr
see Thonhill		
Thornman, William	62	Acc
Thornton, Ann	68	Chr
Anthony	305	Ldn
Benja. G.	306	Frf
Charles	927	Crl
Charles	297	Ldn
Charles	27	Stf
Coats	421	Msn
Eleanor B.	674	Glc
Elianor B.	81	Clp
Frances	99	Spt
Fras.	673	Glc
Fras., jr.	673	Glc
George	60	Stf
George A.	83	Clp
Henry	65	Acc
Henry	127	Acc
Henry	73	Spt
Henry	3	Wod
Henry, estate	927	Crl
James	25	Stf
James B.	928	Crl
Jas. R.	673	Glc
Jno.	83	Clp
Jno., Jnr.	847	Hnv
Jno., Snr.	900	Hnv
Jno. A.	83	Clp
John	65	Acc
John	127	Acc
John	129	Acc
John	876	Cmp
John	927	Crl
John	68	Spt
John, of Jonn.	65	Acc
Jonathan	130	Acc
Joseph	390	Ags
Joseph	2	Rcm
Joshua, Junr.	129	Acc
Kendall	127	Acc
Kendall, Isld.	129	Acc
Littlebury	498	Frn
Lucy	100	Spt
Lydia	9	Wod
Maryanne	519	Prw
Mildred	87	Spt
Molly	128	Acc
Peter	255	Amh
Peter	930	Crl
Peter P.	299	Amh
Peter P.	306	Amh
Philip	927	Crl
Philip	598	Frd
Presley	787	Wst
Priscilla	674	Glc
Rd.	673	Glc
Reuben	80	Clp
Reuben	94	Spt
Saml.	389	Ags
Starling	487	Frn
Sterling	69	Chr
Thomas	500	Prw
Thomas	9	Wod
Thomas G.	927	Crl
Thos.	609	Mnt
Thos.	477	Pra
William	128	Acc
William	869	Cmp
William	876	Cmp
William	106	Spt
William	666	Sss
William, Gild.	130	Acc
William I.	587	Pre
William M.	126	Cmb
Wm.	585	Brk
Wm.	83	Clp
Wm., Senr.	674	Glc
see Pettyford, Thoiston, Thomnton		
John	841	Nrf
Thorowgood, Eliza	812	Nrf
Thorp, Allen	115	Hnr
Charity	870	Sth
Frances	931	Crl
George W.	210	Alb
Jacob	390	Ags
Lewis, Jr.	456	Grn
Lewis, Sr.	456	Grn
Moses	37	Rcm
Pleasant	112	Hnr
Will.	867	Sth
William	484	Bdf
William	675	Br
William	118	Hnr
William	732	Nls
Wm.	387	Ags
Thoup, Thomas	65	Chr
Thrailkeld, William	78	Spt
Thrailkill, Ann	361	Lnc
Thrall, Jno.	361	Lnc
Tho.	362	Lnc
Thrash, John	642	Mnt
Thrasher, Bengamin	810	Hmp
Christr.	661	Btt
Coonrod	662	Btt
Elias	285	Ldn
Fredk.	662	Btt
George	661	Btt
Paul	662	Btt
Peter	662	Btt
Threadkill, Ann	99	Jff
Threcle, James	587	Brk
Threewitts, Ann	667	Sss
Threft see Thrift		
Threildkeld, Danl.	81	Clp
Thresh, John	815	Hmp
Thrielkeld, Willes	81	Clp
Thrielkild, Js.	80	Clp
Thrift, Benja.	674	Glc
Charles	307	Frf
Chs.	278	Ldn
Eliza	394	Rch
Hamilton	309	Frf
Jeremiah	179	Knq
Jeremiah	787	Wst
Jesse	394	Rch
Jessee	674	Glc
John	410	Rch
John, Junr.	410	Rch
Jos.	674	Glc
Margarett	674	Glc
Mary	164	Dnw
Robert	174	Alb
Sarah	163	Dnw
William	471	Mdd
William, jr.	163	Dnw
Wm.	674	Glc
Wm.	278	Ldn
Wm., Senr.	164	Dnw
Throckmorton, Elizh.	884	Yrk
Gabriel	769	Hmp

John	62	Jff	James	588	Pre	Tilton, Daniel	679	Br
Mordecai	534	Frd	Jesse	789	Bck	Tiltoson, Jesse	12	Pwh
Robert	67	Jff	John	588	Pre	Timber, Ths., (F. M.)	82	Clp
Warner	673	Glc	John A.	718	Gch	Timberlake, Aaron	476	Pra
Warner	756	Hmp	Sarah	718	Gch	Austin	875	Hnv
Wm.	575	Brk	Tiberghien, Charles	12	Oho	Benjamin	875	Hnv
Wm., Jr.	517	Frd	Zacheus	12	Oho	Benjamin	770	Nwk
see Thockmorton			Tibs, Jas.	545	Mnn	Chapman	875	Hnv
Throgmorton, Jesse	130	Hnr	Tice, Jacob	656	Mnt	David	547	Frd
Josiah	125	Hnr	John	661	Mnt	David	873	Hnv
Lewis	20	Oho	Tichen, David	915	Hrr	Eppa	412	Fqr
Lucy	132	Hnr	Tidball, Joseph	517	Frd	Harfield	66	Jff
Robt.	131	Hnr	Josiah	396	Fqr	Horace	443	Flv
Sarah	125	Hnr	Tidd, Joseph	833	Hmp	James	929	Crl
Throp, George	476	Pra	William	427	Bth	Jno., Capt.	65	Chr
Thrower, Christopher	763	Brn	Tiddy, Thomson	24	Oho	John	210	Alb
Edward	763	Brn	Tidwell, Reuben	787	Wst	John	353	Fqr
Thrullier, Chs.	921	Nrf	Tiffee, Mary	997	Nrt	John	437	Flv
Thruston, Henry	470	Mdd	Tiffey, Pope	787	Wst	John	770	Nwk
John	470	Mdd	Rachel	787	Wst	John	836	Nrf
Mary	471	Mdd	Tiffy, Chs.	80	Clp	John, Jur.	948	Chc
Ro.	673	Glc	Tignal, Betsey	64	Acc	John, Sr.	951	Chc
Ro., Senr.	674	Glc	Tigner, John	178	Knq	Jos.	803	Nrf
Thu..., Nathan	484	Bdf	Thomas	407	Mds	Lewis	927	Crl
Thurman, Benjamin	210	Alb	Thos.	881	Hnv	Nathan	132	Hnr
David	451	Frn	Tignor, James	996	Nrt	Reubin	873	Hnv
Edmund	524	Prw	Mary	996	Nrt	Richard G. C.	771	Nwk
James	484	Bdf	Philip	996	Nrt	Thos.	872	Hnv
James	5	Wod	Philip, Jr.	997	Nrt	Thos., Snr.	874	Hnv
John	462	Frn	William	605	Frd	Walker	437	Flv
Natham	209	Alb	Tigue, Jacob	65	Acc	William	930	Crl
Peyton	484	Bdf	Nelly	65	Acc	William	543	Frd
Robert	526	Prw	Til..., Richard	485	Bdf	Wm.	801	Nrf
William	174	Alb	Tilas see Til...			Timberlick, Christopher	880	Cmp
William	210	Alb	Tilby, R.	333	Dnw	Timberman, Jno.	545	Mnn
Wm.	309	Frf	Tilden, John B.	541	Frd	Timblick, Frances	29	Hnr
see Thu...			Tilgman, George	541	Frd	Timmon, Collin	477	Pra
Thurmon, Charles	733	Wsh	Till, Henry	298	Rck	Timmonds, John	591	Brk
John	851	Cmp	Tilledge, Richd., Glouces-			Timmons, Charles	592	Brk
Richard [2]	850	Cmp	ter Town	674	Glc	George	163	Dnw
Thurmond, Andrew	53	Chs	Tiller, Daniel	931	Crl	John	28	Stf
Catharine	731	Nls	George	84	Clp	Nicholas	5	Oho
Charles	733	Nls	George	869	Hnv	Peter	587	Frd
Elizabeth	272	Amh	George	252	Shn	Thomas	29	Stf
James	731	Nls	Henry	851	Sth	see Simmons, Tinmons
John	730	Nls	James	716	Gch	Timms, Elisha	257	Ldn
Philip	281	Amh	Mary	189	Shn	Francis	6	Wod
Thomas	731	Nls	Mealy	29	Hnr	Jesse	263	Ldn
William	270	Amh	Richardson	87	Spt	John	4	Wod
William	731	Nls	Saml.	640	Gls	Joseph	247	Ldn
William	733	Nls	William	931	Crl	Wm.	247	Ldn
Thurston, Armstead	179	Knq	William	640	Gls	Timpson, John	884	Yrk
Elizabeth	717	Gch	William	80	Spt	Timson, Billy	20	Hnr
John	209	Alb	William, jr.	260	Amh	Tinch, Sarah	543	Prg
John	716	Gch	Tillery, Samuel	997	Nrt	Tindal, Benjamin	784	Bck
Matthew	717	Gch	Tillet, Wm.	591	Mnr	Hatcher	784	Bck
Robert	178	Knq	Tillett, Elizabeth	277	Ldn	John	779	Bck
William	179	Knq	Francis	54	Jff	Thomas	795	Bck
Wm., Senr.	716	Gch	Geo.	306	Ldn	Tindall, Ann	921	Nrf
Wm. R.	716	Gch	Giles	293	Ldn	James	128	Acc
Thweate, Jno. Jas.	540	Prg	James	308	Frf	Levin	128	Acc
Thweatt, Archer	64	Chs	James	277	Ldn	Tinder, Anthony	80	Clp
Archer	328	Dnw	Samuel	63	Jff	Tindle, Margret	726	Wsh
Benja., Est.	58	Chs	Tilley, John	763	Brn	Tine, Valun	941	Hrr
Burwell	163	Dnw	Sarah	763	Brn	Tiner, Uriah	326	Dnw
Charles	163	Dnw	Tillinger, Henry	667	Mnt	Tines, John	617	Srr
Ephraim	4	Ntt	Tillman, Emanuel	15	Rcm	Timothy	153	Sth
Henry	163	Dnw	Tillott, Thomas G.	617	Srr	Tineson see Timson
John M.	164	Dnw	Tilly, Jno.	303	Ldn	Tinglar, John	221	Pnd
Joseph	163	Dnw	see T...			Tingle, Hannah	507	Prw
Thomas	163	Dnw	Tilman, Daniel	209	Alb	John	908	Hrr
William	535	Prg	Jacob	429	Flv	Mikle	962	Hrr
Thyall, Sally, (free			John	764	Brn	Wm.	543	Mnn
negro)	674	Glc	Luckey	390	Ags	Tingler, Jacob	662	Btt
Tibb, Jno.	545	Mnn	Paul	175	Alb	Tingley, Saml.	3	Rcm
Tibbett, Thomas	193	Shn	Thomas	174	Alb	Tinkle, Danl.	38	Rcm
Tibbs, F., Jr.	545	Mnn	Zachariah	441	Flv	Frederick	38	Rcm
Fran	545	Mnn	Tilson, Lamuel	711	Wsh	Jacob	38	Rcm
G., & Mother	80	Clp	Thos.	711	Wsh	John	38	Rcm
Hester	84	Clp	William	711	Wsh	Peter	38	Rcm

Tinly, John	929	Hrr	Robt.	541	Prg	George	393	Fqr
Tinmons, Elizabeth	5	Oho	Tittle, Henry	25	Oho	Tolly, Christ.	273	Rck
Tinnell, John	732	Nls	Titton see Tilton			John	273	Rck
Robert	732	Nls	Titus, Abnor	234	Ldn	Joseph	273	Rck
Tinner, Patsy	733	Nls	Francis	566	Brk	Saml.	273	Rck
Tinney, Richd.	531	Prg	Item	298	Ldn	Thomas	273	Rck
Tinnisoa, Levi	485	Bdf	Saml.	298	Ldn	Wm.	276	Rck
Tinny, Wm.	884	Yrk	Samuel	234	Ldn	Tolman, Henry	661	Btt
Tinsbloom, Thos.	764	Brn	Tunis	771	Hmp	Tolson, Benjamin	22	Stf
Tinsbloome, Jno.	179	Knq	Tobert, Thomas	274	Ldn	Fielding	507	Prw
William	178	Knq	Tobin, Isaac	82	Clp	George	42	Stf
Tinsley, ---, Mrs.	34	Hnr	Nat.	81	Clp	Thomas	43	Stf
Abraham	407	Mds	Nath.	82	Clp	William	20	Stf
Banester	295	Amh	Nathen	749	Wsh	Tom, Free	453	Mth
Bennett	267	Amh	Tobler, Michael	25	Oho	Tom Acres see Acres		
Caleb	407	Mds	Tobridge, John	824	Hmp	Tomah, John	9	Rcm
Charles	900	Hnv	Toby, William	83	Clp	Philip	19	Rcm
Cornelius	716	Gch	Tod, Samuel	12	Oho	Tomason, Aaron	431	Flv
Daniel	894	Hnv	Thomas	12	Oho	Wm.	431	Flv
David	262	Amh	Todd, Bernard	65	Chr	Tomberlin, William [2]	174	Alb
David	875	Hnv	Betsy	123	Hnr	Tomblin, John, Senr.	374	Fqr
David, jr.	262	Amh	Charles	927	Crl	Samuel	379	Fqr
Edward	271	Amh	Charles, Senr.	931	Crl	Stephen	375	Fqr
Edward, jr.	262	Amh	Edward	687	Br	Thos.	295	Rck
Elizabeth	929	Crl	George	930	Crl	William	374	Fqr
Elizebeth	407	Mds	George	858	Wth	William	599	Frd
George	271	Amh	Henry P.	393	Rch	William, Senr.	375	Fqr
George M.	282	Amh	James	387	Ags	see Tumbling		
Henry	407	Mds	James	118	Hnr	Tombrell, Jno.	922	Nrf
Isaac	264	Amh	Jane	698	Wsh	Tombs, George	894	Hnv
Isaac	277	Amh	Jno.	662	Btt	Jno.	872	Hnv
Jacob	929	Crl	John	164	Dnw	Jno.	896	Hnv
James	262	Amh	John	698	Wsh	Robert	894	Hnv
James	484	Bdf	Joseph	340	Fqr	Robert	60	Stf
Jno.	891	Hnv	Mallory	14	Isw	see Toombs		
John	273	Amh	Miles	11	Hnr	Tombson see Tomleson		
John	717	Gch	Polley	326	Dnw	Tomerson, Elizabeth	175	Alb
John	118	Hnr	Richard	101	Spt	John	210	Alb
Joshua	273	Amh	Samuel	263	Ldn	Tomes, Alexander	174	Alb
Joshua	929	Crl	William	179	Knq	Tomey, Betty	522	Frd
Kisiah	718	Gch	William	530	Prg	Tomilson, Joseph	3	Oho
Lindsay	274	Amh	William	93	Spt	Samuel	17	Oho
Major	11	Pwh	Todhunter, Jno.	290	Ldn	Thomas [crossed out]	14	Oho
Nathl.	848	Hnv	Joseph	529	Brk	Tominson, Thos. J.	18	Hnr
Peter, [his] Est.	891	Hnv	Toel, Peter	852	Cmp	Tomkies, Ann	674	Glc
Pleasant	716	Gch	Tokibens see Tomilson			Jos.	674	Glc
Reuben	480	Frn	Toland, Andrew	588	Brk	Morgan	673	Glc
Reves	111	Hnr	James	686	Br	Tomkins, Chris.	449	Mth
Richard	285	Amh	Tolaven, Zachariah	859	Wth	Eizabeth	174	Alb
Robert	484	Bdf	Tolbert, Charles	723	Wsh	Embro	8	Hnr
Thos.	875	Hnv	Eliza	662	Btt	Henry	23	Hnr
William	273	Amh	Thos.	724	Wsh	Jonathan	406	Fqr
William	407	Mds	Tolbott, Jos.	290	Ldn	Tomleson, Harris	362	Lnn
William [2]	37	Rcm	Tole, Henry	270	Rck	Jane	361	Lnn
Wm.	114	Hnr	Toleman see Toolman			Tomlin, Jno. W.	887	Hnv
Wyatt	854	Hnv	Toler, Absolom	4	Pwh	John	14	Isw
see Rucker			Absolum, jr.	3	Pwh	Moore F.	400	Rch
Tinsly, Thomas	119	Hnr	Anderson	117	Hnr	Richard	499	Prw
Tippete, Thomas	184	Shn	Benjn.	128	Cmb	Robert G.	391	Rch
Tippett, Ezekle	409	Mds	David	639	Gls	Wm.	362	Lnc
James	381	Fqr	Elisha	639	Gls	Tomlinson, Ambrose	295	Amh
James	409	Mds	Geo.	717	Gch	Ambrose, jr.	294	Amh
John	382	Fqr	Godfrey	261	Amh	Joseph	11	Wod
William	356	Fqr	Henry	308	Frf	Mary	259	Ldn
Tipple, Henry	520	Frd	John	111	Hnr	Soloman	673	Glc
Tiry, Nicholas	776	Bck	Lemuel	716	Gch	Thomas	259	Ldn
Roland	776	Bck	Mary	717	Gch	William	295	Amh
Tisdale, Hennery	361	Lnn	Matthew	892	Hnv	William S.	667	Sss
John	361	Lnn	Michum	851	Hnv	Wm.	673	Glc
Reneson	361	Lnn	Plesant	844	Hnv	see Tominson, Tomleson		
Rider	922	Nrf	Richd.	717	Gch	Tompkin, Francis	826	Nrf
Robert	945	Chc	Syntha	872	Hnv	Tompkins, ---, & Murry	20	Hnr
Robt.	389	Ags	Wm.	717	Gch	Bailey	928	Crl
Talton	431	Flv	Zachariah	639	Gls	Benj.	306	Ldn
William	363	Lnn	Toley, Charles	851	Hnv	Bennett	927	Crl
Tishinger, John	229	Shn	Tollar, Elias	127	Hnr	Charles	446	Flv
Tisley, John	59	Stf	Tollcart, Jacob	9	Rcm	Chas.	829	Nrf
William	61	Stf	Tolle, William	278	Amh	Christopher	31	Hnr
Tison, Enos	938	Hrr	Toller, William, jr.	297	Amh	Francis	927	Crl
Titmarsh, Richard	530	Prg	Tolles, George	391	Fqr	George	928	Crl

Martin	81	Clp
Mary	854	Cmp
Mary	65	Chr
Mary	921	Nrf
Richard	928	Crl
Ro.	884	Yrk
Robert	927	Crl
William	175	Alb
William	78	Spt
Wm.	436	Flv
see Tompkin		
Tompson, Danl.	308	Frf
Edmd.	81	Clp
Garland	79	Clp
Henry	308	Frf
Jacob	965	Hrr
James	932	Hrr
James	258	Shn
John	937	Hrr
John	221	Pnd
Mary	16	Hnr
Philip R.	79	Clp
Ths.	82	Clp
William [2]	221	Pnd
Wm. M.	79	Clp
Toms, John	733	Nls
Joseph	732	Nls
Tomson, Benja.	305	Frf
Toncray, Anthony	858	Wth
James	858	Wth
Jno.	543	Mnn
Tonery, John	689	Wsh
Lewis	691	Wsh
Toney, Cary	4	Knw
Charles	835	Bck
Charles	457	Frn
Charles, (SW)	835	Bck
Edmond	801	Bck
Edmund	11	Pwh
Francis	662	Btt
James	456	Frn
John [2]	801	Bck
John	639	Gls
John	1	Pwh
John F.	4	Knw
K.	32	Hnr
Mary	801	Bck
Peter	835	Bck
Poindexter	4	Knw
Richard	13	Pwh
William	834	Bck
William	835	Bck
William	852	Cmp
William	11	Pwh
Tongate, Elizabeth	51	Stf
John	52	Stf
Tongue, Johnzey	421	Fqr
Tonnsen, Ezekiel	961	Hrr
Tony, Edmund	635	Mnt
Tool, Barbary	733	Wsh
John	88	Jff
Joseph	552	Frd
Thomas	104	Jff
Toole, Edwd.	922	Nrf
Tooler, William	210	Alb
Tooley, Charles	288	Amh
John	288	Amh
John	732	Nls
John, jr.	288	Amh
Landon	288	Amh
Tandy	288	Amh
William	174	Alb
Tooll, Arthur	409	Ags
Toolman, Jno.	362	Lnc
Toombes, George	588	Pre
William	587	Pre
William, Senr.	588	Pre
Toombs, Ambrose	931	Crl
Emanuel	65	Chr
Gabriel	928	Crl

Gabriel	930	Crl
Jno.	893	Hnv
Polly	199	Ess
Rittee	930	Crl
Thomas	65	Chr
William	928	Crl
William	65	Chr
Toomery, Wm.	545	Mnn
Toon, Lewis	363	Lnn
Toone, Susan	477	Pra
Tophouse, Francis	795	Hmp
Toping, Nancy	62	Acc
Topper, Henry	764	Hmp
Toppin, Geo.	884	Yrk
Robinson	884	Yrk
Thomas	30	Rcm
Topping, Garrett	63	Acc
James R.	191	Elc
John	191	Elc
Robert	192	Elc
Sally S.	62	Acc
Smith	190	Elc
Torbert, William	393	Fqr
Torbet, Hugh	387	Ags
Jno.	275	Rck
Robt.	390	Ags
Saml.	389	Ags
Thomas	262	Ldn
Torbit, John	389	Ags
Nathl.	410	Ags
Torbone, Andrew	227	Aml
Torrence see Tawrance		
Torreyson, John	504	Prw
Tort see Tart		
Tosh, Jonatn.	662	Btt
Tosspot, Timothy	512	Frd
Tote see Tole		
Totten, Amos	858	Wth
James	813	Hmp
John	858	Wth
Samuel	822	Hmp
Samuel	858	Wth
Totton, James	393	Fqr
Totty, Abner	55	Chs
Arthur	65	Chr
Daniel	54	Chs
Nancy	63	Chs
Wm.	55	Chs
Touber, Frederick	416	Bth
Touchstone, Benjamin	542	Frd
William	546	Frd
Toulson, Bill, a free mulatto	998	Nrt
James, a free mulatto	998	Nrt
Jane	997	Nrt
Mary	922	Nrf
Patrick, a free mulatto	997	Nrt
Richard	996	Nrt
Touns, George	964	Hrr
Tousand, William	588	Pre
Tousnend, Geo.	387	Ags
Toup, George	522	Brk
Tourman, John	716	Gch
Richd.	716	Gch
Tousant, ---, & Tuckfield	46	Stf
Tout, Adam	226	Shn
Toute, Philip	226	Pnd
Towberman, Henry	216	Pnd
Peter	235	Ldn
Towbler, Jacob, Junr.	859	Wth
Jacob, Senr.	859	Wth
Towel, John, jr.	388	Ags
John, sr.	388	Ags
Towell, Mark	363	Lnc
Tho.	361	Lnc
Towl, Roger	870	Cmp
Towler, Barnabas	484	Bdf
Benjamin	484	Bdf

Benjn.	164	Dnw
Elisha	483	Bdf
Elizabeth, Ms.	65	Chr
Luke	940	Chc
see T...ler		
Towles, George	81	Clp
Henry	81	Clp
Henry	408	Mds
Henry	104	Spt
Henry, Sr.	81	Clp
J., (clk Lan. ct)	368	Lnc
Jas.	361	Lnc
Joseph	82	Clp
Joseph	408	Mds
Mary	81	Clp
Oliver	362	Lnc
Portuse	361	Lnc
Rolly	103	Spt
Sto.	361	Lnc
Stokely	103	Spt
Stokesley	997	Nrt
Therit	92	Spt
Thomas	997	Nrt
William	103	Spt
Towlin, Hugh	792	Hmp
Towlington, Matthew	13	Oho
Towndsand, Elizabeth	430	Bth
Towndsend, Solomon	422	Bth
William	431	Bth
Towner, Adam	307	Frf
Jacob [2]	306	Ldn
Townes, Allen	226	Aml
Armstead T.	227	Aml
John	227	Aml
John L.	227	Aml
Lucy	226	Aml
Townley, Jane	179	Knq
John	214	Ess
John	8	Pwh
Townlin, Joseph	497	Frn
Towns, Laban	764	Brn
Townsand, Daniel	362	Lnn
Joseph	362	Lnn
William	362	Lnn
William	363	Lnn
Townsel, Charles	732	Nls
see Townson		
Townsen, Charles	731	Nls
James	936	Hrr
see Townson		
Townsend, Elizabeth	997	Nrt
Henry	859	Wth
John, Junr.	859	Wth
John, Senr.	859	Wth
Joseph	591	Frd
Levin	127	Acc
Nancy	816	Nrf
Richard	862	Cmp
Susannah	65	Acc
Zadock	129	Acc
Townshead see Peyton		
Townsley, James	668	Mnt
Joseph	668	Mnt
Man	210	Alb
Robt.	668	Mnt
Wm.	668	Mnt
Townson, John	907	Hrr
Nathan	731	Nls
see Townsel, Townsen		
Towson, Charles	180	Alb
Toylon, John	24	Oho
Trabue, Jacob	61	Chs
John	61	Chs
Mary	11	Pwh
Polley	57	Chs
Tracewell, Edward	591	Frd
George	592	Frd
Tracey, Danl.	922	Nrf
Henry	15	Oho
James	395	Fqr

William	401	Fqr
William	639	Gls
Trackwell, Joshua	570	Mnr
Tracy, Bazel	674	Br
George	675	Br
James	81	Jff
Joshua	683	Br
Prince	717	Gch
Solomon	484	Bdf
William	485	Bdf
William, Sr.	484	Bdf
Wm.	242	Ldn
Trader, Archibald, Jun.	130	Acc
Archibald, Sen.	130	Acc
Arth., Jr.	546	Mnn
Arthur	545	Mnn
Geo.	470	Mdd
Hannah	130	Acc
Henry	129	Acc
Jno.	545	Mnn
Littleton, Junr.	62	Acc
Littleton, Senr.	63	Acc
Nancy	64	Acc
Patience	63	Acc
Sacker	130	Acc
Staler	576	Frd
Staton	129	Acc
William	64	Acc
William, Senr.	129	Acc
Trager, William, sen.	417	Bth
Tragle, Thos.	674	Glc
Trail, Ashbud	297	Amh
Charles	492	Frn
Charles	731	Nls
Edward	168	Shn
Jane	921	Nrf
Nathan	101	Jff
Trainer, Michl.	390	Ags
Trainham, John	931	Crl
Trammel, Garard	295	Ldn
Gerrard	312	Ldn
Trammell, Gerd., Jr.	310	Frf
Gerd., Senr.	310	Frf
Lettice	307	Frf
Thomas	306	Frf
Washg.	310	Frf
Tranbanger, Davd.	703	Wsh
Travalian, Thomas	210	Alb
Travel, George	442	Bth
Travers, Henry	997	Nrt
Jos. H., has Slaves in		
York County	884	Yrk
Traverse, Benja.	856	Sth
Britain	856	Sth
Edwin	856	Sth
Jno.	856	Sth
Jno.	872	Sth
Travice, Thos.	390	Ags
Travillion, Edwd.	674	Glc
Jno.	674	Glc
Mildred	674	Glc
Travis, Britain	139	Sth
Charles	666	Sss
John	677	Br
Trayler, John	163	Dnw
Traylor, Arbin	62	Chs
Archer	65	Chs
Edward	53	Chs
Edward	13	Ntt
James	65	Chr
Jno.	541	Prg
Joel	163	Dnw
John [crossed out]	163	Dnw
Joseph	55	Chs
Meal	54	Chs
Peler	362	Lnn
Robert	874	Cmp
Robert	163	Dnw
Sandal	54	Chs
Thomas	55	Chs

Wm. [2]	54	Chs
Wm.	10	Ntt
Wm. N.	54	Chs
see Taylor, Trayler, Trayor		
Traynum, Mildred	65	Chr
Trayor, Danl.	388	Ags
Treacle, William	997	Nrt
Treadway, Moses	588	Pre
Treakle, Dem.	362	Lnc
Lea.	362	Lnc
Treble, George	930	Crl
see Trible		
Tredway, Thomas	68	Chs
Tree, George	64	Acc
Treehorn, James	129	Acc
Treelock see Trulock		
Treet, Henry	269	Ldn
Jeremiah	424	Bth
Trehern, James	764	Brn
Tremier, Henry	536	Frd
Tremley, Jno.	545	Mnn
Tremly, Ben	545	Mnn
Trenary, Samuel	543	Frd
Trenis, Peter F.	661	Btt
Trenor, James	661	Btt
Trent, Alexander	800	Bck
Alexander	588	Pre
Benja.	66	Chs
E.W.	11	Hnr
Henry	485	Bdf
Henry	437	Flv
Henry	12	Pwh
Joseph	11	Hnr
Josiah	5	Pwh
Nicholas	484	Bdf
Obabadiah H.	484	Bdf
Thomas	840	Bck
William	227	Aml
William	484	Bdf
Zachariah	864	Cmp
Trenten, Joseph	811	Hmp
Trents, John A.	117	Cmb
Stephen W.	119	Cmb
Treppet, Caleb	544	Mnn
Treppett, Govey	544	Mnn
Treshorier, George	571	Brk
Tresler, Charles	416	Bth
Philip	220	Shn
Tressam, Robert	269	Rck
Tressler, Henry	661	Btt
Tretlepoo, Conrod	568	Brk
Tretlipo see Trttipo		
Trevelian, John	716	Gch
Trevilian, Thos.	867	Hnv
Trevillian, Thomas	928	Crl
Trevor see Trenor		
Trewhitt, Mary Ann	3	Ntt
Trewin, M.	30	Hnr
Treyhern, Sarah	259	Ldn
Thomas	261	Ldn
Thomas	311	Ldn
Trezvant, John	666	Sss
Tribbet, John	276	Rck
Tribbey, Jno.	314	Ldn
Jos.	281	Ldn
Thomas	309	Ldn
Thos.	314	Ldn
Trible, Ann	215	Ess
George	209	Ess
John	215	Ess
see Treble		
Tribo, Abram	390	Ags
Trice, Ann	179	Knq
Frances	471	Mdd
James	777	Bck
Tandy	800	Bck
Thomas	471	Mdd
Tricher, James	220	Kng
Wm.	220	Kng
Trickey, Christopher	524	Prw

Trickle, Joshua	773	Hmp
Triell, David	732	Nls
Triest, Edy	923	Nrf
Trigg, Abraham	628	Mnt
Abram	858	Wth
Clement	13	Knw
Daniel	648	Mnt
Flemming	640	Gls
Frany B., Mrs.	690	Wsh
John	484	Bdf
John J.	721	Wsh
Thomas	101	Spt
William	484	Bdf
William	688	Wsh
Trigge, James	182	Shn
Trimble, Alexr.	307	Rck
James	389	Ags
James	224	Pnd
Jas.	696	Wsh
John	388	Ags
John	389	Ags
Matthew	677	Br
Mo... [crossed out]	311	Rck
Moses	306	Rck
Moses	696	Wsh
Robt.	389	Ags
Walter	389	Ags
Trimper, Laurence	405	Ags
Trine, Jacob	684	Br
Trinkle, Christopher	621	Mnt
Triplet, Hedgeman	4	Wod
James	498	Prw
Robert	4	Wod
Triplett, Chs.	80	Clp
Daniel	716	Gch
Daniel	303	Ldn
Danl.	82	Clp
Eliza.	233	Ldn
Enoch	233	Ldn
Francis	303	Ldn
Francis C.	787	Wst
George	308	Frf
James	385	Fqr
James	317	Ldn
James S.	79	Clp
Jno.	82	Clp
Jno.	276	Ldn
John	342	Fqr
John, Jr.	83	Clp
John, Jr.	342	Fqr
Js. L.	310	Frf
Martha	264	Ldn
Mecaijah	262	Ldn
Nathan	294	Ldn
Nathaniel	380	Fqr
Peter	81	Clp
Reuben	260	Ldn
Ruben	242	Ldn
Sias	265	Ldn
Stephen	315	Ldn
Thomas	256	Amh
Thomas	233	Ldn
Thomas	240	Ldn
William	384	Fqr
William	522	Frd
Wm.	82	Clp
Wm.	233	Ldn
Wm.	250	Ldn
Trisler, George	514	Frd
Kitty	516	Frd
Mary	514	Frd
Tristoe, Jesse	40	Stf
Thomas	25	Stf
Thomas, of C.	40	Stf
Trisy, John	936	Hrr
Tritapers see Trttipo		
Trivy, Jacob	293	Rck
Joseph	293	Rck
Trobough, Adam	7	Rcm
John	7	Rcm

Trock, John	746	Wsh
Trokes, David	325	Dnw
Trone, Peter	514	Prw
Troop, Thomas	501	Prw
Trotter, Barbara	558	Frd
Benjamin	735	Brn
Catharine	735	Brn
Elin	735	Brn
George	163	Dnw
Isaac	388	Ags
James	390	Ags
James	735	Brn
Richd.	735	Brn
William	558	Frd
William	428	Msn
Troublefield, Richd.	538	Prg
Solomon	667	Sss
Trouce, Wm.	17	Hnr
Troupe, Henry	485	Frn
Trout, Abram	475	Frn
Casper	32	Rcm
David	389	Ags
David	475	Frn
Geo.	546	Mnn
George	20	Rcm
Henry	522	Frd
Henry	639	Gls
Michael	20	Rcm
Michael, (Jr.)	23	Rcm
Noah	713	Wsh
Philip	519	Frd
Valentine	23	Rcm
see Tout		
Trouts, Daniel	165	Shn
Troutwine, Fredrick	431	Rnd
Trowbridge, Bethwell	558	Frd
Dav.	545	Mnn
Jessee	546	Mnn
Samuel	558	Frd
Trowbrige, Saml.	546	Mnn
Trower, Henry, Sr.	476	Pra
Jno.	13	Hnr
Lucy	771	Nwk
Trowers, J.W.	922	Nrf
Troxale, Dan'l.	285	Rck
Troxel, Peter	388	Ags
Troxtell, Daniel	698	Wsh
Troy, Jas.	546	Mnn
Thomas	220	Kng
Trttipo, Wm.	281	Ldn
Trubough see Tribo		
Trucks, Henry	489	Bdf
True, Arthur	544	Mnn
James	97	Spt
John	931	Crl
Joseph	92	Spt
Martin	210	Alb
Richard	308	Frf
William	355	Fqr
William	31	Stf
Trueax, William	680	Br
Truehart, Lewis	891	Hnv
Wm.	882	Hnv
Trueheart see Trusheart		
Truelow, James	439	Flv
Trueman, Mark	121	Hnr
Robert	921	Hrr
see Warrenor		
Truhet, William	873	Cmp
Truitt, Justice	130	Acc
Trullinger, John	668	Mnt
Mary	668	Mnt
Trulock, Isaac	703	Wsh
Truly, Saml.	227	Aml
Truman, Robert	484	Bdf
see Tauman, Trueman, Tunman		
Trumbo, Andrew	216	Pnd
Jacob	29	Rcm
Jacob	1	Wod
John	31	Rcm

Trumnels, Wm.	219	Kng
Trumond, Mary	944	Chc
Trump, Danl.	37	Rcm
Jacob	387	Ags
Saml.	608	Mnt
Trusel, Thos.	262	Ldn
Trusheart, Bathurst	15	Pwh
Truslar, William	732	Nls
Trusler, John	732	Nls
Joseph	732	Nls
Lewis	306	Frf
Peter	662	Btt
Trusley, James	720	Wsh
Trusloe, Benjamin	61	Stf
Truslow, Arnstead	25	Hnr
Thomas	219	Kng
Zachariah	220	Kng
Truss, Thos.	806	Nrf
Wm.	476	Pra
Trussel, Rhodam	29	Stf
Wm.	262	Ldn
Trust, Jonas	405	Ags
Trusty, Samuel	617	Srr
Truzedell, John	9	Oho
Wm.	9	Oho
Trydle, Mary	307	Frf
Tuck, Anthony	299	Rck
Mary	928	Crl
Tucker, ---	326	Dnw
Abel	227	Aml
Abram	543	Prg
Absolam	227	Aml
Amey	164	Dnw
Anderson	227	Aml
Anderson	1	Pwh
B.	26	Hnr
Benjamin, Jr.	333	Dnw
Benj,.	227	Aml
Berryman	163	Dnw
Berryman T.	163	Dnw
Boswell	227	Aml
Branch	19	Ntt
Charles	282	Amh
Charles	43	Stf
Charles, jr.	284	Amh
Clary	209	Ess
Coleman	164	Dnw
Colsten	164	Dnw
Daniel	163	Dnw
Daniel	831	Hmp
Daniel	881	Hnv
David	164	Dnw
David	880	Hnv
David, jr.	734	Brn
David, Sr.	734	Brn
Dolley	164	Dnw
Drury	880	Hnv
Elisha	880	Hnv
Elisha	888	Hnv
Elizabeth	888	Hnv
Elizabeth	907	Hrr
Elizabeth	538	Prg
Epps	65	Chr
Erasmus	782	Hmp
Fleming	944	Chc
Frances	330	Dnw
Frances	7	Ntt
Garlant	34	Hnr
Gedion, Jnr.	878	Hnv
Geo.	543	Mnn
Godfrey	2	Ntt
Hartwell	735	Brn
Henry	546	Mnn
Henry	707	Wsh
Henry	717	Wsh
Henry St. Geo.	517	Frd
Henry St. Geo.	540	Frd
Herbert	18	Ntt
Hudson	538	Prg
Isaac, Senr.	163	Dnw

James	763	Brn
James	889	Hnv
James	427	Msn
James	1	Pwh
Jas.	543	Mnn
Jesse	485	Bdf
Jesse	3	Pwh
Jesse	9	Pwh
Jesse	537	Prg
Jno.	83	Clp
Jno., Jr.	83	Clp
Jno., jr.	2	Ntt
Jno. E.	13	Ntt
Jno. P.	179	Knq
John	294	Amh
John	735	Brn
John	163	Dnw
John	409	Mds
John	805	Nrf
John	1	Pwh
John, M.h.	734	Brn
Joseph	163	Dnw
Joseph	782	Hmp
Joseph	588	Pre
Josephus	782	Hmp
Josiph	904	Hrr
Js.	922	Nrf
Judith	277	Amh
Leroy	735	Brn
Lew	362	Lnn
Littleberry	3	Pwh
Littlebury	163	Dnw
Littleton	83	Clp
Margtt.	819	Nrf
Martha C.	163	Dnw
Martin	6	Pwh
Mary	226	Aml
Mary [2]	164	Dnw
Mary	879	Hnv
Mary	128	Hnr
Mary Ann	735	Brn
Matthew	294	Amh
Matthew, jr.	2	Ntt
Matthew, Senr.	18	Ntt
Merryman	65	Chr
Michael	334	Dnw
Michl.	907	Hrr
Miles	771	Nwk
Moses	83	Clp
Nathaniel	943	Hrr
Nathaniel B.	64	Chr
Other	880	Hnv
Peter	544	Prg
Pleasant	885	Hnv
Pleasant	1	Pwh
Rebeca	907	Hrr
Reuben	532	Prg
Richard	766	Hmp
Robt.	16	Ntt
Robt., Senr.	15	Ntt
St. Geo., J's City (W)	884	Yrk
Sally	333	Dnw
Sally	3	Pwh
Sarah	880	Hnv
Stephen	82	Clp
Stephen	83	Clp
Stephen	406	Fqr
Stith	163	Dnw
Susannah	287	Amh
Thomas	782	Hmp
Thomas	1	Pwh
Thomas	531	Prg
Thomas W.	781	Hmp
Thos.	227	Aml
Ths.	81	Clp
Toisman	731	Nls
Warsham	362	Lnn
William	295	Amh
William	483	Bdf
William	929	Crl

William	22 Oho
Wilson	7 Hnr
Wim.	889 Hnv
Wm.	83 Clp
Wm.	546 Mnn
Wm. N.	17 Ntt
Wood	164 Dnw
Wood	588 Pre
Wright	735 Brn
Wright	163 Dnw
see Creekmur	
Tucket, Micl.	546 Mnn
Wm.	546 Mnn
Tuckett, Margt.	546 Mnn
Tuckfield, ---, Tousant &	46 Stf
Tuckle, Sam	544 Mnn
Tuder, Robert	763 Brn
Tudor, Bartee	164 Dnw
Henry	667 Sss
Jesse	667 Sss
Landram	667 Sss
Lewis	667 Sss
Richard	164 Dnw
Robert	11 Knw
Tuel, James	106 Spt
Phillip	102 Spt
Tufts, Abijah	673 Glc
Tuggle, James	717 Gch
John [2]	588 Pre
Thomas	588 Pre
Thomas T.	588 Pre
Tuieford, Purnell	130 Acc
Tuley, Elizabeth	800 Hmp
Tull, Levi	922 Nrf
Tulloh, David	865 Hnv
Tullon, Saml.	713 Wsh
Tulloss, Joshua	353 Fqr
Rhodham	382 Fqr
Ursula W.	352 Fqr
Tully, Betsey	597 Brk
John	227 Aml
Tuly, Joseph	527 Frd
Joseph, [his] (quarter)	584 Frd
Tumbelson, Irbis	710 Wsh
Tumblenn, Saml.	840 Nrf
Tumbleston, Nathaniel	400 Fqr
Tumbling, James	801 Nrf
Tumlinson, James	761 Wsh
Tummels see Trumnels	
Tune, George D.	393 Rch
James	396 Rch
Jessee	222 Ess
Lewis	397 Rch
Thomas	411 Rch
Traverse	397 Rch
Tungate, William	300 Amh
Tuning, Peter, Mulo.	179 Knq
William	846 Hnv
Tunis, ---	917 Nrf
Tunkhouser, Jacob	226 Shn
Tunman, Benja.	80 Clp
Tunnel, Charles	62 Acc
Elizabeth	65 Acc
James	130 Acc
Scarburgh	127 Acc
William	128 Acc
see Turnel	
Tunnell, Eliza.	127 Sth
Tunnels see Trumnels	
Tunstal, Thomas	770 Nwk
Tunstall, Benjamin	763 Brn
Lucy	921 Nrf
Robert	470 Mdd
Tunstill, Stokes	6 Pwh
Tupman, William	928 Crl
Turberville, Gawin C.	219 Kng
Gawin C.	787 Wst
John	787 Wst
John, Est.	788 Wst
John, quar.	309 Frf
Turbifill, William	362 Lnn
Turbifull, Seth	736 Brn
Turce, Benja.	79 Clp
Tureman, Charles	674 Glc
Gilbee	215 Ess
Rd.	674 Glc
Turk, Mary	387 Ags
Robert	180 Alb
Saml.	662 Btt
Thos.	387 Ags
Turkyhiser, Leo.	543 Mnn
Turley, Charles	309 Frf
Giles	4 Rcm
James	305 Frf
Jas.	249 Ldn
John	243 Ldn
Robert	858 Wth
Sampson	308 Frf
Sampson	4 Rcm
William	360 Fqr
Turlington, Arthur	63 Acc
Aser	64 Acc
James	182 Elc
John	64 Acc
Joseph	63 Acc
Sarah	129 Acc
Turly, Nathan	12 Knw
Samuel	12 Knw
Turman, Charles	655 Mnt
Turn, John	575 Brk
Turnable, Roger	770 Brn
Turnan, Patrick	683 Br
Sharlot	7 Hnr
Turnbull, Abigal	472 Frn
Bethlehem	507 Prw
Charles	333 Dnw
John	800 Hmp
Lewis	472 Frn
Rebec.	183 Elc
Robert	736 Brn
Sarah	413 Fqr
Turnell, Major	127 Acc
Turnen, George	13 Oho
Turner, ---, Mrs.	331 Dnw
...	306 Rck
A.W.	132 Hnr
Adam	289 Rck
Admire	484 Bdf
Admire, jr.	484 Bdf
Alexander, [his] Est.	219 Kng
Alexr.	269 Ldn
Ambrose	129 Hnr
Andrew	63 Acc
Andrew	817 Bck
Andrew	606 Frd
Andrew, of A	64 Acc
Andw.	607 Frd
Ann	736 Brn
Ann	928 Crl
Ann	179 Knq
Anne	456 Grn
Anthony	18 Hnr
Anthony	88 Jff
Barny [?]	852 Sth
Benja.	115 Hnr
Benjamin	483 Bdf
Benjamin	997 Nrt
Benjamin	666 Sss
Betsey	878 Hnv
Billey	391 Fqr
Branston	64 Acc
Caleb H.	588 Pre
Carfield	210 Alb
Cary	222 Ess
Celia	21 Isw
Charles	736 Brn
Charles	769 Nwk
Charlotte	852 Sth
Christian	879 Sth
Clara	524 Frd
Daniel	929 Crl
Daniel	500 Frn
Daniel	166 Shn
Daniel	666 Sss
David	18 Rcm
David	666 Sss
Dolley	884 Hnv
Donaldson	456 Grn
Donaldson	666 Sss
Edmund	141 Sth
Edward	604 Frd
Edward	94 Spt
Edwd., (W)	884 Yrk
Edwin	162 Sth
Eilegach, jr.	483 Bdf
Eley	22 Isw
Elias	39 Isw
Elias	33 Rcm
Elijah, sr.	483 Bdf
Eliza.	336 Dnw
Elizabeth	16 Isw
Elizabeth	39 Stf
Ellzey	15 Wod
Evan	800 Hmp
Eve	88 Spt
Ezekiel	387 Ags
Ezekiel	727 Wsh
Fanny	666 Sss
Francis W.S.	731 Nls
Geo.	405 Ags
George	927 Crl
George	928 Crl
George	80 Clp
George	83 Clp
George	451 Frn
George	488 Frn
George	219 Kng
Green	456 Grn
Henry	276 Amh
Henry	187 Elc
Henry	14 Pwh
Henry	477 Pra
Henry S.	65 Jff
Heming	210 Alb
Hemmen	182 Alb
Hezekiah	84 Clp
Hezekiah	604 Frd
Hugh	430 Rnd
Jacob	127 Sth
Jacob	161 Sth
Jacob	858 Sth
James	483 Bdf
James	489 Bdf
James	817 Bck
James	929 Crl
James	402 Fqr
James	717 Gch
James	456 Grn
James	876 Hnv
James	730 Nls
James	731 Nls
James	732 Nls
James	419 Rnd
James	29 Rcm
Jane	545 Mnn
Jas.	361 Lnc
Jas.	722 Wsh
Jas. L.	661 Btt
Jeremiah	408 Mds
Jesse	483 Bdf
Jesse	289 Ldn
Jesse	361 Lnn
Jesse	588 Pre
Jno.	82 Clp
Jno.	272 Ldn
John	64 Acc
John	483 Bdf
John	513 Brk

Name	No.	Abbr.
John	569	Brk
John	787	Bck
John	819	Bck
John	928	Crl
John	196	Ess
John	390	Fqr
John	416	Fqr
John	419	Fqr
John	473	Frn
John	572	Frd
John	717	Gch
John	456	Grn
John	779	Hmp
John	122	Hnr
John	123	Hnr
John	18	Isw
John	23	Isw
John	438	Mth
John	470	Mdd
John	2	Rcm
John	29	Rcm
John	156	Sth
John	788	Wst
John, Esqr.	548	Brk
John, jr.	586	Brk
John, Jr.	489	Frn
John, Jun.	26	Isw
John, (Otter)	485	Bdf
John, Sr.	489	Frn
John, (Stanton)	484	Bdf
John, 3d.	578	Brk
John W.	456	Grn
Joseph	24	Isw
Joseph	88	Jff
Joseph	130	Sth
Joshua	524	Frd
Joshua	9	Isw
Josiah	489	Frn
Jubel	484	Bdf
Laisis [Lewis?]	874	Hnv
Larkin	81	Clp
Lemuel	858	Sth
Lennard	210	Alb
Lewis	484	Bdf
Lewis, F.N.	666	Sss
Major	470	Mdd
Marten	408	Mds
Martha	858	Sth
Martin	24	Hnr
Mary	516	Brk
Mary	930	Crl
Matthew	16	Isw
Meadow	483	Bdf
Mildred	456	Grn
Moses	65	Acc
Nancy	525	Prw
Nathan	140	Sth
Nathaniel	64	Acc
Newsam	16	Isw
Nicholas	822	Bck
Nicholas, (FB)	477	Pra
Olive	852	Sth
Olive	616	Srr
Patsey	83	Clp
Patsy	119	Spt
Terson	456	Grn
Peter	8	Isw
Peter	227	Pnd
Peter	160	Sth
Phillip	780	Hmp
Ransom	40	Isw
Reuben	928	Crl
Reuben	930	Crl
Richard	63	Acc
Richard	297	Amh
Richard	483	Bdf
Richard	596	Frd
Richard	876	Hnv
Richard	219	Kng
Richard	408	Mds

Name	No.	Abbr.
Robbert	210	Alb
Robert	275	Amh
Robert	241	Ldn
Robert T.	770	Nwk
Robt.	21	Isw
Rowland T.	50	Stf
Saml.	112	Hnr
Sampsn., (FB)	477	Pra
Samuel	298	Amh
Samuel	329	Dnw
Samuel	396	Fqr
Samuel	731	Nls
Samuel	140	Sth
Samuel	858	Sth
Sarah	348	Fqr
Sarah	731	Nls
Shores	450	Frn
Shores P.	489	Frn
Simeon	516	Brk
Simon, Jr.	456	Grn
Simon, (Minr.)	456	Grn
Simon, Sr.	456	Grn
Solomon	127	Sth
Stephen	56	Chs
Stephen	732	Nls
Stephen D.	65	Chr
Susanna	770	Nwk
Temperance	850	Sth
Terrisha	731	Nls
Terrisha	733	Nls
Terrisha, Jr.	730	Nls
Thomas	597	Frd
Thomas	456	Grn
Thomas	39	Isw
Thomas	219	Kng
Thomas	509	Prw
Thomas	844	Sth
Thomas	15	Wod
Thomas B.	456	Grn
Thos.	4	Hnr
Thos.	609	Mnt
Thos.	884	Yrk
Van	875	Sth
Walter	883	Hnv
Wiley	40	Isw
Wilie	21	Isw
Wilson	716	Gch
William	174	Alb
William	291	Amh
William	484	Bdf
William	372	Fqr
William	718	Gch
William [2]	731	Nls
William	34	Rcm
William	666	Sss
William	667	Sss
William, Ju.	732	Nls
William, Jun.	9	Isw
William, Snr.	844	Hnv
Willis	152	Sth
Willis	617	Srr
Wilson	477	Frn
Wim., Jnr.	861	Hnv
Wim., S of W.	890	Hnv
Wm.	764	Brn
Wm.	63	Chs
Wm.	716	Gch
Wm.	727	Wsh
Zach	546	Mnn
Zephenh.	82	Clp
see Adams, Barber, Black, Christian, Clarke, Dixon, Hutchings, Moore, Morehead, Parish, Pinn, Richardson, Williamson		
Turnley, Edward	68	Spt
Francis	86	Spt
John	67	Spt
Turnor see Minor		
Turns, Joseph	869	Cmp

Name	No.	Abbr.
Turpin, Archer	8	Pwh
Daniel	484	Bdf
Horatio	8	Pwh
Philip	485	Bdf
Philip, Est.	66	Chs
Thomas	485	Bdf
Thomas	470	Frn
Thomas, Dr.	12	Pwh
Thos., (Overseer for Watts Estate)	661	Btt
William	829	Bck
Wm.	66	Chs
Turreil, Elizabeth	420	Fqr
Turren, Parmenos	794	Nrf
Turrentine, John	698	Wsh
Turt, George	255	Shn
Turvey, Daniel	7	Wod
John	7	Wod
Tush, Margaret	255	Shn
see Turt		
Tusing, Christian	196	Shn
George	196	Shn
John	226	Shn
Nicholas	226	Shn
Philip	226	Shn
Tusinger, Daniel	238	Shn
Tussar, Hy.	922	Nrf
Tussell, David	5	Rcm
Tussinger, Philip	31	Rcm
Tuter, John	743	Wsh
Tutt, Archibald	80	Clp
Benja.	80	Clp
Chs.	82	Clp
Gabl.	80	Clp
Gabl., Jr.	84	Clp
James	83	Clp
Jno.	81	Clp
John	404	Fqr
Js. L.	80	Clp
Lewis	80	Clp
Mildred	81	Clp
Richard J.	89	Spt
Richd. J.	82	Clp
Tuttle, Joel	545	Mnn
Mally	389	Ags
Tutweiler, Catharine	7	Rcm
Henry	3	Rcm
John	7	Rcm
Tweedy, Jas.	297	Rck
Twidy, Joseph, Sr.	869	Cmp
Twiford, George	63	Acc
James	62	Acc
Revel	62	Acc
Robert	63	Acc
Teagle	813	Nrf
Twigg, Samuel	86	Jff
Twiner see Turner		
Twinley, Chs.	83	Clp
Twinney, John	769	Nwk
Twisdall, Mary	80	Clp
Twitchett, Catharine	8	Rcm
Twopence, James, (FB)	483	Bdf
Nancy	470	Mdd
S., F.N.	179	Knq
Ursley	853	Cmp
see Tepence		
Twyman, Anthony	409	Mds
George	210	Alb
George	83	Spt
James	409	Mds
Joseph	210	Alb
Wm.	409	Mds
Wm., Jr.	409	Mds
Tye, Abner	163	Dnw
Tyers, ...	331	Dnw
Susan	336	Dnw
Tyger, James	423	Rnd
John	424	Rnd
Tyler, ---, Doctor	36	Hnr
Allan	111	Hnr

Name	No.	Abbr.	Name	No.	Abbr.	Name	No.	Abbr.
Ann	922	Nrf	William	731	Nls	Manuel	485	Frn
Benjamin	515	Prw	Zachariah	733	Nls	Masaniah	485	Frn
Catharine	931	Crl	Tyree, Batts	770	Nwk	Margt.	281	Ldn
Charles	522	Prw	Dickey	770	Nwk	Mary	19	Isw
Chs.	922	Nrf	Elisabeth	769	Nwk	Mary	869	Sth
Chs., Junr.	307	Frf	Francis	769	Nwk	Nathaniel	667	Sss
Daniel	485	Bdf	Henry	770	Nwk	Peterson	667	Sss
Daniel	886	Hnv	Jacob	280	Amh	Price	221	Kng
Edward	580	Frd	James	770	Nwk	Rebecca	667	Sss
Edward	777	Hmp	John	943	Chc	Samuel	495	Frn
Edwd.	307	Frf	Mary	769	Nwk	Samuel	14	Oho
Elizabeth	891	Hnv	Richard	869	Cmp	Seth	485	Frn
Francis	717	Gch	Richard	770	Nwk	Thos.	850	Hnv
Geo.	717	Gch	Thomas	769	Nwk	Thos.	10	Hnr
George	81	Spt	William	285	Amh	Thos.	114	Hnr
George D.	730	Nls	William	769	Nwk	Thos.	124	Hnr
George G.	518	Prw	William	770	Nwk	William	485	Frn
Henry	308	Frf	William	587	Pre	William	22	Oho
Henry	507	Prw	Tyroe, John	417	Bth	Willie	875	Sth
James	439	Bth	Tyry, Hyrum	501	Frn	Unger, John	567	Brk
Jane	29	Hnr	John	501	Frn	Unglebee, Wm.	281	Ldn
Jarvis	787	Hmp	Tyser, Cornelius	997	Nrt	Unroe, John	662	Btt
John	717	Gch	Tyson, Catharine	38	Stf	Unsild, John [2]	104	Jff
John	35	Hnr	Mathias	14	Wod	Updegraff, Israel	2	Oho
John	122	Hnr	Patty	306	Frf	Jno.	546	Mnn
John, Ser.	938	Chc	Tyus, Edwin	456	Grn	Josiah	2	Oho
Jones	113	Hnr	Elizabeth	667	Sss	Updike, Rufus	309	Ldn
Keeling R.	927	Crl	John	163	Dnw	Updyche, Amen	485	Bdf
Peggy	203	Ess	Joseph	666	Sss	Saml.	485	Bdf
Richd.	717	Gch	Pinkey	666	Sss	Updyke, Danl.	84	Clp
Rosanah	727	Wsh	Sally	164	Dnw	see Upetyke		
Sam, has Slaves in York County, J's City (W)	884	Yrk				Upetyke, John	84	Clp
Saml.	308	Frf	--- U ---			Upp, Jno.	301	Ldn
Sarah	115	Hnr				Upperman, John	78	Jff
Skelton	891	Hnv				John	91	Jff
Thos. G. S.	25	Stf	Umberfield, Elifet	500	Prw	Upshaw, Edwin	179	Knq
William	539	Frd	Umberger, Henry	859	Wth	James	931	Crl
William	502	Prw	Henry, Junr.	859	Wth	Jeremiah	208	Ess
Wim.	868	Hnv	Henry, Senr.	859	Wth	John H.	222	Ess
Tylor, Absolom	409	Mds	John [4]	859	Wth	Upshur, James	131	Acc
Benjamin	895	Hnv	Leonard [2]	859	Wth	John B.	66	Acc
Charles	896	Hnv	Phillip [3]	859	Wth	Upton, Archd.	288	Ldn
Daniel	878	Hnv	Umberhower, Philip	76	Jff	John	823	Nrf
Edmund	872	Hnv	Umbles, Richard	775	Bck	Loyd	579	Mnr
Elizabeth	892	Hnv	Umphris, Robt.	760	Wsh	Saml.	546	Mnn
Francis	873	Hnv	Umpstot, Jacob	823	Hmp	see Edmunson		
Henry	873	Hnv	Peter	825	Hmp	Urick, Matthias	582	Frd
James	426	Msn	Umseter see Museler			Urie, Wm.	678	Glc
Jno.	895	Hnv	Undanwood see Lindamoood			Urise, George	814	Hmp
John	285	Amh	Underdunk, Henry	95	Jff	Urmy, Abram	662	Btt
John	457	Grn	Underfield see Umberfield			Christn.	662	Btt
John	242	Ldn	Underhill, Henry	326	Dnw	Jacob	662	Btt
Patsey	389	Ags	James	66	Acc	Urner see Wener		
Plesant	895	Hnv	John	456	Grn	Urqueart, Mary	880	Cmp
Robert	891	Hnv	Nancy	667	Sss	Urquehart, Alexander	68	Jff
Salley	895	Hnv	Thomas	66	Acc	Hugh	67	Jff
Samuel	875	Hnv	Thos., Capt.	66	Acc	Urquhart, James	439	Flv
Steven	409	Mds	William	66	Acc	Jno.	868	Sth
Wm. B.	304	Ldn	Underwood, Claiborne	667	Sss	John	8	Isw
Tynes, Beck of, (F.N.)	30	Isw	Elijah	410	Mds	Urton, James	391	Fqr
Charles, (F.N.)	12	Isw	Elizh.	145	Sth	James	240	Ldn
Dick, (F.N.)	36	Isw	Francis	718	Gch	John	372	Fqr
Ephraim, (F.N.)	36	Isw	Geo.	718	Gch	John	391	Fqr
Henry	24	Isw	Geo.	546	Mnn	Thomas	377	Fqr
Jim, (F.N.)	31	Isw	Gideon	410	Mds	William	392	Fqr
Lewis, (F.N.)	31	Isw	James	280	Ldn	Usely, Federick	9	Knw
Obediah	871	Cmp	Jas.	718	Gch	Usher, David	391	Ags
Prince, (F.N.)	36	Isw	Jno.	310	Frf	Ussery, Ann [2]	363	Lnn
Randal, (F.N.)	31	Isw	John	391	Ags	Betty	210	Ess
Robt.	2	Isw	John	718	Gch	John	210	Ess
Sally, (F.N.)	36	Isw	John	25	Isw	John	363	Lnn
Tyre, David	129	Cmb	John	132	Sth	Pleasant	363	Lnn
James	210	Alb	John	92	Spt	Samuel, jr.	363	Lnn
John	733	Nls	John	667	Sss	Samuel, sr.	363	Lnn
Jonathan	210	Alb	John	788	Wst	Thomas	210	Ess
Jones	892	Hnv	Joseph	656	Mnt	Ustick, John G.	690	Wsh
Joseph	877	Hnv	Joseph	22	Oho	Thos. W.	759	Wsh
Nathaniel	732	Nls	Joyner	19	Isw	Utes, George	33	Rcm
Reuben	731	Nls	Littleton	667	Sss	George	34	Rcm
						Utezler, Catharine	24	Rcm

Name	No.	Co.	Name	No.	Co.	Name	No.	Co.
Christian	29	Rcm	Ann	4	Hnr	Vincent	806	Hmp
Christian, (Jr.)	33	Rcm	Ann	885	Yrk	William	805	Hmp
Henry	10	Rcm	Geo., (FB)	477	Pra	Vanfosen, Jacob	391	Ags
Utley, William	1	Pwh	Jacob	477	Pra	Jesse	391	Ags
Utly, Henry	718	Gch	Jane	333	Dnw	VanGilder, Jac.	547	Mnn
Hezekiah	718	Gch	John	175	Shn	Vangover, Caleb	477	Pra
John	718	Gch	John B.	931	Crl	Wm.	477	Pra
Josiah	718	Gch	Joseph	771	Nwk	Vanhise, William	163	Shn
Lilly	718	Gch	Lucy	330	Dnw	William	165	Shn
Nancy	718	Gch	Luke	848	Cmp	Vanholt, Jos.	923	Nrf
Obediah	718	Gch	Mann, free negro	70	Chs	Vanhorn, Abraham	944	Hrr
Reuben	718	Gch	Patsy	27	Hnr	Garret	237	Ldn
Utter, Hezekiah	166	Shn	Peter, free negro	70	Chs	Garrett	237	Ldn
William	84	Clp	Peter, jr.	56	Chs	Isaac	529	Frd
Wm.	935	Hrr	Zachariah	363	Lnn	James	271	Ldn
Utterback, Anny	84	Clp	see Tine, Volentine			Jno.	257	Ldn
Elias	377	Fqr	Valintine, Edw.	391	Ags	Jno., Jr.	237	Ldn
Elijah	419	Fqr	Vallendingham, John	311	Frf	Job	955	Hrr
Harman	419	Fqr	Wm.	311	Frf	John	605	Frd
Henry [2]	84	Clp	Vallenger, C.W.	311	Frf	John	60	Jff
Jacob	84	Clp	Vanander, Jane	276	Ldn	Joseph	67	Jff
James	84	Clp	Vanausdale, Abraham	785	Hmp	Thomas	257	Ldn
John	377	Fqr	Vanausdall, Abraham	827	Hmp	William	509	Frd
Joseph	84	Clp	Garrett	785	Hmp	William	955	Hrr
Nathaniel	419	Fqr	Peter	784	Hmp	Vanison, Elizabeth	485	Bdf
Thomson	84	Clp	VanBibber see Bebber			Vanlandingham, Francis	998	Nrt
William	388	Fqr	Vanbiber, Sarah E.	453	Mth	Molley	998	Nrt
see Utter			Vanblara, Andrew	7	Wod	Thomas	998	Nrt
Utz, Solomon	84	Clp	VanBuskirk see Buskirk			William	998	Nrt
Utzs, Abraham	409	Mds	Vance, Andrew	536	Frd	Vanlear, Jacob	391	Ags
Absolom	409	Mds	Andw.	707	Wsh	Jno.	644	Mnt
Aron	409	Mds	Benjn.	21	Rcm	Vanlier, Jacob, jr.	391	Ags
Daniel	410	Mds	Christley	40	Rcm	Vanmaples, John	475	Frn
Elizebeth	409	Mds	Hugh	663	Btt	Vanmeter, Abisha	511	Brk
Ephaham	410	Mds	James	718	Wsh	Abrm.	510	Brk
George	410	Mds	James D.	542	Frd	Abrm.	519	Brk
Julias	410	Mds	John	578	Mnr	Asael	519	Brk
Lewis	410	Mds	John	222	Pnd	Isaac	511	Brk
Michael	409	Mds	John	194	Shn	Isabel	511	Brk
Simeon	409	Mds	John	719	Wsh	John	511	Brk
see Uzts			John	860	Wth	Joseph	510	Brk
Uzts, Adam	409	Mds	John, Jur.	719	Wsh	Joseph	678	Br
Uzzel, John	24	Isw	Margaret	14	Rcm	Josiah	510	Brk
Rose, (F.N.)	39	Isw	Robert	563	Frd	Nathan	513	Brk
Uzzell, Thomas	25	Isw	Robert	222	Pnd	Solomon	174	Shn
			Robert	430	Rnd	William	522	Frd
			Salley	326	Dnw	VanMeter, Abraham	6	Oho
--- V ---			Saml.	702	Wsh	Vanmetre, Abraham	97	Jff
			Saml.	719	Wsh	VanMetree, Henry	421	Msn
			Samuel	438	Bth	John	430	Msn
Vabler, Adam	577	Brk	Sarah	438	Bth	Vanney, ---, Mrs.	30	Hnr
Vaden, Ammonet	62	Chs	Solomon	42	Rcm	Vannost, Ann	923	Nrf
Danl.	60	Chs	Thos.	663	Btt	Vannoy see Vancoy, Vanoy		
George	62	Chs	William	519	Frd	Vanort, Jacob	592	Frd
George, Est.	60	Chs	Wm.	277	Rck	Vanover, Henry	663	Mnt
Marshall	56	Chs	Vancill, Edmund	649	Mnt	Vanoy, Benjn.	423	Rnd
Marshall	62	Chs	Vancol, George	310	Frf	Vanpelt, Benjamin	40	Rcm
Matilda	953	Chc	Vancoy, Aaron	421	Rnd	Jacob	515	Brk
Page	56	Chs	Jacob	420	Rnd	Joseph	485	Bdf
Polley	62	Chs	see Vanoy			Joseph	310	Ldn
Stoman	62	Chs	Vandegraft, Rebecca	663	Btt	Peter	14	Rcm
Wilson	60	Chs	Thos.	663	Btt	Rd.	310	Frf
Wm.	63	Chs	Vandegriff, Ebenr.	547	Mnn	Vansciver, Josiah	294	Ldn
Wm. H.	54	Chs	Vanderall, Nelson	1	Hnr	Wm.	245	Ldn
see Vaiden, Voden			Vandervert, John	547	Mnn	Vansecole, H.	391	Ags
Vadler see Sadler			Nics.	547	Mnn	Vanseyco see Syoe		
Vaiden, Elisabeth	771	Nwk	Vandevall, Danl.	12	Hnr	VanSickle see Sickle		
Elisabeth, jr.	771	Nwk	Vandevanter, Isaac	312	Ldn	Vansickler, Philip	310	Ldn
Henry	771	Nwk	Jno.	307	Ldn	Vanstavern, Nicholas	285	Amh
Isaac	771	Nwk	Jos.	312	Ldn	Vanvactor, Joseph	81	Jff
Jacob	940	Chc	Vandeveere, George	484	Frn	Vanzandt, Joshua	268	Rck
Jeremiah	771	Nwk	VanDevender, Nicholas	24	Oho	Vanzant, Richard W.	89	Jff
Joseph	956	Chc	Vandewall, Ann	119	Hnr	Vardeir, James	94	Jff
Micajah	772	Nwk	Vandigraft, Christopher	789	Hmp	Vardy, James	577	Frd
Sims	941	Chc	Vandine, Jno.	663	Btt	Varley, Thomas	4	Oho
Thomas	771	Nwk	Vandiver, Elizabeth	806	Hmp	Varner, Barbary	216	Shn
see Vaden			Jacob	805	Hmp	Dan	547	Mnn
Vale, John	680	Wrw	John	808	Hmp	David	185	Shn
Valentine, ...	335	Dnw	Lewis	822	Hmp	Jacob	89	Jff
Angilco	951	Chc	Samuel	806	Hmp	John	183	Shn

Jos.	547	Mnn	Mary	311	Frf	William	364	Fqr
Martin	547	Mnn	Mary	719	Gch	William, Sr.	369	Fqr
Philip	181	Shn	Meredith	522	Prw	Willis	107	Cmb
Philip	216	Shn	N. M.	719	Gch	Wm.	923	Nrf
Varnier, Jno.	69	Chs	Nelson	165	Dnw	Vaught, Christian [2]	860	Wth
Varnon, Richard	410	Mds	Nicholas	14	Ntt	David	860	Wth
Varnum, Asa	733	Nls	Patrick, overseer for			George [2]	860	Wth
George W.	733	Nls	Jno. Y. Tabb	165	Dnw	Henry	860	Wth
Vashon, Fanny, (FB)	477	Pra	Peter	85	Clp	Jacob	860	Wth
Geo.	490	Pra	Peter	165	Dnw	John	860	Wth
Vass, ---, Brown &,			Peter, jr.	165	Dnw	Simeon	169	Shn
& Co.	156	Knq	Peterson	164	Dnw	Vaugn, Josh., Jr.	663	Btt
Alexr., Estate	85	Clp	Polly	84	Clp	Josh., Sr.	663	Btt
James	36	Stf	Pryor	771	Nwk	Mitchel	663	Btt
Mary	99	Spt	Reuben	85	Clp	William	100	Spt
Phillip	78	Spt	Reubin	363	Lnn	Vault, Pheby	642	Mnt
Rice	573	Mnr	Richard	85	Clp	Vause, William	806	Hmp
Saml.	276	Rck	Richard	589	Pre	Vaut, Christian	640	Gls
Thomas	75	Spt	Richd.	14	Ntt	Vauter, Benjamin	931	Crl
Vasser, Etheld.	876	Sth	Robert	226	Aml	Ludwel	66	Chr
John	855	Sth	Robert	485	Bdf	Vawter, Benja.	201	Ess
William	226	Aml	Robert	456	Grn	Boulware	202	Ess
Vasseur, Towsard	332	Dnw	Robert	44	Isw	Edward	813	Bck
Vast, Reuben	211	Alb	Russel	84	Clp	Edward	202	Ess
Vaughan, Absalom	465	Dnw	Sally	931	Crl	James	200	Ess
Almond	85	Clp	Saml.	164	Dnw	John	589	Pre
Ann	542	Prg	Sarah	334	Dnw	Richard	71	Spt
Asa	226	Aml	Seymore	137	Sth	Thomas	830	Bck
Asa	1	Ntt	Shad.	137	Sth	William	570	Mnr
Ashley	66	Chr	Shadrick	846	Hnv	V.Buskirk, John	814	Hmp
Benjamin	931	Crl	Thomas	456	Grn	Veach, Alexr.	567	Brk
Benjamin	857	Hnv	Thomas	14	Ntt	Benj.	939	Hrr
Bland	931	Crl	Thos.	154	Sth	Jesse	173	Shn
Caty	180	Knq	Thos. W.	226	Aml	William	173	Shn
China	931	Crl	Ths., Jr.	84	Clp	Veah, Gideon	437	Bth
Chs.	85	Clp	Uriah	45	Isw	see Viah		
Craddock	719	Gch	Vincent	85	Clp	Veal, Amos	253	Ldn
Crafford	363	Lnn	Vincent	561	Frd	Anthony	298	Rck
Danl.	17	Ntt	William	66	Chr	Chs.	253	Ldn
David [Daniel?]	335	Dnw	William	733	Nls	David	663	Btt
David	336	Dnw	William, (Conm)	66	Chr	Saml.	511	Brk
David	363	Lnn	William K.	589	Pre	Thomas	662	Btt
Drury	165	Dnw	Willis	165	Dnw	Wm.	253	Ldn
Edwd.	923	Nrf	Wily	180	Knq	Wm.	574	Mnr
Eliza.	226	Aml	Wm.	85	Clp	see Vears		
Ellinor	931	Crl	Wm.	188	Elc	Veale, ---	923	Nrf
Enoch	165	Dnw	Wm.	6	Ntt	Densey	832	Nrf
Ephraim	164	Dnw	Wm., (H)	12	Ntt	Wm. C.	477	Pra
Eve	85	Clp	Wm., (Tay)	165	Dnw	see Veah		
Francis	65	Chr	Wm., (Whead)	165	Dnw	Vealey, Michael	485	Bdf
Francis	98	Cmb	Zedikiah	65	Chr	Vealy, Isaac	485	Bdf
Freeman	165	Dnw	see Baughan, Riddle, Vaugn			Vears, Jno.	252	Ldn
Gabriel	164	Dnw	Vaughn, Averit	737	Brn	see Near		
George	733	Nls	Beverly	120	Spt	Veech, John	211	Alb
Griffin	65	Chr	David	764	Brn	Veeker, Jos.	923	Nrf
Henry	165	Dnw	Frances	667	Sss	Vegus, Paul	547	Mnn
Henry	771	Nwk	George	737	Brn	Veil, Izeral E.	21	Hnr
Henry	137	Sth	Henry	943	Chc	Veinia, Fatis	8	Hnr
Herbert	164	Dnw	Henry, Sr.	954	Chc	Vellines, Amstead	15	Isw
James	165	Dnw	Herod	737	Brn	Francis	15	Isw
James	719	Gch	Irene	737	Brn	Isaac	13	Isw
James B.	477	Pra	James	737	Brn	John	3	Isw
Jas.	7	Ntt	James	955	Chc	Velvin, John	617	Srr
Jesse	165	Dnw	James	13	Hnr	Vena, Darcus	413	Rch
Jessee	65	Chr	James	130	Hnr	George	413	Rch
Jno., jr.	12	Ntt	James	436	Mth	Hannah	413	Rch
Jno., Senr.	13	Ntt	James, B.	736	Brn	Hannah, Junr.	413	Rch
John	332	Dnw	Janes	764	Brn	Humphrey	413	Rch
John	640	Gls	John	6	Pwh	James	413	Rch
John	180	Knq	John	177	Shn	Joseph, Junr.	413	Rch
John	363	Lnn	John H.	737	Brn	Joseph, Senr.	413	Rch
John	589	Pre	Micajah	737	Brn	Judy	413	Rch
John, (LE)	66	Chr	Moody	737	Brn	Judy, Junr.	413	Rch
Joseph	108	Cmb	Nelson	116	Spt	Molly	413	Rch
Judith	471	Mdd	Peggy	764	Brn	Richard	413	Rch
Ledford	678	Glc	Richard	944	Chc	Samuel	392	Rch
Lemuel	44	Isw	Richd.	737	Brn	Venable, A. B.	333	Dnw
Majr.	863	Hnv	Robt.	125	Hnr	A. B.	21	Hnr
Maria A.	771	Nwk	Stephen	737	Brn	Abm., jr.	440	Flv
Mary	226	Aml	Thos.	759	Wsh	Abm., Sr.	441	Flv

Abraham B.	589	Pre	Moseley	484	Frn	Viele, T. P.	24 Hnr
Charles	14	Knw	Patty	59	Chs	Viena, Danl.	5 Hnr
Charles	589	Pre	Philip, Senr.	59	Chs	see Veinia	
Elizabeth	589	Pre	Rainey	65	Chs	Vier, Rowlin	733 Nls
James	412	Bth	Reuben	845	Hnv	Vigar, William	42 Rcm
John H.	589	Pre	William	822	Bck	Viger, Sarah, Est.	788 Wst
Joseph	65	Chr	William	85	Clp	Vigers, James	733 Nls
Josiah	781	Bck	Vestal, David	79	Jff	James, Ju.	733 Nls
Josias	509	Prw	William	79	Jff	Vigle, Philip	10 Wod
Nathaniel	589	Pre	see Veslet			Villars, Edward	21 Oho
Rachel	525	Frd	Veste, Saml.	226	Aml	James	21 Oho
Richard N.	65	Chr	Via, David, Jr.	490	Frn	Villenar, Christian	853 Cmp
Richard N.	589	Pre	David, Sr.	490	Frn	Vincent, Benja.	456 Grn
Robert	589	Pre	Hezakiah	211	Alb	Cornelius	532 Frd
Saml. W.	589	Pre	James	498	Frn	Enoch	547 Mnn
Samuel	589	Pre	John	493	Frn	Frs.	923 Nrf
Samuel W.	589	Pre	John	494	Frn	Hamlin	456 Grn
William	412	Bth	Jonathan	211	Alb	James	3 Knw
William L.	589	Pre	Josiah	494	Frn	James, Senr.	2 Knw
Womack	589	Pre	Mcajah	211	Alb	Joseph	583 Frd
Venceller, John	546	Brk	Menoah	211	Alb	Manoah	363 Lnn
Vendevener, George	219	Pnd	Obediah	211	Alb	Martha	516 Brk
Jacob	215	Pnd	Peyton	942	Chc	Mary	547 Mnn
Mary	226	Pnd	Roling	211	Alb	Michl.	456 Grn
Veney, Ned	410	Mds	Wade	211	Alb	Nathan	124 Cmb
Polly	410	Mds	William	211	Alb	Parlato	923 Nrf
Venia see Veinia			William	495	Frn	Sampson	325 Dnw
Venilia, E.	5	Hnr	Viah, John	437	Bth	Susan	456 Grn
Venneau, Jno.	923	Nrf	see Veah			William	456 Grn
Vennom, George	1	Oho	Viale, Geo.	823	Nrf	Vincero, Sabia	594 Mnr
Ventrus, Jno.	923	Nrf	Viar, Clarecy	879	Hnv	Vincin, Charles	478 Frn
Venus, Henry	391	Ags	Edmund	888	Hnv	John	473 Frn
Jno.	298	Rck	Josias	879	Hnv	John	945 Hrr
Verble, Christopher	11	Rcm	Lucy	879	Hnv	Thomas	478 Frn
Verges, Peter D., (W)	885	Yrk	Robert	879	Hnv	Vines, Ann	391 Ags
Verlander, Joseph	128	Hnr	Robert, Snr.	884	Hnv	Frank	855 Sth
Vermelion, Nicodemus	868	Cmp	Wim.	888	Hnv	John	391 Ags
Vermillion, ---	311	Frf	Vicars, Anne	519	Prw	Margret	758 Wsh
Levi	638	Mnt	Thomas	401	Fqr	Robert	855 Sth
Vernon, Daniel	236	Ldn	Vice see Via			Thos.	391 Ags
Ebenezer	66	Chr	Vick, Benja.	867	Sth	Viney, Betsy	122 Hnr
Isaac	211	Alb	Councel	155	Sth	Vineyard, Betsy	284 Rck
James	65	Chr	Council	160	Sth	Geo.	637 Mnt
James	259	Ldn	Elijah	149	Sth	John	116 Spt
Jno.	259	Ldn	Elisha	149	Sth	Vingard, William	410 Mds
Jonathan	66	Chr	Exum	870	Sth	Vinos, Saml.	923 Nrf
Richard	66	Chr	Howell	456	Grn	Vins, John	733 Nls
Robert	66	Chr	Hubbard	456	Grn	Vinson, Edward	942 Hrr
Verona, Joseph	416	Fqr	Jacob	870	Sth	John	678 Glc
Verrel, John	164	Dnw	James	148	Sth	Vint, John	215 Pnd
Verser, Danl.	1	Ntt	James	869	Sth	Vinyard, Christn.	663 Btt
Veslet, Edwd.	544	Brk	Jim	148	Sth	Jacob	663 Btt
Vess see Oess			Joel	870	Sth	Jno.	663 Btt
Vessells, Elijah	66	Acc	John	150	Sth	Peter	663 Btt
Ephraim, Senr.	131	Acc	Jordan	150	Sth	Violet, James	505 Brk
Isaac	131	Acc	Joseph	860	Sth	Jemimah	233 Ldn
see Vessels			Josiah	137	Sth	Jno.	232 Ldn
Vessels, Arthur	131	Acc	Mary	127	Sth	Thomas	233 Ldn
Ephraim, Jun.	131	Acc	Ned	149	Sth	see Veslet	
Ephraim, of Ja.	131	Acc	Phereby	871	Sth	Violett, Elijah	240 Ldn
James	131	Acc	Pilgrem	148	Sth	Hugh	311 Frf
John	131	Acc	Richard	153	Sth	John	240 Ldn
Peggy	131	Acc	Richd.	127	Sth	Nesley	310 Frf
Rose	131	Acc	Sharper	877	Sth	Thompson	228 Frf
William, Mis.	131	Acc	Silas	875	Sth	Thompson	229 Frf
William, of Ja.	131	Acc	Simon	150	Sth	Thompson	311 Frf
Vest, Charles	485	Frn	William	151	Sth	Thompson [2]	323 Frf
Charles	845	Hnv	Williams	131	Sth	William	311 Frf
Drucilla	485	Bdf	Vickars, Elias	610	Mnt	Virlander, John	180 Knq
Edward	748	Wsh	William	14	Rcm	Robert	180 Knq
Fancy	748	Wsh	Vickers, Eli	791	Nrf	Virmillion, Jacob	315 Ldn
Henry	59	Chs	Nancy	272	Ldn	Vivas, John	421 Fqr
James	64	Chs	Thomas	35	Stf	Vizonneau, And. T.	328 Dnw
John	485	Bdf	William	610	Mnt	Voden, Frances	164 Dnw
John	330	Dnw	Wm.	239	Ldn	Peter	164 Dnw
John	485	Frn	Vickery, Ann	923	Nrf	see Vaden	
John	494	Frn	Saml.	923	Nrf	Vogle, George	209 Shn
John D.	490	Frn	Victor, John	109	Spt	Voimilion, Jno. W.	249 Ldn
Littlebury	484	Frn	Vidal, Wm. Geo., Ur-			Vokes, Peter	828 Hmp
Littlebury	122	Hnr	banna	471	Mdd	Volentine, Archabald	330 Dnw

Name	Pg	Co.	Name	Pg	Co.	Name	Pg	Co.
James	165	Dnw	George	316	Frf	Robert	934	Crl
Jane	363	Lnn	Henry	759	Wsh	Robert	487	Frn
Phebe	165	Dnw	James	425	Bth	Robert	889	Hnv
William	331	Dnw	James	347	Fqr	Robert	243	Ldn
see Valentine			James	878	Hnv	Robert	294	Ldn
Vollentine, James	121	Hnr	James	860	Wth	Sarah	722	Gch
Vollin, Jno.	311	Frf	John	441	Bth	Susana	885	Hnv
John	363	Lnn	John	375	Fqr	Tho., Jr.	549	Mnn
Vollintine, Elizabeth	120	Hnr	John	11	Oho	Thomas	363	Fqr
John	120	Hnr	John	717	Wsh	Thomas	665	Mnt
Voress, Garret	512	Brk	John	759	Wsh	Thomas B.	22	Isw
Voris, Ruth	511	Brk	Jonas	651	Mnt	Thos. N.	315	Frf
Voshall, James	326	Dnw	Joseph	417	Bth	Ths.	548	Mnn
Voss, Jane	85	Clp	Joseph	429	Bth	William	777	Bck
John	521	Prw	Joseph	11	Oho	William	66	Chr
Nichs., Estate	85	Clp	Mathew	441	Bth	Wm., Jr.	654	Mnt
Robert B.	85	Clp	Mord.	675	Glc	Wm., Sr.	653	Mnt
William	594	Frd	Noel	153	Sth	Wyatt	884	Hnv
see Vass			Richard, Sr.	946	Chc	Zepheniah	19	Rcm
Vought, Wiliam	3	Wod	Robert	642	Gls	see Waide, Wayde		
Vowell, Ebenezer	512	Frd	Thomas	420	Bth	Wadkin, Benjamin	18	Wod
Jno. C.	311	Frf	Thos.	429	Msn	Perry	678	Br
Vowles, ---, & Briggs	35	Stf	William	4	Oho	Wadkins, Nicholas	392	Ags
John	347	Fqr	Waddy, D.R.	926	Nrf	Richard	94	Jff
Voyart, Leml.	923	Nrf	E.S.	925	Nrf	William	388	Fqr
Wm.	923	Nrf	Wade, Alice	884	Hnv	Wm.	550	Mnn
Voynard, Joseph	326	Dnw	Ambrose	719	Gch	Wadle, Jacob	555	Brk
Vyckers, Edwd.	923	Nrf	Anderson	485	Frn	Wadmore, William	783	Bck
			Anderson	592	Pre	Wadsworth, Rob.	554	Mnn
--- W ---			Andrew	876	Hnv	Wafel, Cloe Ann	54	Stf
			Bradley	485	Frn	Wafer, Thomas	722	Gch
			Casselton	485	Frn	Wafter, John	939	Hrr
W..., ...	249	Aml	Dabney	885	Hnv	Wager, John	68	Jff
...	250	Aml	Dan	548	Mnn	Mersey	92	Jff
...	926	Nrf	Daniel	577	Frd	Waggener, Andw.	525	Brk
B...	472	Mdd	Daniel	719	Gch	Andw., ju.	525	Brk
Elizabeth	53	Chs	Daniel	737	Nls	John	570	Brk
George	59	Stf	Daniel	593	Pre	Peter	314	Frf
H...y	924	Nrf	David	488	Bdf	Waggie, Philip	42	Rcm
James	225	Aml	David	767	Brn	Waggioner, James	90	Clp
Thos.	168	Dnw	David	773	Nwk	Waggoner, Adam	217	Pnd
W...dward, Lin	166	Dnw	Dolly	100	Cmb	Geo.	395	Ags
W...dy, William	249	Aml	Edward	569	Mnr	George	34	Rcm
W...htman, Js.	927	Nrf	Eliz.	549	Mnn	Jacob	393	Ags
W...i..., William	488	Bdf	Elizabeth	593	Pre	Jacob	666	Btt
W...lker, James	366	Lnn	Esther	100	Cmb	Jacob	819	Hmp
W...ls see Wiles			Fanney	495	Frn	Jacob	425	Rnd
W...ne, John	166	Dnw	Garland	651	Mnt	Jas.	664	Btt
W...s, William, jr.	166	Dnw	Geo.	548	Mnn	John	952	Hrr
W...te, Randal	168	Dnw	George	904	Hrr	John	637	Mnt
Wa..., Benjamin	488	Bdf	Gideon	774	Nwk	John M.	820	Hmp
Wa...en, Priscilla	618	Srr	Hampton	883	Hnv	Jos.	298	Rck
Wabbleton, Benjm.	955	Chc	Hezekiah	278	Ldn	Joseph	217	Pnd
Elizabeth	898	Hnv	Hezh.	549	Mnn	Lewis	215	Pnd
Thomas	943	Chc	Jacob	487	Bdf	Margaret	499	Prw
Waddal, Sally	593	Pre	Jacob [?]	488	Bdf	Mary	114	Hnr
Waddel, Alexander	692	Br	Jerimiah	487	Bdf	Michal	216	Pnd
Waddell, Carter	593	Pre	Jno.	880	Hnv	Peggy	599	Frd
Dennis	592	Pre	John	392	Ags	Peter	394	Ags
Edward	592	Pre	John	486	Bdf	Waggy, Abraham	224	Pnd
Jacob	590	Pre	John	316	Frf	Wagley, John	95	Jff
James G.	405	Ags	John	538	Frd	Wagner, Jac.	548	Mnn
John	593	Pre	John	904	Hrr	Jno.	553	Mnn
Mary	406	Ags	John	654	Mnt	Wagnor, John	933	Hrr
Walker	592	Pre	John, Jur.	431	Bth	Wagoner, John	206	Ess
William	592	Pre	John, Sen.	431	Bth	Wahab, John	395	Ags
Waddey, George P.	998	Nrt	Joseph	885	Yrk	Waid, Aggy	131	Hnr
Molley	1000	Nrt	Leonard	431	Bth	Alley	120	Hnr
Shapley N.	998	Nrt	Littleberry	884	Hnv	Ambrose	128	Hnr
Walter B.	368	Lnc	M.	30	Hnr	John	117	Hnr
Waddil, Elisabeth	772	Nwk	Martin	774	Nwk	Landy	121	Hnr
Mary	774	Nwk	Mary	167	Dnw	Richard	998	Nrt
Waddill, Nathl.	19	Ntt	Mary	249	Ldn	Thomas	121	Hnr
Waddle, Alexander	423	Bth	Nancey	376	Fqr	Thos.	116	Hnr
Andw.	651	Mnt	Nancy	737	Nls	William	933	Hrr
Barbary	652	Mnt	Nelson	852	Sth	Wyatt	121	Hnr
Davd.	688	Wsh	Otho	431	Bth	Waide see Warde		
David	652	Mnt	Pleasant	773	Nwk	Waigley, Geo.	306	Ldn
Elizabeth	417	Bth	Rebecca	613	Mnt	Wail, C.	30	Hnr
			Richard	542	Frd	Josiah	26	Isw

Mary	25	Isw	John	486	Bdf	Hannah	820	Hmp
Nicholas	6	Isw	Moses	488	Bdf	Henry	949	Chc
Wainright, Cornelius	166	Dnw	Waldrop, Jno.	894	Hnv	Henry	238	Shn
Geo.	4	Ntt	Wale, Geo.	364	Lnc	Humphrey	180	Knq
John	166	Dnw	Wales, Elisha	329	Dnw	Isaac	861	Wth
Wainwright, Polly	816	Nrf	Waleva see Wallace			Jacob	696	Br
Wairce, Patrick	732	Wsh	Walfong, Michael	732	Wsh	Jacob D.	180	Knq
Wait, Jasper	548	Mnn	Walford, Edwd.	16	Hnr	James	175	Alb
John	11	Oho	Walher see Walker			James	541	Brk
Jos.	552	Mnn	Walingford, Margaret	96	Jff	James	664	Btt
Joseph C.	412	Mds	Walke, Anthony, Sr.	480	Pra	James	675	Br
see Wayt			Anthy., Jr.	478	Pra	James	782	Bck
Waite, Isma	68	Acc	Anthy., (of A.)	478	Pra	James	501	Frn
Obed	599	Brk	Hannah	250	Aml	James	457	Grn
Waiteman, John	613	Mnt	Roger	924	Nrf	James	796	Hmp
Waitman see Weightmore			Thomas	794	Bck	James	11	Oho
Waits, Federick P.	123	Hnr	Wm.	477	Pra	James, (Doctr.)	786	Bck
Jessee	99	Spt	Walkeep, John	432	Msn	James, (J)	785	Bck
Mary	665	Btt	Walker, ---	327	Dnw	James, (M)	822	Bck
Richard	4	Hnr	Aaron, (W)	886	Yrk	James, Major	841	Bck
Wake, Ann	471	Mdd	Abel	537	Frd	Jane	951	Chc
Christopher	471	Mdd	Adam	863	Wth	Jane	394	Fqr
Robert	471	Mdd	Alexander	739	Brn	Jane	457	Grn
William	471	Mdd	Alexander	944	Chc	Jane	508	Prw
Wakefeild, Jas.	840	Nrf	Alexander	108	Spt	Jas.	363	Lnc
Wm.	821	Nrf	Alexr. [2]	294	Rck	Jas.	550	Mnn
Wakefield, Geo.	924	Nrf	Andrew	689	Br	Jesse	1000	Nrt
Mary	334	Dnw	Andrew	796	Hmp	Jesse	1	Pwh
Wakely, Jacob	22	Oho	Andw.	666	Btt	Jessee	665	Btt
James	22	Oho	Ann	766	Brn	Jessee	739	Brn
Richard	22	Oho	Ann	789	Wst	Jno.	666	Btt
Thomas	22	Oho	Ann, & Ovsr.	412	Mds	Jno.	677	Glc
Thomas, Jr.	22	Oho	Austin	721	Gch	Jno.	893	Hnv
Wakeman, John	203	Shn	Benedict	788	Wst	Jno.	14	Hnr
Walace, Charles	406	Ags	Benj.	263	Ldn	Jno.	294	Rck
Walbin, John	945	Hrr	Benja. H.	457	Grn	Jno.	296	Rck
Walburn, Edward	926	Hrr	Benjamin	856	Cmp	Jno., Sr.	66	Btt
Walden, Ambrose	472	Mdd	Benjamin	998	Nrt	Jno. M., esq.	280	Rck
Amy	332	Dnw	Bolling M.	166	Dnw	Joel	490	Frn
Anderson	251	Aml	Burwell	501	Frn	Joel	721	Gch
Betsey	326	Dnw	Catharine	998	Nrt	John	135	Acc
Charles	181	Knq	Charles	859	Cmp	John	211	Alb
Drewry	619	Srr	Charles	724	Wsh	John	391	Ags
Edward	178	Alb	Charles, Jr.	641	Gls	John	696	Br
George	933	Crl	Charles, Sen.	641	Gls	John	739	Brn
Henry	861	Cmp	Cupid	739	Brn	John	807	Bck
Jesse	619	Srr	Dailey	861	Wth	John	86	Clp
John	226	Aml	Daniel	274	Ldn	John	332	Dnw
John	79	Spt	Daniel	366	Lnn	John	205	Ess
Katy	933	Crl	Danl. G.	810	Nrf	John	317	Frf
Lewis	182	Knq	David	332	Dnw	John	641	Gls
Lewis	472	Mdd	David	675	Glc	John	676	Glc
Lucy	182	Knq	David	772	Nwk	John	113	Hnr
Richard	933	Crl	Edward	767	Brn	John	599	Mnr
Richd.	181	Knq	Edward	952	Chc	John	10	Oho
Richd., Senr.	182	Knq	Edward	537	Frd	John	426	Rnd
Saml.	128	Hnr	Edward	3	Oho	John	282	Rck
Scilla	619	Srr	Edwd.	942	Chc	John	886	Yrk
Tho.	89	Clp	Edwd. M.	927	Nrf	John, C.	412	Mds
Thomas	641	Gls	Eleanor	721	Gch	John, R.	412	Mds
Thomas	28	Rcm	Eliza.	666	Btt	John, Sr.	412	Mds
William	225	Aml	Elizabeth	415	Bth	John F.	457	Grn
William	181	Knq	Elizabeth	875	Cmp	John M.	819	Bck
Wm.	677	Glc	Elizabeth	720	Gch	John M.	942	Chc
Wright	619	Srr	Elizabeth	888	Hnv	John M.	456	Grn
see Wa...en			Elveston P.	6	Knw	John M.	672	Sss
Walder, Henry	962	Hrr	Fanny, (W)	886	Yrk	John T.	118	Spt
Walding, Charles	50	Stf	Florence	772	Nwk	Jos.	259	Ldn
Waldo, Jediah	930	Hrr	Francis	221	Kng	Joseph	833	Bck
John J.	939	Hrr	Francis	471	Mdd	Joseph	1000	Nrt
Phips	930	Hrr	Garrett	315	Ldn	Joseph	431	Rnd
Waldon, Frances	218	Ess	Geo. R.	18	Ntt	Joseph	280	Rck
James	209	Ess	George	225	Aml	Joseph	112	Spt
James	318	Frf	George	438	Mth	Josiph	279	Rck
Waldrin, Nancy	647	Mnt	George	583	Mnr	Julas	640	Gls
Waldrip, James	860	Wth	George	506	Prw	Leven	500	Prw
Waldrom, George	226	Pnd	George, Jr.	666	Btt	Lewis	578	Frd
Waldron, Benjamin	856	Cmp	George, Sr.	666	Btt	Littleton	135	Acc
Benjamin, Sr.	488	Bdf	George R.	487	Bdf	Lucy	182	Knq
George	10	Knw	Gorge	450	Frn	Major	682	Br

Mansfield	676	Glc	Wm.	666	Btt	Thomas, Qr.	412	Mds
Margaret	213	Alb	Wm.	238	Ldn	Thos.	327	Dnw
Margte.	924	Nrf	Wm.	798	Nrf	Thos.	798	Nrf
Martha	666	Btt	Wm.	810	Nrf	Thos., jr.	798	Nrf
Martin	676	Glc	Wm.	294	Rck	Ths.	86	Clp
Mary	886	Yrk	Wm.	725	Wsh	William	698	Br
Merry	412	Mds	Wm., Sr.	267	Rck	William	102	Cmb
Micajah	713	Wsh	Wm. W.	721	Gch	William B.	36	Stf
Molley	998	Nrt	Wyatt	938	Chc	Wm.	392	Ags
Molly	789	Wst	Yancy	10	Hnr	Wm.	664	Btt
Moses	472	Mdd	see Brown, Patrick, Prewett,			Wm.	327	Dnw
Nat.	810	Nrf	W...lker, Waller			Wm.	272	Rck
Nelson	666	Btt	Walkup, Andw.	267	Rck	Wm.	553	Mnn
Oliver	643	Gls	Arthur	263	Rck	Wm., Jr.	550	Mnn
Patrick	182	Elc	Joseph	614	Mnt	Walle, Isaac	91	Clp
Peggy	739	Brn	Saml.	262	Rck	Wallen, Mary	789	Nrf
Peter	550	Mnn	Samuel	309	Rck	see Weller		
Philip	182	Knq	Susan	271	Rck	Waller, Absalom	66	Spt
Philip	283	Rck	see Walkeep, Walker			Aylett	106	Spt
Polly	67	Acc	Wall, Armd.	91	Clp	Benj., (W)	885	Yrk
Pres.	364	Lnc	Conrad	609	Mnt	Benjamin	456	Frn
Randolph	839	Bck	David	165	Dnw	Benjamin, jr.	69	Spt
Randolph	12	Knw	David S.	768	Brn	Benjamin, Sr.	66	Spt
Rane	819	Bck	Edward	409	Rch	Bowker	70	Spt
Rebecca	137	Acc	James	618	Srr	Charles	383	Fqr
Reuben	664	Btt	James A.	457	Grn	Christopher	496	Frn
Richard	364	Lnn	John	513	Frd	Curtis	75	Spt
Richard	401	Rch	John	628	Mnt	Dabney	79	Spt
Ro.	676	Glc	Mary	457	Grn	Drew	851	Sth
Robert	286	Amh	Michael	668	Sss	Edward W.	24	Stf
Robert	642	Gls	Rebecca	618	Srr	Edwd.	677	Glc
Robert M.	488	Bdf	Sarah	166	Dnw	Elijah	511	Frd
Robt.	166	Dnw	William B.	457	Grn	Eliza M.	180	Knq
Robt.	926	Nrf	Wm.	91	Clp	Hampton	19	Ntt
Saml.	440	Flv	Wallace, ---, Russel &	21	Hnr	Jno.	551	Mnn
Samuel	354	Fqr	Abia	803	Nrf	John	180	Knq
Samuel	762	Hmp	Anderson	406	Ags	John	77	Spt
Sarah	952	Chc	Andrew	176	Alb	John	885	Yrk
Sarah	412	Mds	Asa	803	Nrf	Joseph	66	Spt
Shedrack	721	Gch	David	190	Elc	Levy	851	Sth
Solomon	354	Fqr	David	3	Rcm	Lewis	383	Fqr
Southey	135	Acc	Fatha	548	Prg	Martha, (W)	885	Yrk
Spencer	394	Fqr	Gust. B.	222	Kng	Pomfrett	91	Spt
Spencer	676	Glc	James	393	Ags	Primus	925	Nrf
Spencer	999	Nrt	James	303	Rck	Robt.	20	Ntt
Susan	999	Nrt	James	103	Spt	Sally	79	Spt
Theoh.	167	Dnw	James, (W)	886	Yrk	Sam	551	Mnn
Thomas	212	Alb	James W.	420	Fqr	Sylvanus	382	Fqr
Thomas	486	Bdf	Jamima	482	Pra	Thomas	102	Spt
Thomas	488	Bdf	Jas.	663	Btt	Walker	885	Yrk
Thomas	875	Cmp	Jesse	10	Ntt	William	522	Frd
Thomas	933	Crl	Jesse	668	Sss	William	68	Spt
Thomas	999	Nrt	Jno.	10	Ntt	William, jr.	21	Stf
Thomas	413	Rch	John	393	Ags	William E.	81	Spt
Thomas	789	Wst	John	4	Knw	Wm.	551	Mnn
Thorton	263	Ldn	John	10	Oho	Wm.	885	Yrk
Thos.	567	Mnr	John	95	Spt	Wm., Jur.	551	Mnn
Thos. R.	481	Pra	John	38	Stf	see Lewis, Walles		
Walter	861	Wth	Joseph	436	Bth	Walles, William, sr.	54	Stf
William	132	Acc	Josiah	798	Nrf	Wallhall, Rd., est.	56	Chs
William	791	Bck	Luke	428	Msn	Wallin, William	732	Wsh
William	859	Cmp	Mary	824	Nrf	Wallington, Jas.	676	Glc
William	66	Chr	Mathew	437	Bth	Nathl.	675	Glc
William	99	Cmb	Mattw.	926	Nrf	Read	675	Glc
William	412	Fqr	Michael	412	Mds	Wallins, Lewis	733	Wsh
William	642	Gls	Michl.	221	Kng	Wallis, Behethelon	86	Clp
William	547	Mnn	Nancy	431	Msn	Benj.	752	Wsh
William	579	Mnr	Richard	177	Alb	George	86	Clp
William	999	Nrt	Robert	767	Brn	Hannah	91	Clp
William	178	Shn	Robt.	393	Ags	Hew	364	Lnn
William	58	Stf	Robt.	664	Btt	James	957	Chc
William, Jr.	999	Nrt	Saml.	395	Ags	James	861	Wth
William, Mn.	764	Brn	Saml.	664	Btt	John	312	Frf
William, Senr.	590	Pre	Saml.	272	Rck	Joseph	364	Lnn
William J.	486	Bdf	Saml.	161	Sth	Malley	365	Lnn
William M.	788	Wst	Sarah	538	Prg	Phillip	959	Chc
William P.	766	Brn	Sol.	794	Nrf	Rob.	549	Mnn
William T.	590	Pre	Solomon	482	Pra	Robert	63	Chs
Winnifred	1000	Nrt	Tho.	803	Nrf	Sarah	849	Cmp
Wm.	515	Brk	Thomas	796	Hmp	Tabitha	70	Acc

Thos.	658	Mnt	Walter	402	Fqr	Thomas	776	Bck
William	401	Fqr	William	420	Fqr	Thomas	180	Knq
William	365	Lnn	William	232	Shn	Thomas	591	Pre
Willm.	647	Mnt	William	720	Wsh	Thomas, jr.	182	Knq
Wm., jr.	90	Clp	William	863	Wth	Thomas H.	124	Cmb
Wm., Senr.	88	Clp	William S.	171	Shn	Thomas M.	124	Cmb
see Willis			Willm.	631	Mnt	Thomson	211	Alb
Wallon, Isaac R.	457	Grn	see Watters			William	67	Chr
Wallop, John	136	Acc	Walthal, Francis	812	Bck	William	181	Knq
Skinner	132	Acc	James	807	Bck	William, Snr.	181	Knq
William	132	Acc	James	812	Bck	William S.	118	Cmb
Walls, Adam	665	Btt	Richard	778	Bck	Wim.	865	Hnv
Andrew	225	Aml	Thos.	167	Dnw	Wm.	664	Btt
Elisabeth	772	Nwk	Walthall, Archer, [his]			Wm.	767	Brn
James	515	Frd	Est.	65	Chs	see Wallon, Waltus, Watson		
Jas.	550	Mnn	Bartlet	249	Aml	Waltus, John	212	Alb
Jesse	774	Nwk	Benja.	68	Chs	Wamack, Burwell	534	Prg
John	225	Aml	Benja.	69	Chs	Hubbard	531	Prg
Js.	552	Mnn	Daniel	225	Aml	Nancy	534	Prg
Lucy	394	Ags	Francis	250	Aml	Peyton A.	540	Prg
Richard	773	Nwk	Francis	65	Chs	Phebe	534	Prg
Sally	265	Rck	Henry	64	Chs	Pleasant	334	Dnw
Thomas	773	Nwk	Jno.	65	Chs	Sarah	949	Chc
see Wells			John	249	Aml	William	531	Prg
Wallthall see Wallhall			Peter	249	Aml	Wamble, Jesse	859	Sth
Waln, Joseph	556	Frd	Rebecca	250	Aml	Wammock, Jacob	365	Lnn
Walpert, Casper	94	Jff	William	249	Aml	Wamner, William	250	Aml
Walpool, Lucy	737	Brn	William	7	Pwh	Wamock, Mary A.	17	Hnr
Walraven, Josiah	317	Ldn	Wm.	58	Chs	Wamoth, John	998	Nrt
Nathan	78	Jff	Wm.	63	Chs	Wampler, Chirstopher	862	Wth
Walsh, Patrick	416	Bth	see Wallhall			George	862	Wth
Samuel	10	Isw	Waltham, William	25	Isw	George, Jur.	863	Wth
Walson, Isaac	209	Shn	Walther, William	19	Hnr	George, M.	863	Wth
Waltar, Ann	32	Hnr	Walthrop, Jesse	225	Aml	Henry	863	Wth
Walten see Wallin, Wallins			Joseph	225	Aml	Jacob	862	Wth
Walter, Henry, Junr.	175	Shn	Waltman, Jacob [2]	284	Ldn	John	863	Wth
Henry, Senr.	174	Shn	Jno.	284	Ldn	Joseph	862	Wth
Jacob	289	Rck	Walton, Angelica	765	Brn	Lovis	863	Wth
James	201	Shn	Anthony	778	Bck	Michael	862	Wth
John	133	Acc	Anthony	182	Knq	Peter	863	Wth
John	524	Frd	David	457	Grn	Wamps, Frances	819	Hmp
John T.	594	Frd	Edmund	212	Alb	Wamsley, David	965	Hrr
Laurence	525	Frd	Edward	126	Cmb	John	443	Bth
Martin	175	Shn	Elias R.	766	Brn	Samuel	957	Hrr
Richard	69	Acc	Eliza.	457	Grn	Wanaker, George	567	Frd
Saml.	551	Mnn	Elizabeth	182	Knq	Wanless, Catharine	354	Fqr
William	167	Dnw	Geo.	20	Ntt	Ralph	425	Bth.
see Waller, Wallis			George	768	Brn	Stephen	445	Bth
Walters, A.J.	926	Nrf	George	123	Cmb	Wansley, Adam	10	Wod
Betty	50	Stf	George	28	Hnr	Wanton, Edwd.	11	Hnr
Charles	22	Stf	George	180	Knq	Waple, George N.	401	Rch
Daniel, Senr.	232	Shn	Henry	457	Grn	Waples, Samuel	71	Acc
Danl., Junr.	232	Shn	Isaac, Sr.	457	Grn	War, Thomas	488	Bdf
Dyer	265	Ldn	Isham	212	Alb	Warad, James	187	Shn
Edward	344	Fqr	Ison	211	Alb	Warbettson, Jno.	318	Ldn
Geo.	314	Ldn	James	180	Knq	Warble, Mathias	89	Jff
George	631	Mnt	Jehugh	211	Alb	Warburton, Ro., (W)	885	Yrk
Henry	428	Rnd	Jesse	225	Aml	Ward, ---, Mrs.	927	Nrf
Isaac	513	Brk	Jno.	180	Knq	Aaron	588	Brk
Jacob	395	Ags	John	211	Alb	Abbury B.	366	Lnn
Jacob	631	Mnt	John	213	Alb	Abm.	552	Mnn
Jacob	165	Shn	John	767	Brn	Ann	175	Alb
Jacob	213	Shn	John	837	Bck	Benja.	317	Frf
James	312	Ldn	John	18	Hnr	Benjamin	13	Isw
James	314	Ldn	John	198	Shn	Benjn.	8	Ntt
John	545	Brk	Joshua	768	Brn	Berjamin	768	Brn
John	91	Clp	Josiah	66	Chr	Betsey	588	Brk
John	641	Gls	Langhorn	803	Bck	Cabeb	817	Nrf
John	862	Wth	Littleton	765	Brn	Caleb	479	Pra
Joseph	176	Alb	Martha	591	Pre	Chesley	861	Wth
Landy	90	Clp	Minchun	121	Cmb	Daniel	908	Hrr
Mark, jr.	21	Stf	Nancy	126	Cmb	Danl.	91	Clp
Mark, Sr.	22	Stf	Nelson	876	Hnv	Dicy	367	Lnn
Mary S., (Y)	885	Yrk	Richard	861	Wth	Edmund	851	Cmp
Michael	863	Wth	Richmond	213	Alb	Edward	797	Hmp
Michl.	544	Brk	Richmund	212	Alb	Elizabeth	67	Acc
Pearce	232	Shn	Robert, Sr.	123	Cmb	Elizabeth	66	Chr
Richard	402	Fqr	Salley	132	Hnr	Francess	36	Isw
Samuel	428	Rnd	Sharad	225	Aml	Gedion	479	Pra
Sarah	62	Stf	Simeon	590	Pre	Henry	212	Alb

Henry	250	Aml	see Waid			Warman, Cathre.	552	Mnn
Henry	90	Clp	Warde, Anne	314	Frf	Fran.	552	Mnn
Henry, jr.	88	Clp	Danl.	651	Mnt	Warmouth, Cress	92	Clp
Jacob	420	Rnd	Warden, Arthur	794	Nrf	Warmox, Alex.	90	Clp
James	588	Brk	Elisha	345	Fqr	Warmsley, Daniel	62	Stf
James	849	Cmp	Jas.	479	Pra	James	418	Rnd
James	861	Cmp	John	515	Frd	Joseph	418	Rnd
James	786	Hmp	John	2	Hnr	Matthew	421	Rnd
James	411	Mds	Julia	794	Nrf	Samuel	418	Rnd
James	649	Mnt	Samuel	5	Oho	Wm.	423	Rnd
James	925	Nrf	Timothy	553	Mnn	Warn, Walter	788	Wst
James	181	Shn	Warder, Harry	928	Hrr	Warner, Adam	226	Pnd
Jesse	820	Hmp	Jessee	505	Prw	Peter	219	Pnd
Jessee	768	Brn	Philip, Jr.	519	Prw	Carter	938	Chc
Jno.	480	Pra	Walter	520	Prw	Danl.	306	Rck
Jno., (B Smyth)	481	Pra	William	510	Prw	Dennis	405	Fqr
Joel	503	Brk	Wardin, Thomis	606	Mnt	Geo.	312	Ldn
Joel	832	Hmp	Wardlan see Wardlaw			George	68	Acc
John	212	Alb	Wardlaw, Michl.	299	Rck	George	220	Pnd
John	445	Bth	Wm. [?]	297	Rck	Iverson	796	Bck
John	779	Hmp	Wardlow, Margaret	457	Grn	Jacob	136	Acc
John	812	Hmp	Wardrobe, David	788	Wst	Jacob	487	Bdf
John	88	Jff	Ware, Ann	182	Knq	John	89	Clp
John	3	Knw	Elizabeth	101	Jff	John	773	Nwk
John	366	Lnn	Elizabeth	418	Rnd	John	216	Pnd
John	789	Wst	Federick	737	Nls	Leonard	282	Ldn
John	862	Wth	George	593	Brk	Nancy	2	Hnr
John, (Capt.)	858	Cmp	Humpy.	208	Ess	Philip	520	Brk
John, Senr.	867	Cmp	James	262	Amh	Rebeca	834	Nrf
Johnathan	768	Brn	James	535	Frd	Saml.	911	Hrr
Joseph	588	Brk	James	722	Gch	Susan	55	Stf
Joseph	770	Brn	James	794	Hmp	Thomas	861	Wth
Joseph	2	Knw	James	98	Spt	Uriah	590	Mnr
Joseph	24	Oho	Jno.	675	Glc	William	134	Acc
Joshua	666	Btt	John	722	Gch	Willm.	622	Mnt
Joshua	472	Mdd	John	57	Jff	Wm.	514	Brk
Langston	1	Knw	John	182	Knq	Zebulon	220	Pnd
Loyd	797	Hmp	John, jr.	280	Amh	Warrall, ---, Docte.	35	Hnr
Loyd, Jur.	797	Hmp	John, Senr.	300	Amh	Warran see Worroer		
Martha	167	Dnw	Joseph	556	Frd	Warrell, James	335	Dnw
Martha D.	21	Ntt	Kit	28	Hnr	Thomas	334	Dnw
Mary	875	Cmp	Mary	438	Flv	Warren, Bazell	718	Wsh
Mary	593	Pre	Milly	318	Frf	Benjamin	890	Hnv
Mary	482	Pra	Nathaniel	933	Crl	Drewry P.	618	Srr
Mary	484	Pra	Nicholas	180	Knq	Edwd.	841	Nrf
Mary	485	Pra	Penny	471	Mdd	Fred	925	Nrf
Nathan	1	Ntt	Pleasant	395	Ags	George	167	Dnw
Plesent	750	Wsh	Rachel	214	Ess	Hannah	618	Srr
Polly	11	Knw	Ralph	100	Jff	Henry	883	Hnv
Rawland	8	Knw	Reuben	471	Mdd	Henry	998	Nrt
Richd.	244	Shn	Robert	182	Knq	Isaac	925	Nrf
Robert	3	Knw	Robert	471	Mdd	J.B.	925	Nrf
Robt.	10	Ntt	Saml.	471	Mdd	Jacob, Mulo.	181	Knq
Robt.	37	Rcm	Tho.	548	Mnn	James	167	Dnw
Saml.	313	Ldn	Thomas	737	Nls	James	788	Nrf
Samul	769	Brn	William	270	Amh	James	618	Srr
Seth	855	Cmp	William	860	Wth	James H.	618	Srr
Seth	1	Knw	William, jr.	297	Amh	Jane	938	Chc
Thomas	221	Ess	William, jr.	182	Knq	Jas.	837	Nrf
Thomas	316	Frf	William, Senr.	181	Knq	Jas. B., [his]		
Thos.	289	Ldn	see Wear			(Plantn.)	480	Pra
Thos.	478	Pra	Warely, Andrew	23	Rcm	Jesse	671	Sss
Uriah	861	Wth	John	20	Rcm	Jno.	924	Nrf
William	250	Aml	Waren, Jeremiah	40	Rcm	Jno., Sr.	925	Nrf
William	765	Brn	Sarah	2	Rcm	John	595	Mnr
William	522	Frd	Wareaburg, John	299	Rck	John	773	Nwk
William	591	Frd	Warfeild, Sylvanus	789	Hmp	John	827	Nrf
William	2	Isw	Warfield, John	705	Wsh	John	503	Prw
William	14	Knw	Warford, James	308	Ldn	John	515	Prw
William	862	Wth	Jno.	308	Ldn	John	846	Sth
Wm.	90	Clp	Wm.	251	Ldn	John	876	Sth
Wm.	962	Hrr	Waring, Fanny	28	Stf	John, senr.	618	Srr
Wm.	14	Knw	Jno.	207	Ess	Jonah	788	Nrf
Wm.	817	Nrf	Robert P.	198	Ess	Josiah [crossed out]	788	Nrf
Wm.	821	Nrf	Wm., jr.	223	Ess	Lear	789	Nrf
Wm.	927	Nrf	Wm., Sr.	223	Ess	Lemuel	618	Srr
Wm., 1st.	926	Nrf	Wm. L.	207	Ess	Lettleton	829	Nrf
Wm., Sr.	766	Brn	Wark, Catherine	55	Jff	Mary	480	Pra
Zachariah	501	Prw	Warker, Elizabeth	317	Frf	Moses	3	Wod
Zachr.	314	Frf	Warkin, Valentine	35	Rcm	Peggy	847	Sth

Pleasant, F. N.	669	Sss	Amelia	845	Sth	William	50	Stf
Randal	167	Dnw	Andr.	152	Sth	Wathall, Francis M.	594	Pre
Rebecca	169	Shn	Arthur	845	Sth	Thomas	592	Pre
Rebecca	618	Srr	Bayley	48	Stf	Watkin, William	19	Wod
Samuel, Jr.	618	Srr	Bd., Judge	315	Frf	Watkins, Abner	118	Cmb
Samuel, Senr.	618	Srr	Bushrd.	314	Frf	Abner	125	Cmb
Thos.	167	Dnw	Butler	222	Kng	Ann	670	Sss
Thos.	924	Nrf	Diana	4	Rcm	Archibald	836	Bck
Thos., (Son Joe)	618	Srr	Edwd.	317	Frf	Aron	877	Cmp
Thos., (Son John	618	Srr	Esther	848	Sth	Beck of, (F.N.)	21	Isw
William	597	Frd	Fairfax	58	Jff	Benajah	14	Pwh
see Wa...en, Waren			George	932	Crl	Benja.	719	Gch
Warrenberg, Andrew	862	Wth	George	788	Wst	Benja.	722	Gch
Warrenor, Ann	122	Hnr	Henry	526	Frd	Benja.	181	Knq
Danl.	131	Hnr	Henry	221	Kng	Benjamin	21	Isw
John	122	Hnr	Henry	518	Prw	Benjn.	12	Pwh
Mordica	131	Hnr	Henry, jr.	223	Kng	Betsy Ann	592	Pre
Polley	131	Hnr	Henry T.	222	Kng	Catharine	678	Wrw
Sally	121	Hnr	James	876	Sth	Charles	792	Bck
Saml.	131	Hnr	Jane	120	Spt	David	312	Frf
Trueman	131	Hnr	John H.	222	Kng	David	12	Pwh
Warrick, John	421	Bth	John T. A.	76	Jff	Ebinezer	656	Mnt
Robt.	664	Btt	Joseph	315	Frf	Edward	168	Dnw
William	422	Bth	Lawrence A.	606	Frd	Edward	6	Pwh
Warrin, Abijah	905	Hrr	Lity	3	Hnr	Edward	13	Pwh
Warriner, James	867	Cmp	Lucy	95	Jff	Edward, Aged 100		
John	799	Bck	Martha	87	Clp	years	14	Pwh
William	781	Bck	Nedham L.	221	Kng	Elijah	907	Hrr
Warring, Booth M.	20	Ntt	Peggy	860	Sth	Elizabeth	907	Hrr
Warrington, Jno.	924	Nrf	Rebecca	876	Sth	Elizabeth	618	Srr
John	132	Acc	Richd. H. L.	64	Jff	Enoch	169	Shn
Kaziah	68	Acc	Saml.	86	Clp	Frances	591	Pre
Shadrach	135	Acc	Samuel	64	Jff	Frances	679	Wrw
Southey	135	Acc	Sarah	859	Sth	Francis	423	Msn
Stephen	67	Acc	Thos.	789	Wst	Francis	594	Pre
Susannah	69	Acc	Warner	534	Frd	Francis, Senr.	594	Pre
William	132	Acc	Warner	221	Kng	George	66	Chr
Warror, John	16	Hnr	Washington J.	521	Prw	George	107	Cmb
Wartenbe, Francis	675	Br	Whiting	534	Frd	Henry	907	Hrr
R...	697	Br	William	402	Rch	Henry A.	66	Chr
Warters, James	735	Nls	Wm.	152	Sth	Henry W., Capt.	13	Pwh
John	736	Nls	Wm. A.	789	Wst	James	277	Ldn
William	68	Jff	Zeb.	866	Sth	James	670	Sss
Warthen, David	533	Prg	see ---, Drumwright			Jas.	552	Mnn
John	533	Prg	Waskey, Jno.	289	Rck	Jesse	3	Isw
Theodrick	362	Fqr	Wasky, Christ.	284	Rck	Jno.	663	Btt
Walter	533	Prg	Wason, Alexander	3	Rcm	Jno.	2	Hnr
Wartman, Laurence	252	Shn	William	424	Msn	Jno.	547	Mnn
Warton, Samle.	23	Oho	Wat, Nancy	737	Nls	Joel	66	Chr
Warts see Waits			Thomas	737	Nls	Joel, (Colo.)	826	Bck
Warwick, A. B.	734	Nls	Watckins, William, jr.	66	Chr	John	264	Amh
Andrew, Ser.	421	Bth	Water see Whater			John	800	Bck
Andrew L.	418	Bth	Waterfeild, Jacob	14	Isw	John	167	Dnw
Ann	363	Lnc	Waterfield, Augustus	70	Acc	John	22	Isw
Ben.	363	Lnc	Betsey	70	Acc	John	181	Knq
Daniel	11	Hnr	Peter	270	Amh	John	367	Lnn
Jacob	429	Bth	Waterman, Alexr.	265	Ldn	John	734	Nls
James	878	Cmp	Asher	1	Rcm	John	590	Pre
John	276	Amh	Charles	6	Oho	John	668	Sss
Nelson R.	737	Nls	John	907	Hrr	John, Capt.	66	Chr
Neomy	734	Nls	Waters, Elijah, bound for a			John D.	772	Nwk
William	261	Amh	term of years	447	Bth	Joseph	182	Knq
Wm.	767	Brn	Geo.	926	Nrf	Joseph	594	Pre
Wm.	363	Lnc	George	15	Oho	Joseph D.	720	Gch
Wasam, Nicholes	739	Wsh	James	132	Acc	Levi	919	Hrr
Wasdin, Jas.	140	Sth	Jno.	549	Mnn	Mansfield	68	Chs
Wash, James	865	Hnv	John	66	Acc	Mary	722	Gch
Nathan	177	Alb	John	440	Bth	Mathas	945	Hrr
Wim.	866	Hnv	John	933	Crl	Micajah	304	Rck
Washam, Jos.	729	Wsh	Margaret	502	Prw	Moses	664	Btt
Robert	729	Wsh	Molly	136	Acc	Moses	666	Btt
see Washian			Molly	43	Stf	Moses	861	Cmp
Washburn, Isaac	941	Hrr	Richard	933	Crl	Moses	877	Cmp
Robert	938	Hrr	Shelah	170	Shn	Peter	852	Hnv
Thomas	938	Hrr	Silas	45	Stf	Philip	219	Ess
Washer, Martha	167	Dnw	Susan	167	Dnw	Philip	180	Knq
Rhuben	885	Yrk	Thomas	132	Acc	Philip	591	Pre
Washian, William	718	Wsh	William	134	Acc	Polly	630	Mnt
Washington, ... B., [his] (O.S.)			William	250	Aml	Rebecca	21	Isw
[Overseer?]	63	Jff	William	48	Stf	Reuben	670	Sss

Richard	8	Hnr
Richd.	181	Knq
Rob.	178	Elc
Robert	800	Bck
Robert	857	Cmp
Robert	870	Cmp
Robert	878	Cmp
Robert	69	Chs
Robert	618	Srr
Robt.	21	Isw
Samuel	14	Pwh
Samuel	591	Pre
Silas	824	Bck
Silas	590	Pre
Spencer	805	Bck
Step.	553	Mnn
Thomas	67	Chr
Thomas	830	Hmp
Thomas	611	Mnt
Thomas	6	Pwh
Thos.	720	Gch
Thos.	869	Hnv
Thos. B.	719	Gch
William	176	Alb
William	817	Hmp
William	46	Isw
William	737	Nls
William M.	66	Chr
Wim.	891	Hnv
Wm.	259	Ldn
Wm.	886	Yrk
see Watckins		
Watkinson, Cornelius	69	Acc
Wats, Molley	999	Nrt
Spencer	999	Nrt
Watsan, John	328	Dnw
Watsin, Elizabeth	7	Pwh
Watson, Aaron	6	Oho
Abner	592	Pre
Aggy	11	Hnr
Alexander	282	Amh
Allen	594	Pre
Ann	678	Wrw
Archibald	52	Stf
Arthur	134	Acc
Augustus	592	Pre
Benjamin	590	Pre
Benjamin A.	590	Pre
Caleb	71	Acc
Caleb	925	Nrf
Custis	68	Acc
Daniel	75	Jff
Dav.	549	Mnn
Dav.	552	Mnn
David	456	Grn
Drury	590	Pre
Edward	277	Amh
Edwd.	926	Nrf
Elijah	69	Acc
Elizabeth	167	Dnw
Enock	591	Pre
Ephraim	67	Acc
Francis	558	Frd
Geo.	549	Mnn
Geo., Jr.	549	Mnn
Henry	354	Fqr
Henry	555	Frd
Henry	61	Jff
Hugh	124	Cmb
James	68	Acc
James [2]	212	Alb
James	487	Bdf
James	573	Frd
James	589	Pre
James	46	Stf
James G.	86	Clp
Jas.	480	Pra
Jas. G.	547	Mnn
Jesse	367	Lnn
Jno.	549	Mnn

Joel	717	Wsh
Johm	51	Stf
John	69	Acc
John	133	Acc
John	137	Acc
John	182	Alb
John	220	Alb
John [2]	211	Alb
John	212	Alb
John	488	Bdf
John	404	Fqr
John	493	Frn
John	27	Hnr
John	76	Jff
John	84	Jff
John	8	Oho
John	593	Pre
John	498	Prw
John, Junr.	589	Pre
John P.	177	Alb
Joseph	489	Bdf
Joseph	852	Hnv
Joseph	592	Pre
Joseph, Jur.	846	Hnv
Josiah	593	Pre
Josias	518	Prw
Larner	414	Mds
Levin	69	Acc
Littleberry	594	Pre
Mary	464	Frn
Mary	472	Mdd
Mary	400	Rch
Mary	51	Stf
Matthew	3	Mnn
Moses	560	Frd
Nancy	69	Acc
Nancy	15	Hnr
Nancy	594	Pre
Polly	766	Brn
Richard P.	178	Alb
Richd. D.	514	Brk
Robert	137	Acc
Robert	766	Brn
Robert	669	Sss
Sampson	66	Acc
Samuel, (Son of Jno.)	589	Pre
Sarah	665	Btt
Sarah	86	Clp
Sarah	552	Mnn
Sarah	554	Mnn
Severn	69	Acc
Stephen	925	Nrf
Thomas [2]	486	Bdf
Thomas	550	Brk
Thomas	316	Frf
Thomas	8	Hnr
Thomas	74	Jff
Thomas	293	Ldn
Thos.	505	Brk
Thos.	12	Hnr
Thos.	727	Wsh
Walter	211	Alb
Walter	515	Frd
Wilkerson	801	Bck
William	66	Acc
William	68	Acc
William	176	Alb
William	180	Alb
William	211	Alb
William	487	Bdf
William	800	Bck
William	404	Fqr
William	560	Frd
William	558	Frd
William	22	Oho
William	51	Stf
William, of P	69	Acc
William, Sho.	131	Acc
William, Sr.	805	Bck
Wm.	553	Mnn

Wm.	9	Ntt
see Walson		
Watt, Elizabeth	296	Rck
George	26	Hnr
Hugh	881	Hnv
James	829	Bck
Watten, Moses	238	Shn
Watter see Walter		
Watterman, Elkanah	481	Pra
Joel	479	Pra
Kedar	484	Pra
Mary	484	Pra
Watters, David	484	Pra
Eliza.	484	Pra
Jno.	273	Ldn
William	317	Frf
see Walters		
Watterson, Agness	663	Mnt
Jos.	663	Mnt
Robert	477	Pra
Thos.	630	Mnt
Wattes, William	641	Gls
Watthall, Branch	590	Pre
Christopher	593	Pre
Francis	593	Pre
Henry	593	Pre
John	590	Pre
Watton, Jno.	548	Mnn
Saml.	237	Shn
see Walton		
Watts, ---, Estate	652	Btt
---, Estate	661	Btt
---, Mrs.	664	Btt
Abraham	830	Nrf
Ann	91	Clp
Benjamin	290	Amh
Caleb	272	Amh
Charles	177	Alb
Charles	364	Lnn
Charles	471	Mdd
Charles	735	Nls
Curtis	267	Amh
Daniel	181	Knq
Danl.	814	Nrf
David	132	Acc
David	212	Alb
Densey	830	Nrf
Ed.	655	Btt
Edward	573	Mnr
Elijah	212	Alb
Fanny	413	Mds
Frederick	86	Clp
Geo. K.	166	Dnw
Hoid	413	Mds
Jacob	212	Alb
James	488	Bdf
James	180	Knq
James	240	Ldn
John	181	Knq
Jane	552	Mnn
Jas.	549	Mnn
Joel	829	Nrf
John	212	Alb
John	273	Amh
John	488	Bdf
John	413	Fqr
John	471	Mdd
Kauffman	180	Knq
Margaret	30	Stf
Mary	879	Cmp
Mary	168	Dnw
Mary	815	Nrf
Milly	30	Stf
Philip	911	Hrr
Phillip	176	Alb
Ralph	471	Mdd
Robt.	86	Clp
Robt.	825	Nrf
Saml.	188	Elc
Samuel	291	Amh

Sarah	926	Nrf
Sary	413	Mds
Spencer	364	Lnc
Stephen	285	Amh
Tho.	191	Elc
Thomas	213	Alb
Thomas	412	Fqr
Thomas	180	Knq
Thomas	293	Ldn
Thos.	828	Nrf
Thos., jr.	830	Nrf
Tressy	29	Stf
Washington	67	Chs
William	134	Acc
William	262	Amh
William	330	Dnw
William	453	Frn
William	9	Knw
William	413	Mds
William L.	735	Nls
Wm.	835	Nrf
see Walls		
Waugh, Alexa.	313	Frf
Alexander	413	Mds
Alice	62	Stf
Andrew	167	Dnw
Charles S.	85	Clp
Edward	261	Amh
Elizabeth	222	Kng
Elizabeth	61	Stf
Jacob	421	Bth
James	297	Amh
James	422	Bth
James	314	Frf
James	791	Nrf
Lewis T.	316	Frf
Margarett	85	Clp
Mary	421	Bth
Micajah	5	Knw
Richd.	88	Clp
St. Clair	421	Bth
Samuel	422	Bth
Singleton	588	Brk
Wm.	550	Mnn
see Haugh, Waughp		
Waughp, Jas.	828	Nrf
Wax, Henry	664	Btt
Jacob	688	Wsh
Margarett	665	Btt
Waxler, Sarah	811	Hmp
Way, Edward	594	Frd
Elijah	547	Frd
Henry	389	Fqr
James	76	Jff
Saml.	247	Shn
William	999	Nrt
Wayde, Sally	213	Ess
Wayland, Adam	411	Mds
Catherine	411	Mds
Cornelias	411	Mds
Joel	411	Mds
John	411	Mds
Joseph	392	Ags
Lewis	392	Ags
Wayman, Henry	413	Mds
Henry, Jr.	413	Mds
John	91	Clp
John	413	Mds
Joseph	87	Clp
Lewis	413	Mds
Waymann, Thomas	13	Oho
Waymere, Henry	696	Wsh
Wayne see Whayne		
Waysman, Peter	396	Ags
Wayt, George	212	Alb
Nathanael	11	Oho
Twyman	179	Alb
see Wait		
Waytt, John	406	Ags
Wead, John	746	Wsh
Weaden, Sarah	404	Rch
Weadon, Jane	237	Ldn
Margaret	241	Ldn
Richd.	238	Ldn
Weaglesworth, Mary	932	Crl
Weakly, Francis	29	Rcm
Joseph	90	Clp
Wean, Abra.	284	Ldn
see Mcean		
Weane see Wease		
Wear, James	718	Wsh
John	718	Wsh
Wearen, Reuben	694	Wsh
Wearing, Thomas	527	Prw
Wears, Robert	316	Ldn
Wm.	277	Ldn
see Vears		
Wease, Daniel	421	Rnd
George	423	Rnd
Henry	667	Btt
Jacob	423	Rnd
Jacob	431	Rnd
John	214	Pnd
Soloman	224	Pnd
see Wiase		
Weast, Jno.	298	Ldn
Weathe... red, William	736	Nls
Weatherby, Jane	390	Fqr
Weatherford, Charles A.	67	Chr
Daniel	67	Chr
John	67	Chr
Patsy	66	Chr
Samuel	67	Chr
Stephen	67	Chr
William	67	Chr
Weatherholt, Adam	861	Wth
Peter	922	Hrr
Weatherholtz, Peter	416	Rnd
Weatherhults, Henry	227	Shn
John	227	Shn
Weatherly, James	72	Spt
Weathers, Benjamin	672	Sss
Eliza.	398	Rch
Epd.	390	Rch
Geo.	393	Ags
Geo.	885	Yrk
George	392	Rch
James	90	Clp
Jesse, (est.)	88	Clp
John	396	Rch
John	669	Sss
John	789	Wst
Mary	671	Sss
Sterling	670	Sss
William	390	Rch
Weatherspoon, Francess	722	Gch
Weatherston see Shelton		
Weaver, Aaron, (FB)	479	Pra
Abraham	771	Hmp
Ambrose	414	Mds
Andw.	393	Ags
Anthony, a free mulatto	998	Nrt
Aron	413	Mds
Ben.	364	Lnc
Benjamin	789	Wst
Benjn.	435	Flv
Billy	364	Lnc
Casper	187	Shn
Catharine	12	Rcm
Charles	12	Rcm
Chrisley	200	Shn
Christian	518	Frd
Conrod	253	Shn
Danl.	561	Brk
Danl.	89	Clp
Darky	363	Lnc
David	172	Shn
Elijah	403	Rch
Elliott	789	Wst
Elizabeth	535	Frd
Elizt.	393	Ags
Ephraim	90	Clp
Frederick	205	Shn
Geo.	291	Ldn
George	200	Shn
Hen.	548	Mnn
Henry	304	Amh
Henry	25	Rcm
Jac.	552	Mnn
Jac.	554	Mnn
Jacob	396	Ags
Jacob	527	Brk
Jacob	366	Fqr
Jacob	463	Frn
Jacob	549	Frd
Jacob	641	Mnt
Jacob	198	Shn
Jacob, Senr.	344	Fqr
Jacob, Senr.	577	Frd
James	368	Fqr
James	439	Flv
James	789	Wst
Jas.	553	Mnn
John	393	Ags
John	394	Ags
John	569	Brk
John	385	Fqr
John	464	Frn
John	524	Frd
John	577	Frd
John	413	Mds
John	655	Mnt
John	592	Pre
John	788	Wst
John, jr.	394	Ags
John P.	392	Ags
Jonas	413	Mds
Jos.	553	Mnn
Leanard	665	Btt
Lucy, a free mulatto	999	Nrt
Mary	439	Flv
Mason	252	Ldn
Mathew	862	Cmp
Mathias	414	Mds
Matthias	89	Clp
Michael	200	Shn
Moses	414	Mds
Nancy	363	Lnc
Nanny	363	Lnc
Nanny	364	Lnc
Peter	391	Ags
Peter	413	Mds
Peter	269	Rck
Peter, Sr.	392	Ags
Philip	515	Frd
Priscilla	592	Pre
Richd.	363	Lnc
Saml.	392	Ags
Samuel	876	Cmp
Samuel	385	Fqr
Samuel	274	Ldn
Sp.	364	Lnc
Thomas	689	Br
Thomas	590	Pre
Thomas	789	Wst
Thomas, a free mulatto	998	Nrt
William	861	Cmp
William	345	Fqr
William	413	Mds
William	246	Shn
William	788	Wst
Wm.	738	Brn
see Weawer, Wever		
Weawer, Jesse	819	Nrf
Web, Daniel	498	Frn
Daniel	227	Shn
George	772	Nwk
Haridesh	231	Shn

Jacob	482	Frn	Susanna	998	Nrt	Wm.	720	Gch
Jno.	301	Rck	Tapley	827	Nrf	Wm.	549	Mnn
John	447	Bth	Tarlton F.	526	Frd	Weckem, John	704	Wsh
John	483	Frn	Tho.	363	Lnc	Wecker, Frank	124	Hnr
Joseph	482	Frn	Thomas	67	Chr	Wedderbourne, Eliza.	180	Knq
Judith	34	Hnr	Thomas	948	Hrr	Lydia	180	Knq
Richd.	231	Shn	Thomas	647	Mnt	Weden, Augustine	511	Prw
Samuel	482	Frn	Thomas	1000	Nrt	Richard	511	Prw
Sarah	483	Frn	Thomas	115	Spt	Wedewitt, John	24	Hnr
Smith	458	Frn	Vincent	1000	Nrt	Weebb, Elizabeth	367	Lnn
Smith	482	Frn	Warren	457	Grn	Weeden, Augustin	86	Clp
Theoderick	483	Frn	William	807	Bck	Frederick	675	Glc
Webb, ---	926	Nrf	William	839	Bck	Frederick	446	Mth
Armistd.	886	Yrk	William	643	Gls	John	88	Clp
Benajah	36	Rcm	William	46	Isw	Wm., Senr.	676	Glc
Benj.	960	Hrr	William	180	Knq	Weedon, Augustine	222	Kng
Benja.	910	Hrr	William	1000	Nrt	Caty	223	Kng
Betsy	2	Hnr	William	391	Rch	George	353	Fqr
Charles	69	Acc	William, Jr.	815	Bck	John	354	Fqr
Charles	363	Lnc	William, Senr.	815	Bck	Sally	40	Stf
Conrad	774	Nwk	William B.	83	Spt	Weekes, John H.	88	Clp
Conrade	13	Ntt	Wm.	80	Clp	Weekley, ...	168	Shn
Edmund	874	Cmp	Wm.	815	Nrf	Jacob	167	Shn
Edward	998	Nrt	Wm., (Doctr.)	222	Ess	John	411	Mds
Eliza	180	Knq	Zachh.	88	Clp	John, Jr.	411	Mds
Elizabeth	840	Bck	see Weebb, Welb			Robert	166	Shn
Elizabeth	913	Hrr	Webber, Adam	857	Cmp	Weeks, Benjamin	34	Stf
Ewel	999	Nrt	Henry	859	Cmp	Elijah	488	Bdf
Farmer	722	Gch	James	68	Spt	Elisha	115	Hnr
Foster	886	Hnv	John	863	Cmp	Eliza.	481	Pra
General	208	Ess	John B.	105	Jff	Elizabeth	223	Shn
Geo.	834	Nrf	Joseph	719	Gch	Emanuel, senr.	15	Ntt
George	642	Gls	Martin	858	Cmp	George	486	Bdf
Hartwell	327	Dnw	Mary	719	Gch	Jno.	544	Prg
Herdimon	538	Prg	Mary B.	125	Cmb	Jno., Sr.	285	Rck
Isaac	133	Acc	Peter	860	Cmp	Job	10	Oho
Isaac	738	Brn	Philip	226	Aml	Katy	166	Dnw
Isaac	1000	Nrt	Thomas	865	Cmp	Margaret	526	Prw
James	176	Elc	Webley, Geo.	549	Brk	Richd.	15	Ntt
James	214	Ess	John	180	Knq	Thomas	371	Fqr
James	180	Knq	William C.	180	Knq	Thomas	670	Sss
James	607	Mnt	Webster, ---, & Poor	21	Hnr	William	488	Bdf
James	591	Pre	Anthony	225	Aml	William	327	Dnw
James	392	Rch	Arch.	249	Aml	William	336	Dnw
James	302	Rck	Brewis	515	Prw	William	525	Prw
James P.	886	Hnv	Charles	67	Chr	William	254	Shn
Jerre	394	Ags	Daniel	475	Frn	Wm.	10	Ntt
Jno.	925	Nrf	Daniel	498	Prw	Weer see Wier		
John	809	Bck	Daniel	501	Prw	Weese, Peter	727	Wsh
John	874	Cmp	David	720	Gch	Weet, John	10	Isw
John	642	Gls	Edwd.	249	Aml	Randal	10	Isw
John	913	Hrr	George	934	Crl	Weidmeyer, John M.	110	Spt
John	998	Nrt	George	480	Frn	Weiford, John	405	Ags
John	591	Pre	Henry	667	Btt	Mary	405	Ags
John	538	Prg	Hezekiah	591	Frd	Weightmore, John	608	Mnt
John	400	Rch	Isaac	119	Hnr	Weimer, Jacob	392	Ags
John	670	Sss	Jacob G.	641	Gls	Weir, And.	301	Rck
John, Jr.	641	Gls	James	464	Frn	Hugh	277	Rck
John F.	1000	Nrt	James	515	Prw	John	298	Rck
John S.	774	Nwk	Jas.	551	Mnn	Mark	292	Rck
Joseph	595	Brk	Jesse	474	Frn	Robert	206	Ess
Judith F.	31	Hnr	John	250	Aml	Weireg, Lewis	30	Hnr
Julas	642	Gls	John	511	Prw	Weirs, Jas., Sr.	666	Btt
Kinchen	457	Grn	John	19	Wod	Weisiger, Danl.	67	Chs
Lewis	774	Nwk	John, Jr.	475	Frn	David	68	Chs
Micajah	457	Grn	John, Sr.	475	Frn	Samuel	68	Chs
Micliger	543	Prg	Luke	474	Frn	Wekut, Joseph	958	Hrr
Mourning	879	Sth	Miles	226	Aml	Welb, Wm.	2	Oho
Nancey	814	Bck	Peter	226	Aml	Welbourne see Whilber		
Nancy	69	Acc	Philip	515	Prw	Welburn, Drummond	136	Acc
Nat	550	Mnn	Sam	395	Rch	John	66	Acc
Nutter	960	Hrr	Saml.	667	Btt	William	132	Acc
Rewben	437	Flv	Samuel	439	Btt	Welch, Alexander	360	Fqr
Robt., (FN)	92	Clp	Samuel	474	Frn	Benj.	928	Hrr
Sally	215	Ess	Sarah	225	Aml	Betsey	999	Nrt
Sally	788	Nrf	Tabitha	250	Aml	Biddy	67	Chr
Saml.	717	Wsh	Thomas	313	Frf	Clary	35	Stf
Samuel	1000	Nrt	William	225	Aml	Daniel	999	Nrt
Sarah	804	Nrf	William	457	Frn	Daniel, Jr.	1000	Nrt
Stephen	643	Gls	William	475	Frn	Danl.	667	Btt

Dempsey	825 Hmp	Alexr., Senr.	167 Dnw
Dominic	488 Bdf	Amon	674 Br
Fanny	198 Ess	Augt.	553 Mnn
Henry	180 Alb	Benedict	680 Br
Henry	15 Isw	Benjamin	2 Knw
Isaac	815 Hmp	Bolling	168 Dnw
Isaiah	89 Clp	Buckner	168 Dnw
Jacob	4 Knw	Burwell	165 Dnw
James	486 Frn	Caleb	674 Br
Jamima	825 Hmp	Carter	330 Dnw
Jane	411 Fqr	Charles	19 Oho
Jno., Son of Natl.	87 Clp	Charles P.	19 Oho
John	349 Fqr	Claiborne	739 Brn
John	379 Fqr	Coleman	251 Aml
John	427 Rnd	Cornelius, etc.	315 Frf
John	269 Rck	Daniel	21 Oho
John	195 Shn	David	165 Dnw
John	215 Shn	Drury	167 Dnw
Jon.	90 Clp	Ducket	21 Oho
Levi	14 Knw	Elizabeth	167 Dnw
Natl., Estate	87 Clp	Elizabeth	919 Hrr
Peyton	486 Bdf	Elizabeth	536 Prg
Rebeccah	291 Ldn	Freeman	671 Sss
Richard	4 Knw	Giles	168 Dnw
Robt.	307 Rck	Harrisson	168 Dnw
Sarah	759 Hmp	Henry	685 Br
Sylvester, Jr.	370 Fqr	Henry	539 Frd
Sylvester, Senr.	378 Fqr	Henry	480 Pra
Thomas	486 Bdf	James	11 Knw
Thos.	290 Rck	James	789 Wst
William	67 Acc	James	429 Rnd
William	369 Fqr	Jarrald	165 Dnw
William	815 Hmp	Jeremiah	336 Dnw
William, Senr.	418 Fqr	Jesse	689 Br
Wm.	716 Wsh	Jesse	165 Dnw
see Wilch		Jesse	20 Oho
Weld, Edwd.	924 Nrf	Jno.	315 Frf
Samuel	16 Wod	Jno.	550 Mnn
Welder, John	812 Nrf	Joel	167 Dnw
Jos.	812 Nrf	Joel	18 Hnr
Welding, Phebe	132 Acc	John	249 Aml
Weldon, George	595 Frd	John	595 Frd
James	533 Frd	John	1 Pwh
Welds, Sary	789 Wst	John	862 Wth
Weldy, Geo.	721 Gch	Joseph	739 Brn
Weley see Welsy		Joseph	168 Dnw
Welford, Robert	112 Spt	Joseph	527 Prw
Welhite, Elias	640 Gls	Katey	166 Dnw
Joel	642 Gls	Kitty	595 Frd
Welker, James M.	258 Ldn	Lawrence	488 Bdf
Well, Thomas	948 Hrr	Levi	213 Alb
see Webb		Levie	10 Wod
Wellar, Peter	11 Oho	Michael	249 Aml
Weller, Jacob	26 Rcm	Michl., Senr.	60 Chs
Terence	789 Nrf	Mills	31 Isw
see Wallen		Moses	862 Wth
Welles, David	130 Hnr	Nathaniel	326 Dnw
Moses	130 Hnr	Nathl.	315 Frf
William	130 Hnr	Nicholas	19 Oho
Wellford, John S.	101 Spt	Paschal	327 Dnw
William	111 Spt	Randal	167 Dnw
Welling, John	25 Oho	Rd.	317 Frf
Wellons, Ann	139 Sth	Reubin	668 Sss
Anthony	139 Sth	Richard	689 Br
John	161 Sth	Richard	519 Frd
John	854 Sth	Richard	25 Oho
Mary	856 Sth	Richd.	658 Mnt
Robert	139 Sth	Robert	668 Sss
William B.	670 Sss	Robert	13 Wod
Willie	138 Sth	Saml. H.	326 Dnw
see Willons		Saml. S.	168 Dnw
Wells, ---	329 Dnw	Samuel	212 Alb
Absalem	692 Br	Sarah	178 Alb
Absalem	697 Br	Sarah	335 Dnw
Adam, Senr.	167 Dnw	Susan	167 Dnw
Alexander	677 Br	Susanna	167 Dnw
Alexander	683 Br	Tho.	553 Mnn
Alexander	685 Br	Thomas	1 Ntt
Alexr.	166 Dnw	Thomas	21 Oho
Alexr., jr.	166 Dnw	Thomas	527 Prw

Thomas	671 Sss
Thos.	548 Mnn
Thos.	814 Nrf
Thos.	837 Nrf
Thos. B.	249 Aml
Tilmon	165 Dnw
William	212 Alb
William	165 Dnw
William	21 Oho
William	22 Oho
William	112 Spt
Wm. S.	885 Yrk
see Walls, Wills	
Wels, Richd.	547 Mnn
Welsh, Elizabeth	56 Jff
George	113 Spt
Henry	2 Rcm
Jacob	392 Ags
Jacob	87 Jff
James	666 Btt
James	520 Frd
Jno.	665 Btt
John	577 Brk
John	583 Brk
John	76 Jff
John	84 Jff
Richard	76 Jff
Robert	501 Prw
see Weltch, Wilsh	
Welsham, Danl.	555 Brk
Henry	523 Brk
Welshhans, David	98 Jff
Jacob	106 Jff
Joseph	69 Jff
Welshhauntz, William	15 Rcm
Welshhaus see Welshhans	
Welsy, William	441 Bth
Welt, Peter	22 Rcm
Weltch, John	218 Pnd
Weltner, Jno.	549 Mnn
Jno., Jr.	550 Mnn
Welton, Job	806 Hmp
Wemms, Mason L.	499 Prw
Wenbright, Martin	225 Pnd
Wendell, Barbary	211 Shn
Mary	263 Rck
Wm.	264 Rck
Wender, Edmond	480 Pra
Nancy	364 Lnc
Philip, Senr.	525 Prw
Wendon, Harry	421 Msn
James	422 Msn
Wener, Jacob	14 Rcm
Weneruck, Michael	862 Wth
Wengurdner, Charles	132 Hnr
Wennor, Wm.	284 Ldn
Went, James	222 Kng
Wentz, Thos.	284 Rck
Weram, John	710 Wsh
Werley, Henry	393 Ags
Jacob	393 Ags
Saml.	396 Ags
Werner, Joseph	491 Frn
Wernor, Aaron	664 Btt
George	665 Btt
Werringer, Augt.	551 Mnn
Wert, Andw.	667 Btt
see West	
Werts, Adam	297 Ldn
Cunrod	297 Ldn
Jacob	283 Ldn
Jno.	667 Btt
Peter	285 Ldn
Wm.	667 Btt
Wm.	300 Ldn
Wesbrook, John	334 Dnw
Wescott, Wright	816 Nrf
Wesenberger, Jacob	569 Brk
Wesley, Archd.	707 Wsh
Wessen, Anderson	765 Brn

Name	No.	Co.	Name	No.	Co.	Name	No.	Co.
Buckner	737	Brn	John	785	Bck	Wm., Jr.	479	Pra
Edward	767	Brn	John	811	Bck	Wm., Sr.	479	Pra
Isaac, jr.	767	Brn	John	939	Hrr	Zerob'le.	133	Acc
Isaac, Sr.	768	Brn	John	656	Mnt	see Oess, Weet, Wist		
John, jr.	765	Brn	John	22	Rcm	Westbrook, Burwell	130	Sth
John, Sr.	764	Brn	John	144	Sth	Charles	4	Ntt
Littleton	765	Brn	John, BS	134	Acc	David	130	Sth
Sterling	766	Brn	John, Jr.	656	Mnt	Dianah	146	Sth
Washington	765	Brn	John, of M	68	Acc	Jane	851	Sth
Wessmen, Philip	222	Shn	John, of P	68	Acc	Joel	161	Sth
Wesson, Elvire	618	Srr	John, of R.	30	Stf	Thomas	364	Lnn
West, Aaron, f. negro	315	Frf	John, of W.C.	24	Stf	Thomas	874	Sth
Abel, Junr.	70	Acc	John, PP	71	Acc	William	380	Fqr
Abel, Senr.	70	Acc	John, (S.)	797	Bck	Westbrooks, William	734	Nls
Abraham	70	Acc	John, Senr.	868	Cmp	Westcut see Westlut		
Ader	70	Acc	John W.	867	Cmp	Westenhouse, John	584	Brk
Alexander	953	Hrr	Jonathan	66	Acc	Wester, Giles	879	Sth
Ambrose	677	Glc	Jos.	676	Glc	Jonathan	158	Sth
Ann	67	Acc	Jos.	363	Lnc	Matthew	880	Sth
Ann	749	Wsh	Joseph	35	Hnr	Westerhouse, Peter	131	Acc
Anthony	67	Acc	Js.	548	Mnn	Western, Nancy	789	Wst
Benja.	184	Elc	Js., Jr.	550	Mnn	Susan	789	Wst
Benjamin	354	Fqr	Littleberry	54	Chs	Westfal, Cornelius	953	Hrr
Benjamin	892	Hnv	Luke	250	Aml	Zachariah	913	Hrr
Benjamin	472	Mdd	Margret	471	Frn	Westfale, Isaac	419	Rnd
Bransford	734	Nls	Mary	826	Bck	see Westfall		
Caleb	791	Nrf	Mary	835	Bck	Westfall, Alexander	8	Wod
Charles	666	Btt	Mary	62	Chs	Christian	9	Rcm
Charles	953	Hrr	Michael	805	Nrf	Jacob	951	Hrr
Charles	37	Stf	Mildred	116	Spt	Jacob	2	Wod
Christopher	677	Glc	Mitchel	67	Acc	James	423	Rnd
Clabon	794	Bck	Nathl.	482	Pra	Joel	948	Hrr
Clabon, S.J	812	Bck	Nancy	70	Acc	Michal	214	Pnd
Danl.	406	Ags	Nancy	179	Alb	Westfold, Andrew	910	Hrr
Edmund	933	Crl	Nathen	944	Hrr	John	910	Hrr
Edwd.	676	Glc	Nicholas	270	Amh	Westlake, Benjmin	681	Br
Eliza.	675	Glc	Obadiah	487	Bdf	Westlick, Thomas	641	Gls
Elizabeth	40	Stf	Peggy	70	Acc	Westlut, Josiah	394	Ags
Elizabeth	52	Stf	Peggy	483	Pra	Westmoreland, Robt.	166	Dnw
Enos	549	Mnn	Peter	70	Acc	Weston, Benj.	6	Isw
Esther	135	Acc	Peter	130	Hnr	Elizabeth	803	Nrf
Fed	12	Ntt	Peter	736	Nls	Jno., (Capt.)[Copl.?]	450	Mth
Francis	735	Nls	Phebe	877	Sth	Joseph	395	Ags
Geo. W.	317	Frf	Rachel	69	Acc	Joshua	315	Frf
George	487	Bdf	Rebecca	944	Chc	Sally, (free mulatto)	676	Glc
George	641	Gls	Reuben	487	Bdf	Saml., Sr.	814	Nrf
George	740	Wsh	Rewbin	14	Hnr	Wm.	395	Ags
George	754	Wsh	Richard	933	Crl	Westra, Mary	869	Sth
George M.	897	Hnv	Robert	955	Chc	Westray, Benjamin	43	Isw
Henry	666	Btt	Robert	676	Glc	Joseph	19	Isw
Henry	676	Glc	Robt.	12	Isw	Lemuel	19	Isw
Hugh	314	Frf	Sally	677	Glc	Sally	19	Isw
Hugh	14	Wod	Saml.	549	Mnn	Westwood, Amelia	665	Btt
Isaac	70	Acc	Soloman	71	Acc	Jno. S.	179	Elc
Isaac	754	Wsh	Susanna [2]	737	Nls	Worh.	180	Elc
Isaac, Senr.	656	Mnt	Sybell	312	Frf	Wetheral, Anthony	512	Frd
J.	33	Hnr	Tho.	363	Lnc	Wetherall, Elizebeth	412	Mds
James	133	Acc	Tho.	550	Mnn	Wetherford, Ann C.	367	Lnn
James	313	Frf	Thomas	134	Acc	Joseph	367	Lnn
James	929	Hrr	Thomas	675	Glc	William	367	Lnn
James	737	Nls	Thomas	45	Isw	Benjm.	367	Lnn
James	301	Rck	Thomas	63	Jff	Wetherington, Thomas	927	Hrr
James	140	Sth	Thos.	20	Hnr	Wetherley, Martha	234	Ldn
James	97	Spt	Thos.	483	Pra	Wethers, Benjamin	55	Stf
James	115	Spt	Thos., (B.S.)	675	Glc	Charles	62	Stf
Jas.	677	Glc	Tilman, H.	664	Btt	George	55	Stf
Jenmy	70	Acc	Washington	663	Btt	James	56	Stf
Jesse	868	Cmp	Whiler	15	Hnr	Margaret	61	Stf
Jno.	313	Frf	William	926	Hrr	Thomas	51	Stf
Jno.	26	Hnr	William	62	Jff	Wetsell, George	239	Shn
Jno.	309	Ldn	William	25	Rcm	Wetzal, Christopher	11	Rcm
Jno.	548	Mnn	William	143	Sth	Jacob	30	Rcm
Jno.	926	Nrf	William	31	Stf	John	30	Rcm
Jno.	301	Rck	William	54	Stf	Martin	30	Rcm
Jno. L.	19	Hnr	William	14	Wod	Peter	30	Rcm
Jno. S.	871	Hnv	Wm.	677	Glc	Wetzel, Catharine	507	Frd
Jobe	953	Hrr	Wm.	24	Hnr	Christopher	507	Frd
John	486	Bdf	Wm.	309	Ldn	John	572	Frd
John	683	Br	Wm.	798	Nrf	Wever, Adam	96	Jff
John	780	Bck	Wm.	285	Rck	Henry	958	Hrr

Mengh.	545	Brk	Wheeler, Ben	551	Mnn	Whhelsoll, Adam	420	Msn
William	366	Lnn	Benjamin	178	Alb	Whichard, Jno.	483	Pra
Wey, John	36	Stf	Davd.	737	Wsh	Whidbee, Jas.	832	Nrf
Weymoth, Jno.	363	Lnc	Dianna	182	Knq	Whiddon, Mary	808	Nrf
John	999	Nrt	Francis	177	Alb	Whiffeild, Richd., (W)	886	Yrk
Weymouth, John	185	Elc	Francis	737	Wsh	Whilber, Mary	828	Nrf
Wm. W.	19	Hnr	Gabriel	488	Bdf	While, York	124	Hnr
Whale, Lawson	85	Clp	George	865	Cmp	Wm.	750	Wsh
Timothy	85	Clp	Hannah	998	Nrt	Whilehurst, Oden	29	Rcm
Whalen, Thomas	486	Bdf	Harrison	487	Bdf	Whiles, Jesse	315	Frf
Whaley, Anne	317	Frf	Henry H.	3	Oho	Whilton, Richard	257	Amh
Charles	518	Prw	Ignatius	312	Frf	Whimble, George	133	Acc
Elijah	311	Frf	James	675	Br	Richard	133	Acc
George	316	Frf	James	90	Clp	Whip, Daniel	825	Hmp
Henry	312	Frf	James	12	Knw	Peter	82	Jff
Janes	54	Jff	Jessee	103	Spt	Whipple, David	667	Mnt
Levi	253	Ldn	Jno.	552	Mnn	Jno.	896	Hnv
Whalin, Allin	609	Mnt	John	212	Alb	Milley	876	Hnv
Sally	6	Pwh	John	488	Bdf	Wim.	896	Hnv
Valtn.	612	Mnt	John	314	Frf	Whirley, Henry	488	Bdf
Whaling, Ann	49	Stf	John	4	Oho	Zacheriah	487	Bdf
Posey	47	Stf	John	738	Wsh	Matthew	486	Bdf
Wm.	87	Clp	John, Junr.	66	Chr	Whiscaroer, Fredk.	88	Clp
Whaly, Patsey	27	Hnr	John, Snr.	66	Chr	Harman	88	Clp
Whann, Robert	540	Frd	John H.	12	Oho	Martin	88	Clp
Wharton, Augustus	128	Cmb	Joshua	176	Alb	Robt.	88	Clp
Bagwell	132	Acc	Luke	924	Nrf	Whisenhunt, Jacob	706	Wsh
Benja.	85	Clp	Micajah [2]	176	Alb	John	705	Wsh
Benjamin	933	Crl	Moses	765	Brn	Peter	706	Wsh
Beverly	89	Clp	Moses	104	Spt	Whisler, Danl.	6	Rcm
Charles	68	Acc	Nathan	341	Fqr	Henry	4	Rcm
James, Senr.	178	Shn	Natty	83	Spt	Hy.	285	Rck
Jno.	85	Clp	Oliver	710	Wsh	Isaac	598	Brk
John	137	Acc	Oliver, Junr.	737	Wsh	Jacob	4	Rcm
John	91	Clp	Patty	411	Rch	John	42	Rcm
John, jr.	88	Clp	Robert	815	Bck	Whisman, Peter	392	Ags
John, jr.	95	Spt	Robert	289	Ldn	Whisonhunt, Caly	706	Wsh
Joseph	91	Clp	Samuel	693	Br	George	745	Wsh
Leonard	88	Spt	Samuel	66	Chr	Whissin, Joseph	210	Shn
Margaret	92	Clp	Samul	4	Oho	Whissleman, Michael	19	Rcm
Meredeth	89	Clp	Senah	411	Rch	Whistler, Molly	27	Hnr
Rebecca	414	Fqr	Stephen	737	Wsh	Sawney	472	Mdd
Reuben	932	Crl	Thomas	314	Frf	Whit, Shaderick	739	Brn
Robert	94	Spt	Thomas	998	Nrt	Whitacre, Benj.	317	Ldn
Susannah	67	Acc	Thos.	318	Frf	George	400	Fqr
Thomas	97	Spt	William	66	Chr	James	860	Wth
William	96	Spt	William	524	Prw	Jno.	260	Ldn
Zacharh.	575	Brk	William	3	Rcm	John	395	Fqr
Whater, Patsey	68	Chs	Wm.	758	Wsh	Joshua	554	Frd
William	545	Frd	see Haile, Whalon, Wheelis			Robert	341	Fqr
Whayne, Charles	181	Knq	Wheelhouse, David	165	Dnw	Whitaker, Edwd.	189	Elc
Dianna	182	Knq	Wheeling, Wim.	886	Hnv	Eliza	119	Spt
Wheadon, Mary	29	Isw	Wheelis, Jno.	667	Btt	Frances	679	Wrw
Wheakley, Wm.	282	Ldn	Wheelton, Arthur	132	Acc	James	933	Crl
Whealer, John	176	Alb	Arthur, Sen.	136	Acc	James	934	Crl
Mosess	2	Hnr	Charles	136	Acc	James	861	Wth
Wheat, Eli	488	Bdf	Elisha	136	Acc	Joseph	861	Wth
James M.	575	Brk	John	135	Acc	Lemuel	7	Oho
Joseph	487	Bdf	Joshua	133	Acc	Nancy	934	Crl
Levi	176	Alb	Polly	137	Acc	Rebec.	178	Elc
Reazin	175	Alb	Smith	135	Acc	Zelia.	683	Wrw
Zacheriah	486	Bdf	Wheetley, George	682	Br	see Campbell		
Wheatley, Danl.	87	Clp	Isaac	678	Br	Whitby, Burwell	764	Brn
James	351	Fqr	Joseph	680	Br	John	766	Brn
Jno.	312	Frf	Wheiler, William	734	Nls	Robert	767	Brn
John	136	Acc	Wheldon, George [2]	789	Wst	Wm.	766	Brn
John	374	Fqr	John	392	Rch	Whitcomb, Rebecca	772	Nwk
Lucrecia	351	Fqr	Whelenough, Henry	544	Brk	White, ---, & Shelton	23	Hnr
Susanna	342	Fqr	Wheler, Alice	1000	Nrt	Aaron C.	932	Crl
William	414	Fqr	Rebicah	5	Hnr	Abraham	401	Rch
Wm.	87	Clp	Wherrey, Silas	288	Ldn	Abram	436	Mth
Wheaton, Benjamin	220	Pnd	Wherry, Jesse	68	Chs	Adgate	924	Nrf
John	417	Fqr	Whesson, John	573	Frd	Alexander	14	Oho
John	19	Oho	Whet, Luretta	939	Chc	Alexander	1	Wod
Robert	361	Fqr	Whetis, John	124	Hnr	Alexr.	690	Wsh
Wheelan, Waltr.	188	Elc	Whetsal, Adam	125	Hnr	Ambrose	932	Crl
Wheelar, Bazel	4	Wod	Whetsell, John	434	Msn	Ambrose	890	Hnv
Wheelbarger, David	15	Rcm	see Whhelsoll	706	Wsh	Anderson	56	Stf
Matthias	7	Rcm	Whetstone, John	596	Brk	Andrew	817	Bck
Matthias, (Jr.)	7	Rcm				Andrew	9	Oho

Andrew	239	Shn	Henry	111	Spt	John, (of James)	387	Fqr
Ann	30	Stf	Hessy	133	Acc	John, (of Wm.)	407	Fqr
Ann	59	Stf	Horace	933	Crl	John, (S. Mason)	393	Fqr
Ann, of A.	133	Acc	Hugh	179	Alb	John, (son of Will)	66	Chr
Ann, Senr.	68	Acc	Hugh	734	Nls	John, Sr.	767	Brn
Anne	379	Fqr	Isaac	396	Ags	John, (WW)	66	Chr
Anthony D.	618	Srr	Isaac	543	Frd	John A.	90	Clp
Arthur	262	Amh	Isaac	735	Nls	Jonathan	600	Frd
Augustine	399	Fqr	Isaac	421	Rnd	Jonathan	861	Wth
Barrott	875	Hnv	Isaiah	453	Frn	Jos.	294	Ldn
Batley	222	Kng	Jacob	137	Acc	Jos., esq.	300	Rck
Ben	550	Mnn	Jacob	486	Bdf	Josabed	312	Ldn
Ben., (W)	886	Yrk	Jacob	488	Bdf	Joseph	373	Fqr
Benj.	936	Hrr	Jacob	25	Hnr	Joseph	545	Frd
Benj.	294	Ldn	Jacob	365	Lnn	Joseph	923	Hrr
Benja.	845	Sth	Jacob	477	Pra	Joseph	735	Nls
Benjamin	680	Br	Jacob	419	Rnd	Joseph	299	Rck
Benjamin	222	Kng	James	134	Acc	Joshua	56	Chs
Benjamin	861	Wth	James	136	Acc	Joshua	60	Chs
Benjamin H.	640	Gls	James	211	Alb	Joshua [2]	41	Rcm
Bridget	67	Acc	James	393	Ags	Josiah	301	Ldn
Cabeb	802	Nrf	James	487	Bdf	Josiah	317	Ldn
Carr	367	Fqr	James	933	Crl	Juday, (F. Negroe)	420	Fqr
Carter, jr.	366	Lnn	James	388	Fqr	Judith	17	Hnr
Carter, Sr.	366	Lnn	James	396	Fqr	Judith	1000	Nrt
Chapman	211	Alb	James	400	Fqr	Lemuel	669	Sss
Clement	544	Frd	James	640	Gls	Lettice	344	Fqr
Crenshaw	213	Alb	James	801	Hmp	Levi	294	Ldn
Dabney	447	Flv	James	268	Ldn	Lewis	934	Crl
Daniel	176	Alb	James	281	Ldn	Lewis	735	Nls
Daniel	362	Fqr	James	437	Mth	Lucy	884	Hnv
Daniel	388	Fqr	James	803	Nrf	Maria	332	Dnw
Daniel	58	Stf	James	274	Rck	Maria	506	Frd
Daniel B.	70	Spt	James	59	Stf	Martha, Mrs.	67	Chr
Danl.	294	Ldn	James	618	Srr	Mary	664	Btt
Danl.	300	Rck	James	668	Sss	Mary	168	Dnw
Dav.	548	Mnn	James	688	Wsh	Mary	34	Isw
David	433	Flv	James	1	Wod	Mary	407	Rch
David	547	Frd	James, of Southy.	132	Acc	Mary	881	Sth
David	430	Rnd	James, Sr.	488	Bdf	Matthw	262	Rck
Davis	161	Sth	Jas., jr.	802	Nrf	Merritt M.	305	Amh
Debora	537	Brk	Jeremiah	487	Bdf	Michal	571	Frd
Dick	547	Prg	Jesse	538	Frd	Milly	116	Spt
Edith	884	Hnv	Jessee	676	Glc	Mitchell	401	Fqr
Edward	551	Frd	Jessee	721	Gch	Mordecai	573	Frd
Edwd.	447	Mth	Jno.	664	Btt	Moses	885	Hnv
Elijah	933	Crl	Jno.	675	Glc	N.	24	Hnr
Elisha C.	811	Nrf	Jno.	677	Glc	Nathaniel	531	Brk
Eliza	812	Nrf	Jno. [2]	269	Ldn	Nathaniel	774	Nwk
Eliza	927	Nrf	Jno.	450	Mth	Nelley	330	Dnw
Eliza.	675	Glc	Jno. C.	443	Mth	Nicholas	412	Bth
Elizabeth	680	Br	John	487	Bdf	Obediah	492	Frn
Elizabeth	910	Hrr	John [2]	688	Br	Penelope	365	Lnn
Elizabeth	440	Mth	John	766	Brn	Philip	999	Nrt
Elizabeth	447	Mth	John	377	Fqr	Pleasant	433	Flv
Elizabeth	1	Pwh	John	399	Fqr	Polly	69	Acc
Ezekiel	589	Frd	John	435	Flv	Presley J.	87	Clp
Ezekiah	14	Hnr	John	566	Frd	Randolph	814	Nrf
Frances	735	Nls	John	576	Frd	Rebecah	294	Ldn
Francis	836	Hmp	John	642	Gls	Rebecca	677	Glc
Francis	619	Srr	John	780	Hmp	Rebecca [4]	699	Sss
Garrett	176	Alb	John	920	Hrr	Resen	549	Mnn
Geo.	924	Nrf	John	11	Knw	Reuben	412	Mds
Geo.	926	Nrf	John	222	Kng	Richd.	441	Mth
Geo.	482	Pra	John	364	Lnn	Richd.	924	Nrf
Geo., jr.	223	Kng	John	412	Mds	Richd.	15	Ntt
George	133	Acc	John	582	Mnr	Richd.	717	Wsh
George	696	Br	John	925	Nrf	Robert	568	Frd
George	932	Crl	John	2	Oho	Robert	854	Hnv
George	124	Hnr	John	4	Oho	Robert	891	Hnv
George	37	Stf	John	7	Oho	Robert	268	Ldn
George, Senr.	222	Kng	John	217	Pnd	Robert	262	Rck
George, (yr.)	222	Kng	John	520	Prw	Robert, J.	280	Ldn
Gorden	395	Ags	John	240	Shn	Robert, Jr.	517	Frd
Grafton	547	Mnn	John	84	Spt	Robert B.	517	Frd
H.	4	Hnr	John	617	Srr	Robert N.	839	Hmp
Hanry, (F. Negroe)	417	Fqr	John	789	Wst	Robt.	717	Wsh
Henry	134	Acc	John, [his] Estate	131	Hnr	Sally	934	Crl
Henry	933	Crl	John, H	641	Gls	Sally	520	Frd
Henry	207	Shn	John, Jr.	412	Mds	Sally	924	Nrf

Saml.	603	Btt
Saml.	25	Hnr
Samuel	882	Cmp
Samuel	66	Chr
Samuel	332	Dnw
Samuel	9	Knw
Samuel	143	Sth
Samuel S.	933	Crl
Sarah	539	Frd
Soloman	133	Acc
Soloman	137	Acc
Solomon	7	Oho
Susanah	750	Wsh
Tarply	128	Hnr
Thomas	344	Fqr
Thomas	99	Jff
Thomas	104	Jff
Thomas	221	Kng
Thomas	317	Ldn
Thomas	595	Mnr
Thomas F.	487	Bdf
Thomas, Jr.	407	Fqr
Thos.	900	Hnv
Thos.	924	Nrf
Thos.	228	Shn
Ths.	23	Hnr
Ursula	934	Crl
Valontine	416	Bth
Warner	563	Frd
Warren	669	Sss
Washington	760	Wsh
Whtn.	189	Elc
William	177	Alb
William	486	Bdf
William	487	Bdf
William	932	Crl
William	68	Chr
William	399	Fqr
William	364	Lnn
William	366	Lnn
William	998	Nrt
William	592	Pre
William	526	Prw
William	789	Wst
William, Carpr.	71	Acc
William, (LE)	67	Chr
William, Shoemr.	68	Acc
William, Junr.	134	Acc
William, of Wm.	133	Acc
William S.	132	Acc
William S.	593	Pre
Willian	940	Hrr
Wim.	866	Hnv
Wim.	883	Hnv
Wm.	406	Ags
Wm.	440	Flv
Wm.	936	Hrr
Wm.	959	Hrr
Wm.	960	Hrr
Wm.	294	Ldn
Wm.	315	Ldn
Wm.	317	Ldn
Wm.	548	Mnn
Wm.	550	Mnn
Wm.	479	Pra
Wm.	734	Wsh
Wm., Junr.	66	Acc
Wm. B.	441	Mth
Zachariah	735	Nls
see While, Whit, Whitt		
Whitecar, James	882	Cmp
Whitee, Rachel	23	Oho
Whitefield, Benja.	130	Sth
Hannah	137	Sth
Jane	871	Sth
John	131	Sth
John	161	Sth
Pat	669	Sth
Peter	870	Sth
Reuben	151	Sth

Rich. [Mich.?]	131	Sth
Seymore	149	Sth
Sharper	150	Sth
Suky	871	Sth
Viney	151	Sth
Whiteford, Hugh	396	Fqr
Whitehair, Chris.	552	Mnn
Geo.	552	Mnn
Whitehaurst, Wm. R.	805	Nrf
Whitehead, ---	332	Dnw
Andw.	650	Mnt
Anthony	148	Sth
Bartholomew	278	Amh
Benjamin	833	Bck
Benjn.	109	Cmb
Burcher	277	Amh
Clar.	159	Sth
Clarissa	924	Nrf
Dudley	478	Pra
Elizabeth	112	Spt
Francis	860	Wth
Gray	671	Sss
Isham	670	Sss
James	153	Sth
Jas.	479	Pra
Jereh.	166	Dnw
Jesse	40	Isw
John	90	Clp
John	590	Pre
John	159	Sth
Joseph	168	Dnw
Js., Dr.	925	Nrf
Maelin	668	Sss
Mariam	872	Sth
Mark	671	Sss
Nat.	161	Sth
Nelson	89	Clp
Richard	293	Amh
Stephen	822	Bck
Swepson	831	Nrf
Swepson, [his](Pltnn.)	478	Pra
William	671	Sss
Wm.	155	Sth
Whiteherst, Jno., (of Jno.)	483	Pra
Whitehill, Josh.	664	Btt
Whitehorn, Edward	672	Sss
John	670	Sss
Laurence	670	Sss
Phillamon	671	Sss
Thomas	671	Sss
William	671	Sss
William, Sr.	671	Sss
Whitehurst, Ann	484	Pra
Batn., (of Richd.)	481	Pra
Batson	479	Pra
Batson	480	Pra
Batson	482	Pra
Caleb	478	Pra
Chas., Sr.	484	Pra
Chas., (of Jh.)	482	Pra
Christr.	481	Pra
Cornelius	790	Nrf
Daniel	483	Pra
David, (of Jona.)	481	Pra
David, (of L)	484	Pra
Dennis	478	Pra
Edwd.	808	Nrf
Eliza, of So.	484	Pra
Enoch	478	Pra
Frances	483	Pra
Geo.	479	Pra
Geo.	481	Pra
Henry	479	Pra
Hillary	485	Pra
Jas.	482	Pra
Jas., (Drumr.)	484	Pra
Jas., (of Jas.)	483	Pra
Jas., (of Jno.)	484	Pra
Jas., (of Sm.[?])	484	Pra

Jesse, (FB)	480	Pra
Jno.	477	Pra
Jno.	480	Pra
Jno., (of Chas.)	484	Pra
Jno., (of Jno.) [2]	483	Pra
Jno., (of L.)	484	Pra
Jno., (of S)	479	Pra
Jno., (Pungo)	484	Pra
John	88	Clp
John	808	Nrf
Jona.	477	Pra
Joshua	478	Pra
Joshua, Sr.	480	Pra
Kedar	484	Pra
Major	479	Pra
Mary	809	Nrf
Mary	483	Pra
Moses	480	Pra
Nancy	481	Pra
Nathn.	483	Pra
Nathn., of R.	483	Pra
Obed	484	Pra
Oden	479	Pra
Rachel	479	Pra
Richd.	485	Pra
Richd., of Js.	483	Pra
Sarah	483	Pra
Simon	479	Pra
Tully	482	Pra
Tully, (AB)	483	Pra
Tully, (BB)	485	Pra
Tully, (Pungo)	484	Pra
Willis	482	Pra
Willo.	479	Pra
Wm.	924	Nrf
see Whilehurst, Whitetehurst		
Whitehust, Hillary	839	Nrf
Whiteing, Beverley	64	Jff
Hannah	80	Jff
Whiteker, Isaac	709	Wsh
Jas.	724	Wsh
Richd.	724	Wsh
see Whitecar, Whitteker		
Whitelaw, James	112	Hnr
Whiteley, Francis	403	Fqr
John	487	Bdf
William	486	Bdf
Whitelock, George	788	Wst
James	544	Brk
Judy	295	Rck
Mary	3	Oho
Michael	947	Hrr
Whiteman, Able	925	Hrr
Daniel	938	Hrr
Edward	925	Hrr
Henry	924	Hrr
James	282	Rck
Jane	760	Hmp
John	804	Hmp
Saml.	275	Rck
Whitemore, Wm. G.	739	Brn
Whiten, Mw.	665	Btt
Whitenick, Benjn.	667	Btt
Whitenough see Whelenough		
Whites see Whetis		
Whitesberry, George	695	Wsh
Whiteside, James	392	Ags
Moses	301	Rck
Whitesides, Benjamin	297	Amh
Whitetehurst, Hillary	479	Pra
Whitfeild, Atkinson	45	Isw
Copeland	17	Isw
John	14	Isw
Samuel	25	Isw
Sarah, (W)	885	Yrk
Wilkinson	12	Isw
Whitfield, Benja.	150	Sth
Edwd.	139	Sth
Geo.	827	Nrf
John	179	Elc

Name	No.	Code
Littleberry	670	Sss
Milly	148	Sth
William	670	Sss
see Whiffeild, Whitefield		
Whitham, Joseph	11	Oho
William	17	Oho
Whithrow see Withrow		
Whitico, ---, Mrs.	35	Hnr
Whiting, Dolly	934	Crl
Francis	365	Fqr
Francis	675	Glc
Francis	95	Jff
Fras.	534	Frd
Geo.	534	Frd
Jno.	926	Nrf
Jno. B.	676	Glc
John	222	Kng
John R.	185	Shn
Lettice	472	Mdd
Lewis B.	522	Prw
Lucy C.	675	Glc
Matthew	522	Prw
Skaife	675	Glc
Thomas	373	Fqr
see Washington		
Whitington, Rebecca	75	Jff
see Wittington		
Whitis, John	21	Hnr
Whitlach, John	4	Oho
Joseph	26	Oho
Whitley, Daniel	2	Isw
Elisha, Jun.	3	Isw
Elisha, Jun.	20	Isw
Elisha, Sen.	15	Isw
Joel	13	Isw
Mary	39	Isw
Randal	21	Isw
Rebecca	39	Isw
Robt.	725	Wsh
Timothy	34	Isw
William	20	Isw
see Whittey		
Whitlock, Charles	888	Hnv
Chs.	23	Hnr
Henry	80	Spt
J.B.	33	Hnr
Jas.	890	Hnv
John	121	Hnr
Martha	890	Hnv
Mary	203	Ess
Matthew	887	Hnv
Mitchel	721	Gch
Nathl.	890	Hnv
Sally	721	Gch
Thomas	774	Bck
Thomas	933	Crl
Thomas	590	Pre
see Whittock		
Whitlocke, John	131	Hnr
Whitlow, Andrew S.	857	Cmp
Chancey	823	Bck
Elizabeth	120	Hnr
George	120	Hnr
Henry	866	Cmp
Joseph	823	Bck
William	860	Cmp
William	29	Hnr
William	593	Pre
see Whillow		
Whitman, Andrew	861	Wth
Matthew	419	Rnd
Whitmer, Christo.	554	Brk
Whitmire, Frederick	194	Shn
George	567	Brk
Jacob	565	Brk
Michael	785	Hmp
Valentine	194	Shn
Wm.	565	Brk
Whitmore, Abraham	14	Rcm
Catharine	296	Ldn
Chas.	166	Dnw
Danl.	7	Rcm
David	12	Rcm
David	38	Rcm
Frances	533	Prg
Jacob	7	Rcm
James	533	Prg
John	532	Prg
John	9	Rcm
John	19	Rcm
John	38	Rcm
John Y.	166	Dnw
Martin	7	Rcm
Michael	14	Rcm
Peter	20	Rcm
Sally	334	Dnw
William	590	Frd
Wm.	166	Dnw
Wm. C.	12	Ntt
Whitmyer, Jacob	565	Brk
Whitney, Jane	881	Sth
John	131	Sth
Joshua	131	Sth
Mary	157	Sth
Mary	879	Sth
Whitsby, Elizabeth	110	Spt
Whitsel, Abram	395	Ags
John	395	Ags
Peter	395	Ags
Peter	861	Wth
Whitsell see Whhelsoll		
Whitson, John	61	Jff
Whitt, Abijah	620	Mnt
Archd.	620	Mnt
Benja.	721	Gch
Rachel	281	Ldn
Richard	608	Mnt
Whitteker, William	4	Knw
Whitter see Whtter		
Whittey, John	727	Wsh
Whittington, Arthur	136	Acc
Carrol	671	Sss
James	488	Bdf
Joseph	583	Frd
Lewis	456	Grn
Stark	488	Bdf
Thomas	999	Nrt
Thomas, Ser.	487	Bdf
William	486	Bdf
see Whttington, Whtton		
Whittle, Conway	925	Nrf
Fortescue	925	Nrf
Whittock, Thos.	739	Brn
Whitton, Berry	301	Amh
Mary	290	Amh
William	487	Bdf
William, (BM)	488	Bdf
see Whilton, Whtter, Whtton		
Whitwise see Whitmire		
Whitworth, Jacob	226	Aml
Jerrimiah	592	Pre
Mary H.	249	Aml
Thomas	482	Frn
William	592	Pre
Whitzel, Abrm.	269	Rck
George	15	Oho
Whitzell, Martin	4	Oho
Whombleduff, John	86	Jff
Whordom, Nehemiah	999	Nrt
Whorley, Joshua	69	Chr
Reynard	69	Chr
Whorton, John	487	Bdf
Whtie see White		
Whtter, John	486	Bdf
Whttington, Thomas	487	Bdf
Whtton, Elisha	488	Bdf
Wiand, Mary	212	Alb
Wiant, Henne	955	Hrr
Philip	303	Rck
Wiase, John	423	Rnd
see Wease		
Wiat, Edmon	431	Rnd
James, Sr.	444	Mth
Mary	439	Mth
Wiatt, Ann	677	Glc
Conquest	370	Fqr
Fanny	677	Glc
Floary	21	Hnr
Jacob A.	393	Fqr
James	366	Fqr
Jas.	677	Glc
Jas., Senr.	676	Glc
Jno. R.	677	Glc
John	848	Cmp
John	604	Frd
Mary	675	Glc
Peter	677	Glc
Thomas	848	Cmp
Wibel, Frederick	291	Rck
Wice, Adam	39	Rcm
Catharine	39	Rcm
David	42	Rcm
John	12	Rcm
John	19	Rcm
John	23	Rcm
John	39	Rcm
Wicham, John	521	Brk
Wichard, Mary	484	Pra
Philip	483	Pra
Wicke, William	168	Dnw
Wickem see Wechem		
Wicker, Fanney	890	Hnv
James	889	Hnv
Wim.	887	Hnv
Wickers, Peter	291	Rck
Wickersham, Enoch	552	Frd
Jona.	525	Brk
Wickert see Wikert		
Wickham, John	33	Hnr
John	117	Hnr
Levi A.	514	Frd
Mareen	68	Jff
Nathl.	660	Mnt
Wickins, Corprew	481	Pra
Jas.	482	Pra
Jno.	482	Pra
Wickliff, David	382	Fqr
Wickline, George	573	Mnr
Jacob	594	Mnr
Jacob, jr.	594	Mnr
Wicks, Eliza	544	Prg
Wm.	547	Prg
Wicoff, Cornelius	695	Br
James	691	Br
Joachim	688	Br
Widgen, Isaac	480	Pra
Jno.	480	Pra
Widick, Henry	34	Rcm
Widner, Jno., Junr.	692	Wsh
John	697	Wsh
John F.	692	Wsh
Michael	696	Wsh
Nancy	665	Btt
Wier, Hannah	663	Btt
Wiers, Richard	909	Hrr
see Weirs		
Wigal, Sebastian	622	Mnt
Wigfield, Thomas	364	Fqr
Wiggens, Peter	18	Oho
Wiggenton, Benjamin	487	Bdf
William	354	Fqr
see Wiggnt.		
Wiggins, Charity	685	Br
Dolly	672	Sss
Ned	853	Sth
Sarah	364	Lnc
Wilson	671	Sss
Wigginton, Benja.	316	Frf
Elizabeth	526	Prw
Henry	316	Frf

James	314	Frf	John	688	Br	John, Jr.	411	Mds
James	532	Frd	Samuel	695	Br	Joseph	411	Mds
James	791	Nrf	Wilcut see Wekut			Mary	411	Mds
John [?]	488	Bdf	Wilde, Davd.	706	Wsh	Saml.	91	Clp
John	526	Prw	Wilder, Jas.	714	Wsh	Wilhoite, Gabl.	89	Clp
Peter	517	Prw	John	328	Dnw	Wm.	89	Clp
see W...i..., Wiggenton			Joseph G.	328	Dnw	Wilins, Wm.	954	Hrr
Wiggnt., ---	271	Frf	Michael	363	Lnc	Wilk..., Samuel	486	Bdf
Wigington, Benja.	86	Clp	Sarah	714	Wsh	Wilkeison, Eliza	543	Prg
Jno.	86	Clp	Wildman, Amos	277	Ldn	Wilkenson, Asel	10	Wod
Mary	86	Clp	Jacob	279	Ldn	Joseph	299	Ldn
Wigle, George	592	Mnr	James	279	Ldn	Thomas	116	Cmb
John	641	Mnt	Joseph	278	Ldn	Wilkerson, Augt.	221	Kng
Michael	563	Brk	Martin	277	Ldn	Burwell	668	Sss
Philip	594	Brk	Wildon, Jacob	247	Ldn	Edwd.	249	Aml
Wiglesworth, Claboun	69	Spt	Wilds, Armsted.	924	Nrf	Francis	824	Bck
John	82	Spt	see Wiles			Gabriel	907	Hrr
John, jr.	69	Spt	Wildy, William	1000	Nrt	Henry	531	Prg
Joseph	79	Spt	Wile, Henry	552	Mnn	Henry	668	Sss
Nancy	66	Spt	Wiles, Anna	803	Nrf	James	809	Bck
Robert	76	Spt	Conley	394	Ags	Jesse	489	Bdf
Susanna	76	Spt	Fredrick	803	Nrf	Joel	669	Sss
Thomas	86	Spt	George	425	Rnd	John	176	Alb
Wigley, James	789	Wst	James	925	Nrf	John	212	Alb
Wigner, Daniel	960	Hrr	Jno.	924	Nrf	John	213	Alb
John	960	Hrr	John	425	Rnd	John	487	Bdf
Saml.	947	Hrr	Malachi	481	Pra	John	221	Kng
Wignor, Joseph	966	Hrr	Malachi	482	Pra	John	364	Lnn
Wikel, John	394	Ags	Reuben	480	Pra	John	366	Lnn
Wikerson, William	334	Dnw	Thos.	482	Pra	John	669	Sss
Wikert, Henry	18	Oho	William	425	Rnd	Joseph	487	Bdf
Wikle, Danl.	394	Ags	see Wells			Lewis	802	Bck
Geo.	394	Ags	Wiley, ...elley	304	Rck	Lovel	593	Pre
Geo., jr.	394	Ags	...hn, j.	304	Rck	Marshall	223	Kng
Philip	394	Ags	Alexr.	634	Mnt	Mary	175	Alb
Wil..., George	486	Bdf	Allen	89	Clp	Nathl., [his] Est.	223	Kng
Wilahelm, Peter	664	Btt	Catey	167	Dnw	Nicholas	487	Bdf
Wilam, James, (F.Ne- groe)	345	Fqr	Christeen	251	Shn	Parsons	487	Bdf
Wilbarger, Henry	392	Ags	George	312	Frf	Peter	114	Hnr
Jacob	392	Ags	George	272	Rck	Rachel	258	Ldn
Wilber, Henry	477	Pra	George, Senr.	314	Frf	Reuben	222	Kng
Jas.	485	Pra	Hugh	235	Ldn	Richard	886	Hnv
Moses	480	Pra	Isable	91	Clp	Robert	223	Kng
Wilbon, Jane	813	Bck	James	413	Bth	Sally	223	Kng
Thompson	793	Bck	James	317	Frf	Stephen	222	Kng
Wilborn, Harris	457	Grn	James	642	Gls	Thomas	591	Pre
Simon	485	Pra	Jno.	292	Ldn	Thos.	166	Dnw
Wilborne, Fanny	672	Sss	Jno.	304	Rck	Turner	591	Pre
James	669	Sss	John	692	Br	William	838	Bck
John, Jr.	671	Sss	Joseph	103	Jff	William	699	Wsh
John, Sr.	672	Sss	Joseph	292	Ldn	William B.	20	Hnr
Jones	668	Sss	Joseph	304	Rck	Willm.	223	Kng
William	668	Sss	Laban J.	818	Hmp	Wm.	739	Brn
Wilborn, Robert	125	Cmb	Littleton	314	Frf	Wm.	445	Flv
Robert	591	Pre	Mary	555	Frd	Wm.	263	Ldn
Willm.	183	Elc	Nancy	416	Bth	Wm.	732	Wsh
Wilburn, Robert	642	Gls	Robert	267	Rck	Wm. S.	223	Kng
William	641	Gls	Robert, Ju.	416	Bth	Wyatt	670	Sss
William	6	Pwh	Robert, Ser.	416	Btn	Wilkes, John	772	Nwk
Wilch, Nathaniel	412	Mds	Robt.	663	Btt	Reuben	772	Nwk
Wilcher, Caleb	274	Amh	William	597	Frd	Richd.	7	Ntt
John	301	Amh	William	61	Jff	Wilkeson, Grace	583	Frd
Joseph	286	Amh	Wilfong, Henry	226	Pnd	Wilkey, Jno.	313	Frf
Richard	301	Amh	Jacob	222	Pnd	Wilkilson, Samuel	53	Chs
Wilcker, William	41	Rcm	Jos.	548	Mnn	Wilkins, Alfrid	540	Prg
Wilcocks, James	412	Rch	Wilhelm, Adam	277	Rck	Ambrose	547	Prg
Wilcot, Reib.	550	Mnn	Eliz.	551	Mnn	Amos	25	Hnr
Wilcox, Geo.	364	Lnc	Fred	552	Mnn	Betsy	813	Nrf
Mary	599	Brk	John	547	Brk	Catharine	999	Nrt
Samuel	34	Stf	Michl.	277	Rck	Fredrick	803	Nrf
Stephen	796	Hmp	Pet.	551	Mnn	George	999	Nrt
Susannah	806	Bck	Wilhite, Joshh.	88	Clp	Godfrey	213	Shn
Thomas	272	Amh	Wilhoit, Daniel	411	Mds	Haynie	1000	Nrt
Timothy	579	Frd	David	412	Mds	Henry	796	Nrf
William	499	Prw	Elijah	412	Mds	James	166	Dnw
Wilcoxen, Rezen	313	Frf	Elizebeth	411	Mds	James	243	Ldn
Wilcoxon, Anthony	692	Br	George	412	Mds	James	773	Nwk
Fielder	698	Br	Jeremiah	411	Mds	Jeptha	553	Mnn
George	689	Br	Joel	91	Clp	Jno.	675	Glc
			John	411	Mds	Jno.	677	Glc

Jno.	481	Pra	Minor	366	Lnn	Alex.	392	Ags
John	67	Acc	Phebe	367	Lnn	Alexander	764	Brn
John	765	Brn	Richard	366	Lnn	Alexander	190	Shn
John	55	Jff	William	556	Brk	Amelia	23	Isw
John	772	Nwk	William	66	Chr	Andrew	640	Gls
John	213	Shn	Will, Georg	237	Shn	Andrew	119	Hnr
John D.	738	Brn	George, Sen.	237	Shn	Ann	181	Knq
John L.	737	Brn	Henry	253	Shn	Ann	924	Nrf
Joseph	457	Grn	John	486	Bdf	Ann	20	Ntt
Liddy	335	Dnw	John	513	Frd	Ann	672	Sss
Nathan F.	676	Glc	John	237	Shn	Anna	472	Mdd
Peter	1000	Nrt	John, Junr.	236	Shn	Anne	414	Fqr
Richard	404	Rch	John, Snr.	236	Shn	Archibd.	504	Brk
Robt.	794	Nrf	see Wice			Arthur	878	Sth
Sally	676	Glc	Willard, Abner	592	Pre	Bartlet	773	Nwk
Thomas	562	Frd	Geo.	551	Mnn	Bazil	311	Frf
Thomas	234	Ldn	Henry	551	Mnn	Bazil, Jr.	311	Frf
Thos.	480	Pra	Henry	590	Pre	Benj. [?]	549	Prg
William W.	456	Grn	Huriah	593	Pre	Benja.	532	Prg
Willis	823	Nrf	Jac.	551	Mnn	Benjamin	765	Brn
Wm.	676	Glc	William	590	Pre	Benjamin	130	Hnr
Wm., Sr.	481	Pra	Willaroy, Abraham C.	479	Pra	Benjamin	172	Shn
Wm. B.	483	Pra	Willas, George	68	Acc	Benjamin	212	Shn
see Goodrich			Willatt, Waitman	134	Acc	Benjamin	21	Stf
Wilkinson, Aylce	78	Spt	Willcox, Hamlin	950	Chc	Benjn.	395	Ags
Carter	124	Cmb	Henry	954	Chc	Bennett	729	Wsh
Cary	945	Chc	Jno. V.	546	Prg	Benonie	103	Spt
Eligah	947	Chc	Jno. V.	332	Dnw	Betsy	77	Spt
Frances	480	Pra	John V., & Co.	332	Dnw	Betty	326	Dnw
Gabriel G.	958	Hrr	Joice	942	Chc	Bolly	218	Ess
Galleo	8	Pwh	Major	951	Chc	Britain	129	Sth
George	78	Spt	Thomas	951	Chc	Bulis	741	Wsh
George, (lawyr.)	774	Nwk	Thomas	332	Dnw	Burwell	738	Brn
James	774	Nwk	Willcoxon, George	688	Br	Burwell	153	Shn
James	8	Pwh	Willeford, Bala	618	Srr	Caleb	790	Nrf
James	104	Spt	Willerson, John	947	Chc	Carter	471	Mdd
James, (P)	773	Nwk	Willes, Annel	600	Mnr	Catharine	817	Bck
Jas.	824	Nrf	Henry	569	Mnr	Cathrine	394	Rch
Jno.	264	Ldn	John	641	Gls	Chas.	166	Dnw
Jno.	18	Ntt	Willet, David	664	Btt	Chloe	509	Prw
Jno., jr.	58	Chs	Polly	509	Prw	Christopher	180	Knq
Jno., sr.	62	Chs	Willets, Jno.	551	Mnn	Clairissa	330	Dnw
Joel	721	Gch	Saml.	551	Mnn	Clark	550	Mnn
John	135	Acc	Willett, Aquila	107	Jff	Clement	168	Dnw
John	311	Frf	Aquilla	54	Jff	Daniel	486	Bdf
John	361	Fqr	Aquilla	108	Jff	Daniel	430	Flv
John	14	Pwh	Aquilla	109	Jff	Daniel	552	Frd
John	526	Prw	Aquilla	110	Jff	Daniel	789	Nrf
John	877	Sth	David	919	Hrr	Davd.	756	Wsh
Joseph	53	Chs	George	134	Acc	David	410	Ags
Joseph	930	Hrr	John	67	Acc	David	738	Brn
Joshua	407	Fqr	Jonathan	501	Prw	David	90	Clp
Levin	135	Acc	Nancy	919	Hrr	David	167	Dnw
Martha	25	Hnr	Richd.	300	Ldn	David	459	Frn
Nancy	940	Chc	William, Jun.	134	Acc	David	541	Frd
Nat.	875	Sth	Willey, Edward	89	Clp	David	642	Gls
Nathon	939	Hrr	Gabl.	90	Clp	David	367	Lnn
Ns.	925	Nrf	Jacob	524	Frd	David	773	Nwk
Peter	57	Chs	Jas.	549	Mnn	David	1000	Nrt
Robert	456	Grn	Malachi	807	Nrf	David	543	Prg
Robt.	56	Chs	Wm.	89	Clp	David G.	366	Lnn
Sarah	56	Chs	Wm.	547	Mnn	David G., resid'g in Lunen-		
Sarah	774	Nwk	Wm.	550	Mnn	burg	168	Dnw
Snelling	66	Chr	Willia, Jno.	926	Nrf	Deborah	737	Nls
Stephen	6	Ntt	William, John	918	Hrr	Doctor	392	Ags
Susanna	772	Nwk	Martha	540	Prg	Drew	159	Sth
Susannah	135	Acc	Matthew	67	Chr	Drury, jr.	533	Prg
Thomas	944	Chc	Williames, Jos.	836	Nrf	Drury, Ser.	539	Prg
Thomas	8	Pwh	Williams, ---, Widow	581	Frd	Dudley	773	Nwk
Thos.	292	Ldn	Abner	312	Ldn	E.O.	514	Brk
William	135	Acc	Abraham	178	Shn	Ebenezer	576	Frd
William	717	Wsh	Abraham	115	Spt	Edmund	167	Dnw
see Wilkeison, Wilkerson			Abram	641	Gls	Edward	486	Frn
Wilks, Archibald	487	Bdf	Abram	452	Mth	Edward	591	Pre
Benjn.	652	Mnt	Abram	618	Srr	Edward	417	Rnd
Burwell	738	Brn	Absolom	932	Crl	Edward, jr.	790	Nrf
Henrietta	739	Brn	Absolum	364	Lnn	Edward M.	945	Chc
Jessee	66	Chr	Agathy	869	Sth	Edwd.	675	Glc
Joseph	739	Brn	Agnes	365	Lnn	Edwin	130	Sth
Minor	458	Frn	Aler.	313	Frf	Elenor B.	400	Rch

Eli	133	Acc	James	225	Aml	John	152	Sth
Eli	144	Sth	James	394	Ags	John	854	Sth
Eli	668	Sss	James	405	Ags	John	95	Spt
Elija	999	Nrt	James	486	Bdf	John	618	Srr
Elijah	60	Jff	James	768	Brn	John	708	Wsh
Elijah	12	Knw	James	86	Clp	John	735	Wsh
Elisha	749	Wsh	James	328	Dnw	John	740	Wsh
Elisha, jr.	442	Bth	James	81	Jff	John	757	Wsh
Elisha, Jr.	447	Bth	James	313	Frf	John, jr.	764	Brn
Elisha B.	412	Bth	James	535	Frd	John, jr.	166	Dnw
Eliza	880	Nrf	James	601	Frd	John, Senr.	166	Dnw
Eliza.	182	Knq	James	721	Gch	John B.	531	Prg
Eliza.	132	Sth	James	221	Kng	John M.	619	Srr
Elizabeth	433	Bth	James	367	Lnn	John R.	738	Brn
Elizabeth	738	Brn	James	772	Nwk	John S.	601	Frd
Elizabeth	589	Frd	James	998	Nrt	Jonas, Jr.	366	Fqr
Elizabeth	831	Nrf	James	541	Prg	Jonas, Senr.	366	Fqr
Elizabeth, (M)	738	Brn	James	505	Prw	Jonathan	11	Knw
Elizt.	395	Ags	James	144	Sth	Jonathn., (free Ne-		
Ellender	454	Mth	James	157	Nrf	groe)	351	Fqr
Ellice	295	Ldn	James	91	Spt	Jordan	875	Sth
Enos	287	Ldn	James	862	Wth	Jos. G.	8	Ntt
Ephraim	675	Br	James, este.	89	Clp	Josa.	666	Btt
Faithy	886	Yrk	Jane E.	563	Frd	Joseph	395	Ags
Felix	569	Mnr	Jared	566	Frd	Joseph	738	Brn
France	854	Hnv	Jaret	442	Bth	Joseph	640	Gls
Francis	312	Frf	Jas.	552	Mnn	Joseph	515	Prw
Francis	10	Hnr	Jas.	788	Nrf	Joseph	13	Rcm
Francis	439	Mth	Jas.	18	Ntt	Joseph	84	Spt
Francis	35	Rcm	Jas.	544	Prg	Joseph	100	Spt
Fredrick	332	Dnw	Jas., (Pun...)			Joseph	1	Wod
Frederick	641	Gls	[Pungo?]	485	Pra	Joseph, Jur.	862	Wth
Fredrick	795	Nrf	Jemima	353	Fqr	Joseph, Ser.	862	Wth
Frs.	926	Nrf	Jenkin	862	Wth	Joshua	318	Frf
Geo.	517	Brk	Jenney	776	Bck	Josiah	6	Hnr
Geo.	471	Mdd	Jere.	876	Sth	Josiah	619	Srr
George	738	Brn	Jeremiah	640	Gls	Juliet	998	Nrt
George	312	Frf	Jeremiah	19	Oho	Kinchen	158	Sth
George	313	Frf	Jeremiah, (Est)	67	Chr	Kinchen	851	Sth
George	378	Fqr	Jesse	316	Frf	Lee	317	Frf
George	917	Hrr	Jesse	353	Fqr	Levi	862	Wth
George	738	Nls	Jesse	159	Sth	Lewallin	496	Frn
George	999	Nrt	Jno.	666	Btt	Lewis	679	Glc
George	498	Prw	Jno.	61	Chs	Lewis	265	Rck
George	144	Sth	Jno.	251	Ldn	Lewis	853	Sth
George	703	Wsh	Jno.	264	Ldn	Lewis	41	Stf
George, Ju.	640	Gls	Jno.	308	Ldn	Limus	312	Frf
George, Sen.	641	Gls	Jno.	161	Sth	London	159	Sth
Hannah	268	Ldn	Jno. C.	86	Clp	Lucey	6	Hnr
Hannah	272	Ldn	Joel	565	Frd	Lucy, Sr.	768	Brn
Hatton	813	Nrf	John	394	Ags	Ludwell	669	Sss
Hazael	412	Bth	John	738	Brn	Magalean	788	Wst
Henry	177	Alb	John	829	Bck	Marg	900	Hnv
Henry	667	Btt	John	328	Dnw	Margaret	136	Acc
Henry	642	Gls	John	184	Elc	Margrett	641	Gls
Henry	16	Hnr	John	216	Ess	Martha	295	Ldn
Henry	5	Oho	John	341	Fqr	Martin	67	Chr
Henry	530	Prg	John	388	Fqr	Mary	440	Bth
Henry	728	Wsh	John	392	Fqr	Mary	768	Brn
Hepsaber	312	Ldn	John	486	Frn	Mary	776	Bck
Herbert	165	Dnw	John	518	Frd	Mary	792	Bck
Hezekiah	392	Ags	John	642	Gls	Mary	815	Bck
Hillery	291	Ldn	John	721	Gch	Mary	365	Lnn
Hubbard	533	Prg	John	456	Grn	Mary	481	Pra
Hubbard	543	Prg	John	919	Hrr	Mary	157	Sth
Hugh	212	Alb	John	964	Hrr	Mary	852	Sth
Hugh	640	Gls	John	122	Hnr	Mary	854	Sth
Isaac	765	Brn	John	130	Hnr	Mary	877	Sth
Isaac	330	Dnw	John	94	Jff	Meredith	773	Nwk
Isaac	336	Dnw	John	180	Knq	Milburn	486	Bdf
Isaac	13	Wod	John	364	Lnn	Milchy	878	Sth
Isaac	862	Wth	John	738	Nls	Mildred	546	Prg
Isaac H.	86	Clp	John	807	Nrf	Miles	738	Brn
Isaiah	862	Wth	John	998	Nrt	Mills	924	Nrf
Isham	472	Mdd	John	13	Oho	Molly	925	Nrf
Jacob	835	Bck	John	22	Oho	Moses	855	Cmp
Jacob	533	Frd	John	14	Pwh	Nancy	765	Brn
Jacob	845	Hnv	John	499	Prw	Nancy	117	Spt
Jacob	59	Jff	John	515	Prw	Nathan	151	Sth
Jacob	739	Wsh	John	295	Rck	Nathaniel, sr.	40	Stf

Name	Ref	Co.
Nathaniel P.	23	Stf
Nehemiah	712	Wsh
Nelson	175	Alb
Nicholas	488	Bdf
Nicholas	857	Sth
Owen	763	Hmp
Patience	846	Sth
Paul M.	91	Clp
Pawel	15	Pwh
Pearson	43	Stf
Peggy	66	Chr
Peter	738	Brn
Peter	312	Frf
Peter	364	Lnc
Peter [2]	31	Rcm
Peter	62	Stf
Peter	741	Wsh
Pheby	114	Hnr
Phil	128	Hnr
Philip	249	Aml
Philip	181	Knq
Philip	656	Mnt
Philip	249	Shn
Philip, Jr.	642	Gls
Philip, Sr.	642	Gls
Phillip	767	Brn
Phillip	669	Sss
Polley	326	Dnw
Presley	312	Frf
Prisly	298	Ldn
Queen	330	Dnw
Rachel	159	Sth
Rd.	316	Frf
Rebek.	166	Dnw
Reubin	668	Sss
Richard	57	Jff
Richard	364	Lnn
Richard	597	Mnr
Richard	861	Wth
Richard	862	Wth
Richard, Sr.	367	Lnn
Richd.	120	Hnr
Richd.	540	Prg
Richd.	541	Prg
Richd.	709	Wsh
Richd., Sr.	531	Prg
Richd. C.	405	Ags
Richd. E.	154	Sth
Robert	767	Brn
Robert	833	Bck
Robert	67	Chr
Robert	866	Sth
Robert H.	365	Lnn
Robin	788	Wst
Robt.	165	Dnw
Robt. C.	17	Ntt
Roger	486	Bdf
Roger	869	Cmp
Salley	288	Amh
Salley	180	Knq
Sally	594	Frd
Sam	554	Mnn
Saml.	125	Hnr
Saml. G.	7	Ntt
Samuel	488	Bdf
Samuel	768	Brn
Samuel	111	Cmb
Samuel	82	Jff
Samuel	275	Ldn
Samuel	210	Shn
Samuel	862	Wth
Samuel, Jur.	98	Cmb
Samul	486	Bdf
Sarah	96	Jff
Sarah	160	Sth
Seth	924	Nrf
Soloman	840	Bck
Solon.	872	Sth
Spratley	127	Sth
Susanna	870	Sth

Name	Ref	Co.
Tamar	381	Fqr
Tarleton	108	Cmb
Tarlton	839	Bck
Taylor	949	Chc
Tho.	92	Clp
Thomas	435	Bth
Thomas	447	Bth
Thomas	680	Br
Thomas	871	Cmp
Thomas	875	Cmp
Thomas	315	Frf
Thomas	462	Frn
Thomas	482	Frn
Thomas	785	Hmp
Thomas	182	Knq
Thomas	527	Prw
Thomas	31	Rcm
Thomas	176	Shn
Thomas	618	Srr
Thomas	788	Wst
Thomas O.	60	Jff
Thos.	765	Brn
Thos.	167	Dnw
Thos.	438	Mth
Thos.	801	Nrf
Thos.	925	Nrf
Thos.	265	Rck
Thos.	741	Wsh
Tully	804	Nrf
W.C.	33	Hnr
W.W.	316	Frf
Walter	487	Bdf
Warner	809	Bck
William	286	Amh
William	684	Br
William	536	Frd
William	457	Grn
William	365	Lnn
William	366	Lnn
William	472	Mdd
William	1000	Nrt
William	549	Prg
William	6	Rcm
William	231	Shn
William	244	Shn
William	157	Sth
William	115	Spt
William	25	Stf
William	619	Srr
William	788	Wst
William, (PP)	487	Bdf
William, Ser.	789	Wst
William F.	1000	Nrt
William M.	774	Nwk
Williams, LS.	768	Brn
Willm.	185	Elc
Wim. C.	856	Hnv
Wm.	664	Btt
Wm.	767	Brn
Wm.	86	Clp
Wm. [3]	675	Glc
Wm.	721	Gch
Wm.	959	Hrr
Wm.	120	Hnr
Wm.	363	Lnc
Wm.	257	Ldn
Wm.	289	Ldn
Wm.	297	Ldn
Wm.	796	Nrf
Wm.	481	Pra
Wm.	264	Rck
Wm.	137	Sth
Wm.	156	Sth
Wm., (BW)	482	Pra
Wm., (KJ)	485	Pra
Wm. L.	741	Wsh
Zebulon	738	Brn
Zedekiah	786	Hmp
see McWilliams, OWilliams,		
Spillman, W..., William,		

Wilms, Wms.
Williamson, ---, Jarvis

Name	Ref	Co.
&	2	Hnr
Abraham	565	Frd
Alexander	934	Crl
Ann	485	Pra
Archabald	862	Cmp
Archer	3	Hnr
Arthur	146	Sth
Arthur	672	Sss
Basil	71	Jff
Benja.	315	Frf
Benjamin	472	Mdd
Betsy	812	Nrf
Caleb, Jr.	481	Pra
Caleb, Sr.	481	Pra
Caldwell	850	Cmp
Charles	66	Chr
Chas.	483	Pra
Chas., (B.Smyth)	484	Pra
Chas., (of T)	482	Pra
Christr.	479	Pra
Clement	666	Btt
Cornelius	826	Hmp
Dab.	113	Hnr
Damy [?]	202	Shn
Danl., FN)	14	Rcm
David F.	618	Srr
Debrix	870	Cmp
Edd.	112	Hnr
Eleazar	17	Oho
Francis	485	Pra
Gaius	797	Nrf
Geo.	125	Hnr
Geo.	478	Pra
Geo., Capt.	14	Pwh
George	249	Aml
George	34	Hnr
Henry	487	Bdf
Henry	478	Frn
Henry	481	Pra
Hillary	481	Pra
Isaac	524	Frd
Jacob	89	Jff
Jacob	592	Pre
Jacob	22	Rcm
James	406	Ags
James	919	Hrr
James	19	Oho
James	670	Sss
James, jr.	487	Bdf
James, sr.	488	Bdf
Jas.	481	Pra
Jas., (of Chas.)	481	Pra
Jas., of Tully	479	Pra
Jno.	667	Btt
Jno.	879	Hnv
Jno.	478	Pra
Jno.	483	Pra
Jnon. [2]	926	Nrf
John	514	Brk
John	777	Bck
John	518	Frd
John	33	Hnr
John	112	Hnr
John	119	Hnr
John	810	Nrf
John	20	Oho
John	590	Pre
John	592	Pre
John	845	Sth
John	699	Wsh
Jonathan	458	Frn
Joseph	366	Lnn
Joseph	481	Pra
Joseph	618	Srr
Joseph	668	Sss
Joshua	488	Bdf
Joshua	479	Pra
Josiah	480	Pra

Js.	924	Nrf	Elizabeth	720	Gch	Nancy, Sen.	34	Isw
Js.	926	Nrf	George	29	Isw	Nathl.	4	Isw
Leml.	482	Pra	Hannah	924	Nrf	Parker	8	Isw
Leml., Jr.	482	Pra	Isaac	86	Clp	Philodelphia, a free woman		
Leonard H.	488	Bdf	Isaiah	486	Frn	of couler	721	Wsh
Leticia	67	Chr	Jas.	677	Glc	Rebecca	619	Srr
Littleton	768	Brn	Joel	181	Knq	Robt.	176	Elc
Lodawick	485	Pra	John	89	Clp	Thomas C.	261	Ldn
Lucy	845	Sth	John	364	Lnn	William	488	Bdf
Malachi	484	Pra	John	618	Mnt	William	328	Dnw
Margarett	511	Frd	John, (F.Negroe)	371	Fqr	William	335	Dnw
Mary	24	Oho	John J.	181	Knq	William, resid'g in		
Matthew, (est.	672	Sss	Joseph	450	Frn	Petersburg	168	Dnw
Moses	19	Oho	Joseph	720	Gch	Willis H.	736	Nls
Moses	481	Pra	Joshua	414	Mds	Wm.	15	Ntt
Moses, Sr.	478	Pra	Lewis	108	Spt	Wm.	858	Sth
Moses B. ... [Sindo?			Mark	497	Frn	see Wells		
Blind. ?]	480	Pra	Nancy	959	Chc	Willson, ... [G...?]	306	Rck
Nancy	486	Bdf	Preston	415	Fqr	Daniel	250	Aml
Peggey	533	Prg	Rebecca	721	Gch	Davd.	298	Rck
Peter	587	Brk	Reuben	87	Clp	Edward	365	Lnn
Rachael	860	Sth	Rich	96	Jff	Jacob	313	Ldn
Ralph	521	Frd	Robert	180	Knq	James	252	Ldn
Richd.	137	Sth	Sandy	89	Clp	James	265	Ldn
Robert	481	Pra	Susan	720	Gch	James	267	Rck
Sam	587	Brk	Thomas	29	Isw	James	306	Rck
Samuel	674	Br	William	772	Nwk	Jno.	238	Ldn
Samuel	766	Hmp	William	41	Stf	Jno.	305	Ldn
Samuel	5	Knw	Wm.	85	Clp	John	489	Bdf
Sarah	119	Hnr	Wm.	719	Gch	John	292	Rck
Thomas	19	Oho	Wm.	116	Hnr	John	297	Rck
Thomas	592	Pre	see Wallis, Welles			John	299	Rck
Tully	480	Pra	Williss, Joseph	846	Hnv	Joseph	294	Ldn
Turner	457	Grn	Willoby, William	37	Rcm	Joseph	316	Ldn
William	390	Fqr	Willock, Thos.	924	Nrf	Mary	946	Chc
William [2]	691	Br	Willons, Ann	856	Sth	Matthew	297	Rck
William	822	Bck	see Wellons			Moses	265	Ldn
William	831	Bck	Willoughby, Andw.	719	Wsh	Robert	277	Ldn
William	181	Knq	Henry	105	Spt	Robert	365	Lnn
William	533	Prg	Jas.	105	Spt	Saml.	292	Rck
Willis	860	Sth	John L.	829	Nrf	Saml.	305	Rck
Willoughby	31	Isw	Joseph	83	Spt	Stephen	309	Ldn
Wm.	6	Oho	Joshua	734	Nls	Thos. T.	225	Aml
Wm.	19	Oho	Mary	925	Nrf	Wm.	284	Rck
Wm.	478	Pra	Mat	927	Nrf	Wilmor see Witmor		
Wm.	485	Pra	Mathew, Colo.	706	Wsh	Wilmore, Ann	182	Knq
see Bonner, Chandler, For-			Thos.	811	Nrf	Christopher	181	Knq
tune, Morriss, Simmons,			Thos.	478	Pra	James	305	Amh
Wmson., WmSon.			Thos.	105	Spt	John	181	Knq
Willians, Cunm.	940	Hrr	William	67	Spt	William	305	Amh
Lemuel	823	Nrf	Willoy, John	809	Nrf	Winston	181	Knq
Notty C.	272	Ldn	Wills, Abrm.	429	Rnd	Wilmot, Thomas	67	Chr
Wilson	835	Nrf	Anthony	158	Sth	Wilmoth, John	419	Rnd
Williard, John	870	Cmp	Benj.	273	Ldn	Nicholas	420	Rnd
Willias, Wm.	931	Hrr	Charles	24	Hnr	Thomas	420	Rnd
Williford, Charles	131	Sth	Charles	132	Hnr	Thomas, Jr.	421	Rnd
Jesse	139	Sth	Collin C.	124	Hnr	Wilmott, William	506	Frd
Johnson	140	Sth	Edmd.	15	Ntt	Wilms, Elish.	934	Hrr
Thos.	850	Sth	Elias	281	Amh	Enoch	964	Hrr
Will.	869	Sth	Goodrich	126	Sth	Nathaniel	964	Hrr
Wm.	146	Sth	Henry W.	5	Isw	Thomas	934	Hrr
Willingham, George	404	Fqr	Ignatius	486	Bdf	Wilsan, Sally	30	Hnr
James	402	Fqr	Jacob	15	Rcm	Wilsford, John	886	Yrk
James	404	Fqr	James	17	Isw	Wilsh, Edw.	395	Ags
John, Jr.	401	Fqr	James	738	Nls	Wilsher, Benjamin	413	Mds
John, Senr.	401	Fqr	James, Ju.	736	Nls	Joseph	413	Mds
William	400	Fqr	Jane	431	Flv	Wilshimer, Catherine	99	Jff
Willis, ---, Doctor	863	Cmp	Jesse, (F.N.)	13	Isw	Wilshire, Sarah	83	Jff
Abner	728	Wsh	Jno.	18	Hnr	Wilson, ---, & Patson	264	Rck
Amis	737	Wsh	John	437	Flv	...	249	Aml
Ann	720	Gch	John	736	Nls	Abraham	182	Knq
Bayly	512	Prw	John B.	487	Bdf	Abraham	102	Spt
Benjn.	659	Mnt	Jos.	812	Nrf	Abram	749	Wsh
Bennet	497	Frn	Josiah	2	Isw	Adam	674	Br
Betsy	27	Hnr	Justin	486	Bdf	Ailibab	218	Pnd
Byrd C.	72	Spt	Langley C.	619	Srr	Alex	181	Knq
Carver	76	Jff	Matt	878	Sth	Alexander	681	Br
Chars.	88	Clp	Matt.	681	Wrw	Alexr.	665	Btt
David	460	Frn	Matthew	432	Flv	Allen	109	Cmb
David	617	Mnt	Nancy	26	Isw	Allexander	121	Cmb

Amzry W.	807	Nrf	Hugh	275	Rck	John	271	Rck
Andrew	683	Br	Isaac	89	Clp	John	193	Shn
Andrew [2]	11	Knw	Isaiah	643	Gls	John	150	Sth
Andrew	181	Knq	Isbell	336	Dnw	John	617	Srr
Andrew	221	Pnd	J.S.	553	Mnn	John	738	Wsh
Ann	365	Lnn	Jacob	587	Frd	John	749	Wsh
Anne	796	Nrf	Jacob	521	Prw	John	860	Wth
Arch.	553	Mnn	Jacob	419	Rnd	John	885	Yrk
Archibald	397	Fqr	Jacob	209	Shn	John, Jr.	413	Mds
Arther	548	Mnn	James	395	Ags	John A.	175	Alb
Asa	486	Bdf	James	486	Bdf	Jonathan	877	Sth
Barbara	433	Bth	James	535	Brk	Jonthn.	633	Mnt
Ben	547	Mnn	James	595	Brk	Jos.	553	Mnn
Ben, (of M)	553	Mnn	James	679	Br	Jos.	662	Mnt
Benj.	964	Hrr	James	803	Bck	Joseph	937	Hrr
Benja.	156	Sth	James	933	Crl	Joseph [2]	941	Hrr
Benjamin	22	Oho	James	374	Fqr	Joseph	4	Oho
Benjn.	126	Cmb	James	441	Flv	Joseph	590	Pre
Benjn.	166	Dnw	James	534	Frd	Jos.	298	Rck
Benjn.	427	Rnd	James	642	Gls	Joseph	268	Rck
Betty	405	Rch	James	676	Glc	Joseph	10	Rcm
Caleb	796	Nrf	James	14	Knw	Joseph, (Stanton)	487	Bdf
Cary, mulatto	677	Glc	James	366	Lnn	Joshua	632	Mnt
Charles	954	Chc	James	420	Msn	Josiah	550	Mnn
Charles	583	Mnr	James	586	Mnr	Josiah	617	Srr
Charles	4	Ntt	James	736	Nls	Js.	548	Mnn
D.	392	Ags	James	4	Oho	Js.	549	Mnn
Daniel	222	Kng	James	266	Rck	Js.	925	Nrf
Daniel	789	Wst	James	267	Rck	L., for E.O. Branch	65	Chs
David	135	Acc	James	279	Rck	Lettilia	554	Brk
David	391	Ags	James	881	Sth	Leroy	181	Knq
David	518	Frd	James	81	Spt	Lizy	333	Dnw
David	9	Knw	James	102	Spt	Lodowick	55	Chs
David	14	Knw	James	52	Stf	Mary	924	Nrf
David	472	Mdd	James	617	Srr	Mary	15	Ntt
David	999	Nrt	James	749	Wsh	Mary	218	Pnd
David H.	537	Frd	James	861	Wth	Martha	6	Wod
Dianitia	335	Dnw	James, jr.	558	Brk	Mat	548	Mnn
Dick	739	Brn	James, Jr.	617	Srr	Mathew	393	Ags
Drury	54	Chs	James, Jun.	817	Hmp	Matthew	488	Bdf
Ealizabeth	218	Pnd	James, Sen.	817	Hmp	Matthew	126	Cmb
Edward	65	Chs	James, Ser.	558	Brk	Matthew	55	Jff
Edward	490	Pra	Jane	666	Btt	Meshac	925	Nrf
Edward Rion	8	Knw	Jane	642	Gls	Molly	364	Lnc
Edwd.	837	Nrf	Jas.	14	Knw	Montgomery	269	Rck
Edwd.	477	Pra	Jas.	553	Mnn	Moses	595	Frd
Eleanor	297	Rck	Jas., (jun.)	788	Nrf	Moses	56	Jff
Elizabeth	433	Bth	Jas., (Mst.)	287	Rck	Moses	426	Rnd
Elizh., (W)	886	Yrk	Jas., Sr.	665	Btt	Moses	293	Rck
Fil	736	Nls	Jas., (Sr.)	796	Nrf	Nancy	425	Bth
Fisher	457	Grn	Jeremiah	734	Nls	Nancy	28	Isw
Francis	406	Ags	Jeremiah	76	Spt	Nancy	808	Nrf
Francis	191	Shn	Jno.	62	Chs	Nathaniel	176	Alb
Fredrick	803	Nrf	Jno.	317	Frf	Nathaniel	178	Alb
G.	549	Mnn	Jno.	548	Mnn	Nathaniel	488	Bdf
Geo.	553	Mnn	Jno.	551	Mnn	Nathaniel	67	Chr
Geo.	925	Nrf	Jno.	2	Ntt	Nathaniel	811	Hmp
Geo.	926	Nrf	Jno., (Black Smith)	663	Btt	Nathaniel	1000	Nrt
George	137	Acc	Jno., Sr.	666	Btt	Nathnl.	298	Rck
George	393	Ags	Jo., (B. Smith)	664	Btt	Neal	791	Nrf
George	165	Dnw	John	135	Acc	Peggy	796	Nrf
George	951	Hrr	John	393	Ags	Peggy	405	Rch
George	28	Hnr	John	394	Ags	Peter	643	Gls
George	13	Knw	John	433	Bth	Peter	632	Mnt
George	144	Sth	John	693	Br	Peter, (FB)	18	Ntt
Goodridge	594	Pre	John	738	Brn	Rachel	394	Ags
Green	645	Mnt	John	860	Cmp	Rebeca	550	Mnn
Green, Sr.	662	Mnt	John	329	Dnw	Reben	181	Knq
H.B.	548	Mnn	John	184	Elc	Richard	272	Amh
H.H.	550	Mnn	John	959	Hrr	Richard	98	Cmb
Hannah	595	Brk	John	82	Jff	Richard	798	Hmp
Hannah	67	Chr	John	96	Jff	Richd.	681	Wrw
Henry	55	Chs	John	1	Knw	Rob.	183	Elc
Henry	585	Mnr	John	234	Ldn	Rob.	549	Mnn
Henry	4	Oho	John	413	Mds	Robert	562	Mnr
Henry	24	Oho	John	636	Mnt	Robert, jr.	182	Knq
Henry, Jr.	11	Oho	John	654	Mnt	Robert, mulatto	677	Glc
Henry L.	762	Hmp	John	13	Oho	Robert, Senr.	181	Knq
Holt	835	Nrf	John	591	Pre	Robert B.	366	Lnn
Hugh	58	Jff	John	421	Rnd	Robt.	395	Ags

Name	No.	Co.
Robt.	665	Btt
Robt.	89	Clp
Robt.	271	Rck
Sally	333	Dnw
Sally	791	Nrf
Sally	478	Pra
Sameul	219	Pnd
Saml.	136	Acc
Saml.	395	Ags
Saml.	523	Brk
Saml.	663	Btt
Saml.	552	Mnn
Saml.	634	Mnt
Saml.	794	Nrf
Saml.	837	Nrf
Saml.	746	Wsh
Sampson	617	Srr
Samuel	486	Bdf
Samuel	677	Br
Samuel	681	Br
Samuel	116	Cmb
Samuel	19	Oho
Samuel	617	Srr
Samuel B.	120	Spt
Sarah	542	Frd
Sarah	632	Mnt
Sarah	405	Rch
Sarah	51	Stf
Severn	137	Acc
Solomon	790	Nrf
Spicer	413	Mds
Stacy	526	Frd
Stephen	536	Brk
Susanna	433	Bth
Tatem	796	Nrf
Tho.	89	Clp
Tho.	547	Mnn
Tho., (GR)	805	Nrf
Thomas	488	Bdf
Thomas	67	Chr
Thomas	165	Dnw
Thomas	558	Frd
Thomas	68	Jff
Thomas	734	Nls
Thomas	590	Pre
Thomas	427	Rnd
Thomas, Jr.	348	Fqr
Thos.	409	Ags
Thos. [2]	665	Btt
Thos.	5	Hnr
Thos.	547	Mnn
Thos.	797	Nrf
Thos.	924	Nrf
Thos.	710	Wsh
Thos., (of G.)	550	Mnn
Tobias	235	Ldn
Walter	553	Mnn
Wiley	222	Kng
William	393	Ags
William	488	Bdf
William	523	Brk
William	690	Br
William	934	Crl
William	532	Frd
William	574	Frd
William	642	Gls
William	799	Hmp
William	830	Hmp
William	3	Knw
William	223	Kng
William	413	Mds
William	12	Oho
William	218	Pnd
William	219	Pnd
William	7	Pwh
William	427	Rnd
William	405	Rch
William	412	Rch
William	82	Spt
William	617	Srr

Name	No.	Co.
William	860	Wth
William B.	421	Rnd
Willis	110	Cmb
Willis	186	Elc
Willis	793	Nrf
Willis	617	Srr
Willm.	666	Btt
Wm.	392	Ags
Wm.	533	Brk
Wm.	664	Btt
Wm.	56	Chs
Wm.	547	Mnn
Wm.	549	Mnn
Wm.	553	Mnn
Wm.	633	Mnt
Wm.	828	Nrf
Wm.	26	Oho
Wm.	277	Rck
Wm.	287	Rck
Wm., (Boatyard[?])	274	Rck
Wm., (D)	396	Ags
Wm., Esqr.	393	Ags
Wm., (hill)	279	Rck
Wm., (Mjr.)	394	Ags
Wm., (Revd.)	396	Ags
Wm., 34d.	553	Mnn
Wm., (W)	886	Yrk
Wm., (Y)	795	Nrf
Wm. B.	2	Ntt
Wm. F.	427	Rnd
Zachariah	932	Crl
Zachuriah	209	Shn
see Anderson, Harris, Lucas, Price, Row, Shehorn, Wil..., Winson		
Wilt, Henry	78	Jff
Wilts, Micl.	552	Mnn
Wiltshire, John	592	Pre
Wily, William	13	Knw
Wimans, Isaac	940	Hrr
Wimber, Coleman	137	Acc
William	137	Acc
Wimbish, Thos.	65	Chs
Wimer, Adam	536	Frd
Charles	663	Btt
George	217	Pnd
George	212	Shn
Henry	218	Pnd
Jacob	225	Pnd
John	212	Shn
Philip	217	Pnd
Wimmer, Catherine	55	Jff
Elizabeth	476	Frn
Jacob	476	Frn
John	476	Frn
Wims, Samuel	212	Alb
William	212	Alb
Win, George	6	Hnr
Joseph	175	Alb
Winance, Ezekiel	966	Hrr
Winanger, Davd.	757	Wsh
John	757	Wsh
Winbright, Michal	218	Pnd
see Winebright		
Wince, Jno.	292	Ldn
Winchester, Maria	2	Hnr
Windburn, Eliza.	855	Sth
Windell, Augustine	213	Shn
Augustine, Jr.	217	Shn
Chaty	216	Shn
George, Jr.	216	Shn
John	213	Shn
John, Jr.	216	Shn
John, (B.F.)	213	Shn
John, Sen.	216	Shn
Peter	213	Shn
Peter	253	Shn
Philip	216	Shn
Winder, Betsey	71	Acc
Edmund	442	Mth

Name	No.	Co.
James	450	Mth
Jno.	450	Mth
John	70	Acc
Richd.	446	Mth
Zerobl.	67	Acc
Winders, Alex	553	Mnn
Windham, George	585	Frd
Kinchen	457	Grn
Mary	141	Sth
Moses	808	Nrf
Windle, John	515	Frd
Margarett	511	Frd
Samuel	509	Frd
Windleback, Hy	599	Mnn
Windleberry, John	596	Mnr
Windner, John, Jur.	696	Wsh
Window, John	443	Bth
Windsbury, Jacob	253	Shn
Windsey, James	66	Acc
Windson, Thomas	523	Prw
Windsor, Asa	370	Fqr
Benjamin	5	Knw
Charaty	401	Fqr
Charles	6	Knw
George	793	Hmp
John	506	Prw
Jonathan	404	Fqr
Nathaniel	315	Frf
Rd. S.	313	Frf
Saml.	506	Prw
Sarah	313	Frf
Thomas	680	Br
Thomas	568	Frd
Wine, Adam	396	Ags
Danl.	8	Rcm
George	9	Rcm
Hoshua	61	Stf
Jesse	39	Rcm
John	5	Rcm
John	236	Shn
Michael	236	Shn
William	118	Spt
Wineberry, John, Jnr.	176	Alb
Winebright, Michal	217	Pnd
see Winbright		
Wineburg, Jacob	299	Ldn
Wineburry, John	176	Alb
Winecoop, Philip	259	Ldn
see Wynkoop		
Winegar, Davd.	299	Rck
Wm.	297	Rck
Winegarner, Adam	316	Ldn
Henry	316	Ldn
Herbert	317	Ldn
Winegord, Peter	29	Rcm
Wineman, Fredk.	666	Btt
Winemiller, Henry	419	Rnd
Wines, Jacob	299	Ldn
Saml.	21	Rcm
Susanna	445	Bth
Winfield, Curtis	670	Sss
Edward	739	Brn
Ephraim	672	Sss
Harris	671	Sss
Henry	672	Sss
John	670	Sss
William	670	Sss
William	671	Sss
Winfieled, Edward	766	Brn
Winfree, Archer	63	Chs
Christopher	854	Cmp
Henry	65	Chs
Isaac	3	Ntt
James	68	Chs
James W.	67	Chs
Jno. E.	3	Ntt
John	12	Pwh
Major	63	Chs
Marvil	60	Chs
Mathew	61	Chs

Nelson	63	Chs	Jno.	899	Hnv	Franes.	940	Hrr
Rewbin	65	Chs	Jno.	272	Ldn	James	268	Rck
Val, jr.	57	Chs	John	179	Alb	see Wise		
Val, sen.	62	Chs	John	370	Fqr	Wireman see Wiseman		
Valentine, jr.	60	Chs	John	364	Lnn	Wires, Daniel	959	Hrr
Wm.	55	Chs	John, jr.	366	Lnn	Wirick, George	862	Wth
Winfrey, Austin	773	Nwk	Joseph	364	Lnn	see Wyrick		
Henry	797	Bck	Lydal	364	Lnn	Wirte, William	7	Hnr
Jno. T.	878	Hnv	Mary	381	Fqr	Wirth, Spencer	789	Wst
Major	773	Nwk	Minor	390	Fqr	Wirts, Catharine	22	Rcm
Mary	130	Cmb	Minor	365	Lnn	Wisco, Richard K.	34	Hnr
Stephen	484	Frn	Minor, Jr.	415	Fqr	Wisdom, Cradock	110	Cmb
William	774	Nwk	Mumford	366	Lnn	Tavenor	75	Spt
Wing, George	233	Shn	Orsamus	366	Lnn	Wise, Agnus	35	Acc
Wingard, John	106	Jff	Peter	844	Hnv	Barbara	20	Hnr
Wingate, James	788	Hmp	Peter	590	Pre	Betsey	67	Acc
Winger, Andw.	757	Wsh	Tavner	932	Crl	Calep	25	Oho
Ann	6	Rcm	Thos.	435	Flv	Clark	86	Clp
Benjn.	38	Rcm	Wm.	272	Ldn	Cuthbert	91	Clp
Henry	6	Rcm	see Jones			Elianor	91	Clp
Joseph	15	Rcm	Winneford, George	860	Wth	Eliza	330	Dnw
Peter	757	Wsh	Jeffrey	860	Wth	Geo. D.	815	Nrf
Wingfeild, John	461	Frn	Winning, Saml.	579	Brk	George	304	Amh
Lewes	457	Frn	Winright, John	886	Yrk	George	103	Jff
William	461	Frn	Winsel, Geo.	286	Ldn	George, Senr.	67	Acc
Wingfield, Ann	294	Amh	Jno.	285	Ldn	Jacob	547	Mnn
Charles	177	Alb	Winset, Benjamin	223	Kng	Jacob	224	Pnd
Charles	290	Amh	Winsett, Frances	507	Prw	James	87	Clp
Charles	788	Bck	Winslow, Jos.	924	Nrf	John	69	Acc
Christophe	875	Hnv	Lucy	334	Dnw	John	405	Ags
Christopher	177	Alb	Winson, Wm.	548	Mnn	John	413	Fqr
Elizabeth	876	Hnv	Winstead, Daniel	999	Nrt	John	1000	Nrt
Francis	176	Alb	Elizabeth	999	Nrt	John	224	Pnd
Jno.	860	Hnv	Griffin	171	Shn	Mannen	88	Clp
John [2]	176	Alb	Holland	999	Nrt	Margt.	24	Hnr
Joseph	176	Alb	James	999	Nrt	Martin	214	Pnd
Joseph B.	275	Amh	Salley	999	Nrt	Mathias	861	Wth
Joseph C.	873	Hnv	William	999	Nrt	Molly	886	Yrk
Mary	848	Hnv	Winstine, Wm.	131	Hnr	Peter	286	Ldn
Matthew	176	Alb	Winston, Benjamin A.	855	Cmp	Peter	839	Nrf
Nancy	177	Alb	Edmund	264	Amh	Sally	134	Acc
Reuben	177	Alb	Edmund	840	Bck	Saml.	86	Clp
Robert	175	Alb	Henry R.	848	Hnv	Samuel	425	Msn
Thomas	303	Amh	Horatio G.	873	Hnv	Sebostean	223	Pnd
Thos., Jnr.	848	Hnv	Isaac	116	Hnr	Soloman	67	Acc
Thos., Snr.	898	Hnv	Isaac, Jr.	87	Clp	Soloman, Senr.	66	Acc
Wim.	857	Hnv	Isaac, Sr.	87	Clp	Susannah	68	Acc
Wingo, Allen	250	Aml	Jacob	867	Hnv	Tho.	185	Elc
Archer	226	Aml	Jno.	22	Hnr	Thomas	243	Ldn
Fielding	226	Aml	Jno. G.	664	Btt	Thomas	364	Lnn
Garland	7	Ntt	Peter	892	Hnv	Tully	71	Acc
Henry	8	Ntt	Pleasant	932	Crl	Tully R.	815	Nrf
Horatio	67	Chr	Robt.	15	Hnr	William	168	Shn
James	455	Frn	Saml.	226	Aml	Wm.	447	Mth
John	249	Aml	Samuel J.	896	Hnv	Wm.	282	Rck
John	456	Frn	Sarah	860	Hnv	see Wice, Wyse		
John, jr.	250	Aml	Susanna	899	Hnv	Wisecarver, Henry	571	Frd
John, (WW)	225	Aml	Walter C.	87	Clp	Wisehart, Benjn.	611	Mnt
Miles R.	3	Ntt	Wim.	898	Hnv	Jno., Jr.	612	Mnt
Polley	454	Frn	Wim. O.	860	Hnv	John	627	Mnt
Thomas	5	Ntt	Wm. B.	11	Hnr	Thomas	611	Mnt
see W...			see Winstine			Wiseheart, James	314	Frf
Wingrove, Jno.	260	Ldn	Winter, William H.	526	Prw	Wisely, Daniel	862	Wth
Winiburg, Jacob	313	Ldn	Wintermire, Philip	105	Jff	Wiseman, Benj.	927	Hrr
Winkfield, John	570	Frd	Winters, Daniel	16	Oho	Caleb	554	Mnn
Richard	789	Wst	Henry	930	Hrr	Caleb	8	Wod
Winkle, John	598	Mnr	James	293	Ldn	George	299	Rck
Winkler, Lau.	548	Mnn	James	17	Oho	Isaac	594	Mnr
Winn, Banester	366	Lnn	John	77	Jff	Isaac, j.	564	Mnr
Benjamin	932	Crl	John	631	Mnt	John	928	Hrr
Buckner	365	Lnn	Matthias	925	Hrr	John	574	Mnr
Cretia	366	Lnn	Powles	278	Rck	John	175	Shn
Edmund	366	Lnn	Thos.	631	Mnt	John	258	Shn
Elisha	366	Lnn	Winterton, John	769	Hmp	Joseph	576	Mnr
Freman	365	Lnn	Wintz, Jacob	85	Clp	Lewis	393	Ags
Harison	736	Wsh	Peter	91	Clp	Thomas	919	Hrr
Harrison	742	Wsh	Wire, Benj.	935	Hrr	Wm.	584	Mnr
Horatia	367	Lnn	Christo.	288	Rck	see Wissman, Wizeman		
James	365	Lnn	George	522	Frd	Wisemon, Philip	240	Shn
Jane	20	Ntt	George	947	Hrr	Wisenberg, C.	395	Ags

Name	No.	Co.	Name	No.	Co.	Name	No.	Co.
Wisenberger, Geo.	573	Brk	Wmson., Chas., Senr.	166	Dnw	Wolfenbarger, Joseph	421	Bth
George	571	Brk	Geo.	17	Hnr	Wolfenberger, Benjamin	860	Wth
Wiser, Henry	638	Mnt	Isaac	166	Dnw	Wolff, Jacob	457	Grn
Jemima	926	Nrf	Phobe	65	Chs	Wolford, Jacob	861	Wth
Michael	372	Fqr	Saml.	10	Hnr	John	833	Hmp
Wisewell, Adam	599	Brk	Stephen	166	Dnw	Lewis	861	Wth
Wishart, Alexr.	88	Clp	WmSon., Edmund	279	Amh	Wolfrom, Adam	154	Sth
William	223	Kng	Elizabeth	259	Amh	Wolingford, James	96	Jff
Wisher, Catey	136	Acc	James	209	Ess	Nicholass	96	Jff
Wisie see Wisco			Ludah	280	Amh	Wolker, Sarah	22	Pnd
Wisman, Elizebeth	861	Wth	Nathan	301	Amh	Wollard, Isaac	292	Ldn
George	862	Wth	Salley	442	Flv	Jno.	291	Ldn
John	861	Wth	Wm.Son, Saml.	207	Ess	Jno.	297	Ldn
Wisner, Peter	572	Brk	Wodley, John	472	Mdd	see Woolard		
see Wimer			Wodring, Abm.	552	Mnn	Wolff, Abraim	592	Mnr
Wisom, Thomas	952	Che	Dan	552	Mnn	Wolraven, Jonas	80	Jff
Wisong, Jacob	487	Bdf	Jac.	552	Mnn	Wolsey, Thos.	558	Brk
Jacob	488	Bdf	Jno.	552	Mnn	Woltz, George	589	Mnr
Wissman, George	218	Shn	Nic.	552	Mnn	Jacob	663	Btt
John	231	Shn	Wodrow, Andrew	756	Hmp	Jno.	665	Btt
Nicholas	218	Shn	Wofter, George	949	Hrr	Wolverton, Eliz.	553	Mnn
Wist, Edmon	940	Hrr	Wolair see Molair			James	788	Hmp
Willo.	482	Pra	Woldrige, Peter, jr.	89	Clp	Joel	777	Hmp
see West			see Worldridge			Woly see Wollf		
Wiswell, Isrl.	87	Clp	Wolf, Augustine	551	Mnn	Womack, Anna	106	Cmb
Witcher, Wm.	91	Clp	David	909	Hrr	Anthony H.	16	Ntt
Witezal, George	7	Rcm	David	931	Hrr	Archibald	592	Pre
Jacob	18	Rcm	Geo.	551	Mnn	Charles	106	Cmb
John	7	Rcm	George	426	Msn	Eady	592	Pre
Peter	7	Rcm	Henry	217	Shn	James W.	591	Pre
Peter	8	Rcm	Henry	756	Wsh	Jno.	64	Chs
Witezel, Anthony	10	Rcm	Jac.	551	Mnn	Massanello	593	Pre
Witheroe, James	432	Msn	Jac., Jr.	551	Mnn	Polley	69	Chs
Witherow, Isaac	662	Mnt	Jacob	811	Hmp	Robert V.	593	Pre
Withers, Allen	46	Stf	Jacob	596	Mnr	Tignal	590	Pre
Augustine	387	Fqr	Jacob, Jr.	908	Hrr	William, Junr.	590	Pre
Charles	413	Fqr	Jacob, Senr.	908	Hrr	William, Senr.	590	Pre
David W.	168	Dnw	James	908	Hrr	William L.	593	Pre
Edward	25	Stf	Jas.	665	Btt	see Venable		
Enoch D.	340	Fqr	Jeremiah	739	Wsh	Womacks, Daniel	488	Bdf
Enoch K.	340	Fqr	Jno.	266	Ldn	Womble, Henry	14	Isw
George W.	366	Fqr	Jno. [2]	286	Ldn	Joseph	142	Sth
James	87	Clp	John	936	Hrr	Joshua	142	Sth
James	400	Fqr	John	575	Mnr	Lemuel	35	Isw
Jesse	413	Fqr	John	756	Wsh	Wombwell, Zach.	619	Srr
John	87	Clp	John [2]	862	Wth	Wommack, Jas. B.	146	Sth
John	349	Fqr	Leonard	627	Mnt	Wommock, John	146	Sth
Joseph	62	Jff	Lewis	553	Mnn	Womsley, John	223	Pnd
Lewis	340	Fqr	Michle	940	Hrr	Wonder, Boston	579	Brk
Matthew K.	419	Fqr	Micle	948	Hrr	Wonycott, Nicholas	827	Nrf
Nathl.	165	Dnw	Peter	941	Hrr	Woo..., James	305	Ldn
Sarah	413	Fqr	Sam	551	Mnn	Sarah	789	Wst
Spencer	90	Clp	Simon	132	Hnr	Wood, ---	925	Nrf
Thomas	167	Dnw	Thomas	908	Hrr	Adam	91	Clp
Thos. T.	223	Kng	Wm.	285	Ldn	Alexander	586	Frd
William	412	Fqr	see Wolff, Woulfe			Andw.	925	Nrf
Withrow, Archd.	300	Rck	Wolfe, Ambrose	545	Frd	Ann	159	Sth
William	864	Cmp	Andrew	392	Fqr	Archibald	8	Oho
William	533	Frd	Andrew	4	Rcm	Bailey	575	Mnr
William	575	Mnr	BenJamin	8	Hnr	Benja.	915	Hrr
Wm.	590	Mnr	Charity	599	Brk	Benjamin	177	Shn
Witmor, Thos.	665	Btt	Geo.	595	Brk	Bennet	678	Wrw
Witsford, Oney	884	Hnv	George	506	Frd	Bossel	289	Ldn
Witt, Burgess	736	Nls	George	3	Rcm	C.D.	924	Nrf
David	737	Nls	Henry	20	Rcm	Caleb	926	Nrf
David, Jur.	737	Nls	Jacob	536	Frd	Carolus	66	Chr
Elizabeth	486	Bdf	Jacob	542	Frd	Charlotte	407	Rch
Jesse	486	Bdf	Jacob	427	Msn	Charlotte, a free mu-		
John	486	Bdf	Jacob	430	Msn	latto	1000	Nrt
William	737	Nls	Jacob	19	Rcm	Chas.	364	Lnc
Wittington, Joseph	596	Frd	Jacob, Senr.	537	Frd	Comfort	606	Frd
Witts, Dennett	736	Nls	John	395	Ags	Cornelius	516	Frd
Wittshire see Wiltshire			John	543	Frd	Darnald	86	Clp
Wizeman, George	904	Hrr	Lewis	508	Frd	David	212	Alb
Wizenall, Barney	106	Jff	Mary	925	Nrf	David	213	Alb
Mary	107	Jff	Michl.	579	Brk	David	367	Lnn
Wms., Abriham	218	Ess	Peter	340	Fqr	Dickinson	91	Clp
Samuel	98	Cmb	Peter	582	Frd	Drury	212	Alb
Wmson, Person	457	Grn	Ths.	87	Clp	Edmund	825	Bck
WmSon, Orpson	215	Ess	Valentine	19	Rcm	Edmund	866	Cmp

Name	Ref	Loc
Edmund	618	Srr
Edward	212	Alb
Edwd.	665	Btt
Elenor	245	Shn
Elijah	318	Frf
Elijah	919	Hrr
Eliza	114	Hnr
Elizabeth	877	Cmp
F. Jno.	664	Btt
Frances	471	Mdd
Francis	486	Bdf
Frankey	799	Nrf
George	366	Lnn
George, jr.	367	Lnn
Harrison	176	Alb
Henry	176	Alb
Henry	177	Alb
Henry	178	Alb
Henry	884	Hnv
Henry	11	Knw
Hezakiah	211	Alb
Isaac	530	Frd
Isaac, jr.	486	Bdf
Isaac B.	177	Alb
James	175	Alb
James	278	Amh
James	177	Elc
James	410	Fqr
James	123	Hnr
James	411	Mds
James	19	Oho
James	14	Wod
James H.	278	Rck
Jas.	549	Mnn
Jas.	550	Mnn
Jenny	115	Hnr
Jeremiah	486	Bdf
Jesse	486	Bdf
Jesse	864	Cmp
Jesse	176	Shn
Jessee	176	Alb
Jessee	177	Alb
Jessee	738	Nls
Jessee, Jnr.	177	Alb
Jessee	722	Gch
Jno.	665	Btt
Jno.	666	Btt
Jno.	676	Glc
Jno.	551	Mnn
Jno.	680	Wrw
Joel	868	Sth
John [2]	176	Alb
John	212	Alb
John	86	Clp
John	185	Elc
John	317	Frf
John	432	Flv
John	494	Frn
John	788	Hmp
John	931	Hrr
John	956	Hrr
John	958	Hrr
John	23	Hnr
John	367	Lnn
John	411	Mds
John	613	Mnt
John	1000	Nrt
John	407	Rch
John	177	Shn
John	242	Shn
John	885	Yrk
John, a free mulatto	1000	Nrt
John F.	132	Cmb
Joseph	88	Clp
Joseph	549	Frd
Joseph	958	Hrr
Joseph	313	Ldn
Joseph	1000	Nrt
Joseph, Sr.	664	Btt
Josh.	666	Btt
Joshua	177	Shn
Laurence	848	Sth
Lewis	590	Frd
Lewis	507	Prw
Lucy	177	Alb
Margaret	177	Shn
Margt.	26	Hnr
Mark	289	Ldn
Martha	177	Alb
Mary	211	Alb
Mary	380	Fqr
Mary	854	Sth
Mary	855	Sth
Matt.	676	Glc
Matt.	681	Wrw
Matt., Jur.	681	Wrw
Moses	178	Shn
Mourning	292	Amh
Nancy	80	Acc
Nancy	135	Acc
Nancy	109	Spt
Nehemiah, Jur.	177	Shn
Nehemiah, Senr.	177	Shn
Nelly	26	Hnr
Nicholas	212	Alb
Owen L.	66	Chr
Parchenus	2	Rcm
Patsey	869	Cmp
Paul	868	Cmp
Rice	175	Alb
Richard	735	Nls
Richard	736	Nls
Richard	737	Nls
Robert	212	Alb
Robert	213	Alb
Robert	932	Crl
Robert	590	Frd
Robert	131	Sth
Sally	220	Ess
Sally	27	Hnr
Saml.	394	Ags
Saml.	86	Clp
Saml.	722	Gch
Saml.	471	Mdd
Saml. B.	471	Mdd
Samuel	822	Bck
Samuel	869	Cmp
Samuel	735	Nls
Samuel	736	Nls
Samuel	738	Nls
Scarburgh	80	Acc
Silas	120	Spt
Soloman	176	Alb
Stephen	465	Frn
Stephen	367	Lnn
Susanna	21	Ntt
Susannah	292	Amh
Susannah	394	Rch
Tandy	3	Knw
Thomas	66	Chr
Thomas	465	Frn
Thomas	124	Hnr
Thomas	90	Jff
Thos.	217	Ess
Thos.	432	Flv
Thos., Sr.	432	Flv
William [2]	177	Alb
William	178	Alb
William	212	Alb
William	263	Amh
William	409	Fqr
William	892	Hnv
William	365	Lnn
William	575	Mnr
William	738	Nls
William	1000	Nrt
William	204	Shn
William	735	Nls
William, Ju.	89	Clp
Wm.	664	Btt
Wm.	666	Btt
Wm.	675	Glc
Wm.	677	Glc
Wm. [?]	287	Rck
Zachariah	213	Alb
see Branch, Tucker, Woo...		
Woodal, David	826	Bck
Isaac	826	Bck
Obediah	826	Bck
William	826	Bck
William	67	Chr
Woodall, Jacob	881	Cmp
Jamimy	459	Frn
Patey	459	Frn
Samuel	875	Cmp
Shadrick	857	Hnv
William	459	Frn
Woodard, Chars., jr.	90	Clp
Chars., Sr.	90	Clp
Edmunds	739	Brn
Elizh.	90	Clp
Fanny	509	Prw
Geo.	482	Pra
Henrietta	509	Prw
Henry	482	Pra
Horatio	481	Pra
James	90	Clp
Jesse	482	Pra
Jesse	41	Stf
Jno.	482	Pra
John	938	Hrr
John	844	Sth
Josh., jr.	90	Clp
Josiah	482	Pra
Juannah H.	18	Hnr
Polly	509	Prw
Presly	30	Stf
William	409	Fqr
Wm.	154	Sth
Wm., jr.	92	Clp
see Woodward		
Woodards, Tempce.	869	Sth
Wooday, William	487	Bdf
Woodby, John	693	Wsh
Woodcock, Eliza.	334	Dnw
Frances	544	Frd
Henry	468	Frn
Henry	127	Hnr
Isaac	943	Chc
John	468	Frn
Robert	487	Bdf
Russel	331	Dnw
Samuel	336	Dnw
Wooddle, John	394	Ags
Wooddy, Elisha	883	Hnv
Elizabeth	882	Hnv
James	894	Hnv
John	492	Frn
Nancy	126	Hnr
Saml.	66	Chs
Wm.	883	Hnv
Wim., Jnr.	882	Hnv
Wooden, Catharine	42	Rcm
Woodey, Wm.	304	Ldn
Woodfin, Elisha	112	Cmb
George	66	Chr
James	131	Hnr
John	830	Bck
Nancy	131	Hnr
Samuel	3	Pwh
Susanah	130	Hnr
Woodford, Frances	27	Rcm
John	579	Frd
John T.	934	Crl
Joseph	272	Ldn
Mark C.	931	Crl
Thomas	486	Bdf
William	486	Bdf
William	218	Pnd
William, jr.	934	Crl
William C.	934	Crl

Wm.	272	Ldn	Joseph	391	Ags	Ronny	443	Flv
Woodfork, Cuffy	126	Hnr	Joseph	392	Ags	Sally	720	Gch
Woodgad, Leweasy	927	Hrr	Josiah	496	Frn	Saml. T.	440	Flv
Lewis	927	Hrr	Jremiah	696	Br	Samuel	6	Pwh
Woodgard, H.	928	Hrr	Mary	682	Br	Stephen	111	Cmb
Woodhouse, Arthur S.	478	Pra	Micajah	212	Alb	Stephen	720	Gch
Chas. M.	478	Pra	Michael	738	Nls	Tarleton	117	Cmb
Frances	483	Pra	Molley	392	Ags	Tarlton	177	Alb
Frances	484	Pra	Richard	177	Alb	Tarlton	591	Pre
Henry	484	Pra	Richard	494	Frn	Thomas	720	Gch
Horatio	482	Pra	Richd.	562	Brk	Thomas	6	Pwh
Jas.	483	Pra	Robert	495	Frn	William	813	Bck
Jas., (of Jas.)	484	Pra	Robert	7	Oho	Wm.	719	Gch
Jno., Sr.	479	Pra	Robert, Jr.	496	Frn	Wm.	720	Gch
Jno., (W.N.)	485	Pra	Robert, Sr.	496	Frn	see Bugg, Layne, Ramsey		
Jona.	478	Pra	Robt.	551	Mnn	Woodville, John	87	Clp
Jona., Jr.	478	Pra	Sameul	224	Pnd	Woodwad, Mary	824	Nrf
Thos.	483	Pra	Saml.	664	Btt	Woodward, Andw.	314	Frf
Wm. D.	478	Pra	Samuel	426	Bth	Bartlet	772	Nwk
Wm. M.	483	Pra	Samuel	430	Bth	Benja.	721	Gch
Woodland, Isaac	676	Glc	Stephen	435	Bth	Benedt.	395	Ags
Sarah	672	Sss	Thomas	802	Bck	Bennet	21	Stf
Solomon	676	Glc	Thomas	223	Pnd	Charles	116	Hnr
Woodleif, Lucy	329	Dnw	Usley	732	Wsh	Chas.	802	Nrf
Woodlen, Robert	642	Gls	William [2]	177	Alb	Elizabeth	488	Bdf
Woodley, Andrew	20	Isw	William	212	Alb	Fielder	715	Wsh
Hannah	22	Rcm	William	213	Alb	Frances	18	Ntt
John	28	Isw	William	26	Rcm	Freeder [?]	750	Wsh
Mary	472	Mdd	William	717	Wsh	Geoe.	91	Clp
Saml.	681	Wrw	Wm.	548	Mnn	Hanley	206	Ess
see Wodley			Woodside, James	713	Wsh	Henry	774	Nwk
Woodlief, Eliza	326	Dnw	John	825	Nrf	Henry	795	Nrf
John	535	Prg	Woodsides, William	350	Fqr	Jacob	732	Wsh
Thos.	167	Dnw	Woodsom, Charles	959	Chc	James	562	Frd
Woodling, Matthew	789	Wst	Woodson, Anderson	861	Cmp	Jeremh.	721	Gch
Woodman, Thomas	64	Jff	Anthony W.	590	Pre	Jno.	19	Hnr
see Bloxam			Benjn.	109	Cmb	Jno.	161	Sth
Woodram, Archibald	641	Gls	Blake B.	125	Cmb	John	790	Nrf
John	774	Nwk	Booker	118	Cmb	John	795	Nrf
Woodriff, George, P.	765	Brn	Booth	720	Gch	John	732	Wsh
Woodroad see Woodwad			Booth	722	Gch	John W.	795	Nrf
Woodrom, Richd.	566	Mnr	Charles	957	Chc	Joseph	396	Ags
Woodroof, David, jr.	274	Amh	Charles	119	Cmb	Joseph	775	Nwk
David, Senr.	274	Amh	Charles	591	Pre	Joshua	720	Gch
Elizabeth	274	Amh	Charles	860	Wth	Joshua	802	Nrf
William	269	Amh	Drury	116	Cmb	Js.	924	Nrf
Woodroofe, David	7	Oho	Elizabeth	721	Gch	Nat.	719	Gch
Woodrooff, Hardin	840	Bck	Elizabeth	591	Pre	Martha	774	Nwk
Woodrow, Benjamin	174	Shn	Fredk., Majr.	13	Pwh	Mason	804	Nrf
Isaac	88	Clp	Fs. Charner	100	Cmb	Philemon	206	Ess
Isaac	562	Frd	Henry	104	Cmb	Rachel	169	Shn
Mary	854	Cmp	Jacob	871	Cmp	Richd.	217	Ess
Woodruff, Benja.	457	Grn	Jacob	722	Gch	Richmond	773	Nwk
Edmund	457	Grn	Jacob, Senr.	593	Pre	Saml.	719	Gch
George, Sr.	765	Brn	Jesse, Capt.	6	Pwh	Sterling	167	Dnw
George B.	766	Brn	John	177	Alb	Thomas	110	Spt
Henry	457	Grn	John	871	Cmp	Thos.	225	Aml
John	457	Grn	John	108	Cmb	Warwick	773	Nwk
Nathl.	457	Grn	John	127	Cmb	Wm.	89	Clp
William	457	Grn	John	721	Gch	Wm.	18	Hnr
see Woodriff			John	722	Gch	see W...dward, Woodard		
Woodrum, Wm.	721	Gch	John	846	Hnv	Woody, Benj.	306	Ldn
Woods, Andrew	56	Jff	John	129	Hnr	Benjamin	175	Alb
Andrew	7	Oho	Joseph [2]	720	Gch	Benjamin	822	Bck
Benjamin	124	Hnr	Joseph	722	Gch	Elizabeth	736	Nls
Edmund	802	Bck	Joseph, jr.	249	Aml	George	734	Nls
Edward	446	Bth	Joseph, jr.	720	Gch	Henry	822	Bck
Francis	22	Oho	Joseph, Sr.	249	Aml	John	175	Alb
George	734	Wsh	Josiah	719	Gch	Reubin	178	Alb
George M.	177	Alb	Mariah	722	Gch	Sarah	736	Nls
Henry	551	Mnn	Miller	129	Cmb	Thomas	735	Nls
James	418	Bth	Miller, jr.	121	Cmb	Woblam [William?]	736	Nls
James	645	Mnt	Miller, snr.	109	Cmb	see W...dy		
James	737	Nls	Milner	720	Gch	Woodyard, David	527	Prw
John	802	Bck	Patrick	429	Flv	Jabez	527	Prw
John	734	Wsh	Patrick	443	Flv	James	11	Wod
John, Jr.	495	Frn	Phebe	849	Hnv	Jeremh.	315	Frf
John, Jr.	668	Mnt	Philip	719	Gch	Jesse	15	Wod
John, Sr.	494	Frn	Pryar	177	Alb	Newton	506	Prw
Jos.	735	Wsh	Robt.	720	Gch	Presly	521	Prw

William	527	Prw	Wootton, John	801	Bck	Eliza.	250	Aml
Woolard, Wm.	291	Ldn	Willis	683	Wrw	Essex	593	Pre
see Wollard			Worberton, Wm.	116	Hnr	George	250	Aml
Woolcord, James	247	Ldn	Worce, Plesent	732	Wsh	Green	9	Ntt
Wm.	247	Ldn	Word, Benjamin	480	Frn	Henry	367	Lnn
Wooldredge, Richard	865	Cmp	Benjamin H.	773	Bck	Henry	4	Ntt
Wooldridge, Archer	66	Chs	Daniel	480	Frn	Jno.	11	Ntt
Charles	792	Bck	Jesse	480	Frn	John	250	Aml
Daniel	15	Pwh	John H.	851	Cmp	Ludson	166	Dnw
Danl.	59	Chs	Josiah	489	Bdf	Miles	64	Chs
George	800	Bck	Thomas	825	Bck	Thos.	249	Aml
Henry	784	Bck	Thomas H.	120	Cmb	Thos.	251	Aml
James	136	Acc	Thos. D.	109	Cmb	William	590	Pre
John	793	Bck	William	850	Cmp	William H.	589	Pre
John	812	Bck	see Worce			Wm.	64	Chs
John	869	Cmp	Worell, James	409	Fqr	Wm.	13	Ntt
John	13	Pwh	Work, David	691	Br	Wm. B.	12	Ntt
Joseph	823	Bck	Workman, Isaac	641	Gls	Worson, James	74	Jff
Lucy	591	Pre	Isaac	267	Ldn	Worstell, Isaac	13	Oho
Seth	13	Pwh	Isaac	297	Ldn	Worstley, Jno.	295	Ldn
Simon	591	Pre	James	2	Knw	Worth, Charles	665	Btt
Thomas	820	Bck	Peter	836	Hmp	Jno.	665	Btt
Thomas	836	Bck	Wm.	549	Mnn	John J.	124	Hnr
Thomas	12	Pwh	Wm.	550	Mnn	Thos.	663	Btt
Thomas, Sen.	136	Acc	Worlay, Nathl.	646	Mnt	Worthain, Catharine	472	Mdd
Thomas, senr.	782	Bck	Worldley, John	821	Hmp	Wortham, Charles	932	Crl
Thos.	60	Chs	Worldridge, Peter	90	Clp	Peter	249	Aml
Wm.	870	Cmp	see Woldrige			Ricd. C.	23	Hnr
Woolf, Elisebeth	739	Wsh	Worledge, Jeremh.	87	Clp	Worthan, Thos.	543	Prg
Henry	85	Jff	John	87	Clp	Worthington, Robert	103	Jff
Jacob	738	Wsh	Worley, Daniel	483	Frn	Samuel	739	Brn
Jacob, Senr.	739	Wsh	Davd.	705	Wsh	Wortman, Peter	681	Br
Larance	739	Wsh	Elijah	484	Frn	Phoebe	681	Br
Lawrance	226	Pnd	Finch	491	Frn	Wortmiller, John	216	Pnd
Michael	739	Wsh	Fredrick	751	Wsh	Worton, Molly	677	Glc
Philip	217	Pnd	James	818	Bck	Saml., Jr.	793	Nrf
Rees	4	Wod	Joseph	476	Frn	Woster, John	316	Frf
see Woo...			Joseph	430	Msn	Wotson, John	216	Pnd
Woolfolk, Achilles	932	Crl	Nathen	705	Wsh	Woulfe, George	15	Oho
Frances	934	Crl	Thos.	703	Wsh	Peter	15	Oho
John, jr.	75	Spt	William	491	Frn	Peter, Jr.	15	Oho
John, Sr.	80	Spt	Wm.	535	Brk	Woworth, Margaret	816	Nrf
John C.	932	Crl	see Werley			Wray, Andrew	473	Frn
John G.	932	Crl	Worly, Vallentine	861	Wth	Catharine	765	Brn
Joseph	934	Crl	Wormeley, Eleanor	472	Mdd	Charles	932	Crl
Joseph	870	Hnv	Mary	535	Frd	Chas.	478	Pra
Richard	934	Crl	Ralph	472	Mdd	Diana.	180	Elc
Sarah P.	933	Crl	Wormington, James	806	Nrf	Francis	767	Brn
Spilsby	932	Crl	see Wornington			Henry	874	Cmp
Woolford, John	431	Rnd	Wormley, Ralph, (F.			James	473	Frn
Woolfork, John	76	Spt	Negroe)	340	Fqr	James, Jr.	473	Frn
Woolland, William	393	Rch	Wallace	350	Fqr	John	764	Brn
Woollard, John	411	Rch	Wormsley, Thos.	480	Pra	John	473	Frn
John, Junr.	396	Rch	Wormsly, David	915	Hrr	John	582	Mnr
Joseph	413	Rch	Wornald, James	239	Ldn	Nancy	766	Brn
Richard	392	Rch	Worndrill, Fdk.	506	Brk	Reubin	767	Brn
Woollery, Henry	772	Hmp	Wornington, John	788	Nrf	Sally	250	Aml
Woollingham, Wm.	5	Oho	Wornom, Nancy	1000	Nrt	Tabitha	766	Brn
Woollum, John	19	Oho	Thomas	998	Nrt	Tabitha, jr.	768	Brn
Wools, George, Jnr.	68	Jff	William	1000	Nrt	Thomas	591	Mnr
Woolsey, Abner	766	Brn	Worrell, Carey	858	Sth	Wm.	478	Pra
Wm.	767	Brn	Elijah	149	Sth	Wreghington, Geo.	811	Nrf
Woolverton, Charles	806	Hmp	James	155	Sth	Wren, Ben.	152	Sth
Woolwine, Jacob	225	Pnd	John	222	Kng	John	72	Spt
John, Christiansburg	642	Mnt	Lewis	149	Sth	Peter	306	Ldn
Philip	595	Mnr	Mary	869	Sth	Robert	14	Pwh
William	860	Wth	Patsy	846	Sth	Sanford	290	Ldn
Woolwire, Elizt.	405	Ags	William	222	Kng	Travis	237	Ldn
Wooseley, John	672	Sss	Wm.	858	Sth	William	77	Spt
Wooten, Edward	668	Sss	Worrin, Drewry	460	Frn	Wm.	440	Flv
Wooter, Issabella	488	Bdf	Elijah	498	Frn	Wm. C., Jr.	445	Flv
Wootin, Jack, F.N.	670	Sss	Jesse	498	Frn	see Daily		
Jonn.	665	Btt	Thomas	497	Frn	Wrench, John	47	Isw
Wooton, Jincy	592	Pre	Zackariah	497	Frn	Wrenn, Ann	670	Sss
Samuel	593	Pre	Worroer, James	598	Brk	Charles	8	Isw
Thomas	144	Sth	Worseley, Wm.	393	Ags	Francis	392	Fqr
William	798	Bck	Worsham, ...	69	Chs	Henry	457	Grn
William	592	Pre	Charles	250	Aml	James	313	Frf
William T.	592	Pre	Daniel	250	Aml	James	317	Frf
Wootten, Nancy	15	Isw	David	366	Lnn	James	364	Lnn

James A.	670	Sss	George	765	Brn	Jonathan	572	Frd
Jesse	669	Sss	George	871	Cmp	Jonathan	582	Frd
Jno., Junr.	316	Frf	George	473	Frn	Jonathon	426	Msn
John	312	Frf	George	576	Frd	Jos.	797	Nrf
John	313	Frf	George	581	Frd	Jos.	824	Nrf
John	396	Fqr	George	289	Rck	Joseph	393	Ags
John	365	Lnn	George	710	Wsh	Joseph	486	Bdf
John	618	Srr	George	788	Wst	Joseph	467	Frn
John	669	Sss	Grief	487	Bdf	Joseph	785	Hmp
Jones	456	Grn	Hannah	364	Lnn	Joseph	364	Lnn
Joseph	668	Sss	Henry	137	Acc	Joseph, jr.	393	Ags
Josiah	35	Isw	Henry	932	Crl	Joseph, Sr.	468	Frn
Priscilla	619	Srr	Henry	774	Nwk	Joshua	485	Pra
Rebby [?]	18	Hnr	Henry, Jun.	17	Isw	Joshua, (of Jere)	483	Pra
Richard	670	Sss	Henry, Sen.	20	Isw	Josiah	766	Brn
Richd.	313	Frf	Hyrum	473	Frn	Judith	773	Nwk
Robert	314	Frf	Isaac	68	Acc	Killis	736	Nls
Samuel	397	Fqr	Isaac	187	Shn	Larken	87	Clp
Thomas	316	Frf	Jacob	485	Frn	Lewis	676	Glc
Thomas	363	Fqr	Jacob	7	Pwh	Lucey	833	Bck
Thomas	35	Isw	James	538	Brk	Marg.	225	Aml
Thomas	364	Lnn	James	785	Bck	Martha	768	Brn
Thomas	618	Srr	James	332	Dnw	Mary	487	Bdf
Thomas	668	Sss	James	219	Ess	Mary	792	Bck
William	365	Lnn	James	416	Fqr	Mary	813	Bck
William	669	Sss	James	476	Frn	Mary	681	Wrw
William, jr.	365	Lnn	James	513	Frd	Mary	885	Yrk
Wrey, Benjamin, Jr.	463	Frn	James	734	Nls	Matthew	486	Bdf
Benjamin, Sr.	463	Frn	James	850	Sth	Matthias	29	Rcm
Elias	463	Frn	James	75	Spt	Menous	737	Nls
Wricks, Daniel	619	Srr	James, Jr.	734	Nls	Merritt	768	Brn
Wright, Alexander	734	Nls	James, (W)	886	Yrk	Moses	737	Nls
Alexander	182	Shn	James T.	850	Cmp	Moses, jr.	300	Amh
Andrew	734	Nls	Jamima	91	Clp	Moses, Senr.	300	Amh
Ann	138	Sth	Jas.	509	Brk	Nancy	435	Bth
Ann	114	Spt	Jas.	677	Glc	Nancy	765	Brn
Ant.	313	Ldn	Jesse	590	Brk	Olaver	478	Frn
Anthoney	486	Bdf	Jessee	889	Hnv	Parsons	364	Lnn
Austin	736	Nls	Jessee	738	Nls	Patterson	313	Ldn
Bazel	418	Rnd	Jno.	666	Btt	Peggey	488	Bdf
Benedict	788	Wst	Jno.	287	Ldn	Peter	665	Btt
Benjamin	280	Amh	Jno.	305	Ldn	Peter	885	Yrk
Benjamin	734	Nls	Jno.	310	Ldn	Phobe	68	Chs
Bennett	287	Amh	Jno., Jr.	650	Mnt	Pleasant	249	Aml
Burditt	40	Stf	John	225	Aml	Polly	735	Nls
Catharime	793	Bck	John	303	Amh	Pryor	776	Bck
Charles	488	Bdf	John	488	Bdf	Pryor	591	Pre
Charles	877	Cmp	John	785	Bck	Pryor, Senr.	591	Pre
Charles	315	Frf	John	932	Crl	R...d	542	Frd
Charles	860	Wth	John	944	Chc	Reuben	225	Aml
Charles	884	Hnv	John	88	Clp	Reuben	932	Crl
Chars. D.	88	Clp	John	168	Dnw	Reuben	669	Sss
Danl.	927	Nrf	John	330	Dnw	Richard	932	Crl
David	487	Bdf	John	400	Fqr	Richard	774	Nwk
David	932	Crl	John	418	Fqr	Richard	860	Wth
David	364	Lnn	John	473	Frn	Robert	225	Aml
David	924	Nrf	John	550	Frd	Robert	432	Bth
Dolly	268	Ldn	John	553	Frd	Robert	856	Cmp
Dothry	735	Nls	John	792	Hmp	Robert	871	Cmp
Dudly	885	Yrk	John	364	Lnn	Robert	932	Crl
Edward	133	Acc	John	411	Mds	Robert	364	Lnn
Edward	400	Fqr	John	418	Mds	Robert	735	Nls
Edward	180	Knq	John	623	Mnt	Robert	591	Pre
Edward R.	403	Rch	John [2]	734	Nls	Robert, Sr.	871	Cmp
Edwd.	885	Yrk	John	735	Nls	Robt.	87	Clp
Elijah	134	Acc	John	826	Nrf	Robt.	292	Rck
Elijh.	88	Clp	John	392	Rch	Sam.	886	Yrk
Eliza	788	Wst	John	288	Rck	Saml.	538	Brk
Eliza.	334	Dnw	John	207	Shn	Saml.	313	Ldn
Elizabeth	400	Fqr	John	692	Wsh	Samuel	768	Brn
Elizabeth	542	Frd	John	886	Yrk	Samuel	555	Frd
Elizabeth	888	Hnv	John, (...)	487	Bdf	Samuel	67	Jff
Ellis	487	Bdf	John, Jr.	839	Bck	Samuel	591	Pre
Enoch	473	Frn	John, Jr.	478	Frn	Samuel	593	Pre
Fanny	675	Glc	John, junr.	618	Srr	Samuel	861	Wth
Flamstead	794	Bck	John, (P)	487	Bdf	Silvy	871	Cmp
Francis	485	Pra	John, (W)	886	Yrk	Stepher	825	Nrf
Geo.	926	Nrf	John, Senr.	618	Srr	Stephn.	926	Nrf
Geo. W.	438	Flv	John, Sr.	474	Frn	Sterling	738	Brn
George	68	Acc	John, T.K.	411	Mds	Thomas	134	Acc

Name	Pg	Co.
Thomas	487	Bdf
Thomas	219	Ess
Thomas	467	Frn
Thomas	478	Pra
Thomas	110	Spt
Thos.	250	Aml
Thos.	87	Clp
Tobias	737	Wsh
William	225	Aml
William	250	Aml
William	933	Crl
William	400	Fqr
William	451	Frn
William	473	Frn
William	589	Frd
William	2	Hnr
William	64	Jff
William	91	Jff
William	181	Knq
William	734	Nls
William	736	Nls
William	207	Shn
William	788	Wst
William, Jnr.	137	Acc
William, Senr.	137	Acc
Willis	933	Crl
Willis	867	Sth
Wim.	877	Hnv
Wim., Jnr.	888	Hnv
Winfeild	411	Mds
Winny, (W)	886	Yrk
Wm.	285	Ldn
Wm.	302	Ldn
Wm.	313	Ldn
Wm.	814	Nrf
Wm.	483	Pra
Wm.	430	Rnd
Wm.	850	Sth
Wm.	885	Yrk
Wright	469	Frn
see Bailey, Bond, W...i...		
Writenhouse, Isaac	946	Hrr
Writesman, Jno.	664	Btt
Writt, Isabella	402	Fqr
Hannah	396	Fqr
Writtenhouse, Josha.	69	Clp
Nicholas	412	Mds
Wroe, Benjamin	592	Frd
Jane	789	Wst
John	398	Rch
Samuel	410	Rch
William	999	Nrt
Wuren, Judith	890	Hnv
Wyan, Peter	35	Rcm
Wyans, Jacob	1	Oho
Wyant, David	394	Ags
Wyat, Thomas	579	Mnr
Wyatt, Ann	440	Bth
Aylscy	454	Frn
Billey	328	Dnw
C...	595	Frd
Catharine	472	Mdd
Edward	167	Dnw
Fanny	933	Crl
George, Snr.	182	Knq
Hubbard	167	Dnw
Hubbard	457	Grn
Jacob	283	Ldn
James	520	Prw
James	886	Yrk
Jno.	55	Chs
John	66	Chr
John	453	Frn
John	365	Lnn
John	772	Nwk
Joseph	66	Chr
Joseph	466	Frn
Joseph	471	Mdd
Joshu	832	Nrf
Major	471	Mdd
Overstreet	365	Lnn
Reuben	414	Bth
Richd.	182	Knq
Shadrach	822	Nrf
Smith	182	Knq
Spivey	834	Nrf
Theo.	409	Ags
Theophilous	721	Gch
Thomas	565	Mnr
Thomas, Snr.	181	Knq
Thos.	55	Chs
William	933	Crl
William	181	Knq
William	518	Prw
William P.	934	Crl
Wm.	55	Chs
Wyche, Benjamin	671	Sss
Elizabeth	766	Brn
Henry	457	Grn
James	768	Brn
John	766	Brn
Wycoff, Cornelius	246	Ldn
Elizabeth	415	Fqr
Wyercup, Adam	512	Brk
Garret	512	Brk
Wyett, Peggy	69	Acc
Susannah	70	Acc
Wyhier, Francis	25	Oho
Wykoff, Cornelius	574	Frd
Peter	81	Jff
Wylie, Andw.	585	Mnr
Hugh	67	Chr
John [2]	596	Mnr
Robert	568	Mnr
Thomas	562	Mnr
Thos.	585	Mnr
William	568	Mnr
see Roberts		
Wyne, Fielding	364	Fqr
John	345	Fqr
Leroy	362	Fqr
Lucey	345	Fqr
Molley	345	Fqr
Nata	411	Fqr
William	345	Fqr
Wynes, James	404	Fqr
Wynkoop, Cornelius	259	Ldn
see Winecoop		
Wynn, Cathrine	673	Sss
Ephraim	671	Sss
Gray	671	Sss
Harrison	668	Sss
John	767	Brn
Joicy	737	Brn
Josiah	596	Frd
Mary C.	326	Dnw
Patrience	332	Dnw
Peter	737	Brn
Peterson	671	Sss
Robert	737	Brn
Scott, F.N.	673	Sss
Susanna	672	Sss
Thomas	330	Dnw
Thomas	512	Prw
William	672	Sss
Winnifred	669	Sss
Wm. R.	737	Brn
Wynne, Humphrey	679	Wrw
John	680	Wrw
Joshua	168	Dnw
Peter	668	Sss
Robt., jr.	166	Dnw
Robt., Senr.	167	Dnw
Thos.	681	Wrw
Wm.	166	Dnw
Wm.	885	Yrk
see W...ne		
Wyrick, Andrew	863	Wth
George	863	Wth
John [2]	863	Wth
Henry	863	Wth
Martin [2]	863	Wth
Nicholas	863	Wth
see Wirick		
Wyse, Jac.	549	Mnn
Wysong, Fayette	663	Btt
Jacob	105	Jff
Joseph	56	Jff
Joseph, Jr.	465	Frn
Joseph, Sr.	465	Frn
Michael	56	Jff
Vallintine	466	Frn

--- Y ---

Name	Pg	Co.
Yager, Adam	414	Mds
Benjamin	414	Mds
Daniel	414	Mds
Ephraham	415	Mds
Godfrey	415	Mds
Jacob	249	Shn
James	414	Mds
Joel	415	Mds
John, Jr.	415	Mds
John A.	414	Mds
John H.	414	Mds
John, P.W.	415	Mds
John W.	414	Mds
Jos.	249	Shn
Michael	414	Mds
Nathl.	92	Clp
Philip	33	Rcm
William	415	Mds
Yakeley, John	577	Frd
Yakle, Christian	2	Rcm
Yale, Jno.	5	Ntt
John	367	Lnn
Yancey, Charles	178	Alb
Charles	784	Bck
Jeremiah	178	Alb
Jewnias	178	Alb
Joel	869	Cmp
John	35	Rcm
Layton	24	Rcm
Yancy, Agathy, & Daught.	92	Clp
Elia.	92	Clp
Geoe.	92	Clp
Jechenias	92	Clp
Kaianaugh W.	92	Clp
Majar	92	Clp
Philimon	935	Crl
Richd. H.	92	Clp
Robert	105	Cmb
Robt.	92	Clp
Tho.	92	Clp
Thornn.	92	Clp
Unity	93	Clp
Walter	856	Hnv
Wm.	92	Clp
Yankey, Michal	215	Pnd
Yantes, Nicholas	863	Wth
Yarborough, Susanna	169	Dnw
Yarbraugh, ---	326	Dnw
Yarbrough, Elisha	900	Hnv
Joel	934	Crl
Jeremiah	935	Crl
Joseph	367	Lnn
Yargus see Yerfost		
Yarington, Anena	204	Ess
Yarnall, Mordecai	2	Oho
Yarrington, Patsey	872	Hnv
Vincent	472	Mdd
Yatemon, Thos. M.	446	Mth
Yates, Abner	18	Rcm
Amos	549	Brk
Amos	576	Brk
Benjamin P.	740	Brn

Boswell
Elias 93 Clp
Enoch 489 Bdf
Geoe., Capt. 397 Ags
Geoe., Senr. 93 Clp
Isaac 93 Clp
James 240 Ldn
James 489 Bdf
Jas. G. 93 Clp
John 93 Clp
John 489 Bdf
John 934 Crl
John 93 Clp
John 547 Frd
John 82 Jff
Joseph 741 Wsh
Joseph 93 Clp
Mary 831 Hmp
Mary 93 Clp
Michael 678 Glc
Michl. 75 Spt
Paul 93 Clp
Richard 93 Clp
Richd. 775 Nwk
Robert 93 Clp
Sarah 223 Kng
Susan 934 Crl
Susan 677 Glc
Thomas 678 Glc
William 11 Oho
William 489 Bdf
Wm. 558 Brk
Wm. 739 Brn
Wm. 93 Clp
Wm. 677 Glc
Yeager, George 815 Nrf
John 423 Rnd
Jos. 224 Pnd
Nicholas 554 Mnn
Peter 422 Msn
William 425 Msn
Yearby, Richard 422 Rnd
Yeargan, John 514 Frd
Sanuel 213 Alb
Yearlin, Saml. 740 Brn
Yearman, Austin 4 Hnr
Charles 866 Hnv
Jno. 865 Hnv
Yearnel, Joseph 866 Hnv
Yearout, Abraham 534 Brk
Chas. 397 Ags
Danl. 397 Ags
Isaac 397 Ags
Jacob 396 Ags
Yeatman, Henry L. 397 Ags
James 789 Wst
Jennings 789 Wst
John, Jur. 789 Wst
John, Senr. 789 Wst
John H. 789 Wst
Meredith 399 Rch
Thomas 789 Wst
Thomas 399 Rch
Thomas, Jur. 789 Wst
William 789 Wst
William, Jr. 406 Rch
Yerby, Geo. W. 401 Rch
Jesse 364 Lnc
Jud. 365 Lnc
John M. 365 Lnc
Tho. 407 Rch
William, Jr. 365 Lnc
William, Jr. 368 Lnc
Wm. 369 Lnc
Wm., Jr. 364 Lnc
Yerce, John 364 Lnc
Yerfost, Jacob 931 Hrr
Yergain, ---, Widow 236 Shn
Yerie, John 634 Btt
Yerkes, Joshua 964 Hrr
82 Jff

Yerkis, Josiah 97 Jff
Yew, Caty 570 Frd
Yews, Charles 332 Dnw
Yinger, Gasper 787 Hmp
Yirkle, Henry 237 Shn
see Zirkle
Yoak, John 423 Rnd
Yoakam, Micheal 421 Rnd
Wm. 422 Rnd
Yoe, Peter 572 Frd
Yohoo, Henry 25 Oho
Jacob 25 Oho
John 23 Oho
Peter 25 Oho
Peter, Jr. 25 Oho
Yohow, Henry 23 Oho
Yokem, Michael 234 Shn
Yonley, Thomas 781 Hmp
Yonson, George 863 Wth
Palsor 863 Wth
Yonts, John 863 Wth
Peter 863 Wth
Yontz, Conrod 96 Jff
John 100 Jff
Yopp, Mary 365 Lnc
Wm. 667 Btt
York see James
Yorkshire, John 396 Ags
Thos. 397 Ags
Yost, Anthony 39 Rcm
Casper 406 Ags
Charles 6 Rcm
Christeen 255 Shn
George 738 Nls
Henry 554 Mnn
Henry 863 Wth
Jac. 554 Mnn
Jacob 738 Nls
Jacob 2 Rcm
Jacob 5 Rcm
Jno. 554 Mnn
Jno., Jr. 554 Mnn
John 564 Brk
John 643 Gls
Margeret 318 Frf
Peter 570 Brk
Peter 573 Brk
Peter 554 Mnn
Tobias 1000 Nrt
Wm. 554 Mnn
Youille, Wm. 294 Rck
Young, Adam 596 Brk
Alexander 863 Wth
Alexr. 248 Ldn
Alexr. 609 Mnt
Andrew 692 Br
Andw. 397 Ags
Ann 138 Acc
Ann 92 Clp
Anthony 542 Frd
Archd. 317 Ldn
Bagwell 138 Acc
Ben. 541 Brk
Benj. 246 Ldn
Catharine 541 Brk
Catharine 514 Frd
Cathe. 92 Clp
Charles 934 Crl
Charles 168 Dnw
Charles 2 Knw
Chas. 560 Brk
Comfort 138 Acc
Christopher 18 Rcm
Clem 367 Lnn
Cornelious 945 Chc
Creasey 917 Hrr
Crisley 105 Jff
Cunrod 313 Ldn
Daniel 667 Btt
Davd. 729 Wsh

David 178 Alb
David 310 Ldn
Devalt 571 Frd
Dunkin 489 Bdf
Edmond 594 Pre
Edward 945 Chc
Edward 168 Dnw
Edwd. 927 Nrf
Elijah 594 Pre
Elizabeth 935 Crl
Elizabeth 568 Frd
Elizabeth 831 Nrf
Fountin 728 Wsh
Francis 169 Dnw
Francis 356 Fqr
Frederick 516 Frd
Frederick 37 Rcm
G... [written over "An..."] 299 Rck
Geo. 396 Ags
Geo. 310 Ldn
George 93 Clp
George 530 Frd
George, Guilfd. 138 Acc
Henry 209 Ess
Henry 457 Grn
Henry 796 Hmp
Henry 6 Knw
Henry 182 Knq
Henry 396 Ags
Hugh 396 Ags
Isaac 816 Nrf
Israel 300 Ldn
Jacob 667 Btt
Jacob 85 Spt
James 397 Ags
James 682 Br
James 935 Crl
James 336 Dnw
James 373 Fqr
James 487 Frn
James 818 Hmp
James 91 Jff
James 596 Mnr
James 775 Nwk
James 594 Pre
James 294 Rck
James 298 Rck
James 116 Spt
James 679 Wrw
James 729 Wsh
James, jr. 935 Crl
Jane 576 Mnr
Jas. 836 Nrf
Jno. 310 Ldn
John 138 Acc
John 266 Amh
John [2] 396 Ags
John 424 Bth
John 686 Br
John 934 Crl
John 943 Chc
John 168 Dnw
John 398 Fqr
John 489 Frn
John 785 Hmp
John 55 Jff
John 14 Knw
John 18 Rcm
John 72 Spt
John 709 Wsh
John, BS 138 Acc
John G. 686 Br
Johnson 594 Pre
Jonathan 71 Acc
Jonn., & Broths. 92 Clp
Jos. 4 Hnr
Joseph 935 Crl
Joseph 57 Jff
Joseph 26 Rcm
Joshua 450 Frn

Joshua	538	Prg	William, SS	138	Acc	Zell, Thomas	667 Btt
Julianna	667	Btt	William H. [H. Wil-			see Zoll	
Laban	682	Br	liam?]	775	Nwk	Zemerle, Jacob	703 Wsh
Leanard	667	Btt	Willm.	667	Btt	Jacob, Jur.	703 Wsh
Leonard	935	Crl	Winnefred	168	Dnw	Zentmeyer, John	656 Mnt
Lucy	67	Chr	Wm. [2]	396	Ags	Zian, John	752 Wsh
Lucy	19	Hnr	Wm.	406	Ags	Zickelfooze, George	587 Mnr
Mary	425	Bth	Wm.	561	Brk	Ziglar, Powell	667 Btt
Mary	176	Shn	Wm.	123	Hnr	Zilling, John	634 Mnt
Mary, in Hampton has Slaves			Wm.	554	Mnn	Zills, Marcus	672 Sss
in York County	887	Yrk	Wm.	574	Mnr	Miles	672 Sss
Mat.	397	Ags	Wm.	303	Rck	Rebecca [2]	672 Sss
Mathew	872	Cmp	Wmson.	168	Dnw	William	672 Sss
Matthew	539	Brk	WmSon.	209	Ess	Zimaman, Christly	249 Shn
Matthias	6	Knw	see Bowers, Johnston, Pugh			Zimbro, Geo.	397 Ags
Michael	863	Wth	Youngblood, Andrew	564	Brk	Peter	397 Ags
Mickelberry	935	Crl	Younger, Geo.	813	Nrf	Zimerman, Danl.	93 Clp
Nathan	863	Wth	Humphry	6	Oho	John	93 Clp
Nathaniel	934	Crl	James	203	Ess	Mary	93 Clp
Nathl.	13	Isw	Nehemiah	6	Oho	Zimmemon, Christopher	415 Mds
Natt, (Y)	887	Yrk	Wm.	203	Ess	George	328 Dnw
Natt.	789	Wst	see Thomas, Yinger			Joshua	415 Mds
Nics., Sr.	667	Btt	Younghusband, Elizh.	125	Hnr	Mary	415 Mds
Patrick	734	Wsh	Youngman, Jenry	326	Dnw	Zimmer, Lewis	332 Dnw
Patrick	748	Wsh	William	326	Dnw	Zimmerm..., Jacob	756 Hmp
Peter	450	Frn	Younkin, Ralph	284	Ldn	Zimmerman, Abraham	13 Rcm
Philip	3	Oho	Yount, Benjn.	21	Rcm	Christo.	397 Ags
Powers	939	Chc	Jacob	9	Rcm	Geo.	318 Frf
Richard	138	Acc	Joseph	396	Ags	Jacob [2]	397 Ags
Richard	19	Hnr	Younts, Wm.	756	Wsh	Jacob	318 Frf
Richd.	681	Wrw	Yowel, John	93	Clp	Michael	71 Jff
Robert	138	Acc	Lewis	93	Clp	Stophel	397 Ags
Robert	797	Hmp	Merry	93	Clp	Wm.	667 Btt
Robert	597	Mnr	Yowell, Abraham	415	Mds	see Simmerman	
Robert	863	Wth	Christopher	415	Mds	Zimmermon, Jno.	318 Frf
Saml.	530	Brk	Elijah	415	Mds	Zimmers, Catharine	37 Rcm
Saml.	92	Clp	Jacob	415	Mds	Michael	38 Rcm
Saml. W.	267	Ldn	John	415	Mds	Zimmimom, George	331 Dnw
Samuel	92	Clp	Pendleton	415	Mds	Zimmomon, Elizabeth	315 Ldn
Samuel	459	Frn	Samuel	415	Mds	Zinn, Geo.	554 Mnn
Samuel	509	Frd	William	415	Mds	Jac.	554 Mnn
Samuel	863	Wth				Jno.	554 Mnn
Susanna	596	Mnr				Michl.	554 Mnn
Thomas	575	Brk	--- Z ---			Wm.	197 Shn
Thomas	334	Dnw				Zirkle, Benjamin	37 Rcm
Thomas E.	594	Pre				Danl.	197 Shn
Thos. [2]	396	Ags	Zacerman, Thomas	561	Brk	George	237 Shn
Thos.	550	Prg	Zachary, Crawford	11	Ntt	Jacob	196 Shn
Thos.	758	Wsh	Wm.	9	Ntt	John	197 Shn
Thos., (N.C.)	397	Ags	Zackman, Anthy.	531	Brk	John	199 Shn
Tinsley	169	Dnw	Zahary, Benjamin	415	Mds	John	27 Rcm
Tony, (FN)	69	Chr	Zane, Ebenezer	2	Oho	Lewis, (Jr.)	25 Rcm
Walter	72	Spt	Henry	906	Hrr	Lewis, (Sen.)	
William	138	Acc	Noah	2	Oho	see Yirkle	667 Btt
William	869	Cmp	Zanes, Lewis	21	Rcm	Zoll, Jacob	
William	935	Crl	Zans, John	397	Ags	see Zell	667 Btt
William	169	Dnw	Zearley, Francis	318	Frf	Zolman, Wm.	584 Brk
William	2	Knw	Zediker, Enoch	613	Mnt	Zuck, Jacob	
William	181	Shn	Zegen see Czegan			Zucker see Tucker	64 Jff
William	31	Stf	Zelia, ---, Madm.	927	Nrf	Zumbro, John	

366